INVESTMENTS

a global perspective

OPTION CONVENTIONS

XP = Exercise price
COP = Call option's price
POP = Put option's price
h = Hedge ratio

UNIVERSAL GREEK SYMBOLS

σ = Standard deviation of x = $\sqrt{VAR(x)}$

ρ = Correlation coefficient = $\sigma_{xy}/\sigma_x\sigma_y$

Σ = Summation sign

CAPM, CHARACTERISTIC LINE, AND APT

RFR = Risk free rate, a nominal (not real) return
M = Market portfolio
α = Intercept of characteristic line in returns
β = Slope of characteristic line in returns
e = Residual error term
RP = Risk premium in Jensen regressions = $(r - RFR)$
A = Intercept of characteristic line in risk premiums (Jensen)
B = Slope of characteristic line in risk premiums (Jensen)
u = Residual error term (Jensen)
F_{it} = Risk factor i observed at time period t in generating function from APT
a = alpha intercepts in single-factor return generating function from APT
b = beta sensitivity (slope) in return generating function from APT
x_i = Weight of i = Proportion of asset i in a portfolio

COMMON STOCK SYMBOLS

EPS = Earnings per share
DIV = Cash dividends per share = $(1 - RR)(EPS)$
RR = Retention rate
ROE = Return on equity
k = Risk-adjusted discount rate = Investors' expected return
g = Growth rate
$MGFR$ = Margin fraction = Proportion of down payment

FUTURES AND FOREIGN EXCHANGE SYMBOLS

SP = Spot price
FP = Future price

MUTUAL FUNDS

$NAVPS$ = Net asset value per share

Put A New Twist On Time-Value-of-Money, And $5 In Your Pocket.

You will learn a great deal in this book about the Time-Value-of-Money. TI wants to help you learn the "value of time and money" with a great offer on the BAII PLUS™ financial calculator.

Save time. The easy-to-use features of the BAII PLUS will speed you through calculations such as net present value, internal rate of return, time-value-of-money, and more. And because the BAII PLUS is available at most stores where calculators are sold, you won't spend time searching for it.

Save money. You don't have to spend a lot of money because the BAII PLUS is priced to fit your budget. Plus, for a limited time, TI will put an extra $5 in your pocket.

Take advantage of this offer on the BAII PLUS today, and get the most value out of your time and money.

TEXAS INSTRUMENTS

BAII PLUS Rebate Terms and Conditions

This offer is valid only for BAII PLUS purchases between January 1, 2001 and May 1, 2003. All claims must be postmarked by July 31, 2003. Allow 8 to 10 weeks for processing. All purchases must be made in the U.S. or Canada. Rebates will be sent only to addresses in the U.S. and Canada and paid in U.S. dollars. Not redeemable at any store. Send this completed form along with the retail or on-line receipt (original or copy) and the UPC bar code to the address indicated. This original mail-in certificate must accompany your request and may not be duplicated or reproduced. Offer valid only as stated on this form. Offer void where prohibited, taxed, licensed, or restricted. Limit one rebate per household or address. Texas Instruments reserves the right to discontinue this program at any time and without notice.

AD067.99

© 2000 TI.   ™ Texas Instruments Incorporated

Yes! I Want $5 Back On My Purchase of the BAII PLUS.

INVESTMENTS

a global perspective

JACK FRANCIS

Department of Economics and Finance
Bernard Baruch College

ROGER IBBOTSON

Department of Finance
Yale School of Management

Prentice Hall

Prentice Hall
Upper Saddle River, New Jersey 07458

Library of Congress Cataloging-in-Publication Data
Francis, Jack Clark.
  Investments: a global perspective/Jack Francis, Roger Ibbotson.
      p. cm.
  Includes bibliographical references and index.
    ISBN 0-13-890740-4
      1. Investments. 2. Securities. 3. International finance. 4. Investments, Foreign. I.
Ibbotson, Roger G. II. Title.

HG4521 .F685 2001
332.6—dc21   2001036327

AVP/Executive Editor: Mickey Cox
Editor-in-Chief: PJ Boardman
Managing Editor (Editorial): Gladys Soto
Assistant Editor: Cheryl Clayton
Editorial Assistant: Melanie Olsen
Media Project Manager: Bill Minick
Marketing Manager: Joshua P. McClary
Marketing Assistant: Christopher Bath
Managing Editor (Production): Cynthia Regan
Production Editor: Carol Samet
Production Assistant: Dianne Falcone
Permissions Coordinator: Suzanne Grappi
Associate Director, Manufacturing: Vinnie Scelta
Production Manager: Arnold Vila
Manufacturing Buyer: Diane Peirano
Design Director: Pat Smythe
Art Director: Janet Slowik
Interior Design: Jill Wood
Cover Design: Janet Slowik
Cover Illustration/Photos: Mike Shepard/Shannon Associates LLC, Pierre Tremblay/
Masterfile, Reid Ken/FPG
Manager, Print Production: Christy Mahon
Composition: Pre-Press Company, Inc.
Full-Service Project Management: Pre-Press Company, Inc.
Printer/Binder: Courier-Westford

10 9 8 7 6 5 4 3 2 1
ISBN 0-13- 890740-4

To Harry Markowitz

ABOUT THE AUTHORS

Jack Clark Francis was born in Indianapolis, Indiana, and received his bachelors and M.B.A. degrees from Indiana University. He then enlisted in the U.S. Army, was commissioned as a lieutenant, graduated from paratrooper school, was a company commander, and served on active duty for two years. After the service, he earned his Ph.D. in finance from the University of Washington in Seattle. Francis was a member of the finance faculty of the University of Pennsylvania's Wharton School of Finance for five years. He was a Federal Reserve economist for two years; he did monetary economics research, participated in monetary policy discussions, and spoke at numerous meetings for bankers. Currently, he is professor of Economics and Finance at Bernard M. Baruch College in New York City. Dr. Francis authors and co-authors over 20 books published by McGraw-Hill, Prentice-Hall, John Wiley, and Irwin Publishing Companies. Professor Francis's research usually focuses on investments and banking. He has had dozens of research articles published in numerous academic, business, and government journals. He serves as an expert witness, consultant, and has been a member of the board of directors of a few corporations. He lives in Stamford, Connecticut. Jack recently purchased a greenhouse and is endeavoring to learn how to grow flowers.

Roger G. Ibbotson is professor in the Practice of Finance at Yale School of Management. He also is chairman of Ibbotson Associates in Chicago, New York, and Tokyo, which provides investment consulting, software, data, and financial publishing for financial institutions. His book with Rex Sinquefield, *Stocks, Bonds, Bills, and Inflation*, updated in annual *Yearbooks* (published by Ibbotson Associates), serves as the standard reference for information on investment market returns. He has also co-authored two books with Gary Brinson, *Global Investing*, and *Investment Markets*. In addition, he has co-authored *U.S. Treasury Yield Curves* and is currently working on *The Equity Risk Premium.*

Professor Ibbotson conducts research on a broad range of financial topics, including investment returns, mutual funds, international markets, portfolio management, and valuation. He is a regular contributor and editorial board member to both trade and academic journals. He is the recipient of many awards including the Graham and Dodd Scrolls in 1979, 1982, 1984, and 2001 and AIMR's James R. Vertin Award in 2001.

Professor Ibbotson has served as a consultant to many companies in the financial and investment industries. He serves as a partner at Zebra Capital Management, LLC and on numerous boards, including Dimensional Fund Advisors' funds. He frequently speaks at universities, conferences, and other forums. He received his bachelor's degree in mathematics from Purdue University, his M.B.A. from Indiana University, and his Ph.D. from the University of Chicago where he taught for more than 10 years and served as executive director of the Center for Research in Security Prices.

CONTENTS IN BRIEF

Part 1 *INTRODUCTION* *1*

Chapter 1   The Investment Setting   3
Chapter 2   Rates of Return   18
Chapter 3   Introduction to Valuation   37
Chapter 4   Analysis of Financial Statements   65
Chapter 5   Primary Securities and Their Issuers   93
Chapter 6   The Global Stock Market   125
Chapter 7   Statistical Analysis and the SML   159
Chapter 8   Efficient Capital Markets and Anomalies   187
Chapter 9   Futures and Options   228

Part 2 *INVESTMENT INDEXES* *269*

Chapter 10   Creating Price Indexes   270
Chapter 11   Selected Investment Indexes   295
Chapter 12   Using Indexes   332

Part 3 *PORTFOLIO THEORY* *365*

Chapter 13   Asset Allocation   366
Chapter 14   Portfolio Analysis   398
Chapter 15   CAPM and APT   437
Chapter 16   Investment Performance Evaluation   475

Part 4 *INTERNATIONAL INVESTING* *507*

Chapter 17   Foreign Exchange   508
Chapter 18   Global Investing   530

Part 5 *FIXED INCOME INVESTMENTS* *559*

Chapter 19   Global Bond Markets   560
Chapter 20   Market Interest Rates   595
Chapter 21   Horizon Risk and Interest Rate Risk   626
Chapter 22   Credit Risk   656

Part 6 *EQUITY SHARES* *687*

Chapter 23   Equity Valuation—A Micro View   688
Chapter 24   The Issuer's Earning Power   719
Chapter 25   Stock Valuation Issues   743
Chapter 26   Technical Analysis   777

Part 7   *Derivatives and Alternative Investments*   **797**

    Chapter 27   Futures   798
    Chapter 28   Options   835
    Chapter 29   Alternative Investments   867

Appendix   *A1*

Glossary   *G1*

Index   *I1*

CONTENTS

PREFACE

Part 1 *INTRODUCTION*   *1*

CHAPTER 1   The Investment Setting   3

    What Is Investing?   3
    Gambling   *4*
    Speculation   *4*
    Investing   *5*

    The Assets of Choice   6

    The Global Market   6
    Where the People Are   *6*
    Where the Income Is   *7*

    Where the Capital Is   8
    The World's Equity Capital   *9*
    The World's Bond Market   *10*
    The World's Real Capital and Human Capital   *10*

    The U.S. Financial Markets   12
    The U.S. Market for Equities   *13*
    The U.S. Market for Bonds   *14*

Appendix: Opportunities and Salaries in Investments   16

CHAPTER 2   Rates of Return   18

    The Investors' Goal   18

    The One-Period Rate of Return   20
    Measuring Realized One-Period Rates of Return   *22*
    Measuring Average Rates of Return   *24*
    Assessing Risk   *26*

    The Required Rate of Return   29
    The Largest Investors in the World   *31*

CHAPTER 3   Introduction to Valuation   37

    The Time Value of Money: One-Period Models   38

    The Time Value of Money: Multiperiod Models   40

    Making Buy-Sell Decisions   45

Long Positions, Short Positions, and Rates of Return   46
The Short Position   46
The Return from a Short Position   47
Complications with Short Positions   48
Gain-Loss Illustrations for Long and Short Positions   49

A More Realistic Valuation and Investment Procedure   50

A Model of Price-Value Interaction   51
The Liquidity Traders and the Information Traders   51
Comparing Differences Between Prices and Values   52
The Information Content of Prices   53

Passive versus Active Investment Management   54
Active Investment Management   54
Passive Investment Management   55

Hedging and Arbitrage   55
Perfect Hedges   56
Imperfect Hedges   57

Arbitrage   57
Arbitrageurs Enforce the Economic Law of One Price   58
Everyone Benefits from Arbitrage   58

Appendix: Formulas for Valuing Perpetual Cash Flows   63

CHAPTER 4   Analysis of Financial Statements   65

The Financial Statements   65
The Balance Sheet   66
The Income and Expense Statement   66
The Statement of Cash Flows   67
Sources of Financial Statements   69

Common-Sized Financial Statements   70
Common-Sized Balance Sheet   70
Common-Sized Income and Expense Statement   70

Analysis of Sales and Competition   72

Financial Ratios with Meaningful and Relevant Values   73
Computing and Interpreting Financial Ratios   73
Solvency (or Liquidity) Ratios   74
Turnover Ratios   74
Coverage Ratios   76
A Cash Flow Ratio   77
Financial Leverage Ratios   78
Profitability Ratios   79
Per Share Data for the Common Stock   80

Analyzing and Interpreting Ratios   81
The DuPont Analytical Framework   81
Interpreting Ratios with Standards of Comparison   83
Potential Problems with Financial Analysis   84

CHAPTER 5   Primary Securities and Their Issuers   93

   Money Market Securities and Their Markets   93

   U.S. Treasury Bills   94
   Certificates of Deposit   95
   Banker's Acceptances   96
   Federal Funds   96
   The LIBOR Market   96
   Eurodollars   97
   Repurchase Agreements (Repos)   97
   Commercial Paper   97

   Fixed-Income Securities   98

   Some Bonds Pay Coupons—and Some Do Not   98
   Features of Bond Issues   99

   U.S. Government Securities   101

   Nonmarketable U.S. Treasury Issues   101

   Marketable U.S. Treasury Securities   101

   Municipal Bonds Issued Within the United States   106

   General-Obligation (GO) Bonds   107
   Limited-Obligation Bonds   107
   Insured Municipal Bonds   107

   Corporation Bonds   108

   Secured Bonds   108
   Unsecured Bonds   109

   Equity Securities   109

   Common Stock   110

   Stockholders' Rights   110
   Stock Splits and Dividends   113
   Other Aspects of Common Stock   113

   Preferred Stock   116

   The Rights of Preferred Stockholders   116
   Other Aspects of Preferred Stock   118
   Types of Preferred Stock   119

CHAPTER 6   The Global Stock Market   125

   The Global Stock Market   126

   Brokerage Services   126

   Full-Service Brokers   128
   Discount Brokers Provide Limited Service   129
   Many Electronic Brokers Provide Self-Service   129

   Transacting   131

   Types of Trading Orders   131
   Trading on Margin   132

Investment Banks Make Primary Markets   134

Four Functions Performed by Investment Bankers   134
Electronic Investment Bankers   136
Full Disclosure Is Required in the United States   136

The New York Stock Exchange (NYSE)   138

NYSE Operations   138
NYSE Market-Makers   139
NYSE Listing Requirements   140

The Nasdaq Market   141

Nasdaq Operations   142
The CQS, the ITS, and The Law of One Price   143

The Third and Fourth Markets in the United States   145

The Third Market   145
The Fourth Market in the United States   145

Electronic Communication Networks   146

Order-Crossing Networks   146
Electronic Order-Working Systems   147

Evolving Stock Exchanges   149

Reg ATS Exchanges   150
Modernization and Consolidation   150

Liquidity   151

Transaction Costs   151
International Survey of Transaction Costs   153

CHAPTER 7   Statistical Analysis and the SML   159

The Basic Random Variable   159

Unmargined Returns   160
One-Period Return Calculations   160
Analysis of Margined Investment Returns   161
Margined Returns After Transaction Costs   161
Selecting a Sample   162

Probability Distributions of Returns   162

The Expected Rate of Return   162

Risk Estimates   164

Sources of Risk   165

Constructing Probability Distributions   166

Subjective and Objective Probability Distributions   166
Rates of Return Are More Appropriate
Measures Than Dollar Changes   166

The Stability of Probability Distributions   166

Probability Distributions of Rates of Return Tend To Be Stable   167

Selecting Dominant Assets   168

The Characteristic Line   169

Market Returns: The Characteristic Line's Independent Variable   170
Asset Returns: The Characteristic Line's Dependent Variable   172
Estimating a Characteristic Line's Statistics   172
The Characteristic Line's Unexplained Residual Returns   175

Interpreting the Characteristic Line   176

The Covariance Statistic   176
The Correlation: A Goodness-of-Fit Statistic   177
Beta: A Regression Slope Coefficient   177
Alpha: A Regression Intercept Term   178
Partitioning an Asset's Total Risk   178
Getting Statistics from the Internet   180

The Security Market Line (SML)   180

Appendix: Skewness   185

CHAPTER 8   Efficient Capital Markets and Anomalies   187

Information Hypotheses   188

Evidence Supporting the Weakly Efficient Hypothesis   190

Filter Rules   190
Serial Correlation Tests   191
Runs Tests   193

Anomalies in the Weakly Efficient Hypothesis   193

Day-of-the-Week Effects   193
The January Effect   194
Conclusions About the Weakly Efficient Markets Hypothesis   196

Tests of the Semi–Strong Efficient Hypothesis   197

Stock and Bond Market Adjustments to Federal Announcements   198
The Impact of Information   198
About Information and Market Prices   199

The Effects of Stock Splits and Stock Dividends   199

The Fama, Fisher, Jensen, and Roll (FFJR) Study   200
Analyzing the Residual Errors   201

The Size Effect—Another Anomaly   205

Interrelationship Between the January and Size Effects   205
International Evidence   206

The Growth-Value Anomaly   206

Fama and French (F&F) Analyze the P/B Ratio   208
Capaul, Rowley, and Sharpe's International Study   211
*Concluding Remarks About the Semi–Strong
Efficient Markets Hypothesis*   211

Tests of the Strongly Efficient Markets Hypothesis   213

Evaluating the Performance of Mutual Funds   213
Inside Information   214
Conclusions About the Strongly (Perfectly) Efficient Markets Hypothesis   217

CHAPTER 9   Futures and Options   228

Forward Contracts   229

Futures Contracts   229

Basic Characteristics of Futures   229
Gains and Losses on Futures Positions and Account Administration   233
Speculating with Futures   235
Hedging with Futures   238
The Futures Prices and Other Trading Data in Newspapers   240
Regulating Financial Futures in the United States   241

Characteristics of Puts and Calls on Equities   242

Characteristics of Stock Options Traded
on Options Exchanges in the United States   243
Markets for Options   244

Gain-Loss Illustrations for Call Positions   244

Gain-Loss Illustration of Call Buyer's Position   244
Illustration of Call Writer's Position   248

Gain-Loss Illustrations for Put Positions   249

Gain-Loss Illustrations for a Put Writer   251
Perspectives on Options   252

Choosing Between an Option or a Position in the
Underlying Stock   253

Advantages Derived from Using Options   253
One Major Advantage of the Short Sale over Buying a Put   255
Zero-Sum Game   256

Determinants of Put and Call Premiums   256

The Length of Time Remaining in the Option's Life   256
The Riskiness of the Underlying Asset   256
The Market Price of the Underlying Asset   259
The Exercise Price   259
Rate of Interest   259
Cash Dividend Payments   259

Appendix: Warrants, Embedded Options, and Convertibles   265

Part 2 *INVESTMENT INDEXES*   **269**

CHAPTER 10   Creating Price Indexes   270

Constructing a Stock Market Indicator   271

First Principles for Constructing an Indicator of Market Prices   271
Contrasting Two Well-Known Stock Market Indicators   273

Maintaining a Price Index   278

Maintaining the DJIA   278
Maintaining the S&P500 Index   278
Conclusions About DJIA and S&P500   279

The One-Period Return for an Index   **279**

The Geometric Mean Return (GMR)   **281**
Different Investment Goals   *282*
Contrasting the Arithmetic Mean Return with the Geometric Mean Return   *283*

Computing Returns over Multiple Periods   **285**

The Consumers Price Index (CPI)   **287**

Purchasing Power Risk   **287**
Measuring Inflation   *287*
Nominal Returns Exceed Real Returns   *288*
A Handy Approximation   *288*
Empirical Research   *289*
Hyperinflation   *289*

CHAPTER 11   Selected Investment Indexes   295

Long-Term Returns for Major Asset Classes   **296**
Ibbotson's Seven Basic Indexes   *296*
Wealth Accumulation   *299*
Risk and Returns   *301*
Ten-Year Average Returns for the Basic U.S. Indexes   *302*

Analyzing Total Returns (TRs) from the Seven Basic Indexes   **303**
The Reinvestment Return Component of Total Returns   *303*
Bullish and Bearish Returns   *305*
Intertemporal Stability of Volatility   *306*
Cross Correlations Between the Investment
Indexes and Serial Correlations   *309*

Historical Risk Premia   **311**
Bond Horizon Premia   *313*
Bond Default Premia   *313*
Equity Risk Premia   *315*

Ibbotson's Historically Derived Inflation Premiums   **316**
Inflation-Adjusted Common Stock Returns   *316*
Inflation-Adjusted Long-Term Corporate Bond Returns   *317*
Inflation-Adjusted Government Bond Returns   *318*
Inflation-Adjusted U.S. Treasury Bill Returns   *318*

International Stock Market   **318**
The MSCI Indexes for Non-U.S. Stock Markets   *319*
Correlations Between Developed and Emerging Markets   *325*
Investing in Emerging Markets   *325*
Survivorship Bias   *327*

CHAPTER 12   Using Indexes   332

Investment Companies   **332**
Mutual Fund Investing   *333*
Characteristics of All Mutual Funds   *335*

The Economics of Portfolio Management   336

Mutual Fund Fees   336
Economies of Scale   339
The Management Fees of Index Funds   339
Portfolio Turnover   340
Mutual Funds That Fail   341

Two Other Types of Investment Companies Under U.S. Law   341

Advantages of Investing in Stock Market Index Portfolios   342

Disadvantages of Investing in Indexed Common Stock Portfolios   345

The Trade-off Between Transactions Costs and Tracking Errors   346

Exchange-Traded Funds (ETFs)   347

Differences Between SPDRs and Traditional S&P500 Index Funds   347
Advantages of SPDRs over Traditional S&P500 Index Funds   348
Cloning SPDRs   349

International Stock Market Index Funds   350

The Futures Contract on the S&P500 Index   351

Options on Stock Market Indexes   353
Bond Index Funds   359

Part 3 *PORTFOLIO THEORY*   **365**

CHAPTER 13   Asset Allocation   366

The Asset Allocation Process   367

Phase 1—Create a Written Policy Statement   368
Step 1—Gain Understanding   368
Step 2—Expectations   371
Step 3—The Policy Statement   372

Phase 2—Managing the Money   375
Step 4—Forecasting   375
Step 5—Allocating Assets   376
Step 6—Investing the Allocated Funds   379
Step 7—Performance Reports and Feedback   379

Using Indexes to Explain Investment Behavior   382
Analyzing Large Pensions   382
The Ibbotson-Kaplan Study   383

Appendix: Personal Taxes   390

CHAPTER 14   Portfolio Analysis   398

Simple Diversification   398

Diversifying Across Industries   400

Superfluous Diversification   401

An Introduction to Markowitz Diversification   402

Markowitz Concept One: The Weights Sum to One 403

Markowitz Concept Two: A Portfolio's Expected Return 403

Markowitz Concept Three: The Objective 404

Markowitz Concept Four: Portfolio Risk 404

Revisiting the Covariance and the Correlation Coefficient 406
Markowitz Portfolio Analysis with a Two-Asset Portfolio 406
Perfectly Positively Correlated Returns in Figure 14-2A 407
Uncorrelated Assets in Figure 14-2B 409
Perfectly Negatively Correlated Returns in Figure 14-2C 409
Portfolio Analysis Using Markowitz Diversification 409
Markowitz Portfolio Analysis with More Than Two Assets (N>2) 410
Financial Interior Decorating 410

Rethinking the First Markowitz Concept 410

Negative Weights Represent Short Sales 410
The Investment Opportunities Are Represented by Convex Curves 413
Selling Short Creates Valuable Investment Opportunities 414

Markowitz Concept Five: The Asset Allocation Line 415

Return and Risk Formulas That Are Linear 416
Borrowing and Lending Portfolios Pinpointed on the AAL 417
The Slope of the AAL Provides an Index of Investment Desirability 419
Combining the AAL with Markowitz's Efficient Frontier 420

Investor Preferences 421

An Introduction to Utility Theory 422
Indifference Curves in σ-E(r) Space 423
Making Investment Decisions 427

Appendix A: Derivation of Two-Asset Portfolio Risk Formulas 432

Appendix B: Mathematical Portfolio Analysis 433

Appendix C: Two Statistics Theorems 436

CHAPTER 15 CAPM and APT   437

Investment Opportunities in Risk-Return Space 437

Borrowing and Lending at a Risk-Free Rate of Interest 438
The Market Portfolio (M) 438
Separation Theorem 440

Capital Asset-Pricing Model (CAPM) 440

Assumptions Underlying Portfolio Theory 440
Assumptions Underlying the CML, SML, and CAPM 440

Rationale for the Security Market Line (SML) 441

Restating the SML 443
Overpriced and Underpriced Assets 444
Negative Correlation with the Market Portfolio, M 444
*The Discontinuity Between Expected
Value Theory and Historical Data* 445

Relaxing the CML and SML Assumptions   445
Different Risk-Free Interest Rates for Borrowing and Lending   445
Transaction Costs Create Friction   445
General Uncertainty or Heterogeneous Expectations   446
Different Tax Rates for Capital Gains   446
Indivisibilities   447
Conclusions About the Simplifying Assumptions   447

Criticism and Tests of the SML   447
The Liquidity of the Investments   447
Econometric Analysis of Empirical Data   447
Econometric Problems with the Characteristic Line   448

Arbitrage Pricing Theory (APT)   450
Two Equally Risky Streams of Cash Flows   450
The Arbitrage Pricing Theory Line   453
Overpriced and Underpriced Assets   453
An Arbitrage Portfolio   455
The Formal Definition of an Arbitrage Opportunity   456
Implications of the APT   456

A Two-Factor APT Model   456
Three Highly Diversified Portfolios   457
The APT Model   458
The Arbitrage Portfolio   458
The k-Dimensional APT Hyperplane   461

Comparing APT with the SML   462
The SML Is Equivalent to the One-Factor APT Model   462
APT Employs Fewer Assumptions Than SML   462

Empirical Tests of the APT   463
First-Pass Times-Series Regressions   463
Second-Pass Cross-Sectional Regression   463
Priced Risk Factors   464
An Empirical Study by Roll and Ross   464
Four Factors Are Identified   464
Chen's Empirical Tests   465

Appendix: Mathematical APT 474

CHAPTER 16   Investment Performance Evaluation   475

Mutual Fund Data   476
The Investment Goals of Mutual Funds   477
Closed-End Funds Are Different   477

Mutual Funds Performance   477
Are Mutual Funds Markowitz Efficient Investments?   478
Scrutinizing Mutual Funds' Goal Statements   478

Analyzing a Portfolio Manager's Style   480
*Using Factor Analysis to Attribute
Mutual Funds' Asset Allocations   480*

Rolling Style Analysis 481
Benefits from Using Quantitative Management Style Analysis 481

Two Hypothetical Mutual Funds 482

SHARPE's Portfolio Performance Measure 482

Creating Investment Opportunities 484

TREYNOR's Performance Measure 485

An Investment's Alpha 488

Explanation of an Investment's Alpha 489
Caveats About Alphas 490

Performance Statistics from Mutual Funds 491

Analyzing Performance Statistics 491
Which Mutual Fund Is Best? … Worst? 495
General Discussion of the Performance Measurement Tools 495

Evaluating Timing Decisions 496

Do Winners Repeat? 497

Part 4 *INTERNATIONAL INVESTING*   **507**

CHAPTER 17   Foreign Exchange   508

Common Markets and Economic Unions 509

Foreign Exchange Rate Fluctuations 510
Economic Unions 510
The European Monetary Union (EMU) 510

The Fundamental Elements of a Foreign Exchange Transaction 512

Spot and Forward Markets 512
Components of Investor's Total Return 516
Risks Undertaken by International Investors 516

Three Foreign Exchange Parity Relationships 519

Relative Purchasing Power Parity (PPP) 519
Irving Fisher's Two Inflation-Based Theories 522
Interest-Rate Parity 523
Simplified Summary of Equilibrium Condition 525

CHAPTER 18   Global Investing   530

International Risks 530

Sovereign Risk 530
International Liquidity Risk 531
International Information Risk 534
Foreign Exchange Risk 534

Simple International Diversification 536

Portfolio Analysis of Two-Country Diversification 537

International Efficient Frontiers 540

Correlation Coefficients Between Different Countries 542

The Behavior of Correlations Between Nations' Financial Markets 542
Fundamental Reasons for Low Intercountry Correlations 543

**Do Multinational Corporations (MNCs)
Provide International Diversification? 544**

Depository Receipts 545

American Depository Receipts (ADRs) 545
Global Depository Receipts (GDRs) 547

International Investment Companies 548

Categories of International Investment Companies 548
International Index Funds 548
Homemade International Diversification 549

International Asset-Pricing Models 549

The International Security Market Line (ISML) 549
International Arbitrage Pricing Theory (IAPT) 550

Part 5 *FIXED-INCOME INVESTMENTS*   **559**

CHAPTER 19 Global Bond Markets   560

A Brief Tour of the Global Bond Market 561

The U.S. Bond Market 563

U.S. Government Agency Bonds 564
Corporate Bonds in the United States 564
Bond Markets in the United States 565

Sectors of the Industrialized World's Bond Markets 567

International Bonds 568

Foreign Bonds 569

The Eurobond Market 569

The Primary and Secondary Markets for Eurobonds 570
Bearer Bonds Versus Registered Bonds 571
Eurodollar Bonds 572

Accrued Interest 573

Dirty Bond Prices Experience an Ex-Coupon Price Drop-off 573
Day-Counting Conventions 574
Compounding Conventions 574

The Yield-to-Maturity (YTM): A First Look 575

The Compounded Yield-to-Maturity (YTM) 576
Comparing Various YTMs for a Bond 577
*Conditions Required for an Investor to Earn a Bond's
Expected YTM 578*
The Reinvestment Rate Effects a Bond's Realized YTM 579

**Relationships Among a Bond's YTM, Its Price,
and Its Other Return Measures 579**

A Bond's Holding Period Return   579
The Inverse Relationship Between a Bond's Price and Its YTM   580
Other Measures of Bonds' Yields   580

Brady Bonds Aid Emerging Countries   584

International Bond Index Statistics   585
The Components of International Bond Returns   586
Correlations Between International Bond Returns   587
Markowitz Analysis of International Bond Portfolios   588

Managing International Bond Investments Actively   589

CHAPTER 20   Market Interest Rates   595

The Level of Market Interest Rates   596
Irving Fisher's Theory About the Level of Interest Rates   596
Realized Real Returns (rrr)   599
Conclusions About Prices and Interest Rates   600
Other Factors Influence Market Interest Rates   601

Yield Spreads   604
Measuring Yield Spreads   604
Yield Spreads Open and Close with the Business Cycle   605

The Term Structure of Interest Rates (The Yield Curve)   606

Three Theories About Yield Curves   608
Horizon Premium Theory   608
The Market Segmentation Theory   610
The Expectations Theory   610
Arbitrage Maintains the Expectations Model   613

Appendix: Alternative Formulations of the Yield Curve   621

CHAPTER 21   Horizon Risk and Interest Rate Risk   626

The Present Value of a Bond   626

Coupon and Horizon Effects   627
Par Versus Price   627
Convexity in the Price-Yield Relationship   631
The Coupon Effect   632
The Horizon Effect   632

Hedging Fixed-Income Instruments   634
Reinvestment Risk   635
Hedging Bond Price Fluctuation Risk   636
Derivation of Formula for Macaulay's Duration (MAC)   638

Macaulay Duration (MAC)   640
Contrasting Time Until Maturity and Duration   640
MACLIM Defines a Boundary for Macaulay Duration   641
*Duration Provides a Linear Approximation to the
Curvilinear Price-Yield Relationship   643*

Interest Rate Risk   644

Problems with Duration   646
Duration Wandering and Portfolio Rebalancing   646
Changes in the Term Structure of Interest Rates   647
Alternative Duration Measures   647

Horizon Analysis   649

CHAPTER 22   Credit Risk   656

Corporate Bankruptcy   656
U.S. Bankruptcy Law Specifies a Procedure and a Priority of Claims   657
Boston Chicken on the Precipice of Bankruptcy in 1998–99   659

Securities Quality Ratings   659
Definitions of Quality Ratings   661
Average Returns Vary with Quality Ratings   662
Junk Bond Investing   663
Using MDA to Discriminate Between Bankruptcy Candidates   665

Financial Ratios Help Determine Bond Quality Ratings   667
Coverage Ratios   668
Cash Flow Ratios   668
Profitability Ratios   669
Financial-Leverage Ratios   670

The Economic Significance and Size of the Issuer   670
The Issuer's Industry   670
The Issuer's Competitors   671

Protective Provisions in a Corporation's Indenture   671
Collateral Provisions   672
Subordination Provisions   672
Sinking-Fund Provisions   672
Other Protective Provisions   673
Other Protective Devices   674

Credit Risk and Quality Rating Changes   674

Analysis of Rating Migration Risk   676
A BBB-Grade Bond's Variance in Value   676
Credit Derivatives Usually Have Skewed Probability Distributions   678
Analyzing a Portfolio of Credit Derivatives   678

Part 6 *EQUITY SHARES*   687

CHAPTER 23   Equity Valuation—A Micro View   688

Dividends and Dividend-Discount Models (DDMs)   688
Payment Models for Cash Dividends Per Share   688
The Present Value of a Stream of Constant Cash Dividends   689
Model-Building Assumptions   690
The Present Value of a Stock for Finite Holding Periods   691
The Two-Stages-of-Growth DDM   693
A Common Criticism of the DDM   695

Forecasting   696
Structural Changes in the Payment of Cash Dividends   696

Restating a Share's Present Value in Terms of Its Earnings   698
Modeling the Relationship Between Earnings and Dividends   698
The Reformulated Present Value Model   699
Dividend Policy Is Irrelevant for Most Firms   699
Dividend Policy Affects the Values of Growth Firms and Declining Firms   700

The Price-Earnings Ratio   702
Fluctuations in Stock Prices, Earnings,
and the Price-Earnings (P/EPS) Ratios   703
Analyzing the Price-Earnings (P/EPS) Ratio   705
Price-Earnings (P/EPS) Ratios of Stocks That Pay No Cash Dividends   707
The (k-g) Spread   709

Financial Analysis Through Time   710

Analysis of Growth Investing   710

CHAPTER 24   Measuring Earning Power   719

The Information Content of Cash Dividends   719
Asymmetric Information   720
Reactions to Cash Dividend Payments   720

Forecasting Earnings Per Share   721
Surveys of Forecasts   721
How Expert Are the Experts?   721
Whisper Earnings   722

Surprising Changes in Earnings Affect Stock Prices   722
The Foster-Olsen-Shevlin (FOS) Event Study   723
Interpreting the Results   725

Ambiguities in Accounting Earnings   725
Contrasting Two Income Statements for
the Same Firm in the Same Year   726
The Quality of Earnings   731

Cash Flows   733
Cash Flow from Operations   733
A Firm's Statement of Cash Flows   733
Cash Flows Available to Equity Shareholders   735
The Difference Between Cash Flows Available
to Equity Shareholders and Economic Income   736
Problems with Cash Dividends   736

CHAPTER 25   Stock Valuation Issues   743

The Impact of Inflation on Equity Prices   744
What Stock Market Data Tells Us About Inflation   744
Other Empirical Observations About Inflation   745
Two Yardsticks for Timing the Stock Market   745
The S&P500 Cash Dividend Yield   747

The S&P500 Price-Earnings Ratio 747
Assessing the Buy-Sell Guidelines 748
Problems with the Buy-Sell Guidelines 749

Investment Implications of the Baby Boom 750

The Life-Cycle Theory of Savings 750
Zhiwu Chen's 1990 Forecast 751

Investment Implications of Common Stock Buybacks 752

Increasing Labor Productivity and What It Implies for Investment 752

Industry Analysis 754
The Product Life-Cycle Model 754
Financial Analysis of an Industry 756

The Internet Stocks' Bubble 756

Clicks Versus Bricks 757
Winner-Take-All 759
The Power Law 760
Slippery Slopes Around the Winner's Peak 761
Price-Earnings Ratios for Internet Stocks 762

Valuing Common Stock as a Call Option 762

The Springdale Corporation: A Hypothetical Valuation Case 764
Option Theory and the Prices of Corporate Securities 765

The Price/Book Value Ratio 769

Analysis of the PBV Ratio 770
Over-and Underpriced Stocks 770
Tobin's q Ratio 771

CHAPTER 26   Technical Analysis   777

Theoretical Foundation of Technical Analysis 778

The Dow Theory 779
What Is the Dow Theory? 779
Testing the Dow Theory 780

Bar Charts 781
A Head-and-Shoulders Top Pattern Within a Bar Chart 781
Other Patterns 781

Charting the Volume of Shares Traded 782
Support and Resistance Levels 784
Congestion Areas 785
Selling Climaxes and Speculative Blowoffs 786
The Confidence Index 786

Moving Average Analysis 787
Construction of a Moving-Average Chart 787
Interpreting Charts with a Moving Average 787
Empirical Tests of Moving-Average Rules and Congestion Areas 789

Behavioral Finance 789

Part 7 DERIVATIVES AND ALTERNATIVE INVESTMENTS   **797**

CHAPTER 27   Futures   798

Mechanics of Commodities Trading   799
In the Pits   799
The Commodity Board   800
Price Fluctuation Limits   800
Clearing House Guarantees   801
The Mechanics of Trading Commodity Futures   801
Open Interest   803
Electronic Markets   803

Regulating Futures   804

Prices and Pricing Relationships   805
Price Convergence   805
*The Relationship Between Spot and Futures Prices for Storable
Commodities   808*
The One-Period Returns from Futures   809
Margin Requirements   809
Marking to the Market Daily with Cash and/or T-Bills   810

Hedging   810
The Perfect Hedge   810
Buying Hedges   810
Selling Hedge   811
Basis Risks   811
Spreading with Futures   812
The Economic Effects of Hedging and Spreading   812

Theories About Spot and Futures Price Converge   812

Universal Pricing Principle for Forwards and Futures   813
The PV of Forwards and Futures   814
Financial Futures   815

Pricing Futures Contracts on U.S. Treasury Bills   815
A T-Bill Example   816
Economic Forces That Align Prices   817
The Cost of Marking to the Market on T-Bill Futures   818
Using a Carrying-Cost Model to Price T-Bill Futures   818

Pricing a Futures Contract on a Stock Market Index   820
Index Arbitrage   820
Pricing Futures on a Stock Market Index   823
Using Futures Can Yield Substantial Savings in Commissions   824

Appendix: Futures Options   830

CHAPTER 28   Options   835

Introduction to Binomial Option Pricing   836
The One-Period Binomial Call-Pricing Formula   836
A Multiperiod Binomial Call-Pricing Formula   838

The Black-Scholes Call-Option-Pricing Model   840
The Black-Scholes Call-Valuation Formula   840
The Hedge Ratio   843
Risk Statistics and Option Values   845

The Put-Call Parity Formula   845
Pricing Put Options   847
Checking Alignment of Put and Call Prices on an Underlying Stock   848

The Effects of Cash Dividend Payments   848

Options Markets   851

Synthetic Positions Can Be Created from Options   851
The Synthetic Long Position   851
The Synthetic Short Position   853
Other Synthetic Positions   854

Writing Covered Calls   855

Straddles   856

Spreads   858
Spreading Vocabulary   858
Strangles   858
Bull Spread   860
Bear Spreads   861
Butterfly Spreads   861

CHAPTER 29   Alternative Investments   867

Real Estate   867
Returns form Real Estate Investments   868
Conclusions About Real Estate   871
Real Estate on the Internet   872

Hedge Funds   872
The Hedge Fund Industry   873
The Performance of Hedge Funds   874
Hedge Funds on the Internet   878

Gold Bullion and Physical Silver   879

APPENDIX: PRESENT VALUE TABLES   A-1
GLOSSARY   G-1
INDEX   I-1

PREFACE

This book is co-authored by two finance professors who both teach either introductory investments, advanced investments, global investments, asset allocation, securities analysis, portfolio analysis, or a derivatives course every semester. We have experience teaching undergraduate courses, M.B.A. courses, Ph.D. courses, seminars for money managers, and speaking to investor groups. This experience was gained in the U.S. and other countries. Our thinking has also been shaped by consulting work and knowledge we gained while working as expert witnesses. This book evolved from these experiences. We also collaborated extensively and passed the manuscript back and forth many times.

The book is designed to be used in an undergraduate or M.B.A investments course. The chapters needed for an introductory course can be covered in one semester. Or, the entire book can be used for a two-term course. We grouped the chapters into homogeneous sections to give instructors the flexibility to choose and sequence chapters to accommodate their needs. Advanced courses can focus primarily on the chapters in the back half of the book. The Instructors Manual contains suggested course outlines for: (1) an introductory course; (2) a two-semester sequence; (3) a security analysis course; and (4) a portfolio analysis course.

A finance professor at Yale, Roger Ibbotson is also the CEO of an investment consulting firm named Ibbotson Associates employing 150 people at offices in Chicago and New York City. For over two decades, Ibbotson Associates has developed investment databases and software that is sold to investment professionals around the world. These products use market data to perform exercises discussed in this book. Samples of this "industrial strength" software that compute regression lines and work out Markowitz efficient frontiers are available on a CD-ROM accompanying this book.

UNIQUE THRUSTS

This book reflects four views that differentiate it from other investments textbooks.

- First, we think there is one securities market—a global market. Focusing on a single securities market overlooks important opportunities. Chapter 6, "The Global Stock Market," Chapter 17, "Foreign Exchange," Chapter 18, "Global Investing," and, Chapter 19, "The Global Bond Market," explore multi-national material not found in similar books.

- Second, price indexes play an important role in our book. Chapter 10, "Creating Price Indexes," and Chapter 11, "Selected Investment Indexes," define price indexes in more depth than other finance books. Chapter 12, "Using Indexes," shows how price indexes provide the basis for some of the world's largest mutual funds, most popular options, and most popular futures contracts. Chapter 13, "Asset Allocation," explains a portfolio theory based on price indexes.

- Third, technology is reshaping investing. For instance, Electronic Communications Networks (ECNs) are changing the way securities markets around the world operate. Chapter 6 delves into these and similar developments more deeply than other books.

- Fourth, computers are a powerful tool that is increasingly available to investors. Prentice-Hall helps us demonstrate this point by providing a Web site to accompany this book. The CD-ROM from Ibbotson Associates is a supplement from the business sector. And, Professor Holden's Excel spreadsheets are professional quality tools. Without cluttering the book with "computerese," at various points throughout the book we highlight projects an investor might wish to pursue with these computer tools.

SUPPLEMENTS

We worked with Prentice-Hall to assemble a package of ancillary materials. Instructors should contact their local Prentice-Hall sales representative to request the following:

- **Ibbotson Associates** sells an elaborate database containing statistical and graphical software. The software data has been condensed into a **CD-ROM** that enhances the book with real-world applications. This software that been used by investments professionals for decades.

- The **Instructor's Solutions Manual** was written by Marianne Plunkert, University of Colorado. This ancillary includes chapter outlines, end of chapter solutions and CFA exam questions.

- Marianne Plunkert has also compiled a **Test Bank** of multiple choice and short answer questions. These questions have been shared from our own examinations, as well as the Association for Investment Management and Research (AIMR) exams.

- The **Prentice-Hall Custom Test Manager** is the computerized version of the test bank. This Windows-based program allows instructors to create their own exam questions, evaluate and track student results.

- The **Prentice-Hall Learning on the Internet Partnership (PHLIP)** is a text-specific Web site for this title. The PHLIP site contains investment information, solved exercises, current events, downloadable learning aids, and more.

- Our **Companion Web Site (CW)** offers an **On-line Study Guide,** plus other downloadable supplements for both instructors and students. The On-line Study Guide, created by David Cleeton, Oberlin College, offers a variety of testing modules: Multiple Choice, True/False Questions and Essays, plus Chapter Objectives.

- **Lecture Presentations,** prepared by Pamela Hall, Western Washington University, outlines chapters, highlights examples, and reproduces important text graphs and tables in **PowerPoint.** Available to download from our Companion Web site.

- **Spreadsheet Modeling in Investments to accompany *INVESTMENTS* by Francis/Ibbotson** is a book and browser accessed CD-ROM. Craig Holden, Indiana University, has developed a tool that teaches students how to build financial models, not just templates, in Excel. Spreadsheet Modeling exercises are called attention to by icons throughout our text.

ACKNOWLEDGMENTS

The authors are grateful to many people for their gracious assistance. The folks listed below contributed graphs, tables, data, computer programs, examples, end-of-chapter questions, end-of-chapter problems, valuable criticism, helpful suggestions, and inspiration that contributed materially to this book.

Mr. Tsien-Shien Tu of Dolphin Management in NYC, Prof. Francis's ex-student

Mr. Chia-Hung Cheng, Prof. Francis's ex-research assistant and, now, a financial analyst

Mr. Cheng-Chieh Chang, Prof. Francis's research assistant

Professor Sheng-Yung Yang, Ph.D., an ex-student of Prof. Francis

Mr. Andrew F. Winning, Vice President at MLPF&S, an ex-student of Prof. Francis

Prof. Hans R. Stoll of Vanderbilt University in Nashville, TN

Mr. James Lam, Director, Enterprise Risk Solutions, at Oliver, Wyman & Co. in NYC

Mr. Robert DiClemente, Managing Director at Salomon Brothers in NYC

Mr. Laurence J. Price, VP at Salomon Brothers in NYC, Prof. Francis's ex-student

Mr. Eric H. Sorensen, Ph.D., Managing Director at Salomon Brothers in NYC

Mr. Joseph J. Mezrish, Ph.D., VP at Salomon Brothers in NYC who moved to Morgan-Stanley in 1998

Ms. "Emily" Jing Jia at Salomon Brothers in NYC

Mr. Joseph Kosinsky at Baruch College

Mr. David Smith, Vice President, Bayerische Landesbank, NYC

Professor Terrence Martell of Baruch College

Professor Gayle DeLong of Baruch College

Mr. Gary Gastineau at John Nuveen & Company in NYC

Yogesh V. Borkar at ValueQuest/TA LLC in Marblehead, MA

Professor Richard W. Taylor, Ph.D., CFA, from Arkansas State University

Mr. Ian McKenney at Ibbotson Associates in Chicago

Mr. Leo Brand, Associate Director, Standard & Poor's, New York City

Ms. Sachiko Matsuo at Nikko Securities Co. International Inc. in NYC

Mr. Xiaoyin Li, Vice President at Nikko Securities Co. International Inc. in NYC

Professor Ralph Lim at Sacred Heart Univ

Susan Mangiero, Ph.D., at General Electric

Professor Lawrence Harris from Univ. of Southern California

Russell Gregory-Allen, Ph.D., of TIAA-CREF in NYC

Prof. Miles Livingston from University of Florida in Gainesville

George Sofianos, Managing Director, NYSE

Professor Robert Neal at Indiana University

Professor Catherine Bonser-Neal at Indiana University

Professor Peter Ritchken, Case Western Reserve University, Cleveland, Ohio

Mr. John C. Braddock, Director of Private Client Relations, CIBC Oppenheimer, NYC

Nick Barcia, Ph.D., Head of Risk Solutions, FAME Information Services, NYC. Francis's ex-student

Douglas S. Rolph, Federal Reserve Bank, Kansas City

Professor J. Gregg Whittaker, Ph.D., William Jewell College in Missouri

Aidan McNulty, VP at Morgan Guaranty Bank, NYC

Prof. Dongcheol Kim, Rutgers University in New Jersey

Peter J. Klein, First Vice President, Paine Webber in New York, Prof. Francis's ex-student

Robert B. Greenwald, Vice President, Smith Barney in New York, Prof. Francis's ex-student

Douglas A. Carucci, Director of Research, Credit Suisse First Boston in NYC, Prof. Francis's ex-student

Professor Kishore Tandon, Baruch College, NYC

Professor Linda Allen, Baruch College, NYC

Terrence Burns, Vice President, Assoc. for Investment Management and Research (AIMR), Charlottesville, VA

Laurie Goodman, Ph.D., Senior Vice President, Paine Webber, NYC

Les Gulko, Ph.D., Poloma Partners, Greenwich, CT, Prof. Ibbotson's ex-student

Professor Robert T. Daigler, Department of Finance, Florida International University, in Miami

Daniel Staehle, CPA, CFA, Capital Markets Examiner, Office of Comptroller of Currency

Mark Wimer, Ibbotson Associates, Chicago

Mark Thorpe, Vice President, Ibbotson Associates, Chicago

Dominic Falaschetti, Ibbotson Associates, Chicago

Clay Singleton, Ph.D., Vice President, Ibbotson Associates, Chicago

Professor Craig W. Holden, Finance Department, Indiana University–Bloomington, Indiana

Timothy Falcon Crack, Ph.D., London

Harry Markowitz, Nobel laureate, our friend, and a continual inspiration

We didn't write this book alone. We are indebted to these gracious people.

OUR PUBLISHER

Prentice-Hall is a multi-faceted organization that executed several key roles adroitly. Paul Donnelly was the acquisitions editor who authorized the publishing contract for this project. Paul and Mike Elia, our development editor, got this project started. They also coached us along the way and kept the project moving ahead. Mickey Cox replaced Paul Donnelly as acquisitions editor and "carried the ball" to the completion of the project. Melanie Olsen, editorial assistant; Gladys Soto, managing editor; and, Josh McClary, marketing manager, performed a diverse list of essential tasks. Much of what Melanie, Gladys, and Josh did was essential "behind-the-scenes work" and we admire the results they produced. After the manuscript was finished, Carol Samet, project manager, took charge of the production process. Carol supervised Pre-Press Company in East Bridgewater, Massachusetts, and other individuals. Carol and the staff at Pre-Press labored punctiliously to smooth out more authors' errors than we care to discuss. P.J. Boardman was editor-in-chief throughout the development of the entire book. It was a pleasure to work with this highly capable publishing team.

Jack Clark Francis
Stamford, Connecticut

Roger Ibbotson
New Haven, Connecticut

PART 1

INTRODUCTION

THE INVESTMENT SETTING

Millions of nonprofessional investors "play the market." These investors typically manage their own small portfolio, most work to increase their wealth, but some invest just for fun. In contrast to the millions of non-professional investors, a few thousand professional money managers earn their livelihoods by charging fees to manage other people's money. The professional money managers work actively at managing one or more multimillion- or multibillion-dollar portfolios. Most professionals specialize in a certain class of assets, such as common stocks, corporate bonds, government bonds, futures contracts, options, foreign exchange, commodities, etc. This book addresses the interests of all these investors. Virtually any investor that would rather have more money than less money can gain insight from this book.

This introductory chapter defines investments and reviews types of investment activities that are essential components of the chapters that follow. Table 1-1 provides an overview of the categories of assets covered in this book. Before discussing Table 1-1, however, let us consider what an investment is.

WHAT IS INVESTING?

Suppose a person commits a certain amount of money today with the expectation that it will return some larger amount in the future. This economic venture could be a gamble. It could be a speculation. It might also be an investment. Tax law, contract law, and codes of ethics require us to define investing with care.

The length of the **holding period,** the time between signing a purchase order and selling the item, helps us determine whether something is an investment or something else masquerading as an investment asset. Whether an investment of money is short-term or long-term and whether it is productive or unproductive, whether it is legal or illegal, and whether it is a rational or irrational activity are all criteria useful in separating investing from other economic activities that are sometimes confused with investing.

Gambling

Gambling differs from speculating and investing in fundamental respects. First, a gamble is over more quickly than a speculation or an investment. A roll of the dice or the turn of a card quickly determines the outcome of a gamble. Second, law-abiding people and rational people gamble for entertainment, not as a source of income. Third, gambling is not a bet on an economic endeavor: Gambling creates risk *artificially,* via the rules of the game. Fourth, gambling creates risk without providing any commensurate expectation of economic benefit. Honest gamblers cannot expect a high rate of return to compensate them for exposing themselves to risk. Dishonest games and legal state lotteries are designed to profit at the expense of honest gamblers. Gambling is discussed here in the same context as investing to *clarify* these differences, not to imply similarity.

Speculation

Speculations typically last longer than gambles but have briefer holding periods than investments. A speculation usually involves purchasing a salable asset with the hope that its price will increase rapidly, providing a quick profit. Speculators try to buy low and sell high. Contrary to the folklore, profitable speculators smooth price fluctuations as they make purchases at the low prices and sell at the high prices. An unprofitable speculator can destabilize market prices as he or she buys at a high price and sells at a lower price, but if such inept transactions occur often they will bankrupt the speculator. If a speculator is to survive, she or he must usually execute profitable trades (buy low and sell high) and thus stabilize the swings in market prices.

EXAMPLE   SPECULATING ON COMMON STOCK IPOS

Buying an **initial public offering (IPO)** of common stock on the day it first goes public in hopes of selling the shares a day or two later at a higher price is a popular speculation. Over a sample of 1,526 IPOs, Jay Ritter reports the average speculators' return was 14.3% during the first day after a common stock has an IPO. However, Figure 1-1 shows that 3-year investments in the same stocks did not fare so well.

Figure 1-1 illustrates five series of cumulative average returns (CARs)—from five portfolios that contain the same 1,526 stocks—over the 36 months following the IPOs. The portfolio of raw returns erroneously suggests the IPOs are good speculations and good investments. Note what happens after some appropriate adjustments were made to their returns.

Adjusted returns were computed by deducting the stock returns from matching corporations to determine if the IPOs really performed better than their counterparts.

$$\begin{pmatrix} \text{Adjusted return for} \\ \text{stock } i \text{ in month } t \end{pmatrix} = \begin{pmatrix} \text{Raw return from} \\ \text{stock } i \text{ in month } t \end{pmatrix} - \begin{pmatrix} \text{Simultaneous return from a} \\ \text{matching corporation's stock} \end{pmatrix}$$

The matching firms are exchange-listed stocks that match each IPO, to some extent, by industry and market capitalization. Figure 1-1 shows that although all five portfolios were on average good 1-day speculations immediately after their IPOs, after adjustments were made to the raw returns, the four adjusted portfolios appear to be poor investments. Further examination of the *individual stocks* reveals they all did not earn 14.3% on the first day after their IPO. Some IPOs earned much more than 14.3%, and some suffered large first-day losses. Ritter's study shows us: first, that it is important to distinguish between speculating and investing; second, that it is worthwhile to do good financial analysis; and, third, that IPOs are risky speculations and risky investments.

FIGURE 1-1 Cumulative Average Returns (CARs) from 1,526 Firms over the 3 Years Following Their IPOs

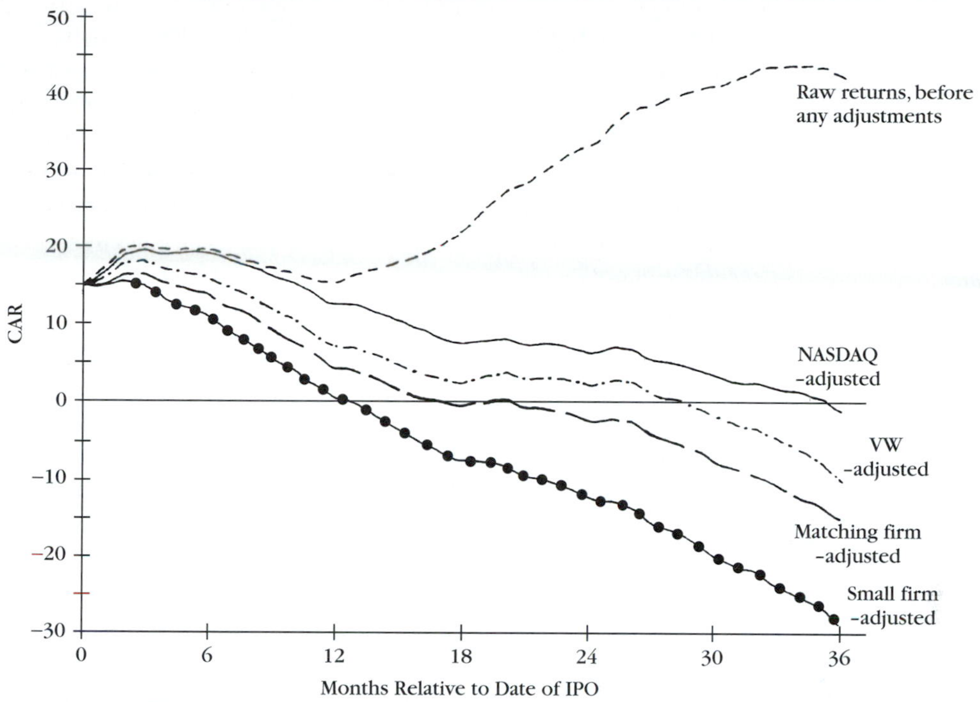

On average, all five portfolios were profitable 1-day speculations. After adjusting the portfolios' raw returns to facilitate more meaningful comparisons, the adjusted NASDAQ, value weighted (VW), matching firm, and small firm portfolios of IPO stocks were not good investments.

SOURCE: Ritter, Jay R. "The Long-Run Performance of Initial Public Offerings," *Journal of Finance,* 46, no. 1 (March 1991): 3–27, Fig. 1.

Investing

The U.S. Treasury defines an *investment* to be a market asset that has a holding period longer than 1 year.* Devising a rigid rule like this is fraught with problems. For instance, would you consider the sale of a U.S. Treasury bill that was originally issued with a maturity of 3 months to be a speculative transaction? Of course not. To differentiate between gambling, speculating, and investing, it is sometimes more logical to consider the investor's original intention than to measure the investor's holding period. Furthermore, what is initially undertaken as a short-term speculation can turn into a long-run investment as additional information becomes available.

---

* The Internal Revenue Service (IRS) is the branch of the U.S. Treasury that collects income taxes. The IRS arbitrarily defines price appreciation gains from investments that last longer than 1 year to be long-term gains that are taxable at a lower income tax rate than the ordinary income from wages and salaries. The preferential **long-term capital gains tax rate** appears to have grown out of the belief that speculation is harmful to the society's welfare. The idea is that the higher tax rate on shorter-term investments is appropriate to discourage speculation. Later chapters show how society benefits from the behavior of speculators.

TABLE 1-1	Some Major Asset Classes Discussed in the Chapters That Follow	
Local Investment	**Multinational Investment**	**Examples**
	Primary Securities	
Domestic stock	International stock	Common stock, preferred stock
Domestic bonds	International bonds	Government bonds, corporate bonds
Domestic money market securities	International money market securities	Treasury bills, commercial paper, bankers' acceptances
	Derived Instruments	
Domestic portfolios	International portfolios	Mutual funds, closed-end funds, hedge funds
Domestic options	International options	Put and call options
Domestic futures	International futures	Forward contracts, futures contracts
Domestic currency	International currencies	Foreign exchange
	Physical Assets	
Domestic real estate	International real estate	Homes, buildings, farm land
Domestic collectibles	International collectibles	Paintings, stamps, coins
Domestic precious metals	International precious metals	Gold and silver

THE ASSETS OF CHOICE

This is a comprehensive book that explores many different equity securities, debt securities, mutual funds, contingent claims, and physical assets. Table 1-1 enumerates some major **asset classes** we will discuss.

Each asset of choice is explained, measures of profit and loss are defined, measures of risk are reviewed, historical performance statistics are presented, and portfolios and derivative instruments that can be formed from the underlying primary assets are analyzed. This book's examples and statistics will become out-of-date, but the economics is timeless.

Table 1-1 lists several international investments.

THE GLOBAL MARKET

Large multinational companies like DaimlerChrysler and Sony have their securities traded on several markets outside the United States and on several different markets within the United States. Telecommunications are blurring the lines between countries and helping to create a global securities market. Securities issued by large international corporations are traded 24 hours a day someplace in the world.

Where the People Are

Figure 1-2 is an unusual-looking map of the world that represents the principal countries in proportion to their populations. China and India dominate this map because they have the largest populations. Population and world influence have been closely related throughout history. The world population map shows why China, despite its poverty, is perceived as a global power.

There is much empty space in the world. The empty space is disproportionately contained in rich countries like Australia, Canada, and the United States. This does not mean spaciousness creates wealth. Crowded countries like Japan and the United Kingdom are also wealthy. Great accumulations of wealth and power may be found also in crowded cities like New York, London, and Tokyo. The opportunities to make money and exchange ideas in large

FIGURE 1-2 World Population Map

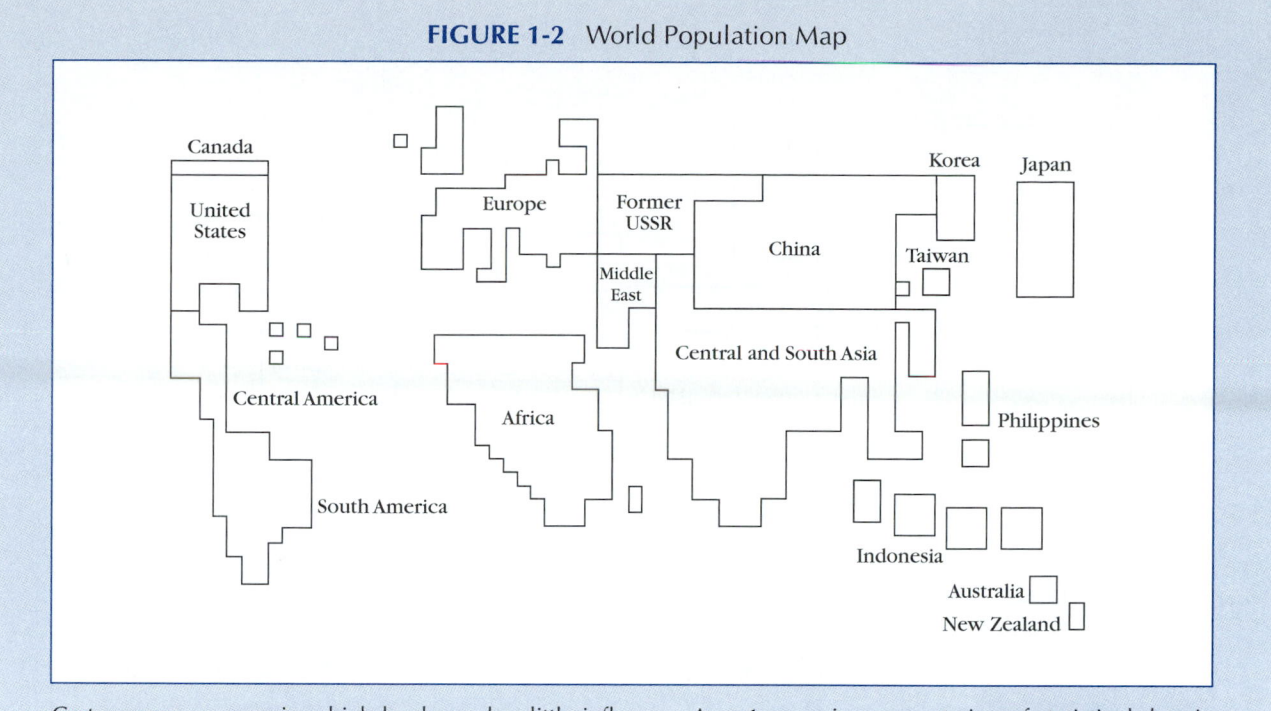

Cartograms are maps in which land area has little influence. A **cartogram** is a presentation of statistical data in geographic distribution on a map. Each country's size in the map is proportional to its population.

cities attracts all kinds of people, poor people among them. Cities do not create poverty, however; they provide opportunities. Population centers enable human skills to be matched to economic needs efficiently.

Where the Income Is

Figure 1-3 is another unusual map—a world income map. Each country is drawn in proportion to its gross national product (GNP), a measure of a nation's income. High-income areas like Europe are larger than Africa, even though Africa is a more populous area and has a larger land area than Europe. Small geographic areas that have advanced economies, like Taiwan and Hong Kong, are larger than poverty-stricken countries of greater physical size. The large sizes of the United States, Europe, and Japan in Figure 1-3 reflect the large national incomes of these industrialized nations.

Figures 1-2 and 1-3 do not tell us how well the people are faring. The per capita gross domestic product (GDP) data in Table 1-2 make a consistent comparison of the incomes of average individuals in different nations. GDP and GNP are very similar measures of a nation's income.

As a measure of a person's welfare, per capita GNP has shortcomings. First, per capita GNP does not consider each country's cost of living. Table 1-2 shows that Luxembourg, Japan, Switzerland, and the Scandinavian countries have the highest GNPs per capita, but these are expensive places to live. After making adjustments for each country's cost of living to create purchasing power parity (PPP) between the countries, the United States turns out to be a better place for the average person to live than most of the countries in Table 1-2 that have higher per capita GNPs. Second, a nation's average per capita GNP ignores income inequalities within nations. Hungary and Mexico are examples of countries that have similar

FIGURE 1-3 World Income Map

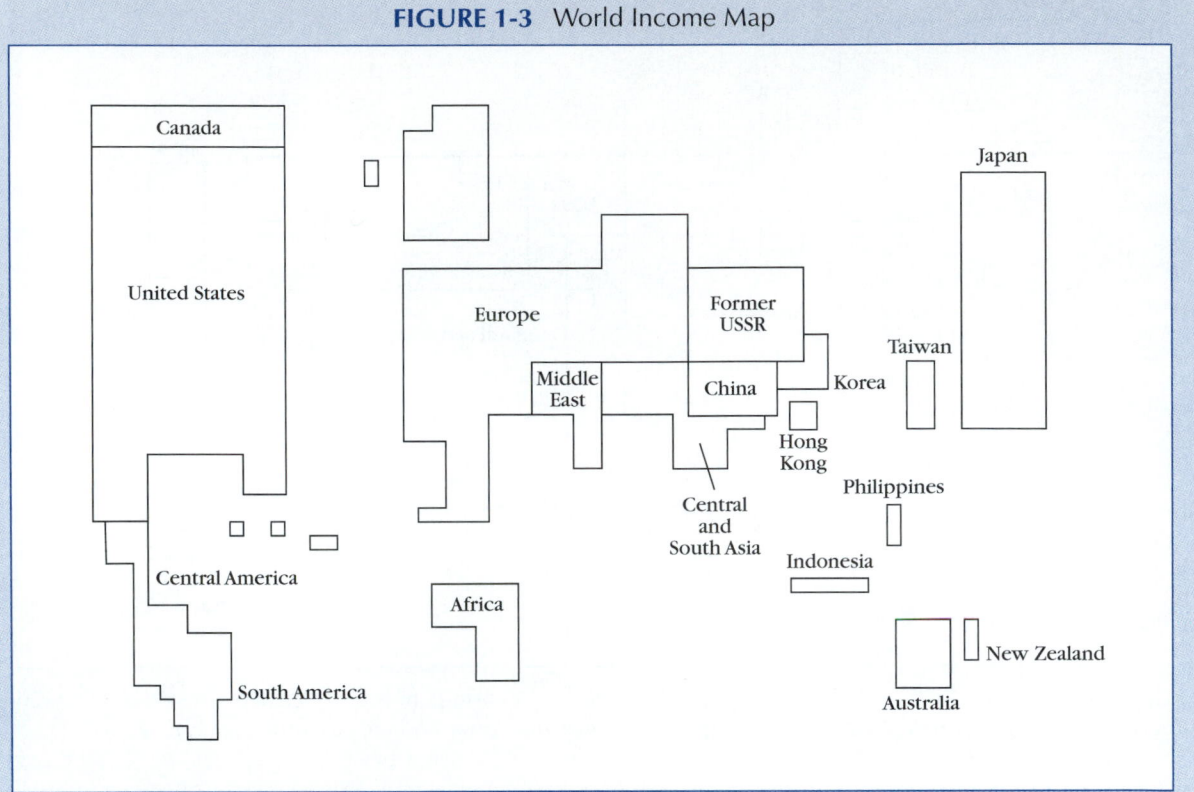

Geographic areas are not reflected in this cartogram. Each country's size in the map is porportional to its national income, as measured by its Gross Domestic Product (GDP).

GNPs per capita. However, Mexico is a place where both abject misery and sudden fortune are found. In contrast, Hungary does not have much of either. Third, every country has regions that are rich and regions that are poor.

Even if it is measured accurately, a person's income is not a perfect wealth indicator. A true measure of wealth should reflect the extent to which the individual has the ability to enjoy living. Climate, natural beauty, cultural amenities, personal health, and personal freedom are determinants of a person's wealth and well-being, but they are not included in GDP measurements. These qualities are hard to measure and comparable data are unavailable. Of the many components of wealth, money amounts are the most readily measurable, most widely available, and most comparable. As a result, in this book we use per capita GNP, the market values of assets, and other money amounts to measure the well-being of a person, community, nation, or the world.

WHERE THE CAPITAL IS

The world's capital can be divided into three subcategories:

1. *Financial capital* such as stocks (or equities) and bonds.
2. *Real capital* such as land, buildings, silver, and gold.
3. *Human capital* such as workers and their job skills.

TABLE 1-2	Population and Income Data for Selected Nations			
Country	Population, in millions	Country's GDP, US$ billions	GDP per capita, in US$	GDP per capita, adjusted for PPP, in US$
Luxembourg	0.4	17.4	37,346	33,119
United States	263.2	8,230.9	29,326	29,326
Norway	4.3	146.2	34,815	26,771
Switzerland	7.0	264.6	35,897	25,902
Denmark	5.2	174.9	32,179	25,514
Iceland	0.3	8.2	27,292	24,836
Japan	125.6	3,783.7	33,212	24,574
Canada	29.6	581.7	20,064	23,761
Belgium	10.2	250.5	23,820	23,242
Austria	8.1	212.3	25,549	23,077
Netherlands	15.5	377.5	23,280	22,142
Germany	81.7	2,135.7	25,470	22,049
Australia	18.1	351.9	21,202	21,949
France	58.1	1,433.9	23,789	21,293
Italy	57.3	1,172.3	19,913	21,265
Ireland	3.6	83.2	21,104	20,634
Finland	5.1	124.8	23,314	20,488
United Kingdom	58.6	1,357.2	21,740	20,483
Sweden	8.8	226.9	25,746	20,439
New Zealand	3.7	53.1	17,272	17,846
Spain	39.2	533.3	13,530	15,990
Portugal	9.9	105.9	10,184	14,562
Korea	45.1	297.9	9,622	14,477
Greece	10.5	120.4	11,438	13,192
Czech Republic	10.3	55.0	5,050	13,087
Hungary	10.2	47.4	4,461	9,875
Mexico	90.5	415.5	4,298	7,697
Poland	38.6	150.2	3,509	7,487
Turkey	61.6	198.7	2,979	6,463

SOURCE: OECD Web site, 1999. The population data are from 1995–96. The GDPs are from 1998, based on 1998 prices and exchange rates. The GDP per capita data are from 1997, based on 1997 exchange rates. Since the data are from different years, GDP per capita does not equal GDP divided by the country's population.

This book focuses on the first category to a greater extent than the latter two, but we need to understand the part each plays in the global economy.

The World's Equity Capital

The **market capitalization** or *total cap* of a corporation's aggregate common stock (or equity) is measured by multiplying the home country's price per share times the number of shares outstanding. Stock markets are located in areas where equity capital accumulates. Figure 1-4 shows that the world's equity capital is concentrated in the high-income countries of North America, western and central Europe, and the Pacific Rim, mostly in Japan. Figure 1-4 was constructed by using one day's foreign exchange rates to convert the values from different countries to one common currency.

FIGURE 1-4 Global Stock Market Capitalization[a] in 2000

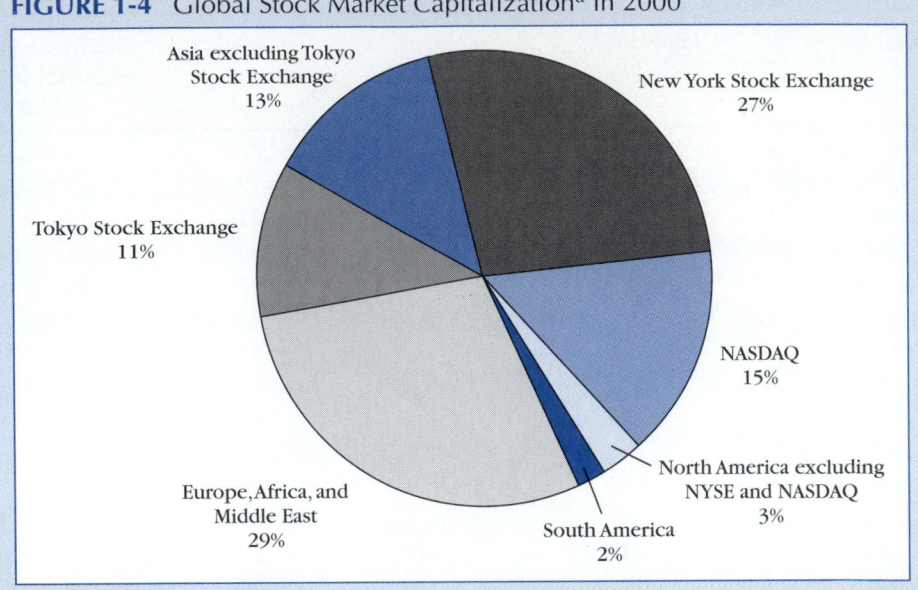

The Tokyo Stock Exchange (TSE) slipped from having the world's largest stock market total capitalization in 1990 to a distant third place in 2000. The NYSE's share of the world's stock market rose from second to first place. In 2000 Nasdaq was the second largest market in North America and in the world. Chapter 6 investigates the stock market. Chapters 25 through 28 focus on common stock analysis.

[a]Market capitalization equals price per share times number of shares outstanding.

SOURCE: International Federation of Stock Exchanges, Paris, France. Visit the Web site: www.fibv.com.

Several dozen underdeveloped countries have small equity accumulations and no stock market. Several dozen developing countries have considerable wealth accumulations and small, new **emerging markets** where common stocks are traded.

The market price of equity capital is more volatile than the prices of other forms of capital. Figure 1-4 shows that in 1999 the U.S. equity market was the most valuable in the world. But, in 1989–90 Japan's stock market was worth more than the U.S. market. Changes can be rapid, and the changes never stop.

The world's stock market is a large and vivid indicator of changes in wealth, but the bond market's aggregate value is larger.

The World's Bond Market

The market capitalization of the world bond market is slightly larger than the total cap of the world stock market. Figure 1-5 shows the United States is the largest borrower in the world. The most noteworthy aspect of the world bond market is that, in nearly every country of the world, the largest issuers of bonds are governments. Governments seem to be perennial deficit spenders.

The World's Real Capital and Human Capital

Economists estimate that the combined value (market capitalization) of all stock and bond holdings in the world is worth a little less than the world's real estate. When the value of precious metals (silver and gold) and jewelry are added to the value of real estate, the value of

FIGURE 1-5 The World Bond Market, Measured by (A) the Issuing Sectors and (B) Regions of the Major Issuers

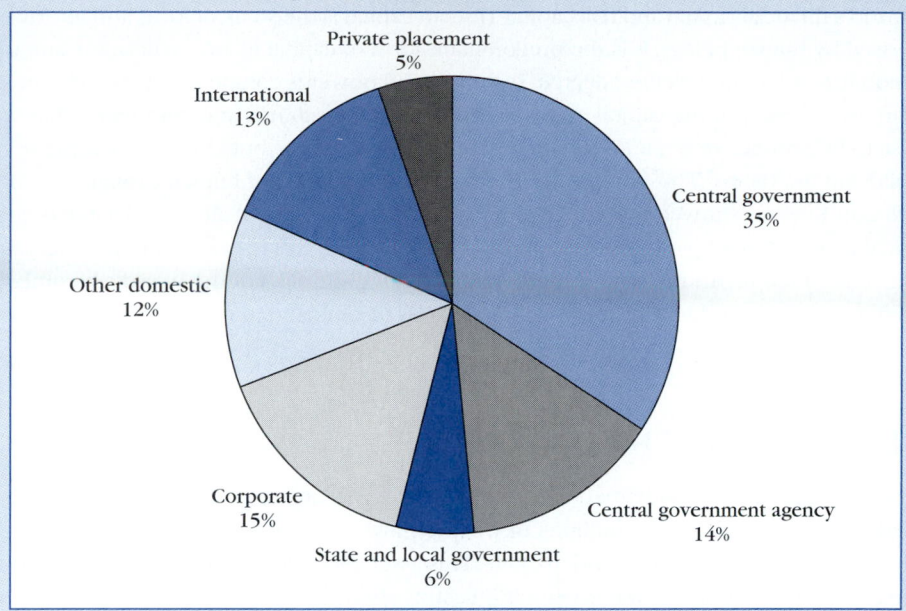

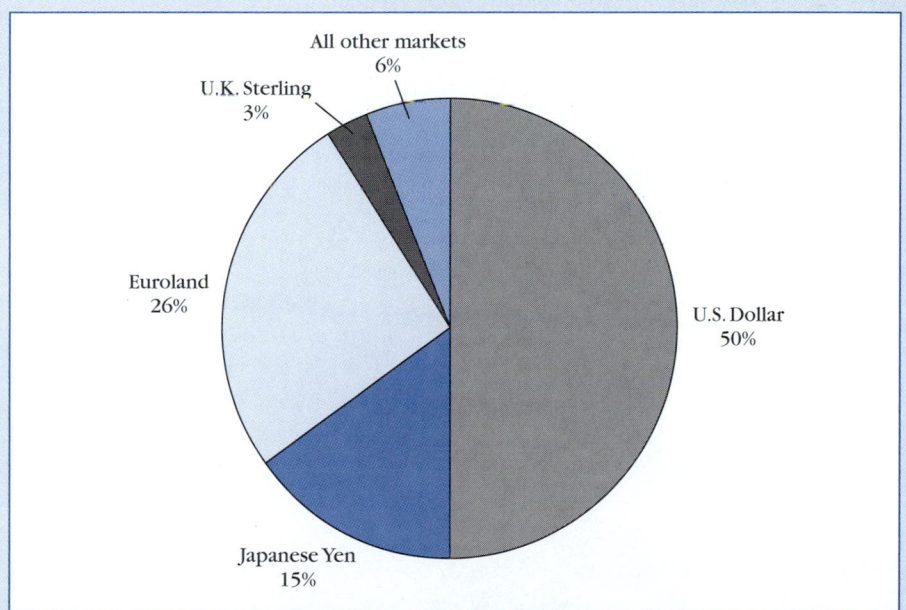

Ignoring the nationalities of the issuers, governmental bodies issued 57% of the world's outstanding bonds market value. The aggregated issuers from all sectors of the United States issued half of the world's outstanding debt. Measured in U.S. dollars and U.S. dollar equivalents, the world's total bond market capitalization at the end of 1998 was $25.5 trillion.

SOURCE: Salomon Smith Barney, "How Big Is the World Bond Market?" New York, 7 April 2000, Fig. 1. Reprinted with permission of Robert DiClemente, Managing Director.

the world's real assets significantly exceeds the aggregate value of the world's financial assets.

Furthermore, the world's human capital is worth much more than the combined value of the world's financial capital and real capital. Human capital is the stock of ideas and information possessed by human beings. It is the predominant form of capital in any civilization, and today it is mobile to an unprecedented degree. Technological power is composed of little else besides human capital. Most of the capital embodied in the tools, machines, and computers that workers use to be productive is not in the physical tools and machines, but in the knowledge of how to build and use them.[1] This book is designed to contribute to your human capital.

Simon Kuznets showed that the income from the ownership of all financial assets and all physical assets is roughly 20% of the world's total income.[2] That means that income paid to employees—income from human capital—represents about 80% of the world's income. This percentage appears to be stable across long periods of time and in many different countries.

THE U.S. FINANCIAL MARKETS

Figure 1-6 suggests that residential real estate is one of the largest investments made by many United States citizens. In fact, millions of people have much more invested in their homes than they have in the stock or bond markets. This asset allocation might change in the future. During the past 10 years common stock investments in the United States, stated as a percentage of household assets, have steadily increased while the value of real estate held declined slightly.[3]

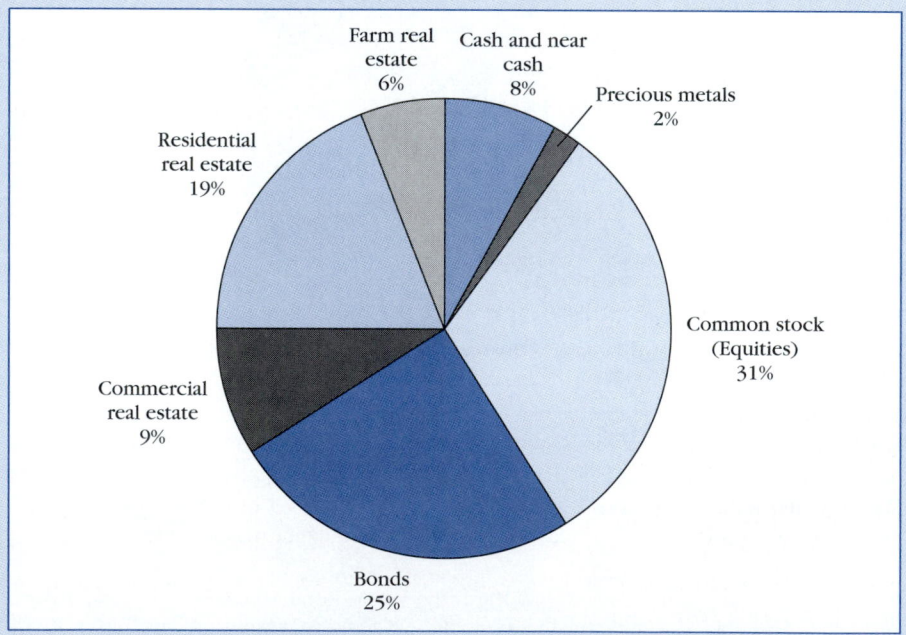

FIGURE 1-6   Investable Wealth in the United States, $49.3 Trillion in 1998

Farm real estate 6%
Cash and near cash 8%
Precious metals 2%
Residential real estate 19%
Common stock (Equities) 31%
Commercial real estate 9%
Bonds 25%

Securities investing has increased in popularity to the point that the market value of all securities surpassed the market value of all real estate in the United States.

The U.S. Market for Equities

Common stock investors can be dichotomized into two categories—individual investors and institutional investors. Although the individual (household) investors and "institutional investors" in the United States manage roughly equal proportions of the U.S. equities, their impacts on the nation's equity market are different.

Individual Investors. There are over 50 million *individual investors* in the United States. The typical individual owns only a few stocks. The aggregate value of a typical household's holdings is about $15,000.[4] Over 80% of the households in the United States have less than $100,000 invested in the stock market. Because of the modest amounts of money they each manage and the unrelated investment styles they adopt (such as liquidity motivated trades, chasing hot tips, "playing the market"), the millions of household investors have a small impact individually and a small aggregate impact on the U.S. equities market. One large institutional investor manages more money than a million small individual investors.

Institutional Investors. In contrast to the millions of household investors in the United States, who are mostly amateurs, there are a few thousand professional investors called **institutional investors.** In spite of their smaller number, institutional investors control most of the "dollar votes" and have a larger impact on securities prices than the individual investors.

Institutional investors in the United States include pension funds (controlling 24.9% of the market value of equities in the United States), mutual funds (16.2%), life insurance companies (4.7%), trust departments of commercial banks (3.4%), property and casualty insurance companies (1.3%), closed-end fund managers (0.3%), brokers and dealers (0.3%), savings (thrift) institutions (0.2%), and commercial bankers (0.1%), among others. In 1998 institutional investors managed 59.2% of the market value of equities in the United States. Household investors controlled the remaining 40.8%.[5] Households own much of the money that is managed by institutional investors, but many households turn control of their invested funds over to institutions that charge annual management fees typically in the range from 1% to 3% of the market value of the investments.

In 1997 the seven largest institutional investors in the United States managed more than $300 billion apiece. Moreover, we find that the 166 largest institutions each managed more than $10 billion.[6] To put this into perspective, suppose these 166 portfolios of over $10 billion apiece allocated their funds equally among 200 different holdings. In this scenario, every institution's holdings of each of these 200 securities would be over $50 million. Most of these institutional investors remain hidden from public view because most of them rarely, if ever, give public interviews.

Large institutional investors are unable to invest in small firms because managing a tiny investment requires as many resources as are needed to manage a large investment, but the tiny portfolio weights of small investments do not permit them to contribute much profit to a portfolio worth billions of dollars. In other words, small investments are not big enough to pay their own way in most large portfolios.

A **block** trade is a single transaction of 10,000 or more shares of stock. As a result of their large positions in individual stocks, institutional investors frequently buy and sell stocks in large blocks. During 1997 the NYSE executed an average of 11,191 blocks of stock per trading day.[7] Block trades generated 50.9% of the volume of shares traded at the NYSE. Individual investors rarely trade in blocks; they usually trade an **odd lot** (one trade of less than 100 shares) or a **round lot** (a multiple of 100 shares).

After studying the U.S. stock market, Robert Schwartz wrote:

The marketplace today is dominated by institutional investors. The investment managers can alter their decisions and submit orders with electronic speed.

Programs are now being run that bring basket orders directly to the exchange floor, where they can execute with considerable market impact....[8]

The U.S. Market for Bonds

Figure 1-7 shows the U.S. Treasury issued 21% of all bonds outstanding in the U.S. *Agencies* of the U.S. federal government like Fannie Mae (FNMA), Ginnie Mae (GNMA), Freddie Mac (FHLMC), and the Tennessee Valley Authority (TVA) issued bonds that have the implied backing by the U.S. government. This off-the-U.S.Treasury-balance sheet financing by agencies of the federal government created 27% of the nation's bond market capitalization. **Municipal bonds (munis)** issued by the governments of states, cities, and other local government-sponsored bodies comprise another 9% of the issued bonds. To summarize: governmental bodies within the United States issued a total of 57% of the nation's outstanding bonds.

Corporations issued 24% of the bonds outstanding in the United States and used the proceeds of these bond issues to expand their business. Other domestic bond issuers sold 5% of the bonds. Foreign governments and foreign businesses issued 14% of the total. A category of international bonds called "Eurobonds" comprises a large and rapidly growing segment of these international issues. **Eurobonds** are underwritten by an international syndicate and offered simultaneously to investors in various countries. When a foreign government or a foreign corporation issues Eurobonds into the U.S. bond market that are denominated in U.S. dollars, the bonds are called **Eurodollar bonds.** For example, if the Sony Corporation issued U.S. dollar–denominated bonds in the United States, they would be Eurodollar bonds or Eurobonds.

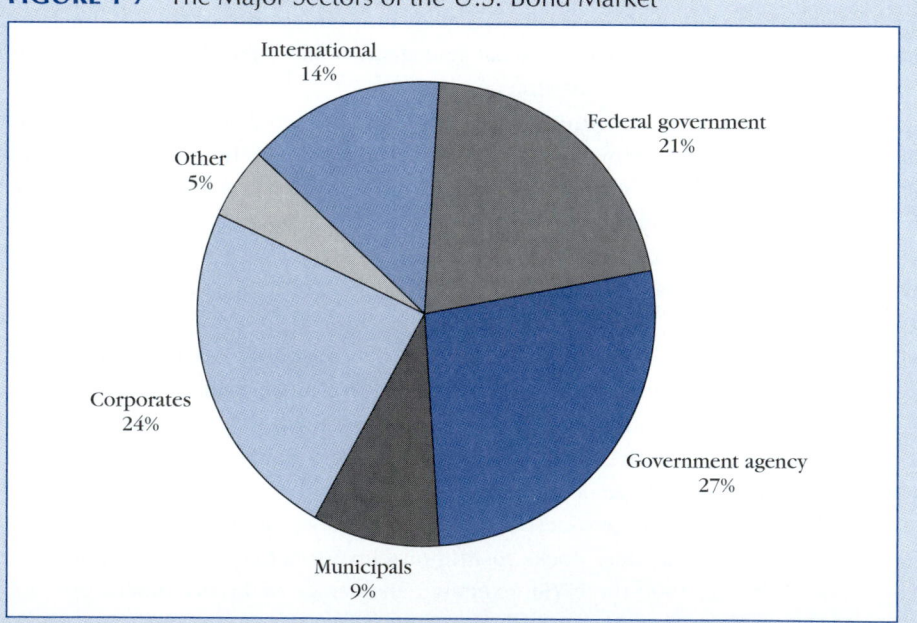

FIGURE 1-7 The Major Sectors of the U.S. Bond Market

Federal, state, and local governments and governmental agencies issued 57% of the bonds issued in the United States. Corporations issued 24% of the nation's total. Bond investing is the focus of Chapters 19 through 22.

SOURCE: Salomon Smith Barney, *How Big Is the World Bond Market?,* New York, 7 April, 2000, Fig. 1.

THE BOTTOM LINE

As mentioned at the beginning of this chapter, the holding period begins on the purchase date and ends on the sale date; it measures the length of time funds are committed to an investment. The length of an investment's holding period is helpful in determining whether it is a gamble, a speculation, or a true investment. These three activities are fundamentally different and should be managed differently.

There are over 50 million individual investors in the United States and the typical individual owns only a few stocks. Because of the modest amounts of money they each manage and the idiosyncratic investment styles they adopt, the millions of household investors have a small individual impact and a small aggregate impact on the U.S. equities market. One large institutional investor manages more money than a million individual investors.

Institutional investors in the United States include pension fund managers, mutual fund managers, life insurance companies financial executives, the officers who run the trust departments of commercial banks, the financial executives at property and casualty insurance companies, closed-end fund managers, brokers and dealers, the financial executives at savings (thrift) institutions, and commercial bankers, among others. In 1997 institutional investors managed 56% of the market value of equities in the United States. Household investors controlled the remaining 44%.

Table 1-1 lists categories of assets and highlights some of the major choices awaiting investors. Stay tuned for details.

ENDNOTES

[1] The economic theory of human capital is summarized in three books written by the Nobel prize-winning economist who fathered the subject. See Gary S. Becker, *Human Capital,* 2nd ed. (Chicago: University of Chicago Press, 1975). See also Becker's books *The Economics of Discrimination* and *The Economic Approach to Human Behavior,* both published by the University of Chicago Press.

[2] Simon Kuznets, *Modern Economic Growth* (New Haven, CT: Yale University Press, 1966) 168–170.

[3] See J. Tracy, H. Schneider, and Sewin Chan, "Are Stocks Overtaking Real Estate in Household Portfolios?," *Current Issues* 5, 5 (April 1999): p. 2.

[4] See Securities Industry Association, *Securities Industry Factbook 1998.* New York, p. 67. See also New York Stock Exchange, *Fact Book 1997.* New York, p. 59.

[5] Securities Industry Association, *Securities Industry Factbook 1999.* New York, p. 71.

[6] To obtain the names and investment details about each of these investors see "America's Top 300 Money Managers," *Institutional Investor* (July 1998): 87–99.

[7] New York Stock Exchange, *Fact Book 1997.* New York, p. 95.

[8] Robert A. Schwartz, *Reshaping the Equity Markets.* (Burr Ridge, IL: Business One Irwin, 1993), 18.

Opportunities and Salaries in Investments

The financial services industry includes commercial banking (Chase Manhattan, Bank of America), investment banking (Merrill Lynch, Goldman Sachs), insurance companies (Prudential, Metropolitan), mutual funds (Fidelity, Janus), pensions (corporations, governmental units), and related fields. Millions of jobs are available in the financial services industry.

A 1999 compensation survey by the Association for Investment Management and Research (AIMR) reported the respondents' 1999 base salary compensation, anticipated 1999 cash bonus, and their actual 1998 noncash compensation (stock options, etc.). These three components can be added to obtain an estimate of the total compensation package. Salaries for people in the 90th percentile are included to give an indication of compensation for high-level performers. Table 1A.1 presents compensation packages broken down by employment organizations. Table 1A.2 contains compensation packages broken down by job function.

Visit the Prentice-Hall Web site for employment information that is updated periodically.

TABLE 1A.1   Estimates of Median Salaries for Different Types of Organizations

	Investment Counseling Firm	Bank	Security Broker/ Dealer	Insurance Company	Mutual Fund Management Company	Plan Sponsor/ Endowment/ Foundation	Pension Consulting Firm
1999 Median Salary	$113,150	$ 90,000	$ 90,000	$107,000	$110,000	$ 92,750	$ 80,000
1999 Median Bonus	$ 50,000	$ 30,000	$ 85,000	$ 35,000	$ 70,000	$ 11,000	$ 12,500
1998 Median Non-Cash Compensation	$ 9,000	$ 10,000	$ 8,000	$ 5,000	$ 20,000	$ 200	$ 2,000
Median Total Compensation	$185,000	$128,000	$185,000	$150,000	$196,000	$104,200	$ 95,000
90th Percentile	$682,264	$365,111	$757,108	$430,769	$814,603	$294,412	$256,250

SOURCE: Association for Investment Management and Research and Russell Reynolds Associates, *1999 Investment Management Compensation Survey*, p. 12. This table is excerpted from a 121-page document available on the Web site of the AIMR at: www.aimr.com.

TABLE 1A.2 Estimates of Median Compensation by Job Function

	1999 Median Salary	1999 Median Bonus	1998 Median Noncash Compensation	Median Total Compensation	90th Percentile
CEO	$150,000	$100,000	$20,000	$253,500	$1,250,000
COO/CAO	$125,000	$ 50,000	$25,000	$225,000	$ 872,727
CIO	$125,000	$ 45,000	$18,000	$188,000	$ 794,419
Head of Equities	$143,000	$ 75,000	$25,000	$257,000	$1,165,000
Head of Fixed Income	$135,000	$ 75,000	$20,000	$230,500	$1,035,000
Portfolio Manager Domestic Equities	$100,000	$ 40,000	$10,000	$153,000	$ 533,571
Portfolio Manager Global Equities	$135,000	$ 70,000	$15,000	$211,000	$ 672,500
Portfolio Manager Domestic Fixed Income	$100,500	$ 42,350	$ 7,000	$158,000	$ 484,231
Portfolio Manager Global Fixed Income	$120,000	$ 55,000	$ 7,000	$185,000	$ 526,000
Strategist	$100,000	$ 35,000	$10,000	$155,000	$ 492,500
Director of Research	$120,000	$ 50,000	$10,000	$180,000	$ 588,000
Securities Analyst Domestic Equities	$ 87,400	$ 50,000	$ 4,500	$140,250	$ 490,000
Securities Analyst Global/ International Equities	$ 90,000	$ 40,000	$ 1,000	$150,000	$ 394,444
Securities Analyst Domestic Fixed Income	$ 90,000	$ 35,000	$ 2,000	$130,000	$ 330,333
Securities Analyst/ Global/ International Fixed Income	$100,000	$ 40,000	$ 5,000	$155,000	$ 350,000
Market/Sales Client Service	$ 95,000	$ 50,000	$10,000	$168,000	$ 515,417
Pension Officer/Asset Allocator/ Manager of Outside Managers	$ 83,000	$ 15,000	$ 4,000	$104,000	$ 298,824
CFO/Treasurer/ Controller	$ 90,000	$ 25,000	$10,000	$123,000	$ 287,500
Trader	$ 65,000	$ 25,000	$ 400	$ 97,467	$ 395,000

SOURCE: Association for Investment Management and Research and Russell Reynolds Associates, *1999 Investment Management Compensation Survey*, pp. 14 and 15. This table is excerpted from a 121-page document available on the Web site of the AIMR at: www.aimr.com.

RATES OF RETURN

Investors frequently discuss how many dollars they gain or lose from an investment. It is more meaningful to discuss the investment's rate of return. The **rate of return** *is the single most important outcome from most investments. This chapter shows how to measure the rates of return from various investments and illustrates ways to use rates of return.*

Rates of return from various types of stocks and bonds are computed, compared, and contrasted in this chapter. Analyzing these rates of return helps us understand the ways in which different classes of assets perform and reveals fundamental economic relationships between diverse categories of investments.

Rates of return can be broken down into components called risk premiums. Investment analysts can assess the risks inherent in an investment and determine what risk premiums (rate of return components) make up the asset's required rate of return. Required rates of return can be tabulated for different categories of assets and used to expedite investment decision-making

Investors want to maximize their returns or wealth, but uncertainty makes investing a risky business. The right information can reduce this ambiguity. This chapter provides information about investment analysis, investment management and risk management that helps you maximize your return without assuming unnecessary risk. We begin with a clear statement about what investors want to achieve.

THE INVESTORS' GOAL

Whether they are managing their own or other people's money, the goal of investors and investment managers is to maximize what they get back relative to what they put into an investment. The goal is to maximize either the rate of return or the investment's *terminal value*. Rate of return maximization and maximization of terminal wealth are equivalent objectives. Note in the following that Eqn. 2-2 is simply Eqn. 2-1 rearranged. Anything that maximizes Eqn. 2-1 will also maximize Eqn. 2-2.

$$\left(1 + \text{Rate of return}\right) = \left(\frac{\text{Terminal value of the invested funds}}{\text{Present value of the investment}}\right) \qquad \text{(2-1)}$$

$$\left(\begin{array}{c}\text{Terminal value} \\ \text{of the invested} \\ \text{funds}\end{array}\right) = \left(\begin{array}{c}\text{Present value} \\ \text{of the investment}\end{array}\right)\left(1 + \text{Rate of return}\right) \qquad \text{(2-2)}$$

IS JODY MAXIMIZING HER RETURN OR HER WEALTH?   EXAMPLE

Suppose Jody invests $100 in a U.S. Treasury bill that matures in 1 year and earns an annual interest rate of 5 percent. Jody's investment will grow to a terminal value of $105.

$$\text{Goal 1: Increase } \left(1 + 5\%\right) = \left(\frac{\text{Terminal value of \$105}}{\text{Present value of \$100}}\right)$$

$$\text{Goal 2: Increase } \left(\begin{array}{c}\text{Terminal value} \\ \text{of \$105}\end{array}\right) = \left(\text{Present value of \$100}\right)\left(1 + 5\%\right)$$

If Jody becomes dissatisfied with a 5% return and wants to earn more, it does not matter whether she pursues Goal 1 or Goal 2. The two equations here are equivalent.

Some people claim that wealth-maximizing investors are performing greedy activities and this harms society. Unless the investor violates the law, those accusations are false; U.S. securities laws prohibit harmful activities. The **Securities Act of 1933** and the **Securities and Exchange Act of 1934** forbid investors and investment managers from engaging in fraud, theft, security price manipulation, and insider trading. Other U.S. laws prohibit environmentally hazardous operations, unfair hiring practices, false advertising, and other harmful activities. All these laws are backed by fines and prison sentences.

Law-abiding wealth maximization is beneficial to the investor and to the general population:

◆ Wealth-maximizing investors operating honestly seek out securities issued by firms producing high-quality goods and services that buyers want. Thus, capital is used to benefit the general population.

◆ Investors can attend stockholders' meetings and urge their firm's management to do research and development in search of improvements.

◆ Wealth-maximizing business activities help a nation compete internationally, likely creating new job opportunities or easier jobs. A profitable corporation provides goods and/or services that it markets at competitive prices and sells at locations and times that are convenient for consumers.

The people who harm society are the ones who violate the law or act unethically. Rational investors are wealth-maximizers who ultimately make the world a better place to live.

A REALITY CHECK   ETHICS

The Need for Ethics in Investment

Would you hand over your money to a shady firm or invest it in a rigged market? Obviously, some level of ethics is essential for investment activity. Ethics is concerned broadly with the standards for right and wrong in all areas of life. The two ethical concepts most relevant to investment are *trust* and *fairness*. Because investment firms serve as intermediaries, they have certain duties to investors. Specifically, they act as *agents* and *fiduciaries*, whom investors trust to act in their interest and safeguard their assets. In addition, the aim of regulation in investment is to ensure both efficiency and fairness. Fairness means not only the absence of fraud and manipulation but also a "level playing field."

A characteristic feature of professionals is specialized knowledge. We ask physicians and attorneys, for example, to employ their knowledge for our benefit, and the same is true of investment professionals, who often become agents. An agent is a person who is engaged to act on behalf of another, called the **principal.** An **agent** is expected to be loyal, to act with due care, and to keep information confidential. In particular, agents should avoid *conflicts of interest*, which are situations in which a personal interest actually interferes or could potentially interfere with serving the interest of a principal. A conflict of interest can prevent an agent from exercising unbiased judgment in serving a patient, client, or principal.

Fairness is an issue in financial markets mainly because of *asymmetries* in information, bargaining power, and resources. Of course, not all asymmetries are unfair. A savvy stock trader should be allowed to exploit superior information—but not inside information! In general, decreasing asymmetries, by such means as requiring a prospectus for a new stock offering, increases both efficiency and fairness. In actual practice, however, it is difficult to determine when an unlevel playing field is unfair.

John R. Boatright, *Professor of Business Ethics*

THE ONE-PERIOD RATE OF RETURN

An investment's **rate of return** measures the degree of success or failure of the investment. It measures the change in an investor's wealth with respect to time. We will learn several rate of return measures. The one we use the most measures the return over one holding period. The one-period rate of return can be derived by rearranging Eqn. 2-1 (p. 19), as shown in Eqn. 2-3.

DEFINITION — **THE ONE-PERIOD RATE OF RETURN**

An investor's single-period rate of return is the total income the investor receives during the holding period, relative to the initial investment at the beginning of the holding period.

$$\begin{pmatrix} \text{One-period} \\ \text{rate of} \\ \text{return, } r \end{pmatrix} = \left[\frac{(\text{Terminal value}) - (\text{Present value})}{(\text{Present value})} \right] = \left[\frac{\text{Holding period income}}{\text{Purchase price}} \right]$$

(2-3)

EXAMPLE — **TYLER'S ONE-PERIOD RETURN FROM A SHARE OF COCA-COLA STOCK**

If Tyler buys a share of Coca-Cola's common stock for $54 on June 6 of one year and sells it on June 6 of the next year for $64, his price change (capital gain) income was $10 and the holding period was 1 year.

If the stock paid a cash dividend of 80 cents during that year, Tyler's total income from the stock is $10.80 (= $10 + $0.80) and the investment's terminal value is ($54 + $10 + $0.80 =) $64.80 at the end of the holding period. Tyler's rate of return for his 1-year investment is 20%.

$$\begin{pmatrix} \text{One--period} \\ \text{rate of return,} \\ r = .2 = 20\% \end{pmatrix} = \left[\frac{(\text{Terminal value, \$64.80}) - (\text{Initial value, \$54})}{(\text{Initial value, \$54})} \right] = \frac{\$10.80}{\$54} \quad \textbf{(2-3a)}$$

Alternatively, the Coke stock's annual return can be computed as follows:

$$\begin{pmatrix} \text{One--year} \\ \text{rate of return,} \\ r = .2 = 20\% \end{pmatrix} = \left[\frac{(\text{Price change, \$10}) + (\text{Cash dividend, \$0.80})}{(\text{Purchase price, \$54})} \right] = \frac{\$10.80 \text{ Income}}{\$54 \text{ Invested}} \quad \textbf{(2-3b)}$$

JODY'S ONE-PERIOD RETURN FROM A U.S. TREASURY BOND   EXAMPLE

Jody paid $900 for a U.S. Treasury bond (T-bond) that matures in 16 years and will repay its face (**par**) value of $1,000. Jody sold the bond for $910 1 year after she bought it. The T-bond paid $35 of coupon interest during the year Jody owned it. The terminal value of her 1-year investment was ($910 + $35 =) $945. Using Eqn. 2-3a, Jody's one-period rate of return was 5%.

$$\begin{pmatrix} \text{One--period} \\ \text{rate of return,} \\ r = .05 = 5\% \end{pmatrix} = \left[\frac{(\text{Terminal value, \$945}) - (\text{Initial value, \$900})}{(\text{Initial value, \$900})} \right] = \frac{\$45}{\$900}$$

The T-bond's 1-year return can also be computed as follows, applying Eqn. 2-3b:

$$\begin{pmatrix} \text{One--year} \\ \text{rate of return,} \\ r = .05 = 5\% \end{pmatrix} = \left[\frac{(\text{Price change, \$10}) + (\text{Coupon interest, \$35})}{(\text{Purchase price, \$900})} \right] = \frac{\$45 \text{ Income}}{\$900 \text{ Invested}}$$

TIM'S RATE OF RETURN FROM A 6-MONTH T-BILL   EXAMPLE

Tim wants a safe investment for 6 months. His research reveals that U.S. Treasury bills (T-bills) are short-term bonds that are issued with maturities of 3 months, 6 months, and 1 year. T-bills make no interest payments to their investors. T-bills are sold at a discount from their face (par, principal, maturity, terminal) value and they provide their investors with price appreciation income as their market price rises through time until the bond reaches its maturity value.

Tim paid $9,800 for a 6-month T-bill that has a terminal value of $10,000. His 6-month rate of return was 2.04%. Using Eqn. 2-3a, it looks like this:

$$\begin{pmatrix} \text{6--month} \\ \text{rate of return,} \\ r = .0204 = 2.04\% \end{pmatrix} = \left[\frac{(\text{Terminal value, \$10,000}) - (\text{Initial value, \$9,800})}{(\text{Initial value, \$9,800})} \right] = \frac{\$200}{\$9,800}$$

If we use Eqn. 2-3b, the T-bill's 6-month return can be computed as follows:

$$\begin{pmatrix} \text{6--month} \\ \text{rate of return,} \\ r = 2.04\% \end{pmatrix} = \left[\frac{(\text{Price change, \$200}) + (\text{Zero interest income})}{(\text{Purchase price, \$9,800})} \right] = \frac{\$200 \text{ Income}}{\$9,800 \text{ Invested}}$$

Since there are two 6-month periods in one year, Tim's 6-month return can be annualized to determine that his equivalent 1-year rate of return is 4.12%.

$$(1.0204)(1.0204) = (1.0204)^2 = (1.0412) = (1 + 4.12\%) = (1 + \text{Annualized rate of return})$$

DECADES OF HISTORICAL RETURNS

Figure 2-1 traces how a $1 investment in large-company stocks, small-company stocks, long-term government bonds, Treasury bills, and a hypothetical asset that returns the inflation rate performed. The dollar was invested in a market index for each of these five asset classes on December 31, 1925. Cash dividends from stocks and coupon interest from bonds were all reinvested. Transactions costs (taxes and commissions) were not deducted, except in the small-stock index starting in 1982.

A logarithmic scale is used on the vertical axis of Figure 2-1. Years are measured on the horizontal axis. Using a logarithmic scale facilitates direct comparisons of behavior at different point in time. No matter where it is measured on the graph, the same vertical distance represents the same percentage change. The logarithmic scale allows the viewer to concentrate on rates of return without worrying about the number of dollars invested.

Figure 2-1 shows that stocks suffered more than the bonds did during the Depression in the early 1930s. However, the riskier stocks earned higher average rates of return than the bonds to compensate investors for taking the larger risks.

U.S. Treasury bills offered the lowest risk and the lowest returns of any asset class in Figure 2-1. After inflation is deducted from the T-bill returns, the real (inflation-adjusted) T-bill returns were not much above zero.

Table 2-1 contains statistics summarizing the five price indexes in Figure 2-1 and two other security price indexes. These statistics were calculated from the one-period rates of change and rates of return realized over the 1926–99 sample period.

Measuring Realized One-Period Rates of Return

One-period rates of change can be calculated for the price indexes shown in Figure 2-1 by adapting Eqn. 2-3 (p. 20) to include time period subscripts and by letting INDEX denote the price index's end-of-period value.

$$r_t = \frac{\left(\begin{array}{c} \text{Change in price index} \\ \text{during the period} \end{array} \right)}{\left(\text{Beginning value of index} \right)} = \frac{\left(\text{INDEX}_t - \text{INDEX}_{t-1} \right)}{\text{INDEX}_{t-1}} \tag{2-4}$$

If the underlying securities paid no cash income, the one-period rate of change equals a one-period rate of return. For the stocks and bonds that paid cash income, the one-period rate of return equals a price plus cash flow relative adapted from Eqn. 2-3b (p. 21) as shown in Eqn. 2-5 where CF_t represents the cash flow received during time period t:

$$r_t = \frac{\left(\begin{array}{c} \text{Change in price index} \\ \text{during the period} \end{array} \right) + \left(\begin{array}{c} \text{Cash–flow income} \\ \text{during the period, if any} \end{array} \right)}{\left(\text{Beginning value of index} \right)} \tag{2-5}$$

$$= \frac{\left(\text{INDEX}_t - \text{INDEX}_{t-1} \right) + \left(CF_t \right)}{\text{INDEX}_{t-1}}$$

FIGURE 2-1   Wealth Indices for Average U.S. Investments in Different
Asset Classes Compared to Inflation, 1926–99

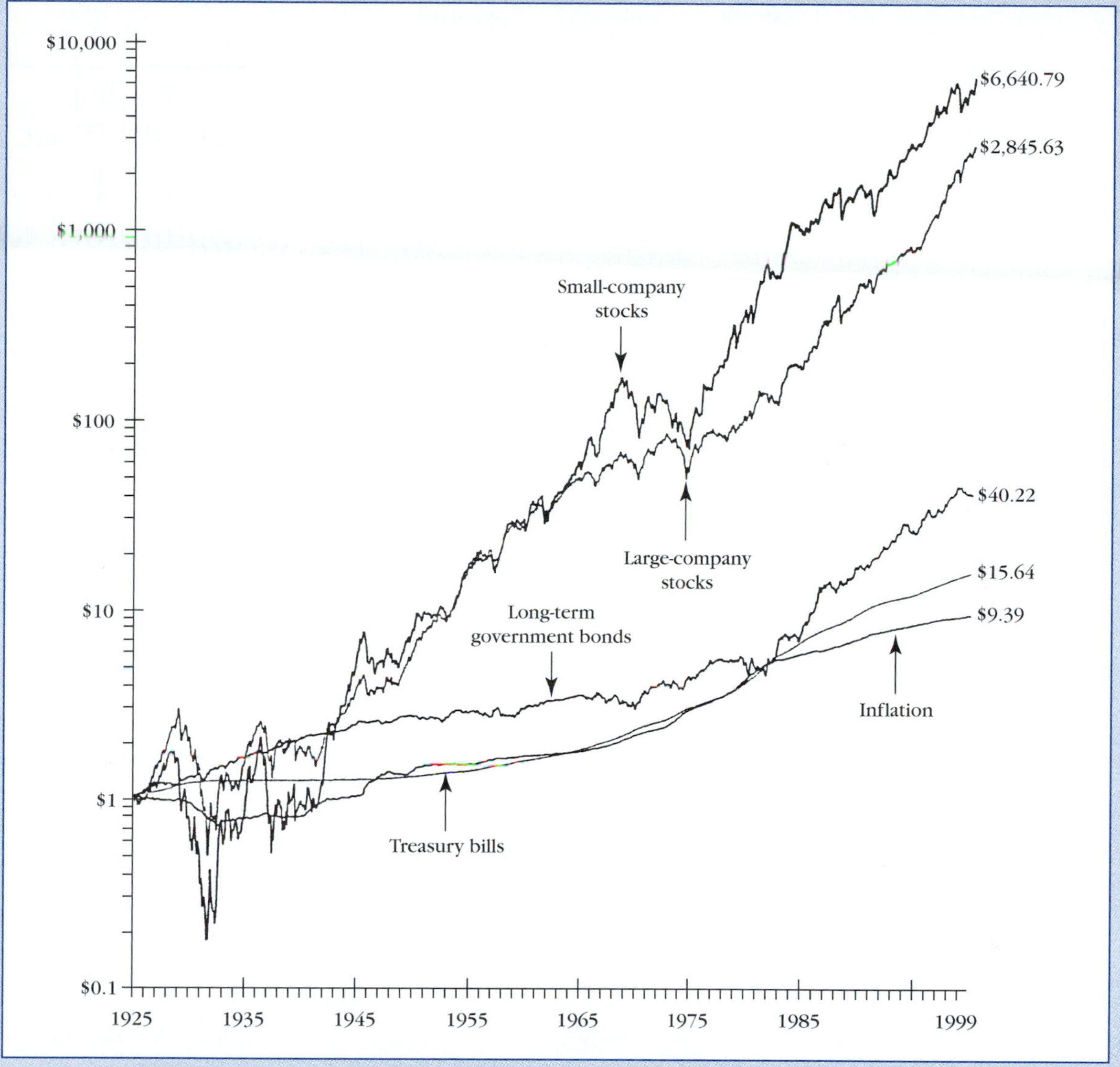

SUMMARY: The historical paths of $1 invested on December 31, 1925 in four asset classes are contrasted with the inflation rate in the U.S. Consumers Price Index (CPI). An investment in U.S. Treasury bills yielded the smoothest (least risky) growth path with the lowest average rate of return. T-bill returns exceeded the rate of inflation by a small margin. In some years (1973–80) inflation advanced faster than T-bills, so T-bill investors lost purchasing power. A dollar invested in a diversified portfolio of small company stocks provided the highest average returns, and it was also the most erratic (riskiest) asset class. The risk and return of the other asset classes were between T-bills and the small company stocks. The historical path of an investment is heavily dependent on its asset class.

SOURCE: *Stocks, Bonds, Bills, and Inflation: 2000 Yearbook,* Ibbotson Associates, North Michigan Avenue, Chicago, IL 60601, Graph 2–1, p. 28, based on copyrighted works by Ibbotson and Sinquefield. All rights reserved. Used with permission.

Ibbotson Associates Web site is: www.ibbotson.com.

TABLE 2-1   **Average Annual Rate of Return and Risk Statistics for Asset Classes and Inflation in the United States, 1926–99**

Series	Geometric Mean	Arithmetic Mean	Standard Deviation	Distribution
Large-company stocks	11.3%	13.3%	20.1%	
Small-company stocks	12.6	17.6	33.6	
Long-term corporate bonds	5.6	5.9	8.7	
Long-term government	5.1	5.5	9.3	
Intermediate-term government	5.2	5.4	5.8	
U.S. Treasury bills	3.8	3.8	3.2	
Inflation	3.1	3.2	4.5	

−90%   0%   90%

SUMMARY: Statistics for six asset classes and the inflation rate in the United States summarize the long-term results from a sample period that includes war and peace; inflation and deflation; booms, recessions, and one depression.

From 1926 through 1999 inclusive, a diversified portfolio of common stocks issued by small corporations yielded an arithmetic average rate of return of 17.6%, a geometric mean rate of return of 12.6%, with a standard deviation of 33.6%. The small-company stocks subjected their investors to the greatest risk (the widest probability distribution) of any asset class in the Table. At the opposite extreme, the U.S. Treasury bills yielded an arithmetic average rate of return of 3.8%, a geometric mean return of 3.8%, and experienced a standard deviation of 3.2% (the narrowest probability distribution). There is a noticeable tendency for the average rate of return to increase directly with the riskiness of the asset class.

SOURCE: *Stocks, Bonds, Bills, and Inflation: 2000 Yearbook*, Ibbotson Associates, North Michigan Avenue, Chicago, IL 60601, Table 2-1, p. 33, based on copyrighted works by Ibbotson and Sinquefield. All rights reserved. Used with permission.

 The Ibbotson Associates Web site is: www.ibbotson.com.

Measuring Average Rates of Return

The arithmetic average rates of return in Table 2-1 summarize a great deal of information and provide a good way to compare the performance of different investments. The **arithmetic mean return (AMR)**, sometimes denoted $\bar{r}$, is an average of historical one-period rates of return computed as follows:

$$AMR = \bar{r} = \left(\frac{1}{T}\right) \sum_{t=1}^{T} r_t = \left(\frac{1}{T}\right) (r_1 + r_2 + \ldots + r_T) \tag{2-6}$$

where T denotes the terminal time period.

The arithmetic mean of historical annual returns should be measured over a representative sample period. A representative sample might cover one complete business cycle, measured from either peak to peak or from trough to trough.

The *compound average rate of return* is similar to the arithmetic mean return; Table 2-1 shows their values differ only slightly. The compound average rate of return is also called the **geometric mean return,** denoted **GMR,** where *GMR* is the geometric mean return computed over *T* successive time periods.

$$(1 + GMR)^T = (1 + r_1)(1 + r_2)(1 + r_3) \ldots (1 + r_T) \tag{2-7}$$

The GMR formula is restated equivalently as follows:

$$GMR = \sqrt[T]{(1 + r_1)(1 + r_2)(1 + r^3) \ldots (1 + r_T)} - 1 \tag{2-7a}$$

The geometric mean return can also be defined in terms of the beginning and ending index values:

$$(1 + GMR)^T = \left(\frac{\text{INDEX}_T}{\text{INDEX}_0}\right) \tag{2-8}$$

COMPUTING AVERAGE RATES OF RETURN

EXAMPLE

A 3-year investment earned $r_1 = 20\%$ in Year 1, $r_2 = -10\%$ in Year 2, $r_3 = 5\%$ in Year 3, and Year 3 was the terminal time period, $T = 3$. The investment's arithmetic mean return was 5%. Applying Eqn. 2-6, we see that

$$AMR = \bar{r} = \left(\frac{1}{T}\right)\sum_{t=1}^{T=3} r_t = \left(\frac{1}{3}\right)(r_1 + r_2 + r_3) = \left(\frac{1}{3}\right)(20\% - 10\% + 5\%) = \left(\frac{1}{3}\right)(15\%) = 5\%$$

The geometric mean return from this 3-year investment is 4.28%, as shown when we apply Eqn. 2-7a:

$$GMR = \sqrt[T]{(1 + r_1)(1 + r_2)(1 + r_3)} - 1$$

$$= \sqrt[3]{(1 + 20\%)(1 - 10\%)(1 + 5\%)} - 1$$

$$= \sqrt[3]{(1.2)(0.9)(1.05)} - 1$$

$$= \sqrt[3]{1.134} - 1 = 1.0428 - 1 = 0.0428 = 4.28\%$$

If $100 is invested in a bank and left there to compound annually for 3 years, and $113.40 is withdrawn at the end of year 3, the deposit earned a compound average rate of return of 4.28% per year. Using Eqn. 2-8, we see that

$$(1 + GMR)^T = (1.0428)^3 = \left(\frac{\$113.40}{\$100.00}\right) = \left(\frac{\text{INDEX}_T}{\text{INDEX}_0}\right)$$

If the $100 bank deposit had compounded annually at a rate of 5.0%, a larger terminal balance of $115.7625 could have been withdrawn.

$$(1 + GMR)^T = (1.05)^3 = \left(\frac{\$115.7625}{\$100.00}\right) = \left(\frac{\text{INDEX}_T}{\text{INDEX}_0}\right)$$

The arithmetic average rate of return is not a compounded average rate of return, but the geometric mean return is. Since compounded interest grows more rapidly than simple (non-compound) interest, the geometric mean return will never be larger than the arithmetic mean return (*AMR*) from the same investment: $AMR \geq GMR$.

Assessing Risk

This book equates **risk** with variability of return. In other words, an asset is perceived as being riskier when its one-period rates of return fluctuate over a wider range. The statistical **variance** can be used to measure an asset's variability of return, or risk.

Variance. The variance is represented by the symbols σ^2 and *VAR(r)*. Computationally, the variance equals the average of the squared deviations from the arithmetic mean return as shown in Eqn. 2-9 where the *T* successive rates of return are $r_1, r_2, r_3, \ldots, r_T$ and $\bar{r}$ stands for the arithmetic average rate of return. Eqn. 2-9a provides an example.

$$\sigma^2 = VAR(r) = \left(\frac{1}{T}\right) \sum_{t=1}^{T} (r_t - \bar{r})^2 \tag{2-9}$$

$$= \left(\frac{1}{T}\right) \left[(r_1 - \bar{r})^2 + (r_2 - \bar{r})^2 + \ldots + (r_T - \bar{r})^2 \right]$$

Standard Deviation. The **standard deviation** of the rates of return equals the square root of the variance of returns and is sometimes represented by the lower-case Greek letter sigma, σ.

$$\sigma = \text{Standard deviation} = \sqrt{VAR(r)} \tag{2-10}$$

The variance and the standard deviation both measure variability of return; they are equivalent measures of total risk.

EXAMPLE   COMPUTING THE VARIANCE AND STANDARD DEVIATION OF RETURNS

Reconsider the 3-year investment (Example, p. 25) that earned $r_1 = 20\%$ in Year 1, $r_2 = -10\%$ in Year 2, and $r_3 = 5\%$ in Year 3. This investment's arithmetic mean return was 5% and $T = 3$ years. Applying Eqn. 2-9:

$$\sigma^2 = VAR(r) = \left(\frac{1}{T}\right) \sum_{t=1}^{T} (r_t - \bar{r})^2$$

$$= \left(\frac{1}{T}\right) \left[(r_1 - \bar{r})^2 + (r_2 - \bar{r})^2 + (r_3 - \bar{r})^2 \right]$$

$$= \left(\frac{1}{3}\right) \left[(0.20 - .05)^2 + (-0.10 - .05)^2 + (0.05 - .05)^2 \right] \tag{2-9a}$$

$$= \left(\frac{1}{3}\right) \left[(0.15)^2 + (-0.15)^2 + (0)^2 \right]$$

$$= \left(\frac{1}{3}\right) \left[0.0225 + 0.0225 + 0 \right]$$

$$= \left(\frac{1}{3}\right) \left[0.045 \right] = 0.015$$

The standard deviation of returns equals the square root of the variance. Applying Eqn. 2-10:

$$\sigma = \text{Standard deviation} = \sqrt{VAR(r)}$$

$$= \sqrt{VAR(r)} = \sqrt{0.015}$$

$$= 0.12247 = 12.247\%$$

Risk Rankings. Although the standard deviation and variance have different numerical values, ranking their associated σ and σ^2 values results in the same risk rankings.

The Variances of Risky Assets 1, 2, and 3	Standard Deviations of Assets 1, 2, and 3	Explanations of Risk Rankings
$VAR(r_1) = 0.16$	$\sqrt{VAR(r_1)} = \sqrt{.16} = \sigma_1 = .40$	Asset #1 is the riskiest asset using either risk surrogate.
$VAR(r_2) = 0.09$	$\sqrt{VAR(r_2)} = \sqrt{.09} = \sigma_2 = .30$	The second riskiest asset is asset #2, in terms of either risk surrogate.
$VAR(r_3) = 0.04$	$\sqrt{VAR(r_3)} = \sqrt{.04} = \sigma_3 = .20$	The third riskiest asset is asset #3, regardless of which risk surrogate is used.

Advantages of σ. There are several ways to measure the variability of return from an asset. The *range* from the highest to the lowest returns in an asset's probability distribution is one possible risk measure. Because the range is based on only two extreme values, statisticians prefer the standard deviation. It offers the following advantages:

Advantage 1. The standard deviation, σ, considers every outcome. Unlike the range, the standard deviation does not ignore any relevant information.

Advantage 2. The standard deviation is well known among statisticians. As a result, many hand calculators and computers are programmed to calculate σ.

Advantage 3. The standard deviation measures the wideness of the probability distributions in the right-most column of Table 2-1 (p. 24). This measure of dispersion around the arithmetic mean corresponds to the verbal "variability of return" definition of risk used in finance.

Advantage 4. The standard deviation is not only a statistic that is widely used in finance, it is also widely used in mathematics, econometrics, biometrics, psychometrics, and other applications.

INTERPRETING HISTORICAL RETURN AND RISK

It is possible to glean useful information from realized (historical) investment returns. The following describes how this relates to each major type of investment.

Large-Company Common Stocks. Figure 2-1 and Table 2-1 show that, on average, common stocks earn higher returns than bonds of all types. The reason for this lies in the bankruptcy law. U.S. law says that if a court declares a corporation bankrupt, the firm must close down and auction off all assets. The bankruptcy law's **Absolute Priority Rule (APR)** goes on to stipulate that, after the bankruptcy auction, all creditors must be paid in full before the firm's common stockholders can receive any liquidation proceeds. Common stockholders in a bankrupt firm usually receive nothing because there is usually nothing left after the creditors are all paid. Common stockholders' **residual claim** under the bankruptcy law makes stock a riskier investment than bonds issued by the same corporation. This relatively high level of bankruptcy risk explains why a corporation's common stockholders demand the highest average rate of return of any security issued by a firm. The additional return of several percentage points per year that a corporation must pay to induce investors to buy its stock rather than its bonds is an **equity risk premium;** this risk premium stems from the APR in bankruptcy law.

Small-Company Stocks. The common stocks issued by small corporations outperformed all other categories of investments in Table 2-1. Nevertheless, it is easy to lose almost everything invested in a small corporation. For instance, Figure 2-1 shows that small stocks were hit harder than any other *asset class* during both the Depression of the early 1930s and the international stock market crash of October 1987.

   Long-run statistics show that the percentage of small firms that go bankrupt exceeds the percentage of large companies that go bankrupt. Investors recognize this size difference and require a **size premium,** or **small-stock premium,** in the form of a higher rate of return, to entice them to invest in the riskier small corporations instead of large corporations. The small-stock premium is about 1.5%, or 1.5 percentage points per year, of additional return over what the stocks issued by large corporations earn. A **basis point** (BP) is $\frac{1}{100}$ of 1%. So, the small-stock premium of 1.5% equals 150 basis points (150 BPs).

Long-Term Corporate Bonds. Since the wealth of the world's largest economy backs the U.S. Treasury, Treasury bonds are sometimes called **default-free bonds**. Unlike U.S. Treasury bonds, some corporation bonds go bankrupt each year. Bankruptcy risk makes corporate bonds riskier than Treasury bonds and, as a result, to attract investors corporations must always pay higher average rates of return than the U.S. Treasury. The rate of return from a bond issued by a corporation must include a **default premium** to induce investors to accept the bankruptcy risk. This default premium equals about $\frac{40}{100}$ of 1% (40 BPs) of additional annual rate of return that a corporate bond must pay above the rate paid by a Treasury bond with the same number of years to maturity.

Long-Term U.S. Treasury Bonds. Risk-averse investors prefer U.S. Treasury bonds over corporate bonds because the Treasuries involve no default risk. The long-term Treasury bonds used to prepare Figure 2-1 and Table 2-1 mature, on average, 20 years after their IPO (initial public offering) date. Since these long-term T-bonds involve no default premium, their required rate of return averages about 40 BPs below the required rate of return for corporate bonds with the same time horizon.

Intermediate-Term U.S. Treasury Bonds. The intermediate-term Treasury bonds used to prepare Table 2-1 mature, on average, about 5 years after their issue date—clearly a much shorter time than 20-year average maturity for the long-term T-bonds. The intermediate-term Treasury bonds' shorter investment horizons cause them to experience smaller price fluctuations than long-term Treasury bonds that are identical in every other respect. Bond investors demand a **horizon premium** of several basis points to induce them to invest in the riskier long-term Treasury bonds instead of the intermediate-term Treasury bonds.

U.S. Treasury Bills. Since all U.S. Treasury bills mature in less than 1 year, they need not pay a horizon premium to attract longer-term investors. And, since the U.S. Treasury is unlikely to default, U.S. Treasury's T-bills need not pay a default premium. T-bills are so riskless they are sometimes called *risk-free assets* and their interest rate is called the **risk-free rate.** There is probably no security in the world that exposes an investor to less risk than a T-bill does.* Their negligible variability of return attracts a clientele of investors who are highly risk-averse and are happy to own T-bills even though their average returns are very low.

Opportunity Cost. Economic resources have alternative uses. The **opportunity cost** of an economic resource is determined by what it could earn in its highest paying alternative use. Opportunity costs include more than out-of-pocket expenses. For example, the cost of school includes not only the cost of books and tuition; it also includes the student's foregone wages.

Cash has an opportunity cost. The *opportunity cost of cash* equals the rate of return the cash could have earned had it been invested in a higher-paying alternative. Table 2-1 lists the opportunity costs of holding cash instead of investing in alternative categories of assets. For instance, Table 2-1 shows that the opportunity cost of holding cash instead of investing in the stock market equals an arithmetic average rate of return of 13.3% per year that was missed. Opportunity costs are not obvious expenses like out-of-pocket costs. Investors who ignore the subtle opportunity costs are not likely to make the best investment decisions.

THE REQUIRED RATE OF RETURN

Investors who are seeking to maximize their rate of return—or, equivalently, wealth—should only enter into investments promising expected returns that exceed the investor's "cost of capital." The **cost of capital** can be interest expense paid for borrowed capital, cash dividend payments that a stock issuer pays to its stockholders, or an opportunity cost. The cost of capital is denoted k and is often called the **required rate of return** because, as shown in Table 2-2, this is the minimum rate of return that an investment must earn to increase the investor's wealth. The cost of capital or required rate of return is a *hurdle rate* that all investment returns should exceed before the investor commits his or her funds to the investment.

Table 2-1 lists historical costs of capital (realized returns) for six categories of assets. The differences between these realized returns (costs of capital) were called equity risk premiums in the previous discussion, Interpreting Historical Return and Risk.

TABLE 2-2   Does the Investment's Return Exceed the Investor's Required Return, k?

Compare k and r to Determine . . .	. . . the Expected Impact on the Investor's Wealth
$\left(\begin{array}{c}\text{Investor's}\\\text{required rate}\\\text{of return, }k\end{array}\right) < \left(\begin{array}{c}\text{Investment's}\\\text{rate of}\\\text{return, }r\end{array}\right)$	Wealth increases
$\left(\begin{array}{c}\text{Investor's}\\\text{required rate}\\\text{of return, }k\end{array}\right) = \left(\begin{array}{c}\text{Investment's}\\\text{rate of}\\\text{return, }r\end{array}\right)$	No change in wealth
$\left(\begin{array}{c}\text{Investor's}\\\text{required rate}\\\text{of return, }k\end{array}\right) > \left(\begin{array}{c}\text{Investment's}\\\text{rate of}\\\text{return, }r\end{array}\right)$	Wealth decreases

* In 1997 the U.S. government began issuing *Treasury inflation-protected securities (TIPS)*. As explained in Chapter 5, these Treasury bonds and U.S. savings bonds are indexed to inflation to remove purchasing power risk.

TABLE 2-3   Combining Risk Premiums to Compute a Security's Required Rate of Return (Cost of Capital)[a]

Required Rate of Return (k)	Sum of	Appropriate Risk Premiums
For Treasury bills, $k = 4.5\%$	4.5% =	Risk-free rate (RFR)
For Treasury Notes, $k = 5.5\%$	4.5% =	Risk-free rate (RFR)
	+1.0% =	+Intermediate horizon premium
	5.5% =	Total = required rate of return
For Treasury bonds, $k = 5.9\%$	4.5% =	Risk-free rate (RFR)
	+1.4% =	+Long horizon premium
	5.9% =	Total = Required rate of return
For corporate bonds, $k = 6.3\%$	4.5% =	Risk-free rate (RFR)
	+1.4% =	+Long horizon premium
	+0.4% =	+Default premium
	6.3% =	Total = Required rate of return
For large-cap stocks, $k = 13.0\%$	4.5% =	Risk-free rate (RFR)
	+1.4% =	+Long horizon premium
	+7.1% =	+Equity risk premium
	13.0% =	Total = Required rate of return
For small-cap stocks, $k = 14.5\%$	4.5% =	Risk-free rate (RFR)
	+1.4% =	+Long horizon premium
	+7.1% =	+Equity risk premium
	+1.5% =	+Size premium
	14.5% =	Total = Required rate of return

SOURCE: Adapted from *Stocks, Bonds, Bills, and Inflation 1999 Yearbook—Valuation Edition*, pp. 10, 18, 23, and 256, published annually by ▲ Ibbotson Associates, Chicago, IL 60601.

[a] The Term Structure of Interest Rates is examined in Chapter 20.

Table 2-3 shows how the various risk premiums add up to the cost of capital that is appropriate for each asset category.

The cost of capital and the cost of capital components that are appropriate for any given market vary as the economic conditions affecting that market change. As a result, it is necessary to periodically update cost of capital statistics to reflect current market conditions.

EXAMPLE

THE REQUIRED RATE OF RETURN FOR TIM'S 6-MONTH TREASURY BILL, USING ANNUAL RATES

In the Example involving Tim's return from the U.S. Treasury bill (p. 21), the 6-month T-bill's return was annualized to determine the equivalent 1-year return, $r_{\text{T-bill}} = 4.12\%$. The top section of Table 2-3 suggests a required rate of return (cost of capital, opportunity cost) of $k = 4.5\%$ for T-bills. Tim's return of 4.12% is $[k - r_{\text{T-bill}} = 4.5\% - 4.12\% = 0.38\%]$ 38 basis points (BPs) below his required rate of return. A basis point is $\frac{1}{100}$ of 1%. Since Tim's risk-free rate of return is a little too low to increase his wealth ($4.5\% = k > r_{\text{T-bill}} = 4.12\%$), he should consider alternative investments.

COMPUTING TYLER'S REQUIRED RATE OF RETURN FOR AN INVESTMENT IN COCA-COLA'S COMMON STOCK

EXAMPLE

Before making a long-term investment in Coca-Cola's common stock (see p. 20) Tyler wants to compare his return of 20% from Eqn. 2-3a with a required rate of return that is appropriate for Coca-Cola. Tyler needs to determine if the investment will increase his wealth.

Coke is one of the largest corporations in the world; its stock is listed on the New York Stock Exchange (NYSE) with a ticker symbol of KO. Table 2-3 indicates investors add the risk-free rate (RFR), the long horizon premium, and the equity risk premium to find the required rate of return for a common stock issued by a large corporation.

$$
\begin{pmatrix} \text{Risk–Free} \\ \text{Rate, 4.5\%} \end{pmatrix} + \begin{pmatrix} \text{Long horizon} \\ \text{premium, 1.4\%} \end{pmatrix} + \begin{pmatrix} \text{Long–term equity risk} \\ \text{premium for a large} \\ \text{NYSE stock, 7.1\%} \end{pmatrix} = \begin{pmatrix} \text{Required rate} \\ \text{of return for Coke} \\ \text{stock, } k = 13.0\% \end{pmatrix}
$$

Tyler's return of $r_{KO} = 20\%$ from Eqn. 2-3b is 700 BPs points above the $k = 13.0\%$ required rate of return from Table 2-3 for a long-term investment in a NYSE stock like KO.

$$r_{KO} - k_{KO} = 20.0\% - 13.0\% = 7.0\% = 700 \text{ basis points (BPs)}$$

If Coke stock continues to earn $r_{KO} = 20\%$, it is an investment that will make Tyler wealthier. If the long-run return from Coke stock turns out to be less than its required rate of return, the Coke stock is a bad investment that will decrease Tyler's wealth.

The Largest Investors in the World

Pension funds comprise the most significant group of investors in the world. A number of large pensions in the United States individually have more money invested than millions of personal investors.

Most pensions shroud their portfolios in secrecy because they do not want to take a chance an investment might embarrass them. For example, Mr. Ford would not want the public to know if Ford Motor Company pension invested millions in GM stock. If such an investment became public, it might hurt Ford's sales.

Table 2-4A lists governmental agencies* and corporations that own and control the largest pensions. Most of the employers that pay for pensions—**pension sponsors**—do not manage their pensions' assets; they hire professional money managers to manage them. Table 2-4B lists some of the largest investment management firms (hired money managers), ranked by the market value of managed assets.

The typical pension management fee is slightly less than 1% of the market value of the assets managed per year. A representative pension invests 60% of

---

* U.S. federal law requires municipalities, schools, and corporations to invest segregated assets in their pension funds to pay in advance for their employees' retirements. Federal law does not require the federal government to provide advance funding for its pension funds. As a result, the two biggest pension funds are the federal government employees pension fund (for postal workers, retired military people, and bureaucrats) and the Social Security system, and neither of these pensions have any assets set aside to pay their trillion-dollar pension liabilities.

TABLE 2-4 Largest Pension and Money Managers, US $ Millions

Table 2-4A U.S. Pension Fund Portfolios

Rank	Pension Fund	Assets
1	California Public Empl. Ret. Syst. (CalPERS)	$155,823
2	New York State Common	$111,369
3	California State Teachers	$98,437
4	Florida State Board	$93,152
5	General Motors	$91,000
6	Federal Retirement Thrift	$85,309
7	New York State Teachers	$81,523
8	Texas Teachers	$79,377
9	New Jersey Division	$74,927
10	General Electric	$71,456
11	New York City Retirement	$63,065
12	Lucent Technologies	$62,267
13	IBM	$61,810
14	SBC Communications	$60,953
15	Wisconsin Investment Board	$57,692
16	Boeing	$57,370
17	Ford Motor	$55,700
18	Bell Atlantic[a]	$54,275
19	Ohio Public Employees	$52,760
20	North Carolina	$52,618
21	Ohio State Teachers	$55,399
22	Michigan Treasury	$51,127
23	Pennsylvania School Employees	$47,279
24	New York City Teachers	$44,315
25	University of California	$41,948
26	Washington State Board	$41,095
27	Minnesota State Board	$40,953
28	Georgia Teachers	$38,540
29	Virginia Retirement	$35,208
30	Lockheed Martin	$34,765

SOURCE: *Pensions and Investments*, 24 January 2000, 30 and "International and Global Assets Up 30% for Year," *Pensions and Investments*, 10 July 2000, 15–39. Also see "America's Top 300 Money Managers," *Institutional Investor*, July 2000, 94–125.
[a]Bell Atlantic is now called Verizon.

Table 2-4B Money Managers[b]

World Rank	U.S. Rank	Money Manager	Headqtr. Country	Assets
1	3	State Street Global	USA	$102,880
2	4	Capital Guardian	USA	$85,638
3	2	Barclays Global Investors (BGI)	UK	$62,600
4	8	Morgan Stanley Dean Witter Inv.	USA	$56,426
5	10	Putnam Investments	USA	$33,520
6	21	Janus	USA	$31,564

[b]These money managers manage pension fund portfolios and other portfolios too.

World Rank	U.S. Rank	Money Manager	Headqtr. Country	Assets
7	13	J.P. Morgan	USA	$28,835
8	NA	UBS Asset Management	Switzerland	$25,369
9	113	Bank of Ireland	Ireland	$24,397
10	NA	Deutsche Asset	Germany	$24,265
11	25	Templeton Worldwide	USA	$22,545
12	132	GM Investment	USA	$22,370
13	NA	Schroder Investment	UK	$22,083
14	15	Scudder Kemper	USA	$20,695
15	32	Rowe Price-Fleming	USA	$20,017
16	1	Fidelity Investments	USA	$16,602
17	131	Oechsle International	USA	$16,602
18	58	Lazard Asset Management	USA	$16,040
19	53	GE Asset Management	USA	$14,477
20	63	Baring Asset Management	Netherlands	$13,230
21	86	Brandes Investment	USA	$12,992
22	112	Grantham, Mayo Van Otterloo	USA	$12,501
23	47	Sanford C. Bernstein	USA	$10,891
24	17	TIAA-CREF	USA	$10,300
25	7	Alliance Capital	USA	$10,056
26	NA	Prudential	USA	$9,917
27	NA	Delaware International	USA	$9,725
28	NA	Marathon-London	UK	$8,900
29	5	Merrill Lynch	USA	$8,734
30	148	Marvin & Palmer	USA	$7,663

its assets in common stocks, 30% in bonds, and the remaining 10% in real estate and foreign securities, but the asset allocation varies over a wide range from one pension to the next.

A REALITY CHECK

ETHICS

Ethics and Pension Funds

For most of us, the golden years depend on the management of our pension funds. The **Employee Retirement Income Security Act (ERISA)** of 1974 recognizes this important responsibility by making the managers of private pension plans *fiduciaries*. However, the fiduciary duties of plan managers are not always clear.

The managers of *defined benefit* plans (which guarantee a fixed income in retirement) have a duty to maintain funds sufficient to cover future obligations. A company's own securities should not be overrepresented, so that the employees' retirement is not tied to the employer's fortunes. Some defined benefit plans become *overfunded*. Should the company be permitted to divert excess funds for other purposes (*reversion*)? On one hand, a bountiful fund reflects a company's sound management, and better use of the money might benefit employees (who would not receive the extra amount anyway). Besides, the overfunding can be reduced eventually by lower future contributions. On the other hand, reversion deprives employees of the possibility of extra benefits and creates greater risk of underfunding in the future. Employees also lose when plans are raided to pay for takeovers.

Defined contribution plans (in which employee and employer contributions accumulate in individual accounts) involve three fiduciary duties:

1. Plan managers must offer at least three funds with different characteristics along with sufficient information for employees to make sound choices.
2. Like mutual fund advisors, they must seek to maximize the risk-adjusted return of each fund in accord with its characteristics. (This includes adequate diversification so that the company's own securities are not overrepresented.)
3. Plan managers have a fiduciary duty to vote a fund's stock solely in the beneficiaries' interests. This duty creates a difficult conflict of interest if, for example, a takeover opposed by management would increase a fund's returns. How should a plan manager vote the company stock held by a fund?

John R. Boatright, *Professor of Business Ethics*

THE BOTTOM LINE

INTERNET CONNECTION

See the Web site of Professor Campbell at Duke University for text, statistics, and graphs of worldwide economic and political data. The Web site also has an extensive glossary of financial words and terms. Visit: www.duke.edu /~charvey

Over the long run investors want to maximize their invested wealth. Over the short run, investors usually look at the rate of return because that facilitates comparing different investments. Wealth maximization and return maximization are equivalent goals.

The one-period rate of return is what statisticians call the basic random variable of investments work; it is the most frequently analyzed random variable. The arithmetic mean of the one-period rates of return is not a compounded return. The geometric mean return is an average rate of return that is compounded over multiple time periods. Since compounded interest grows faster than noncompounded interest, the geometric mean return will never be larger than the arithmetic mean return from the same investment, $\bar{r} = AMR \geq GMR$.

Table 2-1 displays the probability distributions of returns, historical average return, and risk statistics for six categories of domestic U.S. investments and the inflation rate. Figure 2-1 illustrates the time paths of these price indexes. This table and this figure summarize important characteristics about decades of stock and bond investing.

This chapter introduced two rate of return concepts:

◆ Realized returns are historical data.
◆ The required rate of return is a hurdle rate that all investments should surpass.

The required rate of return appropriate for an investment equals the largest of: (1) the investor's cost of capital (such as the interest rate paid for borrowed funds), (2) the opportunity cost of holding cash (Table 2-1), or (3) the sum of whatever risk premiums are appropriate for the investment (Table 2-3).

QUESTIONS

Q2-1 (Rate of return) (i) Write the formula for the one-period rate of return for an investment in a corporate bond, ignoring transactions costs and taxes.

Q2-2 (Opportunity cost) What is meant by an "opportunity cost"? Refer to Table 2-1 to determine the opportunity cost of holding cash instead of investing in long-term government bonds.

Q2-3 (Risk premium) Lynette is expecting her investment in Endosonics stock, a small cap company that trades on the NASDAQ, to return 18% this year. Use the information provided in Table 2-3 in this chapter to determine if this appears to be a good investment for her.

Q2-4 (Wealth maximization) True, false, or uncertain: Society is harmed by the selfish goal of wealth maximization on the part of investors. Explain.

Q2-5 (Gambling, speculation, and investment) The late 1990s gave rise to what is known as "day-trading." A day trader generally pays a sum of money that allows him or her to occupy a seat in a room that is equipped electronically to display bid-and-ask price information on stocks and to trade in those stocks for his or her own account. Day traders generally try to profit from small spread changes in the bid-and-ask prices—i.e., spreads of 5, 10, or 15 cents per share. Would you classify day traders as gamblers, speculators, or investors? Explain your reasoning.

Q2-6 (Variance) What is the variance of returns on a savings account that earns a guaranteed 3% per annum at an FDIC-insured bank?

Q2-7 (Investment vehicles) Contrast an investment in U.S. Treasury bills with an investment in the common stock of small corporations. (a) What are the relative advantages of the T-bill investment? (b) The disadvantages?

Q2-8 (Return definitions) Explain the differences between historical returns and required returns.

Q2-9 (Risk premiums) How does the risk premium on a corporate bond differ from the risk premium on a U.S. Treasury bond?

Q2-10 (Cost of capital) When estimating a cost of capital by looking at historical data, what factors need to be considered?

PROBLEMS

P2-1 (One-period return) Mike Winters purchased 100 shares of Ball Corporation stock for $48 a share and sold it a year later for $55 a share. He received dividends of $0.60 a share during the year. What was his 1-year holding period return?

P2-2 (One-period return) Johanna purchased 200 shares of Vintage Petroleum, Inc. (VPI) for $16 a share. At the end of the first quarter, she received dividends of $0.08 a share, but the price of the stock had dropped to $12 a share, and she decided to liquidate her holdings. What was her holding period return on this investment?

P2-3 (Terminal value) Leah Chien invested $2,000 in a certain stock and earned a total rate of return of 22% on her investment in one year. What was her ending wealth?

P2-4 (Annualized HPR) Justin paid $9,900 for a 3-month Treasury bill that had a terminal value of $10,000. (a) What was his holding period return (HPR) or one-period return on this investment? (b) What was his annualized rate of return?

P2-5 (Annualized HPR) Derrick paid $9,750 for a 6-month Treasury bill that had a terminal value of $10,000. (a) What was his holding period return (HPR) on this investment? (b) What was his annualized rate of return?

P2-6 (One-period returns) The following information is provided for GAP, Incorporated, which trades on the NYSE:

Fiscal year ending January 31	Close price	Annual dividend
1994	$23.75	$0.09
1995	$18.625	$0.10
1996	$23.50	$0.11
1997	$31.25	$0.13
1998	$28.50	$0.13
1999	$33.375	$0.13

Calculate the rate of return a shareholder, who purchased the stock on January 31, 1994, earned for each of his five 1-year holding periods, ignoring commissions and taxes. What was his geometric mean rate of return?

P2-7 (Average return, variance, and standard deviation) Use the information in Problem 2-6 to calculate the shareholder's arithmetic mean return and the standard deviation of the returns.

P2-8 (Required rate of return) Use the data provided in Table 2-3 of this chapter and the calculations for GAP, Incorporated above to determine if you would consider GAP a good investment. Explain your answer.

P2-9 (Average return, variance, and standard deviation) The following data is available on the returns of the Smith-Tinker Corporation (STC) for the past 4 years:

Year	Return
1	10%
2	−1%
3	15%
4	12%

Calculate the (a) arithmetic mean return on STC stock, (b) the variance of the returns on STC stock, and (c) standard deviation of the returns on STC stock.

P2-10 (Real returns) Use the data provided in Table 2-1 in this chapter to determine the inflation-adjusted returns for each asset class listed in the Table. Which asset class provided the highest real returns?

CFA EXAM QUESTIONS

The following questions are adopted from the 1997 CFA Sample Exam, Level I. The first two questions utilize the following information:

The annual rate of return for JSI's common stock has been:

	1993	1994	1995	1996
Return	14%	19%	−10%	14%

1. What is the arithmetic mean rate of return for JSI's common stock over the 4 years?
   A. 8.62%
   B. 9.25%
   C. 14.00%
   D. 14.25%

2. What is the geometric mean rate of return for JSI's common stock over the 4 years?
   A. 8.62%
   B. 9.25%
   C. 14.21%
   D. It cannot be calculated because of the negative return in 1995.

3. A portfolio realized a 10 percent return in year 1 and a −10 percent return in year 2. The geometric mean return for the 2-year period is:
   A. −0.500%.
   B. 0%.
   C. 0.990%.
   D. 0.995%.

FURTHER REFERENCES

Markowitz, Harry, *Portfolio Selection*. New York: Wiley, 1959.

In Chapters 3 and 4 the Nobel laureate provides an easy-to-read yet rigorous exposition of finite probability. Only simple algebra is used.

Francis, Jack Clark, and Richard Taylor, Schaum's Outlines, *Investments,* 2nd ed. New York: McGraw-Hill, 2000.

This paperback booklet is a learning aid that contains numerous solved investment problems. The order of the chapters does not correspond to the chapter order of any investment book. For example, Schaum's Chapter 4 is relevant to this textbook's Chapter 2.

INTRODUCTION TO VALUATION

Determining an investment's price is usually easy. You can ask the seller. Securities prices are also available in many newspapers, on some television channels, and on several Web sites. It is more difficult to determine the value *of an investment than it is to find its* price.

Value *is a measure of worth. Investors compare a security's price to its value to find out if it is underpriced or overpriced. A value estimate is needed every time an investor contemplates buying or selling an investment.*

*There are several ways to estimate the value of an investment. This chapter presents the discounted **present value** model. (Other valuation models are presented in later chapters.) The discounted present value model assumes money has **time value.** Money has time value because borrowers pay interest to lenders to induce them to make loans.*

THE TIME VALUE OF MONEY　　　　**DEFINITION**

Interest is the rent on borrowed money. Interest causes money to have a terminal value in the future that differs from its present value. For example, if $1 is deposited in a Federal Deposit Insurance Corporation (FDIC)–insured bank account at the present time at an interest of 5%, the investment will have a terminal value of $1.05 after 1 year.

$$(\text{Present value})(1 + \text{Interest rate}) = (\text{Terminal value})$$

$$(\$1.00) \qquad (1 + 5\%) \quad = \quad (\$1.05) \qquad (3\text{-}1)$$

This shows how money has time value.

After the discounted present value model is introduced, examples of how to estimate the values of a stock, a bond, and a rental property are presented. Once you have an estimate of the investment's value, you can compare its price with its value and decide whether you think it is underpriced, overpriced, or priced appropriately. The concepts introduced in this chapter are fundamental to all forms of investing and are essential to return or wealth maximization.

Security price fluctuations may appear chaotic, but they aren't. These fluctuations typically result from the market's reactions to the random arrival of new information. The valuation techniques in this chapter not only help you decide whether to buy or sell, they also help you understand what causes securities prices to fluctuate randomly. Studying the market mechanism also makes you realize that when you buy or sell you become part of the economic forces that move securities prices in a manner that benefits the nation. The benefits society gains from investors are explained in this chapter.

After discussing buying and selling we turn to hedging, a way of reducing risk, and arbitrage. Arbitrage is a form of hedging that earns profits and aligns prices in accordance with something called the economic "law of one price." Buying a security, selling a security, hedging with a security, and arbitraging a security all have some impact on the security's price. Informed buying, selling, hedging, and arbitraging tends to make the price of a security move closer to its value. This chapter provides some initial discussion of the efficiency with which securities prices pursue their values.

THE TIME VALUE OF MONEY: ONE-PERIOD MODELS

The rate of return in Chapter 2's Eqn. 2-3 (p. 20) can be rearranged to equal the time value model, Eqn. 3-1, which was introduced earlier in this chapter.

$$\left(\begin{matrix} \text{One-period} \\ \text{rate of return, } r \end{matrix} \right) = \left[\frac{(\text{Terminal value}) - (\text{Present value})}{(\text{Present value})} \right] \tag{2-3}$$

$$\left(\begin{matrix} \text{One-period} \\ \text{rate of return, } r \end{matrix} \right) = \left[\frac{(\text{Terminal value})}{(\text{Present value})} \right] - 1$$

$$(1 + r) = \left[\frac{(\text{Terminal value})}{(\text{Present value})} \right]$$

$$(\text{Present value})(1 + r) = (\text{Terminal value}) \tag{3-1}$$

Eqn. 2-3 and Eqn. 3-1 are mathematically and economically equivalent because the interest rate on the investment (money loaned to, say, a bank) in Eqn. 3-1 equals the lender's one-period rate of return defined in Chapter 2's Eqn. 2-3. The one-period rate of return and the time value models are also related to the present value model.

Eqn. 3-1 is rearranged below to show how to determine the **present value** of an investment.

$$(\text{Present value})(1 + r) = (\text{Terminal value}) \tag{3-1}$$

$$(\text{Present value}) = \frac{(\text{Terminal value})}{(1 + r)} \tag{3-2}$$

Equivalent Models. The one-period rate of return formula, Eqn. 2-3 in Chapter 2, was rearranged above to be the time value model in Eqn. 3-1. Time value Eqn. 3-1 was then rearranged to become present value Eqn. 3-2. Financial analysts take comfort from the fact that these different financial models are compatible with each other.

The rate of return sometimes differs from the discount rate. This difference is acknowledged by rewriting present value Eqn. 3-2 as Eqn. 3-2a:

$$\left(\begin{array}{c}\text{Market-determined}\\\text{present value, or price}\end{array}\right) = \frac{(\text{Terminal value})}{(1 + k)} \tag{3-2a}$$

Eqns. 3-2 and 3-2a will be identical if the discount rate equals the rate of return ($k = r$).[1] Alas, the real world is full of uncertainty, people have differences of opinion, different people have different resources with which to work, and disequilibrium frequently prevails. As a result, situations in which a discount rate differs from a rate of return ($k \neq r$) are common:

♦ **Asset is overpriced:** If $k > r$ the present value of the asset will be below its price.

♦ **Asset is underpriced:** If $k < r$ the present value of the asset will be above its price.

JIM VALUES KO USING DIFFERENT DISCOUNT RATES   **EXAMPLE**

James Clark purchased Coca-Cola stock for $54 per share. He sold KO (Coke's NYSE ticker symbol) 1 year later for $64 to realize a capital gain of $10 and a cash dividend of 80 cents per share. Jim's total income from the stock is $10.80. Eqn. 2-3b from Chapter 2 indicates that Jim's rate of return is 20%.

$$\left(\begin{array}{c}\text{One-year}\\\text{rate of return,}\\ r = 20\%\end{array}\right) = \frac{\$10.80\text{ Income}}{\$54\text{ Invested}} = \left[\frac{(\text{Price change, }\$10) + (\text{Cash dividend, }\$0.80)}{(\text{Purchase price, }\$54)}\right]$$

Jim's one-period rate of return can be analyzed equivalently as follows:

$$r = 20\% = \left[\frac{(\text{Terminal value, }\$64.80) - (\text{Present value, }\$54)}{(\text{Present value, }\$54)}\right]$$

$$= \left[\frac{(\text{Terminal value, }\$64.80)}{(\text{Present value, }\$54)}\right] - 1$$

Jim analyzed the investment in KO under different assumptions about his required rate of return (opportunity cost, discount rate, cost of capital):

Underpriced. If Jim's required rate of return is $k = 19\%$, he will think the stock was underpriced at $54 and be happy to buy it (value = $54.45 > $54 = price).

$$\left(\begin{array}{c}\text{Present}\\\text{value, }\$54.45\end{array}\right) = \frac{(\text{Terminal value, }\$64.80)}{(1 + k)} = \frac{(\text{Terminal value, }\$64.80)}{(1.19)}$$

Priced Correctly. If Jim's required rate of return and the stock's rate of return are identical, $k = 20\% = r$, he will think the stock was priced correctly at $54 and it will not be profitable for him to buy it (value = $54 = price).

$$\left(\begin{array}{c}\text{Present}\\\text{value, }\$54\end{array}\right) = \frac{(\text{Terminal value, }\$64.80)}{(1 + k)} = \frac{(\text{Terminal value, }\$64.80)}{(1.20)}$$

Overpriced. If Jim's required rate of return is $k = 21\%$, he will think the stock is overpriced at $54 and he will recommend that people who own the stock sell it (value = $53.55 < $54 = price).

$$\binom{\text{Present}}{\text{value, \$53.55}} = \frac{(\text{Terminal value, \$64.80})}{(1 + k)} = \frac{(\text{Terminal value, \$64.80})}{(1.21)}$$

Conclusion: An investor's required rate of return is an important determinant of the investor's behavior.

Table 2-3 in Chapter 2 (p. 30) showed how risk premiums add up to determine the required rate of return that is appropriate for an investment. Table 2-3 demonstrates why the required rate of return is sometimes called the **risk-adjusted discount rate.**

THE TIME VALUE OF MONEY: MULTIPERIOD MODELS

DEFINITION

THE PRESENT VALUE MODEL

The present value model can value investments that span more than a single time period.

$$\text{Present value, or } PV = \frac{CF_1}{(1 + k)^1} + \frac{CF_2}{(1 + k)^2} + \dots + \frac{CF_T}{(1 + k)^T} \quad \text{(3-3)}$$

CF stands for cash flow—either inflows or outflows. The subscripts and exponents are time period indicators. The **terminal time period,** when the last **cash flow** occurs, is denoted T. For U.S. Treasury bonds the cash flows are known with certainty in advance and a riskless discount rate is used. For risky investments we use expected cash flows and a risk-adjusted discount rate.

Since a corporation might survive indefinitely, it is sometimes assumed that the terminal time period is $T = \infty$.

$$PV = \sum_{t=1}^{\infty} \frac{\text{Cash flow}_t}{(1 + k)^t} = \frac{CF_1}{(1 + k)^1} + \frac{CF_2}{(1 + k)^2} + \frac{CF_3}{(1 + k)^3} + \dots \quad \text{(3-3a)}$$

The valuation model just discussed says the value of a series of cash flows equals the discounted present value of all future cash flows. These cash flows are expected to arrive at the end of successive time periods denoted $t = 1, t = 2, t = 3, \dots, t = T$. The term k represents the required rate of return that is appropriate for the investment. The cash flows could be cash dividends from a common stock, coupon interest from a bond, rent from a piece of real estate, the asset's selling price, or other cash flows. The following examples show how to use this model to determine what an investment is worth.

COMPUTING THE PRESENT VALUE OF A BOND

EXAMPLE

Most bond investors obtain two types of cash flows: (1) periodic coupon interest payments and (2) repayment of principal when the bond matures. Georgia restated present value Eqn. 3-3 in a manner that is appropriate to value an annual coupon 3-year U.S. Treasury note she is thinking about buying.

$$PV = \frac{\text{Coupon}_1}{(1 + YTM)^1} + \frac{\text{Coupon}_2}{(1 + YTM)^2} + \frac{\text{Coupon}_3 + \text{Par}}{(1 + YTM)^3}$$

(3-4)

The terms in Eqn. 3-4 are discussed below.

◆ **Discount rate:** The discount rate used to value bonds is a fluctuating market interest rate called the **yield-to-maturity**, or **YTM**. A bond's yield-to-maturity is the discount rate that equates the present value of all future cash flows to the bond's current market (purchase) price. The YTM is the compound rate of return a bond investor expects to earn from holding the bond until it matures. From Table 2-3 in Chapter 2 (p. 30)* we see the Treasury note's appropriate discount rate (required rate of return) is 5.5%.

◆ **Par:** A bond's par value is also known as its face value, or principal. The par value and the date when it is scheduled to be repaid (**maturity date, expiration date**) are printed on the bond and cannot be changed during the bond's life. If a bond with a par value of $1,000 repays its principal in 3 years, this terminal cash flow occurs at $T = 3$ years.

◆ **Coupon:** The coupon payment (or simply, the coupon) is the product of the coupon rate and the face value. If the coupon rate is 6%, the bond pays [($1,000)(0.06) =] $60 on the last day of each year of its 3-year life. Substituting these values into Eqn. 3-4 leads Georgia to conclude the bond's present value is $1,013.489:

$$PV = \frac{\$60}{(1 + .055)^1} + \frac{\$60}{(1 + .055)^2} + \frac{\$60 + \$1,000}{(1 + .055)^3}$$

$$= \$56.872 + \$53.907 + \$902.710 = \$1,013.489$$

If Georgia can buy this bond at a price below $1,013.489 it is a good investment, because she is buying it for less than its worth.

THE PRESENT VALUE OF A PERPETUITY

DEFINITION

Perpetual stocks and bonds typically pay fixed cash flows forever, but they never repay the principal. Buying a perpetuity is like buying a perpetual annuity that can be sold to another owner. Perpetuities are valued with the following formula:

---

* YTMs and the term structure of interest rates are examined further in Chapters 20 and 21.

$$PV = \sum_{t=1}^{\infty} \frac{\text{Cash flow}_t}{(1 + k)^t} \qquad \text{(3-5)}$$

$$= \frac{CF_1}{(1 + k)^1} + \frac{CF_2}{(1 + k)^2} + \frac{CF_3}{(1 + k)^3} + \frac{CF_4}{(1 + k)^4} + \dots$$

$$= \frac{CF}{k} \qquad \text{(3-5a)}$$

Eqn. 3-5a can be used to value a preferred stock that pays perpetual fixed cash dividends.* As shown in Eqn. 3-5b, the yield-to-maturity (YTM) is the discount rate that is appropriate to value a bond that pays coupon interest payments perpetually and never repays the principal.

$$PV = \frac{\left(\begin{array}{c} \text{Annual} \\ \text{coupon} \end{array}\right)}{YTM} \qquad \text{(3-5b)}$$

EXAMPLE

ESTIMATING THE VALUE OF A CONSOL

The British government issued perpetual bonds called Consols. These perpetuities pay a constant coupon to infinity and the principal is never repaid. The present value of a Consol is computed by substituting its cash flows into the *PV* formula for a perpetuity:

$$PV = \sum_{t=1}^{\infty} \frac{\text{Cash flow}_t}{(1 + YTM)^t} = \frac{\text{Coupon}_1}{(1 + YTM)^1} + \frac{\text{Coupon}_2}{(1 + YTM)^2} + \frac{\text{Coupon}_3}{(1 + YTM)^3} + \dots = \frac{\text{Coupon}}{YTM} \quad \text{(3-5c)}$$

Jeff is a chemist who lives in London; he is considering investing in a Consol at a time when they have a yield-to-maturity (market interest rate) of 5.9%. He computes the present value of a Consol that pays an annual coupon of £70 as follows:**

$$PV = \frac{CF}{k} = \frac{\text{Annual coupon}}{\text{Yield--to--maturity}} = \frac{£70}{0.059} = £1,186.44$$

Jeff correctly concludes that if the Consol is available at a price below £1,186.44 it is a good buy, but if its price is over £1,186.44 he won't buy it because it is overpriced.

EXAMPLE

ESTIMATING THE VALUE OF A SHARE OF STOCK

A share of stock is worth the discounted present value of all future cash flows the investor expects to receive from it, as previously shown in Eqn. 3-3.

$$PV = \frac{CF_1}{(1 + k)^1} + \frac{CF_2}{(1 + k)^2} + \dots + \frac{CF_T}{(1 + k)^T}$$

---

* An Appendix at the end of this chapter shows how to derive the present value formula for a series of equal-sized perpetual cash flows. See equation (F11) on page 64.

** Foreign exchange is the topic of Chapter 17. There we investigate what happens if Jeff resides outside Great Britain and must exchange currencies.

Eqn. 3-3 can be equivalently restated as Eqns. 3-6 and 3-7 to reflect the cash flows investors receive from a share of stock.[2]

Brenda is thinking about purchasing a share of stock in a small corporation that, based on the risk premiums in Table 2-3 from Chapter 2 (p. 30), she thinks should earn a required rate of return of $k = 14.5\%$. Brenda expects to be able to sell the stock for $40 after collecting cash dividends of $2 per share at the end of each of the next 2 years. The present value of this stock is $33.783 per share.

$$PV = \sum_{t=1}^{T=2} \frac{\text{Cash dividend}_t}{(1 + k)^t} + \frac{\text{Selling price}}{(1 + k)^2} \tag{3-6}$$

$$= \frac{\$2}{(1.145)^1} + \frac{\$2}{(1.145)^2} + \frac{\$40}{(1.145)^2}$$

$$= \$1.7467 + \$1.5255 + \$30.510 = \$33.783 \tag{3-6a}$$

Brenda makes a wealth-maximizing decision to buy the stock if she can get it for less than $33.783.

ESTIMATING THE VALUE OF A SHARE OF STOCK THAT HAS A CONSTANT PERPETUAL GROWTH RATE

EXAMPLE

Jana is wondering whether or not she should pay the market price of $51.50 for a stock issued by a large NYSE-listed corporation that is currently paying an annual cash dividend of $3 per share. Jana believes this dividend will grow at a rate of $g = 3\%$ per year for as far ahead as she can see. Table 2-3 in Chapter 2 suggests that $k = 13.0\%$ is an appropriate risk-adjusted discount rate to use in valuing the stock.

$$PV = \sum_{t=1}^{T=\infty} \frac{(\text{Cash dividend}_0)(1 + g)^t}{(1 + k)^t} + \frac{\text{Selling price}}{(1 + k)^T} \tag{3-7}$$

$$= \sum_{t=1}^{T=\infty} \frac{(\$3.00)(1 + 3\%)^t}{(1 + 13.0\%)^t} + \frac{\$51.50}{(1 + 13.0\%)^T} \tag{3-7a}$$

Rather than using the computationally cumbersome Eqns. 3-7 and 3-7a to find the present value of an infinite sum, Jana uses the simpler, but mathematically equivalent, Eqns. 3-7b and 3-7c.

$$PV = \frac{\text{Cash dividend at time } t = 1}{(\text{Discount rate} - \text{growth rate})} = \frac{DIV_0(1 + g)}{(k - g)} \tag{3-7b}$$

$$= \frac{CF}{k - g} = \frac{DIV_0(1 + g)}{(k - g)} = \frac{\$3(1.03)}{.130 - .03} = \frac{\$3.09}{.10} = \$30.90 \tag{3-7c}$$

Eqn. 3-7c shows that the stock is worth $30.90 per share.* Based on these calculations Jana decides not to buy the stock because it is overpriced by ($51.50 − $30.90 =) $20.60 per share.

---

* An Appendix at the end of this chapter shows how to derive the simplified present value formula for a perpetual cash flow. See equation (F8) on page 64.

EXAMPLE   ESTIMATING THE VALUE OF A SHARE OF PERPETUAL PREFERRED STOCK

Alecia is considering paying the market price of $50 for a share of preferred stock that will pay an annual cash dividend rate equal to 4.5% of its $100 face value per share forever. This $4.50 annual cash dividend is fixed, $g = 0$. Alecia will never receive the stock's $100 principal. Some financial research leads Alecia to conclude that $k = 13.0\%$ is an appropriate risk-adjusted discount rate to use in valuing this preferred stock. Applying Eqn. 3-5a, we see:

$$PV = \frac{CF}{k}$$

$$= \frac{DIV_0}{k} = \frac{\$4.50}{.130} = \$34.615$$

The stock's perpetual stream of constant cash dividends is worth $34.615 per share.* Alecia maximizes her wealth by deciding not to buy the stock, because it is overpriced by ($50 − $34.62 =) $15.38 per share.

EXAMPLE   ESTIMATING THE VALUE OF A REAL ESTATE INVESTMENT

Walter is thinking about buying a home and renting it for an annual net rental income of $10,000, after maintenance expenses and property taxes are deducted from the gross rent. He thinks he can sell the house for $110,000 in 3 years. Since most investments are worth the discounted present value of their future cash flows, Walter substitutes these values into present value Eqn. 3-3 to obtain Eqns. 3-8 and 3-8a. After investigating the home and talking to some real estate assessors and financial analysts, Walter decides that his required rate of return (cost of capital) is $k = 10\%$. If Walter discounts the net cash flows he is forecasting at 10%, the rental property has a present value of $107,513.

$$PV = \frac{\left(\begin{array}{c}\text{Net rental}\\\text{income}\end{array}\right)}{(1 + k)^1} + \frac{\left(\begin{array}{c}\text{Net rental}\\\text{income}\end{array}\right)}{(1 + k)^2} + \frac{\left(\begin{array}{c}\text{Net rental}\\\text{income}\end{array}\right) + \left(\begin{array}{c}\text{Selling}\\\text{price}\end{array}\right)}{(1 + k)^3} \tag{3.8}$$

$$PV = \frac{\$10,000}{(1 + .10)^1} + \frac{\$10,000}{(1 + .10)^2} + \frac{\$10,000 + \$110,000}{(1 + .10)^3} = \$107,513$$

Walter decides to make an initial offer for the house of $90,000. If necessary, he plans to offer successively higher bids up to a maximum bid of $107,513. If Walter can buy the house for less than $107,513, he can expect to earn more than his required rate of return of $k = 10\%$.

The examples above illustrate ways to compute the value of different investments. After the value of an investment is determined, you make rational buy-sell decisions by comparing its price to its value.

---

* An Appendix at the end of this chapter shows how to derive the simplified present value formula.

MAKING BUY-SELL DECISIONS

Millions of nonprofessional investors wonder what determines securities prices and why they fluctuate. They don't understand that a security's value determines its price. Professional investors know how to make value estimates and use them to make buy-sell decisions, and they know that their investment decisions are what makes securities prices fluctuate. To see how value estimates determine securities prices, consider the buy-sell decision rules in the following box. These simplified buy-sell rules would be appropriate to use if the investor could compute the value of the investment with certainty.

BUY-SELL RULES UNDER THE ASSUMPTION OF CERTAINTY　　　**DEFINITION**

The Buy Rule: If a security's price is below its value, it is **underpriced** and the investor should be buying and holding the security to profit from price gains that are expected. If the market price of security i at the tth instant in time is denoted $Price_{i,t}$ and its economic value is represented by $Value_{i,t}$ then the Buy Rule says:

$$\text{If:}\quad Price_{i,t} < Value_{i,t} \quad \blacktriangleright \quad \text{Consider buying}$$

The Don't Trade Rule: If the market price of asset i at the tth instant in time *equals* its value, then that asset is priced correctly—its price and value are not expected to change until new information arrives. No profit is likely to be made from buying or selling an asset that is **correctly priced.**

$$\text{If:}\quad Price_{i,t} = Value_{i,t} \quad \blacktriangleright \quad \text{Don't trade}$$

The Sell Rule: If market price of security i at time t is above its value at the tth instant, the security is **overpriced.** To avoid losses expected to occur when the security's price falls down to its value, consider selling such overpriced securities. If the security is not owned, then it may be "sold short" in order to profit from the expected price decline. "Short sales" are introduced later in this chapter (p. 46).

$$\text{If:}\quad Price_{i,t} > Value_{i,t} \quad \blacktriangleright \quad \text{Consider liquidation, or a short sale}$$

Buy-sell decisions suggested by the rules above provide the economic force that keeps securities prices moving in pursuit of their values. Selling overpriced securities drives their prices down. Buying underpriced securities bids their prices higher. These economic forces are always aiming at a moving target, however, because securities values keep changing as new information arriving continuously alters the securities values.

The buy-sell rules just cited are overly simplified because in this world of uncertainty it is impossible to know exactly the value of an asset. Some investors enjoy a **competitive advantage.** Some investors are better educated than others, some investors have access to more financial information than others, and some investors get the information sooner than others. A few investors enjoy all of these competitive advantages.

It is rational behavior for an investor to act as if a security's price equals its value, because prices are often determined by experts enjoying a competitive advantage. It takes courage for an investor to state that a security is over- or underpriced and bet against a market made up of anonymous experts who may have deep pockets.

Assessing the values of securities is so difficult that some securities analysts are paid millions of dollars per year for providing and explaining their value estimates of a few securities.[3] For example, an expert automotive analyst might only be responsible for following Audi, DaimlerChrysler, Ford, GM, Honda, Toyota, Volkswagen, Volvo, and a few other automakers. An analyst who can correctly predict which direction the prices of these stocks will move most of the time will develop a "track record" (professional reputation) for making good predictions and a "following" of profit-seeking traders will seek this automotive analyst's views. If some stock brokerages and investment banks think that employing a respected securities analyst will generate trading commissions for their firm in excess of $1 million per year, they will be happy to pay that analyst $1 million per year. If that analyst later finds that he or she can generate trading commissions for the firm in excess of $2 million per year, that analyst will likely demand a pay raise to equal that—and have little difficulty getting any one of several employers to pay it.

LONG POSITIONS, SHORT POSITIONS, AND RATES OF RETURN

Buying securities believed to be underpriced and holding them in anticipation of price appreciation is the simplest and most popular investment strategy. Buying a security creates an investment position called a **long position.** The rate of return from a long position was introduced in Chapter 2 as Eqn. 2-3b.

$$\begin{pmatrix} \text{Long position's} \\ \text{rate of return, } r \end{pmatrix} = \frac{\text{Price change } + \text{ Cash flow (if any)}}{\text{Price at beginning of holding period}} = \frac{(P_1 - P_0) + CF}{P_0} \qquad \textbf{(3-9)}$$

Here r stands for the one-period rate of return, P_0 is the market price of the security at the beginning of the time period, P_1 denotes the security's price at the end of the time period, and $(P_1 - P_0)$ is the price change during the single time period. CF represents the cash flow from a cash dividend, coupon interest, rent, or other source that occurred during the time period—which can be days, weeks, months, quarters of a year, or a year.

EXAMPLE   **STEVE'S RATE OF RETURN FROM A LONG POSITION**

If Steven Douglas bought a share of stock for $64, sold it for $66.50 a year later, and collected cash dividends of $3.90 during his 1-year holding period, his rate of return was 10%. Applying Eqn. 3-9, he finds:

$$r = \frac{(P_1 - P_0) + CF}{P_0} = \frac{\$2.50 + \$3.90}{\$64} = \frac{\$6.40}{\$64} = 10\%$$

The Short Position

The **short position** is not as simple as the long position. A **short sale** occurs when one party sells a second party a security the first party does not own. The first party borrows the security from a third party to accomplish delivery. Securities brokerages carry millions of dollars worth of stock in their inventories and are happy to lend shares to short sellers. Short sellers usually "short" a stock or a bond because they expect its price to fall and want to profit from the expected price decline. To profit from the price fall, the short seller sells borrowed shares to a second party who buys them to create a long position in the security. As mentioned, buyers take the long position because they expect to profit from a price rise. Thus, a short sale requires a short seller who is **bearish** (expects a price decline) and a long buyer who is **bullish** (expects price appreciation) about the same security at the same time. A brokerage firm that has multiple offices and several brokers in each office will be able to match up a short seller and long buyer—without the two traders ever knowing each other's names. Commission income provides the incentives for the brokerage firm to match seller and buyer and to lend the shares the short seller needs to deliver to the long buyer. This process keeps working because the brokers earn commissions even if the investors lose money.

After the short seller borrows the securities from a third party to deliver to the long buyer, the short seller waits (and hopes) for the market price of the borrowed securities to fall. If and when it falls, the short seller will purchase the shares at the lower price to cover the short position. If the price falls, the short seller profits by the difference between the price paid for the shares used to repay the third party and the earlier price at which the short seller sold the security short. When the price falls, the long buyer suffers a loss because the price rise that was expected turns out to be a price decrease.

The only difference between short and long positions is the timing of the purchases and sales. A long buyer buys first and sells later. A short seller sells first and buys later.

Ignoring the commissions, the short seller's gain equals the long buyer's loss (or vice versa, if the security's price rises after the short sale). Short sellers can open their bearish positions at any price they select and they may maintain that position for as long as their broker can find a third party to loan them securities to sell short. Figure 3-1 is a newspaper excerpt showing market data on short selling.

The Return from a Short Position

The rate of return from a short seller is defined below:

$$r = \frac{(\text{Price change}) - \text{Cash flow (if any)}}{\text{Price at beginning of short position}} = \frac{(P_0 - P_1) - CF}{P_0} \qquad \textbf{(3-10)}$$

The difference between Eqn. 3-10 and Eqn. 3-9 (p. 46) is that the quantities in the numerators have their signs reversed.

STEVE'S RETURN FROM A SHORT POSITION   **EXAMPLE**

Steven Douglas first sold a share of stock short at a price of $64 per share, later purchased a share of the stock for $66.50 to repay the share lender and took $3.90 from his wallet to reimburse the share lender for the cash dividend of $3.90 that went to the share's new buyer. Steve's rate of return from this short sale was a negative 10%, because the price of the stock rose $2.50 while he was short, and because the $3.90 cash dividend came out of Steve's pocket. Applying Eqn. 3-10 makes this clear:

$$r = \frac{(P_0 - P_1) - CF}{P_0} = \frac{-\$2.50 - \$3.90}{\$64} = \frac{-\$6.40}{\$64} = -10\%$$

The price change = $(P_0 - P_1) = (\$64 - \$66.50) = -\$2.50 = \$2.50$ loss from the price rise. Comparing Eqns. 3-9 and 3-10 reveals that a short position is the mirror image of a long position.

FIGURE 3-1 "Short-Selling Highlights," *Wall Street Journal*, 22 March 2000, B12

SHORT-SELLING HIGHLIGHTS

Largest Short Positions

Rank		Mar. 15	Feb. 15	Change
	NYSE			
1	Qwest Comm Int'l	75,993,604	72,997,555	2,996,049
2	At&T	74,216,583	69,387,948	4,828,635
3	Sprint (Pcs Grp)	65,490,493	79,492,948	−14,002,455
4	VodafoneGrp(Ads)	61,938,122	65,300,068	−3,361,946
5	Walt Disney-Hldg	60,746,141	58,845,710	1,900,431
6	America Online	54,528,042	61,665,635	−7,137,593
7	Lucent Technologies	47,408,985	39,394,215	8,014,770
8	Nortel Networks	41,791,043	33,806,519	7,984,524
9	Time Warner (Hldg)	34,392,577	40,295,634	−5,903,057
10	Pfizer	32,851,919	16,813,732	16,038,187
11	Wal-Mart Stores	32,244,310	33,951,697	−1,707,387
12	Columbia/HcaHlth	31,722,058	32,209,396	−487,338
13	Kmart	31,093,503	33,396,771	−2,303,268
14	TELDeMexico(Ads)	29,008,399	31,096,795	−2,088,396
15	Bell Atlantic	28,136,197	23,043,174	5,093,023
16	Alcatel	23,535,678	4,478,995	19,056,684
17	Schwab (Charles)	21,254,433	14,080,429	7,174,004
18	TelefonicaSA(Adss)	21,200,986	15,667,145	5,533,841
19	LoralSpace&Comm	21,074,014	17,446,530	3,627,484
20	Compaq Computer	21,006,497	20,734,725	271,772
	AMEX			
1	Nasdaq-100 Trust	27,152,790	32,973,660	−5,820,870
2	Standard&PoorsDep	23,390,245	20,927,374	2,462,871
3	TransWorldCommon	12,468,806	12,614,176	−145,370
4	Standard&PoorsMid	7,131,187	5,943,630	1,187,557
5	Echo Bay Mines Ltd	5,404,580	5,389,118	15,462

Largest Changes

Rank		Mar. 15	Feb. 15	Change
	NYSE			
1	Alcatel	23,535,678	4,478,995	19,056,684
2	Pfizer	32,851,919	16,813,732	16,038,187
3	LABCorpofAmerHld	19,199,126	8,023,045	11,176,081
4	Pharmacia+upjohn	15,201,365	5,244,029	9,957,336
5	Lucent Technologies	47,408,985	39,394,215	8,014,770
6	Nortel Networks	41,791,043	33,806,519	7,984,524
7	Schwab (Charles)	21,254,433	14,080,429	7,174,004
8	BP Amoco P.L.C.	18,261,918	11,237,655	7,024,263
1	EMC	9,617,379	31,139,685	−21,522,306
2	Sprint (Pcs Grp)	65,490,493	79,492,948	−14,002,455
3	America Online	54,528,042	61,665,635	−7,137,593
4	Firstar	5,634,643	11,908,155	−6,273,512
5	Kroger Company	18,435,890	24,645,200	−6,209,310
6	Time Warner (Hldg)	34,392,577	40,295,634	−5,903,057
7	Conoco Cl-A	7,813,609	11,848,138	−4,034,529
8	SBC Commun	8,452,511	12,434,754	−3,982,243
	AMEX			
1	Standard&PoorsDep	23,390,245	20,927,374	2,462,871
2	Standard&PoorsMid	7,131,187	5,943,630	1,187,557
3	Diamonds	3,637,778	2,619,448	1,018,330
4	B2B Internet Holdrs	997,300	0	997,300
1	Nasdaq-100 Trust	27,152,790	32,973,660	−5,820,870
2	Organogenesis	4,233,814	5,560,059	−1,326,245
3	Webs Index Japan	1,076,468	2,271,698	−1,195,230
4	Spdr Energy Sel Xle	1,046,449	2,026,096	−979,647

NYSE Short Interest
(In millions of shares)

[chart: values 3400–4200; months M A M J J A S O N D J F M, 1999–2000]

Short Interest Ratio
(NYSE)

[chart: values 2–5; months M A M J J A S O N D J F M, 1999–2000]

Largest Short Interest Ratios

The short interest ratio is the number of days it would take to cover the short interest if trading continued at the average daily volume for the month.

		Mar. 15 Short Int	Avg Dly Vol-a	Days to Cover
	NYSE			
1	Madeco S.A. (Ads)	2,253,998	28,020	80
2	Brooke Group Ltd	1,912,262	24,045	80
3	CompanhiaSiderurg	2,090,769	26,915	78
4	Telecom Nz-Adss	4,493,172	74,005	61
5	Total System Svcs	2,099,206	36,940	57
6	PhoenixInvestPartn	1,126,804	22,100	51
7	PhilippineLdtelGds	1,840,900	36,400	51
8	Pillowtex	3,839,414	78,485	49
9	RoyalGroupTechLtd	1,333,665	29,865	45
10	NTLAustriBnk(Ads)	1,026,767	23,000	45
11	AMF Bowling	3,232,981	73,170	44
12	WHX (Hldg Co)	4,981,479	115,220	43
13	Knight Ridder	17,671,763	417,015	42
14	BankatlanticBanc	3,355,208	80,920	41
15	Titanium Metals	2,525,494	65,410	39
16	Amerus Life Hldg	1,158,948	30,435	38
17	UnitedAssetManage	4,315,735	118,815	36
18	Quebecor Printing	1,380,521	40,890	34
	AMEX			
1	Webs Index Mexico	1,942,549	23,590	82
2	SevenSeasPetrol	3,001,212	91,150	33
3	TransWorldComm	12,468,806	407,740	31
4	Plains Resources	908,602	32,515	28
5	Britesmile	675,470	31,365	22

a-Includes securities with average daily volume of 20,000 shares or more. r-Revised. n-New.

Issues that split in the latest month are excluded.

The largest percentage increase and decrease sections are limited to issues with previously established short positions in both months.

Largest % Increases

Rank		Mar. 15	Feb. 15	%
	NYSE			
1	FletcherCHEnerAds	1,000,100	100	1,000,000.0
2	FletcherCHBldgAds	1,000,950	995	100,498.0
3	Huntingdon Life Sci	2,223,200	3,000	74,006.7
4	First Philippine Fnd	430,900	2,000	21,445.0
5	Taiwan Equity Fund	530,126	7,016	7,456.0
6	Meristar Hotels	381,100	6,400	5,854.7
7	TNP Enterprises	1,064,818	21,209	4,920.6
8	NUI	494,362	10,323	4,688.9
9	Pacific Gulf Props	473,739	12,508	3,687.5
10	Source Capital	330,631	10,475	3,056.4
11	Center Trust	319,025	21,709	1,369.6
12	KoreaElecPwr(Ads)	1,011,192	78,611	1,186.3
13	Safety-Kleen	3,766,171	296,933	1,168.4
14	Telecom-Adss	4,493,172	410,612	994.3
15	Moore Ltd	515,610	50,041	930.4
16	CompCervUnidasS.A	2,096,883	210,500	896.1
17	FreseniusMedcalAds	286,793	29,638	867.7
18	Amer Med Sec Group	297,811	31,500	845.4
19	Sealed Air Pfd A	290,327	37,911	665.8
20	Aurora Foods	1,527,900	220,550	592.8
	AMEX			
1	Insite Vision	501,369	669	74,843.0
2	Texas Biotech	913,589	227,029	302.4
3	GlobalLightTelecom	849,553	413,965	105.2
4	Intermagnetics Gen	1,426,155	715,504	99.3
5	Biotech Holdrs Trust	1,844,470	1,054,642	74.9

Largest % Decreases

Rank		Mar. 15	Feb. 15	%
	NYSE			
1	KimcoRlty7.50%	1	308,269	−100.0
2	MuniyieldNYInsured	27	343,400	−100.0
3	Campbell Res	503	255,147	−99.8
4	Novo-Nordisk (Ads)	3,398	375,649	−99.1
5	Broadwing Ser B	3,946	262,000	−98.5
6	Icici Ltd Ads	28,246	616,637	−95.4
7	Conectiv	149,678	2,567,786	−94.2
8	Swisscom AG	25,537	356,778	−92.8
9	Home Props of NY	106,976	995,427	−89.3
10	Harte-Hanks Comm	103,318	528,250	−80.4
11	Sierra Paci Res	466,587	2,200,896	−78.8
12	Lincoln Ntl F(Incm)	77,569	364,525	−78.7
13	Pohang Iron & Steel	305,938	1,359,801	−77.5
14	Endesa S.A. (Adss)	363,820	1,588,478	−77.1
15	Natl Fuel Gas	153,954	653,033	−76.4
16	Peoples Energy	153,373	550,774	−72.2
17	RougeIndusts(Hldg)	311,411	1,101,089	−71.7
18	ScottishPowerPlc	321,979	1,131,614	−71.5
19	EnhanceFinSvcsGrp	156,611	510,776	−69.3
20	EMC	9,617,379	31,139,685	−69.1
	AMEX			
1	Selfcare	125,135	450,291	−72.2
2	Webs Index Japan	1,076,468	2,271,698	−52.6
3	Spdr Indus Sel Xli	717,696	1,425,222	−49.6
4	Spdr Energy Sel Xle	1,046,449	2,026,096	−48.4
5	Organogenesis	4,233,814	5,560,059	−23.9

Complications with Short Positions

Short sales can be more complicated than they seem. First, if a common stock that has been sold short pays a cash dividend while on loan to the short seller, the short seller must pay an equivalent amount of cash to the third party that lent the shares. Second, the short seller may

be required to put up "margin money" equaling as much as 100% of the value of the borrowed shares as collateral for the third party who lends the shares. **Margin** money is a good-
faith deposit the investor is required to put up to guarantee performance—in this case, to
guarantee the borrowed shares will be repaid. Higher margins require larger investments that
lower the investor's expected rates of return.*

Gain-Loss Illustrations for Long and Short Positions

The gain-loss positions for long and short positions are illustrated in Figure 3-2. The horizontal axis shows the market price of the underlying security or other asset. Above the origin the
graphs' vertical axes trace dollars of profit; dollars of loss are below the origin. The gain-loss
graph for the long position in Figure 3-2A has a slope of $+1$, indicating that the long position
makes a dollar of profit (loss) for each dollar that the market price rises (falls). The profit-loss
graph for the short position in Figure 3-2B has a slope of -1, indicating a dollar of loss
(profit) for the short seller for each dollar that the market price rises (falls).

The long buyer enjoys both an unlimited potential for gains and limited liability. *Limited
liability* means the owner of a long position can do no worse than lose all invested funds,
$r = -100\%$. The owner of a long common-stock position enjoys limited liability because, for

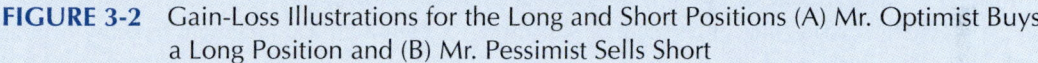

FIGURE 3-2   Gain-Loss Illustrations for the Long and Short Positions (A) Mr. Optimist Buys
a Long Position and (B) Mr. Pessimist Sells Short

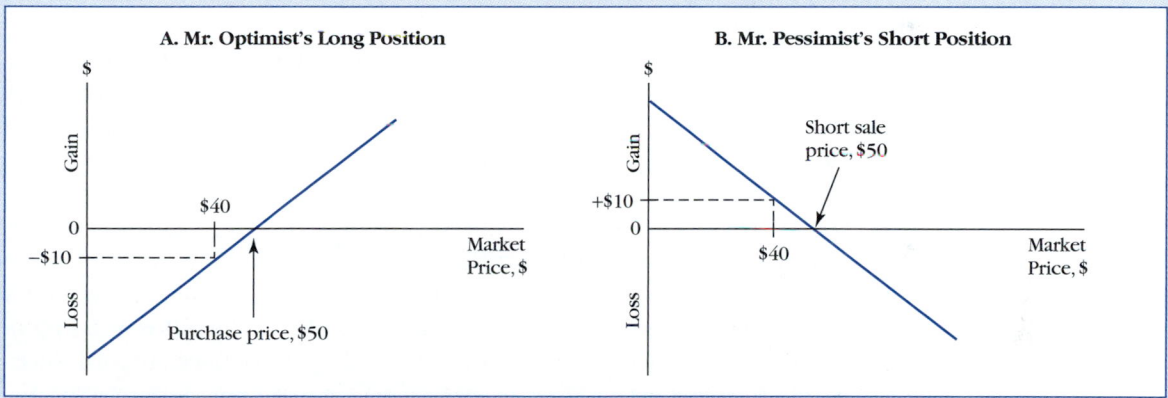

(A) Mr. Optimist pays $50 to create a long position in a share of stock. If the stock's price rises above $50 he profits
from the price gain. If the stock's price falls below $50, Mr. Optimist's losses mount in a one-to-one
correspondence with the price decline. (B) Mr. Pessimist sells a stock short at $50 per share. If the stock's price falls
below $50, his short position profits in a one-to-one correspondence with the price decline. If the price rises above
$50, Mr. Pessimist suffers losses from the price gain.

---

* Brokerage houses require small individual investors to make an up-front cash deposit of P_0 before the institution through which they are executing their trade will permit them to make a short sale. This 100% margin is a negative initial outflow of cash. If the individual investor is named Rockefeller, DuPont, Ford, or is
 some other "substantial individual," some lesser initial deposit between zero and P_0—margins are negotiable—will be acceptable to the brokerage. At the other extreme, institutional investors like Merrill Lynch
 or Citigroup can make short sales for their own account without posting any up-front guarantee money.
 This allows the institutional investors to enjoy initial cash inflows (instead of outflows) from their short
 sales. The one-period rate of return from a no-money-invested position is not defined.

example, if a corporation goes bankrupt and leaves debts of $10,000 per share, the investor is not liable for the debts.

The gains from short selling are limited to a maximum gain of $+100\%$; this occurs if the underlying asset becomes worthless so it costs the short seller nothing to cover the short position (repay the borrowed securities). But, short sellers' losses are unlimited if the price of the underlying security rises infinitely high.

Short sales have been conducted on the floors of securities exchange around the world for decades. The volume of short sales is reported daily in the financial newspapers under the heading "Short Interest." As explained in the newspaper excerpt shown on page 48, the **short interest** is the total number of shares that brokers have listed in their accounts as being sold short. The short interest is usually below 5% of the total volume of shares traded, and stock exchange members do most of the short selling.

ETHICS   A REALITY CHECK

Why the Law Is Not Enough

Law heavily regulates investment activity. So why not let the law be our only guide? Certainly, much that is unethical in investment is also illegal, and so the law is a good starting point. However, the law is also a rather blunt instrument with draconian penalties. A person skirting the edge of the law can end up in prison. Taking the high road is much safer! In addition, broad rules of law cannot substitute for sound ethical judgment in many situations. The law may prohibit conflicts of interest, for example, without being able to define the concept. Ethical standards may be a more certain guide.

The law can be our only guide only if we know it thoroughly. Some people run afoul of the law out of ignorance, others because they apply it incorrectly. Furthermore, the law changes. Legislatures and courts often develop new law in response to moral concerns, so that what is legal one day may be illegal the next. Many people who considered their actions to be legal though perhaps immoral have ruefully discovered otherwise. The law is sometimes slow to correct wrongs, but it eventually responds.

The law is not intended to be a complete guide but is designed to work in tandem with industry self-regulation and professional responsibility. The law permits some industry groups, such as the National Association of Securities Dealers, to be **self-regulating organizations (SROs),** which set general standards for their own members. In turn, SROs adopt more specific rules and expect firms to make them yet more precise. Professional groups, such as the Association for Investment Management and Research, require adherence to a code of professional ethics. This delicate balance of regulation on different levels could not work if everyone believed "If it's legal, then it's okay."

Finally, clients do not expect investment professionals to adhere merely to a legal minimum but, instead, to aspire to an ethical ideal.

John R. Boatright, *Professor of Ethics*

A MORE REALISTIC VALUATION AND INVESTMENT PROCEDURE

Ideals that seem clear in theoretical discussions are sometimes not so clear when we try to apply them. The valuation process, for instance, is more complex than suggested by the present value formula and the buy-sell rules given on pages 40 and 45. Problems result from the

FIGURE 3-3 A Flowchart of the Endless Valuation Process

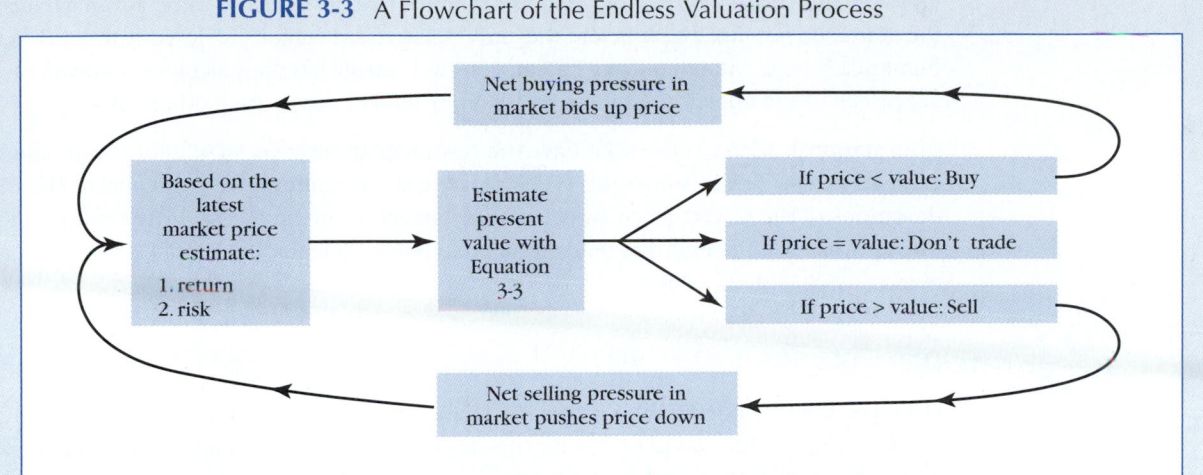

Security analysts assess a security's risk and required rate of return, estimate its present value, and compare the security's price to its value to determine if it is priced correctly. This process should be repeated every time new information about the security arrives and every time its price changes.

fact that a security's risk—and, thus, also its value—can change. For example, expanding or shrinking the security issuer's product line, new competitors, corporate borrowing, changes in the law, and many other things can alter the riskiness of a security.

Securities analysts continually reevaluate the securities they follow. The valuation process is more realistically represented in Figure 3-3, which illustrates a never-ending loop of reassessing the value, comparing the price and the value, and then reconsidering the buy-sell decision based on the latest value estimates. Every new piece of information may change the security's value. Since new information arrives continuously, the value changes continuously. The buying and selling pressures in the marketplace keep market prices in motion as they pursue ever-changing values.

A MODEL OF PRICE-VALUE INTERACTION

The minute-to-minute, hour-to-hour, day-to-day, and week-to-week prices of most securities fluctuate randomly. These short-term fluctuations do not represent meaningless chaos; they result from a rational market mechanism.

The Liquidity Traders and the Information Traders

To see how the market mechanism works, consider two groups of investors that influence securities prices differently.

Liquidity Traders. A huge percentage (perhaps over 90%) of the trades in the world are liquidity trades. Liquidity traders base their decisions to buy on the arrival of an income tax refund, an inheritance, a lottery winning, or some other random good fortune that bestows excess liquidity upon them. Liquidity traders sell an investment when they need to pay a medical bill, buy a new furnace for their house, finance a child's education, or need liquidity for some other reason. Such traders may ignore the distinction between an investment's price and its value, they usually do not buy and sell at times that are selected to be advantageous, and they often do not investigate before they invest. There are millions of liquidity trades, but their numerically large amount of daily trading does not usually have any significant impact on market prices. These numerous random transactions tend to cancel each other out.

Information Traders. Those who have the resources to discover new information and form estimates of securities values are called **information traders.** They recognize significant deviations of the market price away from the general estimate of a security's value and then buy and sell in a manner that tends to (1) maximize their trading profits, and, (2) align the market price with its value.

STUDY CHECK

DOLLARS BUY SHARE VOTES

Have you ever wondered who makes the stock prices move? Consider the *1999 New York Stock Exchange Fact Book's* estimate (pp. 56–57) that almost 70 million individuals owned NYSE stocks directly or indirectly, and the median value of the average investor's portfolios was $15,500. Contrast the average investor with the typical pension fund manager described in Table 2-4A and the associated box about pension funds in Chapter 2.

QUESTION: Is it possible that only a few hundred large pension funds in the United States have more impact on stock market prices than the millions of individual NYSE investors?

ANSWER: Consider, say, a $50 billion pension fund. Dividing the median individual's portfolio value into the aggregate value of a $50 billion pension shows this one large pension has as many "share votes" as ($50 billion/$15,500 =) 3,225,806 individual investors. Additionally, the pension funds probably do more information-based trading, which moves stock prices, while the individual investors probably do more liquidity-motivated trades, which have little impact on prices. These facts suggest that a few hundred large pension funds in the United States have a greater impact on stock market prices than millions of individual investors. Interestingly, the pensions receive very little news coverage.

Comparing Differences Between Prices and Values

Market prices pursue consensus estimates of securities values. If *most* securities analysts' value estimates for a given stock happen to be very similar at some point in time, then the *consensus value estimate* will be narrowly defined. That is, the security's price will probably fluctuate in a narrow range around its well-defined consensus value. But the securities analysts' estimates of another stock's value may vary over a wide range. In this case, that stock's price will fluctuate around its value wildly because great uncertainty exists about its consensus value.

Figure 3-4 depicts a security whose value, which is represented by the dashed straight lines, declines instantaneously when some bad news about the security arrives. The curves in Figure 3-4 graphically represent prices that stray away from this security's value with varying degrees of pricing efficiency.

The price path labeled "Weakly efficient price, I" in Figure 3-4 illustrates how the security's price might fluctuate when only a few investors are making rational buy-sell decisions. In other words, many liquidity traders and only a few information traders determine the weakly efficient stock's price. The curve labeled "Semi–strongly efficient price, II" illustrates how the security's price fluctuates slightly above and below its value in a market composed of numerous information traders and only a few liquidity traders.

The dashed "Value" line coincides with the "Perfectly efficient, Value = Price, III" line in Figure 3-4 because the security's price never deviates from its value. A perfectly efficient mar-

FIGURE 3-4 Illustration of Three Different Hypothesized Price-Value Relationships as Time Passes and the Security's Value Changes at Time *t*: (I) Weakly efficient price, (II) Semi–strongly efficient price, (III) Perfectly efficient price

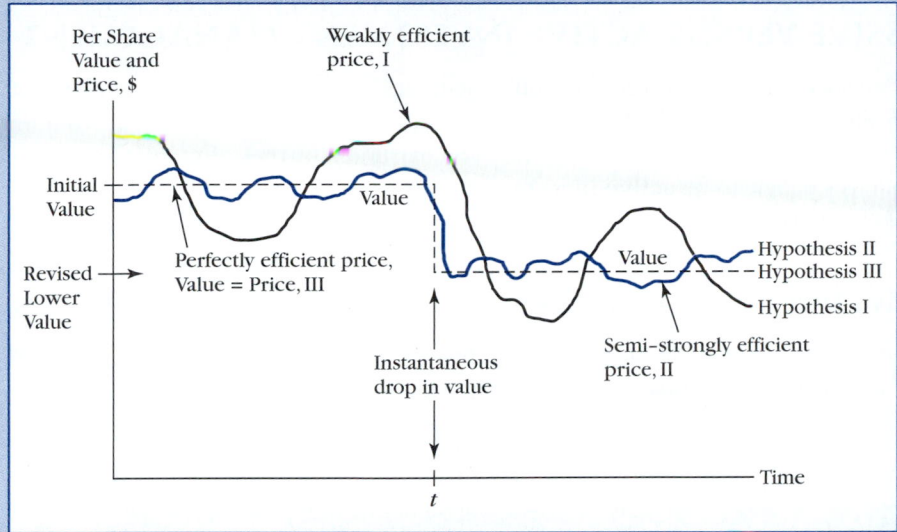

A weakly efficient price fluctuates randomly as it moves far above and far below the value of the security. A semi–strongly efficient price fluctuates randomly too, but not as far above and below the security's value as a weakly efficient price because investors use more information to form semi-strong efficient prices. A perfectly efficient price never deviates from the security's value as the two values fluctuate randomly together through time.

ket occurs when investors that control large amounts of money are doing financial research and making rational buy-sell decisions.

The Information Content of Prices

Consider an alternative interpretation of Figure 3-4. The three different price paths in Figure 3-4 can be interpreted as illustrations of three hypotheses about the amount of information used to determine the prices:

◆ (Hypothesis I) A **weakly efficient price** reflects all historical information, but no current information and no insider information. In other words, a weakly efficient price only reflects what is already obvious, but nothing new or subtle.

◆ (Hypothesis II) A **semi–strongly efficient price** reflects all historical information and all current information, but no insider information. In other words, a semi–strongly efficient price reflects more information than a weakly efficient price.

◆ (Hypothesis III) A **perfectly efficient price** reflects all historical information, all current information, and all insider information. Essentially, a perfectly efficient price reflects everything that is knowable.

Chapter 8 investigates hypotheses I, II, and III to determine which provides the best description of reality. If securities prices impact new information inefficiently, as suggested by hypotheses I, securities analysts can earn fortunes. They could reap large profits by finding underpriced securities, buying them, and holding them in long positions while their prices rise. Furthermore, they could gain by finding overpriced securities, selling them short, and holding them in short positions to profit from their falling prices.

PASSIVE VERSUS ACTIVE INVESTMENT MANAGEMENT

Although securities markets in the United States appear to be efficient,[4] they are not perfectly efficient. There is evidence that expert securities analysts can profit from finding undervalued and overvalued securities.[5] The existence of these lucrative opportunities encourages people to be **active investment managers** that analyze securities and buy and sell them to maximize trading profits.

Active Investment Management

Securities analysis is at the heart of active investment management. Here's an example of how an analyst might estimate the value of a share of common stock.

EXAMPLE   ESTIMATING COCA-COLA COMMON STOCK'S VALUE PER SHARE

A securities analyst's estimates from January 2000 of the earnings per share, cash dividend payout ratio, cash dividends per share, risk-adjusted discount rate,* and present value of all cash flows from purchasing a share of KO's common stock and selling it late in 2003 are below.

Part A: The present value in January 2000 of 4 years of cash dividends per share is $2.18.

Year	Estimated Earnings Per Share, $ (Assume 13% per year growth starting 2000)	×	Estimated Cash Dividends Payout, % (Assume long-run target is 40%)	=	Estimated Cash Dividends Per Share, $ (Assume incr. +$0.04 per year)	×	13% (from Table 2-3) Present Value Factor	=	Present Value of Estimated Cash Dividend
1998 (Actual)	$1.42		42%		$0.60		N. A.		0
1999 (Actual)	$0.98		65%		$0.64		N. A.		0
2000 (Estim.)	$1.45		47%		$0.68		.88495		$0.6018
2001 (Estim.)	$1.64		44%		$0.72		.78314		$0.5639
2002 (Estim.)	$1.85		41%		$0.76		.69305		$0.5267
2003 (Estim.)	$2.09		38%		$0.80		.61331		$0.4906

2000 present value of forecasted cash dividends: $2.18

---

*   Determining the appropriate risk-adjusted discount rate to use when finding the present value of an asset is the subject of Table 2-3 in Chapter 2. The Example below Table 2-3 suggests 13.0% is the appropriate discount rate for Coca-Cola's stock. Additional models to predict an appropriate required rate of return (expected return, discount rate) are the subject of Chapter 15.

Part B: The January 2000 present value of the expected selling price per share of $83.60 in 2003 is $54.64.

Year	Estimated Earnings Per Share	×	Forecasted Price-Earnings Ratio	=	Expected Value[a] Per Share	×	13% Present Value Factor	=	E (present value per share)
2003	$2.09		40 times		$83.60		.61331		$51.27

[a]The expected value refers to a weighted average that uses the probability of the possible prices as weights. The expected value (mathematical expectation) concept is introduced in Chapter 7.

Part C: The 2000 estimate of the value per share for Coke's stock in the year 2000 is $53.45.

(Part A: $2.18) + (Part B: $51.27) = Part C: $53.45 = E (present value per share)

Eqn. 3-3 (p. 40) suggests the value of KO was $53.45 per share in early 2000. Coca-Cola's market price actually fluctuated between $43 and $70 during 2000.

The Coca-Cola illustration above is an example of the common stock valuation issues addressed in Chapters 23 through 25.

Passive Investment Management

Respectable financial economists have published considerable empirical evidence suggesting that the prices of securities fluctuate in a semi-strongly efficient manner. The **efficient markets** concept has become popular and intellectually respectable. Passive investors have read the research and reasoned that if many investors are highly informed and some degree of consensus exists about securities' values, then doing securities analysis to find undervalued stocks is too much trouble, involves too many risks, and high-salaried security analysts are too costly. Millions of passive investors found an easier, less risky, and cheaper way to invest in diversified portfolios: "index funds." An *index fund* is a mutual fund that buys a diversified portfolio of stocks that is designed to track some selected stock market index. Different index funds choose to mimic different stock market indexes.

Instead of working to find undervalued stocks to buy, index fund managers purchase every stock in the appropriate securities market index. The Standard & Poor's 500 Stocks Composite Index is the most popular stock market index to emulate. Over 100 mutual funds have as their stated investment objective to invest in the same stocks that are in the S&P500 index so they can perform as it does. Vanguard Index 500, the oldest and largest index fund, is indexed to the S&P500 and for decades has managed billions of dollars from passive investors. In the United States there are dozens of common stock mutual funds indexed to various stock market indexes and dozens of bond mutual funds indexed to different bond market indexes.

HEDGING AND ARBITRAGE

Hedging is a popular risk-reduction strategy. Hedging also provides the basis for arbitrage. Investors love to discover securities pricing inefficiencies, because they can then use arbitrage to profit from them.

While millions of investors have no idea what "arbitrage" means, informed professional arbitrageurs can reap handsome profits and can help shape security prices. An arbitrage position is an "imperfect" hedge. We begin by exploring perfect hedges and imperfect hedges, and then turn to arbitrage in greater detail.

Perfect Hedges

There are many reasons to hedge. Hedges are usually undertaken to reduce the losses from adverse price movements. The simplest hedge is the perfect hedge, from which no profits or losses can be earned. Suppose you buy a long position of 100 shares of Coca-Cola's common stock (KO). At the same time, you sell 100 shares of KO short. Regardless of whether the price of KO stock goes up or down, the gains and losses from your long and short positions will cancel each other out so that it will be impossible for your two-position portfolio to make or lose money. A long position and an identical short position undertaken together establish a **perfectly hedged portfolio.** The long and short positions completely offset each other and result in a portfolio containing two positions that earns the same returns as a portfolio completely invested in cash.

Figure 3-5 is a gain-loss graph illustrating a perfect hedge. This figure combines the long position from Figure 3-1A and the short position from Figure 3-1B in the same asset at identical purchase and sale prices. Figure 3-5 represents an investor who purchased a long position of 1 share of Ford Motor Company's common stock at $44 per share and simultaneously

FIGURE 3-5 Gain-Loss Diagram for a Perfectly Hedged Position in Ford Stock

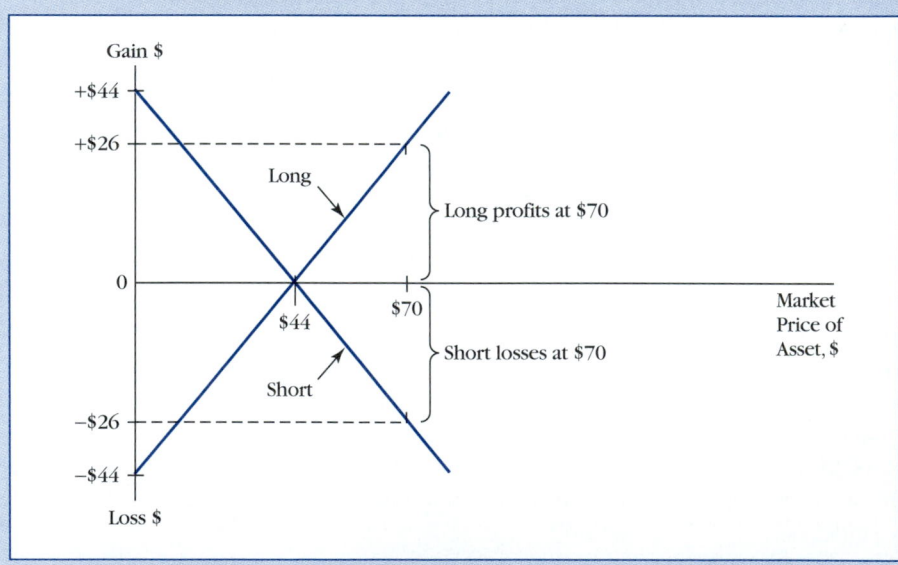

A long position in Ford stock is purchased at $44 per share. The investor also sells Ford stock short at $44 per share. If Ford Motor Company goes bankrupt and its stock price falls to zero, the loss on the long position is $44 per share. The simultaneous gain from the short position is $44 per share. If Ford's stock price falls to zero, the perfectly hedged portfolio earns net profits of zero. In bankruptcy, the portfolio's net losses are also zero.

sold 1 share of Ford short at $44 per share.* The hedger is perfectly hedged because for any market price the gain and the loss from the two positions always sums up to zero. Figure 3-5 shows that if the market price of the hedged asset rises to $70 per share, the $26 profit on the long position will be exactly offset by the loss of $26 on the short position. Gains or losses from price changes are impossible in a perfect hedge. Perfect hedges are used to eliminate risk while still maintaining a desired position.

SELLING SHORT AGAINST THE BOX

DEFINITION

Mr. Finn invested in the Queasy Corporation and he expects the price of the corporation's stock to drop substantially in the near future. QUESTION: How can Mr. Finn avoid losses on the stock he owns without liquidating his investment?

ANSWER: Mr. Finn can sell Queasy stock short to establish a hedge that will reduce the price losses he anticipates. If the stock's price falls, the losses on Mr. Finn's long position are offset by gains on his short position. If his long and short positions are of equal value, he can hedge away 100% of his losses. If Mr. Finn kept the long position shares in a safe-deposit box at his bank or his broker's office, he did what is called *selling short against the box*.

Imperfect Hedges

Some hedges are perfect and some aren't. A hedge is imperfect if the dollar commitments to the long and the short positions are not perfectly balanced, and/or if the short sale price is not equal to the purchase price for the long position. Figure 3-6 illustrates an **imperfect hedge.** The size of the dollar commitments to the long and the short positions cannot be illustrated in a gain-loss graph; assume the dollar commitments are equal. The hedge is imperfect because its short sales price, denoted P_S, exceeds the purchase price for the long position, denoted P_L.

The imperfect hedge in Figure 3-6 will yield a constant profit equal to the excess of the short sale price over the purchase price. The imperfect hedge in Figure 3-6 will earn a gain of $(P_s - P_L)$ dollars per share whether the price of the underlying stock rises or falls.

A caveat is in order: If the short sale price is less than the purchase price for the long position ($P_s < P_L$), that type of imperfect hedge will generate nothing but losses.

ARBITRAGE

ARBITRAGE

DEFINITION

Investors can make **arbitrage** profits by creating an advantageous imperfect hedge. Arbitrage involves buying a long position and selling a short position in the same asset, or different but related assets, to profit from unrealistic price differentials.

---

* The long and short positions do not always have to be of equal dollar magnitude to create a perfect hedge. For instance, an investment of half as many dollars in a perfectly negatively correlated offsetting position that has twice the price volatility could result in a perfect hedge. The analytical tools needed to analyze more sophisticated hedging techniques are introduced in later chapters.

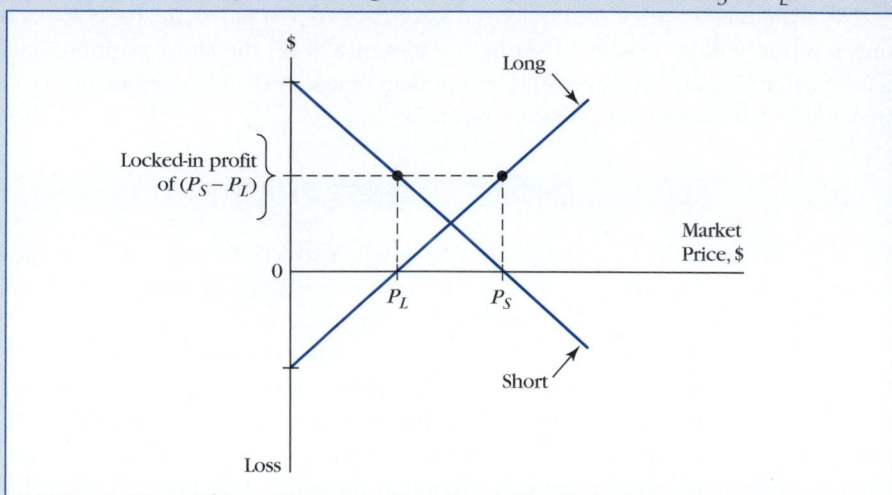

FIGURE 3-6 An Imperfect Hedge with a Locked-In Gain of $(P_S - P_L)$

An imperfect hedge is used to earn arbitrage profits. Suppose KO's stock is simultaneously selling for $40 in London and $41 at the NYSE. Arbitrageurs buy the stock in the market where it is cheapest; and, as their long positions increase, the low purchase price of $P_L = \$40$ in London is bid up to a higher level. Simultaneously, arbitrageurs sell short in the market where the security is overpriced; and, as their short selling continues, the high short-sale price of $P_S = \$41$ at the NYSE is driven down. The short sale price and the price paid for the long position are thus driven toward each other until $(P_S - P_L)$ shrinks to zero.

Arbitrageurs Enforce the Economic Law of One Price

Any time the same good is selling at different prices, arbitrage can be profitable. Profit-seeking arbitrageurs enforce the economic **law of one price** by buying the stock in the market where its price is lowest and selling in another market where the stock's price is higher. Arbitrageurs will go on buying and bidding up the low price and, simultaneously, selling at the higher price and driving that price down, until the prices are the same in all free markets. The price may never be exactly identical in all markets because of transaction costs such as brokers commissions, foreign exchange fees, governmental foreign exchange controls, telephone costs, and other economic frictions that slow arbitrage and erode arbitrage profits. However, with the exception of these transaction costs (typically only a few cents per share), a given share of stock should sell for the same price everywhere in the world. (See Figure 3-6.)

Everyone Benefits from Arbitrage

Arbitrageurs enforce the law of one price as they pursue arbitrage profits. Arbitrage makes the prices of a security traded around the world respond rationally, efficiently, and uniformly to new information. Such price behavior is beneficial because market prices are what determine how nations' resources are allocated. Those who have a desperate need for something are willing to bid its price high, and things that have high prices are conserved and used carefully. Plentiful goods typically sell at low prices, so they are more likely to be used less sparingly.

For an example of how arbitrage allocates resources in an optimal manner, suppose a bountiful wheat harvest in the United States drives the price of wheat down to a low level. At the same time, suppose a shortage of wheat in China drives wheat prices to high levels there. Profit-seeking arbitrageurs will take note of these price differences and hastily buy wheat in the United States and ship it to China. Arbitrageurs' U.S. purchases will drive up the low prices of wheat in the United States and their Chinese sales will push down the high prices of wheat in China. The higher wheat prices in the United States will keep wheat from being fed to hogs or wasted. The lower wheat prices in China will make it possible for the people to eat well and be healthy.

Arbitrage is at work all around us, all the time, but most people don't notice it. The law of one price keeps something that is needed desperately (for instance, heating oil in the Antarctic) from being wasted where the good is in plentiful supply at a low cost (for example, Saudi Arabian oil). Price speculators and arbitrageurs help allocate society's resources in many ways. Speculators buy a good (such as heating oil) at a time when no need exists (during the summer in Mexico) and store it until a widespread need drives its price up (during the winter in Canada). Thus, profit-maximizing speculators and arbitrageurs enforce the law of one price and allocate resources both geographically and through time to the place and time where those goods will be the most useful for the welfare of the population.*

DEFINITION

RISK ARBITRAGE

Economists invented the word *arbitrage* long ago. They use the word to define a profitable transaction that involves no risk and, in many cases, requires zero investment. This is the classic definition of arbitrage. In recent decades, some speculators and the news media have begun to use the word—but sometimes in a different way. The phrase *risk arbitrage* began appearing in newspapers during the 1980s. Since classic arbitrage is a riskless process, "risk arbitrage" confuses financial economists, who think the phrase is an oxymoron—like "jumbo shrimp."

Risk arbitrageurs sometimes speculate on merger activities. The risk arbitrageur might seek to profit by selling short the shares of the acquiring corporation and simultaneously buying a long position in the shares of the corporation expected to be acquired. This strategy can be profitable because the acquirer typically pays a premium for the target stock of 15% to 30% over its pre-merger price and, when the merger is completed, the acquirer's stock price typically drops slightly. This strategy is not as clever as classic arbitrage because: (1) the stocks' prices do not always behave as expected, (2) most merger negotiations break down before the merger is consummated, (3) the risk arbitrageur must invest money at risk, and, (4) when the acquiring corporation and the target corporation are dissimilar, the law of one price is not relevant. Nevertheless, stories about risk arbitrage do sell newspapers and books.[6]

THE BOTTOM LINE

The present value model can be used to estimate the value of an investment. These value estimates can be used as the basis for wealth-maximizing investment decisions. The buy-sell investment decision rules explain how to use the value estimate. Every time a piece of new information arrives it has the power to change the value estimate. Figure 3-3 is a flowchart illustrating a never-ending series of investment decisions that keep securities analysts busy.

---

* Short selling is also used by hedgers and arbitrageurs in developing the arbitrage pricing theory (Chapter 15), in foreign exchange markets (Chapter 17), in futures markets (Chapters 9 and 27), and in options markets (Chapters 9 and 28).

The market prices of securities fluctuate in a way that may appear to be senseless, but these movements are not senseless; these price fluctuations convey evidence that securities prices are pursuing continuously changing values. Changing estimates of the value are what motivate investors to either buy and bid up, or, sell and push down, the price of a security. Some investors pursue their investment management activities actively. At the same time many rational investors prefer to invest passively in an index fund to reduce the hard work and risks associated with active investment management.

Short sales are not always undertaken in search of speculative gains. Short sales may also be used to hedge away the risk in a long position, to maintain corporate control, or a short sale might be part of an arbitrage that aligns unrealistic price differentials. Thus, arbitrageurs, risk-averse hedgers, and risk-taking speculators can all be short sellers.

As informed professional investors buy and sell securities and profit by arbitraging, market prices adjust to reflect the latest information available in the world. Efficiently priced securities are socially desirable because they help allocate the planet's scarce resources to where they are needed most. Thus, profit-seeking speculators, short sellers, hedgers, and arbitrageurs are doing work that also improves the welfare of people in the general population.

QUESTIONS

Q3-1 (Risk-adjusted discount rate) Why must a securities analyst have estimates of a security's risk and return before preparing estimates of the security's value? Explain your answer in terms of the present value model. *Hint:* Use Eqn. 3-3 and Table 2-3.

Q3-2 (Continuous equilibrium) Should the value of a security remain stable in equilibrium? What might change the value of a security? How often might such changes occur?

Q3-3 (Efficient markets theory) Define the phrase "efficient price." Give an example.

Q3-4 (Market information) Suppose the chairman of the board of General Motors (GM) appeared on the late night news of every television station in the United States and announced that GM had discovered oil wells beneath every parking lot that the corporation owned. Assuming the gentleman would not distort the truth, how would his announcement affect the market price of GM stock? Would the price of GM move upward in a trend as more and more investors learned of the GM discovery each day and then bid the stock's price up day after day as they reached their decisions to buy the stock after a learning lag? Explain how you think the market would react to such a public announcement.

Q3-5 (Conceptualizing short selling) Are short sellers primarily risk-taking speculators or risk-averse hedgers? Explain.

Q3-6 (The head count versus the money count) There are millions of part-time investors in the world. But there are only about 35,000 members of the Association for Investment Management and Research (AIMR) in the world. These AIMR members constitute a significant proportion of the full-time professional investment managers. Given that there are hundreds of millions of nonprofes-sional investors and, in contrast, only several thousand professional investors, which group do you think dominates the market? How can the professional investors have any impact on security prices when they comprise only a tiny fraction of 1% of the investing population? Explain.

Q3-7 (A reflecting barrier) Assume the stock of Fictitious Corporation is selling for $18.75, but the professionals' consensus of its true economic value is $19.50. Is it likely that the professionals will trade and, therefore, adjust the price so that it is equal to its economic value? Explain.

Q3-8 (Passive versus active management) If you were managing a billion-dollar pension fund portfolio, do you think you would be wiser for you to: (a) pursue a passive investment policy of indexing the billion dollars so that you could earn 10% per annum over the long run, or (b) pursue an active investment management program that required you to spend many thousands of dollars annually on securities analysis and brokerage commissions in order to earn 12% per year rate of return over the long run? Explain your decision.

Q3-9 (Cash dividends paid on short stock) John Malone was bearish about the stock issued by American Telephone & Telegraph (ATT). He expected the price of ATT to fall significantly within the next 3 months. So, Malone sold 100 shares short. Malone's stock broker arranged to loan Malone's account the 100 shares to deliver with the understanding that these shares would be replaced with other ATT shares later. A month after Malone opened his short position ATT announced a cash dividend of $1.32 per share. How will this cash dividend affect people like Mr. Malone who have sold ATT stock short?

Q3-10 (Arbitrage) What is the "law of one price"? Give an example.

PROBLEMS

P3-1 (Rates of return) Calculate the one-period rates of return for an investor who: (a) buys a share of the Ace Corporation's common stock for $40, holds the stock in a long position for 6 months while collecting a $2 cash dividend, and sells it for $42; and (b) sells a share of Ace common stock short at $40 per share, holds the short position open for 6 months while Ace pays a $2 cash dividend, and covers the short position at $42 per share.

P3-2 (Present value of an annuity) Edie Evans is considering purchasing a 20-year, 10% annuity that pays $8,000 at the end of each year. How much will she be required to pay for this annuity?

P3-3 (Present value of a stock) Mr. Clay is considering investing in the common stock of the Quonset Company. He has estimated the following cash flows for a 5-year holding period:

Year	Cash Flow
1	$2
2	3
3	4
4	4
5	2 + 73 = $75 = E(dividend + price)

If Mr. Clay's projections are accurate, and, if the appropriate return over this period for the stock is 14%: (a) What should he pay today for a share for Quonset? (b) If Quonset is currently selling for $52, what should Mr. Clay do?

P3-4 (Stock price forecasting) The stock of the ABC Company is currently selling for $30. If the stock is held for 10 years, the following dividend payments are expected: years 1–5, $2; years 6–10, $3. What must the stock's selling price be in 10 years for an investor to earn a 12% return before taxes?

P3-5 (Present value) Find the present value of the following cash flows. Assume a rate of return of 14%.

Year	Cash Flow
1	$100
2	−50
3	200
4	400
5	−300

P3-6 (Present value) Elaine R. Fox has been offered an investment opportunity that currently will require an initial investment of $50,000. In 5 years, she can liquidate the investment for $100,000. If Fox makes the investment, what annual rate of return will she earn on a pre-tax basis?

P3-7 (Bond pricing) A $1,000 bond has a coupon rate of 10%, with annual interest payments and will mature in 10 years. If its yield-to-maturity is currently 12%, (a) at what price is the bond selling? (b) If this were a perpetual bond—i.e., had no maturity—at what price would it sell?

P3-8 (Constant growth model) Mark Simms is trying to decide whether to invest in a certain stock that is currently selling for $13.75. The stock recently paid an annual dividend of $0.75 a share, but Mark believes this dividend will grow at an annual rate of 8% for the foreseeable future. If Mark requires a 12% return on this, should he buy it at the current price?

P3-9 (Real estate valuation) Te Cheih is considering the purchase of a condominium in the ski resort of Vail, Colorado. He believes he can rent the condo to net $50,000 a year after paying for maintenance expenses, condo fees, and property taxes. He estimates the condo will be worth $350,000 in 5 years. If he wants to earn 18% on this investment, what is the maximum price he should offer?

P3-10 (Short selling) Jim Collins sold 100 shares of Texaco short at $65. He covered his short position by repurchasing the shares for $50, but Texaco paid a $0.45 a share dividend while his short position was open. (a) Ignoring commissions, calculate Jim's net profit or loss on this transaction. (b) What was his return on this investment?

CFA EXAM QUESTIONS

The following three questions are adopted from the 1999 CFA Sample Exam, Level I:

1. Which of the following assumptions does the constant growth dividend discount model require?

   I. Dividends grow at a constant rate.

   II. The dividend growth rate continues indefinitely.

   III. The required rate of return is less than the dividend growth rate.

   A. I only.
   B. III only.
   C. I and II only.
   D. I, II, and III.

2. Which of the following assumptions imply(ies) an informationally efficient market?

   I. Many profit-maximizing participants, each acting independently of the others, analyze and value securities.

II. The timing of one news announcement is generally dependent on other news announcements.

III. Security prices adjust rapidly to reflect new information.

IV. A risk-free asset exists, and investors can borrow and lend unlimited amounts at the risk-free rate.
   A. I only.
   B. I and III only.

   C. II and IV only.
   D. I, II, III, and IV.

3. If an investor's required return is 12%, the value of a 10-year maturity zero-coupon bond with a maturity value of $1,000 is *closest* to:
   A. $312.
   B. $688.
   C. $1,000.
   D. $1,312.

DO YOUR RESEARCH

Reconsider the numerical example from this chapter of how to estimate the value per share for Coca-Cola's common stock in light of the more recent information that has become available since this estimate was printed. What do you currently estimate the value of a share of Coca-Cola stock will be 4 years in the future? Show the calculations used in preparing your estimate. *Hint:* To get financial statements for free, call Coca-Cola's headquarters in Atlanta, Georgia at 404-676-2121 and ask to have an annual report mailed to your home.

FURTHER REFERENCE

Dumas, Bernard, and Blaise Allaz, *Financial Securities: Market Equilibrium and Pricing Methods.* Cincinnati: South-Western, 1995.

Chapter 1 of this theoretical finance textbook reviews the factors that determine prices in securities markets.

ENDNOTES

[1] See Merton H. Miller and Franco Modigliani, "Dividend Policy, Growth, and Valuation of Shares," *Journal of Business*, 34, no. 4 (October 1961): 411-33. This is a classic article coauthored by two Nobel Prize–winning economists.

[2] The theory behind this model is established by Merton H. Miller and Franco Modigliani, "Dividend Policy, Growth, and the Valuation of Shares," *Journal of Business,* 34, no. 4 (October 1961): 411-33.

[3] See Molly Baker, "Some Analysts Enter the Land of Big Bucks," *Wall Street Journal,* 2 July 1996, C1. The article discusses a growing number of security analysts who earn multimillion-dollar annual incomes. The article quotes a financial recruiter named Mr. Goldstein as saying that "Now even your fairly average analysts are getting between $500,000 and a million dollars (per year), whereas a few years ago it was only top analysts that made that much." (Parenthetical words added.) Also see "The Power Broker," *Business Week*, 15 May 2000, 70-82. This 12-page article about Jack B. Grubman, Vice-President/Telecommunications Analyst, Salomon Smith Barney in New York, says Mr. Grubman's annual compensation is $20 million per year, and he receives higher-paying job offers from other firms.

[4] Eugene F. Fama, "Efficient Capital Markets: A Review of Theory and Empirical Work," *Journal of Finance*, 25 (May 1970): 383-417.

[5] See Sanjoy Basu, "The Investment Performance of Common Stocks Relative to Their Price-Earnings Ratios: A Test of the Efficient Markets," *Journal of Finance*, 22, no. 3 (1977): 663-82. See also Robert J. Shiller, "Do Stock Prices Move Too Much to Be Justified by Subsequent Changes in Dividends?" *American Economic Review*, 71 (June 1981): 421-36. See also Lawrence H. Summers, "Does the Stock Market Rationality Reflect Fundamental Values?" *Journal of Finance*, 41, no. 3 (1986): 591-600. Also see Eugene F. Fama and Kenneth French, "Permanent and Temporary Components of Stock Prices," *Journal of Political Economy*, 96, no. 21: 246-73. Furthermore, see Carlo Capaul, Ian Rowley, and William F. Sharpe, "International Value and Growth Stock Returns," *Financial Analysts Journal* (January-February 1993). Chapter 7 discusses these studies and others that document market inefficiencies.

[6] See Keith Moore, *Risk Arbitrage—An Investors Guide*. (New York: Wiley, 1999).

Formulas for Valuing Perpetual Cash Flows

This Appendix shows how to derive simplified formulas to value a stream of consecutive cash flows that continue to perpetuity. The symbol k stands for a risk-adjusted discount rate, g is a growth rate, and the subscripts are time period counters. The present value (PV) of a common stock model is determined first. Then, a bond valuation model is derived.

Valuing a Stock with a Constant Rate of Growth

If cash dividends per share grow at some constant rate, denoted g, then dividends received t time periods in the future (d_t) are related to current dividends (d_0) as shown below.

$$d_t = d_0(1 + g)^t \text{ for } t = 1, 2, 3, 4, \ldots \text{ time periods}$$

This dividend relationship can be substituted into the well-known present value per share model below to obtain Eqn. F1 (F stands for formula).

$$PV_0 = \sum_{t=1}^{\infty} \frac{d_t}{(1 + k)^t}$$

$$PV_0 = \sum_{t=1}^{\infty} \frac{d_0(1 + g)^t}{(1 + k)^t} \tag{F1}$$

When d_0 is a constant, it follows that $\Sigma d_0 x = d_0 \Sigma x$. This relation means Eqn. F1 may be rewritten as:

$$PV_0 = d_0 \sum_{t=1}^{\infty} \frac{(1 + g)^t}{(1 + k)^t} \tag{F2}$$

Expanding the infinite sum in Eqn. F2 yields:

$$PV_0 = d_0 \left(\frac{(1 + g)^1}{(1 + k)^1} + \frac{(1 + g)^2}{(1 + k)^1} + \frac{(1 + g)^3}{(1 + k)^3} + \cdots \right) \tag{F3}$$

Multiplying F3 by $(1 + k)/(1 + g)$ yields F4.

$$PV_0 \left(\frac{1 + k}{1 + g} \right) = d_0 \left(1.0 + \frac{(1 + g)^1}{(1 + k)^1} + \frac{(1 + g)^2}{(1 + k)^2} + \frac{(1 + g)^3}{(1 + k)^3} + \cdots \right) \tag{F4}$$

Subtracting F3 from F4 results in F5.

$$\left(\frac{1+k}{1+g} - 1.0\right)PV_0 = d_0 \tag{F5}$$

Making the realistic economic assumption that $k > g$ allows the preceding equation to be rearranged as shown below.

$$\left[\frac{(1+k) - (1+g)}{1+g}\right]PV_0 = \left(\frac{k-g}{1+g}\right)PV_0 = d_0 \tag{F6}$$

Multiplying the right-hand side of F6 by $(1+g)$ yields F7.

$$PV_0(k-g) = d_0(1+g) = d_1 \tag{F7}$$

where $d_0(1+g)^1 = d_1$ denotes the next time period's cash dividend per share. Eqn. F8 can be obtained by rearranging F7 as follows.

$$PV_0 = \frac{d_1}{k-g} \tag{F8}$$

Eqn. F8 computes the value of a share of stock that grows at a constant perpetual rate.

Valuing a Bond with a Constant Perpetual Coupon

Eqn. F1 from above is rewritten with coupons substituted in place of cash dividends to obtain Eqn. F9. Eqn. F9 gives the present value of a perpetual bond that never repays its principal.

$$PV_0 = \sum_{t=1}^{\infty} \frac{\text{Coupon}_0(1+g)^t}{(1+k)^t} \tag{F9}$$

Eqn. F9 can be simplified to become F10 the same way that F1 was simplified to F8 above.

$$PV_0 = \frac{\text{Coupon}_1}{k-g} \tag{F10}$$

Since bond coupons are fixed we can delete the time subscripts and assume:

$\text{Coupon}_1 = \text{Coupon}_2 = \text{Coupon}_3 = \ldots = \text{Coupon}.$

Fixed coupons also imply that $g = 0$. Thus, we can simplify Eqn. F10 to F11.

$$PV_0 = \frac{\text{Coupon}}{k} \tag{F11}$$

Eqn. F11 gives the present value of a bond that pays fixed coupons perpetually. Eqn. F11 can also be used to value an annuity or other stream of fixed perpetual cash flows.

Eqns. F8 and F11 are computationally simple and easy to remember.

ANALYSIS OF FINANCIAL STATEMENTS

*A company's financial statements provide essential information about the firm. Analyzing them focuses attention on the advantages and disadvantages of investing in one security relative to another. This venerable approach to security analysis is called **fundamental analysis.** Fundamental analysts employ, along with other tools, financial ratios to investigate the issuer of the securities and its securities. Financial ratios are computed to assess the prospects for the firm's securities and to help the investor decide if the securities are over or underpriced.*

The Coca-Cola Corporation's financial statements are analyzed in this chapter. KO was selected because most people are familiar with some of its products and because the firm is complicated enough to be worthy of advanced discussions.

*Figure 3-4 in Chapter 3 (p. 53) introduced the **efficient market theory,** which hypothesizes that security prices reflect almost all public information. According to this theory, publicly disseminated financial statements contain nothing of any value. This means that even though you may learn some fascinating facts about KO as you read this chapter, some professional security analysts already discovered those facts and, if they had any value, traded on them.*

THE FINANCIAL STATEMENTS

A financial statement is a source of historical and current information about a firm. Large public corporations publish quarterly financial statements; small firms may issue only annual statements; a closely held corporation may not issue any financial statements at all to the public. A firm's financial statements are studied by bankers when the firm applies for a loan, suppliers of raw materials when the firm purchases on credit, investors who are evaluating the firm's securities, and acquisition-oriented firms considering a merger, among others. In each case a firm's financial statements and financial ratios are likely to be evaluated from a different perspective.

Financial statement analysis is the dissection and study of a firm's financial statements from different perspectives in order to gain insights about the firm's relative strengths and weaknesses. The firm's past performance, as represented by its historical financial statements, can provide a basis from which to forecast the future.

The three main financial statements are:

The balance sheet

The income and expense statement

The statement of cash flows

Most of the data used to calculate financial ratios come from these statements. Statements from consecutive years provide a basis for comparison between the firm's activities in those years, as well as for making projections.

The Balance Sheet

A **balance sheet** represents an accounting picture of all the firm's assets, liabilities, and stockholders' equity at one instant in time.

Total assets = Liabilities + Stockholders' equity

The stockholders' **equity** section of the balance sheet measures the firm's **net worth** or the **book value** of the owners' equity computed in accordance with **generally accepted accounting procedures (GAAP).** Most firms align their *fiscal year* (accounting year) with the calendar year, so it ends on December 31.

Table 4-1 shows the Coca-Cola Corporation's balance sheets for three consecutive fiscal years. (The *lines* (or rows) in Table 4-1 are numbered so these balance sheet items can be referred to and used to compute financial ratios later in this chapter.) KO is the world's largest producer of the syrups from which soft drinks are produced. KO also owns Minute Maid orange juice and is a major stockholder in Coca-Cola Enterprise (NYSE ticker symbol CCE), the largest soft drink bottler in the world. KO is also a major investor in Coca-Cola Amatil (Australia), Coca-Cola Beverages (Italy), Coca-Cola of New York, Coca-Cola of Canada, and other large bottling companies around the world (see balance sheet line A7). KO uses its bottlers as cushions between itself and the market for soft drinks to smooth out fluctuations in KO's profits. In addition, KO buys and sells multimillion-dollar bottling businesses to supplement its profits from its core (syrup) business.

The Income and Expense Statement

Balance sheets report the *stocks* of assets and liabilities that existed within a firm at one point in time. In contrast, income statements report *flows* that occurred during the accounting period (or between two points in time). The **income and expense statement** is sometimes nicknamed the **profit and loss statement** (or P and L) because the profits or losses are at the bottom line of the statement. The income and expense statement, commonly shortened to *income statement,* contains information such as the firm's income sources and itemized expenses. The following equation summarizes the income and expense statement.

Sales − Total expenses = Income or Loss

KO's Income Statements for the years 1997 through 1999 are shown in Table 4-2.

TABLE 4-1	Balance Sheet of Coca-Cola Corporation (KO), December 31, 1997–99 (in $ millions)			
Account Item		1997	1998	1999
	Assets (uses of funds)			
A1	Cash	$ 1,737	$ 1,648	$ 1,611
A2	Marketable securities	106	159	201
A3	Accounts receivable	1,639	1,666	1,798
A4	Inventories	959	890	1,076
A5	Other current assets	1,528	2,017	1,794
A6	*Total current assets*	$ 5,969	$ 6,380	$ 6,480
A7	Investments	6,501	8,549	8,916
A8	Property, plant, and equipment	3,743	3,669	4,267
A9	Goodwill	668	547	1,960
A10	*Total assets (TA)*	$16,881	$19,145	$121,623
	Liabilities and Equity (sources of funds)			
L1	Accounts payable			
	Other current liabilities:	$ 3,249	$ 3,141	$ 3,714
L2	Notes payable	3,074	4,462	5,112
L3	Income taxes payable	1,056	1,037	769
L4	*Total current liabilities*	$ 7,379	$ 8,640	$ 9,856
L5	Long-term debt	801	687	854
L6	Other liabilities	1,001	991	902
L7	Deferred tax	426	424	498
L8	*Total long-term liabilities*	$ 2,250	$ 2,102	$ 2,254
E1	Common stock at par value of $0.25 per share	861	865	867
E2	Paid in surplus (Price paid over par)	1,527	2,195	2,584
E3	Retained earnings (Earnings not paid out)	16,468	18,488	19,222
E4	Treasury stock (Repurchased shares, at cost)	(11,582)	(13,145)	(13,160)
E5	Shareholders' equity	$ 7,274	$ 8,403	$ 9,513
A10	*Total liabilities and equity*	$16,881	$19,145	$ 21,623

The Statement of Cash Flows

KO's Statement of Cash Flows is shown in Table 4-3. **Cash flows** are the net cash left after all reinvestments within the firm have been deducted. A company's cash flow is not affected by accelerated depreciation rules, arbitrary inventory valuation rules, or accrual methods of accounting like the income measures that are determined using GAAP. The latitude in which GAAP is reported makes accounting income more ambiguous than a firm's clear-cut cash flows. This is why many financial analysts prefer to focus on a firm's cash flow rather than its accounting income. Cash flow cannot be manipulated by corporate financial managers who take full advantage of permissible accounting practices in an effort to report deceptive accounting profits.*[1]

KO is in a cash business. KO's cash flows have averaged over $2 billion per year in recent years. This huge discretionary cash flow enables management considerable leeway in conducting the affairs of the corporation and exploiting profitable opportunities. These cash

---

* Deriving and using "Cash Available to Equity Shareholders" to value common stock is the topic of section 24–5 of Chapter 24.

TABLE 4-2 **Income and Expense Statements for Coca-Cola Corporation, December 31, 1997, 1998, and 1999 (in $ millions)**

Account	Item	1997	1998	1999
I1	Sales	$18,868	$18,813	$19,805
I2	*less:* Cost of goods sold	6,015	5,562	6,009
I3	*equals:* Gross profit	$12,853	$13,251	$13,796
I4	*less:* Selling, administrative, and general expenses	7,852	8,284	9,814
I5	*equals:* Earnings before interest and tax[a]	$ 5,001	$ 4,967	$ 3,982
I6	Interest expense	47	58	77
I7	Other expenses (income)	(1,101)	(289)	86
I8	*less:* Total expenses (income)	$ (1,054)	$ (231)	$ 163
I9	*equals:* Earnings before tax	$ 6,055	$ 5,198	$ 3,819
I10	*less:* Corporate income taxes	1,926	1,665	1,388
I11	*equals:* Net income after taxes	$ 4,129	$ 3,533	$ 2,431
I12	*less:* Cash dividend payments	1,387	1,480	1,580
I13	*equals:* Addition to retained earnings	$ 2,742	$ 2,053	$ 851
	Per Share Data for Common Stock			
P1	Number of shares outstanding, millions	2,477	2,467	2,469
P2	Market price per share of stock	$72–$51	$89–$54	$71–$47
P3	Earnings per share (EPS) after tax	$1.67	$1.43	$.98
P4	Cash dividends per share	$.56	$.60	$.64
P5	Price-earnings (P/E) ratio	32–47 times	36–56 times	48–72 times

[a]**Earnings before interest and taxes**, or **EBIT**, is sometimes also referred to as the firm's **operating income**.

flows are used primarily for internal reinvestment within the firm, joint ventures with bottlers, repurchase of KO common stock, and cash dividend payments. The table below provides a summary of the detailed cash flows in Table 4-3.

Coca-Cola's Cash Flows (in $ millions)			
	1997	1998	1999
Operations:	4,033	$3,433	$3,883
Investment activities	(1,082)	(1,557)	(1,551)
Free cash flow	2,951	1,876	2,332
Financing:			
Share repurchases	(1,262)	(1,563)	(15)
Other financing activities	(1,833)	230	(456)
Exchange	(134)	(28)	(28)
Increase (decrease) in cash	304	(89)	(37)

SOURCE: Coca-Cola Annual Report for 1999, p. 33.

In 1997 the Financial Accounting Standards Board (FASB) began requiring that, in addition to reporting their accounting income, U.S. companies must report their "comprehensive income." *Comprehensive income* supplements accounting income by including adjustments for the company's gains or losses from bond holdings, foreign currency translation adjustments, adjustments to overseas asset and liability accounts, and adjustments in the firm's pension liabilities. The comprehensive income of Coca-Cola fluctuates much more than its

TABLE 4-3   Statement of Cash Flows for KO, December 31, 1997, 1998, and 1999 (in $ millions)

Account Item		1997	1998	1999
	Operating Activities			
F1	Net income	$4,129	$3,533	$2,431
F2	Depreciation and amortization	626	645	792
F3	Deferred income taxes	380	(38)	97
F4	Equity income, net of dividends	(108)	31	292
F5	Foreign currency adjustments	37	21	(41)
F6	Other noncash items	(984)	(209)	869
F7	Net change in operating assets and liabilities	(47)	(550)	(557)
F8	*Net cash provided by operating activities*	4,033	3,433	3,883
	Investing Activities			
F9	Acquisitions and investments	(1,100)	(1,428)	(1,876)
F10	Purchases of investments and other	(459)	(610)	(518)
F11	Proceeds from disposal of assets	1,999	1,036	176
F12	Purchases of property, plant, and equipment	(1,093)	(863)	(1,069)
F13	Proceeds from disposals of property, plant, and equipment	71	54	45
F14	Other investing activities	82	(350)	(179)
F15	*Net cash used in investing activities*	(500)	(2,161)	(3,421)
	Financing Activities			
F16	Issuances of debt	155	1,818	3,411
F17	Payments of debt	(751)	(410)	(2,455)
F18	Issuances of stock	150	302	168
F19	Purchase of stock for treasury	(1,262)	(1,563)	(15)
F20	Dividends	(1,387)	(1,480)	(1,580)
F21	*Net cash used in financing activities*	(3,095)	(1,333)	(471)
F22	Effect of exchange rate changes	(134)	(28)	(28)
	Cash and Cash Equivalents			
F23	Net increase (decrease) during the year	304	(89)	(37)
F24	Balance at beginning of year	1,433	1,737	1,648
F25	*Balance at end of year*	$1,737	$1,648	$1,611

accounting income because KO's (and many other firm's) accountants did not report some significant transactions until it became mandatory.[2]

Sources of Financial Statements

The Securities Act of 1933 and the **Securities and Exchange Act of 1934** require publicly traded companies in the United States to make full disclosure of their financial statements and related information. A phone call or letter to most large corporations is all that is needed to obtain their financial statements, periodic forms required by the SEC, and other information in first class mail for free. Investors in lesser-developed countries do not enjoy such disclosures.

Investors with access to the Internet can obtain free financial statements quicker from the SEC's Electronic Data Gathering Analysis and Retrieval (EDGAR) System at: www.sec.gov.

Upon reaching the EDGAR Web site you may conduct searches for companies, mutual funds, executive compensation, SEC digests, information on current SEC rulemaking, and other information. A more detailed Web site address for the SEC's EDGAR is: www.sec.gov/edgarhp.htm. The SEC's spelling of Coke's name is "COCA COLA CO" and EDGAR uses the following CIK code to locate the firm's financial statements faster: 0000021344.

The SEC's EDGAR Web site is not very user-friendly. Two private firms named EDGAR Online (www.edgar-online.com) and FreeEDGAR (www.freeedgar.com) distribute the same information in a way that is easier to use. Both sites allow you to establish watch lists and will send you e-mail alerts when a company or fund on your watch list files a report. EDGAR Online charges $9.95 for immediate delivery of their information. Immediate delivery is free at FreeEDGAR. Additional information is available on a fee basis.

Hoover's On-Line (www.hoovers.com) provides information about thousands of companies, but some of this information is only available on a fee basis. PR Newswire (www.prnewswire.com) is a site where hundreds of companies post their news releases; access is free. Yahoo!Finance Web site (http://quotes.yahoo.com) provides stock quotes, financial news, earnings projections, and a far-reaching set of reference materials for companies and industries, plus links to other useful sites. Vendors and databases that sell financial information about individual firms for fees include CompuServe, Standard and Poor's, Moody's, Value Line, Disclosure, Dow Jones News Retrieval, and Lexis-Nexis.

Coca-Cola's corporate Web site is: www.thecoca-colacompany.com. This Web site contains the most recent financial statements and additional information about the corporation and its products.

Financial statements become out-of-date soon after the ink dries. But, thanks to the Internet, you need never be without up-to-date information.

COMMON-SIZED FINANCIAL STATEMENTS

Financial statements that express the value of each item as a percentage of some common base number are called **common-sized statements.** A firm's annual sales or its total assets are routinely used as base numbers. Common-sized financial statements are useful when comparing the financial statements of firms that differ in size, one firm's financial statements from different years, or when comparing companies from two or more countries that use different currencies.

Common-Sized Balance Sheet

KO's **common-sized balance sheet** is in Table 4-4; every value is stated as a percentage of total assets. Total assets is used as the common denominator because it is the largest quantity on a balance sheet and because it equals the accumulated uses of funds within the firm. Table 4-4 shows, for instance, that in 1998 KO financed 45.1% of its total assets with current liabilities (credit obtained from suppliers and other short-term sources). This and other financial ratios are interpreted later in this chapter and in other chapters.

Common-Sized Income and Expense Statement

A *common-sized income and expense statement* is shown in Table 4-5. Every value has been standardized by dividing it by total revenue. The raw data used to compute KO's common-sized values in Table 4-5 came from Table 4-2. Note that in line C22 KO's gross margin exceeds 60% of sales; this is a large profit margin.

TABLE 4-4   KO's Common-Sized Balance Sheet, December 31, 1997–99, Stated as Percentage of Total Assets

Account Item		1997	1998	1999
	Assets			
C1	Cash	10.3%	8.6%	7.5%
C2	Marketable securities	0.6	0.8	0.9
C3	Accounts receivables	9.7	8.7	8.3
C4	Inventories	5.7	4.6	5.0
C5	Other current assets	9.1	10.5	8.3
C6	*Total current assets*	35.4	33.3	30.0
C7	Investments and assets	38.5	44.7	41.2
C8	Property, plant, and equipment	22.2	19.2	19.7
C9	Goodwill	4.0	2.9	9.1
C10	*Total assets*	100.0%	100.0%	100.0%
	Liabilities and Equity			
C11	Accounts payable	19.2%	16.4%	17.3%
C12	Other current liabilities	24.5	28.7	28.3
C13	*Total current liabilities*	43.7	45.1	45.6
C14	Long-term debt	4.7	3.6	3.9
C15	Other liabilities	5.9	5.2	4.2
C16	Deferred taxes	2.5	2.2	2.3
C17	*Total long-term liabilities*	13.1	11.0	10.4
C18	Shareholder's equity	43.1	43.9	44.0
C19	*Total liabilities and equity*	100.0%	100.0%	100.0%

TABLE 4-5   KO's Common-Sized Income Statement, 1997–99, Stated as Percentage of Sales

		Percentage of Total Revenues		
Income and Expense Items		1997	1998	1999
C20	Sales	100.0%	100.0%	100.0%
C21	Cost of goods sold	31.9	29.6	30.3
C22	Gross profit	68.1	70.4	69.7
C23	Selling, administration, and general expenses	41.6	44.0	49.6
C24	Earnings before interest and tax (EBIT)	26.5	26.4	20.1
C25	Interest expense	0.2	0.3	0.4
C26	Other expense (income)	(5.8)	(1.5)	0.4
C27	Total expense (income)	(5.6)%	(1.2)%	0.8%
C28	Earnings before taxes	32.1%	27.6%	19.3%
C29	*less*: Income taxes	10.2	8.9	7.0
C30	*equals*: Net income	21.9	18.8	12.3
C31	*less*: Cash dividend payments	7.4	7.9	8.0
C32	*equals*: Retained earnings	14.5	10.9%	4.3%

ANALYSIS OF SALES AND COMPETITION

KO is one of the largest corporations in the world. It manufactures syrups for the following soft drinks and distributes them to bottlers around the world.

Coke products (about 70% of total sales)

Classic Coke	Decaffeinated Diet Coke	Diet Cherry Coke
Diet Coke	Cherry Coke	

Non-Coke soft drinks (about 21% of total sales)

Sprite	Diet Sprite	Mello Yello
Fanta	Mr. PiBB	Lift
TAB	Fresca	Barq's
Nestea	POWERaDE	Specialty local drinks

Food sales (fruit juices generate about 9% of sales)

Minute Maid juice	Fruitopia	Hi-C

In 1999 KO products comprised 18% of the nonalcoholic soft drinks purchased throughout the world. KO's worldwide sales expanded at a rate of 6% per year over the last decade. Earnings per share grew at a compounded annual rate of 4.8% over the last decade.

KO sells its products in 200 different countries. Figure 4-1 illustrates how the company's worldwide unit sales volume breaks down by geographic areas. Although North America provides the largest share of KO's aggregate sales (32%), only 21% are in the United States, where the corporation is headquartered. Strengths of the company are its multinational

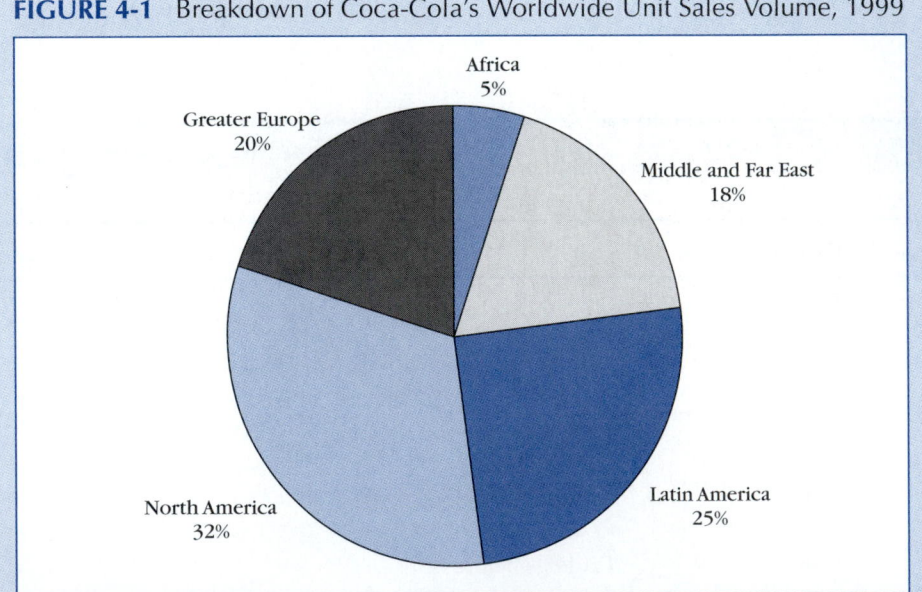

FIGURE 4-1 Breakdown of Coca-Cola's Worldwide Unit Sales Volume, 1999

The Coca-Cola Corporation has an efficient multinational production and distribution system. Only 21% of KO's total sales take place in the United States, where the company is headquartered.

diversification and its differentiated list of drinks. KO executives forecast a continuation of past growth. Although this rosy outlook is plausible, corporate executives do not usually discuss their firm's problems publicly.

KO's main competitor is PepsiCo, whose Pepsi-Cola, Diet Pepsi, Slice, 7UP, Diet 7UP, Mountain Dew, Diet Mountain Dew, and Tropicana provide about half of PepsiCo's total sales. PepsiCo also manufactures snack foods—Doritos, Tostitos, Frito-Lay, Chee-tos, Ruffles, and others—that provide the other half of the firm's sales. Although Pepsi's sales are split between beverages and snack foods, beverages are less profitable. As a result, top management at PepsiCo might be more focused on their more profitable snack foods than on competing with KO.

PepsiCo competes effectively with KO in the U.S. market for soft drinks, but KO dominates the larger international market. Cadbury Schweppes is the third largest soft drink manufacturer in the world; this much smaller firm produces R.C. Cola. None of KO's competitors enjoy its level of brand recognition, worldwide market penetration, profitable bottling arrangements, and annual cash flows averaging over $2 billion.

KO's so-called "food products" are the firm's weakness. KO's food products are fruit juices. Minute Maid provides 9% of KO's total sales, but no profits. In contrast, PepsiCo's Tropicana orange juice business is profitable.

FINANCIAL RATIOS WITH MEANINGFUL AND RELEVANT VALUES

A **financial ratio** uses two values that are meaningfully related to produce new information that has additional value. Financial ratios are used to quantify, summarize, and interpret financial data.

Tables 4-4 and 4-5 are both tables of ratios, since percentages are a kind of ratio. These ratios provide insights because they involve meaningfully related values. For instance, adding line items C13 and C17 in Table 4-4 reveals that creditors financed 56% of KO's total assets in 1999.

Computing and Interpreting Financial Ratios

Financial ratios can be grouped into homogeneous categories:

- ◆ **Solvency ratios** or **liquidity ratios** measure a firm's ability to meet its short-term obligations.

- ◆ **Turnover ratios** measure the rate of activity within various areas of the firm.

- ◆ **Coverage ratios** measure the extent to which the firm's earnings are able to pay (cover) interest expense and repayment of debt.

- ◆ **Leverage ratios** measure the extent to which the firm has been financed by creditors and is, therefore, a measure of the firm's financial risk.

- ◆ **Profitability ratios** measure the productivity of money invested in the firm.

- ◆ **Per share data** focuses on quantities that affect the common stock's market price per share.

- ◆ **Growth ratios** measure the contributions of various items to the firm's development.

- ◆ **Risk analysis ratios** measure variability within various sectors of the firm.

The following sections show how the ratios are calculated. The alphanumeric symbols in the equations refer to the individual line numbers from KO's financial statements in

Tables 4-1, 4-2, 4-3, 4-4, and 4-5. Interpretations of the ratio's value accompany some of the definitions given. Most financial ratios have descriptive names that provide good clues about how to calculate the ratio and interpret its numerical value.

Solvency (or Liquidity) Ratios

The **current ratio** and the **quick ratio** are widely used measures of a firm's solvency. The computations in Table 4-6 show that KO's current ratio indicates it had $0.66 of current assets for every dollar of liabilities coming due in 1999. This ratio indicates that KO did not have quite enough current (liquid) assets to pay its bills.

The quick ratio is similar to the current ratio, but because the numerator in the quick ratio includes only those most liquid assets that can be *quickly* turned into cash, it is a more discriminating measure of solvency. The *quick assets* include all current assets except inventory.

The quick ratio in Table 4-6 indicates that in 1999 KO had 55 cents of quick assets for every dollar of liabilities coming due that year. The quick ratio of $0.55 suggests that if the firm's inventory became worthless because of spoilage, damage, an act of God, or any other reason, KO does not have enough other current assets to pay its current liabilities in a timely manner.

Even though KO's quick ratio indicates it might lack current assets, the corporation enjoys cash flows that average over $2 billion per year (Table 4-3), assuring the firm it will be able to pay its bills on time. What we cannot see in the quick ratio is that KO is using its huge cash flow to conserve on its cash holdings; cash is a nonearning asset that should be minimized when possible.

Studying KO's solvency ratios did not reveal the complete story about the company's solvency; an important source of cash was found elsewhere. More generally, we note that many valuable insights are not in only a few ratios.

Turnover Ratios

Turnover ratios, also called *efficiency ratios* or *activity ratios*, measure business activity within a firm. The idea underlying all turnover ratios is that inactive assets might be nonearning assets. Once nonearning assets have been pinpointed, actions can be taken to employ or eliminate them.

The receivables turnover ratio is used to ascertain the liquidity of accounts receivable. If the credit customers are all paying their bills on time, the accounts receivable should be turning over frequently. The receivables turnover ratio is defined in Table 4-7. Here again, the alphanumerics refer to line items from KO's financial statements (Tables 4-1 and 4-2).

KO's annual credit sales are not known; therefore, its accounts receivable were used as an estimate of credit sales. Table 4-7 shows that KO's accounts receivable turned over 11.02 times in 1999. If a firm's accounts receivables turned over every month, they would turn over 12 times a year. Therefore, it appears that KO's receivables turned over slightly less than once per month. Whether or not a receivables turnover of 11.02 times per year is too fast or too

Table 4-6	**Solvency Ratios (Liquidity Ratios) with Values for Coca-Cola**				
Name of Ratio	Ratio in Words	Source Symbols	1997	1998	1999
Current ratio	Current assets / Current liabilities	A6 in Table 4-1 / L4 in Table 4-1	0.81	0.74	0.66
Quick ratio	Current assets − Inventory / Current liabilities	A6 − A4 in Table 4-1 / L4 in Table 4-1	0.68	0.64	0.55

Table 4-7	Turnover Ratios with Values for Coca-Cola				
Name of Ratio	Ratio in Words	Source Symbols	1997	1998	1999
Receivable turnover	$\dfrac{\text{Annual credit sales}}{\text{Accounts receivable}}$	$\dfrac{\text{I1 in Table 4-2}}{\text{A3 in Table 4-1}}$	11.51	11.29	11.02
Collection period	$\dfrac{\text{Accounts receivable}}{\text{Average day's sales}}$	$\dfrac{\text{A3 in Table 4-1}}{(\text{I1 in Table 4-2})/365 \text{ days}}$	31.71 days	32.32 days	33.14 days
Inventory turnover	$\dfrac{\text{Annual sales (valued at cost)}}{\text{Average inventory (valued at cost)}}$	$\dfrac{\text{I2 in Table 4-2}}{\text{A4 in Table 4-1}}$	6.27	6.25	5.58
Asset turnover	$\dfrac{\text{Annual sales}}{\text{Total assets}}$	$\dfrac{\text{I1 in Table 4-2}}{\text{A10 in Table 4-1}}$	1.11	0.98	0.92
Equity turnover	$\dfrac{\text{Annual sales}}{\text{Equity}}$	$\dfrac{\text{I1 in Table 4-2}}{\text{E5 in Table 4-1}}$	2.58	2.24	2.08

slow cannot be determined without knowing the company's credit policies and the payment customs within its industry.

Another way to assess the liquidity of accounts receivable is to compute the number of days in a firm's *collection period*. This ratio helps gauge the speed at which bills are collected.

$$\left(\begin{matrix}\text{Collection} \\ \text{period}\end{matrix}\right) = \frac{\text{Accounts receivable}}{\text{Average day's sales}} = \frac{\text{Accounts receivable}}{\text{Annual sales/365 days}}$$

$$= \frac{\text{A3 in Table 4-1}}{(\text{I1 in Table 4-2})/365 \text{ days}} = \frac{\$1,798}{\$19,805/365 \text{ days}}$$

$$= \frac{\$1,798}{\$54.26 \text{ sales per day}} = 33.1 \text{ days in 1999}$$

KO's average day's credit sales would ideally be used to compute its collection period. Since KO's credit sales are not known, its accounts receivable were used as an estimate of credit sales. Table 4-7 shows that KO's average collection period was 33.1 days during 1999, compared to 32.3 days in 1998. The firm did a slightly (but not significantly) better job of collecting its bills in 1998 than it did in 1999.

ESTABLISHING FINANCIAL RATIO GUIDELINES FOR COCA-COLA   **EXAMPLE**

KO's 1999 collection period of 33.1 days would be considered slow if KO extended credit terms of 2/15, net 30.* But if KO were in the business of retailing fresh vegetables, then 33.1 days would be too long to let customers' bills go unpaid. It would seem more appropriate for retail buyers of a perishable good to pay cash for their purchases, so the accounts receivable would be near zero. The optimal value for accounts receivable turnover depends on the product being sold and on competitors' credit terms. The manager of accounts receivable at Coke should find out what credit terms Pepsi and other competitors are granting to their customers when establishing Coke's credit policies.

In the final analysis, Coke is selling syrup to bottlers that it owns. Thus, KO has an unusually high degree of control over its collections.

---

* Terms of 2/15, net 30 days mean that customers purchasing goods on credit are invited by the supplier to take a 2% cash discount if and only if they pay for the goods within 15 days after delivery. If the 2% cash discount is not taken within 15 days, the supplier expects full payment within 30 days.

The *inventory-turnover ratio* gauges how efficiently the firm is using its inventory. It is preferable to measure the firm's sales at the cost-of-goods-sold (at wholesale, not retail) when computing this ratio because inventories are entered in the firm's books at their (wholesale) cost in most industries. If retail sales are divided by the inventory valued at cost, the resulting value would overestimate the true value.

Table 4-7 shows that in 1999 KO turned its inventory over 5.58 times per year, a bit slower than in 1998. We need more information before we can say whether KO's inventory is out of control.

EXAMPLE   ESTABLISHING INVENTORY-TURNOVER GUIDELINES

If KO manufactured liquor and had an inventory turnover of 5.58 times per year, the company must be producing their product so hastily that it isn't fit to drink. If the firm is in the fresh vegetable business, inventory that is 2 months old is garbage. An industry average inventory turnover would make an appropriate yardstick with which to interpret KO's inventory turnover.

An entire book devoted to financial statement analysis delves deeper into inventory turnover than this chapter's brief review can. For example, in-depth inventory analysis breaks total inventory down into raw materials inventory, finished goods inventory, and other components that might be appropriate, and it then analyzes each component separately.

The *asset-turnover ratio* in Table 4-7 measures how productive the firm's total assets (TA) are at producing final sales. The values of a firm's asset-turnover ratio should be compared to those of its competitors. The turnover of total assets per year varies from a low value in the neighborhood of once per year for smokestack industries to over a dozen times a year for businesses that own no tangible assets (advertising agencies).

The *equity-turnover ratio* measures the relationship between the dollar values of a firm's sales and its equity. KO's sales were 2.08 times larger than its equity (net worth) in 1999. The 1998 and 1997 values were a little higher, so it appears KO's equity turnover is falling.

Coke's equity turns over faster than its assets because the firm uses financial leverage (borrowed money). The equity-turnover ratio is dissected further later in this chapter, after we become acquainted with financial leverage ratios.

Coverage Ratios

As mentioned earlier, coverage ratios measure how many times a firm's annual earnings cover debt-servicing charges such as interest, sinking-fund payments, or lease payments. The **times-interest-earned ratio,** a widely used coverage ratio, measures the firm's "operating income" relative to its interest payments. For example, if a firm's operating income is twice as large as its interest expense, the firm's times-interest-earned ratio equals 2: The company earned enough to cover its interest expense twice.

A firm's **operating income** is earnings from its ordinary operations. KO's operating income is earned by manufacturing and distributing nonalcoholic soft drinks. Extraordinary income (such as gains income from selling a used truck for more than its book value) is not included in KO's operating income. Nonoperating costs such as interest expenses and taxes are not deducted in determining operating income either. Operating income is sometimes called its **earnings before interest and taxes (EBIT).** In terms of the line numbers in the Income and Expense Statement (Table 4-2), KO's operating income equals line (I1) less [(I2) + (I4)], as shown in Table 4-8.

Table 4-8	**Coverage Ratios with Coca-Cola's Values**				
Name of Ratio	Ratio in Words	Source Symbols	1997	1998	1999
Times-interest-earned	$\dfrac{\text{Annual operating income}}{\text{Annual interest payment}}$	$\dfrac{\text{I1} - (\text{I2} + \text{I4}) \text{ in Table 4-2}}{\text{I6 in Table 4-2}}$	106.40	85.64	51.71
Pretax fixed charge coverage	$\dfrac{\text{Gross income} + \text{interest expense}}{\text{Interest expense}}$	$\dfrac{\text{I9} + \text{I6 in Table 4-2}}{\text{I6 in Table 4-2}}$	129.83	90.62	50.60
Cash flow to long-term-debt	$\dfrac{\text{EBIT} + \text{depreciation}}{\text{Annual interest payment}}$	$\dfrac{\text{I5} + \text{F2 in Tabs. 4-2 \& 4-3}}{\text{I6 in Table 4-2}}$	119.72	96.76	62.00

Interpretation of Coverage Ratio. The 1999 KO's times-interest-earned ratio indicates that the firm's operating income (or EBIT) of $3,982 covered its debt servicing (interest) expenses 51.7 times. This means Coke's income can fall 98.07% [= $1-1.93\% = 1-1/(51.7$ times)] before it will be insufficient to cover the interest on the firm's debts. KO has more than ample coverage.

Bond-quality rating agencies like Moody's and the Standard & Poor's Corporation look closely at the times-interest-earned ratio when deciding what quality rating to assign to an issue of bonds. A firm with a times-interest-earned ratio of only 1.1, for instance, would have very little "cushion" against insolvency if its earnings decreased. Such a firm bond's would probably be assigned a low (perhaps junk) bond-quality rating.

Different Definitions for a Ratio. Each financial analyst has his or her own favorite version of each ratio. This flexibility exists because most financial ratios can be meaningfully redefined. The times-interest-earned ratio, for example, can be reformulated in a different but meaningful manner. Instead of using the firm's operating income (or EBIT) in the numerator of the times-interest-earned ratio, some security analysts prefer to use the firm's *pretax gross income*. Pretax gross income is defined to include the firm's net income plus income taxes plus annual interest charges; it equals lines I9 + I6 in Table 4-2. The *pretax-fixed-charge-coverage ratio* divides the firm's annual interest charges into pretax gross income, as shown in Table 4-8.

There are additional coverage ratios. Some financial analysts choose to narrowly define the interest expense in the denominator of the pretax-fixed-charge-coverage ratio to include only interest expense. Other financial analysts define interest expenses liberally to include all debt-service charges, lease payments, and any cash dividends that may be payable on preferred stock.

Several different variations of the same ratio may be useful for different purposes. Defining ratios in this accommodating manner is permissible as long as the ratios that are compared are defined consistently. As a result of this definitional flexibility, an infinite number of financial ratios can be defined—far too many to discuss in one chapter.

A Cash Flow Ratio

Two quantities from a firm's Income and Expense Statement can be added to obtain a measure of its cash flow.*

---

* A straightforward corporate cash flow is defined here; this definition ignores changes in networking capital and other complex considerations. Coca-Cola's cash flow from its annual reports is in Table 4-3. Different definitions of cash flow have been introduced, and more will follow. The cash flow available to common stock investors is defined in Chapter 24.

EBIT. As mentioned above, a firm's normal operating income (NOI) before taxes is sometimes called earnings before interest and taxes (EBIT). Using the item numbers in Table 4-2, KO's EBIT equals item I1 less items I2 and I4. For 1999 it is [($19,805) − ($6,009) − ($9,814)] = $3,982.

Depreciation. **Depreciation** is an allowance for fair wear and tear on plant and equipment. **Amortization** is an allowance for obsolescence in computer programs and patents. Depreciation and amortization are similar noncash expense items that are deducted from a firm's revenue. Repairs need not actually be made—even though the bookkeeping entry deducting depreciation or amortization expense has been permanently recorded in the firm's books. Depreciation and amortization are financially useful because they reduce the firm's income taxes. Through the income tax deduction and resulting decreased tax bill, depreciation and amortization generate an indirect cash flow that can be used to pay interest expense, to repair the firm's physical assets, or for anything else. Depreciation and amortization are allocations of the cost of assets over their useful productive lives. KO's depreciation and amortization are buried out-of-sight in the cost-of-goods-sold section of its income statement (line I2 of Table 4-2), but some financial detective work will uncover them in the firm's statement of cash flows (line F2 of Table 4-3). KO's depreciation and amortization totaled $792 million in 1999.

KO's 1999 cash flow is its EBIT of $3,982 plus $792 of depreciation, totaling $4,774. Once a firm's cash flow has been calculated, another coverage ratio called the **cash-flow-to-long-term-debt ratio** can be calculated. KO's long-term debt—debt that need not be repaid within 1 year—is $854 million for 1999. Table 4-8 shows that KO's declining, but still high, cash-flow-to-long-term-debt ratios suggest the firm could suffer a large decrease in cash flow without defaulting on its interest payments.

Financial Leverage Ratios

Leverage ratios gauge the extent to which a firm finances its operations with borrowed money. As its name suggests, the *total-debt-to-total-asset ratio* is a leverage ratio that indicates what percent of a firm's assets are financed by creditors. Table 4-9 shows that 56% of Coke's total assets were financed with borrowed money in 1999.

The numerator of the *total-debt-to-equity ratio* is the same as the numerator in the preceding equation, but dividing by equity instead of total assets gives the ratio a different perspective on the firm's indebtedness.

The total debt to equity computation in Table 4-9 indicates that in 1999 creditors put up 127.3% as much money as the owners of the Corporation had invested in the business.

Table 4-9	Leverage Ratios with Values for Coca-Cola				
Name of Ratio	Ratio in Words	Source Symbols	1997	1998	1999
Total-debt-to-total-asset	$\dfrac{\text{Total debt}}{\text{Total assets}}$	$\dfrac{\text{L4 + L8 in Table 4-1}}{\text{A10 in Table 4-1}}$	0.57	0.56	0.56
Total-debt-to-equity	$\dfrac{\text{Total debt}}{\text{Equity}}$	$\dfrac{\text{L4 + L8 in Table 4-1}}{\text{E5 in Table 4-1}}$	131.7	127.8	127.3
Long-term-debt-to-equity	$\dfrac{\text{Long-term debt}}{\text{Equity}}$	$\dfrac{\text{L8 in Table 4-1}}{\text{E5 in Table 4-1}}$	0.31	0.25	0.24
Long-term-debt-to-capitalization	$\dfrac{\text{Long-term debt}}{\text{Capitalization}}$	$\dfrac{\text{L8 in Table 4-1}}{\text{L8 + E5 in Table 4-1}}$	0.24	0.20	0.19
Total-asset-to-equity	$\dfrac{\text{Total assets}}{\text{Equity}}$	$\dfrac{\text{A10 in Table 4-1}}{\text{E5 in Table 4-1}}$	231.7	227.8	227.3

KO's total debt of $12,110 million in 1999 seems huge. However, much of this borrowing is interest-free accounts payable such as utility bills and money owed to raw materials suppliers. Any firm that did not utilize these interest-free loans would not be maximizing profit.

The *long-term-debt-to-equity ratio* focuses on the firm's long-term borrowing. Long-term debt is usually lent under more rigid requirements than short-term credit and, therefore, it limits the borrower's financial flexibility. Table 4-9 shows that KO's long-term-debt-to-equity ratio is a modest 24% in 1999.

Capitalization, a firm's permanently committed capital funds, is the sum of its permanently maintained current liabilities, long-term debt, preferred stock, and stockholders' equity. Current liabilities are not long-term obligations; they must all usually be repaid within less than 1 year. For KO, see lines L8 and E5 in Table 4-1.

The *long-term-debt-to-capitalization ratio* assesses the fraction of a firm's permanent capital obtained from long-term lenders. KO's long-term debt of $2,254 combined with its $9,513 of equity adds up to $11,767 of *permanent capital* in 1999. Table 4-9 shows that the $2,254 of long-term debt is 19% of KO's permanent capital.

Total-asset-to-equity ratio is another ratio that evaluates the structure of a firm's indebtedness. In 1999 KO owned 2.273 times as much assets as it had in equity; this can only occur with significant indebtedness. KO's large profits are analyzed next to determine if the corporation should be able to support this level of debt without problems.

Financial ratios are sometimes calculated with market values instead of book values; this is especially true for leverage ratios. Current market values are often more realistic and relevant than historical book values.

Profitability Ratios

Profitability ratios compare a firm's earnings with various factors that generate earnings. **Net profit margin** measures each sales dollar's contribution to net income.

Table 4-10 shows that KO's net after-tax profit margin was 12% of each sales dollar in 1999. Common sense suggests that after-tax net profit margins of 12% are good for a product that is not much more than sugar water. However, in 1997 and 1998 KO's after-tax net profit margins had the much higher values of 22% and 19%.

Rate of **return on assets** measures net income after taxes as a percentage of the company's total asset investment. KO's rate of return on total assets means that a dollar's worth of

---

NET PROFIT MARGIN GUIDELINES   **EXAMPLE**

A net profit margin of 12% would be very low for a ritzy jewelry store like Tiffany's, an exclusive New York City department store like Bergdorf-Goodman, or Harrods department store in London (where Her Majesty shops). These thickly carpeted stores have beautiful display cases and mannerly sales clerks who are well dressed. The profit margins are high to cover these accoutrements. It is common for luxury retailers to sell their goods for 2, 3, or more times the wholesale price paid for the good, yielding net profit margins of 20% to 30% of sales after the high overhead expenses are deducted. At the other extreme, large retail supermarket chains operate on low markups and thin net profit margins of 1% or 2%. These examples make it clear that an appropriate standard of comparison is needed to interpret a profit margin.

Coke's closest competitor, Pepsi, is not an entirely appropriate standard of comparison because Pepsi's total sales include as much snack food sales as soft drink sales. A perfect standard of comparison for Coke does not exist.

Table 4-10   Profitability Ratios with Values for Coca-Cola

Name of Ratio	Ratio in Words	Source Symbols	1997	1998	1999
Net profit margin	$\dfrac{\text{Net income}}{\text{Sales}}$	$\dfrac{\text{I11 in Table 4-2}}{\text{I1 in Table 4-2}}$	0.22	0.19	0.12
Return on asset (ROA)	$\dfrac{\text{Net income}}{\text{Total assets}}$	$\dfrac{\text{I11 in Table 4-2}}{\text{A10 in Table 4-1}}$	0.24	0.18	0.11
Return on equity (ROE)	$\dfrac{\text{Net income}}{\text{Equity}}$	$\dfrac{\text{I11 in Table 4-2}}{\text{E5 in Table 4-1}}$	0.57	0.42	0.26
Long-term capital's pretax rate of return	$\dfrac{\text{Interest + Pretax earnings}}{\text{Capitalization}}$	$\dfrac{\text{I6 + I9 in Table 4-2}}{\text{L5 + E5 in Table 4-1}}$	0.75	0.58	0.37

assets yielded about 11 cents of after-tax earnings in 1999. Asset-intensive businesses like steel mills usually have low rates of return on their huge investments in assets. Profitable service companies (advertising agencies, public relations firms, and personnel agencies) may be able to earn high rates of return on their assets because they rent everything and own virtually no assets. In view of its substantial investment in bricks-and-mortar assets, KO's return on total assets of 11% is high, although not as high as previous years. All of the profitability ratios in Table 4-10 are down in 1999. Even though 1999 was a profitable year for Coke, it was not as profitable as the previous years.

Rate of **return on equity** (ROE) measures the rate of pretax earnings a firm earns on its owners' equity. If a firm is debt-free, its rate of return on assets and its rate of return on equity are equal. Any differences between the two ratios is attributable to the use of financial leverage. Comparing KO's 1999 return on assets of 11% with its return on equity of 26% in the same year indicates that the company employed borrowed money advantageously to leverage (multiply) the rate of return to its stockholders. Financial leverage magnifies both positive and negative rates of return on assets. Financial leverage is counter-productive when a firm is suffering losses (earning negative returns on assets). KO's consistently high positive rates of return on equity represent one of the forces that pushes its stock price up.

Long-term capital, also called *permanent-capital* or simply capitalization, is a firm's permanently committed capital funds. It is the sum of the values of long-term debt, plus preferred stock, plus common stock. *Long-term capital's pretax rate of return (LTCPTROR)* is a profitability measure that is popular at bond-quality rating agencies. A firm's earnings before taxes plus its interest expense payments equals the total amount of income available to make interest payments.

LTCPTROR is computed for KO in Table 4-10; it is 37% in 1999. The LTCPTROR ratio states the firm's taxable income as a percentage of its permanent capitalization. Comparing with current market interest rates, if this ratio does not exceed current rates of interest, the company is not earning enough to pay its debts. This will result in low bond-quality ratings and, if the situation does not improve, lead to default. KO's pretax ROR on long-term capital is at a comfortably high level.

Per Share Data for the Common Stock

Common stock investors are concerned about variables that affect the market price of their shares. **Earnings per share (EPS)** after income taxes is one of the most important determinants of a common stock's value, because it measures the earning power that supports the stock's market price. Table 4-11 shows that each share of KO's common stock earned $0.98 after taxes in 1999, down from $1.67 in 1997 and $1.43 in 1998.

Table 4-11	Per Share Data for the Common Stock with Values for Coca-Cola				
Name of Ratio	Ratio in Words	Source Symbols	1997	1998	1999
Earning per share (EPS)	$\dfrac{\text{Net income}}{\text{No. of common shares outstanding}}$	$\dfrac{\text{I11 in Table 4-2}}{\text{P1 in Table 4-2}}$	1.67	1.43	0.98
Cash dividend per share (CDPS)	$\dfrac{\text{Total corporate dividend}}{\text{No. of common shares outstanding}}$	$\dfrac{\text{I12 in Table 4-2}}{\text{P1 in Table 4-2}}$	0.56	0.60	0.64
Payout ratio (POR)	$\dfrac{\text{Cash dividends per share}}{\text{Earning per share (EPS)}}$	$\dfrac{\text{P4 in Table 4-2}}{\text{P3 in Table 4-2}}$	0.336	0.419	0.653
Retention rate (RR)	$\dfrac{\text{Retained earnings}}{\text{Net income}}$	$\dfrac{\text{I13}}{\text{I11}}$	0.664	0.581	0.350
Price-earning (P/E)	$\dfrac{\text{Market price per share, P}}{\text{Earning per share (EPS)}}$	$\dfrac{\text{P2 in Table 4-2}}{\text{P3 in Table 4-2}}$	32-47	36-56	48-72

The **payout ratio** measures the percentage of earnings that a corporation pays out as cash dividends. In 1999 KO's Board of Directors elected to pay out 65.3% of the corporation's $2,431 million of net income (or, equivalently, $0.64 out of each share's earnings of $0.98) as cash dividends to the common stockholders. *Cash dividend per share* equals the corporation's total outlay for cash dividends divided by the number of shares of common stock outstanding at the time the dividend is declared.

The **retention rate (RR)** measures the fraction of after-tax corporate earnings that are retained within the firm to finance expansion—or **retained earnings (RE)** stated as a fraction of net income. The retention rate also equals the reciprocal of the payout ratio: (Retention ratio) = 1 − (Payout ratio).

The **price-earnings ratio (P/E)**, also called the *P-E ratio* or *earnings multiplier,* equals a stock's market price per share divided by its earnings per share (EPS). Table 4-11 shows that during 1999 KO stock was selling at 48 times its earnings per share at the lowest point, and as high as 72. Many corporations' stock sells for smaller multiples, for reasons that are considered in later chapters.

ANALYZING AND INTERPRETING RATIOS

Some financial ratios contain additional information that can be obtained by dissecting the ratio. This section shows how to break down the return on equity (ROE) formula into meaningful components.

The DuPont Analytical Framework

Analysis of ROE. Investors are concerned about their corporation's growth because growth usually translates into stock price appreciation. Breaking down the return on equity (ROE) formula from Table 4-10 reveals insights into KO's determinants of growth:

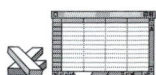

$$\text{Return on equity } (ROE) = \frac{\text{Net income}}{\text{Equity}} = \frac{NI}{EQ} = \frac{I11}{E5}$$

$$= \frac{\$2,431}{\$9,513} = .255 = 25.5\% \text{ in 1999}$$

Dividing both the numerator and the denominator of the ROE ratio by the firm's sales allows us to look at ROE through its components:

$$ROE = \frac{NI}{EQ} = \frac{Sales}{EQ} \times \frac{NI}{Sales} = (\text{Equity turnover}) \times (\text{Net profit margin})$$

Table 4-12A uses the ROE formula above to analyze some of Coke's data.

There are different ways to restate the ROE formula algebraically, and each way yields identical numerical results. The formula above expresses the original ROE formula in terms of two other meaningful ratios. To extract further information, we can break down the equity turnover into fundamental components.

$$\left(\begin{array}{c}\text{Equity} \\ \text{turnover}\end{array}\right) = \frac{Sales}{EQ} = \frac{Sales}{\text{Total assets}} \times \frac{\text{Total assets}}{EQ} = \left(\begin{array}{c}\text{Total asset} \\ \text{turnover}\end{array}\right) \times \left(\begin{array}{c}\text{Financial} \\ \text{leverage ratio}\end{array}\right)$$

TABLE 4-12   DuPont Analysis of Coca-Cola's Return on Equity (ROE)

Table 4-12A Two-Part Decomposition of ROE

Summary: Column (1) × Column (2) = Column (3).
(Asset turnover) × (Profit margin) = (Return on equity).

Year	Sales/Equity	NI/Sales	ROE
1990	2.66	13.50%	35.91%
1991	2.73	13.98%	38.17%
1992	3.36	12.73%	42.80%
1993	3.05	15.58%	47.47%
1994	3.09	15.78%	48.79%
1995	3.34	16.57%	55.38%
1996	3.03	18.70%	56.73%
1997	2.59	21.88%	56.76%
1998	2.24	18.78%	42.04%
1999	2.08	12.27%	25.52%

Table 4-12B Three-Part Decomposition of ROE

Summary: Column (1) × Column (2) × Column (3) = Column (4).
(Asset turnover) × (Financial Leverage) × (Profit margin) = (Return on equity).

Year	Sales/TA	TA/Equity	NI/Sales	ROE
1990	1.10	2.41	13.50%	35.91%
1991	1.14	2.40	13.98%	38.17%
1992	1.18	2.84	12.73%	42.80%
1993	1.16	2.62	15.58%	47.47%
1994	1.17	2.65	15.78%	48.79%
1995	1.20	2.79	16.57%	55.38%
1996	1.16	2.63	18.70%	56.73%
1997	1.12	2.32	21.88%	56.76%
1998	0.98	2.28	18.78%	42.04%
1999	0.92	2.27	12.27%	25.52%

The two components from the equity turnover ratio above are substituted into the ROE formula to restate the ROE in terms of three components:

$$ROE = \frac{NI}{EQ} = \frac{Sales}{EQ} \times \frac{NI}{Sales} = \left(\begin{array}{c} Equity \\ turnover \end{array} \right) \times \left(\begin{array}{c} Net\ profit \\ margin \end{array} \right)$$

$$= \frac{Sales}{TA} \times \frac{TA}{EQ} \times \frac{NI}{Sales} = \left(\begin{array}{c} Total\ asset \\ turnover \end{array} \right) \times \left(\begin{array}{c} Financial \\ leverage\ ratio \end{array} \right) \times \left(\begin{array}{c} Net\ profit \\ margin \end{array} \right)$$

In the three-part decomposition illustrated with KO's data in Table 4-12B, Column 1 shows how KO's asset turnover rose and then fell during the 1990s; Column 2 documents KO's continual usage of debt to obtain financial leverage; Column 3 shows how KO's profit margin rose and then fell during the decade; Column 4 traces the upward push that KO's financial leverage applies the firm's positive annual profit margins to increase its ROE.

The ratios in Table 4-12 indicate that KO's managers were making profitable decisions. ROE components are also useful in analyzing a firm's growth.

Analysis of Growth. Price appreciation in a corporation's common stock depends on various factors. First, growth that is financed internally depends on the amount of earnings retained in the firm. The retention ratio (RR) measures the fraction of a corporation's earnings that are reinvested internally.

Second, a corporation's growth rate depends on the rate of return on equity (ROE) from funds invested in the firm. Defining the earnings growth rate as shown below reveals how the ROE and RR determine growth that is financed from retained earnings.[*]

Growth rate $= RR \times ROE$

Substituting the three-part ROE ratio from Table 4-12B into the growth rate equation above results in the following model:

$$Growth\ rate = RR \times \frac{Sales}{TA} \times \frac{TA}{EQ} \times \frac{NI}{Sales}$$

Substituting RR $=$ RE/NI into the equation above:

$$Growth\ rate = \frac{RE}{NI} \times \frac{Sales}{TA} \times \frac{TA}{EQ} \times \frac{NI}{Sales} = \frac{RE}{EQ}$$

$$= \left(\begin{array}{c} Retention \\ ratio \end{array} \right) \left(\begin{array}{c} Total\ asset \\ turnover \end{array} \right) \left(\begin{array}{c} Financial\ leverage \\ ratio \end{array} \right) \left(\begin{array}{c} Profit \\ margin \end{array} \right)$$

Now we see how the variables affecting ROE and the growth rate can be restated to highlight the way different financial variables affect a common stock's growth in value. For example, the equation above reveals that if the profit margin increases, the firm can continue growing at the same rate while reducing its debt. This approach to ratio analysis is called the **DuPont Analysis** because it was pioneered by the DuPont Corporation decades ago.[3]

Interpreting Ratios with Standards of Comparison

Financial analysts typically undertake two comparisons to analyze the level and trend of a ratio. Cross-sectional comparisons and time-series comparisons are used.

---

[*]   This earnings growth rate analysis ignores expansion financed with funds from external equity sources.

Cross-Sectional Standards. A firm's financial ratios can be compared to other firm's ratios or industry average ratios when appropriate data are available. Making different **cross-sectional comparisons** can reveal strengths and/or weaknesses in one firm relative to other firms.[4]

Industry ratios are derived by averaging over the financial ratios of competing firms. Although the individual firms in any given industry typically have substantially different ratios, their average ratios provide good indications of the normal *level* of the financial ratios of firms producing similar products. Industry average financial ratios for dozens of different industries are published by financial information companies like Moody's, Standard & Poor's, Fitch, Value Line, Duff and Phelps, Dun & Bradstreet, and others.

By comparing the financial ratios of the firm being analyzed with the ratios of competing firms that are poorly or well managed, a financial analyst may be able to detect differences that explain the problems and successes.

Time-Series Standards. A firm's own ratios from other years can provide a useful standard for comparisons. Such **time-series comparisons** may highlight trends or changes that occurred in the firm. Table 4-12 provides an example of time-series financial data for KO that can help the financial analyst search for trends and relationships within the firm. Figure 4-2 shows a sample of Standard & Poor's time-series analysis of KO. Standard & Poor's and the competing financial services purvey this and more detailed financial analyses on thousands of different companies.

Looking at time-series financial data for a firm might reveal relationships and trends that are not easy to discern when viewing data from a single time period. By comparing data for several consecutive years an analyst can ascertain whether changes to seem to be a one-time change, a trend, or a business-cycle fluctuation.

Potential Problems with Financial Analysis

Analyzing financial statements is a valuable way to gain information, but not without pitfalls. Inflation, vague accounting guidelines, and mergers are a few of the many problems that can undermine the value of financial statements.

Inflationary Distortions. Inflation can distort financial statements and the ratios calculated from those statements. For example, if several consecutive years of financial statements from a single corporation are compared, the comparison could be clouded by inflated prices in the financial statements from different years. Inflation can be a particular problem with the balance sheet, where some fixed assets are reported at their historical costs. Historical costs can become irrelevant and even misleading after several years of double-digit inflation. Furthermore, some generally accepted accounting procedures (GAAP) mandate depreciating a fixed asset while its market value is appreciating. In countries like Brazil, Israel, and Mexico, which have had serious inflation problems (see Table 10-6 in Chapter 10), accountants and financial analysts find it necessary to make explicit inflation adjustments to financial statements.

The Vague Definition of Accounting Income. The generally accepted accounting principles (GAAP) used to define a firm's income are not as exact as they may appear. Whether the firm's accountants use straight-line or accelerated depreciation, last-in-first-out (LIFO) or first-in-first-out (FIFO), or some other inventory valuation technique, and whether sales are recognized as occurring when the order is signed by the customer or when the customer makes the final payment, are important accounting decisions that

FIGURE 4-2   Standard & Poor's Time-Series Analysis of Coca-Cola Company

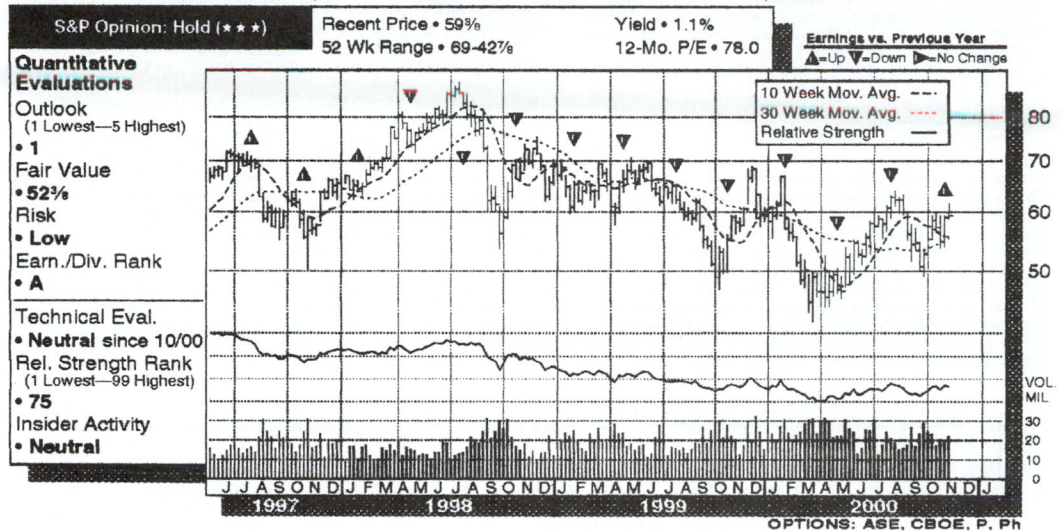

STANDARD &POOR'S
STOCK REPORTS

Coca-Cola

NYSE Symbol **KO**

In S&P 500

04-NOV-00

Industry:
Beverages
(Non-Alcoholic)

Summary: Coca-Cola is the world's largest soft-drink company and has a sizable fruit juice business. Its bottling interests include a 40% stake in NYSE-listed Coca-Cola Enterprises.

S&P Opinion: Hold (★ ★ ★)

Recent Price • 59⅜
52 Wk Range • 69-42⅞

Yield • 1.1%
12-Mo. P/E • 78.0

Earnings vs. Previous Year
▲=Up ▼=Down ▶=No Change

Quantitative Evaluations

Outlook
(1 Lowest—5 Highest)
• **1**

Fair Value
• **52⅜**

Risk
• **Low**

Earn./Div. Rank
• **A**

Technical Eval.
• **Neutral** since 10/00

Rel. Strength Rank
(1 Lowest—99 Highest)
• **75**

Insider Activity
• **Neutral**

10 Week Mov. Avg. – – –
30 Week Mov. Avg. ......
Relative Strength ——

OPTIONS: ASE, CBOE, P, Ph

Overview - 22-AUG-00

Revenues should rise at a high single-digit rate in 2000, as 5% to 6% higher volumes and 5% to 7% higher concentrate prices outweigh unfavorable currency exchange translations. Weakening foreign currencies may reduce earnings by 2% to 3%. Operating margins should widen, aided by operating efficiencies and initial benefits of the company's organizational realignment and headcount reductions. A modest rise in equity income is seen, reflecting an improved earnings outlook for bottlers. Rising free cash flow should allow for debt reduction and a resumption of share repurchases. We anticipate that EPS before special items will rise 10.7% in 2000, to $1.45, from 1999's $1.31. Our estimate includes the net effect of reductions in bottler concentrate inventories and realignment savings for 2000. For the longer term, a return to EPS growth in excess of 15% is possible.

Valuation - 22-AUG-00

We continue our hold opinion on the shares, reflecting concerns about KO's ability to achieve its long-term volume growth objectives as the company implements a massive organizational realignment. While its new decentralized operating structure should improve KO's ability to operate in local markets, we believe the risk of near-term business disruptions warrants a more cautious stance. As far as KO's international troubles are concerned, we believe the worst may be over, as key international markets continue to improve and stabilize. In addition, the 1999 acquisition of Cadbury Schweppes beverage brands in 161 countries worldwide has enhanced international growth prospects. Despite trading recently at 34X our 2001 EPS estimate, a significant premium to the S&P 500, we believe KO's superior margin structure and dominant market position make the shares a worthwhile holding.

Key Stock Statistics

S&P EPS Est. 2000	1.45	Tang. Bk. Value/Share	3.18
P/E on S&P Est. 2000	40.9	Beta	0.77
S&P EPS Est. 2001	1.75	Shareholders	394,603
Dividend Rate/Share	0.68	Market cap. (B)	$147.1
Shs. outstg. (M)	2479.8	Inst. holdings	51%
Avg. daily vol. (M)	3.963		

Value of $10,000 invested 5 years ago: $ 24,479

Fiscal Year Ending Dec. 31

	2000	1999	1998	1997	1996	1995
Revenues (Million $)						
1Q	4,391	4,428	4,457	4,138	4,194	3,854
2Q	5,621	5,379	5,151	5,075	5,253	4,936
3Q	5,543	5,195	4,747	4,954	4,656	4,895
4Q	—	4,931	4,458	4,701	4,443	4,333
Yr.	—	19,805	18,813	18,868	18,546	18,018
Earnings Per Share ($)						
1Q	-0.02	0.30	0.34	0.39	0.28	0.25
2Q	0.37	0.38	0.48	0.52	0.42	0.35
3Q	0.43	0.32	0.36	0.40	0.38	0.32
4Q	—	-0.02	0.24	0.33	0.30	0.26
Yr.	—	0.98	1.42	1.64	1.38	1.18

Next earnings report expected: late January

Dividend Data (Dividends have been paid since 1893.)

Amount ($)	Date Decl.	Ex-Div. Date	Stock of Record	Payment Date
0.170	Feb. 17	Mar. 13	Mar. 15	Apr. 01 '00
0.170	Apr. 19	Jun. 13	Jun. 15	Jul. 01 '00
0.170	Jul. 20	Sep. 13	Sep. 15	Oct. 01 '00
0.170	Oct. 18	Nov. 29	Dec. 01	Dec. 15 '00

A Division of The McGraw-Hill Companies

(continued)

FIGURE 4-2 Standard & Poor's Time-Series Analysis of Coca-Cola Company *(continued)*

STANDARD
&POOR'S
STOCK REPORTS

The Coca-Cola Company

04-NOV-00

Business Summary - 22-AUG-00

The Coca-Cola Company is the world's largest producer of soft drink concentrates and syrups, as well as the world's largest producer of juice and juice-related products. Finished soft drink products bearing the company's trademarks have been sold in the U.S. since 1886, and are now sold in nearly 200 countries. Sales and operating profit in 1999 by geographic region were distributed as follows: North America (38% of revenues, 32% of profits), Greater Europe (23%, 23%), Middle & Far East (26%, 23%), Latin America (10%, 18%), and Africa (3%, 4%).

The company's business may be the most focused and efficient of any in the world, and is, quite simply, the production and sale of soft drink and non-carbonated beverage concentrates and syrups. These products are sold to the company's authorized independent and company-owned bottling/canning operations, and fountain wholesalers. These customers then either combine the syrup with carbonated water, or combine the concentrate with sweetener, water and carbonated water to produce finished soft drinks. The finished soft drinks are packaged in authorized containers bearing the company's well-known trademarks, which include Coca-Cola (best-selling soft drink in the world, including Coca-Cola classic), caffeine free

Coca-Cola (classic), diet Coke (sold as Coke light in many markets outside the U.S.), Cherry Coke, diet Cherry Coke, Fanta, Sprite, diet Sprite, Barq's, Surge, Mr. PiBB, Mello Yello, TAB, Fresca, PowerAde, Minute Maid, Hi-C, Fruitopia, and other products developed for specific markets, including Georgia ready to drink coffees. KO has equity positions in approximately 42 unconsolidated bottling, canning and distribution operations for its products worldwide, including bottlers that accounted for about 58% of the company's U.S. unit case volume in 1999.

In the third quarter of 1999, the company completed the $970 million acquisition of Cadbury Schweppes plc beverage brands in 161 countries worldwide (excluding the U.S.), representing 85% of the world's population. Brands acquired include Schweppes and Canada Dry mixers (such as tonic water, club soda and ginger ale), Crush, Dr. Pepper, and certain regional brands. The proposed acquisition of these brands in several remaining countries is still undergoing regulatory review.

KO enters into forward exchange contracts, and purchases currency options (principally European currencies and Japanese yen) to reduce the risk that its eventual dollar net cash inflows resulting from sales outside the U.S. will be adversely affected by changes in exchange rates.

Per Share Data ($)

(Year Ended Dec. 31)	1999	1998	1997	1996	1995	1994	1993	1992	1991	1990
Tangible Bk. Val.	3.06	3.19	2.67	2.18	1.77	1.79	1.55	1.34	1.55	1.31
Cash Flow	1.30	1.67	1.89	1.59	1.36	1.14	0.97	0.83	0.70	0.60
Earnings	0.98	1.42	1.64	1.40	1.19	0.99	0.84	0.71	0.60	0.51
Dividends	0.64	0.60	0.56	0.50	0.44	0.39	0.34	0.28	0.24	0.20
Payout Ratio	65%	42%	34%	36%	37%	39%	40%	39%	39%	39%
Prices - High	70⅞	88⅞	72⅝	54¼	40¼	26¾	22⅝	22¾	20½	12¼
- Low	47¼	53⅝	51⅛	36⅛	24⅜	19½	18¾	17¾	10¾	8⅛
P/E Ratio - High	72	63	44	39	34	27	27	32	34	24
- Low	48	38	31	26	21	20	22	25	18	16

Income Statement Analysis (Million $)

	1999	1998	1997	1996	1995	1994	1993	1992	1991	1990
Revs.	19,805	18,813	18,868	18,546	18,018	16,172	13,957	13,074	11,572	10,236
Oper. Inc.	4,774	5,612	5,627	4,394	4,546	4,090	3,485	3,080	2,586	2,237
Depr.	792	645	626	479	454	382	333	310	254	236
Int. Exp.	337	277	258	286	272	199	178	171	185	231
Pretax Inc.	3,819	5,198	6,055	4,596	4,328	3,728	3,185	2,746	2,383	2,014
Eff. Tax Rate	36%	32%	32%	24%	31%	32%	31%	31%	32%	31%
Net Inc.	2,431	3,533	4,129	3,492	2,986	2,554	2,188	1,884	1,618	1,382

Balance Sheet & Other Fin. Data (Million $)

	1999	1998	1997	1996	1995	1994	1993	1992	1991	1990
Cash	1,812	1,807	1,737	1,658	1,315	1,531	1,078	1,063	1,117	1,492
Curr. Assets	6,480	6,380	5,969	5,910	5,450	5,205	4,434	4,248	4,144	4,143
Total Assets	21,623	19,145	16,940	16,161	15,041	13,873	12,021	11,052	10,222	9,278
Curr. Liab.	9,856	8,640	7,379	7,416	7,348	6,177	5,171	5,303	4,118	4,296
LT Debt	854	687	801	1,116	1,141	1,426	1,428	1,120	985	536
Common Eqty.	9,513	8,403	7,311	6,156	5,392	5,235	4,584	3,888	4,426	3,774
Total Cap.	10,865	9,514	8,560	7,573	6,727	6,841	6,125	5,090	5,611	4,650
Cap. Exp.	1,069	863	1,093	990	937	878	808	1,083	792	642
Cash Flow	3,223	4,178	4,755	3,971	3,440	2,936	2,521	2,194	1,872	1,600
Curr. Ratio	0.7	0.7	0.8	0.8	0.7	0.8	0.9	0.8	1.0	1.0
% LT Debt of Cap.	7.9	7.2	9.4	14.7	17.0	20.8	23.3	22.0	17.6	11.5
% Net Inc.of Revs.	12.3	18.8	21.9	18.8	16.6	15.8	15.7	14.4	14.0	13.5
% Ret. on Assets	11.9	19.6	24.9	22.4	20.7	19.9	19.0	17.9	16.6	15.8
% Ret. on Equity	27.1	45.0	61.3	60.5	56.2	52.4	51.8	45.7	39.6	39.3

Data as orig. reptd.; bef. results of disc. opers. and/or spec. items. Per share data adj. for stk. divs. as of ex-div. date. Bold denotes diluted EPS (FASB 128). E-Estimated. NA-Not Available. NM-Not Meaningful. NR-Not Ranked.

Office—1 Coca-Cola Plaza, N.W., Atlanta, GA 30313. **Tel**—(404) 676-2121. **Website**—http://www.thecoca-colacompany.com **Chrmn & CEO**—D. N. Daft. **Pres & COO**—J. L. Stahl. **EVP's**—J. E. Chestnut, C. S. Frenette, J. R. Gladden, C. Ware. **SVP & CFO**—G. P. Fayard. **Secy**—S. E. Shaw. **Investor Contact**—Larry M. Mark. **Dirs**—H. A. Allen, R. W. Allen, C. P. Black, W. E. Buffet, D. N. Daft, S. B. King, D. F. McHenry, S. Nunn, P. F. Oreffice, J. D. Robinson III, P. V. Ueberroth, J. B. Williams. **Transfer Agent & Registrar**—First Chicago Trust Co. of New York, Jersey City, NJ. **Incorporated**—in Delaware in 1919. **Empl**—37,400. **S&P Analyst:** Richard Joy

Published with advance written permission from Standard & Poor's. *Caveat:* Such information quickly becomes out of date and irrelevant to those making investment decisions. Investors should use up-to-date information.

modify a company's financial statements and its taxable income. (These issues are examined in Chapter 24.)

Consolidated Financial Statements. Corporations often own subsidiary corporations that must be accounted for on the balance sheet of the parent corporation. For instance, Coca-Cola Company (NYSE ticker symbol KO) is a parent company that owns (1) the famous Coca-Cola trademark and the recipe for the syrup used to make the soft drinks, (2) billions of dollars worth of minority interests ranging from 20% to 50% in bottling subsidiaries named Coca-Cola Enterprises (NYSE ticker symbol CCE) and Coca-Cola Amital, and (3) interests of less than 20% in other large bottling subsidiaries around the world. KO actually exercises more than a minority ownership control in the bottling subsidiaries because KO also controls the product they bottle. Because it does, some accountants argue that KO should show all of these bottling affiliates on its consolidated balance sheet. Such a consolidation would more than double KO's total assets and cut KO's return on assets (ROA) nearly in half. KO has not violated any generally accepted accounting principles or done anything wrong. However, some accountants argue that the consolidated balance sheet released to the public by KO reports its subsidiary interests in a misleading manner.[5]

Buying Goodwill in a Merger. The purchase of one company by another can create problems when their financial statements are consolidated. Intangible assets like "goodwill" often appear on the consolidated balance sheet.

Coca-Cola's trademark is an intangible asset that has a *book value* of $1 on the balance sheet; it is more likely to be worth $1 billion. Coke's controller would probably defend the $1 book value by saying it is a conservative assessment. There is no way of determining the value of an asset that is not traded frequently in a liquid market. It is the accounting convention to equate goodwill with the excess of the purchase price over the book value and amortize it over no more than 40 years.

THE BOTTOM LINE

The balance sheet, income and expense statement, and statement of cash flows are the three basic financial statements that provide the raw data with which to compute financial ratios.

Investors can use many different categories of financial ratios, including solvency ratios, coverage ratios, turnover ratios, profitability ratios, cash flow ratios, leverage ratios, growth ratios, and ratios for analyzing per share data. Ratios are interpreted by doing cross-sectional comparisons with other firms doing the same type of business. Time-series comparisons with the firm's own historical data can also provide benchmarks to aid the financial analysis.

The financial ratios covered in this chapter do not comprise an exhaustive list of ratios. Some financial analysts use the ratios cited but restate them slightly differently. Furthermore, when analyzing firms in some industries (for instance, banking) analysts employ ratios that are peculiar to a specific industry. Inflation, the differences between differing types of inventory accounting, and mergers can create headaches for financial analysts.

We will learn more about the investment characteristics of KO in the chapters that follow.

QUESTIONS

Q4-1 (Limitations of financial analysis) NewKid is a new firm in a high-tech industry, having made its debut 18 months ago. The average age of firms in the same industry is 5 years. The financial analyst for the firm has found that NewKid's total asset turnover is very low relative to the industry average. Is this necessarily a concern for NewKid's management? Explain.

Q4-2 (Coverage ratios) What is the purpose of the coverage ratios? What information are these ratios supposed to convey? Who is most interested in coverage ratios?

Q4-3 (Assessing business risk) Would you expect airline companies like Delta, American, or United to have the same business risk as a big public utility like American Telephone and Telegraph? Explain.

Q4-4 (Rate of growth) In the past decade the Coca-Cola Corporation has earned, say, a 25% rate of return on equity (ROE). Does this mean that the corporation is growing in value at 25% per year? Explain.

Q4-5 (Stock split) In 1979 the IBM Corporation declared a 4-for-1 stock split that gave every stockholder 3 new shares of common stock in addition to every share they owned before the split. Thus, there were 4 times as many shares of IBM stock outstanding after the split as there were before the split. One of the objectives of the split was to reduce the level of IBM's stock price from $300 per share to $75 per share. The price reduction was accomplished. How would this split have affected the earnings per share and cash dividends per share? How would this split have affected the aggregate values of earnings and dividends that each individual shareholder could claim? Explain.

Q4-6 (Liquidity analysis) Explain why a current ratio that is much higher than the industry average can be just as bad as a current ratio that is much lower than the industry average.

Q4-7 (Financial ratio analysis) Consider the following three categories of people who use ratios to analyze corporations' financial statements: (a) potential investors, (b) the managers who run the corporation, and (c) suppliers of raw materials who are asked to extend credit to the corporation. Do these three categories of financial analysts have different interests? If so, on which ratios might each category of analyst tend to focus?

Q4-8 (Cash flow statement) Classify each of the following as a cash flow from operations, a cash flow from investing activities, or a cash flow from financing activities: (a) the firm buys a new piece of equipment; (b) the firm pays cash for additional inventory; (c) the firm buys back shares of its common stock; (d) the firm sells inventory at a loss; (e) the firm pays dividends on its common stock; (f) the firm pays off its accounts payable; (g) the firm sells some equipment it no longer needs.

Q4-9 (Cross-sectional standard of comparison) The values of the various financial ratios tend to vary from firm to firm. Nevertheless, the competing firms within each industry seem to have values for their financial ratios that tend to cluster around unique industry average values. What accounts for the differences in these industry average values? Give a specific example to illustrate your answer.

Q4-10 (DuPont analysis) Firm A and Firm B both have a return on assets of 12%; however, Firm A's return on equity is only 15% while Firm B's return on equity is 18%. What factor explains this difference?

PROBLEMS

P4-1 (Current account ratios) The current assets and liabilities of the Ultima Beauty Shop Supply Corporation are listed below along with some operational information regarding the firm.

Current assets		Current liabilities	
Cash	$ 10,000	Accounts payable	$40,000
Accounts receivable	72,000	Accrued expenses	30,000
Inventories	80,000		
Total	$162,000	Total	$70,000

Ultima's inventory of beauty-aid supplies are used to fill telephone orders received by their beauty salons. The orders are delivered within one working day of the receipt of the phone order. Ultima has annual sales of $600,000, and its cost of the goods sold is $320,000. It is the custom in the beauty salon products industry for the salons to pay cash on delivery (COD) for the goods. Ultima's chief executive officer and primary stockholder pays all of his bills in a timely fashion so that he is able to take advantage of any cash discounts that are available. Ultima's accounts payable and accrued expenses include rent, employees' wages, utility bills, and taxes that are currently due.

a. Calculate Ultima's (i) current ratio, (ii) quick ratio, and (iii) inventory turnover ratio.

b. Assume that 10% of Ultima's sales are made on credit and calculate its accounts receivable turnover and average collection period.

c. Do you think Ultima's current assets and liabilities are well managed? Explain.

Use the following income statement and balance sheet information for the Mohawk Manufacturing Corporation to answer Problems 4-2 and 4-3:

Mohawk Manufacturing Corporation, Income Statement for the Years Ending December 31, 2000 and December 31, 1999

	2000	1999
Sales	$960,000	$870,000
less: Cost of goods sold	600,000	500,000
equals: Gross profit	$360,000	$370,000
less: Operating expenses	320,000	300,000
equals: Earnings before interest and taxes	$ 40,000	$ 70,000

Mohawk Manufacturing Corporation, Balance Sheet as of December 31, 2000

Current assets	$200,000
Fixed assets	500,000
Total assets	700,000
Current liabilities	$100,000
Long-term liabilities (at 9% interest)	300,000
Net worth	$300,000
Total liabilities and net worth	$700,000

P4-2 (Income statement analysis) (a) Construct a common-size income statement for Mohawk Manufacturing. (b) Calculate the annual percentage change for each item on Mohawk's income statement. (c) Why do you think Mohawk's 2000 earnings before interest and taxes (EBIT) decreased from the 1999 level?

P4-3 (Balance sheet analysis) Assume that Mohawk pays $27,000 per year in interest expense, is in the 30% income tax bracket, and pays out 40% of its after-tax earnings as cash dividends. (a) Construct a common-size balance sheet for Mohawk. (b) Calculate Mohawk's total asset turnover, net profit margin, financial leverage ratio, and return on equity. (c) After considering all the information, what do you expect Mohawk's growth rate in earnings will be in 2001, assuming the firm does not raise any more capital externally?

P4-4 (Common stock share data ratios) The Dopler Company had $2.40 in earnings per share and paid $0.30 in dividends per share during 2000. Dopler was selling for $24.00 a share at the end of 2000. (a) What was Dopler's dividend payout ratio for 2000? (b) What was Dopler's P/E ratio at the end of 2000? (c) Explain in words what the P/E ratio means to Dopler's shareholders.

P4-5 (Financial ratio interrelationships) In 2000, the International Telecommunications Corporation had a total debt-to-asset ratio of 45%, a total asset turnover ratio of 0.29, and a net profit margin of 17%. At the end of 2000, total assets were $7,130,000. (a) What were International Telecommunication's sales in 2000? (b) What was International Telecommunication's return on assets in 2000? (c) What was the return on equity for International Telecommunications in 2000?

P4-6 (DuPont Analysis) The Seenew Company is evaluating its performance over the past 3 years. The following information is available:

	1 year ago	2 years ago	3 years ago
Net profit	$ 15,000	$ 13,000	$ 12,000
Sales	$1,000,000	$900,000	$800,000
Total assets	$ 500,000	$300,000	$200,000
Total equity	$ 250,000	$200,000	$175,000

a. What has been the trend in the return on equity for Seenew over the past 3 years?

b. To what do you attribute the trend in the return on equity over the past 3 years? (*Hint*: Use the DuPont Analysis.)

P4-7 (Financial ratios) The Mystery Corporation had an inventory turnover of 5 times, a gross profit margin of 40%, and its cost of goods sold was $3,650. Determine Mystery's sales and its ending inventory balance.

P4-8 (Industry comparisons) The balance sheet and income statement for Telform Corporation are below.

Balance Sheet as of December 31, 2000

Assets		Liabilities and Equity	
Cash and marketable securities	$ 100,000	Accounts payable	$ 500,000
Accounts receivable	700,000	Other current liabilities	185,000
Inventory	950,000	Total current liabilities	$ 685,000
Total current assets	$1,750,000		
Plant, property, and equipment	$2,500,000	Long-term debt	1,300,000
Total assets	$4,250,000	Total liabilities	$1,985,000
		Common stock	$ 800,000
		Additional paid-in capital	950,000
		Retained earnings	515,000
		Total liabilities and equity	$4,250,000

Income Statement for the Year Ending December 31, 2000

Sales	$6,500,000
Cost of goods sold	3,800,000
Gross profit	$2,700,000
General selling and administrative expenses	1,200,000
Operating profit	$1,500,000
Interest expense	800,000
Earnings before tax	$ 700,000
Taxes	280,000
Earnings after tax	$ 420,000

The financial analyst for Telform has identified the following industry averages:

Current ratio	2.35
Quick ratio	1.40
Inventory turnover	5.50
Accounts receivable turnover	9.0 times
Average collection period	40 days
Fixed-asset turnover	2.55
Total-asset turnover	1.60
Total debt-to-assets	0.38
Times-interest-earned	2.10
Net profit margin	7.2%
Return on assets	11.5%
Return on equity	18.3%

a. Calculate the ratios necessary to evaluate Telform's liquidity and discuss how Telform is doing relative to the industry.

b. Calculate the ratios necessary to evaluate Telform's asset management and discuss how the firm is doing relative to the industry.

c. Calculate the ratios necessary to evaluate Telform's debt management and discuss how the firm is doing relative to the industry.

d. Calculate the ratios necessary to evaluate Telform's profitability and discuss how the firm is doing relative to the industry.

P4-9 (Sustainable growth rates) The following data was collected for two firms operating in the same industry:

	Firm A	Firm B
Sales	$500,000,000	$510,000,000
Total assets	$200,000,000	$250,000,000
Total debt	$ 75,000,000	$ 60,000,000
Net income	$ 20,000,000	$ 26,250,000
Dividend payout ratio	30%	31%

Assume neither firm will use additional external financing and use the DuPont system to determine which one can be expected to experience greater growth. What factors contribute to this?

P4-10 (Risk analysis) Consider the following data for two firms operating in the same industry:

	BigCorp	SmallComp
Sales (10-year average)	$ 950,000,000	$36,360,000
Standard deviation of sales	$ 150,000,000	$ 8,000,000
Operating income (10-year average)	$ 500,000,000	$20,000,000
Standard deviation of operating income	$ 60,000,000	$ 5,000,000
Current year data		
Sales	$1,000,000,000	$40,000,000
Operating income	$ 600,000,000	$22,000,000
Interest expense	$ 140,000,000	$ 6,000,000
Total debt	$ 250,000,000	$ 6,000,000
Long-term debt	$ 175,000,000	$ 2,000,000
Preferred stock	$ 10,000,000	0
Common equity	$ 625,000,000	$35,000,000

Calculate the following ratios for each firm: (a) total debt-to-assets, (b) total debt-to-equity, (c) long-term debt-to-equity, (d) long-term debt-to-capitalization, and (e) times-interest-earned. Based on these calculations, discuss the relative levels of financial risk for the two firms. (Hint: Look up "Coefficient of Variation" in a statistics book.)

CFA EXAM QUESTIONS

The following three questions are adopted from the 1999 CFA Sample Exam, Level I:

1. A company's current ratio is 2.0. If the company uses cash to retire notes payable due within one year, would this transaction increase or decrease the current ratio and asset turnover ratio?

Current Ratio	Asset Turnover Ratio
A. Increase	Increase
B. Increase	Decrease
C. Decrease	Increase
D. Decrease	Decrease

2. Other things being equal, two companies have substantially different dividend payout ratios. After several years, the company with the lower dividend payout ratio is *most likely* to have:
   A. lower inventory turnover.
   B. higher inventory turnover.
   C. less rapid growth of earnings per share.
   D. more rapid growth of earnings per share.

3. An analyst applies the DuPont system of financial analysis to the following data for a company:

Equity turnover	4.2
Total asset turnover	2.0
Net profit margin	5.5%
Dividend payout ratio	31.8%

The company's return on equity is *closest* to:
  A. 1.3%.
  B. 11.0%.
  C. 23.1%.
  D. 63.6%.

4. (1994 CFA Exam, Level II)

Introduction

Aspen Pharmaceuticals (Aspen) is a major worldwide producer of prescription drugs with an outstanding record of sales and earnings growth. During the past 18 months, however, the company's profit growth has slowed and its stock price has underperformed market averages. Two factors have been advanced to explain these developments: increasing price discounts to large managed-care buyers and concern about possible "reforms" that the U.S. Congress may mandate later this year.

Aspen has just announced its plan to acquire 100% of the common stock of Pharmacy Services, Inc. (PSI). PSI is much smaller than Aspen but is a leading factor in mail-order delivery of pharmaceuticals and also provides related cost-containment services. Aspen's stock is currently selling at $30 per share and PSI at $25 per share. Both companies are United States–based and their shares are traded on the New York Stock Exchange.

Table 1 Aspen Pharmaceuticals Balance Sheet as of December 31, 1993 ($ millions)

Assets	
Current assets	$4,500
Property, plant, and equipment	5,000
Total Assets	$9,500
Liabilities and Stockholders' Equity	
Current liabilities	$3,500
Long-term debt	1,000
Deferred taxes	1,000
Shareholders' equity[a]	4,000
Total Liabilities and Equity	$9,500

[a]1 billion shares outstanding

Income Statement for Year Ended December 31 ($ millions except per share data)

	1993 Actual	1994 Estimated
Sales	$10,000	$10,500
Cost of goods sold	(2,000)	(2,500)
Marketing and administration	(2,700)	(2,700)
Depreciation	(200)	(200)
Interest	(100)	(100)
Research	(1,000)	(1,000)
Pretax income	$ 4,000	$ 4,000
Income tax expense	(1,200)	(1,200)
Net income	$ 2,800	$ 2,800
Earnings per share[a]	$2.80	$2.80
Dividends per share	$1.10	$1.14

[a]1 billion shares outstanding

Table 2 Pharmacy Services, Inc. Balance Sheet, December 31, 1993 ($ millions)

Assets	
Current assets	$1,000
Property, plant, and equipment	200
Total Assets	$1,200
Liabilities and Stockholders' Equity	
Current liabilities	$ 300
Long-term debt	300
Stockholders' equity[a]	600
Total Liabilities and Equity	$1,200

[a]100 million shares outstanding

Income Statement for Years Ended December 31 ($ millions except per share data)

	1993 Actual	1994 Estimated
Sales	$ 2,500	$ 3,360
Cost of goods sold	(2,130)	(2,880)
Marketing and administration	(80)	(110)
Depreciation	(20)	(20)
Interest	(20)	(20)
Pretax income	$ 250	$ 330
Income tax expense	(100)	(130)
Net income	$ 150	$ 200
Earnings per share[a]	$ 1.50	$ 2.00
Dividends per share	None	None

[a]100 million shares outstanding

  A. Calculate the internal (also called implied, sustainable, or normalized) growth rate of *both* Aspen and PSI.
  B. Briefly discuss *two* limitations of the internal growth rate as a predictor of long-term growth.

DO YOUR RESEARCH

(Industry comparisons) Select a firm you wish to analyze and go to the following Web site address: www.quote.yahoo.com. Enter the ticker symbol for your firm to get the most recent quotes. Click on "profile" to get further information on the company, including a business summary. Within "profile," click on "ratio comparisons" to obtain ratios for your company, the industry, the sector, and the S&P500. Which of the latter three comparison figures do you think is most valid for you to use to evaluate your firm's performance? Why? How has your firm performed based on this comparison?

FURTHER REFERENCES

Bernstein, Leopold A. and John J. Wild. *Financial Statement Analysis: Theory, Application, and Interpretation*, 6th ed. Burr Ridge, IL: Irwin, 1998.

An easy-to-read accounting-oriented book that discusses traditional financial statement analysis in detail.

Cottle, Sidney, Roger F. Murray, and Frank E. Block. *Security Analysis*, 5th ed. New York: McGraw-Hill, 1988.

This is a classic book about fundamental security analysis.

Foster, George. *Financial Statement Analysis*, 2nd ed. Englewood Cliffs, NJ: Prentice-Hall, 1986.

A statistical analysis–oriented book that presents new approaches to financial statement analysis which, in some cases, are grounded in economic theory.

Fraser, Lyn M. *Understanding Financial Statements*, 4th ed. Upper Saddle River, NJ: Prentice Hall, 1994.

This little book provides an easy-to-read, well-organized explanation of financial statement analysis that is supplemented with helpful examples.

Higgins, Robert C. *Analysis for Financial Management*, 5th ed. Burr Ridge, IL: Irwin, 1998.

This is an excellent nonmathematical finance-oriented book. It has outstanding chapters on analyzing growth (Chapter 4) and analyzing risk (Chapter 8).

Klein, Peter J. *Security Analysis*. New York: Wiley, 1998.

This seven-chapter security analysis book is easy-to-read and fundamentally comprehensive. Mr. Klein was Professor Francis's MBA student; he is now a First Vice President at PaineWebber in New York City.

Revsine, Lawrence, Daniel W. Collins, and W. Bruce Johnson. *Financial Reporting and Analysis*. Upper Saddle River, NJ: Prentice Hall, 1999.

This comprehensive volume provides nonmathematical discussions. The coauthors are all accountants and this common viewpoint is reflected in the book.

Walton, Peter, Ed. *European Financial Reporting*. San Diego, CA: Academic Press, 1995.

This collection of articles by experts from around the world traces the evolution of accounting and financial reporting in the major industrialized countries of the world.

ENDNOTES

[1] For additional information about cash flow and security analysis, see Kenneth S. Hackel and Joshua Livant, *Cash Flow and Security Analysis*, 2nd ed. (Burr Ridge, IL: Irwin, 1995).

[2] For details about comprehensive income reporting, see "FASB Rule Will Offer Walk on Wild Side," *Wall Street Journal*, 30 September 1997, C1.

[3] For additional discussion of the factors that contribute to the sustainability of a firm's growth, see Robert C. Higgins, *Analysis for Financial Management*, 5th ed. (Burr Ridge, IL: Irwin, 1998), Chapter 4.

[4] George Foster, *Financial Statement Analysis*, 2nd ed. (Englewood Cliffs, NJ: Prentice-Hall, 1986). Chapter 3 discusses cross-sectional analysis of financial statements in more detail.

[5] For more details about Coca-Cola's consolidated balance sheet, see Paul R. Brown, "Financial Reporting and Disclosure for Equity Analysis," *Practical Issues in Equity Analysis* (Charlottesville, VA: Association for Investment Management and Research, 2000), 23–24, especially Table 3.

PRIMARY SECURITIES AND THEIR ISSUERS

Stocks, bonds, and money market securities are issued by businesses and governments to raise funds. These securities provide opportunities for savers and investors to channel billions of dollars into investments every year. Knowing the identity of a security's issuer provides a clue about the use of the proceeds from the issue: Businesses usually issue stocks and bonds to raise funds to finance their expansion, and governments usually issue debt securities to raise funds to pay for deficit spending.

Law, economics, and finance books explore the securities discussed in this chapter. Some highly paid professionals spend their lives analyzing and trading each type of security. Clearly, it is not possible to squeeze everything known about each security into one chapter. This chapter lays a foundation for later chapters.

Money market securities are examined first. Then a variety of bonds are reviewed. Common and preferred stocks are the focus of the last sections of this chapter. The chapter concludes by contrasting the primary securities.

MONEY MARKET SECURITIES AND THEIR MARKETS

Money market securities are debts that mature in less than 1 year from the date they originated. Both companies and governments issue money market securities to raise cash. Only issuers that are assigned high-quality credit ratings by Standard & Poor's, Moody's, Fitch Investment Service, Duff and Phelps, and the other credit rating services are able to get investors to buy these short-term IOUs. Because of the short lengths of time until maturity and their high-quality credit ratings, money market securities involve only moderate default risk. These securities are actively traded at or near their face value and consequently they are sometimes called *cash equivalents*.

Businesses and governments that borrow less than several million dollars every year and/or originate new borrowings less than once a year do not generate enough sales revenue from subscribers to make it profitable for credit rating agencies like Standard & Poor's or

Moody's to continually reevaluate these issuers and publish up-to-date ratings. Nonrated issuers cannot borrow by issuing money market securities. Consequently, small businesses and small governments that are not rated borrow from banks, life insurance companies, and other financial intermediaries.

The **money market** is an informal telephone network where professional traders from large corporations quickly execute multimillion-dollar transactions every minute of every trading day. It is a fast-moving market used by large organizations that have excellent reputations. Small firms, medium-sized firms, and local firms are not able to sell money market securities, because investors do not want to buy securities from an issuer that does not have a well-known international reputation for fair dealing. Table 5-1 lists money market securities.

U.S. Treasury Bills

The U.S. Treasury has issued more debt than any other organization in the world. Most of the U.S. government's federal debt is financed by short-term bonds called **Treasury bills,** also known as T-bills.

The Treasury offers new T-bills at public auctions, selling them on a **book entry basis:** The transaction is recorded in a computer and the investor receives a receipt instead of a security. Treasury bills are offered by the U.S. Treasury Department in denominations of $1,000, $10,000, $15,000, $50,000, $100,000, $500,000, and $1 million.

T-Bill Pricing Conventions. T-bills with initial maturities of 91 days (13 weeks) and 182 days (26 weeks) are auctioned weekly. Auctions for T-bills with 364 days (52 weeks) until maturity are held monthly. Competitive bids at the weekly T-bill auctions are submitted in the form of percentage **price discounts** from the T-bill's maturity value.

Suppose the U.S. Treasury offers a 6-month (26 weeks) T-bill with a $10,000 maturity value for sale at an 8% price discount. The 8% price discount is sometimes called the *bank discount*, referring to the commercial banks and investment banks that normally trade money market securities. An 8% discount means the Treasury is offering the T-bills for sale at a price of $9,595.56—not $9,200 as you might think. The $9,595.56 price is less than 8% below the $10,000 face value because, although there are 365 days in the calendar year, it is the convention to assume there are 360 days in one year for money market calculations.

T-Bill Price Quotations. Figure 5-1 shows T-bills' price quotations from a newspaper. The maturity date of each issue of T-bills is in the first column. Each number of days until maturity

TABLE 5-1 Components of the U.S. Money Market

Component	Outstanding, in $ billions
Commercial paper	$715.0
Banker's acceptances	$ 14.0
Short-term Treasury securities	$371.2
Term Eurodollars	$149.4
Repurchase agreements	$272.1
Large certificates of deposits (CDs)[a]	$616.1
Small certificates of deposits (CDs)[b]	$958.3

[a]Large-denomination CD means a bank time deposit greater than $100,000.
[b]Small-denomination CD means a bank time deposit less than $100,000.
SOURCE: *Economic Report of the President,* U.S. Government Printing Office, February 1999, pp. 408–409, data for September 1998.

FIGURE 5-1 Newspaper Excerpt Showing Treasury Bill Price Quotations

TREASURY BILLS

Maturity	Days to Mat.	Bid	Asked	Chg.	Ask Yld.	Maturity	Days to Mat.	Bid	Asked	Chg.	Ask Yld.
Feb 17 '00	1	5.20	5.12	+0.15	5.19	Jun 01 '00	106	5.60	5.58	+0.07	5.75
Feb 24 '00	8	5.24	5.16	+0.46	5.24	Jun 08 '00	113	5.60	5.58	+0.05	5.76
Mar 02 '00	15	5.22	5.14	+0.09	5.22	Jun 15 '00	120	5.58	5.56	+0.04	5.74
Mar 09 '00	22	5.27	5.19	+0.16	5.28	Jun 22 '00	127	5.61	5.59	+0.03	5.78
Mar 16 '00	29	5.21	5.13	+0.17	5.22	Jun 29 '00	134	5.60	5.58	+0.03	5.78
Mar 23 '00	36	5.28	5.24	+0.16	5.34	Jul 06 '00	141	5.60	5.58	+0.03	5.78
Mar 30 '00	43	5.32	5.28	+0.12	5.39	Jul 13 '00	148	5.57	5.55	+0.05	5.76
Apr 06 '00	50	5.35	5.31	+0.15	5.42	Jul 20 '00	155	5.63	5.61	−0.01	5.83
Apr 13 '00	57	5.34	5.30	+0.18	5.42	Jul 27 '00	162	5.61	5.59	−0.01	5.81
Apr 20 '00	64	5.52	5.50	+0.11	5.63	Aug 03 '00	169	5.66	5.64	+0.01	5.87
Apr 27 '00	71	5.53	5.51	+0.10	5.65	Aug 10 '00	176	5.69	5.67	−0.03	5.91
May 04 '00	78	5.50	5.48	+0.12	5.62	**Aug 17 '00**	**183**	**5.73**	**5.72**	**−0.03**	**5.97**
May 11 '00	85	5.54	5.52	+0.07	5.67	Sep 14 '00	211	5.77	5.75	−0.02	6.01
May 18 '00	**92**	**5.57**	**5.56**	**+0.07**	**5.72**	Oct 12 '00	239	5.83	5.81	−0.02	6.08
May 25 '00	99	5.60	5.58	+0.06	5.75	Nov 09 '00	267	5.87	5.85	+0.01	6.14
						Dec 07 '00	295	5.88	5.86	+0.01	6.17
						Jan 04 '01	323	5.85	5.83	+0.03	6.15
						Feb 01 '01	351	5.82	5.81	+0.03	6.15

SOURCE: *Wall Street Journal*, 16 February 2000, C15.

published in the second column is 2 days less than the time between the date of the newspaper quotation and the T-bill's expiration date. This discrepancy results from the so-called **skip-day convention.**

Column 3 of Figure 5-1 contains the T-bills' *bid yield*, the highest rate of interest that potential buyers offered to pay for the security that day. The *asked yield* in column 4 is the lowest interest rate that potential sellers offered to accept for their T-bills on that trading day.* The fifth column contains the T-bills' percentage change in price from the previous trading day. The last column in Figure 5-1 gives the asked yield, the annualized bond-equivalent-yield if the T-bill is purchased at its asked price and held until it matures, at the *end* of the trading day.

Certificates of Deposit (CDs)

A certificate of deposit, or **CD,** with denominations as small as $50 is sold by many banks to retail clients to obtain their personal savings. These small CDs are **non-negotiable** because they cannot be bought and sold in any secondary market. A **secondary market** is a market where investors trade existing securities.

Negotiable certificates of deposit, or **negotiable CDs,** are a receipt from a commercial bank for a deposit of $100,000 or more, with provisions attached. One provision is that the deposit will not be withdrawn from the bank before its maturity date. This time restriction could severely limit the usefulness of CDs if a money market dealer does not agree to make an active secondary market in negotiable CDs. The liquidity provided by this secondary market overcomes depositors' objections to the penalty for early redemption. If the bank's deposits are insured by a governmental agency such as the Federal Deposit Insurance Corporation (FDIC), and the CD's denomination does not exceed the limit of the FDIC's insurance, the CD is an extremely safe investment.

As the name suggests, the buyers of large-denomination negotiable CDs can negotiate their interest rate and their maturity date with the bank accepting the deposit (selling the CD). Large depositors can obtain either fixed or **floating rate CDs.** Floating rate CDs

---

* Since bond prices and interest rates move inversely, the highest bid yield is derived from the lowest price that potential buyers bid for the T-bill. Likewise, the lowest asked yield corresponds to the highest asked price at which potential sellers offered to sell.

promise to pay some negotiable amount—for instance, 100 basis points (BPs) over the London interbank offer rate (LIBOR). *Euro CDs* are denominated in foreign currencies and are actively traded in London. *Term CDs* have maturities from 2 to 5 years. **Yankee CDs** are negotiable CDs issued by non-U.S. banks operating in the United States that enable them to pull in U.S. dollar deposits.

Banker's Acceptances

Banker's acceptances (BAs) are primarily used to expedite foreign trade between importers and exporters that do not know each other. The bank of the exporter guarantees that acceptable goods will be shipped on time. The importer's bank guarantees that full payment will be made when the buyer receives the goods. The importer's bank that signs (accepts) a banker's acceptance assumes legal responsibility for payment in full on the date stipulated on the banker's acceptance. This payment guarantee from a large international bank makes the banker's acceptance a *liquid money market security*. Banker's acceptances are liquid because, if the buyer or seller defaults, whoever owns a banker's acceptance on the date it matures can collect from the bank that accepted (guaranteed) it.[1]

To summarize: A banker's acceptance is a loan, a bank order promising to pay a specified amount of money to another bank on a maturity date that occurs within 1 year. In return for fees plus the interest on the loan, one bank signs, and thereby *accepts*, the banker's acceptance from another bank. Foreign trade departments of large international banks deal in each other's banker's acceptances daily.

Federal Funds

Overnight loans between commercial banks are called **federal funds loans,** or **fed funds.** The fed funds market is an informal, interbank network in which bankers call each other on the phone to borrow or lend funds. In the United States thousands of transfers of banks' funds are handled every business day over a wire transfer system called the **Fed wire.** The Fed wire is run by the U.S. government's Federal Reserve System, called **the Fed.** Fed funds arise when a commercial bank (or other financial intermediary) holds required reserves in excess of the Federal Reserve's minimum legal reserve requirement. Fed funds are simply bank reserves that are loaned for 1 day at a time by banks with excess reserves to banks without sufficient reserves to meet their legal minimum reserve requirement. Typically, large city banks are borrowers of fed funds and small country banks are the lenders.

The interest rate on the 1-day fed funds interbank loans is called the *fed funds rate. Term fed funds* are fed funds loans that last for more than 1 day.

The LIBOR Market

As in the United States, English law requires banks to maintain minimum required reserves. Also, like the American banks, English banks borrow and lend bank reserves to and from each other to meet their government's minimum reserve requirements. The market for bank reserves in Britain is an informal, interbank network in which bankers simply call each other up to borrow or lend funds—again, like the United States. Even the overnight interest rates are similar. British banks pay the **London Interbank Offer Rate,** called LIBOR, which is similiar to the Fed Funds rate in the United States.

In addition to the market for overnight bank reserves, active markets in 3-month, 6-month, and 9-month LIBOR funds are operated by the large London banks. Since the large English banks (such as HSBC, Barclays Bank, and National Westminster Bank) have offices around the world, LIBOR has become the **reference rate** on which a wide range of multinational loan transactions are based.

Eurodollars

Eurodollars are U.S.–dollar denominated bank deposits that are deposited outside the United States. These deposits can be made in a non-U.S. bank or in a foreign branch of a U.S. bank. Eurodollar deposits are typically large denomination time deposits of less than 1 year duration; they are sometimes used to escape regulation by the U.S. Federal Reserve Board, the Internal Revenue Service, or other regulatory agencies. U.S. dollar–denominated bank deposits are accepted at banks around the world.

European certificates of deposit (CDs), or *Eurodollar CDs*, developed as a substitute for Eurodollar deposits; they are like ordinary CDs except that the deposit of U.S. dollars goes into a non-U.S. bank. Eurodollar CDs have an advantage over Eurodollar time deposits because they can be turned into cash in an active secondary market before they mature without incurring a penalty for early redemption.

Repurchase Agreements (Repos)

Repurchase agreements, nicknamed *repos,* are instruments used by large securities dealers to help finance part of their multimillion-dollar inventories of marketable securities for a few days. For example, suppose Merrill Lynch ends a day of trading with an unexpected increase of $10 million in its inventory of marketable securities. Merrill needs to finance this additional $10 million inventory overnight. The securities dealer pays a finder's fee to a *repo broker* to induce that broker to find an investor with $10 million cash to invest overnight. The securities dealer borrowing $10 million overnight sells securities to that investor and simultaneously agrees to repurchase the same securities the next day at a slightly higher price. This slightly higher price represents the interest income for the overnight investor who invested in the repo. The investor buying the repo is essentially making a short-term loan to the repo seller (the securities dealer); the securities dealer's inventory is the loan's collateral.

Repos that last longer than overnight are called *term repos*; they can span 30 days or even longer. The money market trading desks of many large banks arrange repos and earn fee income from such repo brokering.

A *reverse repo*, called simply a *reverse*, provides a way for someone to borrow securities (instead of money) for a day or two. A reverse requires the securities borrower to find a securities lender. The borrower buys the desired securities from the lender and promises to sell them back the next day. If the securities lender happens to need an overnight loan, that makes it easy to execute a reverse repo.

The market interest rates on a repo is called the *repo rate*. Figure 5-2 is a newspaper excerpt displaying the money market interest rates that existed one day.

Commercial Paper

Commercial paper refers to short-term, unsecured promissory notes with maturities from 5 to 270 days. This paper is backed only by the issuer's credit rating; no collateral is provided. Commercial paper is only issued by large international companies, international banks, large finance companies, and some large municipalities. The denominations start at $100,000.

In the United States consumer credit corporations like General Electric Credit Corporation (GECC), General Motors Acceptance Corporation (GMAC), Ford Motor Credit Corporation, and Chrysler Credit Corporation are large borrowers in the commercial paper market.

FIGURE 5-2 Newspaper Excerpt Showing Money Market Rates at the Close of One Trading Day

MONEY RATES

Tuesday, February 15, 2000

The key U. S. and foreign annual interest rates below are a guide to general levels but don't always represent actual transactions.

PRIME RATE: 8.75% (effective 02/03/00). The base rate on corporate loans posted by at least 75% of the nation's 30 largest banks.

DISCOUNT RATE: 5.25% (effective 02/02/00). The charge on loans to depository institutions by the Federal Reserve Banks.

FEDERAL FUNDS: 6 % high, 5 1/4 % low, 5 1/4 % near closing bid, 5 1/2 % offered. Reserves traded among commercial banks for overnight use in amounts of $1 million or more. Source: Prebon Yamane (U.S.A) Inc. FOMC fed funds target rate 5.75% effective 2/2/00.

CALL MONEY: 7.50% (effective 02/03/00). The charge on loans to brokers on stock exchange collateral. Source: Reuters.

COMMERCIAL PAPER: placed directly by General Electric Capital Corp.: 5.75% 30 to 48 days; 5.82% 49 to 83 days; 5.87% 84 to 106 days; 5.90% 107 to 144 days; 5.98% 145 to 210 days; 6.04% 211 to 270 days.

EURO COMMERCIAL PAPER: placed directly by General Electric Capital Corp.: 3.27% 30 days; 3.35% two months; 3.44% three months; 3.50% four months; 3.57% five months; 3.64% six months.

DEALER COMMERCIAL PAPER: High-grade unsecured notes sold through dealers by major corporations: 5.77% 30 days; 5.85% 60 days; 5.90% 90 days.

CERTIFICATES OF DEPOSIT: 5.34% one month; 5.43% two months; 5.51% three months; 5.79% six months; 6.18% one year. Average of top rates paid by major New York banks on primary new issues of negotiable C.D.s, usually on amounts of $1 million and more. The minimum unit is $100,000. Typical rates in the secondary market: 5.82% one month; 6.00% three months; 6.25% six months.

BANKERS ACCEPTANCES: 5.75% 30 days; 5.81% 60 days; 5.87% 90 days; 5.92% 120 days; 5.97% 150 days; 6.00% 180 days. Offered rates of negotiable, bank-backed business credit instruments typically financing an import order.

LONDON LATE EURODOLLARS: 5.88% - 5.75% one month; 6.00% - 5.88% two months; 6.13% - 6.00% three months; 6.19% - 6.06% four months; 6.25% - 6.13% five months; 6.31% -

6.19% six months.

LONDON INTERBANK OFFERED RATES (LIBOR): 5.8800% one month; 6.0900% three months; 6.3200% six months; 6.78125% one year. British Banker's Association average of interbank offered rates for dollar deposits in the London market based on quotations at 16 major banks. Effective rate for contracts entered into two days from date appearing at top of this column.

EURO LIBOR: 3.32000% one month; 3.48938% three months; 3.69000% six months; 4.08000% one year. British Banker's Association average of interbank offered rates for euro deposits in the London market based on quotations at 16 major banks. Effective rate for contracts entered into two days from date appearing at top of this column.

EURO INTERBANK OFFERED RATES (EURIBOR): 3.319% one month; 3.487% three months; 3.692% six months; 4.081% one year. European Banking Federation-sponsored rate among 57 Euro zone banks.

FOREIGN PRIME RATES: Canada 6.75%; Germany 3.25%; Japan 1.375%; Switzerland 4.125%; Britain 6.00%. These rate indications aren't directly comparable; lending practices vary widely by location.

TREASURY BILLS: Results of the Monday, February 14, 2000, auction of short-term U.S. government bills, sold at a discount from face value in units of $1,000 to $1 million: 5.510% 13 weeks; 5.760% 26 weeks.

OVERNIGHT REPURCHASE RATE: 5.87%. Dealer financing rate for overnight sale and repurchase of Treasury securities. Source: Reuters.

FREDDIE MAC: Posted yields on 30-year mortgage commitments. Delivery within 30 days 8.37%, 60 days 8.42%, standard conventional fixed-rate mortgages: 6.875%, 2% rate capped one-year adjustable rate mortgages. Source: Reuters.

FANNIE MAE: Posted yields on 30 year mortgage commitments (priced at par) for delivery within 30 days 8.40%, 60 days 8.48%, standard conventional fixed-rate mortgages; 7.40%, 6/2 rate capped one-year adjustable rate mortgages. Source: Reuters.

MERRILL LYNCH READY ASSETS TRUST: 5.33%. Annualized average rate of return after expenses for the past 30 days; not a forecast of future returns.

CONSUMER PRICE INDEX: December, 168.3, up 2.7% from a year ago. Bureau of Labor Statistics.

SOURCE: *Wall Street Journal*, 16 February 2000, C17.

FIXED-INCOME SECURITIES

Figure 5-3 illustrates maturity differences between the money markets and the capital markets. Money market securities mature within 1 year. Money market debt securities and money market preferred stock are actively traded. *Capital market securities* have maturities ranging from 1 year to infinity. Long-term debt securities, preferred stock, and common stock are traded in the capital markets.

Some Bonds Pay Coupons—and Some Do Not

Fixed-income securities include all debt securities issued by governments and businesses. Most fixed-income securities are marketable legal contracts that promise their investors interest payments each year plus repayment of the principal at maturity. Many different interest payment arrangements exist. **Coupon-interest** payments that are made periodically until the bond matures are most common. Some debt securities make fixed quarterly coupon payments, most make fixed semiannual coupon payments, some make fixed annual coupon payments, some pay periodic coupons that fluctuate in amount, and some do not ever pay any coupon interest. Bonds that never pay coupon interest payments are called **zero coupon bonds,** or **zeros.**

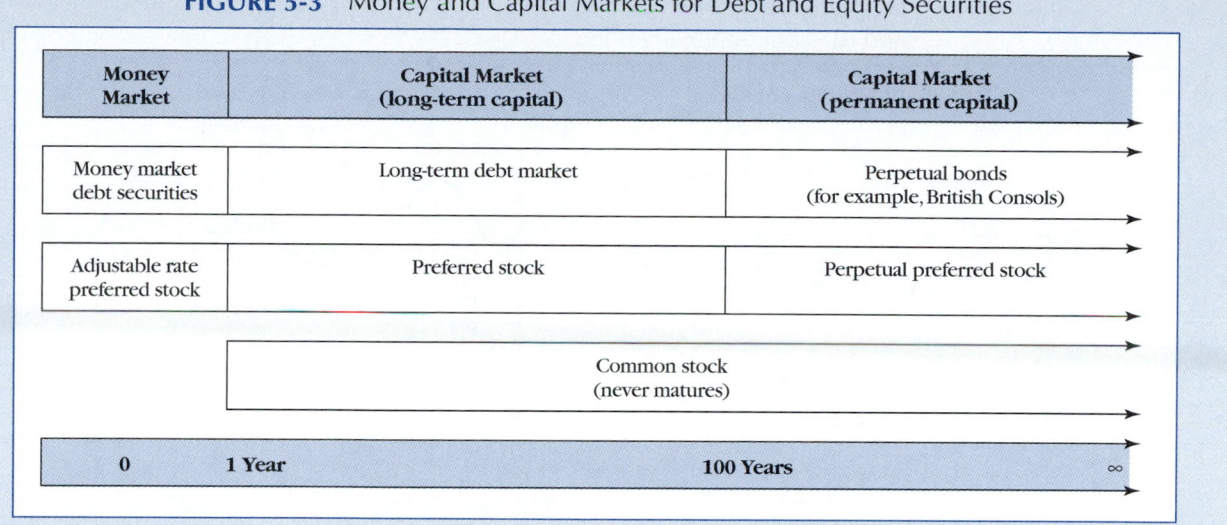

FIGURE 5-3   Money and Capital Markets for Debt and Equity Securities

Money-market securities mature within 1 year or less from their issue date. Bonds, preferred stock, and common stock with maturities ranging from 1 year to infinity are issued in the capital markets.

There are two types of debt securities: those that make *implicit* interest payments and those that make *explicit* interest payments. Figure 5-4 compares and contrasts the price behavior of debt instruments that make their interest payments implicitly—**original issue discount (OID) bonds**—with instruments that make explicit interest payments—**coupon-paying bonds**. We further define each below

Original-Issue Discount (OID) Bonds. Money market securities are examples of OID instruments that make implicit interest payments. If the issuer does not default, those who bought OID bonds enjoy price appreciation until the bonds mature and repay the principal (face value, par value), as shown in Figure 5-4A. The rise in price from the discounted purchase price up to the maturity value (face value) is an *implicit interest payment* that the issuer pays the investor.

Coupon Bonds. The second major category of fixed-income securities makes explicit cash payments periodically. Coupon-paying bonds are issued at their face values, not at a lower OID price. After they are issued their prices fluctuate. As Figure 5-4B illustrates, sometimes a bond's price rises to a **premium** and sometimes it falls to a **discount** relative to the bond's face value.

Features of Bond Issues

Federal government bonds, bonds issued by municipalities, corporate bonds, and money market securities can be described in terms of certain meaningful features.

Coupon Payments. The *coupon rate* is multiplied by the face (par, principal) value of a bond to determine its annual coupon payment. Coupons are fixed payments paid, usually semiannually, as long as the bond issuer is solvent. Money market securities, zero coupon bonds, and certain other debt instruments pay no coupons. **Floating-rate bonds** pay coupons that vary from payment to payment. Not every fixed-income security pays a fixed cash income stream; some never make any explicit interest payments. In spite of these differences, each cash payment arrangement is fixed throughout the life of a fixed-income security.

FIGURE 5-4 Different Market Price Behaviors for (A) Original-Issue Discount Bond and (B) Coupon-Paying Bond

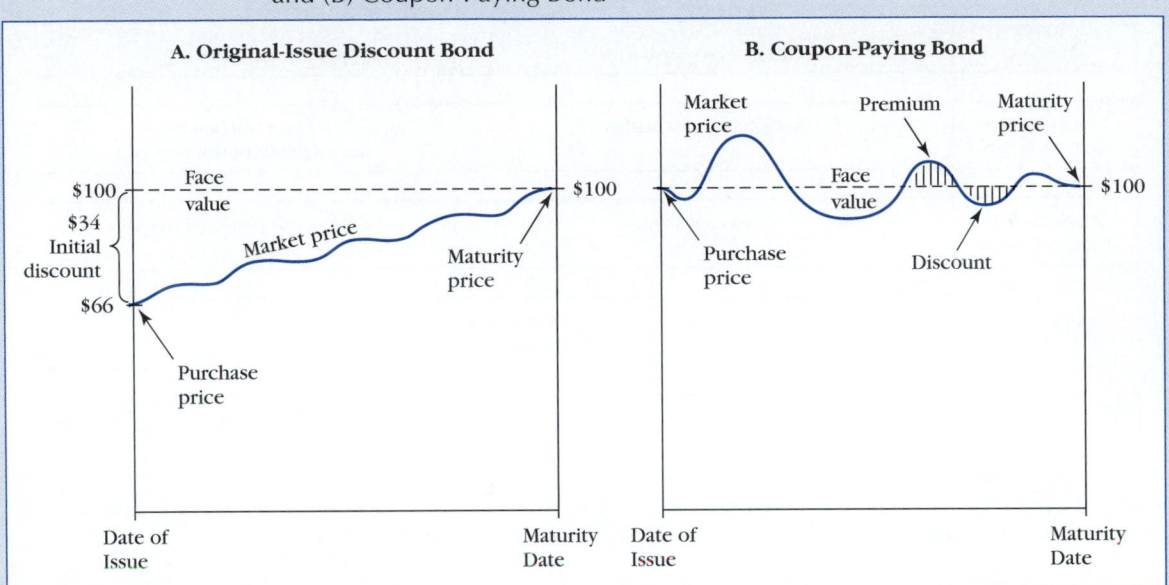

An original-issue discount (OID) bond is a zero coupon bond that is issued at a deep discount from its face (par) value, appreciates to its face value at maturity, and provides implicit interest income in the form of price appreciation. A coupon-paying bond is issued at its face value and matures at its face value. Between its issue and maturity dates the market price of a coupon-paying bond may fluctuate above and/or below its face value.

Bond Maturities. Bonds are often categorized in terms of the time that elapses until they mature. As mentioned earlier, money market securities mature in less than 1 year from their issue date. Short-term bonds mature in 1 to 5 years, medium-term bonds in 5 to 10 years, and long-term bonds have lives of 10 or more years. In 1993, Walt Disney Company pushed the record on U.S. corporate bond maturities up to 100 years, although the bond issue is callable after 30 years.

Callable and Convertible Bonds. "Call options" and "convertibility options" are referred to as **embedded options** because they cannot be separated from the bond. These embedded options affect the value of the bond to which they are attached.*

A *call provision* may or may not be attached to a bond issue. This option allows the bond issuer to call in (redeem) the bond at a specified call price before it matures. Variability of return that results from call provisions is called *contraction risk*, because calling in a bond *contracts* its life. To induce investors to expose themselves to contraction risk, bond issues with call provisions must pay interest rates that are several basis points higher than noncallable bonds that are identical in every other respect.

Convertible bonds have embedded options that permit investors who buy corporate bonds to convert the bonds into the issuer's common stock under certain conditions. Investors like conversion privileges because, if the stock's price rises substantially, bond

---

* The effect of call provisions on bond pricing are analyzed by treating the callable security as a noncallable bond with a call option attached. Likewise, conversion provisions are analyzed by treating the convertible bond as a nonconvertible bond with an equity call option attached. Embedded options are analyzed in the Appendix to Chapter 9.

investors may capture some of those gains by converting their bonds into stock. To obtain this option to convert, a bond investor must buy a bond that offers a slightly lower interest rate than a nonconvertible bond which is identical in every other respect.

Sinking Fund. To retire bonds in an orderly manner, a bond issuer may pay a certain amount each year into a **sinking fund** to be used to redeem the bonds. These payments are made to a sinking fund agent—for example, a bank—that accumulates the funds until they are needed. The sinking fund agent uses the funds to purchase the outstanding bonds when they mature, according to a previously specified schedule, when they are selling below their par (face) value, or under other conditions.

U.S. GOVERNMENT SECURITIES

Figure 1-5A in Chapter 1 and Table 19-1 in Chapter 19 show that governments are the largest borrowers in most countries. The U.S. Treasury issues marketable and nonmarketable debt.

Nonmarketable U.S. Treasury Issues

About one-third of the U.S. public debt consists of nonmarketable issues. The characteristics of these bonds are that:

> They cannot be traded in any market

> They are not transferable or negotiable

> They cannot be used as collateral for a loan

> They can be purchased and redeemed only from the U.S. government

Most of these nonmarketable securities are the Series EE U.S. **savings bonds** and Series HH U.S. savings bonds. Most banks in the United States sell Series EE bonds.

Series EE savings bonds are 30-year Treasury bonds issued with maturity values $50, $75, $100, $200, $500, $1,000, $5,000, and $10,000. Series EE bonds pay no coupons; they are sold at deep original-issue discounts (OIDs) from their face values and pay implicit interest. Series HH U.S. savings bonds are offered in denominations of $500 and larger. They cannot be purchased directly; they can only be obtained by exchanging EE bonds and/or exchanging the interest payments from other U.S. savings bonds for HH bonds. Series I U.S. savings bonds were introduced recently; they contain features to nullify the effects of inflation.

Marketable U.S. Treasury Securities

U.S. Treasury bills were discussed earlier in this chapter. This section considers other types of Treasury securities that mature in 1 year or longer and are traded actively in capital markets. These longer-term bonds are not OID bonds like T-bills. The characteristics of the bonds considered in the following discussions are:

> They are issued and redeemed at their par (face, principal) value

> They make periodic coupon interest payments throughout their lives

> Their market prices fluctuate up to a premium and drop down to a discount relative to their face values (as illustrated in Figure 5-4B)

Bid and asked prices of marketable Treasuries are published daily in newspapers around the world. T-bond prices are quoted in thirty-seconds of 1% of the bond's par (face, maturity) value; these fractional price quotations are written with colons. For instance, 70:16 stands for

TABLE 5-2	Characteristics of Marketable U.S. Treasury Securities			
Features	T-Bill	T-Note	T-Bond	Savings Bond
Original maturities	0–1 year	1–10 years	10–30 years	0–30 years
Money market	Yes	No	No	No
Original-issue discount	Always	Never	Never	Series EE, not HH
Coupon payments	Never	Always	Always	Series HH, not EE
Actively traded	Always	Always	Always	Never
Callable	Never	Never	Some issues	Never
Price quotations	Figure 5-1	Figure 5-6	Figure 5-6	Sales brochures

$70\frac{16}{32}$, which represents 70.5% of par (not 70.16%). Treasury bond dealers could transact in decimal prices. But they prefer "lumpy" prices, quoted in thirty-seconds of 1%, that facilitate extracting slightly larger bid-asked spreads (trading fees) from each transaction.

Treasury Notes and Bonds **Treasury notes** make fixed coupon payments semiannually. For example, a $10,000 T-note with a coupon rate of 7% pays coupons of $350 every 6 months. T-notes mature between 1 and 10 years from their initial issue date. The U.S. Treasury issues T-notes periodically.

   Treasury bonds have the longest maturities of all Treasury securities, from 10 to 30 years. Table 5-2 contrasts characteristics of marketable Treasury securities.

   Some issues of T-bonds are **callable:** The Treasury can call them in before maturity. For example, the T-bonds paying a coupon rate of $11\frac{3}{4}$% and maturing in November 2014 are quoted in financial newspapers as: $11\frac{3}{4}$ Nov 09-14. These bonds are callable at the discretion of the U.S. Treasury at 6-month intervals starting with November 2009 and ending 6 months before maturity, November 2014.*

U.S. Federal Agency Securities. Agencies of the U.S. government are quasi-government institutions that are allowed to issue their own debt obligations. In most cases the government makes no explicit guarantee that the interest and principal of these federal **agency bonds** will be paid. That is why these agency bonds pay slightly higher yields than U.S. Treasury bonds. However, it would be poor political and economic policy for a government to allow any of its agencies to default on their obligations. In several instances the U.S. Treasury provided the funds needed to prevent such an embarrassment.** The income from federal agency bonds is subject to federal, but not state and city, income taxes.

   The U.S. government agencies that have the largest debts outstanding are three mortgage finance corporations: (1) Government National Mortgage Association (GNMA), or Ginnie Mae; (2) Federal National Mortgage Association (FNMA), or Fannie Mae; and (3) Federal Home Loan Mortgage Association (FHLMA), or Freddie Mac. Ginnie Mae, Fannie Mae, and Freddie Mac invest in home mortgages that are insured against default by the U.S. government. Table 5-3 contrasts the federal government's debt with the aggregate (agency and nonagency owned) mortgage debt in the United States.

   The market for federal government and federal agency bonds is an exciting international market, as the *Wall Street Journal* story (Figure 5-5 on page 104) suggests.

---

* The Appendix to Chapter 9 and Chapter 28 show how to assess the value of the call option embedded in a callable bond.

** Since the U.S. government does not accept full legal responsibility for the debts of its agencies, these debts are called **off-balance-sheet financings** of the government. Table 5-3 shows that these off-balance-sheet debts slightly exceed the U.S. Treasury's publicly acknowledged national debt.

TABLE 5-3 U.S. Debt Market Data, in U.S. $ billions						
Category	1994	1995	1996	1997	1998	1999
Aggregate mortgage debt	4373	4603	4899	5216	5728	6181
U.S. Treasury debt	3466	3609	3755	3778	3724	3623

SOURCE: *Federal Reserve Bulletin,* published monthly by U.S. government. Table 1.54 on p. A35, Table 1.57 on p. A37, and Table 1.59 on p. A40.

Zeros. Some investors cannot buy marketable U.S. government securities because the smallest denomination ($1,000) is too large. To profit from this and some related situations, brokerages started purchasing multimillion-dollar blocks of Treasury Bonds and *stripping* the coupons away from the principal (corpus) of the bonds. The brokerages then sold small-denomination debt certificates that were backed by the pool of stripped coupons and principals from U.S. Treasury bonds. Essentially, the Treasury bonds were sold in pieces equal to their individual cash flows, or in combinations of several simultaneous cash flows. The brokerages profited from selling these stripped debt certificates at a slightly higher price than they had paid and, in so doing, created convenient denominations for small investors. These stripped certificates are single-payment Treasury-backed bonds.

In 1985 the U.S. Treasury introduced zeros called **Separate Trading of Registered Interest and Principal of Securities,** or **STRIPS.** Under the STRIPS program, Treasury bonds are eligible to have their coupons and corpus registered separately in a book-entry system at the Federal Reserve to facilitate transfers between investors. The U.S. Treasury's STRIPS program took the zeros business away from the brokerages that created zeros.

Investors buy the zeros at a deep original-issue discount (OID) from their maturity value: The price gain equals the investor's interest income. Figure 5-4A illustrates price fluctuations for zero coupon bonds. Investors receive nothing for months or years, until the maturity date of the zero arrives.

THE PRESENT VALUE OF A 12-YEAR ZERO

EXAMPLE

Consider a zero created by stripping the coupons off a Treasury bond with a $10,000 face value. The T-bond originated in July 2002 and matured in July 2014. In July 2002 an investor could buy this zero for $4,969.69.

$$\left(\begin{array}{c} \text{Zero's present value (purchase} \\ \text{price) in July 2002 is } \$4,969.69 \end{array} \right) = \left(\frac{\left(\begin{array}{c} \text{Face value, payable at zero's} \\ \text{maturity in July 2014, } \$10,000 \end{array} \right)}{(1.06)^{12 \text{ Years}}} \right)$$

The zero produces an average annual rate of return of 6% per year over its 12-year life, if held to maturity. The implicit interest income of ($10,000 − $4,969.69 =) $5,030.31 is received when the zero matures.

The disadvantage of investing in zero coupon bonds is that taxable investors must pay income taxes on their implicit interest income each year—even though they do not receive any coupons or cash inflows of any kind. In other words, zero coupon bonds cannot be used to delay income tax payments: Only their taxable income is postponed.

FIGURE 5-5 Newspaper Excerpt: The Markets Are Open Around the World, and Around the Clock

Bond Professionals Go 'Round-the-Clock

CREDIT
MARKETS

By GREGORY ZUCKERMAN
Staff Reporter of THE WALL STREET JOURNAL

Drew Ertman never had a chance to finish dinner on Nov. 13. In the middle of a sumptuous meal with colleagues from Morgan Stanley & Co. at a chic midtown New York restaurant, Mr. Ertman headed for a phone and spent 30 minutes talking with Asian investors. Later that night he was jolted from sleep by a series of calls from Hong Kong and Tokyo.

Morgan Stanley was in the middle of helping to underwrite a $500 million global offering for Federal National Mortgage Association, known as Fannie Mae, and as a bond professional, Mr. Ertman is getting used to these disruptions.

The reason: More than ever before, bonds are being traded at all hours, and by all nationalities.

Unlike a similar offering that may have taken place just a few years ago, the terms of the Fannie Mae deal were announced at 3 p.m. EST, even as traders were finishing up their plans for the evening. And a conference call with Fannie Mae officials took place at 11 p.m. EST, while most of Wall Street was asleep.

Even as stock-market investors marvel at an increase in after-hours trading of stocks and dream of the day when shares are traded seamlessly around the clock, the bond market is already there.

"The U.S. Treasury securities market is the birthplace of 24-hour trading," boasts Heather Ruth, president of PSA Bond Market Trade Association (formerly Public Securities Association).

In fact, the Fannie Mae transaction has become almost standard fare. Today, bond deals are regularly launched in New York, London or Japan and traded in every time zone.

There are several reasons for the nonstop activity, but none is more important than the strengthening links between global economies and the increasing flows of capital around the world.

"With the enhancements made in recent years, more people than ever are doing multicurrency global trading," says Christopher Leary, director of fixed income at SunAmerica Asset Management.

The emergence of global offerings has made bonds a 'round-the-clock business.

"Increasingly, you have domestic deals placed overseas, and foreign deals in the U.S.," says Mark Seigel, the head of world-wide bond syndication at Morgan Stanley. "So capital markets, and more particularly new issues, are increasingly global by nature, which in itself leads to more transactions."

Money isn't the only thing flowing around the world in greater volume. So is information. "With the growing use of e-mail, voice mail, CNN and other innovations of technology, professionals are on call 24 hours a day," says a bond trader.

The increasing hunger for bonds, specifically U.S. Treasurys, on the part of foreign governments and institutions is another reason for the evolution of the after-hours market. Although central banks and foreign investors do most of their trading in New York, they remain active during their own 9-to-5 workdays in various other markets. And that trend will almost certainly continue as foreign parties become larger players in

the U.S. Treasury market. Today, foreign investors control as much as 40% of Treasurys, according to some estimates.

At the same time, there's more competition in the bond market than ever before, especially among hedge funds desperate to match the lofty gains of their stock-trading brethren. As a result, there is more pressure to obtain the best prices and react immediately to news, forcing them to trade all night.

The increase in after-hours trading has forced bond investors and dealers to change the way they do business. Major Wall Street firms have long passed their order book around the globe: after New York it goes to Tokyo, then to London and back to New York for the start of the next day's trading. But many bond players are beefing up their staffs in foreign locales, or linking up with foreign institutions, in major ways.

For instance, government bond house Cantor Fitzgerald Inc. has tripled its employees in Asia in just the past year, and plans not only to hire more workers, but also to open more offices in the near future.

"Everyone in Treasurys is already going 24 hours," says Stuart Fraser, who runs fixed-income and futures trading at the firm.

More hedge funds have all-night trading desks. And few New York bond traders or money managers leave for home without pagers that alert them to sudden price moves or breaking news. Others are installing computer terminals at their homes.

Few seem to enjoy the intrusion, which until just two years ago was still uncommon.

"I've resisted it so far, but I live close enough so they can call me if anything happens—and they do," grumbles a bond professional.

SOURCE: "Bond Professionals Go 'Round the Clock," *Wall Street Journal,* 25 November 1996, C18.

Newspaper Price Quotations for Treasuries. Figure 5-6 shows how the market prices for U.S. government bonds are quoted in a newspaper. (The U.S. T-bill quotations appear in Figure 5-1.)

FIGURE 5-6   Newspaper Excerpt Showing the Day's Prices for U.S. Government Bonds[a]

TREASURY BONDS, NOTES & BILLS

Thursday, February 17, 2000

Representative Over-the-Counter quotations based on transactions of $1 million or more.

Treasury bond, note and bill quotes are as of mid-afternoon. Colons in bid-and-asked quotes represent 32nds; 101:01 means 101 1/32. Net changes in 32nds. n-Treasury note. Treasury bill quotes in hundredths, quoted on terms of a rate of discount. Days to maturity calculated from settlement date. All yields are to maturity and based on the asked quote. Latest 13-week and 26-week bills are boldfaced. For bonds callable prior to maturity, yields are computed to the earliest call date for issues quoted above par and to the maturity date for issues below par. *-When issued.

Source: Telerate/Cantor Fitzgerald

U.S. Treasury strips as of 3 p.m. Eastern time, also based on transactions of $1 million or more. Colons in bid-and-asked quotes represent 32nds; 99:01 means 99 1/32. Net changes in 32nds. Yields calculated on the asked quotation. ci-stripped coupon interest. bp-Treasury bond, stripped principal. np-Treasury note, stripped principal. For bonds callable prior to maturity, yields are computed to the earliest call date for issues quoted above par and to the maturity date for issues below par.

Source: Bear, Stearns & Co. via Street Software Technology Inc.

GOVT. BONDS & NOTES

Rate	Maturity Mo/Yr	Bid	Asked	Chg.	Ask Yld.
5½	Feb 00n	99:31	100:01	....	4.35
7⅛	Feb 00n	100:00	100:02	−1	4.89
5½	Mar 00n	99:30	100:00	−1	5.39
6⅞	Mar 00n	100:03	100:05	−1	5.36
5½	Apr 00n	99:29	99:31	....	5.60
5⅝	Apr 00n	99:29	99:31	−1	5.69
6¾	Apr 00n	100:04	100:06	−1	5.68
6⅜	May 00n	100:03	100:05	−1	5.62
8⅞	May 00n	100:23	100:25	....	5.44
5½	May 00n	99:27	99:29	−1	5.77
6¼	May 00n	100:02	100:04	−1	5.72
5⅜	Jun 00n	99:25	99:27	....	5.77
5⅞	Jun 00n	99:31	100:01	....	5.74
5⅜	Jul 00n	99:22	99:24	−1	5.93
6⅛	Jul 00n	100:00	100:02	−1	5.96
6	Aug 00n	99:30	100:00	−1	6.00
8¾	Aug 00n	101:09	101:11	−1	5.95
5⅛	Aug 00n	99:14	99:16	−1	6.09
6¼	Aug 00n	100:00	100:02	−1	6.12
4½	Sep 00n	98:29	98:31	−1	6.23
6⅛	Sep 00n	99:29	99:31	−1	6.16
4	Oct 00n	98:14	98:16	....	6.22
5¾	Oct 00n	99:19	99:21	−1	6.25
5¾	Nov 00n	99:18	99:20	−1	6.26
8½	Nov 00n	101:17	101:19	−1	6.24
4⅝	Nov 00n	98:22	98:24	−1	6.28
5⅝	Nov 00n	99:14	99:16	−1	6.28
4⅝	Dec 00n	98:16	98:18	−1	6.35
5½	Dec 00n	99:08	99:10	−1	6.32
4½	Jan 01n	98:07	98:09	−1	6.39
5¼	Jan 01n	98:29	98:31	−2	6.38
5⅜	Feb 01n	98:31	99:01	−1	6.40
7¾	Feb 01n	101:08	101:10	−1	6.37
11¾	Feb 01	105:02	105:04	−2	6.35
5	Feb 01n	98:18	98:20	−2	6.40
5⅝	Feb 01n	99:06	99:08	−1	6.39
4⅞	Mar 01n	98:09	98:11	−1	6.43
6⅜	Mar 01n	99:28	99:30	−1	6.43
5	Apr 01n	98:09	98:11	....	6.45
6¼	Apr 01n	99:22	99:24	−2	6.46
5⅝	May 01n	98:30	99:00	−1	6.47
8	May 01n	101:23	101:25	−1	6.47
13⅛	May 01	107:24	107:26	−2	6.44
5¼	May 01n	98:13	98:15	−2	6.51
6½	May 01n	99:30	100:00	−2	6.49
5¾	Jun 01n	98:29	98:31	−1	6.54
6⅝	Jun 01n	100:01	100:03	−1	6.54
5½	Jul 01n	98:15	98:17	−2	6.58
6⅝	Jul 01n	100:01	100:03	−1	6.55
7⅞	Aug 01n	101:24	101:26	−1	6.58
13⅜	Aug 01	109:14	109:16	−2	6.59
5½	Aug 01n	98:12	98:14	−2	6.53
6½	Aug 01n	99:26	99:28	−1	6.59
5⅝	Sep 01n	98:13	98:15	−2	6.64
6⅜	Sep 01n	99:17	99:19	−2	6.64
5⅞	Oct 01n	98:22	98:24	−2	6.66
6¼	Oct 01n	99:09	99:11	−3	6.66
7½	Nov 01n	101:08	101:10	−3	6.68
15¾	Nov 01	114:19	114:23	−3	6.63
5⅞	Nov 01n	98:20	98:22	−3	6.66
6⅛	Dec 01n	99:00	99:01	−4	6.68
6¼	Jan 02n	99:06	99:08	−3	6.66
6⅜	**Jan 02n**	**99:14**	**99:15**	**−4**	**6.67**
14¼	Feb 02	113:27	113:31	−5	6.65
6¼	Feb 02n	99:05	99:07	−4	6.67

Rate	Maturity Mo/Yr	Bid	Asked	Chg.	Ask Yld.
4¼	Jan 10i	99:17	99:18	−1	4.30
6½	Feb 10n	99:14	99:15	−5	6.57
11¾	Feb 05-10	119:25	119:29	−5	6.96
10	May 05-10	112:29	113:01	−4	6.98
12¾	Nov 05-10	126:25	126:31	−5	6.96
13⅞	May 06-11	134:12	134:18	−4	6.95
14	Nov 06-11	137:07	137:13	−4	6.95
10⅜	Nov 07-12	120:04	120:10	−5	6.94
12	Aug 08-13	131:28	132:02	−5	6.94
13¼	May 09-14	142:13	142:19	−3	6.93
12½	Aug 09-14	138:06	138:12	−3	6.92
11¾	Nov 09-14	134:03	134:09	−4	6.86
11¼	Feb 15	142:16	142:22	−4	6.70
10⅝	Aug 15	137:14	137:20	−4	6.69
9⅞	Nov 15	130:22	130:28	−3	6.67
9¼	Feb 16	125:02	125:08	−2	6.66
7¼	May 16	106:05	106:07	−1	6.62
7½	Nov 16	108:25	108:27	−1	6.62
8¾	May 17	121:14	121:20	....	6.63
8⅞	Aug 17	122:30	123:04	+1	6.62
9⅛	May 18	126:07	126:13	+1	6.61
9	Nov 18	125:11	125:17	+3	6.60
8⅞	Feb 19	124:10	124:16	+4	6.59
8⅛	Aug 19	116:24	116:28	+5	6.58
8½	Feb 20	121:03	121:09	+5	6.57
8¾	May 20	124:01	124:07	+6	6.57
8¾	Aug 20	124:06	124:12	+6	6.57
7⅞	Feb 21	114:30	115:02	+7	6.55
8⅛	May 21	117:28	118:00	+8	6.54
8⅛	Aug 21	118:00	118:04	+8	6.54
8	Nov 21	116:25	116:29	+9	6.53
7¼	Aug 22	108:19	108:21	+9	6.51
7⅝	Nov 22	113:00	113:04	+11	6.51
7⅛	Feb 23	107:10	107:12	+11	6.50
6¼	Aug 23	97:08	97:10	+11	6.47
7½	Nov 24	112:18	112:22	+15	6.46
7⅝	Feb 25	114:08	114:12	+15	6.46
6⅞	Aug 25	105:07	105:09	+16	6.45
6	Feb 26	94:19	94:21	+16	6.43
6¾	Aug 26	103:30	104:00	+16	6.43
6½	Nov 26	100:27	100:29	+15	6.43
6⅝	Feb 27	102:15	102:17	+17	6.43
6⅜	Aug 27	99:12	99:14	+17	6.42
6⅛	Nov 27	96:10	96:12	+18	6.41
3⅝	Apr 28i	90:29	90:30	+3	4.18
5½	Aug 28	88:12	88:14	+19	6.39
5¼	Nov 28	85:07	85:09	+18	6.37
5¼	Feb 29	85:11	85:13	+20	6.36
3⅞	Apr 29i	94:31	95:00	+1	4.17
6⅛	Aug 29	97:06	97:07	+21	6.33
6¼	May 30	100:12	100:13	+21	6.22

U.S. TREASURY STRIPS

Mat.	Type	Bid	Asked	Chg.	Ask Yld.
May 00	ci	98:23	98:23	+2	5.64
May 00	np	98:24	98:24	+1	5.56
Aug 00	ci	97:07	97:07	+1	5.94
Aug 00	np	97:07	97:07	+1	5.96
Nov 00	ci	95:23	95:23	+1	6.10
Nov 00	np	95:21	95:22	+1	6.17
Feb 01	ci	94:03	94:03	+2	6.30
Feb 01	np	94:02	94:02	−1	6.33
May 01	ci	92:13	92:14	....	6.51
May 01	np	92:11	92:12	....	6.56

Mat.	Type	Bid	Asked	Chg.	Ask Yld.
Feb 13	ci	42:17	42:23	+6	6.66
May 13	ci	41:29	42:02	+6	6.65
Aug 13	ci	41:09	41:14	+7	6.64
Nov 13	ci	40:21	40:26	+7	6.63
Feb 14	ci	40:02	40:07	+9	6.62
May 14	ci	39:14	39:19	+9	6.62
Aug 14	ci	38:27	39:00	+9	6.61
Nov 14	ci	38:09	38:14	+9	6.60
Feb 15	ci	37:24	37:30	+10	6.58
Feb 15	bp	37:31	38:05	+13	6.54
May 15	ci	37:07	37:12	+11	6.57
Aug 15	ci	36:21	36:26	+12	6.56
Aug 15	bp	36:26	37:00	+13	6.53
Nov 15	ci	36:04	36:10	+13	6.55
Nov 15	bp	36:10	36:15	+13	6.52
Feb 16	ci	35:20	35:25	+12	6.53
Feb 16	bp	35:27	36:01	+14	6.49
May 16	ci	35:04	35:09	+13	6.52
May 16	bp	35:20	35:25	+15	6.43
Aug 16	ci	34:19	34:24	+13	6.52
Nov 16	ci	34:05	34:10	+13	6.50
Nov 16	bp	34:14	34:20	+14	6.44
Feb 17	ci	33:23	33:28	+13	6.48
May 17	ci	33:08	33:14	+14	6.46
May 17	bp	33:14	33:19	+16	6.43
Feb 17	ci	32:25	32:31	+15	6.45
Aug 17	bp	32:30	33:04	+16	6.42
Nov 17	ci	32:12	32:17	+15	6.44
Feb 18	ci	31:28	32:01	+16	6.43
May 18	ci	31:13	31:18	+16	6.43
May 18	bp	31:16	31:21	+16	6.41
Aug 18	ci	30:30	31:03	+16	6.42
Nov 18	bp	30:15	30:21	+16	6.42
Nov 18	ci	30:17	30:22	+16	6.41
Feb 19	ci	30:03	30:08	+16	6.40
Feb 19	bp	30:06	30:11	+16	6.38
May 19	ci	29:20	29:25	+16	6.40
Aug 19	ci	29:05	29:11	+16	6.40
Aug 19	bp	29:11	29:17	+16	6.36
Nov 19	ci	28:23	28:28	+16	6.40
Feb 20	ci	28:11	28:17	+16	6.38
Feb 20	bp	28:15	28:21	+16	6.36
May 20	ci	27:30	28:04	+16	6.37
May 20	bp	28:01	28:07	+16	6.36
Aug 20	ci	27:17	27:22	+16	6.37
Aug 20	bp	27:21	27:26	+16	6.35
Nov 20	ci	27:10	27:16	+16	6.33
Feb 21	ci	26:29	27:02	+16	6.33
Feb 21	bp	27:00	27:05	+16	6.31
May 21	ci	26:16	26:21	+16	6.33
May 21	bp	26:18	26:23	+16	6.31
Aug 21	ci	26:03	26:09	+16	6.32
Aug 21	bp	26:06	26:11	+16	6.31
Nov 21	ci	25:27	26:00	+16	6.30
Nov 21	bp	25:27	26:01	+16	6.29
Feb 22	ci	25:13	25:18	+14	6.30
May 22	ci	25:00	25:06	+14	6.30
Aug 22	ci	24:21	24:26	+14	6.30
Aug 22	bp	24:27	25:00	+13	6.26
Nov 22	ci	24:09	24:14	+14	6.30
Nov 22	bp	24:13	24:18	+14	6.27
Feb 23	ci	23:31	24:04	+14	6.28
Feb 23	bp	24:02	24:08	+14	6.26
May 23	ci	23:20	23:25	+14	6.28
Aug 23	ci	23:10	23:16	+13	6.27
Aug 23	bp	23:20	23:25	+14	6.21
Nov 23	ci	23:01	23:06	+13	6.26
Feb 24	ci	22:23	22:28	+13	6.25
May 24	ci	22:13	22:18	+13	6.24
Aug 24	ci	22:03	22:08	+12	6.23
Nov 24	ci	21:27	22:00	+12	6.22
Feb 24	bp	21:31	22:04	+13	6.19
Feb 25	ci	21:20	21:25	+12	6.19
Feb 25	ci	21:23	21:28	+12	6.18
May 25	ci	21:12	21:17	+12	6.18
Aug 25	ci	20:31	21:04	+12	6.19
Aug 25	bp	21:02	21:07	+12	6.18
Nov 25	ci	20:22	20:27	+12	6.19
Feb 26	ci	20:10	20:15	+12	6.20
Feb 26	bp	20:18	20:23	+12	6.15
May 26	ci	20:00	20:05	+12	6.20
Aug 26	ci	19:22	19:27	+12	6.20
Aug 26	bp	19:29	20:02	+13	6.16
Nov 26	ci	19:15	19:20	+12	6.19
Nov 26	bp	19:21	19:26	+12	6.15
Feb 27	ci	19:10	19:15	+12	6.14
Feb 27	bp	19:13	19:17	+12	6.14

[a]See Figure 5-1 for the T-bill quotations.

SOURCE: *Wall Street Journal*, 16 February 2000, C17.

If the securities are coupon-paying notes or bonds, the leftmost column of Figure 5-6 gives the coupon rate. The next column gives the maturity date of the issue; the lower-case letter n signifies an issue of Treasury notes.

Because T-bills and STRIPS pay no coupons, their maturity date is in the leftmost column of Figures 5-1 and 5-6, respectively, instead of the second column. The number of days until the T-bill matures is in the second column of Figure 5-1. The second column of STRIPS data in Figure 5-6 tells whether the cash flow comes from the stripped bonds' coupon income (*ci*) or *notional principal* (*np*). Notional principal is a synonym for face (par) value.

The bid and asked prices are in the third and fourth columns of Figure 5-6. For coupon paying bonds the **bid price** is the highest dollar price (stated as a percentage of face value) that any potential investor is willing to pay. The **asked price** or **offer price** is the lowest price that any potential seller is willing to accept. The column headed *Chg.* shows the amount of price change from the previous trading day's closing price to that day's closing price. The rightmost column headed *Yield* contains the YTM (bond equivalent yield) the investor will earn if the security is purchased at the current asked price and held to maturity.*

Inflation-Indexed U.S. Treasury Securities. The purchasing power of coupon interest payments and the principal repayment received by a bond investor is diminished by inflation. To help investors protect themselves against purchasing power risk, the U.S. government issues **Treasury inflation-protected securities (TIPS)**. In 1997 the first issue of 10-year T-notes indexed to the U.S. government's Consumer Price Index (CPI) was followed by the sale of inflation-indexed U.S. savings bonds. TIPS pay interest rates that are a few hundred basis points (BPs) lower than similar Treasury securities because they reduce the risk that their investors will lose purchasing power to inflation. Purchasing power risk is reduced by periodically adjusting the bonds' principal and interest payments to reflect percentage changes in the Consumers Price Index (the inflation rate).

The U.S. Treasury hopes to achieve three gains by issuing TIPS: (1) lower the inflation-adjusted cost of financing the federal debt, (2) increase the savings rate in the U.S., and (3) make it possible to discern the expected rate of inflation by comparing the inflation-indexed bond yields to the yields of bonds that are not inflation-indexed. British, Canadian, and other governments offered such bonds and have been able to finance a small part of their national debt with them.[2]

MUNICIPAL BONDS ISSUED WITHIN THE UNITED STATES

Taxes take away a significant portion of many investors' wealth every year. Municipal bonds are investments that offer investors partial tax-exemption.

Municipal bonds are issued by states, counties, parishes, cities, towns, boroughs, villages, and special tax districts of municipal corporations (such as toll bridge authorities, college dormitory authorities, and sewer districts, among others). U.S. tax law stipulates that coupon income from municipal bonds, called *munis*, is exempt from federal income taxes. This tax exemption does not apply to capital gains. Because of their tax exemption, munis are most popular with investors in the highest income tax brackets.

---

* International bond traders must learn additional vocabulary. For example, British traders use the word *bond* where U.S. traders would use the word *stock*, and vice versa. The international bond market is discussed in more detail in Chapter 19.

The three quantities below are interrelated:

◆ Market interest rate on a muni bond

◆ Market interest rate on a fully taxable bond that is comparable to the muni in terms of risk, callability, and other factors

◆ The investor's income tax rate.

$$\left(\begin{array}{c}\text{Yield on}\\\text{a taxable}\\\text{bond}\end{array}\right) = \left(\begin{array}{c}\text{Yield on comparable}\\\text{tax–exempt}\\\text{municipal bond}\end{array}\right)\Big/\left(\begin{array}{c}1.0 - \text{(Muni buyer's}\\\text{income tax rate)}\end{array}\right) \qquad (5\text{-}1)$$

Eqn. 5-1 can be used to approximate the interest rates that will make the investor indifferent between tax-exempt and taxable bonds. Since bond investors consider factors other than after-tax coupon yields, the equation above can only offer approximate suggestions.

GERALDO'S MUNICIPAL BOND YIELD   **EXAMPLE**

Geraldo is in the 33% income tax bracket and he is indifferent to investing in either (1) a tax-exempt municipal bond that yields 10%, or (b) a taxable corporate bond that yields 15% and involves the same level of risk as the muni. The computation shows that Geraldo is indifferent because both bonds yield the same after-tax return of 10%.

$$\left(\text{Yield on taxable bond, 15\%}\right)\left(\begin{array}{c}100\% - \text{(Geraldo's}\\33.3\%\text{ income tax rate)}\\= 66.6\% = 0.666\end{array}\right) = \left(\begin{array}{c}\text{Yield on tax–exempt}\\\text{muni, 10\%}\end{array}\right)$$

Geraldo would probably prefer the taxable corporate bond if it yielded more than 15%. He would probably prefer the tax-free muni if it yielded more than 10%.

General-Obligation (GO) Bonds

In the United States municipal bonds can be either general-obligation (GO) bonds or limited-obligation bonds. **General-obligation (GO) bonds** are often called *full faith and credit bonds*. GO bonds are issued by municipalities that have unlimited power to tax to meet their obligations and can promise to pay without any payment limitations. GO bonds are usually less risky investments than limited-obligation bonds.

Limited-Obligation Bonds

Limited-obligation bonds are bonds issued by a municipality that is limited in raising revenues to pay its debts. **Revenue bonds** are the most significant form of limited-obligation bonds. Revenue bonds, entitled only to the revenue generated by a specific property that is providing a public service, are used to finance municipally owned projects like toll bridges, toll roads, water works, sewage disposal systems, and dormitories for state colleges.

Insured Municipal Bonds

Investors tend to shy away from bonds involving default risk. Risk-aversion makes it difficult for municipalities whose bonds did not receive high ratings from Standard & Poor's and

Moody's bond rating services to sell their bonds. The American Municipal Bond Assurance Association (AMBAC), Municipal Bond Insurance Association (MBIA), and several other insurance firms sell bond insurance to municipalities that do not merit the highest credit ratings.

Standard & Poor's, Moody's, and the other bond rating services agree to give municipal bonds insured by *muni bond insurance companies* the same quality rating that the bond issue's bond-insurer has been given, because the insurer guarantees the bond issue's payments. This insurance makes it easier for municipalities that do not merit the highest credit ratings to (1) procure high-quality credit ratings, (2) find buyers for their bonds, and (3) sell their bonds at lower rates of interest.

CORPORATION BONDS

Corporate bonds are the "senior securities" of a firm. That's because the **Federal Bankruptcy Act** in the United States, for instance, requires bankrupt firms to pay off their debts before the equity investors can be repaid for the amount they invested in the firm.* Other countries have similar laws.

The **Trust Indenture Act of 1939** also protects corporate bond investors in the United States; it requires each corporate bond issue in the United States to have an **indenture contract** (or *deed of trust*) specifying all terms of the issue. The terms of the issue specify details about the coupon interest payments, collateral provisions, sinking fund provisions, and the option to convert the bonds into the issuer's stock, among other **protective provisions.** U.S. law says the indenture must also appoint a **trustee** to ensure that the bond issuer upholds all provisions of the indenture. The trustee is a "hired watchdog" to protect the bond investors. One of the costs of issuing bonds in the United States is that the law stipulates that the bond issuer pays the trustee. The issuer pays the trustee to sue the issuer if the issuer does not perform in accordance with the protective provisions in the bond issue's indenture contract.

Secured Bonds

If the indenture contract for a corporate bond issue in the United States provides for a "lien" on designated property, that bond issue is **secured** or **collateralized.** The **lien** gives secured bond investors the right to sell the pledged property (collateral) and use the proceeds from that sale to satisfy the debt's unpaid interest and/or principal. Collateral makes bonds more attractive to investors. In reality, the collateral is seldom sold when a bond issue defaults. The company is usually reorganized by issuing new junior securities (such as unsecured bonds or preferred stock) to replace the defaulted bonds. The presence of a lien on underlying assets has value, however, because it strengthens the bondholders' claim during the reorganization process in bankruptcy court.

There are several categories of collateralized bonds. A bond issue secured with a lien on real property or buildings is a **mortgage bond.** If all the assets of the firm are collateral under the terms of the indenture, it is called a **blanket mortgage**. The total assets need not be pledged; only some of the land or buildings of the company may be mortgaged. A mort-

---

* In the United States the original Bankruptcy Act was modified by the liberal **Bankruptcy Reform Act** of 1978 and then the not-so-liberal Bankruptcy Reform Act of 1984. The 1984 Act primarily curtailed some liberal provisions that pertained to consumer bankruptcy.

gage can be a first mortgage, second mortgage, or subsequent mortgage, each with its respective priority of claim on the assets of the firm in case of default. A first mortgage is the most secure (senior) because in a bankruptcy proceeding it enjoys first claim to assets; all later mortgages are *subordinated mortgages*. Likewise, a third mortgage is subordinate (junior) to a second mortgage. An **open-end mortgage** means that more bonds can be issued on the same mortgage contract. When the collateral deposited with the trustee of a bond issue consists of stocks and bonds issued by other companies, the secured bonds are called **collateral trust bonds.**

Unsecured Bonds

Unsecured bonds are called **debenture bonds,** or simply **debentures.** The bond issue's indenture contract contains no collateral provision to protect debenture investors. Debentures are considered a claim on *earnings*, not on assets. Debenture bondholders are called "general creditors" in the United States. **General creditors** include raw material suppliers and the public utilities, for example. In the event of bankruptcy the claims of general creditors are junior to the claims from collateralized creditors. In a typical bankruptcy auction, all unpledged assets remaining after payment of the secured debts are available to pay the claims of the general creditors.

The presence or absence of collateral has a significant effect on the interest rate that bond investors can expect. Because collateralized bonds are less risky than debentures, if all other factors equal, they will offer investors a lower expected return.

EQUITY SECURITIES

Equity securities represent a claim on the earnings and assets of a corporation. **Common stock** is the first security issued in a new corporation and the last security retired in bankruptcy. Every corporation has common stock, but not every corporation has **preferred stock.** Preferred stock is a hybrid security that combines a mixture of ownership and creditorship privileges.

Preferred and common stock have no maturity dates, no claims on specific corporate assets, and no claims on specific sources of corporate earnings. If preferred stockholders and common stockholders receive income from their investments, it is in the form of capital gains (or losses) and/or cash dividends. Both domestic and international investors who invest in common stock or preferred stock earn the one-period rates of return introduced as Eqn. 2-3 in Chapter 2.

YOSHI'S 9-MONTH RATE OF RETURN FROM NISSAN COMMON STOCK   EXAMPLE

Yoshi, a Tokyo resident, bought a share of Nissan common stock for 1,591 yen at the Tokyo Stock Exchange. The share paid him cash dividends of 72 yen before he sold it for 1,566 yen 9 months later. Yoshi's capital loss was (¥1,566 − ¥1,591 =) 25 yen, and his total income was (−¥25 + ¥72 =) 47 yen over his holding period. Yoshi's rate of return was 2.95%.

$$r = \frac{\text{Price change} + \text{Cash dividends}}{\text{Beginning of the period price}} = \frac{(P_1 - P_0) + CF}{P_0} = \frac{-¥25 + ¥72}{¥1,591} = .0295 = 2.95\%$$

ETHICS   **A REALITY CHECK**

Ethics and the Individual Investor

Insofar as investment professionals are agents, they have a duty to act in their clients' interests. However, brokers and planners are sometimes merely sellers of products, and so their responsibility is not always clear. At a minimum, though, they should avoid deceptive sales practices, including misrepresentation and inadequate disclosure. Brokers have an obligation to recommend only *suitable* investments, which take into account a client's situation and objectives. Excessive trading in a client's account in order to generate brokerage commissions is a prohibited practice called **churning.**

Each of these obligations raises questions of definition. What is suitability or excessive trading, for example? In general, we can employ a *reasonable person* standard: Would a reasonably intelligent, informed investor hold a false belief because of a broker's claims (deception), purchase a security knowing what the broker does (suitability), or trade as actively (churning)? At issue is the *objectivity* of the investment professional's judgment, which may be compromised by a conflict of interest, as when a broker or planner receives a higher commission for selling certain products.

These problems are common in agency relationships. In particular, agents are tempted by *opportunism*, which is shirking a duty to act in another's interest and benefiting oneself instead. **Moral hazard** is a situation in which one gains the benefits of a decision while others bear the costs.

One solution for agency problems is *monitoring* or close watching, but this may be costly. (An investor usually engages a broker to avoid the trouble of managing a portfolio.) Other solutions include removing the incentives or aligning them with the principal's. For example, churning can be avoided by basing commissions on the size of the portfolio or its returns. Some planners charge clients a flat fee instead of collecting commissions for selling products. Moral hazard is addressed in insurance by copayments and deductibles that make beneficiaries share the cost of their decisions.

John R. Boatright, *Professor of Business Ethics*

COMMON STOCK

Because it has the last claim (lowest priority in bankruptcy) on the issuing firm's earnings and assets, common stock is the most junior security that corporations issue. The probability of a common stockholder getting anything from a bankrupt firm is near zero. If the corporation is profitable, however, the common stockholders enjoy an unlimited potential for dividend income and price appreciation. This potential for wide variability of return makes common stock the riskiest security issued by every corporation.

Stockholders' Rights

Certain rights and privileges accrue to owners of common stock.

Right to a Stock Certificate. When investors buy common stock, they can obtain certificates as proof of their ownership. A stock certificate states the number of shares purchased, the par value per share (if any), and the **transfer agent** for the issue. When stock is purchased, the new owner and the number of shares bought are noted in the stock record book of the transfer agent. As a result, there is little reason for most investors to have stock certificates prepared. The **registrar** for the issue checks to verify that the transfer agent made no errors. Most stock exchanges allow the same party to be both the transfer agent and registrar, if the issuer agrees.

Voting Rights. Common stockholders own the corporation; they are entitled to elect the firm's board of directors and vote on major issues that affect their corporation. Most stockholders do not attend their corporation's stockholder meetings; they vote by mail. Stockholders not interested in voting can delegate their vote(s) via proxy. A **proxy** grants a specified third party, usually a top corporate executive, the stockholder's authority to vote in any way the proxy holder wishes at a meeting of the stockholders. If a corporate executive is able to gain control of enough proxy votes, that executive can vote the decisions they favor into effect, even though that executive might not own any shares in the corporation. Proxy votes are more important than they might seem.

For many issuers of common stock the "one share, one vote" rule applies. However, many other corporations implement this rule with **cumulative voting,** which permits a stockholder to have as many votes as shares owned multiplied by the number of directors being elected. The stock owner may cast all these cumulative votes for only one director or divide them among several. Cumulative voting allows for stockholders with a significant minority of shares to gain representation on the board of directors.

CUMULATIVE VOTING   **EXAMPLE**

Several states in the United States require cumulative voting. The following formula explains the number of *shares needed* to elect a certain number of *favored directors*. For example, suppose the shareholder wants 2 favored directors elected, the total slate of *directors to be elected* numbers 10, and the *number of voting shares outstanding* is 100,000: The formula shows that under cumulative voting, the ownership of at least 18,183 shares of stock is required to guarantee election of 2 favored directors.

$$\begin{pmatrix} \text{Shares} \\ \text{needed} \end{pmatrix} = \frac{\begin{pmatrix} \text{Favored} \\ \text{directors} \end{pmatrix}\begin{pmatrix} \text{Number of voting} \\ \text{shares outstanding} \end{pmatrix}}{[(\text{Directors to be elected}) + 1]} = 1$$

$$= \frac{(2 \text{ directors})(100{,}000 \text{ shares})}{[(10 \text{ directors}) + 1]} + 1 = \frac{200{,}000}{11} + 1 = 18{,}183$$

The Right to Buy and Sell. Investors buying stock in a firm can have the firm send the shares to them. Or, they can have their broker hold the shares for them at the broker's office, usually for no charge. If the securities are registered (rather than bearer) securities that are kept at the brokerage, they will be kept there in the brokerage's name, not the investor's name. It is common to keep registered securities in the name of the brokerage. In the United States this practice is called keeping the securities in the *street name* (referring to the brokerage's name on Wall Street). Arguments for and against leaving securities in a street name at the broker's office are listed in Table 5-4.

The Preemptive Right. The preemptive right grants existing stockholders the right-of-first-refusal on any new stock their corporation issues. This means old investors are guaranteed the right to maintain their *previous fraction* of total outstanding shares in the corporation if new shares are issued. The preemptive right, if exercised, prevents dilution of the old stockholders'

TABLE 5-4	Should You Hold Your Securities in a "Street Name" with Your Broker or Take Possession of Them Yourself?

Favoring Use of Street Name	Against Using Street Name
You cannot lose your securities or get them stolen. This is especially true if they are **bearer** (as contrasted with **registered**) **securities**.[a]	You will be unable to buy commission-free securities through some direct corporate cash **dividend reinvestment plan (DRIP)** that might be available to you.[b]
You can easily sell your securities with just a phone call.	It might be easier to negotiate a discounted brokerage commission from a competing broker if you held the shares.
Cash dividends and/or interest income can be automatically swept into an interest-earning cash account in your name at your brokerage.	Moving your securities to another brokerage can take weeks (or even months).
Using "street name" allows the brokerage to cut costs by reducing its paperwork a little.	It might be of some educational value for a child who receives securities as a gift to see and touch the certificates.

[a] To reduce the opportunities for illegal tax evasion, the U.S. federal government canceled the tax-exemption of bearer municipal bonds after 1981. Today most municipals, federal government bonds, and domestic corporates are registered under the book entry system. The remaining domestic bearer bonds in the United States will probably disappear eventually, but bearer bonds still flourish in international finance.

[b] Some DRIPs are free, and some are not. A typical DRIP charges employees of the stock's issuer a $5 fee plus 10 cents per share each time they buy their employer's stock. Thus, for 100 shares the fees are [$5 + (10 cents)(100 shares)=] $15. On-line brokerage firms like Ameritrade, Datek Online, and Fleet Financial charge the public fees of less than $15 to buy 100 shares of some stocks.

---

ownership control. Most, but not all, issues of stock in the United States contain the preemptive right.

Right to Information. The **Securities Act of 1933** requires U.S. issuers to make "full disclosure of all relevant information" to any interested party. For example, corporations whose stock is publicly traded in the United States are required to send their stockholders quarterly and annual financial reports. Stockholders can demand and get more information, such as minutes from the board of directors meetings, lists of stockholders, and detailed financial reports. In some of the lesser-developed countries, stockholders are not legally entitled to receive much information from the corporations in which they invest. Such corporate concealment facilitates corporate corruption, discourages public investment in corporations, and, indirectly, hinders that nation's prosperity.

The Right to Receive Cash Dividends. At their periodic meetings, boards of directors typically discuss, among other issues, the question of whether to pay cash dividends, and, if so, how much. Cash dividend payments are not guaranteed. It was once thought that the market price of a corporation's shares tended to increase when the firm maintained stable cash dividend payments; that idea is less prevalent today.[3] Now most companies determine their cash dividend policy according to their growth expectations for the firm. Fast-growing corporations tend to pay small cash dividends, or no cash dividends, to retain as much capital as possible to finance the growth internally. For example, some well-known U.S. corporations like America Online (AOL), 3Com, Amgen, AMR, Applied Materials, CNA Financial, Cisco Systems, Compaq, Federated Department Stores, Microsoft, Toys "R" Us, and WorldCom have gone years without paying cash dividends in order to finance the firm's growth internally with its own retained earnings. In contrast, some firms that are growing more slowly pay out a large portion of their earnings in dividends.

Stock Splits and Dividends

In addition to their cash dividend payments, many corporations pay out stock dividends, and some split their stock.

Paying Stock Dividends. Some corporations pay dividends in shares instead of cash. When a *stock* dividend is paid, one account is increased and another is decreased equally within the net worth section of the corporation's balance sheet. Except for this accounting entry, stock dividends and stock splits are identical. Both transactions leave the corporation's assets, liabilities, and total net worth unchanged.

Splitting the Stock. When a company divides its common stock shares, it is said to have had a **stock split.** If a corporation had 2 million shares of stock outstanding and split them 2-for-1, it would then have 4 million shares outstanding. In a stock split, the corporation must change the par value of every share of its common stock, but this does not change its paid-in surplus accounts, retained earnings, or total net worth. If the firm's stock had a par of $1 per share before the split, then the 2-for-1 split would give it a par value of 50 cents per share.

A common rationale given for stock splits is that the corporation's directors wanted to reduce the stock's market price.[4] The split divides the market price per share in proportion to the split. For example, a $100 per share stock will sell at $50 after a 2-for-1 split, just as a $100 per share stock will sell at $50 after a 100% stock dividend. In both cases there will be twice as many shares outstanding, and thus the total market value of the firm is unchanged.* Most research shows that stock splits and stock dividends have no significant effect on the value of the firm.[5] (The effect of stock dividends and splits is analyzed in Chapter 8.)

Other Aspects of Common Stock

Par Value Per Share. **Par value** is an arbitrary value assigned to a share of stock. Many issues have no par value. Most corporations set a par value on their stock at a level below the price the shares will command on the market; $1 per share is a popular par value. The par value of a stock today tells us nothing about the value of the shares.

Book Value Per Share. A share's **book value** is computed by dividing a corporation's net worth (aggregate book value) by the number of shares of common stock outstanding. For some corporations, book value per share gives an indication of the net assets per common share and, thus, can affect its stock price.[6] Table 5-5 contains book value, par value, and other data for comparison with the market price of Coca-Cola's common stock. Comparing the three values in Table 5-5 reveals substantial disparities between them. Similar comparisons with other corporations suggest if the three values *are* related, it is a weak and ambiguous relationship.

Stock Price Quotations. Figure 5-7 shows a newspaper excerpt listing the previous trading day's NYSE stock prices. The two leftmost columns of Figure 5-7 present the stock's highest and lowest prices during the previous year, not including the current day. The abbreviated name of each issuing corporation, the stock's ticker symbol, and the most recent annual cash

---

* Infrequently, a stock issuer might declare a reverse split. A 1-for-2 reverse split, for example, would exchange 1 new share for each 2 shares that existed before the split. Stocks trading at prices below $10 per share sometimes have reverse splits to raise their share prices.

TABLE 5-5   **Comparison of Annual Time-Series Data on Coca-Cola Corporation's Par Value, Book Value, Market Prices, and Other Data**

Year	Book Value Per Share	Cash Dividend Per Share	Earnings Per share	Range of Market Price	Shares of Common Outstanding	Par Value Per Share
1999	$3.85	$0.64	$0.98	$70.88–47.31	2,472 million	$0.25
1998	$3.19	$0.60	$1.42	$88.94–53.63	2,466	$0.25
1997	$2.67	$0.56	$1.64	$72.63–51.13	2,471	$0.25
1996	$2.18	$0.50	$1.40	$53.12–34.87	2,481	$0.25
1995	$1.77	$0.44	$1.19	$40.25–24.37	2,525	$0.25
1994	$1.80	$0.39	$0.99	$26.75–19.50	2,580	$0.25
1993	$1.55	$0.34	$0.84	$22.62–18.75	2,604	$0.25
1992	$1.34	$0.28	$0.71	$22.75–17.75	2,634	$0.25
1991	$1.55	$0.24	$0.60	$20.50–10.75	2,666	$0.25
1990	$1.31	$0.20	$0.51	$12.25–8.12	2,674	$0.25
1989	$1.10	$0.17	$0.43	$10.12–5.37	2,768	$0.25
1988	$1.05	$0.15	$0.36	$5.62–4.37	2,916	$0.25
1987	$1.06	$0.14	$0.31	$6.62–3.50	3,018	$0.25
1986	$0.93	$0.13	$0.31	$5.62–3.25	3,094	$0.25

dividend per share (if any were paid) are in columns 3, 4, and 5. The lowercase letters refer to footnotes that provide details (for instance, *pf* indicates an issue of preferred stock). Columns 6 and 7 contain each stock's cash dividend yield and price-earnings ratio. The volume of shares traded (in hundreds) during the previous trading day are in column 8. Columns 9, 10, and 11 contain the previous day's high, low, and closing prices. The change in the closing price between the last two trading days is in the rightmost column of Figure 5-7. The National Association of Security Dealers Automated Quotations (NASDAQ) presents the prices of over-the-counter (OTC) stocks using the identical format. Coca-Cola (ticker KO) and its bottling subsidiary named Coca-Cola Enterprises (ticker CCE) are listed in Figure 5-7.

Classified Common Stock. Two categories of **classified common stock** are Class A and Class B. Class A is typically stock that pays cash dividends and is *sold* to the public (outside investors) to raise capital, but its investors might have zero or diminished voting power. Class A stock can be similar to preferred stock but still be common stock.

Class B stock is usually voting stock *held* by management (inside investors) that is entitled to zero or reduced cash dividends. The top managers of the corporation usually take Class B stock as payment for founding, merging, or reorganizing the corporation. The voting power management gets from its Class B stock, combined with its management authority, can give top executives of a corporation total control of the firm—without investing any money. These executives are free to set their own salaries and fringe benefits.[7] As a result, "Killer Bs" is a disparaging nickname applied to some issues of Class B stock. Top executives who are unable to run the corporation profitably or who are endeavoring to drain the corporation's wealth into their own pockets use classified common stock to achieve their goals. Incompetent or dishonest top executives who want to protect their corporate positions put substantial effort into obtaining Class B shares for themselves.

In recent years classified common stock has been used by the top management of a corporation to stop corporate raiders from tendering an unwanted offer to buy a controlling interest in their corporation. By granting themselves Class B stock that has voting power, a

FIGURE 5-7 Newspaper Excerpt Showing the Previous Trading Day's Stock Price Quotations from NYSE

	52 Weeks Hi	52 Weeks Lo	Stock	Sym	Div	Yld %	PE	Vol 100s	Hi	Lo	Close	Net Chg
s	65 1/8	37 1/2	Clorox	CLX	.80	2.0	32	7282	41 11/16	40 1/4	40 5/8	– 3/8
n	41 5/8	26 1/4	CMS EngyTr		1.74e	6.4	...	120	27 15/16	26 3/4	27 1/4	– 1/16
	24	10 9/16	Coachmen	COA	.20	1.7	6	460	11 13/16	11 9/16	11 13/16	+ 1/8
n	27 15/16	21 3/8	CstlCpInc		1.66	6.5	...	31	25 7/8	25 1/4	25 11/16	+ 3/16
	45 1/4	31 1/16	Coastal	CGP	.25	.6	18	22986	42 11/16	41 9/16	42 3/8	+ 7/16
▲	302	260	Coastal pfA		1.19	.4	...	1	310	310	310	+ 8
	25 7/8	22 1/16	CslFnl TOPrS		2.09	8.9	...	20	23 7/16	22 15/16	23 7/16	+ 5/16
	16 13/16	7 1/4	Coastcast	PAR		...	12	153	15 11/16	14 3/4	14 15/16	– 11/16
	70 7/8	47 5/16	CocaCola	KO	.64	1.2	55	34171	55 7/16	53 1/4	53 3/4	– 1 15/16 ←
	22 1/2	12 1/2	CCFemsa ADR	KOF	.12e	.6	...	4471	19 1/8	18 7/8	19	– 1/8
	37 1/2	16 13/16	CocaColaEnt	CCE	.16	.8	cc	10288	26 11/16	25 7/8	26 9/16	– 1 3/8
	5 11/16	**3 1/16**	**Coeur dAMn**	**CDE**		**...**	**dd**	**2273**	**4 1/16**	**3 7/8**	**4 1/16**	**+ 1/4**
	7 1/8	3 3/8	Coeur dAMn pf		1.49	34.1	...	155	4 7/16	4 3/16	4 3/8	+ 3/16
	14 1/4	10	♣CohenStrsTR	RFI	.96a	8.8	...	119	10 15/16	10 11/16	10 15/16	+ 3/16
	18 5/8	3 7/8	ColeNtl A	CNJ		...	dd	77	6 7/16	6 1/8	6 3/8	+ 1/16
▼	48	31 5/8	ColesMyer	CM	1.32e	4.1	...	43	31 7/8	31 1/2	31 7/8	– 3/8
s	66 3/4	41 5/16	ColgatePalm	CL	.63	1.1	37	14930	56 3/4	55 1/8	55 3/8	– 5/16
	91	85 1/2	ColgatePalm pf		4.25	4.9	...	z10	86 1/2	86 1/2	86 1/2	– 1 3/8
	7 5/8	3 15/16	CollnsAikman	CKC	.71	14.6	dd	146	4 15/16	4 3/4	4 7/8	+ 1/8
	15	8 1/2	ColonlBcgp	CNB	.44f	4.9	8	938	9 1/4	8 15/16	9	– 1/16
	8 9/16	6 1/16	♣ColonlHiInco	CXE	.48	7.3	...	259	6 9/16	6 1/2	6 9/16	– 1/16
	10 1/2	7 7/8	♣ColonlIntmk	CMK	.89	11.0	...	55	8 1/8	8 1/8	8 1/8	– 1/16
	6 3/4	4 15/16	♣ColonIntHi	CIF	.70a	12.6	...	331	5 5/8	5 9/16	5 9/16	...
	11 9/16	8 3/8	♣ColonlInvMun	CXH	.60f	6.8	...	13	8 7/8	8 3/4	8 7/8	+ 1/8
	8 3/16	5 3/8	♣ColonlMuni	CMU	.44	8.0	...	366	5 9/16	5 7/16	5 1/2	– 1/8
	28 7/8	21 3/4	♣ColonlProp	CLP	2.40f	9.9	...	282	24 1/2	24 3/16	24 3/16	– 5/16
	25	15 5/8	♣ColonlProp pfA		2.19	11.5	...	64	19 1/4	18 7/8	19	– 1/16
	66 5/16	43 7/8	ColumEngy	CG	.90	1.4	21	8013	64 15/16	62 1/2	62 9/16	– 2 7/16
	32 7/16	16 67/128	ColumHCA	COL	.08	.4	21	41931	23 1/16	22 1/8	22 11/16	– 7/16
	26	21 3/4	ClmbsSo A	CSJ	2.09	9.1	...	20	23 1/4	22 5/8	23	+ 1/16
	43	**11 1/4**	**Comdisco**	**CDO**	**.10**	**.3**	**cc**	**17189**	**40 5/8**	**37 1/16**	**39 7/8**	**+ 2 9/16**
	26 1/8	21	ComEd TOPrS		2.12	9.3	...	62	23	22 13/16	22 13/16	...
	70	39 7/16	Comerica	CMA	1.60f	3.9	10	5201	40 15/16	39 11/16	40 9/16	– 1/16
	18 5/8	6 7/16	CmfrtSysUSA	FIX		...	6	374	7 7/16	7 1/8	7 3/8	+ 3/16
	44 41/64	34	ComrcBcpNJ	CBH	.98b	2.8	16	461	34 7/8	34	34 11/16	– 1/4
	26 3/4	22 3/4	CommCap pfT		2.19	9.6	...	23	22 7/8	22 3/4	22 3/4	– 5/16
	29 3/16	20 3/4	♣CommrcGpInc	CGI	1.12	4.0	10	444	28 1/2	27 1/4	28 1/4	+ 15/16
	25 7/16	13 1/4	ComrclFed	CFB	.28	2.0	8	1080	13 7/8	13 5/8	13 3/4	– 1/16
	19 9/16	10 1/2	ComrclIntech	TEC	.60	3.2	17	186	18 11/16	18 1/8	18 5/8	+ 3/8
	34 3/16	19 11/16	CmrclMtls	CMC	.52	1.7	10	107	31 13/16	31 1/8	31 5/16	+ 1/16
	13 13/16	9 7/16	CmrclNetRlty	NNN	1.24	12.2	9	682	10 1/4	10	10 1/8	– 1/16
	46 3/8	16 3/4	Commscope	CTV		...	26	15784	34 1/4	31 15/16	33 1/2	+ 1 3/8
	30 7/16	21	CmntyBkSys	CBU	1.00	4.7	9	46	21 1/8	21 1/16	21 1/16	– 1/16
▲	9 1/2	4 1/4	Copel ADS	ELP	.28e	2.9	...	4309	9 3/4	9 1/16	9 11/16	+ 5/16
←	**45 1/4**	**8 3/8**	**CompnhiaSidr**	**SID**	**1.51e**	**4.8**	**...**	**1514**	**31 1/4**	**30 1/2**	**31 1/4**	**+ 1 1/2**
	44 7/16	18 1/4	♣Compaq	CPQ	.10f	.4	78	171599	26 3/4	25 5/8	25 13/16	– 5/8
	11 7/8	4 7/8	CompUSA	CPU		...	dd	12229	9 11/16	9 1/2	9 5/8	...
	79 7/16	32 1/8	CptrAssoc	CA	.08	.1	54	26860	74 3/8	72 5/8	72 3/4	...
	94 15/16	52 3/8	CptrSci	CSC		...	37	10349	83 5/8	80 5/16	81 3/4	– 2 1/16
	21 7/8	12 5/16	♣CptrTask	TSK	.05	.3	15	215	15 5/16	14 3/4	14 13/16	– 1/2
	19 7/8	12 1/8	CompxInt A	CIX	.25e	1.3	12	232	18 7/8	18 5/8	18 7/8	+ 3/8
	37 1/16	15 3/8	Comsat	CQ	.20	1.2	54	685	17	16 1/2	16 5/8	– 3/8
	25 7/16	17 5/16	ComsatCap pfA		2.03	10.1	...	97	20 3/16	20	20 1/16	– 1/16
	5 7/8	**2 3/16**	**ComstkRes**	**CRK**		**...**	**dd**	**4540**	**3 15/16**	**3 1/2**	**3 7/8**	**+ 7/16**
▼	32	18 3/16	ConAgra	CAG	.81	4.4	25	29695	18 11/16	17 7/8	18 1/4	– 5/16
	25 9/16	22 1/2	ConAgraCap pfA		2.25	9.5	...	44	23 15/16	23 3/4	23 3/4	– 3/16
▼	20 3/16	16 3/4	ConAgraCap pfB		1.37e	8.2	...	62	16 3/4	16 1/2	16 3/4	– 1/8
	25 15/16	24	ConAgraCap pfC		2.34	9.6	...	58	24 1/2	24 3/8	24 7/16	...
	7 3/16	3 3/16	♣ConeMills	COE		...	dd	232	4	3 7/8	4	– 1/16
	25 1/2	15 5/16	Conectiv	CIV	.88	5.7	dd	2694	15 11/16	15 5/16	15 3/8	– 3/8
	43	26 5/16	Conectiv A	CIVA	3.20	11.8	...	171	27 3/16	26 3/8	27 1/8	+ 13/16
	9 7/16	2 5/8	Congoleum A	CGM		...	5	99	3 3/8	3 3/8	3 3/8	...
	31 1/4	**19 1/2**	**Conoco A**	**COCA**	**.76**	**3.5**	**19**	**17385**	**21 3/4**	**20 1/2**	**21 3/4**	**+ 1 5/16**
n	**29 3/8**	**19 5/8**	**Conoco B**	**COCB**	**.19**	**.9**	**...**	**24591**	**21 13/16**	**20 3/4**	**21 1/2**	**+ 1 3/8**
n	25 1/2	21	Conseco TOPrS		2.36	10.8	...	159	22	21 7/8	21 15/16	+ 1/16
	37 7/8	14 1/16	Conseco	CNC	.60	3.8	5	10279	16 1/8	15 5/8	15 3/4	– 7/16
	26	20	Conseco pfG		2.25	11.1	...	180	20 13/16	20 1/4	20 1/4	– 1/4
	46 3/8	21 3/16	ConsecoFel PRIDES		3.50	15.9	...	95	22 11/16	22	22	– 7/8
	26 1/4	19 7/8	Conseco pfT		2.29	11.0	...	64	20 15/16	20 3/4	20 7/8	– 1/16
	26 3/4	18 1/4	Conseco pfV		2.18	11.1	...	282	20 1/8	19 5/8	19 11/16	– 3/8

SOURCE: *Wall Street Journal*, 17 February 2000, C6.

corporation's managers control the firm and inhibit corporate takeovers that are unfriendly to the incumbent management.*

Each issue of classified common stock assigns different liquidation and voting rights to the classes of stock it creates. Issues of classified stock can be custom-made, so they differ considerably.

HENRY FORD'S FAMILY

EXAMPLE

Ford Motor Company Class B common stock, owned by the Ford family, controls about 40% of the corporation's voting power. The Ford family's Class B stock only comprises about 15% of the aggregate market value of all outstanding stock in the Ford Motor Company. Each share of Class B stock grants the Ford family 8 votes, which are used to elect interested family members to the corporation's board of directors and otherwise control of the firm that was founded by their illustrious ancestor.

---

* In 1924 the New York Stock Exchange stopped listing issues of nonvoting, classified stock. In total disregard of the NYSE's rule, General Motors Corporation came out with what it called its Class E stock when it acquired the Electronics Data Systems (EDS) Corporation in 1984. The prospect of not being able to trade GM shares would deny the NYSE so much brokerage income that the Exchange immediately reevaluated its admirable policy of delisting corporations that issued classified stock. Generating commission income seemed more important than maintaining the "one-stock-one-vote" principle that is the basis for what the U.S. State Department proudly calls "shareholders' democracy." A few years later the NYSE forbid new listings (which typically trade in low volume) from having classified stock while permitting the large, old firms like GM to continue trading classified stock. Officers of the Securities and Exchange Commission (SEC) made public statements in favor of the "one-share-one-vote" principle, but the SEC did not mandate a national policy on the matter.

Tracking Stocks. **Tracking stocks** are equity securities issued by corporations that want separate listings for one or more divisions of the firm. The first tracking stocks were issued during the mid-1980s when General Motors (GM) created separate shares for its glamorous subsidiaries—Electronic Data Systems (EDS) and Hughes Electronics. Donaldson, Lufkin, and Jenrette (DLJ) has a tracking stock for its electronic brokerage, DLJdirect. The Ziff-Davis Corporation has stock outstanding on its ZDNET subsidiary. Tracking stocks promise investors convenient ways to own high-flying growth stocks without taking the risks typically associated with small, rapidly growing firms. Initial studies indicate that the tracking stocks are poor investments that do not deliver what their investors hoped. It seems that the management of a corporation cannot alter the corporation's aggregate stock market price merely by carving the corporation's equity ownership up into pieces.[8]

An IPO. A new issue of common stock is called an initial public offering (IPO). Figure 5-8 shows a newspaper announcement called a **tombstone** from the *Wall Street Journal* for Teligent Incorporated's IPO of 5,000,000 shares of stock at $50 per share. The investment banking firms listed at the bottom of the tombstone comprise the **syndicate** organized temporarily to buy the shares from Teligent Inc., resell them to the investing public at a slightly higher price, and split the profit from the distribution. Since the name of Merrill Lynch & Co. is at the first syndicate member in the list, that firm is the manager of this particular IPO syndicate.

PREFERRED STOCK

Although it is a form of equity investment, preferred stock is a hybrid security that has some of the characteristics of debt, such as fixed-income. Investors buying preferred stock have legal priority (seniority) over common stockholders with respect to earnings and, in bankruptcy, with respect to their claim on assets. Preferred stockholders are in a junior position relative to the corporate bondholders. Preferred stockholders typically receive a greater after-tax rate of return on their investment than bondholders in compensation for the greater risk they bear.* However, they usually receive a lesser rate of return than the common stockholder because they assume less risk than the common investors. Unlike common stock, preferred stock is usually limited in the amount of cash dividends it can receive. If the firm is prosperous, the preferred stock receives only the preferred's stipulated dividend; all the residual earnings go to the firm's common stockholders. In terms of corporate control, if an issue of preferred has any voting rights, the preferred stockholder usually is in a better position than the bondholder. Common stockholders have the most control since they are almost *always* given full voting rights.

The Rights of Preferred Stockholders

Preferred stock investors have many rights, but fewer than common stockholders do. Since preferred stockholders stand to gain more from cash dividends than from capital appreciation, cash dividends are important to preferred stock investors.

Cumulative Cash Dividends. Most of the preferred issues outstanding pay **cumulative cash dividends.** Cumulative means omitted dividends accumulate and are not lost. If the corporation omits a preferred dividend payment, or any part of it, the omitted dividend is not

---

* Preferred stockholders may receive smaller rates of return than bondholders on a pretax basis because of the tax-advantaged dividends earned by corporate owners of preferred stock.

FIGURE 5-8 Tombstone for IPO of Common Stock

This announcement is under no circumstances to be construed as an offer to sell or as a solicitation of an offer to buy any of these securities. The offering is made only by the Prospectus Supplement and the Prospectus to which it relates.

April 3, 2000

5,000,000 Shares

Teligent™

Teligent, Inc.

Class A Common Stock

Price $50 Per Share

Copies of the Prospectus Supplement and the Prospectus to which it relates may be obtained in any State or jurisdiction in which this announcement is circulated from only such of the under-signed or other dealers or brokers as may lawfully offer these securities in such State or jurisdiction.

Merrill Lynch & Co.

Goldman, Sachs & Co.

Salomon Smith Barney

Credit Suisse First Boston

Chase H&Q	**Deutsche Banc Alex. Brown**	**Lehman Brothers**
Friedman Billings Ramsey	Robertson Stephens	PaineWebber Incorporated
Morgan Stanley Dean Witter		Prudential Volpe Technology Group A unit of Prudential Securities
BB&T Capital Markets A division of Scott & Stringfellow		Ladenburg Thalmann & Co. Inc.

The syndicate of investment banking firms listed at the bottom of the tombstone banded together temporarily to underwrite and distribute an initial public offering (IPO) of common stock priced at $250 million to raise capital for the Teligent Corporation. Table 6-2 in Chapter 6 provides details about investment banking firms.

SOURCE: *Wall Street Journal*, 13 April 2000, C25.

lost but must be made up in a later year before any dividends can be paid to the common stockholders. In the United States preferred stockholders are legally entitled to dividend payments, the way bond investors are entitled to coupon interest, regardless of whether or not the corporation has any earnings.

Noncumulative Dividends. The less popular noncumulative preferred stock is entitled to its promised rate of cash dividends only if the issuing corporation earns enough to cover that year's dividend payment. If the firm's earnings are insufficient some year, the preferred stockholders will not get a cash dividend that year. Missed dividends will not be paid in future years—they are not cumulative. To protect noncumulative preferred investors from being exploited by common stockholders who want to keep all the corporation's earnings for their common stock dividends, the law in most countries forbids a corporation from paying cash dividends to its common stock if it has missed a preferred cash dividend during that dividend payment period.

Fixed and Adjustable Dividends. Some issues of preferred stock pay adjustable rates of cash dividends that fluctuate to reflect changing market conditions. Adjustable (floating rate) cash dividends are unusual. Preferred cash dividends are usually a stipulated dollar amount per year. For example, the Mississippi Power Company issued 150,000 shares of perpetual preferred stock that has a par value of $100 per share. These preferreds have a per share cash dividend which is fixed at $12 per year and will never change.

Federal Income Tax Exemption. In the United States the same corporation's income can be taxed at three times:

◆ The partially owned subsidiary corporation pays income taxes on its operating earnings.

◆ The parent corporation pays income taxes on the cash dividend income from its investment in the stock of the partially owned subsidiary.

◆ The investor in the parent corporation pays personal income taxes on income from the parent corporation.

Triple taxation inhibits corporate investment and the nation's economic development. To reduce triple taxation the U.S. Internal Revenue Service (IRS) exempts from federal income taxes 70% of intercorporate cash dividend payments paid by both common and preferred stock. This means, for instance, that if another corporation invests in the Mississippi Power Company's preferred stock that pays cash dividends of $12, only 30%, or $3.60 of each $12 dividend, is taxable if it is paid to a corporate investor. As a result of the intercorporate cash dividend exemption in the United States, corporations are the biggest preferred stock investors. Some other federal governments provide similar tax exemptions.

Voting Rights. Decades ago most people thought that, as long as holders of preferred stock received their cash dividends, they should have no voice in managing the company. More recently, there has been a trend to give preferred shares full voting rights. Moreover, nonvoting preferred stock may become voting stock if preferred dividend payments are missed for a stated length of time.

Additional Rights. Preferred stockholders have some of the same rights as common stockholders. Preferred stockholders have the right to receive a stock certificate if they want it, the right to buy and sell their security anytime they wish, and the right to receive information about the issuer.

Other Aspects of Preferred Stock

Preferred's Par Value. Most preferred stock has a par value. When it does, the dividend rights and call prices are usually stated in terms of the par value. These amounts are stated explicitly if the preferred has no par value. As with common stock, preferred with a par value has no advantage over preferred that has no par value.

Call Feature. Relative to common stock financing, the cash dividend guarantee of preferred stock increases the issuing corporation's vulnerability to adverse conditions and reduces its financial flexibility. That's why corporations that issue preferred usually want to call in their preferred shares if they become able to do so. As with a bond redemption, a preferred stock redemption is allowed only after a public announcement is made in advance of such action, and a call premium of from 5% to 20% of par is usually paid for the stock that is called.

Redemption. Nearly every issue of preferred stock is redeemable in one way or another. Most issues of preferred have either a sinking fund or a call provision that permits the issuer to purchase the shares before they mature. Some issues contain conversion provisions. Convertible preferred stock allows the issuer to encourage investors to convert their preferred stock into common stock by making it profitable for the investor to convert. The main reason issuers want to redeem is because financing costs (interest rates) decline after the preferred stock is issued.

Types of Preferred Stock

Participating preferred stock, like a participating bond, is uncommon.[9] Both are entitled to a fixed rate of cash dividends (or coupon interest) and, in addition, a share of the earnings available to be paid to the common stock.

Issues of preferred stock with adjustable rather than fixed rates of cash dividend are called adjustable-rate preferreds. Typically, these issues had their dividend rates tied to LIBOR or the market interest rates on Treasury Bonds and were adjustable quarterly to reflect current market interest rates. Some issues allowed their rate of cash dividend payments to fall no lower than some specified floor, such as 7.5%, and rise no higher than some ceiling, such as 15.5%. Corporate investors bought most of the adjustable-rate preferred stocks because U.S. tax law makes 70% of intercorporate cash dividends tax-exempt.[10]

Money market preferred stock (MMPS) is reissued with a new cash dividend rate so frequently it behaves like an adjustable rate preferred. The MMPS typically has a brief life— some issues have lives of only 7 weeks.* MMPS are typically offered in large denominations, such as $100,000, because they are targeted at large corporate investors. These issues are often sold at a **Dutch auction** in which potential buyers bid for the stock by offering to accept a certain rate of cash dividends for the short life of the MMPS. The entire issue is sold at the lowest dividend rate bid that will provide shares for all the bidders submitting the lowest bid and all feasible bids above it.[11]

One way investment bankers seek profitable new business is by creating new hybrid securities. Most of these products fail to trade in sufficient volume to generate profits for their creators, and they are never issued again.

THE BOTTOM LINE

Money Market Securities. Although money market securities come in many forms, they all mature in less than 1 year and involve very little default risk. All money market securities pay

---

* Federal income tax laws in the United States allow corporate investors that hold a preferred stock investment 46 days or more to be exempt from federal income tax on 70% of the cash dividends received. This intercorporate tax-exemption explains why some corporations invest in preferred stock—and, in particular, the short-term MMPS.

low rates of interest and are actively traded in liquid markets. Dealers carry inventories of money market securities, and brokers that work for the money market dealer firms help them make a liquid market.

Treasury bills are money market securities issued by the U.S. federal government; other countries offer similar securities. Manufacturing and service corporations, banks, and governments issue commercial paper, negotiable CDs, banker's acceptances, federal funds, Eurodollar loans, repos, and other money market instruments. The prices of most money market securities are based on the bank discount pricing conventions.

Implicit Versus Explicit Interest Payments. Instead of paying coupon interest, most money market securities and other longer-term debt securities make no explicit interest payments to their investors. U.S. Treasury bills and zero coupon bonds, for instance, make implicit interest payments by issuing debt securities at original-issue discounts (OIDs) from their maturity values. The gradual price gains these discounted securities experience, as their prices rise from their discounted issue price up to their maturity values, provides income for their investors. More frequently, fixed income securities make periodic interest payments in the form of coupon interest payments.

Fixed-Income Securities. Debt securities come in many forms. The securities issued by the U.S. Treasury have maturities ranging from 3-month Treasury bills to maturities as long as the 30-year Treasury bonds. Bonds issued by various agencies are also supported by the U.S. government. Because they involve the risk of bankruptcy, a wide range of credit ratings, and different issuer objectives, corporate bonds are more diverse than government bonds. Examples include the 100-year bonds issued by a few corporations during the 1990s and the subordinated debentures that have been issued by corporations for decades.

Most municipal bonds fit into two major categories—general-obligation (GO) bonds or limited-obligation bonds. GO bonds are backed by the full faith and credit of the issuing municipality. Limited-obligation bonds do not enjoy such strong support from the issuing municipality. Revenue bonds, one popular kind of limited-obligation bonds, are used to finance projects like toll bridges or public swimming pools. Revenues from the project are the only source of money available to pay off revenue bonds.

Securities issued by the U.S. Treasury are generally considered to be default-free. Corporate bonds are riskier because there is always the possibility the corporation might go bankrupt. Protective provisions in the indenture contract that governs the terms of a corporate bond issue can furnish significant protection to investors if the issuer becomes financially embarrassed. Collateral or a sinking fund, for instance, can provide protection for bond investors in a bankruptcy proceeding.

Equity Securities. The common stockholder has the right to receive a certificate to evidence share ownership, to receive dividends, to vote at the stockholders' meetings, and, in many states, the preemptive right to maintain a proportionate share in the corporation's assets, earnings, and voting control. But, in return for these advantages the common shareholders are forced to accept (1) a residual claim on the corporation's earnings after all other bills have been paid and (2) the last claim on the assets if the corporation goes bankrupt. If the corporation prospers, however, these residual rights can become lucrative as its stock price soars.

Some issues of preferred stock have infinite lives while other issues are scheduled to mature and repay their principal within a few months. Unlike common stockholders, preferred stockholders participate in the corporation's earnings to only a limited extent. Most preferreds also promise a fixed rate of cash dividends, although some issues pay cash dividends that are adjustable. If the preferred issue is cumulative, any cash dividends that are missed may be collected eventually, unless the issuer goes bankrupt. Some issues of preferred

TABLE 5-6	Contrasting Different Categories of One Corporation's Securities with U.S. Treasury Bonds			
Types of Security	Risk	Expected Return	Control	Liquidity
Coke's common stock	Most, 1	Most, 1	Most, 1	2
Coke's preferred stock	2	2	2	3
Coke's bond	3	3	3	Least, 4
U.S. Treasury bond	Least, 4	Least, 4	Least, 4	Most, 1

stock allow their owners to vote at the stockholders meeting in the event that the preferred dividends are in arrears.

Table 5-6 is a company-specific comparison of U.S. Treasury bonds and different types of securities issued by the Coca-Cola Corporation.* The four securities rankings with respect to risk (probability of default), expected return (probable gain), control (voice in management), and liquidity (marketability) are contrasted. These rankings are representative of thousands of other corporations.

QUESTIONS

Q5-1 (Money market securities) List and describe five characteristics that all money market securities have in common.

Q5-2 (Discount instruments) What is meant when a security is said to be a "discount instrument"?

Q5-3 (Call provisions) Is a call provision in the indenture helpful or detrimental to bond investors? Explain.

Q5-4 (Municipal bonds) What characteristics of municipal bonds are unique and important to the potential investor?

Q5-5 (T-bill pricing) True, false, or uncertain: The ask price on a $10,000 Treasury bill that matures in 6 months is quoted at a discount of 5%. This means that an investor can purchase the Treasury bill for $9,500. Explain.

Q5-6 (Zero coupon bonds) What are STRIPS, and why are they issued?

Q5-7 (U.S. government agency bonds) What are agencies of the U.S. government, and agency bonds?

Q5-8 (Preferred and common stock) Compare and contrast common and preferred stock.

Q5-9 (Stock splits and dividends) "Stock dividends and stock splits have no effect on the value of a company." True, false, or uncertain? Discuss.

Q5-10 (Preferred dividend payments) "If a corporation is in arrears on its preferred cash dividend payments, it is in danger of being sued in bankruptcy court by its preferred shareholders." True, false, or uncertain? Explain.

PROBLEMS

P5-1 (OIDs) The Burton-Heally Corporation has an issue of zero coupon bonds that have a $1,000 face value and mature in 12 years. The current price on these bonds is $360. What average annual rate of return would an investor

earn if he purchased the bonds at the price today and held them to maturity?

P5-2 (Cumulative voting) Kaiser Aluminum has 79,115,000 shares outstanding and a 6-member board of directors.

---

* Tax laws that exempt intercorporate cash dividend payments from income taxes, the tax-free coupons on municipal bonds, the existence of certain tax-exempt investors, the existence of different classes of common stock issued by the same corporation and other complications make Table 5-6 less than totally descriptive. The table should be viewed as an introductory framework for comparing the securities issued by a single corporation and Treasury bonds. Securities issued by different corporations are not described by Table 5-6 because, for instance, some junk bonds are riskier and pay a higher return than the common stock issued by some blue-chip corporations. More comprehensive risk-return relationships are topics for later chapters.

Kaiser is holding an election for 3 of its seats. How many shares does an investor need to control to insure that a person of her choice is elected to one of these seats if (a) noncumulative voting is used? (b) cumulative voting is used?

P5-3 (After-tax preferred stock returns) The Archstone Corporation has an issue of preferred stock that pays an annual dividend of $2.07 and is selling for $30 $\frac{7}{8}$. Calculate the after-tax, 1-year holding period return that each of the following two investors would receive, assuming that the investor purchases the stock at its current price and that the stock's price is unchanged at $30 $\frac{7}{8}$ at the end of 1 year.
  (a) Trudy, an individual investor who pays taxes at the marginal tax rate of 28%.
  (b) NationsBest Insurance Corporation, which has a marginal tax rate of 39%.

P5-4 (After-tax bond returns) Sally is an investment officer at a life insurance company that is in the 25% marginal corporate income-tax bracket. Which of the following two securities will provide the company's portfolio with the higher yield to maturity if neither defaults?

Alternative A: A new issue of AAA-grade corporate bonds selling at par with a coupon rate of 10%.

Alternative B: An issue of AAA-grade preferred stock with an 8% cash dividend rate.

Hint: Consider the tax exemption on intercorporate cash dividends in the United States and some other countries.

P5-5 (After-tax bond yields) John Stone is considering the purchase of one of the following bonds: a 7% annual coupon municipal bond or a 12% annual coupon corporate bond. Mr. Stone is in the 33% tax bracket. If both bonds are selling at par, have similar maturities, and are equally risky, which bond should he purchase? Explain.

P5-6 (One-period rate of return) Alice purchased a $1,000 face value bond issued by the United Motors Corporation (UMC) for $1,050. The bond matures in 2006, but Alice sold the bond for $1,032 after holding it for 1 year and collecting $110 in coupon interest. What was Alice's one-period rate of return, ignoring transactions costs and taxes?

P5-7 (One-period rate of return) A bond issued by the Zall Company sold for $910 on January 1, 1999. One year later, the price of the bond was $980. (a) If this bond paid $70 in interest during the year, what was its one-period rate of return? (b) What would the 1-year rate of return be if the Zall bond had sold for $800 a year later?

P5-8 (Cumulative voting common stock) Gulton Inc. has a thousand shares of common stock outstanding and its common stockholders are going to elect 6 new members to the corporation's board of directors. Gulton has a total of 12 members on its board. How many shares does a single stockholder who is acting independently have to own to be able to elect one director (a) if Gulton has noncumulative voting? (b) if Gulton has cumulative voting? *Beware*: This problem contains one sophistical fact that should be ignored.*

P5-9 (Stock's return in a stock split) The common stock of the Biddle Corporation had the following end-of-year prices and cash dividend record for 3 consecutive years.

Year	Price	Dividend
$t + 1$	$50	$2.00
$t + 2$	$30	$1.00
$t + 3$	$45	$1.50

(a) Calculate the one-period rate of return for Biddle for years $t + 2$ and $t + 3$. (b) Recalculate the rate of return for Biddle for the same 2 years assuming a 2-for-1 stock split took place during year $t + 2$.

P5-10 (Rates of return) Mr. Dowd recently sold 200 shares of Baltic Corporation's stock for $35 per share. (a) If he purchased the stock 1 year ago for $30 per share, and, during the year, received a $2 dividend per share, what one-period rate of return did he earn? (b) Assume Mr. Dowd is in a 30% tax bracket for both capital gains and cash dividend income. What one-period rate of return did he earn on an after-tax basis? *Note:* Beware of sophistry; there is some irrelevant data in this problem.

P5-11 (Intercorporate cash dividends) The Albacore Corporation owns some preferred stock issued by another corporation that pays a fixed cash dividend rate of 10%. Assume that the corporate income tax rate is 34%. What after-tax rate of return will Albacore obtain from its preferred stock investment? Show your computations and explain them.

---
* Some experienced case writers advocate the use of sophistry in cases, because real life contains sophistry. That the total number of directors is 12 is an irrelevant piece of information in solving this problem.

CFA EXAM QUESTIONS

1. (1998 CFA Sample Exam, Level 1) All else equal, which of the following bonds *most likely* would sell for the highest price (or lowest yield)?

   A. Putable debenture.
   B. Callable debenture.
   C. Putable mortgage bond.
   D. Callable mortgage bond.

2. (1986 CFA Sample Exam, Level 1) Preferred stock:
   A. Is actually a form of equity.
   B. Pays dividends not fully taxable to U.S. corporations.
   C. Is normally considered a fixed-income security.
   D. All of the above.

3. (1999 CFA Sample Exam, Level 1) The following are quotes for a U.S. Treasury bond:

Bid	Asked
102:2	102:5

If the face value of the bond is $1,000, the price an investor should pay for the bond is *closest* to:
   A. $1,020.65.
   B. $1,021.56.
   C. $1,025.00.
   D. $1,026.25.

FURTHER REFERENCES

Fabozzi, Frank J. and T. Dessa Fabozzi, Eds. *The Handbook of Fixed Income Securities*, 4th ed. Burr Ridge, IL: Irwin, 1995.

 A collection of informative essays written by experts on debt securities and preferred stock. A little algebra is used in describing some of the securities.

Fabozzi, Frank J., T. Dessa Fabozzi, and Sylvan G. Feldstein. *Municipal Bond Portfolio Management*, Burr Ridge, IL: Irwin, 1994.

 This volume provides a comprehensive discussion of municipal bonds. No mathematics is used in this investigation of municipal bond analysis.

Francis, Jack Clark and Richard Taylor. *Investments*, 2nd ed. Schaum's Outlines. New York: McGraw-Hill, 2000.

 This paperback booklet is a learning aid that contains numerous solved investments problems. The order of the chapters does not correspond to the chapter order of any investment book. For example, Schaum's Chapters 1, 2, 3, 5, and 6 are relevant to this textbook's Chapter 5.

Ross, Steve A., Randolph W. Westerfield, and Jeffrey Jaffe. *Corporate Finance*, 4th ed. Chicago: Irwin, 1996.

 Chapter 14 of this managerial finance textbook discusses common stock, preferred stock, and bonds in an informative fashion. Easy-to-understand numerical examples are provided.

Stigum, Marcia. *The Money Market*, 3d ed. Homewood, IL: Dow Jones-Irwin, 1990.

 A detailed, nonmathematical explanation of money market securities and the markets where they are traded. This volume presents the historical development and additional details of the money market securities. Stigum's book contains about one detailed chapter on every money market discussed in this chapter.

Stigum, Marcia. *Money Market Calculations: Yields, Break-Evens, and Arbitrage.* Homewood, IL: Dow Jones-Irwin, 1981.

 As the title implies, this book explains the vocabulary, presents the formulas, and shows how to perform the calculations to determine the price quotations and yields for various kinds of debt securities in a manner that conforms to the accepted financial conventions.

ENDNOTES

[1] For more detail about banker's acceptances, see J. S. G. Wilson, *Money Markets: The International Perspective* (London: Thomson Business Press, 1993).

[2] For more details about inflation-indexed bonds see Stanley Fischer, "The Demand for Indexed Bonds," *Journal of Political Economy* (June 1975). Also see Richard Roll, "U.S. Treasury Inflation-Indexed Bonds: The Design of a New Security," *The Journal of Fixed Income*, 6, no. 3 (December 1996), 9–28. See R. McFall Lamm, Jr., "Asset Allocation Implications of Inflation Protection Securities," *Journal of Portfolio Management*, 24, no. 4 (Summer 1998), 93–100.

[3] Merton Miller and Franco Modigliani, "Dividend Policy, Growth and the Valuation of Shares," *Journal of Business* (Oct 1961): 411–33.

[4] For an interesting discussion about why corporations split their stock, see Chris J. Muscarella and Michael R. Vetsuypens, "Stock Splits: Signaling or Liquidity?" *Journal of Financial Economics*, 42, no. 1 (1997).

[5] Chapter 8 reviews a classic study by E. Fama, L. Fisher, M. Jensen, and R. Roll, "The Adjustment of Stock Prices to New Information," *International Economic Review* 20, no. 2: 1–21.

[6] Some empirical evidence suggests that book value per share has some effect on stock prices. See B. Rosenberg, K. Reid, and R. Lanstein, "Persuasive Evidence of Market Inefficiency," *Journal of Portfolio Management* (spring 1985): 9–16. More recently, see E. Fama and K. French, "The Cross-Section of Expected Stock Returns," *Journal of Finance* (June 1992). For evidence that the book value/market value ratio is irrelevant see Dongcheol Kim, "A Re-Examination of the Firm Size, Book-To-Market, and Earnings-Price in the Cross-Section of Expected Returns," *Journal of Financial and Quantitative Analysis* 32, no. 4 (December 1997): 463–89.

[7] Investigations into classified common stock have been done by R. C. Lease, J. J. McConnell, and W. H. Mikkelson, "The Market Value of Control in Publicly Traded Corporations," *Journal of Financial Economics* (April 1983). Lease, McConnell, and Mikkelson found that the market prices of shares that had superior voting rights sold for a few percent higher price than shares that had inferior voting rights. Also see H. DeAngelo and L. DeAngelo, 1985, "Managerial Ownership of Voting Rights: A Study of Public Corporations with Dual Classes of Common Stock," *Journal of Financial Economics* 14 (1985): 33–69; M. Partch, "The Creation of a Class of Limited Voting Common Stock and Shareholders' Wealth," *Journal of Financial Economics* 18, no. 2: 313–40.

[8] For details about tracking stocks, see Matthew T. Billett and Anand M. Vijh, "Long-Term Returns from Tracking Stocks," Unpublished Research Paper from Tippie College of Business, University of Iowa, March 2000.

[9] For detailed studies of preferred stock, see J. S. Bildersee, "Some Aspects of the Performance of Preferred Stock," *Journal of Finance* (December 1973): 1187–1201. Also D. B. Smith, "A Framework for Analyzing Non-Convertible Preferred Stock," *Journal of Financial Research* (Summer 1983): 127–39. See also Emanuel Derman, "A Theoretical Model for Valuing Preferred Stock," *Journal of Finance* (September 1983): 1133–55. See also E. H. Sorensen and C. A. Hawkins, "On the Pricing of Preferred," *Journal of Financial and Quantitative Analysis* (November 1981): 515–28.

[10] For details about investment strategies employing adjustable rate preferred stock, see Bernard J. Winger, Carl R. Chen, John D. Martin, J. William Petty and Steven C. Hayden, "Adjustable Rate Preferred Stock," *Financial Management* 15, no. 1 (spring 1986): 48–57.

[11] For an empirical analysis of so-called dividend-stripping (or cash-dividend-capture) investment strategies, see Theoharry Grammatikos, "Dividend Stripping, Risk Exposure, and the Effect of the 1984 Tax Reform Act on the Ex-Dividend Day Behavior," *Journal of Business* 62, no. 2 (April 1989): 157–73.

Those wishing to learn more about auction-type market processes should consult Michael J. Alderson, Keith C. Brown, and Scott L. Lummer, "Dutch Auction Rate Preferred Stock," *Financial Management* 16, no. 2 (1987): 68–73; and Paul R. Milgrom and Robert J. Weber, "The Theory of Auctions and Competitive Bidding," *Econometrica* 50 (September 1982). See also R. Engelbrecht-Wiggans, M. Shubik, and R. Stark, editors, *Auctions, Bidding, and Contracting: Uses and Theory* (New York: New York University Press, 1983).

THE GLOBAL STOCK MARKET

This chapter is about stock markets and Chapter 19 is about bond markets. These chapters require special vocabulary.

A MARKET—AND RELATED CONCEPTS

A **market** is a place or communications network that puts buyers and sellers in contact so they can transact business.

A market has **informational efficiency** if it allocates resources to their most productive uses. Informational efficiency requires that market participants have access to the information that shapes market prices.

A market that minimizes the participants' transactions costs has **operational efficiency.** Some markets are more operationally efficient than other markets, and the prices of some goods can be more informationally efficient than the prices of other goods traded in the same market.

In 1997 the International Finance Corporation (IFC) compiled data on 24 developed stock markets, 70 emerging markets, and 77 small stock markets in other countries. Some of the surveyed stock markets are more than 400 years old (Germany), while others are new (Tanzania in 1998). The number of companies listed on a stock exchange ranges from two (Macedonia) to 5,840 (India). The market capitalization varies from US $2 billion (Guatemala) to US $10 trillion (NYSE). Trading on inside information is permitted at some exchanges, while it is illegal at others. Discussing all these stock markets would fill several volumes with repetitious discussions of fundamental forms that differ primarily with respect to their locations, securities listings, and transactional statistics.

This chapter focuses on a few equity markets that are developing along different lines—primarily within the United States. Various brokerage services, competing primary markets, diverse secondary markets, the third and fourth markets, and an assortment of electronic communication networks (ECNs) are examined.

THE GLOBAL STOCK MARKET

The aggregate market capitalization of all equity shares in the world grew at an average rate of 14.8% per year, from $9.6 trillion in 1990 to over $35 trillion in 2000, measured in U.S. dollars. Figure 1-4 in Chapter 1 and Table 6-1 in this chapter show that, while the world's stock market grew, the Tokyo Stock Exchange's (TSE's) share of the global market shrunk from 30.5% in 1990 to 12.7% for the year 1999. In 1990 the TSE had the largest stock market capitalization (price per share times shares outstanding) in the world. By 2000 the TSE's market share had fallen to third place. This change highlights the fact that financial capital is a *highly mobile* factor of production.

North America increased its share of the world's stock market from 28.0% in 1990 to 50.28% in 1999. The U.S. economy flourished during the 1990s and that helped the New York Stock Exchange (NYSE) become the largest stock market in the world. The National Association of Securities Dealers Automated Quotation (Nasdaq) became the second largest equity market in the world.

A striking change that *cannot* be perceived in Figure 1-4 and Table 6-1 are the job losses at stock exchanges around the world. Large stock exchanges, in London, Tokyo, and Paris, and some smaller exchanges automated many experienced employees out of their jobs. An increasing number of stock market mergers also wiped out jobs.

Table 6-1 enumerates components of the world stock market and highlights their disparities. The difference in the total capitalizations of the NYSE and the stock exchange in Colombo is striking. The **market turnover ratios** at the individual stock exchanges, stated as a percentage of total shares listed on the exchange, varies over a wide range too, because (1) different stock exchanges measure turnover differently and (2) some markets are more active than others.

Stock markets are active in every time zone of the world. Figure 17-2 in Chapter 17 illustrates how foreign exchange markets operate around the world and around the clock; stock markets work the same hours. To summarize: New technology permits fewer people to manage an increasing number of transactions faster, the market shares of the individual marketplaces are changing rapidly, and a global stock market is coming together.

BROKERAGE SERVICES

Brokerage services are provided by brokers and dealers. **Brokers** are commission sales people that are employed by a **dealer** like Merrill Lynch. Brokers have no money invested in the brokerage house's (dealer's) inventory of securities. Brokers help create markets in securities by buying and selling from their employer's inventory. Dealers own inventories of different securities that turn over continuously. The dealer's capital invested in inventories is at risk.

Investors give their buy and sell orders to brokers. Practically every brokerage firm extends credit (margin accounts) to clients because they want their clients to be able to use the borrowed money to do more trading and generate more commission income for the brokerage. Brokerage firms will hold the clients' securities in safekeeping and collect cash dividends without charging for the service. The following discussion considers three competing types of stock brokerage services: full-service brokers, discount brokers, and electronic brokers.

TABLE 6-1   Market Capitalizations of Domestic Companies and Turnover Rates at Stock Markets Around the World

Time Zone	Exchange	February 2000, in US $ millions	Market Share of World's Capital	1998 Turnover Ratio[a]
North America	Amex[b]	126,307.0	0.33%	231.6%
	Bermuda	1,324.4	0.00%	NA
	CDNX	20,057.0	0.05%	NA
	Chicago	322.0	0.00%	13.9%
	Mexico	156,835.2	0.41%	26.8%
	Montreal	1,219.8	0.00%	7.7%
	Nasdaq	5,829,402.1	15.13%	257.7%
	NYSE	10,216,607.8	26.52%	69.9%
	Toronto	860,266.6	2.23%	59.1%
	Subtotal:	17,212,341.9	44.69%	
South America	Buenos Aires	64,266.8	0.17%	51.3%
	Lima	13,084.8	0.03%	22.7%
	Rio de Janeiro	238,235.1	0.62%	14.8%
	Santiago	71,484.0	0.19%	7.5%
	Sao Paulo	240,669.3	0.62%	66.4%
	Subtotal:	627,740.0	1.63%	
Europe, Africa, Middle East	Amsterdam	670,314.5	1.74%	71.4%
	Athens	180,705.5	0.47%	82.7%
	Barcelona (TSV)	404,087.1	1.05%	11.0%
	Barcelona (REV)			73.3%
	Bilbao (TSV)	427,500.9	1.11%	9.5%
	Bilbao (RFV)			66.7%
	Brussels	156,157.9	0.41%	27.8%
	Copenhagen	104,765.5	0.27%	65.3%
	Germany	1,551,746.5	4.03%	137.9%
	Helsinki	377,240.8	0.98%	54.5%
	Irish	66,496.4	0.17%	59.9%
	Istanbul	111,021.6	0.29%	143.4%
	Italy	837,737.1	2.17%	102.3%
	Johannesburg	232,998.5	0.60%	27.0%
	Lisbon	79,720.1	0.21%	82.2%
	Ljubljana	2,901.0	0.01%	30.3%
	London	2,827,406.6	7.34%	47.0%
	Luxembourg	36,361.8	0.09%	4.2%

(continued)

[a]Stock exchanges use different definitions and calculation methods to compile turnover statistics. This means that all turnover figures cannot be compared between the various stock exchanges. Following the classification adopted by the European Federation of Stock Exchanges, the FIBV has split its members among two main groups: those adopting the Trading System View (TSV) and those adopting the Regulated Environment View (REV). TSV exchanges count as turnover only those transactions that pass through their trading systems or that take place on the exchange's trading floor. REV exchanges include in their turnover figures all transactions subject to supervision by the market authority (transactions by member firms, and sometimes nonmembers, with no distinction between on- and off-market and transactions made into foreign markets reported on the national market). Therefore, comparisons are not valid between stock exchanges belonging to different groups.

[b]The market capitalization of American Exchange was not available in February 2000. Thus the number listed is from 1998.

TABLE 6-1   Market Capitalizations of Domestic Companies and Turnover Rates at Stock Markets Around the World (continued)

Time Zone	Exchange	February 2000, in US$ millions	Market Share of World's Capital	1998 Turnover Ratio[a]
	Madrid (REV)	455,579.1	1.18%	170.3%
	Malta	2,004.2	0.01%	NA
	Oslo	60,798.4	0.16%	66.1%
	Paris (TSV)	1,523,585.3	3.96%	65.7%
	Paris (REV)			228.5%
	Stockholm	503,452.0	1.31%	70.0%
	Switzerland	631,166.7	1.64%	100.4%
	Tehran	19,433.5	0.05%	5.8%
	Tel-Aviv	81,133.9	0.21%	33.7%
	Vienna	30,280.8	0.08%	41.7%
	Warsaw	36,745.0	0.10%	57.8%
	Subtotal:	11,411,340.7	29.63%	
Asia, Pacific	Australian	400,592.7	1.04%	52.7%
	Colombo	1,453.9	0.00%	16.5%
	Hong Kong	634,970.6	1.65%	61.9%
	Jakarta	49,385.4	0.13%	56.8%
	Korea	258,203.7	0.67%	207.0%
	Kuala Lumpur	176,258.6	0.46%	29.8%
	New Zealand	24,222.1	0.06%	48.0%
	Osaka	2,756,294.1	7.16%	9.0%
	Philippines	38,636.9	0.10%	32.2%
	Singapore	171,001.0	0.44%	63.9%
	Taiwan	440,752.3	1.14%	314.1%
	Thailand	43,019.1	0.11%	68.8%
	Tokyo	4,271,043.7	11.09%	34.1%
	Subtotal:	9,265,834.0	24.06%	
	Total:	$38,517,256.6	100.00%	

The global stock market is comprised of many nations' stock markets. The components of the global stock market vary in terms of their locations, size, age, turnover rates, and other characteristics. The NYSE was the largest single marketplace in the world by 2000. But, since any marketplace can be replaced by a computer program, the individual stock markets are less important today than they were in the past.

SOURCE: International Federation of Stock Exchanges, Paris, France. Visit the Web site: www.fibv.com.

Full-Service Brokers

The stockbrokers (registered representatives, account executives, consultants) at most **full-service brokerage** firms are college graduates who sit at their own desks. In addition to taking buys and sell orders, extending margin credit to customers, holding the clients' securities in safekeeping, collecting cash dividends, full-service brokers also give free investment research and perform "hand-holding" services. The *hand-holding* services include pleasant telephone conversations, investment counseling, an occasional "free lunch," birthday cards, and other niceties.

Merrill Lynch, Goldman Sachs, PaineWebber, Morgan Stanley Dean Witter, and Salomon Smith Barney (a unit of Citigroup) are the most widely recognized full-service brokers in the United States. Merrill Lynch is the largest, employing 14,000 brokers. Full-service brokers charge commissions totaling $30–$150 for one small common stock transaction, with quantity discounts available for larger transactions.

> **CHURNING**   **DEFINITION**
>
> A broker's hand-holding activities sometimes include an illegal activity called "churning." A client's account is **churned** when a broker turns it over to generate commission income with little regard to whether the client profits from the trades. Although churning is illegal in the United States, it is difficult to prove churning took place if the broker obtains the client's verbal approval for each trade.

Discount Brokers Provide Limited Service

Many discount brokers are not college graduates and they work in spartan offices. Discount brokers simply take orders from their clients; they furnish little or no investment advice. If the discounters provide any investment research, it will likely be in the form of published reports from Moody's or Standard & Poor's. Most discounters provide no hand-holding services and, as a result, there is little opportunity for churning. Like most brokers, the discounters extend margin credit, hold clients' securities in safekeeping, and accumulate the client's cash dividends and interest income. Charles Schwab & Company, Quick & Reilly, Muriel Siebert, Jack White & Company, Fidelity Investments, and Vanguard Brokerage Services (VBS) are the largest discount brokers in the United States, and there are many smaller discount brokers. Commissions at the discount brokers range from $20 to $50 for one small common stock trade. Quantity discounts are available.

Many Electronic Brokers Provide Self-Service

Electronic brokers take buy and sell orders over the Internet. Most provide no hand-holding The investor/client might not even speak with a human as a self-service transaction is executed. Some electronic brokers provide printed investment research; if so, it might be free or there may be a modest charge. The best-known electronic brokers are listed in the following Example.

ELECTRONIC BROKERS   **EXAMPLE**

Access VBS (unit of Vanguard Brokerage Services in Valley Forge, Pennsylvania)

Accutrade (Omaha, NE)

Ameritrade is a large Omaha, NE firm with very low fees.

American Express Financial Direct (Minneapolis, MN)

Archipelago is a Chicago firm owned by Terra Nova, which is owned by a group that includes Goldman Sachs; Merrill Lynch; J. P. Morgan, Morgan Stanley Dean Witter, E*Trade; Instinet; a GE subsidiary named CNBC, BNP Paris Group, and American Century.* Archipelago partners with the Pacific Stock Exchange.

Attain (electronic order processor)*

Brass Utility, or **Brut,** is owned by Automated Securities Clearance, Merrill Lynch, Morgan Stanley Dean Witter, Lehman Brothers, DLJ, Knight/Trimark Group, Bear Stearns, Susquehanna, Cantor, and Sun Microsystems.*

CyberCorp.Com in Austin, TX supports day traders; it was purchased by C. Schwab.

Island ECN is a large order matching system owned by Datek Online of Iselin, NJ, TA Associates, and Bernard Arnault of LVMH.*

Discover Brokerage (a San Francisco unit of Morgan Stanley Dean Witter)

DLJdirect (Jersey City, NJ, unit of investment banker Donaldson, Lufkin & Jenrette [DLJ])

E*Trade (headquartered in Palo Alto, CA)

Fidelity Brokerage (unit of Fidelity mutual funds in Boston)

Hull Group in Chicago owns shares in Archipelago, Wit Capital, Optimark, TradePoint, TradeWeb, Bridge Information and, in turn, is owned by Goldman Sachs.

Market XT is owned by Salomon Smith Barney, Lehman Brothers, Polaris Venture Partners, Madoff Technologies, and Morgan Stanley Dean Witter.*

Merrill Lynch OnLine began operations in 2000; it was the last large broker to go on line.

NexTrade (electronic order processor)*

Jack White Online (San Diego subsidiary of Jack White & Company)

Quick & Reilly (NYC subsidiary of the well-known discounter of the same name)

REDIBook is owned by Spear, Leeds, and Kellog; Lehman Brothers, DLJ, TD Waterhouse, Charles Schwab, CSFB, Fidelity, National Discount Brokers, PaineWebber, Bank of America, and Fleet Securities.*

Charles Schwab is a San Francisco subsidiary of the well-known discount broker.

Siebert (NYC subsidiary of the discounter Muriel Siebert)

SURETRADE (Lincoln, RI)

Tradebook is owned by Bloomberg Corporation in NYC.*

Tradepoint is owned by Morgan Stanley Dean Witter, Instinet, J. P. Morgan, Hull Group, and UBS Warburg.

Timber Hill Group (Greenwich, CT)

Wall Street Access (NYC)

Waterhouse Securities is owned by Toronto-Dominion Bank.

Wells Trade (Houston, TX operation owned by Wells Fargo)

Some electronic brokerages are simple little ventures while others are large sophisticated operations that have powerful backers. Note that Goldman Sachs, Merrill Lynch, J. P. Morgan, and Morgan Stanley Dean Witter have each invested in several competing electronic brokerages; this was apparently done to give them interests in whatever new technology develops.

Electronic brokers charge fees that range from almost free to $35 per trade, and their market share of the business is growing. Almost all brokers give quantity discounts.

---

*   In 1996 the SEC issued its Order Handling Rule, which allows several order handling systems to become electronic communications networks (ECNs). ECNs are discussed later in this chapter.

TRANSACTING

When an investor calls a broker about executing a transaction, two questions are likely to arise:

♦ The broker will ask what type of order the client wishes to place.

♦ The broker may offer to lend money to the client to facilitate a larger transaction.

Types of Trading Orders

A trade begins when an investor gives a broker an order to buy or sell. As they endeavor to maximize their trading gains and/or minimize their costs, investors can select from several different types of trading orders.

A **market order** tells the broker to buy or sell some specified security as soon as possible at the current market price. Market orders are the simplest, most common type of order. They are executed immediately with virtual certainty because there are no conditions attached to these orders that might delay their execution.

A **limit order** is an order to buy or sell, with a restriction on the minimum price to be received or the maximum price to be paid. Limit orders are sometimes called *limit or better orders*. If the limit order cannot be executed immediately, the order is recorded in the market-maker's *limit order book* (LOB) and held for future execution if and when the limit price or a more advantageous price is attained. Limit orders can be combined with other requirements to create more complex orders. For instance, if the client attaches an expiration time to a limit order, the order may expire before it is executed. A problem with limit orders is that occasionally a limit order may be passed over without being executed: The security's market price may move past the limit price without being noticed by the market-maker in a fast moving market.

Stop orders *to buy* are written at prices above the current market price. Stop orders *to sell* are written at prices below the current market price. A stop order is activated and becomes a market order when the market price reaches the *stop price*. For example, a stop order to "Sell 100 KO stop 56" becomes a market order to sell 100 shares of Coca-Cola if the stock's price falls to $56. This order might also be called a *stop loss order to sell*. One advantage of using stop orders is that they are converted to market orders and market orders are always executed.

There are two dangers from using stop orders. The first is that the execution price cannot be known in advance. The order to "Sell 100 KO stop 56" might be executed at 56, 55½, 55, or less. The second danger is that the investor might be **whip-sawed** in a volatile market. A trader gets whip-sawed if he buys during a small rise that is followed immediately by a larger price fall that throws him for a loss, or if he sells during a small drop and then watches with regret as a larger price rise occurs immediately after he sells.

The **stop limit order** is a variation on the stop order: It is activated when the stop price *or a better price* is attained. When a stop limit order is activated, it is converted into a *limit order* rather than a market order. A stop limit order can be executed after the security's market price moves advantageously past the stop price, but the order will not be executed at a price that is worse than its limit price. For instance, consider a stop limit order to "Buy 100 KO at 60 stop, limit 64." A limit order to buy 100 shares of KO would be activated if KO's price rose to $60. This limit order might be exercised at $61 or $62, but it will not be exercised above its limit price of $64. Thus, if the security's price quickly rises above $64 without being noticed by the market-maker, that stop limit order will never be executed.

A *scale order* requires buying or selling part of the order at each price as the market falls (scales down) or rises (scales up). Scale orders are clerically cumbersome and not all brokers will accept them. The *fill or kill order*, or *FOK order*, has a specific price at which the order must be executed—otherwise the order is immediately canceled. FOK orders are much simpler to execute than scale orders.

Timing instructions can be attached to the orders. A **good till canceled (GTC) order** remains in effect until it is canceled. A **day order** must be filled on the day the order is issued or it will be canceled automatically. **Market on close orders** can only be executed at the day's closing price. It is impossible to list every existing type of order because some markets provide special types of orders that are not used in other markets.

Trading on Margin

New customers at securities brokerages are asked if they want to open a cash account or a margin account. Investors opening a **cash account** need only furnish their name, address, and social security number, because they must pay cash for their securities. Opening a **margin account** (See page 49) involves a longer application, because a margin account provides the client the opportunity to buy securities on credit.*

When investors buy securities on margin (credit), the shares paid for with the investor's money are collateral that is similar to the equity or down payment on an installment purchase agreement.[1] The Federal Reserve Board of Governors controls the amount that investors may borrow in U.S. markets to purchase securities. If the Federal Reserve Board stipulates a 50 percent *initial minimum margin requirement*, for instance, the investor must pay cash for at least 50 percent of the market value of the securities when they are initially purchased. The Federal Reserve's initial minimum margin requirements for retail clients' (individual investors) common stock purchases have varied from 10% in 1929 to 100% in the 1940s and have been 50% in recent years. Margin requirements also limit the amount of money brokerage firms can borrow to finance their inventories of securities, but institutional investors have different rules (lower margin requirements) than their retail clients. To make things even more complicated, the margin requirements for stocks, bonds, options, and futures contracts all differ.

To see how margins work, assume the initial margin requirement for a retail investor is 50% and an investor wishes to purchase 100 shares of a $100 stock. To pay for this [(100 shares)($100 per share) =]$10,000 investment the investor pays $5,000 cash for 50 shares and uses the 50 paid shares as collateral for a $5,000 loan from the brokerage. The $5,000 loan is used to pay for 50 additional shares. In the United States brokerages charge the **brokers' call rate** for margin loans. We will consider the investor's position after investing $5,000: (1) if the shares increase 50% to a price of $150, and (2) if the price of the shares price drops 50% to $50.

1. A 50% Gain. If the investor's shares increase in value from $100 to $150, his or her total profit will be $50 profit per share, times 100 shares, or $5,000 before interest, commissions, and taxes. Compare this $5,000 gross gain with $50 profit per share times only 50 shares, or a $2,500 gross profit, if the investor had not bought on margin. The investor's gains were larger because margin was used—as shown in the following T-account.

Assets	Liabilities and Net Worth
Market value $10,000	$5,000 debit balance (borrowed)
	$5,000 equity (initial margin)
	$10,000 total

---

* Investors who open a margin account are required by the NYSE to make a minimum initial deposit in the account of $3,000; this is enough for Merrill Lynch, for example. In contrast, Goldman-Sachs requires over $1 million as a minimum deposit to open an account. Minimum-account-size policies affect the kind of clientele the brokerage serves.

The investor's gross gain of $5,000 equals a 100% return on an investment of $5,000 of cash for the initial margin. Favorable financial leverage magnified the 50% gain in the stock's price to a [($5,000 gain)/($5,000 margin) =] 100% return on equity.

2. A 50% Loss. What if the investor's shares decreased 50% from a purchase price of $100 to only $50 per share? In this case, the current market value of the investment drops from $10,000 to $5,000. As a margin buyer, the investor has a [($50 per share loss)(100 shares) =] $5,000 loss. If the investor had not bought on margin and, instead, paid cash for only 50 shares, then the loss would have been $50 per share times 50 shares, or $2,500. Buying stock on 50% margin doubled the investor's loss. The investor's position after the stock's price falls to $50 is summarized in the following T-account.

Assets	Liabilities and Net Worth
Market value $5,000	$5,000 debit balance (borrowed)
	Zero equity (remaining margin)
	$5,000 total

The investor's total loss of $5,000 equals 100% of the $5,000 cash investment (initial margin). Financial leverage magnified the -50% price change into a -100% return on equity (all equity wiped out). In addition, margined investors must pay interest on the funds they borrow. Ignoring the interest expense, margins allow investors to magnify their gross profits and losses by the reciprocal of the margin requirement (2 times if the margin requirement is $\frac{1}{2}$, or 3 times if it is $\frac{1}{3}$).*

Margin Calls. If a margined stock decreases in value sufficiently, the investor will receive a **margin call** *(maintenance call, maintenance margin call)*. When this occurs the broker informs the client that it is necessary to put up more margin money as soon as possible. If the investor cannot come up with the additional cash within a day or two, the broker liquidates enough of the investor's securities to bring the equity (maintenance margin) in the account up to the required minimum. Liquidating the margined client's shares is easy for the brokerage firm because customers must keep their margined securities at the broker's office as collateral for their loan. If anything is left in the margin account after the margin call, forced sale of the stock, and loan repayment, the investor receives that remaining balance. By how much must the stock decrease in value before there is a margin call? Stock exchanges answer this question by stipulating a maintenance margin requirement.

According to the NYSE's **maintenance margin requirement,** a margin call must occur when the remaining equity in the account is less than 25% of the market value of the account. Stated differently, after the initial purchase is finished, a client's total loans can never exceed 75% of the market value in the account. For the investor we have just followed, a margin call would be required when the market value of the $10,000 margined purchase of common stock falls below $6,666.66 because the investor's $5,000 loan is not allowed to exceed 75% of the market value of $6,666.66.

$6,666.66	Account's total market value = (100 shares)($66.666 per share)
$\times$ 75%	Times: Maximum percentage allowed = $\times(1 - 25\%)$
$5,000.00	Minimum maintenance margin requirement

---

* Margin trading includes both margin buying and short selling on margin. Short selling was introduced in Chapter 2. For details about margin requirements, see John P. Geelan and Robert P. Rittereiser, *Margin Requirements and Practices*, 4th ed. (New York: New York Institute of Finance, 1998).

Some brokers set higher maintenance margin requirements than the 25% minimum set by the NYSE.*

INVESTMENT BANKS MAKE PRIMARY MARKETS

How do securities originate? Corporations and governments make **initial public offerings (IPOs)** of stocks and bonds into the **primary market.** Corporations and governments that already have outstanding securities sometimes raise additional capital by having a new issue of seasoned securities. **Investment bankers** find buyers for IPOs and *new issues* of previously outstanding securities.

There are a few thousand investment banking firms in the United States; most are too small to mention. Almost all large full-service brokerage firms in the United States are also investment banking firms. Table 6-2 lists details about the largest investment banks in the United States. Large investment bankers headquartered outside the United States include Credit Suisse First Boston Corporation (Switzerland), Nomura Securities (Japan), Daiwa Securities (Japan), Yamaichi Securities (Japan), Deutsche Morgan Grenfell (Germany), Banque Paribas (France), HSBC (London), Barclay's BZW (London), SBC Warburg Dillon Read (Swiss Bank Corporation, Switzerland), and NatWest (London), among others.

Four Functions Performed by Investment Bankers

Investment bankers begin each initial public offering (IPO) by (1) consulting with the issuer; then they (2) carry out the administrative duties, (3) underwrite the issue, and finally (4) distribute the securities to investors.

(Step 1) Consulting. An investment banking firm that reaches an underwriting agreement with an issuer is called that IPO's originator. The originator analyzes the client's needs and suggests a financing plan. What type of security should be issued? What amount of funds are needed? When should the new securities be issued?

In addition to consulting with the client, the originator of an IPO also manages two temporary groups. First, members of the **underwriting syndicate** share the financing and underwriting risk; these syndicates range from 5 to 200 investment banking firms, depending on the size of the issue. Second, the selling group is made up of investment banks and brokerage firms that agree to sell the securities to investors. Figure 5-8 in Chapter 5 (p. 117) shows a tombstone announcing an IPO that lists the investment banks comprising that selling group.

(Step 2) Administration. The originating investment banker ensures the IPO is done legally, helps obtain all necessary governmental permissions, has the prospectus printed, and makes the appropriate announcements.

(Step 3) Underwriting. An investment banker *underwrites* an issue by guaranteeing the issuer will receive a prespecified amount of cash for the new securities. The time from when the underwriting syndicate purchases an IPO from the issuer to when the selling group sells the entire issue to investors is a very risky period for the underwriters. During these days or weeks

---

* In the United States the Federal Reserve Board's Regulation T, called the **initial margin requirement,** is effective only when the stock is sold short or on an initial margin purchase. After the initial purchase margin requirement has been met, the Federal Reserve's initial margin requirement becomes irrelevant and the transaction is governed by the **maintenance margin requirement** at the brokerage or stock exchange (whichever is less is the binding constraint).

TABLE 6-2	**Rankings of Largest Investment Banks in the United States by Two Different Criteria—by Capital and by Employees**					
Rank by Capital	Firm	Total Consolidated Capital $ millions	Total Assets $ millions	No. of Employees	No. of U.S. Offices	Rank by Employees
1	Merrill Lynch & Co.	$60,544	$328,071	49,000	800	1
2	Morgan Stanley Dean Witter	39,699	366,976	47,000	475	2
3	Lehman Brothers	37,684	192,244	6,100	18	13
4	Credit Suisse First Boston	31,197	278,584	NA	NA	NA
5	Goldman, Sachs & Co.	31,097	250,491	15,361	41	8
6	Salomon Smith Barney	28,147	224,746	34,393	506	3
7	Bear Stearns Cos.	22,218	177,393	9,276	23	10
8	Donaldson, Lufkin & Jenrette	9,267	109,012	8,500	14	11
9	PaineWebber	8,535	62,000	19,262	310	4
10	Deutsche Bank Alex. Brown	7,149	111,178	4,616	24	15
11	Banc of America Securities	3,572	51,573	4,365	39	17
12	Nomura Holding America	3,429	32,635	NA	NA	NA
13	Warburg Dillon Read	3,109	137,368	NA	NA	NA
14	Ameritrade	2,825	3,783	2,369	8	25
15	Charles Schwab & Co.	2,729	29,299	17,200	340	6
16	TD Waterhouse Holdings	2,548	13,802	4,148	164	20
17	Prudential Securities	2,497	40,671	16,368	308	7
18	Chase Securities	2,492	33,610	2,003	9	30
19	SG Cowen Securities Corp.	1,968	38,120	NA	NA	NA
20	J.P. Morgan Securities	1,883	77,661	2,156	14	27

SUMMARY: Merrill Lynch has more capital and more employees than any other investment banking firm in the world. Merrill Lynch accepts new accounts that are as small as $3,000. Goldman Sachs ranks fifth in terms of total consolidated capital, but ranks eighth in terms of employees. Goldman refuses to accept new accounts of less than $1 million.

SOURCE: *Institutional Investor* (April 2000): 123–26.

the underwriters expose themselves to the risk that adverse market conditions might force the underwriters to sell the issue at a lower price than they paid the issuer for the new securities.*

Setting the "right" price for an IPO is important. The price cannot be too high; this might cause losses because the underwriters could not sell the securities. The right price is not so low it would be unnecessarily costly to the issuer. It is understood that investment bankers usually underprice an equity IPO about 15%, as shown in Figure 1-1 in Chapter 1 (p. 5). About a 15% price rise typically occurs on the first day after an equity IPO goes public. The IPO's first-day gain motivates investors to buy new securities, but this average gain is not guaranteed.[2] The prices of some new issues fall.

(Step 4) Distribution. Investment bankers sell the typical security issue to many different investors. Occasionally the investment banker acts as an intermediary and brings an entire issue to one large investor for a **private placement.**[3]

---

* In 1992 Merrill Lynch was unable to sell their entire IPO of Bradlees stock and First USA's stock before the market prices of these two issues fell below Merrill's IPO price. Goldman Sachs was left holding some shares of an IPO of Hook-SuperRx at a market price that was below Goldman's IPO price in 1992. Also in 1992, Morgan Stanley wound up holding some shares in its IPO of Owens-Illinois after the stock's price dropped below Morgan's IPO price. See *Wall Street Journal*, 12 August 1992, C1. Such losses are not rare.

STUDY CHECK

THE PRIMARY MARKET

QUESTION: Where is the primary market for an IPO that is originated by and managed by the New York City office of Merrill Lynch?

ANSWER: The primary market has no set location. The location might be in the issuer's offices, in the investment banker's offices, at a dinner party in London, in an airplane, or wherever the issuer and the investment banker reach a deal.

INTERNET CONNECTION

Web Sites of Exchanges and Investment Bankers

NYSE: www.nyse.com

NASD: www.nasd.com and www.investor.nasd.com

Chicago Stock Exchange's (CSX's): www.chicagostockex.com

European Association of Securities Dealers Automated Quotations (EASDAQ): www.easdaq.com

International Federation of Stock Exchanges: www.fibv.com

For information about large and small investment banks, see: www.ipo.com

Freidman, Billings, Ramsey Group: www.fbr.com

The ECN named Island has a Web site with an open order book at: www.island.com

The difference between the investment banker's cost and sale price is called the **spread.** Four percent of the market value is a normal spread for an issue of bonds. Preferred stock and common stock are riskier; these spreads range from 5% to 16%.[4]

Electronic Investment Bankers

DLJdirect, an internet subsidiary of Donaldson, Lufkin, and Jenrette (acquired by Credit Suisse First Boston), started distributing IPOs over the Internet in the late 1990s. Some small new electronic investment banking firms also started operations during the late 1990s and others followed. Virginia-based Freidman, Billings, Ramsey Group; E*Offering (partially owned by E*Trade), W. R. Hambrecht; OpenIPO (started by W. R. Hambrecht, partially owned by Instinet); Chase Hambrecht and Quist; Epoch Partners (backed by Charles Schwab, T. D. Waterhouse, Ameritrade, and some venture capital firms); E-InvestmentBank (started by Wedbush Morgan Securities); Wit Soundview; Wit Capital; and Vostock (a joint venture between Wit and ITG) are competing on-line investment banks. Many of these e-underwriters started by letting a larger investment bank underwrite the IPO and then they helped the larger investment bank distribute part of the issue over the Internet. As additional capital is invested in on-line investment banks they will be able to do their own underwriting. Some large investment banks listed in Table 6-2 will distribute over the Internet too, or they will acquire one of the new firms listed here.

W. R. Hambrecht's OpenIPO allocates shares by price according to a *Dutch auction system*. Potential buyers place orders showing the highest price they are willing to pay, and the investment banker fills all the orders at the single highest price at which it can just sell the entire issue of securities. MuniAuction in Pittsburgh has successfully completed municipal bond auctions over the Internet.

Full Disclosure Is Required in the United States

The U.S. government's Securities and Exchange Commission (SEC) requires that most primary issues be accompanied by a 10- to 20-page booklet called a **prospectus** that must be given to every prospective investor before they invest. Every prospectus must **fully disclose** all the information listed in Table 6-3 and must be approved by the SEC . This approval is not, however, an endorsement of the investment value of the securities; it implies only that the information in Table 6-3 has been disclosed. Figure 6-1, an excerpt from the *Wall Street Journal*, reproduced here, is a daily list of the forthcoming IPOs.

The following types of security issues are not required to register with the SEC and issue a prospectus:

Regulated agencies. Issues made by governmental bodies and some companies that are regulated by the governmental agencies.

Small Issues. Small issues of less than $15 million offered to local (intrastate) investors.

TABLE 6-3   Full Disclosure of Information as Required by the SEC

 1. Issuer's articles of incorporation
 2. Purpose for which the proceeds of the issue will be spent
 3. Offering price to the public
 4. Offering price for special groups, if any
 5. Fees promised to developers and/or promoters
 6. Underwriter's fees
 7. Net proceeds to the issuer
 8. Information on the issuer's products, history, and location
 9. Copies of any indentures affecting the new issue
10. Names and remuneration of officers employed by the issuer
11. Details about any unusual contracts, such as a managerial profit-sharing plan
12. A detailed statement of capitalization
13. Detailed Balance Sheet
14. Detailed Income & Expense statements for 3 preceding years
15. Names and addresses of the issuer's officers, directors, and the underwriters
16. Names and addresses of anyone owning more than 10 percent of any class of stock
17. Details about any pending litigation
18. A copy of the underwriting agreement
19. Copies of legal opinions on matters related to the issue

Secondary issues. When one investor sells securities to another investor (so issuer receives no cash).

Private offerings. When securities are offered to one or more small groups of informed investors (for instance, management buyouts) who are not speculators.

Private placements. Under the SEC's Rule 144A U.S. and non-U.S. corporations are allowed to place securities privately with professional investors without SEC approval.

Money market securities. Securities that mature in less than 270 days from their initial issue. Exemption from the SEC's registration procedure does not grant the issuer or underwriter any immunity from legal action if fraud is involved.

The U.S. government requires full disclosure to enable investors to estimate the value of new securities. Prices determine how resources are allocated. The United States supports free markets because the market allocates goods where they will do the most good for the most people—to the highest bidder. Free-market capitalism is based on the belief that price controls, subsidies, or government intervention will misallocate resources to benefit a minority at the expense of the majority.

After an investment banker issues securities in the primary market, the outstanding shares can begin trading in the **secondary market.** Three types of secondary security markets that exist in the United States are considered in the following sections:

1. The NYSE, an organized exchange in New York City that is run by dealers
2. NASDAQ, an electronic market in which dealers compete with each other
3. Electronic communication networks (ECNs), electronic securities exchanges where firms like Archipelago, Island, Instinet, SelectNet, Tradebook, Brass Utility (Brut), ITG, and others compete over the Internet

FIGURE 6-1 Newspaper Excerpt: Forthcoming IPOs

NEW SECURITIES ISSUES

The following were among yesterday's offerings and pricings in U.S. and non-U.S. capital markets, with terms and syndicate manager, based on information provided by Dow Jones Newswires. (A basis point is one-hundredth of a percentage point; 100 basis points equals a percentage point.)

CORPORATE

Freddie Mac—$3 billion offering of three-month reference bills was auctioned. Terms: maturity: Aug. 17, 2000; issue price: 98.362; yield: 6.588% (money-market yield); stop-out discount rate: 6.48%; Cusip: 313396C43.

EQUITY

Carbo Ceramics Inc. (CRBO)—offering of 1.725 million common shares was priced at $27 each through underwriters led by Lehman Brothers.

EUROBOND

Berne—180 million Swiss francs of domestic public bonds with the following terms, lead manager UBS Warburg said: maturity: June 13, 2010; coupon: 4.5%; issue price: 101.00; payment date: June 13, 2000; subscription date: June 5, 2000; yield: 4.3744%; spread to swaps: bid minus 15 basis points; denominations: 5000 Swiss francs; listing: SWX from June 6, 2000. Interest is payable annually.

Caixa Geral de Depositos Finance—$750 million offering of five-year floating-rate notes with the following terms, lead managers CSFB (books) and Deutsche Bank said. Terms: maturity: May 26, 2005; coupon: three-month London interbank offered rate plus 12.5 basis points; issue price: 99.875; reoffer price: 99.875; payment date: May 26, 2000; debt ratings: Aa3 (Moody's Investors Service Inc.); denominations: $1,000, $10,000, $100,000; listing: Luxembourg; interest: quarterly. The bonds are being sold under the borrower's Euro medium-term note program.

Comptoir des Entrepreneurs—300 million euros at three-month euro interbank offered rate plus 20 basis points due November 30, 2001, at 100.035, via CDC, Credit Agricole Indosuez and Natexis Banque Populaire. Fees 0.08.

Hellenic Republic Agricultural—230 billion Greek drachma of zero-coupon due May 22, 2003, at 82.55, via BNP Paribas, Eurobank and National Bank of Greece, reoffer, 82.55%. Fees not listed.

SOURCE: "New Securities Issues" section from the *Wall Street Journal,* 17 May 2000, C22.

THE NEW YORK STOCK EXCHANGE (NYSE)

This section concentrates on the case in which an investor calls a securities broker and places an order to buy or sell a New York Stock Exchange (NYSE) listed stock. The NYSE lists about 3,000 common and preferred stocks issued by American corporations, approximately 300 foreign stocks, and about 250 American Depository Receipts (ADRs); the numbers fluctuate from month to month. As discussed in Chapter 19, the NYSE also trades bonds issued by the corporations it lists.*

NYSE Operations

The trading floor of the NYSE is crowded with personal computers at the trading posts of each of its approximately 460 specialists. About eight NYSE-listed stocks are assigned to each specialist's trading post. Around the perimeter of the trading floor are about 1,500 trading booths with telephones to transmit orders and sales confirmations between the brokerages' offices and the exchange floor.

The NYSE has had 1,366 members since 1953. In 1999 a NYSE membership (seat) sold at a record high of 2.5 million; in 1977 a seat sold for as low as $35,000. In most years there are over 100 transfers of exchange memberships as members die, retire, or go bankrupt. Practically all exchange members are either specialists or floor brokers.**

---

* The NYSE's Automated Bond System (ABS) provides trading in the bonds of its listed firms, but this trading is not liquid and not free from arbitrage opportunities. For details see Adam K. Gehr and Terrence F. Martell, "Pricing Efficiency in the Secondary Market for Investment-Grade Corporate Bonds," *Journal of Fixed Income* (December 1992): 24–38. The NYSE seems to have focused its resources on becoming a global stock market and has given less attention to its bond and derivatives markets.

** Floor brokers can be divided into subcategories such as pure floor brokers (or $2 brokers), commission brokers, floor traders, and odd-lot dealers. Floor traders and odd-lot dealers are practically extinct. The subcategories all work to create liquidity on the exchange floor.

Floor Brokers. Over 900 of the 1366 seats on the NYSE are owned by **floor brokers** who buy and sell securities for the clients of brokerage houses or trade for their own accounts. Floor brokers receive orders via phone from brokerages (NYSE member firms) that employ their services; they walk onto the trading floor, execute the transaction at the appropriate market-maker's (specialist's) post, and then phone the brokerage for which they are acting as agent to confirm the trade and provide details about the execution.

Specialists. The specialists make more money, on average, than other NYSE members. Specialists must earn the right to be a specialist by accepting the obligation to make a fair and orderly market in which only small price changes occur from transaction to transaction in the stocks assigned to them. To keep the market in a stock fair and orderly when there are more buy orders than sell orders, specialists must either raise the market price of the security they control, or sell out of their own inventory to meet the excess demand. When there are more sell orders than buy orders, specialists must either lower the price of stock or buy for their own account (inventory).

A spcialist must have a seat on the exchange, abilities as a dealer, be selected by the NYSE Board, and meet the minimum capital requirements. The NYSE's approximately 460 specialists have banded together to form about 25 different specialist firms to diversify their risks, share capital, and achieve economies of scale in their administrative work.[5] In 1999 a NYSE specialist firm named LaBranche was the first to issue shares to the public.

Every NYSE specialist keeps a separate **limit order book (LOB)** for each stock in which they make a market. These LOBs are kept in the specialist's computer. The LOBs record buy and sell orders from potential traders. Figure 6-2 shows a computer screen view of a hypothetical LOB that lists the limit orders to buy and sell one stock. The information in the LOB includes the customers' names, the quantity they each want to buy or sell, and the price at which they want to execute their transaction stated at $1/8$ of $1 (or 12.5¢) intervals. A specialist's LOB contains the list of potential trades that, essentially, outlines the supply and demand curves that determine the market price of the security. This valuable information helps specialists earn trading profits.[6]

NYSE Market-Makers

The NYSE is a continuous auction market in which stock exchange members called **specialists** post bid and ask prices for several stocks in which they make a market. Specialists must stand at assigned posts on the trading floor and be **market-makers** who are always ready to buy at their **bid price** and sell at their **ask (offer) price.** Every stock is assigned to one specialist who is the monopolistic market-maker for that stock on the floor of the NYSE.

A specialist is a broker and a dealer. As a **broker** the specialist executes orders for other NYSE members for the bid-ask spread; no risk is involved. As a **dealer,** the specialist buys and sells shares of the stock in which they specialize for their own account (inventory) and invest their capital at risk.

Bid-Ask Spread. A stock's *bid-ask spread* ranges from as little as a few cents to as much as a few dollars per share, and averages about 25 cents.[7] Since a specialist buys from every seller and sells to every buyer on the NYSE floor, a specialist earns the bid-ask spread on every NYSE transaction. A specialist may earn additional income by buying for their inventory at a low price and selling at a higher price.

Decimalization. The minimum share price change permissible at an exchange is called a **tick.** The NYSE cut its tick size from one-eighth to one-sixteenth of a dollar in 1997. The NYSE and Nasdaq reduced their tick sizes to 1 cent per share in 2000. Decimalization is expected to reduce bid-ask spreads and customers' trading costs.[8]

FIGURE 6-2 Computer Screen Showing a Market-Maker's Limit
Order Book (LOB) for a Hypothetical Stock

BID: $42 and ?/8				ASKED: $42 and ?/8			
0/8	4 Wentz			0/8			
	9 Mirandi						
	3 Dalton						
1/8	1 Sullivan			1/8			
	4 Jacoby						
1/4	3 McGovern			1/4			
3/8	2 Gabelli			3/8			
1/2				1/2			
5/8				5/8	3 Dart		
3/4				3/4	2 Wu		
					4 Zachs		
					2 Theodakis		
7/8				7/8	5 Emerson		
					9 Moran		
					4 Fallon		

A market-maker's (for example, a NYSE specialist's) book lists the quantities of shares desired and the bid prices from potential investors and the quantities of shares offered and the asked prices from potential sellers who have phoned in their limit orders for a specific stock.

NYSE Listing Requirements

All firms that are listed on an organized exchange must apply to be listed.* Table 6-4 compares the listing requirements for the NYSE with those of an over-the-counter (OTC) stock exchange, Nasdaq.

Although the NYSE has tended to be a laggard in stock market technology, it does have its Super Designated Order Turnaround (SuperDOT) system. SuperDOT expedites executions of small market orders and limit orders by routing them directly from NYSE member firms to the

---

* Some large, exchange-listed companies have their shares listed on more than one exchange. In addition, stock exchanges also grant **unlisted trading privileges (UTPs)** to selected stocks. For example, the so-called **third market** in the United States is an OTC market in NYSE-listed stocks that have UTPs at the several stock exchanges. (The third market is discussed later in this chapter.) Global depository receipts (GDRs) provide another example; they have UTPs at some stock exchanges around the world. (GDRs are discussed in Chapter 18.)

TABLE 6-4	Contrasting NYSE and Nasdaq Listing Requirements for Domestic U.S. Corporations[a]		
Criteria		NYSE	Nasdaq
Minimum taxable annual income		$2.5 million	0
Minimum net tangible assets		$18 million	$2 million
Minimum publicly held shares of stock		$1.1 million	$100,000
Minimum market value of publicly held shares of stock		$18 million	$3 million
Minimum number of investors owning round-lots (100 shares)		2,000 investors	300 investors
Market-makers		1 specialist	At least 2 specialists

[a]International corporations must meet substantially larger size requirements.

SOURCES: *NYSE Fact Book 1997, NASDQ Fact Book 1997*

specialists, thus bypassing the floor brokers. NYSE specialists usually let their computers execute SuperDOT transactions automatically. It is easy to imagine that NYSE specialists could be automated out of their jobs by computers, if the specialists would permit the technology to develop.

A **block** trade is a single transaction that involves 10,000 or more shares. Table 6-5 shows that block trading at the NYSE increased steadily between the 1960s and 1980s, but it seems to have leveled off during the 1990s. NYSE specialists do not get involved with huge blocks of NYSE-listed stock that go outside the NYSE to block positioners.

BLOCK POSITIONERS

DEFINITION

Special broker/dealers called **block positioners** evolved to line up multiple buyers to purchase large blocks. Block positioners routinely process block transactions without changing the market price of the issue significantly. These dealers have the capital to carry a block in inventory for a few days and the connections to distribute it. People sometimes say that block positioners operate in the *upstairs market*, which refers to their offices in high-rise buildings near the NYSE in Manhattan. Block positioners charge small commissions; fees of a few cents per share are available to institutional investors that trade blocks periodically. In contrast, small investors who trade round lots and odd lots typically incur commission rates of 1% to 6% to buy or sell, because economies of scale are not possible with small transactions. Some large blocks are executed with international clients after the NYSE closes and, as a result, there is no public record of these transactions.

THE NASDAQ MARKET

This section considers an investor who calls a securities broker and places an order to buy or sell a stock that is listed in the electronic **over-the-conter (OTC) market** called **Nasdaq.** During the 1930s the OTC dealers in the United States asked the federal government for

TABLE 6-5   NYSE Block Transactions

Year	Blocks Per Year	Average Number of Block Trades Per Day	Total Shares for Year Through Block Trades (in millions)	Percent of Year's Total Volume Through Blocks
1965	2,269	9	48	3.1%
1970	17,134	68	451	15.4%
1975	34,277	136	779	16.6%
1980	133,597	528	3,311	29.2%
1985	539,039	2,139	14,222	51.3%
1990	843,365	3,333	19,682	49.6%
1995	1,963,889	7,793	49,736	57.0%
1998	3,518,200	13,961	82,657	48.7%

SOURCE: *New York Stock Exchange Fact Book*

legislation to provide a self-regulating organization (SRO). Congress enacted the **Maloney Act** of 1938 to allow the OTC market to establish private trade associations that regulated themselves under the supervision of the SEC. To date only one association of OTC dealers has registered with the SEC—the **National Association of Securities Dealers** (NASD). The NASD is an SRO that provides for securities trading between its members at reduced commissions. Reduced commissions for members provide an incentive for every OTC dealer to join the NASD. Nasdaq (pronounced Naz-dak) is an acronym for National Association of Securities Dealers Automated Quotations.

Nasdaq lists over 6,400 common and preferred stocks issued by about 5,500 American corporations, approximately 320 foreign stocks, and about 140 American Depository Receipts (ADRs). It listed over 15% of the world's stock market capitalization in 2000.

Nasdaq Operations

Nasdaq is a complex communications network serving the OTC stock market. About 61,000 Nasdaq computer terminals are connected to Nasdaq's mainframe computer via phone lines. These computer terminals can obtain current bid-and-ask prices for all Nasdaq stocks. Bid-and-ask stock price quotations are updated continuously in Nasdaq's mainframe computer by about 540 competing Nasdaq market-makers that deal in any stocks they select. This system enables an investor's broker to screen competing market-makers (dealers) for the trading opportunities with the lowest price plus commission cost. Trades cannot be executed through Nasdaq's computer.[9] When an investor's broker finds a Nasdaq dealer with a bid or an ask price at which they want to transact, the investor's broker must call the *dealer* to execute the transaction.

Nasdaq centralizes a geographically dispersed market into one mainframe computer. When a NASD broker or dealer anywhere in the world inquires about the price of a security, Nasdaq instantly provides bid-ask price quotations from competing dealers located thousands of miles apart. Nasdaq's supporters claim it is not a *fragmented market* because its bid and ask prices are centrally reported through one mainframe computer. Nasdaq is, however, fragmented in a different sense, because it lacks a **central limit order book (CLOB)** along the lines of the limit order book (LOB) in Figure 6-2. If Nasdaq had a CLOB it could direct investors to the *national best bid or offer (NBBO) price*.

STUDY
CHECK

NASDAQ

QUESTION: Where is the Nasdaq market located?

ANSWER: Any location from which a Nasdaq dealer with a laptop computer can communicate with Nasdaq's mainframe computer in Trumbull, CT.

Nasdaq is designed to handle up to 20,000 stocks, but currently lists only about 6,500 actively traded stocks. Not all OTC stocks are listed on Nasdaq because some are not traded actively enough to be in the computer system. Comparing Nasdaq's listing requirements with the NYSE's in Table 6-4 reveals that Nasdaq makes markets for some stocks the NYSE considers too inactive to list.

Nasdaq's excess computing capacity could be put to use by including the exchange-listed stocks. In 1999 Nasdaq merged with the American Stock Exchange (AMEX). In 2000 Nasdaq announced plans to cross-list stocks with stock exchanges in Europe (London and Frankfurt), the Stock Exchange of Hong Kong, Nasdaq Canada in Montreal, the Australian Stock Exchange, and the Osaka Stock Exchange in Japan. Nasdaq is positioning itself to trade 24 hours a day and is establishing telecommunications connections that allow its market-makers to compete with the NYSE specialists.

The CQS, the ITS, and The Law of One Price

The SEC accelerated stock exchange competition in the United States by mandating that the **Consolidated Quotation System (CQS)** report current transactions from the NYSE, OTC market, American Stock Exchange (AMEX), regional stock exchanges in the United States, and the so-called "third market." Centrally reporting all trades through the CQS helps investors find the best prices, but the CQS cannot perform executions. To facilitate executions the SEC urged the NYSE to create the **Intermarket Trading System (ITS)**, an electronic trading network that links the various U.S. markets and facilitates intermarket trading. The NYSE created the ITS, but it has not updated the ITS to give outsiders rapid access to NYSE-listed stocks. As a result, Nasdaq supplemented the ITS with an electronic communications network (ECN) named Primex which gives faster access to NYSE-listed stocks. Combining the price information from the CQS with the executions available through the ITS and Primex allows stock price arbitrageurs to enforce the law of one price. Such arbitrage reduces market fragmentation within the U.S. stock markets and accomplishes much of the national market transparency that a national CLOB could achieve if one existed.

STUDY
CHECK

DOES THE NYSE OR NASDAQ DO IT BETTER?

It is not difficult to make a market in a stock that enjoys continuous high-volume trading—like most NYSE-listed stocks. It is difficult to make a market in a stock that is traded inactively—like many small Nasdaq stocks. An inactively traded stock issued by a small corporation needs a market-maker that is required to make a continuous market in the stock. But the NYSE refuses to list stocks issued by small corporations that are traded inactively; as shown in the NYSE's listing requirements in Table 6-4. In contrast, Nasdaq's market-makers compete with each other to make markets in hundreds of small stocks that are traded inactively.

QUESTION: Do you think dealers who compete voluntarily through Nasdaq provide the best way to make markets in stocks? Or, do you think the NYSE's monopolistic market-makers provide the general public with better service and/or execution prices?
ANSWER: No consensus exists.

The National Quotation Bureau (NQB)

To be included in Nasdaq's widely publicized *national daily list*, a stock must have at least two market-makers, a minimum of 1,500 stockholders distributed throughout the country, and command significant investor interest. OTC stocks that are not traded actively enough to be included in Nasdaq's national daily list are listed with the **National Quotation Bureau (NQB)**. In 1999 the NQB installed a computer that quotes prices for thousands of stocks and bonds and has the capacity for thousands more. NQB prices are derived from OTC dealers' most recent trades. Since some NQB stocks are not actively traded, in some cases, NQB prices can be weeks old.

Today the NQB's pink electronic listings for 3,600 stocks include:

◆ Domestic U.S. micro-cap stocks

◆ Shares in foreign corporations that do not meet U.S. standards permitting them to be listed on an organized exchange

◆ ADRs and GDRs for the stocks of firms like Rolls Royce, Volkswagen, Nestlé, and Siemans that do meet the accounting standards for an organized exchange in the United States

Today the NQB's yellow electronic listings for 2,500 bonds include:

◆ High-yield (junk) bonds

◆ Convertible bonds[10]

EXAMPLE   **FINANCIAL INFORMATION PROVIDERS**

Several large firms provide information to support the price discovery process.

Dow-Jones is a New York firm that owns the *Wall Street Journal* and *Barrons* financial newspapers, sells news, and operates an Internet news service. Dow-Jones also provides well-known securities market averages.

Reuters is a British financial information company that delivered its first price quotations to customers via carrier pigeon in 1849. Today Reuters has 255,000 computer terminals around the world and it provides foreign exchange rates, stock prices, bond prices, financial software, and business news. Reuters also owns a securities market named Instinet and a portion of a subsidiary named Archipelago ECN that are discussed below.

Bloomberg has about 75,000 terminals around the world for which each user pays $1,200 per month. Bloomberg purveys real-time financial data, historical financial data, financial software, statistical software, and business news; it also owns an ECN. In 1999 Bloomberg's Tradebook ECN formed an alliance with ITG's POSIT to create SuperECN.

McGraw-Hill owns McGraw-Hill Book Company, Irwin Publishing Company, Standard & Poor's, *Business Week* magazine, Compustat Financial Data, J. J. Kenney Municipal Bond Data, DRI, and many smaller firms. McGraw-Hill sells business and financial data and news on paper and electronically.

Numerous smaller firms compete to purvey financial information.

THE THIRD AND FOURTH MARKETS IN THE UNITED STATES

The third and fourth markets are competitors that strengthen stock markets in the United States by competing in ways that are explained below.

The Third Market

The **third market** is a subset of the OTC market where exchange-listed stocks are traded. The third market competes with organized exchanges like the NYSE and AMEX by offering better bid and ask prices. Nasdaq and the regional stock exchanges are at the core of the third market; they use the Intermarket Trading System (ITS) and other electronic communications networks to execute their third-market transactions. For example, in 1999 the Chicago Stock Exchange (CHX) traded over 90% of the NYSE-listed stocks, over 90% of the AMEX-listed stocks, over 400 Nasdaq stocks, and several stocks listed on other exchanges.*

The majority of CHX's trading volume is from **dual listings** of exchange-listed stocks. CHX attracts much of its growing market share by *paying for order flow*. In contrast to the half-penny transactions fees that the NYSE and AMEX charge to execute orders, CHX often pays brokers one penny per share for bring their orders to the CHX to be executed. In other words, the CHX specialists take a penny per share from their bid-ask spread income and give it to brokers to motivate brokers to give them order flow.

The Fourth Market in the United States

The **fourth market** is made up of telephone lines and telecommunications networks between market-makers, block traders, and institutions. Fourth-market participants bypass the normal dealer services (research, credit, and safekeeping of securities). Buyers and sellers in the fourth market can negotiate with each other over price and quantity. The fourth market is an important part of the secondary market in the United States because it provides competition for the other markets and it has been a leader in innovation.

INSTINET: A PIONEER

DEFINITION

A Reuters subsidiary named **Instinet** has been a successful fourth market firm since 1970. Instinet has offices in New York, London, Paris, Frankfurt, Zurich, Australia, and Asia. Instinet (INSTItutional NETwork) has computer terminals in the offices of over 5,000 subscribers' around the world.** Instinet clients communicate with each other using anonymous identification numbers. Subscribers post limit orders to buy or sell that all other Instinet subscribers can see. Subscribers can negotiate transactions prices and quantities by typing confidential messages and responses into their terminals until a trade is consummated or negotiations break off. Millions of shares are traded in secrecy on Instinet daily. Institutional investors pay commissions that vary from 2 to 8 cents per share on Instinet.

---

*   See Chicago Stock Exchange's (CSX's) Web site for up-to-date details: www.chicagostockex.com. CSX was founded in 1882, changed its name to the Midwest Stock Exchange in 1949, and changed its name back to CSX in 1993.

** Instinet is a registered trademark of the Institutional Networks Corporation, 875 Third Avenue, New York, NY 10022. Phone: 212-310-9500.

SelectNet, a computer network available only to dealers, has competed with Instinet since 1997. SelectNet and Instinet make their quoted prices available to the public to increase the fourth market's transparency.

ELECTRONIC COMMUNICATION NETWORKS (ECNs)

DEFINITION

ELECTRONIC COMMUNICATION NETWORK (ECN)

An **electronic communication network (ECN)** is a computer program that provides a securities distribution channel to compete with securities exchanges, other securities markets, and other ECNs. Most ECNs are parasites on exchanges that list securities and post their prices. ECNs seek profits by trading an exchange-listed security at a slightly better price than the price posted by the listing exchange, or at the same price but with additional services. Crossing networks and electronic order working systems are the two main types of ECNs.

Order-Crossing Networks

An **order-crossing network** is an ECN that endeavors to find and match buy and sell orders. The **market impact cost** of trading is zero when anonymous buyers and sellers who are compatible turn up in the crossing network at the same time. Some crossing networks execute trades at the price of the last reported price on an organized exchange. Others execute trades at a price midway between the bid and ask prices existing on an organized exchange. Some crossing networks use other execution prices.

Traders that use alternative market systems sometimes pay a fixed annual fee; if so, their variable trading costs are zero. Since market impact costs are eliminated, trade execution costs are thereby reduced. Rapid executions can be obtained if the other half of the transaction is already present in the crossing network. And the protections that anonymity offers to block traders, tax evaders, and corporations investing in a competitor's stock are valued by those traders. Since crossing networks are not continuous auction markets (like the NYSE), sometimes the network is not operating when it is needed. Or, even when the crossing network is operating, the other half of the transaction can fail to materialize because the networks provide no market-makers. Lack of continuous liquidity is a major drawback of order-crossing networks.

Some of the more noteworthy order-crossing networks are listed below.

EXAMPLE

ORDER-CROSSING NETWORKS

Instinet, a major fourth market firm mentioned above, operates one of the largest electronic trading networks in the world. Instinet also operates the Crossing Network.

POSIT. The Investment Technology Group's (ITG's) order crossing network is named POrtfolio System for Institutional Trading, or POSIT, and is headquartered in New York City.*

---

* ITG stands for Investment Technology Group in New York. Its Web site is www.itginc.com and its stock is traded on Nasdaq. A NYSE-listed institutional brokerage firm named Jeffries is involved with ITG. A financial firm named BARRA helped develop POSIT originally and still has a license to share in the use of POSIT.

Tradebook. Bloomberg runs a continuous matching system named Tradebook, primarily for Nasdaq stocks.

SuperECN. The complimentary nature of Bloomberg's Tradebook and ITG's POSIT caused these two operations to form an alliance named SuperECN in 1999.

Investor's Liquidity Network. Fidelity Investors in Boston also does order crossing through its Investor's Liquidity Network, or ILN.

E-Crossnet. E-Crossnet was established in London by Merrill Lynch Mercury Asset Management, Barclays Global Investors, and about 20 London-based mutual funds and banks. E-Crossnet is an order-crossing network for institutional investors trading European stocks.

Electronic Order-Working Systems

Several of the large brokerage firms utilize electronic communications networks (ECNs) called **electronic order-working systems,** or *smart systems,* to "work an order" received from a client. *Working an order* involves gathering market information and utilizing it to minimize the market impact and other transactions costs associated with an order to trade securities.

ELECTRONIC ORDER-WORKING SYSTEM   DEFINITION

An electronic order-working system is a smart ECN that works a customer's order to buy or sell by performing one or more of the tasks defined below.

1. **Gathers price information** from many markets and displays the best alternatives for further consideration by the trader
2. **Internalizes order flow** by offsetting desired trades from the firm's own accounts, where possible, against the customers' orders. Crossing orders internally minimizes transactions costs
3. **Time-slices an order** by breaking a large order into small pieces that are executed at intervals throughout the day rather than all at once, to disguise the true size of a large order and minimize its market impact
4. **Monitors portfolio risk** by continuously reevaluating the portfolio's profit-and-loss, leverage, sector risk exposures, and volatility and keeping the trader informed
5. **Executes basket trades** by simultaneously buying and/or selling hundreds of individual stocks in a single aggregate transaction
6. **Allocates small parts of an order** to market segments that have the best prices—essentially, advantageously aggregating a fragmented market
7. **Evaluates different market-makers'** historical order-fill rates and other factors to suggest likely trading possibilities to the trader
8. **Links international markets** by exploiting telecommunications and satellite connections

---

To be utilized, an electronic order-working system must first be loaded with relevant information:

Data about the securities that are to be traded (customers' orders and the brokerage houses' own orders)

The limit order prices

Quantities available to be traded at different prices

Time limitations

Markets where the securities are traded

Historical and current data about trading partners

Additional information the electronic order working system might request while it works the order

The smart system uses this information to seek out markets where the whole transaction or parts of the transaction might be consummated. During its search process the order working system continually gathers newer information that will affect the way trading is managed. The order is typically passed to market-makers, order-crossing networks (Instinet, ILN, POSIT, others), and competing order-working systems around the world that might be able to execute the trade. Feedback is gathered from these competing markets and the computer software utilizes this real-time trading information to decide whether or not to execute all or part of the order. Some systems analyze the stock market's short-term volatility in determining advantageous timing. If the transactions, or at least a portion of them, are not executed within some prespecified time limit, the order-working system might send the remaining part of the order to someplace like the NYSE's SuperDot system, to Nasadaq's small-order executing system (SOES), to a foreign system for immediate execution via computer, or to some designated trading desk to be worked by human traders. Or, the order might be canceled. Some of the more noteworthy smart systems are discussed below.

EXAMPLE   SMART SYSTEMS

QuantEX. The Investment Technology Group (ITG) runs an electronic order working system named QuantEX.

Order Management System. The Order Management System from Instinet competes with QuantEX by working to execute orders in several continuous auction markets around the world, Instinet's order-crossing network, and through Instinet's own trading desks.

Lattice Trading System. Credit Suisse First Boston's Lattice Trading System competes by performing internal order matches while seeking to execute orders in several continuous auction markets.

REDIBook. Large investment banks like Donaldson, Lufkin, and Jenrette (DLJ) and Lehman Brothers and Credit Suisse First Boston (CSFB); the huge Bank of America; the vast Fidelity Investments mutual fund operation; electronic brokerage firms like Charles Schwab and National Discount Brokers and Fleet Securities and TD Waterhouse; and a large NYSE specialist firm named Spear, Leeds, and Kellog (SLK) formed a partnership around REDIBook.

Archipelago Exchange. The Archipelago Exchange started in Chicago as an order working system that ran a continuous auction that routed orders to other systems if better prices are available elsewhere. The firm is owned by a holding company named Terra Nova, and Terra Nova is owned by an impressive list of financial institutions. In 2000 Archipelago became a stock exchange that is registered with the SEC by merging with the Pacific Stock Exchange.

After starting in the United States, ECNs have been migrating around the world.

POSIT. ITG formed an alliance with Societe Generale permitting POSIT to conduct a London auction in stocks from the United States, United Kingdom, and Australia.

Barclays Stockbrokers. Barclays Bank operates Barclays Stockbrokers, which is active in the United Kingdom.

Tradepoint. Morgan Stanley Dean Witter, Instinet, J. P. Morgan, the Hull Group, UBS Warburg, Warburg Dillon Read (owned by UBS), Dresdner Kleinwort Benson, and Credit Suisse First Boston (CSFB) invested in Tradepoint. Tradepoint is dicussed below.

Commerzbank is working to create an electronic market in Germany.

A few ECNs will be able to survive alone by offering highly differentiated services. Both the profit potential and liquidity of an ECN can be increased by increasing its order flow. Most ECNs and stock exchanges want to consolidate to effect this increase.

EVOLVING STOCK EXCHANGES

Electronic stock exchanges are an evolving technology that is difficult to define because some seek to accomplish different goals than others. Several different electronic stock exchanges that are now operating are discussed below.

ELECTRONIC STOCK EXCHANGES

EXAMPLE

Arizona Stock Exchange (AZX). The AZX is a stock market in Phoenix that was formed in 1990; it was formerly called the Wunsch Auction System and is housed in a computer. AZX operates an automated auction market process that seeks to equate supply and demand for a broad list of common stocks a few times each trading day; it is a *periodic call market*. Separate auctions are held for NYSE and Nasdaq stocks. Clients' incoming orders must be submitted as limit orders to buy or sell that are entered in the AZX computer. AZH does not draw on orders from other markets or interact with other markets; it operates independently. To create a **transparent market,** the AZX's limit order book (LOB) is open to all participants. All old orders, all revised orders, and all new orders coming into the AZX's LOB are visible to all participants.

The orders are visible, but the anonymity of every participant is maintained. The AZX system also has a "reserve book" that holds certain orders back so participants cannot see them until prespecified conditions are met (for instance, until some part of the order that is visible in the open order book is executed), and then the reserve orders are transferred into the open order book.

Every time an auction takes place the AZX computes supply and demand curves for each security being auctioned. The intersection of these curves determines the security's market clearing price. Orders to buy and sell at the market clearing price are matched on a time priority basis. All sell orders below the market clearing price and all buy orders above the market clearing price are matched too.

The AZX computer determines auction prices that: (1) most nearly balance supply and demand (as represented by bids and offers in the open order book), (2) maximize the volume of shares traded, and (3) usually differ slightly from the market prices simultaneously determined in active trading markets. The auction price and volume of shares in each security are displayed continuously throughout every auction and participants can revise their prices at any time before the auction ends. To insure that all orders represent serious intentions to trade, a penalty charge is levied on participants who cancel an order during the auction. As a result of these operating procedures, bid-ask spreads and market impact costs are zero. In 1998 about two dozen institutional investors used the AZX system to trade several hundred thousand shares on a typical day.

Primex. Primex is an electronic auction system for stocks that is patterned after the NYSE. Primex is owned by Merrill Lynch, Goldman Sachs, Citigroup's Salomon Smith Barney, Morgan Stanley Dean Witter, and B. L. Madoff. Primex will electronically take customers' orders to buy and sell to the NYSE and also to competing electronic exchanges and private broker-dealers in search of the best available price. It is an interactive system that permits users to haggle for the best prices with users of any other trading system. Nasdaq formed an alliance with Primex in 2000 to obtain faster access to the NYSE stocks.

Tradepoint. Tradepoint is a for-profit electronic exchange that has been operating in the United Kingdom since 1995. It conducts auctions for U.K. equities and operates with a transparent order book. Tradepoint is owned by Instinet (a subsidiary of Reuters), American Century (a large U.S. mutual fund company), Archipelago Holdings LLC (owned by Merrill Lynch, J. P. Morgan, Morgan Stanley Dean Witter, Goldman Sachs, E*Trade, and the Pacific Exchange), Warburg Dillon Read (owned by UBS), and in Europe, Dresdner Kleinwort Benson, and Credit Suisse First Boston (CSFB). In 2000 Tradepoint merged with the Swiss Stock Exchange(SWX) and, a short time later, formed an alliance with the Archipelago Exchange.

JIWAY. In 2000 Morgan Stanley Dean Witter and a stock exchange technology company named OM Gruppen invested €100 million to create a screen-based, cross-border European retail trading platform named Jiway. Jiway is a comprehensive outsourcing service through which stockbrokers can transact with each other in 6,000 different European and American stocks. Jiway auctions off the right to be the designated market-maker for each stock in its system to member firms. Jiway provides custody services, a complete back-office-for-hire service, risk management software, and connections to other Internet traders for its broker clients.

EASDAQ. The European Association of Securities Dealers Automated Quotations (EASDAQ) is a Brussels-based operation patterned after Nasdaq. EASDAQ lists and trades about 50 technology stocks. Nasdaq acquired EASDAQ in 2001.

Reg ATS Exchanges

ECNs and electronic stock exchanges have the potential to displace organized securities markets. The SEC has a rule, nicknamed **Reg ATS,** allowing alternative trading systems (ATS) operating in the United States to register as stock exchanges. In 1999 Island ECN started the lengthy regulatory process to register with the SEC as a stock exchange. In 2000 Archipelago ECN became the Archipelago Exchange by merging with the previously registered Pacific Stock Exchange. The SEC requires registered stock exchanges to report their prices through the Consolidated Quotation System (CQS), operate as a self-regulating organization (SRO), and participate in the intermarket trading system (ITS); it also permits them to trade with NYSE member firms like Merrill Lynch. These privileges can change a tiny ECN into a major market overnight.

Modernization and Consolidation

In 1999 the NYSE and Nasdaq announced plans to demutualize and reorganize as for-profit corporations so they could issue securities to raise the capital to finance their technological development. Nasdaq might become a SuperECN by adding a centralized limit order book (CLOB) with internal order execution capabilities. The NYSE might be forced to create its own ECN, merge with an ECN, or open its floor to ECNs that feed on its order flow.

Electronic technology will continue to accelerate change, trading volume will increase as transactions costs fall, and the pressure on stock exchanges and ECNs to consolidate will increase. Table 6-6 is one snapshot from an ongoing moving picture show that will continue until a global market emerges. Because of numerous regulatory and logistical barriers, these new linkages between the NYSE or Nasdaq and foreign markets will occur gradually.

LIQUIDITY

Perfectly liquid assets are highly marketable; they suffer no price shrinkage if they are sold hastily. The following categories of assets are listed with respect to their liquidity in the United States, starting with the most liquid category first:

1. U.S. dollar bills are perfectly liquid.
2. U.S. Treasury bonds are extremely liquid.
3. NYSE-listed stocks and the largest Nasdaq stocks (e.g., Microsoft) are highly liquid.
4. Most Nasdaq stocks are liquid.
5. Corporate bonds can be traded, but they are not very liquid.
6. Most municipal bonds are somewhat illiquid.
7. Most real estate is illiquid.
8. Art objects and collectibles are very illiquid.

Illiquid assets involve a marketability risk that causes investors to add on a **liquidity premium** to raise their required rate of return.[11] Transactions-cost statistics provide estimates of the appropriate liquidity premium.

Transactions Costs

Total transactions costs include direct and indirect costs. Brokers' commissions, income taxes, transfer taxes, custodial fees, and outlays for research information are *direct transactions costs* that are easy to see. The bid-ask spread, the market impact of the transaction, and opportunity costs are *indirect transactions costs*. Indirect transactions costs are more difficult to measure, and they can exceed the direct transactions costs.

1. **Bid-Ask Spread.** Interest expense to finance the inventory of securities, a risk premium for investing capital at risk, and administrative costs determine the bid-ask spread.
2. **Market Impact.** Buying tends to bid up stocks' prices, while selling tends to drive down their prices. Large transactions move prices further than small transactions. Statistical price volatility provides an estimate of these market impacts of trading.
3. **Opportunity Cost.** Opportunity cost is an implicit cost that results from decay of the information value of a trade incurred when the market moves against the trader while the trader waits to trade. Opportunity cost tends to increase with the time between the decision to trade in the completion of the trade. It is not practical to try to estimate the opportunity cost.

Total transactions costs can range from a small fraction of 1% of the value of the transaction to much of the investor's return in countries that have high capital gains taxes.

TABLE 6-6   Technological Advances Motivatel Stock Exchanges to Consolidate to Obtain Order Flow

Table 6A Consolidations

Exchange Consolidating	Progress on the Consolidation
	Nasdaq Deals
Osaka Securities Exchange (OSE) and Nasdaq Japan Planning Co. (NASD and Softbank)	This joint venture began trading in June 2000. The Nasdaq Japan Planning Co. was established in June 1999 by a joint venture agreement between the NASD and Japan's Softbank Corporation.
Nasdaq and Hong Kong	This co-listing agreement called for trading to start in 2000, but delays slowed progress.
Nasdaq Canada	A co-listing agreement between Nasdaq and Quebec Government was announced 2000. This deal threatens the Toronto Stock Exchange.
Europe	Nasdaq acquired Easdag in 2001.
	NYSE'S Global Equity Market (GEM)
NYSE's Global Equity Market (GEM)	In 2000 the NYSE, Tokyo SE, Paris Bourse, Toronto SE, Amsterdam SE, SE of Hong Kong Australian SE, Brazil's Bovespa, Brussels SE, and Mexico's Bolsa agreed to form a Global Equity Market (GEM) that trades each other's stocks 24 hours per day. The GEM alliance is simpler than Nasdaq's plans to merge trading platforms with other stock exchanges.
	Archipelago Exchange
An ECN named Archipelago and the Pacific Stock Exchange	In 2000 the SEC approved this plan to develop into an exchange that could trade NYSE, NASDAQ, and AMEX stocks electronically through the National Market System (NMS) for U.S. exchanges.
	Euronext
Paris, Amsterdam, and Brussels Exchanges create EURONEXT	This 2000 announcement creates an alliance and a new exchange that started trading and demutualized in 2001.
	Nordic Exchanges (NOREX)
Copenhagen Stock Exchange and OM Stockholm Exchange merged to create NOREX	Trading between Copenhagen and OM Stockholm Exchanges began in June 1999. (Sidelight: OM Stockholm Exchange's software was written by OM Gruppen, an aggressive Swedish software group.)
Lithuania's Tallinn, Latvia's Riga, and Lithuania's National exchanges join NOREX	In 2000 these three Baltic Exchanges signed a letter of intent to join NOREX.
Iceland Stock Exchange and Oslo Exchange join NOREX	Separately, these exchanges signed letters of intent to join NOREX in 2000.
	VIRT-X
Swiss Stock Exchange (SWX) joined with Tradepoint, an ECN	The Swiss Stock Exchange got regulatory approval to merge with an ECN named Tradepoint of the United Kingdom and start trading European stocks in 2001.
	Archipelago Exchange and Virt-x
Virt-x and Archipelago Exchange	If this electronic alliance works out, it could be the first transatlantic stock exchange and the first to trade European stocks in the U.S.

TABLE 6-6B A Noteworthy Failure to Complete a Consolidation

Exchanges That Failed to Consolidate	**International Exchange (iX)**
London Stock Exchange (LSE) and Deutsche Bourse tenatively agreed to merge into iX	This merger between two large exchanges failed in 2000 because German and English shareholders with divergent national interests did not approve. When the iX merger failed other exchanges were suggesting mergers, and a hostile takeover bid from Stockholm's OM Gruppen was in play. Stay tuned for more.
Exchanges That Failed to Consolidate	**Australia & New Zealand**
Australia and New Zealand Stock Exchanges	In 2001, months after the merger was announced, the larger and more rapidly growing Ausralia Stock Exchange (ASX) choked while trying to swallow the New Zealand StockExchange (NZSE). Renewed attempts are plausible.

Eqn. 6-2 measures the one-period rate of return after transactions costs (TC) have been deducted.*

$$r_t = \frac{\text{Price change} + \text{Cash flow (if any)} - \text{Transaction costs}}{(\text{Price at beginning of the holding period})} = \frac{(P_t - P_{t-1}) + CF - TC}{P_{t-1}} \quad \text{(6-2)}$$

The cost of transacting in a market varies inversely with the market's liquidity.

International Survey of Transactions Costs

Salomon Smith Barney (SSB), a subsidiary of Citigroup, is a large investment banking firm with offices around the world. SSB analyzes transactions costs and publishes a monthly survey of statistics from 23 countries. The left half of Table 6-7 contains the indirect transactions costs for large capitalization stocks, the right half contains similar statistics for small capitalization stocks; from one of SSB's monthly reports. These costs are expressed as a percentage of the share's market price, stated in basis points (BPs).

Table 6-7 displays a wide array of indirect transaction costs. The large capitalization stocks are usually traded more actively and more information is available about them than is available about the small issuers. As a result, the transactions costs are typically higher for small corporations' stocks in the same country. Trading costs are characteristically lower in large industrialized nations because they often have more active stock markets, more efficient legal systems, and more political stability than exists in smaller and/or newer nations.

A REALITY CHECK   **ETHICS**

Ethics and Financial Markets

The Securities and Exchange Commission (SEC) is charged with maintaining "fair and orderly markets." This raises two questions: What is fairness? And what to do when fairness conflicts with orderliness?

Fraud and manipulation are two obvious sources of unfairness. Fraud is committed when a trader makes a false statement about, or fails to disclose, a material fact. The underlying idea is that the other party is being deceived. Similarly, a trader who bids up the price of a stock in order to sell at the peak—a once-common form of manipulation—is also guilty of deception by making the stock appear to be more valuable.

Fairness in the sense of a "level playing field" requires that some—but not all!—asymmetries be reduced. All investors should be able to compete on relatively equal terms. This means that they should have *access* to but not necessarily *possess* the same information. Equal access is facilitated by *mandatory disclosure*, as when a corporation is required to publish an annual report. Mandatory disclosure also makes markets more efficient, so that both fairness and orderliness are secured.

Many investment instruments and relationships are *contracts* that commit the parties to a certain course of action. Contractors act fairly when they fulfill the terms of a contract. However, in some situations, the terms cannot be fully specified because of complexity and uncertainty. When two parties cannot anticipate situations that might arise or determine precisely what to do, they form *imperfect* or *relational* contracts that specify certain ends. For example, a broker who has been authorized to trade for a client's account cannot be bound

---

* Consider a 5-year investment in a security. If five annual returns were to be computed, purchase commissions could be added to the denominator for the first year's return. But, purchase commissions should be excluded from the denominator for the last four annual returns.

TABLE 6-7   **Average Buy or Sell (One-Way) Bid-Ask Spreads, Market Impact Cost of Trading, and Total Trading Cost Estimates for Large- and Small-Capitalization Stocks, in Basis Points[a]**

	Large-Capitalization Stocks					Small-Capitalization Stocks				
Countries	(1) No. of Issues	(2) Value, US$ millions	(3) Bid- Ask[b]	(4) Market Impact[c]	(5) Total Cost[a]	(6) No. of issues	(7) Value, US$ millions	(8) Bid- Ask[b]	(9) Market Impact[c]	(10) Total Cost[a]
Canada	98	16.05	23	21	44	240	1.97	63	17	80
United States	387	63.39	11	8	19	2,968	24.42	27	10	37
Australia	39	6.39	19	18	37	131	1.08	52	12	64
Hong Kong	29	4.75	45	27	72	97	0.80	63	28	91
Japan	229	37.51	20	17	37	861	7.09	21	19	40
New Zealand	13	2.13	53	42	95	13	0.11	60	33	93
Singapore	32	5.24	44	34	78	47	0.39	63	35	98
France	34	5.57	10	7	17	156	1.28	33	10	43
Germany	24	3.93	35	8	43	215	1.77	43	33	76
Italy	44	7.21	15	11	26	134	1.10	26	11	37
Netherlands	15	2.46	9	5	14	98	0.81	20	6	26
Spain	10	1.64	8	7	15	71	0.58	21	9	30
Denmark	22	3.60	54	42	96	40	0.33	82	14	96
Norway	28	4.59	32	32	64	35	0.29	59	32	91
Sweden	30	4.91	18	14	32	70	0.58	48	11	59
Switzerland	10	1.64	7	5	12	126	1.04	27	7	34
United Kingdom	75	12.29	27	9	36	547	4.50	79	9	88
Austria	14	2.29	28	27	55	23	0.19	37	14	51
Belgium	15	2.46	27	19	46	41	0.34	59	18	77
Finland	5	0.82	9	10	19	56	0.46	68	17	85
Greece	51	8.35	25	58	83	63	0.52	56	39	95
Ireland	7	1.15	48	139	187	25	0.21	120	48	168
Portugal	10	1.64	12	20	32	19	0.16	26	7	33
Total	1,221	200.0	20	17	37	6,076	50.0	37	14	51

SUMMARY: Salomon's monthly world markets transaction cost survey adds the bid-ask spread (Columns 3 and 8) to the market impact costs of trading (Columns 4 and 9) to obtain the total transaction costs (Columns 5 and 10) for large capitalization and small capitalization stocks. Averaged over all stocks, the small-cap stocks total transactions costs (51 basis points) is considerably above that of the large-cap stocks (37 basis points). Salomon continuously maintains and updates data files for (1,186 large plus 6,237 small totals) 7,423 stocks used to prepare Table 6-7 for clients' use.

[a] Average cost expressed as a fraction of share price, stated in basis points (BPs). One BP equals $\frac{1}{100}$ of 1% of share price. The Total Cost equals Bid-Ask Spread plus Market Impact Cost.

[b] Half of the average bid-ask spread that was posted over the last 20 trading days was used, since deals can usually be executed well within the posted spread.

[c] Volatility cost is computed with SSB's proprietary model that considers the last 63 days of price volatility, the last 10 days of trading volume data, and sector correlations.

SOURCE: Eric H. Sorensen, PhD, Managing Director, and Laurence J. Price, Vice President, *The Salomon Smith Barney Global Equity Impact Cost and Market Liquidity Monitor*, New York City, 13 March 2000, Figures 4 and 5, pp. 13–14.

by a detailed contract. That broker is committed to making a "best effort" attempt to meet the client's objectives.

In general, fairness (equity) in markets contributes to orderliness (efficiency). Sometimes the two conflict, and some of the most difficult public policy decisions involve a trade-off between equity and efficiency.

John R. Boatright, *Professor of Business Ethics*

THE BOTTOM LINE

The world contains small and large stock markets that provide varying amounts of liquidity. Two types of investors use these markets: individual investors (households) and institutional investors. When an institutional investor executes a block trade that is big enough to disturb the market, the institution may use a block positioner to obtain an advantageous execution.

A wide range of brokerage services compete with each other. Full-service brokerage firms take buy and sell orders from investors who are willing to pay high commissions to obtain cordial treatment and other services. Investors who are more cost-conscious employ discount brokers, electronic brokers, or use ECNs.

Most investors give their brokers market orders in order to receive swift and certain executions. Investors willing to wait for executions, or willing to accept the possibility that their order may never be executed, may give their brokers limit orders or complex orders in hopes of executing their trade advantageously.

Brokerage houses find it profitable to extend margin credit to their clients. Margin requirements limit the amount of money that clients can borrow from their brokerage. Trading on margin magnifies the investor's gains and losses.

Investment bankers assist their clients in making initial public offerings (IPOs) of stocks and bonds in the primary market. An investment banker will organize a distribution syndicate, underwrite the issue, and distribute the securities to investors in the primary market. Electronic investment bankers are use the internet to distribute securities.

The NYSE is the largest stock market in the world; it is a continuous auction market where many large corporations are listed. NYSE members called specialists are monopolistic market-makers for the stocks the NYSE assigns to them. Nasdaq is a large electronic market in which competing market-makers from different locations operate a continuous market. Thousands of U.S. and foreign issues are listed on Nasdaq. Some Nasdaq market-makers operate a third market that competes with the NYSE by trading NYSE-listed stocks in the over-the-counter (OTC) market. The fourth market is a communications network where block traders negotiate trades among themselves at prices and commissions that are negotiated.

Electronic communications networks (ECNs) include several categories of market technology. An order-crossing network matches buy and sell orders away from the floor of a securities exchange. Market impact costs are minimized in a crossing network when compatible anonymous buyers and sellers turn up in the crossing network at the same time. Electronic order-working systems are computer programs that utilize telecommunications to gather current market information and use that data to work trading orders toward advantageous executions. The Arizona Stock Exchange (AZX) is an ingenious stock market in a computer: It conducts auctions several times each day while providing a high level of internal transparency to its participants.

Technology is increasing the array of brokerage services, increasing the competition between brokerages, reducing transaction costs, speeding executions, creating new types of stock exchanges, and altering the way investment bankers conduct IPOs. Telecommunications is also integrating the world's disparate stock markets into a global stock market.

QUESTIONS

Q6-1 (Comparison of exchanges and the OTC market) Compare and contrast the way that stock prices are determined in (a) the OTC market with the way they are determined (b) on organized exchanges like the NYSE.

Q6-2 (Brokers and dealers) Discuss the differences between brokers and dealers.

Q6-3 (Brokers' conflicts of interest) Do you see any conflict of interest between a stockbroker's roles as (a) a sales representative working to maximize his or her own commission income and (b) an investment advisor who is trying to give her or his clients advice to maximize their wealth? Explain.

Q6-4 (Market orders) What does it mean to give your broker a "market order"?

Q6-5 (Transactions costs) Transactions costs include impact costs, commission costs, and opportunity costs. Distinguish among each of these component costs.

Q6-6 (Types of orders) Ed Birch sold short 100 shares of AT&T stock at $35 a share. Explain how Ed could use a stop loss order to limit his losses on this transaction. Stipulate whether Ed would use a stop loss buy order or a stop loss sell order and suggest a price that he might specify when placing the order.

Q6-7 (Call markets) What is meant by a "call market" and what types of entities might use them?

Q6-8 (Order-crossing networks) What is an "order-crossing network"? Discuss some of the advantages and disadvantages associated with these networks.

Q6-9 (Margin transactions) There is a chance of a much greater loss when an investor buys a security on margin. Why, then, do investors engage in margin transactions?

Q6-10 (Investment banking) Describe the four functions performed by investment bankers.

PROBLEMS

P6-1 (Initial margin requirement) If the initial margin requirement is 60% and an investor purchases 500 shares of a $40 per share stock, what is the minimum initial margin that is required for this transaction?

P6-2 (Initial margin requirement) Reconsider problem 6-1. If the initial margin requirement were 75%, what minimum margin would be required?

P6-3 (Initial margin requirement) If the margin requirement is 65% and an investor intends to purchase 100 shares of $50 per share stock, what is the minimum down payment he will be required to make? Show your calculations.

P6-4 (Return on a margin transaction) An investor purchased a $100 stock on 55% margin and then its price doubled to $200. The interest rate the brokerage firm charged for the loan to make the margined investment was 10%. No cash dividends were received while the investor held the stock. What was the investor's one-period rate of return on this transaction, net of all costs? Show your calculations.

P6-5 (Margin call) John Jones recently opened a margin account with the Evergreen Investment Company. Evergreen currently has a 65% initial margin requirement and a 35% maintenance margin. Mr. Jones initially purchases 300 share of Micro-Tech stock at $50 per share. By how much must the price of Micro-Tech stock decline before a margin call is required?

P6-6 (Maintenance margin) Consider the information provided in Problem 6-5. If the market price of Micro-Tech falls to $15, how much must Mr. Jones deposit in his brokerage account to maintain the minimum margin requirement?

P6-7 (Return on a margin transaction) If the price of Micro-Tech stock of Problem 6-5 rises to $75 per share, what will Mr. Jones's one-period return be? Ignore commission costs, but assume an interest rate of 12% on borrowed funds, and assume that no cash dividends were received.

P6-8 (Cash transactions) Assume that Mr. Jones used only his available cash (that is, the amount of his own cash he put up to satisfy the initial margin requirement) to purchase the Micro-Tech stock described in Problem 6-5. What would his 1-year return on his investment then be? Ignore commissions.

P6-9 (Effect of dividend payments on returns) Using the information provided in Problem 6-7, recalculate Mr. Jones's annual return assuming that he received a $4 a share cash dividend.

P6-10 (Investment banking profits and losses) Assume that an investment banker has agreed to underwrite an IPO for GNU Corporation and has decided that 1 million shares will be offered to the public at an initial price of $18. The underwriting spread will be 10%. (That is, the investment banker will pay GNU only 90% of the initial offer price for the shares.) Assume that the investment banker incurs $500,000 of administrative expenses associated with the issue. (a) What will GNU's proceeds from the IPO be if the issue ends up selling for only $12 a share? (b) What will the investment banker's gain (loss) be if the issue sells for only $12 a share?

CFA EXAM QUESTIONS

The following two questions are adopted from the 1998 CFA Sample Exam, Level I:

1. Which of the following *best* describes a securities exchange, such as the Paris Bourse, that uses a call auction system to determine prices for a security?
   A. Market makers or specialists are setting prices.
   B. A single market price is established for all executed orders.
   C. Prices are being determined for call options on the security.
   D. Prices are being determined for transactions off the floor of the exchange.

2. Which of the following statements *best* characterizes forward stock markets like the London and Paris markets?
   A. Settlement of transactions takes place infrequently, typically on one day each month.
   B. Share price is not determined, even after a transaction occurs, until a specified date in the future.
   C. Investors buy and sell contracts for future delivery of shares, but the shares themselves do not change ownership.
   D. Stock ownership changes occur on the day of the transaction, but money is not exchanged until five business days later.

3. (1996 CFA Exam, Level III) Alice Blue, HFS's domestic equity manager, carefully monitors such obvious direct trading costs as commissions and spreads, and regularly reports these costs to the HFS Board of Trustees. However, Blue does not attempt to measure the three components of indirect trading costs because she does not believe these costs are significant.
   A. Explain how *each* of the following *three* components of indirect trading costs can be measured *and* explain why the cost of *each* component can be significant:
      i. Impact Cost
      ii. Timing Cost
      iii. Opportunity Cost
   B. Explain the relationship between Impact Cost and Timing Cost when the size of a trade is large.

4. (Adapted from a question on the 1994 CFA Exam, Level III) Mrs. Goode is confused about the costs of trading. "I always thought these were the same as the broker's commission," she says.
   A. Identify and briefly describe *three* sources of noncommission transaction costs.
   B. Identify *three* methods that can be used to help control and/or reduce noncommission transaction costs.

DO YOUR RESEARCH

1. (Bid-ask spreads) Define the bid-ask spread. List the primary factors that determine the size of the bid-ask spread. *Hint:* This requires outside research. For example, see Seha Tinic, "The Economics of Liquidity Services," *Quarterly Journal of Economics* (February 1972): 79–93.

2. (Financial market theory) Why does the theory of financial markets suggest that having more different securities being traded in more different markets might be desirable? This is a difficult question that requires outside research; you will need to read one of the following books. (a) Chi-fu Huang, and R. H. Litzenberger, *Foundations of Financial Economics* (New York: North-Holland Publishing Company, 1988), Chapter 5. (b) Jonathan E. Ingersoll, *Theory of Financial Decision Making* (Totowa, NJ: Rowman and Littlefield Publishers, 1987), Chapter 2. (c) James A. Ohlson, *The Theory of Financial Markets and Information* (New York: North-Holland Publishing Company, 1987), Chapters 2–3.

FURTHER REFERENCES

O'Hara, Maureen. *Market Microstructure Theory*, Cambridge, MA: Blackwell Publishers, 1995.

This is a high-level, comprehensive monograph that fills 275 pages. The book's use of advanced mathematics makes it appropriate for advanced graduate students in finance and economics.

Schwartz, Robert A. *Reshaping the Equity Markets*, Homewood, IL: Business One Irwin, 1993.

This 452-page monograph reviews recent market history, analyzes individual markets, discusses market architecture, and analyzes the impact of these factors on the price determination process.

International Finance Corporation. *Emerging Stock Markets Factbook*. Washington, DC, published annually.

The 1997 edition of the IFC's *Factbook* contains 338 pages of stock market data on 30 emerging markets and 14 frontier markets. The *Factbook* also reported observations on 24 developed markets and 77 other small markets.

ENDNOTES

[1] For more detail about orders, see, Robert A. Schwartz, *Reshaping the Equity Markets* (Burr Ridge, IL: Business One Irwin, 1993), Chapters 2 and 13. Or, see Richard J. Tewles and Edward S. Bradley, *The Stock Market*, 7th ed. (New York: Wiley, 1998); Chapter 13 is titled "Margin Trading."

[2] See Roger G. Ibbotson, Jody L. Sindelar, and Jay. R. Ritter, "The Market Problems with the Pricing of Initial Public Offerings," *Journal of Applied Corporate Finance* 7, no. 1 (spring 1994): 68–70. See L. M. Benveniste and P. A Spindt, "How Investment Bankers Determine the Offer Price and Allocation of New Issues, *Journal of Financial Economics* 24: 343, 362. Also, see K. Rock, "Why New Issues All Are Underpriced," *Journal of Financial Economics* 15: 187–212. Also see Jay R. Ritter, "The Hot Issues Market of 1980," *Journal of Business* (April 1984). More recently, see Laurie Krigman, Wayne H. Shaw, and Kent L. Womack, "The Persistence of IPO Mispricing and the Predictive Power of Flipping," *Journal of Finance* 54, no. 3: 1015–44.

[3] For more details about investment banking, see Ernest Bloch, *Inside Investment Banking* (Homewood, IL: Dow Jones-Irwin, 1986). Also see Hsuan-Chi Chen and Jay R. Ritter, "The Seven Percent Solution," *Journal of Finance* 55, no. 3: 1105–31. Further, see C. W. Smith, "Investment Banking and the Capital Acquisition Process," *Journal of Financial Economics* 15 (January-February 1986): 3–29. See also D. P. Baron, "A Model of the Demand for Investment Bank Advising and Distribution Services for New Issues," *Journal of Finance* 37 (September 1982): 955–76.

[4] See Stephen A. Ross, Randolph W. Westerfield, and Jeffrey Jaffe, *Corporate Finance,* 4th ed. (Chicago: Irwin, 1996), Chapter 19. Also see Richard A. Brealey and Stewart C. Myers, *Principles of Corporate Finance*, 5th ed. (New York: McGraw-Hill, 1996), Chapter 15.

[5] See Lawrence Glosten and Paul Milgrom, "Bid, Ask and Transaction Prices in a Specialist Market with Heterogeneously Informed Traders," *Journal of Financial Economics* 14 (1985): 71–100.

[6] See Hans Stoll, "The Supply of Dealer Services in Securities Markets," *Journal of Finance* 33 (1978): 1133–51. Also see Thomas Ho and Hans Stoll, "Optimal Dealer Under Transaction and Return Uncertainty," *Journal of Financial Economics* 9 (1981): 47–73. The NYSE stopped using 12.5¢ price intervals and decimalized (adopted a 1¢ tick size) in 2001.

[7] For details about the determinants of the bid-ask spread, see Seha Tinic, "The Economics of Liquidity Services," *Quarterly Journal of Economics* (February 1972). For the classic study, see Harold Demsetz, "The Cost of Transacting," *Quarterly Journal of Economics* (October 1968), Figure 1, p. 36. Also see K. Cohen, S. Maier, R. Schwartz, and D. Whitcomb, "Transactions Costs, Order Placement Strategy, and Existence of a Bid-Asked Spread," *Journal of Political Economy* (April, 1981). See also George J. Benston and Robert L. Hagerman, "The Determinants of Bid-Asked Spreads in the Over-the-Counter Market," *Journal of Financial Economics* 1 (December 1974). Also see Lawrence R. Glosten and Lawrence E. Harris, "Estimating the Components of the Bid-Asked Spread," *Journal of Financial Economics* 21, no. 1: 123–42. For a study of the bid-ask spreads on CBOE options, see J. Y. Choi, Dan Salandro, and Kuldeep Shastri, "On the Estimation of Bid-Asked Spreads: Theory and Evidence," *Journal of Financial and Quantitative Analysis* 23, no. 2 (June 1988): 219–30. More recently, see David Lesmond, Charles Trzinka, and Joseph Ogden, "A New Measure of Transaction Costs," 1996 NYU Working Paper FIN-96-32. Furthermore, see James J. Angel, "Tick Size, Share Prices, and Stock Splits," *Journal of Finance* 52 (June 1997): 655–81.

[8] For an insightful discussion about the implications of reduced tick sizes, see James J. Angel, "Tick Size, Share Prices, and Stock Splits," *Journal of Finance* 52, no. 2 (June 1997): 655–81.

[9] For information about settlement and clearance of security trades, see Thomas H. McInish, *Capital Markets: A Global Perspective* (Malden, MA: Blackwell Publishers, 2000), Chapter 4. Or, see Richard J. Tewles and Edward S. Bradley, *The Stock Market*, 7th ed. (New York: Wiley, 1998), Chapter 15.

[10] See "In the Pink," *Open Finance* 37 (Summer 1999): 12–13; published by Sun Microsystems, Palo Alto, CA. Also see "Pink Sheets, Plugging into the Modern Era, Give Their Stock Listings Some Color on the Internet," *Wall Street Journal*, 2 September 1999, C1.

[11] See Yakov Amihud and Haim Mendelson, "Liquidity and Asset Prices: Financial Management Implications," *Financial Management* 17, no. 1 (Spring 1988): 5–15. And, see Yakov Amihud and Haim Mendelson, "Asset Pricing and the Bid-Asked Spread," *Journal of Financial Economics* 17 (1986): 223–49. Also see Y. Amihud and H. Mendelson, "Dealership Market: Market-Making with Inventory," *Journal of Financial Economics* (May-June 1980): 31–53.

STATISTICAL ANALYSIS AND THE SML

The old saying that "a fool and his money are soon parted" is, unfortunately, an appropriate way to describe the unscientific way many people invest. This chapter presents some objective statistical measures to help investors avoid foolish decisions. Scientific tools are introduced to help investors make decisions without using their emotions. The analysis focuses on investments' rates of return.

*Statisticians call the one-period rate of return from a stock or bond a **random variable** because its uncertain value fluctuates randomly from minute to minute and from day to day. Rates of return are important investment outcomes that provide a worthwhile focal point for quantitative investment analysis.*

When comparing and contrasting different investments it would be hasty and oversimplified to simply select the asset that had the highest average rate of return. The riskiness of an investment is too important to ignore.

***Risk** is equated with variability of return. As discussed in Chapter 2, an investment's total risk can be measured statistically with the variance, VAR(r), or the standard deviation, σ. This chapter shows how to divide an investment's total risk into diversifiable and undiversifiable components. Quantitative tools are introduced to help the investor do security analysis and make investment decisions.*

This chapter ends by introducing the Security Market Line (SML). The SML reveals an important relationship between assets' undiversifiable risks in their expected returns.

THE BASIC RANDOM VARIABLE

The one-period rate of return measures the speed at which the investor's wealth increases or decreases. Consider different ways to compute the one-period rate of return.

Unmargined Returns

The price change income (or loss) plus any cash flow income that make up an investment's one-period rate of return is called the **total return,** where r^u stands for the unmargined rate of return.

$$r^u = \frac{\text{Price change} + \text{Cash flow (if any)}}{\text{Price at beginning of the holding period}} = \frac{(P_t - P_{t-1}) + CF}{P_{t-1}} \qquad \text{(7-1)}$$

The unmargined rate of return is the return an investor earns from cash investments (or 100% margin); it is the same one-period rate of return from a long position that was introduced in Chapter 2 as Eqn. 2-3b.

One-Period Return Calculations

Consider the rates of return for the stock and bond investments in Table 7-1.

Last year's historical rate of return from the bond in Table 7-1 was 2.13%.

$$r_t = \frac{P_t - P_{t-1} + CF_t}{P_{t-1}} = \frac{\$940 - \$980 + \$60}{\$940} = \frac{\$20}{\$940} = 2.13\%$$

The investor's expected stock return, denoted $E(r)$, for next year is 12.18%:*

$$E(r_t) = \frac{[E(P_t) - P_{t-1}] + E(CF_t)}{P_{t-1}} = \frac{\$70.50 - \$66.50 + \$4.10}{\$66.50} = \frac{\$8.10}{\$66.50} = 12.18\%$$

$E(r)$ denotes the expected return, $E(P)$ stands for the expected future price in Table 7-1, and $E(CF)$ is the cash flow expected next year.

The investor's expected return for next year from the bond is 12.23%:

$$E(r_t) = \frac{[E(P_t) - P_{t-1}] + E(CF_t)}{P_{t-1}} = \frac{\$995 - \$940 + \$60}{\$940} = \frac{\$115}{\$940} = 12.23\%$$

TABLE 7-1	Annual Data for a Stock and a Bond		
Convention	Description	Stock Data	Bond Data
P_{t-1}	Last year's closing price	$64.00	$980.00
P_t	Current year's closing price	$66.50	$940.00
CF_1	Current year's cash flow income	$ 3.90[a]	$ 60.00[b]
$E(P_2)$	Next year's expected closing price	$70.50	$995.00
$E(CF_2)$	Next year's expected cash flow	$ 4.10[a]	$ 60.00[b]

[a]Cash dividends per share can vary each period.
[b]The coupon interest rate of 6.0% is fixed; the annual coupons are $60.

---

* The expected return is a noncompounded one-period rate of return that is mathematically similar to the arithmetic mean return introduced in Chapter 2's Eqn. 2-6. The $E(r)$ is analyzed further in a multiperiod context in Chapter 10.

Compute last year's *historical* rate of return for the stock in Table 7-1. Solution:

$$r_t = \frac{(P_t - P_{t-1}) + CF_t}{P_{t-1}} = \frac{\$66.50 - \$64.00 + \$3.90}{\$64.00} = \frac{\$6.40}{\$64.00} = 10\%$$

Analysis of Margined Investment Returns

If an investor wants to buy securities with borrowed money the investor can open a **margin account.** A margin account permits an investor to make a down payment that is called the **margin fraction (MGFR),** and borrow the rest of the purchase price from the brokerage. The borrowed amount is called the **debit balance.** Consider a $30 stock that is purchased with $20 of margin:

$$\begin{pmatrix} \text{Investor's} \\ \text{margin, \$20} \end{pmatrix} = \begin{pmatrix} \text{Price of} \\ \text{security, } P = \$30 \end{pmatrix} - \begin{pmatrix} \text{Debit balance, borrowed} \\ \text{from brokerage, \$10} \end{pmatrix}$$

$$\begin{pmatrix} \text{Margin fraction,} \\ \text{MGFR} = 0.666 \end{pmatrix} = \begin{pmatrix} \text{Investor's} \\ \text{margin, \$20} \end{pmatrix} \bigg/ \begin{pmatrix} \text{Price of} \\ \text{security, } P = \$30 \end{pmatrix}$$

The one-period rate of return earned from a margined investment is denoted r^m.

$$r^m = \frac{\text{Price change} + \text{Cash dividend} - \text{Interest}}{(\text{Beginning price})(\text{Margin fraction})} = \frac{(P_1 - P_0) + CF - I}{(P_0)(MGFR)} \tag{7-2}$$

If we ignore interest expense, the relationship between the one-period rate of return from an unmargined and a margined position in the same investment is simple:

$$r^m = \frac{r^u}{MGFR} \tag{7-3}$$

Eqn. 7-3 suggests how using margin can magnify the investor's average return and variability of returns.

Margined Returns After Transaction Costs

Eqn. 7-4 defines the rate of return a margined investor earns after taxes, commissions, and other transaction costs (*TC*).

$$r^m = \frac{\begin{pmatrix} \text{Price} \\ \text{change} \end{pmatrix} + \begin{pmatrix} \text{Cash} \\ \text{dividend} \end{pmatrix} - \begin{pmatrix} \text{Transactions} \\ \text{costs} \end{pmatrix}}{(\text{Beginning price})(\text{Margin fraction})} = \frac{(P_1 - P_0) + CF - TC}{(P_0)(MGFR)} \tag{7-4}$$

A margined investor's interest expense can be included in the transaction costs.*

---

* The rates of return from an arbitrage position (Chapter 15), foreign exchange (Chapter 17), options and futures (Chapters 9, 27–28), and more complicated structures are discussed in later chapters.

Selecting a Sample

To analyze an investment, it is usually easier to compute one-period rates of return using a convenient **differencing interval** than it is to compute one-period returns that correspond to the dates when that asset was purchased and sold. For instance, 10 annual rates of return, 40 quarterly returns, or 120 monthly returns might be used to analyze the same 10-year investment. Investment analysts commonly break the investment horizon into a series of consecutive, nonoverlapping* differencing intervals to calculate rates of return. To get a meaningful sense of an existing investment, it should be observed over a complete business cycle.

DEFINITION

A BUSINESS CYCLE

The length of a business cycle can be measured from peak to peak or from trough to trough. The average business cycle lasts about 7 years, but they vary in length from a few years to over a decade. The recessions are almost always shorter and more breath-taking than the expansions. Every recession in the United States is preceded by a bear market. Sample periods that encompass less than one complete business cycle are likely to be unrepresentative samples that yield biased statistics.

PROBABILITY DISTRIBUTIONS OF RETURNS

After investigating an investment, the investor can usually write down what he or she thinks are plausible rates of return during the investment's holding period and attach a probability to each return. A list of such possible rates of return and their probabilities is called a **probability distribution of returns.** As shown in Figure 7-1, probability distribution can be expressed as either a graph or table.

Figure 7-1 shows a probability distribution of returns for Coca-Cola's common stock Tom wrote down after studying this stock. Figure 7-1A is a continuous graph drawn through five discrete rates of return. Figure 7-1B lists the five discrete possibilities.

The horizontal axis of the graph in Figure 7-1 measures the single-period rates of return. The vertical axis gauges the probability that any given rate of return occurs.

Figure 7-2 illustrates the one 6-month rate of return that comprises Dick's entire probability distribution for a 6-month investment in a U.S. Treasury bill. If Dick holds the T-bill until it matures, he is sure (the probability is 1) of the rate of return he will earn.

THE EXPECTED RATE OF RETURN

The weighted average of all the different rates of return in one probability distribution is called the **expected return;** it is denoted $E(r)$. The vertical line through the center of Coca-Cola's probability distribution of returns in Figure 7-1 illustrates the expected return, $E(r_{Coke}) = 20\%$, that can be computed from Tom's probability distribution of returns.

---

* The time intervals over which the rates of return are calculated should not overlap in order to obtain statistically independent rates of return. Dependent returns would be serially correlated. Statistical dependence is a problem because dependent random variables (in this case, dependent returns) can cause biased estimates of other statistics.

FIGURE 7-1 Tom's Subjective Probability Distribution of Returns for Coca-Cola's Common Stock: (A) Graph, (B) Table

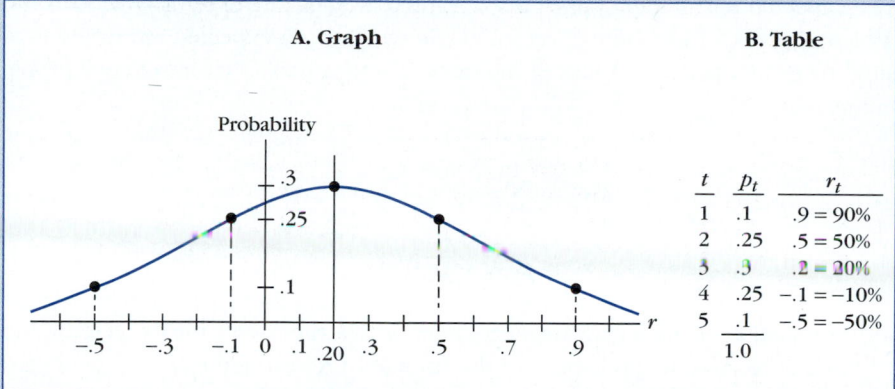

A. Graph

B. Table

t	p_t	r_t
1	.1	.9 = 90%
2	.25	.5 = 50%
3	.3	.2 = 20%
4	.25	−.1 = −10%
5	.1	−.5 = −50%
	1.0	

Tom read everything he could find about Coca-Cola; he tasted Coke, Pepsi, and the competing soft drinks and discussed the soft drink industry with people. After his research Tom wrote down the rates of return, denoted r_t, he thought Coke's stock was likely to earn in the year ahead and the probability, p_t, for each return.

FIGURE 7-2 Dick's Subjective Probability Distribution of Returns for the 6-Month U.S. Treasury Bill with Zero Variability of Return

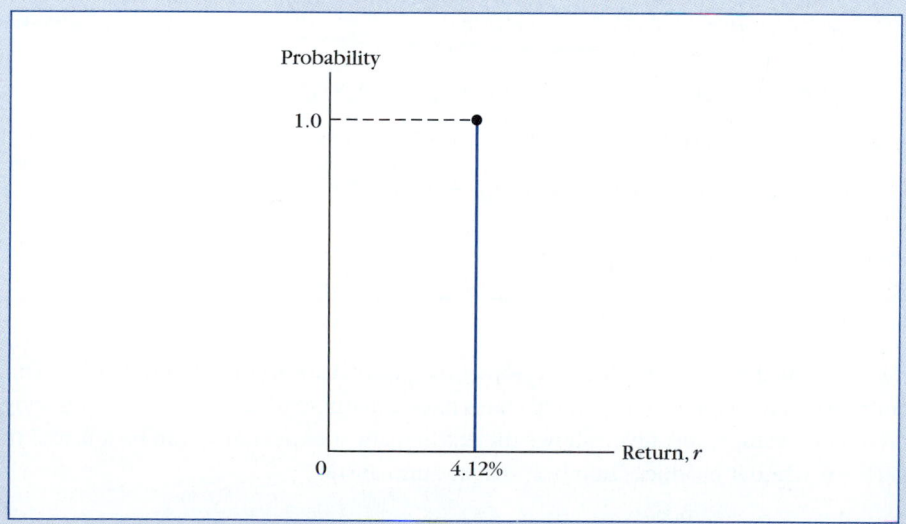

Dick read everything he could find about the securities issued by the U.S. Treasury and discussed them with people. He learned that only one rate of return could be earned if a T-bill is held to maturity. He wrote down this 6-month rate of return of 4.12% and its probability of 1.0. Since it has zero variability of return, it is called a **riskless asset.**

THE EXPECTED RETURN, $E(r)$

The expected return for any asset is a weighted average rate of return that uses the probabilities, p_t, of each rate of return as the weights. An expected return is calculated by summing the products of the rates of return times their respective probabilities, $p_t r_t$.

$$E(r) = \sum_{t=1}^{T} p_t \, r_t \tag{7-5}$$

$$= p_1 \, r_1 + p_2 \, r_2 + \ldots + p_T \, r_T$$

In this equation, $E(\ )$ is a mathematical operator that represents the expected value computations, p_t is the probability of the tth rate of return, and $r_1, r_2, r_3, \ldots, r_T$ are the possible rates of return. The subscripts of t in the formula are counters for each different rate of return. There are $t = 1, 2, 3, \ldots, T$ possible returns, and T denotes the terminal (last) return. If each outcome has the same probability, the *equally likely probabilities* are:

$$p_1 = p_2 = \ldots = p_{T-1} = p_T = (1/T)$$

EXAMPLE   **COCA-COLA STOCK'S EXPECTED RETURN, $E(r)$**

The expected return for Coca-Cola's common stock from Tom's probability distribution in Figure 7-1 is computed as:

$$E(r) = \sum_{t=1}^{T=5} p_t \, r_t = p_1 \, r_1 + p_2 \, r_2 + \ldots + p_T \, r_T \tag{7-5a}$$

$$= (p_1)(r_1) + (p_2)(r_2) + (p_3)(r_3) + (p_4)(r_4) + (p_5)(r_5)$$

$$= (.1)(90\%) + (.25)(50\%) + (.3)(20\%) + (.25)(-10\%) + (.1)(-50\%)$$

$$= .09 + .125 + .06 - .025 - .05 = 0.2 = 20\%$$

Coke's expected return is $E(r_{KO}) = 20\%$.

Mathematical expected values are sometimes unrealistic values. Using census data, for example, married couples in the United States have a mathematical expectation of having 2.2 children. The example just given shows the mathematical expectation can be a useful thinking aid even when it produces numbers that are unrealistic.

RISK ESTIMATES

As seen in Figure 7-2, Dick's 6-month U.S. Treasury bill has zero variability of return. Since we equate risk with variability of return, T-bills are risk-free assets. The wideness of a probability distribution of returns measures variability of return and, therefore, the riskiness of the investment. Tom's probability distribution of returns for Coca-Cola stock in Figure 7-1, for example, illustrates a riskier investment than Dick's probability distribution for the riskless 6-month T-bill in Figure 7-2, because Figure 7-1 is a wider probability distribution than Figure 7-2.

The **variance** of an asset's rates of return is a statistic that measures the asset's "wideness." The variance is represented by the symbols σ^2 and $VAR(r)$. (Eqn. 2-9 in Chapter 2 defines the variance.)

The **standard deviation** equals the square root of the variance; it was introduced at Eqn. 2-10 in Chapter 2. The variance and the standard deviation both measure variability of return; they are *equivalent* measures of total risk.

SOURCES OF RISK

The rates of return from investments fluctuate in a random manner that is hard to predict. Some major sources of risk are defined as:

- ◆ **Market risk** arises from alternating bull and bear market forces.

- ◆ **Interest-rate risk** is the variability of return from an investment that is caused by changes in market interest rates.

- ◆ **Purchasing-power risk** is the variability of return an investor suffers because of inflation (or, less frequently, enjoys from deflation).

- ◆ **Management risk** is that part of an investment's total variability of return caused by alternating profitable decisions and management errors.

- ◆ **Credit risk** is that portion of total risk that results from the possibilities of default or bankruptcy.

- ◆ **Liquidity risk** results from price discounts given or sales commissions paid to be able to sell an asset quickly.

- ◆ **Margin risk** is the variability of return an investor creates by using borrowed funds.

- ◆ **Callability risk** is the variability of return that reflects the possibility that the security may be redeemed (called in) by its issuer before its scheduled maturity date.

- ◆ **Convertibility risk** results from the possibility that the investment in a convertible bond or a convertible preferred stock may be converted into the issuer's common stock.

- ◆ **Foreign country risk** is the variability of return international investors face that can result from expropriation of nonresidents' assets, disadvantageous tax and tariff treatments, unreimbursed destruction of assets that result from hostilities in the foreign country, difficulty in obtaining local information, and other multinational peculiarities.

- ◆ **Foreign exchange risk** is the variability of return that international investors face because the exchange rates at which currencies are traded fluctuate.

- ◆ **Domestic political risk** arises from changes in environmental regulations, zoning requirements, fees, licenses and taxes that cause variability of return.

- ◆ **Industry risk** is the variability of return caused by events that affect competing firms. Product obsolescence is an example of an industry risk.

The uncertainties listed above are the major sources of investment risk. Other risk components will be introduced and investigated in the chapters that follow.

CONSTRUCTING PROBABILITY DISTRIBUTIONS

Investors can analyze variability of returns (risk) scientifically by formulating probability distributions of returns.

Subjective and Objective Probability Distributions

Tom's **subjective probability distribution** for Coca-Cola's stock is illustrated in Figure 7-1. Subjective probability distributions are based on "guestimates" of the outcomes. If Tom knows a lot about Coke's stock, the subjective probability distribution he creates will reflect reality. If Tom does not know much about the investment, his subjective probability distribution may not be much help.

The column to the far right in Table 2-1, Chapter 2 (see p. 24) illustrates seven probability distributions that were prepared from decades of historical data. These **objective probability distributions** are based on historical results. Probability distributions based on historical results are also called **relative frequency distributions.**

Rates of Return Are More Appropriate Measures Than Dollar Changes

Consider a wealth-maximizing choice between two equally risky stocks. Should a wealth-maximizing investor buy the common stock in the box below issued by the Mammoth Corporation to obtain the capital gain of $10 per share? Or, should the investor go for the $5 per share gain from stock issued by the Imperial Corporation?

Price Per Share	Imperial Corporation	Mammoth Corporation
Beginning price	$ 5	$50
Ending price	$10	$60

If you focus on the dollars instead of the returns, you will probably choose the $10 per share gain from the Mammoth Corporation's stock because that is twice as many dollars as the $5 per share gain from the Imperial's stock. If you choose Mammoth, alas, you made a poor decision. Focusing on the rates of return helps you realize that Imperial's stock is the better investment because it offers a 100% rate of return while Mammoth promises only a 20% return. After all, you can invest $50 in 10 shares of Imperial instead of buying 1 $50 share of Mammoth. When you analyze the multiple-share possibilities, you realize that maximizing the rate of return leads to better investment decisions than maximizing the per-share dollar gains. Rates of return provide a common denominator for comparing assets with different prices. Earnings from bonds, real estate, stocks, and other dissimilar assets can be readily compared when they are all stated in terms of their one-period rates of return.

THE STABILITY OF PROBABILITY DISTRIBUTIONS

Suppose that the historical market prices of a stock were recorded at the close of each trading day for 4 consecutive years. Figure 7-3A represents two hypothetical relative frequency (historical probability) distributions representing 4 years of common stock prices. One probability distribution is for the stock's first 2 years, and the other distribution is for the second 2 years.

Probability distributions (relative frequency) of security prices are of little value for two reasons that should be apparent after a glance at Figure 7-3A. First, the distributions are not stable over time. Most stocks' prices increase with the passage of time at about 6.6% per

FIGURE 7-3 Relative Frequency Distributions of a Stock's (A) Market Prices and (B) Rates of Price Change

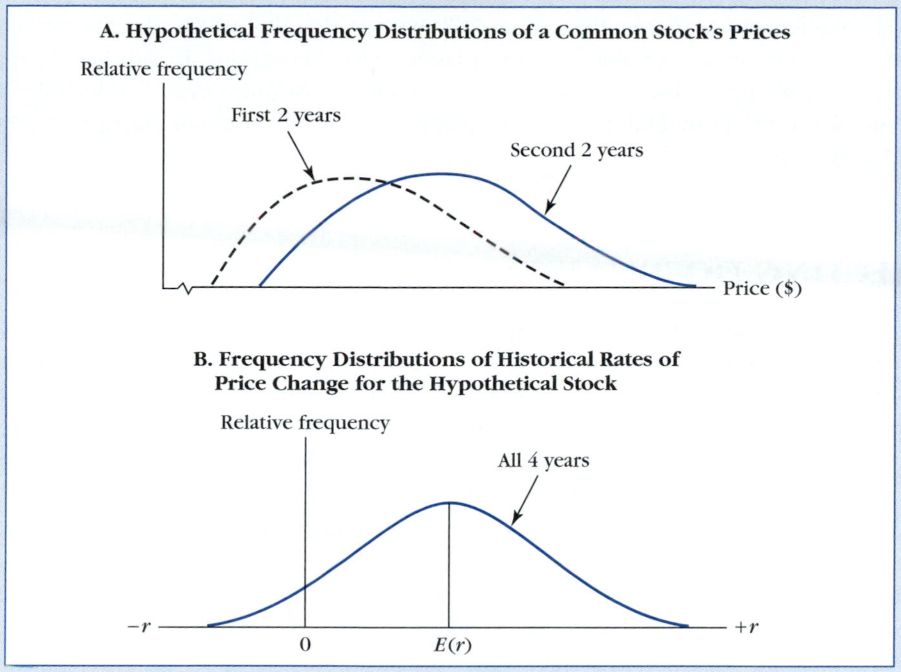

A. Hypothetical Frequency Distributions of a Common Stock's Prices

B. Frequency Distributions of Historical Rates of Price Change for the Hypothetical Stock

The stock's relative frequency distributions (historical probability distributions) of prices in (A) are not stable through time and, therefore, are not useful for forecasting. The stock's relative frequency distribution (historical probability distribution) of rates of price change in (B) *is* useful because it is stable through time.

year.* This upward trend causes each year's relative-frequency distribution to shift to the right and have a higher mean price. Second, the shape of the distribution changes each year. Each year, as the security's price rises, the distribution's tail on the right side grows a little longer. As a security's price trends upward, each year's relative-frequency distribution becomes, in statistical language, more skewed to the right.**

As a result of these two changes, the distributions of security prices are of little value; one year's distribution cannot be used to accurately predict the probability that a certain price will occur in the future. In statistical language, probability distributions of stock prices are not stable through time.

Probability Distributions of Rates of Return Tend to Be Stable

Although the distributions of prices are not stationary, studying these distributions reveals that security prices tend to experience percentage changes that conform to a stable distribution. Percentage price changes are defined in Eqn. 7-6:

---

* The average large stock's price rose at an average rate of about 6.6% per annum during the past 75 years; this ignores the income from cash dividends.

** This paragraph describes a statistical **scaling problem.** It can be shown that $VAR(2P) = 4VAR(P)$. This equation shows that higher-priced stocks (for example, twice as high, or $2P$) have a variance of prices that is four times larger. The standard deviation of a stock that is priced twice as high will have a standard deviation of prices that is doubled, $\sigma(2P) = 2\sigma(P)$. Skewness also experiences scaling problems.

$$r_t = \frac{\text{Price change}}{\text{Price at beginning of holding period}} = \frac{(P_t - P_{t-1})}{P_{t-1}} \qquad \text{(7-6)}$$

The rates of price change that occur daily, weekly, monthly, quarterly, semiannually, or yearly tend to conform to a stable probability (relative frequency) distribution, like the one in Figure 7-3B, if the price changes are drawn from a complete business cycle that includes both bull and bear markets. Including the stock's income from cash dividends changes Eqn. 7-6 to Eqn. 7-1 (p. 160).

SELECTING DOMINANT ASSETS

Dominant assets have the maximum expected rate of return at any selected level of risk or, conversely, the minimum risk of all assets with a given expected rate of return. Six hypothetical assets are shown in Table 7-2 to illustrate the **dominance principle.** Figure 7-4 is a two-dimensional graph with risk on the horizontal axis and rate of return on the vertical axis.* Any vertical line drawn in Figure 7-4 delineates a **risk class,** because all assets on a vertical line have the same standard deviation.

According to the dominance principle, asset T dominates assets B and C because T has less risk at their expected return. Likewise, asset A has the same level of $E(r)$ as asset E but A dominates E because A is has less risk. M dominates B, because M has the largest expected return in its risk class. A wealth-seeking, risk-averse investor would prefer investing in T, M, or A rather than in B, C, or E. Assets B, C, and E are not desirable because they are *dominated*

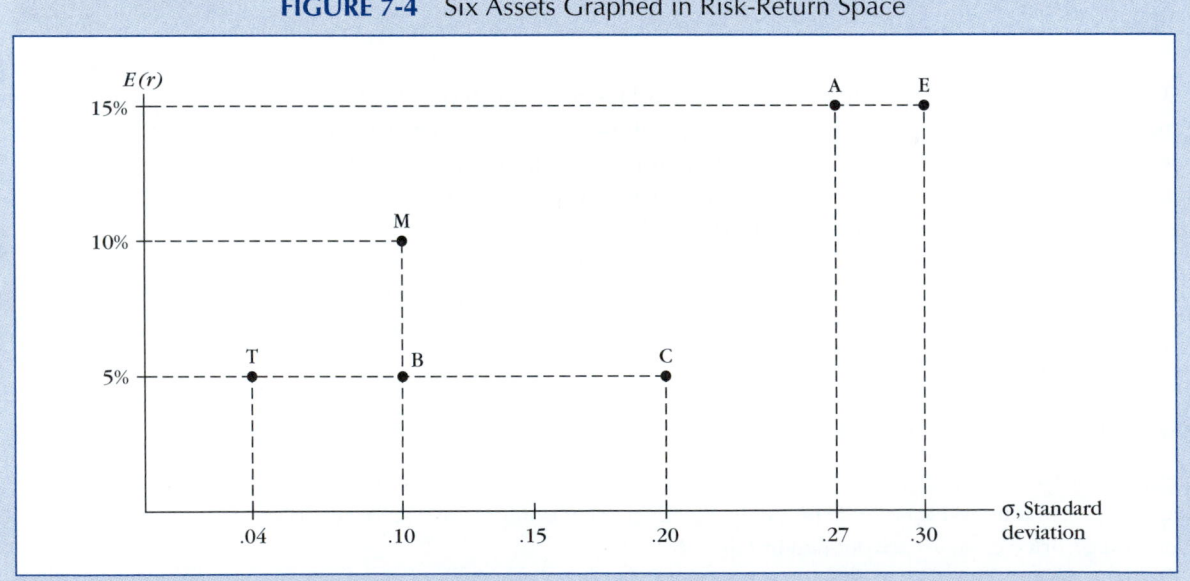

FIGURE 7-4   Six Assets Graphed in Risk-Return Space

Asset B is dominated by assets T and M. Asset C is also dominated by asset T. Asset E is dominated by asset A.

---

* Markowitz portfolio theory is the topic of Chapter 14. Chapter 14 explains how the risk-reducing powers of diversification will cause the individual assets graphed in Figure 7-4 to be dominated by portfolios.

TABLE 7-2	Risk and Return Statistics for Six Investments		
Asset	Expected return, $E(r)$	Risk, σ	Dominated?
M	10%	10%	No
B	5%	10%	Yes, by T and M
C	5%	20%	Yes, by T and B
A	15%	27%	No
E	15%	30%	Yes, by A
T	5%	4%	No

assets. When the dominance principle is combined with information about the investor's tastes for risk and return, it is possible to make even more definitive investment choices.

Consider some *investor preferences*. A *timid* highly risk-averse investor would prefer dominant investment *T* in Table 7-2. An *aggressive* less risk-averse investor would prefer dominant investment *A*. A "*moderately aggressive* investor" will prefer asset *M*.

THE CHARACTERISTIC LINE

When you think of investments as probability distributions of returns you tend to remember them in terms of their expected returns, variances, and other risk statistics like the *beta* and the *residual variance*. Beta and the residual variance are risk statistics that measure an investment's *undiversifiable risk* and *diversifiable risk*. A simple linear regression called the *characteristic line* is used to measure an investment's beta and residual variance.[1]

CHARACTERISTIC LINE   DEFINITION

The **characteristic line** is a line-of-best-fit through some data points. Figure 7-5 graphically depicts three characteristic lines; the data points for these three characteristic lines were omitted to simplify the graph.

A characteristic line is what statistics books call a time-series regression line. The statistical model uses the one-period rate of return from some market index in the time period t, denoted $r_{M,t}$ to explain the simultaneous rate of return from some asset that we will refer to as the *i*th asset. Asset *i* could be a stock, bond, or any other investment. The characteristic line is a tool in the toolbox of many security analysts and is used to estimate the undiversifiable and diversifiable risk of an investment.

$$r_{i,t} = \alpha_i + \beta_i r_{M,t} + e_{i,t} \qquad (7\text{-}7)$$

Eqn. 7-7 defines the characteristic line for asset *i*.[2] The alpha (α_i) and beta (β_i) terms are statistical estimates of the line's intercept and slope, respectively. The $e_{i,t}$ is the unexplained residual return from asset *i* that occurs in time period *t*. Like the residuals in all regression equations, the epsilon ($e_{i,t}$) is a random variable that measures fluctuations above and below the characteristic line. Peek ahead at Figure 7-6 if you want to see the epsilons for KO's stock.

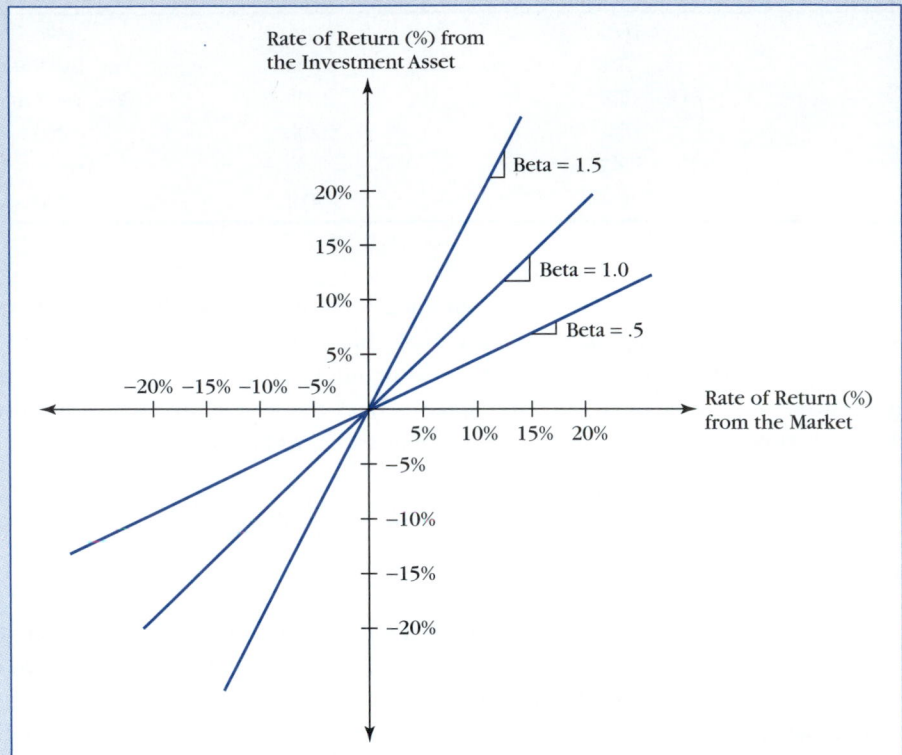

FIGURE 7-5 Characteristic Lines for Assets with High, Medium, and Low Betas

The three characteristic lines show that an investment asset with a beta (slope) coefficient of 0.5, 1.0, or 1.5 tends to vary about one-half, the same amount, or one-and-a-half times as much as a market index like the S&P500 index.

Rearranging Eqn. 7-7 so that the undiversifiable and diversifiable sources of the assets' returns are separated yields the following:

$$r_{i,t} \quad = \quad \beta_i r_{M,t} \quad + \quad \alpha_i + e_{i,t} \tag{7-7a}$$

$$\begin{pmatrix} \text{Total rate} \\ \text{of return} \\ \text{in period } t \end{pmatrix} = \begin{pmatrix} \text{Undiversifiable} \\ \text{return in time} \\ \text{period } t \end{pmatrix} + \begin{pmatrix} \text{Diversifiable} \\ \text{return in time} \\ \text{period } t \end{pmatrix}$$

Figure 7-5 illustrates the characteristic line for three different assets that we might call assets $i, j,$ and k; these three assets have low, medium, and high levels of systematic (undiversifiable) risk.

Market Returns: The Characteristic Line's Independent Variable

The economic forces that move the securities market are measured along the horizontal axis of Figure 7-5. These market rates of return from consecutive time periods, denoted $r_{M,1}, r_{M,2},$ $r_{M,3}, \ldots, r_{M,T},$ are the explanatory variable in the characteristic line. Eqn. 7-8 shows how rates of change in the stock market are calculated if the Standard & Poor's 500 Stocks Composite (S&P500) Index is the explanatory variable.

Eqn. 7-8 measures the percentage change in the S&P500 index during the time interval from the end of period t to the end of $t + 1$. The one-period rate of change in the market index in Eqn. 7-8 is based on common stock income (or losses) from average price changes in the United States; it does not include cash dividends. Cash dividend payments can easily be included, as shown in Eqn. 7-8a.*

$$r_{M,t} = \frac{SP500_{t+1} - SP500_t}{SP500_t} \tag{7-8}$$

$$r_{M,t} = \frac{SP500_{t+1} - SP500_t + \left(\begin{array}{c}\text{Cash dividend from the S\&P500} \\ \text{portfolio of stocks in period } t\end{array}\right)}{SP500_t} \tag{7-8a}$$

Market indexes other than the S&P500 could be used to compute Eqn. 7-8. Once a market index is adopted, it should be used consistently to determine all characteristic lines so they are comparable. Table 7-3 contains quarterly rates of return calculated from the S&P500 Index that are ready to be used as inputs to compute a characteristic line.

TABLE 7-3 Quarterly Market Returns from S&P500 Index, 1995–99

Year	Quarter	S&P500 Index (End of Quarter)	S&P500 Cash Dividends	S&P500 Quarterly Return, Eqn. 7-8a
1995	Q1	500.71	3.14	9.71%
1995	Q2	544.75	3.6	9.51%
1995	Q3	584.41	3.5	7.92%
1995	Q4	615.93	3.55	6.00%
1996	Q1	645.50	3.45	5.36%
1996	Q2	670.63	3.77	4.48%
1996	Q3	687.31	3.89	3.07%
1996	Q4	740.74	3.79	8.33%
1997	Q1	757.12	4.15	2.77%
1997	Q2	885.14	3.33	17.35%
1997	Q3	947.28	4.06	7.48%
1997	Q4	970.43	3.96	2.86%
1998	Q1	1101.75	4.3	13.98%
1998	Q2	1133.84	3.63	3.24%
1998	Q3	1017.05	4.26	−9.92%
1998	Q4	1229.23	4	21.26%
1999	Q1	1286.37	4.01	4.97%
1999	Q2	1372.71	4.18	7.04%
1999	Q3	1282.71	4.44	−6.23%
1999	Q4	1469.25	4.23	14.87%

SUMMARY: Quarterly price change plus cash dividends from the S&P500 index were used to compute market returns with Eqn. 7-8a.

---

* Cash dividend payments change very little from year to year and, so, they have little effect on a stock's risk statistics. The correlation coefficient (a goodness-of-fit statistic) and the beta coefficient (a regression's slope coefficient) for a characteristic regression line are almost identical regardless of whether Eqn. 7-8 or 7-8a is used to compute the explanatory variable.

The explanatory variable defined in Eqn. 7-8 is sometimes called the returns from the **market portfolio,** because this market index is supposed to represent "the market." No market index exists for the market that contains *all* stocks, bonds, futures contracts, options, art objects, pieces of real estate, human capital, and other assets that might be included in a broadly defined market portfolio. More narrowly defined stock market indexes like those discussed in Chapter 11 are usually used for computations with Eqn. 7-8.

Asset Returns: The Characteristic Line's Dependent Variable

The one-period rates of return for an asset's characteristic line are calculated for a series of consecutive time periods with Eqn. 7-1. Statisticians call these returns the **dependent variable,** because their values depend on the values of the explanatory variable—the returns from the market portfolio computed with Eqn. 7-8. The dependent variable is graphed on the vertical axes of Figures 7-5 and 7-6. These consecutive one-period returns are denoted $r_{i,1}$, $r_{i,2}$, $r_{i,3}$, ..., $r_{i,T}$ for asset i. Table 7-1 contains numerical examples of how to compute these one-period rates of return for a stock or a bond.*

Estimating a Characteristic Line's Statistics

The pairs of one-period rates of return for asset i and the market in Table 7-4 are the data inputs that determine the characteristic line for asset i. What security analysts call the characteristic line is called a *regression line* by statisticians. The graph of a simple regression line is determined by the values of two statistics called the **alpha** (α, intercept) and **beta** (β, slope coefficient). Many computer programs will compute the intercept and slope statistics for a regression equation.

The first step in the determination of a characteristic line is to calculate each period's market returns using Eqn. 7-8 and asset returns using Eqn. 7-1. The time periods used for calculating returns on the asset and the market must be simultaneous on a period-by-period basis because the characteristic line model measures the ith asset's concurrent reactions to market forces.

TABLE 7-4   The Raw Data Inputs Used to Compute the Alpha and Beta for Asset *i*'s Characteristic Line

Time Period	Pair of Simultaneous Returns	
$t = 1$	$(r_{i,t=1}, r_{M,t=1})$	
$t = 2$	$(r_{i,t=2}, r_{M,t=2})$	
$t = 3$	$(r_{i,t=3}, r_{M,t=3})$	
$t = 4$	$(r_{i,t=4}, r_{M,t=4})$	
⋮	⋮	
$t = T$	$(r_{i,t=T}, r_{M,t=T})$	← Terminal time period

---

* It is desirable to have at least 30 observations over a sample period from 2 to as much as 10 years when estimating the characteristic line. It is common to use 30 monthly or quarterly observations. Thirty observations are suggested because that is where small sample theory typically ends and the large sample sampling theory begins—for example, the t-distribution may be dropped and the normal distribution used in its place. The reason a decade is suggested as an upper limit for a sample period is because over longer sample periods the asset's risk and return characteristics are more likely to change. If objective historical returns are not available, the analyst must create a subjective probability distribution of returns (p. 166).

TABLE 7-5   Quarterly Raw Data for KO's Characteristic Line, 1995–99

		Unadjusted Data			Adjusted Data		
Year	Qtr.	Ending Price	Cash Dividend	Units	Ending Price	Cash Dividend	Quarterly Return, Eqn. 7-1
1995	Q1	$56.375	$0.220	2	$28.188	$0.110	9.89%
1995	Q2	$63.750	$0.220	2	$31.875	$0.110	13.47%
1995	Q3	$69.000	$0.220	2	$34.500	$0.110	8.58%
1995	Q4	$74.250	$0.220	2	$37.125	$0.110	7.93%
1996	Q1	$82.750	$0.250	2	$41.375	$0.125	11.78%
1996	Q2	$49.000	$0.125	1	$49.000	$0.125	18.73%
1996	Q3	$50.875	$0.125	1	$50.875	$0.125	4.08%
1996	Q4	$52.625	$0.125	1	$52.625	$0.125	3.69%
1997	Q1	$55.875	$0.140	1	$55.875	$0.140	6.44%
1997	Q2	$68.000	$0.140	1	$68.000	$0.140	21.95%
1997	Q3	$61.000	$0.140	1	$61.000	$0.140	−10.09%
1997	Q4	$66.688	$0.140	1	$66.688	$0.140	9.55%
1998	Q1	$77.440	$0.150	1	$77.440	$0.150	16.35%
1998	Q2	$85.500	$0.150	1	$85.500	$0.150	10.60%
1998	Q3	$57.625	$0.150	1	$57.625	$0.150	−32.43%
1998	Q4	$67.000	$0.150	1	$67.000	$0.150	16.53%
1999	Q1	$61.380	$0.160	1	$61.380	$0.160	−8.15%
1999	Q2	$62.000	$0.160	1	$62.000	$0.160	1.27%
1999	Q3	$48.250	$0.160	1	$48.250	$0.160	−21.92%
1999	Q4	$58.250	$0.160	1	$58.250	$0.160	21.06%

[2-for-1 split — bracketing the 1996 Q1 row]

SUMMARY: Coca-Cola's price change plus cash dividend quarterly rates of return were computed with Eqn. 7-1, after adjusting for the 2-for-1 stock split in 1996.

Table 7-5 contains the Coca-Cola Corporation's (KO's) quarterly common stock data used to fit the characteristic line in Figure 7-6C. The price and dividend data can be obtained from public sources.* The analyst may need to make the appropriate adjustments for stock dividends and splits, if any, to avoid distorted returns. KO's data in Table 7-5 shows the kinds of adjustments needed to handle that firm's 1996 stock split.**

The rates of return from the market and KO's simultaneous rates of return are plotted in Figure 7-6C. Each dot in Figure 7-6C represents the rate of return on the asset and the market during one quarter. A line of best fit through these points was estimated statistically by regressing the dependent variable, r_i, onto the independent variable, r_M. Table 7-6 contains statistics that define the KO characteristic line in Figure 7-6C.

---

* The Investor Relations Department at Coca-Cola's corporate headquarters in Atlanta, GA will mail anyone Coke's Annual Report and other financial data about the firm free of charge. Many firms (including KO) publish their financial statements on their Web site. Chapter 4 discusses Internet sources from which financial data on many corporations may be obtained immediately from the SEC (pp. 69–70).

** See Chapter 5 (p.113) and/or Chapter 8 (pp.200–204) about how to adjust for changes in the unit of account caused by stock splits and stock dividends.

FIGURE 7-6 Coca-Cola Common Stock's Characteristic Lines over 5-Year Sample Periods: (A) 1985–89; (B) 1990–94; (C) 1995–99

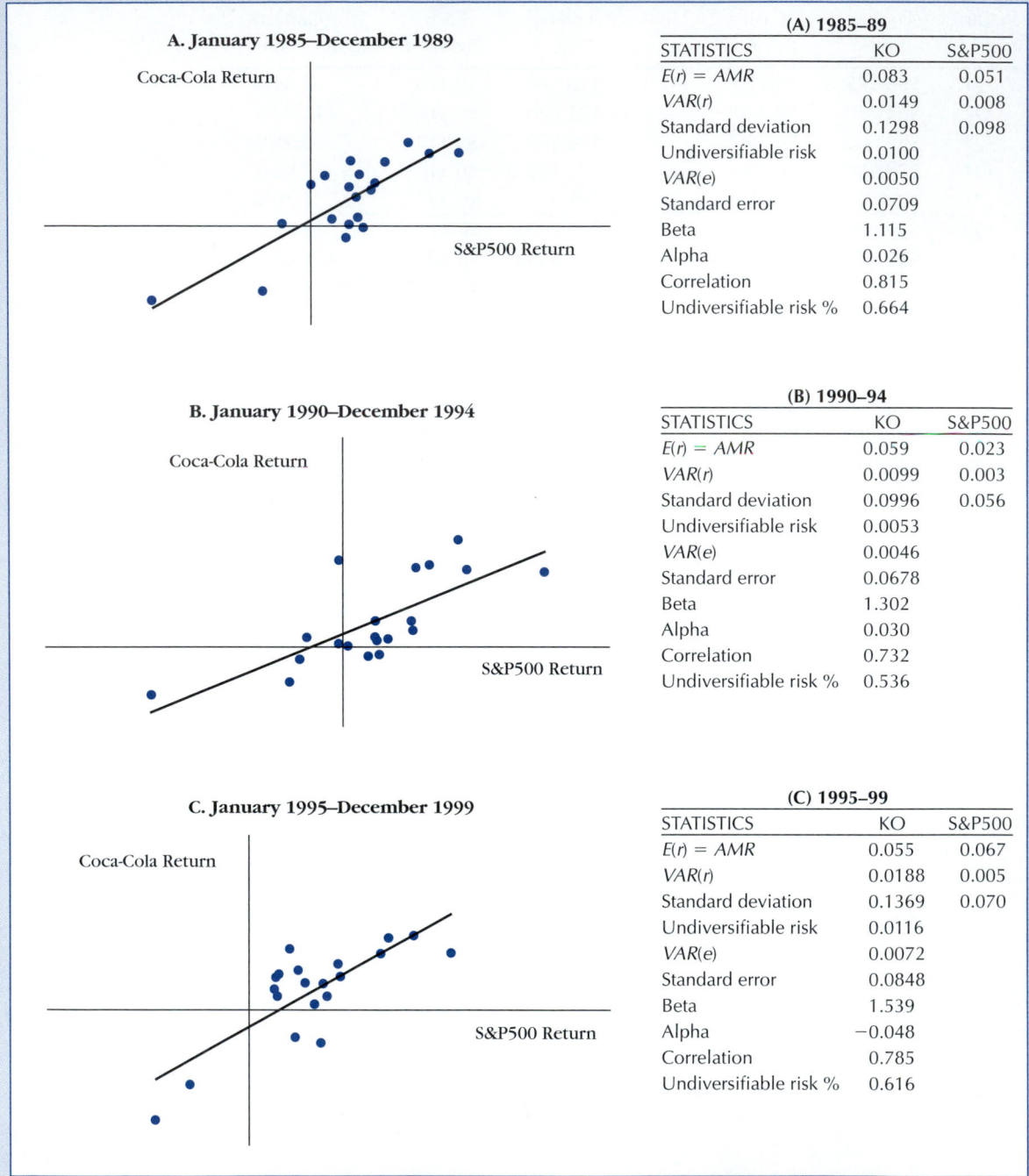

(A) 1985–89		
STATISTICS	KO	S&P500
E(r) = AMR	0.083	0.051
VAR(r)	0.0149	0.008
Standard deviation	0.1298	0.098
Undiversifiable risk	0.0100	
VAR(e)	0.0050	
Standard error	0.0709	
Beta	1.115	
Alpha	0.026	
Correlation	0.815	
Undiversifiable risk %	0.664	

(B) 1990–94		
STATISTICS	KO	S&P500
E(r) = AMR	0.059	0.023
VAR(r)	0.0099	0.003
Standard deviation	0.0996	0.056
Undiversifiable risk	0.0053	
VAR(e)	0.0046	
Standard error	0.0678	
Beta	1.302	
Alpha	0.030	
Correlation	0.732	
Undiversifiable risk %	0.536	

(C) 1995–99		
STATISTICS	KO	S&P500
E(r) = AMR	0.055	0.067
VAR(r)	0.0188	0.005
Standard deviation	0.1369	0.070
Undiversifiable risk	0.0116	
VAR(e)	0.0072	
Standard error	0.0848	
Beta	1.539	
Alpha	−0.048	
Correlation	0.785	
Undiversifiable risk %	0.616	

Figure 7-6C shows that during 1995–99 KO's characteristic line had a beta of $\beta = 1.54$ and an alpha of $\alpha = -4.85\%$ that explained 61.6% of the stock's variability of return—or VAR(r). (A) and (B) are discussed later in this chapter.

TABLE 7-6 Coca-Cola's Market Statistics, 1995–99[a]	
Sample size	20 quarters
Alpha intercept	$\alpha = -0.0485 = -4.85\%$
Beta (slope) coefficient	$\beta = 1.54$
KO's average rate of return	5.46% per quarter
Correlation	$\rho = 0.785$
R-squared = Coefficient of determination	$\rho^2 = .616 = 61.6\%$
KO's $VAR(r)$	0.01875
Residual variance	0.00719
Market's average return (S&P500)	6.70% per quarter
$VAR(r_M)$ for S&P500 index	0.00487
$COV(r_{KO}r_{S\&P500})$	0.0075

[a]Computations use $N = 20$ quarters, not 19 degrees of freedom

The Characteristic Line's Unexplained Residual Returns

Eqn. 7-9 defines the portion of one time period's rate of return from asset i that is left unexplained by the characteristic line. This unexplained residual return is the regression's prediction error during time period t.

$$r_{i,t} - (\alpha_i + \beta_i r_{M,t}) = e_{i,t} \tag{7-9}$$

If $e_{i,t} = 0$, that time period's data point would lay precisely on the characteristic line—the prediction was perfect.

COMPUTING A STOCK'S ALPHA AND BETA   **EXAMPLE**

This shows how to compute the characteristic line statistics for a hypothetical company named U.S. Telephone (UST).

Ten annual returns from UST are used to compute its characteristic line below. UST's covariance of returns with the market is calculated first:

$$COV(r_{UST}, r_M) = \frac{1}{T} \sum_{t=1}^{T} [r_{UST} - E(r_{UST})][r_M - E(r_M)]$$

Year	U.S. Telephone Return, r_{UST}	U.S. Telephone Deviation, $r_{UST} - E(r)$	Market Portfolio, M Return, R_M	Market Portfolio, M Deviation, $R_M - E(r)$	Prob. $(1/T) = p$	Probability × two deviations, $p[r_{UST} - E(r)][r_M - E(r)]$
1	.10	.03	.10	0	.10	(.10)(.03)(0) = 0
2	.2	.13	.30	.20	.10	(.10)(.13)(.20) = .0026
3	−.20	−.27	−.30	−.40	.10	(.10)(−.27)(−.40) = .0108
4	−.10	−.17	−.10	−.20	.10	(.10)(−.17)(−.20) = .0034
5	.30	.23	.50	.40	.10	(.10)(.23)(.40) = .0092
6	.10	.03	.10	0	.10	(.10)(.03)(0) = 0
7	.10	.03	.10	0	.10	(.10)(.03)(0) = 0
8	.10	.03	.10	0	.10	(.10)(.03)(0) = 0
9	−.10	−.17	−.10	−.20	.10	(.10)(−.17)(−.20) = .0034
10	.20	.13	.30	.20	.10	(.10)(.13)(.20) = .0026
	$E(r_{UST}) = .07$		$E(r_M) = .1$		1.0	$COV(r_{UST}, r_M) = .032$

After UST's covariance is determined, its beta and the correlation for its characteristic line can be computed:

$$\text{Beta} = \frac{COV(r_{UST}, r_M)}{VAR(r_M)} = \frac{.032}{.048} = .666$$

$$\text{Correlation} = \frac{COV(r_{UST}, r_M)}{(\sigma_{UST})(\sigma_M)} = \frac{.032}{(.219)(.148)} = .983 = \rho$$

UST's alpha (regression intercept term) is computed from the two expected returns and its beta:

$$\text{Alpha} = E(r_{UST}) - \beta_{UST}E(r_M) = .07 - (.666)(.10) = .07 - .0666 = .0034$$

INTERPRETING THE CHARACTERISTIC LINE

Eqn. 7-7 is the general mathematical form of a characteristic line. Let's compare Eqns. 7-7 and 7-10. Statisticians call the $E(r_i | r_M, a, b)$ term in Eqn. 7-10 a *conditional expectation* because it represents the expected return of asset i conditional on the values of the market's return, the asset's alpha, the asset's beta, and $E(e) = 0$.

Eqn. 7-7 is similar to Eqn. 7-10 except that the residual return is absent from Eqn. 7-10. The mathematics used to determine simple linear regressions guarantees that these residuals sum to zero, $\sum_{t=1}^{T} e_{i,t} = 0$. It follows that the residuals will also have an expected value of zero, $E(e_{i,t}) = 0$, and that is why they are omitted from the conditional expectation in Eqn. 7-10.

$$E(r_i | r_M, \alpha, \beta) = \alpha_i + \beta_i r_M \qquad (7\text{-}10)$$

The statistical components of a characteristic line's alpha and beta are defined below.

The Covariance Statistic

The **covariance** of returns of the ith asset with the market is defined in Eqn. 7-11. Eqn. 7-11a gives the definition using the expected value operator. Eqn. 7-12 provides a more intuitive, but numerically identical, definition of the covariance that uses the correlation coefficient (ρ).

$$COV(r_i, r_M) = \left(\frac{1}{T}\right)\sum_{t=1}^{T}[r_{i,t} - E(r_i)][r_{M,t} - E(r_M)] \qquad (7\text{-}11)$$

$$COV(r_i, r_M) = E\{[r_{i,t} - E(r_i)][r_{M,t} - E(r_M)]\} \qquad (7\text{-}11a)$$

$$COV(r_i, r_M) = \rho_{i,M}\sigma_i\sigma_M \qquad (7\text{-}12)$$

$$0.0075 = (.7850)(0.13693)(0.06978)$$

KO's common stock has a covariance of 0.0075 during the 1995–99 sample.* The covariance measures the degree to which one variable tends to be above or below its mean while another variable is moving above or below its mean. The covariance is a component in other statistics discussed below.

---

* Divisors of $N = 20$ quarters were used for the standard deviations in Eqn. 7-12 instead of $N-1 = 19$ degrees of freedom.

The Correlation: A Goodness-of-Fit Statistic

The *correlation coefficient*, or simply the **correlation,** is represented by the lowercase Greek letter rho, ρ. The correlation is a standardized index number that varies in the interval from $+1$ to -1 and measures how two variables covary. The correlation is also a goodness-of-fit statistic that measures how well the data points fit a regression line. If two variables are *perfectly positively correlated,* ρ equals $+1$ and all the data points lay on a positively sloped regression line. Two variables are *perfectly inversely correlated* when ρ equals -1 and all the data points lay on a negatively sloped regression line. If ρ equals zero, the dependent and the explanatory variables are *uncorrelated.* Two variables that are uncorrelated do not covary together; they are statistically independent of each other. Eqn. 7-13 defines the correlation between asset i and the market portfolio, M:

$$\rho_{i,M} = \frac{COV(r_i, r_M)}{\sigma_i \sigma_M} \tag{7-13}$$

Standard deviations in the denominator of the correlation were defined in Eqn. 2-10 in Chapter 2.

Beta: A Regression Slope Coefficient

The beta coefficient, or **beta,** measures the slope of one asset's characteristic line. The beta coefficient for asset i is represented by the symbol β_i.

$$\text{Beta for asset } i = \beta_i = \frac{\text{Units of rise}}{\text{Units of run}} = \text{Slope of characteristic line for asset } i$$

Eqn. 7-14 defines the beta coefficient mathematically:

$$\beta_i = \frac{COV(r_i, r_M)}{VAR(r_M)} = \frac{\sigma_i \sigma_i \rho_{i,M}}{\sigma_M^2} \tag{7-14}$$

$$= \frac{.0075}{.00487} = 1.54$$

$VAR(r_M)$ represents the variance of the market returns and $COV(r_i, r_M)$ denotes the covariance of returns between the ith asset and the market. Coke's beta of 1.54 indicates that when the market rises (falls) by some particular percent the price of Coke stock tends to simultaneously rise (decline) by 1.54 times the rise in the market.

The Economics of Beta. The beta coefficient is an index of **undiversifiable (market, systematic) risk.** Betas from different assets may be ranked to compare the undiversifiable risk of the assets.

If the beta of asset i is larger than 1, $\beta_i > 1$, then the rates of return from asset i are more volatile than the returns from the market and asset i is classified as an *aggressive asset.* If the beta is less than 1, $\beta_i < 1$, asset i is a *defensive asset;* its rates of return are less volatile than the market's. Figure 7-6 illustrates the characteristic lines for three different assets that have low, medium, and high levels of beta. Figure 7-6C shows that Coca-Cola is a stock with more than an average amount of undiversifiable risk. KO's beta of $\beta_{KO} = 1.54$ indicates that its returns tends to be 54% more (less) than the return on the market average when the market is rising (falling).*

---

* Betas play a key role in the capital asset pricing model (CAPM), a Nobel prize–winning finance theory that is presented in Chapter 15.

The correlation between the typical NYSE stock and the NYSE Index is 0.50. The characteristic line for Coca-Cola has a higher than average correlation of $\rho = .785$, which means that KO's stock returns follow its characteristic line more closely than average.

The Coefficient of Determination. The correlation coefficient squared is called the *coefficient of determination*, ρ^2. Statistics books show that the coefficient of determination measures the percentage of the variance in the dependent variable that is explained by the variance in the explanatory variable. KO's coefficient of determination means that 61.6% $[= 0.616 = 0.785^2 = \rho^2]$ of the total variance in Coke's returns is explained by the market's simultaneous returns.

Alpha: A Regression Intercept Term

Alpha is the intercept term for the characteristic line. Alpha is the value on the vertical axis where the characteristic line intersects that axis. Alpha can also be interpreted to be an estimate of the asset's rate of return when the market is stationary, $r_{M,t} = 0$. The alpha intercept from Eqns. 7-7 and 7-10 is defined in Eqn. 7-15. Coke's alpha is $\alpha_{KO} = -4.85\%$.

$$\alpha_i = \bar{r}_i - \beta_i \bar{r}_M = E(r_i) - \beta_i E(r_M) \text{ for asset } i \tag{7-15}$$

$$\alpha_{KO} = -4.85\% = 5.466\% - (1.54)(6.7\%) \text{ for KO} \tag{7-15a}$$

The statistics above tell us everything we need to know about an asset's characteristic line. This **market model,** or **single-index model,** as the characteristic line is also called, helps us assess the risk characteristics of one asset relative to the market.[3] The statistics in Table 7-6, for instance, indicate that Coca-Cola's common stock is riskier than the average common stock, in terms of total risk and also in terms of undiversifiable beta risk.[*] Because the risk of an asset may change with the passage of time new risk measurements must be made periodically.[4]

Partitioning an Asset's Total Risk

An investment's total risk, measured by its variance of returns, can be partitioned into two components. Eqn. 7-16 shows how to divide the total risk of asset i into a diversifiable part and an undiversifiable part.[**]

$$VAR(r_i) = \text{Total risk of asset } i \tag{7-16}$$

$$= VAR(\alpha_i + \beta_i r_{M,t} + e_{i,t}) \qquad \text{by substituting } (\alpha_i + \beta_i r_{M,t} + e_{i,t}) \text{ for } r_{i,t}$$

$$= 0 + VAR(\beta_i r_{M,t}) + VAR(e_{i,t}) \qquad \text{since } VAR(\alpha_i) = 0$$

$$= \beta_i^2 VAR(r_M) + VAR(e_{i,t}) \qquad \text{since } VAR(\beta_i r_M) = \beta_i^2 VAR(r_M)$$

$$= \begin{pmatrix} \text{Undiversifiable} \\ \text{risk, } \beta_i^2 VAR(r_M) \end{pmatrix} + \begin{pmatrix} \text{Diversifiable} \\ \text{risk, } VAR(e) \end{pmatrix}$$

---

[*]   Statements about the relative degree of total risk are made in the context of a long-run horizon—that is, over at least one complete business cycle. An accurate short-run forecast, which says that some particular company will go bankrupt next quarter, makes it riskier than KO, although KO may have had more historical variability of return.

[**]   In this context, partition is a technical statistical word that means to divide the total variance into mutually exclusive and exhaustive pieces. This partition is only possible if the returns from the market are statistically independent from the residual errors that occur simultaneously, $COV(r_{m,t}, e_{i,t}) = 0$.

The diversifiable risk, $VAR(e)$, is called the **residual variance,** or the *standard error* squared, by statisticians. Diversifiable risk is made up of idiosyncratic fluctuations that are unique to the investment.

Undiversifiable Proportion. The percentage of total risk that is undiversifiable can be measured by the coefficient of determination, ρ^2, the characteristic line's squared correlation:

$$\frac{\text{Undiversifiable risk}}{\text{Total risk of asset } i} = \frac{\beta_i^2 VAR(r_M)}{VAR(r_i)} = \rho^2 \qquad\qquad (7\text{-}17)$$

$$= \frac{(1.54)^2(.00487)}{.01875} = .616 = 61.6\%$$

As shown in Eqn. 7-17, 61.6% of KO's total variance is explained by its characteristic line. This percentage is the undiversifiable proportion of Coke's total risk, because it is explained by the S&P500 index—a market force that influences all market assets simultaneously.

Diversifiable Proportion. The proportion of an investment's total risk that is unsystematic risk equals $(1-\rho^2)$.

$$\frac{\text{Diversifiable risk}}{\text{Total risk}} = \frac{VAR(e)}{VAR(r_i)} = (1 - \rho^2) \qquad\qquad (7\text{-}18)$$

$$= \frac{.0072}{0.01875} = (1 - .616) = .384 = 38.4\%$$

Eqn. 7-18 shows that 38.4% of KO's total variance is residual variance that is left unexplained by the characteristic line. This 38.4% is the diversifiable proportion of Coke's total risk because it is unexplained by the market forces that influence all market assets. Diversifiable risk is made up of idiosyncratic variations that are unique to each asset.

Empirical studies of the characteristic lines of hundreds of stocks listed on the NYSE indicate that the average correlation coefficient is approximately $\rho = .5$.[5] This means that about $\rho^2 = .25 = 25\%$ of the total variability of return in most NYSE securities can be explained by the characteristic line. Comparing KO's stock to the average NYSE stock shows that KO is more systematic than the average stock.

Risk Component	NYSE Average	Coca-Cola
The proportion of systematic (or undiversifiable) risk is ρ^2.	.25 = 25%	.616 = 61.6%
The proportion of unsystematic (or diversifiable) risk is $(1.0-\rho^2)$.	.75 = 75%	.384 = 38.4%
Total risk is 100% of the risk.	1.0 = 100%	1.0 = 100%

COMPARING REGRESSION MODELS

STUDY CHECK

Many statistics textbooks explain a regression formula of the following form: $y = \alpha + \beta x + e$

   QUESTION: How does this common regression model compare with the characteristic line defined in Eqn. 7-7?

   ANSWER: The two regression models are identical mathematically. The characteristic line, Eqn. 7-7, is one of many applications of standard regression analysis.

Getting Statistics from the Internet

Betas, standard deviations, correlations, alphas, and other statistics used by financial analysts may be obtained from the Internet through the following Web sites.

1. Standard & Poor's: www.personalwealth.com
2. CBS Web site for investors is: www.cbsmarketwatch.com
3. *Business Week's* Web site for investors is: www.businessweek.com/investor/
4. Morningstar: www. morningstar.com

Statistics for stocks and mutual funds are available. Most services will ask you to subscribe to gain access to their full offering.

THE SECURITY MARKET LINE (SML)

All types of risk are not equally obnoxious. Undiversifiable risk is more harmful to more people than diversifiable risk because undiversifiable risk is harder to eliminate.

Undiversifiable risk [Beta is an index]	← Harmful and hard to eliminate
Plus: Diversifiable risk [Measured by $VAR(e)$]	← Easy to diversify away
Sum: Total risk [Measured by $VAR(r)$]	

Many investors realize that undiversifiable risk is worse than diversifiable risk. These realizations are reflected in their bid and asked prices. If a stock has a high beta (for instance, $\beta = 1.5$), many investors will not be willing to pay as much for it as they would if it had a low beta of, say, $\beta = 0.5$. As a result, the high-beta stocks have higher expected returns. The formula below illustrates this price adjustment process:

$$\uparrow E(r) = \frac{E(\text{Capital gains or losses } + \text{ cash flow})}{\downarrow \text{Purchase price}}$$

Reverse the directions of the arrows in this formula and, if all other factors are remain fixed, you will see the same logic suggesting that stocks with low betas tend to pay lower expected returns. Figure 7-7 summarizes the economic logic of this. The Security Market Line (SML) illustrates a positive trade-off between undiversifiable risk (indexed by beta) and the expected return a stock must offer to induce investors to buy it. This risk-return trade-off generalizes to include all stocks, bonds, and other investments traded in the capital markets.

THE BOTTOM LINE

Rate of return measures the rate at which the investor is increasing or losing wealth per period; it is often the most important economic outcome from an investment. Risk is related to the variability of the one-period rates of return.

Risk factors that create uncertainty are margin risk, interest rate risk, purchasing power risk, bull-bear market risk, management risk, default risk, liquidity risk, callability risk, convertibility risk, foreign exchange risk, political risk, and industry risk, among others. Risk-averse investors are constantly seeking ways to measure and control their exposure to these risks.

Investment analysts can represent assets as probability distributions of returns (Figures 7-1 and 7-2) that summarize everything known about the asset. The variance (or standard

FIGURE 7-7 The Security Market Line (SML)

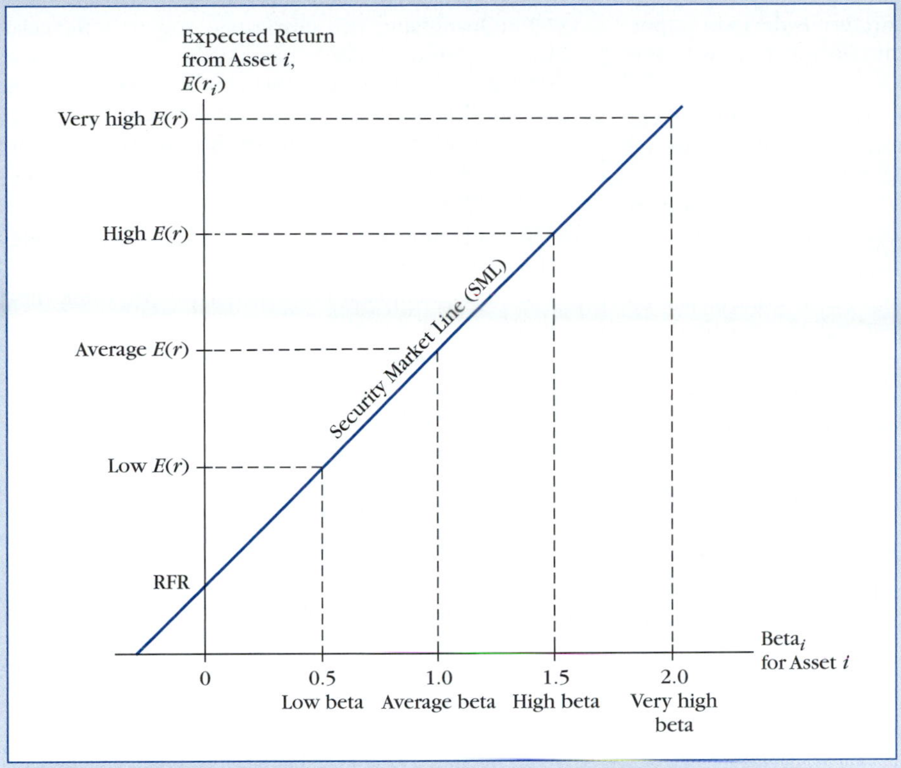

Beta is an index that measures undiversifiable risk. The Security Market Line (SML) illustrates a positive trade-off between beta and the expected return that results from investors' aversion to undiversifiable risk.

deviation) is a quantitative risk surrogate that measures variability of return. Assets' risk and average (expected) return statistics are computed from the data in their probability distributions of returns. These statistics provide market-determined measures that offer a scientific and unemotional approach to security analysis.

The standard deviation (or variance) and expected return statistics from different investment candidates can be analyzed in risk-return graphs (Figure 7-4). Empirical risk-return statistics from a diversified sample of investments will reveal a positive relationship between risk and expected return. This positive risk-return relationship is always present because most investors are risk-averse.

The characteristic line is a simple linear regression. Beta is the slope coefficient of the characteristic line; it is also a gauge of the asset's undiversifiable risk.

The correlation coefficient is a goodness-of-fit statistic that measures how closely the data points fit the characteristic line. Characteristic lines that have high correlations and regression statistics that are stable through time are more useful than characteristic line statistics that do not explain the data very well. Characteristic line can be used to partition an asset's total risk into two meaningful parts—undiversifiable risk and diversifiable risk.

Undiversifiable risk is worse than diversifiable risk because undiversifiable risk is harder to get rid of. The Security Market Line (SML) illustrates a positive trade-off between beta and the expected return that results from rational investors' aversion to undiversifiable risk.

QUESTIONS

Q7-1 (Rate of return) "The rate of return is the most important outcome from an investment." Do you agree with this statement? Explain.

Q7-2 (Past versus future returns) Discuss the differences between historical rates of return and the expected (future) returns on investments. What information does each provide and what role does each play in investor decision making?

Q7-3 (Margin transactions) True, false, or uncertain? The expected rate of return on a margined investment will be higher, but its risk level will equal that of an unmargined investment since the variability of the returns on the assets purchased on margin is unaffected. Explain.

Q7-4 (Expected return) Explain what $E(r)$ measures without using any mathematical symbols or numbers.

Q7-5 (Skewness) Define skewness in a probability distribution of returns without using any mathematical symbols or numbers. Hint: See Appendix to Chapter 7.

Q7-6 (Risk of securities) Generally speaking, is common stocks or corporate bonds the riskier category of investments? Explain your choice.

Q7-7 (Quantitative risk surrogates) You are a financial analyst who has to choose between using two quantitative risk surrogates: (a) the range of returns between the largest and the smallest rates of return, or, alternatively, (b) the variance (or, equivalently, the standard deviation) of the rates of return. Which risk measure would you choose? Defend your choice.

Q7-8 (Relationship between risk and return) Ponder the risk-return relationship documented in Table 7-2 and Figure 7-4 for the dominant investments. Do you think this positive $E(r)$-$VAR(r)$ relationship is coincidental or meaningful? Can you discern any other significant risk-return or risk-income relationships in your life? Feel free to suggest relationships that are unrelated to investing in securities.

Q7-9 (The rate of return concept) The rate of return measure presumes the investment is purchased at the start of each holding period and sold at the end of each holding period in order to compute the capital gain or loss. True, false, or uncertain? Explain.

Q7-10 (Making risky decisions) Making investment decisions based on only the risk and return statistics ignores too much other information. True, false, or uncertain. Explain.

PROBLEMS

P7-1 (Rate of return) Sharon purchased a share of stock on January 14, 1999 for $40 and sold it on January 14, 2000 for $42 after collecting a $2 per share cash dividend. What was her rate of return for this 1-year investment?

P7-2 (Rate of return) Shelly purchased a share of stock on January 14, 1999 for $40 and sold it on July 14, 2000 for $42 after collecting a $2 per share cash dividend. (a) What was her rate of return for that half-year investment? (b) What was Shelly's rate of return over the half-year investment period, stated at an *annualized* rate?

P7-3 (Computing returns) Calculate five annual rates of return for the Consolidated Business Corporation (CBC) using the raw data supplied in Table P7-3.

Table P7-3 Stock Price and Cash Dividends for Consolidated Business Corp.

Year	Year's Closing Prices	Annual Cash Dividends	Annual Returns Calculated with Eqn. 7-1
1995	$ 60.00	$3.00	Insufficient data to calculate
1996	69.00	3.00	[($9.00 + $3.00)/$60] × 100 = 20%
1997	100.50	3.00	
1998	47.25	3.00	
1999	39.53	3.00	
2000	72.10	3.00	
2001	82.52	4.00	

P7-4 (Probability distribution of returns) Draw a historical finite probability distribution of returns for the six rates of return computed in Problem P7-3 for the Consolidated Business Corporation's (CBC's) stock. Label all parts of the graph.

P7-5 (Expected return) Calculate the average (or expected) rate of return and the variance of returns for the CBC stock using the objective historical data from Table P7-3 and the five annual rates of return you calculated for Problem P7-3 plus the one rate of return that was given in the problem. Assume all six rates of return are equally likely so they each have a probability of one-sixth.

P7-6 (Selecting dominant assets) Susan is trying to decide which of the common stocks listed in Table P7-6 she should purchase. What would you recommend?

Table P7-6 $E(r)$ and Risk Statistics for Five Assets

Name of Issuer	Expected Return, $E(r)$	Standard Deviation, σ
Able Corporation (A)	7.0%	3.7%
Baker Inc. (B)	7.7%	4.9%
Charles & Company, Ltd. (C)	15.0%	15.0%
Diamond Corporation (D)	3.0%	3.7%
Energy Design, Inc. (E)	7.7%	12.0%

P7-7 (Semivariance) In his seminal monograph entitled *Portfolio Selection*, Harry Markowitz introduced a quantitative risk surrogate named the semivariance. (See Harry Markowitz, *Portfolio Selection* (New York: Wiley 1959), Chapter 9. Markowitz defines the semivariance, denoted SVR, as follows:

$$SVR = \sum_{i=1}^{N} p_i \left[BAR_i - E(r) \right]^2$$

where BAR_i is the ith below average return. Compare and contrast $VAR(r)$ with $SVR(r)$.*

P7-8 (Skewness computations) The probability distribution in Table P7-8 has been determined for a $100 bond. Calculate the third statistical moment, SKEW, for the bond.

Table P7-8: Probability Distribution Of Returns For a $100 Bond.

3 States of nature	Probability	End price	Coupon	Return
Recession	0.30	$125	$5	30%
Slow growth	0.40	$105	$5	10%
Booming economy	0.30	$85	$5	-10%
Total	1.00			E(r) = 10%

* For additional information about the semivariance see J. C. Francis and S. H. Archer, *Portfolio Analysis*, Englewood Cliffs, NJ: Prentice-Hall, 1979. Chapter 15 is entitled "Semi-Variance Analysis."

P7-9 (Probability distributions) consider the three probability distributions in Table P7-9. (a) Calculate the expected return and the variance of the returns for these three probability distributions. (b) Which of the three investments is the most desirable? Why?

Table P7-9 Probability Distributions for the Returns of Securities A, B, and C

Security A		Security B		Security C	
Probability	Return	Probability	Return	Probability	Return
0.3	10%	0.4	20%	0.3	9%
0.6	12%	0.4	8%	0.5	6%
0.1	−1%	0.2	−5.5%	0.2	22%
1.0		1.0		1.0	

P7-10 (Beta calculation) The following probability distribution of returns has been estimated for the returns on the S&P500 index and the stock of Juxta-Med Prosthetics (JMP) Corporation:

Probability	Return$_{JMP}$	Return$_{S\&P}$
0.2	25%	22%
0.3	22%	18%
0.5	15%	13%
1.0		

Based on this information, calculate a beta for Juxta-Med Prosthetics.

CFA EXAM QUESTIONS

The following questions are adopted from the 1998 CFA Sample Exam, Level I:

1. The standard deviation of Stock A is 0.20. The standard deviation of Stock B is 0.12. The covariance between Stock A and B is 0.0096. The correlation between Stock A and Stock B is:
   A. 0.20.
   B. 0.24.
   C. 0.36.
   D. 0.40.

2. If the correlation coefficient between Baker Fund and the S&P500 Stock Index is 0.70, what percentage of Baker Fund's total risk is specific (i.e., unsystematic)?
   A. 35%.
   B. 49%.
   C. 51%.
   D. 70%.

3. An analyst regresses the excess returns of Stock J against the returns on a market index, M. Using the following regression equation,

   $$r_j = \alpha + \beta_j R_M + e_j,$$

   which of the following statements is/are **true**?

   I. The intercept, α_j, is the amount of Stock J's price movement explained by the market.

   II. The term β_j is the slope of the regression line and is assumed to be constant.

   III. The disturbance term, e_j, is assumed to be uncorrelated with the explanatory variable, r_M, and of zero expectation.

   A. I only.
   B. II only.
   C. II and III only.
   D. I, II, and III.

FURTHER REFERENCES

Markowitz, Harry. *Portfolio Selection.* New York: Wiley, 1959.

Chapters 3, 4, and 5 of this seminal book explicate the finite probability model with elegant simplicity.

Siegel, Jeremy J. *Stocks for the Long Run,* 2nd ed. New York: McGraw-Hill, 1998.

This nonmathematical book contains numerous examples and intuitive graphs that explain important points in an easy-to-read manner.

ENDNOTES

[1] The characteristic line traces its roots back to Harry Markowitz, *Portfolio Selection*, Cowles Foundation Monograph 16, New York: Wiley, 1959. The book's Note 1 on p. 100 contains the first published characteristic line; Markowitz called it an index-model.

[2] The phrase *characteristic line* was introduced in a seminal article by Jack L. Treynor, "How to Rate Management of Investment Funds," *Harvard Business Review* (January-February 1965): 63–75.

[3] Professor Michael Jensen reformulated the characteristic line in a risk-premium form. See M. C. Jensen, "The Performance of Mutual Funds in the Period 1945 through 1964," *Journal of Finance* (May 1968): 389–416. See also M. C. Jensen, "Risk, the Pricing of Capital Assets, and the Evaluation of Investment Portfolios," *Journal of Business* 42 (1969). Jensen interprets the alpha intercept term of the characteristic line, as he formulates it, as an investment performance measure. Smith and Tito suggested that Jensen's performance measure is biased. See Keith V. Smith and Dennis A. Tito, "Risk-Return Measures of Ex-Post Portfolio Performance," *Journal of Financial and Quantitative Analysis* 4 (December 1969): 466.

[4] Empirical studies documenting the intertemporal instability of betas have been published. Marshall Blume, "Betas and Their Regression Tendencies," *Journal of Finance* (June 1975): 785–95. See also J. C. Francis, "Statistical Analysis of Risk Coefficients for NYSE Stocks," *Journal of Financial and Quantitative Analysis* 14, no. 5 (December 1979): 981–97.

[5] An average correlation coefficient was about 0.5 in J. C. Francis, "Statistical Analysis of Risk Surrogates for NYSE Stocks," *Journal of Financial and Quantitative Analysis*, December 1979.

Skewness

Skewness refers to the lopsidedness of a probability distribution. Asymmetric probability distributions are skewed. Symmetrical probability distributions have zero skewness.

Figure 7A-1 illustrates three probability distributions of returns that all have the same $E(r)$ and the same $VAR(r)$, but, in spite of these important similarities, the three are shaped differently. The three probability distributions can all have the same $E(r)$ and same $VAR(r)$ but be shaped differently because the $E(r)$ and $VAR(r)$ statistics overlook skewness. The skewness of returns in the ith investment can be measured with Eqn. 7A-1.*

$$SKEW(r) = \sum_{i=1}^{i=N} p_i [r_i - E(r)]^3 \tag{7A-1}$$

In the formula for the variance, Eqn. 2-9 in Chapter 2, the exponent is 2. Since the variance is based on squared deviations, the variance can only take on positive and zero values. In the skewness equation, Eqn. 7A-1, the exponent is 3. This exponent of 3 allows skewness to take on values that are either positive, zero, or negative.

SKEW will equal zero when a probability distribution is symmetric. Panel (B) of Figure 7A-1 illustrates a symmetric probability distribution. If the probability distribution has a long left tail it is *negatively skewed,* as in panel (C) of Figure 7A-1, and the SKEW statistic will have a negative value. A probability distribution having a long right tail, as in panel (A) of Figure 7A-1, will have a positive SKEW value.

Positive skewness is a quality many investors would like to have in the probability distributions of their investments. In other words, if several different probability distributions of returns all have the same $E(r)$ and the same $VAR(r)$ but are skewed differently, most investors would prefer the probability distribution with more positive skewness. And, if all other factors were equal, most investors would consider the probability distribution that had the most negative skewness to be the least desirable.

The preceding paragraphs should make you wonder if our discussion of the dominance principle illustrated in Figure 7-4 is overly simplified. Since the dominance principle does not consider skewness, you might ask if the principle ignores information that an investor should use to make the best investment choices. The skewness statistic does convey valuable information that should be considered—but only if the probability distributions are asymmetric (skewed). Since most investment candidates being considered have probability distributions that are fairly symmetric, the skewness statistic contains little valuable information and is

---

* Simpler definitions include: Skewness = (Mean − Median), or, alternatively: Skewness = (Mean − Mode). These intuitive definitions yield different values than SKEW, but they will all have the same sign. More generally, skewness is measured by dividing SKEW in Eqn. 7A-1a by the standard deviation cubed to obtain a standardized index of skewness.

therefore often not considered. The dominance principle does not ignore valuable information because most probability distributions of returns are adequately described by their expected returns and variances (or, standard deviations).*

FIGURE 7A–1   Three Probability Distributions of Returns. (a) Positively Skewed; (b) Zero Skewness; (c) Negatively Skewed.

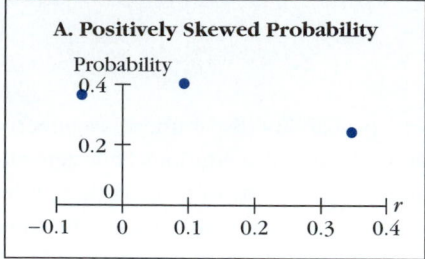

A. Positively Skewed Probability

i	p_i	r
1	0.3659	−0.06
2	0.4	0.1
3	0.2341	0.35

$E(r) = 0.1$
$VAR(r) = 0.024$
Third moment = 0.0022

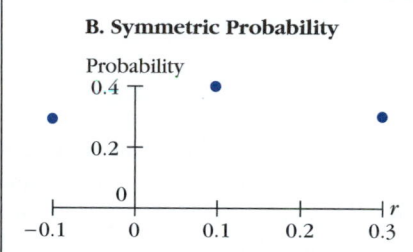

B. Symmetric Probability

i	p_i	r
1	0.3	−0.1
2	0.4	0.1
3	0.3	0.3

$E(r) = 0.1$
$VAR(r) = 0.024$
Third moment = 0

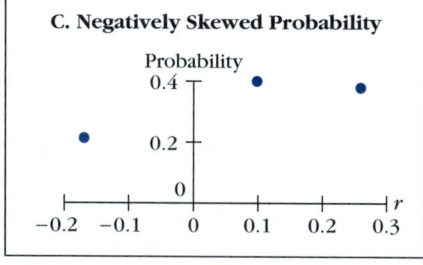

C. Negatively Skewed Probability

i	p_i	r
1	0.216	−0.1666
2	0.4	0.1
3	0.384	0.25

$E(r) = 0.1$
$VAR(r) = 0.024$
Third moment = −0.0028

Skewness measures whether a probability distribution is lopsided or symmetric.

---

* The Central Limit Theorem (CLT) from mathematical statistics deals with sums of random variables. Since portfolios are sums of random variables (stocks, bonds, options, etc.), the CLT is relevant. The CLT says that under plausible assumptions, the probability distributions of returns that describe diversified portfolios tend to be normally distributed. As a result, even if all of the random variables that make up a diversified portfolio are skewed, the portfolio's probability distributions of returns will still tend to be symmetrical. Symmetrically normal probability distributions are fully described by their means and variances. Thus, the CLT suggests we may be able to ignore skewness in diversified portfolios.

EFFICIENT CAPITAL MARKETS AND ANOMALIES

*This chapter investigates the way investors use information. If investors ignore information, the market prices of securities will not react to news announcements. If investors continue to waste information, market prices can drift further from their values. We call securities prices that do not reflect the available information **weakly efficient** prices or **semi-strong** prices. The difference between a security's price and its value is a measure of that security's pricing inefficiency. Figure 3-4 in Chapter 3 illustrates how a weakly efficient price can drift further away from the security's value than a semi-strongly efficient price; this occurs because the weakly efficient price reflects less information than the semi-strong price. Investors who do financial analysis hope to discover pricing ineffi-ciencies and trade actively to profit from their discoveries when the price moves back toward its value.**

*If the price of a security reflects everything that is knowable about the security, we call it a **perfectly efficient** price. A perfectly efficient price is always equal to the security's value, even though the value may change con-tinuously to reflect the random arrival of new information. In other words, the price and value vibrate together in perfect harmony as they react in uni-son to the frequent appearance of news (see Figure 3-4 on page 53).** Smart financial analysts who are active traders will not be able to enrich them-selves in a perfectly efficient market because all the securities are priced cor-rectly. In a perfectly efficient market even expert financial analysts would be well-advised to invest in a mutual fund that is indexed to a securities market index that corresponds with their needs and preferences.*

---

* The Definition box on the first page of Chapter 6 distinguishes between *informational efficiency*, the sub-ject of this chapter, and *transactional efficiency* (see Table 6-7 on page 154).

** Nobel laureate Samuelson defined **continuous equilibrium** the way we defined perfect pricing efficiency. See Paul Samuelson, "Proof That Properly Discounted Present Values of Assets Vibrate Randomly," *Bell Journal of Economics and Management Science* (autumn 1973): 369–74.

INFORMATION HYPOTHESES

Pricing inefficiencies interest investors because a discrepancy between the price and the value of a security provides a profit opportunity. Investment opportunities involving individual securities or entire markets can be categorized into three levels of pricing efficiency; these categories are based on the amount of information the investors in the market use in their valuations.

Hypothesis One: The Weakly Efficient Market Hypothesis. A weakly efficient market exists when the *market prices reflect all historical information.*[1] The participants in a weakly efficient market only utilize historical information. This historical information is attainable from bookstores, libraries, and computer databases for free or for modest outlays.

Hypothesis Two: The Semistrong Efficient Market Hypothesis. A semistrong efficient market is defined to be a market in which *market prices reflect all public information.* Public information includes the historical information mentioned in Hypothesis One plus additional current events information that is more difficult and more costly to obtain. For instance, it might be necessary to purchase reports from Standard & Poors and forecasts from consultants to achieve semi-strong efficient prices.

Hypothesis Three: The Perfectly (or Strongly) Efficient Market Hypothesis. A perfectly efficient market exists when the *market prices reflect everything that is knowable.* In a perfectly efficient market, securities' prices always equal their values as prices and values vibrate randomly together in an immediate and appropriate response to arriving information. Perfectly efficient prices reflect the historical information, the public information, and additional information that is more difficult to obtain. For example, knowable information includes inside information that, in some countries, is illegal for outsiders to utilize.*

Some people are surprised to learn that prices should vibrate randomly; they think that security prices should move smoothly through time. Prices should not move smoothly. A perfectly efficient market is one in which no profits are left after an allowance for the investor's time and research information costs are deducted from the investments' returns. It will be difficult to earn pure economic profits, even for people who have valuable information, because prices adjust rapidly as the information becomes available. These rapid price adjustments cause, not smooth continuity, but *randomness* in the successive price changes of a security. Randomness means that a trendlike series of small upward (or small downward) price moves occurs rarely if at all. If the price is going to change, it should change all at once, rather than in a series of small gradual adjustments. Sudden large price moves are desirable, so long as price movements in the opposite direction do not consistently follow them.[2] Large quick

---

* Based on their inside information, a corporation's board of directors can direct the corporation to buy back some of its own shares (create new treasury stock) and, thereby, impact inside information about what the directors think the stock is worth into market prices. Under U.S. law it would be illegal for one of that corporation's directors (an insider) or an outsider to use the same inside information as a basis for private trading. Corporations' share buybacks and sales permit inside information to be impacted into market prices legally.

FIGURE 8-1   Security Prices React to New Information

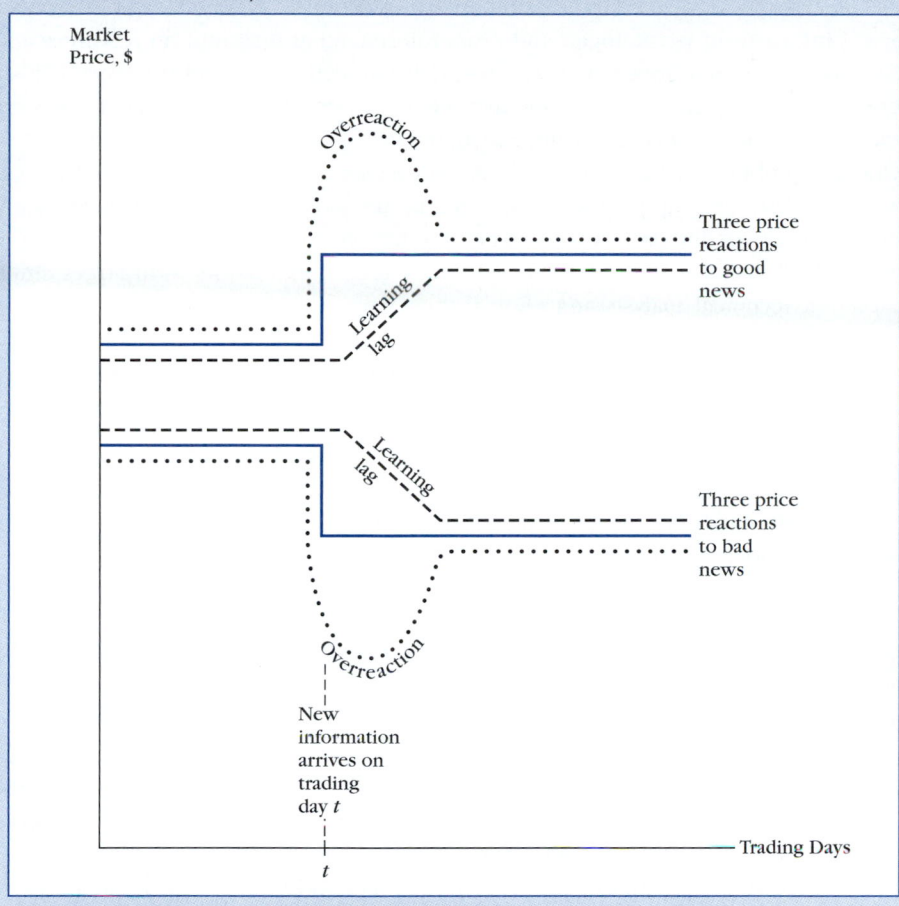

On trading date *t* new information arrives in the market and six different security price paths transpire as investors react to the news in different ways. In a perfectly efficient market (solid line) investors react instantly and impact the new information into prices in one sudden price adjustment. In an inefficient market investors might react with a learning lag (dashed line) or they might overreact (dotted line).

price movements are a good sign the market is not suffering from learning lags. Figure 8-1 illustrates ways that information can shape securities prices.

This chapter reports on investigations of the three efficient markets hypotheses. Each hypothesis is considered separately and evidence supporting the hypotheses is presented; some anomalous evidence is presented as well. You should study this evidence and decide how to interpret it. You should try to reach a conclusion about whether you believe each of the three efficient markets hypotheses, because these conclusions will determine the way you invest. For example, if you reject Hypotheses Two and Three, then it follows logically that you should be an aggressive investor who trades actively. In contrast, if you believe that all three hypotheses are true, then it follows logically that you should be a passive investor who trades infrequently. Empirical evidence supporting Hypothesis One is presented first.

EVIDENCE SUPPORTING THE WEAKLY EFFICIENT HYPOTHESIS

Historical information is cataloged and cross-referenced and should be readily available through books, libraries, universities, and research foundations around the world. This section considers the question: Is it possible that security prices do not reflect all this important historical information that is cheap and easy-to-obtain.

One group of financial researchers focus on past security prices—these folks are called *technical analysts*, or simply *technicians*. Technicians look for meaningful patterns in historical security prices and endeavor to extract predictions from whatever patterns they find. Within the United States millions of investors are technical analysts. Wall Street employs some full-time technical analysts, and a few of them have even risen to the rank of vice president and are in charge of a **technical analysis** department. The discussion below reports the results of empirical tests that are designed to determine if the patterns in security prices reported by technical analysts and other calendar effects (return regularities) really exist.

Filter Rules

An x percent **filter rule** is a mechanical trading rule. Computer programs have been written to read security prices and execute x percent filter rules.

DEFINITION

AN X PERCENT FILTER RULE

The rule is: If the price of a security rises at least x percent, buy and hold the security until its price reaches a peak and then drops at least x percent. When the price decreases from a peak level by x percent, liquidate the long position and sell short as the price starts to fall. Hold this short position while the price falls. Stay short until the price reaches a low point and then turns upward. If and when the price rises x percent above the low point, cover the short position and buy a long position in hopes of profiting from the next price rise.

Different filter rules can be tested by varying the x value. If stock prices fluctuate randomly, filter rules should not outperform similar stocks that are drawn randomly from the same market and held passively in an unmanaged portfolio. Filter rules would be valuable, however, if they could trade profitably on the bull market trends, bear market trends, or any other trends that may exist in the data.

Figure 8-2 illustrates how a 10% filter rule would operate as the price of a stock fluctuates between $18 and $40 over a period of a few years. Note that the stock's price starts rising from a $20 purchase price to a $36 sale price, for a $16 per-share profit during a bullish trend of about 18 months' duration.

Studies have been published using different stocks and different filters.[3] Filters as small as $\frac{1}{2}$ of 1% (x = 0.5) and as large as 50% (x = 50) have been tested. The tests were performed with stock price data gathered at various intervals. One test used daily stock prices over several years. Occasionally, a filter rule earned a return above what would have been earned with a naive buy-and-hold strategy—if the commissions incurred in buying and selling were ignored. However, filter rules can generate large trading commission expenses—especially the trading rules with values of x that are less than 1%. After the commissions were deducted, the filter rules do not outperform a naive buy-and-hold strategy. In fact, some filter

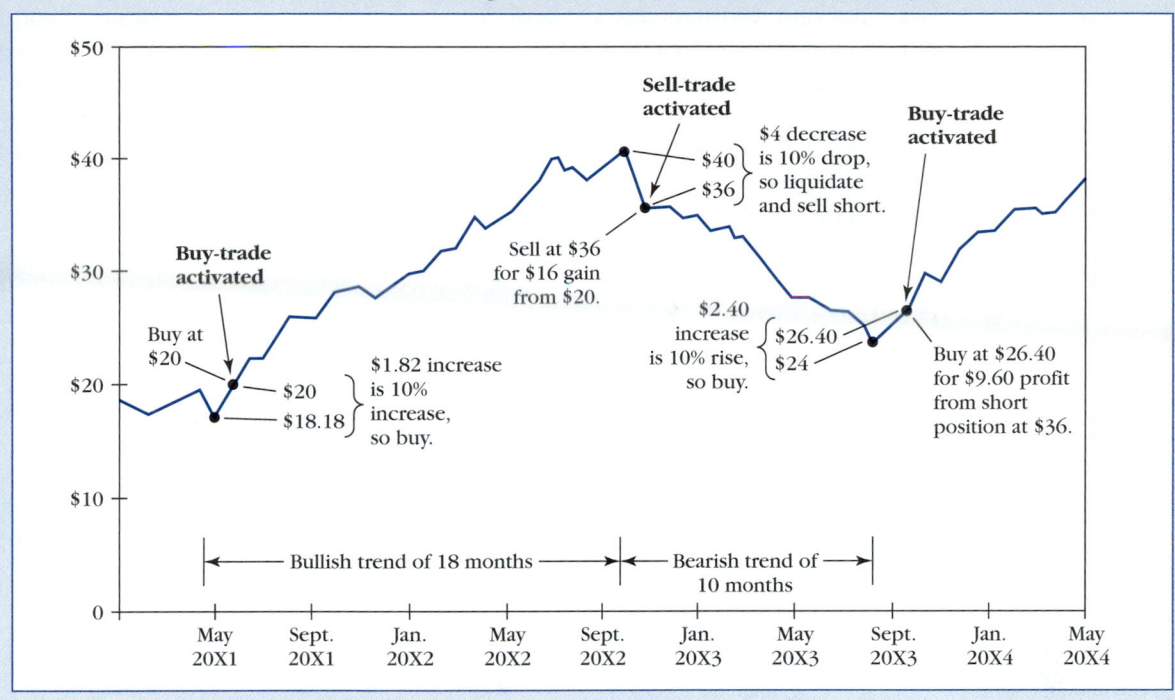

FIGURE 8-2 Using a 10% Filter Rule to Trade a Security

A 10% filter rule issues an order to buy a long position after the price rises 10%. This long position is maintained until the price falls by 10%. Then, the filter rule liquidates the long position and sells the security short to profit from a price decline. This short position is maintained until the price rises 10%.

rules result in considerable net losses after commission expenses are deducted. If there are any price patterns that can be used as a basis for a profitable trading strategy, a wide range of filter rules do not seem able to detect them when tested over hundreds of different stocks and differing sample periods.

Serial Correlation Tests

Some technical analysts claim security prices sometimes move in *trends* as if they possessed *momentum*.* If a security's price follows any trends (has any momentum), filter rules should detect it as they endeavor to profit from trends. Security prices might also follow a pattern of *reversals* in which price changes in one direction tend to be followed by price changes in the opposite direction. Serial correlation can measure reversals.

   Serial correlation (*autocorrelation*) measures the correlation coefficient in a series of numbers with lagged values in the same series. More specifically, serial correlation measures the correlation in a time-series of security prices with the same security's past prices lagged by some preset amount of time. Lags of any length can be employed when searching for significant serial correlations. Serial correlation can detect both trends and reversal patterns.

---

* Physics textbooks tell us: Momentum = (Mass) × (Velocity). Since security prices have zero mass (weight), using the term *momentum* to describe them could mislead someone into thinking substance exists when, in fact, no substance exists.

It is well known that stock prices fluctuate around a long-term upward trend of about 6.6% per year in the United States.* As a result of this upward trend, some positive serial correlation is observed. But these long-term upward trends are not of interest to technical analysts. Technical analysts focus on short-term patterns, not long-run trends. The question examined here is whether patterns in daily price changes or weekly price changes exist and, if so, whether they can be used to earn a trading profit after commissions are deducted.

Figure 8-3 depicts five of an infinite number of patterns that serial-correlation tests can measure. The price fluctuations in Figure 8-3 should provide some understanding of trends and reversals.

Many serial-correlation studies of security prices have been published over the years by financial economists, and these studies have failed to detect daily, weekly, or monthly serial correlations that are significantly different from zero.[4] This is scientific evidence in support of the weakly efficient markets hypothesis.

In 1985 Werner DeBondt and Richard Thaler compared stocks that were losers with stocks that were winners, relative to the aggregate stock market over the past the 3 to 5 years,

FIGURE 8-3 Price Fluctuations for Five Stocks with Different Serial Correlation Coefficients

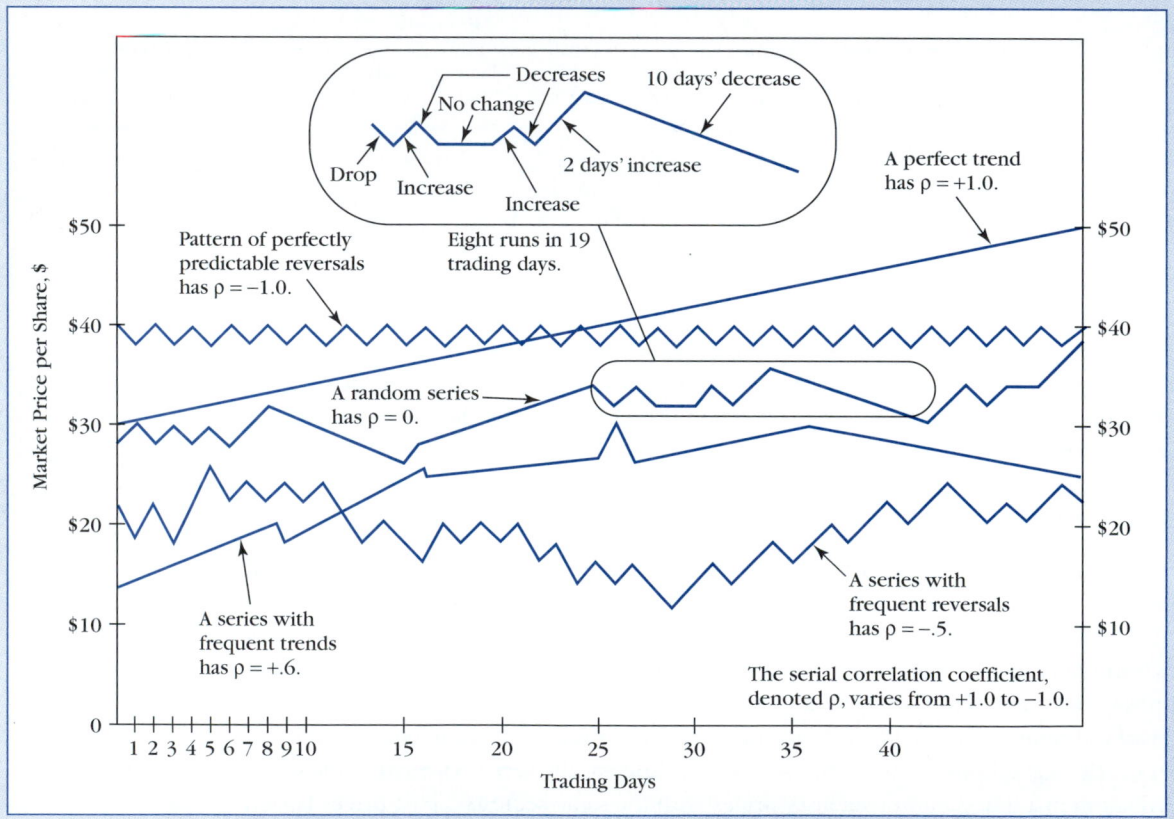

A serial correlation of +1.0 indicates consistent trends are present. A serial correlation of −1.0 documents a pattern of perfect reversals. A serial correlation of zero suggests the movements are random.

---

* See Chapters 10 and 11 of this book for details about the 6.6 % per year price appreciation (ignoring cash dividends) in the S&P500 stock market index.

and produced compelling evidence of long-term stock price overreaction. The DeBondt and Thaler results also yielded negative serial correlations for individual stocks. In 1988 Andrew Lo and Craig MacKinlay reported positive serial correlations for a diversified portfolio of stocks. In 1983 Jennifer Conrad and Gautan Kaul published statistics suggesting that DeBondt and Thaler's negative serial correlations as well as Lo and MacKinlay's positive serial correlations were the result of statistical measurement errors (from bid-ask spreads, nonsynchronous data, price ticks).[5] These conflicting results leave the door open for further research. So far, however, convincing evidence of serial correlation has not been forthcoming.

Runs Tests

It is possible that security prices might change randomly most of the time but occasionally follow trends that filter rules and serial correlations cannot detect. "Runs" tests may be used to determine if there are irregular trends in price changes.

RUNS   **DEFINITION**

A **run** is something that happens in a series of numbers whenever the changes between consecutive numbers switch direction. For example, in a bear market, a security price that declines for 10 consecutive trading days will generate 10 negative daily price changes—or one negative run. A zero run occurs when prices remain flat for a period of time of any duration. The highlighted panel in Figure 8-3 illustrates eight runs—four negative runs, one zero run, and three positive runs—that occurred during the 19 trading days from Day 24 to Day 42 inclusive.

Mathematical statisticians are able to determine how many positive, negative, or zero runs are expected in a series of random numbers. This number of runs is then used for comparison with the actual number of runs in security prices. A series of price changes for a security containing either too many or too few runs (relative to what would be expected in a series of random numbers) is evidence of nonrandom price movements. Scientific runs tests that have been published suggest that the runs in price changes of stocks are not significantly different from the runs in random numbers.

ANOMALIES IN THE WEAKLY EFFICIENT HYPOTHESIS

Impressive scientific evidence supporting the weakly efficient market hypothesis has been published. In addition, some researchers have reported findings that detract from the theory. The following discussion reviews anomalous evidence.

Day-of-the-Week Effects

Table 8-1 shows that, on average, the stock market tends to fall on Mondays and then rise the rest of the week. Since Monday's returns are computed from Friday's closing price until Monday's closing price, a *differencing interval* that spans the weekend, this return regularity is sometimes called the **weekend effect.**

Lawrence Harris took a closer look at the daily returns in the United States. He took the Monday returns that were computed from Friday's closing price until Monday's closing price and dissected them into two parts—the weekend component and the Monday component.

TABLE 8-1	**Average Returns for Each Day of the Week in U.S. Stock Markets**				
	Monday	Tuesday	Wednesday	Thursday	Friday
French's 1953–77 Data	−0.17%	0.02%	0.10%	0.04%	0.09%
Gibbons & Hess's 1962–78 Data	−0.13%	0.00%	0.10%	0.03%	0.08%
Abraham & Ikenberry's 1963–91	−0.12%	0.01%	0.14%	0.11%	0.21%

SOURCES: Kenneth R. French, "Stock Returns and the Weekend Effect," *Journal of Financial Economics 8*, no. 1 (March 1980): 58; Michael R. Gibbons and Patrick Hess, "Day of the Week Effects and Asset Returns," *Journal of Business* 54, no. 4 (October 1981): 582–83; and, Abraham Abraham and David L. Ikenberry, "The Individual Investor and the Weekend Effect," *Journal of Financial and Quantitative Analysis* 29, no. 2 (June 1994): 267.

Harris found that both components were negative, on average. Harris then divided the NYSE's 6-hour trading day into 24 consecutive 15-minute periods and computed 15-minute returns over a sample period of 14 months. Figure 8-4 shows that most of the negative returns on the average Monday occur in the first hour of trading. After the bearish opening hour is finished, Mondays tend to finish up like the other four days of the week.

The weekend (day of the week) effect is also present in other stock exchanges around the world in varying degrees.[6] As shown in Table 8-2, the Japanese stock market is open on Saturday mornings. The Japanese stock market deviates somewhat from the pattern observed in the United States, but this difference does not seem to be substantive. The Japanese market tends to drop on both Monday and Tuesday, with the larger drop occurring on Tuesday. Ignoring the modest Japanese difference, the day of the week pattern is observed in stock markets around the world.

Robert Ariel studied the **holiday effect** that occurs on official national holidays in the United States and, in addition, falls within or adjacent to a weekend.[7] Using daily U.S. stock market returns from 1963 through 1982, Ariel found that returns on the day before the holiday weekends was nine to thirteen times larger than the average daily return. About one-third of the average stock's annual return was earned in the preholiday trading days.[8]

Abraham and Ikenberry suggest that a Friday's return has some predictive power over the following Monday's return.[9] They observe that negative returns on a Friday are usually followed by large negative returns on Monday. Similarly, positive Friday returns are often followed by positive returns on Monday.

No reasons for the various day of the week and the holiday effect can be discerned. They are *anomalies* in the weakly efficient markets hypothesis.

It might seem that the weekend effect presents an opportunity to earn speculative profits. Speculators could buy stocks at their low opening prices on Monday and then sell at them at Friday afternoon's high closing price. However, this speculation would not be profitable because brokerage commissions, income taxes, transfer fees, and related transactions costs would consume the tiny positive daily returns shown in Table 8-1. Any net return that remained would not be sufficient compensation for the risk of holding the stocks from Monday through Friday and hoping they finished the week at a higher price. However, knowing about these effects can be helpful if you are planning to sell or buy anyway.

The January Effect

Table 8-3 shows monthly returns averaged over various sample periods that were tabulated by Michael Rozeff and William Kinney.[10] The data in the table shows that, averaged over 70 years, the average stock's return in January is more than five times larger than the mean

FIGURE 8-4 Cumulative 15-Minute Returns for Each Day of the Week

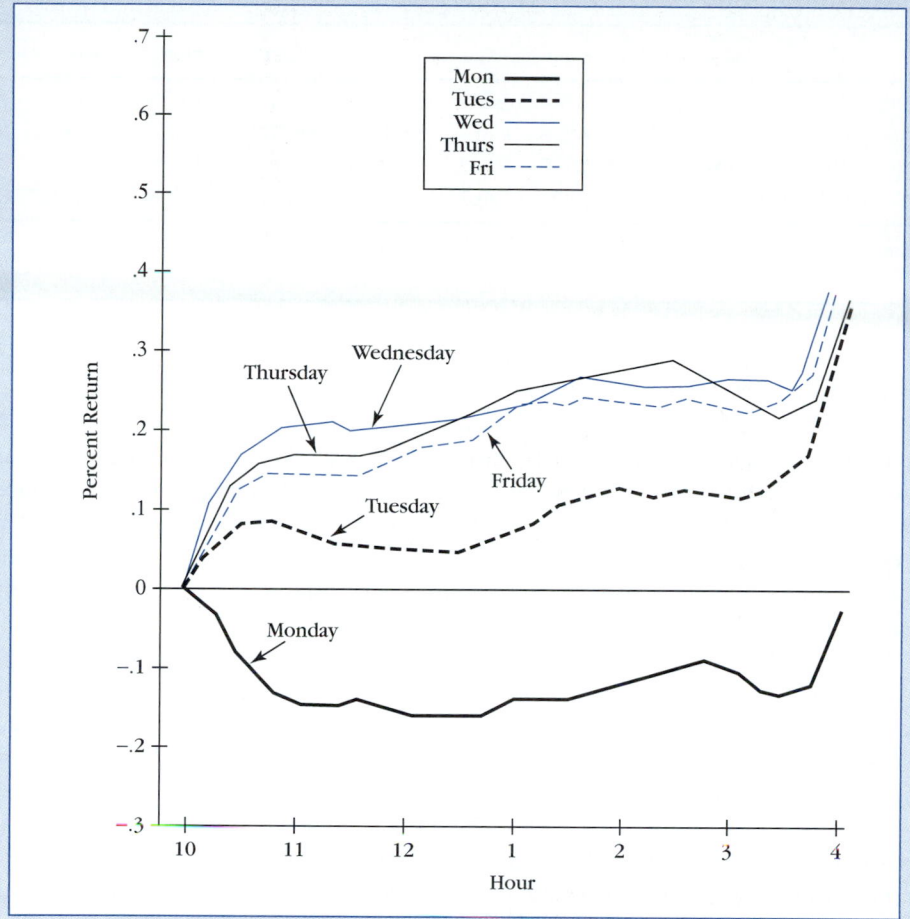

Most weeks get off to a bad start during the first hour of trading on Monday. But, after a bearish start, Mondays usually behave like any other day of the week.

SOURCE: Lawrence Harris, "How to Profit from Intraday Stock Returns," *Journal of Portfolio Management* 12, no. 2 (winter 1986): 63.

TABLE 8-2   Contrasting Average Returns for Each Day of the Week in Tokyo and U.S. Stock Markets, 1970–83

	Monday	Tuesday	Wednesday	Thursday	Friday	Saturday	Average
Japan's Nikkei-Dow Index	−0.02	−0.09	0.15	0.03	0.06	0.12	0.04
Tokyo Stock Exchange Index	−0.01	−0.06	0.12	0.03	0.06	0.10	0.04
S&P500 Index from United States	−0.13	0.02	0.10	0.03	0.08	Close	0.02

SOURCES: Jeffrey Jaffe and Randolph Westerfield, "Patterns in Japanese Common Stock Returns: Day of the Week and Turn of the Year Effects," *Journal of Financial and Quantitative Analysis* 20, no. 2 (June 1985): 263.

TABLE 8-3	Monthly Average Returns in U.S. Stock Market over 4 Different Sample Periods												
Years	Jan	Feb	Mar	Apr	May	June	July	Aug	Sep	Oct	Nov	Dec	Average
1904–28	1.30%	−.97%	.17%	1.22%	.33%	−.58%	.90%	1.02%	1.01%	.42%	1.27%	.10%	.52%
1929–40	6.63%	1.91%	−5.28%	.80%	−3.31%	4.03%	4.97%	4.87%	−5.10%	−5.10%	−1.23%	−3.14%	.19%
1941–74	3.91%	.56%	1.42%	.16%	.17%	−.63%	1.53%	.56%	.02%	.85%	1.00%	2.01%	.96%
1904–74	3.48%	.26%	−.16%	.63%	−.37%	.18%	1.90%	1.46%	−.52%	.07%	.71%	.47%	.68%

SOURCE: Michael S. Rozeff and William R. Kinney Jr., "Capital Market Seasonality: The Case of Stock Returns," *Journal of Financial Economics* 3, no. 4 (October 1976): 388, Table 1.

monthly return obtained by averaging over all 12 months of the year. On average, a large part of the typical common stock's annual return is earned during the month of January. The **January effect** is a larger anomaly in the weakly efficient markets hypothesis than the day of the week or weekend effects. The January effect can yield net trading profits after transactions costs are deducted; it is the most important empirical return regularity (calendar effect) that can be observed with any consistency. The way to profit from the combined holiday effect and January effect is to buy stocks before Christmas and sell them at the end of January.

Many hypotheses about the cause of the January effect have been suggested. Ben Branch suggested that selling stocks in December to establish tax losses could cause the January effect.[11] He showed that investors could sell their depressed stocks in December to establish tax losses, thereby become entitled to tax deductions, then reinvest in January, and, in so doing, fuel the January effect.

The January effect is even stronger outside the United States. Figure 8-5 presents data taken from an international study by Gultekin and Gultekin, comparing the average returns in January with returns averaged over the other 11 months of the year. It shows the January effects from the following seventeen countries:

Australia (Al)	Germany (Gr)	Spain (Sp)
Austria (As)	Italy (It)	Sweden (Sw)
Belgium (Bl)	Japan (Jp)	Switzerland (Sz)
Canada (Cn)	Netherlands (Nl)	United Kingdom (UK)
Denmark (Dn)	Norway (No)	United States (US)
France (Fr)	Singapore (I)	

Conclusions About the Weakly Efficient Markets Hypothesis

The filter rules, serial correlations, and runs tests suggest that technical analysts and short-run traders looking for calendar effects (return regularities) from which to earn easy profits will frequently be disappointed. Some anomalies in the weakly efficient markets hypothesis exist. The day of the week (weekend) effect yielded a small gross profit before transactions costs were deducted, but the returns were not large enough to generate net profits. The January effect is a return regularity based on historical information that historically has been profitable after transactions costs were deducted. The January effect is not what most people would call a get-rich-quick scheme, but it is a serious anomaly in the weakly efficient markets hypothesis.

FIGURE 8-5   Monthly Average Returns from Stock Markets Around the World for January and the Other 11 Months

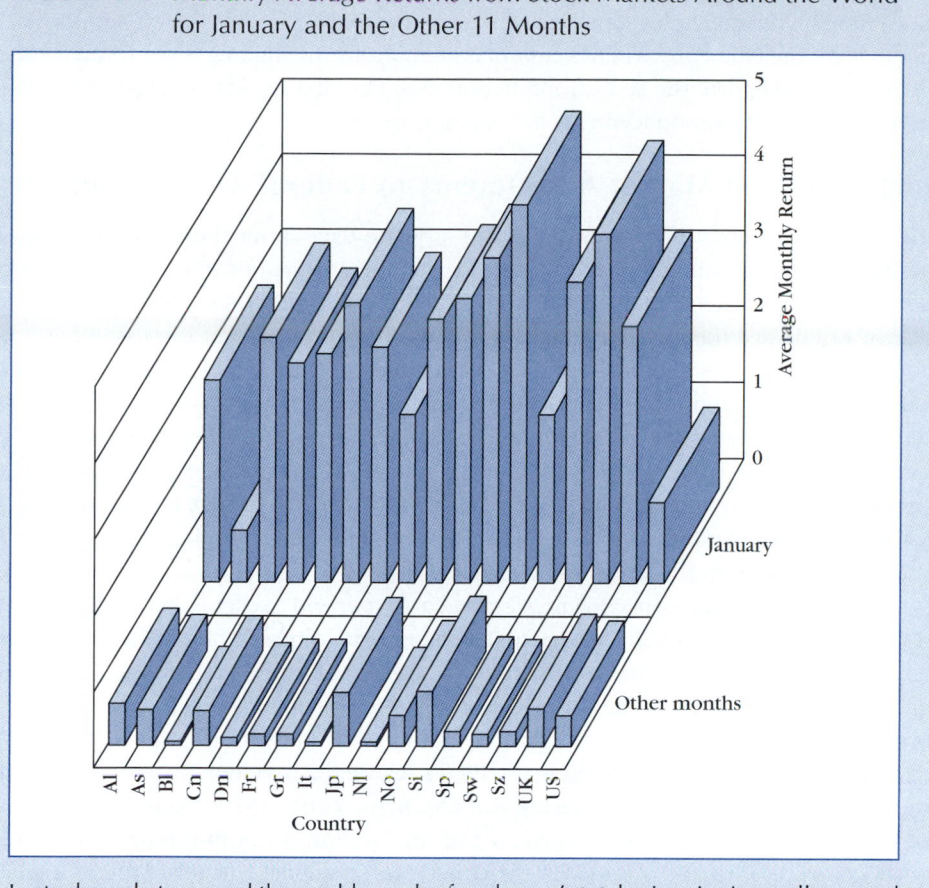

In stock markets around the world, much of each year's total price rise is usually earned during the month of January.

SOURCES: The graph is reproduced from a book by Robert A. Haugen and Josef Lakonishok, *The Incredible January Effect* (Homewood, IL: Dow Jones-Irwin, 1988). The data was taken from a study by M. N. Gultekin and B. N. Gultekin, "Stock Market Seasonality: International Evidence," *Journal of Financial Economics*, December 1983.

The tests we have presented are based on the efficient markets concept that the values of securities should fluctuate randomly. These random fluctuations are expected to result from a market mechanism in which the value of a security changes whenever new information about that security reaches the market. Although this model is empirically testable, indirect tests focusing on random price behavior were employed. The semistrong efficient markets hypothesis examined in the next section uses more direct tests.

TESTS OF THE SEMISTRONG EFFICIENT HYPOTHESIS

Tests of the semistrong efficient markets hypothesis utilize all public information. For instance, all public information includes all historical information in all public libraries, plus all current news in all newspapers and TV shows.

Most semistrong tests utilize financial news announcements as a basis to do an "event study." **Event studies** focus on some event; they observe security prices to see if the prices react rationally when the event of interest becomes public knowledge. If security prices react quickly and efficiently when the event is announced, that finding is interpreted as being evidence that supports the semistrong hypothesis. The first events we study are financial markets' reactions to announcements of economic news.

Stock and Bond Market Adjustments to Federal Announcements

Federal governments routinely compile and tabulate data about their nations' economic activities. Public announcements of the macroeconomic statistics that result are typically made at scheduled times, for example, at 9:30 A.M. on every other Monday. The governments of Great Britain and the United States (and some other countries not discussed here) keep these economic statistics secret until the precise moment they are released to the public. In order to keep these announcements from roiling the financial markets, the U.S. government makes many of its announcements when the nation's financial markets are closed. In contrast, the British government makes its announcements during trading hours. If the statistics that are announced contain valuable new information, the markets react immediately and continuously until that information is impacted into the prices of stocks, bonds, futures contracts, options, and other financial instruments.

A **futures contract** is an agreement between a buyer and a seller to exchange some agricultural or financial commodity at a prespecified price on some selected future delivery date. It is a marketable contract that can be freely traded in a futures exchange at a fluctuating price that is tied to price of the underlying commodity. Chapter 9 investigates futures contracts in detail.

Gwilym, Buckle, Clarke, and Thomas (GBCT) analyzed transaction-by-transaction market data on two futures contracts covering the *Financial Times* Stock Exchange (FT-SE) 100 stocks price index (nicknamed "Footsie") and the Sterling 3-Month Interest rate.[12] These futures contracts are actively traded at the London International Financial Futures Exchange (LIFFE), a major international futures exchange. GBCT analyze 12-minute time spans, which they call *announcement windows*, that start 2 minutes before a public announcement and end 10 minutes after the announcement. Using a sample of 232 announcement days they examine the scheduled macroeconomic announcements of Labor Market Statistics, the Public Sector Borrowing Requirement (PSBR), the Retail Price Index (RPI), the Producer Price Index (PPI), and Retail Sales. GBCT selected these announcements because the financial markets reactions to them were statistically significant over their 3.5-year sample period.

The Impact of Information

GBCT report several informative statistics describing the behavior of the market prices of stock market futures and interest rate futures. First, they tabulate rolling standard deviations at 15-second intervals during their 12-minute announcement windows. Both the stock market and the bond market remain at normal levels during the 2 minutes prior to the announcement. This suggests that there is no information leakage before the announcement. Then, the volatility statistics jump to levels that are several times above normal within the first 15 seconds after the British government's announcements. Within 6 minutes after the announcement the standard deviations drop back to their normal levels and remain there. These standard deviations provide evidence that unusual price volatility occurs for a few minutes after the announcements.

Second, GBCT analyze mean absolute price changes per transaction in the stock and bond futures markets. In transactions time, the mean absolute price changes per transaction jumps to high levels during the first 7 transactions following the government announcements and then declines gradually back to the normal level after approximately 30 transactions. In clock time, the mean absolute price changes per transaction for both the stock and bond futures markets begin reacting to the news release within 15 seconds. The initial reactions are large, decline noticeably after 90 seconds, but remain significantly elevated for approximately 5 minutes for the Footsie contract, and 6 minutes for the Short Sterling contract.

Third, GBCT compute the mean number of transactions per time interval. For the Short Sterling contract, the variable is elevated prior to announcement and remains significant, although declining, throughout the 12-minute observation window. For the Footsie contract, this variable elevates significantly within 15 seconds after the announcement and remains somewhat elevated for most of the following 10 minutes. Essentially, it seems that large price changes occur within the initial 2 minutes after an announcement, but unusual activity that causes gradually smaller price changes persists for several minutes.

Fourth, price continuations and reversals were examined. When prices continue (trend) either upwards or downward after an announcement, this is interpreted as evidence that valuable new information arrived and created an imbalance between supply and demand. In the GBCT study, continuations in the Footsie contract became elevated within 15 seconds after the announcement and remained high for 75 seconds. In transactions time, it took 7 transactions before the continuations returned to normal levels. The price of the Short Sterling contract adjusted more slowly; its continuations remained elevated for 150 seconds, or, until the first 10 transactions after the announcement were completed. Similar studies of the impact of information on financial market prices reached conclusions that differ only slightly.

About Information and Market Prices

Unlike federal governments, corporations do not usually make announcements of their operating results at prescheduled times. Furthermore, investors do not focus as much on the quarterly earnings announcements from one corporation as on the economic news about a major industrial nation. For these reasons, stock prices react to announcements by the issuing corporations more slowly than the financial markets react to announcements made by federal governments.

In separate studies, Patell and Wolfson and Woodruff and Senchak examined the reaction of stock prices to earnings announcements.[13] They found that stock prices adjust more slowly than futures prices, typically taking 14 minutes to begin adjusting to the announcements. They reported that approximately half the adjustment toward a new equilibrium price occurs within 30 minutes after the announcement, and that there are virtually no opportunities for profitable trading remaining 30 minutes after the announcement.

Although the evidence about price reactions to new information is not all perfectly consistent, it strongly suggests that the prices in most financial markets adjust to news announcements quickly. Particularly noteworthy is the fact that all of the studies report price adjustments for industrialized nations that are measured in minutes and seconds, rather than in days or weeks. These fast reaction times mean that if a chart of security prices is updated as frequently as once per day, the information in the chart will be worthless by the time it is recorded.

The next event in our investigation of the semistrong efficient markets hypothesis focuses on stock dividends and splits.

THE EFFECTS OF STOCK SPLITS AND STOCK DIVIDENDS

Stock splits and stock dividends are similar events that do not change the *total* value of the issuing firm's market value or investor's wealth. A 100% stock dividend, or equivalently, a

2-for-1 stock split, results in twice as many outstanding shares of stock and each share being worth half as much.* If security markets process public information efficiently, they will equate share prices with share values and the total value of all the firm's outstanding shares will not be affected by these mere changes in the unit of account. Both events are publicly announced, both affect stock prices, and both provide events with which to test the semi-strong efficient markets hypothesis.

The Fama, Fisher, Jensen, and Roll (FFJR) Study

Eugene Fama, Lawrence Fisher, Michael Jensen, and Richard Roll (FFJR) conducted a classic empirical study of 940 stock splits and stock dividends by NYSE-listed stocks.[14] The study asks if these changes in the unit of account influence investors' one-period rates of return, as initially defined in Eqn. 2-3 from Chapter 2:

$$r = \frac{(\text{Capital gains or loss}) + (\text{Cash dividend, if any})}{\text{Purchase price}} \qquad (2\text{-}3)$$

All the shares of stock were adjusted for the stock splits and stock dividends before the rates of return were calculated. This adjustment ensures that only actual changes in the investor's wealth would be measured rather than the meaningless price changes associated with a stock dividend or split. For example, when a 2-for-1 split or 100% stock dividend occurs, that share's price before the stock dividend or split should be halved so that no changes in the investor's wealth would be erroneously attributed to it when calculating the rate of return. Table 7-5 in Chapter 7 shows how Coke's rates of return were calculated after adjusting for changes in that corporation's unit of account.

Why Split the Stock? Academic researchers have two hypotheses about why stock dividends and splits are popular with corporate boards. First, several researchers have provided evidence in support of the *information-signaling hypothesis.* These researchers have shown that some boards of directors conserve the corporation's cash while passing signals (clues) to the public about future earnings growth by giving their investors stock splits and/or paying stock dividends.[15] It is argued that some investors value the stock more highly because they received a signal from the board that continued growth is expected. The second explanation, the *liquidity hypothesis,* asserts that stocks are split to reduce their market price and thereby make the stock affordable to more small investors.[16] For example, Coca-Cola had 2-for-1 stock splits on May 1, 1992, on May 1, 1996, and on many occasions prior to those dates. (See Table 7-5 in Chapter 7 for Coke's data.) A survey of business executives shows that the liquidity hypothesis is the reason for having a stock split that is cited most frequently.[17]

The Characteristic Line. Residual analysis techniques pioneered by FFJR are used to evaluate rates of return without bias.[18] The FFJR methodology adjusts stocks' one-period returns to compensate for bull- or bear-market price swings. The characteristic line, which was introduced in Chapter 7 and defined in Eqn. 7-7, was calculated for each stock FFJR analyzed:

---

* Accountants and attorneys believe that stock splits are different from stock dividends because of the treatment they receive in the equity section of the balance sheet. With a stock split, the par value per share is decreased to reflect the splitting of the shares; the number of shares outstanding is simultaneously increased so as to leave the total amount in the capital account unchanged. With stock dividends, a portion of retained earnings equal to the value of the stock dividend is transferred from retained earnings to the capital account. Both adjustments are bookkeeping entries that leave total equity and total assets unchanged and have no economic significance to a financial economist.

$$r_{i,t} = a_i + b_i r_{m,t} + e_{i,t} \tag{7-7}$$

where

$r_{i,t}$ = The one-period rate of return from the ith stock in time period t is the dependent variable in the regression

$r_{m,t}$ = The one-period rate of return from the market portfolio in time period t is the independent variable in the regression

a_i = Alpha, or, the characteristic regression line's intercept term

b_i = Beta, or, the characteristic regression line's slope coefficient, or, an index of undiversifiable risk

$e_{i,t}$ = Epsilon, or, the residual return that is unexplained by the regression

t = A subscript that is the time period counter for each stock; it spans a range of 60 months, denoted $t = 1, t = 2, t = 3, \ldots, t = 60$ in the FFJR study.

Each stock's characteristic line was fitted using the 30 months before and 30 months after the change in its unit of account (the event being analyzed). Figure 7-6 in Chapter 7 illustrates Coca-Cola's characteristic line.

Analyzing the Residual Errors

The characteristic line's residual errors, denoted $e_{i,t}$ in Eqn. 7-7, are the focus of this study of stock dividends and splits. The **residual error** is a deviation from the characteristic line. The values of the unexplained residual returns before and after the observed stock split or stock dividend measure abnormal price behavior.

If the residual error at the time of stock split or stock dividend was zero ($e_{it} = 0$), this means the security's actual rate of return equaled what the characteristic line predicted; the change in the unit of account had no positive or negative effects on that month's return. If the residual error was positive ($e_{it} > 0$), the asset's return was above the characteristic line and the stock split or stock dividend (or, perhaps, something else) was apparently boosting returns above what was expected. A negative residual error ($e_{it} < 0$) occurs when the actual rate of return is below the characteristic line because some negative influence is affecting that month's rate of return. If the stock splits and stock dividends create something of value, the residual errors will tend to be positive after the stock dividend or split because the event causes an abnormal increase in the value of the firm's stock.

Averaging the Monthly Residual Errors. The residual errors about the characteristic line result from many influences other than stock splits and stock dividends. Therefore, it is not reasonable to draw general conclusions from the residuals following a split or dividend in a single firm. To overcome this problem, the residual errors were averaged over 940 different stocks for each one of 60 consecutive months before and after the event. This monthly averaging reduces to zero the influences not due to the stock dividend or split. If these average residuals are significantly different from zero in the months after the change in the unit of account, this indicates that the event affected the value of the firm. Eqn. 8-1 defines the average residuals, $\bar{e}_t$, for the tth month before or after the month in which the stock dividend or split occurred:

$$\bar{e}_t = \frac{1}{940} \sum_{e=1}^{940} e_{i,t} = \frac{1}{940}(e_{1,t} + e_{2,t} + e_{3,t} + \ldots + e_{940,t}) \tag{8-1}$$

The *event month* is the month when the stock dividend or split took place. Although all 940 of the stock dividends and splits occurred in different months, FFJR set the event month to be time period zero ($t = 0$) to facilitate adding the residuals. The average residual 6 months before the split month is denoted $\bar{e}_{-6}$ and the average residual 2 months after the split month is $\bar{e}_2$.

Figure 8-6 shows that the residual error averaged over 940 stocks tended to be increasingly positive in the 30 months preceding the stock dividend or split. After the change in the unit of account, the average residuals fluctuate around zero for the next 30 months. The price appreciation occurred before the change in the unit of account, not afterward. Stated differently, the change in the unit of account appears to be the result of the price appreciation, not the cause of the event. Contrary to the popular folklore, those who bought a recently split stock in hopes of earning unusual price appreciation were too late, on average.

FIGURE 8-6 The Average Residual Errors in the Months Before and After a Stock Dividend or Split, Averaged over 940 Stocks

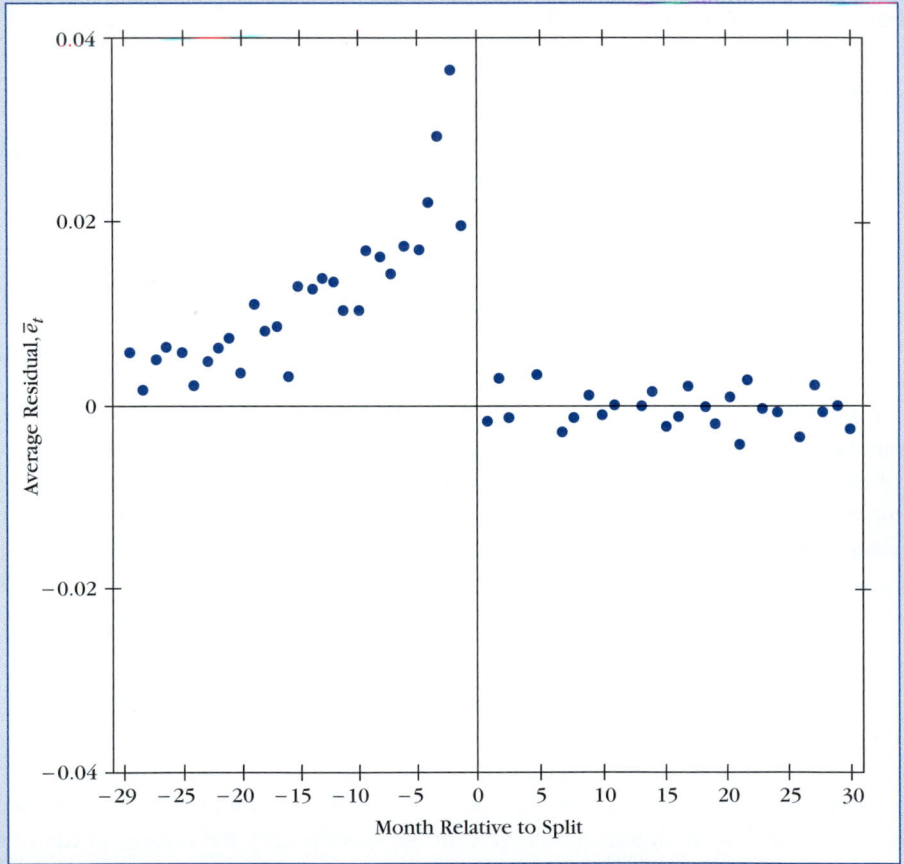

The average residual errors grow to increasing large positive values in the months before the stock dividend or split. But, after the event, average residual errors fluctuating around zero indicate that the price gains that preceded the event ceased.

SOURCE: E. Fama, L. Fisher, M. Jensen, and R. Roll, "The Adjustment of Stock Prices to New Information," *International Economic Review* 20, no. 2 (February 1969): Figure 2a.

Cumulative Average Residuals (CARs). To measure the cumulative month-by-month effect of the stock dividend or split event, the average monthly residuals from Eqn. 8-1 were summed chronologically over (30 + 1 + 30 =) 61 months. Eqn. 8-2 defines cumulative abnormal average monthly residual returns, denoted *CAR*s:

$$CAR = \sum_{t=-30}^{30} \bar{e}_t = \sum_{t=-30}^{30} \sum_{i=1}^{940} e_{i,t} \qquad \text{(8-2)}$$

Note that the CARs graphed in Figures 8-7A, 8-7B, and 8-7C all increase in the months *preceding* the stock split or stock dividend. This preevent increase in the CARs represents the accumulated sum of the preevent average residuals shown in Figure 8-6.

Interpreting the CARs. If a firm declares a stock dividend or split and subsequently fails to raise its cash dividend, that firm disappoints the stock market's expectations. As a result, the corporation's price and returns can be expected to rise before the stock split or stock dividend event and then fall if its cash dividends and underlying earnings fail to continue rising after the stock split. Figure 8-7B shows the cumulative average residuals (CARs) aggregated over all changes in the unit of account when the firms *increased* their cash dividend payments soon after the event. In contrast, Figure 8-7C shows the CARs for firms that had stock dividends or splits and then *decreased* their cash dividend.

More specifically, Figure 8-7B shows that firms that had stock dividends or splits and subsequently raised their cash dividend payments had small positive residuals in the months *after* the stock dividend or split. This is what the market expects will follow a stock split. The owners of securities that split and also increased their earning power enjoyed abnormally high returns, on average, during the months before and after the change in the unit of account.

Unlike the story illustrated in Figure 8-7B, Figure 8-7C tells a story that does not have a happy ending. The firms in Figure 8-7C had stock dividends or splits and then *decreased* their cash dividends. Cash dividend decreases disappoint investors. If the cash dividends decline, the value of the stock usually falls and this causes negative residuals ($e_{it} < 0$). In most cases, the cash dividend reductions were presumably the result of reduced earning power that did not become evident until after the stock dividend or split.

Conclusions About Stock Splits. Jennifer Koski observes that stock splits increase trading activity but, in spite of the increased activity, she suggests stock splits may not really increase the liquidity of the split stocks.[19] Ikenberry, Rankine, and Stice show that in the first year after stocks split they earn an average abnormal return of 7.9%, in the second year after the split they earn abnormal returns of−0.4%, and in the 3 years after the split they earn abnormal returns of−1.3%.[20] In the long run, neither the stocks' liquidity, the market value of the firm, nor investors' returns are changed significantly by stock splits and dividends.

If an investor can correctly anticipate stock dividends and stock splits, the data suggest that it is possible to earn abnormal gains ($e_{it} > 0$). However, the average residuals are zero *after* the announcement date of the stock dividend or split, unless the cash dividends increase further.[21]

The FFJR event study and similar studies provide evidence that stock prices react rationally to public announcements of stock dividends and splits. These empirical studies provide evidence that supports the semistrong efficient markets hypothesis.

FIGURE 8-7   Cumulative Average Residual Errors (CARs) in the Months Before and After a Stock Dividend or Split for (A) 940 Total Splits, (B) 672 Splits Followed by Cash Dividend Increases, And (C) 268 Splits Followed by Cash Dividend Decreases

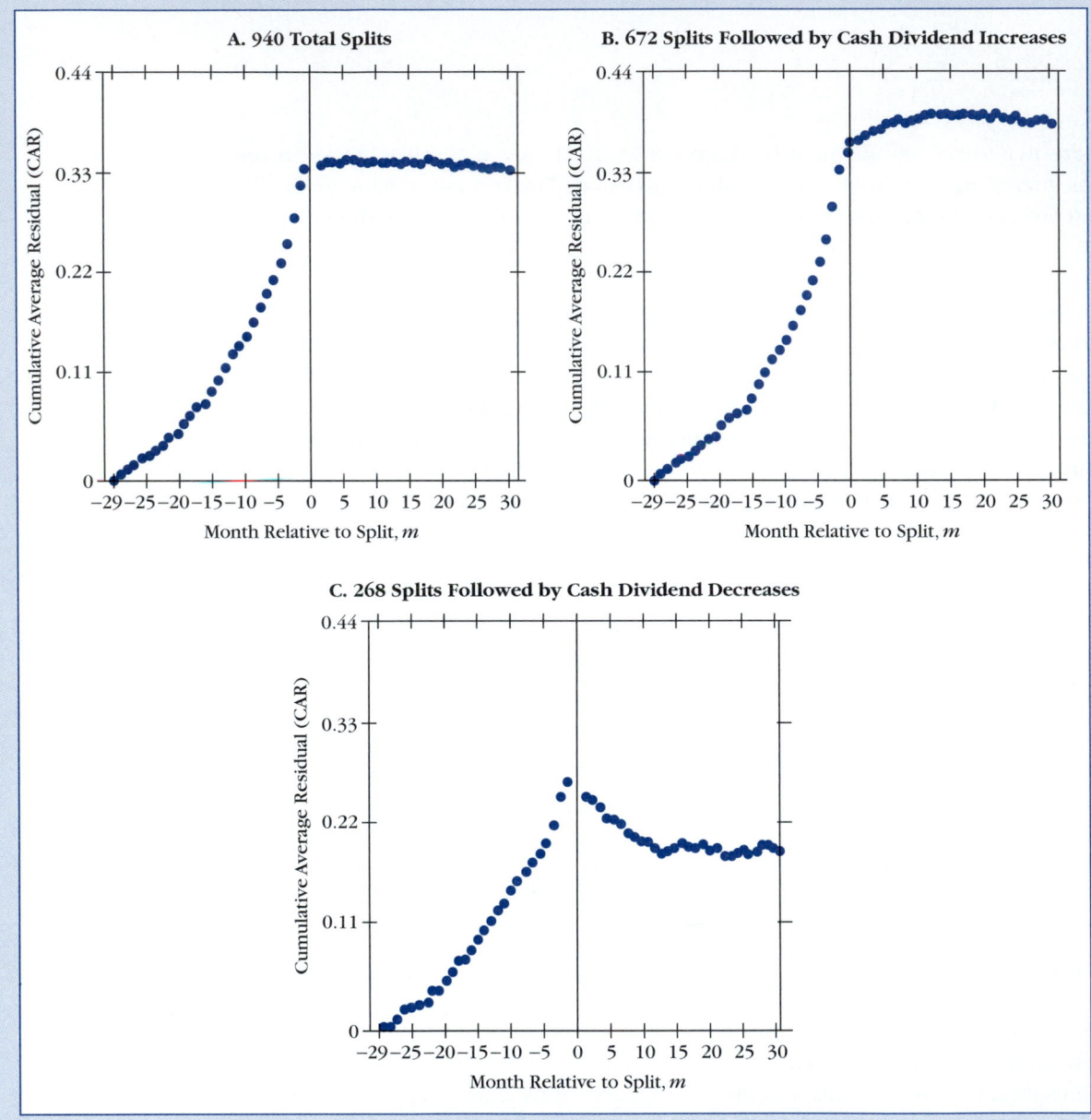

(A) shows that the CARs from the entire sample rose to a peak in the month of the stock dividend or split and leveled off thereafter. (B) shows that corporations that increased their cash dividends after the event month experienced CARs that continued to grow, but at a slower rate, in the months after the event. (C) shows that the CARs from firms that decreased their cash dividend after the event month suffered price declines that shrunk their CARs after the event month.

SOURCE: E. Fama, L. Fisher, M. Jensen, and R. Roll, "The Adjustment of Stock Prices to New Information," *International Economic Review* 20, no. 2, Figures 2b, 3c, and 3d.

THE SIZE EFFECT—ANOTHER ANOMALY

Rolf W. Banz and Marc R. Reinganum published separate empirical studies showing that the stocks issued by small companies earned higher rates of return, on average, than stocks issued by large companies.[22] Banz gathered data on all NYSE stocks and Reinganum gathered data on all NYSE and AMEX stocks and they arrayed their samples by size. The size of the firms was measured by multiplying the number of shares of stock outstanding times the price per share to find each firm's total **market capitalization—or market cap.** After measuring average returns over 10 to 15 years, they found that the portfolios of small-firm stocks earned higher average returns than the portfolios of stocks issued by large companies. Table 8-4 shows daily mean excess returns and the associated beta coefficients for ten decile portfolios arrayed by size.

Banz and Reinganum noted that the small stocks were, on average, riskier than the stocks issued by the large corporations. They realized that the higher returns earned by the small stocks might, therefore, be simply the risk premiums that are fundamental in economic theory. After making risk adjustments, however, they found that a **size effect** still remained. Richard Roll suggested that the riskiness of the stocks might have been measured improperly.[23] Roll pointed out that most small stocks are not traded frequently and, as a result of infrequent price changes, the small stocks' risk measurements might be biased downward. A study by Elroy Dimson confirmed Richard Roll's suspicions that the small stocks' risk statistics were downward biased.[24] Therefore, Reinganum recomputed his risk statistics using an *aggregated coefficients method* Dimson suggested and verified Roll's suspicions of bias in the risk statistics.[25] Reinganum also found the bias was not sufficient to wipe out the size effect when the returns were properly risk-adjusted.[26]

Economic theory provides no reason to expect that stocks issued by small firms should outperform stocks issued by large firms. Since the market capitalization of an exchange-listed corporation is public knowledge, the size effect is an anomaly in the semistrong efficient markets hypothesis.

Interrelationship Between the January and Size Effects

The January effect introduced earlier in this chapter interacts with the size effect. This interaction was documented when Donald Keim examined all NYSE and AMEX stocks over a 17-year sample period and created ten size **decile portfolios** for each month's returns.[27] Each decile portfolio contains 10% of the arrayed sample. Figure 8-8 displays Keim's results. A line was drawn to connect the ten size portfolios for each individual month. With the exception of January, the lines are similar. The line for January depicts an interrelationship between the

TABLE 8-4   Mean Daily Excess Returns and Betas for Size Decile Portfolios

Size decile portfolio	Smallest 1[a]	2	3	4	5	6	7	8	9	Largest 10[b]
Mean excess return[c]	.50	.19	−.03	−.05	−.12	−.19	−.19	−.21	−.29	−.34
Beta	1.0	1.02	1.0	1.0	.94	.88	.90	.83	.83	.82

[a] refers to the 10% of firms that are smallest when arrayed by size.

[b] refers to the 10% of firms that are largest when arrayed by size.

[c] refers to daily portfolio return less the equal-weighted NYSE-AMEX market return. The mean excess returns are multiplied by 1,000.

SOURCE: Marc R. Reinganum, "Misspecification of Capital Asset Pricing: Empirical Anomalies Based on Earnings Yield and Market Values," *Journal of Financial Economics* 9, no. 1 (March 1981): 40, Table 8.

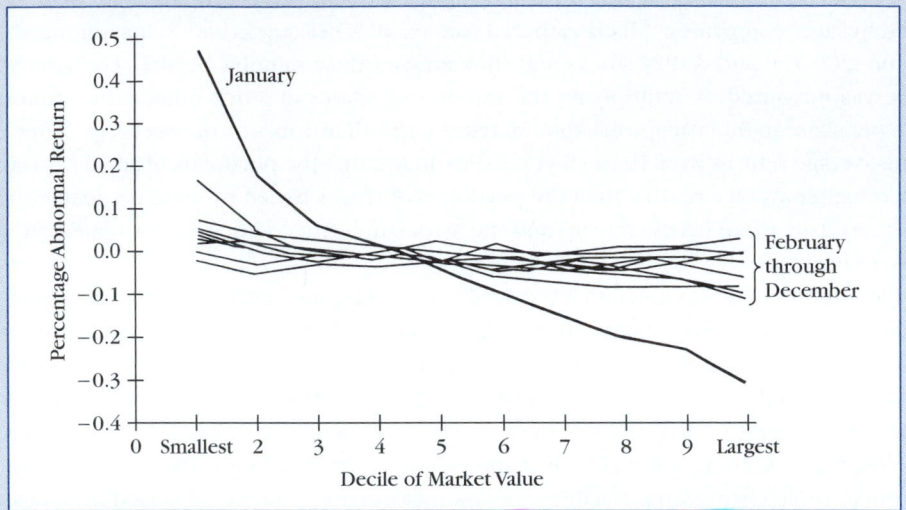

FIGURE 8-8   The Interrelationship Between the Size Effect and the January Effect

The January effect and the size effect interact during January as small cap stocks typically earn higher average returns than large stocks during that month.

SOURCE: Donald B. Keim, "Size-Related Anomalies and Stock Return Seasonality: Further Empirical Evidence," *Journal of Financial Economics* 12, no. 1 (June 1983): 13–32.

size effect and the January effect. The line for January also shows a negative January effect for large firms.

As mentioned earlier in this chapter, the reason that most of the typical stock's returns for an entire year are earned during January is not known.

International Evidence

The interaction between the January effect and the size effect appears to reach around the world.[28] Figure 8-9 illustrates the results of a study of the Japanese stock market conducted by Kiyoshi Kato and James S. Schallheim. The January effect, the size effect, and the interaction between the January and size effects are all visible in Figure 8-9.

THE GROWTH-VALUE ANOMALY

The semistrong efficient markets hypothesis suggests that, if they all have the same information available, money managers who use a particular management style should not be able to consistently outperform the money managers who use some other style of management. It is plausible that a particular money manager who has unique access to valuable information is able to consistently outperform all competing money managers—this would be the result of an *information* advantage, not a management style advantage. Or, it is possible that a person who uses a particular management style will beat the competing management styles *occasionally*. However, as we see in the following discussion, it seems unlikely that one of these management styles should produce results that consistently beat the other management styles.

FIGURE 8-9 Monthly Average Returns from Japan Document the Interaction Between the January and the Size Effects

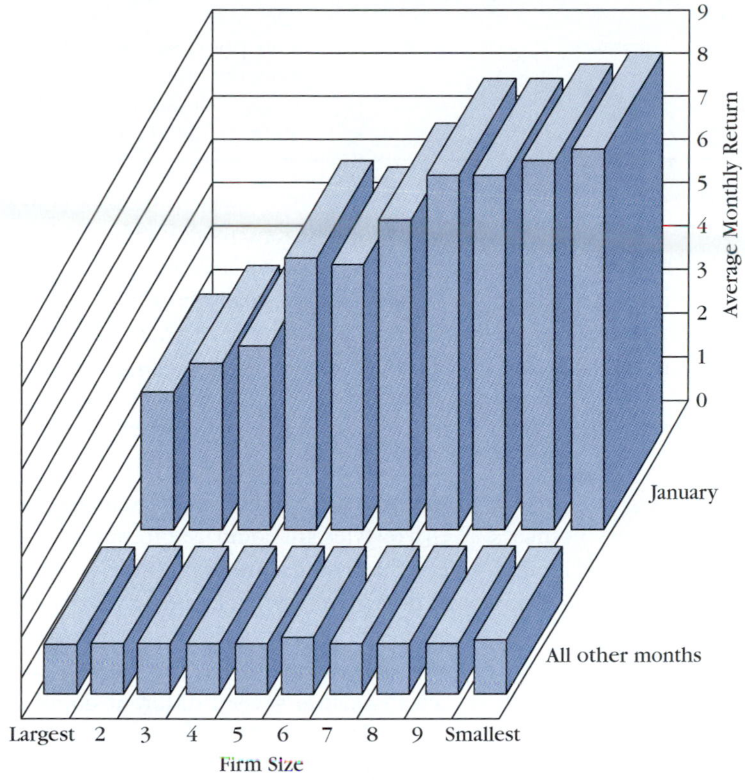

Small cap firms in Japan, like small cap firms in the United States, experience unusually large returns during January, on average.

SOURCE: The graph is reproduced from a book by Robert A. Haugen and Josef Lakonishok, *The Incredible January Effect* (Homewood, IL: Dow Jones-Irwin 1988). Haugen and Lakonishok borrowed the data from a study by Kiyoshi Kato and James S. Schallheim, "Seasonal and Size Anomalies in the Japanese Stock Market" *Journal of Financial and Quantitative Analysis* 20, no. 2 (June 1985): 248.

TWO POPULAR MANAGEMENT STYLES USED BY ACTIVE EQUITY PORTFOLIO MANAGERS   DEFINITION

Value managers typically buy stocks that are issued by firms with low price-earnings ratios, below average earnings growth rates, high cash-dividend yields, and low price-to-book-value (P/B) ratios. Value managers are sometimes called *contrarians* because they often buy stocks that are not popular investments.

Characteristics of Value and Growth Stocks	
Growth Stocks	**Value Stocks**
High earnings per share growth	Low earnings per share growth
Glamorous	Out of favor
High price/earnings ratio	Low price/earnings ratio
High price/book ratio	Low price/book ratio
Low cash dividend yield	High cash dividend yield
Betas tend to be above 1.0	Betas tend to be below 1.0

Growth managers like to buy stocks that are currently enjoying high rates of earnings growth and are expected to continue experiencing high earnings growth. They typically buy **glamour stocks** that are issued by large corporations and have high price-earnings ratios. The stocks they select usually have low cash-dividend yields (Eqn. 8-5), high rates of return on equity, high price-to-book-value (P/B) ratios, and, as mentioned above, high growth rates and high price-earnings ratios.

Value management and growth management are popular equity management styles[29] that are based on contrary premises. The two styles are compared frequently—for example, when investors select mutual funds. What is surprising is that value stock investors have historically outperformed those who invest in growth stocks. Empirical studies of individual stocks[30] and equity mutual funds[31] alike have shown that value investing earns higher (raw and risk-adjusted) returns than investments in growth stocks. The growth managers' relatively weak performance has been shown to exist in several different countries and over extended periods of time.

Partitioning Stocks' Financial Ratios. To make a quantitative distinction between value stocks and growth stocks, investors can use three financial ratios: the stocks' growth rates in earnings, price-earnings ratios, and current yields.

$$\left(\begin{array}{c} \text{Cash dividend yield,} \\ \text{or, Current yield} \end{array} \right) = \frac{\left(\text{Cash dividends per share} \right)}{\left(\text{Market price per share} \right)} \tag{8-5}$$

As explained above, value (growth) managers tend to invest in stocks issued by corporations that have low (high) rates of earnings growth, high (low) current yields, and low (high) P/E ratios. Figure 8-10 illustrates the performance of six diversified common stock portfolios (three growth plus three value) that were selected with the three financial ratios mentioned (growth rates in earnings, price-earning ratios, and current yields). Figure 8-10 also shows how the six portfolios compared with the S&P500 index. The figure shows that three portfolios of value stocks delineated by the three ratios outperforms the analogous growth stock portfolios and the S&P500 index.

Fama and French (F&F) Analyze the P/B Ratio

Instead of using several different ratios, Eugene Fama and Kenneth French (F&F) used only the P/B ratio to discriminate between value stocks and growth stocks:[32]

$$\left(\text{P/B} \right) = \frac{\left(\text{Market price of the stock} \right)}{\left(\text{Book value of the stock} \right)} \tag{8-6}$$

FIGURE 8-10   Cumulative Value of $1 Invested in Value and Growth Portfolios Selected via Three Different Financial Ratios Are Contrasted with S&P500 Index over Time

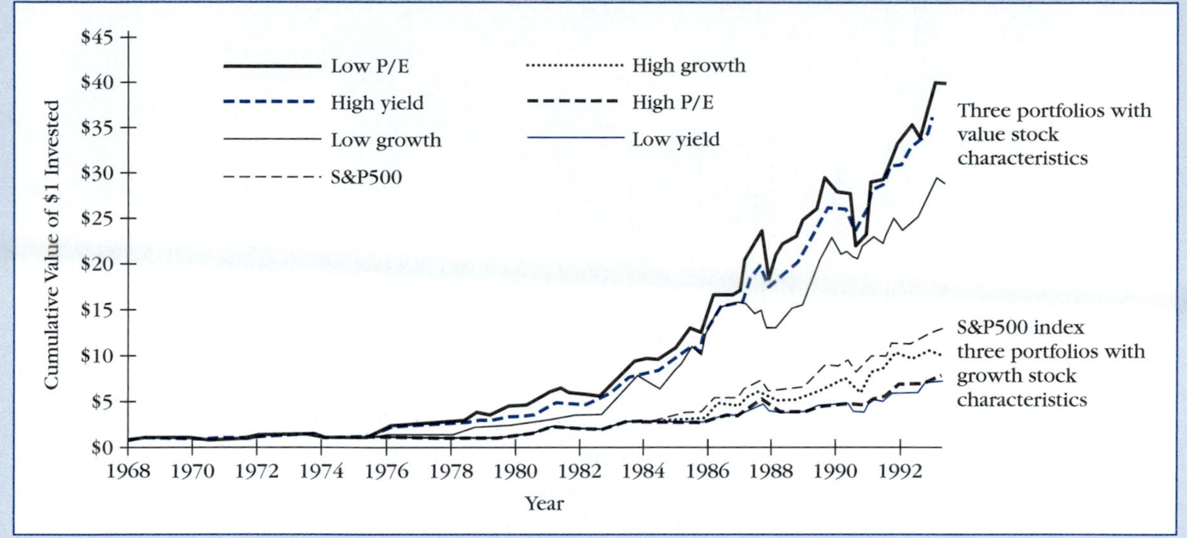

A dollar invested in three portfolios that had low price-earnings ratios, high cash dividend yields, and low growth rates, which are all characteristics of value stocks, outperformed three other portfolios that had growth stock characteristics.

SOURCE: Robert A. Haugen, *The New Finance* (Upper Saddle River, NJ: Prentice-Hall, 1995), Figure 5.3, p. 59. Haugen obtained the data from DeMarche Associates Inc. in Kansas City, MO.

F&F used the P/B ratio to array a sample that includes all nonfinancial firms traded on the NYSE, AMEX, and NASDAQ that also have data available on both the CRSP and Compustat Tapes. F&F partitioned the data from approximately 2,000 firms into the ten P/B deciles shown in Figure 8-11. Each *decile portfolio* contains 10% of the sample. The stocks in the decile portfolios were examined individually to discern if they were growth or value stocks. Although there might be some uncertainty about what kind of stocks are in the middle decile, the decile portfolio with the lowest P/B ratio is unmistakably a portfolio of value stocks. Further, the decile portfolio with the highest P/B ratio is clearly a portfolio of growth stocks.

Figure 8-11 shows that the value portfolio in decile 10 earned more than twice the average return earned by the growth portfolio in decile 1. This disparity between value stocks and growth stocks is too large to be coincidental. At first it seemed that F&F delineated a beat-the-market scheme (anomaly in the efficient markets hypothesis) by simply using the P/B ratio to array stocks. An examination of the risk statistics for the decile portfolios in Figure 8-11 indicated the difference between the returns from F&F's value and growth portfolios might be attributed to differences in riskiness. Lakonishok, Schleifer, and Vishny reported findings that supported F&F's results even after adjusting for the sizes of the firms.[33] Tim Loughran was dubious and performed an exhaustive exploration of firms' P/B ratios.[34] Loughran reports that:

> *The book-to-market effect of Fama and French is shown to be mostly a manifestation of the low returns on small newly listed growth stocks outside of January coupled with a seasonal January effect for value firms. For the largest size quintile (accounting for, on average, 73% of all market value), book-to-market has no*

FIGURE 8-11   Companies Average Returns for Each P/B Decile, 1962–89

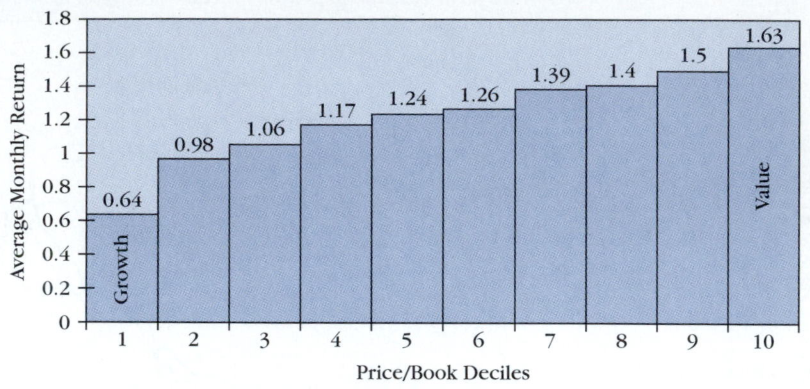

The portfolio of value stocks in Decile 10 earned more than twice the average rate of return earned by the portfolio of growth stocks in Decile 1.

SOURCE: Eugene Fama and Kenneth French, "The Cross-Section of Expected Stock Returns," *Journal of Finance* 46 (June 1992): 427–66.

reliable predictive power for returns during the 1963–1995 period. Further, when value-weighted returns by (P/B) quintiles are reported, growth firms outperform value firms by 140 basis points per year outside of the 1974–1984 subperiod. The explanation for the inconsistency between the academic literature and practitioner experience is that for large firms, in which most managers invest, the book-to-market effect has been statistically insignificant, at least since 1963.[35] [The parenthetical (P/B) ratio was changed to be consistent with the convention used in this book.]

Loughran's results suggests additional research on the P/B ratio might be helpful.

The SP/BARRA Growth and Value Index Funds. In 1992 the Vanguard mutual fund management corporation opened two more index funds named the SP/BARRA Growth Fund and the SP/BARRA Value Fund. Vanguard retains an investment consulting firm named BARRA to divide the 500 stocks in the S&P500 index into two mutually exclusive lists based on the P/B ratio defined in Eqn. 8-6. Two new index funds were created: The SP/BARRA Growth Index Fund contains those 500 stocks that have above high P/B ratios, and the SP/BARRA Value Index Fund contains the corporations with low P/B ratios. These two funds are rebalanced by BARRA semiannually. Table 8-5 contrasts characteristics of the SP/BARRA Growth and Value Indexes on which the two new Vanguard mutual funds are based. Figure 8-12 illustrates how the performance of Vanguard's SP/BARRA Growth and SP/BARRA Value Indexes compare with the performance of the S&P500 index.

Figure 8-12 illustrates the superior long-run performance of the SP/BARRA Value Index over the SP/BARRA Growth Index. People who would rather invest in growth stocks than value stocks point out that significant periods may be found when, contrary to the long-run tendency illustrated in Figure 8-12, growth stocks perform better than value stocks. For example, during the Internet Stock Bubble from January 1995 to February 2000, the SP/BARRA Growth Index beat the SP/BARRA Value Index by an average annual spread of 11.3% (= 31.2% − 19.9%).[36] An international comparison throws more light on this perennial debate between value stock and growth stock investors.

TABLE 8-5	Contrasting the SP/BARRA Growth and Value Indexes	
Characteristic	SP/BARRA Value Fund	SP/BARRA Growth Fund
Number of companies	349	151
Median company's capitalization	$6,090 million	$16,570 million
Average P/E ratio	24.64 times	42.06 times
Average P/B ratio	3.09	10.27
Current (cash dividend) yield	1.9%	0.81%
Return on equity	14.68%	30.32%
Beta	0.93	1.07
Percent of portfolio's value invested in technology stocks	10.40%	26.71%

SOURCE: *S&P500 Directory*, 1999/2000 Edition, Standard & Poor's Corporation, New York, p. 15.

Capaul, Rowley, and Sharpe's International Study

Carlo Capaul, Ian Rowley, and William Sharpe (CRS) analyzed 3 portfolios from each of six countries for a total of 18 portfolios.[37] From the United States they analyzed the S&P500 index and the related SP/BARRA Growth Index and SP/BARRA Value Index described above. In France, Germany, Switzerland, the United Kingdom, and Japan, CRS analyzed indexes that were constructed by the Union Bank of Switzerland (UBS) to match the Morgan Stanley Capital International (MSCI) stock market indexes. In each of these five countries a stock market index was partitioned into a growth stock index and a value stock index using the same market-value weighting and other methodologies used to construct the SP/BARRA Growth and Value Funds. Monthly data from 1981 through 1992 were analyzed.

CRS constructed a monthly growth-value spread for each of the six countries by subtracting the return from the growth (high P/B) portfolio from the simultaneous return that was earned by that country's value (low P/B) portfolio. Table 8-6 shows the average monthly growth-value spreads, standard deviations, and *t*-statistics for the spreads from each of the six countries. The *t*-statistics indicate low confidence levels for the statistics from Germany, the United Kingdom, and the United States. In the other countries and for the world as a whole the monthly growth-value spreads were significantly different in both the economic and statistical sense. CRS also computed risk-adjusted returns for the 18 portfolios they analyzed and reported that the value portfolios provided results that were superior to the market portfolios in all six countries.[38] Value investing seems to outperform growth stock investing in the international arena too.

Conclusions About Growth and Value Stocks. Empirical studies by Chan-Hamao-Lakonishok, Fama-French, and Lakonishok-Schleifer-Vishny indicated that value stocks outperform growth stocks. A portfolio study by Capaul-Rowley-Sharpe and a similar study by Sinquefield provided additional evidence that the unexplained superior returns value managers usually earn constitute an anomaly in the semistrong efficient market hypothesis.

Concluding Remarks About the Semistrong Efficient Markets Hypothesis

The Gwilym, Buckle, Clarke, and Thomas (GBCT) analysis of transactions data on futures indexes supported the semistrong efficient markets hypothesis. Fama, Fisher, Jensen, and Roll's (FFJR's) analysis of stock dividends and splits was also highly supportive of the semistrong efficient

FIGURE 8-12 Comparing the Performances of the SP/BARRA Growth, SP/BARRA Value, and S&P500 Indexes

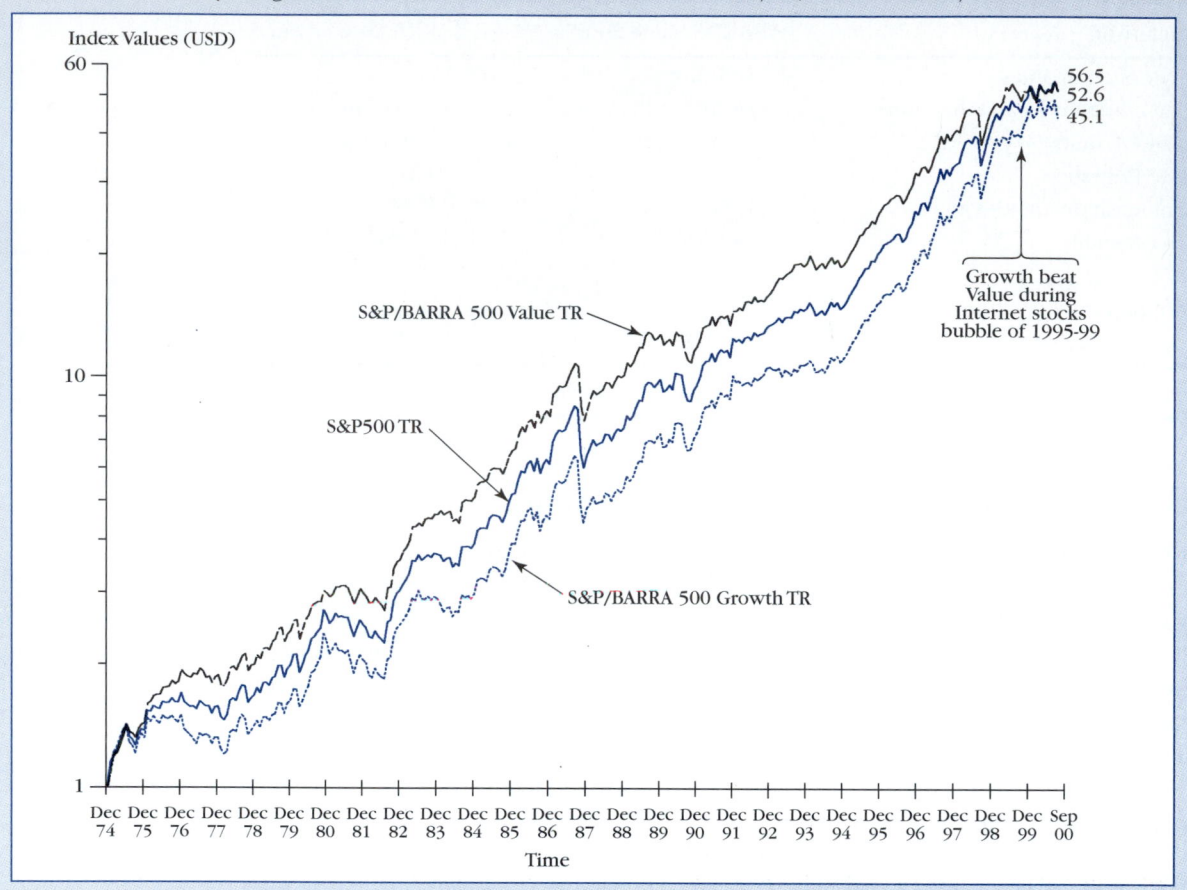

The SP/BARRA Value Index outperformed the S&P500 index, and the S&P500 index outperformed the SP/BARRA Growth Index.

SOURCE: The graph was prepared with data and software from EnCorr, Ibbotson Associates, Chicago, IL.

TABLE 8-6   **Selected Statistics on Monthly Spreads of Value Returns Minus Growth Returns from Six Countries**

Country	Monthly Average Return	Standard Deviation	*t*-statistic
France	0.53	3.86	1.62
Germany	0.13	3.14	0.48[a]
United Kingdom	0.23	3.32	0.81[a]
Japan	0.50	3.76	1.57
United States	0.11	1.99	0.67[a]
Europe	0.23	2.18	1.24
Global	0.29	1.70	1.98

[a]Not significantly different from zero.

SOURCE: Carlo Capaul, Ian Rowley, and William F. Sharpe, "International Value & Growth Stock Returns," *Financial Analysts Journal* (January-February 1993): 27–36, Table IV.

markets hypothesis. However, the size effect and the superior performance of the value-oriented investment managers constitute pieces of anomalous evidence that weight against the semi-strong efficient markets hypothesis.

TESTS OF THE STRONGLY EFFICIENT MARKETS HYPOTHESIS

The strongly efficient markets hypothesis considers everything that is knowable. Public information (books, newspapers, Standard & Poor's publications) is a subset of all knowable information. Everything that is knowable is such a large and rapidly growing set of information that it immediately makes one doubt that all prices in a securities market could continuously readjust to this huge body of knowledge. First, let us investigate to see how the mutual fund industry uses all the available information.

Evaluating the Performance of Mutual Funds

Thousands of mutual funds advertise that money entrusted to them is managed by professional money managers, that they manage millions (or billions) of dollars, that they have years of money management experience, and that they employ some ingenious management methodology. In addition, many of the advertisements contain graphs illustrating how money invested in the fund increased in value over a selected period of time. As a result of these advertisements, many investors get the erroneous impression that all mutual funds are extremely well managed. Let us confront this notion with facts.

Several mutual fund studies that were performed by finance professors at U.S. universities have documented the following list of conclusions:

Large funds typically perform no better than small funds.

High turnover (very actively traded) mutual funds usually perform slightly worse than funds that turn over slowly.

Mutual funds that charge their investors sales commissions (called load fees) perform slightly worse than no-load funds.

Funds with high management fees tend to perform a little worse than funds with low management fees.

The majority of equity mutual funds in the United States are not able to earn rates of return that exceed the returns from no-skill portfolios like the S&P500 index of 500 representative stocks.

Mutual funds are unable to "beat the market" in any meaningful sense.[39]

Professor Burton Malkiel analyzed 21 years of data covering all equity mutual funds and reached the following conclusions:[40]

This study takes a new look at mutual fund returns during the 1971 to 1991 period and utilizes a data set that includes the returns from all mutual funds in existence in each year of the period. Most data sets include all mutual funds currently in existence and, thus, exclude funds that have terminated operations. Our data set permits us to obtain measures of survivorship bias, which we estimate to be substantial. When returns from all times are analyzed, we find that mutual funds have tended to underperform the market, not only after management expenses have been deducted, but also gross of (before) all reported expenses except load fees. [Parenthetical word added.]

. . . In conclusion, this study of mutual funds does not provide any reason to abandon a belief that securities markets are remarkably efficient. Most investors would be considerably better off by purchasing a low expense index fund, than by trying to select an active fund manager who appears to possess a "hot hand." Since active management generally fails to provide excess returns and tends to generate greater tax burdens for investors, the advantage of passive management holds, a fortiori. [Italics added for emphasis.]

In spite of the inability of the mutual fund industry to outperform the security market indexes, there remains a pocket of information that is not fully utilized. "Insiders" possess valuable information.

Inside Information

U.S. law defines an **insider** to be any corporate director, any owner of 10% or more of the corporation's equity shares, or any executive in the corporation who has access to material nonpublic information about the corporation. An unfair **information asymmetry** exists because insiders have access to valuable inside information that is not available to other investors (outsiders). Within the United States, the **Securities Exchange Act of 1934** forbids insiders from keeping any profits they earn from trading their corporation's stock if the stock was held less than 6 months. If the stock was held for over 6 months, the insider may keep the gains. This 1934 Act also prohibits insiders from taking a short position in their corporation's stock. In addition, the Securities and Exchange Commission (SEC) requires insiders to fully disclose their dealings by submitting SEC Form 4 within 10 days after the end of any month in which they trade their corporation's stock. The SEC collects this insider trading information and releases it monthly via the *Official Summary of Insider Transactions* publication.* The Official Summary is released to the public approximately 2 months after the insiders' transactions. Financial service firms collect this information about insider trading as it comes into the SEC and sell it to their subscribers before the monthly *Official Summary* is released.

Figure 8-13 is an excerpt from the *Wall Street Journal* that provides a sample of that newspaper's periodic release of information about trading by insiders. Web sites on the Internet also disseminate information about insider trading.

EXAMPLE — SOURCES OF DATA ABOUT CURRENT INSIDER TRADING

Vickers Stock Research Corporation in New York City (phone 212-482-8300) sells the *Weekly Insider Report* to subscribers.

The Value Line Corporation in New York City sells subscriptions to its *Value Line Investment Survey*. In addition to a financial analysis on each company, this survey also contains information about recent inside trading.

Free insider information is available on the Internet at: www.InsiderScores.com. InsiderScores is owned by PriMark Corporation of Waltham, MA. Additional free Internet information about trading by insiders is available at: www.InsiderTrader.com. InsiderTrader.com is wholly owned by Individual Investor Group, Inc. (Nasdaq ticker symbol: INDI), with offices in New York City. Phone 212-742-2277.

---

* The SEC's Rule 13b requires that anyone who acquires 5 percent or more of the corporation's outstanding stock report these holdings to the SEC. Reporting such holdings under the SEC's Rule 13b is different from and unrelated to reporting insider trading on the SEC's Form 4.

FIGURE 8-13   Insider Trading Spotlight

INSIDER TRADING SPOTLIGHT

Biggest Individual Trades

(Based on reports filed with regulators last week)

COMPANY NAME	EXCH.	INSIDER'S NAME	TITLE	$ VALUE (000)	NO. OF SHRS. IN TRANS. (000)	% OF HLDNG. EXCLD. OPTNS.	TRANSACTION DATES
BUYERS							
Walter Industries	N	R. G. Burton x	P	2,210	262.4	n	04/24-25/00
Cole Natl COM A	N	L. Pollock	P	650	100.0	15.00	04/13-26/00
Calico Commerce	O	A. F. Knapp, Jr	VP	567	35.0	114.00	04/27/00
SMC	O	M. R. Jacque	P	526	128.0	104.00	04/14-25/00
United Capital	A	H. M. Lorber	D	385	30.0	38.00	03/31/00 †
Republic Group	N	P. Simpson	CB	307	26.0	n	04/17/00
Enzon	O	D. S. Barlow	D	281	10.0	w	04/18/00
Cyberian Outpost	O	C. H. Jackson x	D	281	60.0	n	04/18/00
Gentiva Health Services	O	R. S. Troubh	D	227	37.5	201.00	03/07-17/00 †
Grey Advertising	O	R. Reiss	D	210	.5	n	04/13/00
SELLERS							
Wireless Facilities	O	M. Tayebi x	CB	25,330	460.5	10.00	04/28/00
Brocade Coms Sys	O	M. Byrd	O	14,764	102.5	9.00	04/06-07/00
Barpoint.Com	O	M. C. Schilowitz	Z	14,400	1,200.0	57.00	04/06/00
Kopin	O	J. C. Fan	P	7,102	91.0	14.00	02/23-03/01/00
State Street	N	M. N. Carter	CB	5,420	54.7	19.00	04/24-25/00
ADC Telecoms	O	J. J. Boyle III	VP	5,235	101.5	70.00	03/09/00
Kopin	O	M. Zavracky	VP	5,207	66.0	na	02/25-03/01/00
State Street	N	S. Comeau x	VP	5,028	51.0	70.00	04/24-25/00
State Street	N	N. A. Lopardo	O	4,659	47.8	23.00	04/24/00
Honeywell Intl	N	P. M. Kreindler	VP	4,302	77.4	na	04/18-24/00

Companies With Biggest Net Changes

(Based on actual transaction dates in reports received through Friday)

COMPANY NAME	EXCH./SYMBOL	NET % CHG. IN HOLDINGS OF ACTIVE INSIDERS[1] LATEST 12 WEEKS	NET % CHG. IN HOLDINGS OF ACTIVE INSIDERS[1] LATEST 24 WEEKS	LATEST 12 WKS. NO. OF BUYERS-SELLERS	LATEST 12 WKS. MULTIPLE OF HIST. NORM[2]	LATEST 24 WKS NO. OF BUYERS-SELLERS	LATEST 24 WKS MULTIPLE OF HIST. NORM[2]
BUYING							
Acnielsen	N/ART	21	21	7-0	4.7	7-0	2.3
Pennzoil-Quaker State	N/PZL	21	21	4-0	1.0	4-0	1.0
H. B. Fuller	O/FULL	20	20	7-0	1.2	7.0	.6
SELLING							
Lands' End	N/LE	− 93	− 93	0-4	.3	0-4	.7
Aerial Coms	O/AERL	− 75	− 75	0-4	4.0	0-4	2.0
Pogo Producing	N/PPP	− 41	− 41	0-6	2.0	0-6	1.0
General Motors	N/GM	− 39	− 35	1-3	3.0	1-4	2.0
NVR	A/NVR	− 25	− 25	0-3	1.5	0-3	.8

NOTE: Shows purchases and sales by most officers and directors, which must be reported to the SEC and other regulators by the 10th of the month following the month of the trade. Includes both open-market and private transactions involving direct and indirect holdings. Excludes stocks valued at less than $2 a share, acquisitions through options and companies being acquired. w-1000% or more.

n-No prior holdings. r-sale within two weeks of option exercise equal to 90% or more of shares sold. s-Holds other class of stock. x-Reflects shares held indirectly. †-Late filing. *-Base period is less than 3 years.

CB-chairman. P-president. D-director. VP-vice president. O-officer. Z-other.

[1]Ranked by the net change in shares held by those insiders who bought or sold during the last 12 weeks, expressed as a percentage change of only their holdings at the start of the period. Reflects companies for which filings made last week showed some insider activity during the latest 12 weeks. Excluded: companies with total trades valued under $75,000; option-related sales, unexercised options, companies with fewer than three buyers or sellers, or fewer buyers or sellers than the historical average for the period.

[2]Based on the previous three years.

Source: FIRST CALL/Thomson Financial, Boston, MA.

In recent decades the SEC has expanded its definition of insiders to include any insider or outsider who *uses material nonpublic information obtained in breach of a fiduciary trust* to trade in a corporation's securities. This means that both the full-time and part-time employees at all levels of a corporation (for example, a temporary typist) have a **fiduciary responsibility** to the shareholders of the corporation. Even outsiders (called tippees) who receive tips from insiders and trade on that information can be prosecuted for insider trading.[41] In the United States, the **Insider Trading Sanctions Act of 1984** and the **Securities Fraud Enforcement Act of 1988** provide for insider trading penalties of three times any damages that might have been caused, fines up to $1,000,000, and up to 10 years imprisonment.

The perfectly efficient markets hypothesis suggests that all information, both public and nonpublic, is fully reflected in security prices. This idealistic economic situation would result in a perfectly efficient market, where prices and values are always equal as they fluctuate randomly together in response to the arrival of new information. An obvious way to check the validity of the strongly efficient markets hypothesis is to examine the profitability of insider trading to see if the insiders' access to valuable information allows them to earn statistically significant trading profits. The profitability of insider trading should vary directly with the amount of valuable inside information that exists.

Jaffe's Study. Jeffrey F. Jaffe formulated an event study based on insider trades. He gathered 6 years of data from the *Official Summary of Insider Transactions* and measured insiders' trading profits.[42] He also computed risk-adjusted 1-month returns from stocks insiders traded. To delineate the stocks that were being traded most actively by insiders, Jaffe selected a stock for further study if it had three more inside sellers than inside buyers in a month—Jaffe labeled this event a *selling plurality*. Three more insiders buying than selling in the same month was called a *buying plurality*. Jaffe assumed that if the insiders were predominantly net buyers (sellers), it can be inferred that a balance of favorable (unfavorable) inside information motivated the transactions. To test the hypothesis that insiders use valuable information to trade profitably, Jaffe tabulated the monthly residual errors (abnormal returns) for each stock that experienced a plurality of insider trading. After compiling data for thousands of transactions Jaffe summed up the residual returns for every month in which a plurality of insiders emerged.

Table 8-7 shows that 1 month after a plurality of insider trading the insiders' profits before commissions, taxes, and other transactions costs averaged $\frac{98}{100}$ of 1% of the value of the stock. This small return indicates the average insider did not earn enough after 1 month to pay their commission costs. After the stock was held 2 months, the average insiders gained 2.09%. After 8 months, the plurality of insiders' stocks experienced an average price change (gross profit) of 5.07%. If commission costs of 1% to buy and 1% to sell are deducted, the average insider does not seem to be getting rich very rapidly.

TABLE 8-7	Cumulative Average Measures of Insiders' Residual Returns Before Transactions Costs
Months Cumulated	Average Residual Return
1	0.98%
2	2.09%
8	5.07%

SOURCE: Jeffrey F. Jaffe, "Special Information and Insider Trading," *Journal of Business* 47, no. 3 (July 1974): 421, Table 3, third panel.

Jaffe's study suggested the average insider's gains were maximized by holding their positions for about 8 months. Jaffe also investigated what happens when the plurality of insiders increased. Surprisingly, when the plurality reached five, the average insiders' residual return declined slightly below the return earned by a plurality of three or four. Jaffe also reported that outsiders who traded on the same stocks as the insiders. These outsiders had to wait several weeks longer than insiders in order to get their information from the SEC's *Official Summary of Insider Transactions*. Not surprisingly, the outsiders earned residual returns that were a little smaller than the insiders. Jaffe's evidence that, on average, insider trading was not highly profitable aroused responses.[43]

Seyhun's Study. H. Nejat Seyhun analyzed insiders' trading using different sample data and a different research methodology than Jaffe.[44] Seyhun's results suggest that Jaffe's estimates of the insiders' profits might be biased upward. In addition, he examined *outsiders* who traded on inside information purchased from one of the financial services that purveys data about insiders' trading activities. Seyhun found that, on average, outsiders were unable to earn net profits after commissions from their trades.

Meulbroek Study. Lisa Meulbroek analyzed SEC files covering 229 episodes of illegal insider trading.[45] These cases dealt with trading in 218 different companies listed on the NYSE, AMEX, and NASDAQ between 1974 and 1988. She reports that the typical case involved illegal trading in one stock and that the illegal trading usually took place on two or three different days. She says that, "On average, the abnormal return is 3.06% on the day of the insider trade." Meulbroek's research shows that "on inside trading days, stock prices move significantly towards values which incorporate the inside information." Meulbroek's findings provide strong support for those who claim that insider trading helps stock prices reflect all the information that is knowable. In addition, the fact that insiders, on average, can earn trading profits from their inside information is sufficient evidence to refute the strongly efficient markets hypothesis.

Allocating Society's Scarce Resources. The SEC is a federal bureaucracy in the United States staffed with hundreds of lawyers. Law schools train attorneys how to interpret laws and punish law breakers after a crime has been committed. Unlike the law profession, the economics profession does not make many judgments about what is right or wrong or formulate punishments. Many economists believe that free market competition will punish inept people so efficiently that a costly securities law enforcement agency like the SEC wastes the society's resources. Instead of focusing on past crimes, economists are more inclined to look into the future and focus on the way resources are allocated. Economists argue that market prices allocate resources in a free market economy. They point out that if insider trading were permitted, security market prices would reflect more valuable inside information, which would enable a society's resources to be allocated more efficiently. Many respected financial economists conclude that since an optimal allocation of resources benefits everyone, insider trading should be legalized.[46]

Conclusions About the Strongly (Perfectly) Efficient Markets Hypothesis

Jaffe, Seyhun, and Meulbroek provide ample evidence that insiders possess valuable information that gives them a trading advantage over outsiders. But, this information asymmetry is small. Meulbroek reported that on days when insiders were trading illegally the stock's price moved 3.06%, and only 47.56% of this 3.06% average daily price change was attributable to insider trading. Meulbroek's findings suggest, first, insiders do not possess a lot of valuable inside information; and, second, what information the insiders do possess gets disseminated rapidly.[47]

The fact that most mutual funds in the United States cannot outperform a stock market index like the S&P500 over a representative sample period has serious implications. It implies that the professional investment staffs of thousands of equity mutual funds are able to uncover very little valuable information that is not already impacted into prices.

The abnormal returns that Jaffe, Seyhun, Meulbroek, and others attribute to insiders' profitable trading refute the strongly efficient markets hypothesis. But, as we pointed out, on average, insider trading is not very profitable. Thus, although the evidence refutes the strongly efficient markets hypothesis, it would be erroneous to conclude that securities prices ignore substantial amounts of valuable information.

THE BOTTOM LINE

By the time you finish this book, you should reach conclusions about the efficiency of the markets in which you do research or trade. It is important that you develop informed opinions about market pricing efficiency, because these opinions will determine the way you manage investments. If you conclude that all of the anomalies in the efficient markets theory are insignificant, then you believe that the market prices of all securities equal their values.[48] This conclusion implies it would be futile to do security analysis and search for securities that are over- or underpriced. On the other hand, if you think the anomalies in the efficient markets theory are too important to ignore, then you will conclude that it could be profitable to do security analysis and search for securities that are under- or overpriced.

Just because you believe that a securities market is not priced efficiently in some *absolute sense* does not mean that you must also believe that it is inefficient in a more *practical sense*. For example, abundant evidence documenting the January effect may require that you acknowledge this anomaly and, in so doing, that you reject the *absolute* truth of the weakly efficient markets theory. But, as a *practical* matter, you might doubt the January effect is large enough or consistent enough to form the basis for a profitable investment strategy. A numerical example clarifies the distinction between pricing efficiency in an absolute sense and a practical sense.

EXAMPLE | ABSOLUTE EFFICIENCY VERSUS EFFICIENCY IN A PRACTICAL SENSE

An investor who wanted to benefit from anomalies in the efficient markets hypothesis could buy small stocks before the Christmas holiday and hold them past the end of January. This strategy should allow the investor to expect, but not be guaranteed, to benefit from three anomalies at once: the holiday effect, the small stock effect, and the January effect. After deducting modest transactions costs that allow for only one purchase and one sale, Table 8-8 shows how a clever investor could expect to pick up an additional 3.12% (312 basis points) of abnormal annual return from this strategy, beyond what a normal equity investment yields. While 312 BPs is a significant amount, earning an additional return of 312 BPs is not what we call "getting rich quick." Furthermore, the computations in Table 8-8 ignore (1) significant indirect costs that would be incurred in implementing exploiting this anomaly, and (2) the possibility that the January effect might not occur this year. Don't forget, stock prices decline during some Januarys.

TABLE 8-8   Estimating the Net Return Achieved by Combining Three Anomalies Simultaneously for 1 Year (or Less) in U.S. Stock Market

Ariel's adjusted before-holiday effect	0.28%
Plus: Gross returns from Banz-Reinganum size effect (See Chan, Chen, & Hsich)	+1.5%
Plus: Rozeff and Kinney's January effect (3.48% in January − 0.68% in an avg. mo. =)	+2.8%
Less: Buy-sell once per year transactions costs (See Stoll and Whaley)	−1.46%
Equals: Year's net return from a three-simultaneous-anomalies strategy	3.12%

SOURCES: See Robert A. Ariel, "High Stock Returns Before Holidays: Existence and Evidence on Possible Causes," *Journal of Finance* 45, no. 5 (December 1990): 1619, Table II. Also see K. C. Chan, N. Chen, & D. A. Hsich, "An Exploratory Investigation of the Firm Size Effect," *Journal of Financial Economics* 14, no. 3 (September 1985): 451–71. Also see Michael S. Rozeff and William R. Kinney Jr., "Capital Market Seasonality: The Case of Stock Returns," *Journal of Financial Economics* 3, no. 4 (October 1976). Also see Hans R. Stoll and Robert E. Whaley, "Transaction Cost and the Small Firm Effect," *Journal of Financial Economics* 12, no. 1 (June 1983): 57–80.

The point is that you may believe that the January effect, the holiday effect, and the small stock effect all exist in an absolute sense. But, as a practical matter, you may not be willing to stake your reputation as an investments manager on these anomalies by undertaking the strategy outlined in Table 8-8. If so, as a practical matter, you are acting as though the market is efficient.

The *values* of securities fluctuate as they react to the arrival of new information. This chapter provided evidence that the market *prices* of securities continuously pursue their fluctuating values. Figure 3-4 in Chapter 3 and Figure 8-1 illustrate such fluctuations. If the prices of all securities were perfectly efficient, the price and value of every security would vibrate randomly together in response to the arrival of news. But several well-documented anomalies force us to conclude that the markets are not perfectly (strongly) efficient. This situation forces investors to address the following question: How should I manage money in securities markets that are not absolutely efficient at every level but are, nevertheless, still highly efficient? Each person answers this question differently.

Millions of investors who think the anomalies are small manage their investments passively. At the same time, millions of other investors who think the anomalies provide profit opportunities trade actively. Investors who can see some merit in both viewpoints invest part of their portfolio passively while they manage the rest of their portfolio aggressively.

Countless "beat-the-market" ideas exist. Rather than expend the resources to research each of these ideas, economists devised guidelines to help us sort through these "get-something-for-nothing" schemes. One of the better-known guidelines is called the Free Lunch Theorem.

FREE LUNCH THEOREM   **DEFINITION**

There are no free lunches.

People sometimes react to the Free Lunch Theorem by telling how a sales person actually purchased a free lunch for them. However, after the person is reminded that (1) the time they spent listening to the sales pitch had a value of several dollars per hour, and (2) they suffered an intrusion on their privacy when the sales person made follow-up phone calls, the respondent usually concedes that they paid dearly for the free lunch. After someone grasps the Free Lunch Theorem, they are ready for the Generalized Free Lunch Theorem.

DEFINITION

GENERALIZED FREE LUNCH THEOREM

You cannot expect to get something for nothing.

A naive person might try to refute the Generalized Free Lunch Theorem by telling, for example, about how they once happened upon a $100 bill lying on the sidewalk, with no one in sight to whom it might be returned. Reasoning from such a fortuitous example, it is then suggested that occasionally it is possible to get something for nothing. Of course, good luck happens to everyone. So does bad luck. Only people who like to be duped and people who need a membership in Gamblers Anonymous bank on "the luck of the draw."

Economics suggests that decision makers should consider prices. Market prices reflect the knowledge of all market participants. You must either know more or be able to interpret information better than other market participants to be able to earn pure economic profits from trading.

QUESTIONS

Q8-1 (Efficient markets) Consider the following statement made by the famous economist, John Maynard Keynes in 1936.[49] Do you think the view that Keynes espoused has any validity today? Explain.

. . . most of these persons are, in fact, largely concerned, not with making superior long-range forecasts of the probable yield of an investment over its whole life, but with forecasting changes in the conventional basis of valuation a short time ahead of the general public. They are concerned, not with what an investment is really worth to a man who buys it "for keeps," but with what the market will value it at, under the influence of mass psychology, three months or a year hence. . . . For it is not sensible to pay 25 for an investment of which you believe the prospective yield to justify a value of 30, if you also believe that the market will value it at 20 three months hence.

Thus the professional investor is forced to concern himself with the anticipation of impending changes, in the news or in the atmosphere, of the kind by which experience shows that the mass psychology of the market is most influenced.

Q8-2 (Technical analysis) Hermann Rorschach claims to have become an expert technical analyst. Mr. Rorschach asserts that he has been able to make a long series of profitable investments by using patterns that repeat themselves in graphs of stock prices. Evaluate his claims in light of the efficient markets research.

Q8-3 (Market anomalies) Wiley Fohx just came into possession of an after-tax inheritance of $200,000 and is eager to invest it. For 2 years he has been collecting articles from newspapers and popular magazines that describe the January effect, the day-of-the-week effect, the time-of-the-day effect, and the within-the-month effects. Mr. Fohx hopes to be able to earn his living by actively trading $200,000 worth of common stocks at the advantageous times suggested by the articles he has saved that describe return regularities. What advice would you give Wiley?

Q8-4 (Characteristic line) Why should anyone be interested in the unexplained residual terms, denoted $e_{i,t}$, in the simple linear regression model of Eqn. 7-7 for the one-period rates of return from the ith security for time periods $t = 1$, $2, . . . T$?

Q8-5 (Strong-form efficient markets) Executives and other insiders have access to valuable inside information that should enable them to buy stock in the corporation that employs them when its market price is depressed and sell it when the price is elevated and thus make substantial profits. Is this statement true, false, or uncertain? Explain.

Q8-6 (Stock splits) Jake Luna read today in the *Wall Street Journal* that IBM had announced a 2-for-1 stock split and has decided that now would be a good time to buy the stock. How would you respond to Jake's claim?

Q8-7 (Active versus passive management) If you were given the investment management responsibility for a portfolio of common stocks that had a $100 million market value, would you establish a passive or an active investment management system? What are the arguments in favor of each approach? *Hint:* Review pages 52–55 of Chapter 3.

Q8-8 (EMH tests) Many empirical tests of the efficient markets theory use the characteristic line, the capital asset pricing model (CAPM), or some other explicit model from financial theory. Do you see any methodological contradiction in using such theoretical asset pricing models to test the efficient markets theory? Explain. *Hint:* You may want to read more about CAPM in Chapter 15.

Q8-9 (Efficient markets) What implications does the efficient markets theory and the empirical evidence that supports it have for each of the following phenomena? (a) The S&P500 dropped more than 20% in less than a month during the October 1987 international stock market crash. (b) Scientific empirical studies of mutual funds' performance that are reviewed in Chapter 16 show that many mutual funds do not earn risk-adjusted rates of return that are as good as could be obtained by picking stocks with a dart.

Q8-10 (Abnormal returns) A certain mutual fund has been advertising that it was able to earn a 30% return this year while the S&P500 earned only 14%. Does this claim dispute the evidence of efficient markets? Explain.

PROBLEMS

P8-1 (Stock dividends) The Jaring Corporation declared a 200% stock dividend between the second and third quarter. (a) How many shares of stock could be purchased for $150 in each quarter? (b) Calculate the stockholders' one-period rates of return for the second and third quarters from the data below:

Quarters of the Year, Q	$Q = 1$	$Q = 2$	$Q = 3$	$Q = 4$
Beginning market price per share	$150	$150	$50	$50
Cash dividend per share	$ 7.50	$ 7.50	$ 2.50	$ 2.50
Earnings per share	$ 15	$ 15	$ 5	$ 5
Number of shares for $150 of investment	??	??	??	??
One-period rate of return	??	??	??	??

P8-2 (Continuous compounding) If the price of a stock rises from $50 to $55 per share during a month in which no cash dividends are paid, what is the stock's (a) simple non-compounded rate of price change during the month? (b) continuously compounded rate of price change during the month? (c) Why do the two rates of price change differ?

P8-3 (Stock splits) The formula for IBM's characteristic line is $r_{i,t} = +1.04 + 1.021r_{M,t} + e_{i,t}$. (a) Use this characteristic line, the S&P500 returns below, and the IBM returns to calculate IBM's four quarterly predicted returns and the residual returns for 1979.

Year and Quarter	IBM's Quarterly Rate of Return, %	S&P500 Quarterly Rate of Return, %	IBM's Predicted Rate of Return, %	Unexplained Rate of Return Residual, %
1979-1	6.660	7.075		
1979-2	−5.883	2.559	?	?
A 4-for-1 stock split on June 11, 1979				
1979-3	−6.494	7.490	?	?
1979-4	−3.712	−0.110	?	?

(b) Based on your calculations, did IBM's 4-for-1 stock split tend to raise the price of IBM stock?

P8-4 (Filter rule) (a) Assume a stock is currently selling for $42. Using a 5% filter, at what price would you decide to buy and hold the stock? (b) Now assume the stock price peaks at $60 and begins to fall. At what price would you liquidate the long position and sell the stock short if you were using a 5% filter?

P8-5 (Dividends versus capital gains) Assume you own 500 shares of a stock that pays a quarterly dividend of $1.00 a share. (a) If your marginal tax rate is 28%, what will you net after taxes on the dividend income? (b) Assume, instead, that the stock pays no dividends but experienced a $1.00 a share price increase, and that capital gains are taxed at 20%. Calculate your net after-tax gain on the price increase.

P8-6 (Filter rule) John Damien has observed that the price of Sun Microsystems (SUNW) has fallen to $73 a share and is starting to rise again. He has decided to use a 1% filter to time his purchase and subsequent sale of 100 shares of Sun. (a) At what price will John try to purchase the stock, applying the filter rule? (b) Assume that SUNW peaks at $98½ a month after John makes his purchase and begins to fall again. At what price will John try to sell his shares, applying the filter rule? (c) What difficulty, if any, do you think John might have in effecting this strategy?

P8-7 (Runs) The following daily stock price data is available for the Hiprotech Corporation for the month of June 20XX (20 trading days).

Day	Price	Day	Price	Day	Price	Day	Price
1	$86	6	83\frac{1}{2}$	11	$92	16	$105
2	83\frac{1}{16}$	7	$82	12	93\frac{9}{16}$	17	103\frac{3}{4}$
3	$78	8	81\frac{1}{4}$	13	$97	18	$103
4	81\frac{1}{4}$	9	$85	14	98\frac{11}{16}$	19	$110
5	82\frac{3}{4}$	10	87\frac{1}{2}$	15	100\frac{1}{16}$	20	111\frac{1}{2}$

How many runs are observed in the stock prices?

P8-8 (Growth-value anomaly) Consider the following information on two stocks:

	Market Price	Dividend	EPS	EPS Growth— past 5 years
Stock A	$12	$0.50	$2.20	5%
Stock B	$30	$0.25	$1.25	10%

(a) In which of the two stocks would a growth manager prefer to invest? Which would a value manager choose? Why? (b) According to empirical research, which style manager is likely to earn the higher risk-adjusted return?

P8-9 (Growth-value investing) Consider the following information on three stocks:

	Price Per Share	Shares Outstanding	Book Value
Peach Corporation	$30	10 million	$ 75,000,000
Pear Corporation	$25	12 million	$ 50,000,000
Plum Corporation	$18	18 million	$300,000,000

Of the three, which one would be classified as a value stock? Why?

P8-10 (Stock splits) Consider the following information on a stock, both before and after the firm executed a 2-for-1 stock split:

	Before split			After split
	Market Value	Dividends	Shares Outstanding	Dividends
Stock A	$1.40 billion	$10.5 million	20 million	$10.5 million

Calculate the rate of return earned by an investor who purchased 1,000 shares of the stock one year ago at a price of $60 if he sold the stock (a) at the market price of the stock right before the split, and (b) at the market price of the stock right after the split.

CFA EXAM QUESTIONS

The following questions are taken from the 1998 CFA Sample Exam (Level 1):

1. A company announces an unexpectedly large cash dividend to its shareholders. In an efficient market *without* information leakage, the *most likely* expectation is:
   A. an abnormal price change at the announcement.
   B. an abnormal price decrease after the announcement.
   C. an abnormal price increase before the announcement.
   D. an abnormal price change before or after the announcement.

2. The semistrong form of the efficient market hypothesis asserts that stock prices:
   A. may be predictable.
   B. fully reflect all public information.
   C. fully reflect all historical security market information.
   D. fully reflect all relevant information from public and private sources.

The following question is taken from the 1994 CFA Exam (Level III): (Note: the original question has five parts, but only the following three are relevant to this chapter.)

3. Mrs. Goode is very interested in learning about the background for investment decision-making, and has done extensive reading in textbooks as well as the popular investment-oriented press. However, she is confused about a number of terms and concepts, particularly as to how they interrelate. You have been asked to help her make sense out of some of these terms and concepts.
   A. Mrs. Goode has read that there are two traditional approaches to equity valuation: technical and fundamental. Describe *each* of these approaches and discuss the key premise underlying *each* approach.
   B. Mrs. Goode favors the fundamental approach to valuation but has read that the efficient market hypothesis (EMH) presents a challenge to that approach. Briefly describe the *three* forms of the EMH. Identify which of the three forms most directly challenges fundamental analysis and explain your choice.
   C. Recent empirical research has suggested that holding portfolios of stocks classified as "value" (low price/book ratio) as opposed to "growth" (high price/book ratio) in both United States and international markets has resulted in enhanced risk-adjusted returns. Critique the EMH in light of these findings.

The following question is adapted from the 1996 CFA Exam (Level III).

4. Susan Fairfax asks for information concerning the benefits of active portfolio management. She is particularly interested in the question of whether or not active managers can be expected to consistently exploit inefficiencies in the capital markets to produce above-average returns without assuming higher risk.

The semistrong form of the efficient market hypothesis (EMH) asserts that all publicly available information is rapidly and correctly reflected in securities prices. This implies that investors cannot expect to derive above-average profits from purchases made after information has become public because security prices already reflect the information's full effects.

A. Identify and explain *two* examples of empirical evidence that tend to *support* the EMH implication

stated above. Identify and explain *two* examples of empirical evidence that tend to *refute* the EMH implication stated above.

B. Discuss *two* reasons why an investor might choose an active manager even if the markets were, in fact, *semistrong form efficient.*

FURTHER REFERENCES

Fama, Eugene F. "Efficient Capital Markets: A Review of Theory and Empirical Work," *Journal of Finance* (May 1970): 383–417.

This classic paper articulates the efficient markets theory. The paper espouses a worthwhile and insightful way to view security prices.

Fama, Eugene F. "Market Efficiency, Long-Term Returns, and Behavioral Finance," *Journal of Financial Economics* (September 1998): 283–306.

This paper reasserts the efficient markets theory by reviewing the anomalies and attributing them to chance results, overreactions, underreactions, methodological problems, and sample dependent results.

Fama, Eugene F. and Kenneth R. French, "Value Versus Growth: The International Evidence," *Journal of Finance* 53, no. 6 (December 1998): 1975–99.

F&F report that for the 1975–95 period value (high book equity value to market equity value ratio) stocks earned an average of 7.68% per year more than growth (low book value to market value ratio) stocks in 12 of 13 international markets. F&F developed a two-factor arbitrage pricing theory (APT) model with a risk factor for relative distress to explain the difference.

Jacobs, Bruce I. and Kenneth N. Levy. "Disentangling Equity Return Regularities: New Insights and Investment Opportunities," *Financial Analysts Journal* (May-June 1988): 18–43.

This paper provides an easy-to-read review of the previous research and reports some insightful findings from a multivariate statistics investigation of 25 anomalies in the efficient markets hypothesis.

Seyhun, H. Nejat. *Investment Intelligence from Insider Trading.* Cambridge, MA: The MIT Press, 1998.

Seyhun's book summarizes a comprehensive investigation of insider trading. He analyzed thousands of transactions in the United States from 21 years (1975–95) and investigated numerous aspects of insider trading.

Shiller, Robert J. "Do Stock Prices Move Too Much to Be Justified by Subsequent Changes in Dividends?" *American Economic Review* 71 (June 1981): 421–36.

This paper presents empirical evidence that stock market prices vary out of line with their estimated present values.

Shiller, Robert J. *Irrational Exuberance.* Princeton, NJ: Princeton University Press, 2000.

A scholarly review of theory and evidence about the behavior of stock market prices that, if you omit the lengthy footnotes, is a pleasant read.

ENDNOTES

1. This taxonomy of information sets follows Harry V. Roberts, "Statistical Versus Clinical Prediction of the Stock Market," unpublished manuscript. Center for Research in Security Prices, University of Chicago, May 1967. Also see Harry V. Roberts, "Stock Market Patterns and Financial Analysis: Methodological Suggestions," *Journal of Finance* 14, no. 1 (March 1959): 1–10.

2. See Fischer Black, "Toward a Fully Automated Stock Exchange," *Financial Analysts Journal* (July-August, 1971): 29–44.

3. See E. F. Fama and M. E. Blume, "Filter Rules and Stock Market Trading," *Journal of Business,* January 1966 Supplement, 226–41. For more refined results, see Richard J. Sweeney, "Some New Filter Rule Tests: Methods and Results," *Journal of Financial and Quantitative Analysis* vol. 23, no. 3, 285–300. Sweeney was able to modify the x percent filter rule to earn modest net profits from some stocks.

4. See Eugene F. Fama, "The Behavior of Stock Market Prices," *Journal of Business* 38, no. 1 (January 1965): 34–105. Also see Sidney Alexander, "Price Movements in Speculative Markets: Trends or Random Walks," *Industrial Management Review* (May 1961): 7–26. Also see M. G. Kendall, "The Analysis of Economic Time Series, Part I," *Journal of the Royal Statistical Society* 96 (1953): 11–25. Table 11-7 in Chapter 11 of this book presents serial correlations from monthly observations of security price indexes that are not significantly different from zero (except for positive serial correlation in the inflation rates that is irrelevant here).

5. See Werner F. M. DeBondt and Richard M. Thaler, "Does the Stock Market Over-React?," *Journal of Finance* 40 (1985): 793–805. Also see Andrew W. Lo and Craig MacKinlay, "Stock Prices Do Not Follow Random Walks: Evidence from Simple Specification Tests," *Review of Financial Studies* 1 (1988): 41–66. In addition, see Jennifer Conrad and Gautman Kaul, "Long-Term Market Overreaction or Biases in Computed Returns?" *Journal of Finance* (March 1993): 39-63.

6. See Anup Agrawal and Kishore Tandon, "Anomalies or Illusions? Evidence from Stock Markets in Eighteen Countries," *Journal of International Money and Finance* 13, no.1 (February 1994): 83–106. Also see Roger Ignatius, "The Bombay Stock Exchange: Seasonalities and Investment Opportunities," *Indian Economic Review* 27, no. 2 (July-December 1992): 223–27. In addition, see Steven-E. Plaut, "Whose Sabbath Matters?, or, When Does the Weekend Effect Occur?" *Economics Letters* 38, no. 3 (March 1992): 341–44. Furthermore, see Frank de-Jong, Angelien Kemna, and Teun Kloek, "A Contribution to Event Study Methodology with an Application to the Dutch Stock Market," *Journal of Banking and Finance* 16, no. 1 (February 1992): 11–36. Also see Jeffrey Jaffe and Randolph Westerfield, "Patterns in Japanese Common Stock Returns: Day of the Week and Turn of the Year Effects," *Journal of Financial and Quantitative Analysis* 20, no. 2 (June 1985): 261–72.

7. See Robert A. Ariel, "High Stock Returns Before Holidays: Existence and Evidence on Possible Causes," *Journal of Finance* 45, no. 5 (December 1990): 1611–62.

8. Also see Robert A. Ariel, "A Monthly Effect in Stock Returns," *Journal of Financial Economics* 18, no.1 (March 1987): 161–74. Ariel reports that the mean return for stocks is positive only for days immediately before and during the first half of calendar months, and indistinguishable from zero for days during the last half of the month. This "monthly effect" is independent of other known calendar anomalies.

9. See Abraham Abraham and David L. Ikenberry, "The Individual Investor and the Weekend Effect," *Journal of Financial and Quantitative Analysis* 29, no. 2 (June 1994): 263.

10. See Michael S. Rozeff and William R. Kinney Jr., "Capital Market Seasonality: The Case of Stock Returns," *Journal of Financial Economics* 3, no. 4 (October 1976): 379–402.

11. See Ben Branch, "A Tax Loss Trading Rule," *Journal of Business* 50, no. 2 (April 1977): 198–207.

12. See Owain ap Gwilym, Mike Buckle, Andrew Clare, and Stephen Thomas, "The Transaction-by-Transaction Adjustment of Interest Rate and Equity Index Futures Markets to Macroeconomic Announcements," *Journal of Derivatives* 6, no. 2 (winter 1998): 7–17. The GBCT study appears to be the first study to include the prices of every transaction. Studies of United States data utilize only those transactions associated with price changes. This latter set of data contains spurious negative correlation because the price changes bounce between bid and ask prices. For an ingenious method of dealing with this problem, and to see results that are similar to the GBCT findings, see L. H. Ederington and J. H. Lee, "How Markets Process Information: News Releases and Volatility," *Journal of Finance* 48 (1993): 1161–91. Also see L. H. Ederington and J. H. Lee, "The Short-Run Dynamics of the Price Adjustment to New Information," *Journal of Financial and Quantitative Analysis* 30 (1995): 117–34. Ederington and Lee report price adjustment times for interest rate and foreign exchange futures of 40 to 50 seconds, opportunities for profitable trading that last less than 60 seconds, and price volatility remaining elevated for 40 to 60 minutes after announcements in the United States.

13. See J. Patell and M. Wolfson, "The Intraday Speed of Adjustment of Stock Prices to Earnings and Dividend Announcements," *Journal of Financial Economics* 13 (1984): 223–52. Also see C. S. Woodruff and A. J. Senchak Jr., "Intraday Price-Volume Adjustments of NYSE Stocks to Unexpected Earnings," *Journal of Finance* 43 (1988): 467–91.

14. See Eugene Fama, Lawrence Fisher, Michael Jensen, and Richard Roll (FFJR), "The Adjustment of Stock Prices to New Information," *International Economic Review* 20, no. 2 (February 1969): 1–21. The FFJR study was replicated with allowance for shifting beta coefficients and similar results: see Sasson Bar-Yosef and Lawrence D. Brown, "A Re-examination of Stock Splits Using Moving Betas," *Journal of Finance* 32, no. 4 (September 1977): 1069–80. For evidence that changes in the unit of account increase the volatility of a

stock's price, see James A. Ohlson and Stephen H. Pennman, "Volatility Increases Subsequent to Stock Splits: an Empirical Aberration," *Journal of Financial Economics* 14, no. 2 (June 1985): 251-66. James Wiggins demonstrates that the shift in risk statistics following ex-dates decays as the differencing interval used to compute the returns is lengthened. He suggests that there is no statistically significant difference between pre- and postsplit betas. See James B. Wiggins, "Beta Changes Around Stock Splits Revisited," *Journal of Financial and Quantitative Analysis* 27, no. 4 (December 1992): 631-40.

[15] For empirical evidence supporting the signaling hypothesis see Maureen McNichols and Ajay Dravid, "Stock Dividends, Stock Splits, and Signaling," *Journal of Finance* 45, no. 3 (July 1990): 857-79. Also, see Josef Lakonishok and Baruch Lev, "Stock Splits and Stock Dividends: Why, Who, and When," *Journal of Finance* 42, no. 4 (September 1987): 913-32. Also see Michael J. Brennan and Thomas E. Copeland, "Stock Splits, Stock Prices, and Transaction Costs," *Journal of Financial Economics* 22, no. 1 (October 1988): 83-101.

[16] Empirical evidence supporting the liquidity hypothesis has been provided by Chris Muscarella and Michael R. Vetsuypens, "Stock Splits: Signaling or Liquidity? The Case of ADR 'Solo-Splits,'" *Journal of Financial Economics* 42, no. 1 (September 1996): 3-26. The study by Josef Lakonishok and Baruch Lev that is cited in the preceding footnote also provides some evidence supporting the liquidity hypothesis. In contrast, evidence that the percentage of shares owned by individual investors decreases after a stock split has been provided by Gary E. Powell and Kent H. Baker, "The Effects of Stock Splits on the Ownership Mix of a Firm," *Review of Financial Economics* 3, no. 1 (fall 1993): 70-88. Also, Conroy, Harris, and Benet provide evidence that stock splits reduce liquidity. See Robert M. Conroy, Robert S. Harris, and Bruce A. Benet, "The Effects of Stock Splits on Bid-Asked Spreads," *Journal of Finance* 45, no. 4 (September 1990): 1285-95.

[17] For more information about the survey results, see Kent H. Baker and Gary E. Powell, "Further Evidence on Managerial Motives for Stock Splits," *Quarterly Journal of Business and Economics* 32, no. 3 (summer 1993): 20-31.

[18] See John Y. Campbell, Andrew W. Lo, and A. Craig MacKinlay, *The Econometrics of Financial Markets*, (Princeton, NJ: Princeton University Press, 1997), p. 150. Chapter 4 is entitled "Event Study Analysis." For a criticism of the FFJR statistics, see Jennifer Conrad and Gautman Kaul, "Long-Term Market Overreaction or Biases in Computed Returns?" *Journal of Finance* (March 1993): 39-63.

[19] See Jennifer Koski, "A Microstructure Analysis of Ex-Dividend Stock Price Behavior Before and After the 1984 and 1986 Tax Reform Acts," *Journal of Business* 69, no. 3 (July 1996): 313-38.

[20] See David L. Ikenberry, Graeme Rankine, and Earl K. Stice, "What Do Stock Splits Really Signal?" *Journal of Financial and Quantitative Analysis* 31, no. 3 (September 1996): 357-78.

[21] See W. H. Hausman, R. R. West, and J. A. Largay, "Stock Splits, Price Changes, and Trading Profits: A Synthesis," *Journal of Business* (January 1971): 69-77.

[22] See Rolf W. Banz, "The Relationship Between Return and Market Value of Common Stocks," *Journal of Financial Economics* 9, no. 1 (March 1981): 3-18. Also see Marc R. Reinganum, "Misspecification of Capital Asset Pricing: Empirical Anomalies Based on Earnings Yield and Market Values," *Journal of Financial Economics* 9, no. 1 (March 1981): 19-46. In addition, see *Stocks, Bonds, Bills, and Inflation 1999 Yearbook* (Chicago: Ibbotson Associates). Chapter 7 is devoted to size issues.

[23] See Richard Roll, "A Possible Explanation of the Small Firm Effect," *Journal of Finance* 36, no. 4 (September 1981): 879-88.

[24] See Elroy Dimson, "Risk Measurement When Shares Are Subject to Infrequent Trading," *Journal of Financial Economics* 7, no. 2 (June 1979): 197-226.

[25] See Marc R. Reinganum, "A Direct Test of Roll's Conjecture on the Firm Size Effect," *Journal of Finance* 37, no. 1 (March 1982): 27-35. In addition, see this chapter's earlier discussion of the January effect.

[26] See Jonathan B. Berk, "Does Size Really Matter?," *Financial Analysts Journal* (September-October 1997): 12-18. Instead of using market capitalization, Berk uses sales and book value data to measure size. Using these measures, Berk concludes that size does not matter.

[27] See Donald B. Keim, "Size-Related Anomalies and Stock Return Seasonality: Further Empirical Evidence," *Journal of Financial Economics* 12, no. 1 (June 1983): 13-32.

[28] See Mustafa N. Gultekin and N. Bulent Gultekin, "Stock Market Seasonality: International Evidence," *Journal of Financial Economics* 12, no. 4 (December 1983): 475. For data about the size effect internationally, see Rex A. Sinquefield, "Where Are the Gains from International Diversification?" *Financial Analysts Journal* (January-February 1996): 8-14.

[29] *Mutual Fund Fact Book,* 1996 Edition (Washington, DC: The Investment Company Institute), 39.

[30] See L. Chan, Y. Hamao, and Josef Lakonishok, "Fundamentals and Stock Returns in Japan," *Journal of Finance* 46 (1991): 1739-64. Also see Eugene Fama and Kenneth French, "The Cross-Section of Expected Stock Returns," *Journal of Finance* 46 (June 1992): 427-66. Also see Josef Lakonishok, Andrei Shleifer, and Robert Vishny, "Contrarian Investment, Extrapolation, and Risk," *Journal of Finance* 49, no. 5 (December 1994): 1541-78.

[31] See Carlo Capaul, Ian Rowley, and William F. Sharpe, "International Value and Growth Stock Returns," *Financial Analysts Journal* (January-February 1993): 27-36. Also see Rex A. Sinquefield, "Where Are the Gains from International Diversification?" *Financial Analysts Journal* (January-February 1996): 8-14.

[32] See Eugene Fama and Kenneth French, "The Cross-Section of Expected Stock Returns," *Journal of Finance* 46 (June 1992): 427-66.

[33] See Josef Lakonishok, Andrei Schleifer, and Robert W. Vishny, "Contrarian Investment, Extrapolation, and Risk," *Journal of Finance* 49, no. 5 (December 1994): 1541-78.

[34] See Tim Loughran, "Book-To-Market Across Firm Size, Exchange, and Seasonality: Is There an Effect?" *Journal of Financial and Quantitative Analysis* 32, no. 3 (September 1997): 249-68.

[35] See Tim Loughran, "Book-To-Market Across Firm Size, Exchange, and Seasonality: Is There an Effect?," *Journal of Financial and Quantitative Analysis* 32, no. 3 (September 1997): 266-67.

[36] Those who defend value stocks attribute the 1995-2000 results to soaring computer technology stock prices that inflated the SP/BARRA Growth Index during that period. The value stock supporters point out that the March-April 2000 crash in technology stock prices erased the 1995-2000 superior performance of the SP/BARRA Growth Index.

[37] See Carlo Capaul, Ian Rowley, and William F. Sharpe, "International Value and Growth Stock Returns," *Financial Analysts Journal* (January-February 1993): 27-36. For a similar study that provides supporting evidence, see Rex A. Sinquefield, "Where Are the Gains from International Diversification?" *Financial Analysts Journal* (January-February 1996): 8-14.

[38] See Carlo Capaul, Ian Rowley, and William F. Sharpe, "International Value and Growth Stock Returns," *Financial Analysts Journal* (January-February 1993): 27-36, Table VII. CRS computed Sharpe's reward-to-variability ratio for the 18 portfolios. Sharpe's reward-to-variability ratio is explored in Chapter 16.

[39] To learn about the performance of bond mutual funds, see Christopher Blake, Edwin J. Elton, and Martin J. Gruber, "The Performance of Bond Mutual Funds," *Journal of Business* 66, no. 3 (July 1993): 370-403. Also see Edwin J. Elton, Martin J. Gruber, and Christopher Blake, "Fundamental Economic Variables, Expected Returns, and Bond Fund Performance," *Journal of Finance* 50, no. 4 (September 1995): 1229-1956. For information about the performance of common stock mutual funds, see Mark M. Carhart, "On Persistence in Mutual Fund Performance," *Journal of Finance* 52, no. 1 (March 1997): 57-82. In addition, see William N. Goetzmann and Roger G. Ibbotson, "Do Winners Repeat?" *Journal of Portfolio Management* 20, no. 10 (winter 1994): 9-18. Also see Edwin J. Elton, Martin J. Gruber, Sanjiv Das, and Matthew Hlavka, "Efficiency with Costly Information: A Reinterpretation of Evidence from Managed Portfolios," *Review of Financial Studies* 6, no. 1 (1993): 1-22. Also see Burton G. Malkiel, "Returns from Investing in Equity Mutual Funds, 1971-1991," *Journal of Finance* 50, no. 2: 549-70.

[40] See Burton G. Malkiel, "Returns from Investing in Equity Mutual Funds, 1971-1991," *Journal of Finance* 50, no. 2: 570-71.

[41] Insider trading has been defined by both case law and legislated law. To learn about the case law, see the Merrill Lynch, Pierce, Fenner and Smith case involving the underwriting Douglas Aircraft debentures in 1968. For details see the *Wall Street Journal*, 16 August, 1968, 1, and 1 July, 1970, 12. Also, see *Chiarella* v. *United States*, 445 U.S. 222.245 (1980). Also see *Dirks* v. *Securities and Exchange Commission*, 463 U.S. 646.662 (1983). See also *United States* v. *R. Foster Winans, K.P. Felis, and D.J. Carpenter*, 84 Cr. 605 (CES) (S.D.N.Y. 1984). For more discussion of insider trading, see Gary L. Tidwell, "Here's a Tip—Know the Rules of Insider Trading," *Sloan Management Review* (summer 1987): 93-97.

[42] See Jeffrey F. Jaffe, "Special Information and Insider Trading," *Journal of Business* (July 1974): 410-28. Another study of the profitability of insider trading is James H. Lorie and Victor Niederhoffer, "Predictive and Statistical Properties of Insider Trading," *Journal of Law and Economics* (April 1968): 35-51.

[43] For evidence that there is significant information content in stock trading by insiders for outsiders who want to speculate on corporate bond prices, see Sudip Datta, Datta Iskandar, and E. Mai, "Does Insider Trading Have Information Content for the Bond Market?" *Journal of Banking and Finance* 20, no. 3 (April 1996): 555-75. For information about insider trading that is associated with tender offers and other offers to repurchase stock, see D. Scott Lee, Wayne H. Mikkelson, and Megan M. Partch, "Managers' Trading Around Stock Repurchases," *Journal of Finance* 47, no. 5 (December 1992): 1947-61.

[44] See H. Nejat Seyhun, "Insiders' Profits, Costs of Trading, and Market Efficiency," *Journal of Financial Economics* 16, no. 1 (June 1986): 189-212. More recently, see H. Nejat Seyhun, *Investment Intelligence from Insider Trading* (Cambridge, MA: The MIT Press, 1998). Seyhun's book analyzed thousands of transactions in the United States from 21 years (1975-95) and investigated numerous aspects of insider trading. Other researchers who have suggested that outsiders cannot earn anomalous profits after transactions costs are Michael S. Rozeff and Mir A. Zaman, "Market Efficiency and Insider Trading: New Evidence," *Journal of Business* 61, no. 1 (January 1988): 25-44. Seyhun and Rozeff and Zaman realistically deduct larger transactions costs than Jaffe.

[45] See Lisa K. Meulbroek, "An Empirical Analysis of Illegal Insider Trading," *Journal of Finance* 47, no. 5 (December 1992): 1661-99.

[46] Cogent arguments have been made in support of insider trading as a way to increase market efficiency. See Harold Demsetz, "Corporate Control, Insider Trading and Rates of Return," *American Economic Review* 76, no.2 (May 1986): 313-16. Also see Joseph E. Finnerty, "Insiders and Market Efficiency," *Journal of Finance* 31 (September 1976): 1141-48. See George Benston, "Required Disclosure and the Stock Market: An Evaluation of the Securities Exchange Act of 1934," *American Economic Review* (March 1973): 132-55. Try to read Nobel laureate George J. Stigler, "Public Regulation of the Securities Markets," *Journal of Business* 37, no. 2 (April 1964): 117-42. See Harold Demsetz and Kenneth Lehn, "The Structure of Corporate Ownership: Causes and Consequences," *Journal of Political Economy* 93 (December 1985): 1155-77. In addition, see Hayne E. Leland, "Insider Trading: Should It Be Prohibited?" *Journal of Political Economy* 100, no. 4 (August 1992): 859-87. Also see Naveen Khanna, Steve L. Slezak, and Michael Bradley, "Insider Trading, Outside Search, and Resource Allocation: Why Firms and Society May Disagree on Insider Trading Restrictions,"

Review of Financial Studies 7, no. 3 (fall 1994): 575–608. For a rigorous explanation of how insider trading can be harmful to society see Norman S. Douglas, "Insider Trading: The Case Against the 'Victimless Crime' Hypothesis," *Financial Review* 23, no. 2 (May 1988): 127–42.

[47] See Lisa K. Meulbroek, "An Empirical Analysis of Illegal Insider Trading," *Journal of Finance* 47, no. 5 (December 1992): 1675–79.

[48] See Eugene F. Fama, "Market Efficiency, Long-Term Returns, and Behavioral Finance," *Journal of Financial Economics* (September 1998): 283–306. Fama discounts anomalies that he and others reported in previous research and reaffirms efficient markets theory.

[49] See John Maynard Keynes, *The General Theory of Employment, Interest and Money* (New York: Harcourt Brace Jovanovich, 1936), 154–55.

FUTURES AND OPTIONS

Forward, future, and option contracts are called **derivatives** *because their prices are derived from some underlying quantity called simply* **"the underlying."** *The underlying is usually a stock price, a bond price, or a commodity price.*

A **forward contract** *is a bilateral agreement obligating the buyer to purchase the underlying commodity or security from the seller on a given future date for a specified delivery price. The seller is obligated to sell according to the terms of the contract. Forward contracts are arrangements between private parties; they are not actively traded in any market. This differentiates them from* **futures contracts,** *which are actively traded at* **futures exchanges** *until their delivery date arrives. Futures traders earn gains and losses, without ever taking delivery of the underlying goods, as they buy and/or sell futures contracts at fluctuating prices.*

An **option** *is a two-party agreement between an option writer who sells the option and the option's buyer. It gives the option buyer the right to sell or buy the underlying security or commodity at a predetermined exercise price on some designated date, if the option buyer wishes to exercise the option. A* call *is an option to buy. A* put *is an option to sell. The option writer gets paid to carry out the other side of the transaction, as promised in the option agreement. Buyers of puts and calls are not obliged to exercise their options; many options expire unexercised. Options are actively traded at options exchanges and in over-the-counter (OTC) markets. Futures contracts and options are called* **financial instruments,** *which include other marketable contracts that are like securities in some ways and different from securities in other respects. These financial instruments are sometimes called derivatives, as mentioned above, because they derive their values from an underlying quantity.*

This chapter introduces options and futures based mostly on common stocks. When the underlying assets are equities, the futures and options are called equity derivatives. *Chapters 27 and 28 will examine the prices of equity derivatives, and futures and options on other underlying quantities.*

FORWARD CONTRACTS

A forward contract, or a *forward*, is created when someone buys a commodity, security, or other asset for future delivery. The delivery price is fixed at the time of the purchase, but it does not have to be paid until the stipulated delivery date, which can be months or years after the purchase (contracting) date. When a forward contract is being created, the buyer and seller negotiate the price, the quantity, the quality of the goods, the delivery location, and the delivery date. Each forward contract is tailor-made to fit the needs and preferences of the buyer and the seller; hence, each forward contract is unique. After a forward contract is completed, no terms can be changed without the advance, written, mutual consent of the buyer and seller.

Forward contracts are formalized business deals that have been around the world for centuries. A wheat farmer planting his crop can contract to deliver 1,000 bushels to the wheat miller when the crop is harvested at a price that is set at planting time. The buyer (miller) and seller (farmer) are called the **counterparties** to the contract. Sometimes a counterparty to a forward contract defaults. If the goods are not delivered as agreed, there will most surely be a costly and troublesome lawsuit. The risk that the buyer or seller defaults is called **counterparty risk.** Forward contracts are not readily marketable, most are illiquid. Thus, if the wheat farmer wants to get paid before delivery to the wheat mill he will probably not be able to find anyone to buy his wheat forward contract from him. The value of a forward is the discounted value of the delayed payment; the delayed payment is usually assumed to equal the current price of the underlying commodity.

FUTURES CONTRACTS

The futures contract evolved from the forward contract centuries ago in Japan and Europe. The futures contract contains improvements designed to reduce its counterparty risk and increase its liquidity. Agricultural futures on corn and wheat traded at the Chicago Board of Trade in 1865. During the 1970s, financial futures on stock market indexes, bonds, foreign currencies, and other financial quantities started trading at Chicago's futures exchanges. Financial futures are now traded at major financial centers around the world.

Basic Characteristics of Futures

The Futures Contract. A futures contract, or, simply, a *futures*, is a forward contract that has been standardized to increase its marketability. Futures contracts are standardized by making every wheat contract traded on a futures exchange, for example, exactly like every other wheat contract traded on that exchange. Historically, futures were preprinted contracts with three blanks—price, quantity to be delivered, and delivery date—to be filled in and then signed by the buyer and seller. Modern futures exchanges use electronic entries stored in the memory of a computer instead of printed contracts.

Items that can be interchanged because they are identical are *fungible*. The U.S. $1 bills are all fungible. Millions of shares of Coca-Cola common stock are fungible. Futures on the same underlying good that involve the same delivery arrangements are fungible. Fungibility is one aspect in the standardization of futures that contributes to their liquidity.

Taking Delivery. A futures contract's expiration date is usually called its *delivery date*. Buying a futures contract obligates the purchaser to choose between: (1) selling the contract before it reaches its delivery date, or, (2) taking delivery of the underlying goods when the contract expires. Most futures contracts are sold (the position is closed, extinguished) before the delivery date.

Cash Settlement. Buying some futures contracts and holding them until they reach their delivery date entitles the buyer to either receive a **cash settlement** or accept delivery of the underlying asset. The financial futures contract on the Standard & Poor's 500 Index, for example, is a cash-settlement contract because any investor who buys and holds that contract until it expires will receive a cash settlement instead of a portfolio of 500 stocks. Financial futures usually provide for cash settlement; most agricultural futures provide for delivery of the underlying physical goods.

Trading Futures. A futures exchange is a market where futures are bought and sold at fluctuating prices. Active trading overcomes the liquidity problem that exists with forwards.

Members meet on the futures exchange trading floor to buy and sell futures. Buyers and sellers use **open outcry** to negotiate each transaction by shouting and using hand signs that can be observed by anyone on the trading floor.

Every time a futures contract is purchased and resold the transaction can be consummated at a different price. Fluctuating prices are one of the important differences between futures and forwards. The price in a forward contract is fixed and cannot be changed without hiring lawyers to write up a new contract with a new price that is mutually agreed upon by the seller and buyer. Rewriting a forward contract is a procedure that is slow, cumbersome, costly, and sometimes impossible to renegotiate; this is one reason why forwards are illiquid.

The Clearinghouse. A buyer and seller of a futures contract execute a transaction on the trading floor of the exchange and a **clearinghouse** settles the transaction. Futures contracts are designed to be traded without counterparties (the buyer and seller) coming in contact. Every futures exchange has a clearinghouse that inserts itself between buyer and seller. The clearinghouse is an intermediary that will pay the futures seller the contract price and simultaneously sell a different but identical futures contract to the futures buyer. The clearinghouse keeps track of the details of each side of the transaction and communicates separately with the buyer and seller. It reassigns responsibility to make delivery to the latest seller every time the contract is resold.

The last buyer of a futures contract will receive delivery when the delivery date arrives. If the last seller fails to make the promised delivery, the futures exchange's clearinghouse quickly makes delivery to the last buyer and later sues the defaulted seller to recover damages. Willingness of the clearinghouse at the futures exchange to step in and make deliveries is the reason futures buyers always receive deliveries as scheduled. A clearinghouse-guaranteed delivery process removes the counterparty risk and enhances the liquidity of futures.

Both forwards and futures are used around the world. Contract users who (1) are not worried about counterparty risk, (2) do not need a contract that is liquid, and (3) value the flexibility of tailor-making a contract to fit their needs hire attorneys to draw up a forward contract. Users who are more concerned about counterparty risk and/or want liquidity use standardized futures contracts that are traded at prices determined by open outcry at a futures exchange.

The Commodities. Futures contracts on commodities like gold, silver, soybeans, corn, and wheat have been traded for many decades. In the 1970s the exchanges started to trade futures on financial products like bonds, foreign currencies, and stock market indexes. Within 15 years the total annual dollar volume of financial futures exceeded the aggregate value of all trading in the traditional commodities. The total volume of financial futures traded at all futures exchanges around the world keeps growing: It was over $20 trillion in 1997.[1] Table 9-1 lists the most popular commodities and financial instruments and some organized exchanges where they are listed.

| TABLE 9-1 | Popular Derivatives Listed on Organized Exchanges:[a] (A) Agricultural Futures; (B) Currency Futures; (C) Futures on Metals and Energy; (D) Stock and Stock Market Index Futures; (E) Interest Rate Futures; (F) Put and Call Options |

(A)   Agricultural Futures Contracts

Underlying Commodity	Exchange	Trading Unit
Grains and Oilseeds		
Barley	WPG	20 metric tons
Canola	WPG	20 metric tons
Corn	CBT & MCE	5,000 & 1,000 bushels
Flaxseed	WPG	20 metric tons
Oats	CBT & MCE	5,000 & 1,000 bushels
Soybeans	CBT & MCE	5,000 & 1,000 bushels
Soybean meal	CBT & MCE	100 & 20 tons
Soybean oil	CBT	60,000 pounds
Wheat	CBT, KCBT, MPLS, MCE, & WPG	5,000 & 1,000 bushels and 20 metric tons
White wheat	MPLS	5,000 bushels
Livestock and Meat		
Feeder cattle	CME	50,000 pounds
Hogs	CME & MCE	40,000 & 20,000 pounds
Live cattle	CME & MCE	40,000 & 20,000 pounds
Pork bellies	CME	40,000 pounds
Food and Fiber		
Cocoa	CSCE	10 metric tons
Coffee	CSCE	37,500 pounds
Cotton	CTN	50,000 pounds
Domestic sugar	CSCE	112,000 pounds
Orange juice	CTN	15,000 pounds
Rough rice	CRCE	2,000 cwt.
World sugar	CSCE	112,000 pounds
Lumber	CME	160,000 board ft.

(B)   Futures Contracts on Foreign Currencies

Australian dollar	CME	100,000 $A
British pound	CME, MCE	62,500 £, 12,500 £
Canadian dollar	CME	100,000 C$
Euro	CME	125,000 euros
Euro-Sterling	NYBOT	100,000 euros
Euro-U.S. Dollar	NYBOT	200,000 euros
Euro-Yen	NYBOT	100,000 euros
Mexican Peso	CME	500,000 pesos
Japanese yen	CME & MCE	12,500,000 & 6,250,000 Yen
Swiss franc	CME	125,000 SF

(C)   Futures Contracts on Metals and Energy

Brent crude	IPE	1,000 ner bbls.
Copper	CMX	25,000 pounds
Diammonium phosphate	CBT	100 ton

(continued)

TABLE 9-1 *(continued)*

(C)   *Futures Contracts on Metals and Energy*   *(continued)*

Underlying Commodity	Exchange	Trading Unit
Gold—1 kilo	CBT	32.15 troy ozs.
Gold	CMX	100 troy ozs.
Gold—NY	MCE	33.2 fine troy ozs.
Heating oil—No. 2	NYMEX	42,000 gallons
Gas oil	IPE	100 metric tons
Gasoline—unleaded regular	NYMEX	42,000 gallons
Natural gas	NYMEX	10,000 MMBtu
Palladium	NYMEX	100 troy ozs.
Platinum	NYMEX & MCE	50 & 25 troy ozs.
Propane	NYMEX	42,000 gallons
Silver	CBT, MCE, & CMX	1,000 & 5,000 troy ozs.

(D)   *Stock and Stock Market Index Futures*

All Ordinary Share Price Index	STE	AS25 × Index
CAC-40 Stock Index	MATIF	FFr200 × Index
EuroTop 100 Index	CMX	$100 × Index
FT-SE 100 Index	LIFFE	25£ × Index
Individual stocks	LIFFE	Round lots of one stock
G-S Commodity Index (GSCI)	CME	$250 × Index
KR-CRB Index	NYFE	$500 × Index
Major Market Index	CBT	$500 × Index
Mini Value Line Index	KCBT	$100 × Index
NYSE Index	NYFB	$500 × Index
Nikkei 255 Index	CME	$5 × Index
Russell 2000 Index	CME	$500 × Index
S&P500 Index	CME	$250 × Index
S&P Midcap 400 Index	CME	$500 × Index
Toronto 35 Index	TFE	$500 × Index
Value Line Index	KCBT	$500 × Index

(E)   *Interest Rate (Bond Market) Futures*

Canadian bankers' acceptance	ME	1,000,000 C$
Canadian government bonds	CBT	100,000 C$
10-year Canadian government bonds	ME	100,000 C$
3-year Commonwealth T-bonds	SFE	100,000 A$
Eurodollar	CME & MCE	1,000,000 $ & 500,000 $
3-month Eurolira	LIFFE	1,000,000 Itl.
Euromark	LIFFE & CME	1,000,000 DM
Euroswiss	LIFFE	1,000,000 SF
10-year French government bonds	MATIF	500,000 FFr
German government bond	LIFFE	250,000 marks
Italian government bond	LIFFE	200,000,000 Itl.
LIBOR—1 mo.	IMM	$3,000,000
Long Gilt	LIFFE	50,000 £
Sterling	LIFFE	500,000 £
Treasury bills	CME	$1,000,000
30-day interest rate	CBT	$5,000,000

(E)   Interest Rate (Bond Market) Futures   (continued)

Underlying Commodity	Exchange	Trading Unit
10-year T-notes	MCE	$50,000
Treasury bonds	CBT & MCE	$100,000 & $50,000
Treasury notes—2 yr.	CBT	$200,000
Treasury notes—5 yr.	CBT	$100,000

(F)   Put and Call Options

Options on Individual Stocks	CBOE, PSE, AMEX, PHIX	
Stock Index Options		
CAC-40 Stock Index	MATIF	
FT-SE 100 Index	LIFFE, LTOM	
Nikkei 255	CME	
Russell 2,000 Index	CME	
S&P500 Index	CME	
S&P100	CME	
Toronto 35 Index	TFE	
Value Line Index	PHIX	
Foreign Currency Options		
British pound	PHIX, CME	
Deutschemark (Euro)	PHIX, CME	
French franc (Euro)	PHIX, CME	
Japanese yen	PHIX, CME	

[a] Legend of Exchange Symbols

Chicago Board of Trade (CBT)	London Internat. Financial Futures Exchange (LIFFE)
Chicago Board of Options Exchange (CBOE)	Marche A Terme International De France (MATIF)
Chicago Mercantile Exchange (CME)	MidAmerica Commodity Exchange (MCE)
Chicago Rice and Cotton Exchange (CRCE)	Minneapolis Grain Exchange (MPLS)
Coffee, Sugar and Cocoa Exchange (CCSE)	New York Cotton Exchange (CTN)
Commodity Exchange (CMX)	New York Futures Exchange (NYFE)
Financial Instruments Exchange (FINEX)	New York Mercantile Exchange (NYMEX)
Hong Kong Futures Exchange (HKFE)	Philadelphia Stock Exchange (PHIX)
International Monetary Market (IMM)	Singapore International Monetary Exchange (SIMEX)
International Petroleum Exchange (IPE)	Sydney Futures Exchange (SFE)
Kansas City Board of Trade (KCBT)	Tokyo Stock Exchange (TSE)
London Futures and Options Exchange (FOX)	Toronto Futures Exchange (TFE)
London Traded Options Market (LOTM)	Winnipeg Commodity Exchange (WPG)

Gains and Losses on Futures Positions and Account Administration

Futures traders may take either long or short positions. At expiration, futures buyers owning **long positions** are entitled to either take delivery of the underlying goods or, for some futures, to receive a cash settlement of equal value. Those who sold futures have a **short position** that obligates the seller to either make physical delivery or, for some futures, to make cash payments of equal value. Figure 9-1 illustrates the gains and losses from a long and a short position in futures. Note that Figure 9-1 for futures traders looks like the gain-loss graphs for the long and short positions of securities traders shown at Figure 3-2 in Chapter 3.

Table 9-2 contrasts the profitability of holding long and short futures positions in wheat futures. If the gains and losses listed in Table 9-2 were used to construct graphs, they would look like those in Figure 9-1.

FIGURE 9-1 Gain-Loss Illustrations: (A) Long Position, (B) Short Position

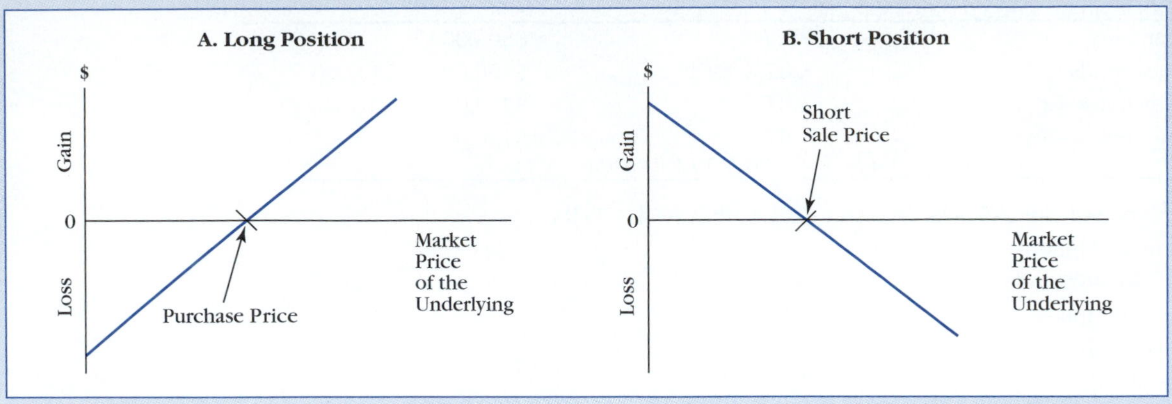

(A) The buyer of a long position obtains a dollar of gain for every dollar of price rise and a dollar of loss for every dollar of price decline. (B) A short sale, which is the inverse of a long position, gains a dollar for each dollar of price decline.

TABLE 9-2 **Profits from Different Positions in Wheat Futures with a $3 Per Bushel Delivery Price Vary with the Price of the Underlying (for a 5,000-bushel wheat contract)**

Market Price of Wheat, Per Bushel	Profit from One Long Wheat Future [Profit from 1 long position in wheat futures purchased at $3 per bushel] = [(per bushel selling price) × (5,000 bushels)] − [$15,000 fixed cost]	Profit from One Short Wheat Future [Profit from 1 short sale of wheat futures at $3 per bushel] = [Fixed revenue from $15,000 short sale] − [cost per bushel] × (5,000 bushels)]
$1 per bushel	−$10,000 = $5,000 − $15,000	+$10,000 = $15,000 − $5,000
$2 per bushel	−$5,000 = $10,000 − $15,000	+$5,000 = $15,000 − $10,000
$3 per bushel	0 = $15,000 − $15,000	0 = $15,000 − $15,000
$4 per bushel	+$5,000 = $20,000 − $15,000	−$5,000 = $15,000 − $20,000
$5 per bushel	+$10,000 = $25,000 −$15,000	−$10,000 = $15,000 − $25,000
$6 per bushel	+$15,000 = $30,000 −$15,000	−$15,000 = $15,000 − $30,000

The owner of a *long futures position* may: (1) wait till the contract expires and take delivery; (2) hold the position and see what happens to its market price; or (3) eliminate (unwind, offset, or liquidate) the long position by selling it. The owner of a *short futures position* may: (1) wait till the contract expires and make delivery; (2) hold the position and see what happens to its market price; or, (3) eliminate (unwind, offset, or liquidate) the short position by buying back the short contract or, equivalently, by purchasing a fungible contract at the futures exchange.

Margin Requirements. Before they can buy or sell futures, the clients of a brokerage firm must open an account. The equity value of a client's brokerage account is called the client's **margin.** When they give their broker an order to buy or sell, most futures traders do not pay for the full amount of their transaction. Instead, they make small down payments called the

initial margin.* Minimum initial-margin requirements are set by the brokerages and commodity exchanges; they range from 3% to 12% of the value of the transaction. Most futures traders put down some initial margin money and trade on that rather than pay for their entire transaction. If a margined futures position suffers significant losses because the price on a long position falls below its purchase price, or the price on a short position rises above the price of the short sale, the trader receives a **margin call** from the broker. The broker asks the client to pay additional margin money called the **maintenance margin** or **variation margin.** Maintenance margins are smaller than initial margins.** If the trader does not quickly give the broker enough cash to meet at least the minimum maintenance margin requirement, the brokerage house will liquidate the client's futures position rather than take a chance that the brokerage might be left holding a trading loss in the client's account.

Speculating with Futures

Speculators are aggressive traders who expose themselves to price fluctuation risk in hopes of earning trading profits.

Speculating in Wheat Futures. To begin, consider a speculative long position in wheat futures. The Chicago Board of Trade's (CBT's) wheat contract stipulates the delivery **unit** to be 5,000 bushels of No. 2 soft red winter wheat, or No. 2 hard red winter wheat, or No. 2 dark northern spring wheat, or No. 1 northern spring wheat. If delivery of acceptable wheat is not made to approved warehouses in Chicago on the stipulated delivery date, a penalty fee must be paid for an unconventional delivery. The CBT's five wheat contracts provide for the same five delivery months every year: March, May, July, September, and December. The contract's minimum price fluctuation, or **tick** size, is one-quarter of one cent ($12.50 for one unit of 5,000 bushels); the CBT deems haggling over lesser amounts not worthwhile.

PROFESSOR SKYLARK SPECULATES ON A WHEAT BLIGHT   **EXAMPLE**

Early in May of last year Professor Skylark started researching a new strain of bacteria, known to cause a blight that spread rapidly, destroying hundreds of acres of wheat in Illinois. Professor Skylark reached the conclusion that if somebody did not find a way to confine the blight before the end of May, it could wipe out a significant part of that year's U.S. wheat crop. He correctly anticipated that the blight might cause the price of wheat to skyrocket. It also occurred to Professor Skylark that there was potential for personal profit if the blight spread. After considering his responsibilities, he saw no harm in calling a commodity futures broker. Without mentioning the blight that had emerged in Illinois, Professor Skylark purchased one September wheat futures at a price of $3.50 per bushel in early May. That CBT contract cost [($3.50 per bushel) $\times$ (5,000 bushels per contract) =] $17,500. However, the professor only had to give the broker a 10% initial margin deposit of $1,750 to buy the contract. A few days after he bought the wheat contract the U.S. Department of Agriculture made an announcement that a wheat blight emerged in Illinois and, as a result, the price of

---

*   Commodity brokerages define a client's margin to be equal to the equity value in the client's account. The equity equals the sum of the following amounts: (1) cash, (2) cashlike securities (namely, U.S. Treasury bills that are left on deposit at the broker's office), and (3) the net total of the unrealized gains on open positions less the unrealized losses (that is, net "paper profits" that may be positive or negative).

** Maintenance margins are approximately 75% of initial margins at most brokerage firms, but this relationship varies from broker to broker. For more discussion of clearinghouses and margins, see John Hull, *Options, Futures and Other Derivatives*, 3d ed. (Englewood Cliffs, NJ: Prentice-Hall, 1997), 20–24.

wheat rose rapidly. Two weeks later the September wheat futures reached $4.00 per bushel and Skylark sold his long futures position for a nice gain:

Professor's selling price in late May:	$4.00 per bushel
Professor's purchase price in early May:	$3.50 per bushel
Professor's gain over 2 weeks:	$0.50 per bushel

Since one CBT wheat contract equals 5,000 bushels, Professor Skylark made [($0.50 gain per bushel) $\times$ (5,000 bushels) =] $2,500 gross profit in 2 weeks. Before commissions and taxes, the professor's investment was worth [($2,500 gain)/($1,750 margin) = 1.43 =] 143% of his initial margin of $1,750.*

Professor Skylark's long position in wheat futures turned out to be very profitable. If the professor's forecast had been wrong and the price of wheat had dropped to $3.00 per bushel, his speculative long position would have lost $0.50 per bushel:

Professor's selling price in late May:	$3.00 per bushel
Professor's purchase price in early May:	$3.50 per bushel
Professor's loss over 2 weeks:	$-$0.50 per bushel

Professor Skylark's 2-week price loss would be [($0.50 per bushel loss) $\times$ (5,000 bushels) =] $2,500. The professor's holding period return would be [($-$2,500 loss)/($1,750 margin) = -1.43 =} -143% of his initial margin of $1,750.

Leverage.   Futures traders can obtain financial leverage by trading on margin. The low initial-margin requirements on futures allow traders to control an underlying quantity worth thousands of dollars by making a small initial margin investment of cash (equity). This leverage magnifies futures traders' profits and losses.

Forward contracts provide no leverage, because the buyers must pay cash on delivery (COD). Table 9-3 contrasts the differences between forwards and futures.

Speculating with S&P500 Index Futures.   The Standard & Poor's 500 Composite Stocks Index (S&P500 index) is called the large stock index in Figure 2-1 and Table 2-1 of Chapter 2. Construction of this index is discussed in Section 10-1 of Chapter 10. In 1982 the Chicago Mercantile Exchange (CME, or "the Merc") started trading a futures contract on the S&P500 index. The S&P500 index futures contract enjoys a huge daily trading volume; it is one of the most successful futures contracts in the world.[2]

The underlying quantity on which the market price of the S&P500 index futures contract is based is the market value of the S&P500 index. The Chicago Merc's futures contract defines its futures price to equal $250 multiplied times the fluctuating S&P500 index's value.

Value of S&P500 index futures contract = (Market value of S&P500 index)($250)   (9-1)

For example, if the S&P500 index had a value of 651, the S&P500 index future would be worth [($250)(651)=] $162,750 per contract until the index changed to some other value. S&P500 index futures owners are not entitled to any cash dividends.

The S&P500 futures contract is a cash settlement contract. The amount of cash received is based on the difference between the most recent market value of the index future, Eqn. 9-1, and the contract's purchase price. Since the futures trades involve no movements of

---

*   Since there are 26 2-week periods in a year, Skylark's 143% gain in 2 weeks is equivalent to an annualized rate of return of $(1+1.43)^{26 \text{ periods}} = 10.611 = 1,061.1\%$ annual rate of gain.

TABLE 9-3   Contrasting Futures and Forward Contracts[a]

	Forwards	Futures
Characteristics		
Regulation by	Contract law	Government agency, e.g., CFTC
Market place	Phones	Organized exchange
Price determination	Fixed price	Fluctuates in continuous public auction
Contract specifications	Tailored	Standardized, fungible
Financial leverage	None, cash on delivery	Provided through margins
Commodities covered	Any commodity	Only listed commodities
Counterparty risk		
Daily settlement	No	Required
Clearinghouse	No	Eliminates default risk
Price fluctuations	Unlimited	Within daily limits
Liquidity		
Delivery date	Tailored	Standardized
Size of contract	Tailored	Standardized
Market accessibility	Only large clients	Available to public
Clearinghouse guarantee	No	Yes, creates liquidity
Transactions costs	Substantial	Tiny
Prices		
Current price	Only estimates	Trading prices posted continuously
Cost of carry: FP=SP+cc	No	Yes
Spot-forward convergence	No	Yes

[a]The pricing characteristics of forwards and futures are discussed more fully in Chapter 27.

physical goods, no cumbersome title transfers, and only a modest initial margin, they are often used for quick speculations on the direction of the U.S. stock market.

Assume a minimum initial-margin payment of 3% of the future's market value must be made to get a broker to execute a trade. If the S&P500 index was 651, the minimum margin payment that a S&P500 index futures buyer would need to give the broker would be [($250)(651)(3%) =] $4,882.50 per contract. If an investor purchased a long position of ten contracts, the minimum margin payment would be [(10 contracts)($4,882.50 per contract) =] $48,825. Such a trade would be highly leveraged, controlling a position having a market value of [($250)(651)(10 contracts) =] $1,627,500 with an initial margin payment of only $48,825. On the downside, using margin magnifies the risk of loss if the market moves adversely. For example, if the S&P500 index value dropped from 651 to 645, the market value of one contract would fall from [($250)(651) =] $162,750 to [($250)(645) =] $161,250. This $1,500 loss could happen in minutes in a rapidly moving market.

LUNCH WITH BRENDA

EXAMPLE

One day in July Brenda felt bullish about the stock market. Before lunch she called her broker and gave him a market order to buy a long position of one September futures contract on the S&P500 index. The S&P500 index was trading at 651 when Brenda purchased her long position worth [($250)(651) =] $162,750. Brenda promised to pay a 3% initial margin requirement of

[($250)(651)(3%) =] $4,882.50 and her broker executed her order. After lunch Brenda phoned her broker and was pleased to learn that the S&P500 index had risen to 653 while she was dining. She gave the broker a market order to sell while the index was still at 653. She got [($250)(653) =] $163,250 for her contract, and her commission costs were $100. Brenda bet on the market and made [($163,250−$162,750)−$100 =) $400 during lunch. The rate of return from a net gain of $400 on an investment of $4,882.50 per contract is 8.19% over a holding period of 2 hours.

$$r = \frac{(\$163{,}250 \ - \ \$162{,}750) + \text{Cash flow} - \left(\begin{array}{c}\text{Transactions} \\ \text{cost}\end{array}\right)}{\text{Purchase price}} \tag{9-2}$$

$$= \frac{\$500 + \text{Zero} - \$100}{\$4{,}882.50} = .0819 = 8.19\%$$

Caveat: Futures speculating is not a game for the weak-hearted. Brenda could have been bankrupted if the market moved quickly in the wrong direction while she was having lunch. On October 19, 1987 the S&P500 index dropped 24%, for example. People who had margined long positions in the S&P500 index contract that day were thrown for huge losses.

Short Sale: If Brenda had bearishly sold the S&P500 contract short at 651 and, after lunch, covered her short position at 653, she would have lost money. She would have had to pay [($250)(653)=] $163,250 to buy back a contract like the one she sold short, suffering a [($162,750 − $163,250) = $500 position loss) + ($100 commissions) =] $600 total loss.

Hedging with Futures

Futures are primarily used for speculating and hedging. Speculators like Professor Skylark and Brenda are willing to take risks to earn larger gains. Hedgers are more interested in avoiding risk than in maximizing their gains.

Selling Hedge. A *selling hedge* is a common strategy used to avoid losses from price declines on physical inventory. For example, a selling hedge can be used to protect a farmer against losses if the market price of the farmer's growing crop declines. Unfortunately, the hedge also limits the farmer's potential profits if the market value of the crop rises.

EXAMPLE   **FARMER BROWN HEDGES HIS GROWING WHEAT CROP**

While planning his crops last year, Farmer Brown added up the cost of his seed, fertilizer, gasoline, and other expenses. After crunching the numbers, Brown concluded that he could profitably produce 20,000 bushels of wheat if he could obtain a price of $4.50 per bushel for his crop when he harvested it in July. While planting his crops on April 2, the price of July wheat futures was $4.50 per bushel. To assure that he could sell his harvest at $4.50 per bushel, Brown sold four wheat futures contracts short at $4.50 per bushel, amounting to (4 contracts × 5,000 bushels =) 20,000 bushels of short wheat futures. The 20,000 bushels of short wheat futures offset (hedged) the 20,000 bushels of physical wheat that was growing in the farmer's field. Farmer Brown's hedge was not designed to earn a large speculative gain; its purpose is to "lock in" the $4.50 per bushel selling price for his crop. This $4.50 per bushel price assures that Farmer Brown will be able to earn the modest profit he needs to operate the farm and feed his family. Various possible outcomes from Farmer Brown's selling hedge are shown in Table 9-4.

TABLE 9-4   Market Values of One Unit (5,000 Bushel Contract) of Farmer Brown's Wheat Hedge at $4.50 Per Bushel

(A) Market Prices of Physical Wheat	(B) Market Value of 5,000 Bushels of Wheat—a long position in physicals	(C) Market Value of One Wheat Futures Contract (5,000 bushels)—sold short at $4.50 per bushel equals: (price change) × (5,000 bushels)	(D) Total Value of Brown's Perfect Selling Hedge— (B) + (C) = (D)
$1 per bushel	$ 5,000	+ $17,500	$22,500
$2 per bushel	$10,000	+ $12,500	$22,500
$3 per bushel	$15,000	+ $ 7,500	$22,500
$4 per bushel	$20,000	+ $ 2,500	$22,500
$4.25 per bushel	$21,250	+ $ 1,250	$22,500
$4.50 per bushel	$22,500	0	$22,500
$5 per bushel	$25,000	− $ 2,500	$22,500
$6 per bushel	$30,000	− $ 7,500	$22,500

THE CONVERGENCE PRINCIPLE

DEFINITION

The market price of a future contract tends to follow (is highly positively correlated with) the price of the underlying commodity as it trades in the cash market (spot price) and these two prices **converge** at the expiration of the futures contract. Convergence of futures and spot prices on the delivery day is the only thing we know in advance about these fluctuating prices.

As Brown harvested his crop in July the cash price of physical wheat fell to $4.25 per bushel and he sold his harvest in the cash (physicals) market for $4.25 per bushel. The futures price converged on the cash price of $4.25 per bushel as Brown sold his harvested crop and he simultaneously purchased four wheat futures contracts at $4.25 per bushel. Buying four wheat contracts eliminated (reversed, offset, unwound) the short futures position that committed him to deliver (4 contracts × 5,000 bushels =) 20,000 bushels of wheat in July at $4.50 per bushel. When the market price of wheat fell, it affected Brown in two ways: first, he realized a net gain of 25 cents per bushel on his short futures position, and, second, he lost 25 cents per bushel on his physical wheat. Excluding the brokerage commissions and taxes, the three transactions (the cash sale and the two futures transactions) provided Farmer Brown the net cash flow of $4.50 per bushel he needed to show a reasonable profit. These events are summarized in Table 9-5. Note that if Farmer Brown had not hedged his harvest against a price change, he would have obtained only $4.25 cents per bushel for his harvested wheat.

About Perfect Hedges. The discussion of Figure 3-5 in Chapter 3 (p. 56) introduced perfect hedges. This chapter's Table 9-5 illustrated how Farmer Brown enjoyed the benefits of a

TABLE 9-5   Summary of Farmer Brown's Transactions

Synopsis	Cash (Physicals) Market	Futures Market	Farmer Brown's Actions
April summary	On April 2 Brown plants wheat with expectation of harvesting 20,000 bushels. He invests $4.50 per bushel in raw materials.	On April 2 Brown sells 20,000 bushels of July futures short at $4.50 per bushel.	Plants crop and establishes a hedge against adverse price fluctuations. These 2 positions are offsetting so that no overall profit or loss is possible.
July summary	Brown sells his July wheat harvest of 20,000 bushels at $4.25 per bushel in the physical wheat market.	Brown reverses his short position; he buys 20,000 bushels (4 contracts) of July wheat futures at $4.25 per bushel.	He harvests his crop and simultaneously lifts his hedge by reversing out of his futures position.
Overall summary	Loss: 25 cents per bushel on physical wheat	Gain: 25 cents per bushel on wheat futures	A perfect selling hedge provided Farmer Brown a net cash flow of $4.50 per bushel.

perfect hedge that shielded him from all price fluctuation risk. **Perfect hedges** are rarely possible. Hedges are usually imperfect for several reasons. First, the long and short positions may not coincide in time. For example, the best time to harvest a crop might occur after the maturity (delivery) date of the futures contract. Second, delivery may have to made at an inaccessible location. A Chicago Board of Trade's (CBT's) wheat contract calls for delivery in Chicago. Chicago could be a costly delivery location for a wheat farmer in Oregon. Third, the specified quality cannot be delivered. For example, suppose a blight discolors Farmer Brown's wheat crop. As a result, he can get only $3.75 per bushel for his 20,000-bushel wheat harvest because discolored wheat is not worth as much as normal wheat. A little blight flawed what seemed like Farmer Brown's perfect selling hedge.

The Futures Prices and Other Trading Data in Newspapers

Figure 9-2 shows market data from one trading day for various futures contracts listed on futures exchanges around the world. The Chicago Merc's future on the S&P500 index is the second contract shown under the heading "INDEX" in Figure 9-2. The first column under each commodity's heading contains the future's expiration dates. The expiration dates for the S&P500 contracts show that new contracts are originated every quarter; the delivery (expiration) months are March, June, September, and December of each year. In June, someone wanting to speculate on the U.S. stock market's fluctuations over the next 9 months should buy a futures expiring in March of the next year.

Activity Statistics. The number of futures contracts that have been opened but not yet eliminated (offset, reversed) since a contract started trading is called the **open interest.** The open interest and the **volume of contracts** traded per day are measures of the usage and trading activity in a contract. Compared to other futures, we see in Figure 9-2 that the open interest in the S&P500 index futures makes it one of the most popular futures in the world. Table 9-6 demonstrates how the volume of contracts and open interest data are tabulated using hypothetical trading data.

FIGURE 9-2 Newspaper Excerpt Showing One Day's Prices from Different Futures Exchanges

Monday, April 17, 2000

Open Interest Reflects Previous Trading Day.

GRAINS AND OILSEEDS

CORN (CBT) 5,000 bu.; cents per bu.

	Open	High	Low	Settle	Change	Lifetime High	Lifetime Low	Open Interest
May	225¾	226¾	223¼	224	− 2¼	261	202½	113,354
July	234	236	232	232½	− 2½	278½	209	189,198
Sept	241½	243¾	240¼	240¾	− 2½	257	215¾	48,295
Nov	247¼	247½	245¾	246¼	− 2½	260	222½	955
Dec	252	253½	249¾	250¾	− 2	279½	225¼	114,170
Mr01	261	261	258½	259	− 2¼	271	233¾	13,488
Dec	266¼	266¼	264	265	− 1¾	272	246½	4,162

Est vol 58,000; vol Fri 89,032; open int 488,996, +591.

OATS (CBT) 5,000 bu.; cents per bu.

	Open	High	Low	Settle	Change	Lifetime High	Lifetime Low	Open Interest
May	123	123¼	122¼	122½	− 1	133	112¾	3,778
July	119¾	120½	119½	119½	− 1	126	110½	8,623
Sept	121¼	121½	120¼	120¼	− 1½	130	115¾	1,878
Dec	128¼	128¼	126½	127	− 2	135	115½	3,677
Mr01	....	....	....	132¾	− 1¾	135	129	336

Est vol 1,000; vol Fri 2,458; open int 18,293, +591.

SOYBEANS (CBT) 5,000 bu.; cents per bu.

	Open	High	Low	Settle	Change	Lifetime High	Lifetime Low	Open Interest
May	528	535	526	531½	− 1	554	432	51,690
July	539½	547½	539½	544	− ½	647	440	75,826
Aug	543¾	551½	543¾	547¼	− 1¼	569	441	8,622
Sept	548½	553	548	549¼	− 1	571½	450	5,666
Nov	553½	560½	552½	556¾	− 1	631	453	43,851
Ja01	563½	567	562	564½	− 1	586	504	3,544
Mar	570	573½	568	571¼	− ¾	591½	502½	2,607

Est vol 46,000; vol Fri 59,313; open int 106,541, −492.

SOYBEAN MEAL (CBT) 100 tons; $ per ton.

	Open	High	Low	Settle	Change	Lifetime High	Lifetime Low	Open Interest
May	167.20	169.20	167.00	167.80	− .30	175.50	127.30	36,287
July	168.40	170.50	168.40	169.20	− .50	176.30	130.00	44,284
Aug	169.70	170.50	168.90	169.20	− .80	176.20	131.00	10,183
Sept	169.70	170.50	168.80	169.40	− .50	176.90	132.00	6,750
Oct	170.20	170.50	168.80	169.70	− .40	177.20	135.00	7,020
Dec	172.20	172.60	171.00	171.80	− .40	180.20	135.50	15,144
Ja01	173.50	173.50	171.80	172.50	− .30	181.00	148.00	1,191
Mar	174.30	174.30	173.30	173.90	− .40	183.00	169.50	2,236

Est vol 15,000; vol Fri 26,756; open int 124,421, −450.

SOYBEAN OIL (CBT) 60,000 lbs.; cents per lb.

	Open	High	Low	Settle	Change	Lifetime High	Lifetime Low	Open Interest
May	18.06	18.23	18.02	18.09	− .08	23.50	15.60	41,672
July	18.38	18.60	18.38	18.46	− .08	22.30	15.95	54,491
Aug	18.65	18.77	18.55	18.62	− .10	21.00	16.12	11,297
Sept	18.80	18.90	18.73	18.76	− .12	21.70	16.27	8,503
Oct	19.06	19.06	18.90	18.91	− .15	22.25	16.42	6,840
Dec	19.35	19.40	19.23	19.28	− .12	20.62	16.75	19,491
Ja01	19.70	19.72	19.50	19.60	− .10	20.08	17.07	8,249
Mar	19.90	20.00	19.75	19.78	− .22	20.38	17.45	2,743
May	20.25	20.25	20.05	20.06	− .17	20.68	17.70	2,743
July	20.40	20.40	20.30	20.31	− .24	20.95	18.00	1,979

Est vol 18,000; vol Fri 18,444; open int 158,218, +259.

WHEAT (CBT) 5,000 bu.; cents per bu.

	Open	High	Low	Settle	Change	Lifetime High	Lifetime Low	Open Interest
May	256	258¼	253	253¼	− 2½	322	246¾	38,143
July	268	270¾	265¼	265½	− 2¾	347	256¾	64,002
Sept	279¾	281	276¼	277	− 1¾	335	266½	10,623
Dec	294½	296	291	291¾	− 2½	345	280½	15,059
Mr01	307	309	304½	305	− 2¼	327	298	3,173

Est vol 19,000; vol Fri 21,024; open int 131,878, +1,228.

WHEAT (KC) 5,000 bu.; cents per bu.

	Open	High	Low	Settle	Change	Lifetime High	Lifetime Low	Open Interest
May	279	299¼	276¾	278¾	− 1¼	340½	272¾	18,415
July	291	294	288¼	289	− 2	366	282	32,721
Sept	300	303	298	298¾	− 1¾	346	291	3,770
Dec	315½	317½	312	313½	− 2	354	302	8,406
Mr01	326	328½	324½	325½	− 1½	344½	318½	788

Est vol 4,171; vol Fri 7,431; open int 64,571, −384.

INTEREST RATE

TREASURY BONDS (CBT)-$100,000; pts. 32nds of 100%

	Open	High	Low	Settle	Change	Lifetime High	Lifetime Low	Open Interest
June	98-19	99-05	97-01	97-05	− 42	99-28	88-22	506,079
Sept	98-21	98-31	97-00	97-02	− 42	99-24	88-19	4,176
Dec	....	....	....	97-03	− 48	99-09	88-31	585
Mr01	....	....	....	97-02	− 46	98-06	88-06	205

Est vol 300,000; vol Fri 584,611; open int 511,045, +7,184.

TREASURY BONDS (MCE)-$50,000; pts. 32nds of 100%

	Open	High	Low	Settle	Change	Lifetime High	Lifetime Low	Open Interest
June	98-07	98-18	96-29	97-00	− 47	99-28	88-25	9,999

Est vol 4,200; vol Tue 5,596; open int 10,006, +284.

TREASURY NOTES (CBT)-$100,000; pts. 32nds of 100%

	Open	High	Low	Settle	Change	Lifetime High	Lifetime Low	Open Interest
June	98-27	99-06	97-26	97-27	− 22	99-30	93-11	629,861

Est vol 180,000; vol Fri 227,154; open int 633,423, −5,016.

5 YR TREAS NOTES (CBT)-$100,000; pts. 32nds of 100%

	Open	High	Low	Settle	Change	Lifetime High	Lifetime Low	Open Interest
June	99-10	99-19	98-275	98-28	− 9.0	00-005	96-10	416,066
Sept	....	....	....	98-28	− 8.5	99-24	97-23	6,396

Est vol 80,000; vol Fri 96,475; open int 422,462, +3,247.

2 YR TREAS NOTES (CBT)-$200,000; pts. 32nds of 100%

	Open	High	Low	Settle	Change	Lifetime High	Lifetime Low	Open Interest
June	99-122	99-20	99-102	99-105	− 1.7	99-225	98-085	42,411

Est vol 6,000; vol Fri 3,479; open int 42,411, −152.

30-DAY FEDERAL FUNDS (CBT)-$5 million; pts. of 100%

	Open	High	Low	Settle	Change	Lifetime High	Lifetime Low	Open Interest
Apr	93.990	93.990	93.985	93.990	....	94.450	93.910	20,800
May	93.87	93.87	93.87	93.87	+ .02	94.20	93.80	15,725
June	93.75	93.75	93.72	93.72	+ .01	94.13	93.66	9,963
July	93.58	93.59	93.57	93.58	+ .02	94.06	93.48	4,780
Aug	93.55	93.56	93.53	93.56	+ .01	93.73	93.47	1,491
Sept	93.51	93.51	93.48	93.51	+ .01	93.64	93.34	1,298

Est vol 4,000; vol Fri 13,180; open int 54,136, +4,465.

MUNI BOND INDEX (CBT)-$1,000; times Bond Buyer MBI

	Open	High	Low	Settle	Change	Lifetime High	Lifetime Low	Open Interest
June	95-14	95-17	94-05	94-07	− 41	96-19	89-08	22,841

Est vol 800; vol Fri 1,379; open int 54,136, +4,465.

Index: Close 95-16; Yield 6.07.

TREASURY BILLS (CME)-$1 mil.; pts. of 100%

	Open	High	Low	Settle	Chg	Discount Settle	Discount Chg	Open Interest
June	....	....	....	94.10	....	5.90	....	705

Est vol 3; vol Fri 33; open int 705, −3.

LIBOR-1 MO. (CME)-$3,000,000; points of 100%

	Open	High	Low	Settle	Chg	Settle	Chg	Open Interest
Apr	....	....	....	93.87	....	6.13	....	16,051
May	93.69	93.70	93.68	93.69	....	6.31	....	18,533
June	93.59	93.59	93.57	93.57	....	6.43	....	3,660
July	93.49	93.50	93.47	93.47	....	6.53	....	2,812
Aug	....	....	....	93.42	....	6.58	....	552
Sept	93.40	93.40	93.40	93.38	....	6.62	....	390
Oct	....	....	....	93.31	....	6.69	....	1,107
Nov	....	....	....	93.26	....	6.74	....	750

Est vol 1,322; vol Fri 4,916; open int 43,895, +1,459.

EURODOLLAR (CME)-$1 million; pts of 100%

	Open	High	Low	Settle	Chg	Yield Settle	Yield Chg	Open Interest
Apr	....	....	....	93.71	....	6.29	....	39,291
May	93.54	93.55	93.54	93.54	....	6.46	....	32,160
June	93.42	93.44	93.41	93.42	....	6.58	....	535,213
July	93.37	93.37	93.34	93.34	....	6.66	....	1,548
Aug	93.30	93.32	93.29	93.29	+ .01	6.71	− .01	1,749
Sept	93.23	93.29	93.22	93.24	....	6.76	....	502,327
Dec	93.08	93.15	93.07	93.10	+ .02	6.90	− .02	415,156
Mr01	93.05	93.14	93.05	93.08	+ .01	6.92	− .01	326,928
June	92.97	93.06	92.97	93.00	+ .01	7.00	− .01	223,357
Sept	92.94	93.03	92.94	92.97	....	7.03	....	184,553
Dec	92.90	92.96	92.89	92.91	....	7.09	....	125,201
Mr02	92.95	93.01	92.94	92.96	....	7.04	....	114,965
June	92.96	93.02	92.95	92.96	....	7.04	....	87,770
Sept	93.00	93.02	92.95	92.96	− .01	7.04	+ .01	84,621
Dec	92.95	92.96	92.89	92.90	− .03	7.10	+ .03	71,549
Mr03	93.01	93.02	92.95	92.95	− .04	7.05	+ .04	62,973
June	92.96	92.99	92.91	92.92	− .05	7.08	+ .05	47,400
Sept	92.95	92.98	92.89	92.90	− .05	7.10	+ .05	48,515
Dec	92.92	92.92	92.84	92.84	− .06	7.16	+ .06	37,673
Mr04	92.94	92.96	92.87	92.87	− .06	7.13	+ .06	33,413
June	92.87	92.91	92.82	92.83	− .06	7.17	+ .06	31,890
Sept	92.86	92.87	92.78	92.79	− .06	7.21	+ .06	25,671

EXCHANGE ABBREVIATIONS
(for commodity futures and futures options)

CANTOR-Cantor Exchange; CBT-Chicago Board of Trade; CME-Chicago Mercantile Exchange; CSCE-Coffee, Sugar & Cocoa Exchange, New York; CMX-COMEX (Div. of New York Mercantile Exchange); CTN-New York Cotton Exchange; DTB-Deutsche Terminboerse; FINEX-Financial Exchange (Div. of New York Cotton Exchange; IPE-International Petroleum Exchange; KC-Kansas City Board of Trade; LIFFE-London International Financial Futures Exchange; MATIF-Marche a Terme International de France; ME-Montreal Exchange; MCE-MidAmerica Commodity Exchange; MPLS-Minneapolis Grain Exchange; NYFE-New York Futures Exchange (Sub. of New York Cotton Exchange); NYM-New York Mercantile Exchange; SIMEX-Singapore International Monetary Exchange Ltd.; SFE-Sydney Futures Exchange; TFE-Toronto Futures Exchange; WPG-Winnipeg Commodity Exchange.

INDEX

DJ INDUSTRIAL AVERAGE (CBOT)-$10 times average

	Open	High	Low	Settle	Change	Lifetime High	Lifetime Low	Open Interest
June	10304	10690	10180	10682	+ 342	11980	9810	16,332
Sept	10465	10817	10450	10817	+ 342	12126	9995	750
Dec	10595	10959	10595	10959	+ 344	12180	8100	1,326

Est vol 20,000; vol Fri 24,749; open int 18,414, −16.
Idx prl: Hi 10583.75; Lo 10232.55; Close 10582.51, +276.74.

S&P 500 INDEX (CME)-$250 times index

	Open	High	Low	Settle	Change	Lifetime High	Lifetime Low	Open Interest
June	136700	141500	134260	141270	+ 4520	157400	98000	378,634
Sept	138400	143400	137900	143220	+ 4620	159500	99000	5,957
Dec	144810	145100	139900	145270	+ 4670	161860	126650	3,467
Mr01	144820	147200	142000	147420	+ 4720	164260	132430	306
June	147300	149400	144200	149670	+ 4770	166660	134280	251
Sept	....	....	....	151920	+ 4820	169060	136130	117

Est vol 94,476; vol Fri 139,906; open int 388,736, +10,285.
Idx prl: Hi 1401.53; Lo 1346.50; Close 1401.53, +44.97.

MINI S&P 500 (CME)-$50 times index

	Open	High	Low	Settle	Change	Lifetime High	Lifetime Low	Open Interest
June	136675	141275	134225	141275	+ 4525	157425	134225	28,399

Vol Fri 90,234; open int 28,407, +3,625.

S&P MIDCAP 400 (CME)- $500 times index

	Open	High	Low	Settle	Change	Lifetime High	Lifetime Low	Open Interest
June	433.00	455.00	428.50	450.25	+ 17.25	513.00	381.45	12,314

Est vol 1,256; vol Fri 958; open int 12,316, +65.
Idx prl: Hi 446.72; Lo 425.65; Close 446.66, +15.72.

NIKKEI 225 STOCK AVERAGE (CME)-$5 times index

	Open	High	Low	Settle	Change	Lifetime High	Lifetime Low	Open Interest
June	19000.	19390.	18950.	19390.	− 385	20750.	16790.	14,743

Est vol 3,940; vol Fri 4,022; open int 14,744, +856.
Idx prl: Hi 20341.50; Lo 18603.87; Close 19008.64, −1426.04.

NASDAQ 100 (CME)-$100 times index

	Open	High	Low	Settle	Change	Lifetime High	Lifetime Low	Open Interest
June	321595	358500	310750	357750	+ 36000	488200	242275	40,846

Est vol 34,331; vol Fri 37,944; open int 40,877, +2,359.
Idx prl: Hi 3530.67; Lo 3107.42; Close 4529.45, +321.49.

MINI NASDAQ 100 (CME)-$20 times index

	Open	High	Low	Settle	Change	Lifetime High	Lifetime Low	Open Interest
June	3207.5	3578.0	3107.5	3577.5	+ 360.0	4884.0	3107.5	18,526

Vol Fri 43,966; open int 18,527, +3,453.

GSCI (CME)-$250 times nearby index

	Open	High	Low	Settle	Change	Lifetime High	Lifetime Low	Open Interest
Apr	198.10	202.50	198.10	na	na	225.40	178.50	686
May	196.00	199.70	196.00	199.20	+ 1.40	220.50	178.50	38,815

Est vol 341; vol Fri 3,370; open int 39,552, +258.
Idx prl: Hi 202.53; Lo 198.17; Close 201.86, +2.13.

RUSSELL 2000 (CME)-$500 times index

	Open	High	Low	Settle	Change	Lifetime High	Lifetime Low	Open Interest
June	457.00	469.50	444.00	465.75	+ 6.50	624.50	419.40	12,988

Est vol 2,309; vol Fri 1,535; open int 12,988, +2.
Idx prl: Hi 459.18; Lo 441.56; Close 459.18, +5.46.

Column 1 lists the delivery month for each futures contract. The opening price, high price for the day, low price for the day, and the day's settlement (closing) price for each futures contract are shown in the second through fifth columns for each contract expiration. The sixth column shows the daily change in the contract's closing price. Columns 7 and 8 show the highest and lowest values the underlying commodity, interest rate, or index achieved since trading was initiated in that contract. The last column shows an activity statistic for the contract called the "Open Interest." The S&P500 index future is under the heading "Index." Multiply the market value of the S&P500 index times $250 to compute the contract's market value.

SOURCE: *Wall Street Journal*, 18 April 2000, C19.

Regulating Financial Futures in the United States

As mentioned, most futures exchanges operate their own clearinghouse. The **Commodity Futures Trading Commission (CFTC)** Act of 1974 establishes an independent federal agency named CFTC to oversee futures exchanges and trading of futures contracts in the United States.

TABLE 9-6	Volume and Open Interest Statistics Computed from Hypothetical Trading Data			
Transaction Number	Trading Activity	Volume	Open Interest	Explanation
1	A buys 10 contracts from B	10	10	A gets long 10 and B gets short the same 10 contracts as trading begins.
2	C buys 20 contracts from B	20	30	Open interest builds as C gets long 20 and B's short position increases to 30.
3	D buys 20 contracts from C	20	30	D buys long position of 20 as C sells (reverses out of) his 20 contracts.
4	B buys 10 contracts from D	10	20	B buys back (reverses out of) 10 of his 30 short contracts as D sells 10 of his 20 long contracts to B.

SOURCE: Adapted from *The Salomon Smith Barney Introductory Guide to Stock Index Futures*, New York City, February 1998, p. 43.

The CBOE, AMEX, PHIX, and PSE clear their option transactions through the **Options Clearing Corporation (OCC)**, which they own. The OCC and the markets for options on common stock are regulated by an agency of the U.S. government called the **Securities and Exchange Commission (SEC)**. (The CFTC has jurisdiction over options on agricultural goods.)

CHARACTERISTICS OF PUTS AND CALLS ON EQUITIES

Various options and combinations of options can be used to achieve many different goals: increase risk, reduce risk, profit if the price of the underlying stock rises, profit if the price of the underlying stock falls, profit if the underlying stock does not change, profit if the price of the underlying stock moves up and down, and so on. No matter what your view of the future path of a stock's price, it is possible to create a configuration of options that will pay off if your view is correct. These profit opportunities can be constructed from the following six elementary building blocks:

1. Buy a long position in the stock.
2. Sell the stock short.
3. Buy a call option on the stock.
4. Sell a call option on the stock.
5. Buy a put option on the stock.
6. Sell a put option on the stock.

DEFINITION   **A CALL OPTION**

A *call* option is a financial contract that gives its owner the right, but not the obligation, to buy the underlying stock. One call grants the *call buyer* the option to purchase one round lot (100 shares) of a specific stock within a specified period of time at a specified exercise price. A buyer that wants an option to buy 200 shares must purchase two calls. The *call writer* gets paid to provide the call buyer the opportunity to buy the underlying stock at the agreed upon terms if the call buyer wishes to do so. Call buyers can exercise their calls—or the calls can be sold in the secondary market rather than being exercised.

A PUT OPTION

DEFINITION

A *put* option gives its buyer (owner) the right, but not the obligation, to sell (put) one round-lot of the underlying stock to the put seller (writer). The buyer of a put must exercise the option at a specified exercise price within a specified period or the option expires and is worthless. Exchange-listed puts are liquid financial instruments that, prior to expiration, can be sold instead of being exercised.

Characteristics of Stock Options Traded on Options Exchanges in the United States

New put and call options are originated by the U.S. options exchanges each month. Originating these options results in different options on the same underlying stock with expirations of 3, 6, 9, and 12 months. Options with different expiration dates on the same underlying stock are traded simultaneously. In the 1990s the American Stock Exchange (AMEX) started listing put and call options called Long-term Equity APpreciation Securities, or **LEAPS,** with expirations as long as 24 months.

Before an option's expiration date, the owner of a put or call may choose to do one of the following four things:

1. **Hold** the option a while longer to see what happens to the price of the underlying stock.
2. **Sell** the option to someone else at the option's current market price and take the resulting gain or loss. This eliminates the option position.
3. **Exercise** the option, eliminating the position.
4. Let the option **expire,** remembering that expired options are worthless.

Most options are used to speculate on price changes or to hedge away risks. As a result, only about 10% of all exchange listed stock options are ever exercised.

There are two parties to every option. One party is the *option buyer*, who pays the option price (premium) to the option seller to induce the seller to write (grant) the option. Option buyers are said to be long options. The counterparty is the *option seller*, who receives the option premium from the option's buyer for writing the option. Option sellers are said to be short options. Options brokers find option buyers and option sellers and act as their agents in consummating transactions. Brokers receive commission income to induce them to arrange option transactions.

Every call and put option has three different prices associated with it:

1. **The price of the underlying asset:** This is the fluctuating market price of the underlying common stock.

2. **The exercise price:** The **strike price,** or contract price, or **exercise price** is the price at which the option writer can be legally required to execute the option. The exercise price never changes during the life of an option.

3. **The option's premium:** The *premium* is the *price* the option buyer pays the option writer to create the option. Later, the option may be resold any number of times at fluctuating premiums that are determined in the secondary market for options.

Options are typically bought and sold by price speculators and risk-averting hedgers, rather than exercised. Most options listed on exchanges expire unexercised. The option writers whose options are never exercised get to keep their premium income for doing nothing more than exposing themselves to the risk of losing money if their options are exercised. The option writers whose options are exercised usually—but not always—lose more than their premium income by fulfilling the provisions of the option they sold.

Contrary to what their name suggests, **European options** are traded in Europe and in non-European countries. European options can be exercised only on their expiration date. **American options** can be exercised on any trading day of their life, up to and including the day they expire. American options are traded in America as well as in other countries.

Markets for Options

The Chicago Board Options Exchange (CBOE) is the largest options exchange in the world. It and other options exchanges are listed in Table 9-1. The American Stock Exchange (AMEX) is not only a stock exchange; it is also the second largest options exchange in the world. The Philadelphia Stock Exchange (PHIX), the oldest stock exchange in the United States, also lists currency options on a half dozen foreign currencies and equity options on dozens of common stocks. The Pacific Stock Exchange (PSE) supplements its stock exchange activities with an options market. Many stock exchanges around the world also trade options.

After you open an option account at a brokerage house, all you need to do is phone your broker to execute an option. Option traders can get current option prices from financial newspapers. Figure 9-3 is a newspaper excerpt listing one day's option prices for various put and call options that are listed on the CBOE.

THE GAIN-LOSS ILLUSTRATIONS FOR CALL POSITIONS

An investor who thinks the price of a stock is likely to move upward might want to buy the stock. Or, instead of buying a long position in the stock, the investor might buy a call on the stock. If the stock's price rises above the call's exercise price, the call buyer can reap price gains by exercising the option to purchase the underlying stock at its exercise price and then by reselling the stock at its higher market price. If the bullish views of the call buyer are erroneous and the price of the stock falls, the call buyer loses only the price (premium) paid for the call.

The gain-loss positions of a call option buyer and a call option writer are depicted in Figure 9-4. Per-share dollar gains and losses are graphed on the vertical axis of Figure 9-4, and the market price of the underlying stock is on the horizontal axis. Contrasting Figure 3-2 in Chapter 3 with this chapter's Figures 9-1 and 9-4 is informative.

Gain-Loss Illustration of Call Buyer's Position

The **intrinsic value** (exercise value) of each position on the date when the call expires is shown in Figure 9-4A by the solid lines that kink at the exercise price. The call option *buyer's*

FIGURE 9-3 Newspaper Excerpt Showing One Day's Market Data for Put and Call Options on: (A) Individual Stocks and (B) Stock Market Indexes[a]

(A) Options On Individual Stocks

LISTED OPTIONS QUOTATIONS

Option/Strike		Exp.	Call Vol.	Call Last	Put Vol.	Put Last
ADC Tel	45	Apr	1193	5 3/4	36	1 7/8
AMFM	85	Apr	...	...	750	26 3/4
AT&T	40	Apr	604	10 3/8	26	1/16
50	45	Apr	22	5 3/4	745	3/4
50	50	Apr	1246	1 13/16	3874	1 7/8
50	50	May	1239	4	2901	3 1/2
50	55	Apr	4889	1/2	779	5
50	55	May	2718	2 1/4	127	6
50	60	Apr	535	1/8	190	9 7/8
50	60	May	2122	1 1/4	25	10
50	65	May	2771	1/2	...	...
Abbt L	30	May	1116	8 1/2	...	...
AdobeS	105	Apr	41	3 1/8	569	9
A M D	50	Apr	914	16	20	1/16
66	60	Apr	814	6 1/8	1048	13/16
66	65	Apr	715	4 1/8	2234	2 1/4
66	75	Apr	1099	2 1/8	437	10 1/2
66	80	Apr	1111	1/4	103	12 1/4
Aetna	50	May	1010	4 7/8	2	2 1/8

Option/Strike		Exp.	Call Vol.	Call Last	Put Vol.	Put Last
53 1/2	55	Apr	596	5/8	225	3
53 1/2	55	May	2006	2 7/8	3	4 3/4
Alcoa	65	Apr	2010	2 7/16	85	7/8
67 9/16	70	Apr	2082	3/4	60	3 7/8
AllegTel	65	May	600	6	...	...
Allste	22 1/2	Apr	1092	5/16	79	1 13/16
20 7/8	25	May	1076	3/8	5	4 1/4
Altera	90	Apr	440	1	1085	14
72 3/16	95	Apr	735	7/16	20	15 1/8
Alza	37 1/2	Apr	40	3	980	1 13/16
Amazon	40	Apr	184	7 3/4	5171	1 5/8
46 7/8	45	Apr	425	4	821	3 5/8
46 7/8	50	Apr	3420	2	2872	5 3/8
46 7/8	50	Jul	179	8 1/2	627	11
46 7/8	52 1/2	Apr	1097	1	248	7 1/8
46 7/8	55	Apr	1303	1 1/8	649	9
46 7/8	60	Apr	286	3/8	1208	14 1/2
46 7/8	60	May	335	3 1/8	545	15 3/8
46 7/8	62 1/2	Apr	52	5/16	564	16 3/8

Option/Strike		Exp.	Call Vol.	Call Last	Put Vol.	Put Last
46 7/8	65	Apr	178	1/4	525	18 7/8
46 7/8	70	Apr	116	3/16	523	23 3/4
A Hess	65	May	...	...	1600	4
AmOnline	45	Apr	2062	9	118	5/16
55	50	Apr	194	6	1913	1
55	52 1/2	Apr	175	3 7/8	745	2 1/16
55	55	Apr	14635	2 3/8	3966	2 13/16
55	55	May	1273	5	1166	4 5/8
55	57 1/2	Apr	4495	1 1/2	1455	4 1/8
55	60	Apr	29408	1	12273	6 3/8
55	60	May	2698	3 1/8	1148	8 1/8
55	60	Jul	869	5 7/8	285	10 7/8
55	62 1/2	Apr	10956	3/4	513	8 3/4
55	65	Apr	1978	3/8	12338	10 3/4
55	65	May	2601	2	470	12 1/4
55	65	Jul	858	4 3/8	182	13 1/8
55	65	Oct	330	6 1/4	2203	15 1/4
55	67 1/2	Apr	896	5/16	206	13 1/4
55	70	Apr	1942	3/16	833	15 1/2

(B) Options On Stock Market Indexes

INDEX OPTIONS TRADING

Friday, April 14, 2000

Volume, last, net change and open interest for all contracts. Volume figures are unofficial. Open interest reflects previous trading day. p-Put c-Call

CHICAGO

NASDAQ-100(NDX)

Strike		Vol.	Last	Net Chg.	Open Int.
Jun	2020p	5	26	+14	47
Jun	2100p	53	35	+20	394
Jun	2200p	40	43	+25	91
Jun	2300p	37	53	+30 1/2	115
Jun	2400p	36	60	+26	363
Jun	2500p	134	100	+51	463
Jun	2600p	34	105	+56 3/8	387
Jun	2700p	28	132	+70 3/4	153
Jun	2800p	47	134 1/8	+52 1/4	186
Jun	2900p	298	206 1/4	+99 1/4	398
Jun	3020p	26	228	+124	118
Jun	3100p	22	257	+120 3/8	663
Jun	3200c	11	482 7/8	−264 7/8	168
Jun	3200p	278	368	+158	781
Apr	3300c	440	108 1/4	−441 3/4	3
Apr	3300p	635	180	+135 1/8	226
Jun	3300c	36	356 5/8	−322 3/8	355
Jun	3300p	12	365	+171 1/2	66
Apr	3320c	37	149	...	...
Apr	3320p	297	134	+100	533
Apr	3340c	18	145 1/2	...	...
Apr	3340p	160	200	+152	185
Apr	3360c	1	128	...	...
Apr	3360p	7	89	+76	13
Apr	3380c	10	136	...	...
Jun	3380p	20	360	...	...
Apr	3400c	60	107	−293	15
Apr	3400p	179	297 3/8	+223 3/4	673
Jun	3400p	44	350 5/8	+123 1/4	399

S & P 500 INDEX-AM(SPX)

Strike		Vol.	Last	Net Chg.	Open Int.
Jun	500p	55	1/16	...	6,592
Jun	700p	30	1/8	...	3,952
Jun	800p	200	5/8	+ 1/2	12,953
Jun	850p	12	3/8	+ 3/16	3,229
Jun	900c	10	532	−90	1,301
Jun	900p	126	1	+ 13/16	15,723
Jun	925p	4	13/16	+ 9/16	1,832
Jun	950p	36	1 5/16	+ 1 1/16	8,176
Jun	975p	5	1 3/8	...	10,305
Jun	1025p	2,280	3	+ 1 3/4	6,011
Jun	1050c	30	310	−91	3,243
Jun	1050p	324	3 1/4	+ 2 7/16	5,576
Jun	1075p	283	6	+ 4 5/8	2,468
Apr	1100p	1,000	1/4	+ 1/8	6,549
May	1100p	254	4	+ 3	3,010
Jun	1100p	290	9 1/4	+ 7	14,475
May	1125c	25	263	...	80
May	1125p	27	2 3/4	+ 1 7/8	238
Jun	1125p	290	7	+ 3 5/8	3,764
Apr	1150p	1,119	1/4	+ 1/8	7,930
May	1150p	26	5	+ 3 9/16	1,400
Jun	1150c	25	280	−30	3,630
Jun	1150p	327	11	+ 7	6,835
Apr	1175p	455	1 1/2	+ 1 3/8	1,424
May	1175p	13	9 1/4	+ 7 1/16	1,876
Jun	1175p	300	12	+ 8 3/4	1,610
Apr	1200c	2	157	−144	56
Apr	1200p	577	2	+ 1 7/8	11,909
May	1200p	278	12	+ 9	11,454
Jun	1200p	208	18	+10 1/4	21,206
Apr	1225p	174	3	+ 2 3/4	4,935
May	1225p	193	12	+ 8	2,454
Jun	1225p	545	21	+11 7/8	6,800
Apr	1250p	454	7	+ 6 3/8	15,697
May	1250c	4	155	−66	4
May	1250p	93	18	+13 3/4	11,308

On each line, (A) lists the day's price for one stock, one strike (exercise) price, an option expiration month, and the volume of trading and last premium for the day for one call and one put on the same stock. Each line of (B) lists either a call or a put on a stock market index. The option's expiration month, strike price, put (*p*) or call (*c*) designator, volume of trading, last premium for the day, net change in the number of open contracts, and an activity measure called the open interest are on each line.

[a]Stock market indexes are discussed in Chapters 10 and 11, and options on those indexes in Chapter 12.

SOURCE: *Wall Street Journal*, 17 April 2000, C28.

FIGURE 9-4 Gain-Loss Graph for the Parties to a Call Option: (A) Call Buyer and (B) Call Writer

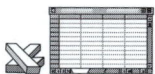

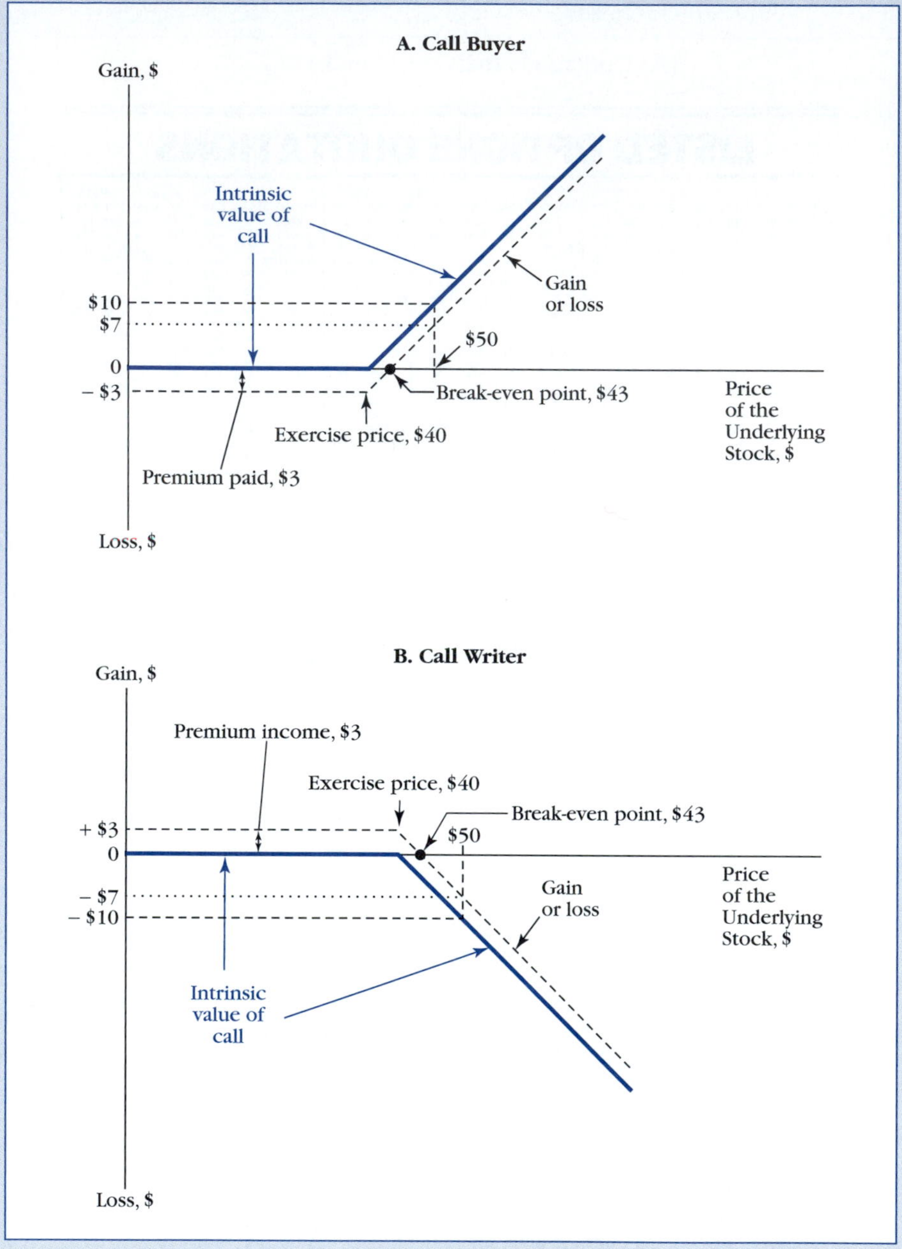

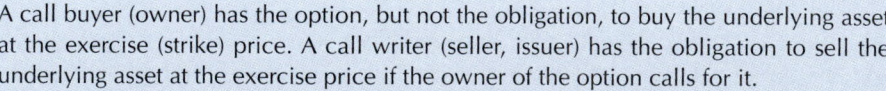

A. Call Buyer

Gain, $

Intrinsic value of call

Gain or loss

$10
$7
0
– $3

$50

Break-even point, $43

Price of the Underlying Stock, $

Exercise price, $40

Premium paid, $3

Loss, $

B. Call Writer

Gain, $

Premium income, $3

Exercise price, $40

Break-even point, $43

+ $3
0
$50

– $7
– $10

Gain or loss

Price of the Underlying Stock, $

Intrinsic value of call

Loss, $

A call buyer (owner) has the option, but not the obligation, to buy the underlying asset at the exercise (strike) price. A call writer (seller, issuer) has the obligation to sell the underlying asset at the exercise price if the owner of the option calls for it.

position has zero intrinsic value when the price of the underlying (optioned) stock is below the option's exercise price. But when the price of the stock rises above the exercise price, the call's intrinsic value rises in one-to-one correspondence with the price of the underlying stock. The *intrinsic value of a call* is either zero or the difference between the stock's price and the exercise price, whichever is greater, as indicated in Eqn. 9-3, where MAX( ) represents selecting the quantity with the maximum value that lies inside the parentheses.*

Intrinsic value of a call = MAX[0, (Stock price − Exercise price)]   **(9-3)**

The intrinsic value ignores brokers' commissions, taxes, and other transactions costs incurred in establishing the call option.[3]

If a call is exercised when the price of the underlying stock equals the sum of the call's exercise price and the call option's premium, that is the point where the option buyer's gain is zero—it is the *break-even point*. At break even:

(Price of stock) = (Exercise price) + (Call option's premium)

A call buyer might exercise an option at the break-even point if the call was expiring; the call's owner thought the price of the underlying security would rise no higher, and the call buyer wanted to recover the premium.

If the underlying stock's market price rises above the break-even point, the call buyer can reap a gain by requiring the call writer to sell the underlying stock at the exercise price, whereupon the call buyer can immediately sell the stock in the market at its current higher price. Alternatively, if the call buyer does not want to buy the underlying stock, the call buyer could sell the option for least its intrinsic value. Eqn. 9-4 defines a call buyer's gain or loss when the option expires:

Call buyer's gain or loss = Intrinsic value of call − Call option's premium   **(9-4)**

The dashed line in Figure 9-4 that is parallel to the call's intrinsic value line traces the call buyer's gain or loss over a range of prices for the underlying stock.

ANALYZING A CALL ON COKE'S STOCK

EXAMPLE

Coke stock is selling for $30 per share. A call option to buy the stock at an exercise price of $40 expires in 6 months and has a current premium of $3 per share. This call's intrinsic value at a stock price of $30 is computed in Eqn. 9-3a.

$$\begin{pmatrix} \text{Call's intrinsic value} \\ \text{per share, 0} \end{pmatrix} = \text{MAX}\left[0, \begin{pmatrix} \text{Stock's market price} \\ \text{per share, \$30} \end{pmatrix} - \begin{pmatrix} \text{Call's exercise price} \\ \text{per share, \$40} \end{pmatrix}\right] \textbf{(9-3a)}$$

Possible gains and losses from the call over a range of possible stock prices are shown in the following table. Figure 9-4A illustrates this example.

---

* If the value of x is larger than the value of y then the solution to MAX(x,y) is written as: MAX(x,y) = x. In the same vein, MAX($-2, -183, -44$) = -2, because negative 2 is the largest of the three values in the parentheses.

KO's Stock Price at Expiration of Call	Intrinsic Value of Call at Expiration	Call Buyer's Gain or Loss on 100 shares
$30	0	(100)(−$3) = −$300
$40	0	(100)(−$3) = −$300
$43	$ 3	$300 + (100)(−$3) = 0
$50	$10	$1,000 + (100)(−$3) = $700
$60	$20	$2,000 + (100)(−$3) = $1,700
$70	$30	$3,000 + (100)(−$3) = $2,700

Illustration of Call Writer's Position

Figure 9-4A makes two things clear. First, if the stock's price stays below the exercise price it will not be profitable for the call buyer to exercise the option and, as a result, the call *writer* keeps the option premium for doing nothing. Second, if the price of the underlying stock rises above the exercise price, the call buyer will find it profitable to exercise the option and the call buyer's gain equals the option writer's loss. The *intrinsic value of a call writer's position* is either zero or the excess of the exercise price over the stock's price, whichever is least, as shown in Eqn. 9-5, where MIN( ) denotes the minimum value that lies within the brackets.*

Intrinsic value of call writer's position = MIN[0, (Exercise price − Price of stock)]   (9-5)

Adding the call's intrinsic value to the income from the call option premium reveals the call writer's intrinsic gain can be either a gain or loss:

Call writer's intrinsic gain = Intrinsic value of call + Call option's premium   (9-6)

The call writer's intrinsic gain is illustrated in Figure 9-4B via the dashed lines that are parallel to the solid lines showing the intrinsic value of the call writer's position. This is the writer's profit before brokers' commissions and taxes are deducted. In spite of the premium income, if the price of the optioned stock rises infinitely high, the call writer's losses rise without limit too.

EXAMPLE   MR. BYER'S AND MS. RHYTER'S CALL ON INTEL IN 1993

In 1993 the price of Intel Corporation's common stock (ticker symbol INTC) fluctuated from $21 to $37 per share and continued upward in the years that followed. During 1993 Mr. Byer purchased a call on INTC from an option seller (writer) Ms. Rhyter. Mr. Byer paid Ms. Rhyter a premium of $2.50 per share ($250 for an option on 100 shares) for a 6-month call with an exercise price of $20 per share. If the market price of INTC's stock rose to $75 before the call expired, Mr. Byer could call the stock from Ms. Rhyter at $20 and earn ($75 − $20 =) $55 per share (less the $2.50 premium yields $52.50 of net gain per share). To enjoy these gains Mr. Byer would have to exercise his call at $20 and then immediately sell the called stock at $75 per share. Since one party's gains become the other party's losses, this outcome would represent a loss of $55 per share for Ms. Rhyter (less $2.50 per share premium income for writing the option). More specifically, if Mr. Byer exercised his call, Ms. Rhyter would have to buy INTC at its market price of $75 and immediately deliver it to Mr. Byer at the exercise price of $20 per share and, in so doing, she would lose $55 of intrinsic value and suffer a total loss of ($55 − $2.50 =) $52.50 per share. Figure 9-4A and B outlines the gains and losses for Mr. Byer and Ms. Rhyter, respectively, and Table 9-7 enumerates them.

---

* If the value of x is larger than the value of y, then the solution to MIN(x,y) is MIN(x,y) = y. For example, MIN(−2, −183, −44) = −183, because −183 is the smallest of the three values in parentheses.

TABLE 9-7	Intrinsic Values of Call Option on Intel's Stock with $20 Exercise Price			
Assumed Price of INTC Stock, denoted P	Intrinsic Value of Mr. Byer's Call = MAX[0, (P − Exercise price,$20)]	Mr. Byer's Gain = Intrinsic Value of Call − Option's Premium, $2.50	Intrinsic Value of Ms. Rhyter's Call = MIN[0, (Exercise Price, $20 − P)]	Ms. Rhyter's Gain = Intrinsic Value of Call + Call Premium
If P = $10 then:	0 => A far out of the money call	−$2.50	0	$2.50
If P = $15 then:	0 => Out of the money	−$2.50	0	$2.50
If P = $20 then:	0 => At the money	−$2.50	0	$2.50
If P = $22.50 then:	0 => At break-even point	$0.0	−$2.50	$2.50 − $2.50 = 0.0
If P = $25 then:	$5 => In the money	$5 − $2.50 = $2.50	−$5	−$5.00 + $2.50 = −$2.50
If P = $30 then:	$10 => In the money	$10 − $2.50 = $7.50	−$10	−$10 + $2.50 = −$7.50
If P = $40 then:	$20 => Deep in the money	$20 − $2.50 = $17.50	−$20	−$20 + $2.50 = −$17.50
If P = $50 then:	$30 => Deep in the money	$30 − $2.50 = $27.50	−$30	−$30 + $2.50 = −$27.50

Ms. Rhyter's bearish call writing position would become profitable if the market price of INTC stock declined to $20 per share, or below. Mr. Byer would lose money if the stock's price was $10 and he called the stock from Ms. Rhyter at $20 per share, because he could only sell it for the low market price of $10 per share. If he behaves rationally, Mr. Byer would not exercise the call when the stock's price was $10 per share; he would simply forfeit the premium of $2.50 per share paid for the option and do nothing. In this case, Ms. Rhyter would keep the per share premium of $2.50 that Mr. Byer to paid her for doing nothing.

Looking back at the prices of Intel stock, we see Mr. Byer's bullish outlook would have paid off nicely because the price of Intel was $37 per share at the end of 1993. If Mr. Byer had bought a 2-year LEAP call on Intel in 1993 with an exercise price of $20 per share, he would have done even better because Intel's price reached a 1995 peak of $78 per share.

GAIN-LOSS ILLUSTRATIONS FOR PUT POSITIONS

The *intrinsic value of a put* is either zero or the difference between the exercise price and the stock price, whichever is larger. Eqn. 9-7 defines a put's intrinsic value.

Intrinsic value of a put = MAX[0, (Exercise price − Price of stock)]   (9-7)

The intrinsic value of a put is the amount the put is worth to the put buyer at the put's expiration. In Figure 9-5A the solid blue line that kinks at the exercise price graphically represents the put's intrinsic value.

The break-even point for the put buyer occurs where the exercise price less the put option premium equals the price of the underlying stock. Break-even:

(Exercise price) − (Price of put) = (Price of the stock)

The put buyer might exercise the option if the price of the underlying stock was between the put's exercise price and the break-even point: Doing so would recover part of the put premium.

FIGURE 9-5 Gain-Loss Graph for the Parties to a Put Option: (A) Put Buyer and (B) Put Writer

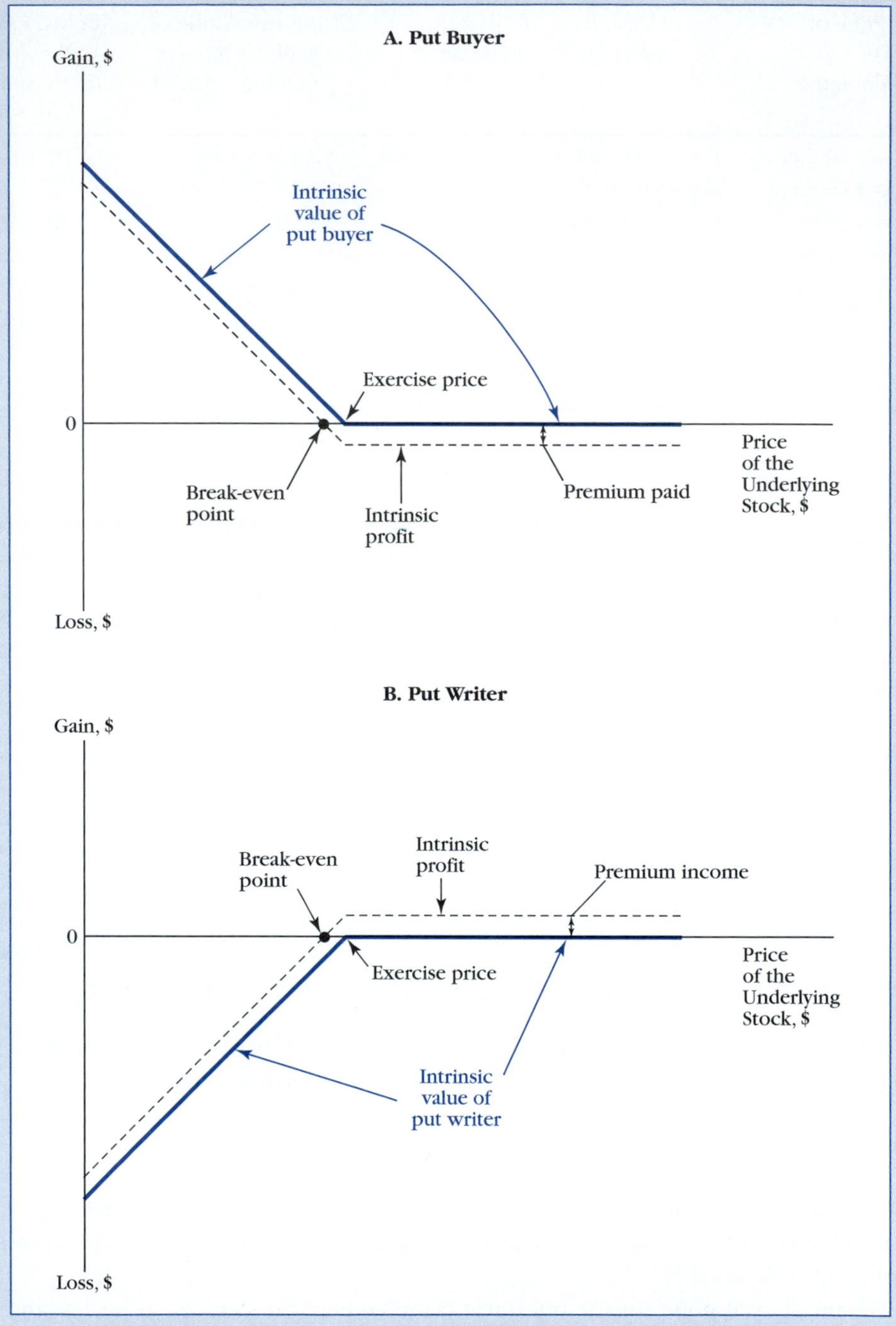

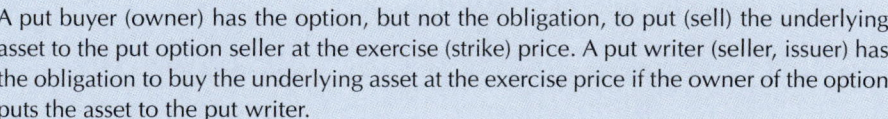

A. Put Buyer

Gain, $

Intrinsic value of put buyer

Exercise price

0

Break-even point

Premium paid

Intrinsic profit

Price of the Underlying Stock, $

Loss, $

B. Put Writer

Gain, $

Break-even point

Intrinsic profit

Premium income

0

Exercise price

Intrinsic value of put writer

Price of the Underlying Stock, $

Loss, $

A put buyer (owner) has the option, but not the obligation, to put (sell) the underlying asset to the put option seller at the exercise (strike) price. A put writer (seller, issuer) has the obligation to buy the underlying asset at the exercise price if the owner of the option puts the asset to the put writer.

If we deduct the put option's premium from its intrinsic value, we see that the put buyer's intrinsic gain can be either a gain or a loss:

Put buyer's intrinsic gain = Intrinsic value of the put − Put option's premium   **(9-8)**

The put buyer's gain is represented in Figure 9-5A by dashed lines parallel to the solid blue intrinsic value of the put line. In our discussions of the value of the put, we have been ignoring, for simplicity, both commission costs and income taxes.

Gain-Loss Illustrations for a Put Writer

A rational put buyer will not exercise the put if the price of the underlying stock rises above its exercise price because, as shown in Figure 9-5A, there is no gain for the put buyer from such an action. If the put buyer behaves rationally, Figure 9-5B shows that when the price of the underlying stock rises above its exercise price, the put option writer gets to keep the put premium for granting an option that will expire unexercised. Eqn. 9-9 defines the intrinsic value of a put writer's position.

Intrinsic value of put writer's position = MIN[0, (Price of stock − Exercise price)]   **(9-9)**

Options writers' gains are always limited to their premium income, but their losses can be much larger. Figure 9-5B shows that if the issuer of the underlying stock goes bankrupt and the stock's price falls to zero, the put writer's maximum loss (negative gain) cannot exceed the exercise price less the income received from the put option premium.

Put writer's gain = Intrinsic value of put writer's position + Price of put   **(9-10)**

The put writer's gains are represented by dashed lines parallel to and above the solid blue intrinsic value line in Figure 9-5B.

STUDY CHECK

INTRINSIC VALUES FOR A PUT BUYER

QUESTION: Mr. Bascomb paid $2 per share for a put on common stock issued by Speed.Com Corporation (SCC). The put's exercise price is $45. (a) What is Mr. Bascomb's maximum loss? (b) What is his maximum gain? (c) What will Bascomb's gain be when the put expires if the stock's price is $50? (d) What will his gain be when the put expires if the stock's price is $40?

ANSWERS:

(a) Limited liability means that the maximum option buyers can lose is their premium; this is $2 per share for SCC.

(b) The maximum a put buyer can gain is the exercise price minus the put's premium, when the price of the underlying stock goes to zero. For SCC this equals: (XP − Premium) = ($45 − $2) = $43 per share net gain, which would occur if SCC goes bankrupt and Bascomb sells the worthless stock for its exercise price.

(c) The put would not be exercised. MAX(0, XP − P) − Premium = MAX(0, $45 − $50) − $2 = −$2 (net loss) See Eqns. 9-7 and 9-8.

(d) The put would be exercised. MAX(0, XP − P) − Premium = MAX(0, $45 − $40) − $2 = $3 (net gain)

STUDY CHECK

QUESTION: Ms. Zalesky received $4 per share for writing a put on Green Lawn Care (GLC) common stock. The put's exercise price is $55. (a) What is Ms. Zalesky's maximum loss? (b) What is her maximum gain? (c) What will Zalesky's gain be when the put expires if the stock's price is $50? (d) What will her gain be when the put expires if the stock's price is $60?

ANSWERS:

(a) A put writer's maximum loss occurs if the underlying stock's price falls to zero. The put buyer would force Zalesky to pay $55 for the worthless stock. $MIN[0, (P - XP)] + Premium = MIN[0, (0 - \$55)] + \$4 = -\$51$ per share net loss.

(b) The maximum an option writer can earn is the premium income of $4 per share, which occurs if the option is never exercised.

(c) The put would be exercised. $MIN(0, P - XP) + Premium = MIN(0, \$50 - \$55) + \$4 = -\$1$ (net loss). See Eqns. 9-9 and 9-10.

(d) The put would not be exercised. $MIN(0, P - XP) + Premium = MIN(0, \$60 - \$55) + \$4 = \$4$ (net gain)

Perspectives on Options

Those who sell a stock short and those who buy put options on a stock have something in common: They both gain from declines in the market prices of the underlying security. If a stock's issuer went bankrupt and the optioned stock's price fell to zero, the gains of those who bought put options on the bankrupt stock would be maximized. An option trader who bought puts on the bankrupt stock could obtain the worthless shares for a price of zero and then put that bankrupt stock to the option writer at the put's exercise price. Since the bankrupt stock cost nothing, the exercise price that the put writer had to give to the put buyer for the bankrupt shares would all be a gain for the put buyer.

If the price of a call buyer's optioned stock falls, or the price of a put buyer's optioned stock rises, these adverse price moves cannot cost these two option buyers more than the premiums they paid for their options. Figures 9-4A and 9-5A illustrate that these two option buyers cannot lose any more than their option premiums, because option buyers enjoy **limited liability.** The limited liability that option buyers enjoy means that put buyers are better off than the short sellers if the price of an underlying stock rises. Similarly, limited liability means that call buyers are better off than investors that have long positions if the price of an underlying stock falls. Call writers gains are limited to the premiums they receive, but they do not enjoy limited liability. If the price of the optioned stock rises to infinity, the call writer's losses also rise to infinity. Put writers face a liability that is limited to the price of the optioned security; and, their gains are limited to the premiums they receive.

The gains (losses) for the put buyers are offset by equal losses (gains) for the put writers. Likewise, the call buyers' gains (losses) are offset by equal losses (gains) for the call writers. These offsetting gains and losses are not obvious in the gain-loss graphs, but they can be summarized by observing that the counterparties in options transactions are participants in a **zero sum game** (further discussed on page 256).

Table 9-8 compares and contrasts the rights and obligations of the parties that buy and sell both call and put options.

TABLE 9-8	**The Rights and Obligations of Buyers and Sellers of Call and Put Options**			
	The option's buyer or owner has:		*The option's writer or seller has:*	
Type of Option	Privilege	Obligation	Privilege	Obligation
Call Option	to buy the underlying security at a profitable exercise price.	to pay the premium to the call writer.	to receive the premium for writing the call.	to sell the underlying security at an exercise price that is unprofitable if asked to do so.
Put Option	to sell the underlying security to the put writer at a profitable exercise price.	to pay the premium to the put writer.	to receive the premium for writing the put.	to buy the underlying security at an exercise price that is unprofitable if asked to do so.

CHOOSING BETWEEN AN OPTION OR A POSITION IN THE UNDERLYING STOCK

An investor who wants to speculate that the price of a stock will change must choose between

Buying an option on that stock

Taking a long or short position directly in the underlying stock

Advantages Derived from Using Options

Purchasing the option can work out better than taking a long or short position directly in the underlying stock for two main reasons, and three other significant reasons, as described here.

Financial Leverage. The investment in an option is limited to the premium paid for it. In contrast, taking a position directly in the stock requires a much larger sum of money (even after allowing for the use of margins). Since less money is invested to acquire an optioned position, it offers more financial leverage than the long or short position. Each dollar invested in an option premium can generate more dollars of gain than each dollar invested directly in the stock that underlies that option. The steeper lines for the options in Figure 9-6A and B illustrates the financial leverage.

Limited Liability. An option buyer can lose no more than the premium if the price of the underlying stock moves adversely. In contrast, the losses associated with a long or short position in the same stock will be larger if the price of the asset experiences a large adverse move. Figure 9-6A shows the potential loss is 100% of the invested funds for both the call and the long position. Do not forget, however, that many more dollars must be invested to establish the long position (even with margins) than to buy a call on the same security. Figure 9-6B shows that the potential losses extend downward to negative infinity for the short sale. The investor's maximum possible dollar losses are almost always less with the option than with the direct position. Those who value the limited liability prefer the options.

Financial leverage and limited liability are the two main reasons to prefer options over taking a position directly in the underlying asset. Additional reasons to like options are discussed below.

No Lost Interest. A third advantage to buying a put over selling short is that short sellers have to give up the use of the proceeds from their short sale without being paid any interest

FIGURE 9-6 Rate of Return Diagrams Contrast: (A) Buying a Call Versus Buying the Underlying Asset; (B) Buying a Put Versus Selling the Underlying Asset Short

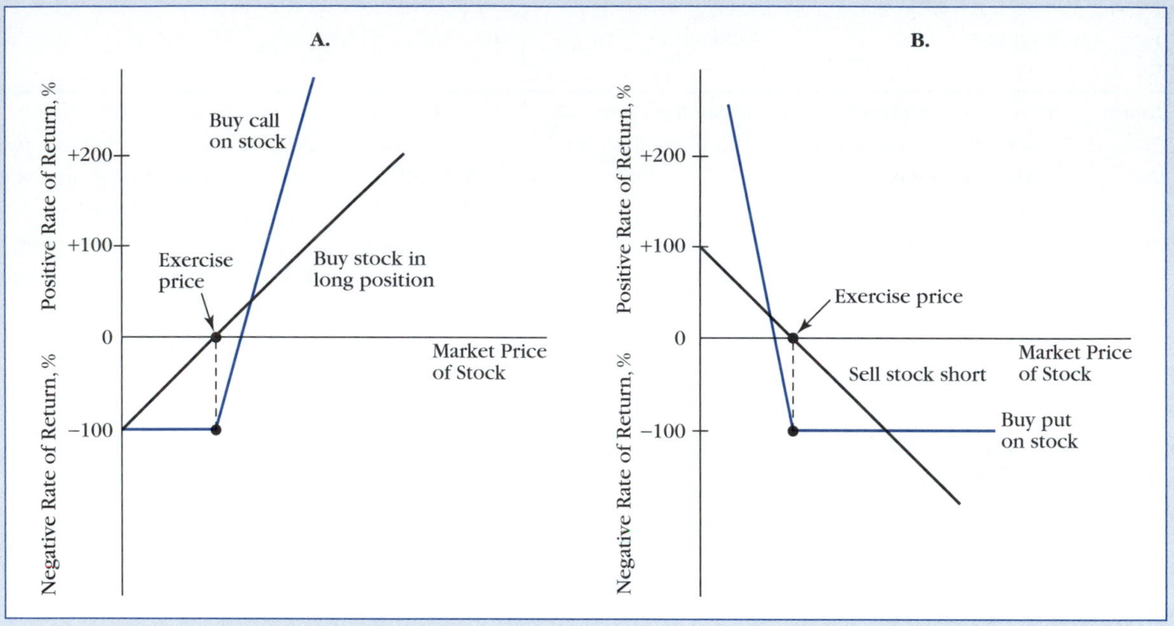

A.

B.

The two main advantages that option buyers enjoy are (1) no more than the option's premium (purchase price) can be lost, and (2) financial leverage that can be advantageous is created by acquiring a position in an asset for a fraction of its market price.

on those funds. The short seller's brokerage typically takes the cash proceeds from the customer's short sale and employs these funds within the brokerage house without paying the short seller any interest on the funds.* There is no lost interest income on untouchable funds to hinder put buyers.

No Cash Dividend Payments. The put buyer does not have to pay cash dividends to a third party. Unfortunately, short sellers must take cash out of their own pockets to make up any cash dividends that the short stock paid to the owners of borrowed shares.

No Time Constraints. Short sales cannot be made on a downtick in some markets—that is, after the stock's price fell from the price in the preceding transaction. A put can be purchased any time.

STUDY CHECK

TWO QUESTIONS ABOUT OPTIONS AND OTHER POSITIONS

Ms. Buhl and Mr. Bare are faced with decisions over whether to buy an option on an underlying stock or take positions directly in the stock itself. Their individual situations are outlined.

---

* Institutional investors like investment banks and commercial banks get to keep the proceeds from their short sales. Although the institutional investors transact most of the dollar volume of securities business, they are few in number relative to the millions of small retail investors. It is the small retail investors (for example, professors and students) who are denied the use of the proceeds from their short sales.

QUESTION 1: *Alpha Corporation's Stock in a Bull Market.*

Ms. Buhl believes that the price of Alpha's stock is going to rise sharply in the near future. She cannot decide whether to buy a long position in Alpha's stock or buy a call option on Alpha's stock. She knows that either will be profitable if the stock's price rises enough to cover the costs incurred to obtain it. Which choice is the most desirable in a bull market?

QUESTION 2: *Omega Corporation's Stock in a Bear Market.*

Mr. Bare thinks the price of Omega's stock will decline sharply in the near future. He cannot decide whether to sell Omega's stock short or buy a put option on the stock. His calculations have shown that either position will be profitable if the price of Omega's stock drops enough to cover the cost of establishing it. Which choice is most profitable in a bear market? *Hint:* Ms. Buhl and Mr. Bare should consult Figure 9-6, the five points discussed previously, and the following point.

One Major Advantage of the Short Sale over Buying a Put

In spite of the five reasons listed previously favoring options, there are circumstances that can make the short sale more desirable than buying a put. Options expire and become worthless if the price of the underlying security does not move favorably during the option's life. In contrast, the long and short positions can be held open for years without incurring any additional transactions costs to renew the position. This factor can pale in significance if the investor is confident that the price of a stock is poised for a profitable short-term move and wants to use the option's financial leverage to maximize the rate of return.

MR. HATTEN, THE UNLUCKY PUT BUYER

EXAMPLE

Mr. Hatten paid $3 per share for a 3-month put on common stock issued by Mullins Corporation (MC). The put's exercise price was $45. During the quarter of a year after he bought the put, the stock's price never fell below the put's exercise price of $45. The put expired unexercised and worthless. Mr. Hatten's bearish enthusiasm for MC's stock price was undiminished. He bought another 3-month put on MC stock. This tale of woe ends after 2 years, during which Mr. Hatten paid $3 per share for each of a series of eight consecutive 3-month puts on MC's stock. During those 2 successive years of put purchases, MC's stock price never fell below the put's $45 exercise price and all eight puts expired unused and valueless. When Mr. Hatten finally gave up his bearish view of MC, he had nothing but frustration to show for the $24 per share he spent on eight consecutive puts on MC.

> Paid $3 per share for 3-month put premiums
> Times: Eight consecutive quarterly purchases
> Total: $24 wasted on 8 unexercised puts on MC

If Hatten had sold MC stock short at $45 per share he would not have made any money, but he would at least still have the $24 per share loss he accumulated from MC put premiums.

In the final analysis, there is no universally correct way to choose between buying an option on a stock or taking a position directly in the stock. Each investment situation is unique and must be judged on its own merits.

Zero Sum Game

The counterparties in options transactions are participants in a *zero sum game*. This means trading a million options does not change society's aggregate wealth. After a million derivatives have been bought and sold, some derivatives traders are wealthier and the other derivatives traders are less wealthy. If the wealthier derivatives traders are better money managers than the less wealthy traders, then trading derivatives reallocates society's wealth in a more optimal manner.

Investors who have superior educations, superior information processing abilities, and/or monopolistic access to valuable information have a *competitive advantage* over other investors. These advantaged investors can increase their wealth by being active investors and from taking unhedged derivative positions. On the other hand, disadvantaged investors will, on average, tend to diminish their wealth by trading actively and by taking unhedged derivatives positions.

DETERMINANTS OF PUT AND CALL PREMIUMS

The profitability of trading in options depends, to a large extent, on the prices of the options. Therefore, it is important to know what determines options prices. The premiums that the put and call buyers pay for their options are determined by six factors: (1) the time remaining until the option expires, (2) the standard deviation of the underlying asset, (3) the market price of the underlying (optioned) asset, (4) the option's exercise (strike) price, (5) the risk-free rate (RFR) of interest, and (6) the cash dividend payments, if any. These factors are discussed below.

The Length of Time Remaining in the Option's Life

Option writers charge larger premiums to write a long-term option than to write a similar option on the same security that expires sooner. Option writers charge higher premiums to write longer-term options because the probability that an option can be profitably exercised by the buyer, and the writer's potential to lose money, increases with the length of time the option expires. Figure 9-7A and B illustrates the impact that time to maturity has on calls and puts, respectively.

The amount by which an option's premium exceeds its intrinsic value measures the option's **time value.** Eqn. 9-11 defines of the time premium embedded in a call option's premium.

$$\begin{pmatrix} \text{Time value of} \\ \text{a call option} \end{pmatrix} = \begin{pmatrix} \text{The call's premium, or,} \\ \text{the market price of the call} \end{pmatrix} - \begin{pmatrix} \text{The intrinsic} \\ \text{value of the call} \end{pmatrix} \qquad \textbf{(9-11)}$$

Eqn. 9-12 defines of the time premium embedded in a put option's premium.

$$\begin{pmatrix} \text{Time value of} \\ \text{a put option} \end{pmatrix} = \begin{pmatrix} \text{The put's premium, or,} \\ \text{the market price of the put} \end{pmatrix} - \begin{pmatrix} \text{The intrinsic} \\ \text{value of the put} \end{pmatrix} \qquad \textbf{(9-12)}$$

Time premiums may be positive or zero, but they are never negative. Time values measure the vertical distance between the intrinsic value and the curves that trace the options' premiums in Figure 9-7A and B.

The Riskiness of the Underlying Asset

Optioned stocks that experience sizable price fluctuations (are very risky) can create profitable opportunities for an option owner to exercise the option. As a result, the price (rate of return)

FIGURE 9-7 The Determinants of Option Premiums: (A) Calls and (B) Puts

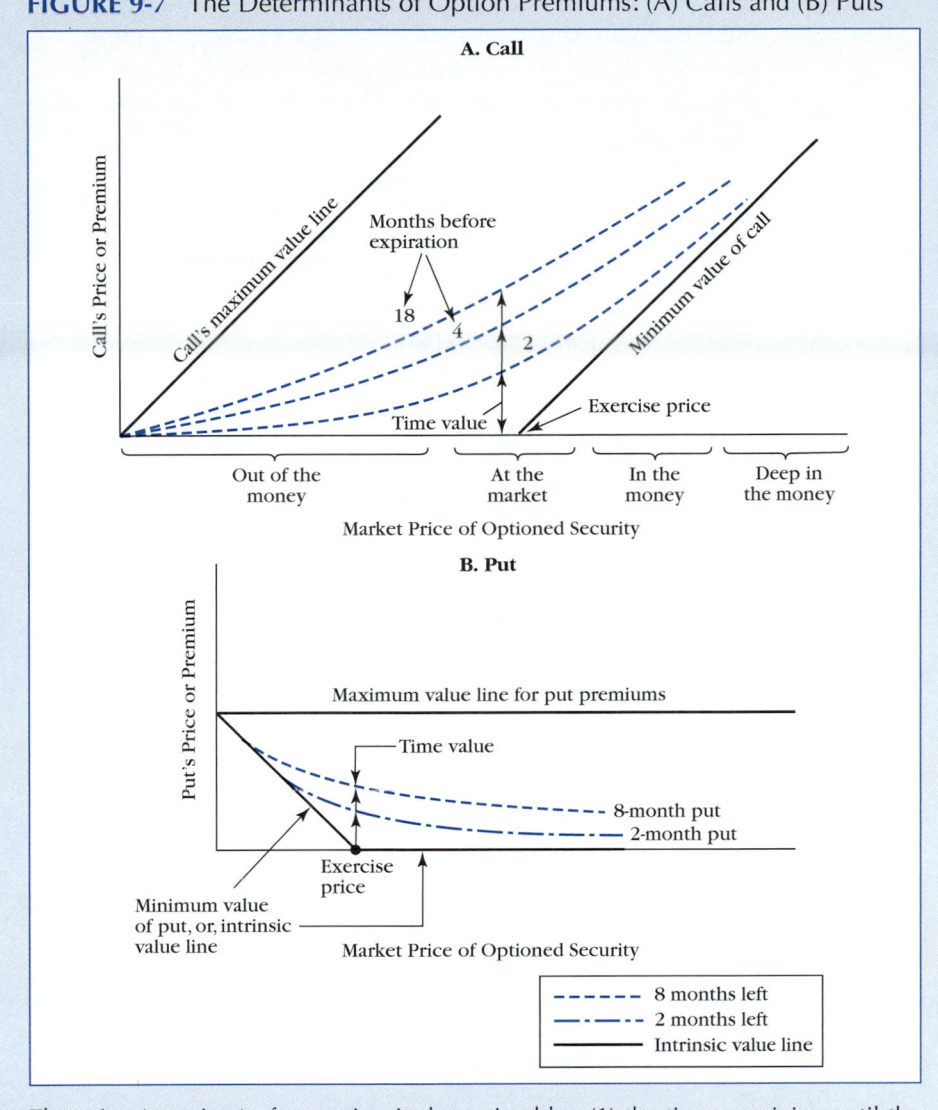

The price (premium) of an option is determined by: (1) the time remaining until the option expires, (2) the standard deviation, measuring the risk of the underlying, (3) the market price of the underlying, (4) the option's exercise price, (5) the risk-free interest rate, and (6) the cash dividend payments. The impact of the risk-free interest rates and any cash dividend payments cannot be seen in the figures above.

volatility of the underlying stock is an important factor determining the value of an option. Option writers assess the volatility (risk) of the underlying stock and charge higher premiums to write options on riskier stocks, because the options on high risk stocks are more likely to be exercised and throw the option writer for a loss than the options on low risk stocks.

Figure 9-8A and B shows probability distributions of stock prices for the ABC and XYZ Corporations, respectively. The different price ranges (widths of the probability distributions) indicate that XYZ is a riskier stock than ABC. Since the exercise prices of the calls on ABC and XYZ both equal their expected stocks' prices, both calls have an equal chance of ending up either out-of-the-money (unprofitable) or in-the-money (profitable).

FIGURE 9-8 Call Premiums Are Affected by Risk: (A) Intrinsic Value of Call and Probability Distribution of ABC's Stock Prices; (B) Intrinsic Value of Call and Probability Distribution of XYZ's Stock Prices; and (C) Contrasting the Premium Curves for Calls on ABC and XYZ Stocks

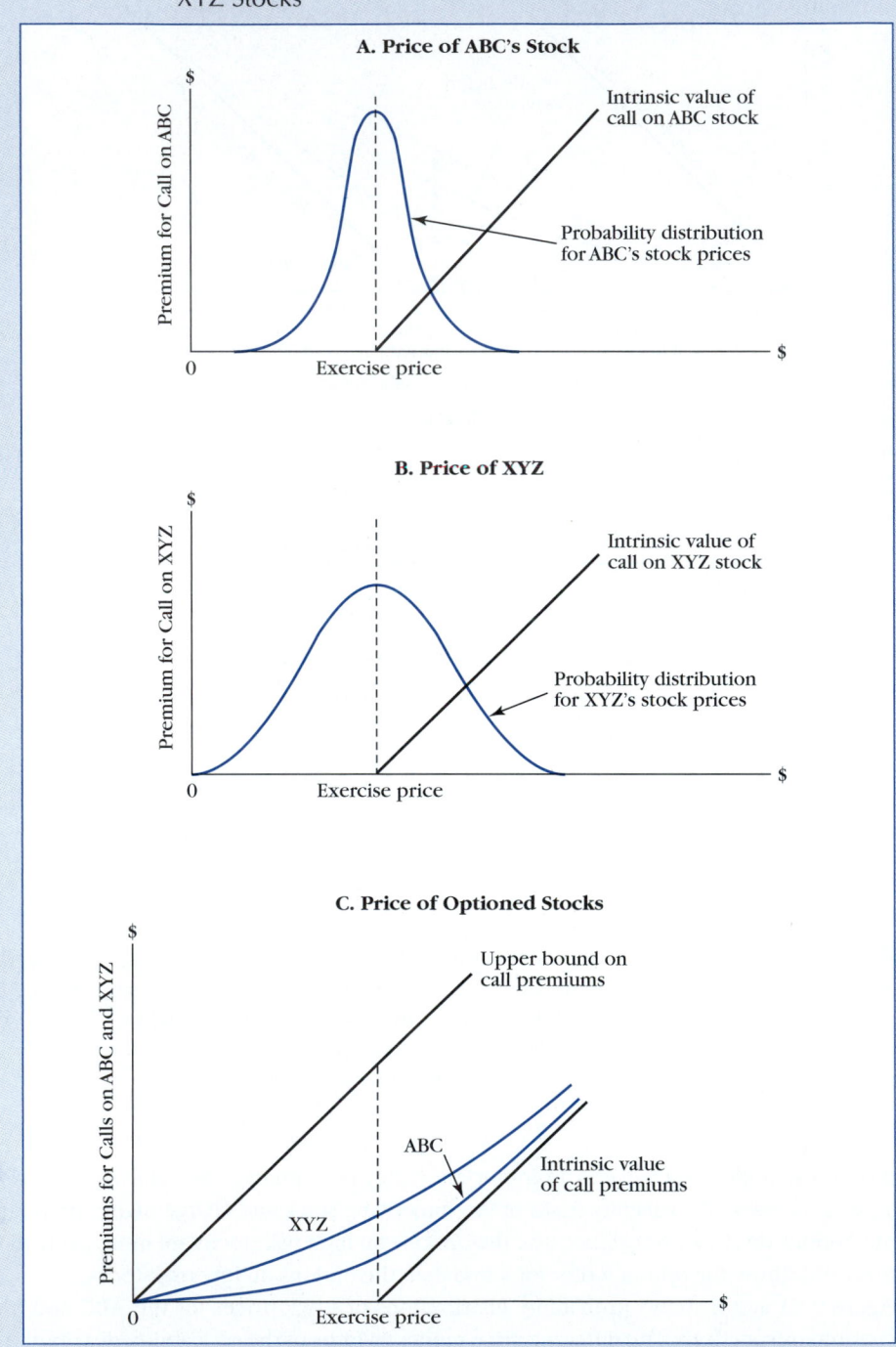

It is more likely to become profitable to exercise an option if the price of the underlying asset fluctuates over a wide range instead of a narrow range.

Figure 9-8A and B shows that the call on XYZ is worth more than the call on ABC because the price of XYZ's stock varies over a wider range (XYZ is riskier). The premium on XYZ's call will exceed the premium on ABC's call if the two stocks and the calls on them were identical in every way except risk.[4] Figure 9-8C illustrates how these facts are reflected in the call option premiums for calls on ABC and XYZ.

Illustrations analogous to those in Figure 9-8 can be used to explain why put options on highly risky stocks are worth more than put options on low-risk stocks.

The Market Price of the Underlying Asset

It takes a larger premium to induce the option writer to assume the risks associated with a high-priced stock because the potential losses are larger than they are with a low-priced stock. Furthermore, a glance at Eqns. 9-3, 9-5, 9-7, and 9-9 reveals that the market price of the underlying stock helps determine the intrinsic values and gains for calls and puts.

The Exercise Price

Call buyers gain when the stock's price rises above the exercise price, and put buyers gain when the stock's price declines below the exercise price. As a result, if the exercise price of a call is lowered while every other detail about the option is held constant, the call's value increases. And, if a put's exercise price is lowered while every other aspect of the option is held constant, the put's value declines. These facts are depicted in the options' intrinsic values, Eqns. 9-3, 9-5, 9-7, and 9-9, and also are illustrated in their gain-loss graphs at Figures 9-4 and 9-5.

Rate of Interest

Interest rates have such a small impact on option premiums it is difficult to observe, but the cause and effect can be explained. Market interest rates affect option prices indirectly through the exercise price via two related routes. First, the discounted present value of the exercise price varies inversely with the level of the interest rate. Second, the discounted present value of the exercise price diminishes as we increase the length of time until the option is exercised. The exercise price impacts the option's intrinsic value in ways that were explained above in Eqns. 9-3, 9-5, 9-7, and 9-9.

In summary, call premiums respond directly, while put prices are inversely related, to the level of the interest rate.

Cash Dividend Payments

The first trading day after a stock pays a cash dividend is called the **ex-dividend** date. The stock's market price drops off on the opening trade of the ex-dividend date, relative to the previous night's closing price, by the amount of the cash dividend payment per share.[5] This *ex-dividend price drop-off* equals the decrease in the paying corporation's capital incurred to pay the cash dividend. The price drop-off reduces the market price and, in turn, that lower price changes the value of options on the stock, as indicated in intrinsic value Eqns. 9-3, 9-5, 9-7, and 9-9.* Essentially, cash dividend payments decrease calls' worth and increase put premiums.

Table 9-9 summarizes the determinants of options' premiums.

---

*   In a later chapter the Black-Scholes formula is suggested as a way to value options. Cash dividend payments do not affect the value of options in the Black-Scholes model because they are ignored to simplify the model's mathematics. See Fischer Black and Myron Scholes, "The Pricing of Options and Corporate Liabilities," *Journal of Political Economy* (May–June 1973): 637–54. However, it is easy to append a cash dividend adjustment factor to the Black-Scholes model. Also see R. Whaley, "Valuation of American Call Options on Dividend Paying Stocks: Empirical Tests," *Journal of Financial Economics* 10 (March 1982): 29–58.

TABLE 9-9   Summary of the Determinants of Options' Premiums (Prices)

Determinants of the Options' Premium (price)	Impact on Put Premium (price)	Impact on Call Premium (price)
Increase in time until option's expiration	Increases	Increases
Increase in variance of underlying asset's price	Increases	Increases
Increase in price of the underlying stock	Decreases	Increases
Increase in exercise price	Increases	Decreases
Increase in interest rates	Decreases	Increases
Increase in cash dividend paid by underlying stock	Increases	Decreases

THE BOTTOM LINE

In the simplest case, investors can gain from price increases by taking a long position, or from price decreases by taking a short position directly in a security.

A derivative is a financial instrument that has its price derived from the price of an underlying asset.

A forward arises when someone buys a commodity, security, or other asset for future delivery. The delivery price is specified at the time of the purchase. Forwards are cash on delivery (COD) contracts; they do not provide an opportunity for the buyer to trade on margin and obtain the associated financial leverage. Forward contracts are simple business contracts that have been used for centuries. They are not liquid because they involve counterparty risk.

Futures contracts are improved forward contracts. All members of an organized futures exchange may trade the futures contracts listed on their exchange. Futures prices are determined in a public marketplace by open outcry or by an electronic limit order book system. A clearing corporation is a middleman that is the buyer in every sale and the seller to every purchaser in all futures transactions, so counterparty risk is nonexistent at futures exchanges. Unlike forward contracts, futures can easily be used for speculating or hedging. Tiny initial margin requirements can be used to magnify the gains and losses from futures positions. Chapter 27 explores futures further.

Financial futures started trading in the 1970s and are already the most popular type of contract traded at most futures exchanges. Futures contracts on government bonds, stock market indexes, and foreign currencies are the most popular financial futures in the world. Many financial futures do not provide for physical delivery; they are cash settled.

Buying options may be more desirable than taking long or short positions in the underlying for two main reasons: Option buyers enjoy limited liability and financial leverage. Put and call premiums (prices) are determined by various characteristics of the underlying, the option's exercise price, and the option's term to maturity. The counterparties in options transactions are participants in a zero sum game because the gains for the option buyers are offset by equal losses for the option writers, or vice versa. Options are discussed further in Chapter 28.

Entering into derivatives transactions is a zero sum game for the average investor. In the long run, only investors with a competitive advantage can expect to gain from trading financial futures.

Warrants, securities that contain embedded options, and convertible securities are examined in an Appendix to this chapter.

QUESTIONS

Q9-1 (Short selling) "Risk-averters do not sell short; short selling is done by speculators." Do you agree or disagree with this statement? Explain.

Q9-2 (Parties to an option) Who are the parties to the sale of put and call options, and what functions are performed by each party?

Q9-3 (Determinants of option premiums) What are the main factors that determine put and call premiums? Describe how each determinant affects the option premium.

Q9-4 (Contrasting warrants and calls) Discuss the differences between warrants and call options on the same corporation's stock. Hint: See chapter's appendix.

Q9-5 (Margin requirements on options) Why do options brokers let options buyers purchase put and call options without requiring them to post a performance bond in the form of an initial margin payment while, in contrast, the same brokers require option writers to make initial margin payments to guarantee their performance?

Q9-6 (Long position versus a call) Compare the following two investments in the Sportee Kayak Boat Company (SKBC): (a) Buy 10 shares of SKBC common stock at $100 a share for a total investment of $1,000. (b) Buy a call option on 100 share of SKBC stock that has a $100 exercise price

for a call premium of $10 a share. The total cost of this call is $1,000 ($10 per share times 100 shares) before commissions. Figure 9-6 illustrates these investment alternatives. Which investment do you prefer? Why? Under what conditions would you prefer the other investment?

Q9-7 (Pricing relationships) When describing investment positions, why are long and short positions called linear positions while puts and calls are called nonlinear positions?

Q9-8 (Futures versus forward contracts) Discuss the differences between futures and forward contracts. What are the advantages and disadvantages of forward contracts?

Q9-9 (Financial futures) Why has the worldwide market in financial futures exploded to become larger than the worldwide market in the much older commodity futures contracts?

Q9-10 (Hedging with futures contracts) Doug Ligget owns a well-diversified portfolio of stocks and would like to hedge against a decrease in value of his portfolio. Explain what position he would take in an S&P500 index futures contract to hedge his position.

Q9-11 (Open interest) What is meant by "open interest" and what information does this number convey?

PROBLEMS

P9-1 (Rate of return on a call option) On July 6, 1973, the only call on the common stock of Texas Instruments (TI) that was being traded on the CBOE was a July call with a $90 exercise price. The optioned stock's price had just fallen to $83 a share (so the TI call was "out of the money.") It was selling for only $1\frac{3}{8}$, or $1.375 per optioned share of stock. Assume you had purchased this July call on July 6, 1973 for $1.375. On July 27, in the short time before the option expired, the price of TI stock shot up to $108.75. (a) What do you estimate the July call of TI's stock was worth when the optioned stock price hit $108.75? (b) What is the percentage gain in the price of the call from $1\frac{3}{8}$ to the July 27th price that you estimated? (*Note*: This remarkable event actually happened.)

P9-2 (Convertible bond valuation) The Carleton Corporation's convertible bonds are selling for $1,100. The bond has a conversion ratio of 50 shares of common stock per bond. Carleton's common stock is currently selling for $25 a share. Equivalent nonconvertible bonds are selling for $1,150. What do you recommend? Hint: See chapter appendix.

P9-3 (Long call position) Sam bought a call with an exercise price of $30. The stock price is currently $29, and the call premium is $6. (a) What is this call's intrinsic value per share when the optioned stock's price is $33? (b) What is

this call's intrinsic value per share when the optioned stock's price is $24? (c) What is Sam's maximum potential loss? (d) What is the maximum potential profit from this call? (e) What is the profit from this call if the price of the stock is $33?

P9-4 (Call buying) Joe sold you a call with an exercise price of $70. The price of the underlying stock is currently $73, and the call's premium is $7 per share. (a) Determine this call's intrinsic value per share under the following expiration conditions: (i) the stock price rises to $82 a share; (ii) the stock price falls to $51 per share. (b) What is the maximum loss you can suffer? (c) What is the maximum amount Joe stands to lose on a per share basis? (d) What is the profit from your call if the price of the underlying stock is $82?

P9-5 (Purchasing a put) Assume you buy a put that has a premium of $3 a share. The price of the underlying stock is $90, and the exercise price is $85 a share. Calculate the following: (a) the put's intrinsic value per share if the stock price is now $97 a share; (b) the put's intrinsic value per share if the stock price is now $79 a share; (c) the maximum amount you could lose on this option; (d) the maximum gain you might make on your put position; (e) the profit if the price of the underlying stock is $79.

P9-6 (Writing a put) Assume you sell a put option for a premium of $7 a share. The stock price is $47, and the exercise price is $50. Calculate the following: (a) the put writer's intrinsic value if the stock price is $51; (b) the put writer's intrinsic value if the stock price is $33; (c) the maximum value you can lose; (d) the maximum value you can make from selling this put if the price of the underlying stock is $135 per share; (e) your profit if the price of the underlying stock is $33.

P9-7 (Buying a put) Tanya buys a European put for a premium of $7 a share. The price of the underlying stock is $76, and the exercise price is $70. (a) Under what circumstances does Tanya earn a profit after she deducts the put option premium but ignores commissions and taxes? (b) Under what circumstances will this put be exercised? (c) Draw a graph that illustrates your answers and label all parts of the graph unambiguously.

P9-8 (Convertible bond) The Bramle Corporation issues a $1,000 par value bond that is convertible into 20 shares of common stock. (a) If Bramle's common stock is selling for $40 per share, what is the conversion value of the bond? (b) If the bond's market price is $955 per bond, what is the conversion premium? Hint: See chapter's appendix.

P9-9 (Speculation with futures contracts) In July, Addison had some spare money from the recent sale of a townhouse and heard a radio commercial that explained he might make a huge return by investing in heating oil futures. The advertisement mentioned that a harsh winter was predicted and that this would increase the demand (and the price) of heating oil. Based on this information, Addison decided to speculate on heating oil futures. (a) What position would he take in the futures contract if he believed the information in the commercial to be accurate? (b) Assume he took his position in one contract, which stipulated the purchase or delivery of 42,000 gallons of heating oil, for February delivery at a price of $0.4574 per gallon, and that the margin requirement was 10% of the value of the contract. How much cash did Addison need to enter this position? (c) Unfortunately for Addison, the winter was unseasonably warm, and the price of heating oil fell to $0.4225 by late January. Addison decided to reverse his futures position at this point. What was his profit (loss) on this transaction? (d) What was his holding period return?

P9-10 (Hedging a stock portfolio) Assume the S&P500 index is currently at 1400 and Cindy holds $1,400 in an S&P500 index mutual fund that pays $12 a year in dividends. Worried that the market will fall, she decides to take a short position in a futures contract on the S&P500 index with a delivery date a year from now and a delivery price of $1,550. Calculate her gains (losses) from her positions at the end of 1 year if the value of her mutual fund is then (a) $1,350, (b) $1,400, (c) $1,450, (d) $1,500, (e) $1,550, (f) $1,600, and (g) $1,650. (*Note*: In reality, the futures contract calls for delivery of $250 times the value of the S&P500 index, and the numbers used in this problem are oversimplified to illustrate a point. In practice, one futures contract in the S&P500 index would hedge a [$250 × 1400 =] $350,000 stock portfolio, a very small portfolio for an institutional investor.)

P9-11 (Hedging against exchange rate fluctuations) The House of Wiebracht (HOW) is an American firm in the business of importing of German beer steins. It anticipates making a payment of 125,000 deutschemarks in December of 2001 to its exporter. Luckily, one futures contract is for 125,000 deutschemarks. (a) What position will HOW take in the futures market in order to hedge against losses from exchange rate fluctuations? (b) If the futures price for December delivery is $0.5565 per mark and the margin requirement is 8%, how much cash will HOW have to deposit with the futures broker when it takes this position?

CFA EXAM QUESTIONS

The following questions were adopted from the 1998 CFA Exam, Level I:

1. A put on Stock X with a strike price of $40 is priced at $2.00 per share; while a call with a strike price of $40 is priced at $3.50. What is the maximum per share *loss* to the writer of the uncovered put and the maximum per share gain to the writer of the uncovered call?

Maximum Loss to Put Writer	Maximum Gain to Call Writer
A. $38.00	$ 3.50
B. $38.00	$36.50
C. $40.00	$ 3.50
D. $40.00	$40.00

2. Which of the following statements describing options is *false*?

   A. A put option's profit increases when the value of the underlying asset increases.

   B. A call option will be exercised only if the market value of the underlying asset is more than the exercise price.

   C. A put option will be exercised only if the market value of the underlying asset is less than the exercise price.

   D. A put option gives its holder the right to sell an asset for a specified price on or before the option's expiration date.

3. Futures contracts *differ* from forward contracts in which of the following ways?

   I. Futures contracts are standardized.

   II. Performance of each party in a futures transaction is guaranteed by a clearinghouse.

   III. Futures contracts require that traders post margin in order to trade.

   A. I and II only.

   B. I and III only.

   C. II and III only.

   D. I, II, and III.

4. (This question is adapted from the 1998 CFA Exam, Level III.) The board of directors of Abco Company is concerned about the downside risk of a $100 million equity portfolio in its pension plan. The board's consultant has proposed temporarily (1 month) hedging the portfolio with either futures or options.

   A. **Contrast** the use of futures to the use of options for hedging the portfolio's equity exposure by discussing:

      i. initial cost.

      ii. effect of implied volatility in pricing.

      iii. sensitivity to movement in value of the underlying.

      iv. risk exposure.

   B. **Contrast** a covered call option strategy with a strategy that combines the current portfolio with a long put option position by discussing the:

      i. effectiveness of the hedges.

      ii. performance of the hedges during a rising market.

      iii. cost of the strategies.

FURTHER REFERENCES

Chance, Don M. *An Introduction to Derivatives*, 3rd ed. Orlando, FL: Dryden Press, 1995, 58–62.

   This easy-to-read textbook provides a good, detailed coverage of options, futures and swaps.

Francis, Jack Clark, William W. Toy, and Gregg Whittaker, Eds. *The Handbook of Equity Derivatives*, Rev. Ed. New York: Wiley, 1999.

   Chapters 1–9 discuss exchange-listed futures, options, and other derivatives. Chapters 10–20 discuss over-the-counter (OTC) equity derivatives. Chapters 21–27 delve into law, taxes, and the design of successful instruments. Very little mathematics is used. The book provides a rare look at the OTC derivatives market, which is larger than the market for exchange-listed derivatives.

Hull, John. *Introduction to Options and Futures*, 3rd ed. Englewood Cliffs, NJ: Prentice-Hall, 1998.

   This textbook provides comprehensive but concise review of futures, swaps, and options.

Jarrow, Robert and Stuart Turnbull, *Derivative Securities*. Cincinnati: South-Western, 1996.

   This mathematically rigorous book provides a comprehensive review of all types of options.

Johnson, R. Stafford and Carmelo Giaccotto. *Options and Futures*, St. Paul, MN: West, 1995.

   This rigorous yet easy-to-read textbook provides a comprehensive review of futures, swaps, and options.

Ritchken, Peter. *Derivatives Markets: Theory, Strategy, and Applications*. New York: HarperCollins, 1996.

   This rigorous textbook provides a comprehensive review of futures and all types of options.

ENDNOTES

[1] Bank for International Settlements, 66th Annual Report, June 1998, Table VIII.6, p. 156.

[2] See C. Sutcliffe, *Stock Index Futures* (London: Thomson Business Press, 1993).

[3] For a discussion of commissions, margins, and how option transactions are taxed, see John Hull, *Introduction to Options and Futures*, 2nd ed. (Englewood Cliffs, NJ: Prentice-Hall, 1995), 187–92. Or see Don M. Chance, *An Introduction to Derivatives*, 3rd ed. (Orlando, FL: Dryden Press, 1995), 50–51 and 58–61.

[4] See Ravi Jagannathan, "Call Options and the Risk of the Underlying Security," *Journal of Financial Economics* 13 (September, 1984).

[5] See Rakesh Bali and Gailen L. Hite, "Ex-Dividend Day Stock Price Behavior: Discreteness Or Tax-Induced Clienteles?" *Journal Of Financial Economics* 47, no. 2 (February 1998): 127–59.

[6] Additional information about warrants is available. For an empirical investigation of issuers' using warrants as compensation to underwriters, see Chee K. Ng and Richard L. Smith, "Determinants of Contract Choice: The Use of Warrants to Compensate Underwriters of Seasoned Equity Issues," *Journal of Finance* 51, no. 1 (March 1996): 363–80. For an argument that adding warrants to the capital structure reduces the systematic risk of equity, see Michael C. Ehrhardt and Ronald E. Shrieves, "The Impact of Warrants and Convertible Securities on the Systematic Risk of Common Equity," *Financial Review* 30, no. 4 (November 1995): 843–56. For an empirical examination of stock price reactions to announced calls, see L. Paige Fields and William T. Moore, "Equity Valuation Effects of Forced Warrant Exercise," *Journal of Financial Research* 18, no. 2 (summer 1995): 157–70. An extension of the binomial model of Cox, Ross, and Rubinstein is developed by Kaushik I. Amin and James N. Bodurtha Jr., "Discrete-Time Valuation of American Options with Stochastic Interest Rates," *Review of Financial Studies* 8, no. 1 (spring 1995): 193–234. For an empirical comparison of models, see Joseph W. Kremer and Rodney L. Roenfeldt, "Warrant Pricing: Jump-Diffusion vs. Black-Scholes," *Journal of Financial and Quantitative Analysis* 28, no. 2 (June 1993): 255–72.

[7] For more information about warrants, see Michael Crouhy and Dan Galai, "Common Errors in the Valuation of Warrants and Options on Firms with Warrants," *Financial Analyst Journal* 47, no. 5 (1991): 89–90. Also see Beni Lauterbach and Paul Schultz, "Pricing Warrants: An Empirical Study of the Black-Scholes Model and Its Alternatives," *Journal of Finance* 45, no. 4 (1990): 1181–1209.

[8] For more details about callable corporate bonds, see Richard S. Wilson and Frank J. Fabozzi, *The New Corporate Bond Market* (New Hope, PA: Fabozzi Publishing Company, 1996).

[9] Convertibles have been well researched. See Anthony K. Byrd, William T. Moore, "On the Information Content of Calls of Convertible Securities," *Journal of Business* 69, no. 1 (January 1996): 89–101. See L. Paige Fields, Eric L. Mais, and William T. Moore, "Conversion-Forcing Security Calls: Wealth Transfers Revisited," *International Review of Economics and Finance* 4, no. 1 (1995): 17–27. See Paul Asquith, "Convertible Bonds Are Not Called Late," *Journal of Finance* 50, no. 4 (September 1995): 1275–89. See Wallace N. Davidson III, John L. Glascock, and Thomas V. Schwarz, "Signaling with Convertible Debt," *Journal of Financial and Quantitative Analysis* 30, no. 3 (September 1995): 425–40. See P. Jalan and Adesi G. Barone, "Equity Financing and Corporate Convertible Bond Policy," *Journal of Banking and Finance* 19, no. 2 (May 1995): 187–206.

Warrants, Embedded Options, and Convertibles

This appendix explores options that are traded less actively than the options discussed in the chapter as well as valuable embedded options that are never traded.

Warrants

Stock purchase warrants, or simply, warrants, are call options to buy shares of common stock. Warrants are like calls in that they are options to buy a specified number of shares at a specified exercise price during some specified time period. Newly created warrants are usually not sold; they are given by the issuing corporation as attachments to a new issue of bonds or preferred stock. The warrants "sweeten" the new issue and make it easier to sell.[6]

Warrant Prices

The *exercise price of a warrant* is the amount the warrant owner must pay to purchase a specified number of the issuer's shares. The *intrinsic value of a warrant* equals the difference between the stock's market price and the warrant option's exercise price on a per share basis, with this difference multiplied by the number of shares of common stock that can be obtained with one warrant. If the difference is a negative number, the intrinsic value of a warrant equals zero:

$$\binom{\text{Intrinsic value}}{\text{of a warrant}} = \text{MAX}\left[0, \left\{\left(\binom{\text{Price of}}{\text{stock}} - \binom{\text{Exercise}}{\text{price}}\right)\binom{\text{Number}}{\text{of shares}}\right\}\right] \qquad \textbf{(9A-1)}$$

PRICING A WARRANT   **EXAMPLE**

A warrant entitling its owner to buy two shares of stock at an exercise price of $50 per share when the market price of the stock is $60 per share has an intrinsic value of $20 per warrant:

$$\binom{\text{Intrinsic value}}{\text{of a warrant}} = \text{MAX}\left[0, \left\{\left(\binom{\text{Price of}}{\text{stock, }\$60} - \binom{\text{Exercise}}{\text{price, }\$50}\right)\binom{\text{Number of}}{\text{shares, }2}\right\}\right]$$

$$= \text{MAX}[0, \{\$20\}] = \$20 \qquad \textbf{(9A-1a)}$$

Comparing the formula above for the intrinsic value of a warrant with the formula for the intrinsic value of a call, Eqn. 9-3, reveals that they are identical if the warrant entitles its owner to one share of the underlying stock. This means that Figure 9-4A for calls is also appropriate for warrants. Furthermore, the six determinants of the premiums for puts and calls on stocks discussed earlier (see pages 256–260) impacts the prices of warrants the same way they effect call premiums.

There are three minor differences between call options and warrants:

◆ Calls and warrants have different writers. The corporation that issues the underlying stock also issues (writes) the warrant, but external third parties write calls.

◆ Warrants dilute the voting power and earnings per share for common stock investors who own a stock when warrants are exercised. Dilution occurs because exercised warrants create new shares of outstanding common stock. The new shares dilute the corporation's earnings per share, cash dividends per share, per share stock price, and the previous owners' proportion of corporate ownership (control via voting).

◆ If the number of shares of stock for each warrant does not equal 1, the correspondence between the price of the underlying stock and the warrant's price (premium) can differ from the one-to-one correspondence that exists for calls.

Warrants are usually listed separately and traded in the same stock exchange as the underlying stock.

The Warrant Agreement

The terms of a warrant are specified in detail in a legal contract called the **warrant agreement.** Most warrants may be exercised at any time within a specified life of between 5 to 15 years. A few warrants have perpetual lives, and some may be exercised only at specific times.

Nondetachable warrants cannot be separated from their associated securities. But *detachable warrants,* which are the most popular, may be actively traded as independent securities.[7]

Callable Bonds Have Embedded Options

Corporations or governments that issued bonds with high coupon rates usually want to try to pay off these high-cost debts as soon as possible. A popular way to prematurely retire an issue of bonds is to insert a call provision in the issue's indenture contract. This **embedded call option** gives the bonds' issuer the option to call in (redeem) the bonds before their maturity date.[8]

When exercised, these calls are usually detrimental to the bond investors. That is because the investors will usually have their principal returned to them at a time when all alternative investments offer disadvantageously low rates of interest. To induce bond investors to buy bonds that have an embedded call provision, bond issuers typically pay interest rates on callable bonds that are 50 to 100 basis points (BPs) more than the rates on equivalent bonds that are not callable. Because bond prices and bond interest rates are inversely related, this means that callable bonds are worth a few dollars less than noncallable bonds that are equivalent is every other respect. Eqn. 9A-2 shows how the price of a callable bond can be resolved into two separate components that can be valued independently.

$$\begin{pmatrix} \text{Price of} \\ \text{callable} \\ \text{bond} \end{pmatrix} = \begin{pmatrix} \text{Price of} \\ \text{equivalent} \\ \text{noncallable} \\ \text{bond} \end{pmatrix} - \begin{pmatrix} \text{Call premium} \\ \text{on embedded option} \\ \text{in the bond} \end{pmatrix} \qquad \text{(9A-2)}$$

The call option premium is deducted from the price of the equivalent noncallable bond because bond investors will pay lower prices (require higher interest rates) for bonds that might be called away from them under disadvantageous market conditions.

Issuers of callable bonds not only give their investors price discounts equal to the value of the call option premium that is embedded in the bonds' prices; they also pay for the call privilege in other ways. Indenture contracts typically provide one or more of the following protective provisions to induce investors to buy callable bonds:

1. The bond issuer is required to wait several years after the bonds' initial public offering (IPO) before exercising its option to call.
2. The bond issuer can exercise the embedded call option only at prespecified call dates during the life of the bond.
3. The bond issuer is required to pay a (penalty-like) call price that is commonly 3% to 5% above the bond's face value if the bonds are retired prematurely. The indenture contract is written so the **call premium** typically declines as the bond issue's expiration date draws near.

Convertible Securities

Convertible securities also contain embedded call options. **Convertible preferred stocks** and **convertible bonds** grant their buyers the option to exchange the stock or bond for another security, usually the common stock of the corporation that issued the convertible securities. Occasionally a convertible bond can be convertible into the issuer's preferred stock.*

Convertible securities can be viewed as a combination of a nonconvertible security and an **embedded call option** on the issuer's stock. As a result, the price of a convertible security equals the sum of the two components:

$$\begin{pmatrix} \text{Price of} \\ \text{convertible} \\ \text{security} \end{pmatrix} = \begin{pmatrix} \text{Price of equivalent} \\ \text{nonconvertible} \\ \text{security} \end{pmatrix} + \begin{pmatrix} \text{Call premium} \\ \text{on the call} \\ \text{issuer's stock} \end{pmatrix} \qquad \text{(9A-3)}$$

Eqn. 9A-3 shows that convertible securities sell at prices that are slightly above the prices of equivalent nonconvertible securities.** The embedded call options are nondetachable; they cannot be traded independently. Most convertible securities are also callable. The buyer of a *callable convertible* has essentially purchased a normal bond or preferred stock and a call option on the issuer's stock, while selling the issuer a call option to redeem the nonconvertible security—all at once.[9] These three components are reflected in the price of a convertible that is callable, as shown in Eqn. 9A-4:

$$\begin{pmatrix} \text{Price of} \\ \text{callable} \\ \text{convertible} \\ \text{security} \end{pmatrix} = \begin{pmatrix} \text{Price of equivalent} \\ \text{nonconvertible} \\ \text{security} \end{pmatrix} + \begin{pmatrix} \text{Call premium} \\ \text{on the call} \\ \text{issuer's stock} \end{pmatrix} - \begin{pmatrix} \text{Call premium} \\ \text{on an equivalent} \\ \text{nonconvertible} \end{pmatrix} \text{(9A-4)}$$

---

* If the country in which the issuer of a convertible security is domiciled treats conversions as a taxable event, that tax law discourages the use of convertible securities by residents of that country. Under U.S. tax law the conversion is not a taxable exchange.

** Some writers claim that the issuers of convertible bonds had a low cost of capital (obtained a "free lunch") because convertible bonds paid lower coupon rates than nonconvertibles, had fewer protective provisions to restrict the issuer, and had a conversion (exercise) price that was above the current stock price. This is a misconception that fails to recognize that the cost of capital for a convertible bond equals the actual interest expense less the premium the convertible investors paid for the embedded call option.

THE COMPONENT VALUES OF THE BLOUGH CORPORATION'S CALLABLE CONVERTIBLE CORPORATE BOND

While considering investing in bonds issued by the Blough Corporation, Ralph learned that none of the bonds have been traded in over 2 years. Because of this illiquidity, Ralph must formulate his own estimate of the bonds' value to determine if they are under- or overpriced. His research reveals that Blough competes with Craig Incorporated, and that the two companies are very similar in many respects.

Craig has noncallable, nonconvertible bonds outstanding with an 11% coupon rate and 6 years remaining until they mature. Blough also has bonds that have 6 years remaining until they expire and that pay a coupon rate of 11%. But, Blough's bonds differ from Craig's in three respects. Blough's bonds are: (1) callable by the issuer; (2) each bond is convertible into one share of Blough's common stock at the investor's option; and (3) Craig's bonds are traded more actively than Blough's bonds.

Ralph has decided to use the "building block" approach suggested by Eqn. 9A-4. He begins by noting that Craig's noncallable, nonconvertible bonds with a $100 face value are currently selling at $101. Then he notes that long-term call options on Blough's stock are selling for premiums of $4 per share at the Chicago Board of Trade. Discussions with a bond analyst at Salomon Smith Barney in New York City lead Ralph to conclude the interest rate call on Blough's bonds is worth $2 per bond. Combining these components leads Ralph to conclude that Blough's inactive bonds are worth $103 apiece:*

$$\begin{pmatrix} \text{Price of} \\ \text{convertible} \\ \text{security, \$103} \end{pmatrix} = \begin{pmatrix} \text{Price of an} \\ \text{equivalent} \\ \text{nonconvertible,} \\ \$101 \end{pmatrix} + \begin{pmatrix} \text{Call premium} \\ \text{on issuer's} \\ \text{stock, \$4} \end{pmatrix} - \begin{pmatrix} \text{Call premium} \\ \text{on an equivalent} \\ \text{nonconvertible,} \\ \$2 \end{pmatrix}$$

Ralph decides to give his bond broker a bid of $100 for the bond and raise his bid a little if necessary.

---

* Some financial intermediaries are legally prohibited from making equity investments, presumably because the equities might be too risky. Some financial intermediaries would prefer to make some carefully selected equity investments that are more profitable than bonds. As fate would have it, bank examiners, insurance company inspectors, and other governmental regulators frequently consider a convertible bond to be a bond rather than an equity investment. Thus, convertible bonds provide the additional advantage of providing financial intermediaries a chance to earn equity rates of return without violating legal restrictions against equity investing that might otherwise encumber them.

PART 2

INVESTMENT
INDEXES

CREATING PRICE INDEXES

Price indexes are designed to summarize the behavior of market prices. The U.S. government's consumer price index (CPI), for example, is based on a shopping basket of 300 heterogeneous goods purchased by urban consumers. The CPI is primarily used to measure inflation in the United States. Standard & Poor's 500 Stocks Composite Index (S&P500) is a well-known stock price index computed from the market prices of 500 stocks issued by large U.S. corporations. The S&P500 index is often used to represent the price of a typical U.S. common stock. Government policymakers and investors use indexes of consumer prices and stock prices to gauge inflation, get a feel for the stock market, and help them make economic policies and decisions.

Government agencies, banks, and financial service corporations maintain thousands of price indicators to track stock prices, bond prices, commodity prices, foreign exchange prices, mortgage prices, options' prices, futures' prices, and other prices.* For example, hundreds of market indexes are continuously updated in the U.S. bonds alone.[1]

This chapter examines the construction of a few popular price indexes. Chapter 11 presents statistics that summarize decades of market data from stock price, bond price, and consumer price indexes. It would take years of experience to become aware of the information that can be obtained quickly from the summary statistics in Chapter 11. Chapter 12 reviews financial products like index funds, index options, and index futures that have become very popular with investors and are based on security price indexes. Chapter 13 introduces asset allocation, which is based on the comparison of different investment indexes. Before proceeding to these topics, however, we start by considering the first principles of sampling and index construction.

---

* The June 9, 1997 issue of *Pensions and Investments,* a biweekly financial newspaper published by Crain Communications in Chicago, contained 16 single-spaced pages listing details about approximately 3,000 indexes of stock markets, bond markets, markets from various countries, ad infinitum.

CONSTRUCTING A STOCK MARKET INDICATOR

A stock market **average** is a weighted or unweighted average stock price. The Dow Jones Industrial Average (DJIA) is a well-known example. Unlike an average price, a price *index number* is a pure number that is void of dollar values or other units of measurement. Indexes are frequently more useful than averages because index numbers are designed to avoid distortions.

Index numbers are usually constructed from a base date value that is 100, 10, or 1. Some past year (average of several years) is selected as the **base year (base period)** to serve as the index's starting point and to impart perspective to a time-series of index numbers. The S&P500 index, for instance, is expressed relative to the average market value during its 3-year base period of 1941 through 1943. The average value of the index during these years was set equal to an arbitrary base value of 10. The S&P500 was constructed in this manner so that when the index was fluctuating above and below the value of 400 in 1991–92, for example, market analysts could easily determine that market prices were (400/10 =) 40 times higher than 50 years before.

In addition to being used to gain time perspective, security price indicators are frequently used as a **standard of comparison** or **benchmark** for evaluating alternative investments. For example, consider two facts. First, the S&P500 is constructed from a representative selection of stocks that is changed infrequently. Second, its value increased at an average rate of 19.3% per year during the 1990s decade.* These facts imply that unless a mutual fund you are considering appreciated more than 19.3% during that decade, that mutual fund's investment managers may not be as skillful as their advertisements suggest. Comparisons like this are useful for rapidly evaluating the performance of investments.

First Principles for Constructing an Indicator of Market Prices

Several factors should be considered when selecting an existing index or designing a new index.

Sample Size. In most cases, the sample should be large enough to be a statistically significant representation of the population of interest. Larger samples tend to give clearer indications of the underlying population. For instance, if you wanted to know how the citizens of the United States liked their current president, you could survey 100, or 1 million, or 100 million citizens. If your sample is too large it might be uneconomical. Or if you are only interested in a narrowly defined group, surveying a large sampler could be irrelevant. Investors studying automobile manufacturer's stocks will not be interested in a small-cap stock price index, for example, because small-cap indexes are based on large samples of stocks issued by small firms and most automobile manufacturers are not small firms.

The disadvantage of small samples is that they are subject to greater **sampling errors** than larger samples are. But, it is not necessary to have a large sample size if the elements in the sample are highly positively correlated. For example, U.S. Treasury bonds that have similar maturities are homogeneous and their market movements are highly positively correlated. The price (or interest rate) movements of one T-bond can reflect the movements of all T-bonds with similar maturities; it would be superfluous to gather data on a large sample of T-bonds that all had similar maturities.

Representativeness. A sample should exemplify the population of interest. This means that all the securities in a representative sample should possess characteristics of interest.

---

* From January 1990 through December 1999 inclusive, the arithmetic mean rate of return was 19.3% at an annual rate if all cash dividends were reinvested and no commissions and no income taxes were paid.

As was true concerning the size of the sample, this guideline about representativeness need not be followed if the elements of the sample are highly positively correlated, or if a narrowly defined index is being constructed. A sample of only one security can be highly representative if the population of interest is made up of highly homogeneous securities. Or, if a substantial portion of the total risk in a securities market is systematic, it will be easy to construct an index that is representative of that market. The S&P500 index and the Dow Jones Industrial Average (DJIA) are relevant. The DJIA is constructed from a small sample of 30 blue chip stocks. In spite of its tiny sample size, the DJIA is highly positively correlated with the S&P500 index of 500 more heterogeneous stocks because the U.S. stock market contains a lot of bull- and bear-market risk that is systematic and undiversifiable.

Weighting. The components in a price indicator are usually assigned weights. A security's weight in a stock price index, for instance, might be made proportional to the total market value of the firm's outstanding shares. The S&P500 index uses such a **market value-weighting** system because it reflects the investment opportunities that exist. For instance, if the market value of Microsoft's common stock comprised 2.9% of the aggregate market value of all 500 common stock used in the S&P500 index, as shown below, then Microsoft would be given a weight of 2.9% in the S&P500 index.

$$\frac{\text{Aggregate market value of Microsoft common stock}}{\text{Aggregate market value of 500 common stocks}} = \left(\begin{array}{c} \text{Microsoft's weight} \\ \text{in S\&P500 index} \end{array} \right)$$

Equal weighting the components in a price indicator achieves a different goal. Equal weights represent equal likelihood of selecting each security in the indicator. Equal weighting is an appropriate way to represent the behavior of investors that have zero skill and, as a result, select stocks irrationally or randomly. Some critics argue that equal weighting gives disproportionately large weights to the securities issued by small companies, because the securities issued by the small companies are given the same weights as securities issued by huge corporations. Equal weighting ignores the fact that the larger companies actually provide more investment opportunities (aggregate market value) in the market.

Either the market-value-weighting or equal-weighting system would provide a good standard of comparison for evaluating the performance of money managers claiming to be expert. Other weighting systems can be used to reflect other characteristics that might be desired in a sample.

Convenient Units. An index should be stated in *convenient units* that facilitate answering questions. Index numbers are usually more convenient to use than average values. The S&P500 index and the Consumers Price Index (CPI) are examples of pure index numbers that are free from unit distortions.

Unlike price indexes, price averages may be distorted by *scale problems* that arise when making large-scale versus small-scale comparisons. For example, consider comparing last year's price gains from all stocks with prices below $5 per share with last year's price gains from all stocks that have prices over $100 per share. This comparison could be simpler and more meaningful if it were made in terms of index numbers or percentages that were void of dollar dimensions.

Uniform Definition. In order to make meaningful comparisons over different periods of time, there should never be a change in the way a price index is computed. In addition, if a popular way to define the indexed quantity exists, that popular methodology should not be corrupted. For example, **total returns (TR)** from stocks or bonds are widely understood to include cash flows from cash dividends and coupon interest, respectively. Returns from stocks or bonds that do not include this cash flow income should not be labeled "total returns"; these returns might be called "percentage price changes" or "returns from price changes." Furthermore, if the returns from stocks or bonds in a price indicator are computed without their cash flow income during one span of time, the cash flow income should not be included when computing returns over other sample periods.

Economical. Computational costs are a shrinking consideration because most clerical work has been computerized. However, economies in gathering and updating data can provide arguments in favor of using small samples. Small samples can offer worthwhile economies in some cases: when data gathering is costly (illiquid foreign markets), the population being observed is located in inaccessible areas (CPI data from all 50 states in the United States), the elements in the population are all highly positively correlated (U.S. Treasury bonds), or some of the data might contain errors (banana prices from a "banana republic" during a period when it was ruled by a crooked dictator).

Timeliness. Ideally, a price indicator will reflect all changes in the underlying prices immediately. A price indicator can only be timely if all components in the indicator are bought and sold continuously. For instance, some price indicators for real estate are not timely because of two problems. First, some real estate price indicators are based on appraised values instead of prices from actual sales, and appraisers tend to understate (smooth) changes in market prices. Second, if a real estate price indicator is based on actual sales prices, that indicator is probably not timely because years typically transpire between sale dates for most pieces of real estate.

Descriptive Title. A price indicator should bear a title that suggests what it represents unambiguously. A misleading title may cause people to use the indicator inappropriately.

Contrasting Two Well-Known Stock Market Indicators

Dow Jones and Standard & Poor's corporations compile and publish dozens of stock market indicators on markets and market sectors around the world. S&P indexes are sold commercially by the Standard and Poor's Corporation. Dow Jones averages are published by Dow Jones & Company, Inc. in its newspapers, *The Wall Street Journal* and *Barron's*. It is instructive to contrast the Dow Jones Industrial Average (DJIA) with the Standard and Poor's 500 Stocks Composite Average (S&P500), since they are both widely used price indicators of the U.S. market for common stocks.

The Dow Jones Industrial Average (DJIA). In 1884 one of the founders of Dow Jones & Company, Charles Dow, started publishing the daily average of eleven stocks in *The Wall Street Journal*; it was called the Dow Jones Industrial Average (DJIA). In 1928 the sample size reached 30, and it remains there today. The companies that Mr. Dow selected for the DJIA were not a representative sample of the stocks that were being traded at that time: He selected stocks that were all issued by large, successful firms. General Electric was in the original DJIA and is still in the average over a century later. Today the staff at Dow Jones selects other large, old, successful firms like Coca-Cola, Exxon, and Boeing to be in the DJIA.

The Dow Jones Industrial Average is a misleading name. It would be more appropriate to call the DJIA the "Dow Jones Blue-Chip Stocks Average" for two reasons. First, small-size, medium-size, and new firms never appeared in the DJIA. Second, some people would say American Telephone and Telegraph (AT&T), one of the DJIA component stocks, is more of a utility stock than an industrial stock. Numeric problems also flaw the DJIA.

The DJIA Divisor. Stock and splits dividends were introduced in Chapter 5 (page 113) and considered in more detail in Chapter 8 (page 200). Both discussions show how changes in the unit of account (1) have a predictable impact on the prices of equity shares and (2) do not change the total market value of all shares outstanding. In this chapter we reconsider stock dividends and splits, because of the way they affect some poorly constructed stock price indicators.

In 1928 the original 30 stocks that comprised the DJIA were simply summed up and that total value was divided by a *divisor* of 30 to obtain the DJIA's value. The frist three columns of Table 10-1 illustrate Dow Jones's original computational methodology with a hypothetical two-stock average that has a divisor of 2.

Stock Splits and the DJIA Divisor.   Not long after the DJIA was started, some of the 30 securities underwent stock splits and some paid stock dividends. To see the problem that such changes in the unit of account can cause for the DJIA, reconsider our simplified two-stock Dow Jones example. Suppose that stock X in Table 10-1 underwent a 2-for-1 split that cut its price from $50 to $25 and doubled the number of shares outstanding (from 10 to 20 million shares). The aggregate market value of all of Corporation X's shares remained unchanged.* As a result of these normal stock price reaction, the average initial price of the two-stock portfolio of X and Y from Table 10-1 increases from [($50 + $10)/2 =] $30 to [($45 + $20)/2 =] $32.50 if the divisor remains at 2. Dow Jones did not want to have an increase from 30 to 32.50 in their stock price average partly because one of the stocks had a stock split.

How could Dow Jones handle its stock dividend and split problem? Perhaps the creators of the DJIA performed an algebra like the one below in search of a new divisor that would keep discontinuities from stock dividends and splits from distorting their stock price average:

$$\left(\frac{\text{Average post-split price with divisor of 2}}{\text{New divisor}}\right) = \left(\begin{array}{c}\text{Average presplit}\\\text{price with divisor of 2}\end{array}\right)$$

$$\left(\frac{\$32.50}{\text{New divisor}}\right) = \$30 \;\rightarrow\; \text{Therefore, the new divisor is } 1.083333$$

In 1928 such calculations might have lead the Dow Jones officials to think they should adjust for stock splits by creating a new divisor. The algebra above shows that replacing the old divisor of 2 from Table 10-1 with the new divisor of 1.08333 in Table 10-2 will keep the stock split from causing a disparity in their initial average prices.** The initial two-stock average computed in Table 10-2 after the stock split has a value of 30, which is identical to the initial two-stock average computed in Table 10-1 before the stock split. In contrast, the two-stock average would not have risen to [($45 + $20)/2 =] $32.50 if the old divisor of 2 was used with the post-split prices.

Over the years the 30 DJIA stocks have undergone various stock splits and stock dividends that changed the DJIA's divisor repeatedly. Each time a stock split occurred, the divisor was reduced to a new value that kept the value of the DJIA unchanged immediately after the split. By 1999 the DJIA's divisor was down to a value of 0.021825395, and it is still shrinking.

The DJIA Points. Stock dividends and splits have drastically altered the divisor used to compute the DJIA. This divisor is an important part of the weighting system that determines the

---

* To see this 2-for-1 stock split more concisely, let *P* represent one stock's price per share and let *N* equal the number of shares of that stock that are outstanding. After the split, the right-hand side of the equation below emerges, but it always equals the value on the left.

   Value before the split = $(P) \times (N) = [(P/2) \times (2N)]$ = Value after the split

   The algebra above shows that the value of an investment in 1 share is unchanged by a 2-for-1 stock split or, equivalently, a 100% stock dividend.

** Every time one of the stocks in the DJIA splits or has a cash dividend in excess of 5%, a new divisor is computed with the formula used here.

TABLE 10-1   Calculating a Two-Stock Average Before a Stock Split

Two Stocks' Data	Start of Period Price	End of Period Price	Millions of Shares Outstanding	Share Weights	Starting Value, $ millions	Ending Value, $ millions
Stock X	$50	$45	10	10/25=.4	$500	$450
Stock Y	$10	$20	15	15/25=.6	$150	$300
Totals:	$60	$65	25	1.0	$650	$750
Average prices:	$60/2=$30	$65/2=$32.50				
Percent change:	$32.50/$30= 1.083 = 1 + 8.3%					
	The presplit average price rose 8.3% using a divisor of 2.					

TABLE 10-2   Calculating a Two-Stock Average After Stock X Is Split[a]

Two Stocks' Data	Initial Stock Price	Ending Stock Price	Millions of Shares Outstanding	Share Weights	Initial Value, $ millions	Ending Value, $ millions
Stock X	$25	$22.50	20	20/35 = .571	$500	$450
Stock Y	$10	$20.00	15	15/35 = .429	$150	$300
Totals:	$35	$42.50	35	1.0	$650	$750
Average prices:	$35/1.083 = $32.31	$42.50/1.083= $39.24				
Percent change:	$39.24/$32.31= 1.214 = 1 + 21.4%					
	The postsplit averaged price rose 21.4%, based on the new divisor of 1.083333					

[a]The Standard & Poor's indexes are computed as shown in the four columns on the right, so stock splits have no effect on these indexes.

value of the DJIA. Instead of assigning equal weights for each stock, as it did in 1928, the DJIA's price-weighting system gives heavier weights to the highest-priced stocks. The prices of the 30 stocks are added up and divided by the most recent tiny value for the divisor to produce a unit of measure Dow Jones arbitrarily calls a **point.**

The DJIA fluctuated from 3,000 up to 11,000 "points" during the 1990s. Dow Jones has suggested that each DJIA "point" represents a few pennies of stock price. This explanation is not very helpful.

Standard & Poor's 500 Stocks Composite Index (S&P500) Standard & Poor's Corporation is a financial information company that developed its first stock market indicators in 1923. The prices of 233 stocks were compiled by hand and used to create 26 industry indexes. By 1941 the list of 233 stocks had grown to 416 stocks, and they were used to create 72 industrial indexes. In 1957 the sample of 416 stocks was expanded to 500 stocks, and they were used to create the Standard & Poor's 500 Stocks Composite Index, which was retabulated by computer every minute throughout each trading day.

S&P500 Weights. The S&P500 employs a market-value weighting system that assigns each security in the S&P500 a weight that is proportional to the market value of all that issue's outstanding shares. Such market value weights correspond to the investment opportunities that exist in the U.S. stock market. This characteristic makes the S&P500 a useful standard of comparison for evaluating the performance of other U.S. common stock investments. For instance, what if someone asks: "Can Fidelity's Magellan Fund outperform picking stocks with an unaimed dart?" The S&P500 index would provide an appropriate standard of comparison to answer this question. The DJIA could also be used for comparison, but because it only contains blue chip stocks, and because it employs a weighting system that does not correspond to Magellan's investments, it would not be as appropriate as the S&P500 index.

The S&P500 is calculated by multiplying the price of each share of stock by the number of shares outstanding to obtain the aggregate market value of all the issues in the index. The value of the S&P500 index at time t is calculated as shown below.

$$SP500_t = \frac{\sum_{i=1}^{500} P_{i,t}N_{i,t}}{\sum_{i=1}^{500} P_{i,B}N_{i,B}} \times 10 = \frac{P_{1,t}N_{1,t} + P_{2,t}N_{2,t} + \cdots P_{500,t}N_{500,t}}{P_{1,B}N_{1,B} + P_{2,B}N_{2,B} + \cdots + P_{500,B}N_{500,B}} \times 10$$

P_{it} represents the market price per share and N_{it} stands for the number of shares outstanding for the ith stock at time period t; the index is calculated over $i = 1, 2, \ldots 500$ issues; and, P_{iB} and N_{iB} denote the market price per share and number of shares of the ith stock used in the computations during the 3-year 1941–43 base (B) period.

The formula above makes it possible to adjust the S&P500 index for stock splits, stock dividends, and/or rights offerings without changing the weighting of a particular issue in the index, or without disturbing the index's value. The simplified three-stock example in Table 10-3 clarifies the computations.

Let us assume that the statisticians at Standard & Poor's made two policy decisions. First, they decided to let Day 1 be the base period. Second, they decided to equate the three-stock index's value to a base index number of 10.

$$\frac{\text{Aggregate market value on day 1}}{\text{Base period's aggregate market value}} \times (\text{Base value}) = \text{Value S\&P three-stock index on day 1}$$

$$\frac{\$350,000,000}{\$350,000,000} \times 10 = (1) \times (10) = 10 = \text{Value S\&P three-stock index on day 1 (base date)}$$

Next, suppose that on Day 2 the prices of stocks X, Y, and Z each increased 10%, to the prices shown in Table 10-4.

TABLE 10-3 Calculation of S&P Three-Stock Index for Base Period (Day 1)

	Share Price	Outstanding Shares	Total Market Value
Stock X	$40	1,000,000	$ 40,000,000
Stock Y	$30	9,000,000	$270,000,000
Stock Z	$20	2,000,000	$ 40,000,000
		Aggregate Value:	$350,000,000

TABLE 10-4 Calculation of S&P Three-Stock Index for Day 2

	Share Price	Outstanding Shares	Total Market Value
Stock X	$44	1,000,000	$ 44,000,000
Stock Y	$33	9,000,000	$297,000,000
Stock Z	$22	2,000,000	$ 44,000,000
		Aggregate Value:	$385,000,000

TABLE 10-5 Calculation of S&P Three-Stock Index After Stock X Splits on Day 2

	Share Price	Outstanding Shares	Total Market Value
Stock X	$22	2,000,000	$ 44,000,000
Stock Y	$33	9,000,000	$297,000,000
Stock Z	$22	2,000,000	$ 44,000,000
		Aggregate Value:	$385,000,000

The value of the S&P three-stock index on Day 2 is computed as:

$$\frac{\text{Aggregate market value on day } t}{\text{Base period's aggregate market value}} \times (\text{Base value}) = \text{Value S\&P three-stock index on day } t$$

$$\frac{\$385,000,000}{\$350,000,000} \times 10 = (1.1) \times (10) = 11 = \text{Value S\&P three-stock index on day 2}$$

The example above shows that from Day 1 to Day 2 the value of the S&P three-stock index increased 10%, from 10 to 11. Cash dividends are not included in the S&P indexes, but all stock dividends and splits are included.

S&P500 and Stock Splits.   Next, let us suppose that on day 2 stock X splits 2-for-1. After the split the price of stock X falls to half the value that was shown in Table 10-4. In addition, the split also doubles the number of shares outstanding, as shown in Table 10-5.

Comparing Tables 10-4 and 10-5 shows that the aggregate market value of stocks X, Y, and Z remains unchanged at $385,000,000 after stock X is split. Therefore, the value of the S&P three-stock index will be 11 immediately before and immediately after the split in stock X. Stock splits do not affect the S&P500 index.

Representative Sample.   In 1996 the S&P500 index's 500 common stocks included 458 NYSE-listed issuers, 6 AMEX stocks, and 36 OTC stocks. The index components change slightly each year. The 500 stocks in the S&P500 equal about 17% of the stocks listed on the NYSE. The S&P500 includes no small stocks and, as a result, the aggregate market value of this sample of 500 large stocks exceeds half of the aggregate market value of all stocks listed on the NYSE and AMEX. In spite of the fact that neither the DJIA nor the S&P500 include any small stocks, the S&P500 is a more representative of diversified common stock investing in the United States than the DJIA. The S&P500 contains all 30 stocks in the DJIA, plus hundreds of other stocks. The S&P500 price index is the large stocks index in Figure 2-1 (page 23) and Table 2-1 (page 24) of Chapter 2.

Timeliness.   The fact that the S&P500 index has 16.6 times more stocks than the DJIA causes the S&P500 index to be slightly less timely than the DJIA. Although the stocks in the S&P500 index are actively traded, some of the component stocks are not traded quite as actively as the 30 blue-chip stocks in the DJIA. As a result, the S&P500 index sometimes reflects the turns in the market a minute sooner than the DJIA. Some active stock market traders value the superior timeliness of the DJIA.

MAINTAINING A PRICE INDEX

It is necessary to revise most market price indicators. The U.S. government takes a survey of consumer spending patterns approximately every 10 years and revises the "market basket" of goods and services that make up the CPI. Stock market indicators experience problems that necessitate more frequent revisions.

Three common problems that require revisions in stock market indicators are:

1. Adjustments for stock dividends and stock splits
2. Changing the number of stocks in the sample
3. Making substitutions to replace securities that become unsatisfactory.

The way these problems affect the DJIA and the S&P500 index are considered next.

Maintaining the DJIA

The way that stock dividends and splits are reflected in the divisor of the DJIA was illustrated in Table 10-2. As a result of the DJIA's price-per-share-weighting procedure, high-priced stocks are more important than stocks that experience constant or decreasing prices. There is no rational advantage to this construction.[2]

Sample Size.   The DJIA has been computed from 30 stocks since 1928. This small sample size permits a few dominant stocks to exert an undue influence on the average. It is surprising that the widespread use of electronic stock price quotations and the falling cost of electronic computations has not motivated Dow Jones to increase its sample size.

Substitutions.   There have been many substitutions in the 30 stocks that make up the DJIA since it was first published. One of the more interesting substitutions involved IBM's stock. IBM was *added* to the DJIA in 1932 and then *deleted* in 1939 in order to make room for American Telephone and Telegraph (ATT). The logic behind this substitution is murky; ATT is a utility stock and the DJIA is not an index of utility stocks. In 1979 IBM was once again *added* to the DJIA. More specifically, Chrysler and Esmark were deleted and replaced by IBM and Merck & Company in 1979. Dow Jones explained this change by saying that the two new stocks were more "blue-chip" than the two that were eliminated. In 1999 the first technology stocks, Microsoft and Intel, were substituted into the DJIA. Microsoft and Intel are also the first over-the-counter stocks ever included in the DJIA.

Maintaining the S&P500 Index

Stock Splits.   The S&P500 index is based on total market values to nullify changes in the unit of account in the indexed stocks. Since the S&P500 is computed from total market values, there is no need to adjust the S&P500 index because of stock dividends and splits.

Sample Size.   The S&P500 sample size has been constant since 1957. There has been no need to increase the sample size because the index adequately represents the stock prices of large U.S. corporations.

Additions and Deletions. Stocks are added or deleted from the S&P500 index when they are listed or delisted, disappear because of mergers or acquisitions, file for bankruptcy, or for other logical reasons.[3] In any event, substitutions in the S&P500 are of only modest importance because the sample is highly diverse and because of the small weight given to each individual stock.

Conclusions About DJIA and S&P500

By most criteria, the S&P500 is a better indicator of U.S. equity markets than the DJIA. But, as suggested earlier in this chapter, despite the different samples that make up the DJIA and the S&P500, and in spite of the aforementioned deficiencies in the DJIA, the DJIA is nevertheless highly positively correlated with the S&P500 index. As we will learn in the chapters that follow, this high positive correlation results from the large amount of undiversifiable risk that exists in the U.S. equity markets. As a result of the high positive correlation between the S&P500 and the DJIA, the painfully simple stock market average constructed by Dow Jones is almost as good an indicator as the respectable S&P500 index.

THE ONE-PERIOD RETURN FOR AN INDEX

Periodic values from a price index can be converted to *price relatives*.

$$\left(\begin{array}{c} \text{Price} \\ \text{relative} \end{array}\right) = \frac{\text{The value of the index in one time period}}{\text{The value of the index in the preceding time period}} = (1 + r) \qquad \textbf{(10-1)}$$

The *percentage change per time period*, denoted r, is embedded in the price relative. If Consumer Price Index (CPI) data is being analyzed, a positive r value is called the rate of inflation and a negative r value equals the rate of deflation. If stock market index data is being analyzed, a positive r value is called the rate of price appreciation and a negative r value is called the rate of price depreciation. The percentage change in an index per unit of time can be computed directly.

$$r = \frac{\left(\text{Value of the index in one time period}\right) - \left(\text{Value of the index in the preceding time period}\right)}{\text{Value of the index in the preceding time period}}$$

The percentage change in the index simply equals the price relative minus 1, $r = $ (Price relative) $- 1$.

The *total one-period rate of return* from a stock market index can be computed by adding the cash dividend income from the index to the change in the value of the index during the same holding period.

$$r = \frac{\left(\begin{array}{c}\text{Value of the index} \\ \text{in one time period}\end{array}\right) - \left(\begin{array}{c}\text{Value of the index in the} \\ \text{preceding time period}\end{array}\right) + \left(\begin{array}{c}\text{The index's cash dividend income} \\ \text{during the holding period}\end{array}\right)}{\text{Value of the index in the preceding time period}} \qquad \textbf{(10-2)}$$

Eqn. 10-2a isolates the cash dividend yield.

$$r = \frac{\left(\begin{array}{c}\text{Value of the index} \\ \text{in one time period}\end{array}\right) - \left(\begin{array}{c}\text{Value of the index in the} \\ \text{preceding time period}\end{array}\right)}{\text{Value of the index in the preceding time period}} + \left(\begin{array}{c}\text{The index's cash} \\ \text{dividend yield}\end{array}\right) \qquad \textbf{(10-2a)}$$

The 1994 closing value of the S&P500 index equals its 1995 opening value, which was 459.27. At the end of 1995 the S&P500 index closed at 615.93, for a gain of (615.93 − 459.27 =) 156.66 during 1995. The percentage change in the S&P500 index during 1995 was a highly bullish 34.11%.

$$r = \frac{\left(\begin{array}{c}\text{Value of S\&P500}\\\text{at end of 1994}\end{array}\right) - \left(\begin{array}{c}\text{Value of S\&P500}\\\text{at end of 1995}\end{array}\right)}{\text{Value of S\&P500 at end of 1994}} = \frac{615.93 - 459.27}{459.27} = 34.11\% \qquad \textbf{(10-2c)}$$

During 1995 the cash dividend yield of the S&P500 index was 3.4693%. Including the year's cash dividend income of 15.93 results in a total annual rate of return of 37.58% for 1995.

$$r = \frac{\left(\begin{array}{c}\text{Value of S\&P500}\\\text{at end of 1994}\end{array}\right) - \left(\begin{array}{c}\text{Value of S\&P500}\\\text{at end of 1995}\end{array}\right) + \left(\begin{array}{c}\text{1995 cash}\\\text{dividend}\\\text{income}\end{array}\right)}{\text{Value of S\&P500 at end of 1994}} = \frac{615.93 - 459.27 + 15.93}{459.27} = 37.58\%$$

$$\textbf{(10-2d)}$$

While 37.58% is a high rate of return, investors that earned 37.58% during 1995 did not do anything worthy of praise. An idiot who picked a diversified portfolio of stocks by throwing an unaimed dart could be expected to have earned 37.58% in 1995. What is noteworthy is that about 80% of the common stock mutual funds in United States earned less than 37.58% during 1995. This comparison highlights the fact that investment indexes can help investors discriminate between good and bad investments.

Some other total returns for the S&P500 index computed as above are:

Years	1926–94	1995	1996	1997	1998	1999
Year's total return from S&P500	NA	37.5%	23.1%	33.4%	28.6%	21.0%
Average annual total return	11.2%	The 1995–99 average was 28.6%.				

The 1926–94 average annual total return was 11.2%. A raging bull market started in U.S. stocks in 1995 and double-digit returns filled the rest of the decade; this internet stocks bubble is examined in Chapter 25. The 1995–99 average annual total return of 28.6% is substantially above the 1926–94 average annual total return of 11.2%. The large stocks index in Figure 2-1 and Table 2-1 from Chapter 2 is the S&P500 index used to compute these returns.

After one-period rates of return are computed, four investment statistics commonly used to describe them are:

◆ The expected return from Chapter 7's Eqn. 7-5

◆ The arithmetic average return from Chapter 2's Eqn. 2-6

◆ The variance (or standard deviation) of returns from Chapter 2's Eqns. 2-9 and 2-10

◆ The geometric mean return (GMR) introduced in Chapter 2's Eqn. 2-7 and discussed next

THE GEOMETRIC MEAN RETURN (GMR)

The geometric mean return (GMR) is an important rate of return measure that differs conceptually from the arithmetic average return, although they occasionally have the same numerical values. The **arithmetic mean return** is mathematically similar to the expected return; because both are additive sums that produce an average rate of return.* Unlike the arithmetic average return and the expected return, the **geometric mean return (GMR)** is a multiplicative quantity that equals the **time-weighted rate of return,** or a **compounded rate of return.** The geometric mean return is usually less than the expected (average) return, but occasionally the two are equal. The geometric mean return is never larger than the expected (average) return for the same investment. Eqn. 10-3 approximates the difference between the expected (average) return and the GMR.[4]

$$\begin{pmatrix} \text{Arithmetic} \\ \text{mean} \\ \text{return } (AMR) \end{pmatrix} \cong GMR + .5VAR(r) \qquad (10\text{-}3)$$

Eqn. 10-3 highlights the fact that the geometric mean return can equal the arithmetic average return only when there is zero risk (no variability of return).**

The GMR can be computed from price relatives or one-period rates of return from T consecutive time periods as shown in Eqn. 10-4:

$$[(1 + r_1)(1 + r_2)(1 + r_3) \ldots (1 + r_T)]^{1/T} = (1 + GMR) \qquad (10\text{-}4)$$

$$\left(\frac{P_1}{P_0}\right) \left(\frac{P_2}{P_1}\right) \left(\frac{P_3}{P_2}\right) \cdots \left(\frac{P_T}{P_{T-1}}\right) = \left(\frac{P_T}{P_0}\right) \qquad (10\text{-}4a)$$

$$\left(\frac{P_1}{P_0}\right) \left(\frac{P_2}{P_1}\right) \left(\frac{P_3}{P_2}\right) \cdots \left(\frac{P_T}{P_{T-1}}\right) = \left(\frac{P_T}{P_0}\right) \qquad (10\text{-}4b)$$

COMPUTING THE CORRECT AVERAGE RATE OF RETURN OVER TWO CONSECUTIVE YEARS

EXAMPLE

If the price of an asset rose from \$40 to \$60 during the year 2001 its rate of return was $r_{2001} = 50\%$. During 2002 if that same asset's price fell from \$60 to \$40 its rate of return was $r_{2002} = -33.33\%$. The asset's arithmetic average rate of return was [(50% − 33.33%)/2 =] 8.335% over these 2 years.

---

* Although the arithmetic mean return and the expected return are both linear additive sums that produce an average rate of return, the arithmetic mean return is statistically different from the expected return unless certain statistical conditions apply. The arithmetic mean return and the expected return are statistically the same only in a random-walk environment in which the returns are independently and identically distributed.

** The variance used in Eqn. 10-3 is the variance around the arithmetic mean return [AMR, or $E(r)$]. Eqn. 10-3 is appropriate if the arithmetic average return and $VAR(r)$ statistics are in decimal form. If the arithmetic average return and $VAR(r)$ statistics are in percentage form, then Eqn. 10-3 must have the decimal point moved two spaces, to become: $(AMR) \cong GMR + 0.005VAR(r)$. Other good approximation formulas exist.

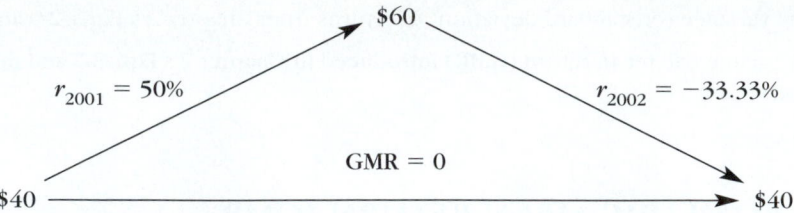

It is naive to say that an asset that was purchased for $40 and sold for $40 2 years later earned a positive rate of return over those 2 years.

This asset's correct rate of return over the years 2001 and 2002 is its geometric mean return *(GMR)*.

$$(1 + r_{2001})(1 + r_{2002}) = (1 + 50\%)(1 - 33.33\%) = (1.5)(.666) = (1 + GMR)^2$$

$$\left(\frac{P_{2001}}{P_{2000}}\right) \left(\frac{P_{2002}}{P_{2001}}\right) = \left(\frac{\$60}{\$40}\right) \left(\frac{\$40}{\$60}\right) = \left(\frac{\$40}{\$40}\right) = (1 + GMR)^2$$

The second root is appropriate for computing the GMR over 2 years. The square root of 1 equals the correct geometric mean return of zero percent per year.

$$\sqrt{1.0} = 1.0^{1/2} = (1 + GMR) = (1 + 0) <==> GMR = \text{zero}$$

The geometric mean return is useful in analyzing and comparing different investment objectives.

Different Investment Goals

Henry Latane published a seminal paper showing that maximizing an investor's terminal wealth at the end of a planning horizon that covers T consecutive time periods, denoted P_T, is equivalent to maximizing the investor's geometric mean return over that time.[5]

$$(1 + GMR)^T = [\text{(Terminal wealth)/(Beginning wealth)}] = P_T/P_0 \qquad \textbf{(10-5)}$$

Nobel laureate Harry Markowitz and others pointed out that Latane's idea about maximizing the geometric mean is a worthwhile investment objective.[*][6]

$$(1 + \text{Maximum } GMR)^T = [\text{(Maximum terminal wealth)/(Beginning wealth)}] = \text{Max}(P_T/P_0)$$

Maximizing the geometric mean return is interesting to investment managers because the approximations in Eqns. 10-3 and 10-3a show how risk, *VAR(r)*, and the arithmetic mean return *(AMR)* interact to determine the geometric mean return.

$$GMR \cong (AMR) - .5VAR(r) \qquad \textbf{(10-3a)}$$

---

[*] Maximizing terminal wealth, maximizing the geometric mean return, and maximizing a logarithmic utility of wealth function are three mathematically and economically equivalent investment goals. Harry Markowitz and other eminent scholars have argued that maximizing these equivalent goals is a logical investment objective.

Eqn. 10-3a shows that maximizing the geometric mean return can be achieved by both maximizing the arithmetic mean (expected) return and minimizing risk. The interrelationship between these goals is a happy coincidence.*

Contrasting the Arithmetic Mean Return with the Geometric Mean Return

The disparity between the arithmetic mean return and the geometric mean return shown in Eqns. 10-3 and 10-3a raises the question: For what purposes should these different return measures be used? The answer is that the GMR should be used for measuring *historical* returns that are compounded over *multiple time periods*. The arithmetic mean return should be used for *future*-oriented analysis, where the use of expected values is appropriate. It is never a good idea to average the arithmetic mean return and the geometric mean return; they measure different quantities in different ways.

CONTRASTING THE ARITHMETIC AND THE GEOMETRIC MEAN RETURN   **EXAMPLE**

Consider paying $100 for a risky security that is equally likely to lose 10% or earn 20% per year. If this $100 investment is held for 2 years, its terminal value will most likely grow to 1.08 times its initial value of $100, which is $108.

$$(1 + GMR)^2 = (1 + r_1)(1 + r_2) = (1 + 20\%)(1 - 10\%) = (1.2)(.9) = 1.08$$
$$= (1 - 10\%)(1 + 20\%) = (.9)(1.2) = 1.08$$

The square root of 1.08 equals one plus the geometric mean return of 3.92% per year.

$$\sqrt{1.08} = 1.08^{1/2} = (1 + GMR) = 1.03923 = 1 + 3.92\% <==> GMR = 3.92\% \text{ per year}$$

This investment's probability distribution of returns is shown in Figure 10-1A. The computations show that this $100 investment's arithmetic mean return is 5.0% per year.

$$\bar{r} = \frac{20\% - 10\%}{2} = \left(20\% - 10\%\right)\left(\tfrac{1}{2}\right) = 5\% = E(r)$$

The lattice at Figure 10-1B enumerates possible outcomes for this risky investment over 2 years. The values in parentheses after each dollar outcome in this figure are probabilities. Figure 10-1C shows that this $100 investment's expected terminal value is $110.25 after 2 years.

Expectations About the Future Should Use the *E(r)*. If the $100 initial investment is compounded forward for 2 years at the expected return of 5%, it will grow to equal the expected terminal value of $110.25.

$$[\$100][1 + E(r)]^2 = [\$100][1 + 5\%]^2 = [\$100][1.05]^2 = [\$100][1.1025] = \$110.25$$

---

* If the returns are normally distributed and the investor has a logarithmic utility function, it can be shown that the GMR maximizing investment is a Markowitz efficient portfolio. For more details, see Gordon J. Alexander and Jack Clark Francis, *Portfolio Analysis*, 3rd ed. (Englewood Cliffs, NJ: Prentice-Hall, 1986), Chapters 2 and 12.

FIGURE 10-1   Analysis of Initial Investment of $100 Over 2 Years: (A) Probability Distribution of 1 Year Returns, (B) Lattice Enumerating Possible Outcomes, (C) Computations for the Expected Terminal Value

(A) Probability Distribution of 1-Year Returns

Outcome	Probability	1-year Rates of Return	Product of P times r
Up	$P(r_{UP}) = .5$	$r_{UP} = +20\%$	10%
Down	$P(r_{DOWN}) = .5$	$r_{DOWN} = -10\%$	−5%
Totals	1.0		$E(r) = 5\%$

(B) Lattice Enumerating All Possible Outcomes

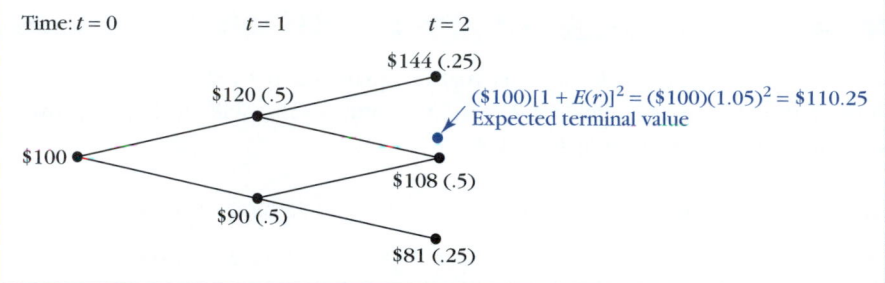

Time: $t = 0$ $t = 1$ $t = 2$

$144 (.25)

$120 (.5)

$100

$108 (.5)

$90 (.5)

$81 (.25)

$(\$100)[1 + E(r)]^2 = (\$100)(1.05)^2 = \$110.25$
Expected terminal value

(C) Computations for the Expected Terminal Value

Price Moves	Probability (P)	Terminal Value (TV)	P times TV
Up twice	.25	($100)(1 + 20%)(1 + 20%) = $144	$36.00
Up and down	.25	($100)(1 + 20%)(1 − 10%) = $108	$27.00
Down and up	.25	($100)(1 − 10%)(1 + 20%) = $108	$27.00
Down twice	.25	($100)(1 − 10%)(1 − 10%) = $81	$20.25
Totals	1.0		$110.25 = E(TV)

(A) contains an investment's probability distribution of annual returns. (B) enumerates 2 years of annual returns from the probability distribution in (A) and compares them with the expected future (terminal) value. (C) shows how the expected terminal value illustrated in (B) is computed.

This example supports the general conclusion that the expected return should always be used to compound the initial investment into the future to find the expected terminal value.

Multi-Period Historical Returns Should Be Used to Compute the GMR. At the end of 2 years, if the financial analyst finds that the initial investment of $100 has grown in value to $108, the geometric mean return over the past 2 years is 3.923% per year.

$$(\$108/\$100)^{1/2} = \sqrt{1.08} = 1.03923 = 1.0 + 3.923\% = 1 + GMR$$

Working this problem backwards, we find that if the GMR is used as the discount rate, the present value of $108 at the end of two periods equals the initial investment of $100.

$$\$108/[1 + GMR]^2 = \$108/(1.03923)^2 = \$100$$

If the arithmetic mean return of 5% is used as a discount rate to find the present value of the terminal value of $108 (or the terminal values of $88 or $144 from Figure 10-1B), the computations will not yield a present value that equals the initial $100 investment.

$$\$108/[1 + E(r)]^2 = \$108/(1.05)^2 = \$97.959$$

The GMR provides the only correct way to take a series of two or more consecutive one-period rates of return from an investment that was made in the past and compute the investment's compound average rate of return.*

COMPUTING RETURNS OVER MULTIPLE PERIODS

Whenever investment returns are measured over more than one time period, it is appropriate to use compounded returns. The future oriented expected return, the historically oriented GMR, any other rate of return, or any interest rate can be compounded.

Essentially, compounding a price relative N times shows the value to which it will grow after N time periods. And, the reverse is true, taking the Nth root of an N-period price relative converts it to a compound average one-period rate of return. The preceding sentence sounds simple. But, let us look at the formulas to make sure we see how this works.

As mentioned above, the *price plus cash dividend relative* for a stock or a stock market index equals one plus the stock's one-period return, symbolically, $[(P_t + DIV_t)/P_{t-1}] = (1 + r_t)$. The same is true of bonds' *price plus coupon relative*, $[(P_t + Coupon_t)/P_{t-1}] = (1 + r_t)$. If no cash flows are involved, the simple *price relative* is appropriate, $P_t/P_{t-1} = (1 + r_t)$.

Three consecutive monthly price relatives can be compounded together to obtain a *quarterly rate of return*, as shown below.

$$(1 + r_{Month\ 1})(1 + r_{Month\ 2})(1 + r_{Month\ 3}) = (1 + r_{Quarter})$$

$$\left(\frac{P_1}{P_0}\right)\left(\frac{P_2}{P_1}\right)\left(\frac{P_3}{P_2}\right) = \left(\frac{P_3}{P_0}\right) = (1 + r_{Quarter})$$

Similarly, twelve consecutive monthly price relatives can be compounded to obtain an *annual rate of return*.

---

* The internal rate of return (IRR) and a bond's yield-to-maturity (YTM) are mathematically identical. But they are different from the geometric mean return (GMR). The YTM formula will occasionally yield the same solution as the GMR formula, but only under certain unusual circumstances. Bonds' yields-to-maturities (YTMs) are a topic covered in Chapters 20 and 21 of this book.

Your authors are aware of the dangers in reasoning from specific examples to general conclusions. The $100 investment in Figure 10-1 is suggestive and intuitive, but provides inadequate proof that the assertions are generally true.

$$(1 + r_1)(1 + r_2)(1 + r_3)(1 + r_4)(1 + r_5)(1 + r_6)(1 + r_7)(1 + r_8)(1 + r_9)(1 + r_{10})(1 + r_{11})(1 + r_{12})$$
$$= (1 + r_{Annual})$$

$$\left(\frac{P_{Jan}}{P_{Dec}}\right)\left(\frac{P_{Feb}}{P_{Jan}}\right)\left(\frac{P_{Mar}}{P_{Feb}}\right)\cdots\left(\frac{P_{Nov}}{P_{Oct}}\right)\left(\frac{P_{Dec}}{P_{Nov}}\right) = \left(\frac{P_{Dec\ of\ year\ N+1}}{P_{Dec\ of\ year\ N}}\right) = \left(1 + r_{Annual}\right)$$

The same annual rate of return can be obtained from a 1-year price relative.

$$\frac{\left(Price\ at\ end\ of\ year\ N + 1\right)}{\left(Price\ at\ end\ of\ year\ N\right)} = \left(1 + r_{Annual}\right)$$

Three annual price relatives can be compounded together to obtain a *compounded 3-year return*. Since the end of one year is the same as the beginning of the next year, no time is lost or unaccounted for when compounding the following series of price relatives:

$$(1 + r_{year\ 1})(1 + r_{year\ 2})(1 + r_{year\ 3}) = (1 + r_{3\ years})$$

Using the 3-year price relative above allows us to compute the third (cube) root to find the *geometric mean return* at an annual rate:

$$(1 + r_{3\ years})^{1/3} = (1 + GMR_{Annualized})$$

For example, consider a hypothetical stock that earned the following three consecutive annual rates of return: $r_{year\ 1} = 11.1\%$, $r_{year\ 2} = -2.2\%$, and $r_{year\ 3} = 3.3\%$. The hypothetical stock's geometric mean rate of return is 3.92% per year:

$$[(1 + r_{year\ 1})(1 + r_{year\ 2})(1 + r_{year\ 3})]^{1/3} = (1 + r_{3\ years})^{1/3} = [(1.111)(0.978)(1.033)]^{1/3}$$
$$= [1.122]^{1/3} = 1.0392 = 1 + 3.92\% = 1 + GMR$$

The hypothetical stock's *arithmetic mean rate of return* per year of 4.07% exceeds its geometric mean annual rate of return of 3.92%:

$$(11.1\% - 2.2\% + 3.3\%)/(3\ years) = 12.2\%/3 = 4.0666\% = \check{r} > 3.9244\% = GMR$$

Eqn. 10-3, applied below, uses the variance of the hypothetical 3-year stock investment, $VAR(r) = .0044663$, to explain the disparity between the arithmetic average rate of return and the geometric mean rate of return:

$$(Arithmetic\ average\ return) \cong GMR + .5VAR(r)$$
$$= .039244 + (.5)(.0044663) = 0.041477 = 4.1477\%$$

Eqn. 10-3's approximation of 4.1477% is about eight BPs above the hypothetical stock's true arithmetic average return of 4.0666%.* Both the multiplicative compound returns and the additive arithmetic average returns (like the expected return) are used in finance.

---

* $VAR(r)$ represents the variance around the arithmetic mean return [AMR, or $E(r)$]. If decimals are used instead of percentages, Eqn. 10-3 should be rescaled by moving the decimal two places as shown below.

$$(AMR) \cong GMR + .005VAR(r) = 3.9244\% + (.005)(44.663\%) = 4.1477\%$$

THE CONSUMERS PRICE INDEX (CPI)

The governments of many countries compile a **Consumer Price Index (CPI).** For example, every month the U.S. Government's Bureau of Labor Statistics computes the value of its CPI.

$$\begin{pmatrix} \text{U.S. CPI in a} \\ \text{given month} \end{pmatrix} = \frac{\text{Price of market basket with fixed weights in a given month}}{\text{Price of the same market basket in the base year}} \times 100$$

The CPI data is derived from point-of-purchase prices of a representative "market basket" of 300 goods and services such as foods, clothing, housing, medical, recreational, travel, and other typical items that have fixed weights determined by a survey of the spending patterns of urban consumers. A new survey is conducted and the 300 components and their weights are updated about once each decade. CPI statistics are reviewed in Figure 2-1 and Table 2-1 in Chapter 2.

Many costs-of-living allowances (COLAs) in the United States are based on the CPI. The Social Security (government pension) checks received by 40 million U.S. citizens, the salaries of millions of government workers, the paychecks of millions of U.S. military personnel, the wages of about 6 million union members, and many people's inflationary expectations are derived from the monthly CPI announcements. Since 1985 the U.S. government's progressive income tax brackets have been indexed to the CPI so that the tax brackets are adjusted upward to keep pace with inflation. In spite of all these price level arrangements, millions of U.S. citizens pay no heed to the rate of inflation.

The CPIs of most countries rarely decline—usually only during a depression. The CPIs of most countries typically inflate almost every month. Inflation causes "purchasing power risk."

PURCHASING POWER RISK

Bonds, savings accounts, life insurance policies, and many other financial assets are **dollar-denominated,** which means they make their required payments in dollars rather than in real goods. For instance, the coupon interest and principal payments promised to most bond investors are fixed dollar quantities that do not increase with inflation. If any inflation occurs, bondholders are repaid in dollars that have less purchasing power over real goods than the dollars they invested in the bonds. The possibility of such losses in purchasing power is called **purchasing power risk.** Purchasing power risk can be larger than an investor realizes if the investor does not understand inflation.

Measuring Inflation

The percentage change in the CPI is the **rate of inflation;** it is denoted *INF*:

$$INF = \frac{\left(CPI \text{ for month } t + 1\right) - \left(CPI \text{ for month } t\right)}{CPI \text{ for month } t} \qquad (10\text{-}6)$$

For example, if the cost of a fixed market basket of goods goes from 200 to 202 in a month, the rate of inflation would be 1.0% in that month.

$$INF = \frac{202 - 200}{200} = \frac{2}{200} = 1.0\%$$

If the CPI increases 1.0% in some month, this monthly rate of 1.0% should be **annualized** as follows to get the annual rate of inflation of 12.68%.*

$$[1 + (1\% \text{ per month})]^{12} = (1.01)^{12} = 1.1268 = (1 + 0.1268) = 1 + 12.68\%$$
$$= 1 + (\text{Annualized INF})$$

If an investor compares the rates of return from their investments to the inflation rate, he or she is on the path to controlling purchasing power risk.

Nominal Returns Exceed Real Returns

When a bank's savings account pays an interest rate of, say, 4%, that is the deposit's "nominal" rate of return. **Nominal rates of return** are money rates of return that we see in advertisements, they are not inflation-adjusted returns.

An investment's **real rate of return** during some time period is calculated by dividing the rate of inflation out of the nominal return. The real return is denoted rr.

$$1.0 + rr = \frac{1.0 + r}{1.0 + INF} \tag{10-7}$$

For example, if a bond earns a 4% nominal rate of return, $r = 4\%$, during a year when the inflation rate is two percent, $INF = 2\%$, the bond's real rate of return is less than 2%.

$$1 + rr = \frac{1.04}{1.02} = 1.0196 \Rightarrow rr = 1.96\%$$

Buying this bond increased the investor's purchasing power 1.96%. The only portion of an investment's nominal rate of return that results in increased consumption opportunities is the real rate of return. The rest of the investment's nominal rate of return is lost to inflation. Investors who believe that the investment in this example yields more than a 1.96% real gain suffer from *money illusion*; they are unaware that inflation erodes the purchasing power of their money.[7]

A Handy Approximation

Eqn. 10-7 can be simplified by multiplying both sides of the equation by the quantity (1.0 + *INF*) and rearranging to obtain the mathematically equivalent Eqns. 10-8 and 10-8a:

$$1.0 + r = (1.0 + rr)(1.0 + INF) \tag{10-8}$$

$$r = rr + INF + (INF)(rr) \tag{10-8a}$$

An easy way to approximate the nominal rate of return is to note that the product of *INF* times *rr* in Eqn. 10-8a will usually be a tiny value that may be ignored with little loss of accuracy. This simplifying assumption allows us to restate Eqn. 10-8a as Eqn. 10-9.**

$$r \cong rr + INF \tag{10-9}$$

---

* Annualizing assumes the same 1.0% continues unchanged for 12 consecutive months. Annualizing an unusual value exaggerates it.
** Eqn. 10-9 is equivalent to Irving Fisher's theory, shown in Chapter 20, Eqn. 20-1 (page 598), about the relationship that should exist between nominal interest rates and the rate of inflation.

Eqn. 10-9a shows how to find the real rate after the values of r and INF are known.

$$rr \cong r - INF \tag{10-9a}$$

When the inflation rate is low, Eqns. 10-9 and 10-9a provide an easy way to calculate the approximate nominal and real rates of return.

Empirical Research

The findings of analysts that studied empirical data discern the impact of inflation on the returns from various categories of securities.

Bodie, Jaffe and Mandelker, and Nelson published three empirical studies showing that both the nominal and the real rates of return from common stocks tended to be negatively correlated with the inflation rate.[8] Their findings support Eqns. 10-7 and 10-9. Fama and Schwert examined the returns from T-bills, T-bonds, corporate bonds, real estate, labor income, and common stocks during 1953–71.[9] Fama and Schwert concluded that only real estate provided investors with a complete hedge against *both* the actual and unanticipated rates of inflation; T-bills and T-bonds were complete hedges against the actual inflation. Fama and Schwert reported that labor income and common stock prices responded to changes in the rate of inflation with lags that were variable and unpredictable. Moosa, Hasbrouck, and Gultekin investigated the ability of common stocks to provide a hedge against inflation; their findings supported the previous studies.[10] Laurence Siegel and David Montgomery investigated pretax returns from 1926 to 1993. The high pretax rates of return they found are much lower in real terms. Siegel and Montgomery suggest that the combined effect of taxes, management costs, and inflation causes the real historical return from bonds and bills to be near zero or negative.[11] Figure 2-1 in Chapter 2 (page 23) supports their findings by showing that during 1946–64 the CPI rose slightly above the T-bill index. The Siegel and Montgomery results also show that while common stocks yield positive real returns averaged over the long run, there are periods as long as 3 years (for instance, 1946–48 inclusive) when common stocks yield negative real returns.

Hyperinflation

Compared to other countries in the world, the United States is free from inflationary problems. The inflation rate in the United States has risen to the low double-digit level a few times. In contrast to the economic stability that U.S. investors enjoyed, some countries have experienced **hyperinflation**; Table 10-6 displays a few examples.

TABLE 10-6   Past and Present Examples of Hyperinflation

Period	Brazil		Israel		Mexico	
	Rate of Change[a]	Index	Rate of Change[a]	Index	Rate of Change[a]	Index
1959		1		1		1
1960–69	44.20%	39	5.22%	2	2.09%	1
1970–79	29.95%	534	31.01%	25	15.28%	5
1980–89	230.03%	81,826,956	104.66%	31,934	65.06%	765
1990–96	719.00%	202,247,470,821,750	13.18%	75,991	21.14%	2,929

[a] Rate of change is the compound annual return for the period indicated.

SOURCE: *International Financial Statistics* (various issues), published by the International Monetary Fund, Washington, DC

Hyperinflation makes it nearly impossible for a business to maintain meaningful financial statements. Business managers must spend time every day determining a profitable selling price for the goods in their firm's inventory. Borrowing and lending money become painfully complicated when prices are changing rapidly. Hyperinflation disrupts a country's capital markets. Several countries that have emerging capital markets suffered spurts of inflation that were not as bad as those in Table 10-6, but the resulting economic instability created serious problems for foreign investors.

THE BOTTOM LINE

It is possible to create a useful price index economically. The number of observations sampled should be large enough to reduce sampling error to an acceptable level. Sampling techniques should be utilized to assure that the sample is sufficiently diverse to be representative of the population of interest and free from bias. The construction of the index should utilize a weighting system that corresponds to user needs. The price indicator should be defined in a consistent manner through time and stated in convenient units. If the price observations that make up a price indicator are gathered from frequent transactions, the information content of the price indicator will be more timely than if the underlying price data is observed infrequently or changes infrequently. Stock splits, stock dividends, mergers, and bankruptcies within the sampled securities make it difficult to maintain consistent stock price indicators.

The S&P500 index does not suffer from the deficiencies in the Dow Jones Industrial Average (DJIA), but the two indicators are still highly positively correlated. The high degree of covariance between these indicators stems from the fact that much of the total risk in the stock market is undiversifiable (bull- and bear-market) risk.

There is a more than one way to compute the average rate of change in investments and price indexes over extended periods of time. The arithmetic mean is the most popular computational method. However, when the arithmetic average is computed over multiple time periods, it produces erroneous values (see pages 281–2). The popular arithmetic mean of one-period returns (AMR) from multiple time periods produces misleading statistics that are biased upward. The geometric mean return (GMR) provides compounded rates of return over multiple periods of time that are correct.

Governments around the world compute Consumer Price Indexes (CPIs) to measure the rate of inflation in their countries. Deflation usually only occurs during depressions. Most countries experience varying rates of inflation most of the time. Inflation erodes the purchasing power of money and other financial assets. The risk of losses to inflation is called purchasing power risk.

In order to minimize purchasing power risk an investor must understand the difference between nominal rates of return and real rates of return. Real rates of return measure the purchasing power that is left after the rate of inflation is removed from nominal returns.

Empirical research shows that real returns from financial assets are diminished by inflation, as suggested by the inflation adjustment formulas. Some countries have suffered rates of hyperinflation that discourage further investing in financial assets and retard the country's economic development.

QUESTIONS

Q10-1 (Designing an index) Discuss the five factors that need to be considered when designing an index.

Q10-2 (DJIA) Discuss some of the problems inherent in the manner in which the DJIA is calculated.

Q10-3 (Price-weighting) Consider the effect of one 10 percent change in one stock's price on the computation of the following hypothetical three-stock portfolio:

		Prices at Time $t = 1$	
Stocks	**Prices at Time $t = 0$**	**Low-Price Change**	**High-Price Change**
Ace	$ 80	$ 80	$80(1.1) = $ 88
Baker	50	50	50
Case	20	$20(1.1) = 22	20
Totals	$150	$152	$158
Divisor	3	3	3
Average	50	50.66	52.66
Percent change in the average		1.3%	5.3%

To what do you attribute the fact that the average rose 1.3 percent when the price of Case's stock rose 10 percent, but the same average rose 5.3 percent when the price of Ace increased 10 percent? What implications do your findings have for the DJIA?

Q10-4 (Stock market indicators) Compare and contrast a stock market average and a stock market index.

Q10-5 (Weighting methods) Compare and contrast the methods used in constructing an equally weighted index and a market-value weighted index.

Q10-6 (Benchmarks) If you were searching for a stock market index to track a portfolio of new, small, growth stocks, what type of index might you use? Explain why.

Q10-7 (Purchasing power risk) Your brother-in-law has made the following statement: "I have safely invested all *my* retirement money in Treasury bills. They are as close to a risk-free investment as I can find. Only fools would invest their funds in the stock market. Stocks are too risky an investment." Comment on his statement.

Q10-8 (DJIA) Consider the 30 stocks that make up the Dow Jones Industrial Average. (You can find them listed in the *Wall Street Journal* every day.) Can you think of a new name that would be more appropriate for the DJIA? Explain your answer.

Q10-9 (Arithmetic average versus geometric average) (a) What is formula for calculating the arithmetic average rate of return on an investment measured over T periods? (b) What is the formula for measuring a geometric mean rate of return on an investment over T periods? (c) What is the difference between these two measures?

Q10-10 (DJIA) On June 7, 1999, the DJIA rose by 109.54 points from the previous day's close. This was an increase of 1.01%. If an investor had a portfolio consisting of the 30 stocks in the DJIA, would she necessarily have earned a return of 1.01% for the day? Why or why not?

PROBLEMS

P10-1 (Calculation of the DJIA) A certain portfolio is comprised of five stocks, with the following market prices:

Stock	Market Price
A	$ 30
B	$ 80
C	$100
D	$ 50
E	$ 20

(a) Assume that you constructed a market indicator for these five stocks in a manner similar to the calculation of the DJIA and called it MYVAL. Calculate MYVAL.

(b) Now assume Stock C is split 2-for-1. Calculate the new divisor for MYVAL.

P10-2 (Weighting) Form a stock price index from the three common stocks listed below. These three stocks issued no additional shares and had no stock dividends or splits. Ignore cash dividend payments when computing this price index.

Stock	Total Shares Outstanding on Both Dates	Base Period Market Price July 1, 1970	More Recent Period Market Price July 1, 2000	Percentage Price Change
Middie	50,000	$40	$60	+50
Mite	10,000	20	70	+250
Maxum	100,000	60	80	+33

(a) If the new three-stock index is value-weighted, what will its value be on July 1, 2000?

(b) If the new three-stock index is price-weighted, what will its value be on July 1, 2000?

(c) If the new three stock index is equally weighted, what will its value be on July 1, 2000?

(d) Compare and contrast the price-weighted, the value-weighted, and the equally weighted index numbers you obtained from the same three stocks and explain why they differ.

P10-3 (Geometric mean return) The following data is supplied for Texaco for 1998:

Quarter	Beginning Price	Ending Price	Dividends Paid
1	$54.375	$60.25	$0.45
2		$59.6875	$0.45
3		$62.5625	$0.45
4		$53.00	$0.45

Calculate Texaco's geometric mean return for the year.

P10-4 (Arithmetic average return) The following yearly data is supplied for the Great Atlantic and Pacific Tea Company, Incorporated (A&P):

Year	Close Price[a]	Dividends Paid
1993	$24.8526	not applicable
1994	$17.2451	$0.80
1995	$22.0773	$0.20
1996	$30.8194	$0.20
1997	$29.067	$0.35
1998	$29.4255	$0.40

[a] Close price is adjusted for stock dividends and stock splits.

What is A&P's arithmetic average return over the 5-year period?

P10-5 (Geometric mean return) Use the data supplied in Problem 10-4 to calculate A&P's geometric mean return. Which measure—the arithmetic average or the geometric mean return—should you use if you want to estimate the expected return on A&P for 1999? Why?

P10-6 (Average returns) Biotech Company's stock has had the following returns for the past 10 years: 20%, −5%, 35%, 5%, 10%, −10%, 25%, 2%, 15%, 18%. Calculate Biotech's arithmetic average return and geometric mean return for the 10-year period.

P10-7 (Inflation-adjusted returns) Consider the following data for 1993:

	Total return
Large company stocks	9.99%
Long-term government bonds	18.24%
Treasury bills	2.90%

The inflation rate for 1993 was 2.75%. Calculate the real returns earned on large company stocks, long-term government bonds, and Treasury bills in 1993.

P10-8 (Arithmetic versus geometric means) Consider the following annual returns reported for a certain stock:

Year	Return
1	10%
2	18%
3	−2%
4	15%

(a) Calculate the arithmetic mean return.
(b) Calculate the geometric mean return.
(c) Which one is a more appropriate measure of the stock's compound average rate of return over the 4-year period?

P10-9 (Price relatives) The following information is given for an aggressive growth mutual fund that pays no dividends:

Date	Net asset value
January 1	$21.28
February 1	$23.50
March 1	$22.75
April 1	$22.92

Calculate the quarterly price relative for the fund. What is the fund's quarterly return?

P10-10 (Inflation-adjusted returns) Carolyn earned a one-year return of 12% on an investment in a mutual fund. Her marginal tax rate was 28%, and the rate of inflation for the year was 4%. Calculate her (a) after-tax nominal rate of return, and (b) her inflation-adjusted after-tax return on the investment.

CFA EXAM QUESTIONS

The following two questions are adopted from the 1999 CFA Exam, Level I:

1. A portfolio of non–dividend paying stocks earned a geometric mean return of 5% between January 1, 1992, and December 31, 1998. The arithmetic mean return for the same period was 6%. If the market value of the portfolio at the beginning of 1992 was $100,000, the market value of the portfolio at the end of 1998 was *closest* to:
   A. $135,000.
   B. $140,710.

C. $142,000.

D. $150,363.

2. The divisor for the Dow Jones Industrial Average (DJIA) is *most likely* to decrease when a stock in the DJIA:

A. has a stock split.

B. has a reverse split.

C. pays a cash dividend.

D. is removed and replaced.

3. (Adapted from a question appearing on the 1997 CFA Exam, Level III) BAC Associates is considering investments in international equities to diversify its U.S.-only stock portfolio. As a benchmark for the international portion of the portfolio, a consultant recommends using *either* a GDP-weighted *or* a market-capitalization-weighted index of all non-U.S. stock markets, such as the Morgan Stanley Capital International EAFE (Europe/Australia/Far East) Index. Discuss *two* reasons that may cause an investor to prefer using a GDP-weighted international equity benchmark rather than a capitalization-weighted international equity benchmark.

FURTHER REFERENCES

Ibbotson, Roger G. and Lawrence B. Siegel, "The World Bond Market: Market Values, Yields and Returns," *The Journal of Fixed Income* 1, no. 1 (June 1991): 90–99.

This empirical study documents changes in market capitalization, yields, and returns that have characterized three decades.

Jorion, Philippe and William N. Goetzman, "Global Stock Markets in the Twentieth Century," *Journal of Finance,* Vol. LIV, no. 3 (June 1999): 953-980.

Price appreciation indexes from 39 stock markets are compiled. The indexes are based on data that reach as far back as the 1920s. The U.S. stock market is found to have achieved the highest uninterrupted real rate of price appreciation of all countries, at 4.3 percent annually from 1921 to 1996. For other countries, the median rate of real price appreciation was 0.8 percent. Several interesting survivorship bias problems are discussed.

Siegel, Jeremy J. *Stocks for the Long Run*, 2nd ed. New York: McGraw-Hill, 1998.

This nonmathematical book contains numerous tables of empirical statistics and intuitive graphs that explain important points about long-run investing in an informative manner.

Stocks, Bonds, Bills, and Inflation, published by Ibbotson Associates, Chicago, IL.

This annual book provides a distilled summary of the raw data, methodology, summary statistics, and concepts for investment managers.

ENDNOTES

[1]   See Frank J. Fabozzi and T. D. Fabozzi, *The Handbook of Fixed Income Securities*, 4th ed. (Burr Ridge, IL: Irwin, 1995). Chapters 39–41 explore indices on fixed income securities.

[2]   See Harold Bierman Jr., "The Dow Jones Industrials. Do You Get What You See?" *Journal of Portfolio Management* 15 (fall 1988): 58–60.

[3]   For details about the Standard & Poor's 500 Stocks Composite Index and investors that use the S&P500 index as a guideline, see *S&P 500 Annual Directory*, published by Standard & Poor's, New York City; this annual paperback had 467 pages in its 1997 edition.

[4]   There are several formulas that are used to approximate the relationship between the arithmetic mean and the geometric mean return (GMR). Eqn. 10-3 is one of the simplest. A good approximation was suggested in a classic article by Henry A. Latane, "Criteria for Choice Among Risky Ventures," *Journal of Political Economy* 67 (April 1959): 144-67. For a discussion of other formulas, see William E. Young and Robert H. Trent, "Geometric Mean Approximations of Individual Security and Portfolio Performance," *Journal of Financial and Quantitative Analysis* 4, no. 2 (June 1969): 179-99. Also see William H. Jean and Billy P. Helms, "Geometric Mean Approximations," *Journal of Financial and Quantitative Analysis* 18, no. 3 (September 1983): 287-94. For criticisms of these approximation see Oliveir de La Grandville, "The Long-Term Expected Rate of Return: Setting It Right," *Financial Analysts Journal* 54, no. 6 (November-December 1998): 77.

[5]   See Henry A. Latane, "Criteria for Choice Among Risky Ventures," *Journal of Political Economy* 67 (April 1959): 144-67.

[6] See Harry M. Markowitz, "Investment for the Long-Run: New Guidance for an Old Rule," *Journal of Finance* 31, no. 5 (December 1976): 1273–86.

[7] Studies of the effect of inflation on stock prices include J. Hasbrouck, "Stock Returns, Inflation, and Economic Activity: The Survey Evidence," *Journal of Finance* 39 (December 1983): 1293–1310. Also see G. W. Schwert, "The Adjustment of Stock Prices to Information About Inflation," *Journal of Finance* 36 (March 1981): pp.15–29. See also R. Stulz, "Asset Pricing and Expected Inflation," *Journal of Finance* 41 (March 1986): 209–24.

[8] Z. Bodie, "Common Stocks as a Hedge against Inflation," *Journal of Finance* 31 (May 1976): 459–70. Z. Bodie and V. I. Rosansky, "Risk and Return in Commodity Futures," *Financial Analysts Journal* (May-June 1980): 27–39. J. Jaffe and G. Mandelker, "The Fisher Effect for Risky Assets: An Empirical Investigation," *Journal of Finance* 31 (May 1976): 447–58. C. R. Nelson, "Inflation and Rates of Return on Common Stocks," *Journal of Finance* 31 (May 1976): 471–83.

[9] See E. F. Fama and G. W. Schwert, "Asset Returns and Inflation," *Journal of Financial Economics* 5 (1977): 115–46.

[10] N. Gultekin, "Stock Market Returns and Inflation," *Journal of Finance* 38 (June 1983): 663–74. J. Hasbrouck, "Stock Returns, Inflation, and Economic Activity: The Survey Evidence," *Journal of Finance* 39 (December 1983): 1293–1310. S. A. Moosa, "Inflation and Common Stock Prices," *Journal of Financial Research* 3 (fall 1980): 115–28. Rene Stulz developed a model in which real returns are negatively related to the inflation rate and the money stock. See Rene Stulz, "Asset Pricing and Expected Inflation," *Journal of Finance* 41 (March 1986): 209–24.

[11] See Laurence B. Siegel and David Montgomery, "Stocks, Bonds, and Bills after Taxes and Inflation," *Journal of Portfolio Management* 21, no. 2 (winter 1995): 17–25.

SELECTED INVESTMENT INDEXES

Each day we hear people asking—on the radio, on TV, or in personal conversations:"How is the stock market doing?" An investor might reply: "The U.S. stock market is down a lot today, because the Hong Kong market collapsed." This chapter investigates the domestic and international market indexes that provide the basis for such statements. Chapter 10 explored the Consumer Price Index (CPI) and two stock market indexes. This chapter investigates a broader range of market indexes.

Chapter 11 has several objectives:

First, we are going to use market indexes to gain knowledge rapidly. Market indexes can impart knowledge that would take decades to gain through actual investing experience.

Second, index data is used to confront theories with facts. If you think common stocks are a good hedge against inflation, stock price indexes and inflation indexes can be used to determine if that is true.

Third, indexes are used to investigate market interrelations. For example, if you think the corporate bond market in Britain leads the stock market in the United States, this chapter introduces indexes to help you confirm or deny that relationship.

Fourth, indexes are used to allocate assets. This chapter provides risk and return data on different stock and bond indexes from around the world that will help you allocate your funds to asset classes.

Fifth, indexes help you look at overall economic relationships. As you seek greater returns by undertaking greater risks, for instance, how far should you go?

Some insightful conclusions can be drawn from market index data. Market indexes explain why millions of investors behave the way they do and also why the efficient markets theory breaks down in some cases. Chapter 12 introduces successful new financial instruments that are based on the market indexes discussed in Chapters 10 and 11. Indexed investment strategies have been important developments during the last two decades. So, hold on to your hat and let some unassuming index numbers show you things you never knew about the world of investing.

The first part of this chapter considers stock and bond indicators for several different categories of U.S. securities. After this, stock market indexes from around the world are examined.

LONG-TERM RETURNS FOR MAJOR ASSET CLASSES

The preceding chapter discussed qualities of market indicators—such as their ability to be representative and unbiased. Using criteria suggested in Chapter 10, we select some well-constructed investment indexes for review in this chapter. This section investigates 74 years of monthly time-series data on seven U.S. price indexes.[1]

Large company stocks (the S&P500 index)

Long-term U.S. Government bonds

Intermediate-term U.S. Government bonds

U.S. Treasury Bills

Small-company stocks

Long-term corporate bonds

Inflation (percent change in the CPI)

Indexes, rather than individual securities, are analyzed because individual securities have idiosyncrasies. For example, if the chief executive officer (CEO) of the XYZ Corporation embezzles millions of dollars from the company, disclosure of this treachery will depress XYZ's stock. This section focuses on price indexes that statistically bury incidents like the XYZ disaster in a diversified portfolio—called a *securities index*—that contains many different securities; the good luck that some other corporation enjoyed offsets the XYZ Corporation's bad luck. Index data makes it possible to discern meaningful trends and relationships between *categories of investments* that would be difficult to detect by comparing the idiosyncratic fluctuations of *individual* securities.

Seven basic indexes are presented first, followed by 10 more indexes derived from the 7 basic indexes. These 17 indexes, compiled by the international investment consulting firm, Ibbotson Associates, headquartered in Chicago, IL, track major investment forces in the United States. Ibbotson data are reproduced in economics and finance books, quoted in news periodicals, subscribed to by many security analysts and numerous portfolio managers, and included in software databases. Over 130 full-time employees continually update and distribute the 7 basic indexes, 10 derived indexes, and thousands of other economic indicators from around the world that are in the Ibbotson database.[2]

Ibbotson's Seven Basic Indexes

Figure 2-1 in Chapter 2 (page 23) illustrates the growth of $1 invested in four of the basic investment indexes and one hypothetical asset that returned the inflation rate. The growth rates shown are *total returns (TRs)* that include income from both unrealized price changes and cash flows. All results assume immediate reinvestment of all coupon interest from bonds and cash dividends from stocks, if any of these cash flows were paid. The returns from the 7 basic indexes and the 10 derived indexes are all computed for a domestic U.S. investor who invests U.S. dollars. Brokerage commissions, income taxes, and other transactions costs are ignored for simplicity.*

---

* Transactions costs are included in the small stock index after 1981.

Table 2-1 in Chapter 2 (page 24) contains statistics summarizing the performance of the 7 basic investment indexes; 5 of these 7 indexes are illustrated in Figure 2-1. The geometric mean returns (GMRs) in the second column of Table 2-1 were discussed Chapter 10 (see pp. 281–286). The arithmetic mean returns (AMRs) and standard deviations in the third and fourth column of Table 2-1 were defined in Chapter 2's Eqns. 2-6 and 2–10. Ex post probability distributions (relative frequency diagrams) are shown in the right-hand column of Table 2-1. These probability distributions have vertical bars at intervals of 5%. Let us now consider each of the 7 indexes in detail.

The Large-Company Stock Index. Standard & Poor's 500 Stocks Composite Index (S&P500) and the cash dividends thereon provide the total return (TR) data for the large company stock index in Figure 2-1 and Table 2-1 of Chapter 2. Construction of the S&P500 index was discussed in the first part of Chapter 10.

Figure 2-1 shows how $1 invested in a diversified portfolio of stocks issued by large U.S. corporations at the end of 1925 grew to $2,845.63, including the reinvested cash dividends, by the end of 1999. This index's 11.3% compound growth rate is composed of a cash dividend yield of 4.5% plus 6.6% per year of capital gains.* Examination of yearly data not in this book reveals that the annual returns fluctuated randomly from a low of −43.3% (<0) in 1933 to a high of 54.0% in 1934. Table 2-1 in Chapter 2 shows that this index of large stocks grew at an arithmetic mean annual return of 13.3% from 1926 through 1999 inclusive, and experienced considerable variability of return.

The Small-Company Stock Index. The small-stock index is computed from the ninth and tenth size deciles (quintile of smallest firms) of all stocks listed on the NYSE and AMEX and selected small-sized OTC stocks.[3]

One dollar invested in the small stock index from the end of 1925 to the end of 1999 grew to $6,640.79. With all dividends reinvested, the compound growth rate was 12.6% per year over 74 years. The annual returns fluctuated randomly from a high of 142.9% in 1933 to a low of −58.0% in 1937. The **Great Crash** that started in September 1929 and kept U.S. stock markets depressed well into the 1930s is clearly visible in Figure 2-1 on page 23. Figure 2-1 also shows that the small-stocks index fluctuated more than the other indexes. The summary statistics in Chapter 2's Table 2-1 show that the small-stocks index provided a lucrative small-stock risk premium (high total return) to compensate investors for bearing the risks associated with small-stock investing. This positive risk-return relationship is part of the foundation of economic theory.

The Long-Term Corporate Bond Index. A dollar invested in the long-term corporate bond index at the end of 1925 grew to a value of $56.77 at the end of 1999. With coupons reinvested, the compounded annual growth rate from the long-term corporate bond index was 5.6%. Year-by-year data that is not reproduced in this book reveals that the annual rates of return fluctuated fairly randomly from a high of 42.6% in 1982 to a low of −8.1% (<0) in 1969. The long-term corporate bond index was not illustrated in Figure 2-1 to keep the graph from being too cluttered. Table 2-1 contains summary statistics comparing this index to alternative indexes. Table 2-1 indicates that the long-term corporate bond index and long-term U.S. Treasury bond index performed somewhat similarly.

The Long-Term Government Bond Index. Figure 2-1 in Chapter 2 shows that $1 invested in the long-term government bond index at the end of 1925 grew, with coupons reinvested, to

---

* The 4.5% cash dividend yield plus 6.6% price appreciation totals (4.5% + 6.6% =) 11.1%, which is less than the 11.3% total return (TR). This discrepancy is caused by reinvestment returns that are discussed in this chapter (pp. 303–305) and Table 11-4 and, less importantly, small cumulative rounding errors.

$40.22 at the end of 1999.* This appreciation represents a compound growth rate of 5.1%.** The total annual returns ranged from a low of −9.2% (<0) in 1967 to a high of 40.4% in 1982.

The interaction of the coupon income and price change components of the long-term T-bond index's total return is interesting. During the 1926 through 1999 period the long-term government bond index suffered many monthly price decreases as market interest rates experienced a long-term upward trend. Price declines exceeded the price rises. To compensate for the price declines, the coupon income component of the T-bond's total return supplied more than 100% of the index's 74-year growth rate of 5.1% per year.

The Intermediate-Term Government Bond Index. The growth path of a $1 investment in the intermediate-term U.S. government bonds index was omitted from Figure 2-1 in Chapter 2 to keep from overcrowding the figure. Summary statistics are in Table 2-1.[†]

A $1 investment at the end of 1925, with coupons reinvested, grew to $43.93 by the end of 1999. The 74-year compound growth rate was 5.2%.[††] Year-by-year detail reveals that the total annual returns ranged from a high of 29.1% in 1982 to a low of −5.1% (<0) in 1994. The 74-year income return averaged 4.7% per year.

The U.S. Treasury Bill Index. Figure 2-1 in Chapter 2 shows that $1 invested in the U.S. Treasury bill index at the end of 1925 grew to $15.64 by the end of 1999; this represents a compound annual growth rate of 3.8%. The total annual returns ranged from a low of zero for the 1938–40 period to a high of 14.7% in 1981. T-bills had the lowest risk and, as economic theory would suggest, the lowest average rate of return of any of the seven basic U.S. indexes.

The T-bill returns were near zero during the 1920s and 1930s, when the U.S. experienced some deflation during its **Depression** (August 1929 to March 1933). From 1941 to 1951, the U.S. Treasury and the Federal Reserve pegged the T-bill rate at a level below the rate of inflation to reduce the cost of financing the federal government deficits caused by World War II. In recent decades, the T-bill returns tracked the inflation rate more closely. Over the 74-year sample period, the T-bill returns exceeded the inflation rate by an average of 60 basis

---

*   A series of individual U.S. Treasury bonds were used in sequence to form the long-term Treasury bond index. As discussed in Chapter 10, this economical sampling procedure was employed since homogeneous long-term U.S. Treasury bonds behave similarly.

** When a bond is purchased between coupon payments, the bond's buyer must compensate the bond's seller for that portion of the coupon payment that was earned since the last coupon payment. This **accrued interest** is calculated as follows:

Accrued coupon payment = [(Semiannual coupon payment) × (Fraction of coupon)] where

$$\left(\begin{array}{c}\text{Fraction}\\\text{of coupon}\end{array}\right) = \frac{\left(\text{Number of days since last coupon payment}\right)}{\left(\text{Number of days from last coupon payment to next coupon payment}\right)}$$

   The accrued interest on corporate and municipal bonds is based on the convention that the year has 360 days and it is made up of 12 months that each have 30 days. This convention is even used for long-term corporate and municipal bonds. The same (unrealistic) convention is also used in the money markets. Unlike the corporates and municipals, the accrued interest on Treasury bonds is based on the actual number of days, as shown above. For more details about computing the long-term government bond index, see *Stocks, Bonds, Bills, and Inflation Yearbook*, 2000 Edition, published by Ibbotson Associates, Chicago, IL, pp. 58–62.

†   As with the long-term T-bond and T-bill indexes, the total returns for the intermediate-term U.S. government bond index are calculated from a series of one-bond portfolios. This economical sampling procedure was employed because U.S. Treasury bonds with similar characteristics behave similarly.

†† The yield-to-maturity differs from the compound growth rate because the two measures are based on two different reinvestment rate assumptions. (1) The yield-to-maturity assumes that all cash flows are invested at whatever each particular bond's yield-to-maturity happens to be, until the next sequential bond investment is made. Then, the next bond's yield-to-maturity is used as the reinvestment rate while that bond is included in the index. (2) The compound growth rate is based on the aggregate sample period's single rate of return, as if all the different short-term bond's were rolled up into one long-term bond and one reinvestment rate was used for 74 years.

points (BPs). One **basis point (BP)** equals one-hundredth of one percent. However, in recent decades the T-bill rate has fluctuated above and below the inflation rate so that the inflation-adjusted T-bill rate was positive during some years and negative during others.*

The Volatility of Interest Rates. Figure 11-1B shows that between the fall of 1979 and the fall of 1982 the volatility (standard deviation) of interest rates in the United States was higher than usual. During this 3-year period the volatility of T-bill rates rose to a level that was approximately 50% above their volatility after 1982 because of some adjustments in the Federal Reserve's monetary policy.**

Inflation in the United States. Figure 2-1 shows that at the end of 1925, if $1 were invested in a hypothetical asset that earned a rate of return that equaled the CPI's rate of inflation, this asset's value would have grown to $9.39 by the end of 1999. The growth in this hypothetical asset represents a compound annual rate of inflation of 3.1%. The rate of inflation ranged from a low of -10.3% (<0) in 1932 to a high of 18.2% in 1946.

The United States experienced deflation during the Depression years, 1926 to 1933. Inflation resumed after 1933 and the CPI attained its pre-Depression 1926 level again in 1945. There was a spurt of inflation after World War II, and then inflation remained at low single-digit levels during the 1950s and 1960s. Inflation accelerated during the 1970s as President Johnson's administration financed the Vietnam war by expanding the money supply rapidly (lightly referred to as "printing money") to pay the federal government's deficits. Inflation in the United States peaked at an annual rate of 24% during the month of August 1973. The Fed reduced the growth rate in the money supply and was able to bring inflation down to a more moderate, but still substantial, rate of about 5% per year during the 1980s. Inflation declined to slightly below 3% during the 1990s.

Wealth Accumulation

One dollar invested in the large-stock index from the end of 1925 to the end of 1999 grew at a compound average rate of 11.3% per year. Although this may not seem like a huge number, it can produce huge long-term results. A compound rate of 11.3% per year means $1 that is continuously reinvested in the large stock index grows to $2,845.63 in 74 years.

$$(1 + \text{Large stock index's return})^{74 \text{ years}} = (1 + 11.3469\%)^{74} = \$2,845.63$$

This marvelous wealth accumulation can be accomplished without using illegal inside information or any other tricks. This accumulation of wealth can be accomplished by simply investing in the popular S&P500 index—our large-stock index in Table 2-1 and Figure 2-1 in Chapter 2—through bull and bear markets.

---

*   Several monthly T-bill returns were negative during the 1933–41 period. These seemingly illogical returns occurred for rational reasons that deserve an explanation. First, cash holdings were subject to personal property tax in some states between 1933 and 1941, while T-bills were tax exempt. Second, a commercial bank in the United States must invest in U.S. Treasury securities in order to be eligible to obtain bank deposits from the U.S. Treasury. Third, nominal interest rates were near zero during the 1933–41 period. Given these three circumstances, excess demand for T-bills occasionally caused T-bills to trade temporarily at premium prices. These premium prices caused negative monthly rates of return when the T-bill prices dropped back to (normal) discounted prices.

**   The 1979–82 period of highly volatile interest rates resulted from changes in the monetary policies adopted by the Federal Reserve. In the fall of 1979 the Fed stopped exerting a smoothing influence over market interest rates and, instead, shifted its focus toward controlling the growth rate in the money supply while letting interest rates fluctuate freely. In the fall of 1982 the Fed abandoned its new controls over the money supply and returned to its previous monetary goals of smoothing some of the volatility out of market interest rates.

FIGURE 11-1 Monthly Rates of Return, 1926–99: (A) Large Company Stock Index; (B) Long-Term U.S. Government Bond Index

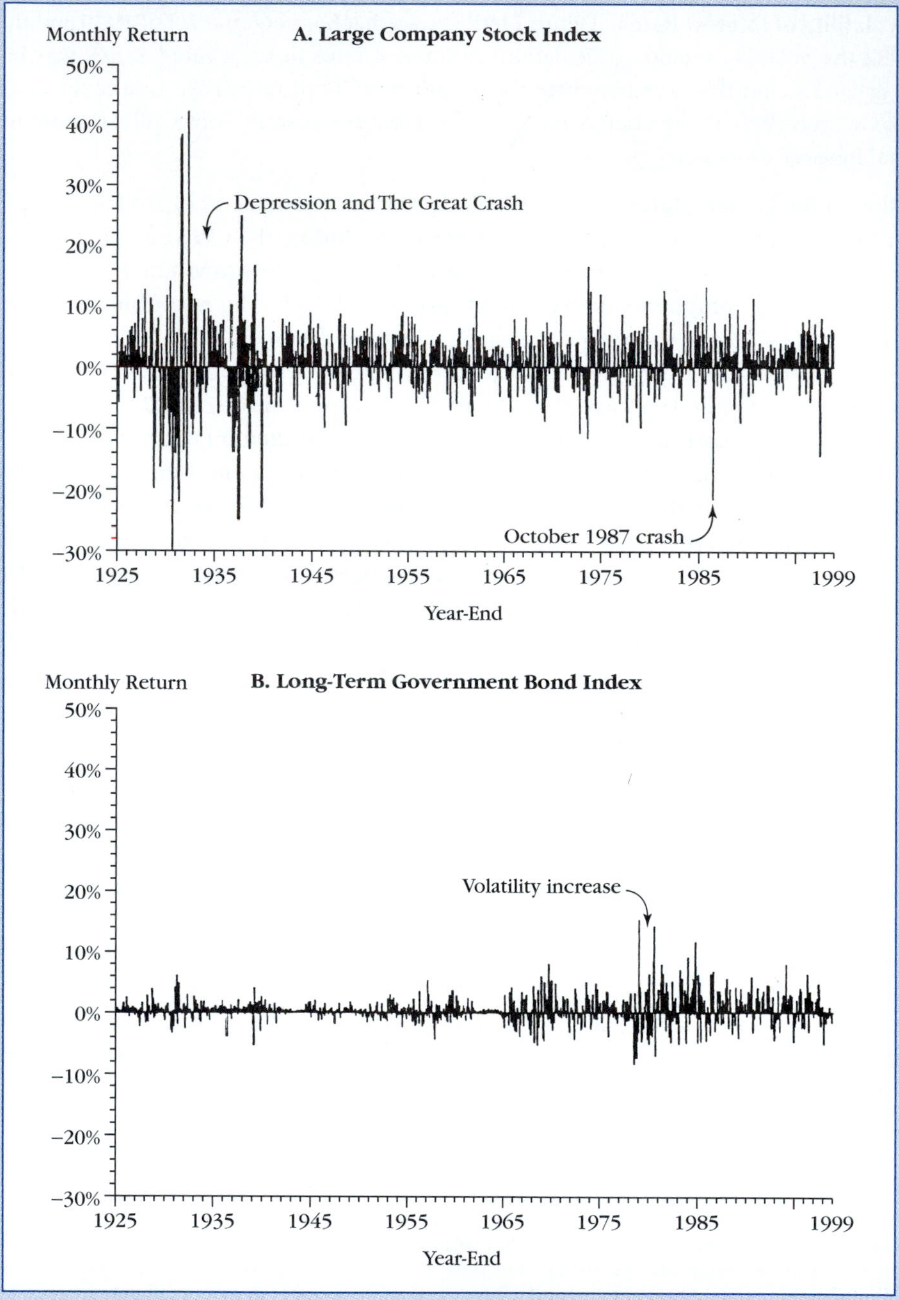

Stock prices are more volatile than bond prices. Over long periods of time both stock and bond price volatilities sometimes change; these changing volatilities are called intertemporally unstable risk statistics.

SOURCE: *Stocks, Bonds, Bills, and Inflation: 2000 Yearbook,* Ibbotson Associates, North Michigan Avenue, Chicago, IL 60601, Graph 6-1, p. 111. Based on copyrighted works by Ibbotson and Sinquefield. All rights reserved. Used with permission.

Inflation means that the $2,845.63 of wealth accumulated in our large-stock index at the end of 1999 will not purchase 2,845.63 times as many goods and services as the $1 invested 74 years before. The Consumer Price Index (CPI) can be used to compute the inflation-adjusted purchasing power of the accumulated wealth.

From the end of 1925 to the end of 1999 CPI inflated at the compound average rate of 3.1% per year. This means that $1 worth of purchases made at the end of 1925 inflated to a purchase price of $9.39 by the time 1999 ended.

$$(1 + \text{Inflation rate})^{74 \text{ years}} = (1 + 3.0728\%)^{74} = \$9.39$$

The inflation-adjusted value of $2,845.63 of accumulated wealth is called the accumulated **real wealth,** calculated as:

$$\frac{\left[1 + \left(\begin{array}{c}\text{Large stock index's} \\ \text{rate of return}\end{array}\right)\right]^{74 \text{ years}} = (1 + 11.3469\%)^{74} = \$2,845.63}{(1 + \text{Inflation rate})^{74 \text{ years}} = (1 + 3.0728\%)^{74} = \$9.39} = \left(\begin{array}{c}\$303.05 \text{ of} \\ \text{accumulated} \\ \text{real wealth}\end{array}\right)$$

After dividing out the purchasing power lost to inflation, accumulated real wealth (purchasing power) increased from $1 invested at the end of 1925 to $303.05 at the end of 1999.

Although inflation reduced the purchasing power of accumulated wealth with a nominal value of $2,845.63 at the end of 1999 to a real value of $303.05, the accumulation is still impressive. Amateur U.S. investors who have average luck can realistically expect to increase their real wealth more than 300 times during a life span of 74 years.

Risk and Returns

Placing risky bets in Las Vegas will most likely decrease your wealth. In contrast, taking carefully selected risks can be rational, wealth-maximizing behavior. For example, allocating assets to riskier asset classes can create wealth. Table 11-1 summarizes risk, return, and accumulated wealth statistics from Figure 2-1 and Table 2-1 in Chapter 2. The positive relationship between the risk and average returns is evident.

TABLE 11-1 Risk, Return, and Accumulated Wealth Statistics for Asset Classes

(1) Asset Class	(2) Accumulated Wealth for 74 Years	(3) Geometric Mean (GMR)	(4) Standard Deviation	(5) Arithmetic Mean (AMR)
Small-company stocks	$6,640.79	12.6%	33.6%	17.6%
Large-company stocks	$2,845.63	11.3%	20.1%	13.3%
Long-term corporate bonds	$ 78.14	5.6	8.7	5.9
Long-term government	$ 40.22	5.1	9.3	5.5
Intermediate-term government	$ 45.57	5.2	5.8	5.4
U.S. Treasury bills	$ 15.64	3.8	3.2	3.8
Inflation	$ 9.39	3.1	4.5	3.2

SOURCE: *Stocks, Bonds, Bills, and Inflation: 2000 Yearbook,* Ibbotson Associates, North Michigan Avenue, Chicago, IL 60601, Graph 2-1 from p. 28 and Table 2-1 from p. 33. Based on copyrighted works by Ibbotson and Sinquefield. All rights reserved. Used with permission.

TABLE 11-2 Arithmetic Mean Risk Premiums for Different Types of Risk

(1) Risk Premium's Name	(2) Definition of Risk Premium	(3) Arithmetic Mean Risk Premium
Small-company premium	(Small-cap return) less (Large-cap return)	17.6% − 13.3% = 4.3%
Equity (C. Stock) premium	(Large-stock return) less (T-bill return)	13.3% − 3.8% = 9.5%
Horizon (Time) premium	(T-bond return) less (T-bill return)	5.5% − 3.8% = 1.7%
Inflation premium	(T-bill return) less (Inflation rate)	3.8% − 3.2% = 0.60%

SOURCE: Calculated by J. C. Francis using data presented in *Stocks, Bonds, Bills, and Inflation: 2000 Yearbook*, Ibbotson Associates, North Michigan Avenue, Chicago, IL 60601, Graph 2-1 from p. 28 and Table 2-1 from p. 33. Based on copyrighted works by Ibbotson and Sinquefield. All rights reserved. Used with permission

---

Table 11-2 decomposes the total returns (TRs) from Table 11-1 into risk premiums. A **risk premium** is an additional rate of return investors expect to receive that induces them to accept the risks associated with a class of assets. Column 3 of Table 11-2 shows that the risk premiums for common stocks and small stocks are large. Investors undertaking the added risks associated with equities instead of bonds, or small-cap stocks instead of large corporations, receive big payoffs in the form of the large wealth accumulations shown in the top two rows of Table 11-1's column 2.

Ten-Year Average Returns for the Basic U.S. Indexes

Table 11-3 breaks the 74-year sample into smaller time frames; it displays 10-year average rates of change for Ibbotson's seven basic total return indexes. The decade by decade perspective shows that in order to accumulate wealth a long-run investor only need participate in one or two periods of truly outstanding performance.

Common stocks enjoyed four bull markets that account for the majority of the wealth that has been accumulated by equity investors in the United States: (1) from 1922 to the beginning of the Great Depression in September 1929 (part of the twenties), (2) 1949–61 (the fifties), (3) mid-1982 to the international stock market crash in October 1987 (the

---

TABLE 11-3 Compound Annual Rates of Return by Decade

Asset Class	1920s[a]	1930s	1940s	1950s	1960s	1970s	1980s	1990s
Large company	19.2%	−0.1%	9.2%	19.4%	7.8%	5.9%	17.5%	18.2%
Small company	−4.5	1.4	20.7	16.9	15.5	11.5	15.8	15.1
Long-term corporate	5.2	6.9	2.7	1.0	1.7	6.2	13.0	8.4
Long-term government	5.0	4.9	3.2	−0.1	1.4	5.5	12.6	8.8
Inter-term government	4.2	4.6	1.8	1.3	3.5	7.0	11.9	7.2
Treasury bills	3.7	0.6	0.4	1.9	3.9	6.3	8.9	4.9
Inflation rate	−1.1	−2.0	5.4	2.2	2.5	7.4	5.1	2.9

[a]The data for this column are based on the period 1926–29, which omits the bullish years of 1922–25 and includes the Great Crash in the last quarter of 1929.

SOURCE: *Stocks, Bonds, Bills, and Inflation: 2000 Yearbook*, Ibbotson Associates, North Michigan Avenue, Chicago, IL 60601, Table 1-1, p. 19. Based on copyrighted works by Ibbotson and Sinquefield. All rights reserved. Used with permission.

eighties), and (4) the 1990s, which were remarkably rewarding years for equity investors. If a stock market investor's wealth merely doubled, tripled, or quadrupled during the best part of any of these bull markets, that unfortunate investor could have expected to earn more by investing passively in a representative stock market index like the S&P500.

Inflation rose to a peak during the 1970s. This rising inflation pushed bond yields higher and set the stage for bond investors to enjoy a colossal bull market. The greatest bond bull market in U.S. history lasted from 1981 to 1994.

ANALYZING TOTAL RETURNS (TRS) FROM THE SEVEN BASIC INDEXES

This section breaks the total returns from Ibbotson's seven basic indexes into appreciation and cash flow components. The returns on these components are observed over different sample periods, the behavior of volatility is analyzed through time, and correlation coefficients are examined.

The Reinvestment Return Component of Total Returns

The total returns from U.S. Treasury bills are simple to compute because T-bills pay no coupon income—the pre-maturity cash flows are zero. A T-bill's rate of price change equals its total return over a holding period, $[(P_t/P_{t-1}) - 1] = r_t$. If the T-bill is held over multiple time periods, the price at the end of one time period is merely reinvested to earn the next period's rate of return.

Coupon paying bonds involve three different kinds of income. First, income from cash flows; second, income from capital appreciation (or depreciation); and, third, income from reinvestment returns. To understand the cash flow component of income, reconsider Eqn. 10-2 from Chapter 10, which is rearranged below to identify the first two bond income sources.

$$r_t = \frac{\text{Index change during holding period} + \text{Cash flow}}{\text{Index at beginning of the holding period}} \tag{10-2}$$

$$= \frac{\left(\text{Index}_t - \text{Index}_{t-1}\right)}{\text{Index}_{t-1}} + \frac{\text{Cash flow}}{\text{Index}_{t-1}}$$

$$= \left(\begin{array}{c}\text{Yield from price} \\ \text{appreciation}\end{array}\right) + \left(\begin{array}{c}\text{Current} \\ \text{yield from} \\ \text{cash flows}\end{array}\right)$$

Consider how consecutive total returns (TRs) that include cash flows interact to determine a multiperiod return. When computing returns over multiple time periods, it is conventional to assume that any cash flow income is reinvested in the underlying asset as soon as the cash is received. As a result, during the second period, third period, and all following time periods the capital gains income and cash flow income that were reinvested generate a third type of income. For the year 1982, for instance, the total return from the coupon-paying intermediate-term U.S. Treasury bond index is composed of the following three components:

Coupon income for 1982 that is reinvested	12.81%
Plus: Price change income (capital appreciation) for 1982	14.23%
Plus: Reinvestment return (interest-on-the-interest)	2.06%
Total: Intermediate-term T-bond index's total return for 1982	29.10%

Since the interest-on-the-interest is easy to overlook, some investors fail to manage this component of income to their advantage.

Table 11-4 shows the annual total returns and component returns from 1971 through 1999 for the large common stocks, long-term U.S. Treasury bonds, and intermediate-term U.S. Treasury bonds indexes. The data in Table 11-4 reveal that whether or not the cash flows are reinvested has a significant impact on the future value of invested funds. Most financial researchers assume that all cash flows are immediately reinvested. In reality, the cash flows may not actually be reinvested. If the cash flows are not reinvested, the investment's returns will be reduced by: (1) the cash flows not reinvested and (2) future interest-on-the-interest the cash flows could have earned if reinvested.

TABLE 11-4 **Yearly Total Returns and the Components of Total Returns for the Large Common Stocks, Long-Term U.S. Treasury Bonds, and Intermediate-Term U.S. Treasury Bonds Indexes, 1971–99, Percent Per Year**

	Large-Company Stocks				Long-Term Government Bonds					Intermediate-Term Government Bonds				
Year	Capital Appreciation Return	Income Return	Reinvestment Return	Total Return	Capital Appreciation Return	Income Return	Reinvestment Return	Total Return	Year-end Yield	Capital Appreciation Return	Income Return	Reinvestment Return	Total Return	Year-end Yield
1971	10.79	3.33	0.19	14.31	6.61	6.32	0.31	13.23	5.97	2.72	5.75	0.25	8.72	5.25
1972	15.63	3.09	0.26	18.98	−0.35	5.87	0.17	5.69	5.99	−0.75	5.75	0.16	5.16	5.85
1973	−17.37	2.86	−0.16	−14.66	−7.70	6.51	0.08	−1.11	7.26	−2.19	6.58	0.22	4.61	6.79
1974	−29.72	3.69	−0.44	−26.47	−3.45	7.27	0.54	4.35	7.60	−1.99	7.24	0.44	5.69	7.12
1975	31.55	5.37	0.29	37.20	0.73	7.99	0.47	9.20	8.05	0.12	7.35	0.36	7.83	7.19
1976	19.15	4.38	0.31	23.84	8.07	7.89	0.80	16.75	7.21	5.25	7.10	0.51	12.87	6.00
1977	−11.50	4.31	0.01	−7.18	−7.86	7.14	0.04	−0.69	8.03	−5.15	6.49	0.06	1.41	7.51
1978	1.06	5.33	0.17	6.56	−9.05	7.90	−0.03	−1.18	8.98	−4.49	7.83	0.14	3.49	8.83
1979	12.31	5.71	0.42	18.44	−9.84	8.86	−0.25	−1.23	10.12	−5.07	9.04	0.12	4.09	10.33
1980	25.77	5.73	0.92	32.42	−14.00	9.97	0.08	−3.95	11.99	−6.81	10.55	0.17	3.91	12.45
1981	−9.72	4.89	−0.08	−4.91	−10.33	11.55	0.64	1.86	13.34	−4.55	12.97	1.03	9.45	13.96
1982	14.76	5.50	1.15	21.41	23.95	13.50	2.91	40.36	10.95	14.23	12.81	2.06	29.10	9.90
1983	17.27	5.00	0.24	22.51	−9.82	10.38	0.09	0.65	11.97	−3.30	10.35	0.35	7.41	11.41
1984	1.39	4.56	0.31	6.27	2.32	11.74	1.42	15.48	11.70	1.22	11.68	1.12	14.02	11.04
1985	26.34	5.10	0.72	32.16	17.84	11.25	1.88	30.97	9.56	9.01	10.29	1.04	20.33	8.55
1986	14.63	3.74	0.10	18.47	14.99	8.98	0.56	24.53	7.89	6.99	7.72	0.43	15.14	6.85
1987	2.03	3.64	−0.44	5.23	−10.69	7.92	0.06	−2.71	9.20	−4.75	7.47	0.19	2.90	8.32
1988	12.41	4.17	0.24	16.81	0.36	8.97	0.34	9.67	9.18	−2.26	8.24	0.13	6.10	9.17
1989	27.26	3.85	0.38	31.49	8.62	8.81	0.68	18.11	8.16	4.34	8.46	0.49	13.29	7.94
1990	−6.56	3.36	0.03	−3.17	−2.61	8.19	0.61	6.18	8.44	1.02	8.15	0.56	9.73	7.70
1991	26.31	3.82	0.42	30.55	10.10	8.22	0.98	19.30	7.30	7.36	7.43	0.67	15.46	5.97
1992	4.46	3.03	0.18	7.67	0.34	7.26	0.45	8.05	7.26	0.64	6.27	0.28	7.19	6.11
1993	7.06	2.83	0.11	9.99	10.71	7.17	0.35	18.24	6.54	5.56	5.53	0.15	11.24	5.22
1994	−1.54	2.82	0.03	1.31	−14.29	6.59	−0.07	−7.77	7.99	−11.14	6.07	−0.07	−5.14	7.80
1995	34.11	2.91	0.41	37.43	23.04	7.60	1.03	31.67	6.03	9.66	6.69	0.45	16.80	5.38
1996	20.26	2.54	0.27	23.07	−7.37	6.18	0.26	−0.93	6.73	−3.90	5.82	0.18	2.10	6.16
1997	31.01	2.11	0.25	33.36	8.51	6.64	0.71	15.85	6.02	1.94	6.14	0.30	8.38	5.73
1998	26.67	1.68	0.24	28.58	6.89	5.83	0.34	13.06	5.42	4.66	5.29	0.25	10.21	4.68
1999	19.53	1.36	0.15	21.04	−14.35	5.57	−0.19	−8.96	6.82	−7.06	5.30	−0.01	−1.77	6.45

SUMMARY: Whether or not cash flows are reinvested has a significant impact on the future value of invested funds. Since the reinvestment component of an investment's total return is often too large to ignore, most financial researchers assume that all cash flows are immediately reinvested. In actuality, the cash flows may or may not be reinvested. If the cash flows are not reinvested, the investment's returns will be reduced by two components: (1) the cash flows, and (2) future interest-on-the-interest from reinvested cash flows.

SOURCE: *Stocks, Bonds, Bills, and Inflation: 2000 Yearbook*, Ibbotson Associates, North Michigan Avenue, Chicago, IL 60601, Table 2-6, pp. 40–41. Based on copyrighted works by Ibbotson and Sinquefield. All rights reserved. Used with permission.

Extended data like that in Table 11-4 contain some surprises. Data not included in Table 11-4 show that for the years 1929–31 inclusive the reinvestment return component of the large common stock index's total returns were negative. These negative reinvestment returns occurred because the reinvested cash dividends were used to buy stocks that were depreciating during the Depression and the stock market's associated crash. Other negative reinvestment return components may also be found for other indexes for similar reasons.

Table 11-4 also throws some light on the October 19, 1987 international stock market crash the *Wall Street Journal* article (Fig. 11-2) says was the worst day in history for common-stock investors. Table 11-4 shows that the stock market index racked up enough gains during the rest of the 1980s to post a handsome return for the decade. The conclusion to be drawn from the October 1987 international stock market crash is that investors should try not to succumb to a panic attack during short-term price fluctuations that, from a larger perspective, may be of lesser importance. Unfortunately, many panicky investors sold near the bottom during October 1987.

Bullish and Bearish Returns

The *Wall Street Journal* article below (Fig. 11-2) focuses on a few special days when the stock market collapsed. Table 11-5 extends this newspaper article's look at spectacularly bad days in the stock market to consider bullish and bearish periods that lasted for 1 year or longer. To see both the short- and long-run points of view in several different financial sectors, holding periods of 1, 5, 10, 15, and 20 years are analyzed. Table 11-5 analyzes 74 nonoverlapping annual, 70 overlapping 5-year, 65 overlapping 10-year, 60 overlapping 15-year, and 55 overlapping 20-year time periods. The table shows the number of times that each index had a positive return, and the number of times that each index was the highest of all seven of the basic Ibbotson indexes. Table 11-5 provides market insights that help investors answer important questions before they invest. For example, investors can: (1) determine in advance of investing the investment vehicles in which they can feel most comfortable during the bad times, (2) get ideas about how long certain kinds of market conditions usually last, and (3) gain insights about how long it will take to achieve their investment goals with alternative asset allocations under the best- and/or worst-case scenarios.

To see what the data mean, consider the 20-year rolling period returns in the bottom panel of Table 11-5. The first of the 20-year rolling period returns was from 1926 to 1945 inclusive. For each successive 20-year rolling period return 1 additional year was added to both the beginning year and the ending year, and then another average rate of return was computed for the next 20-year period. Thus, 18 years from one 20-year period were used again in the next 20-year period. For all asset classes the largest 20-year average annual return, 21.13%, was found to be for small-company stocks from 1942 to 1961 inclusive.

The data in Table 11-5 can be analyzed to obtain some interesting patterns. For instance, note that the number of positive returns, stated as a percentage of the total number of periods that were compiled, tends to increase with the duration of the periods sampled. For the large-common-stocks index, for example, $(54/74 = .729 =)$ 72.9% of the 1-year returns were positive while $(55/55 = 1.0 =)$ 100% of the 20-year periods were positive. These data suggest that as you invest for longer time spans, the probability your wealth appreciates increases.

Table 11-5 provides some evidence supporting what is called **time diversification.** Note that the maximum and minimum annualized returns over holding periods of 1, 5, 10, 15, and 20 years tend to become closer together as the length of the holding period increases. This tendency results from the **mean reverting** returns. If a return is either extremely high or low during one period, it tends to revert back toward its mean return during some later period. As a result of this mean reversion, some people argue that time diversification tends

FIGURE 11-2   NEWSPAPER EXCERPT: "Market Crash? What's That?"

DOW DIARY
A WEEKLY LOOK AT THE AVERAGE IN ITS 100TH YEAR

Market Crash? What's That?

What does a bad day in the stock market feel like? In a sense, people who started investing during the past six years wouldn't know.

Sure, there have been days when the Dow Jones Industrial Average lost a lot of points. But what affects investors' wallets isn't the point change; it's the percentage change. In the 1990s, the biggest one-day percentage loss in the industrial average has been a 3.93% drop on Nov. 15, 1991.

That decline was spurred by a rout in biotechnology stocks and by fears that Congress would cap the rate on credit cards, hurting bank stocks. "A classic cave-in," one trader called it. But in relative terms, it was just a mosquito bite.

The fact is, not one of the 100 greatest percentage losses in the Dow industrials (all 4.27% or more) has occurred in this decade.

The accompanying table shows the five biggest one-day percentage losses in history. The biggest was the historic crash that brought the industrials down 22.61% on Oct. 19, 1987. Among the caus-

The Five Worst Days
Largest one-day percentage drops in the Dow Jones Industrial Average

DATE	POINT LOSS	% LOSS
Oct. 19, 1987	508.00	22.6%
Oct. 28, 1929	38.88	12.8
Oct. 29, 1929	30.57	11.7
Nov. 6, 1929	25.55	9.9
Dec. 18, 1899	5.57	8.7

es of the 1987 crash were rising interest rates, the U.S. bombing of Iranian oil platforms, friction with U.S. trading partners, rampant speculation in the futures markets, and loss of investor confidence after the Dow industrials skidded in September and early October.

The second-worst, third-worst and fourth-worst days occurred within about a week of each other in the crash of 1929. As in 1987, the 1929 crash had been preceded by a boisterous economic and stock-market boom. Speculation by investors who needed to put down only 10% of the purchase price for their stocks fueled the Roaring Twenties bull market, but also aggravated the crash. When their brokers demanded more collateral, investors were forced to sell shares, producing a downward spiral.

The fifth-worst day was Dec. 18, 1889. According to historian Robert Sobel of Hofstra University, the U.S. had suffered some casualties in the Philippines fighting against guerrillas seeking independence, and the British had suffered losses in the Boer War. What's more—as is so often a factor in market declines—interest rates were rising.

—John R. Dorfman

Visit the DJIA Centennial site on the Internet at http://djia100.dowjones.com

SOURCE: "Market Crash? What's That?" *Wall Street Journal*, 9 September 1996, C1.

to average away some of the short-term fluctuations and, in so doing, reduce the risk of long-term investing.[4] This pattern can be observed in Table 11-5.

Intertemporal Stability of Volatility

The Risk-Return Relationship. Figure 11-1 contains two graphs showing how the monthly rates of return from the large-company-stock index and the long-term U.S. Government bond index fluctuated from 1926 through 1999. Figure 11-1A shows that the U.S. stock market was

TABLE 11-5 **Maximum and Minimum Returns over 1-, 5-, 10-, 15-, and 20-Year Holding Periods for Seven Investment Indexes (compounded annual returns in percent)**

Series	Maximum Value		Minimum Value		Times Positive (out of 74 Years)	Times Highest Returning Asset
	Return	Year(s)	Return	Year(s)		
Annual Returns						
Large-company stocks	53.99	1933	−43.34	1931	54	16
Small-company stocks	142.87	1933	−58.01	1937	52	32
Long-term corporate bonds	42.56	1982	−8.09	1969	57	6
Long-term government bonds	40.36	1982	−9.18	1967	53	6
Intermediate-term government bonds	29.10	1982	−5.14	1994	66	2
U.S. Treasury bills	14.71	1981	−0.02	1938	73	6
Inflation	18.16	1946	−10.30	1932	64	6
5-Year Rolling Period Returns				**(out of 70 overlapping 5-year periods)**		
Large-company stocks	28.55	1995–99	−12.47	1928–32	63	22
Small-company stocks	45.90	1941–45	−27.54	1928–32	61	37
Long-term corporate bonds	22.51	1982–86	−2.22	1965–69	67	7
Long-term government bonds	21.62	1982–86	−2.14	1965–69	64	1
Intermediate-term government bonds	16.98	1982–86	0.96	1955–59	70	2
U.S. Treasury bills	11.12	1979–83	0.07	1938–42	70	0
Inflation	10.06	1977–81	−5.42	1928–32	63	1
10-Year Rolling Period Returns				**(out of 65 overlapping 10-year periods)**		
Large-company stocks	20.06	1949–58	−0.89	1929–38	63	20
Small-company stocks	30.38	1975–84	−5.70	1929–38	63	35
Long-term corporate bonds	16.32	1982–91	0.98	1947–56	65	6
Long-term government bonds	15.56	1982–91	−0.07	1950–59	64	0
Intermediate-term government bonds	13.13	1982–91	1.25	1947–56	65	2
U.S. Treasury bills	9.17	1978–87	0.15	1933–42/ 1934–43	65	1
Inflation	8.67	1973–82	−2.57	1926–35	59	1
15-Year Rolling Period Returns				**(out of 60 overlapping 15-year periods)**		
Large-company stocks	18.93	1985–99	0.64	1929–43	60	12
Small-company stocks	23.33	1975–89	−1.30	1927–41	57	44
Long-term corporate bonds	13.66	1982–96	1.02	1955–69	60	4
Long-term government bonds	13.53	1981–95	0.40	1955–69	60	0
Intermediate-term government bonds	11.27	1981–95	1.45	1945–59	60	0
U.S. Treasury bills	8.32	1977–91	0.22	1933–47	60	0
Inflation	7.30	1968–82	−1.59	1926–40	57	0
20-Year Rolling Period Returns				**(out of 55 overlapping 20-year periods)**		
Large-company stocks	17.87	1980–99	3.11	1929–48	55	5
Small-company stocks	21.13	1942–61	5.74	1929–48	55	50
Long-term corporate bonds	10.86	1979–98	1.34	1950–69	55	0
Long-term government bonds	11.14	1979–98	0.69	1950–69	55	0
Intermediate-term government bonds	9.85	1979–98	1.58	1940–59	55	0
U.S. Treasury bills	7.72	1972–91	0.42	1931–50	55	0
Inflation	6.36	1966–85	0.07	1926–45	55	0

SOURCE: *Stocks, Bonds, Bills, and Inflation: 2000 Yearbook*, Ibbotson Associates, North Michigan Avenue, Chicago, IL 60601, Table 2-7, p. 43. Based on copyrighted works by Ibbotson and Sinquefield. All rights reserved. Used with permission.

TABLE 11-6	Annualized Monthly Standard Deviations by Decade, 1926–99							
Asset Class	1920s[a]	1930s	1940s	1950s	1960s	1970s	1980s	1990s
Large company	23.9%	41.6%	17.5%	14.1%	13.1%	17.1%	19.4%	15.8%
Small company	24.7	78.6	34.5	14.4	21.5	30.8	22.5	20.2
Long-term corporate	1.8	5.3	1.8	4.4	4.9	8.7	14.1	6.9
Long-term government	4.1	5.3	2.8	4.6	6.0	8.7	16.0	8.9
Intermediate-term government	1.7	3.3	1.2	2.9	3.3	5.2	8.8	4.6
Treasury bills	0.3	0.2	0.1	0.2	0.4	0.6	0.9	0.4
Inflation rate	2.0	2.5	3.1	1.2	0.7	1.2	1.3	0.7

[a]Based on the period 1926–29.

SOURCE: *Stocks, Bonds, Bills, and Inflation: 2000 Yearbook,* Ibbotson Associates, North Michigan Avenue, Chicago, IL 60601, Table 6-1, p. 114. Based on copyrighted works by Ibbotson and Sinquefield. All rights reserved. Used with permission.

tremendously volatile before and during the crash of the 1930s and again during the October 1987 international stock market crash. Acting independently, the returns from U.S. Treasury bonds were unusually volatile from 1979 through 1982. The 1979–82 interest rate volatility is attributable to monetary policies the Federal Reserve adopted during that period.

Table 11-6 quantifies the volatilities illustrated in Figure 11-1 and other standard deviations as well. The table contains decades-long averages of monthly standard deviations stated at annual rates.* Comparing the average risk and return statistics in Table 11-1 with the standard deviations in Table 11-6 reveals that the positive risk-return relationship suggested by economic theory is durable through time. Even though the risk statistics in Table 11-6 are unstable through time, T-bills consistently are the least risky category and the stocks of small companies are consistently the most risky. These consistent risk-rankings correlate positively with the average returns in Table 11-1.

Econometrics. Although economists and financial analysts are pleased with the support that the empirical risk-return statistics lends to economic theory, statisticians and econometricians are displeased with the erratic standard deviations in Table 11-6. Most statistical estimation procedures assume the standard deviation of a random variable remains constant through time. Intertemporal stability (constancy through time) in a standard deviation is a desirable quality called **homoscedasticity**.

Unfortunately, most of the standard deviations in Table 11-6 are not homoscedastistic through the 1926–99 decades. The stock market indexes and the longer-term bond indexes display a troublesome characteristic that statisticians call *heteroscedasticity*. Statisticians dislike standard deviations that are unstable (heteroscedastistic) because they are apt to yield

---

* The annualized monthly standard deviations (σ_n) are calculated as follows:

$$\sigma_n = \{\, [\, \sigma_1^2 + (1 + \bar{r}_1)^2 \,]^{\,n} - (1 + \bar{r}_1)^{2n} \,\}^{1/2}$$

where n = the number of periods per year (namely, n = 12 for monthly); σ_1 = the 1-month standard deviation; and, $\bar{r}_1$ = the 1-month arithmetic mean return. This formula is from Haim Levy and Deborah Gunthorpe, "Optimal Investment Proportions in Senior Securities and Equities Under Alternative Holding Periods," *Journal of Portfolio Management* (summer 1993): 33. This formula is more exact than the following popular approximation: $\sigma_N = (n)^{1/2} \sigma_1$.

statistical estimates that are erratic and vary from sample to sample in a disconcerting manner.* Investors have the same concerns as the statisticians and econometricians.

Unstable variances can corrupt some important asset-pricing models that are introduced later in this book. Heteroscedasticity causes problems for these asset-pricing models because the models assume economic equilibrium exists. The static nature of equilibrium models means they are ill-equipped to deal with the fluctuating empirical values that arise in real-life disequilibriums. Tools for dealing with unstable risk statistics are suggested later in this book.

Cross Correlations Between the Investment Indexes and Serial Correlations

Financial analysts not only need information about investments' average returns and risk statistics, they can also want to understand any interrelationships that exist. The *correlation coefficient* is a statistic that measures statistical relationships. Correlations measure the way random variables covary (interact). A correlation can also be a goodness-of-fit statistic. For instance, a correlation describes how closely the data points fit around a regression line like the characteristic line in Chapter 7 (pages 169–170).

Definition of Correlation Coefficient. A correlation coefficient is an index number that is represented by the lowercase Greek letter rho, ρ.

$$+1.0 \geq \rho \geq -1.0$$

Eqn. 11-1 defines the **cross correlation,** where

$COV(r_x,r_y)$ = the covariance of returns from assets x and y as defined below

σ_x = the standard deviation of returns from x

σ_y = the standard deviation of returns from y

$$\rho_{xy} = \frac{COV(r_x,r_y)}{\sigma_x \sigma_y} \tag{11-1}$$

Eqn. 11-2 defines the **covariance** of returns, where

$r_{x,t}$ = the one-period rate of return from series x in time period t

$r_{y,t}$ = the one-period rate of return from series y in time period t

$\bar{r}_x$ = the arithmetic mean return of the historical x series

$\bar{r}_y$ = the arithmetic mean return of the historical y series

T = Total number of observations = the number of the Terminal (last) observation

$$COV(r_x,r_y) = \left(\frac{1}{T}\right)\sum_{t=1}^{T}(r_{x,t} - \bar{r}_x)(r_{y,t} - \bar{r}_y) \tag{11-2}$$

Cross- and Serial-Correlations. Table 11-7 contains two different kinds of correlation coefficients. **Cross correlations** measure the predictability of one series, conditional on knowing the value of a different series. In other words, cross correlations measure how two separate series are interrelated. The second kind of correlation coefficient is the **serial correlation,**

---

* Heteroscedasticity and homoscedasticity have implications for statistics that are discussed in many econometrics and statistics textbooks.

TABLE 11-7   Cross Correlations Between Annual Returns from Asset Class Indexes and Serial Correlations, 1926–99

Series	Large-Company Stocks	Small-Company Stocks	Long-Term Corporate Bonds	Long-Term Government Bonds	Intermediate Government Bonds	U.S. Treasury Bills	Inflation
Large-company stocks	1.00						
Small-company stocks	0.79	1.00					
Long-term corporate bonds	0.25	0.10	1.00				
Long-term government bonds	0.19	0.02	0.94	1.00			
Intermediate-term government bonds	0.11	−0.04	0.91	0.91	1.00		
U.S. Treasury bills	−0.02	−0.09	0.21	0.24	0.49	1.00	
Inflation	−0.03	0.05	−0.15	−0.15	0.01	0.41	1.00
Serial correlations[a]	0.01	0.08	0.09	−0.03	0.17	0.92	0.65

[a]The standard error for all estimates is 0.12

SOURCE: *Stocks, Bonds, Bills, and Inflation: 2000 Yearbook,* Ibbotson Associates, North Michigan Avenue, Chicago, IL 60601, Table 6-3, p. 119. Based on copyrighted works by Ibbotson and Sinquefield. All rights reserved. Used with permission.

also called the **autocorrelation.** Serial correlations measure the extent to which the values in one time-series are related to leading or lagged values in the same time-series of data. Stated differently, serial correlations measure how the successive values in a series influence lagged or leading values in that same series. Data that move in *trends* will have *positive serial correlation* coefficients. Data that experiences more *reversals* than random numbers will have *negative serial correlations.* Random numbers have serial correlation coefficients of zero. Figure 8-3 in Chapter 8 (page 192) illustrates various patterns associated with different serial correlation (autocorrelation) values.

Cross Correlations Between Annual Returns.   The matrix of cross correlations in Table 11-7 shows how all the random variables in the table interrelate (covary, interact) with each other. The high positive correlation of 0.79 between the small-company stocks and the large-company stocks shown in Table 11-7 indicates that both categories of stocks tend to vary together closely. The long-term and the intermediate-term bond indexes are highly positively correlated with each other as well. These two long-term bond indexes also have marginally significant positive (slightly above zero) correlations with the two stock market indexes, which suggests that bonds and stocks tend to covary together in a weak but undependable fashion. The T-bills also have statistically significant positive correlations with the two long-term bond indexes, the intermediate-term bond index, and the inflation rate. These relationships arise because the inflation rate affects other variables—directly, and indirectly through intermediate variables. As explained in Eqn. 10-9 in Chapter 10, first, the inflation rate has a direct (positive) impact on all market interest rates; and, second, interest rates vary inversely with bond prices (and, to a lesser extent, with stock prices).

Serial Correlations Between Annual Returns.   The row of serial correlations across the bottom of Table 11-7 shows that the rate of inflation is highly positively serially correlated with itself. This means that inflation moves in trends; it does not zigzag (reverse direction frequently). Figure 2-1 in Chapter 2 (page 23) illustrates the smooth trends in the inflation rate that are suggested by inflation's high positive serial correlation coefficient in Table 11-7. Simple linear projections (extrapolations) of economic variables (like the inflation rate) that have high positive serial correlations usually make good short-run forecasts.

T-bill returns are also highly positively serially correlated through time. This indication of trending behavior results from the previously mentioned facts that (1) the T-bill returns are highly positively cross-correlated with the rate of inflation, and (2) the rate of inflation is highly positively serially correlated with itself.* Inflation's high positive serial correlation feeds the T-bill returns to make them highly positively serially correlated too—as illustrated in Figure 2-1.

The serial correlation coefficients for the stocks and the two long-term bond indexes are not significantly different from zero. This absence of serial correlation suggests that, unlike the trendy inflation rate, the stock returns and the returns from the two long-term bond indexes tend to fluctuate randomly. These random price fluctuations make it difficult to forecast their market prices. As a result, using trend projections or extrapolating simple patterns cannot be expected to yield meaningful forecasts of the prices of stocks or long-term bonds. Nevertheless, stock price chartists and other technical analysts disagree with these scientific statistics and assert they find price patterns that are useful in making predictions.

ASSESSING THE CREDIBILITY OF CONFLICTING SOURCES OF INFORMATION

STUDY CHECK

QUESTION: Which of the following conflicting views do you choose to believe?

(View One) Technical analysts who earn their livings by drawing and interpreting graphs of historical security prices claim they find meaningful patterns in these prices.

(View Two) Academic scholars whose esteem in their profession suffers if they publish poor research claim that no patterns exist and that stock prices fluctuate randomly in the short-run.

ANSWER: The technical analysts' credibility is diminished by the fact that they have an economic incentive to exaggerate their findings, and that the technicians have published no scientific evidence. The academics have an economic incentive to present unbiased findings, and the academics publish supportive scientific statistics to back their claims of randomness.

HISTORICAL RISK PREMIA

This section uses the empirical data on seven basic indexes in Table 2-1 of Chapter 2, which is reproduced in this chapter's Table 11-1, to develop two subcategories of derived returns:

◆ **Risk premia** are inducements to encourage risk-averse investors to take risks. Tables 11-8 and 11-9 contain examples of historical risk premia.

◆ **Real returns** are inflation-adjusted returns that are defined in Chapter 10's Eqns. 10-7 and 10-9a. Table 11-10 contains historical real returns.

The return statistics computed from long-term samples like those in Table 11-1 provide history-based estimates of an asset's risk-adjusted discount rate (required rate of return, cost

---

*   Irving Fisher's venerable theory about the positive relationship between market interest rates and the infla-
      tion rate is the topic of Chapter 20.

TABLE 11-8 **Historical Risk Premia for Bonds from 1926–99 Computed from Arithmetic Mean Returns (AMRs), in percentages**

Historical Bond Returns from Table 2-1 in Chapter 2 and Table 11-1

Long-term (20-year) corporate bond AMR = 5.9%
Long-term (20-year) U.S. Treasury bond AMR = 5.5%
Intermediate-term (5-year) U.S. Treasury coupon note AMR = 5.4%
Short-term (30-day) U.S. Treasury bill AMR = 3.8%

Historical Risk Premia

Long-term horizon premium = (AMR LT T-bond TR) − (AMR T-bill TR) **(11-3)**
$$= 5.5\% - 3.8\% = 1.7\%, \text{ or } 170 \text{ BPs}$$

Default premium = (AMR LT Corp. Bond TR) − (AMR LT T-bond TR) **(11-4)**
$$= 5.9\% - 5.5\% = 0.4\%, \text{ or } 40 \text{ BPs}$$

SOURCE: Calculated from *Stocks, Bonds, Bills, and Inflation: 2000 Yearbook*, Ibbotson Associates, North Michigan Avenue, Chicago, IL 60601, Table 2-1, p. 33. Based on copyrighted works by Ibbotson and Sinquefield. All rights reserved. Used with permission. Ibbotson's Table 2-1 is reproduced as Table 2-1 in Chapter 2 of this book, and in this chapter's Table 11-1.

TABLE 11-9 **Selected Historical Risk Premia for Stocks, 1926–99**

Historical Default-Free Returns from Tables 2-1 and 11-1

Large-company stock's AMR = 13.3%
Small-company stock's AMR = 17.6%
Long-term (20-year) U.S. Treasury coupon bond AMR = 5.5%
Intermediate-term (5-year) U.S. Treasury coupon note AMR = 5.4%
Short-term (30-day) U.S. Treasury Bill AMR = 3.8%

Historical Horizon Premia for Stocks

Long-horizon premium = (AMR Large stock TR) − (AMR LT T-bond TR) **(11-5)**
$$= 13.3\% - 5.5\% = 7.8\%, \text{ or } 780 \text{ BPs}$$

Intermediate-horizon premium = (AMR Large stock TR) − (AMR IT T-bond TR) **(11-6)**
$$= 13.3\% - 5.4\% = 7.9\%, \text{ or } 790 \text{ BPs}$$

Short-horizon premium = (AMR Large stock TR) − (AMR T-bill TR) **(11-7)**
$$= 13.3\% - 3.8\% = 9.5\%, \text{ or } 950 \text{ BPs}$$

Historical Size Premia

Small-stock risk premium = (AMR Small Stock TR) − (AMR Large Stock TR) **(11-8)**
$$= 17.6\% - 13.3\% = 4.3\%, \text{ or } 430 \text{ BPs}$$

SOURCE: Calculated using data from *Stocks, Bonds, Bills, and Inflation: 2000 Yearbook*, Ibbotson Associates, North Michigan Avenue, Chicago, IL 60601, Table 2-1, p. 33. Based on copyrighted works by Ibbotson and Sinquefield. All rights reserved. Used with permission. Ibbotson's Table 2-1 is reproduced as Table 2-1 in Chapter 2 and summarized in this chapter's Table 11-1.

of capital). The formulas in Tables 11-2 suggested ways to dissect the historical returns in Table 11-1 into meaningful components. After various different risk premiums are derived, whatever risk premia are appropriate for a particular asset can be combined to determine the appropriate risk-adjusted discount rate to use in computing that asset's present value. Table 2-3 in Chapter 2 shows how to combine risk premiums.

Bond Horizon Premia

Inflation Premium. Chapter 10 explained how the nominal rate of return, r, can be divided into two components, the real rate (rr) plus an inflation premium (INF). Inserting values into Eqn. 10-9a approximates the real return to be $\frac{60}{100}$ of 1%—or 60 basis points (BPs)—for a U.S. Treasury bill.

$$rr = r - INF = 3.8\% - 3.2\% = 0.6\% \hspace{2cm} \text{(10-9a)}$$

Historical AMR inflation rate, INF, 1926–99	3.2%	= 320 BPs
Plus: Historical real rate of return for T-bills, rr	0.6%	= 60 BPs
Equals: Historical Treasury bill nominal AMR, 1926–99	3.8%	= 380 BPs

Horizon Premium. The prices of long-term U.S. Treasury bonds behave differently than the prices of Treasury bills and, as a result, their returns differ. The **bond horizon premium** defined by Eqn. 11-3 in Table 11-8 measures the additional return that investors demanded historically to induce them to hold T-bonds instead of shorter-term T-bills.[*]

The return from a U.S. Treasury bond equals the sum of two component returns—the riskless short-term rate plus a horizon premium. To measure the return from a long-term Treasury bond, the approximate (5.5% − 3.8% =) 1.7% long-term horizon premium computed from data in Table 2-1 in Chapter 2 is added to the 3.8% nominal return from a Treasury bill to obtain the long-term Treasury bond's historical return of 5.5%.[**]

Short-term Treasury bill's historical AMR	3.8%	= 380 BPs
Plus: Approximate long-horizon risk premium	1.7%	= 170 BPs
Equals: Historical AMR from a long-horizon T-bond	5.5%	= 550 BPs

Bond Default Premia

The return from a long-term corporate bond is composed of the real riskless rate, an inflation premium, the horizon premium, and a default premium. Eqn. 11-4 in Table 11-8 shows that bond default premiums are computed as the difference between the total return (TR) from a long-term corporate bond and the total return from a long-term U.S. Treasury bond. This *total bond default premium* can be further decomposed into three separate subcomponents: the pure bond default premium, callability premium, and the expected default loss.

---

[*] Duration measures the time structure and interest rate risk of a bond. Duration is explored in detail in Chapter 21. Duration, not years to maturity, is the bond characteristic that determines the horizon premium.

[**] Two mutually exclusive assumptions can be made about the reinvestment rate for bonds' cash flows. (1) Coupon income returns can be used to compute the bond's multiperiod return for coupon-paying bonds. Some prefer this approach because the capital appreciation component of a bond's total return (TR) cannot be forecasted accurately. (2) In this book the bond's total return (TR) is used as the reinvestment rate instead of the coupon income return. The TR is the appropriate reinvestment rate for those who assume all coupons are immediately reinvested in the bonds used to create the index. Either approach is acceptable, as long as it is followed consistently.

TABLE 11-10	Arithmetic Average Real Returns and Their Standard Deviations, 1926–99

Formula for a Stock's Real Return, rr

(Stock's real return, rr) = (Stock's nominal return, r) − (Inflation rate, INF)	**(10-9a)**

Stocks Real Return Statistics, rr	Eqn. No.	Standard Deviation of rr
(Large stock rr, 10.0%[a]) = (Large stock r, 13.3%) − (INF, 3.2%)	**(11-9)**	20.3%
(Small stock, rr, 14.1%[a]) = (Large stock, r, 17.6%) − (INF, 3.2%)	**(11-10)**	32.9%

Bonds Real Return Statistics, rr	Eqn. No.	Standard Deviation of rr
(LT corporate bond rr, 2.9%[a]) = (LT corp. bond r, 5.9%) − (INF, 3.2%)	**(11-11)**	10.0%
(LT T-bond rr, 2.5%[a]) = (LT T-bond r, 5.5%) − (INF, 3.2%)	**(11-12)**	10.6%
(IT T-bond rr, 2.3%[a]) = (IT T-bond r, 5.4%) − (INF, 3.2%)	**(11-13)**	7.0%
(T-bill rr, 0.8%[a]) = (LT T-bond r, 3.8%) − (INF, 3.2%)	**(11-14)**	4.1%

[a]Correct answer after rounding errors eliminated and interest on the interest included.

SOURCE: Calculated from *Stocks, Bonds, Bills, and Inflation: 2000 Yearbook,* Ibbotson Associates, North Michigan Avenue, Chicago, IL 60601, Tables 2-1 and 6-8, pp. 33 and 125. Based on copyrighted works by Ibbotson and Sinquefield. All rights reserved. Used with permission. Ibbotson's Table 2-1 is reproduced as Table 2-1 in Chapter 2 of this book and in this chapter's Table 11-1.

Components of the Bond Default Premium. The possibility always exists that a corporate bond issuer defaults. As a result, corporate bonds must pay higher returns than are required of an identical bond that is free from default (credit) risk. If a bond defaults, the *default loss* will be small if only one coupon is paid late or omitted. In the worst case scenario, a bond default results in the complete loss of all coupon income and the entire principal. In any event, even the smallest default loss erodes the bond default premium to an amount that is less than what is computed with Eqn. 11-4.

As a result of default losses, the rate of return that is anticipated from a corporate bond, or a portfolio of corporate bonds, is less than the bond's yield. The expected default loss must be subtracted from the bond's yield. That portion of the bond default premium that remains after default losses are subtracted is a *pure default risk premium*. The expected return from a corporate bond equals the expected return from a U.S. Treasury bond of equal maturity, plus the pure default risk premium.

Callability Risk Is Captured in the Default Risk Premium. Investors buying callable bonds face the risk that market interest rates fall below their bond's coupon rate and, as a result, the bond's issuer redeems (calls in) the bond before its maturity date. An early call prevents the owner of a redeemed bond from keeping the bond's principal invested at its previously higher market interest rate. The bond default premium computed with Eqn. 11-4 inadvertently includes the call risk premium from callable bonds. Empirical observations suggest that call risk premia can vary from as little as 5 BPs on investment grade bonds that are not likely to be called soon to over 30 BPs on lower-grade bonds that are likely to be called in the near future.

FIGURE 11-3   The Expected Return Components for a Noncallable
                  Long-Horizon Bond Issued by a Large Corporation

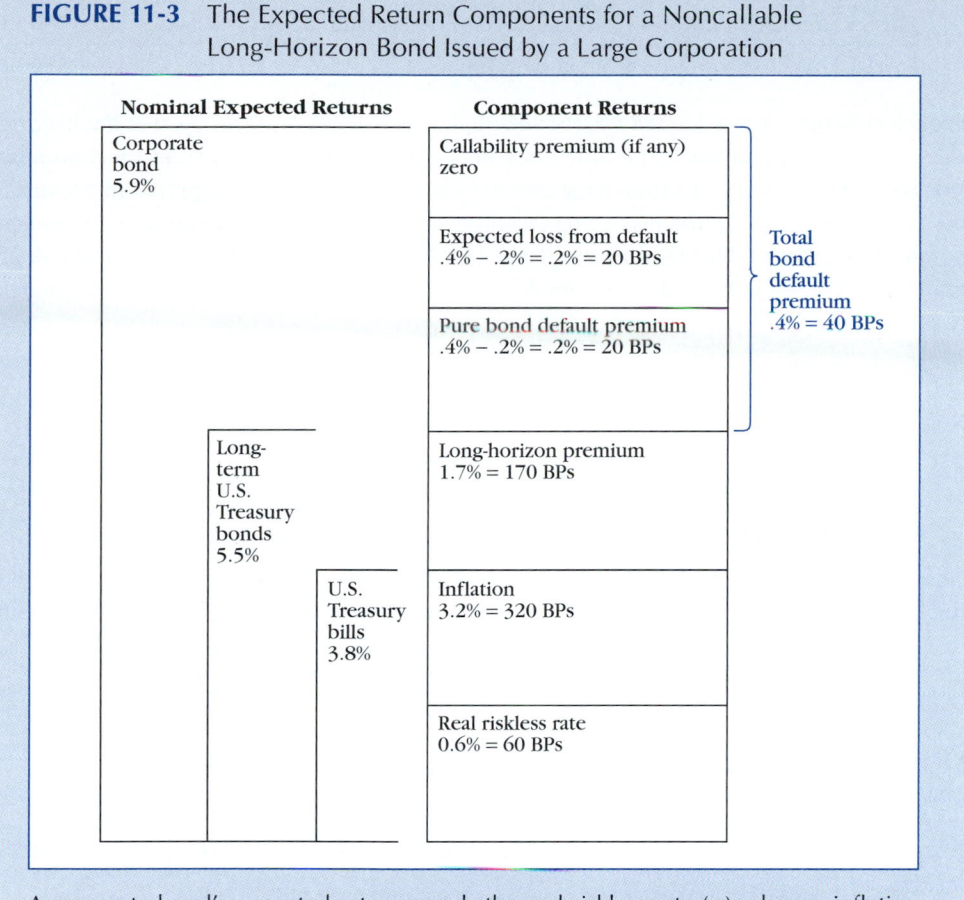

A corporate bond's expected return equals the real riskless rate (*rr*), plus an inflation premium (*INF*), plus an appropriate horizon premium, plus a default premium.

SOURCE: Workbook for AI/RI Global Portfolio Intensive Classroom Program, Alliance-Ibbotson Research Institute; this graph is adapted from Volume Two, p. 31 of Day 13.

Figure 11-3 illustrates how the return components add up to the return that is appropriate of a long-horizon noncallable bond issued by a large corporation.

Equity Risk Premia

Historical Data.   Large-company stock returns are composed of the short-term riskless rate (T-bill return) plus an equity risk premium. Eqn. 11-5 in Table 11-9 shows that the historical equity risk premium equals the amount by which the total return (*TR*) from a large company stock exceeds the total return from a long-term U.S. Treasury bond. Because large company stocks are not directly comparable to bonds, the bond horizon and bond default premia are not used to analyze the components of equity returns. Table 2-1 in Chapter 2 contains historical estimates of some of these arithmetic mean returns (AMRs). Table 11-9 lists risk premia that can be added to obtain risk-adjusted discount rates for computing the present values of equity shares.

The Return from a Large Issuer.   The long-horizon return from a common stock issued by a large corporation, for example, equals an approximate long-horizon equity risk premium of 7.80% that is added to the long-term U.S. Treasury bond return of 5.50%.

Long-term Treasury bond's AMR	5.50%	= 550 BPs
Plus: A large corporation's long-horizon equity risk premia	7.80%	= 780 BPs
Equals: Long-horizon AMR from large-cap equity	13.3%	= 1,330 BPs

Expected Returns from a Small Cap Issuer. Eqn. 11-8 in Table 11-9 shows that the historical small stock risk premium is the difference between the total returns from small company stocks and the total returns from large company stocks. To use this risk premium, reconsider the large corporation in the preceding example. If the issuer were a small-capitalization corporation instead of a large corporation, Table 11-9 shows that an additional small-cap risk premium of 4.30% would be added to obtain an appropriate numerical estimate of the stock's required rate of return.

Long-term Treasury bond's AMR	5.50%	=	550 BPs
Plus: A large corporation's long-horizon equity risk premia	7.80%	=	780 BPs
Plus: A small-cap equity size premium	4.30%	=	430 BPs
Equals: Long-horizon AMR from a small-cap equity	17.60%	=	1,760 BPs

(550 BPs and 780 BPs bracketed = 1,330 BPs)

Note that the AMR of 1,330 BPs = 13.3% for a long-horizon large-cap equity is identical to the sum of the AMR for a long-term T-bond's and the large-corporation equity risk premium.

IBBOTSON'S HISTORICALLY DERIVED INFLATION PREMIUMS

Chapter 10 introduced purchasing power risk and differentiated between real and nominal returns.

Nominal return

Minus: Real return

Equals: Embedded inflation premium

Discussion of Eqn. 10-6 in Chapter 10 explains how the U.S. government's Consumer Price Index (CPI) measures the country's inflation rate (INF). Eqn. 10-7 defined the relationship between nominal returns and real returns, and Eqn. 10-9a showed a short-cut approximation for estimating real returns. Table 11-10 contains nominal and real returns for the United States.

Table 11-10 summarizes arithmetic averages of real returns from a 74-year period. Scrutinizing month-by-month returns not published in this book reveals that occasionally most of the investment portfolios had a positive nominal return, $r_t > 0$, and a negative real return, $rr_t < 0$, in the same month. This means that sporadically those assets' nominal return were less than the inflation rate, $r_t < INF_t$, and the investor lost purchasing power. In other words, most of the asset categories in Table 11-10 provided less-than-perfect hedges against inflation.

The six average mean real returns in Table 11-10 are highly positively correlated with the six standard deviations of the average real returns. This means the positive risk-return trade-off observed with the nominal returns also exists with the real returns.

Inflation-Adjusted Common Stock Returns

Large-Cap Stocks. Table 2-1 in Chapter 2 (page 24) shows that large-company stocks total nominal returns averaged 13.3% annually from 1926 to 1999. In Table 11-10 we see that in inflation-adjusted terms the large-company stocks provided an arithmetic mean return (AMR) of 10.0%. In other words, the average U.S. investor in stocks issued by large corporations enjoyed an increase in purchasing power of 10.0% per year. This return is the difference between the large-company stocks total return and the inflation rate, as shown in Eqn. 11-9 in Table 11-10.

Small-Cap Stocks. In nominal terms, the small companies' total return over the 1926–99 period averaged 17.6% per year. Table 11-10 shows the small-company stocks provided 14.1% increase per year in purchasing power, on average.

The monthly inflation-adjusted small-company stock return equals the amount by which the small-company stocks total return exceeds the inflation rate, as shown by Eqn. 11-10 in Table 11-10. Investors who don't understand that a part of their nominal returns are lost to inflation suffer from what economists call **money illusion.**

DARLA'S MONEY ILLUSION   **EXAMPLE**

Fifty-year-old Darla is scheduled to retire and receive a lump-sum pension payout of $200,000 cash (after her income taxes are paid) on her sixtieth birthday. Darla is excited about spending the $200,000 to buy a car, a boat, and a home of her own.

Purchase	Current Price
Car	$ 30,000
Boat	$ 10,000
Home	$160,000
Total expenditure:	$200,000

If inflation proceeds at 3.0% per year during the decade that Darla works toward retirement, the cost of living will rise [$(1.03)^{10} - 1 = 0.344 =$] 34.4%. This inflation will erode the purchasing power of Darla's cash payout to 74.4% of its current cash value, or [($200,000) $\times$ (.744) =] $148,819.

$$\frac{1}{(1 + INF)^{10 \text{ years}}} = \frac{1}{1.03^{10}} = \frac{1}{1.344} = .744 = 74.4\%$$

Money illusion will cause Darla to be disappointed when he learns she can only buy 74.4% of what she thought she could buy when she was 50 years old. Hopefully, Darla's parents are not as naïve as Darla because, if they are, Darla might be forced to spend her $200,000 pension proceeds to support them.

Inflation-Adjusted Long-Term Corporate Bond Returns

The total nominal annual return from long-term corporate bonds over the 1926–99 period was 5.9%. Table 11-10 shows that, on average, the long-term corporate bonds outpaced inflation by 2.9% per year. In other words, long-term corporate bonds increased investors purchasing power by 2.9% annually, on average. This inflation-adjusted long-term corporate bond return is the difference between the long-term corporate bond total return and the inflation rate, as shown by Eqn. 11-11 in Table 11-10.

DALLAS UNDERWRITING PRICES AN IPO OF CORPORATE BONDS   **EXAMPLE**

Dallas Underwriting Corporation is pricing an initial public offering (IPO) of long-term bonds they are underwriting for the Texas Electric Power Corporation. Dallas Underwriting is using

Ibbotson Associates' historical nominal return of 5.9% as the discount rate to find the bonds' present value.

The inflation rate is currently 100 basis points (BPs) below the inflation rate that existed during the 74-year period when Ibbotson Associates computed the historic nominal interest rate. Dallas Underwriting compensates for this lower inflation rate at the time of the IPO by adjusting the 5.9% historical rate downward by 100 BPs to reflect current market conditions. Dallas Underwriting uses (5.9% − 100 BPs =) 4.9% as the discount rate to find the present value of Central Texas Electric Power Corporation's forthcoming bond issue.

Inflation-Adjusted Government Bond Returns

Long-Term Bonds. The total return from long-term government bonds over the 1926–99 period was 5.5% annually in nominal terms. Table 11-10 shows that, in inflation-adjusted terms, long-term government bonds provided 2.5% annual return. On average, long-term government bonds outpaced inflation over the 74-year sample period by 250 BPs per year. The inflation-adjusted long-term government bond return is the difference between the long-term government bond's total return and the inflation rate, as defined by Eqn. 11-12 in Table 11-10.

Intermediate-Term Bonds. In nominal terms, the total return from intermediate-term government bonds over the 1926–99 period was 5.4% annually. In inflation-adjusted terms, intermediate-term government bonds provided a 2.3% annual real return. Table 11-10's statistics show that, on average, the intermediate-term government bond returns exceeded the inflation rate over the 74-year sample by 230 BPs, as shown in Eqn. 11-13 in Table 11-10.

Inflation-Adjusted U.S. Treasury Bill Returns

The total return from U.S. Treasury Bills over the 1926–99 period was 3.8% per year in nominal terms. In inflation-adjusted terms, Table 11-10 shows that short-term government bonds provided an annual real return of only 80 BPs. These 80 BPs of inflation-adjusted Treasury bill returns are *real riskless returns* that, on average, barely outpaced inflation. The monthly inflation-adjusted long-term government bond return is the difference between the total return from U.S. Treasury bills and the inflation rate, as shown in Table 11-10's Eqn. 11-14.

To maintain their purchasing power, investors should give more thought to the real returns in Table 11-10 than the nominal returns in Table 2-1 in Chapter 2. The importance of focusing on real returns increases as the investor's time horizon grows because the corrosive effects of inflation compound with time.

INTERNATIONAL STOCK MARKETS

Many investors want an international dimension in their investment portfolio. Portfolio theory suggests that international diversification will reduce the risk of a portfolio below what it would be if it were invested in only one country. Furthermore, foreign securities can improve the average return of a portfolio of, say, domestic U.S. securities since several countries in the world are always growing faster than the United States.

Table 6-1 in Chapter 6 (pp. 127–128) and Chapter 1's Figure 1-4 (p. 10) review the world's equity investments. This section reviews empirical statistics on stock market indexes from around the world to help you evaluate these multinational investing opportunities. Table 11-11

TABLE 11-11   International Stock Market Performances, 1970–95

Country	Compound Annual Return	Standard Deviation
Australia	9.5%	29.7%
Austria	11.8%	24.2%
Belgium	15.6%	22.6%
Canada	9.4%	20.8%
Denmark	14.3%	21.7%
France	12.0%	27.3%
Germany	11.8%	23.4%
Hong Kong	21.3%	53.5%
Italy	5.7%	28.9%
Japan	16.4%	27.3%
Netherlands	16.1%	21.2%
Norway	12.8%	32.1%
Spain	8.6%	25.2%
Sweden	15.7%	26.4%
Switzerland	14.0%	22.0%
United Kingdom	12.9%	29.6%
U.S. S&P500 index	11.9%	17.2%
World	11.8%	16.1%

SUMMARY: The market statistics summarize international results before the Euro was introduced. These results are for a tax-exempt U.S. investor investing U.S. dollars and reinvesting the cash dividends free of commission costs and transfer fees. All the statistics except those from the United States were computed from MSCI indexes.

SOURCE: Ibbotson Associates, Chicago, IL.

lists risk and return statistics from Europe and other developed markets. These long-run statistics were compiled before the Euro was introduced in Europe in 1999; they can be compared with more recent—post Euro—data.

Financial markets outside of the United States have not generated as much empirical data as the U.S. securities markets. Even if different stock market indexes could be obtained from disparate stock markets and laid out for comparison over comparable time periods, they would still not be completely comparable. Many of the international indexes that are available are not compatible because they use different formulas to compute the returns, different assumptions about whether cash dividends are reinvested or paid out, and different assumptions about whether taxes and transactions fees are deducted from the returns; furthermore, some local indexes are computed from small and/or unrepresentative samples of securities.

The MSCI Indexes for Non-U.S. Stock Markets

In 1986 an international investment bank named Morgan Stanley purchased a database of stock market indexes that define the variables uniformly to facilitate international comparisons. The Morgan Stanley Capital International (MSCI) databank started with 16 countries' stock markets in 1969 and grew to 50 countries in 1997 and continues to grow. Table 11-12 contains information about the countries underlying the MSCI indexes.

Developed and Emerging Countries. Table 11-12 groups the countries into two categories: developed markets and emerging markets.

TABLE 11-12   Stock Market Information from Markets Underlying MSCI Indexes (U.S. $)

(1)[a] Country	(2) GDP Per Capita, 1996	(3) Total Market Capitalization, 1997	(4) No. of Domestic Companies	(5) No. of MSCI Securities Covered	(6) No. of MSCI Index Securities	(7) MSCI Index Market Capitalization, 1997
Developed Markets						
Australia	$21,976	$322,134	1,135	98	55	$177,637
Austria	26,197	38,224	112	36	24	25,254
Belgium	25,686	134,419	10	36	16	72,729
Canada	19,421	554,124	1,194	118	83	323,258
Denmark	32,832	89,343	242	34	24	64,721
Finland	24,135	87,550	71	28	20	53,519
France	26,296	649,363	767	115	67	449,793
Germany	28,256	821,893	717	129	66	583,541
Hong Kong	24,119	448,128	545	62	35	235,982
Ireland	20,411	47,727	62	22	11	23,652
Italy	21,350	321,045	236	117	53	229,699
Japan	34,413	2,034,178	3,114	542	309	1,864,205
Netherlands	24,833	484,718	197	50	22	342,566
New Zealand	18,735	36,821	128	20	10	21,747
Norway	36,194	72,266	148	29	24	37,800
Singapore	31,684	124,329	285	55	37	66,895
Spain	14,566	232,597	361	57	31	161,900
Sweden	28,221	296,483	223	61	29	173,311
Switzerland	38,638	540,427	261	69	36	421,006
United Kingdom	21,507	2,103,076	1,859	211	132	1,297,646
United States	27,614	9,275,445	703	552	391	6,006,638
Developed market average	$25,311					
Totals:						
EAFE		$9,835,515	11,215	1,882	1,077	$6,383,189
Developed world		$19,665,683	20,072	2,552	1,551	$12,713,085
Emerging Markets						
Argentina	$8,376	$ 60,734	147	33	21	$ 40,786
Brazil	4,453	305,961	550	115	59	160,975
Chile	4,166	82,345	290	60	32	40,396
China	610	164,710	532	48	26	5,942
Colombia	2,002	17,464	123	27	9	8,808
Czech. Rep.	4,625	16,706	10	33	19	9,587
Greece	8,211	38,459	218	58	37	26,737
Hungary	4,186	8,658	45	12	9	6,198
India	342	150,668	5,999	109	65	60,503
Indonesia	981	69,969	256	69	48	34,286

[a] *Column Headings:* (1) Country (and for emerging markets, Country Free) refers to statistics for the entire country (and statistics on the subset of the country's securities that are free for foreign investors to purchase). (2) Gross domestic product per capita is a measure of the average person's annual income. (3) Total market capitalization equals the sum over all companies of: (price per share) × (number of shares outstanding). (4) Number of domestic companies. (5) Number of securities covered by MSCI investigators. (6) Number of securities in MSCI index. (7) MSCI index capitalization equals the sum over all companies in MSCI index of: (price per share) × (number of shares outstanding).

(1)[a] Country	(2) GDP Per Capita, 1996	(3) Total Market Capitalization, 1997	(4) No. of Domestic Companies	(5) No. of MSCI Securities Covered	(6) No. of MSCI Index Securities	(7) MSCI Index Market Capitalization, 1997
Indonesia Free		69,969	256	69	48	34,144
Israel	16,719	46,096	655	74	50	23,919
Jordan	1,168	5,180	133	30	14	1,235
Korea	10,612	131,537	760	164	116	71,775
Malaysia	3,889	150,194	410	113	76	79,577
Malaysia Free		150,194	410	113	76	79,248
Mexico	3,521	159,008	196	57	43	116,596
Mexico Free		159,008	196	54	40	112,297
Pakistan	462	14,137	782	54	33	7,754
Peru	2,443	18,693	239	16	14	11,141
Philippines	1,023	43,019	216	69	35	18,464
Philippines Free		43,019	216	58	30	14,816
Poland	3,227	12,632	66	31	19	6,170
Portugal		41,889	158	40	23	31,463
Russia	2,400	123,623	173	29	14	52,686
S. Africa	3,175	266,774	636	94	55	107,958
Sri Lanka	688	2,415	235	19	10	880
Taiwan	12,778	298,051	382	113	77	187,578
Thailand	2,687	43,610	454	135	62	25,213
Thailand Free		43,610	454	135	62	27,365
Turkey	2,859	53,834	228	85	45	21,316
Venezuela	3,027	21,300	89	19	14	15,718
Emerging market average	$3,944					
Totals:						
Emerging market, free		$2,224,123	14,895	1,663	1,003	$985,033
Emerging market		$2,224,123	14,895	1,677	1,011	$1,120,975
Aggregate world		$21,739,612	34,557	4,116	2,486	$13,754,483

SOURCE: *Morgan Stanley Capital International (MSCI): Methodology and Index Policy* (March 1998): 15, 25. Or, visit: www.msci.com

The classic **emerging market** is new, small, experiences low turnover, and is located in a country where below-average incomes prevail. The four criteria below are usually enough to correctly ascertain whether a market is emerging or developed.

1. With few exceptions, a stock market that is less than 25 years old is an emerging market.
2. Emerging markets typically list a small number of stocks. If a stock market is both small and new, it is almost surely an emerging market.
3. Averaged over all markets, the turnover rates in the emerging markets are only half of the average turnover rate in the developed markets. This means that emerging markets are less liquid than developed markets.
4. Column 2 of Table 11-12 provides income per capita data for each country. Comparing the average GDP per capita for the two categories listed in Table 11-12

reveals that countries with developed markets have average annual incomes that are about six times larger than countries with emerging markets.

Most emerging markets can be easily recognized by using the four criteria cited on page 321, but a few emerging markets violate some of these criteria. For example, some are decades old and list dozens of stocks. If the prospects for such an old medium-sized market are dim, it will usually be called an emerging market. Some writers, however, will call it a developed market. Even the experts disagree on how a few ambiguous markets should be categorized.

Market Indexes. Table 11-13 compares and contrasts five of the MSCI indexes with competing local indexes that are quoted in newspapers around the world. These well-known local indexes are statistically inferior to the MSCI indexes. Consider the Financial Times Stock Exchange (FT-SE) index, nicknamed "Footsie," in Table 11-13. The MSCI Index for London Stock Exchange and Footsie are both market value–weighted indexes, both use total returns (include cash dividend income), and they both adjust appropriately for stock splits and stock dividends. The MSCI samples 132 representative securities, while Footsie is based on the 100 largest-cap stocks. Footsie samples fewer securities from fewer industries and is a less representative indicator. Any local taxes that are withheld from payments to foreign investors are

TABLE 11-13   Comparison of Five Local Indexes with MSCI Indexes

Country, Index	Local Market Index					MSCI Index for Same Market		
	Weighting	Selection Criteria	No. of Securities	No. of Industries	Index % of market	No. of Securities	No. of Industries	Index % of market
Hong Kong, Hang Seng	Market cap	Top 90% by market cap and turnover	33	10	83.3%	35	16	52.6%
Sweden, OMX	Market cap	Highest market cap at Stockholm Stock Exchange	30	15	39.2%	29	16	58.5%
United Kingdom, FTSE-100	Market cap	100 largest cap at London Stock Exchange	100	27	27.3%	132	33	61.7%
Canada, TSE-35	Basket	Blue chips in Canada	35	16	43.4%	83	24	58.3%
Italy, MIB 30	Market cap	Largest 30 that are liquid	30	13	76.4%	53	19	71.5%
Thailand, SET 50	Market cap	Top 50 in market cap and liquidity	50	15	90.4%	62	26	57.8%

SOURCE: *Morgan Stanley Capital International (MSCI): Methodology and Index Policy* (March 1998): Exhibit 2.

deleted in computing the MSCI returns. No other taxes or transaction fees are deducted from the MSCI returns. Footsie is more appropriate for British than for foreign investors because it ignores the international tax considerations confronting foreign investors.

It is often difficult to find computational details about foreign indexes (like Footsie). Details about the MSCI indexes are distributed worldwide on the MSCI Internet Web site and in widely distributed publications. For more details about Morgan Stanley investment banking firm, visit their Web site at: www.ms.com. For information about the MSCI indexes visit: www.msci.com. Or, visit: www.msdw.com, the Morgan Stanley Dean Witter Company Web site. The MSCI indexes on markets around the world are defined uniformly. The MSCI indexes are not only statistically superior to most local indexes, they also expedite multinational comparisons.

Return and Risk Statistics. Table 11-14 shows risk and return statistics for the MSCI indexes tabulated from a 5-year period (1996–2000), for the emerging markets and the developed nations. Tables 11-14 and 11-15 represent domestic investors who are investing local currencies in their homelands; this computational assumption was followed so that foreign exchange considerations are not mixed with investment results.

Both high and low returns can be found in both the emerging and developed markets. Comparing the 25-year statistics in Table 11-11 with the 5-year statistics in Table 11-14 reveals little consistency. It seems that profitable international investing requires investing in the right place at the right time, and the right places keep changing.

The emerging markets statistics are more heterogeneous and more unstable than the statistics from developed markets. In Table 11-14 we see that the 5-year standard deviation of returns averaged over all the developed markets is 23.6% and that the 5-year standard deviation of returns averaged over all the emerging markets is 41.1%. This shows that investing in emerging markets involves more risk than investing in developed markets.

Market Correlations. The four columns on the right of Table 11-14 list the correlation coefficients of each individual country with (1) MSCI's world (all countries) market index, (2) MSCI's Emerging Markets Free (EMF) index, (3) the MSCI's Europe-Australasia-Far-East (EAFE) index, (4) and MSCI's European Monetary Union (EMU) index. The bottom rows of Table 11-14 show average correlation coefficients for each of these four indexes. Note that all four average correlation coefficients for developed markets exceed all four average correlations for emerging markets. This is because the developed markets are more economically integrated than the emerging markets. Stated differently, the developed nations do more trading with each other than the emerging markets nations. This economic integration causes stock prices in the developed countries to covary together and create more undiversifiable risk between the developed markets than exists between the emerging markets. The emerging markets have larger standard deviations of returns, on average, and, in addition, more of their risk is diversifiable (statistically independent, uncorrelated).

STUDY CHECK

QUESTION: Compare the nominal returns from Ibbotson's seven basic U.S. indexes in Table 2-1 in Chapter 2 (or Table 11-1) with the international returns in Table 11-14. Do you think the United States offers better investments than are available internationally?

ANSWER: Table 2-1 (or 11-1) and Table 11-14 involve different kinds of risks and returns. Table 2-1 presents only domestic asset classes within the United States. Table 11-14 presents an international comparison of equity markets. The international markets offer a wider range of opportunities, but greater risks of a more complicated nature must be undertaken to invest internationally. Stay tuned for Table 11-15.

TABLE 11-14   MSCI Return, Risk, and Correlation Statistics Based on 5 Years of Monthly Total Returns, U.S. $ Invested

Country	Annual Return %	Standard Deviation %	World	EMF	EAFE	EMU
Developed Markets						
Australia	6.2	16.6	0.71	0.68	0.71	0.54
Austria	−4.7	19.6	0.57	0.46	0.62	0.65
Belgium	9.4	16.2	0.58	0.19	0.57	0.66
Canada	21.7	19.2	0.8	0.74	0.7	0.66
Denmark	16.8	17.1	0.6	0.43	0.63	0.72
Finland	58.1	32.6	0.6	0.52	0.56	0.58
France	20.4	16.6	0.71	0.54	0.77	0.89
Germany	18.2	18.6	0.67	0.55	0.67	0.83
Hong Kong	11.7	33.6	0.61	0.73	0.55	0.43
Ireland	12.7	15.7	0.68	0.46	0.63	0.56
Italy	17.4	24.0	0.5	0.45	0.53	0.68
Japan	0.2	21.8	0.52	0.49	0.51	0.41
Malaysia	−7.0	47.5	0.45	0.67	0.45	0.39
Malaysia Free	−7.0	48.0	0.45	0.62	0.46	0.39
Netherlands	17.7	17.1	0.74	0.51	0.78	0.8
New Zealand	−4.1	22.2	0.63	0.57	0.65	0.52
Norway	2.9	23.1	0.6	0.61	0.61	0.6
Portugal	16.2	21.5	0.43	0.34	0.5	0.68
Singapore	0.3	32.9	0.62	0.37	0.55	0.4
Singapore Free	−3.0	35.9	0.65	0.77	0.58	0.43
Spain	26.4	22.0	0.68	0.77	0.71	0.74
Sweden	35.7	23.1	0.56	0.54	0.62	0.75
Switzerland	14.8	18.6	0.61	0.51	0.62	0.63
United Kingdom	16.0	12.4	0.74	0.49	0.68	0.65
United States	26.1	15.1	0.7	0.66	0.69	0.62
Average:	12.9	23.6	0.62	0.55	0.61	0.61
Emerging Markets						
Argentina	12.1	32.5	0.52	0.72	0.48	0.45
Brazil	10.5	41.3	0.57	0.71	0.55	0.51
Chile	−4.1	26.3	0.53	0.81	0.47	0.4
China Free	−11.7	49.8	0.3	0.54	0.16	0.07
Colombia	−9.1	35.3	0.18	0.34	0.17	0.13
Czech Rep.	4.4	30.6	0.21	0.43	0.23	0.26
Greece	24.4	32.8	0.34	0.39	0.33	0.47
Hungary	28.2	42.2	0.48	0.59	0.39	0.52
India	6.3	32.4	0.13	0.32	0.16	0.2
Indonesia	−18.3	66.9	0.52	0.62	0.5	0.41
Israel	19.2	24.0	0.38	0.46	0.37	0.52
Jordan	−5.0	14.0	0.22	0.19	0.24	0.16
Korea	−3.8	58.1	0.4	0.31	0.44	0.22

Country	Annual Return %	Standard Deviation %	Country's Correlation with:			
			World	EMF	EAFE	EMU
Mexico Free	17.6	34.7	0.65	0.72	0.57	0.54
Pakistan	−5.2	46.0	0.09	0.34	0.03	0.03
Peru	0.3	27.0	0.31	0.63	0.33	0.33
Philippines	−17.6	41.2	0.59	0.67	0.53	0.44
Poland	4.6	39.4	0.46	0.6	0.43	0.45
Russia	39.9	84.2	0.49	0.64	0.45	0.39
South Africa	−4.6	28.9	0.57	0.71	0.54	0.45
Sri Lanka	−13.7	32.2	0.37	0.5	0.37	0.39
Taiwan	5.6	34.0	0.48	0.68	0.41	0.29
Thailand	−25.6	56.1	0.58	0.64	0.51	0.36
Turkey	29.6	60.2	0.25	0.33	0.25	0.33
Venezuela	7.4	56.2	0.26	0.39	0.25	0.25
Average:	3.7	41.1	0.40	0.53	0.37	0.34

SOURCE: Morgan Stanley Capital International (MSCI) Web site, April 2000; Web site: www.msci.com

Correlations Between Developed and Emerging Markets

Risk-averse investors sometimes analyze the possibilities for international diversification across a number of different countries. How well an international portfolio is diversified depends, in large part, on the correlation between its components.

Table 11-15's data for emerging markets provides a correlation matrix for the emerging market indexes introduced in Table 11-14. Table 11-15 also displays the correlation matrix for the developed markets in Table 11-14. Table 11-15 contains a few more countries than Table 11-14. Although the world contains many more emerging markets than developed markets, many emerging markets are too small or too unstable to support a securities market. As a result, some tiny, new emerging markets do not have enough data to be present in Table 11-15.

Comparing the correlations in tables like 11-15 over successive sample periods (not shown here) reveals that the correlations between emerging markets are not only lower, on average; they are also less stable through time than the correlations between the developed markets. These erratic statistics for emerging markets reflect political and economic instability in many of the countries. The correlations in Table 11-15 indicate that international diversification offers more risk reduction possibilities to multinational investors than is available to domestic investors.[5]

Investing in Emerging Markets

Table 11-14 shows that the greater risks typically associated with investments in emerging markets can be rewarded handsomely or punished harshly. For example, a portfolio of Russian common stocks selected by MSCI statisticians to create a representative market index earned a compounded average rate of 39.9% per year between 1996 and 2000. This average return increased the portfolio's market value more than five times:

$$(1 + r_{Russia})^{5 \text{ years}} = (1 + 39.9\%)^5 = (1.399)^5 = 5.36 \text{ times in 5 years}$$

TABLE 11-15 Matrix of Correlation Coefficients, 1995–2000; Monthly Total Returns U.S. $

Developed Markets

	Code	AU	AT	BE	CA	DK	FI	FR	DE	HK	IE	IT	JP	NL	NZ	NO	SG	ES	SE	CH	GB	US	ACWIxl	EAFE	EMU
Australia	AU	1																							
Austria	AT	0.39	1																						
Belgium	BE	0.27	0.58	1																					
Canada	CA	0.64	0.52	0.26	1																				
Denmark	DK	0.38	0.6	0.54	0.57	1																			
Finland	FI	0.47	0.42	0.34	0.57	0.35	1																		
France	FR	0.47	0.55	0.62	0.62	0.65	0.52	1																	
Germany	DE	0.51	0.58	0.57	0.62	0.66	0.59	0.81	1																
Hong Kong	HK	0.6	0.38	0.14	0.61	0.4	0.35	0.4	0.38	1															
Ireland	IE	0.54	0.63	0.54	0.55	0.61	0.37	0.35	0.49	0.36	1														
Italy	IT	0.36	0.44	0.51	0.4	0.53	0.37	0.43	0.31	0.21	0.37	1													
Japan	JP	0.61	0.32	0.24	0.46	0.29	0.38	0.37	0.56	0.47	0.38	0.21	1												
Netherlands	NL	0.44	0.73	0.7	0.56	0.67	0.48	0.41	0.76	0.46	0.64	0.54	0.43	1											
New Zealand	NZ	0.63	0.52	0.36	0.58	0.46	0.4	0.75	0.46	0.49	0.51	0.29	0.48	0.54	1										
Norway	NO	0.53	0.56	0.35	0.69	0.56	0.49	0.48	0.5	0.42	0.5	0.44	0.29	0.5	0.61	1									
Singapore	SG	0.58	0.31	0.18	0.59	0.29	0.37	0.4	0.32	0.79	0.32	0.2	0.44	0.4	0.58	0.47	1								
Spain	ES	0.55	0.51	0.54	0.52	0.58	0.44	0.73	0.62	0.43	0.53	0.32	0.36	0.63	0.49	0.58	0.58	1							
Sweden	SE	0.44	0.39	0.24	0.59	0.42	0.65	0.69	0.74	0.38	0.33	0.33	0.33	0.63	0.46	0.53	0.53	0.59	1						
Switzerland	CH	0.33	0.57	0.6	0.39	0.59	0.3	0.59	0.52	0.28	0.53	0.4	0.4	0.69	0.57	0.48	0.46	0.6	0.41	1					
United Kingdom	GB	0.63	0.67	0.6	0.58	0.63	0.43	0.57	0.53	0.51	0.63	0.39	0.41	0.74	0.5	0.53	0.57	0.62	0.4	0.61	1				
United States	US	0.59	0.43	0.5	0.77	0.47	0.54	0.55	0.55	0.57	0.63	0.39	0.39	0.59	0.4	0.5	0.61	0.54	0.66	0.52	0.67	1			
ACWI Free ex USA	ACWIxl	0.75	0.63	0.54	0.76	0.64	0.61	0.8	0.73	0.65	0.63	0.58	0.58	0.8	0.67	0.65	0.65	0.73	0.66	0.75	0.75	0.73	1		
EAFE	EAFE	0.72	0.62	0.58	0.7	0.64	0.58	0.8	0.73	0.59	0.63	0.57	0.8	0.81	0.65	0.56	0.61	0.73	0.65	0.67	0.76	0.69	0.99	1	
Euro. Mon. Union	EMU	0.54	0.66	0.68	0.66	0.72	0.63	0.94	0.92	0.43	0.57	0.76	0.76	0.85	0.52	0.6	0.4	0.79	0.75	0.63	0.65	0.62	0.85	0.85	1

Emerging Markets

	Code	AR	BR	CL	CN	CO	CZ	GR	HU	IN	ID	IL	JO	KR	MX	PK	PE	PH	PL	PT	RU	ZA	LK	TW	TH	TR	VE	EMF	KOKUSAI
Argentina	AR	1.00																											
Brazil	BR	0.64	1.00																										
Chile	CL	0.6	0.71	1.00																									
China Free	CN	0.41	0.38	0.48	1.00																								
Colombia	CO	0.32	0.41	0.47	0.05	1.00																							
Czech Republic	CZ	0.34	0.33	0.33	0.24	0.11	1.00																						
Greece	GR	0.33	0.27	0.42	0.04	0.19	0.28	1.00																					
Hungary	HU	0.52	0.48	0.42	0.2	0.22	0.49	0.42	1.00																				
India	IN	0.11	0.23	0.23	0.11	0.02	0.43	0.31	0.29	1.00																			
Indonesia Free	ID	0.4	0.43	0.4	0.33	0.29	0.25	0.3	0.36	0.12	1.00																		
Israel	IL	0.4	0.49	0.56	0.05	0.05	0.22	0.25	0.36	0.46	0.26	1.00																	
Jordan	JO	-0.04	0.05	0.23	-0.05	0.16	-0.19	0.25	0.05	0.25	0.13	0.26	1.00																
Korea @50%	KR	0.12	0.16	0.23	0.11	0.11	0.15	0.18	0.08	0.05	0.36	0.36	0.15	1.00															
Mexico Free	MX	0.71	0.71	0.54	0.11	0.37	0.31	0.32	0.52	0.24	0.16	0.31	0.09	0.53	1.00														
Pakistan	PK	0.21	0.37	0.37	0.26	0.17	0.17	0.12	0.26	0.43	0.16	0.26	0.15	0.09	0.23	1.00													
Peru	PE	0.67	0.62	0.71	0.51	0.37	0.34	0.49	0.43	0.25	0.36	0.47	0.07	0.04	0.49	0.27	1.00												
Philippines Free	PH	0.52	0.43	0.57	0.32	0.52	0.22	0.22	0.39	0.03	0.39	0.17	0.07	0.3	0.44	0.05	0.35	1.00											
Poland	PL	0.44	0.38	0.39	0.05	0.17	0.57	0.32	0.66	0.28	0.31	0.34	-0.05	0.29	0.49	0.08	0.32	0.36	1.00										
Portugal	PT	0.28	0.27	0.23	-0.01	0.06	0.33	0.17	0.32	0.27	0.28	0.31	0.09	0.16	0.29	-0.01	0.33	0.33	0.46	1.00									
Russia	RU	0.41	0.6	0.69	0.28	0.28	0.21	0.23	0.46	0.29	0.58	0.36	0.19	0.13	0.51	0.3	0.43	0.52	0.34	0.29	1.00								
South Africa	ZA	0.62	0.55	0.58	0.5	0.34	0.23	0.35	0.39	0.18	0.47	0.41	0.06	0.36	0.53	0.12	0.48	0.6	0.53	0.37	0.42	1.00							
Sri Lanka	LK	0.34	0.37	0.45	0.23	0.42	0.45	0.21	0.47	0.34	0.37	0.25	0.26	0.22	0.21	0.36	0.38	0.24	0.21	0.36	0.36	0.41	1.00						
Taiwan @50%	TW	0.57	0.57	0.64	0.67	0.23	0.11	0.27	0.29	0.29	0.42	0.22	0.00	0.53	0.26	0.53	0.22	0.37	0.46	0.08	0.53	0.61	0.23	1.00					
Thailand Free	TH	0.47	0.39	0.45	-0.04	0.14	0.15	0.2	0.24	0.00	0.43	0.22	0.06	0.26	0.62	0.2	0.17	0.39	0.34	0.2	0.34	0.65	0.56	0.56	1.00				
Turkey	TR	0.22	0.44	0.37	0.33	0.42	0.06	0.18	0.17	0.16	0.27	0.21	0.39	0.22	-0.02	0.31	0.33	0.15	0.22	0.27	0.09	0.33	0.26	0.06	0.06	1.00			
Venezuela	VE	0.38	0.3	0.37	0.33	0.28	0.18	0.17	0.27	0.27	0.21	0.09	0.16	0.09	0.34	0.28	0.34	0.27	0.09	0.14	0.23	0.29	0.23	0.23	0.06	0.17	1.00		
EMF	EMF	0.74	0.81	0.83	0.55	0.55	0.34	0.43	0.59	0.4	0.64	0.49	0.2	0.36	0.79	0.35	0.68	0.6	0.6	0.37	0.67	0.77	0.5	0.74	0.38	0.4	0.4	1.00	
World ex Japan	KOKUSAI	0.52	0.58	0.53	0.32	0.32	0.18	0.21	0.54	0.21	0.52	0.41	0.21	0.32	0.66	0.1	0.3	0.6	0.47	0.48	0.51	0.55	0.39	0.46	0.56	0.27	0.27	0.73	1.00

SOURCE: Morgan Stanley Capital International (MSCI): Web site, April 28, 2000. Reproduced with advance written permission from MSCI.

These lucrative undertakings are not for the weak-hearted. Note that Russia's standard deviation of returns is also breathtaking. Russia's high standard deviation during the 1996–2000 sample period reflects an economic disaster. Russia experienced an economic collapse in 1998 that more than wiped out its 1996–97 stock market run-up. The discussion of Table 18-1 in Chapter 18 delves into Russia's financial 1998–99 problems.

Survivorship Bias

A few capital markets are long-term survivors, but most are not. Philippe Jorion and Will Goetzmann show that most of the world's capital "markets have been closed or suspended due to financial crisis, wars, expropriations, or political upheaval."[6] Many of the so-called "emerging markets" are actually "reemerging markets." Some estimates of securities' expected returns are based on long-term U.S. data, because the United States appears to have the longest-running stock market in the world. Using U.S. data in this manner imparts an upward survivorship bias to the expected returns.

THE BOTTOM LINE

This chapter introduced and contrasted Ibbotson's seven basic indexes. These indexes traced the investment performance of different categories of U.S. securities. In addition, other indexes were derived from the basic indexes to uncover other facets of investing in U.S. securities. The chapter closed with a review of the Morgan Stanley Capital International (MSCI) indexes from stock markets around the world.

This chapter's statistics summarize over seven decades of investment experience in the United States, about 25 years of data from a number of developed countries, and a smaller number of years of data for emerging security markets around the world. These market statistics will be used to evaluate investment studies examined in the chapters that follow and place them in perspective. In addition, the statistics in this chapter can be used to provide inputs for real-life portfolio analysis problems, calibrate theoretical models with realistic market values, and establish standards for comparison. The tables in this chapter provide a statistical resource that is measured consistently over lengthy sample periods to facilitate the evaluation of investment opportunities.

The empirical results reviewed in this chapter document the following conclusions:

◆ There is a positive relationship between risk and rate of return that permeates the world's financial markets.

◆ The positive risk-return relationships observed in different markets decade after decade provides strong empirical support for the notion that most investors are risk-averters.

◆ Equities are riskier and provide higher returns than debt securities.

◆ Investors with the discipline to reinvest cash flows from their investments can benefit from reinvestment returns that usually increase their total returns.

◆ Inflation is an insidious force that erodes the purchasing power of investors' wealth.

◆ Covariances, cross-correlations, and serial correlations are useful statistical measures of the tendencies of random variables to behave in a certain manner and/or relate to other random variables.

◆ Corporate bond returns contain a default risk premium that elevates their returns above the returns from default-free U.S. Treasury bonds.

◆ Bonds with long-term maturities usually provide higher yields than bonds with shorter maturities.

◆ Over the long run, equities provide higher inflation-adjusted returns than debt securities do.

◆ The default-free U.S. Treasury bills provide yields that are only slightly above the rate of inflation in the United States.

◆ Investing outside the United States is riskier than investing inside the United States.

◆ Investing in emerging markets is usually riskier than investing in developed markets.

◆ Emerging markets' risk premiums await aggressive investors who are and willing to undertake the risks associated with this type of investing.

The conclusions above are suggested by economic theory and, therefore, are not surprising. The chapter's data simply quantifies what theory suggests.

QUESTIONS

Q11-1 (Homoscedasticity and heteroscedasticity) To what do the terms homoscedasticity and heteroscedasticity refer? Which characteristic is more applicable to stock market indexes?

Q11-2 (Serial correlations) What information is provided by serial correlation coefficients? What do the serial correlations provided in Table 11-7 suggest to you about the ability to forecast future stock prices by studying past stock prices?

Q11-3 (Callability risk) What is callability risk? How does it affect investors? How is it accounted for in the risk premia?

Q11-4 (Correlation coefficients) Based on Table 11-15, which provides a matrix of correlation coefficients for various countries, investment in which country's stock would provide the greatest diversification potential to American investors who hold a well-diversified portfolio of U.S. stocks?

Q11-5 (Foreign investments) Table 11-11 provides average returns and standard deviations for 19 developed countries, incorporating exchange rate fluctuations. Based on the information provided, U.S. investors could have earned a greater average annual return by investing in the Hong Kong stock market over the 25-year period, 1970–95, than by investing in the U.S. stock market, even when exchange rate fluctuations are considered. Does it follow, then, that the Hong Kong stocks are the better investment vehicle? Why or why not?

Q11-6 (Time diversification) There is a debate regarding whether or not time diversification actually works. What is meant by "time diversification"? How do the proponents of the case for time diversification believe it works?

Q11-7 (Market indexes) Discuss four uses of market indexes. Why are indexes, rather than individual securities, studied?

Q11-8 (Geometric mean return) Table 2-1 in Chapter 2 reveals that the geometric mean return on long-term corporate bonds was 5.6% for the period spanning 1926 through 1999. Does this mean that the average yield-to-maturity on these bonds was 5.6% over the 72-year period? Why or why not?

Q11-9 (Reinvestment return) At the beginning of 1999, Mike DeLeon invested in an index fund of large-company stocks and was pleased to discover he received some sizable dividend checks each quarter. Mike decided to use these checks to finance a weekend getaway each quarter. At the end of the year, he noted that large-company stocks had offered a total return of 21.04% for the year, as reported in Table 11-4. Did Mike earn this much on his investment? Why or why not?

Q11-10 (Reinvestment return) True, false, or uncertain: An investor's total return will always be larger if he or she reinvests any cash flows received back into the portfolio. Explain.

PROBLEMS

P11-1 (Calculation of an index) A certain index is comprised of five stocks. Information regarding them is presented in the table below:

Stock	Shares Outstanding, base period	Market Price, base period	Current Shares Outstanding	Current Market Price
A	1,000	$10	1,000	$15
B	2,000	$20	4,000	$18
C	3,000	$30	3,000	$22
D	2,000	$40	2,000	$41
E	5,000	$50	5,000	$53

The base value of the index is 100. Calculate the current value of the index.

P11-2 (Risk premia) Use the data from Table 2-1 in Chapter 2 to calculate (a) a historical average equity risk premium, (b) a historical average small-stock premium, (c) a historical average bond default premium, and (d) a historical average bond horizon premium.

P11-3 (Wealth accumulation) Bob Eastman invested $1,000 in a portfolio of stocks 10 years ago that grew at a compound average rate of 17.8% a year. Inflation averaged 3.2% a year over that same period.
(a) How much is his portfolio worth now, in nominal dollars?
(b) How much has Bob accumulated in *real* wealth?

P11-4 (Bond horizon premium) Use the information provided in Table 11-4 and the following data on Treasury bills to calculate the historical bond horizon premium for each of the years 1975–85 inclusive. What conclusions can you draw from your results?

Year	U.S. Treasury Bill Total Returns
1975	5.8%
1976	5.08%
1977	5.12%
1978	7.18%
1979	10.38%
1980	11.24%
1981	14.71%
1982	10.54%
1983	8.8%
1984	9.85%
1985	7.72%

P11-5 (Small-stock risk premium) Use the information provided in Table 11-4 and the following information on small-stock returns to calculate the historical small-stock risk premium for the years 1986 to 1995 inclusive. Can you draw any conclusions from your results?

Year	Small-Stock Total Return
1986	6.85%
1987	−9.3%
1988	22.87%
1989	10.18%
1990	−21.56%
1991	44.63%
1992	23.35%
1993	20.98%
1994	3.11%
1995	34.46%

P11-6 (Money illusion) Elaine has been diligent about saving for her daughter's college education and is pleased to note that she should have $40,000 saved toward it when her daughter graduates from high school in 8 years. Unfortunately, Elaine has not factored inflation into her calculations. If inflation is expected to increase at a rate of 4% a year, how much will Elaine's education account purchase 8 years from now?

P11-7 (Cross-correlation) Use the data provided in Table 11-4 for the time period 1986–95 inclusive to calculate the cross-correlation for the returns of long-term government bonds and large-company stocks. Compare your answer to the data presented in Table 11-7 and discuss any differences between the numbers.

P11-8 (Reinvestment return) In 1996, the total return reported for large-company stocks was 23.07%. The income return was 2.54%, and the capital appreciation return was 20.26%. What was the reinvestment return?

P11-9 (Expected returns) Assume that the 30-day Treasury bill yield is currently 5.2%. Use this information, along with the risk premia data provided in Table 11-9, to determine an expected return on small-cap stocks over the next year.

P11-10 (Real returns) Use the data from Table 2-1 in Chapter 2 and Eqn. 10-7 in Chapter 10 to determine the real returns on large-company stocks, small-company stocks, long-term government bonds, and Treasury bills for the period 1926–99 inclusive.

CFA EXAM QUESTIONS

The following two questions are adopted from the 1998 CFA Sample Exam, Level I:

1. Bill Parsons manages an equity fund with an expected risk premium of 10% and an expected standard deviation of 14%. The rate on U.S. Treasury bills is 6%. Diane Webb, Parson's client, chooses to invest $60,000 of her portfolio in the equity fund and $40,000 in a Treasury-bill money market fund. The expected return on Webb's portfolio will be:
   A. 8.4%.
   B. 10.0%.
   C. 12.0%.
   D. 14.0%.

2. An analyst makes the following calculations about the returns for Stock X and Stock Y:

   $Cov(R_x R_y) = 0.005$

   $\sigma_x = 0.20$

   $\sigma_y = 0.06$

   The correlation coefficient between the returns for Stock X and Stock Y is between:
   A. 0.00 and 0.25.
   B. 0.25 and 0.50.
   C. 0.51 and 0.75.
   D. 0.76 and 1.00.

The following question is an adaptation of a question appearing on the 1994 CFA Exam, Level III:

3. In the past, the chairman of the Investment Committee for the defined-benefit pension plan of Food Processor's, Incorporated has opposed consideration of venture capital investments for inclusion in the pension portfolio. Now, however, he has asked the plan's equity portfolio manager to make a detailed presentation on this subject, including identification of risk and reward potentials. He is aware that several Committee members, who have heard that venture investing produced 35% to 45% annual returns in the 1970s and 1980s, believe that as much as 20% of the plan's assets should be placed in such investments.
   A. Using the capital markets data provided in Table 1, below, as your reference source, **estimate** and **justify** a set of return *and* risk expectations for the venture capital asset class, taking a long-term view.

Table 1   Capital Markets Data

	Total Return 1929–93	Total Return 1984–93	Annualized Monthly Standard Deviation 1984–93	Consensus Forecast Total Return 1994–2000
U.S. Treasury bills	3.7%	6.4%	2.2%	3.5%
Intermediate-term Treasury bonds	5.3%	11.4%	5.6%	5.0%
Long-term Treasury bonds	5.0%	14.4%	11.7%	6.0%
U.S. corporate bonds (AAA)	5.6%	14.0%	8.9%	6.5%
Non-U.S. bonds (AAA)	n/a	15.4%	14.5%	6.5%
U.S. common stocks (S&P500)	9.5%	14.9%	18.0%	8.5%
U.S. common stocks (small-cap)	12.0%	10.0%	19.9%	10.5%
Non-U.S. common stocks (in U.S. $)	n/a	17.9%	23.7%	9.5%
U.S. real estate[a]	n/a	9.3%	2.4%	7.5%
U.S. inflation (annual rate)	3.2%	5.5%	n/a	3.3%

[a]Business, Residential, and Agricultural Appraisal Data

One of your research contacts has provided Table 2 below, a matrix of the projected correlations that their firm expects to prevail among U.S. venture capital investments and the other U.S. asset classes shown.

Table 2   Correlation Matrix

	Venture Capital	Small-Cap Stocks	S&P500 Stocks	Corporate Bonds	Treasury Bills	Real Estate
Venture capital	1.00					
Small-cap stocks	0.50	1.00				
S&P500	0.35	0.80	1.00			
Corporate bonds	0.15	0.25	0.45	1.00		
Treasury bills	−0.10	−0.20	−0.10	0.05	1.00	
Real estate	0.25	0.30	0.35	0.20	0.25	1.00

   B. **Briefly explain** the implication for portfolio diversification of the correlations for venture capital with the five other asset classes shown in Table 2 above.

FURTHER REFERENCES

Ibbotson, Roger G. and Lawrence B. Siegel. "The World Bond Market: Market Values, Yields and Returns," *The Journal of Fixed Income* 1, no. 1 (June 1991): 90–99.

This empirical study documents changes in market capitalization, yields, and returns that have characterized three decades.

Jorion, Philippe and William N. Goetzmann. "A Century of Global Stock Markets," *Journal of Finance* 54, no. 3 (June 1999): 953–80.

Stock price indexes from 39 stock markets are compiled from data that reach as far back as 1920. The U.S. stock market is found to have achieved the highest uninterrupted real rate of price appreciation of all countries, at 4.3% annually from 1921 to 1996. For other countries, the median rate of real price appreciation was 0.8%. Survivorship bias problems are discussed.

Siegel, Jeremy J. *Stocks for the Long Run*, 2nd ed. New York: McGraw-Hill, 1998.

This nonmathematical book contains numerous tables of empirical statistics and intuitive graphs that explain important points about long-run investing in an entertaining and informative manner.

Stocks, Bonds, Bills, and Inflation (SBBI) Yearbook, published annually by Ibbotson Associates, Chicago, IL.

SBBI is updated annually. This chapter provides a distilled summary of the raw data, methodology, and summary statistics discussed in more detail in *SBBI*. Many tables and figures in this chapter were reproduced from the 2000 edition of *SBBI*.

ENDNOTES

[1] For more information about the construction of the indexes, see Roger G. Ibbotson and Rex A. Sinquefield, "Stocks, Bonds, Bills, and Inflation: Year-By-Year Historical Returns," *The Journal of Business* 49, no. 1 (January 1976): 11–47. See *Stocks, Bonds, Bills, and Inflation Yearbook*, annually from 1983 through the present, published by Ibbotson Associates, Chicago. This chapter draws heavily on the 2000 edition of the *SBBI Yearbook*.

[2] The Ibbotson Associates Web site is: www.ibbotson.com.

[3] The small-company stock index was initially developed by Professor Rolf Banz for 1926–81. See Rolf W. Banz, "The Relationship Between Return and Market Value of Common Stocks," *Journal of Financial Economics* 9 (1981): 3–18. Following Banz's guidelines after 1981, returns from the DFA Small Company 9/10 Fund are used.

[4] There is an intellectual debate about how well time diversification (mean reversion) actually works. Those arguing against it include the Nobel laureate Paul Samuelson, "Asset Allocation Could Be Dangerous to Your Health," *Journal of Portfolio Management* (spring 1990): 5–8. Also see Zvi Bodie, Alan Kane, and Alan J. Marcus, *Investments*, 3d ed. (Chicago: Irwin, 1996), Appendix C to Chapter 7, "The Fallacy of Time Diversification," pp. 231–33. In addition to your authors, those arguing that time diversification is beneficial include Steven Thorley, "The Time Diversification Controversy," *Financial Analysts Journal* (May–June 1995): 68–76. Also see Richard Taylor and Donald J. Brown, "On the Risk of Stocks in the Long-Run," *Financial Analysts Journal* (March-April 1996): 69–71. In addition, see Wayne Y. Lee, "Diversification and Time: Do Investment Horizons Matter?" *Journal of Portfolio Management* (spring 1990): 21–26. Time diversification (mean reversion) works better when the returns have negative serial correlations (price reversals). The serial correlations in this chapter's Table 11-5 are near zero, which suggests a random walk.

[5] For detail and supporting views, see C. B. Barry, J. W. Peavy III, and M. Rodriguez, *Emerging Stock Markets: Risk, Return, and Performance*, The Research Foundation of the Institute of Chartered Financial Analysts (Charlottesville, VA, 1997). Additional information about emerging markets is provided throughout this book. Chapter 6 discusses the operation of emerging securities markets. Chapters 17, 18, and 19 discuss global diversification and foreign exchange.

[6] See Philippe Jorion and William N. Goetzmann, "Global Stock Markets in the Twentieth Century," *Journal of Finance* 54, no. 3 (June 1999): 978. Also see Stephen J. Brown, William J. Goetzmann, and Stephen Ross, "Survival," *Journal of Finance* 50 (1995): 853–73.

USING INDEXES

This chapter explains uses for security market indexes like the ones discussed in Chapters 10 and 11. Different investment products that are based on security market indexes are introduced. The material presumes a familiarity with Chapters 8 through 11 inclusive.

*The chapter begins with "investment companies." The legal and economic structure of "investment companies" in the United States are explored and three types of "investment companies" are examined. First, "mutual funds," the most popular type of "investment company," are defined. Second, millions of investors have put money into a group of "investment companies" that invest in the same stocks that make up some selected stock market index. These portfolios of index-component securities are called "**index funds.**" Third, a new kind of "investment company" called an "exchange traded fund" is investigated. Numerous older and more complex portfolios, which comprise the majority of the existing "investment companies," are the subject matter for Chapter 16.*

Following "investment companies," this chapter brings financial futures that are based on financial indexes into the spotlight. As explained in Chapter 9, financial futures are exchange traded futures contracts and options that have a financial instrument as the underlying quantity. This chapter acquaints us with those futures contracts that have stock market indexes as their underlying quantity. Then, put and call options that are tied to a stock market index are considered.

This chapter closes with a discussion of bond portfolios that are designed to mimic a pre-selected bond index. Before discussing these various index-based products, however, we begin by defining that legally regulated category of portfolios called "investment companies."

INVESTMENT COMPANIES

Under U.S. law an **investment company** is a business organization that markets its equity shares to the investing public, commingles the monies from the shares that are sold into a single pool, and uses the pooled funds to buy a diversified list of securities. Investment companies hire professional money managers to administer their investments. Investors who buy shares in an investment company that invests in common stocks compensate their money managers by paying an average management fee of about 1.4% of the market value of the managed funds each year.

The **Investment Company Act of 1940** defines three different types of investment companies:

◆ **Open-end investment companies**, commonly called **mutual funds**, are the most popular. About 10,000 mutual funds exist in the United States. Residents of the United Kingdom call open-end investment companies *unit trusts*, while the Japanese call them *open-type investment trusts*.*

◆ **Closed-end investment companies** are not permitted to sell additional shares or redeem their original shares; thus, they are called closed-end funds. About 500 closed-end funds exist in the United States. Japan's *Securities Investment Trust Law* gives structures like the American closed-end funds the label of *closed-type investment trusts*, while the British call them simply *investment trusts*.

◆ **Unit investment trusts (UITs)** are narrowly defined investment companies that are not allowed to actively trade the securities in their portfolios. The termination date for a UIT is specified when it is created. Only about 100 UITs exist in the United States. America's UITs are sometimes called *authorized investment trusts* in Great Britain. Japan appears to have nothing closely resembling America's UIT.

Mutual Fund Investing

The Investment Company Act of 1940 refers to mutual funds as open-ended investment companies because they are permitted to keep selling more shares as long as investors are willing to buy more shares. In 1999 over half the world's mutual fund assets were held in the United States, and mutual funds were growing more rapidly in the United States than in other areas of the world.**

Required Goal Statements. The Investment Company Act requires mutual funds to publish a statement of the investment objective that their portfolio managers will pursue and to distribute these goal statements to every new investor. This legal requirement is another example of the general tendency of U.S. securities law to require full disclosure of the relevant facts to potential investors. Few other countries require so much disclosure. Based on their goal statements, U.S. mutual funds can be categorized as shown in Table 12-1. Some of these funds offer different fee schedules and, thus, one fund can be considered to be more than one fund.

The Index Funds Are Hidden. Index funds are not visible in Table 12-1 because some index funds invest in a growth stock index, some invest in a value stock index, some invest in an index of foreign stocks, and some invest in bond indexes. Thus, index funds are sprinkled throughout the categories in Table 12-1. Table 12-2 lists some U.S. stock market indexes and characterizes some of the index funds that state their goal is to imitate that index.

---

* Japan's investment trusts come in both open-end and closed-end varieties, and some other varieties too. For details see *Securities Market in Japan, 1996* (Tokyo: Japan Securities Research Institute, 1996), Chapter VIII, entitled "Investment Trusts." Americans typically use the phrase *investment trust* for an account at the trust department of a commercial bank.

** See the *1999 Mutual Fund Fact Book* (Washington, DC: Investment Company Institute, 1999), 102–103. The United States owned 64% of the world's mutual funds in terms of market value, 23% in terms of the number of funds, and is growing faster than the rest of the world by both measures.

TABLE 12-1 **Number of U.S. Mutual Funds Categorized by Their Investment Goals, 2000**

Category of Fund	Funds	Percent
Equity Mutual Funds		
Aggressive growth funds	836	
Growth funds	1,088	
Sector funds	345	
Emerging markets funds	107	
Global equity funds	202	
International equity funds	446	
Regional equity funds	205	
Growth and income funds	684	
Subtotal	3,913	49.7%
Equity and Bond Funds		
Income equity funds	121	
Asset-allocation funds	69	
Balanced funds	290	
Flexible portfolio funds	111	
Income mixed funds	62	
Subtotal	653	8.3%
Fixed Income Funds		
Corporate bond funds—general	86	
Corporate bond funds—intermediate	154	
Corporate bond funds—short term	87	
High-yield funds	209	
Global bond funds—general	93	
Global bond funds—short term	39	
Other world bond funds	41	
Government bond funds—general	126	
Government bond funds—intermediate	92	
Government bond funds—short term	76	
Mortgage-backed bond funds	77	
Strategic income funds	294	
Subtotal	1,374	17.5%
Municipal Bond Funds		
State municipal bond funds—general	534	
State municipal bond funds—short term	72	
National municipal bond funds—general	206	
National municipal bond funds—short term	77	
National tax-exempt money market funds	155	
State tax-exempt money market funds	185	
Subtotal	1,229	15.6%
Money Market Funds		
Taxable money market funds—government	283	
Taxable money market funds—nongovernment	417	
Subtotal	700	8.9%
Total of all fund categories:	7,869	100.0%

SOURCE: Investment Company Institute, Washington, DC

TABLE 12-2 **Popular U.S. Stock Market Indexes and Some Indexed Mutual Funds That Track Them**

	Dow-Jones Industrial Average[a]	Standard & Poor's 500[b]	Russell 2000[c]	Wilshire 5000[d]	NASDAQ 100[e]
Number of Firms	30	500	2,000	7,412	100
Weighting	Price	Market Value	Market Value	Market Value	Market Value
Market Capitalization of Equity (Billions of Dollars)					
Large Firm	240.3	260.6	1,403	282.1	114.4
Mean	64.9	15.298	.592	1.6	5.8
Median	49.8	6,517	.500	.136	2.3
Smallest Firm	5.9	.369	.221	.001	.527
Total	1,946.9	7,649.0	1,184.0	11,635.0	587.1
Listed Exchange (% of Firms)					
NYSE	100.0	92.0	50.6	27.4	.0
AMEX	.0	.4	3.0	8.2	.0
NASDAQ	.0	7.6	46.4	64.4	100.0
Business Sector Share (% of Firms)					
Industrials	93.3	75.2	66.9	69.0	92
Utilities	.0	7.4	6.7	9.6	5
Financial	6.7	15.4	22.5	19.9	0
Transportation	.0	2.0	3.9	1.5	3
Mutual Funds Tracking the Index	DIAMONDS listed on AMEX	SPDRs, iShares, Vanguard Index Trust 500, and over 100 others	Vanguard Small Cap, BT Small Cap, Northern Small Cap	Vanguard Extended Market, Vanguard Total Stock Market	Rydex NADAQ 100 Fund, AMEX NASDAQ 100 shares

[a]Some data are from the Dow Jones Averages, 1997 Annual Report, and other sources. Data is year-end 1997 or later. This table draws on Peter Fortune, "A Primer on U.S. Stock Price Indexes," *New England Economic Journal* (November–December 1998), Table 1, p. 33, Federal Reserve Bank of Boston, Boston, MA.
[b]Data are from www.proinvestor.com. Information date is August 1998.
[c]Data are from www.nussell.com. Information date is June 1998.
[d]Data are from www.wilshire.com, dated March 1998.
[e]Data are from The Nasdaq Stock Market, Nasdaq-100, Information date is March 31, 1997. Nasdaq-100 is skewed toward technology stocks.

Characteristics of All Mutual Funds

Any investor willing to pay an annual management fee of about 1% to 2% of the market value of the assets managed can buy as many shares in a mutual fund as they want. To insure that the value of an investor's shares are accounted for correctly, U.S. law defines accounting conventions that must be used by every mutual fund.

Net Asset Value Per Share (NAVPS). U.S. securities law requires that mutual funds sell and redeem their shares at the day's **net asset value per share**, or **NAVPS**. NAVPS equals the market value of the mutual fund portfolio divided by the total number of shares in the mutual fund outstanding that day.

$$\begin{pmatrix} \text{Net asset value} \\ \text{per share at} \\ \text{time } t, \text{NAVPS}_t \end{pmatrix} = \dfrac{\begin{pmatrix} \text{Current market value of} \\ \text{the fund's total assets}_t \end{pmatrix} \text{less} \begin{pmatrix} \text{Total} \\ \text{liabilities}_t \end{pmatrix}}{\left(\text{Total number of shares outstanding}_t\right)} \qquad \text{(12-1)}$$

After contemplating the NAVPS you realize it changes every time anything in the portfolio experiences a price change. The Investment Company Act of 1940 requires all U.S. mutual funds to compute their NAVPS daily, publish their NAVPS daily, and sell and redeem their shares each day only at that day's NAVPS. In contrast, U.S. law permits shares in closed-end investment companies to be bought and sold at premiums above and discounts below their NAVPS (book value), just like the shares of common stocks.

The Single-Period Rate of Return. Investors obtain three types of income from mutual fund shares:

1. **Disbursed cash flows** are disbursements of cash dividends and/or interest paid to the fund that are passed through to the shareowners. Undisbursed cash flow income is included in (3), below.
2. **Disbursed capital gains** are disbursements of the fund's realized net capital gains (after losses are deducted). Unrealized and undisbursed capital gains and losses are included in (3).
3. **NAVPS change** is the total change in book value that occurs between the close of time periods $t-1$ and t; it is denoted $(\text{NAVPS}_t - \text{NAVPS}_{t-1})$. Most of this *NAVPS change* comes from unrealized capital gains and losses from securities held. In addition, a fund's *NAVPS change* includes realized net capital gains that were not disbursed, undisbursed cash dividend income, and undisbursed coupon interest income. These changes in book value represent owners' equity that has not yet been passed through to the shareowners.

The one-period rate of return for a mutual fund share is defined in Eqn. 12-2.

$$r_t = \dfrac{\begin{pmatrix} \text{Cash flow} \\ \text{disbursements}_t \end{pmatrix} + \begin{pmatrix} \text{Capital gains} \\ \text{disbursements}_t \end{pmatrix} + (\text{NAVPS}_t - \text{NAVPS}_{t-1})}{\left(\text{Purchase price at beginning of period, NAVPS}_{t-1}\right)} \qquad \text{(12-2)}$$

Mutual fund investors can reinvest their disbursed income by buying more shares in the mutual fund. Whether or not a mutual fund's disbursed income is reinvested, mutual fund investors must pay income taxes on each year's disbursed income in the year it is earned. Reinvestment provides no opportunities for income tax evasion.

THE ECONOMICS OF PORTFOLIO MANAGEMENT

The mutual fund industry has operating costs and economies of scale that shape the fees they charge.

Mutual Fund Fees

Mutual funds' fees are complicated by pricing schemes designed to conceal ownership costs from investors and to discourage investors from redeeming their shares. There are several types of mutual fund fees:

1. **Entry fees. Load fees** are one-time front-end sales commissions that U.S. law limits to a maximum of 8.5% of the purchase price, which equals 9.3% (= 8.5%/91.5%) of the invested funds. Load fees are up-front deductions that diminish the investor's initial NAVPS. Thousands of **no-load funds** charge entry fees of zero. And thousands of other funds charge entry fees between zero and 8.5%. Studies show that mutual funds that charge lower entry fee percentages tend to perform slightly better than funds that charge the higher load fee percentages.

2. **Exit fees**. Back-end fees, called exit fees or **redemption fees**, discourage investors from liquidating their investments. Some funds charge *contingent deferred sales charges* (CDSCs) that decline toward zero as the fund is held additional years before liquidation. Most funds charge no exit fees. Investors should usually avoid funds that charge load fees and/or exit fees (although many choose not to).

3. **Management fees**. Management and administrative fees average 1.4% of assets per year for common stock funds, stated as a percentage of the market value of the managed assets. However, management fees vary from as low as $\frac{7}{100}$ of 1% at mutual funds for institutional investors (with a $10 million minimum account size) to a high of about 3.5% per year. Management fees are used to pay the portfolio managers' salaries, trading commissions, office rent, utilities, and other expenses. Studies show that the performance of mutual funds tends to vary inversely with the size of their management fees: Poor managers charge higher fees.

4. **Distribution fees**. The Securities and Exchange Commission (SEC) Rule 12b-1 allows mutual funds to deduct up to 1% of their assets per year to pay distribution fees (sales commissions and promotional expenses). Mutual fund investors gain nothing from 12b-1 fees.

5. **Transaction fees**. Some funds deduct these liquidity fees to cover the costs of buying and/or selling securities. For example, a Vanguard international fund charges 1% of the assets market value to buy and an additional 1% to redeem.

The appropriate fees must be deducted from the investment. To determine an investor's net rate of return the expenses paid every year are deducted in Eqn. 12-2a.

$$r_t = \frac{\begin{pmatrix} \text{Cash flow} \\ \text{disbursements}_t \end{pmatrix} + \begin{pmatrix} \text{Capital gains} \\ \text{disbursements}_t \end{pmatrix} + (\text{NAVPS}_t - \text{NAVPS}_{t-1}) - \begin{pmatrix} \text{12b-1 fee (if paid)} \\ + \text{ Management fee} \end{pmatrix}}{(\text{Purchase price at beginning of time period } t, \text{NAVPS}_{t-1})} \quad \textbf{(12-2a)}$$

Some mutual funds ignore ethical considerations and neglect to deduct their fees in the rates of return they advertise. In other words, some funds use Eqn. 12-2 instead of Eqn. 12-2a and/or they omit the load fee and/or they omit the redemption fee. The various fees listed above do not help the funds' performance. Investors should minimize fee payments. Mark Carhart studied hundreds of mutual funds covering decades and echoed the conclusion reached by other studies: ". . . the investment costs of the expense ratios, transactions costs, and load fees all have a direct, negative impact on performance."[1]

This book's Chapter 16 focuses on evaluating the performance of investment portfolios.[2]

THE NET RATE OF RETURN FROM A MUTUAL FUND   EXAMPLE

Ralph gave $1,000 to the Alchemy mutual fund. Not all of Ralph's $1,000 was invested. Because the fund deducts an up-front load fee of 3%, Ralph's initial investment is $\text{NAVPS}_{t-1} = \$970.$*

---

* The load fee is only deducted from the initial investment. If the investor invests new money in the same mutual fund at a later date, the load fee should not be deducted again from the earlier investment.

After 90 days Ralph liquidated the fund at $\text{NAVPS}_t = \$1,010$. During the one-quarter of a year he owned the fund Ralph received $5 of cash dividend disbursements and a $15 capital gain disbursement. Ralph's gross rate of return of 6.18% for the 90 days is computed with Eqn. 12-2.

$$r_t = \frac{\left(\begin{array}{c}\text{Cash dividend}\\\text{disbursements, \$5}\end{array}\right) + \left(\begin{array}{c}\text{Capital gains}\\\text{disbursements, \$15}\end{array}\right) + \left(\begin{array}{c}\text{NAVPS}_t - \text{NAVPS}_{t-1} =\\\$1,010 - \$970 = \$40\end{array}\right)}{\left(\begin{array}{c}\text{Purchase price at beginning of period,}\\\text{NAVPS}_{t-1} = \$970\end{array}\right)} = 6.18\%$$

After Annual Fees. Assume Alchemy charges no 12b-1 fee. The fund's annual management fee of 0.97 of 1% per year equals 0.2425 of 1% per quarter of a year, or $2.425.

$$r_t = \frac{\left(\begin{array}{c}\text{Cash dividend}\\\text{disbursements, \$5}\end{array}\right) + \left(\begin{array}{c}\text{Capital gains}\\\text{disbursements, \$15}\end{array}\right) + \left(\begin{array}{c}\text{NAVPS}_t - \text{NAVPS}_{t-1} =\\\$1,010 - \$970 = \$40\end{array}\right) - \left(\begin{array}{c}\text{Management}\\\text{fee, \$2.425}\end{array}\right)}{\left(\begin{array}{c}\text{Book value purchased at beginning of}\\\text{90-day period, NAVPS}_{t-1} = \$970\end{array}\right)} = 5.94\%$$

A Closer Look. Since Alchemy charged Ralph a redemption fee of 1.5% (or $15.15), Ralph deducted that outlay from his income (the numerator). Recalling that he initially gave Alchemy $1,000, he added the $30 load fee that was deducted up-front back into the amount he invested (the denominator).

$$r_t = \frac{\left(\begin{array}{c}\text{Cash dividend}\\\text{disbursements, \$5}\end{array}\right) + \left(\begin{array}{c}\text{Capital gains}\\\text{disbursements, \$15}\end{array}\right) + \left(\begin{array}{c}\text{NAVPS}_t - \text{NAVPS}_{t-1} =\\\$1,010 - \$970 = \$40\end{array}\right) - \left(\begin{array}{c}\text{Management fee, \$2.425}\\+ \text{Liquidation fee,}\\\$15.15 + \text{Load fee, \$30}\end{array}\right)}{\left(\begin{array}{c}\text{Purchased at beginning of 90-day}\\\text{period, NAVPS}_{t-1} = \$970\end{array}\right) + \left(\text{Load fee, \$30}\right) = \$1,000 \text{ Initial outlay}}$$

Ralph figures his net rate of return is 1.2425% for the quarter.

$$r_t = \frac{\left(\text{How much did I get out?}\right)}{\left(\text{How much did I put in?}\right)} = \frac{\text{Net income}}{\text{Total investment}} = \frac{\$12.425}{\$1,000} = 1.245\%$$

If Ralph stayed invested longer, the load fee would not be included in the purchase price for later periods.

Mutual funds that invest in small companies and foreign companies typically charge higher-than-average fees. To some extent, these higher fees can be justified because it is more costly to obtain information and trade in stocks issued by small cap (capitalization) companies and foreign companies. However, it is difficult to justify the wide cost variations in these mutual funds with similar goals. Some mutual fund managers charge investors exorbitantly high fees that are unrelated to the services provided.

Most money managers have fee structures with *quantity discounts*. For instance, Vanguard Index Trust 500 Portfolio accepts accounts as small as $3,000 and charges a low management fee of $\frac{18}{100}$ of 1% per year to manage these *retail accounts*. Vanguard Institutional Index 500 Portfolio has $10 million account minimums and charges an even smaller management fee of $\frac{7}{100}$ of 1% per year for investing in the identical S&P500 stocks. The Vanguard Institutional Index 500 Portfolio is available for *institutional accounts* such as pensions, mutual funds, trusts, foundations, endowment funds, and substantial individuals. Mutual funds that charge load fees also grant quantity discounts on their load fees. The disparity between the fees for retail clients and institutional clients is justified because many retail investors make numerous small deposits and withdrawals, require cordial telephone clerks to answer their questions, expect free educational literature, and require other expensive administrative services. Professional money managers that make multimillion fund investments typically require far fewer costly "hand-holding services." Mutual funds' quantity discounts reflect these cost differences, and they also reflect *economies of scale*.

Economies of Scale

It is cheaper to manage one portfolio worth $1 billion than it is to manage several smaller portfolios that have an aggregate value of $1 billion invested in the same securities. Managing large portfolios is cheaper because of quantity discounts on trading commissions and economies of scale in portfolio management.

Quantity Discounts on Commissions. Table 12-3 shows that brokerage commissions, stated as a percentage of the total dollar value of each buy or sell transaction, vary inversely with the size of the transaction. These quantity discounts reflect the fact that a brokerage house's costs for processing a $10,000 trade and a $100,000 trade are about the same.

Economies of Scale in Portfolio Management. Economies of scale arise from operations that have high fixed costs and small variable costs. Both the brokerage industry and the money management industry have high fixed costs and small per unit cost structures. For example, after the offices, computers, and administrative staff needed to manage a $100 million portfolio have been acquired, it does not cost much more to manage another $100 million.

As a result of economies of scale, the Vanguard Index Trust 500 Portfolio can manage a portfolio worth more than $100 billion for management fees of only $\frac{18}{100}$ of 1% per year and be profitable. But, it would be impossible to operate a $1 million indexed portfolio profitably on annual fees of $\frac{18}{100}$ of 1%. One million dollars is enough to buy round (100 share) lots in only about 200 different issues of stock. Odd lots would have to be purchased in most issues to spread $1 million far enough to buy the 500 different issues of stock that make up the S&P500 index. In this example, the high odd-lot commissions defined in Table 12-3 would push the portfolio's costs up to a level too high to be competitive with the dozens of other S&P500 index mutual funds.

The Management Fees of Index Funds

Indexed portfolios do not need to hire a staff of highly paid securities analysts, economists, and portfolio managers. Decisions about what stocks to buy have already been made through the commitment to buy the stocks comprising an index. These savings in operating expenses allow indexed portfolios to charge much lower management fees than actively managed port-folios. The average managed common stock mutual fund subtracts about 1.4% of the market

TABLE 12-3 Brokerage Commission Rates, Stated as a Percent of the Total Market Value of Each Purchase or Sale	
Name of Transaction and Number of Shares	Brokerage Commission Rate, %
Odd-lot transactions involve less than 100 shares	1% to 5%
Round-lot transactions involve 100 share lots	About 1%
A block trade involves 10,000 or more shares	A fraction of 1%

value of the investors' funds as an annual management fee, which pays for its analysts, managers, and promoters. In contrast, Vanguard Index Trust charges its investors an annual management fee of only $\frac{18}{100}$ of 1%. These management fees mean the average managed common stock fund (which does not perform as well as the S&P500 index) falls 1.22% per year further behind the performance of the index fund just on the basis of fees.

Mutual fund	Annual Management Fee
Average actively managed common stock mutual fund's fee	1.40%
Vanguard Index Trust 500 Portfolio's fee	less: 0.18%
Indexers average annual savings on management fees	1.22%

Consider the management fee of $\frac{18}{100}$ of 1% per year relative to the managed mutual funds' average management fee of 1.4% per year. To compare the implications of these fees, contemplate investing money in two different mutual funds, both earning returns before management expenses were deducted of 10% per year each year. A long-run average return of 10% per year is not unreasonable; it is a typical return for an equity mutual fund. Table 12-4 shows the results of investing $100 in each of the mutual funds.

When you think that $100 invested for your retirement at the end of 30 years would be worth ($1,661 − $1,188 =) $473 more simply because you selected a mutual fund with lower-than-average management fees, you become motivated to minimize your mutual funds' fees. Low management fees are one of the advantages gained by investing in most indexed portfolios. However, investors must be constantly vigilant. Over 100 index funds compete by indexing to the S&P500 index and the fees of a few reach as high as $\frac{50}{100}$ of 1%.

Portfolio Turnover

The Standard & Poor's Corporation does not change the 500 stocks included in the S&P500 index frequently. Likewise, the composition of most securities market indexes changes slowly. Since index funds mimic their underlying indexes, the securities in index funds also turn over slowly. For example, the Vanguard Index Trust 500 Portfolio and Fidelity's Market

---

TABLE 12-4 Comparison of Long-Run Investment Implications of Different Mutual Fund Management Fees

	Vanguard Index Trust 500 Mutual Fund	Managed Mutual Fund with Average Management Fee
Assumed gross annual return	10.0%	10.0%
Less: Annual management fee	0.18%	1.4%
Equals: Investor's net return	9.82%	8.6%
After 10 years a $100 investment grows to:		
	($100)(1 + 9.82%)^{10} =	($100)(1 + 8.6%)^{10} =
	($100)(2.55 times) = $255	($100)(2.28 times) = $228
After 20 years a $100 investment grows to:		
	($100)(1 + 9.82%)^{20} =	($100)(1 + 8.6%)^{20} =
	($100)(6.51 times) = $651	($100)(5.21 times) = $521
After 30 years a $100 investment grows to:		
	($100)(1 + 9.82%)^{30} =	($100)(1 + 8.6%)^{30} =
	($100)(16.61 times) = $1,661	($100)(11.88 times) = $1,188

Index Fund are both index funds that have turnover rates of 3% to 4% per year. In contrast, Fidelity's Magellan Fund is an actively managed common stock mutual fund that turns its assets over more than 100% per year in some years. If the Magellan Fund had a turnover rate of 150% in one year, for instance, it turned over its total assets 1.5 times that year. A portfolio's turnover rate is usually calculated at an annual rate:

$$\left(\begin{array}{c} \text{Portfolio's} \\ \text{turnover rate} \end{array} \right) = \frac{MIN(\text{Annual sales, Annual purchases})}{\text{Average value of portfolio's assets during the year}}$$

MIN(Annual sales, Annual purchases) stands for the minimum of sales or purchases, whichever is less, and this amount is divided by the portfolio's average market value. This means Magellan's sales plus purchases during an 8-month period equaled the portfolio's aggregate market value.

Eight months is two-thirds of a year = 2/3 = 100%/150% = 1/(1.5 turns per year)

The slower turnover rates of indexed portfolios generate smaller brokerage commission expenses. Reduced expenses convert into lower management fees and higher investor returns.

Mutual Funds That Fail

Some mutual funds fail during their first year because they are unable to pull in money to manage. Other mutual funds fail during their later years because they managed the investors' money ineptly and the portfolio's total assets shrank. A mutual fund's total assets can shrink, because investors redeem their shares or the net asset value per share (NAVPS) drops. These two forces can work together as continually declining NAVPS cause persistent redemptions.

Some failed mutual funds are liquidated. Other failed mutual funds are merged. Mutual fund families frequently use mergers to hide their embarrassments. During the mid-1990s the Dreyfus family of funds, for instance, merged more than a dozen of its poorly performing mutual funds into other Dreyfus funds that had better records.[3] The names and performance records of the poor performers disappear after the merger. Mutual fund mergers are not publicized, but they are common.

TWO OTHER TYPES OF INVESTMENT COMPANIES UNDER U.S. LAW

In addition to mutual funds, two other types of investment companies are defined by U.S. securities law.

Closed-End Investment Company. A closed-end investment company procures the funds it invests through an initial public offering (IPO) of common stock. After the IPO, the law does not permit a closed-end fund to sell additional shares or redeem outstanding shares—hence the name closed-end. Shares in closed-end funds are listed on stock exchanges like the NYSE and AMEX. Sometimes the market price of a closed-end fund rises to a *premium* above the fund's net asset value per share (NAVPS) and sometimes the market price falls to a *discount* below the fund's net asset value per share. In contrast, U.S. law requires that mutual (open-end) funds can only be sold and redeemed at their NAVPS. Closed-end funds never became as popular as mutual funds.[4]

Unit Investment Trust (UIT). *A unit investment trust (UIT)* is an investment company created for a special purpose. UITs have limited growth potential, which is enforced by prohibitions against issuing new shares. They are closed-end portfolios. A termination date is set for every UIT when it is originated. U.S. law stipulates that UITs must own a specified set of securities for the life of the trust.

A UIT is created when a sponsor (typically, a brokerage or securities exchange) purchases a narrowly defined list of securities and deposits them with a trustee (usually a commercial bank). Sales of redeemable trust certificates to the UIT's investors raises the initial cash that is used to purchase the portfolio's securities. Sponsors usually sell their portfolios at prices that are from half of 1% to 4% above the cost of the securities in the portfolio. This up-front origination fee is what induces sponsors to create UITs. Investors in a UIT obtain a proportional interest in the portfolio's assets and whatever income the portfolio might generate. U.S. law permits only enough buying and selling activity during the life of a UIT to realign changes in the portfolio (caused by security price changes or cash income) with its original composition. Because active trading is forbidden, UITs annual management fees are typically very low—as low as $\frac{15}{100}$ of 1% of the net asset value per year.

Many UITs contain fixed-income securities. If so, the UIT expires when the last bond matures or is sold, or if the portfolio becomes bankrupt. Thus, the life of a UIT containing money market securities is less than 1 year, while a UIT containing longer-term bonds might survive for 30 years. Figure 12-1, an excerpt from the *Wall Street Journal,* discusses some of the ways UITs are promoted.

ADVANTAGES OF INVESTING IN STOCK MARKET INDEX PORTFOLIOS

The oldest and largest indexed mutual fund in the world is Vanguard Index Trust 500 Portfolio; it began in 1976.* It invests billions of dollars in the stocks that make up the Standard & Poor's 500 Stocks Composite Index (S&P500). This mutual fund's weights are identical to the proportions Standard & Poor's assigns to the 500 stocks in its S&P500 Index. Vanguard stays attuned to the S&P500 index's changes so its index fund will perform as closely as possible to the targeted index.

Over sample periods ranging from the past 5 to 20 years the S&P500 index has outperformed more than three-fourths of the professionally managed U.S. mutual funds that invest in common stocks.[5] Mutual funds and other portfolios that target a stock market index outperform most actively managed common stock portfolios for several reasons:

♦ **Management Expenses Are Minimized**. Indexed funds do not hire costly staffs (see pp. 339–340).

♦ **Higher Returns**. Many investors are surprised to learn that the professionally managed portfolios, on average, do not outperform the index funds.[6] Details about mutual fund performance in Chapter 16 shows ads from actively managed funds can be misleading. Some professional money managers are incompetent.[7]

---

* It is difficult to discuss indexed portfolios without mentioning the Vanguard family of mutual funds that is headquartered in suburbs of Philadelphia, Pennsylvania. Vanguard's founder, John Bogle, pioneered no-load (zero sales commission) mutual funds in 1974, and created the first indexed mutual fund in 1976. As a result of accomplishments like these a Princeton University economics professor named Burton Malkiel, in his book entitled *A Random Walk Down Wall Street*, describes Vanguard as "the most pro-consumer financial services company in the world."

FIGURE 12-1   NEWSPAPER EXCERPT: "Smart Plays or Hype? Unit Investment Trusts Are Hot"

YOUR MONEY MATTERS: WEEKEND REPORT

Smart Plays or Hype? Unit Investment Trusts Are Hot

By Suzanne McGee
Staff Reporter of The Wall Street Journal

Some of Wall Street's hottest investments can't be found on a stock exchange. And they're not grabbing headlines in personal-finance magazines. But you're probably hearing a lot about them from your broker.

Unit investment trusts, unmanaged investment portfolios with preset maturities, are being promoted by **Merrill Lynch** & Co., **Travelers Group**'s Smith Barney Inc., Prudential Securities Inc. and a growing number of other brokerage firms for investors seeking performance, diversification and peace of mind.

With investment minimums as low as $250, for individual retirement accounts, they are being sold as a way for the little guy to buy a stake in a collection of securities that only a millionaire could afford to own outright.

Investors are snapping them up. In the first eight months of the year, they steered $24.6 billion into unit investment trusts, compared with $13.4 billion in the year-earlier period. Assets in the trusts soared 88% in 1996 over 1995.

"Our success is the best-kept secret of Wall Street," boasts Ken Swankie, manager of the unit investment trust department at Prudential Securities, a subsidiary of **Prudential Insurance Co. of America**.

But as far as some critics are concerned, many people would be better off with mutual funds or individual stocks. The popularity of unit investment trusts is "a triumph of aggressive marketing to a captive audience," scoffs John Markese, president of the American Association of Individual Investors. "They are fixed portfolios that add costs but not necessarily performance."

Unit investment trusts were designed in the early 1970s to sell bonds, then adapted in the early 1990s as a stock-investment vehicle, competing with index funds.

The stock-market trusts are easy to understand—and sell. A brokerage firm buys large blocks of stock, typically in as few as five or as many as 25 companies. It then puts the shares into a trust, and sells units in that trust to clients.

During the trust's lifespan—from a year to five years—the portfolio usually remains untouched, although dividends may be paid out periodically. The trusts aren't publicly traded, but investors can ask the brokerage firm to buy back the holdings at a price closer to net asset value.

The investments appeal to people puzzled by the stock market's gyrations and the uneven performance of many mutual funds. And the returns on many unit investment trusts have been large enough to keep them from worrying about potential drawbacks.

"You can't sneeze at annualized returns of about 30%," says Alan Hansen, a Portland, Ore., investor. "And I don't have to figure out what kind of investment style my mutual-fund manager has and what he's up to this month."

The most popular unit investment trusts are the "Dow Dogs" products, based on the theory that investors will reap rewards by buying the 10 stocks in the Dow Jones Industrial Average with the highest dividend rates. "Investors are comfortable with household names like this," says Mr. Swankie, who estimates 75% of Prudential's unit trust sales are of its "Select 10" portfolio.

But as investor interest has exploded, so has the list of choices. Want to own a portfolio of fledgling biotechnology stocks? Talk to **Principal Financial Securities** Inc., Dallas, which believes the trusts are a less risky way than individual stocks to bet on this sector.

Zacks Investment Research Inc. has teamed up with Reich & Tang on a 39-stock portfolio based on the picks of top-ranked analysts in The Wall Street Journal's annual All-Star Analysts survey. (Zacks, a Chicago firm whose specialty is tracking brokeragehouse research, crunches the numbers for the Journal's All-Star survey; the paper and its parent, **Dow Jones** & Co., have no involvement in the unit investment trust. Reich & Tang, a New York money-management firm, is a unit of **New England Investment** Cos.)

On the drawing board at Smith Barney: a unit investment trust owning stocks the firm expects to benefit from the aging of the baby-boom generation. Meanwhile, discount brokerage giant **Charles Schwab** & Co., which has sold other firms' unit trusts, is in the midst of launching its own Dow Dogs product, undercutting fees at most other brokers.

Most brokerage firms charge a 1% load for the unit investment trusts they sell, and deduct another 1.75% annually from the net asset value, in 10 monthly installments. Investors who roll over their holdings in subsequent years pay only the annual 1.75% fee.

But that still exceeds management fees of as little as 0.2% at index mutual funds, and an average annual expense ratio of 1.32% at U.S. stock mutual funds, according to Chicago fund researcher Morningstar Inc. Only when measured against funds with big front-end loads of 5% or so, do unit investment trusts come out ahead.

Brokers argue that they earn those fees by removing fear and greed from the investment process, and by imposing a buy-and-hold discipline. Trusts can't be compared to broad index funds, they say, because they are smaller and more-targeted. They are also far cheaper than building a portfolio independently.

"To own a diversified portfolio that has IBM, Hewlett Packard, Caterpillar and names like that is prohibitively expensive for small investors, or they might only afford one share of each," says Stanley Craig, director of sales and marketing for defined funds at Merrill Lynch.

This week, Smith Barney offered investors the first no-load stock unit trust, a $250 million product with stakes in 12 REITs, or real-estate investment trusts. Investors will pay only 0.14% annually in fees, says Laurie Hesslein, head of the unit investment trust division.

"We took advantage of ties between the REIT business and our banking group, and the REITs issued stock directly to us that we put into the trust," cutting costs, Ms. Hesslein says. "This isn't something we could do every day, unfortunately."

Schwab also hopes to slash fees. Its first unit investment trust will carry a deferred fee of 1.25%, falling to 1% in subsequent years. A spokesman says Schwab believes the lower fees will make unit investment trusts more accessible to investors, some of whom are deterred by high costs.

Liquidity is another thorny issue. August Viekman, a broker with MML Investment Services in South Dennis, Mass., who used to sell fixed-income unit trusts, worries investors might find it difficult to redeem their holdings quickly at a fair asset value in a sudden market correction, despite brokers' pledges to do so.

"The problem with a fixed portfolio instead of a typical mutual fund is that you don't have a money manager who's going to sell any stocks that turn sour," he says. "The only recourse is the broker's willingness and ability to redeem the [investors' trust units], and that hasn't been tested."

Tax concerns are easier to tackle. Merrill's Mr. Craig says about two-thirds of the people who buy unit investment trusts keep these holdings in IRAs, where capital-gains taxes aren't an issue. Those who don't invest through tax-favored accounts will benefit from a new letter ruling from the Internal Revenue Service, he says. It will allow investors in one-year trusts to roll over some gains if they reinvest in the next year's trust, Mr. Craig says. They would qualify for the lowest capital-gains tax rate on stocks that are included in the trust for both years, he says.

But Mark Mordoh, a retired theatrical manager in Palm Desert, Calif., worries less about his tax rate than his returns and diversifying his portfolio.

"Without unit trusts, I couldn't buy these blue-chip portfolio names, only a mutual fund where I'd never be sure exactly what I owned," says Mr. Mordoh, a four-year investor in a Dow Dogs portfolio. He devotes much time to chasing small stocks, and "I need that safety net."

SOURCE: *Wall Street Journal*, 10 October 1997, C1.

◆ **No-Load Funds**. Many index funds do not employ sales people to sell their product; they operate as no-load funds. As a result, every penny of the invested money goes to purchase securities for the investor's account.

◆ **Fully Invested**. Actively managed mutual funds hold 2% to 8% of their funds in cash or cash equivalent investments. This liquidity is needed in case a good investment opportunity arises or redemptions occur. Cash is not an earning asset. Indexed portfolios usually stay more fully invested so their portfolios will track the targeted index as closely as possible, they hold tiny liquidity reserves of nonearning cash.

◆ **Slower Turnover**. Investors pay the commission costs their mutual fund generates. Because index funds turn over slowly, they incur small trading commission expenses.

◆ **Tax Efficiency**. U.S. tax law says the capital gain or loss from an asset is not *realized* until the investment is actually sold. Index funds are tax-efficient investments because the slow turnover in the securities comprising indexed portfolios allows investors to carry their capital gains forward as unrealized and untaxed income, which is reinvested tax-free each year until the mutual fund is sold.[8] This tax efficiency is unattainable with an actively managed mutual fund that turns over rapidly. (See Figure 12-2.)

How long an investor holds a portfolio for tax purposes has little to do with how long the investor maintains continuous ownership of the portfolio's securities. If a mutual fund turns over rapidly, it is possible for an investor who owns the fund for decades to have a realized holding period for tax purposes of only a few months' duration. Figure 12-2 shows that the length of time an investor holds a portfolio for tax purposes equals the reciprocal of that portfolio's turnover rate.

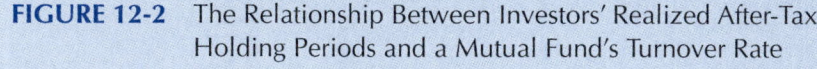

FIGURE 12-2   The Relationship Between Investors' Realized After-Tax Holding Periods and a Mutual Fund's Turnover Rate

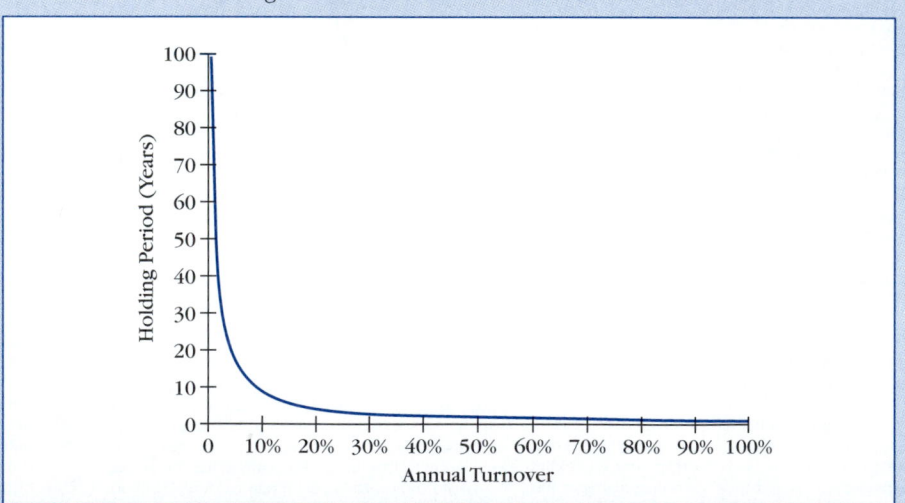

Index funds are tax efficient investments because the slow turnover in the indexed securities allows investors to carry their capital gains forward as unrealized and untaxed income, which is reinvested tax-free each year until the mutual fund is sold.

SOURCE: Robert H. Jeffrey and Robert D. Arnott, "Is Your Alpha Big Enough to Cover Its Taxes?," *Journal of Portfolio Management* (spring 1993): 15–25, Exhibit 3.

Most large institutional investors (pensions, mutual funds, foundations, and endowments) are tax-exempt. However, individuals, insurance companies, and some other investors are taxable.

DISADVANTAGES OF INVESTING IN INDEXED COMMON STOCK PORTFOLIOS

Some indexed portfolios do not mimic their targeted index very closely. **Tracking errors** measure the inability of an indexed portfolio to imitate its target index.

10.68%	Return on a targeted index or asset class
10.50%	Less: Return on the index fund or other replicating portfolio
0.18%	Equals: Tracking error of 18 BPs

For example, suppose the Vanguard Index Trust 500 Portfolio earns a return of 10.50% in a year when its target, the S&P500 index, earns 10.68%. In this example, the Vanguard Index Trust 500 Portfolio's tracking error is 18 basis points (BPs). In fact, the Vanguard Index Trust 500 Portfolio's tracking error is about 18 BPs every year. This is because the portfolio's management fee of $\frac{18}{100}$ of 1% is deducted from the investor's returns. Management fees are a source of positive tracking error for all indexed mutual funds. Tracking errors arising from an index fund's management fees represent poor portfolio management practices if the management fees are large. Vanguard Index Trust 500 portfolio's management fee of $\frac{18}{100}$ of 1% is not a problem because it is lower than most other mutual funds.

An indexed portfolio might not replicate its target index and, as a result, generate tracking errors, for one or more of the following reasons:

1. The portfolio deducts management fees from the investors' returns—a normal practice.
2. The indexed portfolio might not invest in all the stocks that make up the targeted index.
3. The indexer might invest in all the stocks that make up the index, but use a weighting scheme that differs from the weights of the targeted index.
4. Financial service organizations that create and maintain indexes add and delete stocks in their indexes—sometimes without warning. In addition, firms in an index sometimes go bankrupt, and mergers occur. Sometimes managers of indexed portfolios react to changes in their target index with delays. If the market value of a revised index changes before the indexed portfolio is rebalanced to mimic its target index, a tracking error occurs.
5. **Enhanced indexing** refers to attempts by an indexed portfolio's manager to try to "outsmart" the market. For example, in an effort to outperform the targeted index, the manager of an enhanced index fund might *tilt* the indexed portfolio in favor of some securities that the portfolio manager believes to be temporarily underpriced. Or, the portfolio manager might omit a stock believed to be overpriced. If the enhanced indexer's forecast is correct, a negative tracking error indicates the portfolio is outperforming its index. More commonly, incorrect forecasts cause positive tracking errors as the indexed portfolio falls behind its targeted index.
6. Some index portfolios are partially or entirely made up from derivatives of the stocks that comprise the underlying index. Derivatives such as stock index futures have low commission rates that are below the commissions to buy and sell the common stocks in the index. The managers of some indexed portfolios invest in derivatives in an attempt to replicate their target index while minimizing the index fund's commission costs. Awkward attempts to benefit from these differences in commissions can be a source of tracking year.

THE TRADE-OFF BETWEEN TRANSACTIONS COSTS AND TRACKING ERRORS

Common stock brokers typically charge lower commission rates if the investor buys a round lot (a multiple of 100 shares) instead of an odd lot (fewer than 100 shares). Block trades (a single transaction of 10,000 or more shares) enjoy lower commissions than round lot trades. Suggestive commission schedules and quantity discounts are in Table 12-3. Portfolio managers are aware there is a tradeoff between the transactions costs (commission rates) and the tracking errors of their indexed portfolios.

FIGURE 12-3   The Trade-off Between Transactions Costs and Tracking Error for a S&P500 Indexed Portfolio

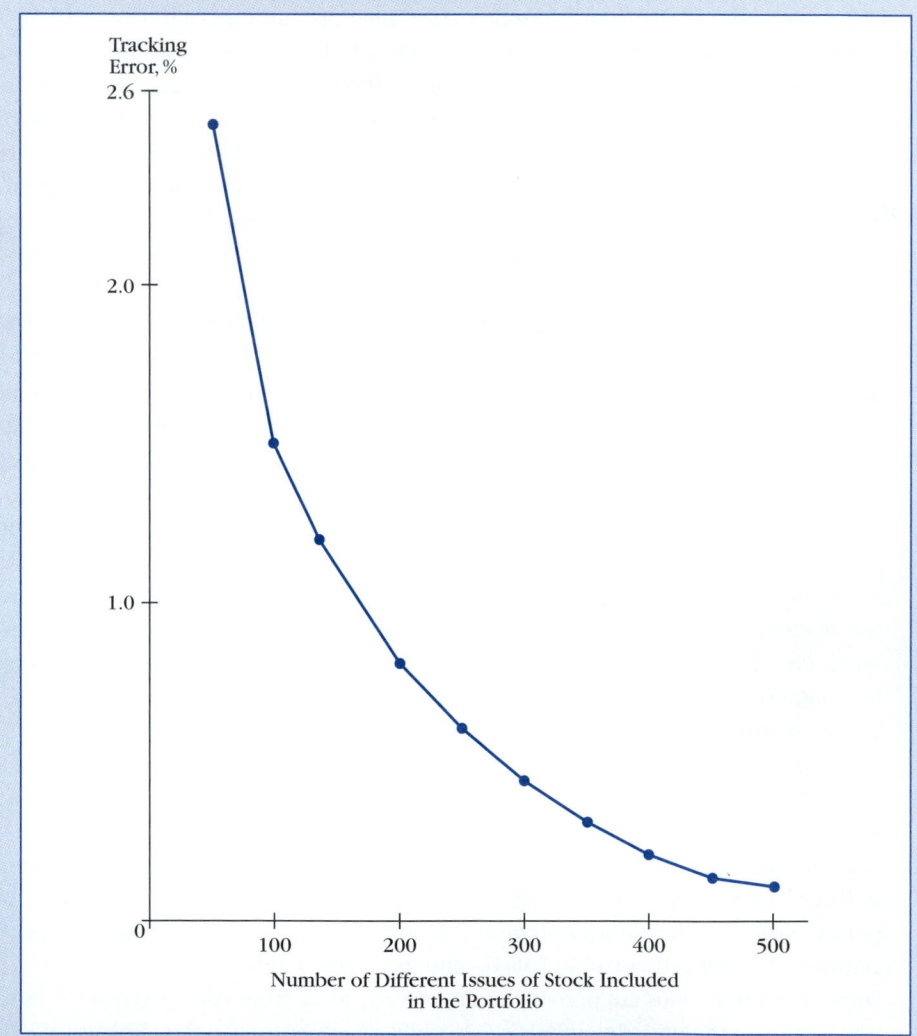

As more of the 500 stocks that comprise the S&P 500 index are added to a portfolio, the portfolio tracks the S&P500 index better. But since smaller positions are carried in each stock as more stocks are added, the portfolio's transactions costs increase as the tracking error decreases.

Figure 12-3 illustrates the relationship between transactions costs and tracking error for a portfolio indexed to the S&P500. If less than the 500 stocks comprising the index bar are in the replicating portfolio, the portfolio's tracking error tends to increase as fewer issues are held. The offsetting consideration is the portfolio's commission expenses. If the portfolio holds fewer issues, the portfolio will be able to execute larger trades and obtain lower commission rates. Although attempts to minimize the portfolio's trading costs are admirable, they are fraught with opportunities for tracking errors.

A multibillion-dollar portfolio does not face the trade-off illustrated in Figure 12-3, because it can buy round lots and/or blocks of all 500 stocks in the S&P500 index. In contrast, a small S&P500 index fund having total capital of only, say, $50 million would not be able to buy round lots of 500 different issues. As a result, the small index fund would be forced to either buy odd lots at high commission costs or to omit some issues from the portfolio. Either way, the risk of tracking error increases.

EXCHANGE-TRADED FUNDS (ETFS)

Prior to 1989, no mutual funds were listed on U.S. stock exchanges. Investors buying mutual fund shares wrote a check to the mutual fund of their choice. When a mutual fund receives an investor's money, it is required by the Investment Company Act of 1940 to sell the shares to the investor at net asset value per share (NAVPS) on the day the money is received. NAVPS were traditionally based on **market-on-close prices**—prices that exist when the market stops trading for the day (at about 4 P.M.). Mutual funds redeem shares based on market-on-close prices too. If a mutual fund share owner phones in an order to sell her shares at 10 A.M. or 1 P.M., for example, the mutual fund accumulates the order and its other clients' orders all day and executes the net total in a single batch transaction at market-on-close prices. If a mutual fund investor wants to buy (sell) on a day when the stock market is rising (falling), the investor is understandably frustrated if the order is placed in the morning and not executed until hours later when the market-on-close prices emerge. The American Stock Exchange (AMEX) responded to these frustrations by creating a new type of exchange-traded fund (ETF) for mutual fund investors who don't want to have their orders executed at the close of the trading day.

In 1993 the AMEX began trading an indexed ETF that is like the Vanguard Index Trust 500 Portfolio in many ways, and superior to it in other ways. A **Standard & Poor's Depository Receipt (SPDR**, pronounced *spider*) is a marketable security that is traded continuously on the AMEX. Unlike traditional mutual funds, when you place an order to buy or sell a SPDR (1) you place your order through a stock broker, and (2) your order is executed immediately. Orders to trade ETFs, like orders to buy stock, are executed as soon as your broker can pass your order to the AMEX's trading floor.

SPDRs offer investors investment opportunities similar to opportunities offered by traditional stock market index funds. SPDRs are indexed to the S&P500 index using the same market-value-weights that Standard & Poor's uses in computing the S&P500 index. SPDRs pays its quarterly cash dividends from the S&P500 stocks, and investors can arrange through their brokers to have the quarterly cash dividend payments used to buy more SPDRs. To make SPDRs competitive with other S&P500 index funds, the organizers endeavor to keep the annual management fees on SPDRs slightly below the fee of $\frac{18}{100}$ of 1% that Vanguard's S&P500 index fund charges retail investors.

Differences Between SPDRs and Traditional S&P500 Index Funds

SPDRs differ from traditional index funds in several respects. First, SPDRs represent ownership in The SPDR Trust, which is not a mutual fund. The SPDR Trust is a unit investment trust

(UIT). The Investment Company Act does not permit UITs to trade actively. UITs may only buy and sell securities to realign their holdings with the investment target they were organized to pursue. A side effect of this restriction is that it minimizes trading commission expenses and tracking errors.

Second, the Investment Company Act defines mutual funds to be open-ended investments that can grow by selling new shares or shrink by redeeming old shares. In contrast, the Act forbids UITs from selling more shares after their initial public offering (IPO). The number of shares issued by a UIT can never change. The AMEX has overcome the legal rigidity that limits the growth of UITs. During a period when investors are net purchasers of SPDRs, new UITs are started to absorb the net inflow of funds. When investors are net sellers of SPDRs, some existing UITs are liquidated to generate the cash to redeem the investors' shares.

Third, unlike traditional mutual funds, SPDRs are listed and traded at an organized stock exchange. An investor can buy and sell odd lots, round lots, or blocks of SPDRs on the trading floor of the AMEX. Unlike some of the more costly index funds, there are no load fees or 12b-1 fees on SPDRs. The entry fees and the exit fees for SPDRs equal the sum of the broker's negotiated commission, plus the bid-asked spread. The common bid-asked spread for SPDRs is about 3 cents per share, but it can vary from 2 to 12 cents.[9]

Advantages of SPDRs over Traditional S&P500 Index Funds

Billions of dollars have flowed into SPDRs since they were listed in 1993, but their aggregate value is still a small fraction of the aggregate value of the traditional S&P500 indexed mutual funds. Benefits available to SPDR investors include:

1. SPDRs can be bought and sold throughout the trading day at market prices that are updated continuously, rather than only at the market-on-close prices.
2. SPDRs may be sold short. If investors want to profit from market declines or hedge long positions in the stock market or perform arbitrage, they may take short positions in SPDRs for as long as they want. Unlike many securities, it is possible to sell SPDRs short on a *down-tick* (a price that decreased on the last transaction), making it easier to sell a SPDR short than a share of stock in a falling market.
3. The Investment Company Act forbids the SPDR Trust (and all other UITs) from using derivatives. As a result, SPDR investors will never be subject to counterparty risks that arise if the portfolio uses derivatives and a derivative's counterparty defaults.
4. Many traditional index funds use derivatives and, from time to time, an index fund misuses derivatives in a manner that creates a tracking error. (Examples of index futures and index options are provided later in this chapter.) Since the Investment Company Act does not permit SPDRs to use derivatives, SPDRs never experience these problems.
5. SPDR investors who execute large transactions are eligible to receive **payment-in-kind (PIK)** when they close their positions. This means that the investor may receive a basket of the underlying stocks instead of cash. PIK can provide tax benefits.
6. SPDR investors may give their brokers all the different kinds of (limit, market, GTC, etc.) orders to buy and/or sell as common stock investors. This gives SPDR investors more alternatives than are available to traditional mutual fund investors, who may transact only at each day's market-on-close price.

SPDRs brought index funds into new territory. In addition to providing all the same benefits as the traditional S&P500 index funds, SPDRs are also useful to hedgers, arbitrageurs, and speculators in arenas where the traditional S&P500 index funds cannot compete.

MAKING SMALL INVESTMENTS

QUESTION: What is the cheapest way for an investor with a modest amount of capital to acquire a diversified position in the 500 stocks that make up the S&P500 index?

ANSWER: Buy one SPDR for less than $200.

Cloning SPDRs

SPDRs were such a good idea the AMEX cloned it. AMEX also developed MidCap SPDRs that are indexed to Standard and Poor's MidCap 400 stocks index. In addition, Select Sector SPDRs are sector funds that are indexed to stock market sectors.

DIAMONDS. An AMEX-listed security named the Dow-Jones Industrial Average MOdel New Deposit Shares (DIAMONDS) competes with the SPDRs. **DIAMONDS** are like SPDRs except that they are indexed to the Dow-Jones Industrial Average instead of the S&P500 index.

Nasdaq-100 Shares. In 1999 the AMEX listed *Nasdaq-100 Shares*. This SPDR-like indexed portfolio is indexed to the Nasdaq-100 index of over-the-counter (OTC) stocks. The Nasdaq-100 index includes many technology stocks like Microsoft, Intel, Oracle, Dell Computer, Yahoo, MCI WorldCom, and Amazon.com. The index also includes many nontechnology OTC stocks like Starbucks, Bed Bath & Beyond, and Northwest Airlines.

Domestic iShares. In 1999 Barclay's Global Investors (BGI), a large institutional money manager owned by Barclays Bank in London, launched an exchange-traded fund (ETF) in Canada called *iUnits*. The iUnits are indexed to the Toronto Stock Exchange Index of 60 stocks (TSE 60). BGI also has an ETF called *iFT-SE 100* trading on the London Stock Exchange. The iFT-SE 100 is indexed to the Financial Times-Stock Exchange (FT-SE, nicknamed "Footsie") index. BGI also launched a number of different ETFs in the United States that trade on the AMEX. These different ETFs, called *iShares,* are indexed to Standard & Poor's, the Russell 1000 Value Fund, and other indexes. The *iShares S&P 500 Fund,* for instance, competes with Vanguard's Index Trust 500 Portfolio and SPDRs.

HOLDRS. In 1998 Merrill Lynch introduced a mutation in exchange-traded funds (ETFs) named HOLding company Depository ReceiptS, or **HOLDRS**. HOLDRS are a series of investment portfolios that are not based on an underlying index. A HOLDR is one ownership share on a basket (portfolio) of stocks issued by 20 different corporations in the same industry. One HOLDRS is a round lot (a HOLDR multiplied by 100) on a basket of stocks issued by 20 different corporations. Some HOLDRS are diversified across 50 different stocks, instead of 20. Separate HOLDRS are outstanding for the Internet, banking, utility, pharmaceutical, semiconductor, and telecom industries. Additional HOLDRS are being issued. Merrill Lynch selects actively traded stocks to go into a HOLDR, and specifies their initial weights in the portfolio. The stocks in a HOLDR are not changed after it is issued, unless two of the shares in a HOLDR merge. Since security analysts and a portfolio manager need not be hired to manage a predetermined HOLDR, its annual management fees are less than $\frac{1}{10}$ of 1% of its market value. Proceeds from an initial public offering (IPO) of HOLDRS are used to buy common stock in different companies and these stocks are held by a trustee, Bank of New York. HOLDRS representing the underlying stocks are exchange traded portfolios listed and traded on the AMEX. HOLDRS may be traded or canceled. Investors may cancel HOLDRS and take possession of the underlying stocks for a fee of no more than $10 per HOLDRS. Since a cancellation is not a sale, it is a nontaxable transaction.

HOLDRS are rigidly defined portfolios that do not provide the flexible structure of a mutual fund, and they are not administratively friendly. If a HOLDR represents an ownership interest in a basket of 20 different stocks, the owner of that HOLDR will receive 20 annual reports per year, 20 quarterly reports each quarter, and numerous proxy statements. If two stocks in a HOLDR merge, accounting for the merger and paying taxes on it will not be simple. Merrill Lynch maintains a Web site (www.holdrs.com) where the owners of HOLDRS can find data on their portfolios, because information about HOLDRS is not as accessible as information on a stock market index.

TIP 35. Although much of the development of exchange-traded funds (ETFs) has taken place in the United States, ETFs originated in Canada. In 1989 the Toronto Stock Exchange (TSE) created the world's first ETF. The Toronto Index Participation (TIP) Fund markets TIP 35s that are invested in 35 liquid Canadian stocks. The TSE followed TIPs with HIPs, which have 100 Canadian stocks in the underlying fund.

INTERNATIONAL STOCK MARKET INDEX FUNDS

Beginning in 1996 exchange-traded mutual funds called **World Equity Benchmark Shares**, or **WEBS**, added an international dimension to index funds. WEBS are ETFs like SPDRs, except that each WEBS mimics a different international stock market index. WEBS each track equity market indexes on a stock market in one of the following 18 countries:

Australia	Hong Kong	Singapore
Austria	Italy	S. Korea
Belgium	Japan	Spain
Canada	Malaysia	Sweden
France	Mexico	Switzerland
Germany	Netherlands	United Kingdom

MSCI Indexes. Morgan Stanley, the large international investment bank, is the majority stockholder in Morgan Stanley Capital International (MSCI). The MSCI stock market indexes were introduced in Chapter 11 (pp. 318–326); they track stock markets in the countries listed above and other countries.

No Foreign Exchange. Morgan Stanley created WEBS. The WEBS portfolios in the selected countries track the selected country's MSCI index. WEBS are 18 *separate* one-country mutual funds that are *U.S. dollar–denominated*. Each WEBS portfolio arranges to convert investors' U.S. dollars into a foreign currency and later return cash dividends and liquidation proceeds in U.S. dollars. WEBS are international no-load stock index funds that are listed and traded actively on the AMEX.

iShares MSCI. Barclay's Global Investors (BGI) was an advisor to the WEBS. And in 2000 took more interest in the WEBS, changing their names to **iShares MSCI**. This change added attractive international mutual funds to the list of domestic iShares BGI already offered in the United States.

BGI's iShares MSCI funds are like traditional indexed mutual funds in many respects:

1. iShares MSCI are open-end investment companies (mutual funds) organized under the Investment Company Act.
2. Since the securities in iShares MSCI are components in an MSCI index, the iShares MSCI funds need not hire costly security analysts, economists, and portfolio managers.

3. The stocks in a stock market index are not changed frequently. As a result, the MSCI-based iShares portfolios turn over slowly and generate small brokerage commission expenses, resulting in higher after-tax returns for iShares MSCI investors.[10]

PRICING iSHARES MSCI

QUESTION: How will the market price per share of iShares MSCI be determined?

ANSWER: According to the Investment Company Act of 1940, the mutual fund must issue and redeem the shares at their NAVPS. During each trading day, however, the market price can fluctuate slightly above or below the NAVPS, which is based on close-of-trading prices.

ACTIVE VERSUS PASSIVE

QUESTION: Are iShares MSCI best suited for active investors or passive investors?

ANSWER: Although active and the passive investors use them for different things, iShares MSCI are similar to SPDRs. Both structures appeal to both active and passive investors.

THE FUTURES CONTRACT ON THE S&P500 INDEX

As mentioned in Chapter 9, the Chicago Mercantile Exchange (CME, or "The Merc") began trading futures contracts on the S&P500 index in 1982. As the newspaper excerpt in Figure 9-2 in Chapter 9 (p. 241) shows, thousands of S&P500 index futures are now traded daily. The underlying quantity from which the S&P500 index futures contract derives its price is the market-determined value of the S&P500 index. The designers of this contract decided to price it at the current value of the S&P500 index multiplied by $250.*

$$\begin{pmatrix} \text{Value of futures contract} \\ \text{on S\&P500 index} \end{pmatrix} = \begin{pmatrix} \textit{Current} \text{ market value} \\ \text{of S\&P500 index} \end{pmatrix}(\$250) \qquad \textbf{(12-3)}$$

For example, if the S&P500 index had a value of 1300, the S&P500 index future would be worth [(1300)($250) =] $325,000 per futures contract. People buying the S&P500 index futures are not entitled to cash dividends. Figures 9-1A and 9-1B in Chapter 9 (p. 234) illustrates gain-loss diagrams for long and short positions in futures. Table 9-1D and Figure 9-2 in Chapter 9 list similar financial futures contracts traded at exchanges around the world.

The S&P500 futures contract serves the needs of risk-taking speculators, risk-averting hedgers, and arbitrageurs. It is a cash settlement contract. The amount of cash received is the difference between the current value of the index future, Eqn. 12-3, and the price at which the contract was originally purchased or sold short.

Futures traders are required to pay some cash up front to get their order executed. In the United States an initial margin payment of 3% of the financial future's market value is usually sufficient "good faith" money to induce a broker to execute a trade. If the S&P500 index was 1300, the minimum margin payment that a S&P500 index futures buyer would need to give the broker would be [(1300)($250)(3%) =] $9,750 per futures contract. If, say, 10 contracts were purchased, the minimum margin payment would be [(10 contracts) × ($9,750 per contract) =]

---

* As explained in Chapter 27, some investors use futures on market indexes to do **index arbitrage** in hopes of profiting from an index's tracking errors. See Ira G. Kawaller, Paul D. Koch, and Timothy W. Koch, "The Temporal Price Relationship Between the S&P500 Futures and the S&P500 Index," *Journal of Finance* 42, no. 5 (December 1987): 1309–29.

$97,500. Traders who want to be highly leveraged like to be able to control a long position with a market value of [($250)(1300)(10 contracts) =] $3,250,000 with an initial margin payment of only (3% of $3,250,000 equals) $97,500.

Leverage (margined investing) is risky because it not only magnifies the size of the transaction, it also magnifies the possible loss if the market price moves adversely. For example, if the S&P500 index value dropped from 1300 to 1100, the market value of one contract would fall from [($250)(1300) =] $325,000 to [($250)(1100) =] $275,000. This ($325,000 − $275,000 =) $50,000 per contract loss could happen in minutes in a fast-moving market. A nonmargin (cash) transaction would presumably be for a smaller amount and, therefore, the potential for losses and profits is reduced.

EXAMPLE   **A DOMESTIC COMMON STOCK MUTUAL FUND'S HEDGE DURING A VOLATILE PERIOD**

Assume financial markets are going through a period of high volatility. The Risk Manager of a large mutual fund meets with the Portfolio Manager on Monday morning to discuss damage control. They fear the Federal Reserve might raise interest rates any time, and that would cause stock prices to drop. To protect the current market value of their fund's investments they decided that for a few days they will use a S&P500 index futures contract to hedge their multimillion-dollar mutual fund's diversified stock portfolio. They sell short millions of dollars' worth of S&P500 index futures on Tuesday morning to fully hedge their mutual fund's portfolio of stocks. This hedge is sometimes called a **futures overlay** because short S&P500 futures positions of equal aggregate market value were placed over the stock portfolio.

Assume the Fed raises the Fed funds rate 25 BPs on Wednesday—as the mutual fund's executives feared. Also assume the mutual fund unwound (lifted) their hedge Wednesday evening. Table 12-5 shows the results of this 2-day hedge. The futures overlay earned a 5.9%

TABLE 12-5   One-Day Returns from a Long Position in a Diversified Stock Portfolio, Short S&P500 Index Futures Position, and the Resulting Insured (Hedged) Portfolio

Trading Day	Monday	Tuesday	Wednesday	Thursday	Friday
Assumed Returns from Fund's Long Position in Stocks[b]	NA[a]	$r_T = 1.1\%$	$r_W = -6\%$	$r_{Th} = 1\%$	$r_F = 2.2\%$
Closing Value for S&P500 Index	1,000	1,010	950	959	980
Returns from Short SP500 Futures Position[c]	NA[a] and NH[e]	$-10/1000 = -1\%$	$60/1010 = 5.9\%$	NH[e]	NH[e]
Returns from Hedged Portfolio[d]	NA[a] and NH[e]	1.1%−1% = 0.1%	−6% + 5.9% = −0.1%	1%	2.2%
Activity	Planning hedge	2-day hedge in place		2-day hedge finished	

[a] "NA" means the day's return is "Not Available" because the previous day's price is not available.

[b] See Eqn. 2-3b and/or Table 7-1 about computing one-period returns for a long common stock position. Two assumptions: (1) The aggregate value of the stock portfolio changed by 1.1%, −6%, 1%, and 2.2% on Tuesday through Friday. (2) the portfolio's value is highly positively correlated (p = +0.95) with the SP500 index. *Note:* Since the correlation was not perfect (p < +1.0) the SP500 index futures do not track the diversified stock portfolio perfectly; the hedge's tracking errors are 0.1% and −0.1% on Tuesday and Wednesday.

[c] As shown in Eqn. 3-10, omitting dividends means the return from the short position in SP500 futures is: $r_t = (SP500_{t-1} - SP500_t)/SP500_{t-1}$

[d] Assume that the hedge has equal dollar amounts in the long stock position and the short futures positions, so the returns from the long and short positions are given equal weights and added together to get the return from the hedged position.

[e] "NH" means "no hedge," the hedge was not in operation this day.

gain and provided an almost perfect hedge for the mutual fund when the stock market dropped 6% on Wednesday. Deducting commission costs of 0.1% to buy and 0.1% to sell and, also, deducting Tuesday's S&P500 futures loss of 1% that occurred because the hedge started one day too soon, the 2-day hedge increased the mutual fund's value 4.6%.

−1.0% loss on Tuesday attributable to S&P500 hedge being established one day too early

+5.9% gain from S&P500 index futures short position on Wednesday

−0.2% = [(0.1% per transaction) × (2 transactions)] = commissions to buy and sell futures

4.6% net gain in portfolio's value from the 2-day hedge

This example shows how hedging can increase a portfolio's value (return) and smooth its fluctuations (reduce risk).

Simple Alternative. You might ask: Instead of setting up a hedge with stock index futures contracts, why not simply liquidate all the stocks Tuesday morning and then buy them back after the market volatility quieted down? To answer the question we need to compare costs. Because the stock brokerage commissions and other expenses incurred in liquidating stocks (such as the market impact of liquidation and the commissions) are much higher than the similar expenses on futures, it is less costly to hedge with stock index futures than it is to sell and repurchase the stock.*

OPTIONS ON STOCK MARKET INDEXES

Index options are puts and calls whose premiums are based on the market value of an underlying stock market index. As shown in Table 9-1F and Figure 9-3B in Chapter 9 (pp. 233, 244), index options are available on stock market indexes around the world.

Index options, like index futures, are not settled by delivering the underlying securities—they are settled in cash. These financial instruments are usually used for speculation, hedging, arbitrage, and as a means to obtain exposure to the underlying securities.

Eqn. 9-3 in Chapter 9 (p. 247) showed that the intrinsic value of a call option on a stock market index equals the amount by which the market value of the underlying market index exceeds the call's exercise price. For example, if the current market value of the S&P500 index is 980, a call on that index that has an exercise price of 975 will have an intrinsic value of 5.

$$\begin{pmatrix} \text{Intrinsic value of call} \\ \text{on S\&P500 index} \end{pmatrix} = MAX\left[0, \left(\begin{Bmatrix} \text{Current value of} \\ \text{S\&P500 index} \end{Bmatrix} - \begin{Bmatrix} \text{Exercise} \\ \text{price} \end{Bmatrix}\right)\right]$$

$$= MAX[0, (980 - 975)] = 5$$

Option buyers routinely bid an option's premium (price) up slightly above its intrinsic value because options have time value. It would be realistic to the S&P500 index call to have a premium above 5; let us assume the premium is 7. The market value of that index option will be $700 (= $100 × 7), because the index option's designers decided to price it at $100 times its premium.

Figures 9-4 and 9-5 in Chapter 9 (pp. 246, 250) illustrate gain-loss diagrams for call and put options on equity shares; these diagrams are also applicable to equity index options on

---

* A portfolio of stocks can be hedged with stock market index futures, stock market index options, SPDRs, DIAMONDS, iShares, or in several other ways. Another example later in this chapter employs the identical mutual fund scenario to construct a hedge that uses index options instead of index futures.

the S&P500. The factors that determine the prices (premiums) of equity options reviewed in Chapter 9 also explain the premiums on stock market index options.

EXAMPLE — A MUTUAL FUND USES PROTECTIVE PUTS TO HEDGE DURING PERIOD OF VOLATILITY

Background. In the preceding example on pages 352–353 we assumed the financial markets were unusually volatile. Because the mutual fund's Risk Manager and Portfolio Manager were afraid the Federal Reserve might raise interest rates and cause a stock market prices to fall, they took a short position in S&P500 index futures contracts to hedge the mutual fund's portfolio against possible losses. Table 12-5 contains a numerical data documenting the success of the futures hedge.

The mutual fund's Risk Manager and Portfolio Manager might have established their hedge with options, instead of using stock market index futures. Given the identical scenario, the mutual fund's managers could also construct the hedge by purchasing put options on a stock market index. Most domestic stock market indexes for a given country are highly positively correlated with each other and with all diversified portfolios of domestic stocks. A market index that is perfectly positively correlated with the portfolio to be hedged would create the best possible hedge, if one existed. As the correlation decreased below +1.0 the risk-reduction power of the hedge diminishes correspondingly.

Assume the S&P500 index is highly positively correlated—a realistic assumption—with the market value of the mutual fund. The mutual fund's managers could purchase put options on the S&P500 index that have an exercise price equal to whatever market index value they want as a "floor" beneath their portfolio's value. Eqn. 9-7 from Chapter 9 is adapted below to show how the put option's intrinsic value (minimum market price) is computed.

$$\left(\begin{array}{c}\text{Intrinsic value of put}\\\text{on S\&P500 index}\end{array}\right) = \text{MAX}\left[0,\left(\left\{\begin{array}{c}\text{Exercise price of}\\\text{S\&P500 index put}\end{array}\right\} - \left\{\begin{array}{c}\text{Current market value}\\\text{of S\&P500 index}\end{array}\right\}\right)\right]$$

The managers of the equity portfolio should select a floor beneath which they cannot tolerate the stock market index to fall and then select puts with an exercise price that protects them from any price decline below that floor. Puts acquired for this purpose are often referred to as **protective puts**, because they protect the value of the hedged portfolio from falling. Figure 12-4 illustrates how a diversified portfolio of common stocks can be hedged with puts on the S&P500 index—or puts on any other index that is highly correlated with the portfolio's market value.

How the Hedge Works. Table 12-5, showing how a 2-day hedge using the S&P500 index futures protected the mutual fund's value, can also be used to illustrate a hedge constructed with protective puts on the S&P500 index. Suppose the mutual fund managers purchase S&P500 index puts with an exercise price equal to the minimum acceptable market index value on Tuesday morning (the same time the hedge with the S&P500 futures in the previous example started). The S&P500 puts' exercise price (the selected floor value) is the point where the protective puts begin paying off if the stock market falls.

If the mutual fund managers wish to fully hedge their portfolio, they need to buy a large number of puts with an aggregate exercise prices equal to the aggregate market value of the mutual fund's total portfolio. If the S&P500 index falls below the floor value, as it did on Tuesday in Table 12-5, the protective puts will pay off. If the portfolio is fully hedged, the index puts will pay gains from a falling market that equal (offset) the falling market value of the mutual fund's stocks. Using protective puts in this manner is sometimes called buying **portfolio insurance**; the premiums paid for the protective puts are like insurance premi-

FIGURE 12-4   Gain-Loss Graphs for: (A) An Insured Portfolio That Is Indexed to S&P500, (B) Buy a Protective Put on S&P500 index, and (C) Components of the Insured Aggregate Position

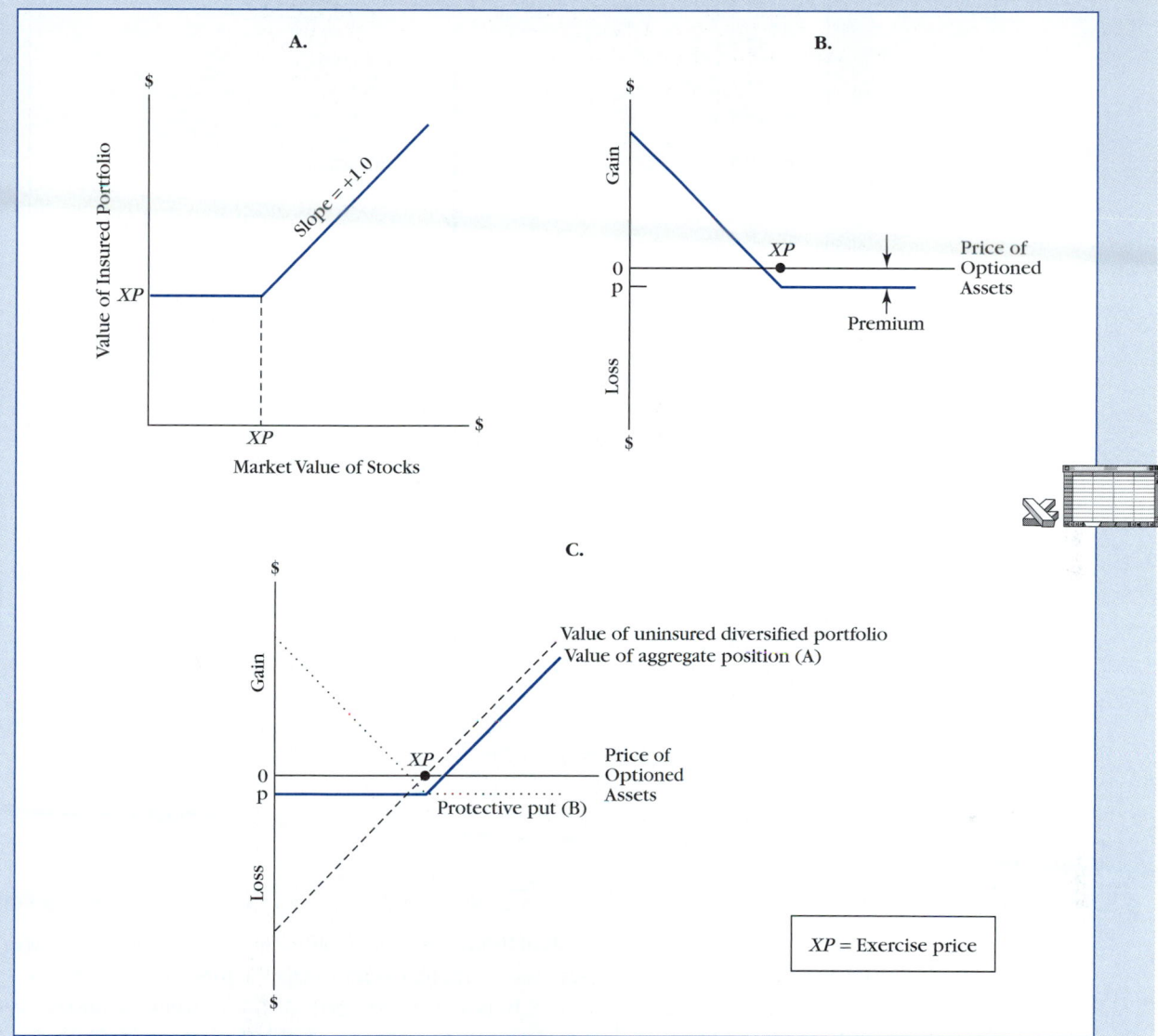

(A) shows the result of combining a long stock position and a protective put. (B) illustrates the put option on the S&P500 index alone. (C) illustrates how the protective put (dotted line) and the long stock position (dashed line) combine to create the insured portfolio (solid lines).

ums paid to insure that the value of the hedged portfolio does not decline below the selected floor value. The higher floor that is selected, the higher the put premiums (cost of the hedge, insurance premiums).

Using options reshapes investor's probability distribution of returns. Figure 12-5 contrasts one-period rates of return from the mutual fund's portfolio of stocks with and without portfolio insurance. The *Wall Street Journal* article (Figure 12-6) tells how portfolio managers use options to hedge stocks in their portfolios.

FIGURE 12-5 Using Protective Puts Reshapes a Mutual Fund's Probability Distribution of Returns

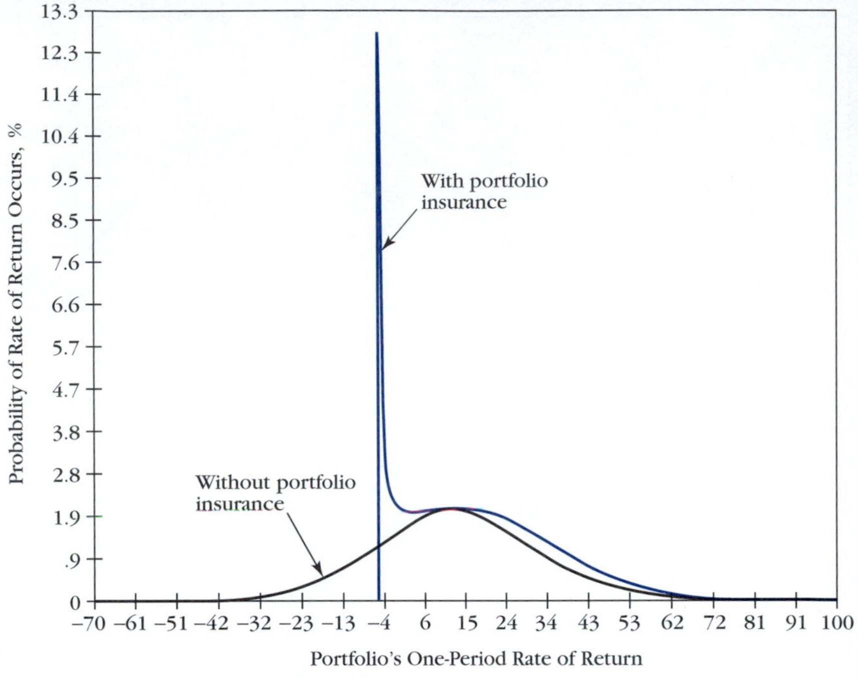

Protective puts reduce (portfolio insurance reduces) the portfolio's downside risk while maintaining its potential for upward gains.

SOURCE: Richard M. Bookstaber and Roger G. Clarke, *Option Strategies For Institutional Investment Management* (Reading, MA: Addison-Wesley, 1983), Figure 5-5, p. 82.

EXAMPLE   THE RYDEX FAMILY OF MUTUAL FUNDS

The Rydex family of no-load mutual funds has created different mutual funds for traders who want to invest in different asset classes and may want to change funds frequently. The *Rydex Nova Fund* is an enhanced index fund that seeks 150% of the movements in the S&P500 index (it has a beta of 1.5 and a correlation with the S&P500 index over 0.9). Rydex Nova uses index futures and options.

The *Rydex Ursa Fund* maintains short positions in S&P500 futures and options to generate returns that are perfectly negatively correlated with the S&P500 index. Ursa is for those who want to diversify away systematic stock market movements.

The Rydex OTC Fund is an enhanced index fund that is indexed to the Nasdaq-100 index. This fund is for investors who want returns from over-the-counter (OTC) technology stocks like Microsoft, Intel, Oracle, and some nontechnical stocks.

Rydex Arktos Fund uses short sales, financial futures, options, and other derivatives to earn returns that are perfectly inversely correlated with the Rydex OTC Fund (and, equivalently, the Nasdaq-100 index).

The *Rydex U.S. Government Bond Fund* seeks to mimic 120% of the price moves of the 30-year T-bond; it uses interest rate options and futures.

FIGURE 12-6 Using Options

Hedging Helps Some Funds Brave Big Sell-Offs

FUND

TRACK

By Karen Damato
Staff Reporter of The Wall Street Journal

Fund manager Howard Schachter isn't popping Excedrins, even though his heavy technology pummeled have been pummeled by earnings worries in recent days.

It's not that the manager of Needham Growth Fund is insensitive to swoons in holdings such as chip-maker Intel, down 7.5% last Friday when it announced an earnings slowdown, or networking company Cabletron Systems, down a whopping 34% Tuesday following similarly disappointing news. Intel has continued to decline, while Cabletron barely budged yesterday.

Rather, Mr. Schachter has limited his fund's risk in these and other volatile stocks by buying options that rise in price when the stocks tumble. In fact, he says a combination of investing savvy and "dumb luck" led his fund to actually make money in its Intel holdings during Friday's bloodbath.

Mr. Schachter's strategy might be called momentum investing for the motion-sick. "What I am trying to do is run a traditional growth fund—in very aggressive stocks that are typically very volatile—but reduce the risk and volatility for my investors," he says.

While Needham Growth is only 18 months old and has just $26 million in assets, the strategy appears to be working. The New York-based fund returned 52% in 1996. It is up 9.7% this year (through Tuesday), taking a pleasantly smooth route to beat the average 5.4% gain among capital-appreciation funds tracked by Lipper Analytical Services of Summit, N.J.

Some other fund managers who buy volatile technology stocks dismiss hedging with options as both costly and unnecessary. Short-term volatility doesn't matter for long-term investors, so the smart thing "is to ignore it," says Glenn Fogle, lead manager of American Century's Twentieth Century Giftrust and Twentieth Century Vista funds.

Says Gary Pilgrim of the PBHG fund group: "If you don't like volatility, don't invest in our funds."

But at least one big fund firm dealing in high-risk stocks, the AIM group in Houston, sees value in selectively hedging with options. AIM stock funds now hedge up to 5% of their holdings, says Scott Lucas, chief equity officer, "and we think it is an important ability for us."

While the AIM group typically has hedges on only a handful of stocks at any one time, those hedges can be useful in protecting against earnings-related shocks, explains Brant DeMuth, AIM's senior options and futures trader. By enabling fund managers to hold onto some stocks that face near-term difficulties, hedging can reduce the funds' realized capital gains and therefore investors' tax bills, he says.

The 50-year-old Mr. Schachter became a fund manager after a long career in stock research and sales, usually puts 90% of his fund assets in three high-growth, high-risk sectors—technology, specialty retailing and health care. By hedging many of his most volatile stocks, he says, "I don't have to worry as much." Currently, hedged stocks include about three quarters of the fund's technology names. Mr. Schachter figures the protection from big tumbles is worth the cost—which he puts at 10% to 15% of big upside moves.

The principal options that the Needham fund and the AIM group use for hedging their stock holdings are "out-of-the-money" puts. A put contract gives the holder the right to sell a stock at a set price by a certain date. With an "out-of-the-money" put, the contract's "strike" price is below the stock's current market price.

For example, Mr. Schachter says he began buying Cabletron shares in mid-April, at around $32. When the stock quickly ran up to $38 or $39, he paid between $1.50 to $2 a share for June puts, giving him the right to unload the stock at $35. About a week ago, with the stock up to $45, he says he paid an additional $2 a share for July puts at a higher $42.50 strike price.

Cabletron stock closed Wednesday at $30.375. But Needham Growth can unload its shares for $42.50 any time between now and the end of July—ensuring a gain of about 20%, even after accounting for the options cost.

In the case of Intel, which peaked at just under $170 last month before tumbling to close at $142.50 yesterday, Mr. Schachter says his fund actually held two sets of puts expiring at the end of this month. About a week ago, near the stock-price peak, the fund manager purchased puts with a $165 strike price. But in that case he didn't sell the previous hedge, a $150 contract, because the price was a skimpy 50 cents.

The upshot on Friday: The two series of options shot up in price, exceeding Needham Growth's loss in Intel common stock and warrants.

Mr. Schachter points to networking company 3Com as a portfolio holding that has been climbing smartly in price, and where the fund has kept rolling over put contracts to lock in most of the gain.

The Needham Growth manager says his hedging strategy won't in itself make the fund a success. "The key is still being in the right stocks, in the right sectors," he says. But with the hedging policy, he says, "corrections don't kill us."

SOURCE: *Wall Street Journal*, 5 June 1997, C1 and C23.

The *Rydex U.S. Government Money Market Fund* is a very safe portfolio that invests in money market instruments that are guaranteed by the U.S. government and/or its agencies.

Rydex Juno Fund uses short positions in interest rate options and futures to achieve price moves that are inverse to the 30-year T-bond, it is designed for investors who want to diversify away interest rate risk.

The *Rydex Precious Metals Fund* is managed to mimic the PHLX Gold/Silver Index, it was designed to appeal to the "gold bugs" and other inflation wary investors.

The 14 different *Rydex Sector Funds* invest in banking, basic materials, biotechnology, consumer products, electronics, energy, energy services, financial services, health care, leisure, retailing, technology, telecommunications, and transportation securities.

The Rydex family of funds uses market index futures, market index options, and other derivatives to achieve their investment goals. Rydex funds are trading-oriented; they permit investors to trade daily (while some stock index mutual funds limit their investors to a maximum of a few trades per year). Rydex requires a $25,000 minimum account balance.

EXAMPLE   DENVER TRADER MAKES INVESTMENTS OVERSEAS

Paul was born in Denver and has never been outside of Colorado. Paul finished his BS in engineering but became interested in finance and is now a part-time MBA student at the University of Colorado's campus in Denver. Paul also works part-time for a large international mutual fund headquartered in Denver.

The Problem: One day the Portfolio Manager asked Paul to invest $5 million of new cash receipts in the Japanese stock market as soon as possible (ASAP). Paul has never studied any foreign language and he knows nothing about foreign exchange. What should Paul do with the $5 million?

Clue: One futures contract on the Nikkei index from the Chicago Mercantile Exchange (CME) is worth $1 million.

Futures Overlay Solution: Within a few minutes Paul should buy $5 million of U.S. Treasury bills for the Janus account and then, also, purchase five contracts on the CME's Nikkei index future contract.

Advantages of Futures Overlay: Investing $5 million in U.S. T-bills earns interest income of, say, 4% at an annual rate. In addition, T-bills will serve as margin (instead of cash) for the purchase of futures contracts. Purchasing $5 million of Nikkei equity index futures provides a fully invested position in a diversified list of Japanese stocks ASAP. The $5 million futures overlay will earn whatever the Nikkei earns or loses plus 4% interest from the T-bills. A Nikkei futures overlay on the $5 million of T-bills will probably earn a rate of return that will outperform similar equity mutual funds. Remember, over a complete business cycle the index funds outperform most mutual funds run by stock pickers. The commissions on futures contracts are small—less than the commissions on stocks. CME futures contracts are very liquid; the Nikkei index contract is more liquid than the underlying Japanese stocks listed on the Tokyo Stock Exchange. After the Nikkei futures overlay is in place the mutual fund's portfolio manager can leisurely unwind some of the Nikkei futures every time he or she finds a good stock to buy in Japan. Foreign exchange problems are absent from this solution because the CME's Nikkei futures contract is denominated in U.S. dollars (like other foreign futures contracts, options, and ADRs). So, Paul needs no foreign language or foreign exchange expertise.

Other Correct Solutions:

1. iShares: Buying Japanese iShares makes sense, but iShares involve higher commission costs.
2. Currency Hedging. Paul's superiors might consider selling Japanese yen (or yen futures) short to hedge the yen currency risk concealed inside every dollar-denominated Japanese equity index future (or option). However, currency hedging may not be cost-effective for a portfolio that has diversified foreign exchange positions that are not correlated.
3. Index Options. Buy liquid U.S. dollar–denominated calls on the Nikkei index in United States.
4. Buying Yen. Buy yen in United States and use the yen to buy $5 million of:

    (a) liquid Japanese equity index futures sold in Japan, or,

    (b) liquid Japanese equity index calls sold in Japan, or,

    (c) Japanese stocks sold in Japan.

Unfortunately, selecting and buying a list of Japanese stocks takes time. Overall, buying yen involves more transactions, more commission costs, and avoidable complications.*

BOND INDEX FUNDS

A *bond fund* is a mutual fund that has the stated objective of investing only in fixed-income securities. Several categories of bond funds exist:

◆ *Treasury bond funds* invest only in long-term securities issued by the U.S. Treasury.

◆ *Tax-exempt funds* seek the tax-exempt coupon income from municipal bonds.

◆ *High-grade corporate bond funds* buy bonds issued by blue-chip corporations.

◆ *High-yield funds* invest in junk bonds. **Junk bonds** are issued by corporations that Moody's, Standard & Poor's, Fitch, and other rating agencies assign quality ratings equivalent to Standard & Poor's BB grade or lower.

◆ *Mortgage bond funds* invest in mortgages and securities issued by the mortgage financing agencies.

◆ *Bond index funds* have the stated objective of investing in bonds in such a manner as to mimic some specified fixed income index.

Investors like bond index funds for many of the same reasons they like stock index funds. Bond index funds charge low annual management fees that range from a low of $\frac{20}{100}$ of 1% to a high of 1.4%. Historical statistics on a bond index or reference rate of interest give a preview of how a bond index fund will behave if history repeats itself.

The market for U.S. Treasury bonds is a huge and highly liquid market; because of that, bond index funds that track Treasury bond indexes are able to track them closely. The markets for corporate bonds and municipal bonds are unfortunately not as liquid. Corporate and municipal bonds trade infrequently, they trade with significant bid-asked spreads, and at times some of them are simply not for sale. These factors make bond index funds that are indexed to a corporate or municipal bond index more likely to experience tracking errors

---

* Equity swaps offer an excellent alternative to the futures overlay, but equity swaps were not discussed. An equity swap means Janus could pay the T-bill interest rate and receive the return on the Nikkei index. Swaps never need to be marked to the market.

than either a bond index fund that is indexed to Treasury bonds or a stock index that tracks an index of liquid stocks listed in a large U.S. exchange.[11]

Hundreds of different bond market indexes exist. Some bond market indexes track narrowly defined categories of bonds—for example, one bond index tracks New York State municipal bonds with maturities of 15 to 20 years. Historically, the two most popular indexes of high-grade bonds were the Lehman Government/Corporate Bond Index and the Salomon High Grade Long-Term Bond Index. In recent years, investing in high-grade bonds has become less popular.

Newer bond indexes that are indexed to different types of bond issues and are more difficult to mimic have become popular. For instance, the Lehman Brothers Aggregate Bond Index is based on more than 5,500 different bond issues that include U.S. Treasury bonds, U.S. government agency bonds (such as mortgage-backed securities), high yield corporates, and high-quality corporate bonds that usually have maturities ranging from 8 to 10 years. The market value of all the bonds that comprise the Lehman Brothers Aggregate Bond Index is about $5 trillion. Vanguard's Total Bond Market Portfolio (VTBMP) is indexed to the Lehman Brothers Aggregate Bond Index (LBABI). But the VTBMP only invests in a representative subset of the 5,500 bond issues that make up the LBABI. The VTBMP manager uses enhanced indexing and is able to outperform the LBABI before expenses. But, after the VTBMP's expenses of about 20 BPs per year are deducted, it falls behind its target index by a few BPs.

THE BOTTOM LINE

Diversified stock and bond portfolios that mimic stock market and bond market indexes, respectively, are popular investments.

The S&P500 index funds, which involve no active management, routinely outperform the majority of the actively managed mutual funds. Since index funds need not employ security analysts, these funds typically deduct low management fees from their investors' returns.

Investors noticed that the index funds usually outperform the actively managed mutual funds and responded by investing billions of dollars in indexed portfolios. Index funds have become popular. The S&P500 index is the most popular index.

Financial innovators sought ways to profit from the growth in index funds. The AMEX developed three exchange-traded funds (ETFs) that can be bought and sold on the trading floor of the exchange, can be margined, and can be sold short:

◆ SPDRs are indexed to the S&P500; they compete with traditional S&P500 index mutual funds like the Vanguard Index Trust 500 Portfolio.

◆ DIAMONDS are indexed to the Dow-Jones Industrial Average.

◆ Nasdaq-100 Shares are indexed to the NASDAQ 100 stocks index.

Morgan Stanley Capital International (MSCI) created stock market indexes on dozens of stock markets around the world. Morgan Stanley then developed index funds named WEBS that are separate mutual funds that are indexed to the MSCI country stock market indexes. Barclay's Global Investors (BGI) took over the WEBS in 2000 and renamed them iShares, which make it possible for investors to invest as little as $400 or as much as $4 million in a diversified portfolio of stocks from markets located around the world.

When a replicating portfolio (index fund) has trouble following its targeted index closely, the disparity is called a tracking error. Tracking errors are common with smaller index funds that do not have enough assets under management to enable them to buy round lots in every security in their target index, to portfolios that invest in illiquid assets, and to enhanced index funds that miscarry in their enhancement attempts. Large index funds that mimic an index comprised of liquid stocks have few problems with tracking errors. For example, the Vanguard 500 Index Trust portfolio consistently earns slightly less than the S&P500 index it tracks because the portfolio's management fee of $\frac{18}{100}$ of 1% is deducted from its returns every year; this annual deduction is the mutual fund's only source of tracking error.

Index funds are popular with passive investors. The high liquidity of SPDRs, DIAMONDS, and iShares makes them useful, also, to investors that trade actively.

Financial futures contracts and options on security market indexes provide opportunities for investors, speculators, hedgers, and arbitrageurs to utilize indexing strategies that are more complex than passively holding an index fund. Equity derivatives based on stock market indexes and interest rate derivatives based on popular reference interest rates have become the highest volume financial instruments traded at exchanges around the world.

QUESTIONS

Q12-1 (Passive investing) Describe the two approaches that a passive investor might use.

Q12-2 (Mutual fund fees) Discuss the four types of fees that mutual fund investors face.

Q12-3 (Mutual fund income) What are the sources of income for mutual fund investors?

Q12-4 (Advantages of indexed portfolios) What advantages do indexed portfolios have over actively managed stock portfolios? What are the disadvantages associated with indexed portfolios?

Q12-5 (Tracking errors) What is a tracking error and what are possible causes of tracking errors?

Q12-6 (Small indexed portfolios) You are trying to decide between two mutual funds that are indexed to the S&P500. One such fund controls $99 million in assets while the other has $500 million in assets. Assuming that both funds have equally talented managers, might there be any advantage to selecting one over the other?

Q12-7 (Standard & Poor's Depository Receipts) What are SPDRs? How do they differ from traditional index funds?

Q12-8 (iShares MSCI) What are iShares? Compare and contrast them to traditional indexed mutual funds.

Q12-9 (Tax advantages of indexed funds) True or False: Investors in an indexed mutual fund may enjoy tax benefits that investors in an actively managed mutual fund will not. Explain.

Q12-10 (Turnover rates) Is it more advantageous to invest in a mutual fund that has a high turnover rate or a low turnover rate? Explain.

PROBLEMS

P12-1 (Mutual fund returns) Sylvia invested $1,000 in a balanced, no-load mutual fund when its net asset value was $18.18 a share. During the year that she held it, the fund distributed dividends and interest income of $0.556 per share and capital gains of $0.3122 per share. The fund's year-end net asset value per share was $23.04. What was Sylvia's return on this investment?

P12-2 (Load funds) Marcus invested $1,000 in a fund that had a 4% load. The net asset value of the fund was $36.04. How many shares of the fund was Marcus able to purchase? How many shares would he have purchased if this had been a no-load fund?

P12-3 (Mutual fund returns) Ji Chang invested $5,000 in an aggressive growth, no-load mutual fund when its net asset value was $32.03. The fund distributed no dividends, but Ji received $3.222 a share in capital gain distributions during the year. At the end of the year, the net asset value of the fund was $26.88. What return did Ji earn?

P12-4 (Net asset values) Consider the data supplied for the following three mutual funds:

Fund	Shares Outstanding	Market Value of Assets	Total Liabilities
A	1,100,000	$25 million	$1 million
B	1,250,000	$100 million	$6 million
C	1,420,000	$50 million	$2 million

Calculate the net asset value per share of each fund.

P12-5 (Turnover rates) Consider the following information collected for three no-load mutual funds:

Fund	Annual Purchases	Annual Sales	Average Assets
A	$80 million	$100 million	$188.0 million
B	$600 million	$750 million	$854.1 million
C	$550 million	$400 million	$601.6 million

All else equal, in which of the above would you prefer to invest? Why?

P12-6 (Tracking errors) The following three mutual funds are indexed to the S&P500, which returned 18.1% this year:

Fund	Annual Return
A	15.2%
B	17.3%
C	12.4%

Calculate the tracking errors for each fund. Which fund appears to be better managed? Why?

P12-7 (Management fees) Bob invested $1,000 in the Big20 Fund. At the same time, Barb invested $1,000 in Index20 Fund. The management fee of the Index20 Fund is 0.5% a year while the management fee of the Big20 Fund is 1.15% a year. Assume that both funds earned a gross return (before management fees) of 12% a year every year for 5 years. Calculate the difference in the wealth of the two investors at the end of the 5-year period.

P12-8 (Loads and redemption fees) Jack and Judy each invested $1,000 in two different mutual funds. Jack's fund charged a 2% load. Judy's fund was a no-load fund, but she had to pay a 1% redemption fee when she sold the shares. Coincidentally, each fund had a net asset value of $20 a share when purchased. Even more coincidentally, a year later both investors had received $1.25 a share in dividends and capital gain distributions, and the net asset value of both funds was $24.00. Calculate each investor's rate of return.

P12-9 (Tax efficiencies) Two funds, ACTIVE FUND and PASSIVE FUND, each earned a 14% return for its investors this year, but 5% of ACTIVE FUND's return came in the form of dividends and short-term capital gain distributions, whereas only 3% of PASSIVE'S return was the result of dividends and short-term capital gain distributions. What would an investor who was in a 28% tax bracket have earned as an after-tax return on each fund? (Assume the investor continues to hold her shares in the fund, so that the gain from the appreciation in the net asset value of each fund is unrealized and, therefore, untaxed.)

P12-10 (SPDRs) On a certain Monday morning, Sally called her broker and placed a limit order to buy shares of an SPDR for $64. Her order was executed that day. At about the exact same time, Sam placed a call to an investment company and indicated that he wanted to sell some of his shares that were invested in the company's money market mutual fund and use the proceeds to purchase shares of its S&P500 Index Fund. The market took a particularly large jump that day. The net asset value of the S&P500 Index fund was $70 at the close of the market. At the end of the year, the close price of the SPDR was identical to the net asset value of Sam's mutual fund, $76. Ignoring dividends and transactions costs, calculate both Sally and Sam's returns on their investments.

CFA EXAM QUESTIONS

1. (1997 CFA Sample Exam, Level 1) If stock prices in general are expected to increase substantially after the transaction is complete, which of the following transactions in the stock index option market would be *most risky* for an investor to undertake?
   A. Writing an uncovered call option.
   B. Writing an uncovered put option.
   C. Buying a call option.
   D. Buying a put option.

The following two questions are adopted from the 1999 CFA Sample Exam, Level 1:

2. *All* of the following statements *typically* characterize the structure of an investment company **EXCEPT**:

   A. an investment company adopts a corporate form of organization.
   B. an investment company invests a pool of funds belonging to many investors in a portfolio of individual investments.
   C. an investment company receives an annual management fee ranging from 3% to 5% of the total value of the fund.
   D. the board of directors of an investment company hires a separate investment management company to manage the portfolio of securities and to handle other administrative duties.

3. Security market indexes are used:

 I. as benchmarks for portfolio performance.

 II. to construct index funds.

 III. as inputs for technical analysis.

 IV. to determine systematic risk.

  A. I and II only.

  B. II and III only.

  C. III and IV only.

  D. I, II, III, and IV.

FURTHER REFERENCES

S&P 500 Directory, published by Standard & Poor's Corporation, New York City.

 This 450-page annual paperback contains facts about the Standard & Poor's 500 Stocks Composite Index, mutual funds that are indexed to the S&P500, derivatives that are based on the S&P500, and strategies that investors use to index their portfolios to the S&P500 index. Only a tiny bit of elementary algebra is used.

Bond Index Bonds. Mossavar-Rahmani Sharmin. Chicago: Probus Publishing Company, 1991.

 This thoughtful book is one of the few dedicated solely to bond index funds. The author is a partner at Goldman-Sachs Asset Management.

ENDNOTES

[1] See Mark M. Carhart, "On Persistence in Mutual Fund Performance," *Journal of Finance* 52, no. 1 (March 1997): 81.

[2] For recent information about the performance of bond mutual funds, see Edwin J. Elton, Martin J. Gruber, and Christopher Blake, "Fundamental Economic Variables, Expected Returns, and Bond Fund Performance," *Journal of Finance* 50, no. 4 (September 1995): 1229–1956. Also see Christopher Blake, Edwin J. Elton, and Martin J. Gruber, "The Performance of Bond Mutual Funds," *Journal of Business* 66, no. 3 (July 1993): 370–403. For information about the performance of common stock mutual funds, see Mark M. Carhart, "On Persistence in Mutual Fund Performance," *Journal of Finance* 52, no. 1 (March 1997): 57–82. And, see Edwin J. Elton, Martin J. Gruber, Sanjiv Das, and Matthew Hlavka, "Efficiency with Costly Information: A Reinterpretation of Evidence from Managed Portfolios," *Review of Financial Studies* 6, no. 1 (1993): 1–22. Also see Burton G. Malkiel, "Returns from Investing in Equity Mutual Funds, 1971–1991," *Journal of Finance* 50, no. 2 (June 1995): 549–72. Less recently, see *Institutional Investor Study of the Securities and Exchange Commission,* vol. 2, Washington, DC, 1971, pp. 328–32. These and similar studies suggest the following general conclusions. Large funds perform no better than small funds, high turnover funds perform slightly worse than funds with low turnover, funds with load fees perform slightly worse than no-load funds, funds with high management fees tend to perform a little worse than funds with low management fees, and mutual funds are unable to "beat the market" in any meaningful sense.

[3] See "Mercy Killings," *Mutual Fund* (April 1997). Also, see "Fund Burials" and "Born Again," *Mutual Fund* (October 1999): 20, 23.

[4] For more information about investing in closed-end funds, see Marcelle Arak and Dean Taylor, "Risk and Return in Trading Closed-End Country Funds: Can Trading Beat Holding Foreign Stocks?" *Quarterly Review of Economics and Finance* 36, no. 2 (summer 1996): 219–31.

[5] For details about the Standard & Poor's 500 Stocks Composite Index and investors that index their portfolios to the S&P500 Index see the *S&P 500 Directory*, a paperback book published annually by Standard & Poor's in New York City.

[6] See Burton G. Malkiel, "Returns from Investing in Equity Mutual Funds, 1971–1991," *Journal of Finance* 50, no. 2: 549–72. Professor Malkiel's empirical data shows that most mutual funds do not perform as well as the S&P500 index. Also see Edwin J. Elton, Martin J. Gruber, Sanjiv Das, and Matthew Hlavka, "Efficiency with Costly Information: A Reinterpretation of Evidence from Managed Portfolios," *Review of Financial Studies* 6, no. 1 (1993): 1–22. In addition, see *Institutional Investor Study of the Securities and Exchange Commission,* Washington, DC, 1971, vol. 2, 328–32. Other scientific studies discussed elsewhere in this book reach similar conclusions.

[7] For details about how poorly some "professionally managed" mutual funds perform, see Timothy Middleton, "The Dead Man Funds," *Mutual Funds* (December 1995): 48–53. Or, see "At Dead-Last Steadman, Past Is Prologue," *Wall Street Journal*, 15 April 1997, C1. One particularly noteworthy point in the article is that, in spite of remarkably bad investment results and management fees as high as 25% per year, some investors continue to throw away their money by buying the worst mutual funds. For a more general discussion of incompetent mutual fund managers, see Mark M. Carhart, "On Persistence in Mutual Fund Performance," *Journal of Finance* 52, no. 1 (March 1997): 57–82.

[8] See Robert H. Jeffrey and Robert D. Arnott, "Is Your Alpha Big Enough to Cover Its Taxes?," *Journal of Portfolio Management* (spring 1993): 15–25. More recently, see R. D. Arnott, A. L. Berkin, and J. Ye, "How Well Have Taxable Investors Been Served by the 1980s And 1990s?," *Journal of Portfolio Management* 26, no. 4 (summer 2000): 84–94. Also see David M. Stein, "Measuring and Evaluating Portfolio Performance After Taxes," *Journal of Portfolio Management* (winter 1998): 117–24.

[9] For details about trading a traditional S&P500 index fund and SPDRs, see James J. Angel, Don M. Chance, Jack Clark Francis, and Gary L. Gastineau, "Comparison of Two Low-Cost S&P 500 Index Funds," *Derivatives Quarterly* (spring 1996).

[10] For an empirical study of WEBS, see Ajay Khorana, Edward Nelling, and Jeffrey J. Trester, "The Emergence of Country Index Funds," *Journal of Portfolio Management* 24, no. 4 (summer 1998): 78–84.

[11] See James Philpot, et al., "Active Management, Fund Size, and Bond Mutual Fund Returns," *Financial Review* 33, no. 2 (May 1998): 115–25.

PART 3

PORTFOLIO

THEORY

ASSET ALLOCATION

An **asset class** is a grouping of securities with similar characteristics and properties. **Asset allocation** focuses on determining the mixture of asset classes that is most likely to provide a combination of risk and expected return that is optimal for the investor. The following portfolios provide examples of allocations to asset classes:

- *Portfolio 1, a 50-50 allocation between stocks and bonds*
- *Portfolio 2, a 60-40 allocation between stocks and bonds*
- *Portfolio 3, a 20-60-20 allocation among real estate, stocks, and bonds*
- *Portfolio 4, a 10-40-20-30 allocation among domestic real estate, domestic stocks, foreign stocks, and domestic bonds*

Asset allocation assumes that allocating investment funds to asset classes should precede other approaches to investment management, such as trying to time the market (buy low and sell high) or "cherry picking" individual securities that are expected to be "winners." Asset allocation does not preclude trying to time the market or pick winners. If an asset allocator has views about specific assets or the market's timing, security selection or market timing may be integrated into the asset allocation process.

The asset allocator might be managing his or her own funds. Or, the asset allocator might have a client who has never invested in the stock market before, who is a multimillionaire that has invested for decades or is an institutional investor with a diversified portfolio worth billions. In each case, the asset allocator's job is to endeavor to get "inside the skin" of the party whose money is being managed.

This chapter describes the asset allocation process in terms of an asset allocator and a client that are different people. It may increase the objectivity of an asset allocator who is managing his or her own funds to think about working for a client. The chapter presents the management process as a series of steps, as a formalized structure that is appropriate whether the asset allocator is managing his or her own investments or someone else's funds.

THE ASSET ALLOCATION PROCESS

Asset allocation should begin with the development of a **strategic asset allocation (SAA)**. SAA identifies asset classes and the proportions for those asset classes that would comprise the *normal* portfolio mix. **Tactical asset allocation (TAA)** comes after SAA, as it involves planning for deviations from the normal asset allocation. TAA establishes policies to govern dynamic reallocations of a temporary nature. After the SAA and TAA plans are complete, market timing or security selection may be integrated into the plans. (Security selection and market timing are discussed in Chapters 23 through 26 inclusive.)

The asset allocator cannot begin working on the SAA and TAA plans until appropriate preparations are completed. Phase 1 of the asset allocation process requires that the asset allocator and the client have a "meeting of the minds." The asset allocator needs to have scheduled meetings with the client to learn the client's wants and needs. The asset allocator and the client must reach an agreement about how the client's funds will be managed. To provide concrete examples, professional asset allocators discuss investment indexes like those presented in Chapters 10 and 11. Security market index data provides a useful basis for discussions, and historical index data like those presented in Chapters 10 and 11 can be used to educate the client about what expectations are reasonable. Phase 1 of the asset allocation process is not complete until the asset allocator/money manager and the client/investor have consummated a written agreement about the investment goals and the policies that will be followed in managing the investor's funds.

Phase 2 of the asset allocation process involves managing the money. In collaboration with the client, the asset allocator (money manager) makes asset allocation decisions and invests the funds. Periodic performance reporting is part of Phase 2. The asset allocator must meet with the client occasionally to find out if the client's investment goals have changed and determine if changes in the investment policies are necessary. Table 13-1 suggests a step-by-step approach to the never-ending asset allocation process.

TABLE 13-1   The Asset Allocation Process

Phase 1—Create a Written Policy Statement

1. The asset allocator and the client continue to have discussions until the asset allocator learns about the client's financial position, goals, constraints, and the investor's preferences in a risk-return context.
2. The asset allocator uses market index data to educate the client and develop realistic expectations within the client, explains the style and methodologies that will be used to manage the invested funds, and continues to try to discern the investor's risk-return preferences.
3. The client and the asset allocator work up a written **policy statement** specifying the goals and the policies to use in managing the client's funds.

Phase 2—Investment Management

4. The asset allocator studies current conditions and prepares estimates about the future.
5. The asset allocator allocates the portfolio's funds to asset classes.
6. Investment orders are issued and executed.
7. The asset allocator makes periodic performance reports, obtains feedback, and revises the investment goals and policies as needed. This means that, after showing the client the results, the asset allocator returns to Step 1.

PHASE 1—CREATE A WRITTEN POLICY STATEMENT

Some clients and some asset allocators are not interested in investing time and effort in the asset allocation process. Some clients want to select a money manager and then leave them alone to do their job. Some money managers want to be selected to manage the money and then be left alone to manage it. Experienced asset allocators have learned to proceed more slowly. Adept asset allocators argue that the client's objectives are much more likely to be achieved if the client and the asset-allocator do not shortcut any steps of the asset allocation process in Table 13-1.

Step 1—Gain Understanding

After the client and the asset-allocator are on a first-name basis, the money manager must ask questions. Individual investors must be willing to reveal intimate facts to their money manager about their age, education, work experience, health, and details about their family and personal life. Institutional investors must be willing to tell the money manager about large deposits or withdrawals that are expected, name strong personalities within the organization, provide the names of any hypersensitive clients that give the institution money to manage, and explain the criteria that will be used to evaluate the money manager's performance. The topics of return and risk should be discussed.[1]

Getting acquainted is not a one-way street. There are also questions that the investor should ask the money manager. The money manager should be prepared to answer questions about the size, education, and experience of the asset allocation staff. The investor might inquire about the library, economic and financial database, and computer resources that the asset allocator employs. Even if the asset allocator is not asked about it, the initial discussions should be used to explain the money manager's investment philosophy to the client. Communications should become relaxed and open, and some bonding and a sense of trust between the client and the money manager should develop.

Just as there is a wide range of investors, there is a wide array of goals and constraints that are appropriate for their investments. An important part of the money management processes is to continue discussions with the client to stay abreast of any changes that might occur. In the initial discussions it is important that the asset allocator and the client discuss the client's financial situation, the length of the client's investment horizon, the investor's tax situation, any legal constraints that might be binding on the client's investing activities, anticipated cash withdrawals or deposits, and the client's liquidity needs.

The Investor's Financial Situation. Institutional investors usually have much larger portfolios than individual investors do. Institutional investors are also more likely to be encumbered with legal constraints than individual investors. Many institutional investors are exempt from taxation of their investment income, but individual investors may be involved in complicated tax situations.

The Investor's Time Horizon. In some cases, it is possible to specify precisely an investor's time horizon. Consider a client investing to fund a contractual liability that must be paid in 2 years. Clearly, this client has a 2-year planning horizon. Most investment horizons are not so easy to perceive.

For some investors, the investment horizon that is appropriate is the time remaining until retirement. For those with long-term dependents, the appropriate investment horizon may extend until after they pass away and the dependent dies.

Foundations and endowments are institutional investors that may have either short-term or long-term investment horizons. Some foundations and endowments have been set up to continue operating a museum, hospital, church, college, or other organization forever. If their portfolio covers their needs, they can take long-term investment positions. However, if the portfolio is inadequate to meet the needs of the foundation or endowment, the organization may be forced to liquidate parts of its principal each year to continue operating. Life insurance companies and well-funded pension funds sometimes have investment-planning horizons that extend decades into the future. It is important to define the investor's planning horizon in as much detail as possible.

Investment Goal. Different clients have different goals. Some clients might wish to maximize their average annual rate of return. In contrast, an inflation-conscious client or a retirement planner might have a goal of earning a real (inflation-adjusted) rate of return that averages 2% per year. The goal of another client might be to accumulate a certain dollar amount by a specific date. Institutional investors typically have a wider range of goals than individual investors.

Foundations and endowments have complicated investment goals. A well-managed foundation or endowment that has adequate funding and intends to operate forever has the simplest situation. It should plan on spending no more than 5% of its total capital each year, while retaining any earnings above 5% per year to maintain the future purchasing power of its principal.[2]

The investment decisions are more complicated for a foundation or endowment that has inadequate funding. Its investment decisions and the expenditure decisions must be determined simultaneously, because portions of the principal must be liquidated periodically to fund the operating budget. Bad investments can further complicate the process. For example, if one-fourth the principal is lost unexpectedly, expenditures will continue unchanged and they must be funded from a principal amount that is suddenly only three-fourths as large.

Defined-benefit pension funds and defined-contribution pension funds are two different kinds of pensions that have different investment goals. **Defined-benefit pension funds** are legally required to pay specified benefits to pensioners until the liability terminates at the death of the pensioner or, for generous pension plans, at the death of the last surviving spouse. This kind of pension fund is legally required to pay all benefits in full and on time. The investment returns needed are reduced by contributions received from the employer, who is called the **pension sponsor**. Table 2-4A in Chapter 2 (p. 32) presents data about some large defined benefit pensions. The needs of each pension differ because the demographic characteristics of the retirees are unique, and because the benefits that each sponsor promised its pensioners differs.

It is easier to manage a **defined-contribution pension fund** than a defined-benefit pension fund because defined-contribution pension funds have no legally defined liabilities. Defined-contribution pension funds are called **profit-sharing plans** if the employer is obligated to give a fixed percent of each year's profits to the pension fund. In unprofitable years, nothing goes into the pension fund. If the sponsor of a defined-contribution bankrupts the pension fund by making bad investments, the pensioners are entitled to nothing. The pensioners cannot sue to obtain benefits from the sponsor of a defined-contribution pension fund that is bankrupt, because no contractual pension liabilities ever existed. As a result, defined-contribution pension funds can be managed as the sponsor wishes and the sponsor bears little responsibility.

The Investor's Tax Situation. Like most countries, the United States has progressive income tax structures for both corporations and people. Progressive income taxes place taxpayers with large incomes in higher tax brackets than taxpayers with lesser incomes. As a result, some investment behavior is tax-motivated. For example, progressive income taxes make people with large incomes become interested in municipal bond investments, because the coupon interest is tax-exempt in the United States.

In the United States the estate of a citizen who is worth less than $1 million at death is not required to pay any estate or inheritance taxes.* The lowest tax bracket in the **Unified Gift and Inheritance Tax** begins at 41% of estates in excess of $1 million, and the tax rate marches upward as the size of the estate increases. (For detail, see Table 13A-4 in this chapter's Appendix.) Inheritance tax makes it worthwhile for wealthy taxpayers to expend resources on tax lawyers, tax accountants, and estate planning. These matters should be discussed as the asset allocator and client formulate their asset allocation plans.

The Appendix to this chapter outlines the structure of U.S. tax laws. Personal income taxes, capital gains taxes, tax-exempt investment income, gift taxes, inheritance taxes, estate taxes, generation-skipping transfers, corporate income taxes, and other tax considerations are discussed in the Appendix.

To minimize the possibility that misunderstandings emerge later, discussions between the asset allocator and the client/investor should gradually progress toward the formulation of a written statement of the client's investment goals.

Legal Constraints. Some wealthy people are limited by laws that constrain the way they can use their wealth. For instance, consider the founder of a successful firm who takes the firm public to turn his or her ownership interest into cash. These entrepreneurial IPOs typically provide cash and/or "letter stock" as payment for the "sweat equity" invested while the firm was a start-up. **Letter stock** is restricted by guidelines that are set forth in a letter the founder signs upon receipt of the letter stock. The founder usually promises not to go into competition with the firm or to sell the letter stock during a **lock-up period** of 2 or 3 years after signing the letter.

IRAs provide a more common example of how investors can be constrained by securities laws and tax laws in the United States. Millions of individual investors in the United States have what U.S. law calls an **Individual Retirement Account**, or **IRA.**** IRAs are personal pensions that provide deferred income taxes if the IRA investor abides by rules that govern their deposits and withdrawals. (For detail, see the discussion of Table 13A-2 in this chapter's Appendix.) Many people retain asset allocators to manage their pension assets.

Employer-sponsored pensions in the United States are governed by the **Employee Retirement Income Security Act (ERISA)** of 1974. ERISA's regulations are administered jointly by the U.S. Department of Labor, the Securities and Exchange Commission (SEC), and the Internal Revenue Service (IRS). The pensions and pension managers listed in Table 2-4 in Chapter 2, for example, are all governed by ERISA. ERISA:

◆ Spells out the conditions under which employees can defer paying taxes on the income from their pension assets until they retire

◆ Stipulates the job longevity required for an employee to gain a vested legal right to the employer's pension benefits

◆ Limits the ability of employers to invest the pension fund they sponsor in their own corporation's securities

◆ Requires that employers maintain adequate funding for the pension benefits they promised to pay

◆ Contains other provisions to protect current and prospective pensioners

---

* The $1 million exclusion is actually being phased in: it started at $650,000 in 1999 and by 2006 it will be increased to $1 million, but for the sake of convenience, we will refer to it as $1 million.

** The U.S. tax law provides for more than one type of Individual Retirement Account (IRA): In addition to the original IRA there is the Roth IRA, the Modified IRA, and the Educational IRA (for children).

Pension funds are the largest investors in the United States; they make lucrative clients for asset allocators.

U.S. law also grants valuable tax exemptions to qualified foundations and endowments. To gain tax exemption, foundations and endowment are required to make significant annual donations to a school, museum, library, or charity. In addition, U.S. law allows benefactors to use their wealth to establish trust accounts at commercial banks to care for loved ones or to fund charities of their choice.

IRAs, employer-sponsored pensions governed by ERISA, the laws governing foundations and endowments, and the laws governing trusts provide examples of the ways in which U.S. investors can be constrained by laws. It is essential for the individual asset allocator managing his or her IRA and the institutional allocator who manages a pension to consider the applicable laws as they formulate investment strategies.

Liquidity. If a client has no liquidity needs, the asset allocator can consider real estate and other illiquid assets. If the client's situation requires liquidity, the portfolio should include investments that are capable of being liquidated on short notice, such as actively traded securities or, if liquidity is extremely important to the client, money market securities.

As mentioned, the client must divulge cash-flow needs to the asset allocator. Large purchases of securities that are made quickly tend to bid up the purchase price, and large sales that are made hastily tend to drive down selling prices. The **market impact costs** associated with large purchases and liquidations can be minimized if the transactions are planned and executed over a period of days or weeks. Planning and patience are especially important ways to reduce transactions costs when transacting with illiquid assets (real estate, art objects, municipal bonds, corporate bonds, emerging markets stocks), multimillion-dollar amounts, and foreign exchange.

Personality Inventory. The National Association of Security Dealers (NASD) gives its thousands of members the following "Know Your Customer Rule":[3]

> *In recommending to a customer the purchase, sale or exchange of any security, a (securities broker) shall have reasonable grounds for believing that the recommendation is suitable for such customer upon the basis of the facts, if any, disclosed by such customer as to his other security holdings and as to his financial situation and needs. [Parenthetical words inserted.]*

To facilitate carrying out this rule, prospective investors opening accounts at brokerage firms in the United States are supposed to supply personal financial information. To help brokers and asset allocators assess the personality of their clients, ascertain the investor's financial goals, and gauge the person's tolerance for risk, many financial service firms provide questionnaires to expedite this information-gathering process.

Step 2—Expectations

Some investors may not always get everything they want from their investments. The asset allocator can manage such frustrations by educating the investor about what is realistic and achievable.

Some investors are unaware of the corrosive effects inflation can have, some hope to select only assets that appreciate in price rapidly, and some want their portfolio to be liquidated before every market collapse. It is normal for investors to ignore inflation and to desire eye-popping investments. But, the asset allocator must disabuse clients of naive expectations if they want their relationship with the client to continue.

The asset allocator must explain to the client what is possible and what is impossible, what the asset allocator will try to accomplish and what the asset allocator will not even attempt to accomplish, and the positive relationship between risk and return.

Market volatility needs to be discussed. The asset allocator should explain to inexperienced clients that *timing the market* is extremely difficult and can never be accomplished without some mistakes. Clients need to be made aware that volatility can be very harmful to in-and-out investors if the transactions are not timed extremely well. The unprofitable **filter rules**, zero **serial correlations**, and **runs tests** suggesting random price changes in Chapter 8 provide arguments against market timing strategies.

Investors should be wary of charts and tables of financial data used in promotional literature. For example, a mutual fund might advertise a high average return earned over a period selected to include unusually good times; marketing departments sometimes—unethically—elect to publish the unrepresentative but flattering statistics. Wise asset allocators use scientifically prepared investment indexes and market statistics like those presented in Chapters 10 and 11 to educate their clients and help them develop realistic investment expectations.

Step 3—The Policy Statement

The client and the asset allocator need to work together to create a written policy statement that carefully sets forth the investment goals and policies. This document provides continual guidance through the asset allocation process and is equally important to the asset allocator managing his or her own investments.

Commiting the policy statement to paper forces the writer to think about goals that might conflict or are not clearly formulated. A written statement provides consistent guidance during stressful periods and can also be used as a performance standard.

The Benchmark. A written policy statement should stipulate a **benchmark** portfolio or market index to guide the asset allocator and serve as a standard for evaluating the asset allocator's performance. Table 12-2 in Chapter 12 lists and describes some popular benchmarks, but *any* consistently defined benchmark that mimics what the asset allocator and the client want to achieve can serve as the target. A good benchmark will provide historical risk and return statistics like those in Chapter 11. Unambiguous statistics reduce the possibility of a misunderstanding between the asset allocator and the client and explicit goals in the policy statement will clarify everyone's expectations. The following two goal policy statements provide examples of clear-cut guidance for an asset allocator:

GOAL POLICY 1. Maintaining a portfolio that has a low standard deviation of annual returns is very important. Earning the low average rate of return which is typically associated with a low-risk portfolio is acceptable. Specifically, to achieve a standard deviation with less than half the standard deviation of the S&P500 index, the investor is willing to accept a modest long-run average annual rate of return of 4% to 5%.

GOAL POLICY 2. The investor is willing to assume stock market risk levels that exceed the standard deviation from the S&P500 index. As compensation for accepting these above-average levels of risk, the investor expects to earn returns that exceed by 100 basis points the total returns (including cash dividends) from the S&P500 index measured over the same time period.

The two policy statements above are stated in terms of risk-and-return measures that do not "tie the hands" or "take away options" available to the money manager. In addition, they will be useful in evaluating the asset allocator's performance.

Constraining Policies. If the investor has beliefs, opinions, preferences, or constraints that must be reflected in the investments that are undertaken, they should be written out. Two different examples of explicit investment policy statements are:

CONSTRAINING POLICY 1. The portfolio should be managed very conservatively. Margin accounts, leverage, and derivative instruments should not be employed.

CONSTRAINING POLICY 2. Since the portfolio must operate under the regulations governing federal savings and loan associations, real estate assets should comprise at least 60% of the total assets.

The investment constraint policies above provide clear-cut guidance to the asset allocator and minimize the possibility that misunderstandings arise between the client and the money manager.

Asset Allocation Policies. In addition to the guidelines above, the client and the asset allocator should construct a numerical policy statement. Normal proportions for each of the portfolio's asset classes should be set forth. Tables 13-2 and 13-3 illustrate desirable policy statements for portfolios that have different objectives and policies.

If an asset allocator does not have views about specific assets or about the direction of the market, the money can be invested in mutual funds that invest in the desired asset classes. For example, Table 13-3 names specific mutual funds.

Panic Attack. Some investors panic when faced with adverse market movements. Emotional investors have converted entire portfolios to cash in a single day in a "flight to safety." Transactions expenses can be costly, but liquidating a portfolio in a collapsing market can be worse than costly—it can be a financial catastrophe.

To get clients to adhere to the established investment guidelines, experienced asset allocators may supplement their tactical asset allocation policy statement with some dynamic

---

TABLE 13-2   A Low-Risk, Low-Return Asset Allocation Policy Statement

Long-Run Objective: Maintain a low exposure to risk (small standard deviation of returns), while earning a single-digit long-run average annual rate of return.

Long-Run SAA and Dynamic TAA Policies:

Investment Category	Long-Run SAA Policy	Range for TAA
U.S. Treasury bills	25%	15% to 35%
U.S. Treasury notes or bonds	25%	15% to 35%
U.S. corporation bonds	25%	15% to 35%
High-grade U.S. preferred stock	25%	15% to 35%
Total:	100%	

Dynamic Asset Allocation Guidelines: At the sole discretion of the asset allocator the strategic proportions (long-run normal mix) allocated to any major asset category may be temporarily reduced or increased to temporary values indicated by the ranges in the table above. Such tactical asset allocations should be used to exploit short-run market disequilibriums that may emerge.

Long-Run Performance Statistics:

Expected rate of return per year	5.5%
Typical range of annual returns	−2% to +13%
Portfolio's standard deviation	11.0%

Constraints: No illiquid assets, no leverage, and no derivatives.

TABLE 13-3 A High-Risk, High-Return Asset Allocation Policy Statement

Long-Run Objective: Undertake substantial risk (standard deviation of returns larger than S&P500 index) to earn a long-run average annual rate of return that exceeds S&P500 index by 100 basis points.

Long-Run SAA and Dynamic TAA Policies:

Investment Category	Long-Run SAA Policy	Range for TAA
Junk bond mutual funds like Pimco "A" High-Yield Fund	30%	Zero to 60%
U.S. and foreign growth stock mutual funds like Janus Worldwide Fund	20%	Zero to 40%
Diversified U.S. large-cap stock mutual funds like Vanguard Index Trust 500 Portfolio	50%	Zero to 100%
Total:	100%	

Dynamic Asset Allocation Guidelines: The strategic proportions allocated to any mutual fund may be temporarily reduced or increased to temporary values that are indicated by the ranges in the table above at the sole discretion of the asset allocator. Such tactical asset allocations should be used to exploit short-run market disequilibriums that may emerge.

Long-Run Performance Statistics:

Expected rate of return per year	13.0%
Typical range of annual returns	−50% to +70%
Portfolio's standard deviation	45.0%

Constraints: Financial leverage and investments in emerging market securities may be used to achieve superior returns.

DEFINITION

PERFORMANCE PRESENTATION STANDARD (PPS)

A **performance presentation standard,** or **PPS**, is a set of ethical principles and guidelines designed to promote uniformity in reporting investment performance data. The investment performance reports and advertisements from different money managers are comparable only if they use the same PPS. The Association for Investment Management and Research (AIMR) has established a high level PPS called **AIMR-PPS** that is used by some of the more ethical North American money managers and other investment professionals to ensure full disclosure and a fair presentation.

More than one PPS exists. The **Global Investment Performance Standards (GIPS)** is a similar, but less demanding, set of guidelines that are designed to serve as a minimum worldwide standard for the presentation of investment performance data. When asset allocators are writing policy statements, selecting benchmarks, and discussing mutual funds their work will be more credible if they use AIMR-PPS than if they use GIPS. However, using GIPS is better than using no PPS at all.

A discussion of AIMR-PPS and GIPS may be found under the topic of "Standards" at the AIMR Web site: www.aimr.com

guidelines, underestimate the portfolio's expected return, and overstate the portfolio's standard deviation. A well-known asset allocation book entitled *Investment Policy* offers the following advice to help an asset allocator deal with an excited client:

> *In investment management, the real opportunity to achieve superior results is not in scrambling to outperform the market, but in establishing and adhering to appropriate investment policies over the long-term—policies that position the portfolio to benefit from riding with the main long-term forces in the market. Investment policy, wisely formulated by realistic and well-informed clients with a long-term perspective and clearly defined objectives, is the foundation upon which portfolios should be constructed and managed over time and through market cycles.*[4]

Phase 2—Managing the Money

After the written policy statement is complete, the asset allocator and the client can reduce the frequency of their meetings. During Phase 2 of the asset allocation process, the asset allocator returns to his or her office to manage the money. In a large asset allocation firm, information in Phase 1 of the asset allocation process may be gathered from the client by someone different than the person who manages the money in Phase 2.

Step 4—Forecasting

Before any assets are allocated the money manager should study current conditions, analyze alternatives, and forecast likely outcomes. The forecast that is needed depends on the way the money manager operates. We briefly review three major approaches to contrast the forecasts that each type money manager uses:

1. **Fundamental security analysts** study financial ratios (Chapter 4), the security issuer's products, the competition, relevant legislation, and related facts about a company in which they are considering investing. Fundamental analysts may analyze several dozen different securities, but they typically prepare their security forecasts for one security at a time.
2. **Technical analysts** study historical market data. They prepare graphs of stock prices and study statistics in hopes of discerning patterns that will repeat themselves in the future. Technical analysts typically analyze dozens of different assets and market indexes, but they typically prepare their forecasts for one asset or one market index at a time.
3. **Risk-return analysts** usually begin by studying the historical means and variances of probability distributions of returns, and the correlations between different investments. As seen in Chapter 7, to forecast future behavior the analyst often updates historical statistics to convert them to expected returns, variances, and correlations. Most asset allocators perform risk-return analysis on stock indexes, bond indexes, real estate indexes, and other asset class indexes rather than analyze individual assets.

Some asset allocators do not rely heavily on technical analysis and/or fundamental analysis. They invest in market indexes like those discussed in Chapters 10 and 11 rather than select individual stocks and bonds. Research findings reviewed later in this chapter suggest that allocating funds to asset classes is more productive than trying to time the market or searching for undervalued securities.

The historical market index statistics in Chapters 2, 10, and 11 are not only useful for educating asset allocation clients and evaluating the performance of money managers; they also provide a starting place when making forecasts of future risk-return statistics.* One of the fastest and least expensive ways to obtain a forecast is to start with historical statistics, study current events, and then adjust the historical statistics to reflect your view of the future.

Preparing forecasts for an asset allocation is fast and economical. Asset allocators overlook the individual stocks, individual bonds, and individual pieces of real estate; instead, they focus on the categories of homogeneous assets. The asset allocator needs the risk-and-return statistics for domestic stock indexes, foreign stock indexes, domestic bond indexes, foreign bond indexes, domestic real estate indexes, foreign real estate indexes, and other indexes for asset classes that are investment candidates.

Step 5—Allocating Assets

The asset allocator begins Step 5 by reviewing the client's policy statement created at Step 3 to get the investment target in mind. Next, the asset allocator considers the expected risk-and-return statistics created in Step 4 to obtain the input data needed to allocate investment money to asset classes.

If the world's capital markets are in equilibrium, the asset allocator can follow the *strategic asset allocation (SAA)*. SAA is also called **policy asset allocation**, the **normal asset mix**, and the **long-run asset allocation**. If the asset allocator perceives some market disequilibrium, then the asset allocator may make a *tactical asset allocation* (TAA) that deviates from the SAA. If the asset allocator produced clear, meaningful dynamic asset guidelines at Step 3 of the asset allocation process (as shown in Tables 13-2 and 13-3), they will provide boundaries on how far the TAA is permitted to deviate from the client's SAA.

Simple Asset Allocation. Tables 13-2 and 13-3 suggest two simple, unconstrained asset allocations. The asset allocator breaks down the total amount to be invested into asset classes. After the asset allocation is completed, it is the asset allocator's responsibility to see that the portfolio's expected return and risk align with the goals set forth in the client's written policy statement. The asset allocator should meet with the client to obtain final approval of the investment plan. In the months after the funds are invested, the asset allocator changes the weights assigned to each asset class infrequently.

Constrained Asset Allocation. Many investors have no control over a significant portion of their investment portfolio. For example, investors may have no discretion over assets in pensions provided by their employers. Such nondiscretionary pensions comprise a large part of many individual investors' portfolios. Likewise, endowments and foundations sometimes receive gifts from benefactors that specify how the benefactor wants the donation invested. Although these assets are desirable contributions, they might also represent suboptimal asset allocations.

When operating under external constraints, the asset allocator must investigate the makeup of the nondiscretionary assets before allocating the discretionary portion of the investable funds. Situations involving major constraints sometimes lead to surprising invest-

---

* The questions we are raising involve whether or not the return and risk statistics from historical samples are linear, unbiased estimators of the future's population parameters. In addition, by dealing with categories of assets, asset allocators are using grouping to reduce errors-in-variables problems that are present when dealing with individual securities. These issues are discussed more rigorously in textbooks about mathematical statistics and econometrics. See Michael D. Intriligator, Ronald G. Bodkin, and Cheng Hsiao, *Econometric Models, Techniques, and Applications* (Upper Saddle River, NJ: Prentice-Hall, 1996), 360–68, 155–58.

TABLE 13-4   Input Statistics for Asset Allocation by a Markowitz Optimizer

Asset Categories	Expected Return, $E(r)$	Standard Deviation, σ
Stocks	14.1%	20.3%
Treasury bonds	6.2%	7.0%
Treasury bills	5.2%	2.7%

ment advice from the asset allocator. Consider a client who confides in her asset allocator that she wants to avoid foreign investments, but 90% of this client's assets are already invested in domestic assets by her employer-managed pension fund. Then, in spite of the client's previously stated wishes, the asset allocator might suggest investing all of the remaining 10% of the assets that are discretionary in foreign securities. To make an asset allocation recommendation like this, the asset allocator would have to spend time educating the client and gaining her trust.

Markowitz Portfolio Theory. Some money managers use Markowitz portfolio theory to allocate assets. To see how this works, suppose the policy statement delineated in Step 3 of the asset allocation process focuses on three asset classes: (1) stocks in large U.S. corporations represented by the S&P500 index, (2) a U.S. Treasury bond index, and (3) an index of U.S. Treasury bill returns. Further, suppose that in Step 4 the money manager forecasted the expected return, risk, and correlations statistics shown in Table 13-4.

The asset allocator inputs the statistics from Table 13-4 into an optimizing computer program that computes the most desirable investments. Figure 13-1 illustrates the locations of the three asset classes used as inputs for the optimizing computer program. Every Markowitz **efficient portfolio** generated has:

◆ The maximum expected return available at its level of risk

◆ The minimum risk at its level of expected return

USING MARKOWITZ PORTFOLIO ANALYSIS TO ALLOCATE ASSETS   EXAMPLE

The Markowitz *efficient frontier* illustrated in Figure 13-1 is the curve connecting an infinite number of desirable portfolios. The efficient portfolios lying on the efficient frontier are computed so that their weights sum to 1, Eqn. 13-1, and each portfolio earns a weighted-average expected return computed with Eqn. 13-2.

$$x_{\text{Stock}} + x_{\text{T-bond}} + x_{\text{T-bill}} = 1 \tag{13-1}$$

$$
\begin{aligned}
E(r_p) &= x_{\text{Stock}} E(r_{\text{Stock}}) + x_{\text{T-bond}} E(r_{\text{T-bond}}) + x_{\text{T-bill}} E(r_{\text{T-bill}}) \\
&= x_{\text{Stock}} (14.1\%) + x_{\text{T-bond}} (6.2\%) + x_{\text{T-bill}} (5.2\%)
\end{aligned} \tag{13-2}
$$

Table 13-5A lists statistics describing the three asset classes used as inputs for this portfolio analysis. Table 13-5B lists the weights of the securities in five portfolios from the Markowitz efficient frontier. Figure 13-1 illustrates the locations of the three input asset classes and the Markowitz efficient frontier. Efficient portfolios that have expected returns of 6%, 8%, 10%, 12%, and 14% are highlighted in Figure 13-1 and their statistics are displayed in Table 13-5B. The formula used to compute the portfolio's risk (standard deviation) is introduced in Chapter 14.

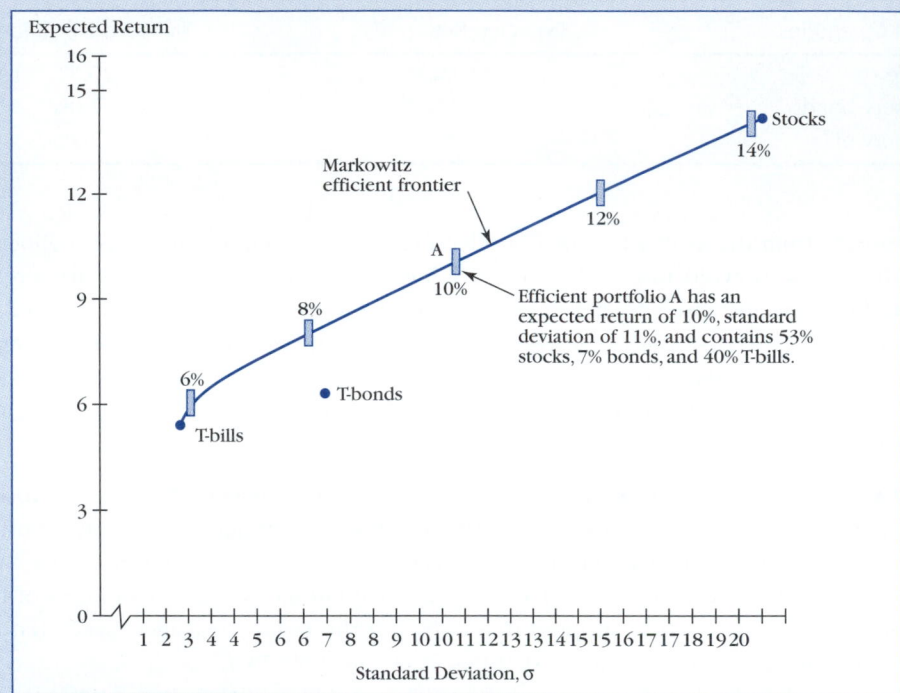

FIGURE 13-1   An Efficient Frontier of Asset Allocations That Is Generated from Three Assets by the Optimizing Computer Program

A computer program computes an infinite number of different asset allocations along the Markowitz efficient frontier. Every efficient portfolio has the maximum return at its level of risk, or, conversely, the minimum risk at its level of return. In Step 5 of the asset allocation process, the money manager selects one efficient portfolio that aligns with the investment preferences set forth in the client's policy statement.

SOFTWARE: Computed and graphed with EnCorr from Ibbotson Associates.

TABLE 13-5   Input Statistics for the Optimizer and Portfolios from the Efficient Frontier: (A) Index Statistics and (B) Five Asset Allocations

| Asset Categories Analyzed | Input Statistics | | Portfolio Weights | | | |
	Expected Return, $E(r)$	Standard Deviation, σ	X_{STOCKS}	X_{BONDS}	X_{BILLS}	Sum of the 3 Weights
A—Index Values for the Three Asset Classes Used as Inputs						
Stocks	14.1%	20.3%	1.0	0	0	1.0
T-bonds	6.2%	7.0%	0	1.0	0	1.0
T-bills	5.2%	2.7%	0	0	1.0	1.0
B—Asset Allocations of Five Portfolios from the Efficient Frontier						
6% efficient portfolio	6.0%	2.98%	.0874	.0218	.8907	1.0
8% efficient portfolio	8.0%	6.56%	.3146	0	.6854	1.0
10% efficient portfolio A	10%	11%	.53	.07	.40	1.0
12% efficient portfolio	12.0%	15.49%	.7640	0	.2360	1.0
14% efficient portfolio	14.0%	20.07%	.9888	0	.0112	1.0

Selecting an Efficient Asset Allocation. To complete Step 5 the money manager selects one of the optimal portfolios on the efficient frontier. The efficient portfolio that is selected should align with the goals and policies written down at Step 3. If the client is extremely risk-averse or needs completely liquid investments, then the optimal portfolio will be at the lower end of the efficient frontier (heavily invested in U.S. Treasury bills). If the client is aggressively seeking to maximize the expected return, all the client's funds might be invested in common stocks at the high-risk end of the efficient frontier.

Step 6—Investing the Allocated Funds

If the money manager invests in an actively traded stock, problems are rare. The money manager simply gives the order to a reputable broker who provides rapid executions and charges low transactions costs. The trade should be confirmed in moments. However, if the client owns assets that must be liquidated to make a new asset allocation, or if the client wants to make a multimillion-dollar investment, then Step 6 becomes a more important part of the asset allocation process.

Liquidating Old Assets. Few clients will arrive at the asset allocator's office with all their assets in cash. Most clients already have an assortment of investments and they are often reluctant to liquidate them. Some investors are reluctant to admit past mistakes and realize their losses; some investors erroneously believe that their tax-deferred investments (IRAs, Keogh plans, 401k plans) cannot legally be liquidated; some are emotionally attached to investments they cannot justify on an economic basis; some investors think they have an asset (a potential "winner") about to begin a period of lucrative price appreciation; and some investors do not have enough confidence in their asset allocator. Any of these circumstances require the asset allocator to work to gain the client's trust and to educate the client.

Large Transactions. If the client is a very wealthy individual or an institutional investor, it might be wise to retain the services of a securities trading firm that specializes in executing large transactions. For example, if 100,000 or more shares of a NYSE-listed stock or 10,000 or more thousand shares of a stock traded only in an emerging nation's securities market are to be traded, the transactions costs could become avoidably high unless the transaction is handled by experienced traders.

Small transactions usually have no market impact. *Market impact costs* arise because large sales tend to depress the security's market price and large purchases tend to bid up its price. Very large transactions can have surprisingly large execution costs because the market impact cost of the transaction can exceed the commission costs. As explained in Chapter 6, the services of a *block positioner* or one of the electronic order working systems may be worthwhile if a client needs to execute a large order. Furthermore, if the money manager can give the trader several days to "work the order" that time can be used to reduce the execution cost of a large transaction.

Step 7—Performance Reports and Feedback

Performance reports showing the current market value of each asset and the aggregate value of the portfolio are typically prepared for the client quarterly. These reports usually cause two problems for the asset allocator if the investor/client is inexperienced. First, if the asset allocator is involved in a dynamic strategy, the TAA weights and the SAA weights will differ. Second, when the portfolio's return over the last 3 months is annualized and compared to its long-run expected annual return, it will almost always differ from the long-run goal. These two deviations from the written policy statement must be explained if the client does not already understand why they occur.

Asset Allocations Can Vary. When clients inquire about differences between tactical asset allocation weights and the portfolio's SAA weights, the well-prepared asset allocator can point to dynamic asset allocation guidelines like Tables 13-2 and 13-3 to explain deviations from the SAA. As long as the asset allocator's TAA has not varied outside the dynamic guidelines in the policy statement that the client helped prepare, the client should not be surprised.

Discussions about deviations from the normal SAA asset mix provide a good opportunity for the asset allocator to educate the client about different asset allocation strategies, such as:

1. **Strategic asset allocation** (SAA) is used to derive long-run asset allocation weights. These weights are not changed when capital market conditions change. When the current weights in a quarterly report deviate from the SAA weights, those deviant weights are eventually realigned with the SAA weights.

2. **Tactical asset allocation** (TAA) produces temporary asset allocation weights that occur in response to temporary changes in capital market conditions. The investor's goals and risk-return preferences are assumed to remain unchanged as the asset weights are occasionally revised to help attain the investor's constant goals. For example, if the asset allocator tries to time the market or believes some sector of the market is over- or undervalued, TAA is the way to act on such views. A *passive asset allocation* will not have any TAA weights; the SAA weights will always be used.

3. **Dynamic asset allocation (DAA)** refers to alterations in the asset weights made in response to changes in the investor's circumstances and/or changes in the market conditions. TAA is one type of DAA. More complex DAAs are presented in Chapters 9 and 27 through 29.

4. **Integrated asset allocation** considers (a) the investor's goals and policies and (b) capital market conditions, and then uses these data as inputs to some kind of optimizer. The *optimizer* could be some mathematical formula (such as constant proportions), or an optimizing computer program to do Markowitz portfolio analysis. The optimizer's solution becomes the new inputs that are reconsidered along with the investor's latest goals and policies and most recent market conditions when revising the asset allocation.

Missing the $E(r)$ Goal. Experienced investors know not to get excited about short-term returns that fluctuate above and below the long-run expected return (SAA goal). Neophyte investors need to be educated when they start observing short-term returns that fluctuate randomly.

As explained in Chapter 11, *mean reversion* is a process whereby security returns tend to fluctuate randomly in the short run but tend to revert back to their long-run means after attaining extreme values. Financial economists debate about mean-reversion in security returns.[5] Explaining mean-reverting returns is an effective way for an asset allocator to help the client understand why the quarterly returns rarely hit their expected (long-run mean) rate of return.[6]

Change and Feedback. Changes in the amount of the client's assets, changes in the client's risk-return preferences, or other factors may require the client and the asset allocator to prepare a new policy statement. The client and the asset allocator should always be prepared to return to Step 1 of the asset allocation process. In addition, it may become necessary to upgrade the client's education, stimulate communications, and nurture trust between the client and the asset allocator. As the *Wall Street Journal* article (Figure 13-2) suggests, asset allocation is not simple.

FIGURE 13-2   NEWSPAPER EXCERPT: Asset Allocation

GETTING GOING/ By Jonathan Clements

The Right Mix: Fine-Tuning a Portfolio To Make Money and Still Sleep Soundly

Plunged into doubt?

Amid the recent market turmoil, maybe you are wondering whether you really have the right mix of investments. Here are a few thoughts to keep in mind:

■ **Taking stock**

If you are a bond investor who is petrified of stocks, the wild price swings of the past few weeks have probably confirmed all of your worst suspicions. But the truth is, adding stocks to your bond portfolio could bolster your returns, without boosting your portfolio's overall gyrations.

How can that be? While stocks and bonds often move up and down in tandem, this isn't always the case, and sometimes stocks rise when bonds are tumbling. That happened in this year's first six months, when U.S. stock-mutual funds soared 10.8%, while taxable bond funds slipped 0.3%, according to Lipper Analytical Services.

Indeed, Chicago researchers Ibbotson Associates figures a portfolio that's 100% in longer-term government bonds has the same risk portfolio as a mix that includes 83% in longer-term government bonds and 17% in the blue-chip stocks that constitute Standard & Poor's 500-stock index.

But while the risk level is similar, the bond-stock mix had better returns over the past 25 years, gaining 10.2% a year, compared with 9.6% for longer-term government bonds alone. The bottom line? Everybody should own some stocks. Even cowards.

■ **Same Great Taste, Even More Filling**

All right, you will buy a few stocks. But you are sticking strictly with blue chips. A good move? Here's another fun fact from Ibbotson Associates.

The Chicago firm calculates that a portfolio that's 100% in the S&P 500 is about as risky as a mix that includes 73% S&P 500, 6% smaller-company stocks and 21% foreign stocks. But the globally diversified portfolio was more rewarding over the past 25 years, climbing 12.9% a year, compared with 12.2% for the S&P 500. If you're going to own stocks, it clearly pays to diversify.

■ **Padding the Mattress**

On the other hand, maybe you're a committed stock-market investor, but you would like to add a calming influence to your portfolio. What's your best bet? You've got a bunch of choices, but none of them is great.

Some investments, like gold and Treasury bills, really help to damp a stock portfolio's ups and downs, but their recent returns haven't been anything to rave about. Other choices, such as bonds and real estate investment trusts, don't crimp returns too much, but they also don't provide a lot of downside protection.

What should you do? When investors look to mellow their stock portfolios, they usually turn to bonds. Indeed, the traditional balanced portfolio, which typically includes 60% stocks

and 40% bonds, remains a firm favorite with many investment experts.

A balanced portfolio isn't a bad bet. But if you want to calm your stock portfolio, I would skip bonds and instead add cash investments such as Treasury bills and money-market funds. Ibbotson calculates that, over the past 25 years, a mix of 75% stocks and 25% Treasury bills would have performed about as well as a mix of 60% stocks and 40% longer-term government bonds, and with a similar level of portfolio price gyrations.

So why do I favor the stock-cash mix? A couple of reasons. First, the stock-cash mix offers more certainty, because you know that even if your stocks fall in value, your cash never will. By contrast, both the stocks and bonds in a balanced portfolio can get hammered at the same time.

Second, a mix of stocks and cash should offer fewer tax hassles. That's partly because a stock-cash combination will kick off less in total interest and dividend income each year than a traditional balanced portfolio, so the stock-cash mix should be more tax efficient. In addition, you can dip into your cash investments without realizing a capital gain, so there are fewer accounting headaches at tax time. That's not the case with stocks or bonds, where a sale usually results in a capital gain or loss that then has to be reported to the Internal Revenue Service.

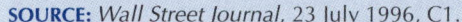

■ **Patience Has Its Rewards, Sometimes**

Stocks are capable of generating miserable short-run results. During the past 50 years, the worst five-calendar-year stretch for stocks left investors with an annualized loss of 2.4%.

Sound grim? In fact, even conservative investments can generate disappointing results over shorter periods. Longer-term government bonds, in their worst five-year stretch during the past 50 years, lost 2.1% a year, while Treasury bills gained just 0.8% a year in their toughest five-year spell.

But while any investment can disappoint in the short run, stocks do at least sparkle over the long haul. As a long-term investor, your goal is to fend off the dual threats of inflation and taxes and make your money grow. And on that score, stocks are supreme.

According to Ibbotson Associates, over the past 50 years, stocks gained 5.5% a year after inflation and an assumed 28% tax rate. By contrast, longer-term government bonds waddled along at just 0.8% a year and Treasury bills returned a mere 0.3%.

* * *

WSJ **Journal Link:** Got a question or complaint about **-com** the Getting Going column? Send your e-mail to editors@interactive.wsj.com. Your comments and queries may appear in the GetGo Exchange, part of The Wall Street Journal Interactive Edition (http://wsj.com).

SOURCE: *Wall Street Journal*, 23 July 1996, C1.

USING INDEXES TO EXPLAIN INVESTMENT BEHAVIOR

Neither fundamental security analysis nor technical analysis plays a large role in asset allocation because, instead of focusing on individual securities, asset allocation focuses on homogeneous classes of assets. To defend the asset allocation against criticisms from fundamental security analysts and technical analysts who feel their skills could enhance the process, asset allocators have published research that demonstrates the power of pure asset allocation.

Analyzing Large Pensions

Gary P. Brinson, L. Randolph Hood, and Gilbert L Beebower (BHB), and, later, Gary P. Brinson, Brian D. Singer, and Gilbert L Beebower published two similar investigations of asset allocation.[7] BHB started by breaking down the asset mixes of 91 pension funds from a 10-year sample period into four mutually exclusive asset classes: cash equivalents, bonds, common stocks, and other assets. BHB decided to ignore the category of "other assets" because they felt that this was not a category of homogeneous assets that could be adequately represented by a financial index. BHB created a "shadow asset mix" for the 91 pensions that used the returns from market indexes to represent the returns from cash equivalents, bonds, and common stocks—the remaining three of the four asset classes. Consider a pension portfolio having the following asset mix in one quarter: 10% of the total assets in cash, 30% in bonds, 40% in stocks, and 20% in other assets (which BHB ignored). BHB concentrated only on the 80% of the total assets by using 80% as a base value to develop their "shadow asset mix." Using the percentages from the example above results in a shadow asset mix of (10%/80% =) 12.5% in cash equivalents, (30%/80% =) 37.5% in bonds, (40%/80% =) 50% in stocks, and a weight of zero is attributed to other assets.

BHB multiplied each pension's shadow asset weights by the returns from three security market indexes every quarter to obtain forecasted quarterly returns for the asset classes in each pension. Under these assumptions, portfolio P earned 9.5% in quarter Q.

	Cash	Bonds	Stocks	Portfolio
Shadow asset weight in portfolio P for quarter Q	12.5%+	37.5%+	50% =	100%
Times: Returns from market index for quarter Q	$\times$ 4%	$\times$ 8%	$\times$ 12%	
Forecasted quarterly returns of portfolio P	0.5%+	3%+	6% =	9.5% = r_{PQ}

Since the shadow asset mix used only market index returns to prepare the forecasts, no security selection or technical analysis or market timing skills are included in BHB's forecasted returns. If portfolio P was rebalanced during the quarter, the shadow asset mix weights were not adjusted to reflect the rebalancing. BHB used their sample of 91 different pensions to compare the 40 quarterly forecasted returns with the same pension's actual returns. The goodness-of-fit statistics for the forecasted versus actual returns are surprisingly high.

Figure 13-3 compares the actual returns from one pension with its forecasted returns. The average correlation coefficient between the 40 actual returns and the 40 returns forecasted by the shadow asset mix was +0.976. This means the average R-squared was ($R^2 = \rho^2 = 0.976^2 = 0.953 =$) 95.3%. The R-squared value (squared correlation) measures the percentage of variation in the pensions' actual returns explained by the forecasted returns. In other words, BHB's shadow asset mix explained an average of 95.3% of the variation in pension returns over 40 quarters. BHB's empirical results provide strong evidence suggesting that (1) asset allocation is the main determinant of the returns from large, highly diversified pension portfolios, and (2) the researchers ignored little useful information by not considering fundamental security analysis and technical analysis in their study.

FIGURE 13-3   Comparison of Actual Quarterly Returns with the Returns from Shadow Asset Mix for a One Representative Pension Fund

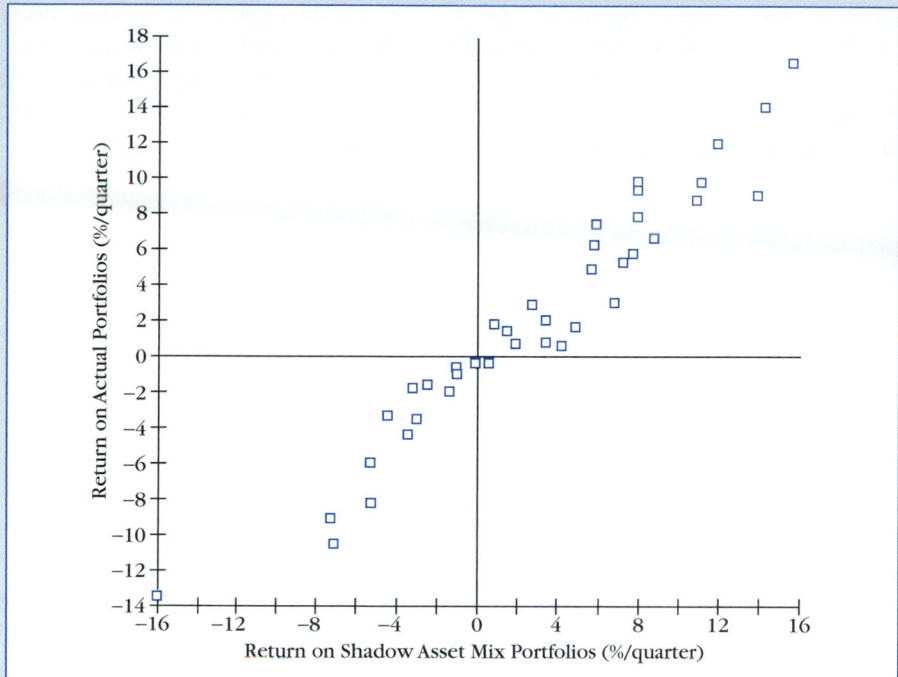

Shadow asset mix portfolios that were created by Brinson, Hood, and Beebower (BHB) were combined with publicly available security market indexes to predict the actual quarterly investment returns through time for one large pension fund at a time. Their findings provide evidence from 91 large pensions studied over 40 quarters that the asset allocation process can explain a large proportion of the variance in investment returns through time even though the process ignores security selection.

SOURCE: Gary P. Brinson, L. Randolph Hood, and Gilbert L Beebower, "Determinants of Portfolio Performance," *Financial Analyst Journal* (July-August 1986). Reprinted with permission from *Managing Investment Portfolios*, 2nd ed. Copyright 1990. Advance written permission from Association for Investment Management and Research, Charlottesville, VA. All rights reserved.

The Ibbotson-Kaplan Study

Roger Ibbotson and Paul Kaplan published a study that supports and extends the BHB findings.[8] Ibbotson and Kaplan (IK) analyzed 10 years of monthly returns on 94 balanced mutual funds and 5 years of quarterly returns on 58 pension funds. IK reported three major asset allocation findings.

First, IK analyzed individual portfolios one-at-a-time in the same time-series context developed by BHB. Like BHB, IK reported that about 90% of the variability of return of the typical portfolio across time is explained by asset allocations. The median coefficient of determination (symbolically, R^2 or ρ^2) was 87.6% for the 94 mutual funds and 90.7% for the 58 pensions.

The second and third thrusts of the IK inquiry were in directions previously not investigated by researchers. Second, IK investigated the cross-sectional differences between the portfolios' returns. They reported that about 40% of the variation in returns across portfolios can be explained by differences in the portfolios' asset allocations. The 60% that remains unexplained can be attributed to differences in security selection, market timing, costs, and other factors that IK did not investigate.

IK's third line of inquiry was directed at determining the impact of asset allocation policies on the level of portfolios' returns. IK reported that about 100% of the level of portfolio returns can be explained by asset allocation policies. This third finding is not surprising in view of Figure 2-1 and Table 2-1 in Chapter 2 (pp. 23 and 24), which document the extent to which the average returns vary between basic asset classes in the United States.

THE BOTTOM LINE

The asset allocation process focuses on allocating the funds to be invested among different asset classes to achieve a combination of risk and expected return that fulfills the investor's preferences. The asset allocation process can be divided into two phases. Phase 1 requires the asset allocator and the client to work together to create a written policy statement. The policy statement guides the remainder of the asset allocation process, and it furnishes a standard against which the performance of the asset allocator can be evaluated.

In Phase 2 of the process the asset allocator manages the client's money. Phase 2 begins with the preparation of needed forecasts. Then the investment funds are allocated to asset classes and the appropriate investment orders are executed. Phase 2 ends with a periodic performance report. The asset allocator and the client discuss the performance report and, if necessary, update the written policy statement.

Asset allocators publish impressive empirical studies. First, they showed that the quarterly time-series returns from large pension funds can be explained with accuracy simply by multiplying the quarterly returns from security market indexes times each pension's asset allocation weights. Second, Ibbotson and Kaplan (IK) report that about 40% of the variation of returns across portfolios can be explained by differences in their asset allocations. Third, IK show that about 100% of the differences in the level of portfolios' returns can be explained by their asset allocation policies.

QUESTIONS

Q13-1 (Asset allocation steps) Briefly discuss the seven steps involved in the asset allocation process.

Q13-2 (Defined-benefit versus defined-contribution pension plans) How does a defined-benefit plan differ from a defined-contribution plan? What effect does this have on the asset allocation of each type of plan?

Q13-3 (Realistic expectations) Mr. Crotchet has recently retired and opted for a lump-sum settlement from his retirement plan. He has come to you with the check for $500,000 and wants you to invest it entirely in a municipal bond mutual fund because he thinks the federal government has no right to his hard-earned money. Mr. Crotchet is in good health and expects to live to be 100. (He is now 65.) His only other income is his monthly social security check of $600. How might you advise Mr. Crotchet?

Q13-4 (The written policy statement) Why is it important to have a written investment policy statement and what pieces of information should be included in one?

Q13-5 (Approaches to financial analysis) Discuss the three different approaches to financial analysis. Which approach do most asset allocators use? Why?

Q13-6 (Allocating assets) Jim just graduated from college at the age of 23 with a degree in computer science and has been offered a job with a major company at a starting salary of $50,000 a year. Jim's parents are in their late 40s and spent most of their savings on Jim's college education, but now that he has finally graduated, they will have some extra money to set aside. They recently attended a financial seminar that emphasized the importance of retirement planning, so they have come with Jim to your office and want you to develop an investment policy for them that will allow them to retire at age 65 and one for Jim as well. Should the asset allocations of the two portfolios be the same? Why or why not?

Q13-7 (Asset allocation strategies) Discuss four different asset allocation strategies.

Q13-8 (Empirical research) True or False: Asset allocators who do not engage in fundamental or technical analysis in order to select individual securities do their clients a disservice. Explain your answer.

Q13-9 (Mean reversion) You recently prepared an investment policy for your client, Mary Donner, a 32-year-old single woman. In your interviews with her, you discerned that she was extremely nervous about having enough money on which to retire, but she was also very risk-averse. Mary is in a good, secure job that adequately meets her needs for current income. Her employer offers a tax-sheltered annuity plan that gives her the choice of a num-

ber of families of mutual funds in which to invest. Upon your advice, she decided to direct this money into a mutual fund that was indexed to the S&P500 index. This quarter, however, the market performed particularly badly, and Mary has noted that she has lost money on this investment. You found ten phone messages on your desk from her when you arrived at work this morning. How will you respond to her panic?

Q13-10 (Asset allocation and taxes) Scott is a 39-year-old entrepreneur who has made it big and enjoys a six-digit annual income that far exceeds his needs as a single man. Sandy is also single. She is 36 years old and earns an annual salary of $34,000, working as a paralegal. Her salary is enough to provide for her current needs and, because she is frugal, she even manages to save a bit each month. Discuss why you would structure the asset allocation of these two investors differently.

PROBLEMS

P13-1 (Asset allocation and taxes) Jill has decided to allocate 15% of her investment monies into a bond fund. She is trying to decide between a corporate bond fund that she believes will offer an average annual return of 9% and a municipal bond fund that she has assessed to be similar in risk to the corporate bond fund and that she believes will offer an average annual return of 6%. If Jill pays taxes at a marginal rate of 31%, which would you recommend?

P13-2 (Inflation and investment returns) Prepare a table showing the purchasing power of $500,000 10, 20, and 30 years from now assuming the annual inflation rate is 4%. Also show the real annual interest income earned on an investment that earns 5% annually under these conditions.

P13-3 (Inflation and purchasing power) Assume inflation is expected to average 3.5% a year for the next 10 years. How will this affect the cost of living? How will it affect the purchasing power of money?

P13-4 (Saving for retirement) Deanna has decided that she can save $2,000 a year for retirement, but she doesn't want to go through the bother of opening an IRA (Individual Retirement Account), since she doesn't qualify to deduct her contributions to the IRA. She instructs you, her advisor, to mingle the money with her other investment funds. Deanna is in the 28% tax bracket. Prepare a schedule to show her the differences in her account values in 10, 20, and 30 years, assuming she can earn an annual pre-tax rate of return of 8% on her investments regardless of whether it is invested through an IRA or held in a regular account. (Assume that all the return earned on the regular account is fully taxable and that Deanna will make her first deposit at the end of the year.)

P13-5 (Saving for retirement) Your sister has asked you to help her with her finances. After discussing her situation with her, you learn that her retirement savings plan involves

putting $100 a month into a savings account. You know that she has the ability to save the money in a tax-sheltered annuity (TSA) instead, but she whines that she doesn't understand all this TSA mumbo jumbo. You explain that the money she puts into a TSA reduces her taxable income and that she will actually end up with more spending money each month by investing the same $100 in a TSA instead of putting the money into a savings account. Even though she asked for your advice, she doesn't seem to believe you, so prepare a comparison for her. Her gross wages are $1,200 a month and she pays taxes at the marginal rate of 28%. Hint: See this chapter's appendix.

P13-6 (Inflation and purchasing power) One of the investment goals of your client (Dottie) is to have enough money saved in 10 years to pay for her daughter's college education. At the present time, the annual cost is $20,000 a year, but you expect inflation to average 3% a year for the foreseeable future. (a) When inflation is considered, how much cash will Dottie need to have available for her daughter to draw on at the beginning of each of her 4 years in college? (b) Dottie wants to have enough money at the end of 10 years to deposit in a separate, low-risk account to pay for her daughter's education. You estimate that such an account will return only 5% a year. What is the minimum amount that Dottie must have accumulated by the end of 10 years to meet this goal?

P13-7 (Realistic expectations) You have a client, Larry Moe, who calls at least once a quarter—whenever a new report on mutual funds is released—with a request that you switch part of his portfolio to a fund that has reported a particularly good performance for the quarter. You have told him that past performance is not necessarily a good indicator of future performance. You have also informed him that each switch constitutes a taxable event—that is, he must pay taxes on the gain when he redeems shares from one fund to buy shares of another, which erodes his annual return. But Larry is from Missouri and needs to be shown. Prepare an example for him, assuming he begins with $25,000 invested in a fund that is expected to return 12% this year (or 3% a quarter) and makes the following changes:

Quarter	Fund	Amount Invested	Expected Annual Return
1	A	$25,000	12%
2	B	?	14%
3	C	?	15%
4	D	?	16%

Compare this result to a buy-and-hold strategy. Larry's marginal tax rate is 28%.

P13-8 (Real dollar returns) Assume the inflation rate is expected to be 3% over the next 5 years. Calculate the real dollar return at the end of 5 years for Investor A, who invests $50,000 in Treasury bills with an expected return of 6% a year and Investor B, who invests $50,000 in an indexed fund with an expected return of 12% per year.

P13-9 (Tax rates and investment allocation) Rich Stevens, a resident of Colorado, has $500,000 to invest. You have recommended he invest 20% in a bond fund, and, more specifically, a Colorado municipal bond fund that is expected to return 7% this year. Rich notes that a corporate bond fund that analysts have assessed as equal in risk to the fund you recommended is expected to return 10%. Rich pays taxes at the marginal rate of 36%. Explain why your recommendation is the better investment for him.

P13-10 (Taxation of capital gains) Heather liquidated some assets this year with the following results:

Asset	Gain (Loss) on Sale	Holding Period
A	$62,000	8 years
B	($11,000)	6 months
C	($32,000)	2 years
D	$ 8,000	8 months

Her marginal tax rate is 28%. Under current tax laws, long-term gains and losses are realized if the assets are held for more than 1 year before they are sold. Long-term gains are taxed at 20%. Calculate Heather's tax liability on her investment income. Hint: See this chapter's appendix.

CFA EXAM QUESTIONS

1. (1998 CFA Sample Exam, Level 1) The portfolio management process consists of the following four steps:

   I. Monitoring of market conditions, relative asset values, and the investor's circumstances.

   II. Formulation of appropriate investment strategies and their implementation through selection of optimal combinations of financial and real assets in the marketplace.

   III. Identification and evaluation of the investor's objectives, preferences, and constraints as a basis for developing an investment policy specific to that investor.

   IV. Adjustment of the portfolio as is appropriate to reflect significant change in any of the relevant variables.

   The proper ordering of these steps (from first to last) is:
   A. I, II, III, IV.
   B. II, I, III, IV.
   C. III, II, I, IV.
   D. IV, I, II, III.

2. (1999 CFA Exam, Level I) Which of the following statements reflects the importance of the asset allocation decision to the investment process? The asset allocation decision:
   A. helps the investor to decide on realistic investment goals.
   B. identifies the specific securities to include in a portfolio.
   C. determines most of the portfolio's returns and volatility over time.

   D. creates a standard by which to establish an appropriate investment time horizon.

3. (This question has been adapted from a question appearing on the 1997 CFA Exam, Level III) Susan Fairfax is president of Reston Industries, a U.S.-based company whose sales are entirely domestic and whose shares are listed on the New York Stock Exchange. The following are additional facts concerning her current situation.

   Fairfax is single, aged 58. She has no immediate family, no debts, and does not own a residence. She is in excellent health and covered by Reston-paid health insurance that continues after her expected retirement at age 65.

   Her base salary of $500,000/year, inflation-protected, is sufficient to support her present lifestyle, but can no longer generate any excess for savings.

   She has $2,000,000 of savings from prior years held in the form of short-term instruments.

   Reston rewards key employees through a generous stock-bonus incentive plan, but provides no pension plan and pays no dividend.

   Fairfax's incentive plan participation has resulted in her ownership of Reston stock worth $10 million (current market value). The stock, received tax-free but subject to tax at a 35% rate (on entire proceeds) if sold, is expected to be held at least until her retirement.

Her present level of spending and the current annual inflation rate of 4% are expected to continue after her retirement.

Fairfax is taxed at 35% on all salary, investment income, and realized capital gains. Assume her composite tax rate will continue at this level indefinitely.

Fairfax's orientation is patient, careful, and conservative in all things. She has stated that an annual after-tax real total return of 3% would be completely acceptable to her if it was achieved in a context where an investment portfolio created from her accumulated savings was not subject to a decline of more than 10% in nominal terms in any given 13-month period. To obtain the benefits of professional assistance, she has approached two investment advisory firms—HH Counselors ("HH") and Coastal Advisors ("Coastal")—for recommendations on allocation of the investment portfolio to be created from her existing savings assets (the "Savings Portfolio") as well as for advice concerning investing in general.

A. **Create** and **justify** an Investment Policy Statement for Fairfax based *only* on the information provided above. Be specific and complete as to objectives and constraints. (An asset allocation is *not* required in answering this question.)

B. Coastal has proposed the asset allocation shown in Table I below for investment of Fairfax's $2 million of savings assets (the "Savings Portfolio"). Assume that only the Current Yield portion of Projected Total Return (comprised of both investment income and realized capital gains) is taxable to Fairfax and that the Municipal Bond income is entirely tax-exempt. **Critique** the Coastal proposal. Include in your answer *three* weaknesses in the Coastal proposal from the standpoint of the Investment Policy Statement you created for her in Part A above.

Table I
Susan Fairfax Proposed Asset Allocation
Prepared by: Coastal Advisors

Asset Class	Proposed Allocation (%)	Current Yield (%)	Projected Total Return (%)
Cash equivalents	15.0	4.5	4.5
Corporate bonds	10.0	7.5	7.5
Municipal bonds	10.0	5.5	5.5
Large-cap. U.S. stocks	0.0	3.5	11.0
Small-cap. U.S. stocks	0.0	2.5	13.0
International stocks (EAFE)	35.0	2.0	13.5
Real Estate Investment trusts (REITs)	25.0	9.0	12.0
Venture capital	5.0	0.0	20.0
Total	100.0	4.9	10.7
Inflation (CPI)— projected			4.0

The next two questions appeared on the 1998 CFA Exam, Level III, and both are based on the following information:

INTRODUCTION

Vincenzo Donadoni and his sister, Maria Barda, have sold their Italian-based business for cash. Donadoni expects to remain a resident of Switzerland; Barda expects to remain a resident of Italy. Both have incurred tax liabilities payable in Italian lira (LIT) as a result of the sale. Donadoni's tax payment, equivalent to 2.0 million Swiss francs (CHF) at current exchange rates, is due in 2 years. Barda, on the advice of her tax consultant, will eliminate her liability by making an immediate charitable contribution of LIT 2.5 billion.

Vincenzo Donadoni

Donadoni, who is 56 and a widower, will act as a consultant to the Italian-based business for the next 2 years and will be paid CHF 125,000 per year. Donadoni's investment portfolio, including his share of the proceeds from the sale of the business, amounts to CHF 13.0 million and has been entrusted to Alpine Invest AG, a Swiss money management firm. He estimates his living expenses to be CHF 250,000 annually, rising with inflation. He needs approximately CHF 1.5 million immediately to renovate his home. His major investment goal is to leave a trust fund of CHF 15.0 million for his three children.

Donadoni achieved success and local fame as a businessman by profiting greatly from large bets on short-term opportunities. An impulsive and opinionated individual, he believes that success depends on taking the initiative. Donadoni intends to actively monitor and participate in the management of his assets, although he has had little direct portfolio management experience. He plans to rely a great deal on Alpine's expertise, but he will not permit Alpine to use derivative instruments or currency hedges.

Maria Barda

Barda, who is 69 and a widow without children, received (gross) LIT 5.0 billion from the sale and will have LIT 2.5 billion remaining after making the charitable contribution. She believes her annual living expense will be about LIT 175 million, rising with inflation. These expenses have been covered by dividends and pension income from the family business and by the income from a small investment portfolio (with a current value of LIT 360 million). This portfolio is invested in Italian government notes and a few high-dividend-yielding stocks. Now that both the dividends and pension from the business have ceased, the small investment portfolio will be combined with the remaining sale proceeds and will be managed by Alpine. Barda, who will leave any assets remaining at her death to a local school, worries that these assets will not be enough to support her in her remaining years. She has no interest in the day-to-day management of her investments. However, she does not want to take a loss in any of the individual securities she owns.

Donadoni and Barda have arranged a meeting with Alpine to discuss their financial situations.

4. Maria Barda's portfolio manager at Alpine states the following to explain how investors should, theoretically, make decisions:

Rational, risk-averse investors will focus on the results of their entire portfolios. When selecting among possible portfolios, a rational risk-averse investor will choose the one with the highest expected return given the inves-

tor's desired level of risk or the one with the lowest level of risk given the desired level of return.

Describe *two* differences between Barda's stated loss aversion and a "rational investor's" risk aversion.

5. **Discuss** *each* of the following elements of an investment policy statement for *both* Vincenzo Donadoni *and* Maria Barda:
   A. Current income requirements.
   B. Total return requirements.
   C. Willingness to assume risk.
   D. Ability to assume risk.
   E. Time horizon.

A total of 10 responses is required.

FURTHER REFERENCES

Gibson, Roger C. *Asset Allocation*, 2nd ed. Burr Ridge, IL: Irwin, 1996.

This easy-to-read the book begins with a nonmathematical review of investment theory. The book proceeds to walk the reader, presumably an individual investor, through the asset allocation process step by step.

Ibbotson Associates, *Stocks, Bonds, Bills, and Inflation,* an annual yearbook, published in Chicago, IL.

This reference book reviews some relevant investment theory and provides a rich repository of empirical data about debt and equity markets in the United States. The historical data is drawn from seven decades and the forecasts of future decades are explained with the help of elementary statistics. The data and the discussion are presented in terms of asset classes that are appropriate for asset allocators.

Ibbotson, Roger G. and Paul D. Kaplan, "Does Asset Allocation Policy Explain 40%, 90%, or 100% of Performance?" *Financial Analysts Journal* 56, no. 1 (January-February 2000): 26–33.

This study analyzes the returns from mutual funds and pension funds with respect to differences in their asset allocation policies. The research reveals that a large part of the variation in both the time-series returns and the cross-sectional returns can be explained by asset allocation policy.

ENDNOTES

[1] For informative publications that address asset allocation process in more detail, see the Association for Investment Management and Research, P.O. Box 7947, Charlottesville, VA 22906.

[2] *The Challenges of Investing for Endowment Funds*, ed. Catheryn E. Kittell, sponsored by The Institute of Chartered Financial Analysts. (Burr Ridge, IL: Dow Jones-Irwin, 1986).

[3] Excerpted from Article 3 of the NASD the Rules of Fair Practice.

[4] See Charles D. Ellis, *Investment Policy*, 2nd ed. Special Edition for CFA Candidates (Burr Ridge, IL: Irwin, 1993), 24–25.

[5] See Richard W. McEnally, "Time Diversification: The Surest Route to Lower Risk?" *Journal of Portfolio Management* (summer 1985): 24–26. For a complete review of this literature, see William Reichenstein and Dovalee Dorsett, *Time Diversification Revisited* (Charlottesville, VA: The Research Foundation of the Institute for Chartered Financial Analysts, 1995). For a more recent argument in favor of time diversification, see Haim Levy and Allon Cohen, "On the Risk of Stocks in the Long Run: Revisited," *Journal of Portfolio Management* 24, no. 3 (spring 1998): 60–69. For an unbiased tutorial see Mark Kritzman and Don Rich, "Beware of Dogma," *Journal of Portfolio Management* 24, no 4 (summer 1998): 66–77.

[6] For historical evidence that stock returns are mean reverting, see J. Poterba and L. Summers, "Mean Reversion in Stock Returns: Evidence and Implications," *Journal Of Financial Economics* (October 1988).

[7] See Gary P. Brinson, Brian D. Singer, and Gilbert L. Beebower, "Determinants of Portfolio Performance II: An Update," *Financial Analysts Journal* (May–June 1981): 40–48. This article updates a similar study by Gary P. Brinson, L. Randolph Hood, and Gilbert L. Beebower, "Determinants of Portfolio Performance," *Financial Analysts Journal* (July–August 1986): 39–44.

[8] See Roger G. Ibbotson and Paul D. Kaplan, "Does Asset Allocation Policy Explain 40%, 90%, or 100% of Performance?," *Financial Analysts Journal* 56, no. 1 (January–February 2000): 26–33. For supporting evidence from England, see David Blake, Bruce N. Lehmann, and Allan Timmermann, "Asset Allocation Dynamics and Pension Fund Performance," *Journal of Business* 72, no. 4 (October 1999): 429–61.

How Taxation Affects Investments in the United States*

Pension funds, mutual funds, foundations, and some other institutional investors are exempt from income taxes. Individual and corporate investors must pay taxes on their investment income.

Personal Taxes

Keeping the tax collector from taking too much of your investment income is a worthwhile challenge. Consider that over a 30-year period the value of a tax-deferred investment will grow to nearly double that of an equal investment whose income is taxed at 28% per year, assuming equivalent pre- and after-tax rates of return. IRA's, 401K's, 403B's and other tax-deferred retirement investment vehicles are popular because they reward tax-deferred investing.

Consider 1998 marginal tax rates in Table 13A-1.

These are the tax rates for ordinary income (such as wages, interest, cash dividends, and distributions from IRA, 401K, and 403B accounts) *after taxable income* is calculated. Taxable income is always less than *gross income,* since *taxable income* at a minimum is gross income less either standard or itemized deductions and personal exemptions.

Assume you are single, self-supporting, and your only income shows up on your 1998 year-end tax Form W-2 as $61,400. Does that mean your federal income tax in 1998 is $13,896.50? No! *Gross income* is $61,400. From this amount you can deduct:

TABLE 13A-1 **1998 Tax Rate Schedules**

Married Filing Jointly or Qualifying Widow(er)					Single				
Over . . .	but not over . . .	the tax is . . .		. . . of the amount over . . .	over . . .	but not over . . .	the tax is . . .		. . . of the amount over . . .
$0	$42,350	———	15%	$0	$0	$25,350	———	15%	$0
42,350	102,300	$6,352.50 +	28%	42,350	25,350	61,400	$3,802.50 +	28%	25,350
102,300	155,950	23,138.50 +	31%	102,300	61,400	128,100	13,896.50 +	31%	61,400
155,950	278,450	39,770.00 +	36%	155,950	128,100	278,450	34,573.50 +	36%	128,100
278,450	———	83,870.00 +	39.6%	278,450	278,450	———	88,899.50 +	39.6%	278,450

* The authors are indebted to Deborah Susan Francis, MBA, CPA, Vice President, Bank of America, for her help with this appendix.

TABLE 13A-2 Determining a Person's Taxable Income

Gross Income	$
minus Adjustments to Gross Income	(___)
equals Adjusted Gross Income	$
minus Itemized Deductions / Standard Deductions	(___)
minus Personal Exemptions	(___)
equals Taxable Income	$

1. Your adjustments (such as deductible IRA contributions)
2. Your standard deduction. Or, if it is higher, you can deduct your total of itemized deductions (including but not limited to some types of state and local taxes, investment and mortgage interest expense, and charitable contributions)
3. Your personal exemption. See Table 13A-2 for a summary.

You have then arrived at *taxable income* to which the tax rates in Table 13A-1 apply.*

VARIABLE ANNUITIES

DEFINITION

Dictionaries define an *annuity* to be a financial contract that pays *fixed*, periodic income payments to its owner (buyer, investor). Buying a fixed annuity is like buying a bond that makes fixed coupon payments each year. A **variable annuity** is an annuity contract that provides periodic income payments that *fluctuate,* because they are linked to the fluctuating market value of an underlying investment portfolio. Variable annuities are tax-advantaged investments that are good purchases when the investor is not legally permitted to invest additional funds in an IRA or a Keogh Plan.

Stock brokers, mutual funds, and life insurance companies sell variable annuities. The purchase price is called the *premium* and is usually paid in a lump sum. Alternatively, the investor can make a series of investments (premium payments) over a period of time called the *accumulation phase*. These premium payments are tax deductible, like the contributions to an IRA shown in Table 13-A2.

The premiums paid for a variable annuity can be used to purchase a bond mutual fund, a stock mutual fund, or may be allocated to several investments. U.S. law permits the investment to grow tax-free until the investor begins taking withdrawals. The Internal Revenue Service (IRS) imposes a 10% penalty tax on withdrawals made before age 59.5. When the investor ends the accumulation phase and begins the *distribution phase*, the distributions are taxed as ordinary income.

When the investor wants to start receiving income payments, he or she *annuitizes* the accumulated investment. Annuitization uses the accumulated investment to purchase a series of monthly, quarterly, or annual annuity payments covering a specified time period. These fluctuating distribution payments may be spread over a specified number of years, or continue until the investor dies. Variable annuities are flexible investments that permit the investor to make a lump-sum withdrawal anytime during the distribution phase.

---

* The U.S. Treasury's Internal Revenue Service (IRS) has a Web site to provide tax information: http://www. irs.ustreas.gov

Variable annuities contain a life insurance policy that promises the investor's beneficiary a *death benefit* if the investor dies. This death payment equals the greater of the market value of the accumulated investment or the premiums paid (less any withdrawals). The annual expense for a variable annuity exceeds the annual expense of a mutual fund by 0.6% to 1.6% because of the cost of this life insurance. The typical variable annuity costs the investor about 2.4% of the market value of the accumulated investment per year.

Average mutual fund's annual management fee	1.4% of the asset value
Plus: Approximate annual term life insurance premium	+1.0% of the asset value
Typical total annual fee for a variable annuity	2.4% of the asset value

In addition, most variable annuities charge a surrender fee if the contract is cashed in within the first few years.

Variable annuities are also called tax sheltered annuities (TSAs).

Alternative Minimum Tax

To make matters more complicated, there is an *alternative minimum tax (AMT)*. The AMT was created to insure the wealthiest individuals paid some tax. Unlike the ordinary income tax, which is indexed annually for inflation, the AMT tax brackets and exemptions remain exactly the same from year to year. Thus, an increasing percentage of the population becomes subject to the AMT annually. The name, alternative minimum tax, is appropriate. The taxpayer first computes his/her taxable income and tax the ordinary way, via Tables 13A-1 and 13A-2, and then the alternative way. He or she then compares the amount of tax computed each way and then must pay the higher amount.

Currently, the wealthiest one million Americans are subject to the AMT. To keep this tax discussion short, let us assume you are not one of the one million richest Americans and move on to more appropriate tax laws.

Capital Gains Tax

Capital assets include stocks, bonds, and real estate held for personal investment purposes (but not your residence). **Capital gains** equal the difference between sales proceeds and cost basis of capital assets. *Long-term capital gains,* from assets held beyond 1 year, are desirable since they enjoy a maximum tax rate of 20%. For individuals in the lowest ordinary income tax bracket, the long-term capital gains tax rate is only 10%. Thus, long-term capital gains are generally taxed at either 20% or 10%, irrespective of the rates at which the taxpayer's ordinary income is taxed. **Short-term capital gains,** from assets held 1 year or less, are considered ordinary income and taxed at the higher ordinary tax rates in Table 13A-1. Investors should seek to maximize the benefits from the long-term capital gains tax rate structure.

Evaluating investments on an *after-tax* basis is a sound principle that should be adhered to by all investors. Unfortunately, many investment managers receive compensation based on pretax investment results, leaving their clients to struggle with the results of rapid portfolio turnover and undisciplined selling methods. Rapid portfolio turnover creates immediate tax consequences for the investor, and selling taxable assets that have low (rather than high) cost basis creates unnecessarily large tax bills. Consequently, there are a growing number of mutual funds offering "tax-managed funds." Taxes really do matter; they can cause up to 40% of pretax investment returns to evaporate.

Tax Treatment: To determine the tax treatment of capital gains and losses, group all short-term gains and losses to arrive at one short-term net total. Then group all long-term gains and losses to arrive at one long-term net total. Be sure to include loss carryovers from prior years in each group; these deductions reduce taxes. Combine the long-term and short-term net totals to determine overall capital gains or loss. The maximum 20% applies only to *net long-term capital gain*. If there is a net overall loss for the year, up to $3,000 of it may be deducted against ordinary income. Net losses in excess of $3,000 are carried forward for the life of the taxpayer to be used against future capital gains and up to $3,000 of ordinary income per year.

JAKE'S YEAR-END INVESTMENT TAX RESULTS

EXAMPLE

S-T gains:	$16,000	L-T gains:	$25,000
Less: S-T losses:	24,000	Less: L-T losses:	2,000
Equals: Net S-T losses:	8,000	Equals: Net L-T gains:	23,000

Jake reports ($23,000 − $8,000 =) $15,000 in net long-term gains on his income tax return. Assuming he is not in the lowest income tax bracket, he is taxed (20% × $15,000 =) $3,000. If Jake had failed to deduct his losses (of $24,000 + $2,000 = $26,000), he would have paid a lot more than $3,000.

Curiously, long-term capital gains for tax purposes do not exist in retirement plans. Obviously, capital gains do occur in IRAs and other retirement plans, but for tax purposes those gains receive no preferential treatment. Income from assets inside retirement plans is not taxed (it is tax-deferred) until it is finally distributed to the account owner. All annual distributions are taxed as ordinary income (Table 13A-1) as they are paid each year. Consequently, preferred long-term capital gains taxes applies only to after-tax/nonretirement-type investment portfolios.

The IRS discourages mutual funds from retaining income within the portfolio by imposing a penalty tax for distributing less than 90% of the mutual fund's total income to investors. Interest income, cash dividend income, and capital gains realized by a mutual fund can be passed through the fund to investors free from taxes in the year the mutual fund earns the income. Regardless of whether or not a mutual fund pays penalty taxes for retaining income internally to help investors defer their income taxes, all income distributions made by mutual funds become the investor's taxable income in the year the fund makes the distribution. Money managers who are aware of and sensitive to the shareholders' desire to maximize after-tax returns as opposed to pretax returns can usually improve after-tax returns. Capital gains distributions from mutual funds are usually made in November or December. Investing in a mutual fund just before a capital gains distribution date makes the new investor subject to taxes on the capital gains the fund realized prior to his or her investing. Investments after that distribution date avoid those taxes.

Wash Sales. A **wash sale** occurs when a taxpayer sells a security in order to claim a tax loss but, thinking they still want the security in their portfolio, buy it back immediately. Wash sales were a great tax-planning idea that was made illegal. Under current tax law, a taxpayer is not allowed to claim a loss if, within a period beginning 30 days before the date of sale and ending 30 days after that date, the taxpayer has acquired, or has entered into an option to acquire, substantially identical securities.

TAX-EXEMPT INVESTING

Opportunities for tax-exempt investing are few, but the most notable ones are municipal bond investments, and to some extent, ownership of a personal residence.

Municipal Bonds. Most municipal bonds are tax-free for federal income tax purposes. A minority of these state and local bond issues are subject to the alternative minimum tax, which is a problem only to those individuals who are alternative minimum taxpayers (their AMT calculation is greater than their ordinary income tax calculation). In general, tax-exempt municipal bonds are also subject to state income taxes if they are *not* issued in the taxpayer's state. For most purposes, however, municipal bonds are tax-exempt and offer an attractive investment option for taxpayers who are in a high tax bracket and not seeking growth in a portion of their portfolio. Equivalent pretax and after-tax rates of return given the four ordinary income tax brackets are shown in Table 13A-3; the values were computed with Eqn. 5-1 in Chapter 5.

Home Ownership. Home ownership is a tax-exempt investment for most taxpayers. Up to $250,000 of the gain from the sale of a home is tax-exempt for single taxpayers ($500,000 for joint taxpayers). Certain qualifications are required to obtain this tax exemption, such as occupying and owning it as a principal residence for at least 2 of the 5 years prior to selling the home. This tax exemption can be used on a continuing basis—but not more frequently than once every 2 years. In other words, the exemption is renewed every 2 years following each home sale. It seems clear that Congress intends home ownership not to be a taxable investment except in some extraordinary circumstances.

Unified Transfer Tax

Besides the federal income tax, the next most significant tax an investor faces is the ***estate tax.*** Technically, it is known as the *Unified Transfer Tax*. It takes a big bite out of estates in excess of $1 million. Tax rates are shown in Table 13A-4.

These brackets are *not* indexed for inflation as are the income tax brackets. The estate tax has especially been criticized for its propensity toward double taxation: after a taxpayer's income is taxed as he or she earns it, the assets acquired with the after-tax income are effectively taxed again at death at the estate tax rates, which reach 55% on taxable estates in excess of $3 million.

The Unified Transfer Tax actually encompasses three types of transfers: estates (following death), gifts (during one's lifetime), and generation-skipping transfers (whether during life or at death).

TABLE 13A-3 Equivalent Taxable and After-Tax Yields from Municipal Bonds

	Equivalent Taxable Yield at Indicated Marginal Tax Rate			
Tax-Exempt Yield	15% Tax Rate	28% Tax Rate	36% Tax Rate	39.6% Tax Rate
4%	4.7%	5.6%	6.3%	6.6%
5%	5.9%	6.9%	7.8%	8.3%
6%	7.1%	8.3%	9.4%	9.9%
7%	8.2%	9.7%	10.9%	11.6%
8%	9.4%	11.1%	12.5%	13.3%

TABLE 13A-4 Unified Rate Schedule

Taxable Amount Equal To or More Than Column (1)	Taxable Amount Less Than Column (2)	Tax on Amount in Column (1)	Rate of Tax on Amount in Excess of Amount in Column (1)
0	10,000	0	.18
10,000	20,000	1,800	.20
20,000	40,000	3,800	.22
40,000	60,000	8,200	.24
60,000	80,000	13,000	.26
80,000	100,000	18,200	.28
100,000	150,000	23,800	.30
150,000	250,000	38,800	.32
200,000	500,000	70,800	.34
500,000	750,000	155,800	.37
750,000	1,000,000	248,300	.39
1,000,000	1,250,000	345,800	.41
1,250,000	1,500,000	448,300	.43
1,500,000	2,000,000	555,800	.45
2,000,000	2,500,000	780,800	.49
2,500,000	3,000,000	1,025,800	.53
3,000,000		1,290,800	.55

Note: There is a 5% additional tax for estates between $10,000,000 and $21,040,000.

Estate Taxes. An exclusion of up to $1 million is available for the estate of every individual; after $1 million, the tax rate begins at 41% and marches upward to 55% at $3,000,000. Actually the $1 million exclusion is being phased in: It is $650,000 in 1999 and by 2002 it will be $1 million, but for convenience here, we refer to it as $1 million. It is *not* indexed for inflation. The tax is known as the **Unified Transfer Tax** because it is technically *not* a tax on assets (which is unconstitutional) but a tax on the *transfer* of assets. As far as tax rates and exclusions are concerned, it is irrelevant whether assets are transferred during a person's lifetime or at death—the tax rates are the same and the available exclusion is the same. Lifetime gifts are added back into one's estate at death so that a cumulative amount of transfers are the total, the $1 million exclusion is deducted to reduce that total, and the tax rates from Table 13A-4 are applied to the reduced total to calculate the final estate tax. All property owned or in any way controlled by the decedent (whether or not owned) is included as part of his/her estate. **Estate planning** constitutes a thriving industry focused on reducing taxable estates and the taxes thereon at one's death.

Estate taxes and income taxes are totally separate, distinct taxes. However, these taxes intersect in an interesting way at a person's death. For example, assume Sam is 95 years old with a sizable estate including a $1 million non–retirement fund portfolio with a cost basis of $100,000. Liquidating his portfolio would create long-term capital gains of $900,000, and, at an income tax rate of 20%, federal income taxes of $180,000. Let's further assume Sam has been diagnosed with terminal cancer. Should he liquidate his portfolio to pay his rapidly growing nursing home and medical bills? No! When Sam dies, his portfolio for *income tax purposes* will receive a stepped-up cost basis (arbitrarily increased by IRS rules) to, say, $900,000, the fair market value on Sam's date of death. This cost basis of $900,000 will eliminate the capital gains tax of $180,000. Sam would be wise to borrow the funds to pay his bills, using his portfolio as collateral. His estate will be reduced by the amount of the loan outstanding at his death and his heirs will be $180,000 wealthier (less any interest due on the loan).

If Sam's portfolio had been a tax-deferred retirement portfolio such as a traditional IRA, the result would be very different. Cost basis step-up rules and capital gains taxes do not apply to tax-deferred portfolios. Whether Sam or his heirs liquidate a $1 million tax-deferred portfolio, 100% would be subject to ordinary income tax rates.*

Gift Taxes. Originally, there was just one transfer tax known as an estate tax—which was assessed at death. To counteract the creative genius of the wealthier segment of the population to reduce their estate taxes by making gifts during life, a gift tax was added to the law which created the *Unified Estate and Gift Tax*. Since accounting for very small gifts seemed both labor-intensive and intrusive, an annual gift tax exclusion was added to the law. For many years the annual *per donee* exclusion was $3,000, then $10,000, and then in 1997 Congress indexed the $10,000 for inflation, but only in increments of $1,000. As of this writing, the annual gift tax exclusion remains at $10,000, allowing each person to give up to $10,000 per year to as many persons as he/she desires without adversely affecting the $1 million estate tax exclusion. In addition to the $10,000, the donor can make unlimited payments of tuition and medical expenses for donees. However, payments must be made directly to the educational institution or medical provider so as not to interfere with either the $10,000 annual gift tax exclusion or $1 million lifetime transfer tax exclusion. Another gift and estate tax exclusion is the one for qualified charitable donations, which is unlimited. Perhaps you are detecting a pattern. The primary method of minimizing one's estate taxes is removing assets from one's estate via gifting. There are other more complex techniques available, but most revolve around gifting in some form.

Generation-Skipping Transfer Tax. Very wealthy families, such as the Rockefellers and DuPonts, were urged by their tax advisors to make gifts directly to grandchildren to avoid one generation's worth of estate taxes. To thwart this, Congress passed a generation-skipping transfer tax in the mid-1980s that essentially assesses an additional 55% (flat tax) on assets transferred in this way. There is a $1,000,000 lifetime exclusion per donor/decedent, which is indexed for inflation. For example, Bill Gates can transfer a total of $1 million to his grandchildren either during his lifetime or at death without the 55% generation-skipping transfer tax being assessed. Many books, treatises, and other documents have been published exploring ways to minimize the effect of this most recent transfer tax.

Corporate Taxes

Coca-Cola's Income and Expense Statement at Table 4-2 in Chapter 4 (p. 68) shows how to compute a corporation's taxable income. Table 13A-5 contains the progressive corporate income tax rates applicable to a corporation's taxable income.

---

* The Roth IRA is an exception to this general rule, but space does not allow for a full discussion of Roth IRAs.

TABLE 13A-5 Corporation Income Tax Rates, 1997

Taxable Income Over . . .	. . . but not over . . .	Pay	+	% on Excess . . .	. . . of the Amount over . . .
$ 0—	$ 50,000	$ 0		15%	$ 0
50,000—	75,000	7,500		25	50,000
75,000—	100,000	13,750		34	75,000
100,000—	335,000	22,250		39	100,000
335,000—	10,000,000	113,900		34	335,000
10,000,000—	15,000,000	3,400,000		35	10,000,000
15,000,000—	18,333,333	5,150,000		38	15,000,000
18,333,333—	....	6,416,667		35	18,333,333

Note: Taxable income of certain personal service corporations is taxed at a flat rate of 35%.

PORTFOLIO ANALYSIS

Speculators are risk-takers who are inclined to sink all their money into one risky investment and hope it pays off. Instead of putting all their eggs in one basket, more risk-averse investors try to reduce their exposure to risk by purchasing a diversified list of different investments called a **portfolio**. *Every investor seems to have a different idea about what should be in their portfolio. This chapter reviews several ideas about how to construct a portfolio, and analyzes the strengths and weaknesses of each. It presumes an understanding of Chapters 2 and 7.*

Most people understand that diversification means not "putting all the eggs in one basket." Few people have a clear idea about whether diversification can really reduce risk. This chapter begins by examining simple theories about how a portfolio should be diversified. Most of the last part of the chapter focuses on a Nobel Prize–winning portfolio theory conceived by Harry Markowitz.[1] Markowitz's portfolio management model uses diversification to reduce risk while maximizing the portfolio's return.

Chapter 15 presents another Nobel Prize–winning theory that extends the Markowitz portfolio theory introduced in this chapter. Chapter 15 traces out the asset pricing implications of Markowitz portfolio theory.

SIMPLE DIVERSIFICATION

The simplest portfolio theory is based on *random diversification*. Suppose you took 1,000 domestic common stocks and computed the standard deviation of each individual stock from one decade of historical returns. In Figure 14-1 the riskiest individual stock is at point Y, and W is the least risky. Further suppose you took the same 1,000 stocks and divided them into 500 mutually exclusive portfolios containing equal amounts of two randomly selected stocks. The riskiest of these 500 random portfolios lies at point Z in Figure 14-1, and X is the least risky 2-stock portfolio. Can you guess what this simple 2-stock diversification accomplishes? The 2-stock portfolios will have a mean standard deviation, denoted σ_2, that is smaller than the mean standard deviation averaged over the 1,000 individual stocks, σ_1.

$$\begin{pmatrix} \text{Mean standard} \\ \text{deviation averaged} \\ \text{over 1,000} \\ \text{individual stocks at} \\ \text{point } \sigma_1 \text{ in Fig. 14-1} \end{pmatrix} = \begin{pmatrix} \begin{pmatrix} \text{1,000 different} \\ \text{individual} \\ \text{stocks} \end{pmatrix} \\ \frac{1}{1,000} \sum_{i=1} \sigma_i \end{pmatrix} = \sigma_1 > \sigma_2 = \begin{pmatrix} \begin{pmatrix} \text{500 different} \\ \text{2-stock} \\ \text{portfolios} \end{pmatrix} \\ \frac{1}{500} \sum_{i=1} \sigma_i \end{pmatrix} = \begin{pmatrix} \text{Mean standard} \\ \text{deviation averaged} \\ \text{over 500 2-stock} \\ \text{portfolios at} \\ \text{point } \sigma_2 \text{ in Fig. 14-1} \end{pmatrix}$$

The $\sigma_1 > \sigma_2$ relationship results from **simple diversification**. You should not do a lot of calculations to verify this relationship; just think about it. It is intuitive.

Next, suppose you randomly divided the same 1,000 stocks into 333 different 3-stock portfolios. Intuition tells you the 3-stock portfolios would be less risky, on average, than the 2-stock portfolios.

$$\begin{pmatrix} \text{Mean standard} \\ \text{deviation averaged} \\ \text{over 333 3-stock} \\ \text{portfolios is at} \\ \text{point } \sigma_3 \text{ in Fig. 14-1} \end{pmatrix} = \begin{pmatrix} \begin{pmatrix} \text{333 different} \\ \text{3-stock} \\ \text{portfolios} \end{pmatrix} \\ \frac{1}{333} \sum_{i=1} \sigma_i \end{pmatrix} = \sigma_3 < \sigma_2 = \begin{pmatrix} \begin{pmatrix} \text{500 different} \\ \text{2-stock} \\ \text{portfolios} \end{pmatrix} \\ \frac{1}{500} \sum_{i=1} \sigma_i \end{pmatrix} = \begin{pmatrix} \text{Mean standard} \\ \text{deviation averaged} \\ \text{over 500 2-stock} \\ \text{portfolios is at} \\ \text{point } \sigma_2 \text{ in Fig. 14-1} \end{pmatrix}$$

The $\sigma_1 > \sigma_2 > \sigma_3$ progression is risk reduction accomplished by the simplest kind of diversification. Ignoring statistical sampling errors, we will find a tendency for the average standard deviations to diminish as more stocks were added to the portfolios. In other words, we expect: $\sigma_1 > \sigma_2 > \sigma_3 > \sigma_4 > \sigma_5 > \sigma_6$. The curved solid line labeled "Random portfolios' average risk" in Figure 14-1 traces out the risk-reduction power of simple, random, naive diversification.

The tendency for the average standard deviations to decrease as we go from 1-stock portfolios to 2-stock portfolios, 3-stock portfolios, 4-stock portfolios, 5-stock portfolios, and 6-stock portfolios is visible in Figure 14-1. Simple diversification is not surprising; the process tends to reduce portfolio risk until about three dozen randomly selected stocks have been added to a portfolio. What is harder to understand, however, is that when more than about three dozen equally weighted stocks are combined into a portfolio, additional simple diversification has virtually no further power to reduce risk. For example, Figure 14-1 shows that the mean standard deviation of a 36-stock portfolio is almost identical to the mean standard deviation of a portfolio that contains 1,000 randomly selected stocks. Can you explain why $\sigma_{36} = \sigma_{1,000}$?

Market forces that affect all assets simultaneously in some systematic manner generate **undiversifiable risk**. Bull markets (optimistic markets), bear markets (pessimistic markets), wars, changes in the level of inflation are examples of risk factors that make part of the total risk in a stock systematic (undiversifiable). **Diversifiable risk** is caused by Acts of God (a hurricane or flood), inventions, management errors, lawsuits, good or bad news affecting one firm, and any other idiosyncratic events that are statistically independent from the more widespread forces that generate undiversifiable risk. Diversifiable risk may be easily diversified away to zero in a portfolio that contains more than about 36 random stocks because the unsystematic pieces of good luck and bad luck from randomly selected assets tend to average out to zero.

After a portfolio increases beyond about 36 randomly selected stocks, the curve in Figure 14-1 tracing the mean portfolio standard deviations becomes a horizontal line. This horizontal line at $\sigma_{40} = \sigma_{400} = \sigma_{1,000}$ measures the undiversifiable risk. Spreading the portfolio's funds randomly over more than approximately 36 stocks cannot be expected to reduce the undiversifiable risk. This is because the diversifiable risk has already been reduced to zero and only undiversifiable risk remains, on average, in a portfolio containing more than 36 random stocks.

Simple diversification is analyzed using random selection and equal weighting to simulate unskilled investing. These naive techniques do not nullify the ability of simple diversification

FIGURE 14-1   Simple Diversification Reduces a Portfolio's Total Diversifiable Risk to Zero and Only the Undiversifiable Risk Remains

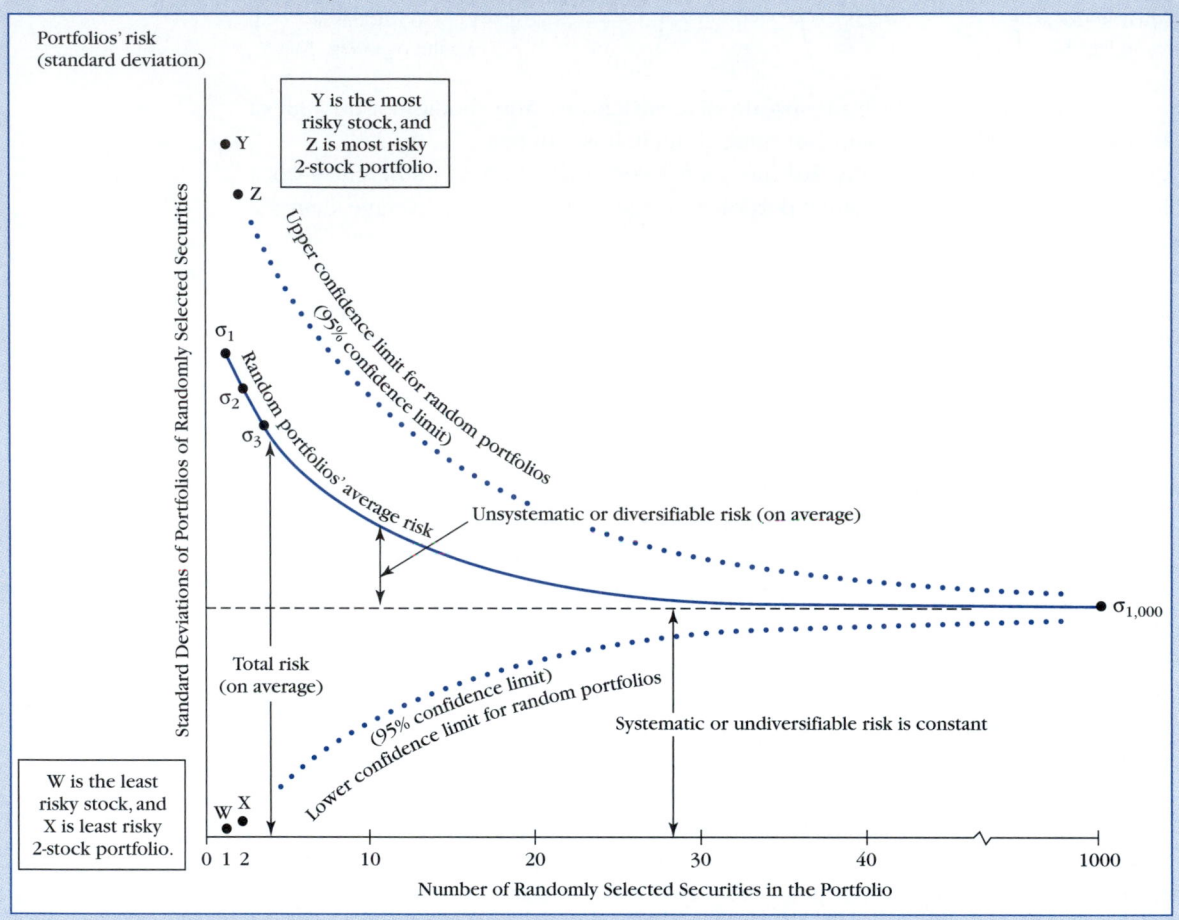

The total risk of a diversified portfolio of stocks can be partitioned into 2 components.

> Undiversifiable (or systematic) risk
>
> Plus: Diversifiable (or unsystematic) risk
> _____
> Equals: Total risk (or total variability of returns)

On average, the total risk of a diversified portfolio tends to diminish as more randomly selected common stocks are added to the portfolio. But, when more than about three dozen random stocks are combined, it is impossible to reduce a randomly selected portfolio's risk below the level of **undiversifiable risk** that exists in the market.

to reduce risk. Figure 14-1 shows that simple diversification over about 36 naively selected assets almost halves risk, on average. Not putting all the eggs in one basket is a simple idea, but a powerful one.[2]

DIVERSIFYING ACROSS INDUSTRIES

Selecting securities from different industries seems like a better idea than random diversification, but, surprisingly, this technique is actually not much better at reducing risk.

TABLE 14-1   Statistics from Various Diversification Techniques

Number of Stocks in Portfolio	Technique Used to Diversify	Minimum Rate of Return	Maximum Rate of Return	Mean Rate of Return	Standard Deviation of Returns
8	Random	−47%	164%	13%	0.22
8	Across industries	−47	158	13	0.22
16	Random	−37	121	13	0.21
16	Across industries	−37	121	13	0.21
32	Random	−31	98	13	0.20
32	Across industries	−29	93	13	0.20
128	Random	−29	76	13	0.19

SOURCE: Lawrence Fisher and James Lorie, "Some Studies of Variability of Returns on Investments in Common Stocks," *Journal of Business* (April 1970): 112, Table 5.

Portfolios containing 8, 16, and 32 NYSE-listed common stocks were formed using two different techniques: (1) simple random selection of stocks and (2) drawing each stock in the portfolio from a different industry. Lawrence Fisher and James Lorie constructed numerous portfolios using both techniques; their portfolio performance statistics are in Table 14-1.

Table 14-1 shows us that the minimum returns, mean returns, and standard deviations for the random 8-stock portfolios, for instance, are *not* significantly different from the same statistics for 8-stock portfolios diversified across eight different industries. Comparing the portfolio performance statistics in Table 14-1 indicates that diversifying across industries is not much better than simple diversification.

SUPERFLUOUS DIVERSIFICATION

The maximum risk-reduction benefits for a portfolio are likely to be attained by spreading the investment funds over several dozen different stocks. Further spreading of the portfolio's assets is **superfluous diversification**. Superfluous diversification will usually result in the following poor investment management practices:

1. **Poor portfolio management**. The manager of a portfolio containing over, say, 100 different stocks cannot hope to be fully informed about all of them. Every stock in the portfolio detracts from the attention the portfolio manager can give to other stocks and other investment candidates.
2. **Lackluster performers**. The search for a large number of different assets will inevitably lead to purchasing investments that do not yield superior returns. It is unrealistic to expect to discover hundreds of underpriced stocks in an efficient market like the New York Stock Exchange every day.
3. **High search costs**. As the number of securities in a portfolio and the number of investment candidates increases, transactions costs and the cost of performing the security analysis increase accordingly.

More money spent on superfluous diversification is not likely to improve the portfolio's performance. Worse, superfluous diversification may lower the portfolio owners' net return after some lackluster investments and increased expenses are considered.

Most mutual funds do not perform as well as the Standard & Poor's 500 index. Superfluous diversification suggests itself as one of the reasons for this poor performance, since most mutual funds own hundreds of different securities.*

AN INTRODUCTION TO MARKOWITZ DIVERSIFICATION

Markowitz diversification can reduce a portfolio's risk below the level of risk that simple random diversification suggests is undiversifiable.[3] To see how it works, consider what happens when two hypothetical common stocks that have negatively correlated rates of return are combined to form a portfolio. The symbol B denotes stock issued by the Black Ink Corporation, and R is for the Red Ink Corporation's stock. When accountants publish their companies financial statements, many print profits in black ink and losses in red ink. As a result, assume that black ink sells well during booms and red ink sells well during recessions. Table 14-2 shows the results over a 4-year period for a portfolio containing ink stocks R and B.

Table 14-2 shows that the portfolio of half B and half R has zero variability of returns over the 4 years. Total elimination of risk was due to the perfect negative correlation of the rates of return of B and R. The returns from B and R move perfectly inversely so that the gains on one stock always offset the losses from the other.

Table 14-2 shows that it is possible to combine risky assets into a portfolio that is riskless. But, riskless portfolios cannot be created from any pair of risky assets, and it can't be accomplished dependably without Markowitz portfolio analysis.

Markowitz's portfolio management model is based on five related concepts. The first concept requires that the weights of the assets in the portfolio sum to 100% of the portfolio's value. Concept 2 says a portfolio's return is the weighted average of the returns from the

TABLE 14-2 Example of Diversification with Two Inversely Correlated Stocks[a]

Asset	Year 1—Economic Boom	Year 2—Deep Recession	Year 3—Start of Recovery	Year 4—Recovery	VAR(r)
Red Ink's returns	−10%	+35%	+15%	+5%	0.0267
Black Ink's returns	+30%	−15%	+5%	+15%	0.0544
50-50 portfolio returns	$\frac{-10\% + 30\%}{2} = 10\%$	$\frac{35\% - 15\%}{2} = 10\%$	$\frac{15\% + 5\%}{2} = 10\%$	$\frac{5\% + 15\%}{2} = 10\%$	Zero

[a] The mean return for Red Ink is 11.25%, $VAR(r_R)$ = .02671875, and σ = .16345 = 16.3458%. The mean return for Black Ink is 8.75%, $VAR(r_B)$ = .054375, and σ = .23318 = 23.318%.

---

* An exception to the tendency of mutual funds toward superfluous diversification is a large, well-known, no-load mutual fund named Janus Twenty. The Janus Twenty Fund is a multibillion-dollar portfolio that invests in only 20 to 30 stocks and, over the long-run, is one of the few mutual funds that beats the S&P500 index. Janus Twenty uses derivatives and takes high risks; it is not for faint-hearted investors.

assets in the portfolio. The third concept dictates that, while seeking assets with the highest returns, the portfolio manager should minimize the portfolio's risk. Concept 4 is an insightful portfolio risk formula showing how the risk of every investment asset combines to determine the portfolio's risk. The portfolio management process ends with Concept 5, which shows how to determine whether or not the portfolio should be financed with borrowed money. The sections below use simple 2-stock examples to explain each concept separately. The step-by-step analysis shows how to find optimal investments.

MARKOWITZ CONCEPT ONE: THE WEIGHTS SUM TO ONE

The investment weights are the **decision variables** that the portfolio manager is paid to determine. Markowitz portfolio analysis assumes that the weights of the assets in a portfolio sum to one. Table 13-5 in Chapter 13, for example, shows that a Markowitz efficient portfolio that earns 10% return has 53% invested in stocks, 7% in bonds, and 40% in T-bills, and these three weights sum up to exactly 100%. It is pointless to account for more or less than 100% of the funds in a portfolio. For example, what does it mean if the weights of all the assets in a portfolio add up to 120%? . . . or, 60%? . . . or anything other than 100%? Eqn. 14-1 states Markowitz Concept One.

$$\sum_{i=1}^{N} x_i = 1 \qquad (14\text{-}1)$$

Eqn. 14-1 is called the *weights equation* because the symbol x_i represents the **weight** or *participation level* of asset i in a portfolio that contains N different assets. For example, if a 2-asset ($N = 2$) portfolio had two-thirds of the funds invested in Asset A and the remaining money invested in Asset B, we say that the weight of Asset A $\left(x_A = \frac{2}{3}\right)$ plus the weight in Asset B $\left(x_B = \frac{1}{3}\right)$ sums to unity. Essentially, $x_A + x_B = \frac{2}{3} + \frac{1}{3} = 1$.

The money in a portfolio may not be invested continuously, but it must be accounted for continuously. For instance, if none of the money in a 2-asset portfolio is invested in stocks or bonds, but is instead all held in cash, let the symbol x_C represent the weight invested in cash. We can write: $x_C = 100\% = 1.0$. We account for all of this 2-asset portfolio's funds by writing: $x_C + x_B = 1 + 0 = 1$. In this case we know that nothing is invested in Asset B ($x_B = 1 - x_C = 0$) because all of the money is invested in Asset C (cash).

MARKOWITZ CONCEPT TWO: A PORTFOLIO'S EXPECTED RETURN

A **portfolio's expected return** is the weighted average of the expected returns of the assets that make up the portfolio. Markowitz Rule Two is stated formally in Eqn. 14-2, which defines the portfolio's expected rate of return, $E(r_p)$, for an N-asset portfolio.

$$E(r_p) = \sum_{i=1}^{N} x_i E(r_i) \qquad (14\text{-}2)$$

$E(r_i)$ denotes the expected rate of return from the ith asset. $E(r)$ was introduced in Chapter 7 as Eqn. 7-5 (p. 164). Security analysts forecast the values for the assets' $E(r_i)$s. Security analysts'

TABLE 14-3 **Statistics for the Admiralty and Bathurst Corporations**

Stock's Issuer	Expected Return, $E(r)$, %	Risk, σ, %
Admiralty	5%	20%
Bathurst	15%	40%

expected return forecasts provide the portfolio analyst with input statistics for Markowitz portfolio analysis.

Table 14-3 gives the risk and return of two common stocks, the Admiralty Machinery Corporation and Bathurst Merchandise Incorporated.

Suppose two-thirds of the portfolio's funds are invested in Admiralty and one-third in Bathurst $\left(x_A = \frac{2}{3}\right)$ and $\left(x_B = \frac{1}{3}\right)$. The formula for the weighted average return from this portfolio is

$$E(r_p) = x_A E(r_A) + x_B E(r_B) \tag{14-2a}$$

This can be equivalently rewritten in terms of one weight since $x_B = 1.0 - x_A$.

$$E(r_p) = x_A E(r_A) + (1 - x_A)E(r_B) \tag{14-2b}$$
$$= x_A(5\%) + x_B(15\%)$$
$$= \tfrac{2}{3}(5\%) + \tfrac{1}{3}(15\%)$$
$$= 0.666(0.05) + 0.333(0.15) = .08333 = 8.33\% \tag{14-2c}$$

The portfolio with two-thirds of its funds invested in Admiralty and one-third in Bathurst has an expected rate of return of $E(r_p) = 8.33\%$.

MARKOWITZ CONCEPT THREE: THE OBJECTIVE

Markowitz Rule Three says the portfolio manager's goal is to select investment weights that add up to an efficient portfolio. An **efficient portfolio** is any combination of assets that has:

1. the maximum expected return in its risk-class, or, conversely,
2. the minimum risk at its level of expected return.

The objective of portfolio management is to simultaneously analyze different assets and determine what weightings of the investment candidates can be combined to form efficient portfolios. The set of all efficient portfolios will be called the efficient frontier. The **efficient frontier** is the locus of points in a two-dimensional graph—in $[\sigma, E(r)]$ space—having the maximum return at each level of risk. The efficient frontier dominates all other investment opportunities.

MARKOWITZ'S CONCEPT FOUR: PORTFOLIO RISK

Eqns. 2-9 and 2-10 in Chapter 2 introduced the variance of returns, $VAR(r)$, and the standard deviation, σ, for a single asset. A portfolio's variance includes the variance of each individual asset and the covariances between the assets. The covariance statistic was introduced at Eqns. 7-11 and 7-12 in Chapter 7 (p. 176).

Let N denote the number of assets that are investment candidates for a portfolio. To perform Markowitz portfolio analysis, the portfolio's variance must be broken down into the variances and covariances that represent the individual risks and interactions between the N candidate assets.

$$VAR(r_p) = \sum_{i=1}^{N}\sum_{j=1}^{N} x_i x_j \sigma_{ij} \tag{14-3}$$

The variance-covariance matrix represented by the double summation in Eqn. 14-3 can be expanded and rewritten equivalently as the matrix below in Eqn. 14-3a:

	Column 1	Column 2	Column 3	Column $N-1$	Column N	
$VAR(r_p) =$	$+\, x_1 x_1 \sigma_{11}$	$+\, x_1 x_2 \sigma_{12}$	$+\, x_1 x_3 \sigma_{13}$	. . . .	$+\, x_1 x_N \sigma_{1N}$	Row 1
	$+\, x_2 x_1 \sigma_{21}$	$+\, x_2 x_2 \sigma_{22}$	$+\, x_2 x_3 \sigma_{23}$	. . . .	$+\, x_2 x_N \sigma_{2N}$	Row 2
	$+\, x_3 x_1 \sigma_{31}$	$+\, x_3 x_2 \sigma_{32}$	$+\, x_3 x_3 \sigma_{33}$	. . . .	$+\, x_3 x_N \sigma_{3N}$	Row 3
	. . . .	. . . .	. . . .	. . . .	. . . .	Row $N-1$
	$+\, x_N x_1 \sigma_{N1}$	$+\, x_N x_2 \sigma_{N2}$	$+\, x_N x_3 \sigma_{N3}$	. . . .	$+\, x_N x_N \sigma_{NN}$	Row N

where x_i = the weight (which might be zero) of the ith asset in the portfolio,

$\sigma_{ii} = \sigma_i^2 = VAR(r)$ = the variance of returns from asset i, and,

$\sigma_{ij} = COV(r_i, r_j)$ = the covariance of returns between assets i and j

Since $x_1 x_2 \sigma_{12} + x_2 x_1 \sigma_{21} = 2 x_2 x_1 \sigma_{21}$ and $x_2 x_2 \sigma_{22} = x_2^2 \sigma_2^2$ we can abbreviate matrix Eqn. 14-3a above as matrix Eqn. 14-3b below:

	Column 1	Column 2	Column 3	Column $N-1$	Column N	
$VAR(r_p) =$	$+\, x_1 x_1 \sigma_{11}$					Row 1
	$+\, 2 x_2 x_1 \sigma_{21}$	$+\, x_2 x_2 \sigma_{22}$				Row 2
	$+\, 2 x_3 x_1 \sigma_{31}$	$+\, 2 x_3 x_2 \sigma_{32}$	$+\, x_3 x_3 \sigma_{33}$			Row 3
	. . . .	. . . .	. . . .	. . . .		Row $N-1$
	$+\, 2 x_N x_1 \sigma_{N1}$	$+\, 2 x_N x_2 \sigma_{N2}$	$+\, 2 x_N x_3 \sigma_{N3}$	. . . .	$+\, x_N x_N \sigma_{NN}$	Row N

Eqns. 14-3, 14-3a, and 14-3b comprise Markowitz Rule Four: They define the **variance-covariance matrix** for a portfolio problem made up of N different investment candidates.* Harry Markowitz did not create the mathematical variance-covariance matrix. But, he was the first to show how to use it to manage money. Table 13-5 in Chapter 13 contains return-and-risk statistics for three categories of assets (stocks, bonds, and T-bills) used to compute the efficient portfolios in Figure 13-1.

---

* Three patterns exist in every variance-covariance matrix. First, every variance-covariance matrix is a square table of numbers that has dimensions of N by N. Second, the variances all lie on a diagonal line from the upper-left corner to the lower-right corner of the square variance-covariance matrix. Restated, symbolically, $\sigma_{ij} = VAR(r_i)$ for $i = j$. Third, the covariances above the diagonal line are the mirror image of the covariances below the diagonal line. Restated, symbolically, $\sigma_{ij} = \sigma_{ji}$ for $i \neq j$. But, there are simplifications in Eqn. 14-3b. Since $\sigma_{ij} = \sigma_{ji}$ each covariance term in Eqn. 14-3b is multiplied by 2 rather than repeating all of the identical covariance terms twice. As a result, the identical covariances that lie below the diagonal line are omitted from Eqn. 14-3b.

Revisiting the Covariance and the Correlation Coefficient

Eqns. 7-11 and 7-12 and Table 7-7 in Chapter 7 (pp. 175–176) introduced the covariance. Eqn. 7-12 showed that the *covariance* is related to the correlation coefficient as shown in Eqn. 14-4, where ρ_{ij} is the correlation coefficient between two random variables, i and j.

$$\sigma_{ij} = \sigma_i \sigma_j \rho_{ij} \tag{14-4}$$

Note that Eqn. 14-4 can be easily solved to obtain a simple definition of the correlation coefficient, $\rho_{ij} = \sigma_{ij}/\sigma_i \sigma_j$.

STUDY CHECK

SUBSCRIPTS

QUESTIONS:

1. Explain in words each pair of equalities in the following relationship:

$$\sigma_i^2 = \sigma_{ii} = \sigma_i \sigma_i = VAR(r_i)$$

2. Explain the following equality in words:

$$COV(r_i, r_j) = \sigma_{ij}$$

3. In the following equality, assume $i = j$ and explain the relationships:

$$\sigma_i^2 = \sigma_{ii} = \sigma_i \sigma_i = VAR(r_i) = COV(r_i, r_j) = \sigma_{ij}$$

ANSWERS: (1) The first relationship shows equivalent statistical symbols that all represent the variance of returns from asset i. (2) The second relationship shows equivalent symbols representing the covariance of returns between assets i and j. (3) Assuming $i = j$, the relationship shows equivalent ways to represent the variance of returns from asset i and the covariance of asset i with itself.

The covariance measures how two variables covary. If two assets are positively correlated, their covariance will also be positive. Most of the common stocks in a country have a positive covariance with each other. These positive covariances and correlations measure, for example, the tendency for all NYSE stocks to trend downward during a bear market and rise more or less together as a bull market progresses.

If two variables are independent, their covariance (and correlation) is zero. For example, the covariance of the stock market and the weather in your hometown is probably zero.

If two variables move inversely, their covariance (and correlation) is negative. For example, the returns from a long position in Coca-Cola's stock are perfectly inversely correlated with the returns from a short position in Coca-Cola's stock, $\rho_{\text{Long, Short}} = -1$. The covariance and the correlation statistics play an important role in Markowitz portfolio analysis.

Markowitz Portfolio Analysis with a Two-Asset Portfolio

Eqn. 14-5 is a simple 2×2 matrix taken from the upper-left corner of the $N \times N$ matrix in Eqn. 14-3b. Eqn. 14-5 defines the standard deviation of returns for a portfolio of two common stocks issued by the Admiralty (A) and Bathurst (B) Corporations that were introduced in Table 14-3.

$$\sigma_p = \sqrt{x_A^2 \sigma_A^2 + x_B^2 \sigma_B^2 + 2x_A x_B \sigma_{AB}} \tag{14-5}$$

Substituting $\sigma_{AB} = \sigma_A \sigma_B \rho_{AB}$ from Eqn. 14-4 into Eqn. 14-5 yields 14-6. Eqn. 14-6 shows how the correlation between the returns from Admiralty and from Bathurst affect the portfolio's risk, σ_p.

$$\sigma_p = \sqrt{x_A^2 \sigma_A^2 + x_B^2 \sigma_B^2 + 2x_A x_B \sigma_A \sigma_B \rho_{AB}} \tag{14-6}$$

Taking Admiralty and Bathurst stocks' standard deviations from Table 14-3 and substituting them into Eqn. 14-6 yields:

$$\sigma_p = \sqrt{x_A^2(0.2)^2 + x_B^2(0.4)^2 + 2x_A x_B(0.2)(0.4)\rho_{AB}}$$

$$= \sqrt{x_A^2(0.04) + x_B^2(0.16) + 0.16 x_A x_B \rho_{AB}} \tag{14-6a}$$

Figure 14-2A, B, C, and D are graphs in σ-$E(r)$ space (the two-dimensional risk-return plane) of Admiralty's and Bathurst's stocks and the portfolios that can be formed from these two stocks. The graphs in Figures 14-2A, B, and C differ because three different values were used for the correlation coefficient between the stocks, $\rho_{AB} = +1, 0,$ and -1. Figure 14-2D is simply a combination of Figures 14-2A, B, and C. These four graphs were prepared by plotting the risk and return of the various portfolios composed of Admiralty and Bathurst stocks for all the positive weights ($x_A > 0$ and $x_B > 0$) that sum to unity ($x_A + x_B = 1$) and for three different values of the correlation coefficient ($\rho_{AB} = +1, 0,$ and -1).

To get a clear sense of what is represented in each of the panels of Figure 14-2, let us verify a few of the points in the graphs by substituting some numbers into Eqns. 14-2a and 14-6 and calculating the portfolio's expected return and risk. For example, the portfolio that has $x_A = \frac{2}{3}$ and $x_B = \frac{1}{3}$ has an expected return of 8.33%, as shown above in Eqn. 14-2c. However, the risk of the portfolio with $x_A = \frac{2}{3}$ and $x_B = \frac{1}{3}$ varies directly with the value of the correlation coefficient, ρ_{AB}, as shown in Eqn. 14-6b below.

$$\sigma_p = \sqrt{x_A^2 \sigma_A^2 + x_B^2 \sigma_B^2 + 2x_A x_B \sigma_A \sigma_B \rho_{AB}} \tag{14-6}$$

$$= \sqrt{\left(\tfrac{2}{3}\right)^2(0.2)^2 + \left(\tfrac{1}{3}\right)^2(0.4)^2 + 2\left(\tfrac{2}{3}\right)\left(\tfrac{1}{3}\right)(0.2)(0.4)\rho_{AB}}$$

$$= \sqrt{0.0175 + 0.0175 + 0.035\rho_{AB}}$$

$$= \sqrt{0.035 + 0.035\rho_{AB}} \tag{14-6b}$$

The following discussion shows how to insert different values of the correlation coefficient ($\rho_{AB} = +1, 0,$ and -1) into Eqn. 14-6b to compute different standard deviations for the portfolio.

Perfectly Positively Correlated Returns in Figure 14-2A

Suppose the correlation coefficient between the rates of return from Admiralty's and Bathurst's stocks is positive unity ($\rho_{AB} = +1$)—the maximum value for any correlation. In this case, we get the linear σ-$E(r)$ relationship in Figure 14-2A. This straight dashed line between the risk and return of assets A and B is derived by first setting ρ_{AB} in the portfolio risk formula to positive unity.

$$\sigma_p = \sqrt{x_A^2 \sigma_A^2 + x_B^2 \sigma_B^2 + 2x_A x_B \sigma_A \sigma_B \rho_{AB}} \tag{14-6}$$

$$= \sqrt{x_A^2(0.2)^2 + x_B^2(0.4)^2 + 2x_A x_B(0.2)(0.4)(+1)}$$

$$= \sqrt{x_A^2(0.04) + x_B^2(0.16) + x_A x_B(0.16)} \tag{14-6c}$$

FIGURE 14-2   Portfolio Analysis with Two Assets that are: (A) perfectly positively correlated, (B) zero correlated, (C) perfectly negatively correlated, and (D) assumed to have three different correlations.

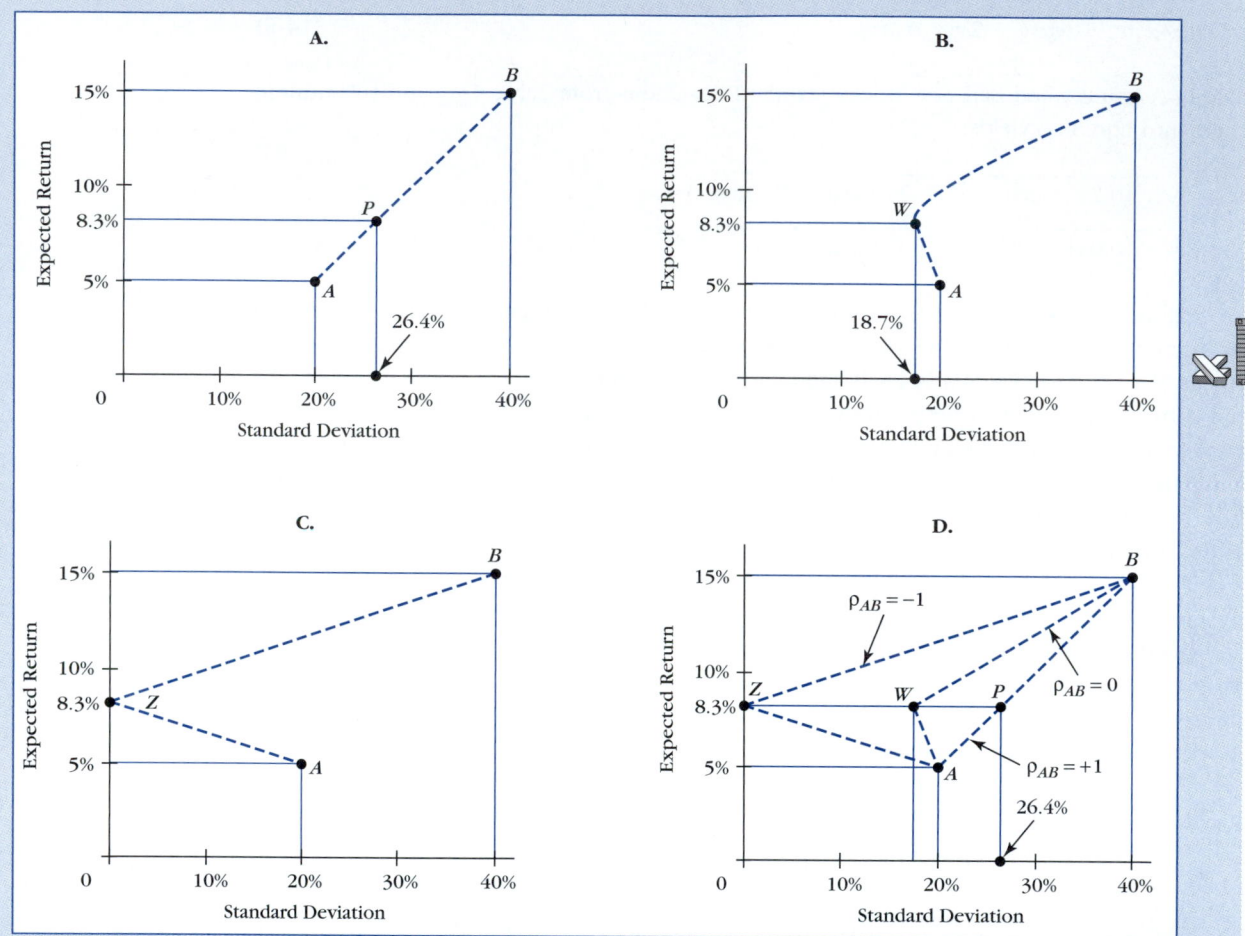

(A) Two assets that are perfectly positively correlated may be combined to form portfolios that lie on the *straight line* APB in risk-return space. (B) If assets A and B are zero correlated they will form portfolios that lie along the *curve* AWB in [σ, $E(r)$] space. (C) Two assets that are perfectly negatively correlated may be combined to form portfolios along two line segments AZ and BZ that come together to form a zero risk portfolio at point Z. (D) Panels (A), (B), and (C) are combined.

Next the values of the two assets' weights are varied inversely from zero to one ($0 < x < +1$) in such a manner that they always sum to positive unity ($x_A + x_B = 1$). Five of the infinite number of pairs are listed below.

Five investment decisions: $(x_A, x_B) = (.2, .8), (.4, .6), (.5, .5), (.6, .4), (.8, .2)$

Varying the weights in this manner allows us to evaluate a range of investment decisions. Finally, the pairs of positive values for x_A and x_B that sum to 1 are substituted into the portfolio risk formula, Eqn. 14-6c, and the portfolio return formula, Eqn. 14-2a. For instance, the portfolio at point P in Figures 14-2A and D has $\rho_{AB} = +1$, $x_A = \frac{2}{3}$ and $x_B = \frac{1}{3}$, an expected return of 8.33%, and a standard deviation of 26.4%. The infinite number of risk and return statistics for the 2-asset portfolio that are derived in this manner trace out the straight dashed line in Figure 14-2A. Crunch some numbers to convince yourself the line in Figure 14-2A should be a perfectly straight line.

Uncorrelated Assets in Figure 14-2B

If the rates of return are zero-correlated, substantial risk reduction benefits can be obtained from diversifying between two stocks. To see this, look at what happens to every version of portfolio risk Eqn. 14-6 when the correlation equals zero, $\rho_{AB} = 0$. The last quantity on the right-hand side of Eqn. 14-6 becomes zero when ρ_{AB} equals zero. This reduces the portfolio's risk level below what it was when this correlation was a positive value.

Uncorrelated returns generate the results illustrated in Figures 14-2B and D. For instance, the portfolio at point W in Figure 14-2B and D has $\rho_{AB} = 0, x_A = \frac{2}{3}$ and $x_B = \frac{1}{3}$, an expected return of 8.33%, and a standard deviation of 18.7%. The portfolio's expected return is unaffected by changing the correlation between assets: This is because ρ_{AB} is not a variable in the portfolio's return formula, Eqn. 14-2a.

$$E(r_p) = x_A E(r_A) + x_B E(r_B) \tag{14-2a}$$

All differences between the portfolios with $\rho_{AB} = +1.0$ and the portfolios with $\rho_{AB} = 0$ are risk differences arising in Eqn. 14-6b. A look at Figure 14-2D shows that portfolios with $\rho_{AB} = 0$ have less risk at every level of expected return than the same portfolios with $\rho_{AB} = +1$.

The correlation coefficients in Table 11-7 in Chapter 11 (page 310) show that common stock price indexes and bond price indexes tend to be uncorrelated. Table 11-15 in Chapter 11 (page 326) displays correlation coefficients between foreign stock market indexes that are low. Some commodity price indexes and foreign exchange rates in the chapters ahead also have low correlations. Substantial risk reductions are available to investors that diversify across these uncorrelated assets.

Perfectly Negatively Correlated Returns in Figure 14-2c

The lowest possible value for a correlation coefficient is -1. When the correlation coefficient in portfolio risk Eqn. 14-6b reaches -1, the last term on the right of the equation assumes its maximum negative value. For certain weights, the portfolio's risk can be reduced to zero when $\rho_{AB} = -1$. For example, for the portfolios created from the Bathurst and Admiralty stocks, Figures 14-2C and D shows that at point Z, where $x_A = \frac{2}{3}, x_B = \frac{1}{3}$, and $\rho_{AB} = -1$, the portfolio's risk falls to zero. For all other weights the portfolio's risk is above zero. Figure 14-2D demonstrates that portfolio risk is always at its lowest level over all portfolio weights when the correlation is at its minimum value of $\rho_{AB} = -1$.

It is difficult to see how two risky assets like Admiralty and Bathurst can be combined in precise proportions to form a *riskless* portfolio like the one at point Z in Figures 14-2C and D. Reconsider the ink manufacturers example in Table 14-2, it demonstrates how two assets that are perfectly negatively correlated can be combined to reduce risk to zero. As a result of the assets' perfect inverse movements, whatever losses one asset has are exactly offset by equal gains from the other asset. That leaves the portfolio with zero variability or return, or riskless.

Portfolio Analysis Using Markowitz Diversification

Figure 14-2D graphically combines Figures 14-2A, B, and C. Summarizing, Figures 14-2A and D show that at point P where $x_A = \frac{2}{3}$ and $x_B = \frac{1}{3}$, for a correlation of $\rho_{AB} = +1$, the portfolio's total risk is $\sigma_p = \sqrt{0.07} = 26.4\%$.

Let us consider two other portfolios that have $x_A = \frac{2}{3}$ and $x_B = \frac{1}{3}$. Figures 14-2B and D illustrate that if $\rho_{AB} = 0$, then $\sigma_p = \sqrt{0.035} = 18.7\%$ at point W. Figures 14-2C and D show that when $\rho_{AB} = -1$ then $\sigma_p = \sqrt{0} = 0$ at point Z.

Figure 14-2D plots all the points (such as P, W, and Z from Figures 14-2A, B, and C) together. Figure 14-2D shows that Markowitz diversification can reduce a portfolio's risk below the undiversifiable level if the portfolio's manager can find securities whose rates of return have low enough correlations.

Markowitz Portfolio Analysis with More than Two Assets (N > 2)

Markowitz portfolio analysis is a scientific way to manage a diversified portfolio. The Markowitz model can analyze the risk and return of many different securities simultaneously, usually via computer. Only two things limit the number of assets analyzed: the size of the computer and the number of securities for which the risk and return statistics are available. Because it is impossible to draw graphs that have more than three dimensions, it is impossible to illustrate portfolio analysis process graphically when more than three assets are analyzed.

Markowitz portfolio analysis is a mathematics problem requiring that different mathematical equations be solved simultaneously. This can be done on a large scale by using a computer program that does quadratic programming. **Quadratic programming (QP)** is a mathematical procedure that minimizes the portfolio's risk at each level of portfolio return.[4] The portfolio's risk is analyzed using the quadratic equation at Eqn. 14-3. Some people that use a computer program to do QP call the program the *optimizer*.

Financial Interior Decorating

Some investment counselors who are not analytical are *financial interior decorators*. They design portfolios of securities to match the investors' personalities. Thus, an elderly gentleman who is naive about financial matters and depends on the income from a modest investment might be advised to invest in low-risk assets like high-grade bonds and public utility stocks, assuming this would minimize his risk. A financial interior decorator would likely give little consideration to the correlation between the assets. However, a Markowitz portfolio analyst might advise the elderly fellow to invest in high-risk, high-return securities that were uncorrelated—to minimize risk and yet get a high rate of return. In spite of the intuitive appeal of the financial interior decorating approach to portfolio management, Markowitz portfolio analysis reveals the fallacy of this unscientific practice.

RETHINKING THE FIRST MARKOWITZ CONCEPT

Let's take another look at Markowitz's Rule One and try to deduce more important implications from Eqn. 14-1.

Negative Weights Represent Short Sales

All the investment opportunities illustrated in Figure 14-2 were computed using *nonnegative weights*, meaning the weights (the x's) can have only positive or zero values. Negative weights are permissible in Markowitz portfolio analysis, as long as they do not violate Markowitz Rule One, Eqn. 14-1, which says all the weights must sum to $+1$ (or 100%).

A negative weight is: $x < 0$. Consider three 2-asset portfolios with a negative weight: $(x_A, x_B) = (1.2, -.2), (-.6, 1.6), (2.5, -1.5)$. When negative weights are allowed to enter the analysis, additional investment opportunities illustrated in Figure 14-3 become feasible. Portfolios with negative weights are called **leveraged portfolios** or *borrowing portfolios*.

The leveraged portfolio possibility lines in Figure 14-3 represent portfolios that include negative weights. The weights in Admiralty (A) and Bathurst (B) corresponding to possible portfolios are graphed along the two vertical lines at the right-hand side of Figure 14-3.

Two economic interpretations of negative weights are possible. First, a negative weight can be used to represent the short sale of a security. Second, a negative weight may indicate that the investor created a leveraged (borrowing, margined) position by printing and selling (issuing) a security that has the same risk and return statistics as the asset that has the negative weight.* Figure 14-3 indicates that the leverage is favorable to the investor's interests when low-return asset *A* is issued (or sold short) to obtain funds to finance a larger position in high-return asset *B*. The leverage is unfavorable when the high-return asset *B* is issued (or sold short) to obtain funds to finance a larger position in the low-return asset *A*. Table 14-4 shows the weights for some portfolios illustrated in Figure 14-3.

FIGURE 14-3   Portfolio Analysis of Opportunities from Admiralty and Bathurst with Negative Weights Allowed

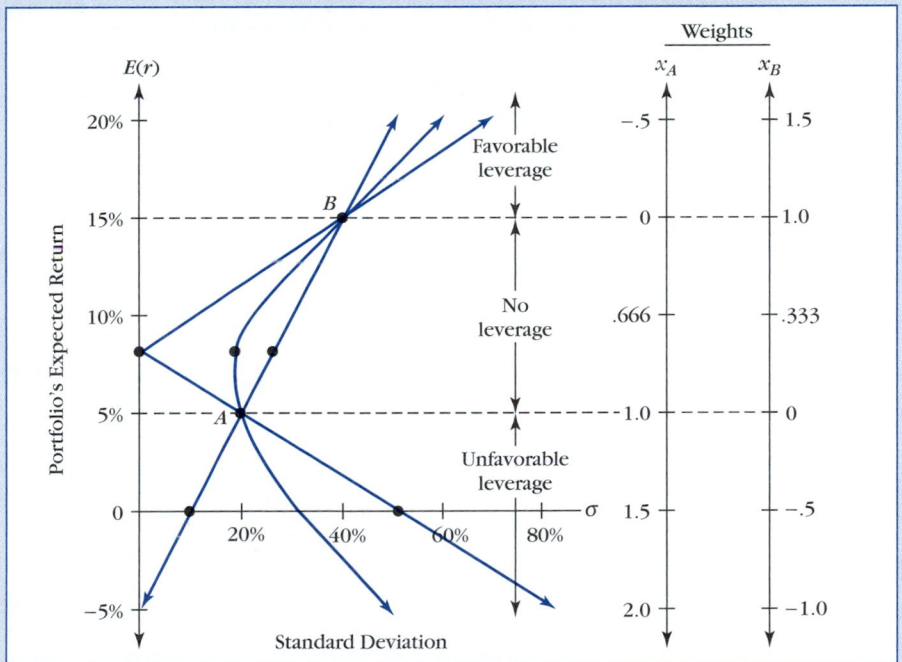

Either x_A or x_B may assume a negative value. But the two weights must always sum to 1, $\sum_{i=1}^{2} x_i = 1$. Any portfolio that contains a negative weight is a leveraged (borrowing) portfolio. Admitting negative weights into the solutions extends the efficient frontiers.

---

* Most short sellers do not get the use of the proceeds paid by the buyer. The short seller's brokerage house typically holds the proceeds from short sales and also requires the short seller to make an *initial margin deposit*. When the short seller closes out the short position and returns the borrowed securities to their lender/owner, the brokerage returns the short seller's margin money plus the proceeds from the short sale. The arrangements of every short sale vary with the short seller's position. When stock exchange specialists, brokerage houses, and investment bankers sell short, they, unlike the nonprofessional investors, get to keep the cash proceeds from their short sales.

TABLE 14-4 Two-Asset Portfolio Analysis with Negative Weights Permitted

(A) Portfolio Possibilities Analyzed for a Perfect Positive Correlation, $\rho_{AB} = +1$

Inputs from Assets A and B		Output For Efficient Portfolios			
Expected Return A	0.05 = 5%	Weight in A	Weight in B	Portfolio Return	Portfolio σ
Expected Return B	0.15 = 15%	1.3	−0.3	2%	14.000
Standard Deviation A	0.2 = 20%	1.1	−.1	4%	18.000
Standard Deviation B	0.4 = 40%	1.0	0	5%	20.000
Correlation, ρ_{AB}	+1.0	.9	.1	6%	22.000
		.7	.3	8%	26.000
		.666	.333	8.3%	26.600
		.5	.5	10%	30.000
		.3	.7	12%	34.000
		.1	.9	14%	38.000
		0	1.0	15%	40.000
		−.1	1.1	16%	42.000
		−.3	1.3	18%	46.000

(B) Portfolio Possibilities Analyzed for Uncorrelated Assets, $\rho_{AB} = 0$

Inputs from Assets A and B		Output for Efficient Portfolios			
Expected Return A	0.05 = 5%	Weight in A	Weight in B	Portfolio Return	Portfolio σ
Expected Return B	0.15 = 15%	1.3	−0.3	2%	28.600
Standard Deviation A	0.2 = 20%	1.1	−0.1	4%	22.300
Standard Deviation B	0.4 = 40%	1.0	0.0	5%	20.000
Correlation, ρ_{AB}	0	.9	.1	6%	18.439
		.7	.3	8%	18.439
		.666	.333	8.3%	18.800
		.5	.5	10%	22.361
		.3	.7	12%	28.636
		.1	.9	14%	36.056
		0	1.0	15%	40.000
		−.1	1.1	16%	44.000
		−.3	1.3	18%	52.300

Some pension funds, some mutual funds, some trust accounts at banks, and some endowment funds are legally prohibited from borrowing or short selling. Essentially, many of the largest investors in the world are not permitted to borrow or sell short. But there are no such prohibitions against negative weights for most individual investors, closed-end funds, and hedge funds; nothing forbids them from borrowing or short selling.

Allowing negative weights to enter portfolio analysis extends the portfolio possibility lines illustrated in Figures 14-2A, B, C, and D. Figure 14-3 has longer lines than Figure 14-2;

(C) Portfolio Possibilities Analyzed for a Perfect Inverse Correlation, $\rho_{AB} = -1$

Inputs from Assets A and B		Output for Efficient Portfolios			
		Weight in A	Weight in B	Portfolio Return	Portfolio σ
Expected Return A	0.05 = 5%	1.3	−0.3	2%	38.000
Expected Return B	0.15 = 15%	1.1	−.1	4%	26.000
Standard Deviation A	0.2 = 20%	1.0	0	5%	20.000
Standard Deviation B	0.4 = 40%	.9	.1	6%	14.000
Correlation, ρ_{AB}	−1	.7	.3	8%	2.000
		.666	.333	8.3%	0.0
		.5	.5	10%	10.000
		.3	.7	12%	22.000
		.1	.9	14%	34.000
		0	1.0	15%	40.000
		−.1	1.1	16%	46.000
		−.3	1.3	18%	58.000

these longer lines represent additional investment opportunities that become available when borrowing and/or short selling are permitted.

The Investment Opportunities Are Represented by Convex Curves

Instead of thinking about $N = 2$ assets, consider $N = 20$ or $N = 2,000$. The risk and return of all stocks, bonds, oil paintings, commodity futures, foreign exchange, gold, jewels, homes, college degrees (human capital), and other individual assets can be graphically represented by dots like those in Figure 14-4.

The quarter-moon-shaped *opportunity set* in Figure 14-4 contains individual assets represented by dots below and to the right of the efficient frontier. The Markowitz efficient frontier is represented by the blue curve from E to F on the upper-left side of the quarter-moon-shaped opportunity set. Only portfolios attain the efficient frontier, because only portfolios benefit from the risk-reducing benefits of diversification. Only portfolio F in Figure 14-4 is likely to be a single-asset efficient portfolio. The quarter-moon-shaped opportunity set in Figure 14-4 represents all the investment opportunities analyzed so far in this chapter.

Note that the quarter-moon-shaped opportunity set in Figure 14-4 is constructed from curves that are all convex toward the $E(r)$ axis. This is because all assets we have considered so far are assumed to have correlation coefficients between +1 and −1. As shown in Figures 14-2 and 14-3, correlations between +1 and −1 result in a locus of portfolios that trace a curve that is convex to the $E(r)$ axis in σ-$E(r)$ space. Figures 14-2 and 14-3 also show that only perfectly positively correlated ($\rho = +1$) assets will generate linear combinations of risk and return; and under no circumstances will a portfolio possibility locus ever curve away from the $E(r)$ axis in σ-$E(r)$ space.[5]

Dominant portfolios are more desirable than dominated (less efficient) portfolios because dominant portfolios have higher rates of return at the selected risk level. Portfolios below the efficient frontier are dominated portfolios. Markowitz diversification generates portfolios that dominate portfolios derived with simple diversification. If Markowitz diversification

FIGURE 14-4   Investment Opportunities Have an Efficient Frontier
                  That Is Convex

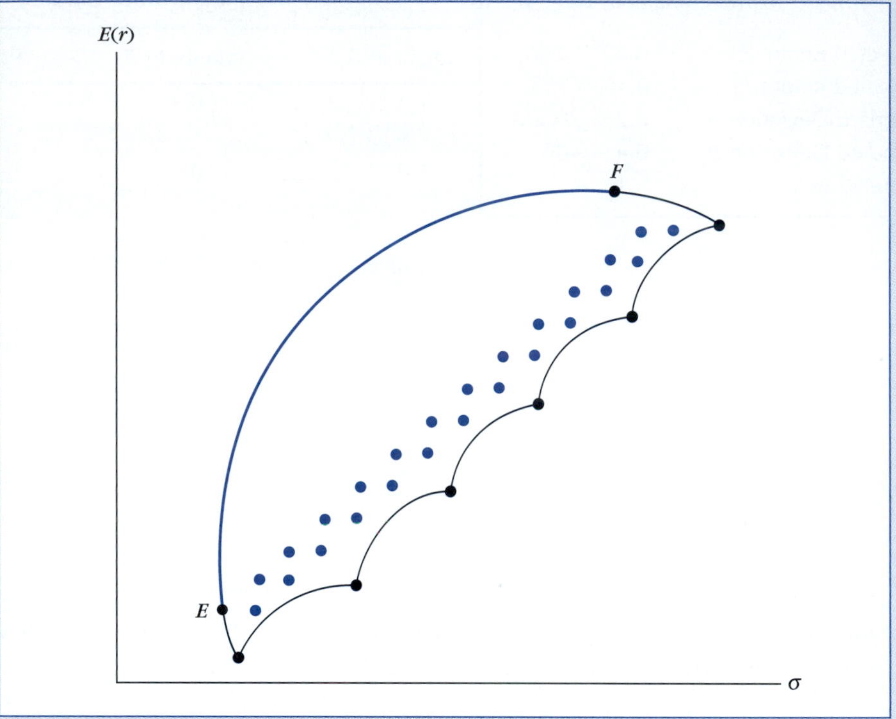

Markowitz portfolio analysis analyzes the risk, return, and covariance of individual assets (the dots) and computes an efficient frontier (curve *EF*) that has the maximum return in every risk-class and the minimum risk at every level of return.

is applied to all assets in the world, the dominant efficient set of portfolios that results will form an efficient frontier curve like the one from *E* to *F* in Figure 14-4.*

Selling Short Creates Valuable Investment Opportunities

If *N* securities are investment candidates for a portfolio, then the number of investment candidates can be doubled to become 2*N* by considering buying long and, at the same time, selling short the same *N* securities. The *N* short positions (represented by negative weights) are opportunities that are negatively correlated with their associated long positions (represented by positive weights). The increased risk-reduction possibilities made available by these negatively correlated investments generates new investments that dominate those available without short sales.

Including short sales not only allows the creation of a more dominant investments, but it also redefines the *minimum variance portfolio* on the efficient frontier at point *E* in Figure 14-4. Consider combining long and short positions of equal market value in one particular asset. The result of combining these two offsetting positions can be seen by adding the one-period rates of return formulas for a long and a short position.

---

*   Appendix B in Chapter 14 shows how to perform mathematical portfolio analysis to find the efficient frontier.

FIGURE 14-5   Contrasting the Efficient Frontier Attainable with and Without Short Sales

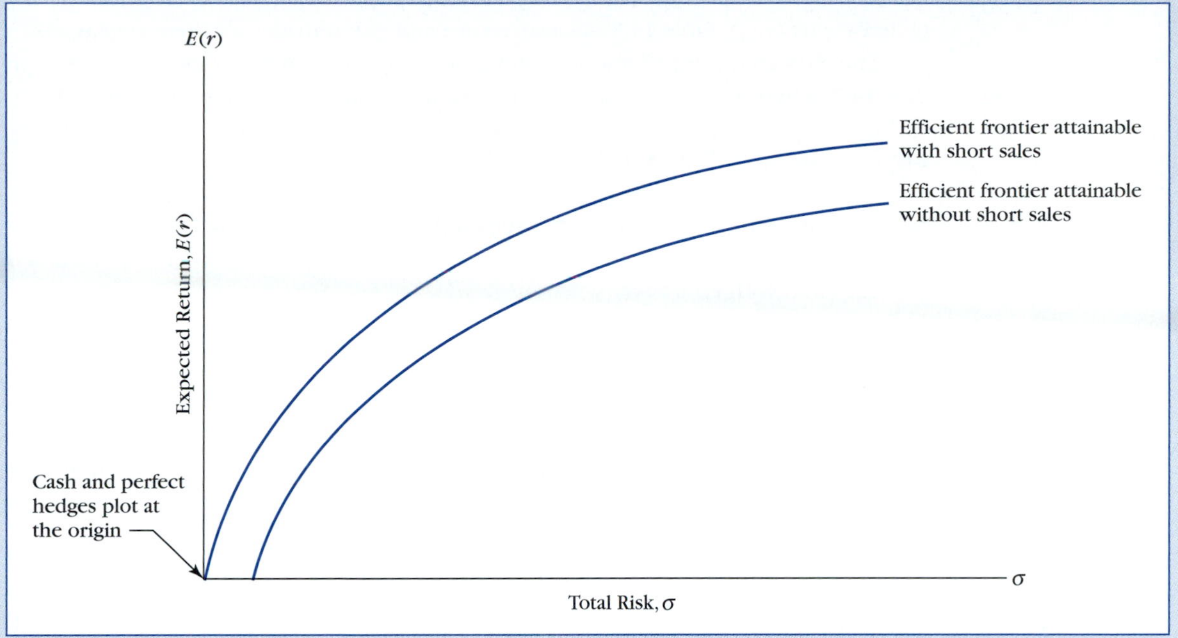

Assets with negative weights can be interpreted to be either assets that were sold short or assets that were issued. Allowing every asset to have both a positive weight (long position) and a negative weight (short position) doubles the number of assets being analyzed and improves the efficient frontier that is possible.

Long position's return +	**Short position's return =**	**Perfect hedge**
$r_L = \dfrac{P_1 - P_0 + CF}{P_0}$	$r_S = \dfrac{P_0 - P_1 - CF}{P_1}$	$r_L + r_S = 0$

As discussed in Chapter 3, combining long and short positions of equal value in the same asset creates a perfect hedge that has zero expected return and zero risk. The zero-return and zero-risk position attained via a perfect hedge is equivalent to holding cash or, alternatively, having no position at all. This position is plotted at the origin in $\sigma\text{-}E(r)$ space. Figure 14-5 shows that this zero-variance-portfolio and the rest of the efficient frontier attainable with short sales dominates the efficient frontier attainable without short sales.

MARKOWITZ CONCEPT FIVE: THE ASSET ALLOCATION LINE

This section extends the Markowitz portfolio models introduced in Figures 14-2 and extended in Figures 14-4 and 14-5 by including additional economic opportunities: the ability to lend and borrow at a risk-free rate of interest (RFR).[6] As the phrase "risk-free rate" suggests, the RFR has zero variance, $VAR(RFR) = 0$. A U. S. Treasury bill that is held to maturity, or, an FDIC-insured savings deposit are riskless assets.

Return and Risk Formulas That Are Linear

Consider a 2-asset portfolio containing 1 asset paying the risk-free rate, *RFR*, and 1 risky asset Q that yields $E(r_Q)$. Table 14-5 suggests return and risk statistics for these two assets.

The expected return for a portfolio containing the two assets in Table 14-5 is given by Eqn. 14-7, where x_Q is the weight of the portfolio's funds invested in risky asset Q.

$$E(r_p) = x_Q E(r_Q) + (1 - x_Q)RFR \qquad (14\text{-}7)$$

Solving Eqn. 14-1 for $x_{RFR} = (1 - x_Q)$ shows the proportion invested at the risk-free rate.

The variance of a 2-asset portfolio composed of risky asset Q and the risk-free asset can be computed with Eqn. 14-8:

$$\text{Var}(r_p) = x_Q^2 \sigma_Q^2 + x_{RFR}^2 \sigma_{RFR}^2 + 2x_Q x_{RFR} \sigma_{Q,RFR}$$
$$= x_Q^2 \sigma_Q^2 + 0 + 0 \quad \text{since } VAR(RFR) = COV(Q,RFR) = 0 \qquad (14\text{-}8)$$

Simplifying Eqn. 14-8 and taking its square root reduces the 2-asset portfolio's risk formula to a simple multiple of the standard deviation of the risky asset.

$$\sigma_p = x_Q \sigma_Q \qquad (14\text{-}9)$$

$$x_Q = \sigma_p / \sigma_Q \qquad (14\text{-}9a)$$

Since Eqns. 14-7 and 14-9 are both linear equations, this means that all portfolios made up of a risky asset like asset Q and a risk-free asset must form straight lines of investment opportunities in σ-$E(r)$ space, as shown in Figure 14-6. The set of investment opportunities in Figure 14-6 is called an **Asset Allocation Line** (**AAL**). The first step in graphically determining the AAL is to solve Eqn. 14-9 for $x_Q = \sigma_p / \sigma_Q$. Next, substitute $x_Q = \sigma_p / \sigma_Q$ into Eqn. 14-7:

$$E(r_p) = x_Q E(r_Q) + (1 - x_Q)RFR \qquad (14\text{-}7)$$

$$= (\sigma_p / \sigma_Q)E(r_Q) + [1 - (\sigma_p / \sigma_Q)]RFR \qquad (14\text{-}7a)$$

$$= RFR + (\sigma_p / \sigma_Q)[E(r_Q) - RFR] \qquad (14\text{-}7b)$$

$$= RFR + \{[E(r_Q) - RFR]/\sigma_Q\}\sigma_p \qquad (14\text{-}10)$$

Eqn. 14-10 defines the general form of the AAL. Substituting the statistical values from Table 14-5 into Eqn. 14-10 yields the AAL shown at Eqn. 14-10a:

$$E(r_p) = RFR + \{[E(r_Q) - RFR]/\sigma_Q\}\sigma_p \qquad (14\text{-}10)$$

$$= 5\% + \{[10\% - 5\%]/10\%\}\sigma_p = 5\% + .5\sigma_p \qquad (14\text{-}10a)$$

TABLE 14-5 Parameters for Two Possible Investments

Asset	Expected Return	Standard Deviation	Variance, *VAR(r)*
Risky asset Q	10%	10%	100
Risk-free asset	RFR = 5%	Zero	Zero

FIGURE 14-6   Investing in Different Combinations of Risky Asset Q and the Risk-Free Rate of Interest Trace Out the Asset Allocation Line (AAL)

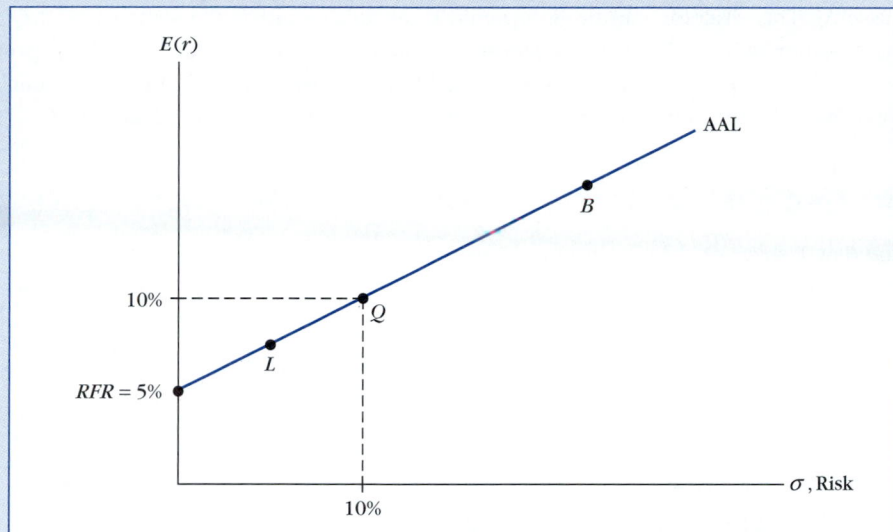

Lending (investing) some money at the risk-free rate (RFR) of 5% and investing the rest in risky asset Q creates the lending portfolio L. Borrowing at RFR = 5% to buy asset Q creates the borrowing portfolio B. Investments L, Q, and B are only three of an infinite number of investment opportunities that lie along the AAL.

Figure 14-6 depicts Eqn. 14-10a; it shows the investment opportunities based on the 2-asset portfolios made up of the risk-free asset and risky asset Q. Portfolios L, Q, and B are three of the infinite number of investment opportunities on the AAL in Figure 14-6. Other AALs can be formed by changing the values of the risk-free rate, and/or the expected return from asset Q, and/or the standard deviation of asset Q listed in Table 14-5.

The AAL is more than a mathematical equation. Financial engineers use Eqns. 14-7, 14-9, and 14-10 to make financial plans and to analyze borrowing and lending opportunities.

Borrowing and Lending Portfolios Pinpointed on the AAL

When the weight of the investment in risky asset Q is positive but less than one, $0 < x_Q < 1$, the remainder, x_{RFR} [$= (1-x_Q) > 0$], of the portfolio's funds are invested in the riskless asset. Any portfolio that has some of its funds invested at the RFR is called a **lending portfolio** because the investor lent funds at the risk-free rate. Point L on the AAL in Figure 14-6, for instance, represents a lending portfolio that has half, $x_{RFR} = \frac{1}{2}$, of its funds lent at the RFR and the other half, $x_Q = \frac{1}{2}$, invested in risky asset Q.

Next, suppose it is possible to go to the bank and either (1) deposit money to earn an interest rate of *RFR,* or (2) borrow and pay the interest rate RFR. Borrowing at the rate *RFR* is represented by a negative weight on the RFR investment ($x_{RFR} < 0$). When x_{RFR} is negative $x_Q > 1$, because portfolio analysis is based on Markowitz Rule One, that the weights always sum to one. Portfolios that have negative values for x_{RFR} and values for x_Q that exceed 1 are called **borrowing portfolios,** or **leveraged portfolios,** or **margined portfolios.** Figure 14-6 illustrates a borrower's position at point B on the AAL.

Suppose portfolio B in Figure 14-6 has $x_{RFR} = -1$ and $x_Q = 2$. The $x_{RFR} = -1 = -100\%$ means the investor borrowed an amount equal to 100% of the portfolio's initial equity investment at an interest rate of RFR. These borrowed funds were combined with the original equity and used to invest an amount equal to $x_Q = 2 = 200\%$ of the portfolio's initial equity value in risky asset Q. This situation can be interpreted to mean that either (1) some of asset Q was purchased on margin, or (2) a riskless debt security paying an interest rate of *RFR* was printed and sold and the bond issue proceeds were used to buy more of asset Q. In either event, this portfolio that is financed with borrowed money is illustrated at point *B* in Figure 14-6.

EXAMPLE | **COMPUTING THE UNDERLYING BORROWING PORTFOLIO B IN FIGURE 14-6**

Assume that 1 share of risky asset Q in Figure 14-6 costs $100 and offers a 50-50 chance of returning either $100 or $120. The following calculations show that the expected return for asset Q is 10%.

$$E(r_Q) = \sum_{i=1}^{2} p_i r_i = p_1 r_1 + p_2 r_2$$

$$= .5\left(\frac{\$100 - \$100}{\$100}\right) + .5\left(\frac{\$120 - \$100}{\$100}\right)$$

$$= .5(0) + .5(20\%)$$

$$= 0 + 10\% = 10\%$$

The standard deviation of returns from portfolio Q is 10%.

$$\sigma_Q = \sqrt{\sum p_i [r_i - E(r)]^2}$$

$$= \sqrt{.5(0 - 0.1)^2 + .5(0.2 - 0.1)^2}$$

$$= \sqrt{.5(0.01) + .5(0.01)}$$

$$= \sqrt{0.01} = 0.1 = 10\%$$

Consider buying portfolio Q with borrowed money. If an investor borrows $100 at *RFR* = 5% and uses that borrowed money to pay $100 for a second share of Q, then $x_Q = 2$ and $x_{RFR} = -1$. When borrowed money is used the investor has a 50-50 chance of receiving $95 or $135 on the $100 of equity that was originally invested, as shown in Table 14-6.

TABLE 14-6 Analysis of Two Possible Investment Outcomes for Asset Q

	Bad	*Good*
Original equity	$100	$100
Principal amount borrowed at 5%	100	100
Total amount invested in *Q*	$200	$200
Return on two shares of *Q*	$200	$240
Repayment of loan principal	(100)	(100)
Payment of interest of 5%	(5)	(5)
Net return on original equity	$95	$135
Probabilities of outcomes	$p_{Bad} = 0.5$	$p_{Good} = 0.5$

The following computations show that borrowing can be used to leverage the expected return on asset Q out to point B in Figure 14-6 is 15%.

$$E(r_B) = \sum_{i=1}^{2} p_i r_i = p_1 r_1 + p_2 r_2$$

$$= .5\left(\frac{\$95 - \$100}{\$100}\right) + .5\left(\frac{\$135 - \$100}{\$100}\right)$$

$$= .5(-5\%) + .5(35\%)$$

$$= -2.5\% + 17.5\% = 15\%$$

The standard deviation of returns of borrowing portfolio B is 20%:

$$\sigma_B = \sqrt{\sum p_i [r_i - E(r)]^2}$$

$$= \sqrt{.5(-5\% - 15\%)^2 + .5(35\% - 15\%)^2}$$

$$= \sqrt{.5(-20\%)^2 + .5(20\%)^2}$$

$$= \sqrt{.5(.04) + .5(.04)}$$

$$= \sqrt{.02 + .02}$$

$$= \sqrt{.04} = .2 = 20\%$$

The results of the preceding calculations are illustrated in Figure 14-6 as portfolios Q and B on the AAL. The practicality of Eqns. 14-7, 14-9, and 14-10 may be checked by substituting the values from this numerical example into them.

The Slope of the AAL Provides an Index of Investment Desirability

The slope, S, of a line equals the units of vertical rise along the line divided by the units of horizontal run corresponding to that rise.

$$S = \frac{\text{Units of vertical rise}}{\text{Units of horizontal run}} = \text{Slope of a straight line}$$

The slope of the AAL in Figure 14-6 is defined below in terms of a hypothetical asset i that lies somewhere on the AAL.

$$S_{AAL} = \frac{E(r_i) - RFR}{\sigma_i} = \frac{\text{Risk premium for asset } i}{\text{Risk from asset } i} = S_i \qquad (14\text{-}11)$$

Consider an economic interpretation for the mathematical slope of the AAL. Eqn. 14-11 shows the slope equals the risk premium for asset i, $[E(r_i) - RFR]$, divided by the units of risk for the asset i, σ_i, where i could be any asset on the AAL. Evaluating Eqn. 14-11 at the point where asset Q lies on the AAL yields:

$$S_{AAL} = \frac{E(r_Q) - RFR}{\sigma_Q} = \frac{10\% - 5\%}{10\%} = \frac{5\%}{10\%} = S_Q = 0.5 \text{ at point } Q$$

Because the slope of any straight line is the same at every point on the line, the slope of the AAL measured at the borrowing (B) portfolio is also .5:

$$S_{AAL} = \frac{E(r_B) - RFR}{\sigma_B} = \frac{10\% - 5\%}{10\%} = \frac{5\%}{10\%} = 0.5 = S_B \; at \; point \; B$$

STUDY CHECK

THE SLOPE OF THE AAL

QUESTION: What is the slope of the straight line through the lending portfolio at point L in Figure 14-6?

ANSWER: Since the slope of any straight line is the same at every point on the line, the slope at point L is the same as the slope at points Q and B in Figure 14-6. Slope$_L$ = Slope$_B$ = Slope$_Q$ = .5.

William Sharpe defined the slope of Eqn. 14-11 to be the **reward-to-variability ratio** because the numerator measures the units of reward for taking the risk in the denominator.[7] Thus, a slope of .5 means that by moving out further along the AAL an investor can gain one-half unit of risk premium for each unit of (standard deviation) risk the investor assumes. The slope (reward-to-variability ratio) of a line through an investment can be interpreted as an *index of desirability* for that asset. An investment becomes more desirable as the steepness (slope) of its AAL increases.

Combining the AAL with Markowitz's Efficient Frontier

Combining the individual investments and the efficient frontier from Figures 14-4 and 14-5 with the AAL model in Figure 14-6 will enable us to graphically rank the desirability of investment alternatives. For example, Figure 14-7 shows three AALs that were generated by drawing three straight lines from the risk-free asset to the three risky assets K, J, and M.

The computations for the slopes of the AALs to assets K, J, and M are ranked below.

$$\frac{E(r_M) - RFR}{\sigma_M} = \frac{15\% - 5\%}{10\%} = .5 > \frac{E(r_J) - RFR}{\sigma_J} = \frac{20\% - 5\%}{45\%} = .33 > \frac{E(r_K) - RFR}{\sigma_K} = \frac{3\% - 5\%}{8\%} = -.25$$

The slopes of the three AALs are: $(S_M = \frac{1}{2}) > (S_J = \frac{1}{3}) > (S_K = -\frac{1}{4})$. Asset M is the most desirable, even though asset J has a higher rate of return, because M has the highest *risk-adjusted return* (slope, index of desirability). Asset K is the least desirable of the three; it has the smallest slope (a negative slope).

The logic of this ranking mechanism can be extended to rank the desirability of any number of different investment candidates—even if they are all in different risk classes. This ability to rank investments is valuable when selecting the most desirable investments from numerous candidates and in evaluating the performance of mutual funds and other possible investments.

Figure 14-7 illustrates the fact that it is possible to delineate the dominant—most desirable in σ-$E(r)$ space—investments by borrowing and lending at the RFR. Borrowing and lending at RFR combined with an investment in one risky asset results in new investment opportunities represented by an AAL. For example, asset M can be used to generate the AAL with the steepest slope; these are the dominant investment opportunities in Figure 14-7. AAL_M provides higher returns at every risk class than the Markowitz efficient frontier that

FIGURE 14-7   Borrowing and Lending at the Risk-Free Rate (RFR) Is Combined with Risky Investments to Create Asset Allocation Lines (AALs) That Can Rank the Desirability of Any Risky Investment Opportunities

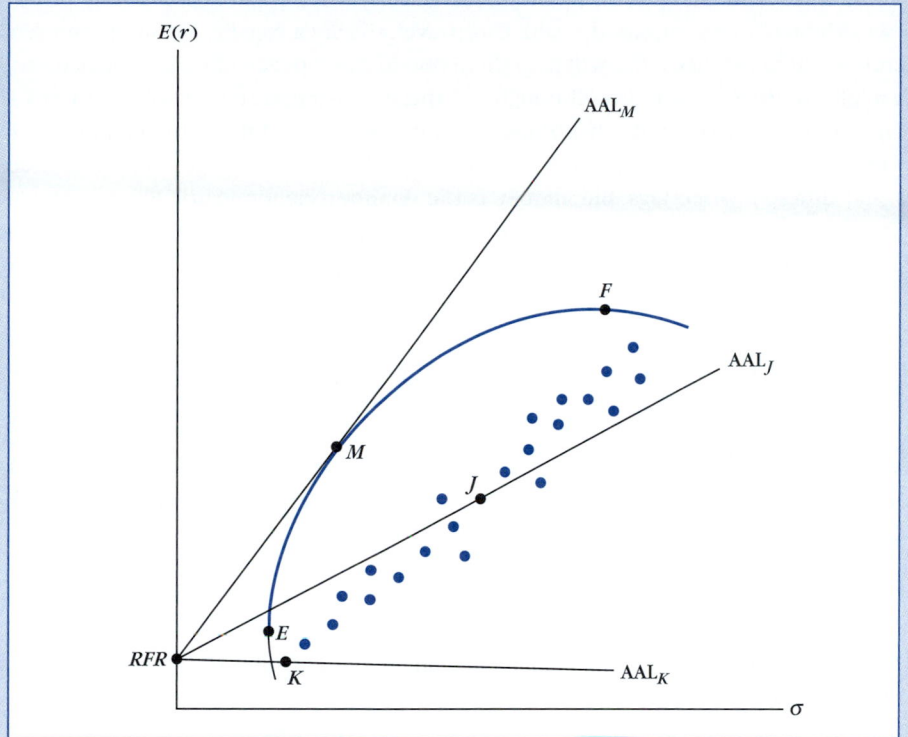

The Asset Allocation Line (AAL) through point *M* dominates the efficient frontier (curve *EF*) without borrowing opportunities. The Asset Allocation Line (*AAL*) through point *M* also dominates the asset allocation line through points *J* and *K*. The slopes of the three AALs are: (Slope of ALL_M is $S_M = \frac{1}{2}$) > (Slope of ALL_J is $S_J = \frac{1}{3}$) > (Slope of ALL_K is $S_K = -\frac{1}{4}$).

curves from point *E* to point *F*, except at point *M* where the AAL and the efficient frontier are tangent. AAL_M also dominates AAL_J and AAL_K and every individual asset (the dots) in Figure 14-7.

INVESTOR PREFERENCES

There are an infinite number of different Markowitz efficient investments illustrated in Figure 14-7. The efficient frontier includes low-risk portfolios with low returns, medium-risk portfolios with mid-level returns, and high-risk portfolios that might pay lucrative returns. How can a portfolio manager select one investment from this infinite number of Markowitz efficient portfolios? A portfolio manager can use intuition, personal preferences, or experience to select one. Or, economic theory provides scientific tools to help with decisions that involve risk.

An Introduction to Utility Theory

In economics, the word **utility** means happiness. Economic utility theory assumes every person seeks to maximize his or her own personal utility (happiness). Economists use utility theory to analyze decision making.

Economics assumes that utility increases directly with wealth. Individuals can spend their wealth on clothes, cars, food, health care, travel, charity, a face-lift, savings for retirement, to purchase circumstances that will help them obtain more peace of mind, or whatever they think might increase their utility. Although it is these consumption goods and services—and not the cash itself—that creates happiness, economics focuses only on the money. The focus is on money because consumption goods all have different advantages, different disadvantages, and different price tags. But, money is the common denominator. Economists do not want to try to determine how many more "utils" of happiness someone gets from eating an apple instead of a peach. Economists simply assume people would rather have more wealth instead of less wealth, and they can spend the money on whatever they think will maximize their utility (happiness).

Since an investment sold for $1,000 cash can provide as much utility as $1,000 of cash in the billfold, financial economists can focus on either the market prices of investments or cash. Changes in the market value of invested wealth that typically occur with the passage of time are the result of positive or negative rates of return during the holding period. The holding period return in Eqn. 14-12 is no different than the one-period rates of return from stocks, bonds, or other investments discussed in previous chapters.

$$r = (W_T - W_B)/W_B \qquad\qquad (14\text{-}12)$$

W_T denotes an investor's terminal (ending) wealth and W_B represents the beginning wealth. Summarizing what we have said about utility theory:

- Utility is some positive function (denoted f) of consumption goods.

- Since consumption goods are purchased with money, consumption is some positive function (called g) of wealth.

- Wealth is increased or decreased directly through (a function h of) the rates of return from investments and, therefore, wealth is a positive function of investment returns.

The following formula express how economists believe an investor's happiness is determined.

Utility $= f(\text{consumption})$		**(14-13)**
$\quad = f\,[g(\text{wealth})]$	since consumption $= g(\text{wealth})$	**(14-13a)**
$\quad = f\,[g\{h(\text{rate of return})\}]$	since wealth $= h(\text{rate of return})$	**(14-13b)**

In the equation, f, g, and h are all increasing mathematical functions that we will not bother to specify here.*

The three functional equations above depict how positive returns are a source of utility (happiness), and negative returns produce disutility (unhappiness), for investors. In a world where there was no uncertainty, investors could maximize their utility by simply selecting the assets that yielded the highest returns. But in the real world the outcomes from an invest-

---

* The functions f, g, and h must all be positive monotone functions. The function h is the inverse of Eqn. 14-12. Many economists believe that functions f and g are logarithmic functions.

ment cannot be known in advance: the future involves uncertainty. In particular, investment returns are risky. Uncertainty makes investment decision making more complex. In the real world, which is an uncertain world, investors must maximize their **expected utility** from their risky investments.

Rational investors are assumed to be risk-averters who obtain disutility from risk. Rational people will buy risky investments only if they expect higher returns (risk premiums) to compensate them for exposing themselves to the risk. Eqn. 14-14 represents the way economists believe investors maximize their expected utility:

$$\text{Maximize: } E[U(r)] = F[E(r),\sigma] \tag{14-14}$$

Eqn. 14-14 says that in an uncertain world investors can maximize their expected utility from investing by focusing on (some function, F, of) investments' expected returns and standard deviations (risk).*

Indifference Curves In σ-$E(r)$ Space

Figures 14-8 through 14-12 illustrate four different families of indifference curves that represent the σ-$E(r)$ preferences of four different investors. **Indifference curves** are sometimes called *utility isoquants*, because an individual derives the same level of happiness all along a given indifference curve. Thus, a person is indifferent (equally happy) at any point on a given indifference curve.

Eqn. 14-14 can be represented graphically as a family of indifference curves by varying the level of expected utility in accordance with the inequality shown at Eqn. 14-15.[8]

$$E[U(r)]_1 < E[U(r)]_2 < E[U(r)]_3 < E[U(r)]_4 \tag{14-15}$$

Let's assign some numerical values to Eqn. 14-15. Suppose that $E[U(r)]_1$ represents a portfolio of one or more investments that provides the investor with 1 util of happiness, $E[U(r)]_2$ represents a second portfolio that provides the investor with 2 utils of happiness, $E[U(r)]_3$ is a third investment that provides 3 utils, and $E[U(r)]_4$ is a fourth investment that yields 4 utils. From these numbers we know the first investment makes the investor less happy than the second investment because it yields fewer utils, the second investment brings the investor less happiness than the third investment, and the third less than the fourth. The exact number of utils that are assigned is an arbitrary number, because economists have never learned how to measure individuals' happiness with any precision.** Nevertheless, let's use these numbers to review more closely the four investors illustrated in Figures 14-8 through 14-12.

Risk-Averse Investors. In Figures 14-8 and 14-9 the two sets of indifference curves slope upward to reflect the σ-$E(r)$ preferences of these two different risk-averse investors. The indifference maps for all risk-averse investors exhibit two characteristics:

◆ The indifference curves slope upward, because risk-averters require higher returns (risk premiums) to induce them to accept greater risks.

◆ The indifference curves grow steeper at higher levels of risk, reflecting investor's diminishing willingness to assume additional risk unless they are paid increasingly large risk premiums. Thus, the steeper curves in Figure 14-8 mean that investor is more risk-averse than the risk-averse investor in Figure 14-9.

---

* Economic theory is based on the entirely plausible assumptions that investors like larger expected returns, $\delta E[U(r)]/\delta E(r) = F_{E(r)} > 0$; and, investors dislike risk, $\delta E[U(r)]/\delta\sigma = F_\sigma < 0$.

** Utils have ordinal significance, but not cardinal significance.

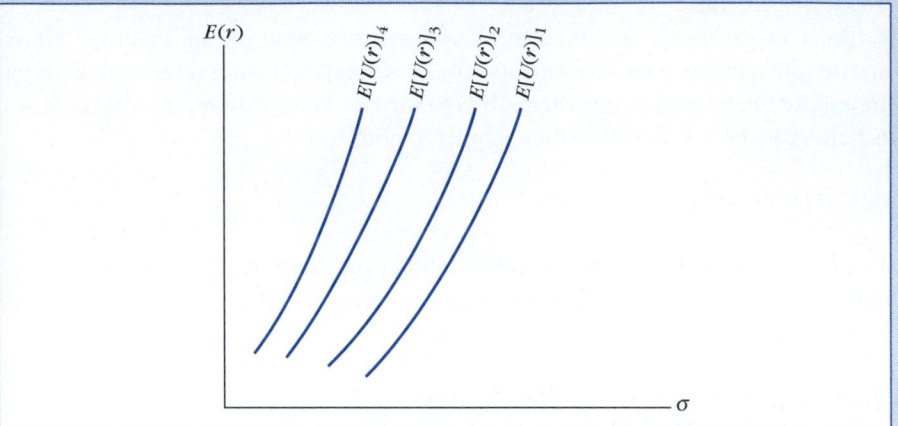

FIGURE 14-8   Indifference Curves in σ-$E(r)$ Space That Reflect a High Degree of Risk-Aversion

Indifference curves are happiness isoquants. All combinations of risk, σ, and return, $E(r)$, along an indifference curve gives the investor the same level of satisfaction.

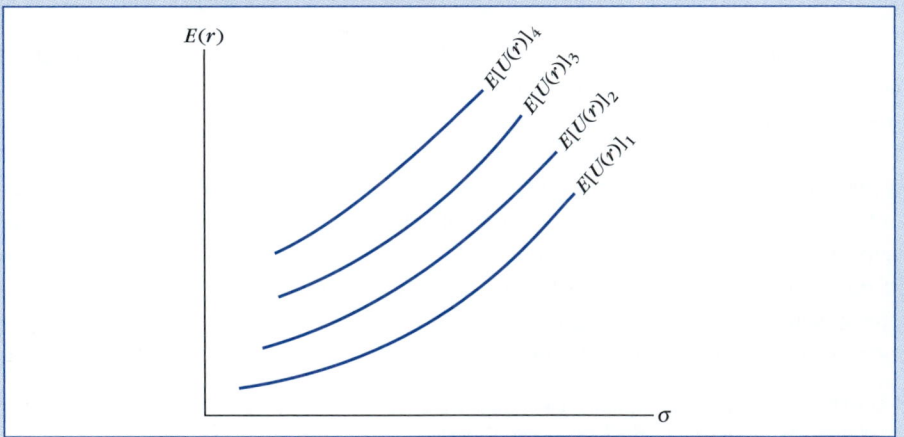

FIGURE 14-9   Indifference Curves In σ-$E(r)$ Space That Reflect a Moderate Amount of Risk-Aversion

Indifference curves that slope upward reflect a distaste for risk. The investor's risk-aversion increases with the steepness of the slope of the curves.

Risk-Loving Investors. The indifference curves sloping downward in Figure 14-10 reflect the σ-$E(r)$ preferences of a risk-lover. Risk-lovers would pay money to enter into risky gambles even though they expected to diminish their terminal wealth if they repeated the gamble a large number of times. Risk-loving is a theoretical possibility, but not a reality because we are only considering rational investors.

Most people who go to Monte Carlo or Las Vegas to gamble are not risk-lovers. Most gamblers are recreational gamblers who gamble amounts of money that they can afford to lose:

FIGURE 14-10   Indifference Curves in *σ-E(r)* Space That Reflect the Preferences of a Risk-Lover

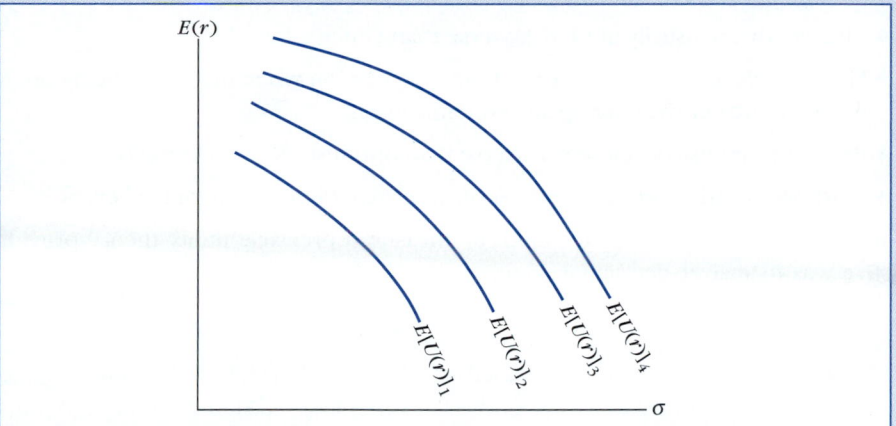

An investor who likes risk would have indifference curves that slope downward. Rational people do not consistently love risk.

FIGURE 14-11   Indifference Curves in *σ-E(r)* Space That Reflect Indifference to Risk

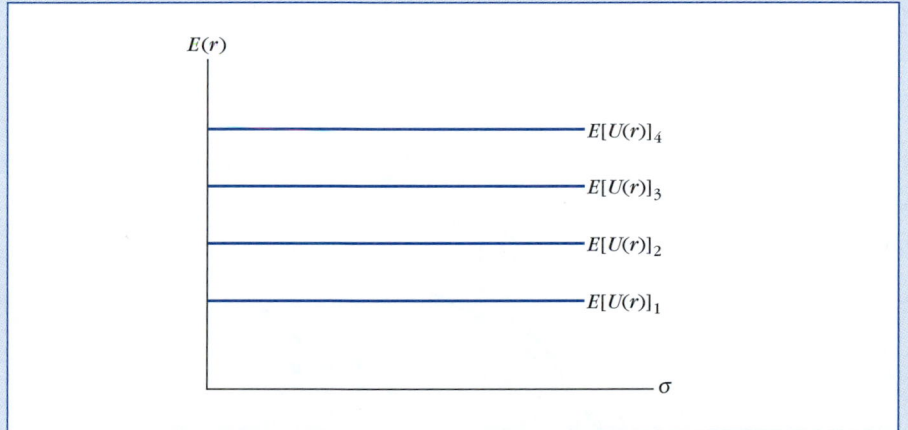

An investor who did not like risk but was not afraid of risk would be risk-indifferent. Risk-indifferent investors have indifference lines instead of indifference curves.

They are not really gambling, they are purchasing entertainment. These recreational gamblers act like risk-averters when they are managing their life savings.

Risk-Indifferent Investors. The indifference map for an investor who is indifferent to risk is illustrated in Figure 14-11. An investor who is indifferent toward risk has an indifference map made up of horizontal straight lines that are parallel. Higher returns bring greater utility, but greater risk does not affect the happiness of a risk-indifferent investor. Some large corporations behave as if they are risk indifferent when they seek to maximize the dollar value of the firm without bringing risk explicitly into their decision-making process.

Determinants of Investor Utility. Factors that determine a person's σ-$E(r)$ preferences are:

◆ The elderly are usually more risk-averse than young adults.[9]

◆ Most people are more risk-averse during a recession when the risk of being unemployed is greater than during an economic boom.

◆ Pessimists are usually more risk-averse than optimists.

◆ Most people are more risk-averse soon after experiencing a traumatic event.[10]

Although utility is subjective and cannot be measured precisely, utility theory provides an objective way to analyze decision-making.

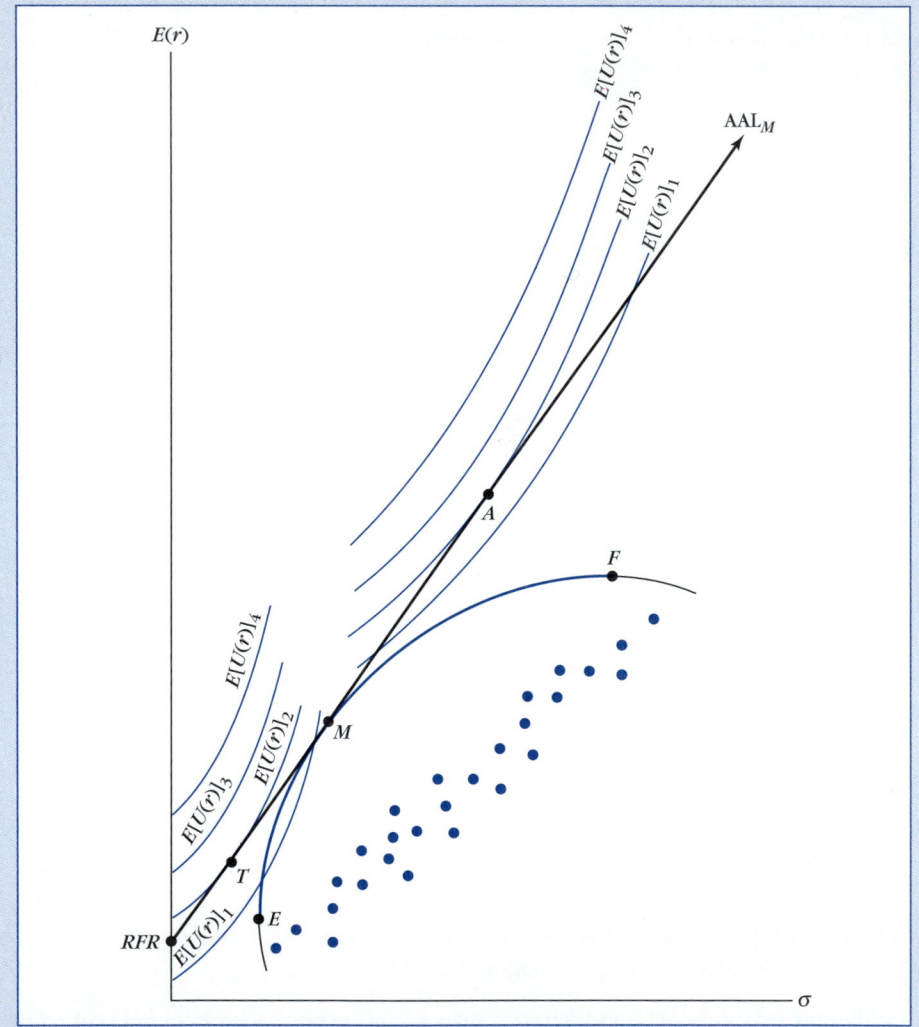

FIGURE 14-12 Two Different Risk-Averters Pick Their Utility Maximizing Investment Off of the Dominant Asset Allocation Line (AAL)

The aggressive risk-averter's highest achievable indifference curve is at Point *A*. The highest indifference curve the timid risk-averter can attain is at Point *T*.

Making Investment Decisions

To maximize expected utility, we must select the most desirable investments. First, let us consider the dominance principle. *Dominant investments* have the maximum return in their risk class. Dominant investments can be discovered by using the AAL model. The AAL that has the steepest slope determines the dominant investments. For example, the AAL that passes through point M in Figure 14-7 dominates the Markowitz efficient frontier (which curves through points E, M and F) and any other AAL that could be constructed from the opportunities in Figure 14-7. While the dominance principle helps eliminate the dominated investments from further consideration, it does not tell us precisely which the numerous investment lying along the dominant AAL is the "best" one.

Let us reconsider utility theory. The indifference curves can pinpoint the one specific investment that will maximize an investor's happiness (utility).

Figure 14-12 is a simplified version of Figure 14-7, which is a composite of the two risk-averters' indifference maps from Figures 14-8 and 14-9. These indifference maps illustrate how different people, when given identical investment opportunities, reach different investment decisions. The timid risk-averter, introduced in Figure 14-8, finds his utility maximized at point T in Figure 14-12, where his second indifference curve, $E[U(r)]_2$, is tangent to the Asset Allocation Line, AAL_M. At point T the timid risk-averter invests half his funds in efficient portfolio M and deposits the other half in an FDIC-insured bank to earn RFR.

The aggressive risk-averter, introduced in Figure 14-9, finds her utility maximized at point A in Figure 14-12, where her second indifference curve, $E[U(r)]_2$, is tangent to AAL_M. The aggressive risk-averter reaches point A by borrowing at the riskless interest rate to leverage herself out to a high-risk point on the AAL. Both risk-averters would have been happier if they could have found investment possibilities lying above their second indifference curves. Unfortunately for these two investors, looking at Figure 14-12, we can see that there were no investment opportunities for them as high as their third or fourth indifference curves. Investment opportunities exist along portions of both investors' first indifference curves, $E[U(r)]_1$, but these investments yield less utility than the higher points they selected on the AAL.

THE BOTTOM LINE

Diversification can reduce portfolio risk. Empirical evidence showed that risk can be reduced by simple random diversification across individual securities without regard to their industry, as well as by selecting securities randomly from different industries. However, Markowitz diversification is a more scientific way to reduce risk.

The fundamental concepts of Markowitz portfolio analysis are:

◆ The weights must sum to 1.

◆ The portfolio's expected return is the weighted average of the returns from the assets which make up the portfolio.

◆ The variance-covariance matrix (portfolio risk equation) shows how the risk of each asset and the interaction between all of the assets work together to determine a portfolio's risk.

◆ Markowitz named the set of portfolios that have the maximum expected return in each risk class, or, conversely, the minimum risk at every level of return, the efficient frontier.

◆ Borrowing and lending at a risk-free interest rate can be combined with an investment in one risky asset to create a capital allocation line (AAL).

◆ The AAL that has the steepest slope (*S*) is more desirable (more dominant, more Markowitz efficient) than the curved efficient frontier that can be attained without borrowing and lending.

After deriving an efficient frontier made up of assets that only have positive weights, a more desirable efficient frontier was derived by broadening the list of investment candidates to include short sales and borrowing that are represented by negative weights. When the investments with positive weights are combined with investments that have negative weights, the risk-reduction potential increases because the investments with negative weights are often negatively correlated with the investments that have positive weights.

Borrowing and lending at the risk-free interest rate was combined with one risky investment to create the AAL. Graphical analyzing the various AALs that could be created revealed that the most desirable (dominant) investments used the risk-free rate to create lending and/or leveraged portfolios.

After investors delineate the efficient portfolios, they still must select a portfolio in which to invest. Portfolio selection is a decision that involves risk which can be analyzed with utility theory.

Portfolio analysis leads to the conclusion that diversification is essential to maximize the utility of a rational, risk-averse, wealth-seeking investor. Markowitz diversification helps the investor attain a higher level of expected utility than any other risk reduction technique. Rational investors will use Markowitz's concepts and be concerned with the correlation between assets, as well as the assets' expected returns and standard deviations.

QUESTIONS

Q14-1   (Portfolio weights) (a) What does portfolio analysis assume about the weights of the assets in a portfolio? (b) Is this assumption necessary? Why or why not?

Q14-2   (Naive diversification) (a) Define simple diversification. (b) Will simple diversification reduce total risk? Explain. (c) Will simple diversification reduce diversifiable risk? Why or why not? (d) Will simple diversification reduce undiversifiable risk? Explain.

Q14-3   (Superfluous diversification) (a) Define superfluous diversification. (b) What problems frequently result from superfluous diversification?

Q14-4   (Efficient frontier) Consider Figures 14-3 through 14-5. Why are all the curves drawn convex (rather than concave) to the expected return axis?

Q14-5   (Diversifiable risk) "Apart from negatively correlated stocks, all the gains from diversification come from 'averaging over' the independent components of the returns and risks of individual stocks. Among positively correlated stocks, there would be no gains from diversification, if independent variations [or, diversifiable risk] were absent." Quotation from Professor John Lintner, "Security Prices, Risk, and Maximal Gains from Diversification," *Journal of Finance* (December 1965): 589 [bracketed words added]. Explain this statement.

Q14-6   (Portfolio analysis) What statistical inputs are required for a portfolio analysis of *N* different assets?

Q14-7   (Variance-covariance matrix) Mathematically expand the following formula for a portfolio's variance of returns for four assets into a form showing all four assets' variances and covariances:

$$VAR(r_p) = \sum_{i=1}^{N}\sum_{j=1}^{N} x_i x_j \sigma_{ij} \quad for \ N \ = \ 4$$

Q14-8   (Diversification) Ivan Dahl read an article about the fact that diversification can reduce risk, so Ivan decided to invest 80% of his investment money in a mutual fund indexed to the S&P500 and 20% of his investment money in a corporate bond fund. Comment on his strategy.

Q14-9   (Indifference curves) Explain why the indifference curves for risk-indifferent investors are simply horizontal parallel straight lines.

Q14-10   (Leveraged portfolios) What are the two economic interpretations of negative weights in portfolio analysis?

PROBLEMS

P14-1 (Calculating investment statistics) Below are the returns for two assets:

State of Nature	r_1	r_2	Probability
Weak growth	15%	15%	$\frac{1}{3}$
Strong growth	30	12	$\frac{1}{3}$
Very strong growth	45	9	$\frac{1}{3}$
Expected returns	30	12	Total 1.0

Calculate the two variances and $COV(r_1,r_2)$. If assets 1 and 2 are combined 50-50 into a portfolio, what is the variance of this portfolio? Show your calculations.

The information in the table below applies to Problems 14-2 through 14-8:

Table P14-2   Data for Problems 14-2 to 14-8

Year	Stock A Returns	Stock B Returns	Stock C Returns
20X1	10%	6%	−5%
20X2	−5	10	15
20X3	−7	12	20
20X4	15	8	25
20X5	20	14	30
20X6	−30	7	−35
20X7	12	8	20

P14-2 (Calculating correlations) Calculate the correlation coefficients between the returns of each pair of the three stocks in Table 14-2 over the 7-year sample period.

P14-3 (Computing standard deviations) Calculate the standard deviations of the returns from the three stocks over the 7-year sample period.

P14-4 (Expected portfolio return) Assume the annual returns given in year 20X7 are the expected returns. What is the expected return from a portfolio made up of 20% in asset A, 40% in B, and 40% in C?

P14-5 (Portfolio risk) Use all seven years of historical data from Table 14-2 to compute the standard deviation of a portfolio made up of 20% in asset A, 40% in B, and 40% in C.

P14-6 (Expected portfolio return) Use all 7 years of historical data from Table 14-2 to compute the expected return for a portfolio of 50% invested in A and 50% in B?

P14-7 (Portfolio risk) Determine the standard deviation of the 2-asset equally weighted portfolio suggested in problem 14-6.

P14-8 (Computing covariances) Determine the covariance of returns between stocks A and B over the 7-year sample. *Hint:* The information from problems 14-2 and 14-3 can be useful.

The information in the table below applies to problems 14-9 and 14-10:

Table 14-9   Data for Problems 14-9 and 14-10

Stock	$E(r)$	Standard Deviation
D	10%	15%
G	18	30

P14-9 (Minimum variance portfolio) Assume the correlation between D and G is 0.1. Determine the minimum standard deviation portfolio for D and G. What is the expected return of that portfolio? *Hint:* The following formula will determine the amount of D for a minimum standard deviation portfolio:

$$x_D = \frac{\sigma_G^2 - \rho_{DG}\,\sigma_D\,\sigma_G}{\sigma_D^2 + \sigma_G^2 - 2\rho_{DG}\,\sigma_D\,\sigma_G}$$

P14-10 (Slope of AAL) If the risky portfolio M has an expected return of 15% and a standard deviation of 20% and the risk-free rate of interest is 8%, what is the slope of the asset allocation line (AAL)? What does this mean to an investor?

P14-11 (AAL calculations) Using the information given in problem 14-10, calculate investors' risk and return assuming they: (a) invested only in the risk-free asset; (b) invested one-half of the portfolio's funds in the risk-free asset and one-half in Portfolio M, and, (c) borrowed 50% of their initial funds for an additional investment and then invested all the funds in Portfolio M?

P14-12 (Elementary portfolio analysis) Use the Markowitz concepts introduced in this chapter to delineate three portfolio possibility curves for the two stocks in Table 14-12. Base these three portfolio possibility curves on the following three assumptions about the correlation between the returns of DI and UST: (a) perfect positive correlation, (b) zero correlation, and (c) perfectly inverse correlation. Draw a graph in $[\sigma, E(r)]$ space showing the three portfolio possibility curves you delineate.

Table P14-12   Risk and Return Statistics for Dynamics International (DI) and U.S. Telephone (UST) Common Stocks

	Expected Return, $E(r)$	Variance, $VAR(r)$	Standard Deviation, σ
Dynamics International	0.2 = 20.0%	0.134	0.366
U.S. Telephone	0.07 = 7%	0.0221	0.14866

CFA EXAM QUESTIONS

The following two questions are adopted from the 1998 CFA Sample Exam, Level I:

1. Use the following expectations for Stocks X and Y for Question 1:

	Bear Market	Normal Market	Bull Market
Probability	0.2	0.5	0.3
Stock X	−20%	18%	50%
Stock Y	−15%	20%	10%

An investor has a $10,000 portfolio consisting of $9,000 in Stock X and $1,000 in Stock Y. What is the investor's expected return on the portfolio?
   A. 18%.
   B. 19%.
   C. 20%.
   D. 23%.

2. Which statement about portfolio diversification is true?
   A. Proper diversification can reduce or eliminate systematic risk.
   B. As more securities are added to a portfolio, total risk is likely to fall at a decreasing rate.
   C. Diversification reduces the portfolio's expected return because diversification reduces a portfolio's total risk.
   D. The risk-reducing benefits of diversification do not occur meaningfully until at least 30 individual securities are included in the portfolio.

3. (1993 CFA Sample Exam, Level I) Which one of the following portfolios cannot lie on the efficient frontier as described by Markowitz?

	Portfolio	Expected Return (%)	Standard Deviation (%)
A.	W	15	36
B.	X	12	15
C.	Z	5	7
D.	Y	9	21

4. (Adapted from the 1995 CFA Exam, Level III) Ambrose Green, 63, is a retired engineer and a client of Clayton Asset Management Associates ("Associates"). His accumulated savings are invested in Diversified Global Fund ("the Fund"). Ambrose has asked you to review the existing asset allocation of Diversified Global Fund. He wonders if a 60/30/10 allocation to stocks, bonds, and cash equivalents would be better than the present 40/40/20 allocation. Green also wonders if the Fund is appropriate as his primary investment asset. To address his concerns you

decide to do a scenario forecasting exercise, using the data in Tables 1 and 2 (shown below) provided by Associates.

Table 1 Associates' Diversified Global Fund—Current Asset Allocation

	Percent of Total Assets				
Asset Class	U.S.	Europe	Far East	Other	Total
Stocks	15%	10%	12%	3%	40%
Bonds	20%	12%	8%	0%	40%
Cash equivalents	10%	5%	5%	0%	20%
Totals	45%	27%	25%	3%	100%

Under the "Degearing" scenario, the U.S.-Europe-Far East trading nations experience an extended period of slow economic growth while they reduce prior debt excesses. This scenario is assigned a probability of 0.50, while *each* of the other two scenarios—"Disinflation" and "Inflation"—is assigned a probability of 0.25. The asset classes shown in Table 1 reflect the diversification strategy used by Associates in managing its Diversified Global Fund.

Table 2 Projected Returns by Economic Scenario, 1996–99 (All data have been weighted to reflect the geographic mix shown in Table 1)

	Scenario		
	"Degearing"	"Disinflation"	"Inflation"
Real economic growth	2.5%	1.0%	3.0%
Inflation rate	1.0%	1.0%	6.0%
Nominal total returns:			
Stocks	8.25%	−8.00%	4.00%
Bonds	6.25%	7.50%	2.00%
Cash equivalents	4.50%	2.50%	6.50%
Real total returns:			
Stocks	5.25%	−9.00%	−2.00%
Bonds	3.25%	6.50%	−4.00%
Cash equivalents	1.50%	1.50%	0.50%

   A. Calculate the expected total returns associated with the existing 40/40/20 asset allocation *and* with the alternative 60/30/10 mix, given the *three* scenarios shown in Table 2. Show your work.
   B. Justify the 40/40/20 asset allocation shown for the Fund in Table 1 versus the alternative 60/30/10 mix and explain your conclusion. In formulating your response, use the data in Table 1 and Table 2, your knowledge of multiple scenario forecasting, and your Part A calculations.

FURTHER REFERENCES

Dumas, Bernard, and Blaise Allaz. *Financial Securities*. London: South-Western, 1996.

> Chapters 2 and 3 review utility theory and portfolio analysis.

Francis, J. C., and Gordon Alexander. *Portfolio Analysis*, 3d ed. Englewood Cliffs, NJ: Prentice-Hall, 1986.

> The AAL and other more sophisticated models are developed. Graphical utility analysis and elementary statistics are used in the chapters.

Markowitz, Harry M. *Portfolio Selection*. New York: Wiley, 1959.

> Chapters 1 through 5 present the foundations for portfolio analysis. Chapters 7 and 8 present different techniques for performing portfolio analysis. Algebra is used.

Michaud, Richard O. *Efficient Asset Management: A Practical Guide to Stock Portfolio Optimization and Asset Allocation*. Boston, MA: Harvard Business School Publishing, 1998.

> A useful summary and critique of old and new statistical work that relates to mean-variance analysis.

Sharpe, William F. "Mutual Fund Performance," *Journal of Business* 39 (January, 1966): 119–38.

> This seminal article uses empirical data and the asset allocation line (AAL) to rank the desirability of mutual funds.

ENDNOTES

[1] See Harry Markowitz, "Portfolio Selection," *Journal of Finance* 12 (March 1952): 77–91.

[2] The discussion of simple diversification is based on research by John Evans and S. H. Archer, "Diversification and the Reduction of Dispersion: An Empirical Analysis," *Journal of Finance* (December 1968): 761–67. W. H. Wagner and S. Lau, "The Effect of Diversification on Risk," *Financial Analysts Journal* (November-December 1971): 52. Edwin J. Elton and Martin J. Gruber, "Risk Reduction and Portfolio Size: An Analytical Solution," *Journal of Business* 30, no. 4 (October 1977): 415–37. Gerald D. Newbould and Percy S. Poon, "The Minimum Number of Stocks Needed for Diversification," *Financial Practice and Education* 3, no. 2 (fall 1993): 85–87. Kristine L. Beck, Steven B. Perfect, and Pamela P. Peterson, "The Role of Alternative Methodology on the Relation Between Portfolio Size and Diversification," *The Financial Review* 31, no. 2 (May 1996): 381–406.

[3] Harry Markowitz, "Portfolio Selection," *Journal of Finance* (March 1952): 89.

[4] Computer programs to perform portfolio analysis and other forms of investment analysis are publicly available. See Richard Bookstaber, *The Complete Investment Book* (Glenview, IL: Scott, Foresman, 1985), Chapter 9. Also see Jack Clark Francis, *Investments Analysis Software* (New York: McGraw-Hill, 1994), Chapters 17–19. And, see the free software that accompanies this textbook.

[5] Ignoring the legal, psychological, and economic limitations, Merton delineated the mathematical limits on the set of investment opportunities. Robert C. Merton, "An Analytic Derivation of the Efficient Portfolio Frontier," *Journal of Financial and Quantitative Analysis* 7, no. 4 (September 1972): 1851–72.

[6] The implications of a 2-asset portfolio comprised of a riskless asset and a risky asset were first explored in a seminal article by Nobel laureate James Tobin. See James Tobin, "Liquidity Preference as Behavior Towards Risk," *The Review of Economic Studies* 26, no. 1 (February 1958): 65–86.

[7] See William F. Sharpe, "Mutual Fund Performance," *Journal of Business* 39 (January 1966): 119–38. This important tool will be investigated in Chapter 16.

[8] For a more detailed discussion of utility analysis and the ways it applies to portfolio analysis, see Gordon J. Alexander and Jack Clark Francis, *Portfolio Analysis*, 3d ed. (Englewood Cliffs, NJ: Prentice-Hall, 1986). Chapters 2, 3, and 12 focus on investors' utility. For empirical estimates of peoples' relative risk aversion, see William B. Riley and K. Victor Chow, "Asset Allocation and Individual Risk Aversion," *Financial Analysts Journal* (November-December 1992): 32–37.

[9] Franco Modigliani, "Life Cycle, Individual Thrift, and the Wealth of Nations," *American Economic Review* (June 1986): 297–313.

[10] See Roy Santanu, "Theory of Dynamic Portfolio Choice for Survival Under Uncertainty," *Mathematical Social Sciences* 30, no. 2 (October 1995): 171–94.

[11] Informative examples of Markowitz portfolio analysis performed graphically may be found in *Portfolio Selection* by Harry Markowitz (New York: Wiley, 1959); see Chapter 7. Or, see Chapter 5 of *Portfolio Analysis,* 2nd ed. by J. C. Francis and S. H. Archer (Englewood Cliffs, NJ: Prentice-Hall, 1979).

Derivation of Two-Asset Portfolio Risk Formulas

The mathematical expectation operator (E) is used to derive the variance-covariance matrix for a 2-asset portfolio below.

$$VAR(r_p) = E[r_p - E(r_p)]^2 \text{ the definition of } VAR(r_p)$$

$$= E\{x_1r_1 + x_2r_2 - [x_1E(r_1) + x_2E(r_2)]\}^2 \text{ by substituting } x_1r_1 + x_2r_2 \text{ for } r_p$$

$$= E\{x_1[r_1 - E(r_1)] + x_2[r_2 - E(r_2)]\}^2 \text{ collecting like terms}$$

$$= E\{x_1^2[r_1 - E(r_1)]^2 + x_2^2[r_2 - E(r_2)]^2 + 2x_1x_2[r_1 - E(r_1)][r_2 - E(r_2)]\}$$

$$= x_1^2E[r_1 - E(r_1)]^2 + x_2^2E[r_2 - E(r_2)]^2 + 2x_1x_2E\{[r_1 - E(r_1)][r_2 - E(r_2)]\}$$

$$= x_1^2VAR(r_1) + x_2^2VAR(r_2) + 2x_1x_2COV(r_1,r_2) \text{ restating definitions}$$

If $i = j$, then $COV(r_i,r_j) = \sigma_{ij} = \sigma_i^2 = VAR(r_i)$. Furthermore, $\sigma_{ij} = \sigma_{ji}$. These conventions allow the last line of the formula above to be restated equivalently as a 2×2 variance-covariance matrix.

$$VAR(r_p) =$$

	Column 1	Column 2	
	$x_1x_1\sigma_1^2 +$	$x_1x_2\sigma_{12}^2 +$	Row 1
	$x_2x_1\sigma_{21} +$	$x_2x_2\sigma_2^2$	Row 2

The 2×2 variance-covariance matrix above can be restated equivalently as the following double summation.

$$VAR(r_p) = \sum_{i=1}^{2}\sum_{j=1}^{2}x_ix_j\sigma_{ij}$$

The results above can be generalized to an $N \times N$ variance-covariance matrix.

Mathematical Portfolio Analysis

Markowitz portfolio analysis performed graphically cannot handle more than four securities. The graphical analysis serves well as an introduction to portfolio analysis and may permit a better understanding of the analysis and of the solution.[11] However, a more efficient solution technique for portfolio analysis that uses differential calculus and linear algebra is explained in this appendix.

A Generalized Calculus Risk Minimization Solution Procedure

Calculus can be used to find the minimum risk portfolio for any given expected return E^*. Mathematically, the problem involves finding the minimum portfolio variance.

$$\text{Minimize} \quad VAR(r_p) = \sum_{i=1}^{n}\sum_{j=1}^{n}x_i x_j \sigma_{ij} \tag{14B-1}$$

This minimum variance should be subject to two Lagrangian constraints. The first constraint requires that the desired expected return E^* be achieved. This constraint is equivalent to Eqn. 14B-2.

$$\sum_{i=1}^{n}x_i E(r_i) - E^* = 0 \tag{14B-2}$$

The second constraint requires that the weights sum to unity. This constraint is equivalent to requiring that the following equation not be violated.

$$\sum_{i=1}^{n}x_i - 1 = 0 \tag{14B-3}$$

Combining the three quantities above yields the Lagrangian objective function of the risk-minimization problem with a desired return constraint:

$$z = \sum_{i=1}^{n}\sum_{j=1}^{n}x_i x_j \sigma_{ij} + \lambda_1\left(\sum_{i=1}^{n}x_i E(r_1) - E^*\right) + \lambda_2\left(\sum_{i=1}^{n}x_i - 1\right) \tag{14B-4}$$

The minimum risk portfolio is found by setting $dz/dx_i = 0$ for $i = 1, ..., n$ and $dz/d\lambda_j = 0$ for $j = 1, 2$ and solving the resulting system of equations for the x_i's. The number of assets analyzed, n, can be any positive integer.

Calculus Minimization of a Three-Security Portfolio

For a three-security portfolio, the objective function to be minimized is:

$$z = x_1^2\sigma_{11} + x_2^2\sigma_{22} + x_3^2\sigma_{33} + 2x_1x_2\sigma_{12} + 2x_1x_3\sigma_{13} + 2x_2x_3\sigma_{23}$$
$$+ \lambda_1(x_1E_1 + x_2E_2 + x_3E_3 - E^*) + \lambda_2(x_1 + x_2 + x_3 - 1) \qquad \textbf{(14B-4A)}$$

Setting the partial derivatives of z with respect to all variables equal to zero yields equation system Eqn. 14B-5:

$$\frac{dz}{dx_1} = 2x_1\sigma_{11} + 2x_2\sigma_{12} + 2x_3\sigma_{13} + \lambda_1E_1 + \lambda_2 = 0$$

$$\frac{dz}{dx_2} = 2x_2\sigma_{22} + 2x_1\sigma_{12} + 2x_3\sigma_{23} + \lambda_1E_2 + \lambda_2 = 0$$

$$\frac{dz}{dx_3} = 2x_3\sigma_{33} + 2x_1\sigma_{13} + 2x_2\sigma_{23} + \lambda_1E_3 + \lambda_2 = 0 \qquad \textbf{(14B-5)}$$

$$\frac{dz}{d\lambda_2} = x_1 + x_2 + x_3 - 1 = 0$$

$$\frac{dz}{d\lambda_1} = x_1E_1 + x_2E_2 + x_3E_3 - E^* = 0$$

This is a system of linear equations, since the weights (x_i's) are all of degree 1. Thus the system may be solved as a system of simultaneous linear equations. The matrix representation of this system of linear equations is shown as matrix Eqn. 14B-6:

$$
\begin{matrix}
& C & & x & = k \\
\end{matrix}
$$

$$
\begin{bmatrix}
2\sigma_{11} & 2\sigma_{12} & 2\sigma_{13} & E_1 & 1 \\
2\sigma_{21} & 2\sigma_{22} & 2\sigma_{23} & E_2 & 1 \\
2\sigma_{31} & 2\sigma_{32} & 2\sigma_{33} & E_3 & 1 \\
1 & 1 & 1 & 0 & 0 \\
E_1 & E_2 & E_3 & 0 & 0
\end{bmatrix}
\begin{bmatrix}
x_1 \\
x_2 \\
x_3 \\
\lambda_2 \\
\lambda_1
\end{bmatrix}
=
\begin{bmatrix}
0 \\
0 \\
0 \\
1 \\
E^*
\end{bmatrix}
\qquad \textbf{(14B-6)}
$$

The system of linear equations above may be solved in several ways. The inverse of the coefficient matrix, denoted C^{-1}, may be used to find the solution (weight) vector x, as shown with matrix notation.

Table 14B-1 Statistical Inputs for Portfolio Analysis of Three Common Stocks

Asset	$E(r_i)$	$VAR(r_i) = \sigma_{ii}$	$COV(r_i, r_j) = \sigma_{ij}$
Homestead	$E(r_1) = 5\% = 0.05$	$\sigma_{11} = 0.1$	$\sigma_{12} = -0.1$
Kaiser	$E(r_2) = 7\% = 0.07$	$\sigma_{22} = 0.4$	$\sigma_{13} = 0.0$
Textment	$E(r_3) = 30\% = 0.3$	$\sigma_{33} = 0.7$	$\sigma_{23} = 0.3$

$$Cx = k$$

$$C^{-1}Cx = C^{-1}k$$

$$Ix = C^{-1}k$$

$$x = C^{-1}k \qquad \text{(14B-7)}$$

The solution will give the N (in this case, $N = 3$) weights in terms of E^*, where the a_i and d_i are constants.

$$x_1 = a_1 + d_1 E^*$$

$$x_2 = a_2 + d_2 E^*$$

$$x_3 = a_3 - d_3 E^* \qquad \text{(14B-8)}$$

For any desired E^* the equations give the weights of the minimum risk portfolio. These are the weights of a portfolio in the efficient frontier. By varying E^* the weights may be generated for the entire efficient frontier. Then the risk, $VAR(r_p)$, of the efficient portfolios may be calculated, and the efficient frontier may be graphed.

As a numerical example, the data from the 3-security portfolio problem indicated in Table 14B-1 is used to obtain the following coefficients matrix.

$$
\begin{bmatrix}
2\sigma_{11} & 2\sigma_{12} & 2\sigma_{13} & E_1 & 1 \\
2\sigma_{21} & 2\sigma_{22} & 2\sigma_{23} & E_2 & 1 \\
2\sigma_{31} & 2\sigma_{32} & 2\sigma_{33} & E_3 & 1 \\
1 & 1 & 1 & 0 & 0 \\
E_1 & E_2 & E_3 & 0 & 0
\end{bmatrix}
=
\begin{bmatrix}
2(.1) & 2(-1) & 2(0) & .05 & 1 \\
2(-.1) & 2(.4) & 2(.3) & .07 & 1 \\
2(0) & 2(.3) & 2(.7) & .3 & 1 \\
1 & 1 & 1 & 0 & 0 \\
.05 & .07 & .3 & 0 & 0
\end{bmatrix}
\qquad \text{(14B-6)}
$$

Multiplying the inverse of this coefficients matrix by the constants vector k yields the weights vector ($C^{-1}k = x$) as shown below.

$$
\overset{C^{-1}}{\begin{bmatrix}
.677 & -.736 & .059 & .789 & -1.433 \\
-.736 & .800 & -.064 & .447 & -2.790 \\
.059 & -.064 & .005 & -.236 & 4.223 \\
-1.433 & -2.790 & 4.223 & .522 & -15.869 \\
.789 & .447 & -.236 & -.095 & .552
\end{bmatrix}}
\overset{k}{\begin{bmatrix}
0 \\ 0 \\ 0 \\ 1 \\ E^*
\end{bmatrix}}
=
\overset{W}{\begin{bmatrix}
x_1 \\ x_2 \\ x_3 \\ \lambda_2 \\ \lambda_1
\end{bmatrix}}
\qquad \text{(14B-6)}
$$

Evaluating the weights vector yields the system of equations below.

$$x_1 = .789 - 1.433E^*$$

$$x_2 = .447 - 2.790E^* \qquad x_1 + x_2 + x_3 = 1 \text{ for any given } E^*$$

$$x_3 = -.236 + 4.223E^*$$

$$\lambda_1 = .522 - 15.869E^*$$

$$\lambda_2 = -.095 + .522E^*$$

The weights in the three equations sum to unity, are a linear function of E^*, and represent the weights of the three securities in the efficient portfolio at the point where $E(r_p) = E^*$. Varying E^* generates the weights of all the efficient portfolios.

Two Statistics Theorems

Theorem One: The Weak Law of Large Numbers

Let $r_1, r_2, r_3, \ldots$ be independent and identically distributed random variables that have finite means and variances. Let S_N define the sum of N random variables: $S_N = r_1 + r_2 + r_3 + \ldots + r_N$. The sum S_N approaches $E(S_N)$ as N increases. Symbolically, let e be any tiny value that is very near zero, then, the probability defined below approaches zero as N increases.

$$\underset{N \to \infty}{\text{Limit Probability}} \left[\left| \left(\frac{S}{N} \right) - E(r) \right| > e \right] \to 0 \text{ for any tiny value of } e > 0.$$

This theorem tells us that as the sample gets larger the sample mean converges on the population mean asymptotically. In other words, if r is an independent and identically distributed random variable and if it has a finite mean $\bar{r}$, then when the sample size N used to compute $\bar{r}$ becomes a very large integer the sample mean statistic will become a very close estimator of the population mean parameter.

Theorem Two: The Central Limit Theorem

Let $r_1, r_2, r_3, \ldots$ be independent random variables that are drawn randomly from a population that has a finite mean, u, and finite variance, σ. Let S_N represent the sum of a sample of size N: $S_N = r_1 + r_2 + r_3 + \ldots + r_N$. The sample mean is: $\bar{r} = S_N/N$. The sampling distribution of the random variable Z approaches a normal distribution with mean zero and variance of positive one as N increases. Symbolically,

$$Z = \frac{\bar{r} - u}{\sigma/\sqrt{N}} \to N(0,1)$$

The random variable z is called the *unit normal variable*. In other words, if r is an independent and identically distributed random variable and if r has a finite mean denoted u and finite variance denoted σ^2, then as the sample size N becomes very large the sample mean $\bar{r}$ will become very close to the population mean parameter ($\bar{r} \to u$) and the sampling distribution of the sample means ($\bar{r}$) will become normally distributed with a mean of u and a standard deviation of $\sigma/\sqrt{N}$. As a result, the standardized variable Z becomes asymptotically normally distributed with a mean of zero and a variance of one as N increases.

CAPM AND APT

This is a chapter about economic equilibriums. An economic equilibrium occurs whenever supply equals demand and, as a result, prices have no tendency to change. The portfolio concepts from Chapter 14 are employed here to develop two similar, but different, equilibrium portfolio theories. *These theories are similar because they are both grounded in portfolio theory, and they have parallel asset pricing implications.*

This chapter's two equilibrium portfolio theories both use quantitative risk surrogates like the variance and covariance, and the concepts of diversifiable risk and undiversifiable risk introduced in Chapters 7 and 14. Chapter 14 explained the variance-covariance formula and the asset allocation line (AAL) that are also used in this chapter.

This chapter's first theory is called the **Security Market Line***, or* **SML***. Some books refer to the SML as the* **Capital Asset Pricing Model***, or* **CAPM***. The SML and the CAPM are the same: both models use undiversifiable risk to explain assets' expected returns. After the SML is introduced, we review some statistical tests that employ market data to test the ability of the theory to describe reality.*

Arbitrage Pricing Theory, or **APT***, is the second major theory introduced in this chapter. The big difference between the APT and the SML is that the APT considers several risk factors, while the SML is based on a single risk factor. After the APT is presented, some empirical tests designated to validate or refute it are reviewed.*

The SML and APT were both developed with the aid of simplifying assumptions. This chapter compares and contrasts the assumptions underlying the two theories.

INVESTMENT OPPORTUNITIES IN RISK-RETURN SPACE

A computer program to do quadratic programming (QP) can analyze numerous assets simultaneously and delineate the Markowitz efficient frontier. Figure 14-4 (p. 414) in Chapter 14 illustrates the *efficient frontier* that can be derived. The sections below anlayze the efficient frontier and establish the background for the Security Market Line (SML).

Borrowing and Lending at a Risk-Free Rate of Interest

The investment opportunities in Figure 14-4 may be extended by considering borrowing and lending. Suppose all investors can borrow or lend any amount at a risk-free rate (*RFR*) of interest. By definition, a riskless asset must have no variability of return, *VAR(RFR)* = 0.

Figure 15-1 illustrates the one-asset allocation line (AAL) that has a steeper slope than any other AAL that can be constructed. If all marketable assets in the world were used to construct Figure 15-1, the AAL with the steepest slope represents a global investor's most desirable portfolio. Hereafter, that most desirable AAL will be called the **capital market line (CML)**.

DEFINITION

THE CAPITAL MARKET LINE (CML)

Figure 15-1 represents the investment opportunities that would exist in equilibrium if investors were Markowitz diversifiers who could borrow or lend at the RFR. The **capital market line (CML)** is formalized in Eqn.(15-1).

$$E(r_i) = RFR + \left(\frac{E(r_M) - RFR}{\sigma_M} \right) \sigma_i \qquad (15\text{-}1)$$

where

$E(r_i)$ = expected return from ith portfolio, whose total risk is σ_i

RFR = risk-free rate of interest

$E(r_M)$ = expected rate of return from the market portfolio

$E(r_M) - RFR$ = Equity risk premium (introduced in Chapter 2)

σ_M = the market portfolio's standard deviation of returns.

Eqn. 15-1 is restated below in conceptual terms.

$$\begin{pmatrix} \text{Total} \\ \text{Return,} \\ E(r_i) \end{pmatrix} = \begin{pmatrix} \text{Reward for} \\ \text{delaying} \\ \text{consumption,} \\ RFR \end{pmatrix} + \begin{pmatrix} \text{Reward for} \\ \text{bearing risk} \end{pmatrix}$$

The Market Portfolio (M)

In equilibrium all assets will be owned by someone. Portfolio M in Figure 15-1 is called the **market portfolio**; it is an equilibrium portfolio containing all assets in the world. The market value weight of asset i in portfolio M equals the proportion x_i^*:

$$x_i^* = \frac{\text{Total market value of the } i\text{th security}}{\text{Aggregate value of all market assets}} \qquad (15\text{-}2)$$

The market portfolio contains all securities in the proportions they are supplied. It is the single portfolio all rational investors prefer to own. M is the most desirable investment because

FIGURE 15-1   The Capital Market Line (CML) Is the Efficient Frontier
When Borrowing and Lending at the Risk-Free Rate (RFR)
Are Permitted

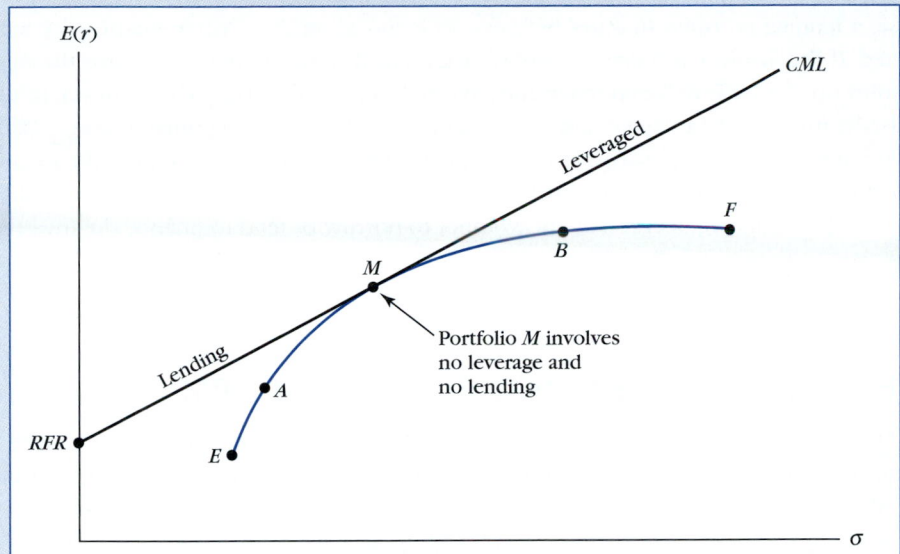

When borrowing and lending at the Risk-Free Rate (*RFR*) is part of portfolio analysis, the
efficient frontier (curve *EF*) is dominated by a new efficient frontier called the Capital
Market Line (*CML*).

it is the single risky asset that can be used to create the dominant Capital Market Line (CML)
in Figure 15-1.

The market portfolio's return is the weighted average return from all capital assets.[1] The
market portfolio is a useful theoretical construct; the return on M is the return that security
market indexes approximate.

A NUMERICAL ESTIMATE OF THE CML

EXAMPLE

Table 2-3 of Chapter 2 (p. 30) shows the authors' estimates of the risk-free rate equals RFR =
4.5% and the equity risk premium equals $E(r_M) - RFR = 7.1\%$. We assume the standard deviation of returns from the S&P500 (large-company stocks) index provides an estimate of the
market portfolio's standard deviation; Table 2-1 of Chapter 2 shows this empirically estimated
standard deviation is $\sigma_M = 20.1\%$. Substituting these values into Eqn. 15-1 yields a numerical
estimate of the CML:

$$E(r_i) = RFR + \left(\frac{E(r_M) - RFR}{\sigma_M}\right)\sigma_i \tag{15-1a}$$

$$= 4.5\% + \left(\frac{7.1\%}{20.1\%}\right)\sigma_i$$

$$= 4.5\% + .353\,\sigma_i$$

The Separation Theorem

Markowitz diversifiers will select portfolio M because that is the only way to reach the dominant investment opportunities on the CML. After the decision to investment in M is made the next question is: How should the investment in M be financed? If the investor is highly *risk-averse,* a lending portfolio that lies between *RFR* and *M* on the CML in Figure 15-1 will be selected. If the investor is more *aggressive*, a leveraged portfolio that lies above the market portfolio on the CML will maximize the investor's expected utility (happiness). In other words, the investor's financing decision is whether to select a lending portfolio ($x_{RFR} > 0$) or a borrowing portfolio ($x_{RFR} < 0$). Note that equilibrium portfolio theory implies the following *separation theorem:* The optimal investment decision (to buy M) is separate and independent from the financing decision about whether to borrow or lend to finance the investment in M.

THE CAPITAL ASSET-PRICING MODEL (CAPM)

The Nobel Prize–winning Capital Asset Pricing Model, or CAPM, is based on simplifying assumptions. Some of these assumptions are needed to justify Markowitz's efficient frontier, the CML, and the SML.

Assumptions Underlying Portfolio Theory

Four assumptions underlie the efficient frontier in Chapter 14's Figure 14-4 (p. 414) and all portfolio theories based on the efficient frontier:

1. The rate of return from an investment is the most important outcome from the investment.
2. Investors' risk estimates are proportional to the variability of return (namely, the standard deviation or variance) they perceive.
3. Investors are willing to base their decisions on only two parameters of the probability distribution of returns: the expected return and the variance (or its square root, the standard deviation) of returns. Symbolically, $E[U(r)] = f\{E(r), \sigma\}$ where $E[U(r)]$ denotes the investors' expected utility from investment returns.*
4. For any risk class, investors prefer a higher rate of return to a lower one. In terms of utility maximization, $dU/dE(r) > 0$. Conversely, among all securities with the same rate of return, investors prefer less rather than more risk. Symbolically $dU/d\sigma < 0$.

Investors who conform to the preceding assumptions prefer efficient portfolios.

Assumptions Underlying the CML, SML, and CAPM

Financial engineers require some of the following assumptions to develop the CML and SML models. All these assumptions must be combined with the CML and SML to create the CAPM and its far-reaching economic implications:

1. Any amount of money can be borrowed or lent at the risk-free rate of interest RFR.
2. The phrases **homogeneous expectations** and **idealized uncertainty** both refer to the assumption that all investors visualize the same expected return, risk, and correlation statistics for any specific asset.

---

* The preceding chapter's Figures 14-8 through 14-12 use utility theory to rationalize the investment preferences of an investor characterized by the four preceding assumptions.

3. All investors have the same "one-period" investment horizon. The CML is not a model that covers more than one time period.
4. All investments are infinitely divisible; fractional shares may be purchased.
5. No taxes or transaction costs for buying and selling securities exist.
6. No inflation and no change in the level of interest rates exist.
7. The capital market is in a static equilibrium in which supply equals demand for all goods.
8. The market portfolio is a Markowitz efficient portfolio that contains all assets in the world in the proportions they exist.

Essentially, the CAPM is based on a list of unrealistic assumptions. The assumptions provide a concrete foundation upon which a theory can be derived by applying the forces of economic logic and mathematics. Without these assumptions, the analysis degenerates into inconclusive arguments. Financial economists base their models on a few simple assumptions. Then a theory is derived with conclusions and implications, which are incontestable, given the assumptions. The final test of a theory should be its predictive power, not the realism of its assumptions.

RATIONALE FOR THE SECURITY MARKET LINE (SML)

The CML was introduced in Figures 14-7 and 14-12 in Chapter 14 (pp. 421, 426). The Security Market Line (SML) introduced in Figure 7-7 of Chapter 7 (p. 181). When the CML and SML are supported by the assumptions just cited, they become equilibrium portfolio theories.

The economic rationale for the SML is based on the way the assets in a diversified portfolio covary. The formula for the variance of a diversified portfolio was introduced in Eqns. 14-3, 14-3a, and 14-3b in Chapter 14. These portfolio variance formulas are equivalently rewritten as Eqn. (14-3c) to focus our attention on the covariances, denoted σ_{ij} for $i \neq j$:

$$VAR(r_p) = \sum_{i=1}^{N} x_i^2 VAR(r_i) + \sum_{\substack{i=1 \\ i \neq j}}^{N} \sum_{j=1}^{N} x_i x_j \sigma_{ij} \tag{14-3c}$$

Note that within the expression for a portfolio's risk are covariances between all pairs of assets that are investment candidates. The essence of Markowitz portfolio analysis is to find securities with low covariances. If all other factors are equal, demand will be high for investments that have a low covariance (undiversifiable comovement) with the market portfolio. Low covariances with the market are desirable because they reduce portfolio risk. In contrast, securities that have high covariance with the market have high undiversifiable risk and will, therefore, experience low demand. High covariances are undesirable because they tend to increase portfolio risk. The prices of securities with high systematic risk will fall, and prices of securities with low systematic risk will be bid up. Since equilibrium rates of return move inversely with the price of the security, securities having high market covariances will have relatively low prices (that is, low relative to their income, but not necessarily low in dollar amounts) and high expected returns. Conversely, securities with low or negative covariances will have relatively high prices and therefore experience low expected rates of return in equilibrium. The resulting relationship is depicted in Figure 15-2A and Eqn. 15-3.*[2]

---

*   The intuitive discussion above assumes that all expected returns, variances, and covariances are constant.

DEFINITION

THE SECURITY MARKET LINE (SML)

Eqn. 15-3 states the security market line (SML) in terms of the covariance between the market portfolio and asset i. A graphical representation of the SML is in Figure 15-2A.

$$E(r_i) = RFR + \frac{E(r_M) - RFR}{VAR(r_M)} COV(r_i, r_M)$$ (15-3)

where

$E(r_i)$ = equilibrium expected return for ith asset

RFR = risk-free rate of interest

$E(r_M) - RFR$ = Equity risk premium (introduced verbally in Chapter 2)

$\dfrac{E(r_M) - RFR}{VAR(r_M)}$ = slope of SML

$COV(r_i, r_M) = \sigma_{iM}$ = covariance of returns between asset i and the market portfolio

The expected return from the SML, $E(r_i)$, is the appropriate discount rate to use when computing the ith security's present value. Stated differently, $E(r_i)$ is the **risk-adjusted discount rate**, **required rate of return, cost of capital**, or capitalization rate that should be used to find the present value of an asset with the amount of systematic risk in asset i.

Figure 15-2A and Eqn. 15-3 say that in equilibrium every asset should be priced so that its expected return is a linear function of its covariance of returns with the market. This means the expected return from any asset should increase as its undiversifiable risk rises. The more risk a security has that cannot be reduced by diversification, the more return investors will require to induce them to hold that asset in their portfolios.

The locus of equilibrium expected returns shown in Figure 15-2A is called the SML. The $[E(r), COV(r_i, r_M)]$ pairs for diversified portfolios and individual securities will lie on the SML. The SML of Figure 15-2A is a separate and distinct relation from the CML shown in Figure 15-1. In equilibrium, an *individual* security's expected return and risk statistics will lie on the SML if the asset is correctly priced. But an *individual* security's expected return and risk statistics lie below the CML. In equilibrium, only *efficient portfolios* lie on the CML. Individual securities cannot reach the CML because they have not had their diversifiable risk reduced via diversification.

Note that the economic process that determines the expected returns of individual securities held in portfolios does not consider diversifiable risk.* This unsystematic portion of an asset's total risk can be ignored because it can be diversified away to zero in a portfolio using simple diversification. (See Figure 14-1 in Chapter 14, p. 400.)

---

* Total risk is the relevant risk for investors who do not diversify. For example, if mom and pop have all their wealth invested in Mom & Pop's Grocery, the *total risk* of that investment is relevant to its owners because their diversifiable risk has not been diversified away. It is a different story for the pension funds in Table 2-4A (page 32).

FIGURE 15-2   Equivalent Security Market Line (SML) Models in Terms of: (A) Covariance and (B) Beta

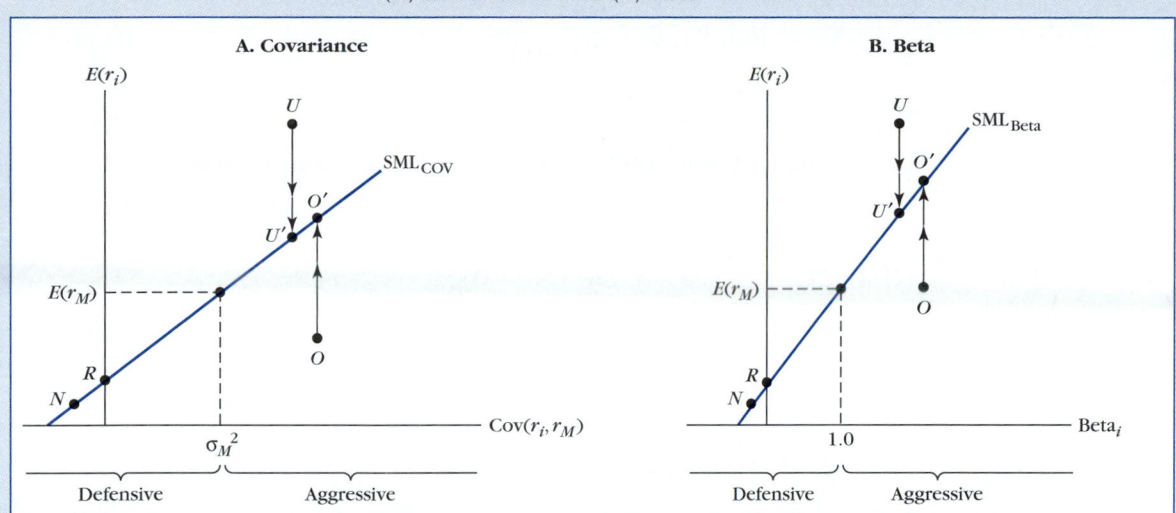

The Security Market Line (SML) can be stated equivalently in terms of either the covariance or the beta because they differ by a factor that is constant throughout the market.

$$\text{Beta}_i = \frac{COV\,(r_i,\,r_M)}{VAR\,(r_M)} = COV\,(r_i,\,r_M)\left(\frac{1}{VAR\,(r_M)}\right) \text{ where } \left(\frac{1}{VAR\,(r_M)}\right) \text{ is a constant factor}$$

Restating the SML

The latter part of Chapter 7 defined the beta regression slope coefficient in Eqn. 7-14 and explained how it is an index of an asset's undiversifiable (systematic) risk. Figures 7-5 and 7-6 in Chapter 7 illustrate the discussion (see pp. 170 and 174). The preceding paragraphs of this chapter suggested that an asset's covariance of returns with the market is also a measure of undiversifiable risk. These two undiversifiable risk statistics are mathematically equivalent. They are interchangeable risk measures that mean two methods of defining the SML exist. In Figure 15-2B the SML is defined in terms of the beta regression coefficient, denoted β_i. The SML stated in terms of the $COV(r_i, r_m)$ is shown in Figure 15-2A. The two representations of the SML are mathematically and economically equivalent. The only difference between these two graphs is in the scaling of their horizontal axes. The horizontal axis of the SML that is stated in terms of the beta coefficient is scaled by a factor of $[1/VAR(r_M)]$ relative to the SML stated in terms of the covariance. This is due to the mathematical relationship between the beta coefficient and the covariance shown in Eqn. 15-4.

$$\beta_i = \frac{COV(r_i, r_M)}{VAR(r_M)}$$

$$= COV(r_i, r_M)\left(\frac{1}{VAR(r_M)}\right) \quad \text{where } \left(\frac{1}{VAR(r_M)}\right) \text{ is a constant over all assets} \qquad \textbf{(15-4)}$$

Thus, the SML of Eqn. 15-3 may be equivalently restated in terms of the beta coefficient, as shown in Eqn. 15-5, by substituting in Eqn. 15-4.

$$E(r_i) = RFR + \frac{E(r_M) - RFR}{VAR(r_M)}COV(r_i, r_M) \tag{15-3}$$

$$= RFR + [E(r_M) - RFR]\frac{COV(r_i, r_M)}{VAR(r_M)}$$

$$= RFR + [E(r_M) - RFR]\beta_i \tag{15-5}$$

Eqns. 15-3 and 15-5 represent the two equivalent SMLs graphed in Figure 15-2.

NUMERICAL ESTIMATE OF THE SML

Table 2-3 of Chapter 2 (p. 30) shows the authors' estimates of the risk-free rate equals $RFR = 4.5\%$ and the equity risk premium equals $E(r_M) - RFR = 7.1\%$. Substituting these values into Eqn. 15-5 yields a numerical estimate of the SML stated in terms of beta.

$$E(r_i) = RFR + [E(r_M) - RFR]\beta_i$$

$$= 4.5\% + 7.1\%\beta_i \tag{15-5a}$$

Overpriced and Underpriced Assets

The SML has asset-pricing implications. Points between the SML and the $E(r)$ axis like point U in Figure 15-2 represent **underpriced securities**. Point U represents a security with an unusually high return for the amount of systematic risk it bears; assets like this will enjoy strong demand that will bid their prices up until their equilibrium rate of return is driven down onto the SML at point U'.

Assets lying between the SML and the systematic risk axis have prices that are **overpriced**. The asset at point O in Figure 15-2, for instance, does not offer sufficient return to induce rational investors to accept the amount of systematic risk it bears. The price of asset O will fall because it will suffer from a lack of demand. The arrows in Figure 15-2 and Eqn. 15-6 illustrate these price adjustments. The prices of such assets will continue to fall until the denominator of the rate-of-return formula is low enough to allow its expected return to reach the SML at point O' in Figures 15-2A and B.

$$\uparrow E(r_O) = \frac{E(\text{capital gains or losses } + \text{ cash flow})}{\downarrow \text{purchase price}}$$

$$= \frac{E(P_t - P_{t-1} + \text{cash flow}_t)}{\downarrow P_{t-1}} \tag{15-6}$$

When an asset lies on the SML it is at equilibrium. Equilibrium prices remain constant until a change in the asset's systematic risk, a change in the RFR, or some other change causes a disequilibrium.

Negative Correlation with the Market Portfolio, M

Point N in Figure 15-2 represents a security with an equilibrium rate of return below the return on risk-free asset's rate, RFR. Capital market theory explains that the price of N is maintained at high levels because it has a negative covariance (beta) with the market. Some gold mining corporations' stocks provide examples of assets with low betas and low average returns like asset N in Figure 15-2.

The Discontinuity Between Expected Value Theory and Historical Data

Portfolio theory asserts that *expected* returns are determined by *expected* risk: The theory is cast in terms of expected values. Although investor expectations are affected by historical data, investors do not confine their thoughts to these historical data as they make their investment decisions. Plans for the future are based on expectations about the future. Thus, a "jump" is made in going from the Security Market Line (SML), which is stated in terms of expectations, to historical data. If the probability distributions of the historical returns have all remained stable over time, then historical average return and variance statistics are unbiased estimates of the expected returns and expected variances. However, if the probability distributions of returns have changed with the passage of time, the historical data will play little or no role in this chapter's theories about expected future values. To perform an empirical test of the equilibrium portfolio theory presented here, investors' expectations must be observed. Observing people's expectations would be a costly exercise, and impossible to do with any accuracy.

RELAXING THE CML AND SML ASSUMPTIONS

This section relaxes the assumptions underlying equilibrium portfolio theory listed on pages 440–441 and considers aligning them more closely with reality.

Different Risk-Free Interest Rates for Borrowing and Lending

Realistically, the interest rate charged for borrowing, B, is higher than the interest rate paid to depositors, D. In Figure 15-3 this is represented by two risk-free interest rates at points D and B representing deposit and borrowing opportunities. The dashed portions of the two lines emerging from points D and B do not represent investment opportunities; they merely clarify construction of the model. Two tangency portfolios, denoted M_D and M_B, are shown for lenders and borrowers, respectively. They replace the single market portfolio, M, that existed when we assumed money could be borrowed or lent at the same riskless rate. The kinked line formed by the solid sections of the two lines and a section of the opportunity locus is the relevant efficient frontier when the borrowing and lending rates differ. As a result, the CML has a curved section between M_D and M_B in Figure 15-3.[3]

Reconsider the mathematical representation of the SML in terms of the covariance, Eqn. 15-3. If different borrowing and deposit rates are assumed then two slightly different SML's emerge; these two SMLs have different vertical axis intercepts. Multiple risk-free interest rates make it difficult to specify the SML.

Transaction Costs Create Friction

Transaction costs such as brokerage commissions, bid-ask spreads, search costs, taxes, fees, and other "market frictions" can be modeled as a "band" below both the CML and SML. The CML and lower edge of the transaction cost band are a few percentage points apart. It would not be profitable for investors to buy and sell securities located between the CML and the lower edge of the band because transaction costs would consume the potential profit that induced the trading. As a result, the markets would never quite reach the theoretical equilibrium.[4]

FIGURE 15-3   The Capital Market Line Bends When the Borrowing (B) and Deposit (D) Rates Differ

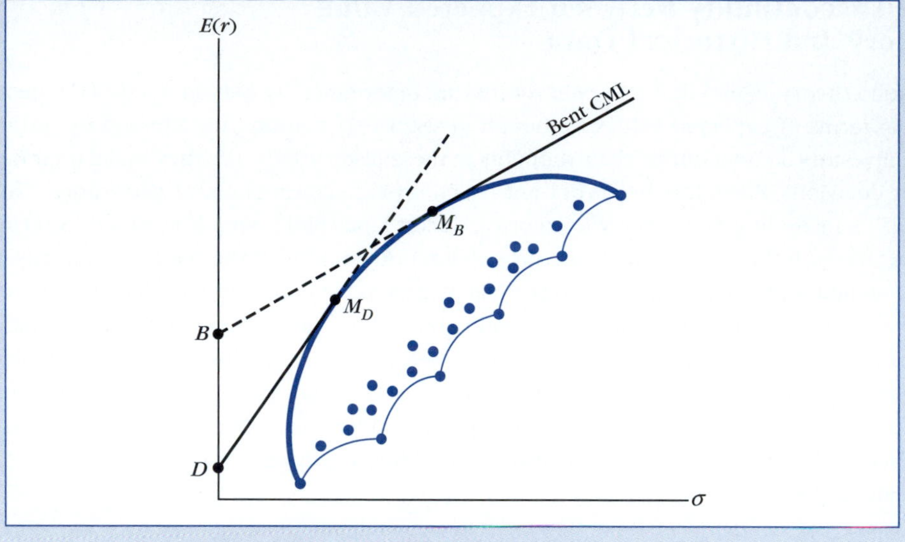

The borrowing rate, denoted B, must exceed the interest rate paid for deposits, denoted D, if a bank is to be profitable. This realistic formulation converts the Capital Market Line (CML) into a CML that bends.

General Uncertainty or Heterogeneous Expectations

Eliminating the simplifying assumptions about *homogeneous expectations* or a *common investment horizon* would require drawing a separate efficient frontier, CML and SML, for each investor. "Fuzzy" curves and lines would result. The more investors' expectations differed, or the more investors' investment horizons differed, the fuzzier all lines and curves become. In effect, the lines would become bands. Because of this uncertainty, the analysis becomes determinate only within limits. Only major disequilibriums will be corrected. Statements could not be made with certainty.[5]

Different Tax Rates for Capital Gains

Most countries in the world have legislated lower income tax rates on capital gains (price appreciation) income than on ordinary (wages and rent) income to encourage business investment. Recognizing that tax rates on ordinary income differ from the tax rates on capital gains income blurs our model's picture of economic equilibrium.

Eqn. 15-7 defines the after-tax rate of return from a one-period investment, where T_G is the capital gains tax rate and T_0 is the tax rate on ordinary income.

$$r^t = \frac{(\text{Capital gains})(1 - T_G) + (\text{Cash dividends})(1 - T_O)}{\text{Market price at beginning of the holding period}} \tag{15-7}$$

If capital gains are taxed at a different rate than ordinary income, every investor would see a slightly different CML and SML in terms of after-tax returns that varied with their tax brackets. As a result, a static equilibrium could not emerge, even if all the other assumptions were maintained.[6]

Indivisibilities

Dropping the assumption that all assets are infinitely divisible changes the SML into a dotted line. Each dot would represent an opportunity attainable with an integral number of shares. This punctuated scenario would make the mathematics intractable.

Conclusions About the Simplifying Assumptions

Simplifying assumptions underlying capital market theory were relaxed one at a time. Each time, the implications of the theoretical model were obscured slightly. If all the simplifying assumptions were relaxed simultaneously, the result would be even less determinate. However, the fact that the theoretical model is not derivable under realistic assumptions does not mean it is worthless. The model still rationalizes complex behavior (such as diversification) and offers realistic suggestions about the directions that prices and returns should follow when they deviate significantly from equilibrium. Theory is a powerful engine for analysis.

CRITICISMS AND TESTS OF THE SML

The market portfolio is an important feature of the characteristic line, the CML, and the SML. Undiversifiable (systematic, market) risk from the market portfolio is the *sole* determinant of expected returns and asset prices in the SML. Some people criticize the elegant simplicity of the Nobel Prize–winning SML by saying the model is too simple. Critics have suggested additional explanatory variables for the SML.

The Liquidity of the Investments

The bid-ask spread, the size of the price mark-down needed to sell an asset, brokerage commissions, transfer taxes, and any other fees that are incurred in selling an investment are called *transactions costs* or *liquidity costs*. A market asset's liquidity varies inversely with its liquidation costs. When discussing a closely held (founder-owned) business, experts describe a large difference between the value of this illiquid business as a going concern and the liquidation value of the same firm.[7] Liquidation costs exceeding 30% of the value of the illiquid firm are sometimes discussed.[8]

Yakov Amihud and Haim Mendelson suggested an **illiquidity premium** be added to the expected return from the SML, as shown in Eqn. 15-8.[9]

$$E(r_i) = RFR + [E(r_M) - RFR]b_i + f[E(\text{Liquidity costs}_i)] \qquad \text{(15-8)}$$

Amihud and Mendelson suggest the illiquidity premium should increase at a decreasing rate as the liquidation costs associated with the investment increase. Several scholars have criticized the SML because it omits liquidity costs.

Econometric Analysis of Empirical Data

The SML is a positive linear relationship in which the assets' market betas explain their expected returns. Beta subsumes all other risk factors. This powerful hypothesis can be tested by performing two stages of regression analysis.

First-Pass Regressions. The characteristic line is a simple linear regression that was introduced as Eqn. 7-7 in Chapter 7 (repeated here); it can be fit using time-series market data from any asset. Tables 7-5 and 7-6 and Figure 7-6 in Chapter 7 (pp. 173–175) contain information about Coca-Cola's characteristic line.

$$r_{i,t} = \alpha_i + \beta_i r_{M,t} + e_{i,t} \tag{7-7}$$

If a sample contains N assets, then N first-pass characteristic line regressions are estimated to obtain those assets' N betas. N average returns are also computed—to provide estimates of the N expected returns.

Second-Pass Regression. After N average returns and N betas have been computed from N characteristic lines, the SML is estimated as the single cross-sectional regression Eqn. 15-9, where b_0 and b_1 are the intercept and slope coefficients, and u_i is the unexplained residual for asset i.

$$\left(\begin{matrix} \text{Average} \\ \text{return}_i \end{matrix}\right) = b_0 + b_1(\text{Beta}_i) + u_i \quad \text{for } i = 1, 2, \ldots N \text{ assets} \tag{15-9}$$

The N first-pass regressions provide the statistical input data for the one second-pass regression.

Econometric Problems with the Characteristic Line

The characteristic line, Eqn. 7-7, is a well-defined model that has numerous practical applications. As a result, it is subject to statistical testing. Empirical estimates of characteristic line statistics reveals that some of the statistics are not constant through time. Marshall Blume points out a tendency for betas to regress toward their mean value of $+1$ from one 7-year sample period to the next 7-year sample period.[10] Betas that behave this way are said to be unstable from sample to sample, to suffer from **intertemporal instability,** or to be **sample dependent**. Jack Francis extended this research by showing that betas, standard deviations, and correlations with the market portfolio were all sample dependent to varying degrees.[11] Frank Fabozzi and Jack Francis provided evidence that this intertemporal instability does not comprise a sufficient problem to negate the value of the models.[12]

Econometric Problems with the SML Contrary to the predictions of the theoretical SML model, some empirical studies reported that anomalous variables have significant explanatory power over the assets' returns, while the assets' betas have little explanatory power.

Anomalous Findings. Eqn. 15-10 it is a cross-sectional multiple regression model that extends the simple regression model of the SML in Eqn. 15-9, where b_0 is the intercept, b_1, b_2, b_3, and b_4 are regression slope coefficients, and u_i is the unexplained residual for asset i.

$$\left(\begin{matrix} \text{Average} \\ \text{return}_i \end{matrix}\right) = b_0 + b_1(\text{Beta}_i) + b_2(B/V_i) + b_3(E/P_i) + b_4(\text{Size}_i) + u_i \tag{15-10}$$

The statistically significant explanatory variables include firms' sizes (total market value of equity), book-value-to-market equity (B/V) ratio, and the earnings-price (E/P) ratio. SML theory does not suggest that (B/V), (E/P), and firm size should have any explanatory power over firms' average returns. Richard Roll suggested the problem with the empirical tests of the SML may be that the researchers did not use an efficient market portfolio, as specified in the assumptions underlying the SML.[13]

In the late 1970s and early 1980s Sanjoy Basu and Marc Reinganum, working separately, reported empirical evidence suggesting that excess returns on common stocks are a continuously increasing function of their earnings-per-share-to-price-per-share (E/P) ratios.[14] Then, in the early 1980s Rolf Banz, Marc Reinganum, and Donald Keim reported that large (small) firms tend to have smaller (larger) average returns than those predicted by the SML.[15] In the early 1990s statistics provided by Eugene Fama and Kenneth French suggested book-value-to-market equity (B/V) as another contradiction to the SML.[16] Empirical findings made it difficult to maintain faith in the theoretical SML as Barr Rosenberg, Kenneth Reid, and Ronald Lanstein; Louis K. C. Chan, Yasushi Hamao, and Josef Lakonishok; Eugene Fama and Kenneth French; James Davis; and S. P. Kothari and Jay Shanken reported finding that firms with greater book-value-to-market equity tended to earn greater risk-adjusted returns.[17] These studies argued that there was a direct relationship between book-value-to-market equity and beta risk-adjusted returns estimated with a multiple regression model like Eqn. 15-10.

The EIV Problem. Most of the empirical research reporting anomalous explanatory variables that contradict the SML were performed without taking sufficient steps to overcome a statistical difficulty called the *errors-in-variables (EIV) problem*. The EIV problem arises because the true beta coefficients are unobservable. Researchers use various estimates as proxies for the true betas.* Puneet Handa, S. P. Kothari, Charles Wasley (HKW), and Dongcheol Kim showed that the EIV problem throws light on the troublesome anomalies reported above.[18] The research by HKW and Kim shows that the EIV problem leads to an underestimation of the importance of the beta as an explanatory variable and overestimation of the cross-sectional regression (CSR) coefficients associated with anomalous explanatory variables that can be observed without error such as firms' sizes, book-value-to-market equity ratios, and E/P ratios.

Several researchers have done work to overcome the EIV problem. Robert Litzenberger and Krishna Ramaswamy, Jay Shanken, and, independently, Dongcheol Kim have suggested altering the commonly used two-pass regression methodology that was reviewed above.[19] (See the previous discussion of Eqns. 7–7 and 15-9 about that methodology.) In addition, Michael Gibbons, as well as Marjorie McElroy and Edwin Burmeister, estimated asset risk factors and their associated risk coefficients jointly.[20] Kim commented on the EIV problem he found in a 1973 paper by Eugene Fama and James MacBeth.[21] Kim used an altered version of the two-pass regression test methodology Fama and MacBeth used and provided his own CSR coefficients. Kim's procedure differed from that of most of the preceding researchers, who usually formed portfolios of similar assets to obtain portfolio average statistics that would reduce the EIV problem.

Kim's Positive Conclusions. Kim pointed out that using individual assets in empirical tests offers several advantages that were not available when using portfolios of assets to minimize the EIV problem.[22] The first advantage is that the methodology avoids arbitrariness. In previous empirical studies the estimated statistics differed with the portfolio formation method and/or the number of portfolios used in the CSR.[23] The second advantage is that the new procedure utilizes all information about the cross-sectional behavior of individual stocks. Some of this information might have been lost if portfolio-grouping techniques had been employed, as has been typically done in preceding research. Third, using all of the individual assets avoids the data-snooping bias suggested by Lo and MacKinlay.[24]

Eqn. 15-9 is an econometric formulation of the theoretical SML shown at Eqn. 15-5. Kim found that massive empirical data he gathered fit Eqn. 15-9 better than it fit a similar model that also contained anomalous variables like Eqn. 15-10. In view of the simplifying assumptions (see pp. 440–441) on which equilibrium portfolio theory is based, and all the negative empirical studies that preceded Kim's findings, Kim's empirical support for the SML is surprising and gratifying.

---

* Betas can be estimated statistically by using a sample of monthly returns over a sample of 36 months, quarterly returns over a sample of 8 years, and many other ways. The SML theory does not give a precise definition of how the betas should be measured.

The remainder of this chapter considers a competing capital market theory that can take anomalous variables like those in Eqn. 15-10 and incorporate them into the theory.

**DEFINITION**

ARBITRAGE REVISITED

We learned in Chapter 3 that the **law of one price** says, after the appropriate foreign currency adjustments are made, a share of Coca-Cola stock sells for the same price at the NYSE, the Chicago Stock Exchange, the London Stock Exchange, and in every other stock market in the world. If the stock's price differed in two markets, *arbitrageurs* would buy the stock in the market where its price is cheap and immediately sell the stock in the market where its price is higher and make an easy profit. This arbitrage would continue to bid up the low price and push down the high price until those prices were pushed together. The point is: Arbitrage becomes profitable whenever the law of one prize is violated.

ARBITRAGE PRICING THEORY (APT)

Stephen Ross formulated various arbitrage arguments into a formal Arbitrage Pricing Theory (APT) that uses any number of risk factors.[25] We begin with the simplest case—the APT model with one risk factor.

Two Equally Risky Streams of Cash Flows

The one-factor APT model assumes the rates of return for all assets are generated by a single systematic risk factor (risk attribute) denoted F, as shown in Eqns. 15-11 and 15-12.

$$r_{1,t} = a_1 + b_1 F_t + e_{1,t} \tag{15-11}$$

$$r_{2,t} = a_2 + b_2 F_t + e_{2,t} \tag{15-12}$$

The single line in Figure 15-4 could illustrate either Eqn. 15-11 or 15-12. *

STUDY CHECK

ARBITRAGE PRICING

QUESTION: Before you read the APT explanation below, can you explain how the assets in 15-11 and 15-12 might be priced correctly?

ANSWER: When assets 1 and 2 are correctly priced the two lines in Figure 15-4 will be identical, if they have identical expected returns, identical intercept terms, $E(r_1) = a_1 = E(r_2) = a_2$, and identical slopes (equal risk), $b_1 = b_2$.

---

* Eqns. 15-11 and 15-12 are two ordinary least squares (OLS) regression lines of the general form: $y = a + bx + e$, which is rewritten as: $r = a + bF + e$. APT is based on some statistical assumptions that are easy to accept. The residuals $e_{1,t}$ and $e_{2,t}$ in Eqns. 15-11 and 15-12 have expected values of zero, $E(e_{1,t}) = E(e_{2,t}) = 0$; and, F_t is a random variable with an expected value of zero, $E(F_t) = 0$.

FIGURE 15-4   The Return Generating Process for a Single-Factor
Time-Series Model

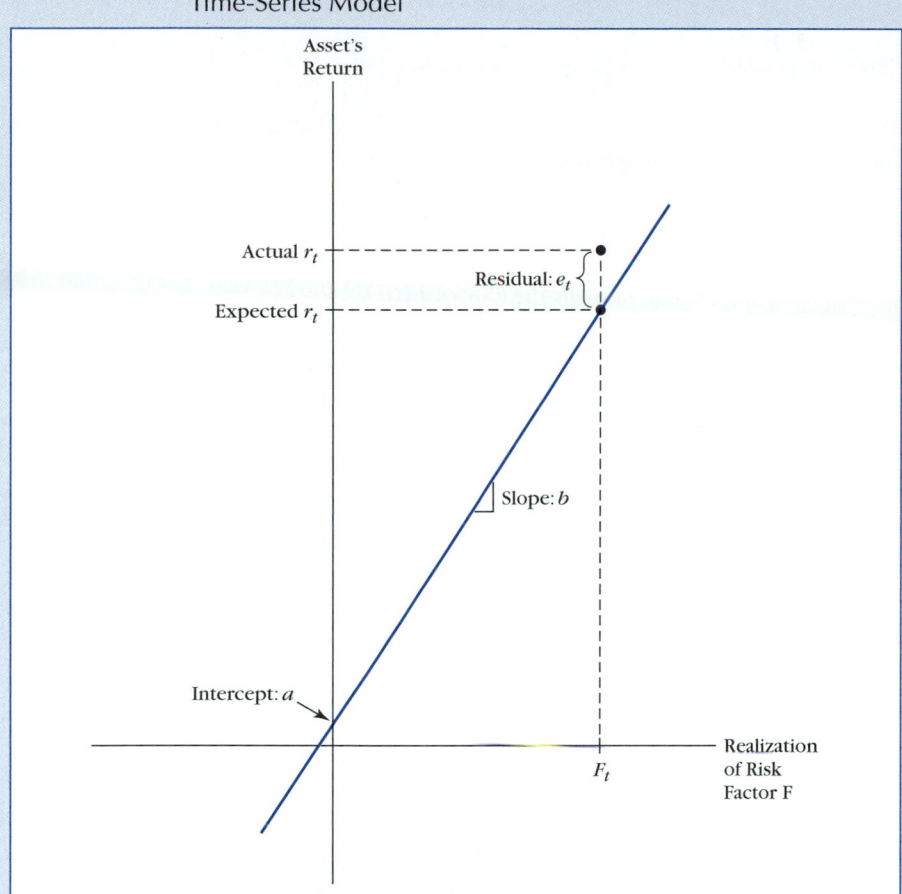

The **return generating process** is a simple time-series regression for one asset. The
asset's rate of return, r_t, is explained by a risk factor with a value denoted F_t during time
period t. The part of the asset's return during time period t left unexplained by the return
generating process is the idiosyncratic residual return, denoted e_t.

Assume the **factor betas** in Eqns. 15-11 and 15-12 are equal, $b_1 = b_2$, as illustrated by the
single line in Figure 15-4. Assuming the betas are equal is a convenient, but temporary, assumption. In a different realistic example, every asset could have a different factor beta (slope)
value. These factor betas measure how sensitive the assets' returns are to shocks from the
common risk factor denoted F. Factor betas are indexes of undiversifiable (systematic) risk.

Think of Eqns. 15-11 and 15-12 as being like the characteristic line at Eqn. 7-7 in Chapter 7
(p. 169) in every way except one. Eqns. 15-11 and 15-12 have one common risk factor,
denoted F, but that common factor must be *different from the market portfolio*, denoted M.
Any random variable other than M can serve as an APT risk factor.

WHY IS THE EXPECTED VALUE OF AN APT RISK FACTOR ALWAYS ZERO?   **EXAMPLE**

An APT risk factor might be gross domestic product (GDP), a market interest rate, the rate
of inflation (INF), the price of a barrel of crude oil, or any other random variable that affects

security prices. If we use gross domestic product (GDP) as an APT risk factor (F), the fluctuation around the mean (expected) value of GDP in time period t is called an *unanticipated change* in GDP.

$$F_t = [GDP_t - E(GDP)] = \text{Unanticipated change in GDP}$$

The expected value of the unanticipated changes in GDP are always zero because deviations around every mean always sum to zero.

$$E(F_t) = E[GDP_t - E(GDP)] = \left(\begin{array}{c} \text{Expected value of} \\ \text{fluctuations around the} \\ \text{mean value of } E(GDP) \end{array} \right) = 0$$

$E(F)$ represents the expected (weighted average) value of F measured across T successive GDP outcomes.

$$E(F) = \sum_{t=1}^{T} p_t F_t = 0$$

$$= p_1 F_1 + p_2 F_2 + p_3 F_3 + \dots p_T F_T = 0$$

$$= E[GDP_t - E(GDP)] = p_1[GDP_1 - E(GDP)] + p_2[GDP_2 - E(GDP)] + \dots + p_T[GDP_T - E(GDP)] = 0$$

and the probabilities (weights) across all the outcomes sum to 1, $\sum_{t=1}^{T} p_t = 1$.

The random variable F is an APT risk factor that has an expected value of zero, $E(F) = 0$. Since b is a constant, it follows that Eqns. 15-11 and 15-12 both contain quantities that have expected values of zero: $bE(F) = E(bF) = 0$. The residuals also have expected values of zero, $E(e_{1,t}) = E(e_{2,t}) = 0$. It follows that these two assets' expected rates of return must equal their intercept terms, as shown in Eqns. 15-13 and 15-14.

$$E(r_1) = a_1 \tag{15-13}$$

$$E(r_2) = a_2 \tag{15-14}$$

Figure 14-1 in Chapter 14 (p. 400) showed that the unsystematic part of assets' total variance could easily be diversified away to zero in a portfolio of a few dozen randomly selected assets. That is why we focus on betas and ignore the residual variances and total variances. Only the beta risk is undiversifiable.

Combining Eqns. 15-11, 15-12, 15-13, and 15-14 above with the additional assumption that assets 1 and 2 have identical betas, $b_1 = b_2$, makes the two assets equally risky. The law of one price tells us that assets with equal betas have the same amount of undiversifiable risk and, therefore, should have identical expected rates of return. Furthermore, as explained above with reference to Eqns. 15-13 and 15-14, they should also have identical expected rates of return and intercept terms, $E(r_1) = a_1 = E(r_2) = a_2$. The scenario described here is an equilibrium situation in which it will not be profitable to perform arbitrage between assets 1 and 2. The single upward sloping line in Figure 15-4 illustrates both Eqns. 15-11 and 15-12. When assets 1 and 2 are correctly priced, the two lines in Figure 15-1 are identical because, as explained above, they have identical expected returns and identical intercept terms, $E(r_1)$ = a_1 = $E(r_2)$ = a_2, and identical slopes, b_1 = b_2. A few pages ahead, Figure 15-6 illustrates what happens when two assets are mis-priced.

The Arbitrage Pricing Theory Line

Eqn. 15-15 defines the **arbitrage pricing theory line** for one risk factor. This equation says that the expected return from risky asset i equals the risk-free rate of return plus a risk premium that is proportional to the asset's sensitivity, b_i:

$$E(r_i) = RFR + b_i\lambda \tag{15-15}$$

An asset's sensitivity is measured by its *factor beta*, or *sensitivity coefficient*, or *factor loading*; it equals the statistical slope coefficient b_i in Eqns. 15-11 and 15-12. The Greek letter lambda, λ, in Eqn. 15-15 can be interpreted to be the **risk premium**, excess rate of return, or the quantity $[E(r_i) - RFR]$ for any asset that has b_i = 1.0. Figure 15-5 illustrates the arbitrage pricing line of Eqn. 15-15.

The arbitrage pricing line shown in Figure 15-5 is a risk-return relationship that is similar to the SML introduced earlier in this chapter. Undiversifiable risk is proportional to the assets' factor betas, b_i; and is measured along the horizontal axis. Assets' expected returns are measured along the vertical axis of Figure 15-5, and the APT Line intersects the vertical axis at the risk-free rate (RFR) of interest. The only difference between the APT Line of Eqn. 15-15 and the SML of Eqn. 15-5 is that their common risk factors must differ. *Only the SML can have the market portfolio, M, as its common risk factor.* The importance of having different risk factors will become apparent when the APT model is expanded to include more than one risk factor.

Overpriced and Underpriced Assets

Consider two assets in the same risk class, like the two assets at points U and O in Figure 15-5. Asset O is overpriced relative to its value, and asset U is underpriced. Figure 15-6 illustrates the two different return generating functions for assets O and U. Assets O and U can be represented by Eqns. 15-11 and 15-12 if we redefine these equations so that Eqn. 15-11 represents the overpriced asset, $E(r_1)$ = a_1 = a_o, and Eqn. 15-12 represents the underpriced asset, $E(r_2)$ = a_2 = a_u. The different alpha intersect values indicate that the two assets are in a disequilibrium, so they will have different expected returns, $E(r_o) < E(r_u)$. Stated differently, assets U and O violate the law of one price because they are both in the same risk class, b_o = b_u, but do not have the same expected rates of return. The supply and demand forces created by arbitrageurs will modify the prices of these assets until an equilibrium is attained in which all assets lie on the APT Line in Figure 15-5.

STUDY CHECK

SOURCES OF RISK

QUESTION: How do the APT return generating functions at Eqns. 15-11 and 15-12 differ from the time-series regression estimates of the characteristic lines in Chapter 7's Eqn. 7-7?

ANSWER: The only difference between Eqn. 7-7 and Eqns. 15-11 and 15-12 is that their common risk factors differ. Only the SML uses the market portfolio, M, as its common risk factor.

FIGURE 15-5   The APT Line for One Risk Factor

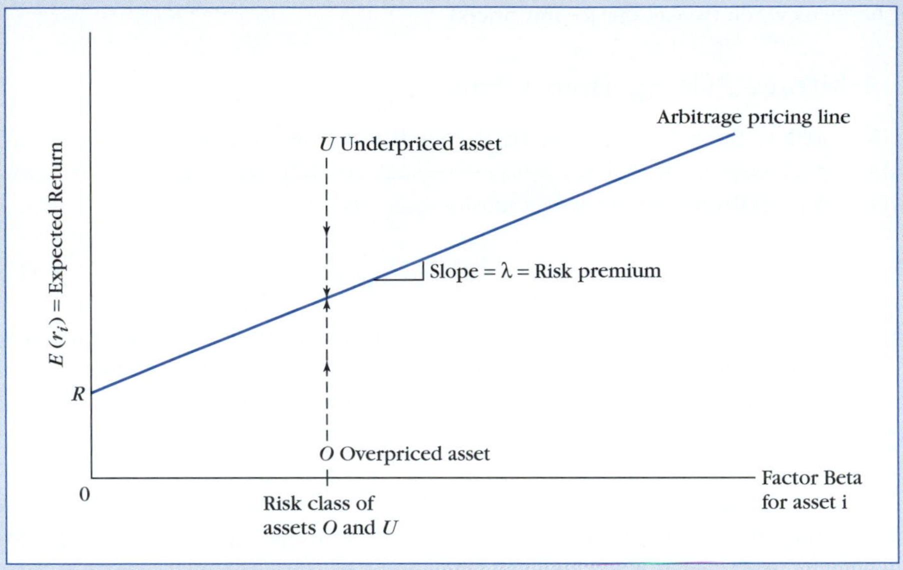

An asset's expected return increases linearly with its beta risk factor. Asset *U* has an unreasonably high expected return for its risk class because the asset is underpriced. The market price of underpriced asset *U* will rise until its expected return drops down onto the APT line, where it is correctly priced. Asset *O* is overpriced and it will experience price declines until its expected return rises up to the APT Line.

Overpriced Assets. Financial analysts will discover that asset O in Figure 15-6 offers investors a lower rate of return than asset U, even though they both involve equal amounts of undiversifiable risk (identical factor betas). Investors are well advised to sell asset O because it is overpriced. The resulting excess supply for asset O will drive down its market price. As the price of asset O is driven down the expected return from asset O will rise. This price-adjustment process is indicated by the arrows in the Eqn. 15-16; the equation defines the expected return for a common stock.

$$\uparrow E(r) = \frac{E(P_{t+1} - P_t + DIV_t)}{\downarrow P_t} = \frac{E(\text{Price change } + \text{ Cash dividend, if any})}{\downarrow \text{Purchase price}} \tag{15-16}$$

Investors will continue to sell asset O until its price is driven down and its expected rate of return rises up to a competitive level on the arbitrage pricing line in Figure 15-5. The upward pointing arrow in Figure 15-5 traces the path that $E(r_o)$ should follow until it reaches equilibrium on the APT Line. These same economic adjustments would push the return generating model for the overpriced asset represented by the dashed line in Figure 15-5 upward until it coincides with the solid line representing the underpriced asset.

Underpriced Assets. Asset U has an unusually high expected rate of return because it lies above the APT Line in Figure 15-5. Investors will buy asset U in order to profit from its abnormally high expected rate of return. As profit-seekers buy asset U to obtain its high return they bid up its price. As the price of asset U is bid higher its expected rate of return will fall. The logic of this economic process can be traced by reversing the direction of the arrows in Eqn. 15-16 above.

FIGURE 15-6   An Arbitrage Opportunity Exists Because Two Equally
Risky Assets Have Different Expected Returns, $E(r_u) = a_u >$
$a_o = E(r_o)$

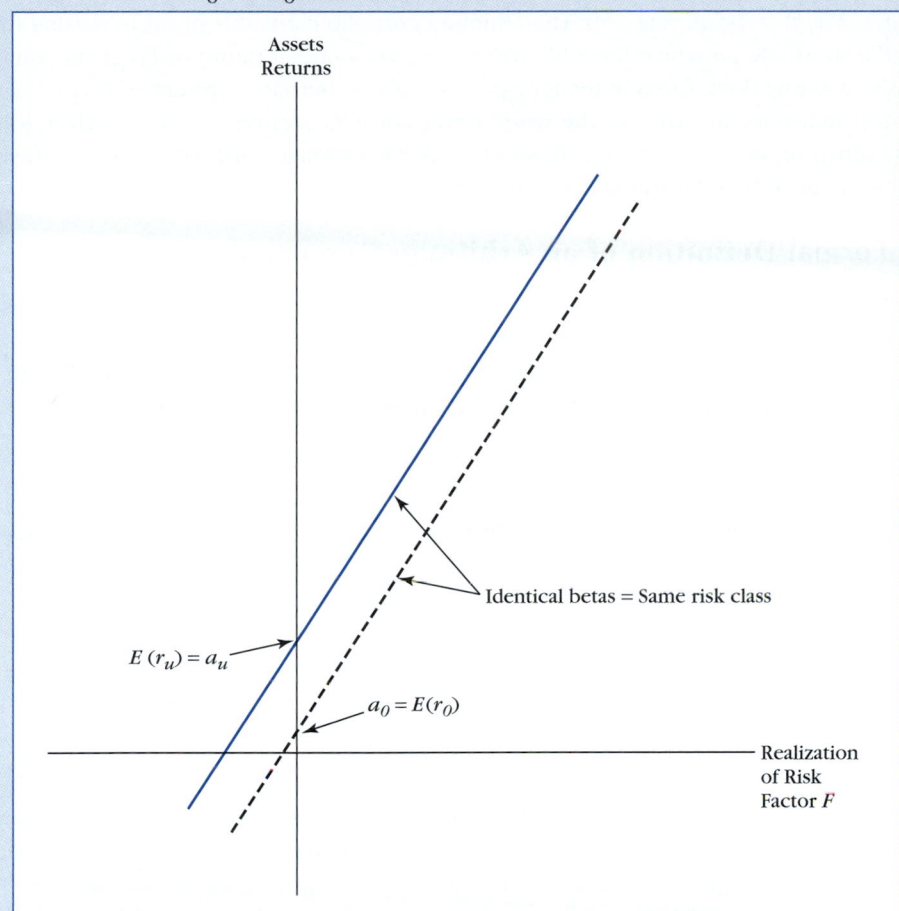

Since the return generating processes for assets O and U have the same slope (equal
betas, identical riskiness), they should have the same expected return. The expected
return (intercept) for asset U is excessively high relative to asset O because asset U is
underpriced. The market price of asset U should rise until its expected return (intercept)
decreases to an equilibrium level that equals $E(r_o) = a_o$. At the same time, $E(r_o) = a_o$
could rise up to equal $E(r_u) = a_u$.

Every asset that plots above the arbitrage pricing line in Figure 15-5 is underpriced,
and *every asset that plots below the APT line is overpriced.*

An Arbitrage Portfolio

To maximize profits, smart investors will sell asset O short and *simultaneously* buy a long
position of equal dollar value in asset U. They will not have one penny of their own cash
invested in their *arbitrage portfolio* made up of a short position in asset O combined with an
equal long position in asset U (more concisely, $P_{O,t=0} - P_{U,t=0} = 0$). They can use the cash

proceeds from the short sale of asset O to buy a long position of equal value in asset U.*
These arbitrageurs will not be exposed to any risk because their arbitrage portfolio is perfectly hedged, with long and short positions of equal value that offset each other's gains and
losses, $VAR(P_O - P_U) = 0$. And finally, the *arbitrage portfolio* will earn a riskless profit of:
$[E(r_U) - E(r_O)]$ = profit rate > 0. The arbitrage portfolio earns this profit by raising funds
from the short sale on which the arbitrageur must pay a rate of return of $E(r_O)$ and, simultaneously, investing these funds in the long position at a higher rate of return of $E(r_U)$.

Most individual investors in the world never consider arbitraging. Nevertheless, it only
takes a few professionals managing multimillion-dollar arbitrage portfolios to sustain the APT
equilibrium condition illustrated in Figure 15-5.

The Formal Definition of an Arbitrage Opportunity

An **arbitrage opportunity** is a perfectly hedged portfolio that can be acquired at a cost of
zero, generates zero cash flows before the position is terminated, and has a positive value
with *certainty* at the end of the investment. An arbitrage opportunity is expressed more formally in Eqns. 15-17, 15-18, and 15-19 below. These three equations are denominated in
money prices.

$$\sum_{i=1}^{N} P_{i,0} = 0 \qquad \text{that is, zero money initially invested at time } t = 0 \tag{15-17}$$

$$\sum_{i=1}^{N} P_{i,T} > 0 \qquad \text{that is, positive profits at time } t = T \tag{15-18}$$

$$\sum_{i=1}^{N} \sum_{j=1}^{N} \sigma_{ij} = 0 \qquad \text{that is, zero risk} \tag{15-19}$$

$P_{i,0}$ is the initial market price of asset i, $P_{i,T}$ is the terminal price of asset i (when the arbitrage
portfolio is liquidated), and $\sigma_{i,j}$ is the covariance of the money prices for assets i and j. These
equations define the arbitrage portfolios that make APT work.

Implications of the APT

If we allow risk factor F in Eqns. 15-11 and 15-12 to be the same as the market portfolio from
the SML, then the SML of Eqn. 15-5 is mathematically equivalent to the APT Line in Eqn.(15-
15). It is reassuring to find that when only one risk factor exists in the world that single factor must be the *market portfolio*, and the single factor APT model turns out to be identical to
the SML.[26] Stated differently, *two completely different theories about asset pricing lead to
identical conclusions and pricing models.*[27]

A TWO-FACTOR APT MODEL

The APT can be extended to include F_1, F_2, F_3, or more independent risk factors that work
together to determine market prices. For example, Eqn. 15-20 is a two-factor return generating function, where

---

* Merrill Lynch, Goldman Sachs, Citigroup, Barclays, and Fidelity can obtain the cash proceeds from their short
  sales. Investors who do not have multimillion-dollar accounts cannot obtain the cash proceeds from their
  short sales.

$r_{i,t}$ = one-period rate of return from ith asset in time period t

a_i = the risk-free rate of return (RFR), which equals the expected rate of return for asset i if all risk factors have a value of zero, $F = 0$

$F_{j,t}$ = jth risk factor (an undiversifiable risk factor, or risk attribute) that affects assets' returns, where $j = 1, 2 \ldots, k$ different undiversifiable risk factors exist. These risk factors all have mathematical expectation of zero, $E(F_{j,t}) = 0$

b_{ij} = sensitivity indicator* (or factor beta) that measures how responsive returns from asset i are to risk factor j

$e_{i,t}$ = random error term for asset i in period t, which measures unexplained residual return, and has an expected value of zero, $E(e_{i,t}) = 0$, and a constant variance, $VAR(e_{i,t})$ = a positive constant.

$$r_{i,t} = a_i + b_{i1}F_{1,t} + b_{i2}F_{2,t} + e_{i,t} \tag{15-20}$$

Think of the first risk factor in Eqn. 15-20 as being, say, the unanticipated change in GDP, denoted $F_{1t} = [GDP_t - E(GDP)]$, and the second risk factor, F_{2t}, as being the unanticipated change in the cash dividend payout ratio for asset i. Observations of these two factors could easily be collected over $t = 1, 2, \ldots T$ time periods. There is nothing special about these two risk factors. Unlike the rigidly defined SML, which is based on only the market portfolio, APT is a more flexible model. APT gives us no clues as to what risk factors are relevant. A statistically oriented financial analyst must do research to find the best explanatory factors.

Three Highly Diversified Portfolios

Consider three risk-averse investors who form portfolios B, C, and D that each contains N assets. In order to solve APT problems mathematically we must assume that the number of assets exceeds the number of risk factors. Thus, this example requires at least N assets $> k$ *risk factors* = 2 risk factors.

Reconsider Figure 14-1 in Chapter 14 (p. 400) and you will see the desirability of having a large number of assets. As N grows larger, the probability increases that the diversifiable risk is diversified away to zero.**[28]

The return from a two-factor portfolio is defined in Eqn. 15-21:

$$r_{p,t} = \sum_{i=1}^{N} x_i[a_i + b_{i1}F_{1,t} + b_{i2}F_{2,t} + e_{i,t}] \tag{15-21}$$

Eqn. 15-22 is the balance sheet identity requiring the assets to equal the liabilities so the weights of all assets ($x_i > 0$) and liabilities ($x_i < 0$) sum to zero. The economic interpretation of the zero sum is that a combination of long and short positions are used to create an arbitrage portfolio that requires no cash investment. This arbitrage portfolio is a **self-financing position**.

$$\sum_{i=1}^{N} x_i = 0 \tag{15-22}$$

---

* The b_{ij} term is called a factor loading if it is estimated using factor analytic procedures; it is called a regression slope coefficient if it is estimated via regression analysis. Eqn. 7-14 (p. 177) provides a mathematical definition of a regression beta.

** If n is a small number we might obtain an APT model composed of rough lines and surfaces with finite thicknesses that has no unique solutions.

In a well-diversified portfolio (when N is large) the unsystematic residual risk diversifies away to zero, as shown in Figure 14-1 in Chapter 14 (p. 400). As the result, Eqns. 15-23 and 15-24 will contain only *systematic risk factors* 1 and 2, respectively:

$$b_{1_p} = \sum_{i=1}^{N \ assets} x_i b_{i1} + 0 \tag{15-23}$$

$$b_{2_p} = \sum_{i=1}^{N \ assets} x_i b_{i2} + 0 \tag{15-24}$$

Eqns. 15-23 and 15-24 define a portfolio containing two kinds of undiversifiable risk, b_{1p} and b_{2p}, plus the zero diversifiable risk that (by definition) will be in the arbitrage portfolio.

Table 15-1 shows the risk and return statistics for the three well-diversified portfolios B, C, and D.

The APT Model

Eqn. 15-25 shows the general form of the APT model that can be derived from the two-factor return generating function of Eqn. 15-20. The factor betas, b_{i1} and b_{i2}, are the *explanatory variables* (*risk factors*) that determine the value of the expected return in Eqn. 15-25a.

$$E(r_i) = \lambda_0 + \lambda_1 b_1 + \lambda_2 b_2 \tag{15-25}$$

$$E(r_1) = 5.629 + 7.777 b_{i1} + 3.703 b_{i2} \tag{15-25a}$$

Eqn. 15-25a shows the specific APT model that can be derived from the numerical values in Table 15-1.

Three points define a three-dimensional plane. Eqn. 15-25a is the formula for a specific three-dimensional plane in $[E(r_p), b_{i1}, b_{i2}]$ space. More specifically, Eqn. 15-25a is an asset-pricing model for the three portfolios in Table 15-1. Figure 15-7 illustrates the APT plane that represents Eqn. 15-25a. Substituting the numerical value for any of the three portfolios in Table 15-1 into Eqn. 15-25a proves numerically that the three points fit on this APT plane.

The Arbitrage Portfolio

Figure 14-1 in Chapter 14 shows that when more than about 36 randomly selected stocks are assembled into a portfolio, the portfolio's unsystematic (diversifiable) risk usually gets averaged away to zero. When dealing with such well-diversified portfolios (if there were no transaction costs to impede trading) the risks and return of every asset would conform to an APT model resembling Eqn. 15-25a and Figure 15-7. Consider a specific case where one asset is mispriced to see how the profit-seeking arbitrageurs realign prices.

TABLE 15-1   Risk and Return Statistics for Three Portfolios

Portfolio	Expected Return	Risk Factor b_{p1}	Risk Factor b_{p2}
B	$E(r_B) = 16\%$	$b_{B,1} = 1.0$	$b_{B,2} = 0.7$
C	$E(r_C) = 14\%$	$b_{C,1} = 0.6$	$b_{C,2} = 1.0$
D	$E(r_D) = 11\%$	$b_{D,1} = 0.5$	$b_{D,2} = 0.4$

FIGURE 15-7   APT Plane for Two-Factor Model

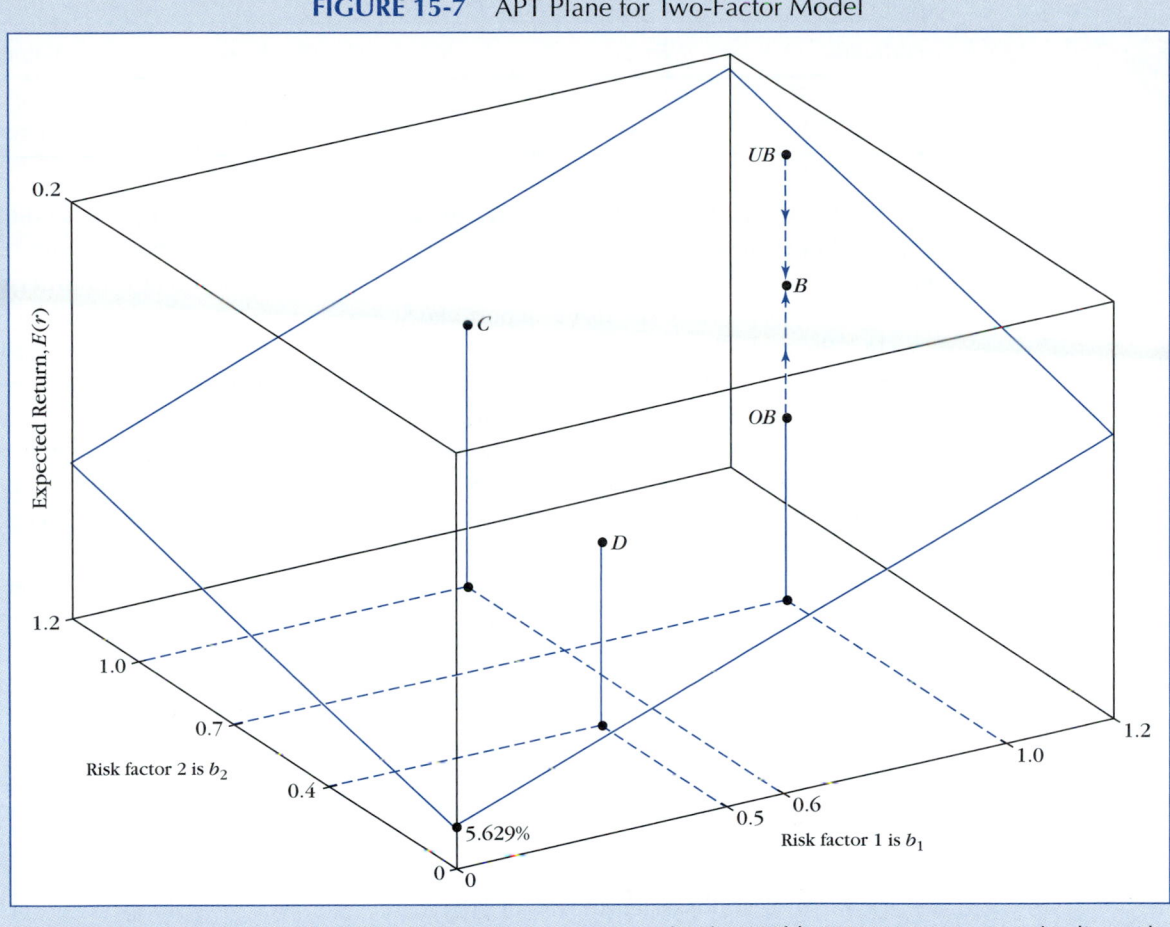

The APT Plane from Eqn. 15-21a is graphed with assets B, C, and D from Table 15-1. Assets B, C, and D lie on the APT Plane because they are priced correctly. The return for risk-free assets is 5.629%. If asset B were underpriced, it would lie at point UB. If asset B were overpriced, it would lie at point *OB*.

Graphic Artist: Timothy Falcon Crack

Suppose an investor who prefers to have more wealth instead of less wealth analyzes portfolio U in Table 15-2 and discovers it is underpriced. To make this discovery the investor had to analyze a portfolio with the same risks, like S. Portfolio S is made up of three equal investments in portfolios B, C, and D from Table 15-1. The two-factor betas and the expected return in Table 15-2 for portfolio S are calculated as follows:

$$E(r_S) = \tfrac{1}{3}E(r_B) + \tfrac{1}{3}E(r_C) + \tfrac{1}{3}E(r_D) \tag{15-26}$$

$$13.66\% = \tfrac{1}{3}(16\%) + \tfrac{1}{3}(14\%) + \tfrac{1}{3}(11\%)$$

$$b_{S1} = \tfrac{1}{3}b_{B1} + \tfrac{1}{3}b_{C1} + \tfrac{1}{3}b_{D1} \tag{15-27}$$

$$0.7 = \tfrac{1}{3}(1.0) + \tfrac{1}{3}(0.6) + \tfrac{1}{3}(0.5)$$

$$b_{S2} = \tfrac{1}{3}b_{B2} + \tfrac{1}{3}b_{C2} + \tfrac{1}{3}b_{D2} \tag{15-28}$$

$$0.7 = \tfrac{1}{3}(0.7) + \tfrac{1}{3}(1.0) + \tfrac{1}{3}(0.4)$$

TABLE 15-2   Risk-Return Statistics for Two Portfolios

Portfolio	$E(r_p)$	b_{i1}	b_{i2}	Definition
S	13.66%	0.7	0.7	$\frac{1}{3}B + \frac{1}{3}C + \frac{1}{3}D$
U	15.66%	0.7	0.7	Underpriced

Portfolios S and U in Table 15-2 have identical risk statistics, but they have different expected rates of return. This violates the law of one price. Since portfolios S and U have identical factor betas (equal risks), smart investors should buy portfolio U in order to get more return for the same risk that is in portfolio S.

In a theoretically ideal market, a smart investor might use the law of one price to earn riskless arbitrage profits. By setting up an imperfect hedge with portfolios S and U, the smart investor can create a profit without investing any money or without taking any risk. Table 15-3 illustrates how a smart investor could sell, say, $100 of portfolio S short and then take the $100 from that short sale and buy a $100 long position in portfolio U. This no-money-invested characteristic of the arbitrage portfolio is shown the second column of Table 15-3, it was formalized above as Eqn. 15-22.

Table 15-3 shows how the shrewd investor set up a riskless *arbitrage portfolio*, denoted A, which has long and short positions with equal betas. These identical long and short positions create a riskless hedge that cannot enjoy gains and cannot suffer losses from any price changes. The zero-systematic-risk characteristic of the arbitrage portfolio is formalized in Eqns. 15-29 and 15-30*.

$$\sum_{p=1}^{p=2} x_p b_{p1} = 0 \qquad \text{No systematic risk of Type 1} \tag{15-29}$$

$$\sum_{p=1}^{p=2} x_p b_{p2} = 0 \qquad \text{No systematic risk of Type 2} \tag{15-30}$$

The third column of Table 15-3 shows that at the end of the arbitrage the closing cash flows sum up a gain for the smart investor. The investor can sell portfolio U and collect the $100 investment plus the 15.66% return for a total of $115.66 cash inflow. At the same time, the smart investor can spend $113.66 to cover the $100 short position in portfolio S and pay the 13.66% interest (or cash dividend) that the person who bought $100 worth of S expects to receive for making that risky investment. After these cash flows, the smart investor earns $2 profit without investing any money or taking any risk. As a result of these actions, arbi-

TABLE 15-3   The Arbitrage Portfolio

Portfolio	Initial Cash Flow	Ending Cash Flow	B_{i1}	b_{i2}
S = short position	+$100	−$113.66	−0.7	−0.7
U = underpriced (long position)	−$100	$115.66	0.7	0.7
A = arbitrage (perfectly hedged)	0	+$2.00	0	0

---

* Note that although they may appear similar at a glance, Eqns. 15-27 and 15-28 are different from Eqns. 15-25 and 15-26 because Eqns. 15-25 and 15-26 are averaging across B, C, and D while (15-27) and (15-28) are summing across the objects in the arbitrage portfolio—namely, portfolios S and U.

trageurs bid up the price of the underpriced portfolio U and thereby drive down its expected return, as indicated in the formula below.

$$\downarrow E(r_U) = \frac{E(\$15.66 \text{ income per period})}{\uparrow \text{Purchase price (bid upward)}}$$

Arbitrage will continue until portfolio U is priced so that it lies on the APT plane in Figure 15-7. In fact, arbitrage will cause the price of every asset to be revised until its expected return and risk statistics align with the APT model of Eqn. 15-25a and the associated APT plane in Figure 15-7.

The k-Dimensional APT Hyperplane

The return-generating process with only two risk factors in Eqn. 15-20 was discussed above for simplicity's sake. Eqn. 15-31 represents a more elaborate return generating process that has *k* risk factors.

$$r_{i,t} = a_i + b_{i1}F_{1,t} + b_{i2}F_{2,t} + \ldots + b_{ik}F_{k,t} + e_{i,t} \tag{15-31}$$

If the environment represented by Eqn. 15-31 existed, arbitrageurs would find it profitable to rearrange prices to conform the *k*-factor APT model in Eqn. 15-32.

$$E(r_i) = \lambda_0 + \lambda_1 b_{i1} + \lambda_2 b_{i2} + \cdots + \lambda_k b_{ik} \tag{15-32}$$

Eqn. 15-32 is the APT in a *k-dimensional hyperplane* that has all the implications previously suggested for the two-factor APT model. The following example box explains the Salomon Smith Barney multifactor arbitrage pricing model.

SALOMON SMITH BARNEY (SSB) WEEKLY RISK ATTRIBUTE MODEL (RAM)   EXAMPLE

Salomon Smith Barney (SSB) is a subsidiary of Citigroup, which publishes two weekly arbitrage-pricing theory newsletters. SSB calls their multidimensional arbitrage-pricing model a Risk Attribute Model (RAM). The SSB newsletters are entitled: (1) **U.S. RAM Monitors This Week** and (2) **Japan RAM Monitors This Week**. The Japanese newsletter is published in conjunction with Nikko Securities, headquartered in Tokyo. These two 8-page weekly newsletters report the latest statistics for nine risk factors:

1. Drift—The market's trend
2. Residual market—Market movements not picked up by other risk factors
3. Economic growth—A measure of macroeconomic activity
4. Credit quality—Default risk
5. Long-term interest rates—Current market interest rates on long-term bonds
6. Short-term interest rates—Current market interest rates on money market securities
7. Inflation shock—Recent changes in inflationary pressures
8. Domestic currency—Either the U.S. dollar or the Japanese yen
9. Small-cap premium—Common stock risk premiums for small capitalization stocks

The Japanese RAM Monitor also reports on a tenth sensitivity named "oil." The project is supervised by an ex-finance professor named Eric H. Sorensen, Ph.D., Managing Director, Salomon Smith Barney, New York City.

COMPARING APT WITH THE SML

The intercept term λ_0 in Eqns. 15-25 and 15-32 equals the rate of return from an asset with zero sensitivity to all the risk factors. In other words, the intercept term, λ_0, is like the risk-free rate of return (RFR). Unlike the SML, the derivation of the APT does not depend on the existence of a risk-free return. If we define the return on a zero beta asset to be the risk-free rate of return, *RFR*, it follows logically that $\lambda_0 = RFR$. Using this equality allows the APT model of Eqn. 15-25 to be equivalently rewritten in the *risk-premium forms* shown as Eqns. 15-25e and 15-25f.

$$E(r_i) - \lambda_0 = \lambda_1 b_{i1} + \lambda_2 b_{i2} \tag{15-25e}$$

$$E(r_i) - RFR = \lambda_1 b_{i1} + \lambda_2 b_{i2} \quad \text{since } \lambda_0 = RFR \tag{15-25f}$$

The lambda coefficient associated with the factor beta (risk sensitivity) for index j, denoted λ_j, measures the increase in expected return the market requires to induce investors to assume one more unit of undiversifiable beta risk from the jth index, denoted b_j. The λ_j coefficient measures the **risk premium** for the risk measured by the factor beta denoted b_j.

The SML Is Equivalent to the One-Factor APT Model

When $b_{i1} = 1$ and $b_{i2} = 0$, then APT Eqn. 15-25 reduces to Eqns. 15-25g and 15-25h.

$$E(r_i) - RFR = \lambda_1 b_{i1} \tag{15-25g}$$

$$E(r_i) = RFR + \lambda_1 b_{i1} \tag{15-25h}$$

Eqn. 15-26h is equivalent to the SML of Eqn. 15-5 when λ_1 is defined in Eqns. 15-33.

$$\lambda_1 = E(r_m) - RFR \tag{15-33}$$

The beta coefficient can be defined to reveal another similarity between the SML and the APT. If b_i is the beta coefficient from the time-series regression line of Eqn. 7-7 in Chapter 7 (p. 169), only one risk factor exists and that risk factor is the market portfolio, M. In this case, the one-factor APT becomes identical to the SML. This equivalence of the APT one-factor model and the SML shows that the two models do not conflict. In fact, the two theories complement each other by using different economic processes to arrive at the same asset-pricing model.[29]

Burmeister and McElroy prepared empirical estimates of a linear factor model under various assumptions.[30] Their econometric work suggests that under some reasonable assumptions the SML can be found nested inside the APT. Wei analyzed the SML and APT models theoretically and showed that they are equivalent under plausible assumptions.[31] Wei went on to extend the SML and APT models and integrate them by including the SML's market portfolio in an APT model.

APT Employs Fewer Assumptions Than SML

An economic theory that is based on a few realistic assumptions is easier to understand than a theory contrived with the aid of numerous assumptions. One argument favoring APT over the SML is that the APT's greater generality is accomplished with fewer simplifying assumptions.

Like the SML, the APT assumes that investors prefer to have more wealth rather than less wealth. Both theories assume that investors dislike risk. The SML and the APT both assume capital *markets are perfect*; this is a fair representation of reality in the United States and a few other securities markets. The common assumptions in this paragraph are all fairly realistic.

The SML assumption that investors have *homogeneous expectations* is also employed in the APT. Homogeneous expectations is a more heroic assumption than the common assumptions in the preceding paragraph

This chapter has discussed the simplifying assumptions underlying the SML. The SML is also based on the following three assumptions: (1) rates of return conform to a normal two parameter probability distribution; (2) a uniquely desirable investment called the *market portfolio* exists; and (3) risk-free borrowing and lending is possible. Some supporters of the APT argue that it is superior to the SML because none of these three assumption is needed to generate the APT.

Although the APT requires fewer assumptions than the more rigidly defined SML, the APT depends on one uniquely unrealistic assumption. The APT's no-money-invested assumption, Eqn. 15-22, presumes that arbitraging short sellers are able to obtain 100% of the proceeds from their short sales to finance the purchase of their long positions.* Realistically, only brokerage houses, market makers at securities exchanges, and investment bankers are able to operate in this manner. Nevertheless, only a few well-funded arbitrageurs are needed to support the APT. And, there are dozens of multibillion-dollar portfolios around the world that are able to create self-financing arbitrage portfolios.

EMPIRICAL TESTS OF THE APT

Empirically testing the APT involves a two-step process that is analogous to the two steps used to test the SML.

First Pass Time-Series Regressions

Trial-and-error statistical testing, factor analysis, or economic logic can be used to delineate what risk factors shape securities prices. Then first-pass time-series regressions must be performed for each candidate investment to estimate its factor betas for each risk factor. Eqns. 15-20 and 15-31 are time-series regression models that must be estimated for each investment candidate.

Second-Pass Cross-Sectional Regression

After the time-series regression Eqn. 15-20 or Eqn. 15-31 is estimated for all the candidate assets a second-pass cross-sectional regression is used to measure the relationship between the average rates of return and the factor betas from the individual assets. This second-pass regression is of the form below, where the u_i is an unexplained residual return for asset i:

---

* Federal Reserve Board margin requirements forbid amateur investors from taking positions with zero funds invested. Since amateur investors must meet margin requirements on both long and short positions, they would not be able to get their brokers to give them the cash proceeds from their short sale. Therefore, amateur investors will never be powerful arbitrageurs. For a discussion of this point see Edward M. Miller, "Arbitrage Pricing Theory: A Graphical Critique," *Journal of Portfolio Management* 18, no. 1 (fall 1991): 72–76.

$$\left(\begin{array}{c}\text{Average return}\\\text{for asset } i\end{array}\right) = \lambda_0 + \lambda_1 \left(\begin{array}{c}\text{First factor}\\\text{beta for asset } i\end{array}\right) + \lambda_2 \left(\begin{array}{c}\text{Second factor}\\\text{beta for asset } i\end{array}\right) +$$

$$+ \lambda_3 \left(\begin{array}{c}\text{Third factor}\\\text{beta for asset } i\end{array}\right) + ... + \lambda_k \left(\begin{array}{c}\text{Kth factor}\\\text{beta for asset } i\end{array}\right) + u_i \quad \textbf{(15-34)}$$

The number of risk factors (denoted k in this chapter's formulas) must be determined empirically since the mathematical APT gives no clue as to the value of k.[32] If the lambda *risk premium*, denoted λ_j for the jth risk factor is significantly different from zero, then jth factor is said to be *priced* or *valued by the market* in the determining market prices.

Priced Risk Factors

The APT risk factors that typically have statistically significant explanatory power over security prices can be grouped into three categories:

- **Macro-economic risk factors** such as the inflation rate, interest rates, the nation's money supply, or the nation's gross domestic product (GDP)

- **Industry risk factors** such as the number of different companies competing to produce the same product in the industry or the growth rate of the product's (industry's) annual sales

- **Company risk factors** such as the degree of indebtedness of each company, the sizes of the companies, or each company's rate of return on assets

An Empirical Study by Roll and Ross

Stephen Ross and Richard Roll (RR) employed factor analytic techniques to analyze 1,260 NYSE-listed stocks divided into 42 groups that contained 30 stocks each.[33] They analyzed one decade of daily stock price returns. After estimating the factor betas (factor loadings) in the first step of their tests, RR performed their second-pass regression. For their second-pass regression, RR computed a separate cross-sectional multiple regression for each of 42 different groups of stocks. At least one cross-sectional regression coefficient, denoted λ_j, for the jth factor beta should be statistically significantly different from zero if the APT is to be substantiated (priced).* RR concluded there were four or fewer significant risk factors.[34]

Four Factors are Identified

Chen, Roll, and Ross (CRR) isolated four factors that significantly influenced securities returns.[35] These factors represented unanticipated changes in four variables:

1. Changes in the rate of inflation, $[\text{INFL} - E(\text{INFL})]$,
2. Changes in the index of industrial production, $[\text{IIP} - E(\text{IIP})]$,
3. Changes in the yield spread between high-grade and low-grade corporate bonds, $[\text{Y. Spread} - E(\text{Y. Spread})]$, a measure of investor confidence,
4. Changes in the slope of the term structure of interest rates, as measured by the difference in between the yields on long-term government bonds and T-bills, $[\text{Slope} - E(\text{Slope})]$.

---

* RR also tested to see if securities' variances had significant explanatory power over the stocks' average returns. Assets' variances should not be important if APT is valid because the diversifiable component of the returns can be diversified away to zero. APT suggests that the only contribution to a portfolio's risk would be made by its factor loadings. RR found that even though variances and average returns were highly correlated the variance did not contribute to the explanatory power of an APT model. This result supports the APT.

Chen's Empirical Tests

Nai-Fu Chen compared the APT and the SML using 15 years of daily stock returns.[36] First, time-series data was analyzed to obtain factor betas and average returns for each stock. Second, cross-sectional regressions of the historical average returns from the sampled stocks were contrasted to both the APT and SML models. Eqn. 15-35 is a second-pass regression estimate of Eqn. 15-34. Eqn. 15-36 is a second-pass regression estimate of the SML in Eqn. 15-9,

where

$$b_{i1}, \ldots, b_{ik} = \text{estimated factor betas (sensitivities)}$$

$$b_i = \text{estimated beta coefficient for stock } i$$

$$e_i \text{ and } z_i = \text{unexplained residual returns}$$

$$APT\text{:}\quad \bar{r}_i = \lambda_0 + \lambda_1 b_{i1} + \cdots + \lambda_k b_{ik} + e_i \tag{15-35}$$

$$SML\text{:}\quad \bar{r}_i = \lambda_0 + \lambda_1 b_i + z_i \tag{15-36}$$

The λ_i on the first factor beta in both Eqns. 15-35 and 15-36 had high statistical significance. It was noteworthy that the simple correlation coefficient between the characteristic line's beta, b_i, and the APT's first factor beta, b_{i1}, was found to be high and positive (in excess of .9) regardless of the market index used to estimate the characteristic line's betas. This finding suggests that the first risk factor resembles the *market portfolio*. In addition, the statistical hypothesis that $\lambda_2 = \lambda_3 = \ldots = \lambda_k = 0$ in Eqn. 15-35 was rejected. Rejecting this hypothesis implies that more than one risk factor should be considered.

Chen conducted a second test using cross-sectional regression Eqn. 15-37.

$$\bar{r}_i = k\hat{r}_{i,APT} + (1 - k)\hat{r}_{i,SML} + e_i \tag{15-37}$$

Eqn. 15-37 relates the historical average return from the ith stock, $\bar{r}_i$, to a weighted average of the stock's average returns that are predicted by the right-hand sides of APT Eqn. 15-35, $\hat{r}_{i,APT}$, and SML Eqn. 15-36, $\hat{r}_{i,SML}$, respectively. Various estimates of Eqn. 15-37 all produced values of k that was in excess of 0.9; this finding implies that APT predicts average returns better than the SML.

Chen formulated a third test using cross-sectional regression Eqns. 15-38 and 15-39, where u_i and w_i are estimates of errors in the residual terms e_i and z_i from Eqns. 15-35 and 15-36, respectively, for the ith stock.

$$z_i = \lambda_0 + \lambda_1 b_{i1} + \cdots + \lambda_k b_{ik} + u_i \tag{15-38}$$

$$e_i = \lambda_0 + \lambda_1 b_i + w_i \tag{15-39}$$

This test was designed to detect unused information about stocks' expected returns that turned up as residue in the error terms e_i and z_i. The tests were based on the idea that if a particular model was valid its random error term should (be *white noise*) contain no additional information. Chen reported that the SML appeared to be econometrically misspecified in most cases. The APT model was able to explain some of the SML's unexplained residual returns. In contrast, the SML was unable to explain anything about the error terms from the APT model.

All empirical tests are open to criticisms for failing to eliminate all biases, failing to adjust for all plausible statistical effects, failing to eliminate any other statistical problems that might be present, and being a joint a test of both the economic model and the statistical methodology. As a result, the statistical tests reviewed here are suggestive but not conclusive.[37]

THE BOTTOM LINE

Conclusions About the CML and SML. The CML and the SML are equilibrium portfolio theories that are based on Markowitz efficient portfolios. The SML is an implication of risk-reduction behavior derived from the CML. The SML can be used to find over- and underpriced market assets.

The characteristic line that was introduced in Chapter 7 is not a theoretical model. It is a simple regression that can be fit using market data from any asset. The characteristic line is not part of this chapter's equilibrium portfolio theory. Coincidentally, the characteristic line aligns with and substantiates the SML theory. Chapters that follow show the characteristic line is also a useful tool in other applications.

The simplifying assumptions underlying the CML and SML were relaxed one at a time. Each time, the implications of the model were slightly obscured. However, the fact that the CML and SML cannot be derived under realistic assumptions does not mean that these models are worthless. The analysis still rationalizes complex behavior that is observed in the financial markets (for example, diversification) and offers realistic suggestions about the directions that prices and returns should follow when they deviate significantly from equilibrium.[38]

Researchers have tried to formulate empirical studies using historical data that would affirm or deny the expectations suggested by the CML and SML. Many of the empirical studies reported during the 1970s, 1980s, and early 1990s were flawed. As a result, some of these studies reported findings that disagreed with the CML and SML models. More recently, more sophisticated econometric studies using larger samples overcame the earlier problems and have been more supportive of equilibrium portfolio theory.

APT Conclusions. The APT is an asset-pricing model that can employ multiple risk factors. Prior to the APT, the Nobel Prize–winning Security Market Line (SML) was the most prominent financial theory to explain the prices of market assets. It is natural to contrast the two important theories.

The APT requires fewer underlying assumptions and admits more different variables into the analysis than the SML. The APT is a more general theory than the SML.

The APT can be shown to be mathematically equivalent to the SML when the market portfolio is the only risk factor in both models. Other similarities show that the two theories do not contradict each other. Moreover, the two theories are similar because both delineate *undiversifiable commonalties* that form the basis for risk premiums in market prices and returns.

Empirical research has isolated four risk factors that significantly influenced securities returns:

1. Unanticipated changes in the rate of inflation
2. Unanticipated changes in the index of industrial production
3. Unanticipated changes in the yield spread between high-grade and low-grade corporate bonds
4. Unanticipated changes in the slope of the yield curve

Different researchers reported other risk factors.

Since APT has been in existence for fewer years than the SML, it has not been tested as extensively. However, the results from initial tests look favorable.[39]

QUESTIONS

Q15-1 (CML and SML) Compare and contrast the CML and the SML. (a) What assets lie on both lines in equilibrium? (b) What assets should never lie on the CML? Explain why.

Q15-2 (Betas) Explain how you would find the beta coefficient for a common stock using historical data. (a) What data would you need? (b) What would you do with the data? (c) For what purpose can you use the beta coefficient?

Q15-3 (Separation theorem) Given the assumptions underlying equilibrium portfolio theory, rationalize the following separation theorem: The investment decision of which asset to buy is a separate and independent decision from the financing decision of whether to borrow or lend.

Q15-4 (CAPM) Underlying the capital asset-pricing model (CAPM) are a set of assumptions that do not describe the "real world" very closely (if at all.) Does this mean that the CAPM is not a good model? Explain.

Q15-5 (Differing risk-free interest rates) What happens to the graphs of the Capital Market Line and the Security Market Line when the assumption that everyone can borrow and lend at the risk-free rate of interest is relaxed? Interpret the results in plain language.

Q15-6 (EIV problem) Describe the EIV (errors-in-variables) problem. Why does it arise and what are the problems that are encountered because of it?

Q15-7 (CAPM versus APT) Compare and contrast the role of the market portfolio in the CAPM with its role in the APT.

Q15-8 (APT risk factors) What does the APT tell us about the risk factors that should determine the size of the average (or expected) returns from market assets?

Q15-9 (Betas) Compare and contrast the beta coefficient from the characteristic regression line with the sensitivity coefficient (or factor loading) in the APT.

Q15-10 (CAPM versus APT) True, false, or uncertain: The capital asset-pricing model (CAPM) and the arbitrage-pricing theory (APT) models are very similar. Explain.

Q15-11 (Unsystematic risk) True, false, or uncertain: While the CAPM assumes that only systematic risk is priced, the APT model assumes that unsystematic risk is also a factor in determining the expected return on an asset. Explain.

Q15-12 (Priced factors) True, false, or uncertain: One advantage of the APT model is that it uses many factors that are known with certainty to affect the returns on assets while the CAPM uses only one factor, the returns on the market portfolio. Explain.

PROBLEMS

P15-1 (Valuation using CAPM) Assume that the return on the market is 14% and that the risk-free rate is 8%. Use the CAPM to determine which of the following stocks are overpriced or underpriced.

Stock	Expected Return, %	Beta
A	17	1.20
B	14	0.80
C	15	1.50
D	16	0.75

P15-2 (Computing portfolio expected returns) A diversified portfolio is composed of the following five stocks:

Stock	Price	Shares Held	Estimated Beta
Z	$10	1,000	0.80
AB	$30	1,000	0.90
QZ	$15	4,000	1.25
DB	$10	1,000	1.05
RST	$ 8	5,000	1.15

(a) What is the portfolio's beta?

(b) What does the CAPM suggest the expected return for this portfolio should be if the expected return on the market is 16%, with a standard deviation of 10%, and the expected risk-free rate is 9%.

P15-3 (Capital Market Line) The market portfolio has an expected return of 14% and a standard deviation of returns of 10%. If the risk-free rate is 8%, what return would you expect to make if you invested 50% of your funds in the market portfolio M and 50% of your funds in the risk-free asset? What would the risk of this portfolio be?

P15-4 (Calculating beta) Assume that the standard deviation of the returns on the market portfolio M is 0.1 and the standard deviation of the returns on asset B is 0.2. Further assume that the correlation coefficient of the returns of asset B and portfolio M is 0.5. (a) What is the value of the covariance of the returns of asset B and portfolio M? (b) What is asset B's beta coefficient?

P15-5 (Applying the CAPM) Finance Professor Mandenaro established a reputation as a respected financial analyst by publishing empirical estimates of the following CAPM:

$$E(r_i) = RFR + [E(r_m) - RFR](\text{beta coefficient})$$

The Edison Electric Utility Corporation (EEUC) has requested a rate increase from its state Public Utility Rate Setting Commission (PURSC) because the corporation's executives feel the 8.5% average annual rate of return EEUC's common stock has been earning in recent years is inadequate. Financial executives at EEUC have heard of the professor's reputation and have retained her to provide the PURSC with expert testimony explaining why the EEUC should be granted permission to raise the prices it charges for electricity. Professor Mandenaro estimates the risk-free rate of interest to be 7%, the expected return on the S&P stock market index to be 11%, and EEUC's beta coefficient to be 0.61. How can the professor use her skills to argue that the EEUC should be granted a rate increase by the PURSC? Show your calculations.

P15-6 (Portfolio betas and CAPM) Ricardo owns a portfolio of stocks that have a market value of $50,000 and an estimated beta of 0.90. (a) If the expected return on the market portfolio is 15% and the risk-free rate is 6%, what is the expected equilibrium return on this portfolio? (b) Assume Ricardo decides to sell one of his holdings that has a market value of $10,000 and a beta of 0.75 and invest the proceeds in another stock that has a beta of 1.3. What is the new expected equilibrium return on his portfolio?

P15-7 (APT expected rates of return) Assume you are evaluating a stock and have a two-factor model. Factor 1 embodies the changes in the rate of inflation and the risk premium related to this factor is 4%. Factor 2 reflects the growth in the unemployment rate and the average risk premium for this is 1%. The average rate of return on the risk-free asset is 5%. The stock you are evaluating has $b_1 = 1.1$ and $b_2 = -0.8$. What is the expected return on your stock according to the APT?

P15-8 (APT expected rates of return) The General Enterprise Corporation (GEC) has a two-factor return generating function. GEC's stock is expected to earn a 4.0% rate of return if the economy is stagnant (i.e., $E(r_{GEC}) = \sigma_{GEC} = 4.0\%$.) In addition, GEC has a sensitivity coefficient for the inflation rate of 0.9 and its sensitivity coefficient for the percentage change in the gross national product (GNP) is 1.1. What rate of return do you expect GEC's stock to earn this year if the rate of inflation is 5.0% and the GNP rises to 5.0%?

P15-9 (APT and stock valuation) The cash dividends per share of the Omega Medical Corporation (OMC) have been growing at an annual rate of 5.0%, and this growth rate is expected to continue unabated in the foreseeable future.

OMC's current cash dividend is $2 a share. The following two-factor model is assumed to be appropriate for OMC:

$$E(r_{OBC}) = 10\% + b_{i1}(2\%) + b_{i2}(7\%)$$

The factor betas for Omega Medical's stock are: $b_{i1} = 1.5$ and $b_{i2} = 0.5$

Use the information above and the present value model to value a share of OMC's stock. Use the dividend discount model for a stream of cash dividends that grows at a constant rate until infinity. *Hint:* See Chapter 23 to review the model used to value a stock with constantly growing cash dividends.

P15-10 (APT and stock valuation) The cash dividends of the Titan Trucking Corporation have been growing at a rate of 25% the last few years. Analysts expect this rate to continue for 5 more years and then expect it to fall to a more normal growth rate of 5% thereafter. The following three-factor model is assumed to be descriptive of stock market conditions:

$$E(r_i) = 9\% + b_{i1}(3\%) + b_{i2}(2\%) + b_{i3}(4\%)$$

The beta coefficients for Titan's stock are as follows:

$$b_{i1} = 1.5 \quad b_{i2} = -0.5 \quad b_{i3} = 0.5$$

If the Titan Trucking Corporation has a current cash dividend of 25 cents per share, what is the present value of one share of its common stock?

P15-11 (APT equilibrium returns) Assume that a two-factor model is descriptive of reality and determine the equation that describes the equilibrium returns for the following three portfolios:

Portfolio	$E(r_p)$	b_{i1}	b_{i2}
Q	11%	1	0.6
R	13%	2	0.1
Z	11%	2	-0.6

P15-12 (Arbitrage opportunities) Use the information in Problem 15-11 and assume the following portfolio called q exists:

$$E(r_q) = 15\% \quad b_{q1} = 2 \quad b_{q2} = -0.25$$

Arbitrage opportunities are present here; show how you can profit from them. *Hint:* Create a portfolio with the same risk factors as q by investing in portfolios R and Z from Problem 15-11.

CFA EXAM QUESTIONS

1. (1999 CFA Sample Exam, Level I) Which of the following statements about the security market line (SML) are true?

    I. The SML provides a benchmark for evaluating expected investment performance.

    II. The SML leads all investors to invest in the same portfolio of risky assets.

    III. The SML is a graphic representation of the relationship between expected return and beta.

    IV. Properly valued assets plot exactly on the SML.

    A. I and III only.

    B. II and IV only.

    C. I, II, and IV only.

    D. I, III, and IV only.

2. (1998 CFA Sample Exam, Level I) Both portfolio X and portfolio Y are well-diversified. The risk-free rate is 8%, and the return for the market is 16%. That is:

Portfolio	Expected Return	Beta
X	16%	1.00
Y	12%	0.25

In this situation, which of the following about portfolio X and portfolio Y is true?

	Portfolio X	Portfolio Y
A.	Overvalued	Properly valued
B.	Properly valued	Undervalued
C.	Undervalued	Properly valued
D.	Properly valued	Overvalued

3. (1998 CFA Exam, Level II) An analyst expects a risk-free return of 4.5%, a market return of 14.5%, and the returns for Stocks A and B that are shown in the Table below.

Table - Stock Information

Stock	Beta	Analyst's Estimated Return
A	1.2	16%
B	0.8	14%

  A. Show on a graph:

    i. where stocks A and B would plot on the Security Market Line (SML) if they were fairly valued using the Capital Asset Pricing Model (CAPM).

    ii. where stocks A and B actually plot on the same graph according to the returns estimated by the analyst and shown in Table 5.

  B. State whether stock A and stock B are undervalued or overvalued if the analyst uses the SML for strategic investment decisions.

4. (1998 CFA Exam, Level II) Modern Portfolio Theory (MPT) may not be directly applicable to "real-world" portfolios because some of the underlying assumptions of MPT do not hold. Discuss the impact of the following on the Capital Market Line (CML):

    i. taxes.

    ii. different borrowing and lending rates.

5. (1998 CFA Sample Exam, Level I) In contrast to the capital asset pricing model, arbitrage pricing theory:

    A. has fewer restrictive assumptions.

    B. uses risk premiums based on micro variables.

    C. requires normally distributed security returns.

    D. specifies the number and identities of specific factors that determine expected returns.

6. (1991 CFA Sample Exam, Level I) A zero-investment portfolio arises when:

    A. An investor has only downside risk.

    B. The law of prices remains unviolated.

    C. The opportunity set is not tangent to the capital allocation line.

    D. A risk-free arbitrage opportunity exists.

7. (1989 CFA Exam, Level III) You are an investment officer at Pegasus Securities and are preparing for the next meeting of the investment committee. Several committee members are interested in reviewing two asset-pricing models—The CAPM and the APT—and their use in portfolio management and stock selection.

    A. Describe both the CAPM and APT, and identify the factor(s) that determines returns in each.

    B. "The APT model is more general than the CAPM." Explain how this observation has meaning in the stock selection process.

8. (1998 CFA Exam, Level II) The Arbitrage Pricing Theory (APT) and the Capital Asset Pricing Model (CAPM) have received much attention from practitioners and academicians for use in asset pricing and valuation.

    A. Explain the difference between APT and CAPM with respect to:

        i. investor utility functions.

        ii. distribution of returns.

        iii. the market portfolio.

    B. Explain *one* conceptual difference between APT and the CAPM other than those listed in Part A.

FURTHER REFERENCES

Alexander, G. J. and J. C. Francis. *Portfolio Analysis*, 3d ed. Englewood Cliffs, NJ: Prentice-Hall, 1986.

Chapters 7 through 10 of this monograph review the capital market theory. Algebra, calculus and statistics are used.

Fama, Eugene F. "Risk, Return and Equilibrium: Some Clarifying Comments," *Journal of Finance* (March 1968): 29–40.

Fama introduced the concept of the market portfolio and clarified some early questions about the equilibrium portfolio theory.

Markowitz, Harry. *Portfolio Selection*, Cowles Foundation Monograph 16. New York: Wiley, 1959.

This easy-to-read book lays out Markowitz's Nobel prize winning portfolio theory. See footnote on page 100 for the first published characteristic line; Markowitz called it a single-index model.

Ross, Stephen A. "Return, Risk and Arbitrage," in *Risk and Return in Finance*, I. Friend and J. Bicksler, eds. Cambridge, MA: Ballinger Press, 1976.

Ross uses only algebra and statistics in this seminal presentation of the APT.

Sharpe, William F. "A Simplified Model for Portfolio Analysis," *Management Science* (January 1963): 277-93. See especially part 4 on the diagonal model.

This published condensation of Sharpe's Ph.D. dissertation extends the footnote on page 100 of Harry Markowitz's 1959 book (see Markowitz above).

Sharpe, William F. "Capital Asset Prices: A Theory of Market Equilibrium under Conditions of Risk," *Journal of Finance* (September 1964): 425–552.

This seminal article by Nobel laureate Sharpe pulls together the findings of Markowitz and Tobin into a unified formulation of equilibrium portfolio theory.

Tobin, James. "Liquidity Preference as Behavior Towards Risk," *The Review of Economic Studies* 26, no. 1 (February 1958): 65–86.

This seminal article by Nobel laureate Tobin developed the asset pricing implications of borrowing and lending at a risk-free interest rate.

Treynor, Jack L. "Toward a Theory of Market Value of Risky Assets." Unpublished manuscript, 1961.

This manuscript is cited in William Sharpe's 1964 paper. Treynor was one of the founders of portfolio theory.

Treynor, Jack L. "How to Rate Management of Investment Funds," *Harvard Business Review* 43, no. 1 (January 1973): 63–75.

Treynor introduced the phrase "characteristic line" in this seminal article about mutual fund performance evaluation using beta.

Le Roy, Stephen F. and Jan Werner, PRINCIPLES OF FINANCIAL ECONOMICS, Cambridge University Press, 2001.

A mathematically rigorous review of investment theories.

ENDNOTES

[1] The market portfolio was developed by Eugene Fama. See Eugene Fama, "Risk, Return and Equilibrium: Some Clarifying Comments," *Journal of Finance* (March 1968): 32–33. Stambaugh shows that empirical tests of the SML are not overly sensitive to the makeup of the market portfolio. See Robert F. Stambaugh, "On the Exclusion of Assets from Tests of the Two-Parameter Model: A Sensitivity Analysis," *Journal of Financial Economics* 10, no. 3 (1982): 237–68.

[2] For an early mathematical derivation of the SML, see W. F. Sharpe, "Capital Asset Prices: A Theory of Market Equilibrium Under Conditions of Risk," *Journal of Finance* 19, no. 3 (September 1964): note 22. Jack L. Treynor also developed the SML in a 1961 paper that was never published. Treynor's paper is entitled "Towards a Theory of Market Value of Risky Assets." For a different formulation of the same model, see Jan Mossin, "Equilibrium in a Capital Asset Market," *Econometrica* (October 1966): 768–83. For a review of derivations of the SML, see Chapters 7 and 8 of J. C. Francis and G. J. Alexander, *Portfolio Analysis*, 3d ed. (Upper Saddle River, NJ: Prentice-Hall, 1986).

[3] See K. L. Hastie, "The Determination of Optimal Investment Policy," *Management Science* (August 1967): B757–B774. Hastie was the first analyst to study relaxing the assumptions. See also, M. J. Brennan, "Capital Market Equilibrium with Divergent Borrowing and Lending Rates," *Journal of Financial and Quantitative Analysis* 6, no. 5 (December 1971): 1197–1206. Brennan shows that, under certain assumptions, a weighted average of the borrowing and lending rates could emerge as a single rate. The assumption that funds are borrowed and lent at a risk-free rate is also addressed by Black's zero-beta portfolio. See Fischer Black, "Capital Market Equilibrium with Restricted Borrowing," *Journal of Business* 45 (1972): 444–45.

[4] See Mark B. Garman and James A. Ohlson, "Valuation of Risky Assets in Arbitrage-Free Economies with Transactions Costs," *Journal of Financial Economics* 9, no. 3 (September 1981): 271–80. Also see Yakov Amihud and Haim Mendelson, "Asset Pricing and the Bid-Ask Spread," *Journal of Financial Economics* 17 (1986): 223–49.

[5] See N. Gressis, G. C. Philippatos, and J. Hayya, "Multiperiod Portfolio Analysis and the Inefficiency of the Market Portfolio," *Journal of Finance* 31, no. 4 (September 1976): 1115–26. For an extension see John E. Gilster Jr., "Capital Market Equilibrium with Divergent Investment Horizon Length Assumptions," *Journal of Financial and Quantitative Analysis* 18, no. 2 (June 1983): 257–68. Several people have analyzed the homogeneous expectations assumption. See A.R. Admati, "A Noisy Rational Expectations Equilibrium for Multi-Asset Securities Markets," *Econometrica* 53, no. 3 (May 1985): 629–57.

[6] See M. J. Brennan, "Taxes, Market Valuation and Corporate Financial Policy," *National Tax Journal* 23, no. 4 (December 1970): 417–27. Brennan's model was extended by R. H. Litzenberger and K. Ramaswamy, "The Effect of Personal Taxes and Dividends on Capital Asset Prices: Theory and Empirical Evidence," *Journal of Financial Economics* 7, no. 2 (June 1979): 163–95. Also see Ronald F. Singer, "Endogenous Marginal Income Tax Rates, Investor Behavior and the Capital Asset Pricing Model," *Journal of Finance* 34, no. 3 (June 1979): 609–16.

[7] See Tom Copeland, Tim Koller, and Jack Murrin, *Valuation*, 2nd ed. (New York: Wiley, 1994): 284. Also see Patrick A. Gaughan, *Mergers And Acquisitions* (New York: Harper Collins, 1991): 606. Furthermore, see Shannon P. Pratt, *Valuing a Business: The Analysis of Closely-Held Companies*, 2nd ed. (Homewood, IL: Dow-Jones Irwin, 1989).

[8] For an informative discussion about transaction costs, see Joseph P. Ogden, David A. Lesmond, and Charles A. Trzcinka, "Do Stock Returns Reflect Investors' Trading Thresholds? Empirical Tests and a New Measure of Transactions Costs," FMA 1995 Competitive Paper Award winner, synthesized in *Financial Management Association Collection* 11, no. 1 (winter 1996): 5–6.

[9] See Yakov Amihud and Haim Mendelson, "Asset Pricing and the Bid-Ask Spread," *Journal of Financial Economics* 17 (1986): 223–49.

[10] See Marshall Blume, "Betas and Their Regression Tendencies," *Journal of Business* 39, no. 1 (June 1975).

[11] See Jack C. Francis, "Statistical Analysis of Risk Statistics for NYSE Stocks," *Journal of Financial and Quantitative Analysis* 14, no. 5 (December 1979): 981–98.

[12] See F. J. Fabozzi and J. C. Francis, "Beta as a Random Coefficient," *Journal of Financial and Quantitative Analysis* (March 1978). Also see F. J. Fabozzi and J. C. Francis, "Stability Tests for Alphas and Betas over Bull and Bear Market Conditions," *Journal of Finance* (September 1977). In addition, see F. Fabozzi and J.C. Francis, "The Effects of Changing Macroeconomics Conditions on Alphas, Betas, and the Single Index Model," *Journal of Financial and Quantitative Analysis* (June 1979).

[13] See Richard Roll, "A Critique of the Asset Pricing Theory's Tests," *Journal of Financial Economics* (March 1977): 129–76.

[14] See Sanjoy Basu, "Investment Performance of Common Stocks in Relation to Their Price-Earnings Ratios: A Test of the Efficient Market Hypothesis," *Journal of Finance* 32 (1977): 663–82. Sanjoy Basu, "The Relationship Between Earnings Yield, Market Value, and Return for NYSE Common Stocks: Further Evidence," *Journal of Financial Economics* 12 (1983): 129–56. Marc R. Reinganum, "Misspecification of Capital Asset Pricing: Empirical Anomalies Based on Earning Yield and Market Value," *Journal of Financial Economics* 9 (1981): 19–46. In 1992 Fama and French showed evidence suggesting that the relation between E/P ratio and average return appeared to be absorbed by the combination of the firm size and book-value-to-market equity variables. Eugene F. Fama and Kenneth R. French, "The Cross-Section of Expected Stock Returns," *Journal of Finance* 47 (1992): 427–65.

[15] See Rolf W. Banz, "The Relationship Between Return and Market Value of Common Stocks," *Journal of Financial Economics* 9 (1981): 3–18. Marc R. Reinganum, "Misspecification of Capital Asset Pricing: Empirical Anomalies Based on Earning Yield and Market Value," *Journal of Financial Economics* 9 (1981): 19–46. Also see Donald B. Keim, "Size-Related Anomalies and Stock Return Seasonality," *Journal of Financial Economics* 12 (1983): 13–32.

[16] See Eugene F. Fama and Kenneth R. French, "The Cross-Section of Expected Stock Returns," *Journal of Finance* 47 (1992): 427–65. E. F. Fama and Kenneth R. French, "Common Risk Factors in the Returns on Bonds and Stocks," *Journal of Financial Economics* 33 (1993): 3–56. E. F. Fama and Kenneth R. French, "The SML Is Wanted, Dead or Alive," Working Paper, University of Chicago, 1995.

[17] See Barr Rosenberg, Kenneth Reid, and Ronald Lanstein, "Persuasive Evidence of Market Inefficiency," *Journal of Portfolio Management* 11 (1985): 9–17. Louis, K. C. Chan, Yasushi Hamao, and Josef Lakonishok, "Fundamentals and Stock Returns in Japan," *Journal of Finance* 46 (1991): 1739–89. James L. Davis, "The Cross-Section of Realized Stock Returns: The Pre-COMPUSTAT Evidence," *Journal of Finance* 49 (1994):

1579–93. S. P. Kothari and Jay Shanken, "Book-To-Value, Dividend Yield, and Expected Market Returns: A Time-series Analysis," Working Paper No. 95-13, University of Rochester, 1995.

[18] See Puneet Handa, S.P. Kothari, and Charles Wasley, "Sensitivity of Multivariate Tests of the Capital Asset Pricing Model to the Return Measurement Interval," *Journal of Finance* 48 (1993): 1543–51. Dongcheol Kim, "The Extent of Nonstationarity of Beta," *Review of Quantitative Finance and Accounting* 3 (1993): 241–54. Dongcheol Kim, "The Errors-in-Variables Problem in the Cross-Section of Expected Stock Returns," *Journal of Finance* 50 (1995): 1605–34. Dongcheol Kim, "A Re-examination of Firm Size, Book-To-Market, and Earnings-Price in the Cross-Section of Expected Stock Returns," *Journal of Financial and Quantitative Analysis* 32, no.4 (December 1997): 463–89.

[19] See Robert H. Litzenberger and Krishna Ramaswamy, "The Effect of Personal Taxes and Dividends on Capital Asset Prices: Theory and Empirical Evidence," *Journal of Financial Economics* 7 (1979): 163–96. Jay Shanken, "On the Estimation of Beta-Pricing Models," *Review of Financial Studies* 5 (1992): 1–33. Dongcheol Kim, "The Errors-in-Variables Problem in the Cross-Section of Expected Stock Returns," *Journal of Finance* 50 (1995): 1605–34.

[20] See Michael R. Gibbons, "Multivariate Tests of Financial Models," *Journal of Financial Economics* 10, (1982): 3–27. Marjorie B. McElroy and Edwin Burmeister, "Arbitrage Pricing Theory as a Restricted Nonlinear Multivariate Regression Model," *Journal of Business and Economic Statistics* 6 (1988): 29–42.

[21] See Eugene F. Fama and James D. MacBeth, "Risk, Return, and Equilibrium: Empirical Tests," *Journal of Political Economy* 81(1973): 607–36.

[22] See Dongcheol Kim, "The Errors-in-Variables Problem in the Cross-Section of Expected Stock Returns," *Journal of Finance* 50 (1995): 1605–34. Also see Dongcheol Kim, "A Re-examination of Firm Size, Book-To-Market, and Earnings-Price in the Cross-Section of Expected Stock Returns," *Journal of Financial and Quantitative Analysis* 32, no. 4 (December 1997): 463–89.

[23] For examples of differences see Eugene F. Fama and Kenneth R. French, "The Cross-Section of Expected Stock Returns," *Journal of Finance* 47 (1992): 427–65. Also see S. P. Kothari, Jay Shanken, and Richard G. Sloan, "Another Look at the Cross-Section of Expected Stock Returns," *Journal of Finance* 50 (1995): 185–224.

[24] See Andrew W. Lo and A. Craig MacKinlay, "Data-Snooping Biases in Tests of Financial Asset Pricing Models," *Review of Financial Studies* 3 (1990): 431–67.

[25] To see the seminal article read Stephen A. Ross, "Return, Risk and Arbitrage," in *Risk and Return in Finance*, ed. Irwin Friend and James Bicksler (Cambridge, MA: Ballinger Press, 1976). Also see Stephen Ross, "The Arbitrage Pricing Theory of Capital Asset Pricing," *Journal of Economic Theory* (December 1976): 344–60. Ross's original paper was simplified by Gur Huberman, "A Simple Approach to Arbitrage Pricing Theory," *Journal of Economic Theory* 28, no. 1 (October 1982): 183–91.

[26] See Robert Jarrow and Andrew Rudd, "A Comparison of the APT and SML," *Journal of Banking and Finance* 7, no. 2 (June 1983): 295–303.

[27] For a discussion of fixed-income factor analytic models, see Ronald N. Kahn and Deepak Gulrajani, "Risk and Return in the Canadian Bond Market," *Journal of Portfolio Management* 19, no. 3 (spring 1993): 86–92.

[28] Articles that derive APT models with modest values of n that are nevertheless accurate include Philip H. Dybvig, "An Explicit Bound on Individual Assets' Deviations from APT Pricing in a Finite Economy," *Journal of Financial Economics* 12 (December 1983): 483–96. Also see Mark Grinblatt and Sheridan Titman, "Factor Pricing in a Finite Economy," *Journal of Financial Economics* 12, no. 4 (December 1983): 497–507. And, see Gregory Connor, "A Unified Beta Pricing Theory," *Journal of Economic Theory* 34, no. 1 (October 1984): 13–31.

[29] See William F. Sharpe, "Factor Models, SMLs, and the APT," *Journal of Portfolio Management* 11, no. 1 (fall 1984): 21–25.

[30] See Edwin Burmeister and Marjorie B. McElroy, "Joint Estimation of Factor Sensitivities and Risk Premia for the Arbitrage Pricing Theory," *Journal of Finance* (July 1988): 721–33.

[31] See K. C. John Wei, "An Asset-Pricing Theory Unifying the SML and APT," *Journal of Finance* (September 1988): 881–92.

[32] See Gregory Connor and Robert A. Korajczyk, "A Test for the Number of Factors in an Approximate Factor Model," *Journal of Finance* 48, no. 4 (September 1993): 1263–91.

[33] R. Roll and S. Ross, "An Empirical Investigation of the Arbitrage Pricing Theory," *Journal of Finance* 35 (December 1980): 1073–1103.

[34] See Stephen J. Brown and Mark I. Weinstein, "A New Approach to Testing Asset Pricing Models: The Bilinear Paradigm," *Journal of Finance* 38, no. 3 (June 1983): 711–43. The study suggests that common stock returns were consistent with the existence of three factors, but the existence of more than three factors was dubious.

[35] See Nai-Fu Chen, Richard Roll, and Stephen A. Ross, "Economic Forces and the Stock Market: Testing the APT and Alternative Asset Pricing Theories," *Journal of Business* (July 1986). Also see R. Roll and S.A. Ross, "The Arbitrage Pricing Theory Approach to Strategic Portfolio Planning," *Financial Analysts Journal* (May-June 1984): 14.

[36] See Nai-Fu Chen, "Some Empirical Tests of the Theory of Arbitrage Pricing," *Journal of Finance* 38, no. 5 (December 1983): 1393–1414.

[37] Professor Gehr published the first APT empirical study; see A. Gehr, "Some Tests of the Arbitrage Pricing Theory," *Journal of the Midwest Finance Association* (1978). For criticisms of the APT empirical tests,

see Jay Shanken, "The APT: Is It Testable?" *Journal of Finance* (December 1982). Also see Phoebus J. Dhrymes, Irwin Friend, and N. Bulent Gultekin, "A Critical Re-examination of the Empirical Evidence on the Arbitrage Pricing Theory," *Journal of Finance* 39, no. 2 (June 1984): 323–46. For replies, see Philip N. Dybvig and Stephen A. Ross, "Yes, the APT Is Testable," *Journal of Finance* 40, no. 4 (September 1985c): 1173–88; R. Roll and S. A. Ross, "A Critical Re-examination of the Empirical Evidence on the Arbitrage Pricing Theory: A Reply," *Journal of Finance* 39, no. 2 (June 1984): 347–50; Jay Shanken "Multi-Beta SML or Equilibrium APT?: A Reply," *Journal of Finance* 40, no.4 (September 1985): 1189–96. Also see Phoebus J. Dhrymes, Irwin Friend, Mustafa N. Gultekin, and N. Bulent Gultekin, "New Tests of the APT and Their Implications," *Journal of Finance* 40, no. 3 (July 1985): 659–74. For evidence that supports the APT, see Bruce N. Lehmann and David Modest, "The Empirical Foundations of APT," *Journal of Financial Economics* 21, no. 2 (September 1988): 213–54. More support can be found in Gregory Connor and Robert A. Korajczyk, "Risk and Return in an Equilibrium APT: Application of a New Test Methodology," *Journal of Financial Economics* 21, no. 2 (September 1988): 255–89. More recently, see Jay Shanken, "The Current State of Arbitrage Pricing Theory," *Journal of Finance* 47, no. 4 (September 1992): 1569–74. For a review of reasons that arbitrage will not work, see Andrei Schleifer and Robert W. Vishny, "The Limits of Arbitrage," *Journal of Finance* 52, no. 1 (March 1997): 35–55.

[38] Equilibrium portfolio theory has been extended to include international securities markets. See Bruno H. Solnik, "An International Market Model of Security Price Behavior," *Journal of Financial and Quantitative Analysis* (September 1974): 537–54. See also a book of readings edited by E. J. Elton and M. J. Gruber, *International Capital Markets* (Amsterdam: North-Holland, 1975). In particular, see Rene Stulz, "On the Effects of Barriers to International Investment," *Journal of Finance* 36, no. 4 (September 1981): 923–34. In addition, see Bruno H. Solnik, *International Investments*, 2nd ed. (Reading, MA: Addison-Wesley, 1991). Also see Roger G. Ibbotson and Gary P. Brinson, *Global Investing* (New York: McGraw-Hill, 1993). Furthermore, see Ephraim Clark, Michel Levasseur, and Patrick Rousseau, *International Finance* (London: Chapman and Hall, 1993).

[39] For empirical tests that clearly favor the APT over the SML, see Nai-Fu Chen, "Some Empirical Tests of the Theory of Arbitrage Pricing," *Journal of Finance* 38, no. 5 (December 1983): 1393–1414. Also see Edwin Burmeister and Marjorie B. McElroy, "Joint Estimation of Factor Sensitivities and Risk Premia for the Arbitrage Pricing Theory," *Journal of Finance* (July 1988): 721–33.

APPENDIX

CHAPTER 15

Mathematical APT

This Appendix shows the mathematical derivation of Eqn. 15-25a and the plane in Figure 15-7. The APT model of Eqn. 15-25 can be rewritten with numerical values for the three portfolios in Table 15-1 as shown in Eqns. 15A-1a, b, and c.

$$E(r_i) = \lambda_0 + \lambda_1 b_{i1} + \lambda_2 b_{i2} \tag{15-25}$$

$$16.0 = \lambda_0(1.0) + \lambda_1(1.0) + \lambda_2(0.7) \tag{15A-1a}$$

$$14.0 = \lambda_0(1.0) + \lambda_1(0.6) + \lambda_2(1.0) \tag{15A-1b}$$

$$11.0 = \lambda_0(1.0) + \lambda_1(0.5) + \lambda_2(0.4) \tag{15A-1c}$$

Eqns. 15A-1a, b, and c are three equations in three unknowns, λ_0, λ_1 and λ_2, which are equivalently rewritten as matrix Eqns. 15A-2 and 15A-3.

$$
\begin{bmatrix} 16.0 \\ 14.0 \\ 11.0 \end{bmatrix} =
\begin{bmatrix} 1.0 & 1.0 & 0.7 \\ 1.0 & 0.6 & 1.0 \\ 1.0 & 0.5 & 0.4 \end{bmatrix}
\begin{bmatrix} \lambda_0 \\ \lambda_1 \\ \lambda_2 \end{bmatrix} \tag{15A-2}
$$

$$\quad R \quad = \quad\quad C \quad\quad\quad \lambda \tag{15A-3}$$

The vector of unknowns λ is evaluated by first finding the inverse of the coefficients matrix, C (this inverse matrix is denoted C^{-1}); then premultiplying C^{-1} times the return vector R yields the values of the vector of unknowns λ as shown in Eqns. 15A-4 and 15A-5:

$$
\begin{bmatrix} -0.9629 & -0.1851 & 2.1481 \\ 2.2222 & -1.1111 & -1.1111 \\ -0.3703 & 1.8518 & -1.4814 \end{bmatrix}
\begin{bmatrix} 16.0 \\ 14.0 \\ 11.0 \end{bmatrix} =
\begin{bmatrix} 5.629 \\ 7.7777 \\ 3.7037 \end{bmatrix} =
\begin{bmatrix} \lambda_0 \\ \lambda_1 \\ \lambda_2 \end{bmatrix} \tag{15A-4}
$$

$$\quad\quad\quad C^{-1} \quad\quad\quad\quad R \quad = \quad \lambda \quad = \lambda \tag{15A-5}$$

The values for the lambdas in matrix Eqn. 15A-4 are used in APT Eqn. 15-25a.

INVESTMENT PERFORMANCE EVALUATION

Suze Orman is an investment adviser whose best-selling books, The 9 Steps to Financial Freedom *in 1997 and* The Courage To Be Rich: Creating a Life of Material and Spiritual Abundance *in 1999, focus on the emotional and spiritual steps she thinks are needed to attain prosperity. This chapter provides no clues about how to evaluate Ms. Orman's approach and recommendations. Rather, this chapter focuses on the more objective investment selection techniques used by stock pickers, market timers, asset allocators, portfolio managers, and other professional money managers.*

Many of the money managers considered in this chapter are **institutional investors**. *Institutional money managers oversee the trust departments of banks, mutual funds, investment advisory services, the investment management departments of insurance companies, and money management firms. Table 2-4 in Chapter 2 (p. 32) lists some of the largest institutional investors in the world but only shows the "tip of the iceberg." The smallest of the 300 money managers listed managed $12,100,000,000.*

The institutional money managers listed in Table 2-4 receive most of the funds they manage from the following owners of investable wealth:

1. **Pensions**:

   a. *Corporate pension funds: For example, General Motors Corporate pension fund has assets of over $90 billion.*

   b. *Government pensions: California Public Employees Retirement System (CalPERS), for example, contains over $155 billion.*

   c. *Individuals' pensions: For instance, John Doe has a tax-sheltered retirement account containing $7,400. Millions of small accounts like this exist in the United States.*

2. **Substantial individuals**: *Members of the Rockefeller, DuPont, Mellon, and Ford families; Arab oil sheiks; and others who have hundreds of millions of dollars to be managed.*

3. **Endowments**: *The University of Texas, for instance, has over $14 billion.*

4. **Foundations**: *The Ford Foundation's $9.4 billion, for example.*

Such people and institutions own their funds, but they have entrusted the day-to-day investment decisions to professional portfolio managers. Before delegating the investment management function, the owner of the invested funds wonders: Which money manager is best? This chapter addresses this question and presents tools that can be used to measure and rank the performance of different money managers. Portfolio performance evaluation tools are useful to investors who want to evaluate their present money managers and prospective new money managers; these tools are also used by the money managers themselves, to appraise and improve their skills.

This chapter uses the characteristic line from Chapter 7, asset allocation line (AAL) from Chapter 14, and the Capital Market Line (CML) and Security Market Line (SML) from Chapters 7 and 15. New models are introduced as well.

Investments' rates of return are needed to evaluate the performance of an investment manager. Many money management services do not make their data available to the public. This chapter analyzes historical mutual fund data because the Investment Company Act of 1940 requires every U.S. mutual fund to reveal details about its operations to the public. This is another example of how U.S. securities law requires full disclosure of information. This disclosure helps the nation's investors allocate the nation's financial resources in a manner that benefits all citizens, even though most citizens do not own mutual funds. Investment capital flows into the most profitable investments. These profits are derived by serving the public's needs and desires efficiently.

Mutual funds were introduced and index funds were examined in Chapter 12. This chapter evaluates the performance of all types of mutual funds. Mutual funds are exempted from income taxes if they distribute all their income annually, diversify their holdings, and disclose their operations.* These uniformities and the alluring mutual funds advertisements makes them an interesting subject for study.

MUTUAL FUND DATA

The Investment Company Act stipulates that mutual fund investors redeem their shares at the current day's net asset value per share (NAVPS). As shown at Eqn. 12-1 in Chapter 12, the **net asset value per share** (NAVPS) equals the market value of the fund's net assets (after

---

* Subchapter M of the U.S. Internal Revenue Code says all income earned by a mutual fund is tax-exempt if the fund: (1) distributes at least 97% of its cash dividend and interest income in the same year it is received, (2) diversifies by placing no more than 5% of its total assets in any one security issue, (3) is registered with the Securities and Exchange Commission (SEC) under the provisions of the Investment Company Act of 1940. Practically every mutual fund meets these provisions.

liabilities are deducted) divided by the total number of shares outstanding. A mutual fund's one-period rate of return per share, which was introduced in Chapter 12's Eqn. 12-2, is repeated as Eqn. 16-1:

$$r_t = \frac{\begin{pmatrix} \text{Cash flow} \\ \text{disbursements}_t \end{pmatrix} + \begin{pmatrix} \text{Capital gains} \\ \text{disbursements}_i \end{pmatrix} + (NAVPS_t - NAVPS_{t-1})}{(\text{Purchase price at beginning of time period } t, \text{ or } NAVPS_{t-1})} \qquad (16\text{-}1)$$

The Investment Goals of Mutual Funds

U. S. law requires that open-end investment companies distribute to the public a one- or two-paragraph statement of the portfolio's investment objective to all investors. Table 12-1 in Chapter 12 (p. 334) uses these goal statements to group 7,869 U.S. mutual funds into 33 categories and shows the number of funds pursuing each type of goal.

Every category of investment goals can be divided into two subcategories: load funds and no-load funds. As explained in Chapter 12, **no-load funds** do not deduct an initial sales commission (load fee) from the amount to be invested.

Closed-End Funds Are Different

Closed-end investment companies resemble mutual funds to the extent that both are investment portfolios that comingle funds from different investors into a pool that is used to purchase diversified investments. However, closed-end funds differ from open-end funds in important respects. First, as the name implies, a closed-end fund cannot sell shares after its initial public offering (IPO)—the initial number of shares in the portfolio can never be increased. Second, the Investment Company Act allows closed-end funds to borrow money, trade options and futures contracts, and to pursue more different investment objectives than the open-end funds. Third, the shares of most closed-end funds are not redeemable at their net asset value, as are mutual fund shares. The shares of the closed-end funds are shares of stock that are listed and traded on stock exchanges at market prices that are usually at a discount, but are sometimes at a premium, relative to their net asset values.

Michael J. Barclay, Clifford G. Holderness, and Jeffrey Pontiff (BHP) present a compelling explanation of widespread discounts in the prices of closed-end funds. BHP report a relationship between funds' discounts from net asset value and the percentage of managerial ownership in closed-end funds. The average price discount for funds with owner/managers is 14%, whereas the average discount for funds with hired managers is only 4%. BHP argue that owner/managers receive private benefits not available to other shareholders and that owner/managers to preserve these benefits by vetoing open-ending proposals.[1] For this and other reasons closed-end funds have never attracted as many investors as mutual funds and often sell at discounts from their net asset value per share (NAVPS).

Closed-end funds are essentially marketable shares of common stock in an investment company. Their one-period rates of return are calculated like common stock returns—with Eqn. 2-3 from Chapter 2. This chapter focuses on mutual fund data.

MUTUAL FUNDS PERFORMANCE

In Chapter 14 Markowitz portfolio theory showed how to create efficient portfolios. Figure 16-1 is from a classic study of the performance of 23 mutual funds relative to the efficient frontier (the curve *EF*). Figure 16-1 has been confirmed with larger and more recent samples.

FIGURE 16-1 The Performance of 23 Mutual Funds Graphed in Risk-Return Space

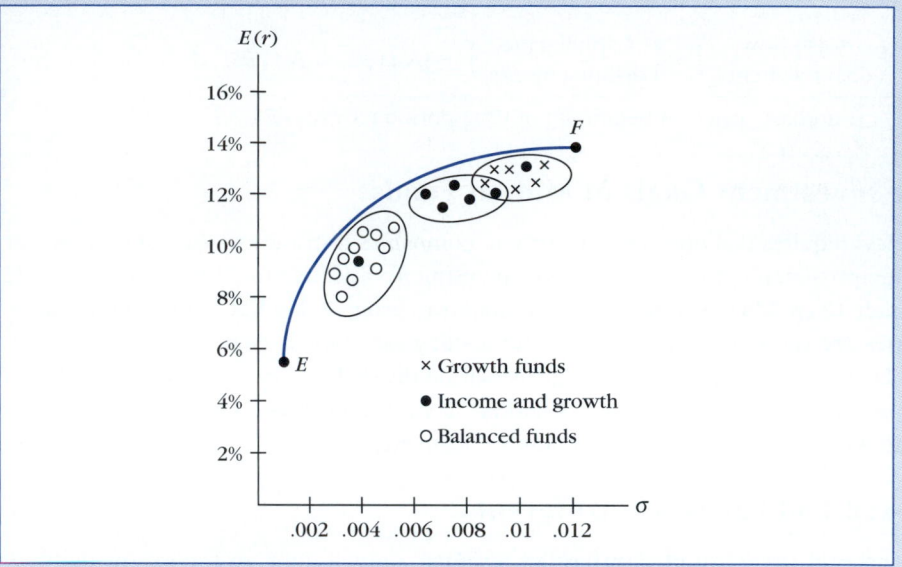

The mutual funds are all inefficient investments, to varying degrees. The 23 funds tend to group themselves into three clusters that correspond, in most cases, to their published investment goals. The investment behavior of a few mutual funds differs from their published goal.

SOURCE: Donald E. Farrar, *The Investment Decision Under Uncertainty* (Englewood Cliffs, NJ: Prentice-Hall, 1962) 73.

Are Mutual Funds Markowitz Efficient Investments?

Figure 16-1 shows that none of the 23 mutual funds are efficient portfolios. Only a few are within 1 percentage point of the efficient frontier. In view of the promises made in mutual fund advertisements, this scientific portfolio analysis is eye-opening.

Figure 16-1 also reveals that the funds tend to cluster into homogeneous groups. Funds that have the published goal of seeking growth and assuming the risk that accompanies higher returns form a cluster above the cluster of less aggressive income-growth funds. The highly risk-averse balanced funds tend to cluster at lower rates of return.

Scrutinizing Mutual Funds' Goal Statements

The Investment Company Act requires mutual funds in the United States to publish a written statement of their investment objective. Farrar classified the 23 funds analyzed in Figure 16-1 into three categories of investment objectives. These three categories are listed here in descending order with respect to the aggressiveness with which the mutual fund's managers seek a high average rate of return and assume risks:

1. Growth funds
2. Growth and income funds
3. Income, growth, and stability funds (balanced funds)

TABLE 16-1   Risk-Return Relationships for Mutual Funds

Risk Class	Range of Betas	Number of Funds	Average Beta	Average Variance	Average Rate of Return
Low	0.5 to 0.7	28	0.619	.000877	9.1%
Medium	0.7 to 0.9	53	0.786	.001543	10.6%
High	0.9 to 1.1	22	0.992	.002304	13.5%

SOURCE: Irwin Friend, Marshall E. Blume, and Jean Crockett, *Mutual Funds and Other Institutional Investors: A New Perspective* (New York: McGraw-Hill, 1970) 150.

TABLE 16-2   Comparison of Mutual Funds' Performances with Their Published Objectives[a]

Beta	Number of Funds Claiming Each Goal				Category's Average Rate of Return			
	Growth	Growth and Income	Income and Growth	Income, Growth, and Stability	Growth	Growth and Income	Income and Growth	Income, Growth, and Stability
0.5 to 0.7	3	5	4	16	6.9%	10.1%	9.7%	9.1%
0.7 to 0.9	15	24	7	7	11.2%	10.0%	10.0%	12.2%
0.9 to 1.1	20	1	None	1	13.8%	9.5%	None	13.5%

[a]The investment objectives are taken from Arthur Wiesenberger Services.

SOURCE: Irwin Friend, Marshall E. Blume, and Jean Crockett, *Mutual Funds and Other Institutional Investors: A New Perspective* (New York: McGraw-Hill, 1970), 150.

Close examination of Figure 16-1 reveals that the funds' stated investment objectives and their performances differed in a few cases. Some mutual funds' stated investment objectives are untruthful and misleading.

Table 16-1 shows the relationship between the two quantitative risk surrogates and the average rates of return for 103 mutual funds. The data in Table 16-1 shows that the betas and standard deviations for the portfolios vary together positively.* Table 16-2 also shows the two risk surrogates are highly positively related with each other and with the portfolios' average rates of return.

Table 16-2 compares the portfolios' published investment objectives with their quantitative risk and average return statistics. The table suggests that the portfolios' standard deviations and beta coefficients were better indicators of the portfolios' actual performance than the goal statements the law requires they publish. More recent research has suggested that "About 40% of the funds examined displayed return patterns that more closely resembled

---

* There is a mathematical reason we would expect the betas and standard deviations to be highly positively correlated. The beta is defined below:

$$\text{Beta}_i = \frac{COV[(r_{i,t}, r_{m,t})]}{VAR(r_{m,t})} = \frac{\rho_{i,m}\sigma_i\sigma_m}{VAR(r_m)} = \frac{\rho_{i,m}\sigma_i}{\sigma_m}$$

Note that as the correlation in the numerator in the far right-hand definition of beta approaches +1.0, the beta becomes a positive linear transformation of the asset's standard deviation, σ_i. In fact, most mutual funds are highly positively correlated; for instance, $\rho_{i,m} = .9$ is a common portfolio correlation.

another category than the one listed in their prospectuses: of those, 9% were seriously mis-classified two or more risk tiers away from their declared categories."[2] Findings that quantitative risk surrogates were more dependable indicators of mutual fund performance than the goal statements published by mutual fund managers spurred development of quantitative style analysis tools.[3]

ANALYZING A PORTFOLIO MANAGER'S STYLE

A portfolio manager's *management style* depends on the segment of the securities market in which the manager invests. Chapter 8, for example, contrasts two popular styles of equity investing—growth stock investing and value stock investing. The mutual fund investment goals listed in Chapter 12's Table 12-1 (p. 334) suggest numerous other investment management styles.

William Sharpe developed a statistical model that analyzes a portfolio manager's style by imputing an asset allocation to the portfolio. After portfolios' asset allocations have been delineated statistically, the portfolio managers' styles become evident. Sharpe uses a statistical tool called *factor analysis* to impute the asset allocations of a heterogeneous sample of hundreds of mutual funds by analyzing a modest amount of public information about each fund.[4] Other approaches to analyzing a portfolio managers' styles exist, but they require more input data than Sharpe's approach.[5]

Using Factor Analysis to Attribute Mutual Funds' Asset Allocations

In 1992 William Sharpe proposed using price indexes for 12 asset classes as the explanatory variables to explain a mutual fund's returns through time, as shown in Eqn. 16-2, where $r_{i,t}$ denotes the one-period rate of return from mutual fund i during time period t.

$$r_{i,t} = b_0 + b_{i,1}F_{1,t} + b_{i,2}F_{2,t} + ... + b_{i,11}F_{11,t} + b_{i,12}F_{12,t} + e_{i,t} \qquad (16\text{-}2)$$

The $e_{i,t}$ is the unexplained residual return from mutual fund i during time period t; the $e_{i,t}$ values have an expected value of zero and can be ignored. The 12 explanatory variables denoted $F_{k,t}$ (for $k = 1, 2, \ldots, 11, 12$ indexes) stand for simultaneous one-period rates of return from different market indexes. The $k = 12$ asset class indexes that Sharpe used are:

Salomon Brothers 90-Day Treasury bill index

Lehman Brothers Intermediate-Term Government Bond Index

Lehman Brothers Long-Term Government Bond Index

Lehman Brothers Corporate Bond Index

Lehman Brothers Mortgage-Backed Securities Index

Sharpe/BARRA Value Stock Index

Sharpe/BARRA Growth Stock Index

Sharpe/BARRA Medium-Capitalization Stock Index

Sharpe/BARRA Small-Capitalization Stock Index

Salomon Brothers Non-U.S. Government Bond Index

FTA Euro-Pacific Ex Japan Index

FTA Japan Index

The twelve beta coefficients (denoted $b_{i,k}$ for $k = 1, 2, \ldots, 11, 12$ indexes) in Eqn. 16-2 are the sensitivities (factor loadings, Sharpe weights) associated with the 12 explanatory variables listed above. Sharpe interprets the $b_{i,k}$ coefficients to be estimates of the weights that fund i invests in asset category k. Sharpe also interprets the sum of the twelve $b_{i,k}F_{k,t}$ products to be a measure of the portfolio manager's style.

The twelve $b_{i,k}$ coefficients (factor loadings, Sharpe weights) are estimated statistically using a constrained procedure that forces their values to remain constant over the estimation period, to be nonnegative, and to sum to 1. These 12 weights can be interpreted to be weights that are statistically attributed to passive investments in 12 different financial market indexes. Sharpe estimated Eqn. 16-2 using 60 consecutive monthly returns from mutual fund i and simultaneous returns from the 12 asset classes to obtain one set of coefficients (weights) for the portfolio. Eqn. 16-2 is economical to estimate because it employs a modest amount of easy-to-obtain public data. The equation typically enjoys high levels of explanatory power over the portfolio's weights. Coefficients of determination (ρ^2 or R^2) with values of 0.7 are common, they mean that Eqn. 16-2 explains 70% of the variance in the mutual fund's returns.

Rolling Style Analysis

Sharpe also pointed out that Eqn. 16-2 can be estimated as a rolling regression to obtain estimates of how a portfolio's asset allocation varies through time. For example, Ibbotson Associates estimates Eqn. 16-2 over 60 months and then deletes the oldest month from the 60-month sample and adds a new month to reestimate the model in the next month. Eqn. 16-2 is estimated iteratively in this manner to obtain a time series of monthly estimates of the 12 $b_{i,k}$ coefficients (portfolio weights). Figure 16-2 illustrates how Ibbotson's statistical estimates of mutual funds' asset allocation weights varied month-by-month over a period of several years.

Figure 16-2 is a Rolling Style Analysis that shows the continually varying monthly weights Ibbotson Associates estimated with Eqn. 16-2 for Fidelity's Magellan Fund over 72 months. Note that some long-term bonds (fixed income securities) crept into this growth stock fund during the mid-1990s. The asset allocation to bonds illustrated in Figure 16-2 is a statistical estimate of Magellan's bond holdings (which, like all statistics, contains sampling errors). Magellan's bond investments actually reached 16.6% of its total assets during 1995. Magellan's bond holdings are surprising since the fund's published investment objective statement declares it is a growth stock fund.

Benefits from Using Quantitative Management Style Analysis

As mentioned above, quantitative style analysis is important because of two moral hazards inherent in portfolio managers' reports:

1. Investment holdings are typically reported months after they are made. For example, Figure 16-2 showed that Fidelity's Magellan Fund, an equity fund, was partially invested in bonds during the mid-1990s. Magellan's bond holdings were made public months after the bonds were purchased—too late for investors to react in a timely manner.
2. Mutual funds can publish statements of their investment goals that may be misleading or even false. For instance, Magellan Fund's published investment goal statement did not say the fund made bond investments. Furthermore, Figure 16-1 and Table 16-2 showed that a small but significant minority of mutual funds do not manage money the way their written goal statements stated they would. Quantitative-style analysis tools provide a way to avoid these moral hazards.

Another benefit from quantitative management–style analysis is that it provides more accurate forecasts of mutual funds risk and return statistics than the subjective comments published by newspapers, magazines, and some financial services.

FIGURE 16-2 The Imputed Asset Allocation Weights for Fidelity's Magellan Fund Vary Each Month

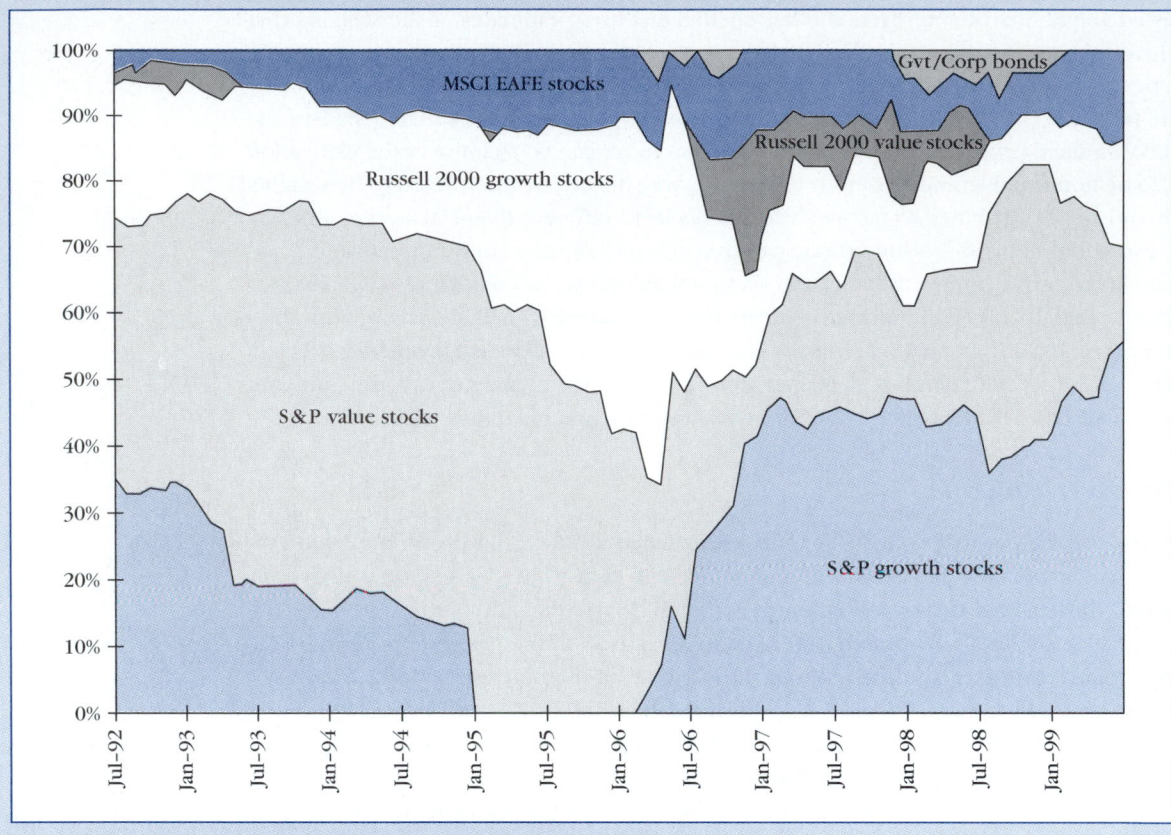

The horizontal axis spans 72 months from the life of the Magellan Mutual Fund. The vertical width of each band at any point represents a statistical estimate of the proportion of a particular asset class within the portfolio at that moment in the 72-month sample. Note that long-term bonds (represented by the grey pattern at top of figure) enter and leave the Fund during the late 1990s. Bonds actually reached 16.6% of total assets during 1995.
SOURCE: Data and software for Rolling Style Analysis from Ibbotson Associates, Chicago, IL.

TWO HYPOTHETICAL MUTUAL FUNDS

Two mutual funds are analyzed to provide a sample of how the computations are performed. Table 16-3 contains 10 annual returns from two hypothetical mutual funds called the Avon Fund and the Blair Fund. The mutual fund returns were computed with Eqn. 16-1. Statistics computed from data in Table 16-3 are used below.

SHARPE'S PORTFOLIO PERFORMANCE MEASURE

Both the risk and return of a portfolio should be considered. Ranking portfolios' returns averaged over several years is oversimplified because such rankings ignore risk. Evaluating risk and return together, as done in Figure 16-1, is a more comprehensive analysis of a portfolio's performance. An index of portfolio performance that is determined by both return and the

TABLE 16-3 Ten Annual Observations on the Avon and Blair Funds

| | Rates of return, r | | | T-Bill's | Risk Premiums, RP = (r−RFR) | | |
Year	Avon	Blair	SP500	RFR	Avon RP	Blair RP	SP500 RP
1	10.0%	10.0%	10.0%	4.0%	6.0%	6.0%	6.0%
2	30.0%	40.0%	30.0%	4.0%	26.0%	36.0%	26.0%
3	−20.0%	−20.0%	−20.0%	4.0%	−24.0%	−24.0%	−24.0%
4	−10.0%	−10.0%	−10.0%	4.0%	−14.0%	−14.0%	−14.0%
5	20.0%	40.0%	20.0%	4.0%	16.0%	36.0%	16.0%
6	10.0%	20.0%	30.0%	4.0%	6.0%	16.0%	26.0%
7	0.0%	−20.0%	−10.0%	4.0%	−4.0%	−24.0%	−14.0%
8	30.0%	20.0%	20.0%	4.0%	26.0%	16.0%	16.0%
9	−10.0%	10.0%	0.0%	4.0%	−14.0%	6.0%	−4.0%
10	20.0%	40.0%	30.0%	4.0%	16.0%	36.0%	26.0%
E(r)	8.00%	13.00%	10.00%	4.00%	4.00%	9.00%	6.00%
Standard Deviation	16.60%	22.40%	17.90%	0.00%	16.60%	22.40%	17.90%
VAR(r)	2.76%	5.01%	3.20%	0.00%	2.76%	5.01%	3.20%

risk, and can also be used to rank portfolios, is needed. Eqn. 16-3 defines a *single parameter portfolio performance index* that is calculated from both the risk and return statistics. William F. Sharpe devised the reward to variability index of portfolio performance, denoted $SHARPE_p$, that is defined in Eqn. 16-3 for portfolio p, where

> $\bar{r}_p$ = average return from portfolio p
>
> σ_p = standard deviation of returns for portfolio p
>
> RFR = risk-free rate of interest

$$SHARPE_p = \frac{\text{Risk premium for } p}{\text{Total risk of } p} = \frac{\bar{r}_p - RFR}{\sigma_p} \qquad (16\text{-}3)$$

The numerator of Eqn. 16-3, $\bar{r}_p - RFR$, is called the **risk premium** for portfolio p. As we have learned, the risk premium is that return above the riskless rate paid to induce investors to assume risk.

The SHARPE performance index is a single number that is determined by both the risk and average return of the portfolio, or other investment, that is being evaluated. Substituting summary statistics from the bottom of Table 16-3 into Eqn. 16-3 yields the following inequality.

$$SHARPE_A = \frac{\bar{r}_A - RFR}{\sigma_A} = \frac{.08 - .04}{.166} = 0.241 < 0.402 = \frac{.13 - .04}{.224} = \frac{\bar{r}_B - RFR}{\sigma_B} = SHARPE_B$$

The inequality $SHARPE_A = 0.241 < 0.402 = SHARPE_B$ indicates that the Blair Fund has a better *risk-adjusted return* than the Avon Fund. Figure 16-3 illustrates how Sharpe's performance index measures the slope of a line from the riskless rate *RFR* to the risky assets. The fact that the portfolios have different average returns and are in different risk classes does not hinder performance ranking with the SHARPE index.[6]

FIGURE 16-3 Illustration of the Reward to Variability (SHARPE) Index of Portfolio Performance for the Avon Fund and Blair Fund

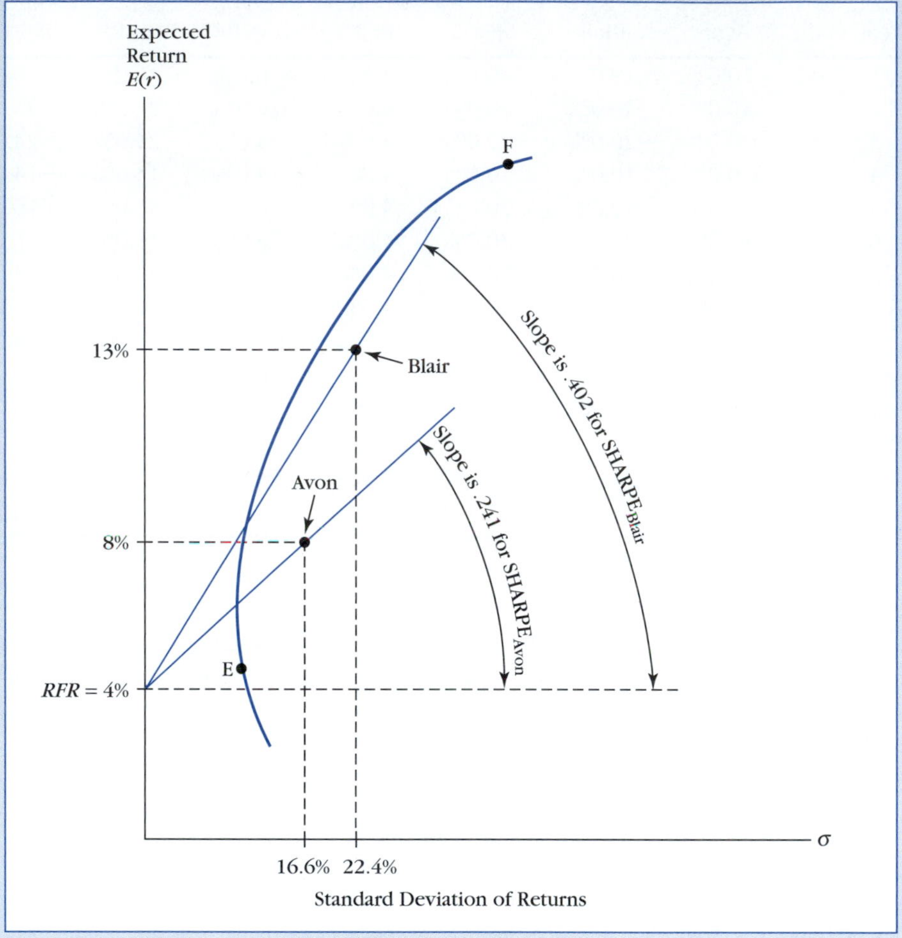

The Blair Fund has more risk premium, $E(r) - RFR$, per unit of risk, σ, than the Avon Fund—symbolically, $SHARPE_A = 0.241 < 0.402 = SHARPE_B$

CREATING INVESTMENT OPPORTUNITIES

The two straight lines passing through the Avon and Blair Funds in Figure 16-3 illustrate realistic investment opportunities. To see how these investment possibilities are created, assume that the investor can borrow or lend at the risk-free rate (RFR), as was done in constructing the capital market lines (CML) illustrated in Figure 14-7 of Chapter 14 (p. 421) and Figure 15-1 from Chapter 15 (p. 438). For example, suppose an investor allocates a proportion of her funds denoted x_{Avon} for investment in the Avon Fund, while the remaining proportion of her funds, $(1 - x_{Avon})$, is invested at the risk-free rate. These two weights should be defined so they sum to 1, $x_{Avon} + (1 - x_{Avon}) = 1$, in order to account for all the money involved in this asset allocation decision. Eqn. 16-4 defines an **asset allocation line (AAL)** for this two-asset portfolio:

$$E\left(r_{\text{Avon}}^{\text{AAL}}\right) = (1 - x_{\text{Avon}})(RFR) + (x_{\text{Avon}})[E(r_{\text{Avon}})] \tag{16-4}$$

$$= RFR + (x_{Avon})\left[E\left(r_{\text{Avon}}^{\text{AAL}}\right) - RFR\right]$$

$$= .04 + (x_{Avon})(.08 - .04)$$

$$= .04 + .04x_{Avon} \tag{16-4a}$$

Eqn. 16-4a measures the expected return for the infinite number of 2-asset portfolios lying on the straight line from *RFR* that runs through the Avon Fund in Figure 16-3.

The variance of a 2-asset portfolio composed of the Avon Fund and the risk-free asset is defined by Eqn. 16-5, which is identical to Eqn. 14-8 in Chapter 14 (p. 416), where the asset allocation line was introduced.

$$Var\left(r_{\text{Avon}}^{\text{AAL}}\right) = x_{\text{Avon}}^2\sigma_{\text{Avon}}^2 + x_{\text{RFR}}^2\sigma_{\text{RFR}}^2 + 2x_{\text{Avon}}x_{\text{RFR}}\sigma_{\text{Avon,RFR}} \tag{16-5}$$

$$VAR\left(r_{\text{Avon}}^{\text{AAL}}\right) = x_{\text{Avon}}^2\sigma_{\text{Avon}}^2 + 0 + 0 \quad \text{since VAR(RFR)} = \text{COV(Avon,RFR)} = 0 \tag{16-5a}$$

Taking the square root of Eqn. 16-5a shows that the 2-asset portfolio's risk formula is a simple linear function of the standard deviation of the risky asset.

$$\sigma_{\text{Avon}}^{\text{AAL}} = x_{\text{Avon}}\sigma_{\text{Avon}} \tag{16-6}$$

Since Eqns. 16-4 and 16-6 are both linear equations, this means that all portfolios made up of a risky asset (like the Avon Fund) and a risk-free asset must form straight lines of investment opportunities in risk-return space, as shown in Figure 14-7 of Chapter 14 (p. 421) and Figure 16-3. These straight lines were introduced in Chapter 14 and called asset allocation lines (AALs). The AAL with the highest SHARPE value is the most desirable investment.

TREYNOR'S PERFORMANCE MEASURE

Jack Treynor conceived an index of portfolio performance that is based on systematic risk, as measured by a portfolio's beta coefficient. To use Treynor's measure, the characteristic line of the portfolio or other assets must be estimated with time-series regression Eqn. 16-7, where

STUDY CHECK

THE ASSET ALLOCATION LINE

QUESTION: What asset allocation line has a higher SHARPE value than any other AAL?

ANSWER: The capital market line (CML) is the AAL with the highest SHARPE value; it dominates all other investments in $[\sigma, E(r)]$ space.

$r_{p,t}$ = rate of return on portfolio p in time period t

$r_{M,t}$ = return on market index in period t

$e_{p,t}$ = random error term for portfolio p in period t, $E(e_{p,t}) = 0$,

α_p = intercept coefficient for portfolio p

β_p = portfolio's beta coefficient

T = terminal time period

TABLE 16-4   Avon and Blair Funds' Characteristic Lines in Returns

(A) Avon's Characteristic Line from Returns

Regression formula: $r_{A,t} = \text{Alpha}_A + \text{Beta}_A r_{M,t} + e_{A,t}$ **(16-7a)**

Alpha: -0.00125 Beta: 0.8125 Correlation: 0.875 VAR(e_A): 0.0065

$$\text{TREYNOR}_A = \frac{r_{A,t} - RFR_t}{\text{Beta}_A} = \frac{8\% - 4\%}{0.8125} = \frac{.04}{.8125} = .049$$ **(16-8a)**

(B) Blair's Characteristic Line from Returns

Regression formula: $r_{B,t} = \text{Alpha}_B + \text{Beta}_B r_{M,t} + e_{B,t}$ **(16-7b)**

Alpha: 0.014 Beta: 1.16 Correlation: 0.924 VAR(e_B): 0.0073

$$\text{TREYNOR}_B = \frac{r_{B,t} - RFR_t}{\text{Beta}_B} = \frac{13\% - 4\%}{1.16} = \frac{.09}{1.16} = 0.078$$ **(16-8b)**

FIGURE 16-4   Characteristic Lines in Returns for the Avon Fund and the Blair Fund

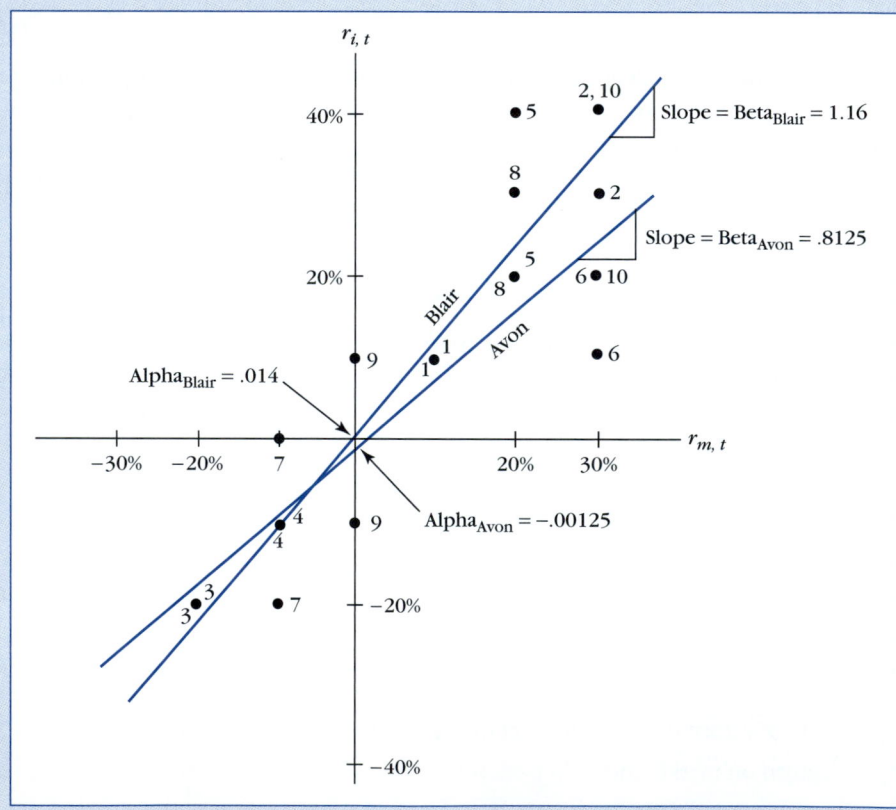

Characteristic lines for the Avon Fund and the Blair Fund are illustrated; they were computed from the data in Table 16-3 to obtain estimates of the two funds' alphas, betas, and average returns.

$$r_{p,t} = \alpha_p + \beta_p(r_{M,t}) + e_{p,t} \qquad t = 1, 2, \ldots, T \text{ time periods} \qquad \text{(16-7)}$$

Eqns. 16-7a and 16-7b in Table 16-4 shows the statistics that were computed for the Avon and Blair Funds from the returns in Table 16-3. Figure 16-4 illustrates the characteristic lines for the Avon Fund and the Blair Funds. Their different slopes (betas) reflect the portfolios' different investment policies toward risk and different amounts of undiversifiable risk.

Chapters 7 and 15 pointed out the beta coefficient from a characteristic line is an index of an investment's undiversifiable risk. Treynor suggested using a portfolio's risk premium relative to its beta. Eqn. 16-8 defines **Treynor's index of return-to-volatility portfolio performance**, denoted TREYNOR$_p$ for the pth portfolio,[7] where $\bar{r}_p$ measures the average rate of return for portfolio p.

The TREYNOR index ranks Blair Fund above Avon Fund because Blair earned a higher reward-to-volatility ratio than Avon.

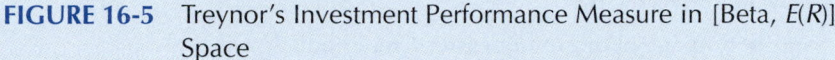

$$\text{TREYNOR}_p = \frac{\text{Risk premium}}{\text{Index of undiversifiable risk}} = \frac{\bar{r}_p - RFR}{\text{Beta}_p} \qquad \text{(16-8)}$$

FIGURE 16-5   Treynor's Investment Performance Measure in [Beta, $E(R)$] Space

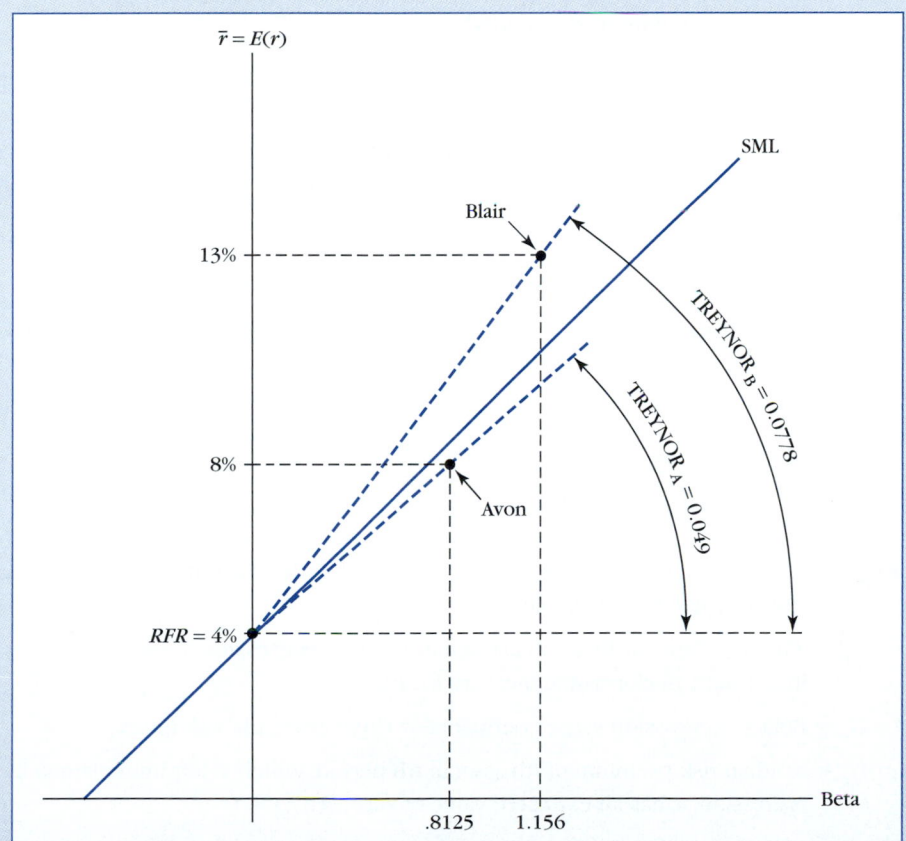

The Blair Fund has more risk premium, $E(r) - RFR$, per unit of undiversifiable (beta) risk than the Avon Fund. Symbolically, TREYNOR$_A$ = .049 < .0778 = TREYNOR$_B$

Eqn. 16-7 is a characteristic line for a portfolio; it is just like the characteristic line for an individual stock or bond introduced at Eqn. 7-7 in Chapter 7.

$$\text{TREYNOR}_A = \frac{\bar{r}_A - RFR}{\text{Beta}_A} = \frac{.08 - .04}{.8125} = 0.049 < 0.0778 = \frac{.13 - .04}{1.156} = \frac{\bar{r}_B - RFR}{\text{Beta}_B} = \text{TREYNOR}_B$$

The TREYNOR ratio measures the desirability of the Avon and Blair Funds in a SML context. As Figure 16-5 illustrates, TREYNOR_p is a measure of the slope of the line from RFR to portfolio p. The TREYNOR lines represent realistic investment opportunities. These investment opportunities are created by assuming money can be borrowed and lent at the risk-free rate, in the same way the CML and SML were created in Chapters 14 and 15.

AN INVESTMENT'S ALPHA

Michael C. Jensen modified the characteristic line of Eqn. 7-7 that was introduced in Chapter 7.[8] The basic random variables in Jensen's model are not the one-period rates of return, they are one-period risk premiums denoted RP in Eqn. 16-9, where

$RP_{i,t}$ = Risk premium for asset i in time period t = the part of the total return that is a reward for risk-taking,

$r_{i,t}$ = one-period rate of return from asset i in period t

RFR_t = risk-free rate of interest in period t

$$RP_{i,t} = r_{i,t} - RFR_t \tag{16-9}$$

Jensen restated the original characteristic line of Eqn. 7-7 in risk premiums, as shown in Eqn. 16-10. Eqn. 16-10 is a simple linear regression of the form: y = a + bx + e, where the x and y variables are risk premiums (RP):

$$r_{i,t} - RFR_t = A_i + B_i(r_{m,t} - RFR_t) + u_{i,t}$$
$$RP_{i,t} = A_i + B_i(RP_{m,t}) + u_{i,t} \tag{16-10}$$

where

$$B_i = \frac{COV[(r_{i,t} - RFR_t)(r_{m,t} - RFR_t)]}{VAR(r_{m,t} - RFR_t)} \tag{16-11}$$

$RP_{m,t}$ = $(r_{m,t} - RFR_t)$ = risk premium for the market index for time period t, the regression's explanatory variable,

A_i = Alpha = The ordinary least squares (OLS) regression intercept is Jensen's investment performance measure for ith asset

B_i = Beta = Regression slope coefficient = Undiversifiable risk index

$u_{i,t}$ = residual risk premium of ith asset in tth period, which is left unexplained by the regression; it has an expected value of zero, $E(u_{i,t}) = 0$

The security market line (SML) is an asset-pricing model that was introduced in Eqns. 15-3, 15-4, and 15-5 and illustrated in Figure 15-2A and B of Chapter 15 (p. 443). The SML in Figure 16-6 is stated in terms of the beta slope coefficient. And even though Jensen's beta, Eqn. 16-11, is computationally different from the original beta systematic risk coefficient of

FIGURE 16-6   The Security Market Line (SML) Restated in Risk-Premium Form with Several Assets' Investment Performance Statistics Indicated

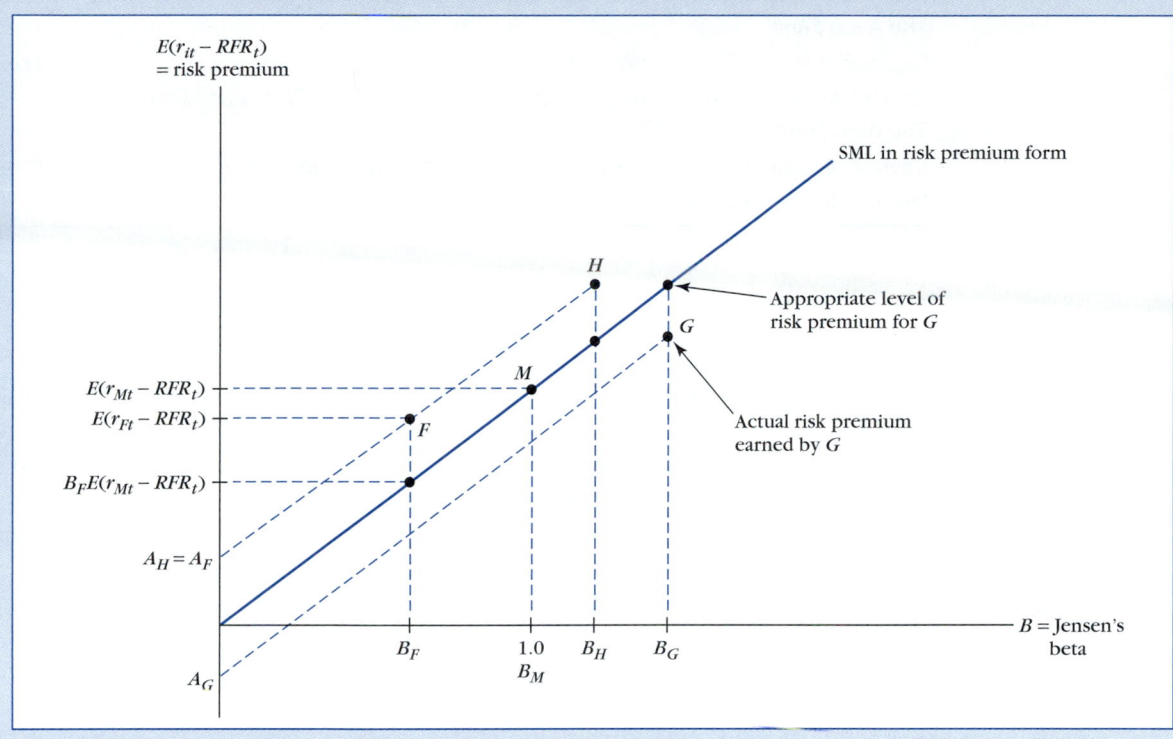

If the characteristic line is formulated in risk premiums instead of returns, $r_{i,t} - RFR_t = A_i + B_i(r_{m,t} - RFR_t) + u_{i,t}$, a slightly different alpha (A = intercept) and beta (B = slope) are computed. Taking the expected value, $E(r_{i,t} - RFR_t) = A_i + B_iE(r_{m,t} - RFR_t)$, reformulates the SML in terms of risk premiums instead of returns. The performance of assets F, G and H (not Avon and Blair) are compared.

Eqn. 15-4 in Chapter 15, these two different betas have very similar numerical values for the same asset. The two betas in Eqns. 15-4 and 16-11 also have the same interpretations as measures of undiversifiable risk.

The mathematical expectation of Eqn. 16-11 is Eqn. 16-12, since $E(u_{it}) = 0$,

$$E(r_{i,t} - RFR_t) = A_i + B_iE(r_{m,t} - RFR_t) \tag{16-12}$$

Eqn. 16-12 is represented graphically in Figure 16-6 as the SML reformulated in risk premiums. Table 16-5 contains the regression estimates of Eqn. 16-10 computed from the data in Table 16-3 for the Avon and Blair Mutual Funds.

Explanation of an Investment's Alpha

The **alpha** intercept from the characteristic line in risk premium form can be interpreted as a measure of the excess returns from the asset. This alpha can have a positive, zero, or negative value; it measures the **excess returns** averaged over the sample period used to estimate the asset's characteristic line regression. If an asset is correctly priced, then it should not yield returns above or below the appropriate risk premium, on average, and the alpha intercept will have a value of zero, A = 0. But if asset F has rates of return that exceed its appropriate risk

---

TABLE 16-5 Characteristic Lines in Risk Premiums (not returns) for the Avon and Blair Funds

The Avon Fund

Regression formula: $(r_{A,t} - RFR_t) = \text{Alpha}_A + \text{Beta}_A(r_{M,t} - RFR_t) + e_{A,t}$ **(16-10a)**

Jensen's Alpha: $- 0.00875$ Beta: 0.8125 Correlation: 0.875 VAR(e_A): 0.0065

The Blair Fund

Regression formula: $(r_{B,t} - RFR_t) = \text{Alpha}_B + \text{Beta}_B(r_{M,t} - RFR_t) + e_{B,t}$ **(16-10b)**

Jensen's Alpha: $+ 0.02062$ Beta: 1.1562 Correlation: 0.924 VAR(e_B): 0.0073

---

premium, on average, so that Eqn. 16-12a is an inequality, then asset F's alpha intercept will be positive.

$$\text{If}\quad E(r_{F,t} - RFR_t) > B_F E(r_{m,t} - RFR_t)\quad \text{then Alpha}_F > 0 \qquad \textbf{(16-12a)}$$

The positive excess return, Alpha $_F > 0$, measures a vertical distance above the SML. This quantity is asset F's excess returns; it is depicted graphically in Figure 16-6. Any individual asset that has a positive alpha has earned an average return that exceeds what is appropriate for its level of undiversifiable (beta) risk.

If asset G is overpriced so that it yields risk premiums that are inappropriately low for its level of systematic risk over some sample period, asset G's alpha will be negative, Alpha $_G < 0$. This undesirable investment situation is mathematically specified by Eqn. 16-12b:

$$\text{If}\quad E(r_{G,t} - RFR_t) < B_G E(r_{m,t} - RFR_t)\quad \text{then Alpha}_G < 0 \qquad \textbf{(16-12b)}$$

Asset G's negative excess return is illustrated in Figure 16-6.

The alpha intercept term in Jensen's characteristic line reformulated in risk premiums can be used to evaluate the performance of individual assets or portfolios. For example, if asset F outperformed the market, this is represented by $A_F > 0$. If hypothetical asset Q earned returns that are exactly appropriate for its level of undiversifiable risk then, $A_Q = 0$. If asset A performed poorly, then $A_G < 0$. These three assets' investment performances could be ranked as shown in the inequality at Eqn. 16-13.

$$A_F > A_Q = 0 > A_G \qquad \textbf{(16-13)}$$

Caveats About Alphas

Consider two assets named H and F. Suppose these two assets' excess returns measured over the same sample period are identical, $A_H = A_F$. Further suppose that asset H has more systematic risk than asset F as shown in Figure 16-6. Can we conclude that these two assets performed equally well simply because their alphas are identical? To see why the answer is "no," reconsider Treynor's investment performance ranking tool, TREYNOR from Eqn. 16-8.

$$\text{TREYNOR}_F = \frac{E(r_{F,t} - RFR_t)}{Beta_F} > \frac{E(r_{H,t} - RFR_t)}{Beta_H} = \text{TREYNOR}_H \qquad \textbf{(16-14)}$$

The inequality at Eqn. 16-14 utilizes Treynor's performance ranking measure to show that asset F's performance surpassed asset H's performance, even though their alphas are identical, $A_F = A_H$. The point is that Jensen's alpha should not be used to *rank* the performance of different assets unless it is adjusted for the assets' risks. Eqn. 16-15 defines the **appraisal ratio**, which is computed by dividing Jensen's alpha by the standard error of the estimate, denoted $SE(u)$, to make it suitable for performance ranking purposes.*

$$\text{Appraisal ratio} = \frac{A_F}{SE(u)_F} > \frac{A_H}{SE(u)_H} \tag{16-15}$$

The first caveat is against using Jensen's alpha for ranking purposes. Jensen's alpha has asset-pricing implications, and it measures excess returns. But it is not suitable for ranking purposes until it has been risk-adjusted, as shown in Eqn. 16-15, to be an appraisal ratio.[9]

The second caveat is about the interpretation of the alpha intercept term from the original characteristic line, Eqn. 7-7 in Chapter 7, that is estimated with rates of return instead of risk premiums. This original alpha is different from Jensen's alpha, $\alpha_i \neq A_i$. The original alpha from Eqns. 7-7 and this chapter's Eqn. 16-7 should not be used for investment performance evaluation; it has no asset-pricing implications.

PERFORMANCE STATISTICS FROM MUTUAL FUNDS

Table 16-6 lists general information and values of the portfolio performance evaluation tools discussed above for 30 U.S. open-end investment companies. The descriptive information in Table 16-6A shows that Fidelity Magellan Fund is the largest fund, it charges a 3% load fee, and that Magellan's published investment objective is to acquire growth stocks. The performance data in Table 16-6B shows that a technology fund named Munder NetNet Fund earned the highest average return, had the highest standard deviation, and had the highest beta of the 30 funds.

Analyzing Performance Statistics

Some investors think the mutual fund with the highest return is the most desirable investment and, following the same logic, the portfolio with the lowest return is the least desirable. Table 16-6B shows that this is not the way the SHARPE, TREYNOR, and Alpha measures rank the desirability of the 30 mutual funds. Why do these rankings differ?

To understand why the mutual fund with the highest average rate of return might not have the highest portfolio performance evaluation scores, consider financially engineering two hypothetical mutual funds. Assume the Yak Fund is a high-risk, high-return fund that has an average annual rate of return of 30% and a standard deviation of 20%. The less aggressive Zebra Fund has an average expected rate of return of 15% and a standard deviation of 5%. Assume money can be borrowed and lent at the riskless rate of 4%.

Possible Investments	Expected Return	Standard Deviation	Description
Yak Fund	30%	20%	High-risk and high-return fund
Zebra Fund	15%	5%	Low-risk and low-return fund
RFR	4%	0	Risk-free interest rate

---

* Treynor and Black suggested dividing Jensen's alpha by the standard error of the estimate (standard deviation of the residual errors) to normalize it. See Jack L. Treynor and Fischer Black, "How to Use Security Analysis to Improve Portfolio Selection," *Journal of Business* 46, no. 1 (January 1973): 66–86.

TABLE 16-6   Portfolio Performance Evaluation Statistics for 30 Mutual Funds (Open-End Investment Companies)[a]

16-6A Marketing Data

Mutual Fund	Net Assets Millions U.S. $	Front-End Load Fee, %	Expense Ratio, %	12b-1 Fee, %	Back-End Exit Fee, %	Annual Rate of Turnover (%)	Published Investment Objective
AIM Constellation A	$17,855	5.5	1.1	0.3	0	62	Aggressive Growth
Dreyfus Growth & Income	$1,495	0	1.1	0	0	102	Growth and Income
Fidelity Magellan	$100,940	3	0.6	0	0	37	Growth
Fidelity Puritan	$21,442	0	0.63	0	0	80	Balanced
Gabelli Asset	$1,982	0	1.36	0.25	0	21	Growth
Guardian Park Avenue A	$2,888	4.5	0.77	0	0	74	Growth
Harbor International	$5,071	0	0.94	0	0	14	Foreign Stock
Income Fund of America	$18,700	5.75	0.59	0.24	0	44	Asset Allocation
Investment Comp of America	$56,228	5.75	0.55	0.22	0	25	Growth and Income
Janus	$46,869	0	0.84	0	0	63	Growth
Janus Twenty	$34,274	0	0.87	0	0	40	Growth
Kemper Technology A	$3,394	5.75	0.93	0	0	59	Specialty: Technology
Lindner Large-Cap Inv	$384	0	0.57		0	53	Growth
Midas	$72	0	2.55	0.25	0	74	Specialty: Precious Metals
MSDW Developing Growth E	$1,143	0	1.7	1	5	172	Small Company
Munder NetNet A	$2,805	5.5	1.59	0.25	0	22	Specialty: Technology
Mutual Beacon Z	$2,912	0	0.78	0	0	68	Growth and Income
Firsthand Technology Value	$3,353	0	1.91	0	0	41	Specialty: Technology
Oppenheimer Growth A	$2,406	5.75	1.05	0.25	0	106	Growth
Putnam Fund for Grth & Inc.	$18,776	5.75	0.79	0.25	0	50	Growth and Income
Rydex OTC Inv	$2,683	0	1.15	0	0	773	Growth
T. Rowe Price Growth Stock	$5,668	0	0.74	0	0	56	Growth
T. Rowe Price Sci & Tech	$12,606	0	0.87	0	0	128	Specialty: Technology
Templeton Developing Mkts	$2,251	5.75	2.11	0.33	0	38	Diversified Emerging Markets
Templeton World A	$9,081	5.75	1.04	0.25	0	36	World Stock
Value Line Spec Situations	$468	0	1.02	0	0	183	Aggressive Growth
Vanguard 500 Index	$102,815	0	0.18	0	0	6	Growth and Income
Vanguard Sm Cp Index	$3,720	0	0.25	0	0	42	Small Company
Vanguard Windsor II	$23,721	0	0.37	0	0	26	Growth and Income
Merrill Lynch Basic Value A	$4,662	5.25	0.54	0	0	18	Growth and Income

16-6B Portfolio Performance Statistics

Mutual Fund	Annual Geometric Mean (%)	Annual Arithmetic Mean (%)	Standard Deviation (%)	Beta	R-Squared	Sharpe	Treynor	Jensen's Alpha (%)
AIM Constellation A	21.87	24.73	27.06	1.08	0.55	0.73	0.18	−1.76
Dreyfus Growth & Income	13.58	14.70	16.01		0.84	0.60	0.11	−6.36
Fidelity Magellan	20.80	22.30	19.24	1.00	0.90	0.89	0.17	−2.44
Fidelity Puritan	13.28	13.81	11.00	0.61	0.89	0.79	0.14	−2.76
Gabelli Asset	20.46	21.55	16.24	0.82	0.83	1.01	0.20	0.23
Guardian Park Avenue A	25.30	27.16	21.92	0.93	0.64	1.01	0.24	2.84
Harbor International	15.58	16.88	17.44	0.72	0.52	0.68	0.16	−1.98
Income Fund of America	11.54	11.91	9.08	0.46	0.72	0.75	0.15	−1.83
Investment Comp of America	20.66	21.61	15.24	0.82	0.95	1.08	0.20	0.24
Janus	27.98	29.85	22.13	0.96	0.70	1.12	0.26	4.38
Janus Twenty	37.38	40.62	30.69	1.15	0.61	1.16	0.31	9.19
Kemper Technology A	37.15	43.43	44.02	1.28	0.39	0.87	0.30	8.91
Lindner Large-Cap Inv	5.23	6.66	17.39	0.72	0.45	0.09	0.02	−11.31
Midas	−25.63	−19.92	32.36	0.74	0.09	−0.77	−0.34	−40.10
MSDW Developing Growth B	24.32	30.66	42.60	1.07	0.24	0.60	0.24	3.16
Munder NetNet A	73.25	91.42	90.13	1.61	0.32	0.96	0.54	30.99
Mutual Beacon Z	15.34	16.19	14.00	0.66	0.67	0.79	0.17	−1.59

Mutual Fund	Annual Geometric Mean (%)	Annual Arithmetic Mean (%)	Standard Deviation (%)	Beta	R-Squared	Sharpe	Treynor	Jensen's Alpha (%)
Firsthand Technology Value	58.33	69.71	65.98	1.30	0.25	0.98	0.50	26.09
Oppenheimer Growth A	24.96	26.83	22.13	0.77	0.43	0.98	0.28	5.37
Putnam Fund for Grth & Inc A	14.48	15.70	16.89	0.86	0.78	0.63	0.12	−5.59
Rydex OTC Inv	47.97	54.14	45.07	1.33	0.46	1.09	0.37	15.45
T. Rowe Price Growth Stock	23.90	25.25	18.31	0.93	0.89	1.10	0.22	1.29
T. Rowe Price Sci & Tech	30.81	36.40	40.06	1.32	0.45	0.78	0.24	3.09
Templeton Developing Mkts A	2.58	6.32	28.65	1.21	0.46	0.04	0.01	−20.20
Templeton World A	15.27	16.54	17.28	0.81	0.66	0.66	0.14	−3.87
Value Line Spec Situations	28.87	32.27	30.75	0.91	0.34	0.88	0.30	7.19
Vanguard 500 Index	23.76	25.14	18.61	1.00	1.00	1.08	0.20	−0.05
Vanguard Sm Cp Index	15.50	17.85	23.76	0.81	0.36	0.54	0.16	−2.70
Vanguard Windsor II	15.91	17.28	18.04	0.86	0.71	0.67	0.14	−4.21
Merrill Lynch Basic Value A	15.64	16.68	15.65	0.78	0.75	0.74	0.15	−3.19
								−0.40
Arithmetic Mean	22.54	25.79	26.92	0.95	0.59	0.75	0.20	0.28
S&P 500 Index	23.81	25.19	18.61	1.00	1.00	1.08	0.20	0.00
30-day T-bill	5.11	5.11	0.15					

[a] All statistics based on 5 years of monthly data (60 observations) ending June, 2000, except for Munder NetNet, which uses 46 months of data.

SOURCES: Ibbotson Associates perfomed the computations. Morningstar provided the raw data. Chicago-based Morningstar, Inc. is a leading provider of investment information, research, and analysis. Its extensive line of Internet, software, and print products provides unbiased data and commentary on mutual funds, U.S. and international equities, closed-end funds, and variable annuities. Established in 1984, Morningstar is a source on key investment issues of the day. For more information about Morningstar, visit www.morningstar.com or call 800-735-0700.

The asset allocation line (AAL) created with Eqns. 16-4 and 16-6 earlier in this chapter are used to engineer an apples-to-apples comparison of these significantly different funds.

First we compare the Yak and Zebra funds and determine that their standard deviations differ by a multiplier of 4. The multiplier of 4 is a leverage factor that tells the investor to borrow 4 times as much as the initial equity (down payment, initial margin) to financially engineer a dominant investment with the same risk. Eqn. 16-6a shows us that if we multiply Zebra's low standard deviation by the value of 4 we create a new portfolio on Zebra's AAL that has the same high standard deviation as the Yak Fund.

$$(\sigma \text{ on AAL}) = (x) \text{ times } (\text{actual } \sigma) \tag{16-6}$$

$$\left(\sigma_{\text{Zebra}}^{\text{AAL}}\right) = (4) \text{ times } (\sigma_{\text{Zebra}} = 5\%) = 20\% = \sigma_{\text{Yak}} \tag{16-6a}$$

An expected return on the asset allocation line (AAL) is computed with Eqn. 16-4 from above. We want to use the same leverage factor of 4 that was used in Eqn. 16-6a. If we use the Zebra Fund's average annual rate of return of 15% and the same multiplier of 4, we obtain an expected return of 48% on the AAL, as shown in Eqn. 16-4a and illustrated in Figure 16-7.

$$E\left(r_{\text{Zebra}}^{\text{AAL}}\right) = \left(1 - x_{\text{Zebra}}\right)(RFR) + \left(x_{\text{Zebra}}\right)\left[E(r_{\text{Zebra}})\right]$$

$$= RFR + \left(x_{\text{Zebra}}\right)\left[E\left(r_{\text{Zebra}}\right) - RFR\right]$$

$$= 4\% + (4)(15\% - 4\%) \tag{16-4a}$$

$$48\% = 4\% + (4)(11\%)$$

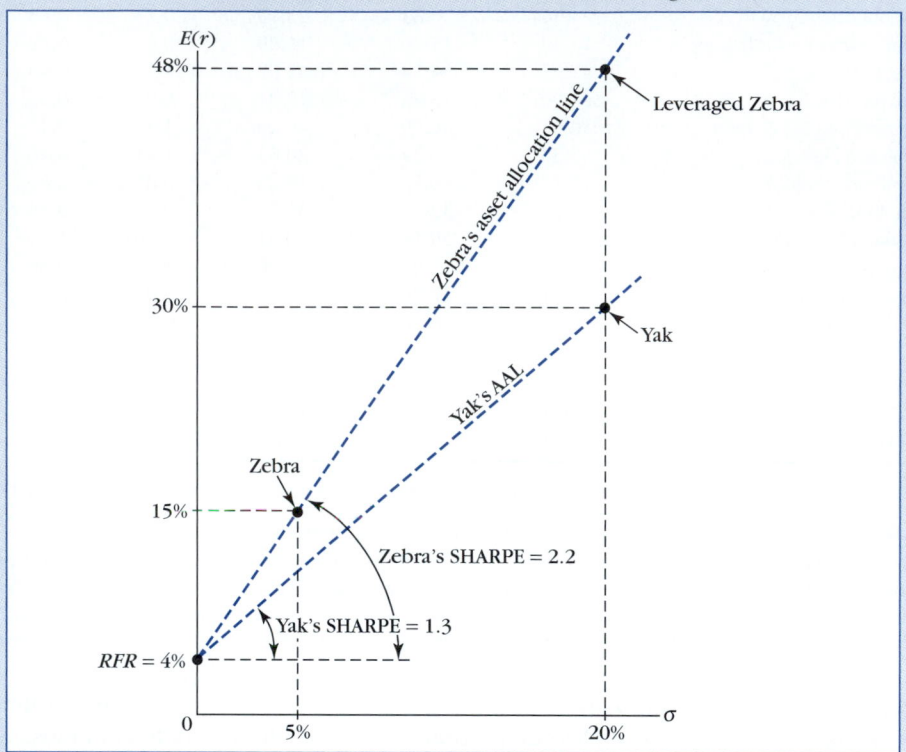

FIGURE 16-7 A Mutual Fund's SHARPE Value Points Out an Investment with a Low Return That Can Be Leveraged into a Dominant Position over Another Asset That Has a Higher Return

The Zebra Fund has a lower average rate of return than the Yak Fund, 15% < 30%. But, financial engineering is used to leverage the Zebra Fund up into a dominant position over the Yak Fund, 48% > 30%.

The investment opportunity we created on Zebra's AAL has the following risk-return statistics: $\left[\left(\sigma^{\text{AAL}}_{\text{Zebra}} \right), E \left(r^{\text{AAL}}_{\text{Zebra}} \right) \right] = [20\%, 48\%]$. Note that this portfolio on Zebra's AAL dominates an investment in the Yak Fund of equal risk: $[(\sigma_{\text{Yak}}), E(r_{\text{Yak}})] = [20\%, 30\%]$. The AAL portfolio is more desirable than the Yak Fund because when Yak Fund and the AAL portfolio are in the same risk-class of $\sigma = 20\%$, the AAL portfolio has a higher expected return (48% > 30%). Borrowing at the risk-free rate of 4% and leveraging the Zebra Fund 4 times creates a leveraged-Zebra-Fund that dominates the Yak Fund in risk-return space at every level of risk. Thus, we see that the Zebra Fund is a better investment than the Yak Fund even though the Yak Fund has a higher average return.

Financial engineering was used to leverage the Zebra Fund into a dominant position over the Yak Fund. Financial engineering can also be used to select an asset with a high TREYNOR value and then leverage that asset into a position in Beta-$E(r)$ space that dominates a higher-return asset that has a lower TREYNOR value. In fact, the AALs in Figures 16-3 and 16-5 illustrate an infinite number of investment opportunities that can be created with financial engineering. The analysis above shows why an investor should pay less attention to the average returns in Table 16-6 and pay more attention to the mutual funds' SHARPE, TREYNOR, and Alpha values.

Which Mutual Fund Is Best? . . . Worst?

Earlier in this chapter, the section entitled "Performance Statistics from Mutual Funds" never said which of the 30 mutual fund in Table 16-6 was best or worst. Table 16-6B shows that the Munder NetNet Fund earned the highest average return, achieved the highest TREYNOR value, and produced the highest excess return (Jensen's alpha) by "cherry picking" Internet stocks during a period when Internet stocks were appreciating rapidly. These impressive results are offset by the undesirable facts that the Munder NetNet Fund has a high load fee of 5.5%, charges high annual expenses of 1.35%, levies a 12b-1 fee of 25 basis points per year, is the riskiest fund in Table 16-6B, has a mediocre SHARPE score because its investments are concentrated in technology stocks, and it will earn a large negative return when the technology sector plunges. We conclude that the Munder NetNet Fund is only for those investors who want its high returns badly enough to put up with the Fund's list of associated undesirable characteristics. Munder NetNet is not suitable for highly risk-averse investors or for investors who foresee a bleak future for technology stocks. Thirteen of the 30 mutual funds in Table 16-6 had higher SHARPE scores than Munder NetNet; this means it is possible to use financial engineering techniques that were applied to the Yak and Zebra Funds in Figure 16-7 to produce 13 leveraged portfolios that dominate the Munder NetNet Fund in a σ-$E(r)$ graph.

Burton Malkiel analyzed a large sample of mutual funds and concluded that:

> *When returns from all funds are analyzed, we find that mutual funds have tended to underperform the market, not only after management expenses have been deducted, but also gross of all reported expenses except load fees.*[10]

Many investors have reached conclusions like Malkiel's and, in response, turned to indexed mutual funds that earned higher returns than 75% of the actively managed mutual funds while charging lower fees.

The Vanguard 500 Index Fund's returns and risk-adjusted returns ranked in the top 20% of the portfolios in Table 16-6B, while the portfolio undertook only average risks. In addition, Vanguard's fees are among the lowest in the mutual fund industry and Vanguard is probably the most ethical company in the mutual fund industry. Table 16-6A shows that the Vanguard 500 Index Fund was one of the largest mutual funds in the United States.

The Midas Fund is a small portfolio that made an unfortunate commitment to precious metal stocks as the prices of gold and silver declined. Midas charges the highest annual fees in Table 16-6A. These facts cause the Midas Fund to earn the lowest rankings for several criteria in Table 16-6A. Scientific studies show that the Midas performance is not surprising; there is an weak inverse correlation between mutual funds' annual expenses and the returns they earn.[11]

General Discussion of the Performance Measurement Tools

When analyzing and comparing the merits of alternative investments, two types of questions are usually considered: (1) asset selection issues and (2) market timing issues.

Asset Selection. Asset selection questions focus on the ability of portfolio managers to "pick winners" and sell "losers." The SHARPE, TREYNOR, and Alpha tools are well suited to evaluating a portfolio's asset selection ability.

Market Timing. Market timing focuses on the ability of portfolio managers to "buy low and sell high," and to how well the managers react to changes in the market's direction. These problems cannot be analyzed within the framework provided by the SHARPE, TREYNOR, and Alpha evaluation tools unless the theoretical (CML or SML) framework is extended.[12]

EVALUATING TIMING DECISIONS

To discern whether a portfolio manager can time the market well enough to profit from bullish upturns and bearish downturns requires special tools. To perform market timing evaluations Treynor and Mazuy[13] supplemented the characteristic line to include a second-order term, as shown in Eqn. 16-16. Eqn. 16-16 is a multiple regression model for portfolio i that is estimated over $t = 1, 2, \ldots, T$ successive time periods.

$$r_{i,t} = \alpha_i + \beta_{1,i}(r_{m,t}) + \beta_{2,i}(r_{m,t}^2) + e_{i,t} \qquad (16\text{-}16)$$

In the equation,

$r_{i,t}$ = rate of return from investment i in tth time period

$r_{m,t}$ = return on market index in period t

$e_{i,t}$ = random error term for investment i in period t, $E(e_i) = 0$,

$_1\alpha_i$ = repression intercept term for investment i

$\beta 1,i$ = beta coefficient for market returns from investment i

$\beta_{2,i}$ = beta coefficient for squared market returns from investment i

t = a time period counter over $t = 1, 2, \ldots, T$ successive periods.

Figure 16-8 illustrates the Treynor-Mazuy model for the case when the second order term contributes positively to the ith asset's return, $b_{2i} > 0$.

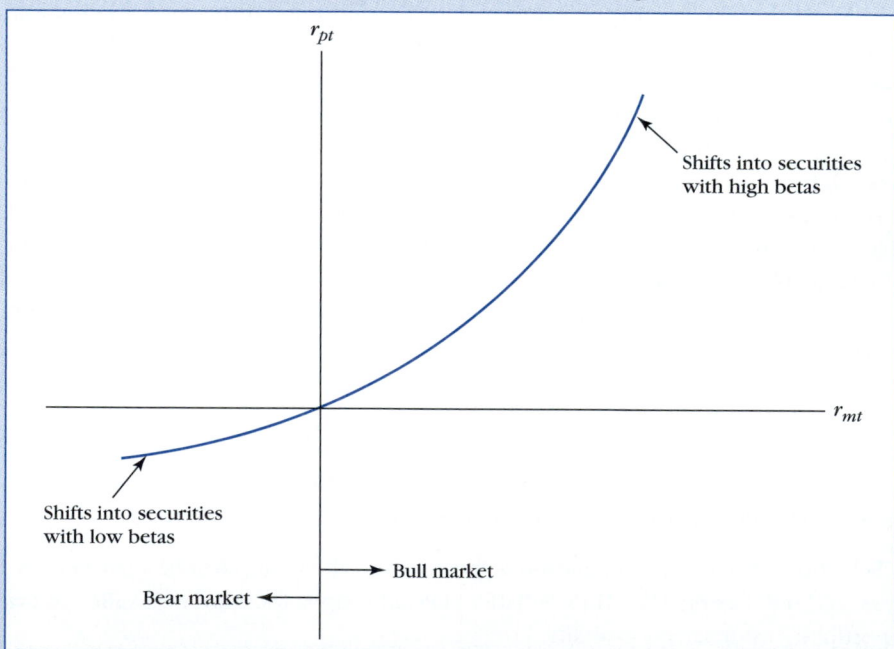

FIGURE 16-8   Curvilinear Characteristic Line for a Portfolio Manager Who Can Often Forecast the Market's Turning Points

The characteristic line can be extended to include a second-order term, as shown in Eqn. 16-16. An adept market timer who has $b_{2,i} > 0$ is illustrated. This market timer shifts the portfolio into high (low) beta securities as a bull (bear) market is beginning.

Suppose that the ith asset is a mutual fund managed by a person who is able to predict bull- and/or bear-market conditions. To maximize the portfolio's gains, this omniscient portfolio manager shifts the portfolio into high beta securities whenever a bull markets begins. When a bearish decline is starting, the clever portfolio manager switches from high beta assets to low beta assets. As a result of such adept market timing decisions, the portfolio would have $\beta_{2,i} > 0$, as illustrated in Figure 16-8.

Three values that the $\beta_{2,i}$ term in Eqn.(16-16) might assume are noteworthy:

1. **Positive $\beta_{2,i}$ coefficients.** Adept market timing decisions would cause the portfolio to have positive $\beta_{2,i}$ values, as illustrated in Figure 16-8.
2. **Zero $\beta_{2,i}$ coefficients.** If a portfolio manager could not outguess the market turns, $\beta_{2,i}$ would equal zero. The $\beta_{2,i}$ term would not have to precisely equal zero to indicate a lack of market timing skill, it only needs to be not significantly different from zero in a statistical (probabilistic) sense.
3. **Negative $\beta_{2,i}$ coefficients.** Suppose a portfolio manager erroneously predicted the market would move up (down) and, therefore, moved the portfolio into high (low) beta assets to benefit from the upturn (downturn). If, in defiance of the erroneous forecast, the market moved down (up), that portfolio manager's $\beta_{2,i}$ coefficient would be negative. In this case the quadratic characteristic line would not be concave toward the asset return axis, as shown in Figure 16-8; instead, it would be concave toward the market return axis.

Treynor and Mazuy estimated Eqn. 16-16 for 57 mutual funds (32 balanced funds and 25 growth funds) over ten annual returns. After finding that 56 of these mutual funds had $\beta_{2,i} = 0$ and only one had a slightly positive value for $\beta_{2,i}$, Treynor and Mazuy concluded that none of the mutual funds in their sample had the ability to foresee either bull- or bear-market conditions. Essentially, all 57 mutual funds appeared to have linear characteristic lines that fit their data better than the quadratic Eqn. 16-16.[14]

DO WINNERS REPEAT?

This chapter's discussion of investment management evaluation begs the question: Are the best performers able to repeat their high level of performance in the future? The question is important because the value of all portfolio performance evaluation tools is greatly increased if the winners of the "performance derby" repeat their performances. The question also has important implications for the efficient market theory. If security markets are perfectly efficient, no investors should be able to turn in winning performances consistently. The remainder of this section considers the question: Do winners repeat?

Several investigations of investment performance have been flawed by a common bias that can arise from the use of a market index for comparison. Many market indexes suffer from **survivorship bias** because the index only contains securities that survived bankruptcy, merger, delisting, and other misfortunes.[15] Goetzmann and Ibbotson published an empirical mutual fund performance evaluation study that mitigated survivorship bias by comparing the funds' within-sample performance rankings through time.[16] Their comparison is superior to comparing the funds' performances to (1) a market index that performs in some manner because survivorship bias helps shape that performance or (2) a within-sample average that is biased because mutual funds that perform poorly are usually closed or disappear because they are merged with more successful funds.

Goetzmann and Ibbotson's database consisted of monthly total returns from a sample of several hundred mutual funds over a 13-year period. Returns were computed after deducting the mutual funds management fees, but front-end load fees, exit fees, and taxes were not taken into count.[17] All cash flows were reinvested monthly. The mutual funds' returns were measured over a 2-year within-sample period for the years 1976–77 to predict the out-of-sample performance for the subsequent 2-year period, 1978–79. Similarly, they used the prior 2 years' performances to predict the subsequent 2-year performances for the periods 1980–81, 1982–83, 1984–85, and 1986–87. Only those funds that existed for the entire 2-year interval were included in the computations. Every mutual fund was categorized as either a winner or a loser, according to whether the fund ranked above or below that 2-year sample's median return.

Table 16-7 shows two-way tables of winners and losers for each 2-year subsample. The combined results are shown in the lower right-hand corner of Table 16-7. Measured over all subsamples, the table shows that if a mutual fund was classified as a winner in a 2-year sample, there are about 60% and 40% chances it will be a winner or a loser, respectively, in the following subsample. Table 16-7 also shows that this repeat-winners pattern occurred in four out of the five 2-year subsamples. While the tendency for winners to repeat their good performances is noticeable, it is not guaranteed. In particular, when the 1980–81 rankings were used to predict the 1982–83 rankings the repeat-winners phenomenon was reversed. This latter finding suggests that the rankings might be based on some common response that varies through time.

It could be argued that high-return mutual funds continued to have high-ranking returns year after year because they were high-risk funds, not because they were winners. To over-

TABLE 16-7 Two-Way Tables of Ranked Raw Mutual Fund Returns over Successive Two-Year Periods

	1978–79 Winners	1978–79 Losers		1980–81 Winners	1980–81 Losers
1976–77 Winners	84	54	1978–79 Winners	110	41
1976–77 Losers	50	88	1978–79 Losers	38	113
	1982–83 Winners	1982–83 Losers		1984–85 Winners	1984–85 Losers
1980–81 Winners	63	96	1982–83 Winners	104	62
1980–81 Losers	96	63	1982–83 Losers	71	95
	1986–87 Winners	1986–87 Losers		Combined Results Successive Period Winners	Losers
1984–85 Winners	125	72	Initial Winners	486 59.9%	325 40.1%
1984–85 Losers	72	125	Initial Losers	327 40.3%	484 59.7%

SOURCE: William N. Goetzmann and Roger G. Ibbotson, "Do Winners Repeat?" *Journal of Portfolio Management* 20, no. 10 (winter 1994): Exhibit 1, p. 11.

come this objection, Goetzmann and Ibbotson replicated their study using risk-adjusted returns. Eqn. 16-10 was used to compute Jensen's alphas over successive 2-year intervals and, thereby, generate risk-adjusted return measures for each subsample. To the extent that alphas are appropriate risk-adjusted return measures, the security market line (SML) suggests that any persistence in the ranking of a mutual funds' alphas results from management skill differences. To investigate this possibility, the mutual funds were categorized as winners or losers depending on whether their alpha was above or below, respectively, the period's median alpha. Table 16-8 shows two-way tables of winners and losers for each 2-year subsample. As with the preceding table, the combined results are shown in the lower right-hand corner of Table 16-8.

The results in Table 16-8 provide further support for the repeat-winners hypothesis. The winner-loser breakdowns in all five subsamples and the aggregate sample are consistent with the persistence hypothesis.

In order to substantiate the findings reported in Tables 16-7 and 16-8, Goetzmann and Ibbotson reformulated their study in several different ways. First, they examined the subset of their funds that are called growth funds, to see if the repeat-winner phenomenon might result from some particular mixtures of stocks and bonds within the portfolios. Using the same investigative procedures, Goetzmann and Ibbotson found that the results reported in Tables 16-7 and 16-8 were equally true for the growth funds. Second, Goetzmann and Ibbotson reformulated their study in terms of 1-year subsamples instead of 2-year subsamples. Using the 1-year subsamples also supported the repeat-winners hypothesis, but the

TABLE 16-8   Two-Way Tables of Ranked Alphas over Successive Two-Year Subsamples

	1978–79 Winners	1978–79 Losers		1980–81 Winners	1980–81 Losers
1976–77 Winners	83	55	1978–79 Winners	105	44
1976–77 Losers	52	86	1978–79 Losers	40	109
	1982–83 Winners	1982–83 Losers		1984–85 Winners	1984–85 Losers
1980–81 Winners	83	75	1982–83 Winners	85	73
1980–81 Losers	75	83	1982–83 Losers	73	85
	1986–87 Winners	1986–87 Losers		Combined Results Successive Period Winners	Losers
1984–85 Winners	126	49	Initial Winners	482 / 62.0%	296 / 38.0%
1984–85 Losers	45	130	Initial Losers	285 / 36.6%	493 / 63.4%

SOURCE: William N. Goetzmann and Roger G. Ibbotson, "Do Winners Repeat?" *Journal of Portfolio Management* 20, no. 10 (winter 1994): Exhibit 2, p. 12.

shorter subsamples yielded weaker support than the 2-year subsamples. Third, Goetzmann and Ibbotson shortened the length of their subsamples to increase the number of observations, even though the shorter intervals contain more statistical noise. They used 1-month subsamples. The monthly results were also supportive of the repeat-winners hypothesis. Fourth, Goetzmann and Ibbotson reformulated their methodology using 3-year subsamples and 4×4 classification tables (instead of the 2×2 tables shown at Tables 16-7 and 16-8). They did not employ subsamples in excess of 3 years because the mutual fund manager might change or the fund's strategy might change over subsamples of much greater length. The raw returns and the alphas displayed in 4-way tables uniformly suggest that quartile rankings from 3-year subsamples have predictive power for quartile ranking in the next 3-year period. Although these results could be due to risk factors that were omitted, timing strategies, or fee-related considerations, they are consistent with the repeat-winner hypothesis.[18]

Burton Malkiel published a study of mutual funds from 1971 to 1991 that was critical of research suggesting it is possible to detect mutual funds that will probably enjoy superior performance in the future.[19] Malkiel argued that while the repeat-winners phenomenon was observable during the 1970s, this phenomenon was not present during the 1980s.

Mark M. Carhart studied mutual fund data from 1962–93 for evidence of persistent mutual fund performance.[20] He reports that "funds with high returns last year have higher-than-average expected returns next year, but not in the years thereafter . . ." Carhart reports a stronger tendency for losers to persist than Goetzmann and Ibbotson. Carhart concludes that mutual funds that perform worst usually continue their bad performances for years.

ETHICS   A REALITY CHECK

ETHICAL ISSUES FOR FUND MANAGERS

A 1994 SEC report observed, the mutual fund industry "will continue to be trusted by investors only if it demonstrates that it maintains the highest possible ethical standards and that it operates free from abusive and fraudulent practices." Although the industry has been criticized for misleading advertising about fund returns, the main ethical concerns are personal trading by fund managers and "soft-dollar" transactions.

Fund managers (advisors) who trade for their own account face potential conflicts of interest. Despite a fiduciary duty to serve a fund's shareholders, advisors can benefit themselves by such practices as *frontrunning* (trading ahead of a fund's purchase) and keeping the best bargains for their personal portfolio. SEC Rule 16j-1 not only prohibits such abuses but requires firms to adopt a code of ethics and take preventive measures (including disclosure requirements). Among the safeguards are blackout periods for personal trading in the securities traded by a fund and bans on short-term trading and short selling of stocks held by a fund. The industry has shied away from a complete ban on personal trading because it would be unfair to fund managers (who have a right to accumulate wealth) and would disadvantage shareholders by not attracting the best management. Advisors who invest along with their funds might even inspire greater confidence, like chefs who eat their own cooking.

Fund managers are obligated to seek the best execution of trades at the lowest cost. However, it is common for advisors to pay a higher commission to a broker in return for in-kind services, such as research, which the advisor would otherwise pay out-of-pocket. Such "soft-dollar" transactions are legal as long as the commission is "reasonable in relation to the value of the brokerage and research services provided" and the arrangement is explained to clients. But an SEC study found abuses, including the use of soft-dollars to pay for rent, theater tickets, and new carpeting. Fraud aside, critics argue that soft-dollar transactions encourage excessive trading and reduce concern about the quality of execution. Defenders argue that the arrangement produces higher returns for clients because the market will punish advisors who misuse soft dollars.

John R. Boatright, *Professor of Business Ethics*

THE BOTTOM LINE

This chapter's discussion of investment performance tools focused on mutual fund data. These tools are also useful to evaluate the performance of other kinds of investments.

About Mutual Fund Investments

The typical mutual fund can perform valuable services for investors, even if the fund's risk-adjusted returns are not high. Consider an average U.S. investor who has a total of $21,000 invested in mutual funds.* Assume this investor purchased only round lots (to avoid paying higher odd-lot commissions) and that these stocks have an average price of $30 per share. Since $30 times 100 shares equals $3,000 per round lot, the average investor could invest in only [($21,000 to invest)/($3,000 per round lot) =] seven different stocks. Figure 14-1 in Chapter 14 showed that seven stocks are too few to minimize the average investor's diversifiable risk. It follows that the average investor could reduce his or her investment risk by investing in a well-diversified mutual fund.

Although mutual funds do not all earn the high rates of return that some advertisements and braggers suggest, they are usually able to reduce their risk to the level of the market's fluctuations. Since the fortunes of the average individual mutual fund investor are not tied to the destinies of only a few securities, the average (small) investor is better off investing in a mutual fund.

A mutual fund can help an investor stay in some preferred risk class, although that risk class is not necessarily the one the fund says it will pursue in its written statement of investment objectives. By examining mutual funds' quantitative risk statistics, investors are more likely to determine the level of risk a fund will maintain.

Analysis of mutual funds' performance suggests that most investors should focus on the funds' load fees, exit fees, 12-b1 fees, and management fees and select funds that charge the smallest fees. The size of these outlays tends to be weakly inversely related to mutual funds' performances; investors' welfare tends to be harmed by these outlays. Investors can earn higher net rates of return, on average, by seeking to minimize mutual funds expenses.

About Portfolio Performance Measures

Ranking portfolios' average rates of return can make an efficient low-risk portfolio appear to do poorly. To evaluate a portfolio adequately, its risk must be considered with its rate of return. If the standard deviation is used, portfolios' standard deviations and average rates of return may be plotted in $\sigma\text{-}E(r)$ space and compared with the efficient frontier. Sharpe's index of portfolio performance measures the risk premium per unit of risk. The SHARPE index considers both risk and return and yields one index number for each portfolio; these index numbers may be used to rank the desirability of heterogeneous portfolios.

---

* Page 67 of the *1999 Mutual Fund Fact Book* shows net assets for the mutual fund industry of $5,525.2 billion in 1998. Page 114 shows a total of 206 million mutual fund shareholders' accounts in 1998. Division yields [($5,525.2 total assets)/(206 million accounts) =] $26,820 per account. Since the total number of accounts includes many pensions and other institutional investors, the average individual person's account was arbitrarily rounded down to $21,000.

TREYNOR uses beta coefficients and average returns to derive an index number suitable for ranking the desirability of assets in Beta-$E(r)$ space. Some analysts prefer the TREYNOR portfolio performance measure because systematic risk is more relevant than total risk in certain applications and because the TREYNOR measure can be used to compare individual assets and portfolios. The TREYNOR performance measure has the disadvantage that its values can be sensitive to the market index used to estimate the investments' betas.

Jensen's alpha measures risk-adjusted returns and is useful for evaluating the performance of both portfolios and individual assets. However, the Alpha is not quite as easy to use for rankings as the other one-parameter performance measures.

The TREYNOR, SHARPE, and Alpha investment performance measures tend to rank mutual funds similarly. Additional tools are available to analyze a portfolio's returns through time and determine if the portfolio manager possesses market timing skills.[21]

Considering the low fees associated with most indexed mutual funds, and the fact that index funds perform better than the majority of actively managed mutual funds, passive investing should not be ignored.

QUESTIONS

Q16-1 (Closed-end investment companies) True, false, or uncertain: All closed-end investment companies redeem their shares at net asset value. Explain.

Q16-2 (Closed-end investment companies versus mutual funds) Compare and contrast closed-end investment companies with mutual funds.

Q16-3 (Taxation of investment companies) How is the income of an open-end investment company taxed?

Q16-4 (Mutual fund performance) True, false, or uncertain: Rankings of portfolios' average returns show that, although the average mutual fund does not outperform the market, a few truly superior funds consistently beat the market. Explain.

Q16-5 (Mutual fund performance) How well does the mutual fund industry perform relative to a naive buy-and-hold investment strategy?

Q16-6 (Mutual fund management) Assume you have been put in charge of a mutual fund with a large staff of fundamental analysts and millions of dollars of assets spread over more than 100 different securities. The fund's gross return is about average for the industry, but its management

expenses are high, so its net yield to its investors is slightly below average. The previous management did not try to specialize as a growth or safety fund, but ran the firm as a general purpose fund. What do you plan to do with your fund? Explain.

Q16-7 (Sharpe's factor analysis model) William Sharpe's factor analysis model that is used to explain the asset allocations of mutual funds is repeated below:

$$r_{i,t} = [b_{i,1}F_{1,t} + b_{i,2}F_{2,t} + \dots b_{i,11}F_{11,t} + b_{i,12}F_{12,t}] + e_{i,t}$$

In this model, how are the $b_{i,k}$ coefficients interpreted? How is the sum of the twelve $b_{i,k}F_{k,t}$ products interpreted?

Q16-8 (Benefits of quantitative management style analysis tools) Discuss the benefits of using quantitative management style analysis tools.

Q16-9 (Jensen's alpha) Discuss three problems that are inherent in Jensen's alpha value.

Q16-10 (The Sharpe and Treynor Indexes) Compare and contrast the SHARPE Index and the TREYNOR Index.

PROBLEMS

P16-1 (Sharpe and Treynor Indexes) Consider the following summary statistics about three investment portfolios.

Portfolio	Average Return	Standard Deviation	Beta	Correlation, ρ
Alpha (A)	7%	3	0.4	0.89
Beta (B)	10	8	1.0	0.91
Gamma (G)	13	6	1.1	0.90
Delta (D)	15	13	1.2	0.95
Epsilon (E)	18	15	1.4	0.88

Assume that the riskless rate of interest is 3%. (a) Which of the portfolios performed the best according to Sharpe's measure? The worst? (b) Which performed the best according to Treynor's performance measure? The worst? (c) Assume that the riskless rate of interest was 6%. Under this new assumption which portfolio ranks the best according to Sharpe's measure? According to Treynor's measure? Show your calculations and draw graphs to illustrate the work. Label all variables in your calculations and graphs.

The information below will be used with Problems 16-2 through 16-7. A regression was run for the five mutual funds using the following model, where

$rp_{p,t}$ = quarterly excess fund return = rate of return from mutual fund p − T-bill rate

$rp_{m,t}$ = quarterly excess market return = rate of return from market portfolio − T-bill rate

A_p = alpha coefficient (Jensen's performance measure) for portfolio p

B_p = beta coefficient for portfolio p

$u_{p,t}$ = error term for portfolio p in period t

$$rp_{p,t} = A_p + B_p rp_{m,t} + u_{p,t} \quad for\ t = 1,2,\dots,T$$

Fund	Alpha Coefficient %	Alpha's Standard Deviation, %	Beta Coefficient	Beta's Standard Deviation, %	R^2	Mean Return, %	Mean Standard Deviation, %
A	−0.24	0.4143	1.08	0.06	.94	1.71	7.42
B	2.03	0.9200	1.62	0.14	.89	3.68	11.71
C	4.27	1.3400	1.45	0.20	.75	6.02	11.25
D	3.46	1.2700	1.36	0.19	.74	5.26	10.78
E	1.18	1.4100	1.30	0.21	.68	3.00	10.64
S&P 500						1.99	6.74
T-bill						2.52	0.76

P16-2 (Jensen's performance measure) Rank the five funds using the Jensen performance measure. Is this a reliable ranking?

P16-3 (Sharpe's performance measure) Rank the five funds with the Sharpe performance measure.

P16-4 (Treynor's performance measure) Rank the five funds using Treynor's performance measure.

P16-5 (Systematic risk) Which of the five funds had the most systematic risk?

P16-6 (Correlation with the market) Which of the five funds is the least correlated with the market?

P16-7 (Correlation with the market) Which of the five funds' returns moved more closely with the market's returns?

The following data will be used for Problems 16-8 through 16-11:

Year and Quarter	Guardian Fund Return, %	Acorn Fund Return, %	S&P 500 Return, %	T-bill Return, %
1983—2	9.42	13.17	11.10	2.04
1983—3	−1.28	−2.72	−0.10	2.14
1983—4	2.70	0.00	0.40	2.13
1984—1	−4.53	−5.78	−2.40	2.14
1984—2	−2.64	−1.09	−2.61	2.50
1984—3	10.13	10.45	9.68	2.50
1984—4	4.95	1.51	1.76	2.63
1985—1	8.23	11.95	9.18	2.29
1985—2	6.33	7.35	7.34	2.15
1985—3	−2.04	−3.70	−4.10	1.78
1985—4	11.15	13.57	17.19	1.90
1986—1	11.64	13.95	14.02	1.79
1986—2	5.48	6.59	5.85	1.61
1986—3	−6.44	−6.66	−6.94	1.33
1986—4	1.58	3.62	5.58	1.46

P16-8 (Sharpe and Treynor measures) Calculate the Treynor and Sharpe performance measures for the Guardian Fund.

P16-9 (Sharpe and Treynor measures) Calculate the Treynor and Sharpe performance measures for the Acorn Fund.

P16-10 (Jensen performance measure) Calculate the Jensen performance measure for the Guardian Fund and the Acorn Fund.

P16-11 (Interpretation of the analysis) Is the Guardian Fund or the Acorn Fund the more aggressive?

CFA EXAM QUESTIONS

1. (1991 CFA Sample Exam, Level I) Which *one* of the following methods measures the reward to volatility trade-off by dividing the average portfolio excess return over the standard deviation of returns?
   A. Sharpe's measure
   B. Treynor's measure
   C. Jensen's measure
   D. Appraisal ratio.

2. (This question has been adapted from a question appearing on the 1996 CFA Exam, Level III) HH counselors has developed five alternative asset allocations (shown in Table II) for client portfolios. Assume that the risk-free rate is 4.5%.
   i. Calculate the Sharpe Ratio for Asset Allocation D. Show your calculations.

ii. Determine the *two* asset allocations in Table II having the *best* risk-adjusted returns, based *only* on the Sharpe Ratio measure.

Table II Summary Data

	Asset Allocation A	Asset Allocation B	Asset Allocation C	Asset Allocation D	Asset Allocation E
Projected Total Return	9.9%	11.0%	8.8%	14.4%	10.3%
Projected After-tax Return	7.4%	7.2%	6.5%	9.4%	7.4%
Expected Standard Deviation	9.4%	12.4%	8.5%	18.1%	10.1%
Sharpe Ratio	0.574	0.524	0.506	?	0.574

3. (1998 CFA Sample Exam, Level I) The correlation coefficient of Portfolio X's returns and the market's returns is 0.95, and the correlation coefficient of Portfolio Y's returns and the market's returns is 0.60. Which of the following statements *best* describes the levels of portfolio diversification?

A. Both Portfolio X and Portfolio Y are well diversified.
B. Both Portfolio X and Portfolio Y are poorly diversified.
C. Portfolio X is well diversified and Portfolio Y is poorly diversified.
D. Portfolio X is poorly diversified and Portfolio Y is well diversified.

FURTHER REFERENCES

Alexander, Gordon and Jack Clark Francis. *Portfolio Analysis*, 3d ed. Englewood Cliffs, NJ: Prentice-Hall, 1986.

Chapter 14 uses advanced statistics and discusses different investment performance evaluation techniques and problems.

Goetzmann, William N. and Roger G. Ibbotson. "Do Winners Repeat?" *Journal of Portfolio Management* 20, no. 2 (winter 1994): 9–18.

The study provides empirical evidence that some mutual fund managers can beat the market averages with some degree of consistency.

Jensen, Michael C., "The Performance of Mutual Funds in the Period 1945–64," *Journal of Finance* (May 1968): 389–416.

An analysis of the performance of mutual funds that uses regression analysis.

Logue, Dennis E. and Jack Rader. *Managing Pension Plans*. Cambridge, MA: Harvard Business School Press, 1998.

This book is rich with pension management definitions, real world problems, and empirical data. Table 8-1 on page 193 indicates that pension fund managers do not manage money as well as the mutual fund managers.

Sharpe, William F., "Mutual Fund Performance," *Journal of Business*, Supplement on Security Prices (January 1966): 119–38.

This risk-return analysis of mutual fund performance uses correlation, regression, and statistical inference.

Spaulding, David. *Measuring Investment Performance*. New York: McGraw Hill, 1997.

The book's 12 chapters and 6 end-of-book appendices show details about how portfolio administrators calculate investment performance measures. Background on standards suggested by trade associations and regulatory bodies is provided.

ENDNOTES

[1] See Michael J. Barclay, Clifford G. Holderness, and Jeffrey Pontiff, "Private Benefits from Block Ownership and Discounts on Closed-End Funds," *Journal of Financial Economics* 33, no. 3 (June 1993): 263–91.
[2] See Dan diBartomeo and Erik Witkowski, "Mutual Fund Misclassification: Evidence Based on Style Analysis," *Financial Analysts Journal* (September/October 1997): 40–41.
[3] For additional evidence, see Barbara Donnelly, "What's in a Name? Some Mutual Funds Make It Difficult to Judge," *Wall Street Journal*, 5 May 1992, C1. Also see Moon Kim, Ravi Shulka, and Michael Tomas, "Wolf in

Sheep's Clothing: Do Mutual Fund Objectives Tell the Truth?" Working Paper, Syracuse University, Syracuse, NY, 1995.

[4] See William F. Sharpe, "Asset Allocation: Management Style and Performance Management," *Journal of Portfolio Management* 18, no. 2 (winter 1992): 7–19.

[5] For a more definitive, but more complicated, research methodology, see Stephen J. Brown and William N. Goetzmann, "Mutual Fund Styles," *Journal of Financial Economics* 43, no. 3 (March 1997): 390.

[6] See William F. Sharpe, "Mutual Fund Performances," *Journal of Business* (January 1966): 125. A few years later Smith and Tito published a study of 38 mutual funds that showed similar results. See K.V. Smith and D. A. Tito, "Risk Return Measures of Ex Post Portfolio Performance," *Journal of Financial and Quantitative Analysis* (December 1969): 464–65. For a similar study, see John G. McDonald, "Objectives and Performance of Mutual Funds," *Journal of Financial and Quantitative Analysis* (June 1974): 319, Table 1. McDonald reported a few departures from the funds' stated objectives and generally unimpressive performances.

[7] See Jack Treynor, "How to Rate Management of Investment Funds," *Harvard Business Review* (January-February 1965): 63–75.

[8] See Michael C. Jensen, "Risk, the Pricing of Capital Assets, and the Evaluation of Investment Portfolios," Ph.D. Dissertation, University of Chicago, 1968. Michael C. Jensen, "The Performance of Mutual Funds in the Period 1945–64," *Journal of Finance* 23, no. 2 (May 1968): 389–416. M. C. Jensen, "Risk, the Pricing of Capital Assets, and the Evaluation of Investment Portfolios," *Journal of Business* 42 (April 1969): 167–247.

[9] For an informative interpretation of the components of an asset's performance, see Eugene F. Fama, "Components of Investment Performance," *Journal of Finance* 27, no. 3 (June 1972): 551–67.

[10] See Burton G. Malkiel, "Returns from Investing in Equity Mutual Funds, 1971–1991," *Journal of Finance* 50, no. 2 (1995): 571.

[11] See Mark M. Carhart, "On Persistence in Mutual Fund Performance," *Journal of Finance* 52 no. 1 (March 1997): 57–82. In addition to the inverse correlation, Carhart also reports that mutual funds that have been poor performers in the past tend to be poor performers in the future.

[12] For details about market timing studies, see Roy D. Henriksson and Robert C. Merton, "On Market Timing and Investment Performance, II. Statistical Procedure for Evaluating Forecasting Skills," *Journal of Business* 54 (October 1981): 513–33. See also Roy D. Henriksson, "Market Timing and Mutual Fund Performance: An Empirical Investigation," *Journal of Business* 57 (January 1984): 73–96. Also see Ravi Jagannathan and Robert A. Korajczyk, "Assessing the Market Timing Performance of Managed Portfolios," *Journal of Business* 59, no. 2, Part 1 (April 1986): 137–235. And see A.R. Admati, S. Bhat Tacharya, P. Pfleiderer and S.A. Ross, "On Timing and Selectivity," *Journal of Finance* 41, no. 3 (July 1986): 715–32.

[13] See Jack L. Treynor and Kay K. Mazuy, "Can Mutual Funds Outguess the Market?" *Harvard Business Review* 44, no. 4 (July-August 1966): 131–36. For a similar model, see F. J. Fabozzi and J. C. Francis, "Mutual Fund Systematic Risk for Bull and Bear Markets: An Empirical Examination," *Journal of Finance* 34, no. 5 (December 1979): 1243–50.

[14] For contrary conclusions, see Zakri Y. Bello and Vahan Janjigian, "A Reexamination of the Market-Timing and Security Selection Performance of Mutual Funds," *Financial Analysts Journal* (September-October 1997): 24–30. Bello and Janjigian add two additional explanatory variables to the Treynor-Mazuy model and report some different conclusions.

[15] See Philippe Jorion and William N. Goetzmann, "Global Stock Markets in the Twentieth Century," *Journal of Finance* 54, no. 3 (June 1999): 978. Also see Stephen J. Brown, William J. Goetzmann, and Stephen Ross, "Survival," *Journal of Finance* 50 (1995): 853–73. And, see Burton G. Malkiel, "Returns from Investing in Equity Mutual Funds, 1971–1991," *Journal of Finance* 50, no. 2 (June 1995): 553. Malkiel provides empirical estimates that survivorship bias is about 150 basis points per year in traditional mutual fund studies.

[16] See William N. Goetzmann and Roger G. Ibbotson, "Do Winners Repeat?" *Journal of Portfolio Management* 20, no. 10 (winter 1994): 9–18.

[17] For a discussion of mutual funds' fees, see Miles Livingston and Edward S. O'Neal, "The Cost of Mutual Fund Distribution Fees," *The Journal of Financial Research* 11, no. 2 (summer 1998): 205–18.

[18] For research findings that support Goetzmann and Ibbotson's results, see Mark Grinblatt and Sheridan Titman, "The Persistence of Mutual Fund Performance," *Journal of Finance* 47, no. 5 (December 1992): 1977–84. Also, see Darryll Hendricks, Jayendu Patel, and Richard Zeckhauser, "Hot Hands in Mutual Funds: Short-Run Persistence of Relative Performance, 1974–1988," *Journal of Finance* 48, no. 1 (March 1993): 93–130.

[19] See Burton G. Malkiel, "Returns from Investing in Equity Mutual Funds, 1971–1991," *Journal of Finance* 50, no. 2 (1995): 549–72.

[20] See Mark M. Carhart, "On Persistence in Mutual Fund Performance," *Journal of Finance* 52, no. 1 (March 1997): 57–82.

[21] For some empirical evidence of superior performance, see Mark Grinblatt and Sheridan Titman, "Mutual Fund Performance: An Analysis of Quarterly Portfolio Holdings," *Journal of Business* 62, no. 3 (July 1989): 393–416. For additional evidence, see Darryll Hendricks, Jayendu Patel, and Richard Zeckhauser, "Hot Hands in Mutual Funds: Short-Run Persistence of Relative Performance, 1974–1988," *Journal of Finance* 48 (March 1993): 93–130. Independently, Lee and Rahman report an evidence of superior timing and selection. They also report a positive correlation between selection and timing in their sample. See Cheng-Few Lee and Shafiqur Rahman, "Market Timing, Selectivity, and Mutual Fund Performance: An Empirical Examination," *Journal of Business* 63, no. 2 (April 1990): 261–78.

PART 4

INTERNATIONAL INVESTING

FOREIGN EXCHANGE

There are over 180 countries in the world. Allowing for the fact that some countries share a common currency, there are about 170 different foreign currencies in the world. These currencies are traded in a global currency market that operates 24 hours a day. The majority of the world's currencies are traded infrequently; most transactions take place in a few popular currencies. The most popular currencies are the Euro, the U.S. dollar, and a few other currencies that are considered to be safe investments.

*The price at which one country's currency can be converted into another's is called the **exchange rate**. For instance, if $1 will purchase 1.1 Euros the exchange rate is $1/€1.1 = 0.909 Euros per U.S. dollar. Although some government's decree that their exchange rate is fixed, most exchange rates continuously fluctuate randomly. After some vocabulary is introduced, the rest of this chapter discusses the determinants of exchange rates.*

As shown in Table 17-1, the currencies market is the largest financial market in the world. Multimillion-dollar transactions are common. It is a decentralized market in which most foreign exchange transactions take place via telephone conversations between the currency traders employed by international banks, foreign subsidiaries of large nonfinancial corporations, and foreign exchange brokers around the world. Only the largest banks in the world have a currency trading desk, where a dozen or more currency traders may work. A single person might staff the currency desk at a smaller institution.* As in most financial markets, written agreements and lawyers are not involved in the trading. Transactions are executed quickly over the phone and settled via telecommunications networks like the Clearing House Interbank Payments System (CHIPS) and the Society for Worldwide Interbank Financial Telecommunications (SWIFT) within 2 business days after the trade. Over $1 trillion in currencies are traded daily in this informal interbank market. In 1998 the world's currency trading occurred in the United Kingdom (32%), United States (18%), Japan (8%), Singapore

---

* Chase Bank, for instance, is a large international bank that in 1998 employed 64 foreign exchange traders in New York City and over 300 foreign exchange (forex, FX, currency) traders around the world.

TABLE 17-1	Estimates of the Average Daily Trading Volume in Selected U.S. Markets in 1996	
U.S. Financial Market		Volume, $US Billions
Foreign exchange traded in United States		$330
U.S. Treasuries		$212
Mortgage-Backed securities		$ 47
U.S. Federal Agency debt (FNMA, GNMA)		$ 40
New York Stock Exchange		$ 16
Corporate debt		$ 10
Municipal bonds		$ 3

SOURCE: Adapted from: "Never Cross a Bond Dealer," *Business Week*, 9 March 1998, 84. *New York Stock Exchange Fact Book, 1996*, pp. 100–101. Also, coauthors' estimates.

(7%), Germany (5%), and the rest of the world (30%); most of it was between large international banks in London, New York City, Tokyo, and Singapore.

Currencies are commodities that are traded in international markets—like agricultural commodities. Most governments endeavor to maintain some controls on their currencies. The international currency market is so huge that no government in the world can control its currency's fluctuating exchange rate, but some governments have devised other types of currency arrangements.

COMMON MARKETS AND ECONOMIC UNIONS

For centuries governments attempted to control the value of their currencies by maintaining a **gold exchange standard** that tied their currency to a specified amount of gold. It was the ratio of the weights of gold that defined the currencies. Under the gold exchange standard **foreign exchange rate risk** was the risk that a country's government decreed that its currency would be exchanged for a different amount of gold in the future than it was in the past. People holding a currency liked a *revaluation* because that increased their gold weight per unit of currency. The people disliked a *devaluation* because that decreased their gold weight per unit of currency.

Since 1970 most national governments abandoned the gold exchange standard. Abandoning the gold standard allowed the ruling powers to expand the country's money supply without being encumbered by the need to purchase gold to back newly created currency. Abandoning the gold standard makes it easier for rulers and politicians to create money to pay for whatever they want. Irresponsible rulers and politicians sometimes increase the country's money supply too rapidly and this often leads to inflation. *Inflation* can occur during a boom or a recession; either way, it erodes the purchasing power of money invested in cash, bonds, and savings accounts. When a nation's money supply is increased there is a lag of 1, 2, or 3 years as the country's rate of inflation responds with a gradual increase. As a result of this lag, high inflation plays havoc with the nation's economy for years after the money supply's rapid growth has been brought under control.

Foreign Exchange Rate Fluctuations

Exchange rate movements are caused by changes in economic relations between countries and market participants' *expectations* of future economic conditions.

Often, however, governments intervene in foreign exchange markets to affect their currency values. Some governments fix their currency values. For example, in 1979 the European Monetary System (EMS) was established. The EMS placed tight bands around member currencies fluctuations with respect to each other, while allowing all member currencies to float freely against the U.S. dollar. A **dirty float** refers to a system in which the financial markets determine exchange rates, but governments are free to intervene and attempt to slow the speed with which exchange rate adjustments take place. As of this writing, the dirty float system is still in effect in the principal industrialized nations—namely, the United States, the United Kingdom, Japan, Germany, France, and Canada. Under this system short-term (minute-to-minute, day-to-day, and week-to-week) fluctuations in foreign exchange rates are random and unpredictable.

The way currencies interact with each other in the long run depends on the political and economic conditions in the countries issuing the currencies. In recent decades the United States and Germany, for instance, have had stable political systems and have kept their currency (money) supplies under control. During the 1980s and 1990s this caused the exchange rates of the U.S. dollars and the German deutschemark to remain fairly stable relative to other currencies in the world. After years of political and economic stability, international businesspeople and central bankers came to view the dollar and deutschemark as currencies that are safe to accept in international trade.

Some governments control their national politics, national economies, and currencies better than others. Table 10-6 in Chapter 10 (p. 289) displays statistics from countries that suffered *hyperinflation*. The table shows that Brazil, Israel, and Mexico expanded their money (currency) supplies so rapidly in some years that they experienced inflation of over 100% per year. As a result of this hyperinflation, their currencies lost substantial purchasing power in relation to other currencies (were severely devalued) in international trade.

Economic Unions

Some countries endeavor to improve their economic welfare by banding together to form a trading group called a **common market**. An **economic union** goes beyond being a common market by also adopting a single common currency. Common markets and economic unions believe they can foster cross-border trade that will spur their economic welfare. Sales increases are expected to facilitate specialized manufacturing, promote technological advances, and increase the flow of foreign capital so member nations prosper.

Economic unions are expected to prosper more than common markets for three reasons. First, when the members of an economic union adopt a common currency this will reduce the number of unproductive foreign exchange transactions in their multinational market. Second, a common currency is expected to spur business competition by facilitating price comparisons within the economic union. Third, it is hoped that adopting a common currency will bond the members of the economic union together more closely.

The European Monetary Union (EMU)

The European Monetary Union (EMU) is a voluntary organization of the nations listed in Table 17-2. On January 1, 1999 the EMU created a new currency called the Euro and took actions to encourage cross-border commerce between its members. From January 1, 1999 until July 1, 2002, those who wished to do so could use the Euro instead of the European cur-

TABLE 17-2   Members of the European Monetary Union (EMU)

Country	Currency Before Euro
11 Original Members	
Austria	Schilling (S)
Belgium	Francs (BF)
Finland	Markka (FmK)
France	Franc (FF)
Germany	Deutschemark (DM)
Ireland	Punt
Italy	Lira (Lit)
Luxembourg	Franc (LuxF)
Netherlands, or Holland	Guilder (Hfl)
Portugal	Escudo (Esc)
Spain	Peseta (Ptas)
Potential EMU Members	**Currency**
United Kingdom (UK)	Pound (£)
Denmark	Krone (DKr)
Norway	Krone (NKr)
Sweden	Krona (SKr)
Switzerland	Franc (SFr)
Greece	Drachma (Dr)

rencies listed in the table. After July 1, 2002 all the member currencies will cease to exist and only the Euro will survive.

Almost every economic undertaking involves uncertainties. First, it is easy for special-interest groups to exaggerate the extent to which a common currency (like the Euro) facilitates cross-border trade between member nations.* Second, the economic unions existing prior to the EMU did not fare well.** Third, cultural differences between EMU member nations that are centuries old will not vanish because the countries adopt a common currency. Fourth, some people have suggested that the cost of the pre-Euro foreign exchange transactions might be less than the administrative (governmental) costs of operating the EMU.

None of the EMU member nations are giving up their national political identities. The only national political powers member nations are turning over to the EMU are their monetary authorities. To increase the probability that their common currency system works, the EMU member nations created the European Central Bank (ECB) to replace the member countries' separate central banks.

The ECB is designed to facilitate economic cooperation between the member nations. Multinational economic unions that existed before the EMU failed because some of the independent central banks of the member nations sometimes pursued conflicting monetary

INTERNET CONNECTION

For the latest information about the EMU and the Euro visit the Web site of the European Central Bank at: www.ecb.int

For up-to-the-minute foreign exchange rate data visit the Web site of the New York Federal Reserve Bank at: www.ny.frb.org Go to the Web site's Statistics section for current foreign exchange prices on various currencies traded in the spot and forward markets.

For foreign exchange rates and other international financial information, see Reuters Web site: http://quotes.reuters.com/

---

* To put foreign exchange in perspective, let us contrast it with using credit cards. Stated as a percentage of sales, it as been suggested that the cost of using foreign exchange in a retail establishment approximates the cost of using credit cards. The widespread use of credit cards implies the cost of using foreign exchange should not be prohibitive. Furthermore, using foreign exchange in large industrial transactions costs even less percentage-wise than using credit cards for the small transactions that occur in retail establishments.

** The Latin Monetary Union (France, Belgium, Italy, Switzerland, and Greece) began in 1865 and fell apart in a few years. The Scandinavian Monetary Union (Sweden, Norway, and Denmark) lasted from 1873 until 1924. The East African Community (Kenya, Tanzania, and Uganda) began in 1967 and ended in 1977.

policies. For example, one member country's central bank might lower interest rates to stimulate lending and economic expansion while a neighboring member country's central bank raised interest rates to fight inflation. These conflicting monetary policies undermined the nations' attempt to share a common currency (money supply). The ECB has the power to enforce inflation, deficit spending, and currency stability controls on all EMU member countries. The only way a member country can pursue independent economic policies is to withdraw from the EMU.[1]

The EMU is an exciting recent foreign exchange development. Whether the EMU succeeds in the long run depends on how the member nations value the gains from membership. In the best case, the Euro will flourish and additional nations will join the EMU.*

FUNDAMENTAL ELEMENTS OF A FOREIGN EXCHANGE TRANSACTION

A *foreign exchange transaction* occurs every time a currency trader buys one currency and pays for it with a different currency. The foreign exchange rate is a fluctuating market price for one currency stated in terms of another currency.

Spot and Forward Markets

Some nations have mandated that their currency trade at a fixed ratio to some popular currency—usually the U.S. dollar or the Euro. If one currency trades at a fixed ratio to another currency, the two currencies fluctuate together. Other countries have freely fluctuating foreign exchange rates. Figure 17-1 is an excerpt from the *Wall Street Journal* showing foreign exchange rates for various currencies on a particular trading day. The Wednesday price for one British pound, for example, was $1.6442. Equivalently, $1 could be purchased for (1/$1.6442 =) 0.6082 pounds in the spot market. In foreign exchange, as in commodities, the **spot market** is also called the **cash market** or the **physicals market**—all three terms are synonyms for the market where physical goods are sold for cash and delivery is immediate. Actually, foreign exchange is delivered within 2 business days. The prices of $1.6442 for 1 pound or, equivalently, 0.6082 pounds for $1, are called foreign exchange prices in the spot market, or **spot prices (SP)**.

Situations sometimes arise in which it is more convenient to purchase foreign exchange for future delivery rather than for current delivery. These are investigated later in this chapter. In such a case, the transaction is said to have occurred in the **forward market**. Figure 17-1 shows that on Wednesday 1 British pound could be purchased for delivery 1 month in the future for $1.6443. This $1.6443 price for delivery a month in the future is called the 1-month **forward price (FP)**. Looking just below the 1-month forward price, we see $1.6443 is also the 3-month forward price. The 6-month forward price is $1.6436 per pound.

Figure 17-1 shows that most currencies traded in the spot market do not also trade in the forward market. Only those few currencies that enjoy a large volume of transactions generate enough foreign exchange trading commission income to motivate foreign exchange market makers (the currency desks at large international banks) to become a currency dealer and make a continuous forward market in the currency. It is unprofitable to make a market in a currency that is traded inactively. But custom-made contracts can be negotiated for currencies that are traded inactively.

---

* A number of Central American and South American nations (Argentina, Brazil, Paraguay, and Uruguay initially) created a "Southern Cone Common Market" named MERCOSUR. Pressure to advance MERCOSUR and other customs unions, common markets, and economic unions that are on the drawing boards around the world will depend on the success of the EMU.

FIGURE 17-1 Currency Quotations Excerpted from a Newspaper

CURRENCY TRADING

EXCHANGE RATES

Wednesday, January 19, 2000

The New York foreign exchange mid-range rates below apply to trading among banks in amounts of $1 million and more, as quoted at 4 p.m. Eastern time by Reuters and other sources. Retail transactions provide fewer units of foreign currency per dollar. Rates for the 11 Euro currency countries are derived from the latest dollar-euro rate using the exchange ratios set 1/1/00.

	U.S. $ equiv.		Currency per U.S. $	
Country	Wed	Tue	Wed	Tue
Argentina (Peso)	1.0002	1.0002	.9998	.9998
Australia (Dollar)	.6636	.6660	1.5070	1.5016
Austria (Schilling)	.07359	.07366	13.589	13.576
Bahrain (Dinar)	2.6525	2.6525	.3770	.3770
Belgium (Franc)	.0251	.0251	39.8379	39.8006
Brazil (Real)	.5583	.5579	1.7910	1.7925
Britain (Pound)	1.6442	1.6377	.6082	.6106
1-month forward	1.6443	1.6378	.6082	.6106
3-months forward	1.6443	1.6378	.6082	.6106
6-months forward	1.6436	1.6372	.6084	.6108
Canada (Dollar)	.6888	.6898	1.4517	1.4498
1-month forward	.6894	.6901	1.4506	1.4491
3-months forward	.6902	.6911	1.4489	1.4469
6-months forward	.6914	.6923	1.4464	1.4444
Chile (Peso) (d)	.001935	.001939	516.75	515.75
China (Renminbi)	.1208	.1208	8.2797	8.2793
Colombia (Peso)	.0005148	.0005167	1942.50	1935.50
Czech. Rep. (Koruna)				
Commercial rate	.02810	.02812	35.593	35.562
Denmark (Krone)	.1360	.1362	7.3514	7.3437
Ecuador (Sucre)				
Floating rate	.00004004	.00004004	24975.00	24975.00
Finland (Markka)	.1703	.1705	5.8717	5.8662
France (Franc)	.1544	.1545	6.4779	6.4719
1-month forward	.1547	.1549	6.4623	6.4559
3-months forward	.1555	.1556	6.4322	6.4282
6-months forward	.1564	.1566	6.3924	6.3862
Germany (Mark)	.5177	.5182	1.9315	1.9297
1-month forward	.5190	.5195	1.9268	1.9249
3-months forward	.5214	.5217	1.9179	1.9167
6-months forward	.5247	.5252	1.9059	1.9041
Greece (Drachma)	.003062	.003064	326.59	326.38
Hong Kong (Dollar)	.1285	.1286	7.7793	7.7790
Hungary (Forint)	.003971	.003970	251.85	251.89
India (Rupee)	.02297	.02296	43.540	43.545
Indonesia (Rupiah)	.0001362	.0001375	7340.00	7275.00
Ireland (Punt)	1.2857	1.2870	.7778	.7770
Israel (Shekel)	.2445	.2457	4.0893	4.0695
Italy (Lira)	.0005230	.0005235	1912.18	1910.38
Japan (Yen)	.009492	.009462	105.35	105.69
1-month forward	.009540	.009511	104.82	105.14

	U.S. $ equiv.		Currency per U.S. $	
Country	Wed	Tue	Wed	Tue
3-months forward	.009633	.009602	103.80	104.15
6-months forward	.009784	.009754	102.21	102.53
Jordan (Dinar)	1.4085	1.4085	.7100	.7100
Kuwait (Dinar)	3.2819	3.2819	.3047	.3047
Lebanon (Pound)	.0006634	.0006634	1507.50	1507.50
Malaysia (Ringgit)	.2632	.2632	3.8000	3.7999
Malta (Lira)	2.4480	2.4474	.4085	.4086
Mexico (Peso)				
Floating rate	.1062	.1063	9.4150	9.4050
Netherland (Guilder)	.4595	.4599	2.1763	2.1742
New Zealand (Dollar)	.5149	.5205	1.9421	1.9209
Norway (Krone)	.1252	.1252	7.9878	7.9883
Pakistan (Rupee)	.01928	.01926	51.875	51.925
Peru (new Sol)	.2857	.2865	3.5005	3.4905
Philippines (Peso)	.02460	.02463	40.650	40.595
Poland (Zloty)	.2451	.2446	4.0800	4.0875
Portugal (Escudo)	.005051	.005056	197.99	197.80
Russia (Ruble) (a)	.03502	.03492	28.555	28.635
Saudi Arabia (Riyal)	.2666	.2666	3.7505	3.7505
Singapore (Dollar)	.5966	.5974	1.6763	1.6740
Slovak Rep. (Koruna)	.02393	.02394	41.788	41.764
South Africa (Rand)	.1636	.1641	6.1135	6.0925
South Korea (Won)	.0008822	.0008877	1133.50	1126.50
Spain (Peseta)	.006086	.006092	164.32	164.16
Sweden (Krona)	.1180	.1182	8.4780	8.4598
Switzerland (Franc)	.6272	.6283	1.5943	1.5917
1-month forward	.6296	.6307	1.5883	1.5856
3-months forward	.6342	.6350	1.5767	1.5749
6-months forward	.6405	.6415	1.5612	1.5588
Taiwan (Dollar)	.03249	.03155	30.775	31.700
Thailand (Baht)	.02676	.02678	37.375	37.335
Turkey (Lira)	.00000183	.00000183	546755.00	546595.00
United Arab (Dirham)	.2723	.2723	3.6730	3.6726
Uruguay (New Peso)				
Financial	.08574	.08558	11.663	11.685
Venezuela (Bolivar)	.001533	.001531	652.50	653.10
		— — —		
SDR	1.3661	1.3667	.7320	.7317
Euro	1.0126	1.0136	.9876	.9866

Special Drawing Rights (SDR) are based on exchange rates for the U.S., German, British, French , and Japanese currencies. Source: International Monetary Fund.

a-Russian Central Bank rate. Trading band lowered on 8/17/98. b-Government rate. d-Floating rate; trading band suspended on 9/2/99.

The 3-month and 6-month forward rates for France, Germany, Japan and Switzerland appearing in the Foreign Exchange column were incorrectly calculated for the period beginning with August 13 and ending with October 7. Corrected data is available from Readers' Reference Service (413) 592-3600.

Key Currency Cross Rates Late New York Trading Jan. 19, 2000

	Dollar	Euro	Pound	SFranc	Guilder	Peso	Yen	Lira	D-Mark	FFranc	CdnDlr
Canada	1.4517	1.4700	2.3869	0.9106	.66705	.15419	.01378	.00076	.75159	.22410	....
France	6.4779	6.5595	10.6510	4.0632	2.9766	.68804	.06149	.00339	3.3538	....	4.4623
Germany	1.9315	1.9558	3.1758	1.2115	.88752	.20515	.01833	.00101	....	.29817	1.3305
Italy	1912.2	1936.3	3144.0	1199.4	878.64	203.10	18.151	....	990.00	295.19	1317.2
Japan	105.35	106.68	173.22	66.079	48.408	11.190	....	.05509	54.543	16.263	72.570
Mexico	9.4150	9.5336	15.480	5.9054	4.3261	....	.08937	.00492	4.8744	1.4534	6.4855
Netherlands	2.1763	2.2037	3.5783	1.3651	....	.23115	.02066	.00114	1.1267	.33596	1.4991
Switzerland	1.5943	1.6144	2.6213	....	.73257	.16934	.01513	.00083	.82542	.24611	1.0982
U.K.	.60820	.6159	....	.3815	.27946	.06460	.00577	.00032	.31488	.09389	.41896
Euro	.98760	....	1.6237	.61943	.45378	.10489	.00937	.00052	.51129	.15245	.68028
U.S.	....	1.0126	1.6442	.62723	.45950	.10621	.00949	.00052	.51773	.15437	.68885

Source: Reuters

For the latest foreign exchange rates visit the Web site of the New York Federal Reserve Bank at: www.ny.frb.org. For current foreign exchange prices on various currencies traded in the spot and forward markets, go to this Web site's Statistics section. Or, see Reuters Web site at: http://quotes.reuters.com/.

SOURCE: *Wall Street Journal*, 20 January 2000, C23.

Expected Foreign Exchange Rate. The expectations hypothesis for foreign exchange states that the foreign exchange spot rate that is expected today ($t = 0$) to exist during the next time period, $E(SP_1)$, equals the value of today's forward rate for delivery next period, FP_1:

$$E(SP_1) = FP_1 \tag{17-1}$$

Suppose, for example, $E(SP_1) = E(\$1.73/\pounds)_1$ represents a spot rate of \$1.73 per British pound that is expected today to exist during the next time period ($t = 1$). Let $FP_1 = \$1.73/\pounds$ signify that today one pound will buy 1.73 U.S. dollars for delivery one time period in the future.

$$E(SP_1) = E(\$1.73/\pounds)_1 = \$1.73/\pounds = FP_1 \tag{17-1a}$$

Eqns. 17-1 and 17-1a would be false if the spot or forward prices were consistently biased in either an optimistic or pessimistic manner.[*]

Premiums and Discounts in Forward Exchange Rates. When the percentage calculated using Eqn. 17-2 is positive, the British pound is selling at a *forward premium* at that moment in time. When Eqn. 17-2 is negative, the pound is selling at a *forward discount*.

$$\begin{pmatrix} \text{A currency's percentage} \\ \text{premium or discount} \end{pmatrix} = \frac{FP_1}{SP_0} - 1.0 = \frac{\$1.73/\pounds}{\$1.66/\pounds} - 1.0 = +0.04 = +4\% \tag{17-2}$$

In the example above the British pound is selling at a forward premium.

If the forward rate (FP_1) equals the future spot rate, $E(SP_1)$, then that currency's forward premium or discount should equal the expected percentage change in the exchange rate, $\frac{FP_1}{SP_0} - 1.0 = \frac{E(FP_1)}{SP_0} - 1.0$, which implies $\frac{FP_1}{E(SP_1)} - 1.0 = 0$. If Eqn. 17-3 does not equal zero, then an expected profit opportunity exists.[**]

$$\text{Expected percentage premium or discount} = \frac{FP_1}{E(SP_1)} - 1.0 \tag{17-3}$$

For example, if $\frac{FP_1}{E(SP_1)} - 1.0 = \frac{\$1.50/\pounds}{\$1.60/\pounds} - 1.0 = -0.06 = -6\%$, then one expects to be able to buy pounds forward for \$1.50 and sell them in the spot market next period for \$1.60 and capture a profit of 10 cents per pound. However, currency investors should be reluctant to trade on values computed with Eqn. 17-3, because it is difficult to measure peoples' expectations of $E(SP_1)$.

---

[*] Three foreign exchange conventions exist. *Convention 1:* State all exchange rates in terms of the U.S. dollar. For example, discuss the number of British pounds per dollar (£/US\$), but not dollars per pound (US\$/£). *Convention 2*: An exchange rate should be stated to exceed one. It is improper to discuss (£/US\$1) = 0.6 but it is proper to discuss (US\$/£1) = 1.666, although they are equivalent. *Convention 3*: When Conventions 1 and 2 conflict, ignore Convention 1. In other words, in the example here, follow Convention 2. Some writers do not bother to follow these conventions.

[**] A currency's forward premium or discount is a percentage difference between the forward and spot exchange rates; it should equal the interest rate differential between bonds that have the same maturity as the currency forward. This interest rate parity relationship can be restated in terms of the expected value of SP_0 one period in the future, $E(SP_1)$, as shown in Eqn. 17-3.

ANALYSIS OF FOREIGN EXCHANGE RISK

EXAMPLE

Consider two people who simultaneously make investments of equal value in an Indian security.

◆ A *domestic investor* in India uses the domestic currency to buy a domestic security.

◆ A *foreign investor* from the United States uses U.S. dollars to make an investment of equal value in the same Indian security.

If the foreign exchange rate between these two investors' currencies fluctuates, they will earn different rates of return from the same security over the same holding period.

The Domestic Investor. The domestic investor's return, r_d is the familiar one-period rate of return that a domestic investor earns after paying for a domestic security with the local currency.

$$r_d = \frac{P_t - P_{t-1} + CF_t}{P_{t-1}} = \frac{(\text{Price change}) + (\text{Cash income})}{(\text{Purchase price})} \tag{17-4}$$

Suppose a domestic Indian investor invests 500 rupees (Rs) in an Indian security that pays no cash dividends or coupon interest and then sells that security 1 year later for Rs550. The Indian investor earns 10%, as shown in Eqn. 17-4a:

$$r_d = \frac{\text{Rs}550 - \text{Rs}500 + 0}{\text{Rs}500} = \frac{\text{Rs}50}{\text{Rs}500} = 10\% \tag{17-4a}$$

The Foreign Investor. If an American investor invests U.S. dollars in the same Indian security, Eqn. 17-5 measures the foreign investor's return, r_f:

$$r_f = \frac{SP_t P_t - SP_{t-1}P_{t-1} + SP_t CF_t}{SP_{t-1}P_{t-1}} = \frac{(\text{Price change}) + (\text{Cash income})}{(\text{Purchase price})} \tag{17-5}$$

The prices are stated in rupees and SP_t denotes the dollar-rupee spot price (current exchange rate) at time t. If the spot price (foreign exchange rate) is 40 rupees for \$1 at the beginning of the investment holding period we represent that as $SP_{t-1} = \$1/\text{Rs}40 = \$0.025$ at time $t-1$. In other words, an American investors must pay 2.5 cents for 1 rupee. This exchange rate translates into a purchase price of $[(SP_{t-1})(P_{t-1})] = (0.025)(\text{Rs}500) = \$12.50$ that the American investor pays for the Indian security.

$$r_f = \frac{(.025)(\text{Rs}550) - (.025)(\text{Rs}500) + (.025)(0)}{(.025)(\text{Rs}500)} = \frac{\$1.25}{\$12.50} = 10\% \tag{17-5a}$$

If the exchange rate (spot price) remains constant, the American earns the same 10% rate of return from the Indian security as the Indian investor, because Eqns. 17-4a and 17-5a are numerically equal.

Most governments allow exchange rates to fluctuate. Consideration of fluctuating exchange rates reveals that the American investor actually makes two separate risky investments. First, the American pays a fluctuating dollar price for rupees in the foreign exchange market. Second, the American uses the rupees to buy an Indian security at a price that fluctuates in the securities market.

Suppose that from the start to the end of the investment holding period (between time $t-1$ and time t) the U.S. dollar depreciates relative to the rupee so that, when the American investor sells the Indian security, the exchange rate is $SP_t = \$1/\text{Rs}36.36 = \$0.0275$ per rupee at time t. Stated differently, the American made a 10% gain on the investment in Indian rupees.

$$r_c = \frac{SP_t - SP_{t-1}}{SP_{t-1}} = \frac{0.0275 - 0.0250}{0.0250} = \frac{0.0025}{0.0250} = 10\% \tag{17-6}$$

In this case the American investor can sell the Indian security for $SP_t p_t = (0.0275)(\text{Rs}550) = \$15.125$. Inserting the fluctuating exchange rate values and the fluctuating stock prices into Eqn. 17-5 results in Eqn. 17-5b:

$$r_f = \frac{(0.275)(\text{Rs}550) - (.025)(\text{RS}500) + (.0275)(0)}{(.025)(\text{Rs}500)} = \frac{\$2.625}{\$12.50} = .21 = 21\% \tag{17-5b}$$

Eqn. 17-5b shows that the American investor's total rate of return is 21%, before commissions, fees, and taxes.

Components of Investor's Total Return

Algebraically restating Eqn. 17-5 in terms of Eqns. 17-4 and 17-6 creates Eqn. 17-5c.

$$(1 + \text{Eqn. 17-5}) = (1 + \text{Eqn. 17-4})(1 + \text{Eqn. 17-6}) \tag{17-5c}$$

$$(1 + r_f) = (1 + r_d)(1 + r_c)$$

$$(1.21) = (1.10)(1.10)$$

Eqn. 17-5c can be simplified to Eqn. 17-7:

$$r_f = r_d + r_c + r_d r_c \tag{17-7}$$

$$21\% = 10\% + 10\% + 1\%$$

Eqns. 17-5c and 17-7 decompose the foreign (American) investor's 21% total return from the investment in an Indian security into a pure gain in the Indian security of $r_d = 10\%$ for either a domestic or foreign investor, plus a foreign exchange gain of $r_c = 10\%$ for the foreign investor, plus a cross-product of $(r_d)(r_c) = (0.1)(0.1) = 1\%$. In most investments the cross-product is small enough to ignore, which permits Eqn. 17-7 to be approximated by Eqn. 17-8.

$$r_f \cong r_d + r_c \tag{17-8}$$

$$21\% \approx 10\% + 10\%$$

The approximation in Eqn. 17-8 highlights the fact that an international investment equals the sum of two separate investments: one investment in the foreign security and another investment in the foreign currency needed to buy the foreign security.

Risks Undertaken by International Investors

Eqns. 14-5 and 14-6 are equivalent risk formulas for a 2-asset portfolio from Chapter 14. Eqn. 14-4 in Chapter 14 (p. 406) explains the covariance term that makes Eqns. 14-5 and 14-6 identical. Eqns. 14-5 and 14-6 can be reformulated as Eqns. 17-9 and 17-9a to analyze the risky 2-asset portfolio for an American investing in Indian rupees and an Indian security. Any investor who undertakes a foreign investment faces three risk factors shown in Eqns. 17-9 and 17-9a.

$$\begin{pmatrix} \text{Total} \\ \text{risk} \end{pmatrix} = \begin{pmatrix} \text{Foreign} \\ \text{currency} \\ \text{risk} \end{pmatrix} + \begin{pmatrix} \text{Foreign} \\ \text{security} \\ \text{risk} \end{pmatrix} + (\text{Covariance risk})$$

$$VAR(r_f) = VAR(r_c) + VAR(r_d) + (\rho_{cd})\sqrt{VAR(r_c)}\,\sqrt{VAR(r_d)} \qquad (17\text{-}9)$$

$$VAR(r_f) = VAR(r_c) + VAR(r_d) + COV(r_c, r_d) \qquad (17\text{-}9a)$$

$VAR(r_f)$ in Eqns. 17-9 and 17-9a is interpreted to be the foreign investor's (American's) total risk. The foreign investor's total risk is the sum of the risk the investor takes in the foreign (Indian) securities market, $VAR(r_d)$, and the foreign currency (rupee) risk, $VAR(r_c)$, plus the covariance between the foreign security's return and the foreign currency's return, $COV(r_c, r_d) = \rho_{cd}\sigma_c\sigma_d$. The covariance can be negative (positive) if the value of the foreign investment and the foreign exchange rates fluctuate inversely (directly). The sign of the correlation between the foreign investment and the foreign exchange rate determines the sign of the covariance in Eqn. 17-9. Table 17-3 provides empirical estimates of the components of Eqns. 17-9 and 17-9a for stock and bond investments from several countries.

Interpreting the Table. Column 1 of Table 17-3 contains the domestic investor's total risk from investing domestically in the country's Morgan Stanley Capital International (MSCI) market index, σ_d. Foreign exchange risk statistics (standard deviations) for a U.S. investor's pure foreign currency investments are in Column 2, σ_c. Column 3 contains the correlation coefficient between the foreign exchange and the MSCI market index investment, with both investments in the same foreign country, ρ_{dc}. The total risk an international investor assumes by buying a foreign country's currency and using that foreign currency to buy that foreign country's MSCI index is in Column 4, σ_f. Column 5 contains the ratio of Column 4 over Column 1. The ratios in Column 5 list the foreign (American) investor's risk divided by the risk a domestic investor would experience from a similar investment, (σ_f/σ_d). When the

TABLE 17-3   Estimates of the Risks Undertaken by U.S. and Domestic Investors in Selected Countries, 1993–99 Inclusive

Country	(1) Domestic Risk, σ_d	(2) Currency risk, σ_c	(3) Correlation, ρ_{dc}	(4) Foreign risk, σ_f	(4)/(1) = (5) σ_f/σ_d
Canada	18.12	4.72	−0.38	17.79	0.98
France	22.83	9.47	0.49	23.89	1.05
Germany	22.92	9.64	0.45	23.91	1.04
Japan	19.67	13.12	0.14	20.03	1.02
Singapore	30.87	6.21	−0.45	30.01	.97
Switzerland	21.89	10.78	0.41	22.86	1.04
Italy	30.04	8.48	0.17	30.47	1.01
United Kingdom	14.76	6.91	0.33	15.09	1.02
United States	15.98	0	1.0	15.98	1.0

SOURCE: MSCI stock market index and foreign exchange data from Ibbotson database (before Euro).

foreign exchange risk is positively correlated with the investment's returns ($\rho_{cd} > 0$), that increases the foreign (American) investor's risk above a domestic investor's risk and causes the ratio in Column 4 to exceed positive 1. A few negative correlations in Column 3 (Canada and Singapore) cause the ratios in Column 5 to be less than $+1$.[2]

EXAMPLE A WORLDWIDE ELECTRONIC TRADING BOOK

The "world map" in Figure 17-2 is annotated to show the hours when major financial markets are open for trading. Dissimilar operating times create international communication problems, motivate the various markets around the world to stay open for longer trading hours, and result in ingenious multinational arrangements.

Consider how a large international bank like Citibank or Chase Bank headquartered in New York City might manage its worldwide foreign exchange operations. Suppose the bank's New York office employs 100 foreign exchange traders who make active markets in 50 currencies. The 50 currencies that the bank continuously carries in inventory and from which its currency traders actively buy and sell were selected by the bank's currency managers; these men and women made an executive decision that the bank would a *make markets* in these 50 currencies. The bank's worldwide foreign exchange inventory is kept as an electronic *trading book*. This trading book is part of a computer network that connects 300 foreign exchange traders working around the world, keeps track of their trades, accounts for the profit or loss on every trade, and accounts for the entire bank's inventories in 50 currencies. At the close of every NYC business day the head NY currency trader phones the bank's head currency trader in Tokyo for a discussion of current market conditions and details about the bank's multimillion-dollar inventory in 50 currencies. After this phone call the head currency trader in NYC passes responsibility for the bank's foreign exchange trading book to the head currency trader in the bank's Tokyo office. The aggregate accounting for the bank's inventories in 50 currencies is electronically passed from NYC to Tokyo by a computer keystroke.

Suppose the Tokyo office of a bank like Chase or Citibank employs 80 foreign exchange traders. At the close of every trading day the head currency trader in Tokyo calls the bank's head currency trader in London to discuss the bank's inventory of 50 currencies. When their phone conversation is finished, the head trader in Tokyo passes responsibility for the bank's foreign exchange trading book and the bank's currency inventory to the head trader in the London. Suppose the London office of a bank like Chase or Citibank employs 90 foreign exchange traders. These 90 foreign exchange traders in London go to work while the bank's Tokyo currency traders are having their evening meal and the NYC traders are still sleeping. At the close of a normal business day in London the aggregate accounting for the bank's inventories in 50 currencies is passed in an electronic instant from London to NYC.

A major international bank like Citibank or Chase Bank might also employ 30 foreign exchange traders who do not work in the bank's NYC, London, or Tokyo offices. These 30 people might work in Zurich, Sao Paolo, Madrid, Singapore, Johannesburg, and other places; they are under the control one of the bank's head currency traders in New York City, London, or Tokyo.

Each trading day responsibility for each large international bank's worldwide foreign exchange trading book is electronically passed around the world once. In this manner the informal, interbank currency market operates around the world and around the clock.*

---

* A large international commercial bank, investment bank, merchant bank, insurance company, and other financial intermediaries probably have separate electronic trading books for foreign exchange, money market securities, common stocks, and bonds.

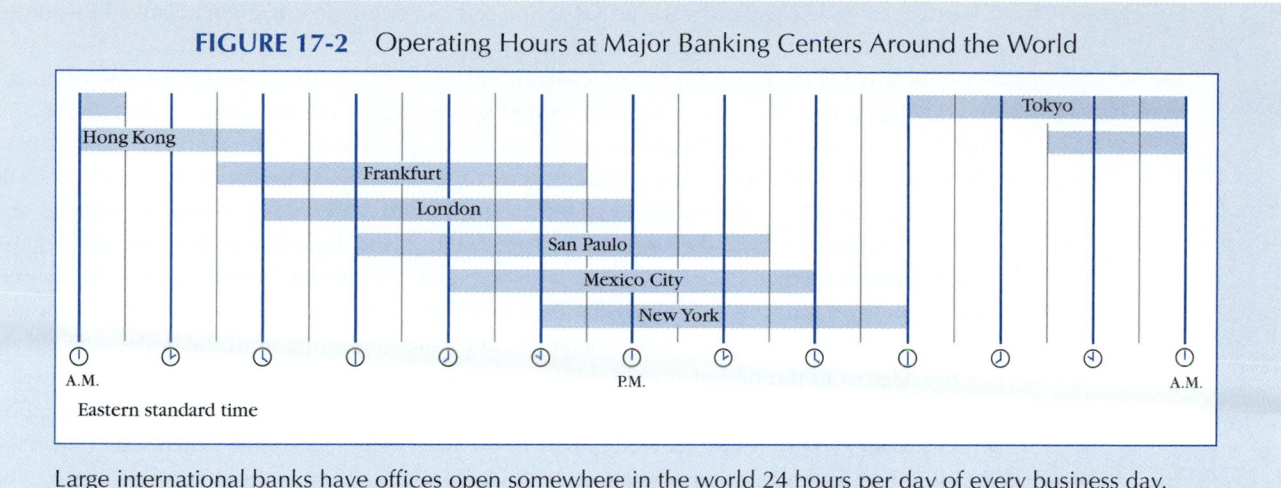

FIGURE 17-2   Operating Hours at Major Banking Centers Around the World

Eastern standard time

Large international banks have offices open somewhere in the world 24 hours per day of every business day.

THREE FOREIGN EXCHANGE PARITY RELATIONSHIPS

Foreign exchange markets are made liquid by the continuous activities of international businesses, currency speculators, and those who make markets in foreign currencies. A large transaction can influence exchange rates in the short run. In the long run, however, foreign exchange rates are determined by fundamental economic relationships between the nations that create the currencies. Economists have studied these economic relationships and developed three parity models to explain foreign exchange rates.

Relative Purchasing Power Parity (PPP)

The **law of one price**, introduced in Chapter 3, states that identical goods should sell at identical prices. The law of one price will tend to equalize the prices of physical commodities that are traded in markets around the world, but it cannot make the price of every particular commodity exactly equal throughout the world. Transportation costs make it profitable for arbitrageurs to equate the prices of physical commodities only after an allowance for shipping costs is deducted.

The law of one price applies to financial quantities more accurately than it applies to physical quantities because international bankers can wire money and securities around the world at negligible cost. As a result, after making the appropriate exchange rate adjustments, at any given moment a share of Coca-Cola stock should sell for the same price in the New York Stock Exchange (NYSE), the London Stock Exchange (LSE), the Tokyo Stock Exchange (TSE), the Hong Kong Stock Exchange (HKSE), and every other stock market in the world. Since the international transportation costs for cash and securities are a negligible percent of large transactions **absolute purchasing power parity** exists in securities markets. If a share of Coca-Cola were priced differently at one exchange than another, arbitrageurs would buy the stock where it was cheapest and sell it in the market where its price was highest. Arbitrageurs would continue to buy at the lowest price and bid that price higher, sell at the highest price and drive that price down, and continue this profitable arbitrage until the law of one price was affirmed.

Relative Purchasing Power Parity (Relative PPP). Relative PPP generalizes the law of one price. It says a basket of identical goods should sell at the same price around the world if no barriers to trade exist and if the goods are priced in a common currency. Relative PPP adjusts for differences between countries' inflation rates.

Relative PPP implies, for example, that if inflation is 4% in the United States and 8% in the United Kingdom, then, the U.S. dollar should appreciate by [(1.08/1.04) − 1.0 =] 3.8% relative to the British pound to maintain economic equilibrium. If the British pound fails to become 3.8% cheaper relative to the American dollar in the foreign exchange market, the goods that the United Kingdom exports to the United States will become overpriced and United States exports to the United Kingdom will become underpriced. If such a pricing disequilibrium emerged, very few people would want to buy British pounds. Instead, many people would want to buy U.S. dollars so they could purchase U.S. goods to ship to the United Kingdom. This foreign exchange disequilibrium would continue until the dollar was bid up 3.8% relative to the pound. If no foreign exchange tariffs or barriers to trade existed, market forces would restore economic equilibrium. This equilibrium relationship between inflation and exchange rates is summarized in Eqn. 17-10, where the subscripts f and d refer to foreign and domestic conditions. These equations assume a U.S. citizen is the domestic investor. The U.S. dollar is the domestic currency and the foreign exchange rate is stated as the number of U.S. dollars for one British pound.

$$\frac{SP_1}{SP_0} = \frac{1 + INF_f}{1 + INF_d} \qquad (17\text{-}10)$$

In Eqn. 17-10,

SP_0 = Spot price = Today's (at time t = 0) price for a foreign currency in the cash (spot, physicals) market. For example, a spot rate of SP_0 = US\$1.666/£1 means one British pound costs US\$1.666.

SP_1 = Future spot rate = The amount of foreign currency that can be purchased for one unit of domestic currency in the cash market one time period in the future. For example, SP_1 = US\$1.73/£1 one year in the future (at time t = 1), this currency price is not observable today (at time t = 0).

INF_f = The inflation rate in the foreign country, for example, 8% per year in the United Kingdom. The subscript f stands for foreign.

INF_d = The domestic inflation rate, perhaps, 4% per year in the United States. The subscript d stands for domestic.

Taking the difference between the nominal rates of inflation in the foreign and domestic countries, as shown in Eqn. 17-11, approximates the percentage change in the spot rate, Eqn. 17-10.

$$\frac{SP_1}{SP_0} - 1 \approx INF_f - INF_d \qquad (17\text{-}11)$$

Consider the implications of PPP for foreign exchange rates in a world where prices were free to fluctuate. If the world's exchange rates fluctuated without any restrictions, foreign exchange rates would reflect the inflation differentials between countries. In this idealized economic environment exchange rates would have no effect on the returns from investments in different foreign countries.

Critique of PPP. PPP has no ability to explain short-run (day-to-day or month-to-month) movements in foreign exchange rates, and very little ability to explain year-to-year changes. Figure 17-3 shows that over a number of decades the exchange rate between the British

FIGURE 17-3 Purchasing Power Parity (PPP) and the Pound/U.K. Dollar Exchange Rate: (A)–Pounds/U.S. Dollars and (B)–Percent Difference

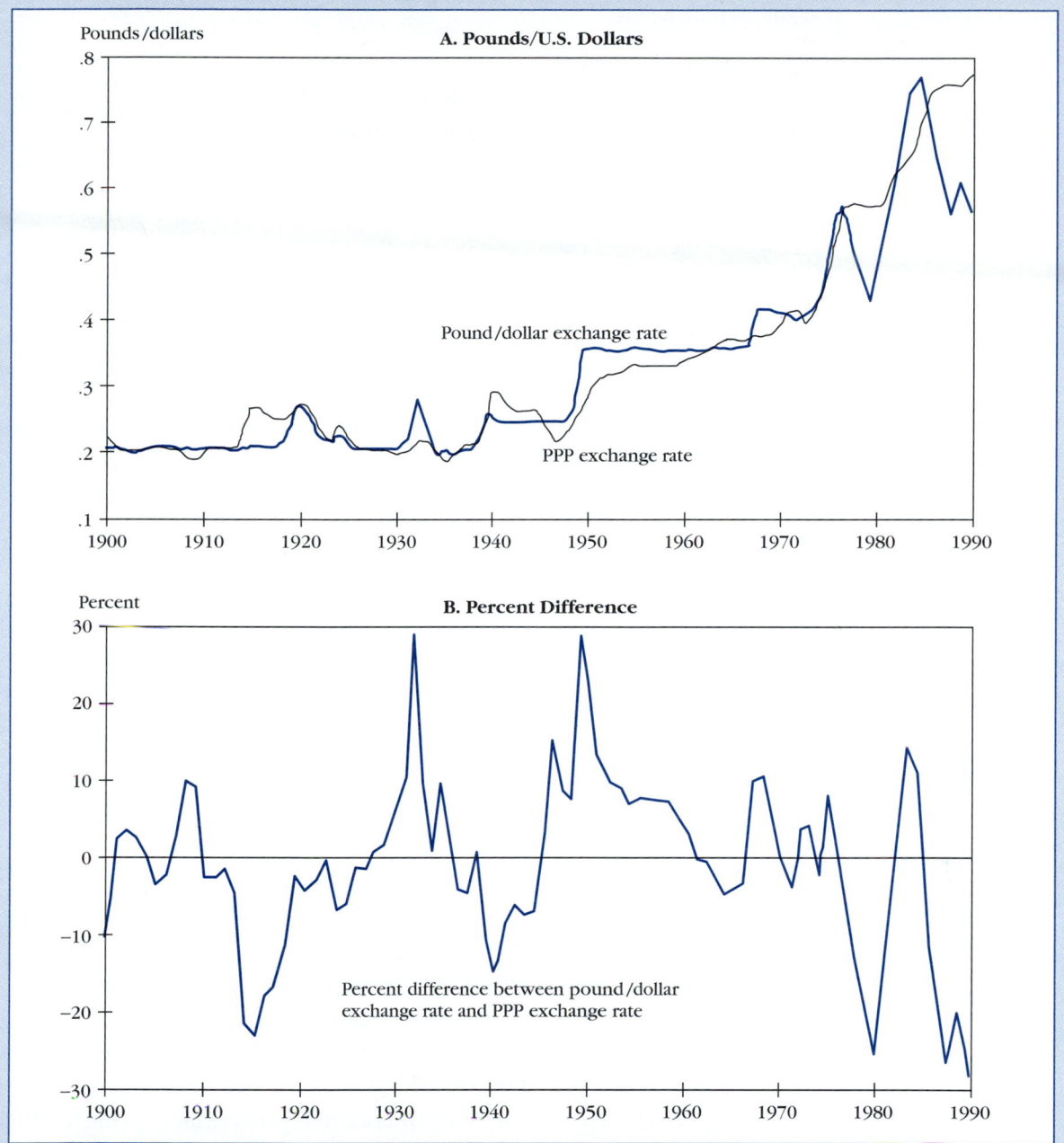

Purchasing Power Parity (PPP) cannot explain small changes or short-term changes in foreign currencies exchange rates. In the long run, however, prices tend toward the fundamental values suggested by PPP.

SOURCE: Craig S. Hakkio, "Is Purchasing Power Parity a Useful Guide to the Dollar?" *Economic Review* 77, no. 3 (Third Quarter 1992): 41, Chart 1. Hakkio's Chart 1 draws on M. H. Lee, *Purchasing Power Parity* (New York: Dekker, 1978).

pound and the U.S. dollar that PPP predicted was sometimes as much as 30% too high or 30% too low. One of the main flaws with PPP lies in our inability to measure inflation.

Most researchers equate the percentage changes in a country's price index with its inflation rate, as shown here:

$$\begin{pmatrix} \text{Rate of} \\ \text{inflation} \\ \text{during some} \\ \text{time period} \end{pmatrix} = \frac{(\text{Price index's ending value})}{(\text{Price index's beginning value})} - 1 = \frac{208}{200} - 1 = .04 = 4\%$$

Using the inflation measure above to implement the PPP theory is flawed in several respects. First, the typical consumer's basket of goods changes continuously over time (less whiskey, more wine), and it is difficult for government researchers to appropriately alter the basket of goods used in their calculations. Second, different baskets of goods are appropriate for each different country. For example, the French drink more wine than Americans, and the Japanese eat more fish than Americans. Third, most inflation measurements are based on historical data that take no cognizance of expected future price changes. However, people typically base their decisions on their inflationary expectations instead of historical inflation rates. In spite of its inability to make valuable short-run predictions, PPP still provides a valuable framework in which to analyze long-run trends in exchange rates.

Irving Fisher's Two Inflation-Based Theories

During the 1930s Yale University economist Irving Fisher pointed out that market (nominal) interest rates we read about in the newspapers can be separated into two components: a constant real rate and the fluctuating expected rate of inflation. This relationship is stated as Eqn. 17-12 for a closed (one-country) economy in which only a single currency is used; hence it is called **Fisher closed.**

$$\left(1 + \begin{bmatrix} \text{Nominal} \\ \text{rate, } r_t \end{bmatrix}\right) = \left(1 + \begin{bmatrix} \text{Real} \\ \text{rate, } rr \end{bmatrix}\right)\left(1 + E\begin{bmatrix} \text{Inflation} \\ \text{rate, } INF_t \end{bmatrix}\right) \tag{17-12}$$

$$\left(1 + \begin{bmatrix} \text{Nominal} \\ \text{rate, } r_t = 7.12\% \end{bmatrix}\right) = \left(1 + \begin{bmatrix} \text{Real} \\ \text{rate, } rr = 3\% \end{bmatrix}\right)\left(1 + E\begin{bmatrix} \text{Inflation} \\ \text{rate, } INF_t = 4\% \end{bmatrix}\right) \tag{17-12a}$$

In these equations,

r_t = The nominal (market) interest rate during time period t, for example, 7.12%

rr = The constant real rate of interest = A inflation-adjusted rate of return that has no time subscript because it is assumed to remain fixed from one time period to the next = approximately: $r_t - INF_t$ = a rearranged Eqn. 17-12, for example, 3%

$E(INF_t)$ = The expected rate of inflation during time period t, for example, 4%. The inflation rate fluctuates from one time period to the next.

Eqn. 17-12's definition of the nominal interest rate can be approximated as sum of the real rate and the expected rate of inflation.

$$\begin{pmatrix} \text{Nominal} \\ \text{rate, } r_t = 7\% \end{pmatrix} \approx \begin{pmatrix} \text{Real rate,} \\ rr = 3\% \end{pmatrix} + \begin{pmatrix} \text{Expected inflation} \\ \text{rate, } E(INF_t) = 4\% \end{pmatrix} \tag{17-13}$$

The Fisher closed in Eqn. 17-13 says that adding a country's real rate ($rr = 3\%$) and its expected rate of inflation ($INF_t = 4\%$) over the same time span approximates that country's nominal interest rate ($r_t = 7.12\%$). Eqn. 17-13 provides an approximation that misses the exact solution in Eqn. 17-12a by ($7.12\% - 7.0\% =$) 12 basis points. Eqns. 17-12 and 17-13 imply that if the expected inflation rate accelerates to, say, 8% in the next time period, $[E(INF_{t+1}) = 8\%]$, then the nominal interest rate should rise to about 11%, if the real rate remains unchanged.

$$r_{t+1} = rr + E(INF_{t+1}) = 3\% + 8\% = 11\%$$

Fisher's model is sometimes criticized for being oversimplified, because it is based on the unrealistic assumption that the real rate (rr) never varies.

Fisher Open. Fisher extended his inflation model to an open economy, which means a model that includes trading between different countries and multiple currencies. In this multicurrency model, differences in nominal interest rates between countries can be explained by differences in the countries' real rates and differences in their inflation rates. Eqn. 17-14 spells out the **Fisher open** model, where

r_f, r_d = The nominal interest rates in the foreign and domestic economies, respectively. For example, $r_f = 11\%$ and $r_d = 7\%$.

rr_f, rr_d = The fixed real rates in the foreign and domestic economies, respectively. For example, $rr_f = rr_d = 3\%$.

$E(INF_f), E(INF_d)$ = The expected inflation rates in the foreign and domestic economies, respectively. For example, $E(INF_f) = 8\%$, $E(INF_d) = 4\%$.

$$\left(\frac{1 + r_f}{1 + r_d}\right) = \left(\frac{1 + rr_f}{1 + rr_d}\right)\left(\frac{1 + E(INF_f)}{1 + E(INF_d)}\right) \tag{17-14}$$

Eqn. 17-15 provides an approximation of the Fisher open model.

$$\left[\left(\begin{array}{c}\text{Nominal} \\ \text{rate, } r_f\end{array}\right) - \left(\begin{array}{c}\text{Nominal} \\ \text{rate, } r_d\end{array}\right)\right] \approx \left[\left(\begin{array}{c}\text{Real} \\ \text{rate, } rr_f\end{array}\right) - \left(\begin{array}{c}\text{Real} \\ \text{rate, } rr_d\end{array}\right)\right] + \left[E\left(\begin{array}{c}\text{Inflation} \\ \text{rate, } INF_f\end{array}\right) - E\left(\begin{array}{c}\text{Inflation} \\ \text{rate, } INF_d\end{array}\right)\right]$$

$$[11\% - 7\%] = 4\% = [3\% - 3\%] + [8\% - 4\%] \tag{17-15}$$

Eqn. 17-15 means that if the two countries real rates are identical, any difference in their nominal rates can be attributed to differences in their expected rates of inflation.

Fisher open is more useful for analyzing long-run relationships than it is as a tool for making short-run forecasts. It has the same flaws as PPP. Furthermore, differences in real rates across countries make the Fisher open model difficult to use.

Interest-Rate Parity

Interest-rate parity means the market returns in two countries are equal when they are denominated in the same currency. When the currencies differ, adjustments must be made to remove the exchange rate effects between the two currencies so that their interest rates on assets of equal risk can be compared in terms of a common currency. Interest-rate parity applies the law of one price to nominal interest rates, after adjusting to remove exchange rate effects.

Interest-rate parity comes in two forms, uncovered and covered. **Uncovered interest-rate parity** is a simple relationship that involves no offsetting "cover" to hedge the position. It occurs when the difference between two countries' nominal interest rates equals the expected future spot rate divided by the current spot rate.

$$r_f - r_d \approx \frac{E(SP_1)}{SP_0} - 1.0 \tag{17-16}$$

Although uncovered interest-rate parity is a useful concept, it is not used to make predictions for three reasons. First, the difference between two countries' nominal interest rates must be measured on equally risky assets. This can be a complex problem if the riskiness of the two countries bonds also involves different levels of sovereign risk. Second, the expected value, $E(SP_1)$, in Eqn. 17-16 is difficult to measure. Third, as with other models, the foreign exchange adjustments required to derive the model in terms of a common currency make using the model cumbersome. The covered interest rate parity model is more useful than the uncovered interest-rate parity model.

Covered interest-rate parity, Eqn. 17-17, is easier to use because no expected values that are difficult to measure are involved and no foreign exchange adjustments are needed.

$$\left(\frac{1 + r_f}{1 + r_d}\right) = \left(\frac{FP_1}{SP_0}\right) \tag{17-17}$$

In this equation,

r_d = The nominal interest rates in the domestic economy, for example, 7% in the United States.

r_f = The nominal interest rates in the foreign economy, for example, 11% in the United Kingdom.

SP_0 = Today's (time $t = 0$) spot price for foreign exchange = For instance, the number of British pounds that can be purchased for immediate delivery for one U.S. dollar. For example, $(\text{£/US\$})_0 = \text{£}0.6024/\text{US\$}1 = 0.6024$ British pounds for US\$1.

FP_1 = Forward price (foreign exchange rate) for a foreign currency that will be delivered one time period in the future (time $t = 1$) to a domestic buyer that is paying for it with the domestic currency = the amount of foreign currency for delivery one period in the future that can be purchased today with one unit of domestic currency. For example, $FP_1 = (\text{£/US\$})_1 = \text{£}0.625/\text{US\$}1 = 0.625$ British pounds per U.S. dollar for delivery in 1 year.

Eqn. 17-17's covered interest-rate parity model can be approximated as Eqn. 17-18:*

$$r_f - r_d \approx \frac{FP_1}{SP_0} - 1.0 \tag{17-18}$$

EXAMPLE   **COVERED ARBITRAGE**

Consider what would happen if the Canadian dollar (C\$)/U.S. dollar (US\$) 1-year forward exchange rate in the United States was $FP_1 = \text{C\$/US\$}_1 = 1.17$, the spot rate was $SP_0 = \text{C\$/US\$}_0 = 1.16$, the interest rate for domestic U.S. borrowers was $r_d = 10\%$, and the foreign

---

* Comparing Eqns. 17-17 and 17-18 shows that the approximate covered interest rate parity model contains an approximation error of (4% − 3.75% =) 26 basis points in this example.

investment in Canadian dollars could earn $r_f = 13\%$. Substituting these four values into Eqn. 17-17 yields an inequality:

$$\left(\frac{1 + r_f}{1 + r_d}\right) = \left(\frac{1 + 13\%}{1 + 10\%}\right) = 1.027 > 1.009 = \left(\frac{FP_1}{SP_0}\right) = \left(\frac{C\$/US\$_1}{C\$/US\$_0}\right) = \left(\frac{1.17}{1.16}\right)$$

U.S. arbitrageurs could profit from the inequality above by borrowing, say, $100,000 at $r_d = 10\%$ for 1 year and immediately converting this U.S. cash into Canadian dollars at the spot rate of $SP_0 = C\$/US\$_0 = 1.16$ to obtain C$116,000. This C$116,000 investment in the Canadian currency might depreciate and wipe out the arbitrage profits, or the Canadian dollars might appreciate and earn additional profits. To hedge away this uncertainty and lock in a riskless profit the U.S. arbitrageur could buy a foreign exchange forward contract guaranteeing the ability to exchange (C$116,000×1.13% =) C$131,080 year-end proceeds for US$112,034 at the forward rate of C$1.17/US$1.

Canadian Dollar Proceeds	Converted into U.S. Dollars
C$116,000	C$131,080
Times: $1 + 13\% = 1 + r_f$	Divided by: $1.17 = C\$/US\$_1$
C$131,080	US$112,034

At the end of the 1-year arbitrage the United States could use the US$112,034 proceeds to repay the U.S. loan of $100,000 plus the 10% interest of $10,000. The remaining (US$112,034 − US$110,000 =) $2,034 is riskless arbitrage profit. In this example, actions of aggressive arbitrageurs would eliminate this riskless arbitrage profit because their actions would affect prices in two ways: (1) An increase in the demand for Canadian dollars today would increase the U.S. dollar cost of Canadian dollars, or reduce the C$/US$ exchange rate; (2) An increase in the supply of Canadian dollars in the forward market would cause an increase in the C$/US$ forward exchange rate. Both price changes act to reestablish the covered interest parity relationship in Eqn. 17-17.

Simplified Summary of Equilibrium Conditions

Figure 17-4 summarizes the inflation, interest rate, exchange rate, and other currency conditions that characterize the economic equilibrium discussed above.

Some currency traders are speculators, and some are arbitrageurs. Speculators can speculate any time they have the money to invest and confidence in their forecast. But, it will not be possible for the arbitrageurs to profit from currency trading when the arbitrage-free equilibrium condition in Eqn. 17-14, are met. Eqns. 17-14, 17-17, and 17-18 define arbitrage-free conditions. Profit-seekers can use the arbitrage-free equilibrium condition in Eqn. 17-17 as a guide to help them discover profitable currency trading opportunities. Furthermore, large deviations from Eqn. 17-17 can be used to earn large arbitrage profits. Profitable trading opportunities will not last very long. When arbitrageurs earn profits, their trading activities tend to move market prices and interest rates toward the arbitrage-free equilibrium conditions, and then the profitable opportunities are gone.

For the arbitrageurs to continually maintain covered interest rate parity, they must be able to transact quickly in the foreign exchange markets and in the foreign bond markets. These conditions are met in the Eurocurrency markets and, as a result, covered interest rate parity prevails there. In markets that are less liquid and/or more regulated than the Eurocurrency markets, Eqn. 17-17 is more likely to be violated.

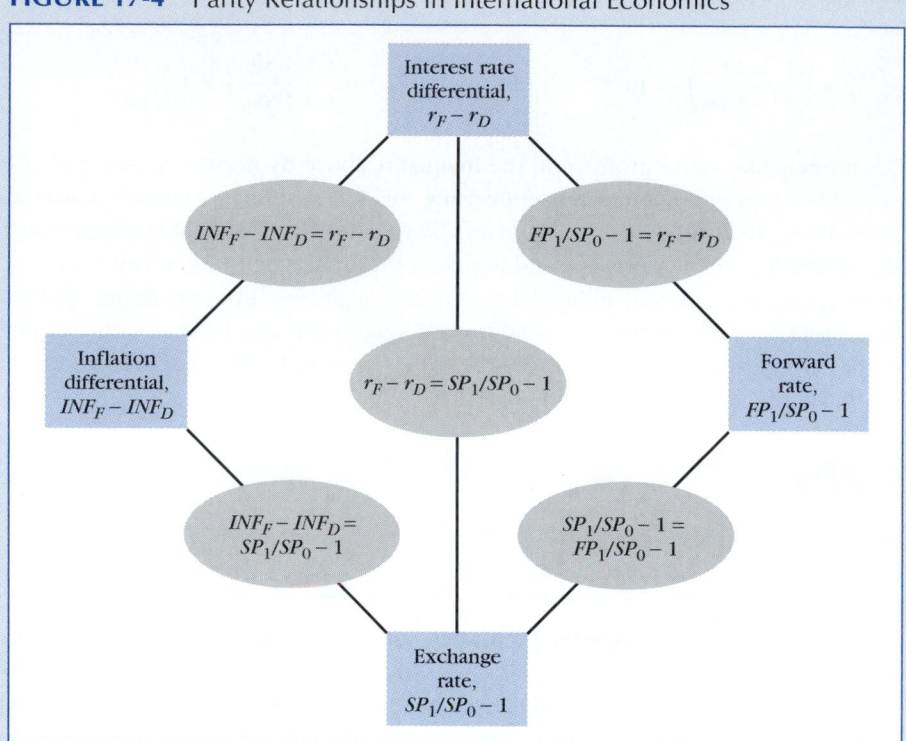

FIGURE 17-4 Parity Relationships in International Economics

Foreign exchange rates are continually shaped and reshaped along the lines suggested by purchasing power parity, the Fisher effect, the international Fisher effect, interest rate parity, and the forward-spot relationship.

THE BOTTOM LINE

When an investor buys a security that is denominated in a foreign currency, two different investments are required in order to consummate the transaction. First, the multinational investor must buy foreign exchange. Second, the foreign exchange is used to pay for the security. Although equal amounts are simultaneously invested in the foreign exchange and the foreign security when an international investment is undertaken, the two separate investments will experience different price fluctuations after they are initiated.

Several European nations are endeavoring to reduce the barriers to international trade by operating a multinational union in which all transactions are executed in a single currency. The participants believe that a common market's use of a common currency will stimulate trade and enable them to enjoy higher levels of prosperity. Such monetary unions have not succeeded in the past. But the European Monetary Union hopes to succeed where predecessors failed by adopting a multinational central bank to coordinate the member nations' economic policies. A customs union exists in Central America and South America, but it is a long way from discussing a common currency.

Three parity relationships have been developed to explain foreign exchange rates. The first, purchasing power parity (PPP), is an equilibrium model. PPP says that identical goods should sell at the same prices around the world, if they are priced in a common currency, and if no barriers to trade exist. Unfortunately, because multiple trade barriers exist, PPP has very little ability to predict short-term changes in exchange rates. However, PPP does provide a useful way in which to analyze long-run trends in international trade. Interest rate parity is the second theoretical model. Interest rate parity occurs when the returns in two countries are equal when denominated in the same currency. It is difficult to determine if the market interest rates in two countries are equal because adjustments must be made to remove the exchange rate effects between the two countries currencies so that their interest rates can be meaningfully compared. The third theory is called covered interest rate parity: it is summarized in Eqn. 17-17. Covered interest rate parity can be evaluated fairly easily and the model can uncover opportunities to earn arbitrage profits. Some foreign exchange traders find all three theoretical models useful.

QUESTIONS

Q17-1 (European Monetary Union) Attempts at monetary unions in the past failed. What contributed to their failures and what advantages does the EMU have to prevent it from failing as well?

Q17-2 (Gold standard) What effect does the abolition of the gold exchange standard have on a government's ability to control its money supply?

Q17-3 (Dirty float) What is meant by "dirty float"? What is a major disadvantage of "dirty float"?

Q17-4 (Risk of foreign investments) What are the three factors that affect the total risk of an investor who purchases a foreign security that is denominated in that same foreign country's currency?

Q17-5 (Expectations hypothesis) Explain the expectations hypothesis for foreign exchange.

Q17-6 (Exchange rates) Assume that the inflation rate in Denmark is 10%, while the inflation rate in the United

States is 3%. What would you expect to happen to the value of the U.S. dollar relative to that of the Danish Krone? Explain.

Q17-7 (Uncovered interest rate parity) Provide three reasons why the uncovered interest rate parity model is not useful in making exchange rate predictions.

Q17-8 (Purchasing power parity) Explain the concept of purchasing power parity. What are the criticisms of it?

Q17-9 (Fisher open model) Assume that the real rate of interest in the United States is identical to the real rate of interest in Britain. What does the Fisher open model suggest is the reason for any observed difference in the nominal interest rates between the two countries? What are the difficulties involved in applying the Fisher open model?

Q17-10 (Interest rate parity) What does covered interest rate parity arbitrage imply about the term structure of forward rates?

PROBLEMS

P17-1 (Interest-rate parity and futures price) On May 14, 2010, the U.S. annual interest rate was 5%, the Japanese interest rate was 3%, and the spot rate for $/Yen was 0.008333. What would be the theoretical futures price on May 14 of the December 10 contract (expiring on December 17, 2010)? (Assume a 360-day year.)

P17-2 (Exchange rates) On October 16, 2000, the Japanese yen was quoted in the spot market at 108.10 yen per dollar. How many dollars would be received in exchange for 1 yen?

P17-3 (Forward premiums and discounts) The exchange rate for Swiss francs per U.S. dollar for delivery in 6 months is $1.75 per S.F. The exchange rate in the spot market is $1.77 per S.F. Is the Swiss franc currently selling at a 6-month forward premium or discount? What is the amount of the premium or discount?

P17-4 (Return on foreign investment) The current exchange rate between the Brazilian real and the U.S. dollar is 1.8655

reals per dollar. Pete Alcade, a telecommunications employee who lives in New York, invested in 100 shares of the preferred stock of Itaubanco at 153.99 reals per share. The stock paid a dividend of 9.50 reals per share at the end of 1 year, and Pete sold the shares for 160 reals. The exchange rate at the time of the sale was 1.7980 reals per dollar. Calculate Pete's rate of return on this investment.

P17-5 (Foreign investment return components) How much of Pete's total return in P17-4 is due to the domestic return on the security? How much is due to the foreign exchange gain?

P17-6 (Purchasing power parity) The current spot exchange rate for US$/Mexican peso is 8.466 peso per U.S. dollar. The expected inflation rate over the coming year is 15% in Mexico and 4% in the United States. What is the expected spot exchange rate, a year from now, according to PPP theory?

P17-7 (Interest-rate parity) The 3-month interest rates in Euro Zone and the United States are 3% and 6% per annum, respectively. The spot rate of the Euro is US$1.1567. The Euro futures price for a contract deliverable in 3 months at the Chicago Mercantile Exchange (CME) is US$1.1751. Can you find any arbitrage opportunity in this case? (Assuming no transaction costs and no short selling limit.)

P17-8 (Risk of a foreign investment) The standard deviation of the returns on the foreign exchange for the U.S. dollar and the Niwot nebu has been estimated to be 5.81%. The correlation coefficient for the returns on the Niwot Total Stock Index Fund and the foreign currency is −0.22. The standard deviation of the returns on the Niwot Total Stock Index Fund is 32.57%. Calculate the total risk, as measured by the standard deviation, faced by an American investor who invests in the Niwot Total Stock Index Fund.

P17-9 (Purchasing power parity) The current spot exchange rate for US$/Euro is US$1.132 per Euro. The expected inflation rate over the coming 2 years is 3% in the Euro Zone and 2% in the United States, annually. What will be the expected spot exchange rate 2 years from now, according to PPP theory?

P17-10 (Purchasing power parity) Assume that the expected inflation rate in the United States is 3.2% and the expected inflation rate in Germany is 12%. Also assume that no foreign exchange tariffs or barriers to trade exist. What should happen to the exchange rate between the U.S. dollar and the German deutschemark? If the current spot exchange rate for the US$/German deutschemark is US$0.6105 per deutschemark, what is the expected spot exchange rate 1 year from now, according to PPP theory?

CFA EXAM QUESTIONS

The following two questions are adopted from the 1999 CFA Sample Exam, Level I:

1. An analyst gathers the following information:

1-year interest rates:	German mark	4%
	U.S. dollar	5%
Spot exchange rate:	DM/$	1.70

   Based on the information above, the forward exchange rate that will satisfy the interest-rate parity condition is *closest* to:
   A. 1.684.
   B. 1.716.
   C. 1.768.
   D. 1.785.

2. Interest-rate parity describes relationships among current:
   A. interest rates and expected future interest rates.
   B. interest rates, expected future interest rates, and spot/forward exchange rate differentials.
   C. intercountry interest rate differentials and spot/forward foreign exchange rate differentials.
   D. intercountry interest rate differentials and expected inter-country future interest rate differentials.

3. (1994 CFA Exam, Level II)
   A. Assuming that the purchasing power parity relation is always satisfied, describe the effect of a difference in the inflation rates of two countries on the exchange rate between their currencies.
   B. Briefly describe *three* reasons why purchasing power parity might not hold in the short run.
   C. Briefly discuss why the concept of purchasing power parity is useful in investment analysis and management even though parity may not be maintained on a continuing basis.

4. (1998 CFA Exam, Level II)
   A. i. Define relative purchasing power parity.
      ii. Explain *one* reason why, assuming relative purchasing power parity holds in the short run, a foreign investor and a domestic investor purchasing the same asset would expect to receive the same real rate of return.
   B. i. Define interest rate parity.
      ii. Explain *one* reason why interest rate parity must hold in the short run.

FURTHER REFERENCES

Baker, James C. *International Finance: Management Common Market, and Institutions.* Upper Saddle River, NJ: Prentice-Hall, 1998.

   This multinational financial textbook provides a comprehensive 18-chapter review of management procedures, market data, and institutional detail encountered in international transactions. Elementary algebra is supplemented with graphs to create an easy-to-read textbook.

Hull, John C. *Options, Futures and Other Derivatives*, 3d ed. Englewood Cliffs, NJ: Prentice Hall, 1997.

This textbook about futures and options provides a comprehensive, yet concise, coverage of the topics. The book's international discussions reflect the author's European background, and it contains numerous real-life examples from the author's considerable consulting experience. Currency options are addressed in Chapter 12.

Shapiro, Alan C. *Multinational Financial Management*, 6th ed. Upper Saddle River, NJ: Prentice-Hall, 1999.

This 26-chapter corporation finance textbook provides a comprehensive review of international financial institutions, foreign currency markets, international risk management procedures, a good discussion of international accounting, international taxes, international banking, and international corporation finance.

Solnik, Bruno. *International Investments*, 3d ed. Reading, MA: Addison-Wesley, 1996.

This 18-chapter textbook discusses many aspects of foreign investing. Chapters 1, 2, and 3 focus on foreign exchange. Chapter 14 delves into currency risk management.

ENDNOTES

[1] For an informative discussion of 10 scenarios in which the European Monetary Union (EMU) might collapse, see "SS Euro—Sinking the Unsinkable," *Euromoney* (April 1998): 32–37.

[2] For additional discussion of foreign exchange risk, see Fischer Black and Robert Litterman, "Global, Portfolio Optimization," *Financial Analysts Journal* 48, no. 5 (September-October 1992): 30–31. Also see Chapter 13, entitled "International Derivatives Exchange-Traded," and Chapter 14, entitled "International Nonexchange-Traded Derivatives," by James C. Baker, *International Finance: Management Common Market, and Institutions* (Upper Saddle River, NJ: Prentice-Hall, 1998). In addition, see Chapter 6, entitled "Currency Futures and Options Markets," Alan C. Shapiro, *Multinational Financial Management*, 6th ed. (Upper Saddle River, NJ: Prentice-Hall, 1999). Furthermore, see Chapter 3, entitled "The Determination of Forward and Futures Prices," John Hull in *Introduction to Futures and Options Markets*, 2nd ed. (Englewood Cliffs, NJ: Prentice Hall, 1995). See also, Gunter Dufey and S. L. Srinivasuler, "The Case for Corporate Management of Foreign Exchange Risk," *Financial Management* (Fall 1983).

GLOBAL INVESTING

The highest returns on investments are available in one country one year and in a different country the next year. As a result, international investing increases each year. In addition, some invest in different countries to obtain the risk-reduction power of international diversification.

Most inexperienced investors avoid international investments until after they have some experience investing domestically. International investing involves all the risks associated with domestic investing, plus additional risks. Foreign exchange risk, introduced in Chapter 17, is one of those risks.

American Depository Receipts (ADRs) and Global Depository Receipts (GDRs) are special securities that make it easier for investors to deal with foreign exchange risk. Specialized mutual funds that accept deposits in the investor's domestic currency and make international investments using foreign currencies provide another way to deal with foreign exchange risk. These international mutual funds also provide international diversification that reduces risk more than investing in a multinational corporation (MNC). These and related issues are discussed in this chapter.

INTERNATIONAL RISKS

In addition to foreign exchange risk, which was the topic of the preceding chapter, **sovereign risk**, international liquidity risk, international information risk, and other factors make multinational investing a challenge.

Sovereign Risk

Investors in a foreign country should evaluate the possibility that the foreign country's government collapses, its legal system is inadequate, its police force is not able to maintain order, the settlement process for securities transactions breaks down occasionally, or other problems arise. Political upheaval can mean:

◆ The new government might seize investments made by foreigners.

◆ The government may repudiate its debts.*

◆ The government might reschedule the payments of its debts without consulting lenders.

◆ Foreign exchange controls that deny foreign investors the right to withdraw their funds may be imposed.

◆ Disadvantageous taxes and tariffs may be imposed.

◆ The government might force nonresident investors to give partial ownership of the investments to local residents or to the local government.

◆ Hostile forces operating within the country might destroy foreign-owned assets.[1]

Euromoney is an international finance magazine. It evaluates sovereign risk and publishes sovereign risk rankings for 180 countries, as shown in Table 18-1. *Euromoney* updates these sovereign risk rankings about twice each year.

Institutional Investor magazine publishes country risk rankings periodically; these cover fewer countries than *Euromoney's* rankings, and do not reveal much about how its rankings are determined. Large international banks and consulting companies also provide sovereign risk analysis but, unlike the magazines, these reports are not accessible to the public and are not as cheap.[2]

Multinational investors deal with sovereign risk as they do other types of risk: They require higher expected rates of return (discount rates, required rates of return) to induce them to accept more risk. Large foreign investors are sometimes able to increase their expected returns before agreeing to make an investment—by extracting guarantees from government officials in countries that are seeking to increase their inflow of foreign capital. Or, a large foreign investor might be able to improve the safety or return from its investment by obtaining financing from within the country that is seeking an external investor. More often, foreign investors increase their expected returns simply by refusing to invest unless they can get higher returns internationally than are available from similar domestic investments—in other words, an **international risk premium** is added to the investment's required rate of return.

International Liquidity Risk

Chapter 6 defined a market's **liquidity risk** to be price discounts and/or sales commissions that must be paid to sell an asset quickly (see p. 151). **Illiquid assets** are not marketable unless deep price discounts are given *and* high sales commissions are paid. International liquidity risk includes these factors and other risks. Table 6-7 in Chapter 6 (p. 154) lists transaction cost statistics from stock markets around the world.

The mature financial markets listed in Table 6-7 are located in developed countries and are usually more liquid than the emerging markets in a less developed country. An emerging financial market often lacks liquidity because it:

◆ Trades only a modest volume with significant intervals between transactions

◆ Is staffed by inexperienced and/or undercapitalized market makers

◆ Has a legal systems that cannot dependably enforce contracts at a reasonable cost

◆ Is unable to clear security transactions quickly

◆ May be unable to provide access to international cash flows, or

◆ May disappoint international investors in other respects

---

* Countries that repudiated their debts in recent years are China (1949), Cuba (1961), North Korea (1964), and Russia (1998).

TABLE 18-1 · Euromoney's Rankings and Computational Detail of Sovereign Risk

March 2000 rank	September 1999 rank	Countries	Total Score 100	Political Risk 25	Economic Performance 25	Debt Indicators 10	Debt in Default or Rescheduling 10	Credit Ratings 10	Access to Bank Finances 5	Access to Short-Term Finances 5	Access to Capital Markets 5	Forfeiting Discount 5
1	1	Luxembourg	98.83	24.39	25.00	10.00	10.00	10.00	5.00	5.00	5.00	4.44
2	2	Switzerland	97.06	24.95	22.12	10.00	10.00	10.00	5.00	5.00	5.00	4.99
3	4	Norway	94.88	23.79	21.18	10.00	10.00	10.00	5.00	5.00	5.00	4.91
4	3	United States	94.04	25.00	19.04	10.00	10.00	10.00	5.00	5.00	5.00	5.00
5	8	Denmark	93.43	23.67	20.23	10.00	10.00	9.58	5.00	5.00	5.00	4.94
6	6	Netherlands	92.69	24.62	18.12	10.00	10.00	10.00	5.00	5.00	5.00	4.95
7	9	Austria	92.61	23.95	18.73	10.00	10.00	10.00	5.00	5.00	5.00	4.93
8	7	France	92.51	24.44	18.10	10.00	10.00	10.00	5.00	5.00	5.00	4.97
9	12	Finland	92.27	23.97	18.58	10.00	10.00	9.79	5.00	5.00	5.00	4.94
10	14	Sweden	92.19	24.11	18.98	10.00	10.00	9.17	5.00	5.00	5.00	4.94
11	5	Germany	92.18	24.61	17.59	10.00	10.00	10.00	5.00	5.00	5.00	4.97
12	10	United Kingdom	91.84	24.83	17.02	10.00	10.00	10.00	5.00	5.00	5.00	4.98
13	15	Belgium	90.74	23.59	18.05	10.00	10.00	9.17	5.00	5.00	5.00	4.93
14	11	Japan	90.25	23.63	18.39	10.00	10.00	9.58	5.00	5.00	4.47	4.19
15	17	Singapore	90.18	23.27	19.44	10.00	10.00	9.58	5.00	5.00	4.24	3.65
		(Ranks 16–159 omitted)										
160	168	Sao Tome and Principe	23.18	5.78	4.47	0.00	10.00	0.00	0.00	2.93	0.00	0.00
161	164	Congo, Dem. Republic	22.82	1.62	3.25	7.21	9.71	0.00	0.00	1.03	0.00	0.00
162	169	Sierra Leone	22.25	1.20	3.14	6.91	9.97	0.00	0.00	1.03	0.00	0.00
163	141	Laos	21.74	3.39	0.00	7.20	10.00	0.00	0.00	1.03	0.11	0.00
164	136	Uzbekistan	21.31	4.54	5.30	9.49	0.00	0.00	0.10	1.67	0.22	0.00
165	163	New Caledonia	21.03	14.30	3.17	0.00	0.00	0.00	0.00	1.55	2.00	0.00
166	170	Guinea-Bissau	19.96	3.53	2.99	2.59	9.82	0.00	0.00	1.03	0.00	0.00
167	157	Angola	19.93	2.28	2.38	5.08	8.56	0.00	0.00	1.64	0.00	0.00
168	146	Djibouti	19.23	2.48	5.38	0.00	10.00	0.00	0.00	1.38	0.00	0.00
169	172	Libya	18.92	8.79	8.57	0.00	0.00	0.00	0.00	1.55	0.00	0.00
170	173	Somalia	18.79	3.47	3.45	0.00	10.00	0.00	0.00	1.03	0.83	0.00
171	166	Myanmar	18.24	3.33	3.79	0.00	10.00	0.00	0.00	1.03	0.08	0.00
172	142	Tajikistan	16.65	1.73	3.91	9.01	0.88	0.00	0.00	1.03	0.08	0.00
173	175	Liberia	16.61	2.05	3.87	0.00	10.00	0.00	0.00	0.69	0.00	0.00
174	171	Antigua and Barbuda	13.28	4.74	6.14	0.00	0.00	0.00	0.00	1.90	0.50	0.00
175	174	Yugoslavia	12.64	0.69	1.57	0.00	10.00	0.00	0.00	0.00	0.38	0.00
176	176	Surinam	11.78	6.78	3.28	0.00	0.00	0.63	0.00	1.03	0.05	0.00
177	177	Cuba	10.41	3.36	5.85	0.00	0.00	0.00	0.00	1.03	0.17	0.00
178	179	Iraq	6.90	2.42	3.67	0.00	0.00	0.00	0.00	0.69	0.13	0.00
179	180	North Korea	3.65	1.72	0.82	0.00	0.00	0.00	0.00	1.03	0.08	0.00
180	178	Afghanistan	1.84	0.00	0.12	0.00	0.00	0.00	0.00	1.72	0.00	0.00

SOURCE: *Euromoney,* March 2000, 106–9.

THE 1999 RUSSIAN CRISIS

EXAMPLE

During the mid-1990s many people thought Russia was on the road to capitalism. From 1996 to 1997 a diversified common stock investment in Russia earned a spectacularly high average return of 142.8% per year. But by 1998 Russia's political system and financial markets were sliding into crisis. Oil revenues were in steep decline, an already-huge budget deficit was ballooning, and Russia's tax collection system has always been a joke. In August 1998 Russia's government defaulted on billions of U.S. dollars' worth of international debt and devalued Russia's currency.

After the ruble was devalued, inflation skyrocketed to 56% in 1999 and Russia developed an economic never-never land that grew stranger each day. The nation had no effective banking system. Most businesses in Russia were bankrupt, but they kept cranking out goods. To keep the electric utility from turning off the lights, the government made up for missed utility payments by giving the electric utility a tax credit. Companies didn't pay their electricity or heating bills either: They used intercompany barter to keep the utility from cutting off their power.

In this bizarre and oddly flexible economy the ruble was used mainly to buy food and other necessities. IOUs, barter, and other contrived mediums of exchange were used in most dealings between companies. Instead of paying cash wages, many companies issued employees cards to be used in company-owned shops and, perhaps, at a local department store. Workers at one bicycle plant received total compensation of one bicycle per month. It was up to the bicycle workers to use their bicycles to barter for rent, food, and clothing. Most Russians keep their savings hidden at home in U.S. dollars. Economists estimated that as many U.S. dollars as rubles were circulating in Russia in 1999. See Table 18-2.

Where was the Russian's money? One answer lies with companies like Russia's biggest oil company and a major employer, Lukoil. The government let Lukoil and its affiliates pay

TABLE 18-2   Russians Improvised Mediums of Exchange

Swapping	U.S. Dollars	Veksels	Chits	Cross-Cancelling
Bartering for goods and services was common; it was often done with the aid of middlemen who charged a commission for helping to strike a deal.	To hedge against further ruble devaluations and a 56% rate of inflation, many Russians keep their savings at home in U.S. dollars.	Veksels are IOUs issued by companies to pay suppliers and taxes. Veksels may later be sold or traded to a veksel broker for half their face value.	Companies issued coupons to workers instead of cash. These chits may be spent only in a company store where prices are high and the selection is limited.	Companies agree with each other and with some units of the government to cross-cancel each other's debts. Offsetting debts was common.

SUMMARY: During 1999 the Russian ruble was worth little, further ruble devaluations were viewed as still possible, the banking system was in collapse, credit was not available, crime was worsening, and inflation was 56%. Russians improvised ways to collect their wages, buy goods, and pay taxes.

SOURCES: For additional details see *Wall Street Journal,* 26 April 1999, R4. Also see *Business Week,* 26 April 26 1999, 50–52.

only half their taxes in cash. Lukoil paid the other half with IOUs, known as *veksels,* which the company pledged to redeem later for oil. Of course, the government didn't need oil, it needed money. Lacking cash, the government gave *veksels* to suppliers as payment for goods and services, and also passed them along to finance the public schools. Noncash forms of payment paid for a large portion of Russia's declining economic activity. A large amount of every Russian citizen's time and energy was spent negotiating, bartering, and trying to arrange mediums of exchange.

All this gave rise to "veksel brokers." Domestic currency brokers bought *veksels* for rubles and resold them to customers who needed to buy food or clothing. The traders typically buy veksels for 50% of their face value, leaving everyone except the currency traders starved for cash.

International Information Risk

Information-gathering should precede and accompany every investment. Information for foreign investments is more difficult to obtain than domestic information because of things like language differences, currency differences, dissimilar systems of weights and measurements, different political systems, international mail taking longer than domestic mail, unfamiliar geography, different financial reporting techniques in each country, and "outsiders'" difficulty in obtaining information. These considerations are important because information has value.

Foreign Exchange Risk

The price of one currency stated in terms of another currency is called an exchange rate. Foreign exchange rates fluctuate randomly and continuously. Chapter 17 showed that one foreign investment could be decomposed into two foreign investments: First the domestic investor purchases a foreign currency. Second, the domestic investor uses the foreign currency to purchase the foreign asset.

Table 18-3 provides a statistical summary of investing in the stock market indexes of 19 different countries from 1970 to 1997 inclusive. The Morgan Stanley Capital International (MSCI) stock market indexes described in Chapter 11 underline the computations.

Table 18-3 contains risk-and-return statistics computed over a 28-year period that preceded the introduction of the Euro. The average returns and standard deviations for each country are computed for investors using five different currencies: U.S. dollars (US$), Japanese yen (Y), German deutschemark (DM), British pound (£), and each market's domestic currency. Table 18-3 documents 95 different international investment strategies and 19 investments made in each country's domestic currency. The table summarizes investments made in each country using four different currencies that create 76 strategies that involve foreign exchange.*

19 countries	95 total investment strategies
Times: 5 currencies	Less: 19 domestic strategies
Equals: 95 total investment strategies	Equals: 76 foreign strategies

The column on the far right of Table 18-3 is headed "Local" and shows the average return and the standard deviation of returns (in parentheses) if the investment was made in the

---

* Since the currencies of the United States, Japan, Germany, and England are used throughout Table 18-3, these four countries' currencies are not foreign in those four countries. The total number of truly international strategies is [(76 international strategies) − (4 artificially international strategies) =] 72 foreign strategies.

TABLE 18-3   Nominal Returns from Investments in the MSCI Stock Market Indexes of 19 Developed Stock Markets, 1970–97 Inclusive

Return from Investing in Country via Currency:

Investment in Country:	U.S.$	Yen	DM[b]	Pound[b]	Local
United States[a]	12.5	8.5	9.7	14.0	12.5
	(16.4)	(22.8)	(23.7)	(23.2)	(16.4)
Japan	13.3	9.3	10.5	14.9	9.3
	(36.3)	(29.3)	(33.9)	(38.9)	(29.3)
United Kingdom	13.8	9.7	10.9	15.3	15.3
	(30.5)	(30.3)	(34.0)	(32.8)	(32.8)
Germany[b]	12.3	8.3	9.5	13.8	9.5
	(30.0)	(27.0)	(26.1)	(27.2)	(26.1)
France[b]	12.3	8.4	9.5	13.9	12.7
	(29.1)	(27.5)	(27.6)	(29.2)	(26.5)
Canada	10.1	6.3	7.4	11.6	11.3
	(16.7)	(24.2)	(22.1)	(19.5)	(16.2)
Netherlands[b]	16.8	12.7	13.9	18.4	14.4
	(18.7)	(21.9)	(22.9)	(23.4)	(22.6)
Italy[b]	6.9	3.2	4.2	8.4	11.0
	(39.6)	(32.2)	(35.9)	(34.3)	(35.9)
Australia	8.5	4.7	5.8	10.0	10.7
	(26.2)	(27.1)	(31.7)	(27.9)	(26.7)
Switzerland	14.6	10.5	11.7	16.1	10.2
	(25.7)	(24.5)	(24.9)	(25.7)	(24.7)
Spain[b]	10.2	6.3	7.4	11.7	13.3
	(32.3)	(29.2)	(29.6)	(32.5)	(28.7)
Hong Kong	19.7	15.5	16.6	21.3	20.8
	(51.8)	(51.8)	(55.2)	(57.2)	(51.7)
Belgium[b]	15.5	11.4	12.5	17.0	14.3
	(23.0)	(20.7)	(20.5)	(23.2)	(22.2)
Denmark	15.2	11.2	12.3	16.8	14.9
	(29.7)	(31.9)	(35.2)	(34.7)	(34.6)
Sweden	16.4	12.3	13.4	18.0	18.2
	(24.2)	(25.8)	(28.1)	(27.8)	(28.1)
Singapore	8.3	5.6	7.8	10.7	7.0
	(32.1)	(30.6)	(34.5)	(36.7)	(31.2)
Austria[b]	11.1	7.2	8.3	12.6	8.3
	(39.5)	(37.0)	(29.9)	(35.0)	(29.9)
Norway	13.2	9.2	10.3	14.7	13.3
	(48.8)	(58.3)	(46.7)	(46.6)	(45.9)
South Africa	5.6	2.9	5.1	8.0	18.0
	(31.8)	(27.8)	(26.1)	(33.9)	(26.3)

[a]Top line for each country: Average return, (Second Line: Standard Deviation)

[b]This country is (currency belongs to) one of the 11 founding members of the European Monetary Union (EMU). After July 1, 2002 the national currency will cease to exist and be replaced by the Euro.

SOURCE: Calculated from Morgan Stanley Capital International (MSCI) annual returns. South African and Singapore data are from the Financial Times/Standard & Poor's Actuaries World Indices over 1981–97 inclusive. Data, software, and computations from Ibbotson Associates, Chicago.

local currency; this column contains no foreign exchange risk. For example, consider the United Kingdom: investing British pounds sterling in the British MSCI stock market index over the 28-year sample yielded an average rate of return of 15.3% and a standard deviation of 32.8%. Continuing with the United Kingdom, the statistics show the results if the same investment were made in a foreign MSCI index using a foreign currency (dollar, yen, or deutschemark); these return-and-risk statistics do contain foreign exchange risk.

Table 18-3 contrasts the effects from investing in a risky domestic asset with investing in a similar risky foreign asset that involves foreign exchange risk. Eqns. 17-5 and 17-7 in Chapter 17 analyzed these effects. Since the currency risk may be positively or negatively correlated with the foreign stock market risk, it can increase or decrease the investment's return and risk.

SIMPLE INTERNATIONAL DIVERSIFICATION

Reconsider *simple diversification* from Chapter 14. Figure 14-1 (p. 400) illustrates how randomly selecting different domestic stocks reduces portfolio risk as additional stocks are added to the portfolio. Figure 14-1 shows that, on average, combining a few dozen randomly selected domestic stocks eliminates diversifiable risk and leaves the portfolio with only undiversifiable risk remaining.

We also looked at diversifying across randomly selected domestic stocks that are each taken from different industries. The summary statistics in Table 14-1 (p. 401) show that *diversifying across industries* within a single country does not reduce portfolio risk any better than simple diversification. Diversifying across industries is no more effective than random diversification because the competing firms in a country tend to be highly positively correlated. Chapter 14's investigation of domestic diversification prepared us for this chapter's investigation of international diversification.

Barriers to Entry. Complications that frustrate international investors can enhance the benefits a portfolio can obtain from multinational diversification.[3] International barriers to entry include language barriers, different time zones, restrictions on the flow of foreign currencies, lack of uniformly prepared financial statements, cultural differences between countries, government restrictions on foreign ownership, and markets that do not provide full disclosure of information.[4] When such barriers exist they cause international **market segmentation** that tends to make international diversification more beneficial. If barriers to international diversification did not exist, the world could move closer to having homogeneous markets. Two conditions must exist simultaneously to have **homogeneous markets**: There can be no barriers to investing or trade between countries, and the economic activity of all countries must be highly positively correlated. Multinational diversification would not be beneficial if the world's capital markets were perfectly homogeneous.

Solnik's Diversification Study. To gauge the benefits obtained from diversification across different countries, Bruno Solnik used stock returns from eight different countries over a 6-year period.* Solnik analyzed weekly data from Belgium (20 stocks), France (65 stocks), Germany (40 stocks), Italy (30 stocks), Netherlands (25 stocks), Switzerland (15 stocks), the

---

* Bruno Solnik was extending the methodology introduced by John L. Evans and Stephen H. Archer in "Diversification and the Reduction of Dispersion: Empirical Analysis," *Journal of Finance* (December 1968). The Evans-Archer results were illustrated in Figure 14-1. Unfortunately, the benefits from Solnik's study cannot be taken too literally because Solnik's study did not make foreign exchange adjustments needed to make the rates of return from different countries comparable. For details, see Bruno H. Solnik, "Why Not Diversify Internationally?" *Financial Analysts Journal* (July-August 1974): 48–54.

United Kingdom (50 stocks), and the United States (65 stocks). Solnik's pre-Euro sample period spanned 6 years. As with the preceding studies of domestic simple diversification and domestic diversification across industries, Solnik's investigation assumes the investor has no ability to select profitable investments. Solnik implemented this no-skill assumption by selecting stocks randomly and assigning each stock an equal weight. He calculated the proportion of variance that could be eliminated from portfolios by increasing the number of randomly selected stocks included in the portfolios. The portfolio variances were averaged for each country's 2-stock portfolios, 3-stock portfolios, 4-stock portfolios, 5-stock portfolios, and portfolios containing successively larger numbers of randomly selected stocks.

Bruno Solnik assumed only U.S. dollars were invested in the stocks from every country and, as a result, his results combine foreign exchange risk with the risk from investing in foreign securities. Essentially, Solnik's study takes the position of a U.S. citizen who is making all investments from the United States. Figure 18-1A, B, and C summarizes Solnik's diversification findings.

To evaluate different ways to diversify, Solnik evaluated different random diversification strategies. Stocks were randomly selected (1) across countries, (2) across industries, and (3) across countries with currency hedging to reduce foreign exchange risk. Panel (A) of Figure 18-1 shows that selection across countries is superior to domestic diversification within the United States. (B) suggests that random selection across countries and across both countries and industries is a superior strategy to diversifying across industries alone. (C) is similar to (A), but in addition (C) shows that a substantial portion of the risk-reducing value of multinational diversification occurs whether or not the portfolio is hedged against foreign exchange losses. The portfolios that are hedged against foreign exchange losses have only slightly less risk than the unhedged portfolio, but these modest hedging benefits are not free. The rate of return from the investing with currency hedges is reduced by transactions costs and by missing those gains in which a hedged position is unable to participate.

Solnik's experiments with random diversification suggest a portfolio need not contain more than about three dozen common stocks to achieve substantial benefits from either domestic or international diversification. Similar studies of the same countries that used more recent data, but data that preceded the introduction of the Euro, reached conclusions like Solnik's.

PORTFOLIO ANALYSIS OF TWO-COUNTRY DIVERSIFICATION

Markowitz's portfolio theory provides a tool to analyze international investing.[5] Consider a U.S. citizen investing in either an international mutual fund that is denominated in U.S. dollars or iShares MSCI.[6] As mentioned in Chapter 12, iShares MSCI are U.S. dollar–denominated indexed mutual funds that invest in foreign stocks. The investments are assumed to be denominated in U.S. dollars to eliminate discussions of foreign exchange from this example. In this two-country model the internationally diversified portfolio has an expected return that is determined by the expected returns from each country and the proportion of funds the investor decides to invest in each country, as shown in the box below.

TWO-COUNTRY PORTFOLIO ANALYSIS   **EXAMPLE**

The expected return from a two-country portfolio is defined in Eqn. 18-1.

$$E(r_p) = (x)E(r_1) + (1-x)E(r_2) \qquad (18\text{-}1)$$

FIGURE 18-1 Results from Various Diversification Strategies: (A) International Diversification, (B) Diversification Across Industries, (C) International Diversification with Foreign Exchange Hedging

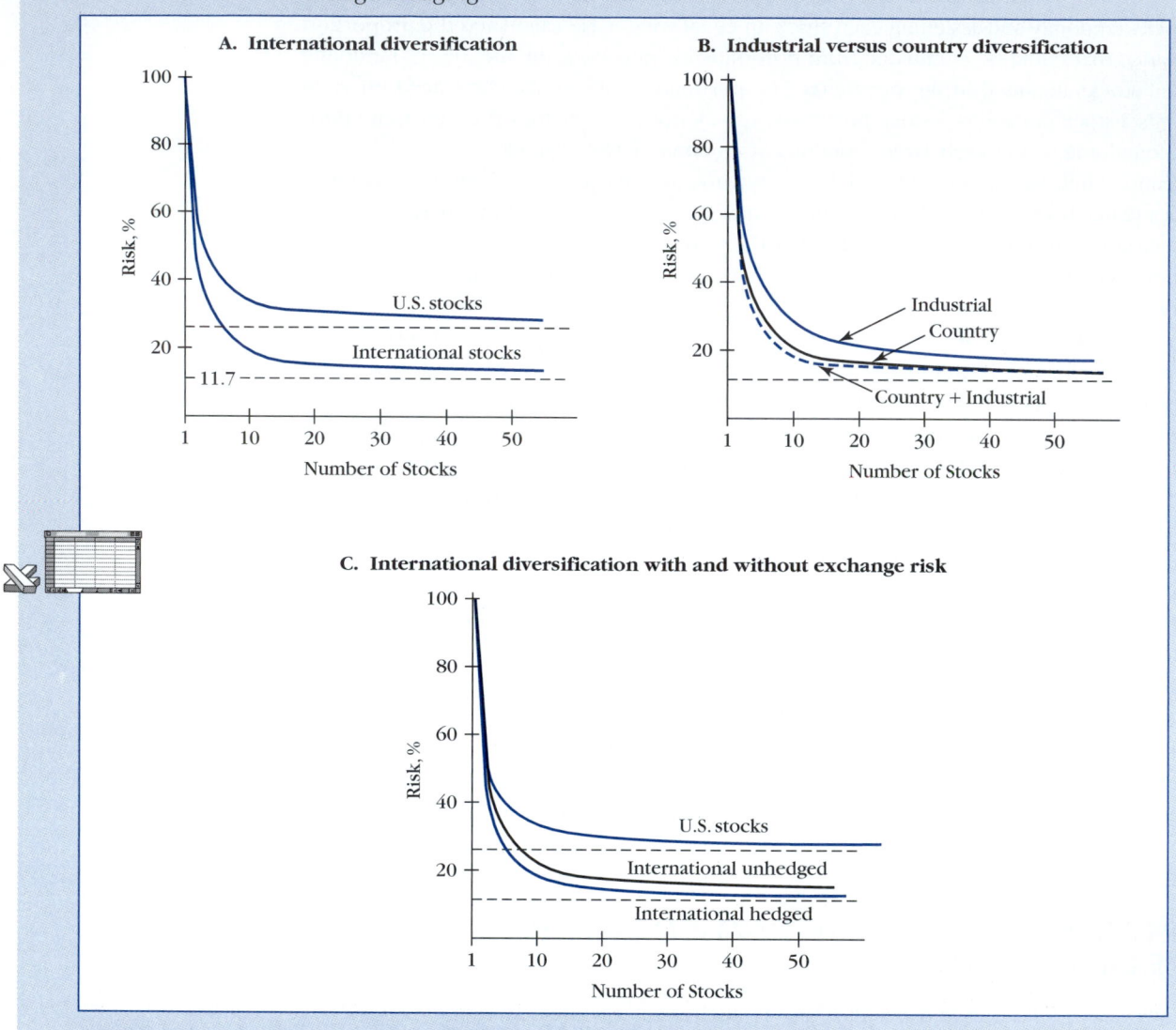

The vertical axis measures the risk (standard deviation) associated with randomly diversifying among a stated number of stocks from the indicated category, stated as a percentage of the risk from the average 1-stock investment. (A) Multinational diversification reduces risk more than domestic diversification. (B) International diversification is slightly more effective when combined with industry diversification. (C) Hedging the foreign-exchange risk in an international portfolio reduces its risk slightly below the portfolio's risk without hedging.

SOURCE: Bruno H. Solnik, "Why Not Diversify Internationally?" *Financial Analysts Journal* (July-August 1974): 48–54, Figures 9, 10, and 11.

Eqn. 18-1 is defined from the perspective of an investor residing in Country 1. As mentioned, the terms are defined to keep foreign exchange risk implicit rather than complicate the analysis by making it explicit. It is possible to make an alternative simplifying assumption. It might also be assumed that the foreign exchange rates between Countries 1 and 2 are pegged so the exchange rate does not fluctuate. Either assumption simplifies the formulas equivalently.

$E(r_p)$ = Expected return from an international portfolio of marketable securities from Countries 1 and 2

$E(r_i)$ = Expected return in Country i

x = Proportion (weight) of the international portfolio's assets invested in Country 1, where $1.0 > x > 0$

$1 - x$ = Proportion (weight) of assets invested in Country 2

$$VAR(r_p) = x^2\, VAR(r_1) + (1-x)^2\, VAR(r_2) + 2x(1-x)\sigma_1\sigma_2\rho_{1,2} \qquad (18\text{-}2)$$

$VAR(r_1) = \sigma_1^2$ = *Variance* of returns in Country 1

$VAR(r_2) = \sigma_2^2$ = *Variance* of returns in Country 2 as seen from Country 1 and adjusted for any changes in foreign exchange rates

$\rho_{1,2}$ = *Correlation* coefficient between the two countries' returns

Computing the Impact of Two-Country Correlations on the Portfolio's Variance

$E(r_1) = E(r_2) = 10\%$ = Expected returns in the two countries

$\sigma_1^2 = \sigma_2^2 = 16\%$ = Variances of returns

$x = 1 - x = 0.50$ = Proportion (weight) of asets invested in each country

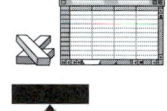

$$E(r_p) = (x)E(R_1) + (1-x)E(r_2) \qquad (18\text{-}1)$$

$$E(r_p) = (0.5)(0.1) + (1.0 - 0.5)(0.1) = 0.1 = 10.0\% \qquad (18\text{-}1a)$$

$$VAR(r_p) = x^2 VAR(r_1) + (1-x)^2 VAR(r_2) + 2x(1-x)\sigma_1\sigma_2\rho_{1,2} \qquad (18\text{-}2)$$

$$= (0.5)^2(0.16) + (1.0 - 0.5)^2(0.16) + 2(0.5)(1.0 - 0.5)\sqrt{0.16}\sqrt{0.16}\,\rho_{1,2} \quad (18\text{-}2a)$$

$$VAR(r_p) = 0.08 + 0.08\rho_{1,2}$$

A numerical illustration of the variance reduction follows:

If the correlation is:	+1.0	+.50	0.0	−.50	−1.0
then $VAR(r_p)$ will be:	0.16	0.12	0.08	0.04	0

Conclusion: As the correlation between the returns from two countries declines from +1 to −1, if all other factors are held constant, the risk of the two-country portfolio declines also.

All this shows that intercountry correlations are important to risk reduction through international diversification. Table 11-15 in Chapter 11 (p. 326) shows the intercountry correlations between stock market indexes from different countries. These correlations can be used to assess the risk-reduction possibilities from international diversification.

Correlations between emerging markets in Table 11-15B are generally lower than the correlations between the developed markets in Table 11-15A. Although no negative correlations are in Table 11-15A, several negative correlations are found between emerging markets. The lowest value is the correlation of -0.19 between the Czech Republic and Jordan. The high positive correlation of 0.77 between the U.S. stock market and its next-door neighbor Canada characterizes the way highly developed markets can move together. Using the correlations from Table 11-15 in Eqn. 18-2 shows that equal investments in emerging countries like the Czech Republic and Jordan, for example, can produce less portfolio variance than investments in developed countries like Canada and the United States. In other words, international diversification can reduce risk—especially when countries with emerging markets are involved.

INTERNATIONAL EFFICIENT FRONTIERS

Markowitz portfolio analysis from Chapter 14 can be used to evaluate international opportunities. The following discussion reviews four different international efficient frontiers. As you may anticipate, more desirable Markowitz efficient frontiers emerge as the number of countries in which investments are made increases.

Table 11-14 in Chapter 11 (pp. 324–325) contains two panels of risk-and-return statistics based on the Morgan Stanley Capital International (MSCI) stock market indexes from various countries. Table 11-14 lists risk-and-return statistics from countries that have emerging stock markets and similar statistics for developed markets. A Markowitz efficient frontier for 21 emerging market countries was computed using statistics in Table 11-14 as input data. And another efficient frontier for 21 countries with developed markets was computed using statistics from Table 11-14 as inputs. The input statistics from Table 11-14 were combined with the correlation coefficients in Table 11-15 in Chapter 11 (p. 326) to compute international efficient frontiers. Four international efficient frontiers are illustrated in Figure 18-2; the efficient frontier computed from the developed markets data is represented by the curve *DD*, and the curve *EE* represents the efficient frontier computed from the emerging markets data.

The curve *UU* in Figure 18-2 is the efficient frontier for the U.S. stock markets. This efficient frontier was computed from 8 different U.S. stock market indexes that have few securities in common. Monthly returns were drawn from the same 11-year period for all countries.

The curve *GG* in Figure 18-2 is the global efficient frontier. The global efficient frontier was computed from the 50 stock market indexes listed here; it dominates the other three international efficient frontiers in Figure 18-2.

Sources of Raw Data for Global Efficient Frontier

8 U.S. Investment sectors	8 Indexes (some overlapping)
21 Emerging market countries	21 Indexes (mutually exclusive)
21 Developing market countries	<u>21</u> Indexes (mutually exclusive)
	50 Indexes

Point *SP* in Figure 18-2 indicates the risk level and average rate of return for the SP500 stock market index. The U.S. efficient frontier dominates the SP500 index because that efficient frontier was computed from the S&P500 and seven other U.S. market indexes. The other indexes sometimes provide more desirable investment opportunities because they might have higher returns, smaller risk statistics, and/or lower correlation coefficients than the S&P500.

The risk-and-return combinations available from investing only in emerging markets dominate most of the U.S. opportunities and all of the developed market opportunities illustrated

FIGURE 18-2   Contrasting Efficient Frontiers Derived from Different
International Opportunities

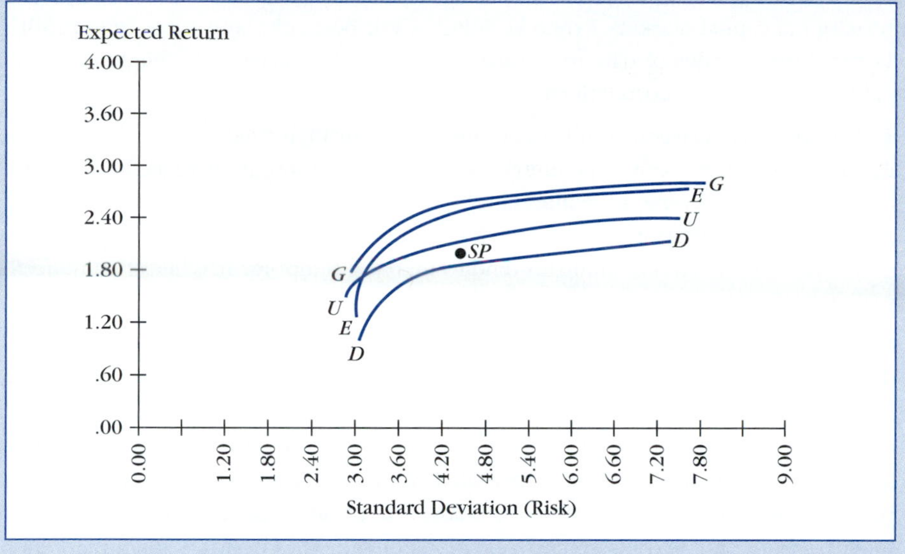

The global efficient frontier, denoted *GG*, dominates all others because it considers all the opportunities. Efficient frontier *EE* is from emerging markets data alone; at the highest returns *EE* dominates *UU*. *UU* is from only the U.S. stock markets. Efficient frontier *DD* is completely dominated; it is computed from markets data from non-U.S. developed countries.

SOURCE: Ibbotson Associates EnCorr database supplied monthly international return and foreign exchange data for investments that were made in U.S. dollars from January 1989 through December 1999. Ibbotson Associates EnCorr Optimizer contains the quadratic program that computed the efficient frontiers.

in Figure 18-2. The emerging markets efficient frontier dominates the efficient frontiers for the developed market for two reasons. First, the correlations between the emerging markets are low, and a few are negative. Second, 11 of the emerging market countries had very high average returns during the period that was sampled. To keep the 11 countries that had extremely high returns from pushing the other emerging markets completely out of the efficient frontier, the weights of these 11 countries were each constrained to a maximum value of 1% of the portfolios. The emerging markets efficient frontier (curve EE) in Figure 18-2 would have had even higher returns if the weight constraints on the 11 emerging countries that had very high returns had been removed.*

International portfolio analysis suggests that Markowitz efficient portfolios will contain investments from different countries.[7] However, government imposed policies that prohibit international capital flows or restrict the use of foreign exchange may make the theoretically optimal portfolios unattainable.

---

*   Weight constraints on the 11 emerging market countries that had very high returns were added because (1) the authors believe that these 11 countries' very high historical rates to return were unsustainable at such high levels, and (2) Markowitz's quadratic programming efficient frontier solutions are sensitive to input statistics with extreme values.

CORRELATION COEFFICIENTS BETWEEN DIFFERENT COUNTRIES

Correlations between countries are a key factor that can improve investment opportunities in international capital markets. Bruno H. Solnik, Cyril Boucrelle, and Yann Le Fur (SBL) analyzed over three decades of data from four countries. SBL's research highlights four conclusions about international correlations:[8]

1. Correlations between countries are not stable through time.
2. The correlations between countries seem to be trending upward as the world's financial markets become more integrated.
3. Standard deviations are also somewhat unstable.
4. Correlations between countries tend to increase temporarily when the financial markets' volatility increases.

SBL analyzed the returns to a U.S. investor who invested U.S. dollars in Germany, France, and the United Kingdom. Figure 18-3 shows what happened when U.S. dollars were invested in Japan. French and German investment results are not illustrated, but they are similar to Japan. Figure 18-3A illustrates four things: (1) the correlation coefficient (left scale) between the U.S. and Japanese stock markets fluctuates (solid wiggling line) through both negative and positive values, (2) a straight line that traces the trend through time of this correlation coefficient, and (3 and 4) the standard deviations of the two country's stock markets (measured by the scale on the right side). Similarly, Figure 18-3B illustrates the correlation coefficient between the U.S. and Japanese bond markets (left scale), a straight line that traces the trend of this correlation coefficient, and the standard deviations of the two country's bond markets (right scale).

The Behavior of Correlations Between Nations' Financial Markets

In Figure 18-3A and B the correlation coefficients between the U.S. and Japanese markets fluctuated over wide ranges. The correlation between the two stock markets fluctuated from as low as −0.35 to as high as 0.60 between 1961 and 1994. Similarly, the correlation between the U.S. and Japanese bond markets fluctuated from a low of −0.18 up to a high of 0.70 between 1963 and 1993. These correlations between two country's financial markets are not what statisticians call efficient statistics (minimum variance statistical estimates of the underlying parameter). Financially speaking, these unstable correlations through time mean that it is necessary to periodically rebalance (recompute and reallocate) international portfolios.

The trend lines in Figure 18-3A and B slope upward, indicating that the values of the correlation coefficients between the U.S. and Japanese markets rose through time. The correlations appear to be trending gradually upward in most of the markets. A tendency for the values of the correlation coefficients between nations' financial markets to rise over time might result from increasingly integrated financial markets and national economies. As telecommunications, faxes, the Internet, and satellites make long-distant communications easier, this trend is expected to continue.

Inspection of Figure 18-3A and B reveals the correlation between the U.S. and Japanese financial markets often increases when either country's financial markets become more volatile. A similar tendency can also be discerned in the values of the correlation coefficients between other countries' financial markets. When financial markets become highly volatile is precisely when risk-reducing diversification is needed most. This last finding is bad news for international investors.

FIGURE 18-3 Intertemporal Comparisons Between U.S. and Japanese Correlations and Standard Deviations: (A), Stock Markets and (B) Bond Markets

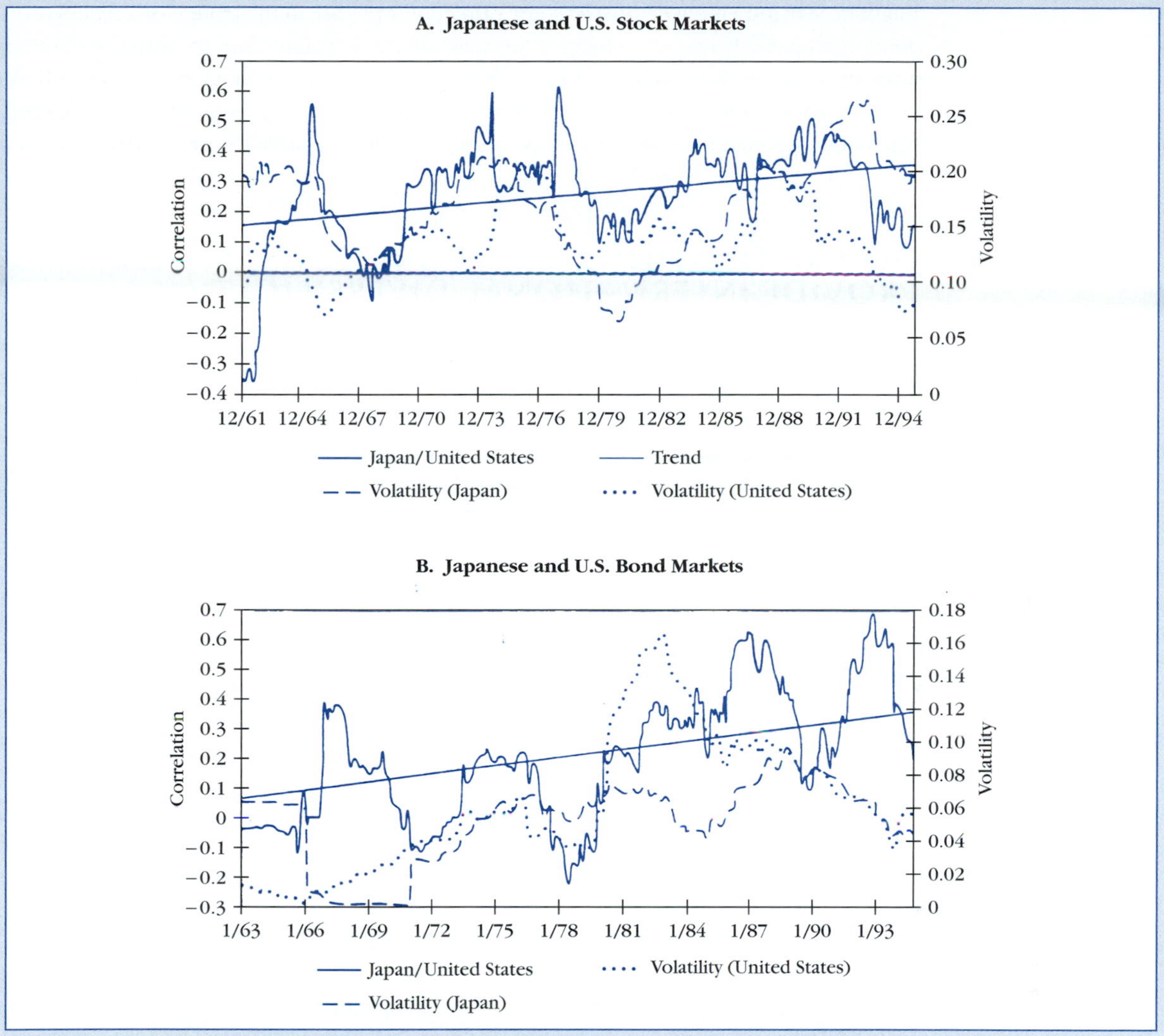

A. Japanese and U.S. Stock Markets

B. Japanese and U.S. Bond Markets

Analyzing the stock and bond markets of several countries suggests four conclusions. The correlations between countries are unstable through time. The correlations between countries seem to be trending upward as the world's financial markets become more integrated. The standard deviations are also somewhat unstable. The correlations between countries tend to increase with market volatility. The U.S.-Japan examples above illustrate these general conclusions.

SOURCE: Bruno H. Solnik, Cyril Boucrelle, and Yann Le Fur, "International Market Correlation and Volatility," *Financial Analysts Journal* (September-October 1996): 20, 28, Figures 1, 5.

Fundamental Reasons for Low Intercountry Correlations

Most intercountry correlations between securities markets are low because different countries and their economic prospects are not tied closely together. Different countries have different political systems (for example, capitalism versus socialism), different currencies (such as the Mexican peso and the Japanese yen), different foreign exchange regulations (for example, fixed versus floating exchange rates), different trade restrictions (such as import and export limitations and/or tariffs), different political alliances (such as socialistic nations and the capitalistic nations), and various other barriers to international trade. Furthermore, different countries may be at different phases in their business cycle (for example, the United States might be starting a recovery just as some other countries are in the trough of a recession), undergoing foreign exchange rate changes (because of different intercountry inflation rates, interest rates, monetary policies, and/or fiscal policies), or in differing military postures (such as peace versus cold war versus active aggression) at any given time. As a result of these differences, the fluctuations in countries' security markets are not highly positively correlated with each other.[9]

DO MULTINATIONAL CORPORATIONS (MNCs) PROVIDE INTERNATIONAL DIVERSIFICATION?

Table 18-4 lists the largest corporations in the world. These giant multinational corporations (MNCs) beg the question: Does investing in a MNC provide a quick and easy route to risk-reducing international diversification?

TABLE 18-4   The Largest Corporations Are Multinational

Rank, April 2000	Company	Country	Market Capitalization, US$ Millions
1	General Electric	United States	534,046.40
2	Cisco Systems	United States	434,066.80
3	Intel	United States	388,089.40
4	Microsoft	United States	346,773.10
5	NTT Docomo	Japan	319,714.30
6	Vodafone Airtouch	United Kingdom	291,934.90
7	Exxon Mobil	United States	277,956.20
8	Wal-Mart Stores	United States	262,231.20
9	Nokia	Finland	241,308.10
10	Citigroup	United States	207,466.80
11	NTT	Japan	207,261.50
12	Oracle	United States	205,607.10
13	Deutsche Telekom	Germany	199,716.40
14	Toyota Motor	Japan	198,011.80
15	Royal Dutch/Shell	Netherland/United Kingdom	195,801.50
16	Lucent Technologies	United States	193,240.80
17	BP Amoco	United Kingdom	191,071.50
18	International Business Machines	United States	191,035.50
19	AIG Group	United States	172,343.70
20	Pfizer	United States	167,431.50
21	Merck	United States	166,648.50
22	Ericsson	Sweden	165,400.30
23	France Telecom	France	158,967.30
24	AT&T	United States	156,742.60
25	Sun Microsystems	United States	153,077.60

SOURCE: *Financial Times*, 4 May 2000. The data is excerpted from the FT500 listing of the 500 largest companies in the world compiled by the *Financial Times* annually.

Researchers investigated MNCs from around the world to see if their investors obtain as much international diversification as they can by investing in a portfolio of stocks from different countries.[10] MNCs did not fare well in this comparison. Variability in the MNCs' stock returns are largely determined by variations in the MNCs' domestic stock markets. Investigating nine countries showed that between 69% and 93% of the countries' MNCs' variability is explained by simultaneous stock market index fluctuations in the MNC's country of domicile.*[11] This means that although only 21% of Coca-Cola's global sales take place in the United States, where the company is headquartered, conditions in the U.S. stock market exert the predominant market influence over KO's stock price.

The most encouraging news came from a related study that showed that as the percentage of a MNC's sales occurring outside its domestic market increases, that MNC's stock price dependency on (correlation with) its domestic stock market tends to decrease.[12] Nevertheless, investing in MNCs like those listed in Table 18-3 does not provide as much international diversification as investing in a portfolio of securities from different countries.

DEPOSITORY RECEIPTS

The remainder of this chapter considers alternative arrangements investors can use to diversify internationally. Depository receipts, for instance, are marketable ownership securities that are used by international investors. Two types of depository receipts are popular: American Depository Receipts (ADRs) and **Global Depository Receipts (GDRs)**.

American Depository Receipts (ADRs)

When a corporation headquartered outside the United States has its common stock traded within the United States, the securities that are traded may be **American Depository Receipts (ADRs)** instead of the foreign corporation's common stock. An ADR is a document that provides evidence of an ownership share in a foreign corporation. To keep the U.S. dollar price of an ADR in a range that is convenient for American investors, one ADR might represent one or more of the underlying foreign shares of stock. ADRs were created by J. P. Morgan in 1927 to remove the foreign exchange complications from international investing, and to generate fee income for the bank that acts as the depository for the ADRs. ADRs trade at brokerage commission rates that frequently equal the commissions charged for domestic transactions. These ADR commissions are typically less than the commissions a small investor must pay to make an investment directly in a foreign security. In addition, trades clear within 3 days in the United States, while some foreign transactions can take weeks to settle.

Origination and Trading of ADRs. ADRs are created by large American commercial banks that have international operations.** New York City banks like Bank of New York, Citigroup's Citibank, and J. P. Morgan are the leaders in the field. The banks create ADRs by purchasing a foreign corporation's securities in the name of a *Section 20 subsidiary corporation* owned by the bank. A Section 20 subsidiary is eligible to conduct investment banking activities in the United States under specific powers granted by the Federal Reserve Board. The parent

---

* Empirical research suggests that buying shares in a large multinational corporation is not a highly effective way to reduce risk via international diversification.
** The phrase *American Depository Share (ADS)* is frequently used interchangeably with the phrase *American Depository Receipt (ADR)*. Technically, the ADS is the instrument that actually is traded, and the ADR is the underlying document that represents a number of ADS.

bank keeps the shares of stock underlying the ADRs in its vault in the bank subsidiary's name. Investors are issued an ADR stating that the bank is holding the underlying shares for the client. For example, an American investor might purchase an ADR evidencing the fact that J. P. Morgan's subsidiary is holding 100 shares of Toyota common stock in the bank's vault. The bank will collect Toyota's cash dividends in Japanese yen and convert the yen to U.S. dollars to pay the American investors their dividends. ADR investors pay a modest fee of a penny or two that is taken out of each security's cash dividend payment. This ADR fee is less than the foreign exchange commissions an investor who received cash dividends in Japanese yen would incur to convert a small amount of yen to dollars. This quarterly fee income for the bank and other custodial fees can motivate an international bank to create a Section 20 subsidiary to provide ADRs.

ADRs covering more than 2,000 corporations from dozens of foreign countries are traded in the United States.[13] Table 18-5 lists some ADRs traded in high volume. Most of the corporations represented by banks' ADRs are large, well-known, and have their ADRs listed at an organized exchange or are in the NASDAQ national market system. On some days more shares of a popular stock (like Toyota) are traded in the United States via ADRs than are traded in Japan.[14] Most ADR investors receive about the same benefits that someone who owned the underlying security would receive without paying any additional brokerage commissions, without losing any marketability, and without transacting in a foreign currency.

TABLE 18-5 ADRs Traded in High Volume

Corporation	Headquarters Country	Traded in U.S. Market
BP-Amoco	United Kingdom	NYSE
B.A.T Industries	United Kingdom	AMEX
Hanson Trust	United Kingdom	NYSE
Glaxo Wellcome	United Kingdom	NYSE
Reuters Holdings	United Kingdom	NASDAQ
Vodafone	United Kingdom	NYSE
Telefonos de Mexico (Telmex)	Mexico	NASDAQ
De Beers Consolidated	South Africa	NASDAQ
Volvo	Sweden	NASDAQ
LM Ericsson	Sweden	NASDAQ
Mitsubishi Corporation	Japan	Pink sheets
Toyota	Japan	NASDAQ
Nestle S. A.	Switzerland	Pink sheets
Royal Dutch Petroleum	Netherlands	NYSE
Unilever	Netherlands	NYSE
Telefonica Nacional de Espana	Spain	NYSE
Korea Telecom	Korea	NYSE
Nokia	Finland	NYSE
Telecomunicacoes Brasileiras (Telebras)	Brazil	NYSE
Compania de Telecomunicacione Chile	Chile	NYSE
News Corp.	Australia	NYSE

SOURCE: Bank of New York in New York City maintains a Web site that provides considerable information about ADRs and GDRs and BNY's European Depository Receipts (EDRs). Visit: www.bankofny.com/adr

ADRs Are Not Problem-Free. ADRs on stocks that are issued by well-known international corporations, sponsored by the issuer, and listed on an organized stock exchange in the United States are highly liquid. Stock issuers that sponsor their own ADR issues provide complete financial statements in foreign languages, and even pay the ADRs' fees. But, many stock issuers do not sponsor the ADRs on their stock.

Investors must pay the ADR fees if the stock's issuer does not sponsor the ADRs. *Unsponsored ADRs* may not provide a complete set of financial statements in English. Furthermore, many ADRs not listed on an organized stock exchange are traded instead in the over-the-counter (OTC) market. Some of these ADRs are traded in an inactive part of the OTC market. Unsponsored ADRs that are issued by obscure corporations and are traded OTC are not very liquid. However, some well-known, large corporations whose ADRs are liquid prefer to have their ADRs traded OTC instead of being listed at an organized exchange—to avoid costly disclosure requirements and stringent accounting conventions that exist in the United States. Corporate control is another problem that can arise with ADRs. Some depository banks are allowed to vote on behalf of the ADR shareholders under certain circumstances.

Other problems may haunt an ADR investor. For example, price volatility may be high in the country where the ADR issuer's corporate headquarters is located. In particular, countries that have small, illiquid, and unregulated emerging securities markets can experience breathtaking stock price volatility. Foreign income is typically subject to more complicated tax regulations than domestic income. Most investors find that it is more difficult to follow the news about a foreign security than to follow domestic news. Finally, as the following example illustrates, ADRs are still subject to exchange rate risk.

A HYPOTHETICAL COLLAPSE FOR AN INVESTMENT IN TOYOTA ADRS   EXAMPLE

Suppose that an American investor invests in Toyota ADRs and any one of the following three hypothetical events occurs: (1) The Japanese yen depreciates by 50% relative to the U.S. dollar, (2) the U.S. dollar appreciates by 100% relative to the Japanese yen, or (3) a catastrophe causes the market price (in yen, on the Japanese stock exchange) of Toyota's common stock to drop 50%. Any one of these three events will cause the U.S. dollar–denominated market value of a Toyota ADR to drop in value by 50%. The American investor need not become involved in any foreign exchange transactions. Nevertheless, the U.S. dollar market value of the investment in Toyota ADRs will be cut in half by any one of the events.

An American investor who is considering international investing might ask if a nightmare like the Toyota example could be avoided by investing in an international mutual fund that is denominated in U.S. dollars. The answer is no. An American investor who spent U.S. dollars to buy shares in a U.S. mutual fund that invested in Japanese stocks that were all simultaneously afflicted by one or more of the unfortunate events in the Toyota example would still lose half of the market value of their U.S. dollar–denominated investment. Eliminating the need for an investor to execute a foreign exchange transaction does not eliminate foreign exchange risk; it merely hides the foreign exchange risk so the investor is not forced to deal with it directly.

Global Depository Receipts (GDRs)

Global Depository Receipts (GDRs), patterned after ADRs and first issued in 1993, are special certificates representing ownership interests created to minimize investors' foreign exchange transactions. Unlike ADRs, most GDRs are not denominated in U.S. dollars. They can be issued in the United States, Europe, Asia, or any country, and can be denominated in any currency. Both ADRs and GDRs can be issued in the United States under the SEC's Rule 144A, which permits foreign equities to be issued without the long and costly registration procedure required for a U.S. corporation.[15]

Only a small fraction of the world's total number of publicly traded foreign corporations are represented by ADRs and GDRs. As a result, instead of limiting themselves to these convenient shares, an investor might also consider investing in international mutual funds. However, neither ADRs nor GDRs nor international mutual funds eliminate foreign exchange risk; they merely perform the foreign currency transactions for the investors.

INTERNATIONAL INVESTMENT COMPANIES

Chapter 12 introduced investment companies that:

> Market their shares to public investors
>
> Commingle the monies obtained from the share sales into a common pool
>
> Use the pool of commingled funds to buy a diversified list of securities
>
> Hire professional money managers to administer the investments.

Each different investment company pursues a different investment goal. Table 12-1 in Chapter 12 (p. 334) shows that some mutual funds specialize in international investments.

Categories of International Investment Companies

There are several categories of U.S. mutual funds that specialize in international investments:

1. **Global funds** are mutual funds that invest in both foreign and domestic securities (Janus Worldwide Fund, Aim "A" Global Aggregate Growth Fund).
2. **International funds** or **foreign funds** invest primarily in foreign securities (Vanguard International Equity Index Funds).
   a. **Regional foreign funds** invest only in foreign securities from specific regions; they typically have names that suggest their regional interest (Fidelity European Fund, or Price New Asia Fund).
   b. **International style funds** invest in categories of foreign securities that are unique in some respect (Fidelity Emerging Markets Fund, Templeton Developing Markets Trust, or Vanguard International Value Fund).
   c. **Foreign index funds** invest only in portfolios that are indexed to international stock market indexes (Vanguard International Equity Index Fund for Europe).
3. **Country funds** confine their investments to a single country, which is usually stipulated in the fund's name (Templeton Russia Fund, Japan Fund, Fidelity Canada Fund, or Korea Fund). Some country funds are mutual funds, but many are what the U.S. law calls closed-end investment companies.[16]

International Index Funds

iShares MSCI, introduced in Chapter 12 (pp. 350–351) are shares in a mutual fund indexed to a stock market index in a single foreign country. Seventeen different iShares MSCI mutual funds track 17 non-U.S. stock market indexes that were created by Morgan Stanley Capital International (MSCI). Essentially, each different iShares MSCI index fund converts investors' U.S. dollar investments into a foreign exchange, buys the stocks that make up the MSCI index for the selected country, manages the iShares MSCI mutual fund to track the MSCI index, collects cash dividends not paid in U.S. dollars and converts them to dollars, sends the dividends to the iShares MSCI investor in dollars, and maintains a stock market listing on the AMEX.* iShares MSCI are diversified portfolios that can be used by *asset allocators* who want to allocate funds to selected countries while avoiding foreign exchange transactions and stock picking in a foreign market.

The Vanguard Group has created index funds based on combinations of several MSCI indexes (Vanguard International Equity Index Fund for Pacific Countries). Other index funds have been created to track different stock markets around the world. For example, index funds based on many of the stock and bond indexes discussed in Chapter 11 exist. These funds have names like SPDRS, iShares MSCI, DIAMONDS, and STOXX.

Homemade International Diversification

Vihang Erunza, Ked Hogan, and Mao-Wei Hung (EHH) analyzed three U.S. stock market indexes, 12 different U.S. industry portfolios, 30 multinational corporations (MNCs), several closed-end country funds, and several ADRs to see how much international diversification a U.S. investor could buy without leaving the U.S. securities markets. EHH varied the weights in these international components to create what they called *augmented portfolios* and then compared these hybrid portfolios to the returns available in foreign markets. They made comparisons with seven developed markets (Australia, Canada, France, Germany, Italy, Japan, and Britain) and nine emerging markets (Argentina, Brazil, Chile, Greece, India, Korea, Mexico, Thailand, and Zimbabwe). By investing U.S. dollars in U.S. securities markets, EHH were able to construct augmented portfolios that mimicked all the developed markets, and all the emerging markets except Chile and Thailand. EHH concluded that the need for U.S. investors to undertake global diversification is exaggerated.[17]

INTERNATIONAL ASSET-PRICING MODELS

Business executives, government regulators, and investors use asset-pricing models like those discussed in Chapter 15 for several tasks. First, asset-pricing models can be used as standards of comparison to evaluate the performance of investments. Second, asset-pricing models indicate the appropriate risk-adjusted discount rate (required rate of return, expected return) with which to compute present values. Third, asset-pricing models are sometimes used by risk managers for risk assessments. Fourth, some rate-setting commissions for public utilities use asset-pricing models to value the stock of a public utility; then, the rate-setting commission decrees that the public utility's customers pay utility usage fees sufficient to support the utility's stock price at a level the asset-pricing model suggests is appropriate. Two international asset pricing models are reviewed below.

The International Security Market Line (ISML)

Let us refer to the *security market line* (SML) introduced in Chapter 15 as the domestic SML. The *international security market line* (ISML) mirrors the domestic theory. Individuals' portfolio behavior is aggregated, clearing assumptions are made, and the same equilibrium

---

* Chapter 11 explained that MSCI added some lesser-developed countries and some emerging market countries to bring its total to 50 country indexes. That chapter also describes these indexes and the empirical data on these 50 MSCI stock market indexes provides a historical view of how representative investments fared in each country.

pricing relationship and risk-return tradeoffs are derived in the ISML. If the international financial markets are fully integrated, international beta coefficients can be calculated as shown in Eqn. 18-3:

$$\begin{pmatrix} \text{An asset's} \\ \text{international} \\ \text{beta} \end{pmatrix} = \begin{pmatrix} \text{The asset's} \\ \text{correlation with} \\ \text{the world's} \\ \text{market portfolio} \end{pmatrix} \begin{pmatrix} \text{The asset's} \\ \text{standard} \\ \text{deviation} \end{pmatrix} \bigg/ \begin{pmatrix} \text{Standard} \\ \text{deviation of the} \\ \text{world's market} \\ \text{portfolio} \end{pmatrix} \tag{18-3}$$

The Morgan Stanley Capital International (MSCI) world market index introduced in Chapter 11, or a similar global index, can be used as a surrogate for the world market portfolio.

If all the individual security betas in each separate country were appropriately averaged, country betas could be computed for every country in the world. Some assets and some countries will have betas larger than 1, and some assets and some countries will have betas less than 1. The problem with the ISML model is that, as discussed earlier in this chapter, the world's financial markets are not fully integrated. The U.S. and Canadian markets are among the most highly integrated markets in the world today, but even these neighboring markets are only *partially integrated*. And some of the emerging markets violate the ISML's idealized assumptions substantially.

As a result of numerous barriers to entry that tend to insulate markets from each other, the economies of every country in the world exhibit a **home bias**.[18] This home bias manifests itself in the form of *international risk premiums* that differ for each country. In other words, if all other factors are equal, international investors require higher returns from foreign investments than they do from domestic investments that are similar.[19]

International Arbitrage Pricing Theory (IAPT)

The ISML needs to consider every asset in the world to determine global equilibrium conditions. We know from Chapter 15 that arbitrage pricing theory is easier to use than the SML because it can be used to analyze either a few or many assets.

The first step in applying the arbitrage pricing theory is to statistically fit the multifactor return-generating function, Eqn. 15-31 (p. 461), for each individual asset that is being considered. Eqn. 15-31 is a time-series model that uses k different risk factors as explanatory variables. These multifactor return-generating functions are then analyzed simultaneously to determine a cross-sectional asset-pricing model that best explains each asset's expected return (required rate of return, discount rate). Eqn. 15-32 in Chapter 15 represent the k-dimensional arbitrage pricing theory (APT) model that summarizes the implications of the multifactor return-generating functions of all the assets that were analyzed. The APT model can readily be extended to international proportions by including appropriate international risk factors.

The international arbitrage pricing theory (IAPT) overcomes some problems that trouble the international capital asset-pricing model (ISML) by bringing anomalous risk factors inside the IAPT so they are analyzed as part of the solution. Country-to-country violations in purchasing power parity can be priced as additional risk factors in the IAPT. And the home bias that the ISML is unable to explain can be utilized as an additional explanatory variable in the IAPT. Figure 18-4 illustrates how the international risk premiums for Germany, Japan, and the United Kingdom varied over a 20-year sample period. Note that foreign exchange (currency) risk is separated out of, and sometimes moves in the opposite direction from, total risk. In particular, Figure 18-4 shows the risk premiums in Germany and the United Kingdom during the mid-1970s and early 1980s.

FIGURE 18-4   The International Risk Premiums for Individual Countries Vary Through Time

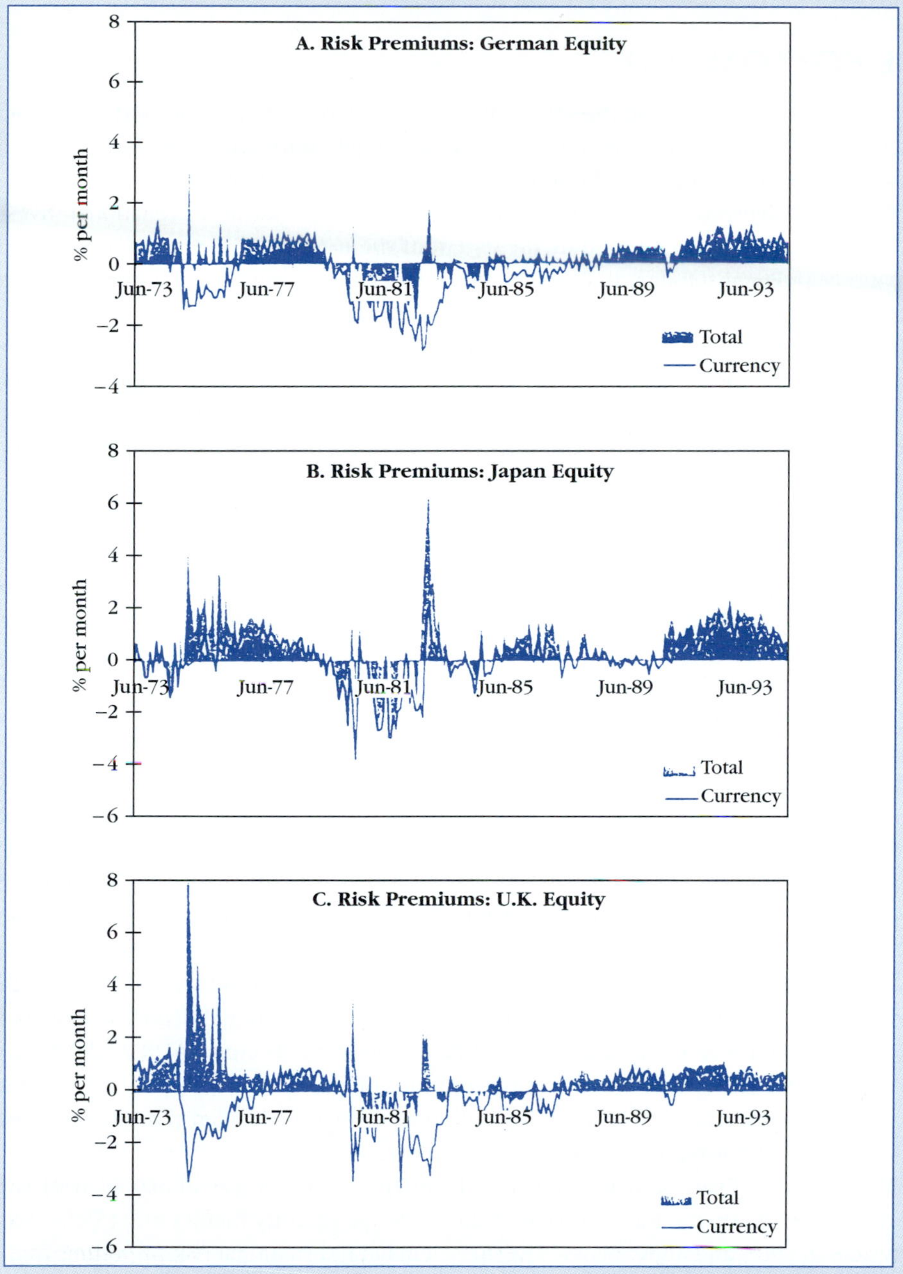

INTERNET CONNECTION

Investment Insurance International is the political risk division of Aon Group Limited. The firm has an interesting Web site about its insurance against international investing risks and sovereign risk: www.aonpoliticalrisk.com

The International Monetary Fund (IMF) provides international financial information through their Web site: www.imf.org

See the Web site of Professor Campbell Harvey at Duke University for worldwide economic and political data. www.duke.edu/~charvey

Information about 500 American Depository Receipts (ADRs) is available through J. P. Morgan's Web site www.jpmorgan.com

Look under Business Sites for adr.com

Information on Latin American stocks, bonds, Global Depository Receipts (GDRs), and ADRs is available through: www.latinstocks.com

Real-time quotes on European stocks, IPOs, and market news can be seen at: www.europeaninvestor.com

English-language stock quotes, financial histories, and investment reports on stocks and bonds issued by thousands of foreign companies is available at: www.wisi.com

Yahoo has foreign language financed links to many different countries. All reports from the United States, Canada, and Britain are in English. See finance.yahoo.com

The currency risk premiums and total risk premiums (currency risk premiums plus market risk premiums) for Germany, Japan, and the United Kingdom experienced significant variations over a 259-month sample period (June 1973 to December 1994). Foreign exchange (currency) risk premiums sometimes moves in the opposite direction from market risk premiums (in particular, during the mid-1970s and early-1980s in Germany and the United Kingdom).

SOURCE: Giorgio De Santis and Bruno Gerard, "How Big Is the Premium for Currency Risk?" *Journal of Financial Economics* (September 1998): 403, Figures 2a, 2b, and 2c.

In the final analysis, the ISML and IAPT are both useful; they can complement each other in international applications.

THE BOTTOM LINE

International investors face all the same risks faced by domestic investors and more: country (sovereign) risk, international liquidity risk, international information risk, foreign exchange risk, and problems arising from different time zones and cultural differences.

Country (sovereign) risk is a fundamental consideration for all international investors. The condition of a nation's economy, the extent of the national government's indebtedness, the nation's political stability, and the effectiveness of the nation's legal system in enforcing contracts are all factors potential investors should consider.

No markets are as liquid and free from fraud as the securities markets in the United States and Europe. Dealing with the liquidity risks can be slow and costly. Liquidity problems can be especially bad in the emerging markets. For example, security price manipulation, which is illegal in some industrialized nations, is permitted in many emerging markets (and some industrialized nations).

Country risk and foreign exchange risk are usually interrelated. The governments that issue the currencies sometimes fix their foreign exchange rates; these pegged exchange rates are not allowed to float freely so the market forces of supply and demand can continually reshape them. But fixing a country's foreign exchange rate does not fix does not fix the problems that destabilize its currency.

Competing against domestic investors who may have inside information, and/or access to public information about their country before foreign investors get it, puts foreign investors at a disadvantage. Some large international banks (like those listed in Table 6-2 in Chapter 6) and some large institutional investors have foreign offices to help manage distant investments. These foreign offices are often partially staffed by local citizens. Foreign nationals may also be able to gather information for their employer. Or, a foreign investor can purchase a highly diversified portfolio of securities in the foreign country without doing much investments research. Buying iShares MSCI and/or shares in international mutual funds provides passively managed international investments.

Investing in multinational corporations (MNCs) provides some worldwide investment exposure. Unfortunately, MNCs do not provide as much international diversification as their worldwide operations might suggest. American depository receipts (ADRs), global depository receipts (GDRs), and international mutual funds provide easy access to the world's security markets. These convenient international investment vehicles can remove the need for the investor to perform foreign exchange transactions.

If the world's financial markets were fully integrated, the international security market line (ISML) should be the mirror image of the domestic security market line (SML). Because of barriers to entry and home biases, investors demand international risk premiums that they add onto their required rate of return before they will make foreign investments. The international arbitrage pricing theory (IAPT) is an asset-pricing model that can endogenize (provide internal solutions for) these risk factors.[20]

The risk-reducing benefits from international investing offsets many of its disadvantages. The correlations between the securities markets in different countries are usually lower than domestic correlations. As a result, multinational investing offers a more dominant Markowitz efficient frontier from which to choose an optimum portfolio.

Empirical research suggests some caveats about using international correlation coefficients. First, the correlations between countries are unstable through time. Second, as international financial markets become more fully integrated the correlations between countries may trend upwards. Third, the correlations between countries tend to increase during periods when the country's financial markets are most volatile. This third problem means the international correlation coefficients may not only be unstable, they may increase as financial markets collapse—the worst possible time.

QUESTIONS

Q18-1   (Foreign exchange risk) Explain what is meant by the statement: "One foreign investment actually involves two separate investments."

Q18-2   (International investment risks) Are there any risks that are peculiar to international investing? Stated differently, what factors, in addition to the usual investment risks, should be of particular concern to the multinational investor?

Q18-3   (Rewards of international investing) What induces investors to invest internationally when they face additional risks that are peculiar to multinational investing?

Q18-4   (Efficient frontier for international investing) Does every international investment opportunity provide the investor with new investment opportunities that dominate the old opportunities in a risk-return analysis? Explain.

Q18-5   (Intercountry correlations) What factors explain why the intercountry correlations between securities markets are low?

Q18-6   (Alternatives to direct foreign investment) Myron Budnick just bought a Toyota and loves the car so much that he wants to invest in the Toyota Corporation's stock. But, Toyota is a Japanese company and Myron does not want to get involved in foreign exchange and the other administrative problems that might arise from a foreign investment. How can Myron buy shares in Toyota without getting involved with any international complications?

Q18-7   (International investment companies) Ralph Jones is interested in multinational diversification but does not have the time or expertise to select individual foreign securities in which to invest. Is there some easier way that Ralph can obtain international diversification?

Q18-8   (Intercountry correlations) Since the value of the intercountry correlation coefficients between securities markets plays such as important role in international diversification, consider the trend in these statistics. Do you think that these correlations should increase, stay the same, or decrease in value with the passage of time? Explain why.

Q18-9   (Investing in MNCs) Susan has heard that there are diversification benefits to be gained from investing internationally. She reasons that if she buys stock of AT&T, which she knows to have operations worldwide, that she should be able to achieve the diversification benefits without having to worry about such things as exchange rate risk. Comment on her observation.

Q18-10   (ADRs) Discuss some of the problems of which an investor who invests in an American Depository receipt needs to be aware.

PROBLEMS

P18-1 through P18-5. The following international security market returns are to be used with Problems 18-1 through 18-5:

Year	United Kingdom	Japan	Canada	Australia	United States
1971	47.99%	46.55%	14.13%	−1.54%	18.16%
1972	3.93	126.56	33.12	21.06	17.71
1973	−23.44	−20.13	−3.11	−12.06	−18.68
1974	−50.33	−15.65	−26.52	−32.97	−27.77
1975	115.06	19.84	15.07	50.71	37.49
1976	−12.55	25.80	9.71	−10.00	26.68
1977	56.49	15.70	−1.37	11.25	−3.03
1978	14.63	53.33	20.55	22.24	8.53
1979	22.20	−11.69	52.55	43.44	24.18
1980	38.80	29.70	22.00	52.20	33.22

P18-1   (Intercountry correlations) Determine the correlation of returns for the United States, United Kingdom, and Japan over the 10-year period. In addition, determine the standard deviation of returns for the three countries over the same period of time. *Hint:* You might want to use a computer program to do statistics.

P18-2   (Intercountry correlations) Determine the correlation between the returns from Australia and Canada over the 10-year period. Also determine the standard deviation of returns over the same time period.

P18-3   (International portfolio risk and return) With the information generated in Problem 18-1 above, determine the expected return and risk (as measured by the standard deviation) for a portfolio of 25% U.K., 25% Japanese, and

50% U.S. stocks. Assume the historical means, standard deviations, and correlation coefficients are the expected values.

P18-4 (International portfolio risk and return) Using the information generated in Problem 18-2, determine the expected return and standard deviation of return for a portfolio of 40% Australian and 60% Canadian stocks. Again, assume the historical statistics are the expected values.

P18-5 (International portfolio risk and return) Using the information generated in Problems 18-1 and 18-2, determine the standard deviation of returns for a portfolio of 50% U.S. and 50% Canadian stocks.

P18-6 (Effect of exchange rates on returns) Currently, the German deutschemark is trading at DM1.8342 per dollar. A year ago, it was trading for DM1.6224 per dollar. If the return on the German stocks had been 17% in the last year, what would have been the net return earned by a U.S. investor?

P18-7 (Total return on a foreign investment) Bob works as an accountant for Soundtrack and attended a finance seminar last year in which the benefits of international diversification were emphasized. He noticed that Aiwa products do particularly well for Soundtrack and decided to invest in the stock, which was selling on the Tokyo exchange for 2,680 yen. The exchange rate at the time was ¥117.60 per dollar. Three months later Aiwa had skyrocketed to 2,990 yen on the Tokyo exchange, but Bob noted that the dollar had appreciated in value against the yen; the exchange rate was then ¥123.50 per dollar, and Bob decided to liquidate his investment. He had received no dividends. What rate of return did he earn on his 3-month investment? How did the appreciation of the dollar affect his return?

P18-8 (ADRs) Rose noticed that an ADR for Nissan stock was selling on NASDAQ for $7.1875. She also noted that on that same day, Nissan closed at 441 yen on the Tokyo stock exchange. She found that the exchange rate was 117.60 yen per U.S. dollar. How many dollars will it take to purchase one share of Nissan on the Tokyo exchange? Is this a market inefficiency? Explain.

P18-9 (Return on a foreign investment) Assume the expected rate of return and standard deviation of returns from investing British pounds in the common stock of Barclays Bank, which is headquartered in England, are 10% and 20%, respectively. Assume also that the pound has been appreciating relative to the dollar at a rate of 5% a year. How much return should a U.S. investor who pays British pounds for stock in Barclays Bank expect?

P18-10 (Return on a foreign investment) While working as a chemist at a laboratory in New York, Rolf Kierulf decided to invest some money in the common stock of his previous employer, Hoffman LaRoche, a large pharmaceutical corporation headquartered in Switzerland. Rolf bought Swiss francs in the United States at the rate of $0.1800 per franc. He purchased Hoffman LaRoche stock at a price of SF26,990 per share. (a) How many dollars per share did Rolf have to pay for the stock? (b) If Rolf sold the stock for SF28,100 3 months later, having received no cash dividends, and the exchange rate at that time was $0.1750 per franc, what rate of return did he earn for the 3 months? (c) How did the dollar/franc exchange rate affect Rolf's return?

CFA EXAM QUESTIONS

1. (1999 CFA Sample Exam, Level I) Which of the following factors affect the correlation coefficients among asset prices in different national capital markets?

   I. Technological specialization.

   II. Cultural and sociological differences.

   III. Independent fiscal and monetary policies.

   IV. Regulations imposed by national governments.
   - **A.** I and IV only.
   - **B.** II and III only.
   - **C.** I, III, and IV only.
   - **D.** I, II, III, and IV.

2. (1998 CFA Sample Exam, Level I) Based on empirical evidence, a U.S. equity money manager who wants to acquire the full benefits of international diversification would be *best* advised to:

   I. Invest directly in foreign stocks.

   II. Invest in U.S. multinational firms.

   III. Hedge his or her portfolio by short selling foreign stocks.
   - **A.** I only.
   - **B.** II only.
   - **C.** II and III only.
   - **D.** I, II, and III.

3. (1996 CFA Exam, Level III) The HFS Trustees have solicited input from three consultants concerning the risk and rewards of an allocation to international equities. Two of them strongly favor such action, while the third consultant commented as follows:

   The risk reduction benefits of international investing have been significantly overstated. Recent studies relat-

ing to the cross-country correlation structure of equity returns during different market phases cast serious doubt on the ability of international investing to reduce risk, especially in situations when risk reduction is needed the most.

A. Describe the behavior of cross-country equity return correlations to which the consultant is referring. Explain how that behavior may diminish the ability of international investing to reduce risk in the short run.

Assume the consultant's assertion is correct.

B. Explain why it might still be more efficient on a risk/reward basis to invest internationally rather than only domestically in the long run.

4. (Adapted from the 1995 CFA Exam, Level III) Ambrose Green is considering selling a portion of his Diversified Global Fund holding in order to create a portfolio that concentrates on country exposures. He now understands that an investor must look at both country/security returns and currency returns when deciding on a specific country in which to invest. You have developed the forecast returns shown in the first two columns of Table 5 below, along with the current 1-year yields available to a U.S. investor in the several Eurodeposit markets.

Table 5

	Forecast Returns (Year Ending 6/30/96)		Current Yields
	Local Market Returns	Exchange Rate Returns	One-Year Eurodeposits
Germany (DM)	6.0%	2.0%	4.0%
Japan (yen)	7.0	−1.0	6.0
U.S. ($)	8.0	0.0	7.0

After examining the Table 5 data, Green suggests that an investment made in Japan, with the currency exposure hedged into Deutschmarks, would maximize his U.S. dollar return expectations. You disagree with Green's suggestion. Instead, you recommend that the investment be made in Germany with the currency exposure hedged into U.S. dollars.

Using Table 5 data, calculate the expected returns for *both* your *and* Green's proposals. Show your work and briefly comment on the result.

5. (Adapted from a question appearing on the 1997 CFA Exam, Level III) Global Equity Managers (GEM) manages international equity portfolios that are invested mainly in developed markets. The Investment Committee of GEM is now considering the possibility of adding emerging markets to existing portfolios.

Scott Simone, a member of the Investment Committee, comments on the ability of emerging markets to reduce the risk of a portfolio that is invested in developed markets:

Emerging market returns tend to be extremely volatile, especially when compared with the return volatility in developed markets. Therefore, adding emerging markets to a portfolio invested in developed markets will increase the overall portfolio risk, not reduce it.

Discuss *two* characteristics of cross-country return correlations for emerging markets that may contradict Simone's conclusions.

FURTHER REFERENCES

Adler, Michael and Bernard Dumas. "International Portfolio Choice and Corporation Finance: A Synthesis," *Journal of Finance* 38, no. 3 (June 1983): 925–84.

This far-reaching paper examines various reasons why the international capital asset-pricing model that would be appropriate if all of markets in the world were fully integrated is, in fact, not fully descriptive of reality.

Bekaert, Geert and Campbell Harvey. "Time-Varying World Market Integration," *Journal of Finance* 50, no. 2 (June 1995): 403–44.

The paper proposes measure of capital market integration arising from a conditional regime-switching model. This measure permits expected returns in countries that are segmented from world capital markets in one part of the sample and to become integrated later in the sample. A number of emerging markets exhibit time-varying integration. Some markets appear to be segmented even though foreigners have relatively free access to their capital markets.

Ferson, Wayne E. and Campbell Harvey. "Sources of Risk and Expected Returns in Global Equity Markets," *Journal of Banking and Finance* 18, no. 4 (September 1994): 775–803.

This paper empirically examines multifactor asset pricing models for the returns and expected returns on 18 national equity markets. The evidence indicates that world market betas do not provide a good explanation of cross-sectional differences in average returns. However, multiple beta models provide an improved explanation of the equity returns.

Frankel, Jeffrey A., Ed. *The Internationalization of Equity Markets*. National Bureau of Economic Research Project Report series. Chicago: University of Chicago Press, 1994.

This book contains a useful introduction by the editor plus eight papers-cum-discussions that were presented at an NBER conference in October, 1993. The book contains wisdom in its chapters and in the discussions.

Grossman, Gene M. and Kenneth Rogoff, Eds. *Handbook of International Economics*, Vol. 3. Amsterdam: Elsevier Publishing, 1995. Chapter 37 entitled "Puzzles in International Financial Markets," by Karen K. Lewis, pp. 1913-71.

Professor Lewis provides a scholarly discussion of the international capital asset pricing model and the home bias in investing that is evident in many countries. Home bias in investing and a review of the literature on that subject is found on pages 1950-66.

Solnik, Bruno. *International Investments*, 3rd ed. (Reading, MA: Addison-Wesley, 1996).

This 17-chapter textbook about international investing introduces the relevant topics and provides good references where additional detailed studies can be found. Elementary algebra and statistics are used.

ENDNOTES

[1] See Gabriel Hawawini, "Market Efficiency and Equity Pricing: International Evidence and Implications for Global Investing." In *International Finance: Contemporary Issues*, Dilip K. Das, ed. (New York: Routledge, 1993): 291-318.

[2] See Richard Cantor and Frank Packer, "Determinants and Impact of Sovereign Credit Ratings," *Journal of Fixed Income* 6, no. 3 (December 1996): 76-91. Also see Claude B. Erb, Harvey R. Campbell, and Tadas E. Viskanta, "The Influence of Political, Economic, and Financial Risk on Expected Fixed Income Returns," *The Journal of Fixed Income* 6, no. 1 (June 1996): 7-30.

[3] For a theoretical analysis of the market value implications of barriers to entry, see Vihang Errunza and Lemma Senbet, "The Effects of International Operations on the Market Value of the Firm: Theory and Evidence," *Journal of Finance* 36 (May 1981): 401-17.

[4] For more details about international investment risks, see Bruno Solnik, *International Investments*, 3d ed. (Reading, MA: Addison-Wesley, 1996). Also see Ian Giddy, *Global Financial Markets* (Lexington, MA: D. C. Heath, 1994). See also Vihang Errunza and Etienne Losq," International Asset Pricing Under Mild Segmentation: Theory and Text," *Journal of Finance* (March 1985): 105-24. In addition, see F. Black, "International Capital Market Equilibrium with Investment Barriers," *Journal of Financial Economics* (December 1974): 337-52.

[5] The implications for the capital asset-pricing model (CAPM) for the international investor have been worked out by Rene Stulz, "On the Effects of Barriers to International Investment," *Journal of Finance* 36, no. 4 (September 1981): 923-34.

[6] This section draws on Herbert Grubel, "Internationally Diversified Portfolios: Welfare Gains and Capital Flows," *American Economic Review* (December 1968): 1299-1314. The investor could be buying iShares MSCI (previously called WEBS), ADRs, international mutual funds that are denominated in U.S. dollars, or in other U.S. dollar–denominated international securities.

[7] For a Markowitz portfolio analysis of international diversification, see H. Levy and M. Sarnat, "International Diversification of Investment Portfolios," *American Economic Review* (September 1970): 668-75. Also see Donald R. Lessard, "World, Country and Industry Relationships in Equity Returns: Implications for Risk Reduction through International Diversification," *Financial Analysts Journal* (January-February 1976): 2-8. For a multiperiod study of the benefits of international diversification, see Robert R. Grauer and Nils H. Hakansson, "Gains from International Diversification: 1968-85 Returns on Portfolios of Stocks and Bonds," *Journal of Finance* 42, no. 3 (July 1987): 721-39.

[8] See Bruno H. Solnik, Cyril Boucrelle, and Yann Le Fur, "International Market Correlation and Volatility," *Financial Analysts Journal* (September-October 1996): 17-34.

[9] For empirical risk-and-return statistics from various investments in foreign countries, see Yasushi Hamao, "Japanese Stocks, Bonds, Bills and Inflation, 1973-1987," *Journal of Portfolio Management* (winter 1989): 20-26. Also see Daniel Wydler, "Swiss Stocks, Bonds and Inflation, 1926-1987," *Journal of Portfolio Management* (winter 1989): 27-32.

[10] See Fayez A. Elayan, Brian A. Maris, and C. Edward Chang, "Stock Market Response to the Formation of Foreign Affiliates by U.S. Corporations," *Journal of Multinational Financial Management* 5. no. 1 (1995): 1–12.

[11] See Bertrand Jacquillat and Bruno Solnik, "Multinationals Are Poor Tools for Diversification," *Journal of Portfolio Management* 4, no. 2 (winter 1978): 8–12.

[12] See Phillipe Jorion, "The Exchange-Rate Exposure of U.S. Multinationals," *Journal of Business* 63, no. 3 (July 1990): 331–45. And, see Phillipe Jorion, "The Pricing of Exchange Rate Risk in the Stock Market," *Journal of Financial and Quantitative Analysis* 26, no. 3 (September 1991): 363–76.

[13] For worldwide usage statistics on ADRs, see Kenneth A. Lopian, "The Reality of Depository Receipts," *Investing Worldwide VI* (Charlottesville, VA: Association for Investment Management and Research (AIMR), 1996), pp. 30–36.

[14] For more details about ADRs, see M. Wahab and A. Khandwala, "Why Not Diversify Internationally with ADRs?" *Journal of Portfolio Management* (winter 1993): 75–82. In addition, see G. Andrew Karolyi and Rene M. Stulz, "Why Do Markets Move Together? An Investigation of U.S.-Japan Stock Return Comovements," *Journal Of Finance* 51, no. 3 (July 1996): 951–86. Furthermore, see Youguo Liang and Mbodia Mougoue, "The Pricing of Foreign Exchange Risk: Evidence from ADRs," *International Review of Economics and Finance* 5 no. 4 (1996): 377–85. And see Stephen R. Foerster and G. Andrew Karolyi, "The Effects of Market Segmentation and Investor Recognition on Asset Prices: Evidence from Foreign Stocks Listing in the United States," *Journal of Finance* 54, no. 3 (June 1999): 981–1014.

[15] For more details, see "New Members for the GDR Club," *Euromoney* (November 1996): 87–89.

[16] See Eric Chang, Cheol S. Eun, and Richard Kolodny, "International Diversification Through Closed-End Country Funds," *Journal of Banking and Finance* 19, no. 7 (October 1995): 1237–63.

[17] See Vihang Erunza, Ked Hogan, and Mao-Wei Hung, "Can the Gains from International Diversification Be Achieved Without Trading Abroad?" *Journal of Finance* (December 1999): 2075–2107.

[18] For a recent empirical study that reconfirms home bias, see Jun-Koo Kang and Rene M. Stulz, "Why Is There a Home Bias? An Analysis of Foreign Portfolio Equity Ownership in Japan," *Journal of Financial Economics* 46, no. 1 (October 1997): 3–28. For a review of the home bias literature, see Karen K. Lewis, "Trying To Explain Home Bias in Equities and Consumption," *Journal of Economic Literature* 37, no. 2 (June 1999): 571–608.

[19] For a book that summarizes much international finance literature, see Jeffrey A. Frankel, ed. *The Internationalization of Equity Markets*. National Bureau of Economic Research Project Report series (Chicago: University of Chicago Press, 1994). Frankel's book contains a useful introduction by the editor plus eight papers-cum-discussions that were presented at an NBER conference in October, 1993. The book contains wisdom in its chapters and in the discussions. Also, see Geert Bekaert and Campbell Harvey, "Time-Varying World Market Integration," *Journal of Finance* 50, no. 2 (June 1995): 403–44. Bekaert and Harvey propose to measure of capital market integration arising from a conditional regime-switching model. This measure permits expected returns in countries that are segmented from world capital markets in one part of the sample and to become integrated later in the sample. A number of emerging markets exhibit time-varying integration. Some markets appear to be segmented even though foreigners have relatively free access to their capital markets. Furthermore, see Wayne E. Ferson and Campbell Harvey, "Sources of Risk and Expected Returns in Global Equity Markets," *Journal of Banking and Finance* 18, no. 4 (September 1994): 775–803. Ferson and Harvey examine multifactor asset-pricing models for the returns and expected returns on 18 national equity markets. The evidence indicates that world market betas do not provide a good explanation of cross-sectional differences in average returns. However, multiple beta models provide an improved explanation of the equity returns. Also see Giorgio De Santis and Bruno Gerard, "How Big Is the Premium for Currency Risk?" *Journal of Financial Economics* (September 1998): 375–412. De Santis and Gerard provide empirical estimates of international risk premiums that vary through time.

[20] See Giorgio De Santis and Bruno Gerard, "International Asset Pricing and Portfolio Diversification with Time-Varying Risk," *Journal of Finance* (December 1997): 1881–1912.

PART 5

FIXED-INCOME INVESTMENTS

GLOBAL BOND MARKETS

Chapter 6 surveyed the global stock market. This chapter explores the world's market for fixed income securities. Much of this chapter's action takes place in bond-trading rooms like the one described by Tom Wolfe in The Bonfire of the Vanities.

> *The writhing silhouettes were the arms and torsos of young men, few of them older than forty. They had their suit jackets off. They were moving about in an agitated manner and sweating early in the morning and shouting, which created the roar. It was the sound of well-educated young white men baying for money on the bond market.*

Wolfe's paragraph provides a fairly accurate portrayal of the bond trading rooms at money center banks around the world.

Salomon Smith Barney is a unit of Citigroup in New York City. Before Salomon Brothers merged with Smith Barney in 1997 and Citigroup in 1998, its highest-paid traders made annual incomes of over $20 million.[1] Bond trading was Salomon Brothers specialty. The Smith Barney and Citibank mergers may reduce the level of compensation and risk-appetite of Salomon bond traders, but a steady stream of multimillion-dollar transactions continues to flow through Salomon Smith Barney's New York City trading room daily.

Not all the action in fixed-income securities takes place on trading floors. At large investment banking firms real-time systems provide current market prices, interest rates, and foreign exchange rates from around the world.* Software to perform sophisticated financial analysis has been developed in-house. Anyone in the world can obtain access to

---

* One of the largest, most modern trading rooms in the world is in the Stamford, CT, North American UBS headquarters building for the Swiss Bank Corporation and SBC Warburg Dillion Read subsidiaries of UBS. The 600-position trading room opened in 1997. For photos and details see Robert Sales, "SBC Warburg and Stamford: The Beginning of a Trend?" *Wall Street Technology* (October 1997): 70–74. Visit the magazine's Web site at: www.wstonline.com.

similar financial computer programs and real-time financial data by paying $1,200 per month to rent a Bloomberg machine.[2] The Bloomberg Corporation is a financial services company headquartered in New York City. The Corporation has over 75,000 Bloombergs (highly specialized financial computer terminals) installed in 91 countries. Michael Bloomberg, who resigned from Salomon Brothers and founded his own firm in 1981, offers financial information and analysis to subscribers. Major investment banking firms like Salomon Smith Barney have fixed-income research departments that employ many MBAs and PhDs in finance, some of whom earn million-dollar annual incomes. Nearly all subscribe to Bloomberg and Reuters and other external suppliers of data and software to supplement their in-house research capabilities.

A BRIEF TOUR OF THE GLOBAL BOND MARKET

During the past two decades the aggregate value of outstanding bond issues in the world have grown at rates as low as 1.5% and as high as 30% per year. An average annual growth rate of 8% per year over the past two decades pushed the aggregate value of all outstanding bonds in the world to $25.4 trillion, measured at prices and exchange rates prevailing at the end of 1998.

The Currency of Issue. Table 19-1 provides data on the world's bond markets. The table divides international bonds into 22 meaningful categories based on their currency of issue. Regardless of the domicile of the investor, the domicile of the issuer, or the location of the bond issue's trading market, bonds that are denominated in U.S. dollars are principally affected by movements in U.S. interest rates. Similarly, bonds issued from anyplace in the world that are purchased by investors in any other country that are denominated in Japanese yen are primarily affected by interest rate movements in the Japanese bond market. The currency of denomination (currency of issue) is an important determinant of the price behavior of every bond because it usually reflects the sovereign risk and the national credit conditions that influence the issue.

Emerging Markets. The detailed information in Table 19-1 is not available for most countries that have emerging markets. This omission does not overlook a large portion of the world's bond market. Table 19-1 shows the European Monetary Union (EMU) and the United States comprise the two largest components of the global bond market.

The EMU. Figure 1-5B in Chapter 1 (p. 11) and Table 19-1 delineate the European Monetary Union's (EMU's) market share by combining the market shares from the 11 initial member nations of the EMU.* Euroland issued 26% of the world debt in 1998, which makes it the world's second largest bond market. Since the EMU is composed of 11 different member nations, it is not highly meaningful to examine the sectors of those 11 different nations as an aggregate. Instead, the sectors of these large national bond markets are discussed separately, even though they are now under one common currency.

---

*   Luxembourg is one of the 11 initial EMU countries, but it was omitted from this chapter's compilation. Since the debt denominated in Luxembourg's franc comprises a tiny fraction of 1% of the world's debt market, this omission is thought to be insignificant.

TABLE 19-1 Characteristics of the World's Major Bond Markets (Nominal Value Outstanding; $US Billions or Equivalent)ᵃ

Bond Market	Total Publicly Issued	Percent of All Public Issues	Central Government	Central Agency & Government Guaranty	State & Local Government	Corporate (Including Convertible)	Other Domestic Publicly Issued	International Bondsᵇ		
								Foreign Bonds	Eurobonds	Private Placement Unclassified
U.S. Dollar	$12,475.7	49.0%	$2,664.5	$3,320.5	$1,148.5	$3,051.8	$608.5	$261.5	$1,423.3	—
Japanese Yen	$3,923.7	15.4	$2,291.7	178.7	113.9	498.0	492.3	86.2	262.9	$699.2
Deutschemark	$2,578.5	10.1	$741.5	40.7	73.5	4.8	1,347.7	$370.4ᶜ	—	536.8
Italian Lira	$1,461.7	5.7	$1,046.7	14.7	—	5.9	263.8	5.1	125.4	—
French Franc	$1,074.7	4.2	$548.8	176.1	2.8	138.7	—	4.7	205.8	—
U.K. Sterling	$789.8	3.1	$451.3	—	0.2	55.4	—	5.6	277.3	—
Dutch Guilder	$441.9	1.7	$184.0	—	1.2	153.4	0.7	2.8	100.6	57.6
Canadian Dollar	$432.2	1.7	$195.6	—	113	72.7	—	0.4	49.9	—
Belgian Franc	$369.0	1.4	$212.0	11.1	—	14.2	81.1	45.2	5.3	—
Danish Krone	$299.6	1.2	$96.3	—	—	—	190.8	—	12.5	—
Spanish Peseta	$283.0	1.1	$210.1	—	17.1	18.3	17.3	20.2	—	—
Swiss Franc	$264.3	1	$33.2	—	20.0	33.5	65.5	112.2	—	29.1
European Currency Unit (ECU)	$217.4	0.9	$74.1	—	—	—	—	—	143.3	—
Swedish Krona	$208.0	0.8	$100.3	—	1.0	10.6	92.1	—	4.0	—
Austrian Schilling	$144.9	0.6	$70.5	2.2	—	4.4	64.8	2.0	—	1.5
Australian Dollar	$124.3	0.5	$49.1	24.6	—	22.6	—	1.4	26.7	—
Greek Drachma	$85.0	0.3	$79.2	—	—	—	—	1.3	4.6	—
South African Rand	$73.1	0.3	$54.4	10.8	1.7	—	—	—	6.2	—
Portuguese Escudo	$68.8	0.3	$35.3	—	1.2	8.3	13.1	10.9	—	—
Finnish Markka	$62.7	0.2	$48.2	—	0.7	4.0	7.4	—	2.4	—
Norwegian Krone	$55.5	0.2	$17.6	3.5	5.7	3.4	23.3	0.4	1.7	—
Irish Pound	$26.8	0.1	$24.0	0.8	—	1.1	—	0.1	0.7	—
New Zealand Dollar	$23.7	0.1	$9.5	1.0	—	2.5	—	0.0	10.7	—
Total	$25,484.4	100.0%	$9,235.7	$3,784.7	$1,500.1	$4,103.6	$3,266.4	$560.0ᵈ	$3,033.9ᵉ	$1,324.1ᶠ
Percentage of All Public Issues	100.0%		36.2%	14.9%	5.9%	16.1%	12.8%	2.2%	11.9%	

ᵃExchange rates prevailing as of December 31,1998: 115.6/US$, DM1.673/US$, 1,653.1/US$, Ffr5.6221/US$, £0.601142/US$, On1.8888/US$, G$1.5305/US$, Bfr34.575/US$, Dkr6.387/US$, Pta142.61/US$, Sfr1.3765/US$, Ecu0.8554/US$, Skr8.061/US$, A$1.62893/US$, Dr262.57/US$, R5.8600/US$, Fmk5.096/US$, Nkr7.60/US$, £0.6724/US$, ATS11.747/US$, Esc171.83/US$, NZ$1.892/US$.

ᵇIncludes straight, convertible, and floating-rate debt.

ᶜThe German bond market does not distinguish between Euro and Foreign International issues.

ᵈIncludes Foreign and Eurobond totals.

ᵉThe German International Bonds are included in the Eurobond total.

ᶠIn addition, an unspecified amount of privately placed issues of the private sectors exists.

SOURCE: "How Big Is the World Bond Market?," Salomon Smith Barney, New York City, April 7, 2000, 1. Reprinted with permission of Robert DiClemente, Managing Director, Salomon, NY.

THE U.S. BOND MARKET

Column three of Table 19-1 and Figure 1-5B in Chapter 1 show that about half the world's out-standing debt is denominated in U.S. dollars. Since only a small proportion of the U.S. dollar–denominated bonds are issued by non-U.S. organizations, it follows that U.S. organizations are the largest borrowers in the world. Figure 19-1A illustrates details about the U.S. bond market.

The U.S. Treasury. Figure 19-1A shows that the federal government sector in Figure 19-1A—namely, the U.S. Treasury—makes up 21% of the U.S. bond market. The U.S. Treasury is the world's largest single borrower; it issues approximately [(49% of world)(21% of U.S.) =] 10.3% of the world's outstanding debt. The U.S. Treasury bond market is not only the largest debt market in the world, it is also the most liquid market for fixed income securities in the world. It is an over-the-counter (OTC) market that operates informally via telephone lines between bond trading desks around the world.

In addition to the U.S. Treasury (21%), agencies of the U.S. government (27%) and state and local governments (9%) also make up large segments of the U.S. debt market. Private enterprise borrows less than the (21% + 27% + 9% =) 57% share of the U.S. debt market attributed to governmental bodies.

FIGURE 19-1   Contrasting Sectors of the Four Largest National Bond Markets

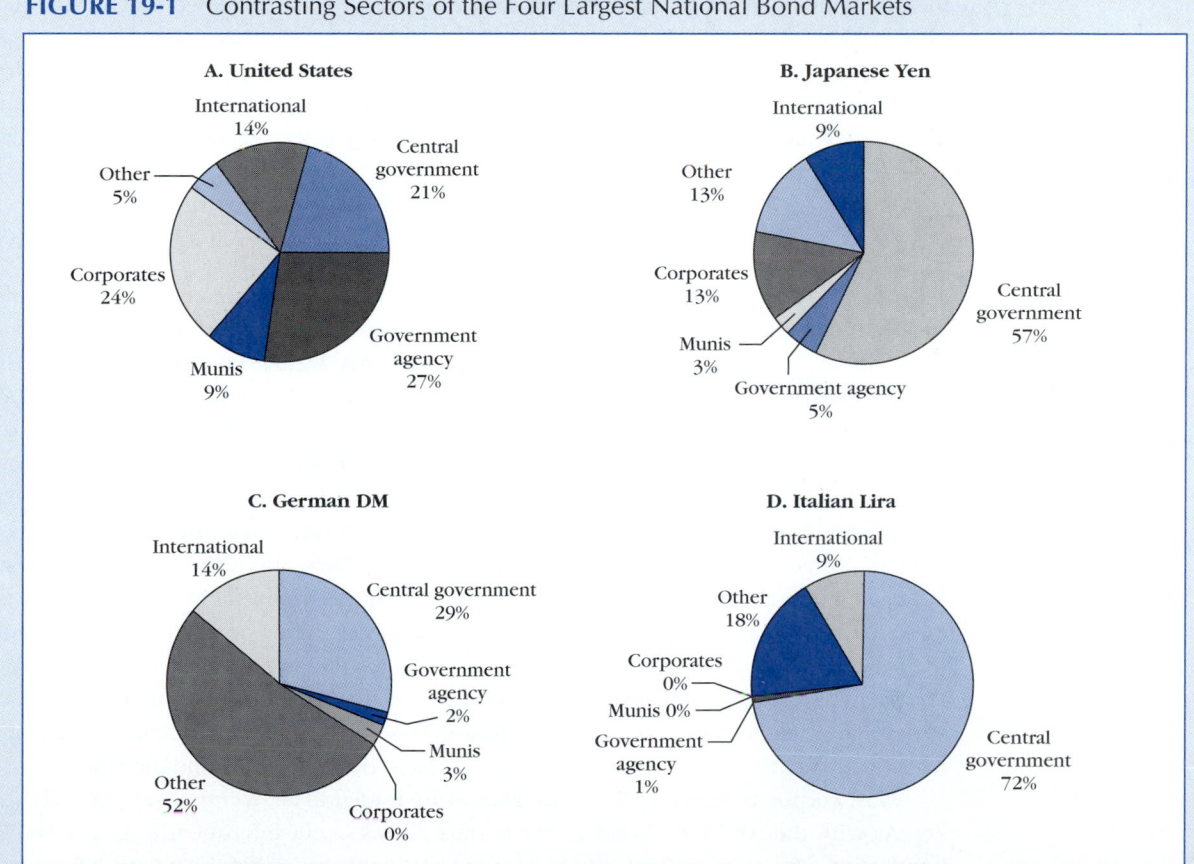

The mix of government bonds versus private sector bonds and domestic bonds versus international bonds varies considerably from one modern industrialized nation to the next.

SOURCE: Data from "How Big Is the World Bond Market?" Salomon Smith Barney, New York City, 7 April 2000.

U.S. Government Agency Bonds

U.S. government agency bonds comprised 27% of the U.S. dollar–denominated bonds outstanding in 1998. This debt arose because, like many other federal governments, the U.S. government participates in "off-balance sheet financing." This means the federal government establishes governmental agencies that are empowered to borrow in the name of the agency. As a result of this creative governmental accounting, the federal government does not show the governmental agency's debts as part of the federal government's debts. The federal government, nevertheless, implicitly guarantees the debts of its agencies. The U.S. government excels at this deceptive practice.

Next to the U.S. Treasury, an agency of the U.S. government called the Federal National Mortgage Association (FNMA, or Fannie Mae) is the largest borrower in the United States. The Government National Mortgage Association (GNMA, or Ginnie Mae) and the Federal Home Loan Mortgage Corporation (FHLMC, or Freddie Mac) are similar large-borrower agencies of the U.S. government. Fannie Mae, Ginnie Mae, and Freddie Mac subsidize home ownership in the United States by issuing low-interest-rate bonds that are implicitly guaranteed by the U.S. government. They use the cash proceeds from their bond issues to buy home mortgages, which bids up the prices of mortgage loans and drives down mortgage interest rates. The bonds are traded in a liquid over-the-counter market.

The terms **structured finance** and **securitization** have similar meanings—both include bonds created by repackaging cash flows from small borrowers with low quality ratings.[3] For example, when Fannie Mae, Ginnie Mae, and Freddie Mac issue *mortgage-backed securities* to raise billions of dollars to buy home mortgages worth about $100,000 apiece, they are said to be *securitizing* home mortgages. Indirectly, the U.S. Treasury stands behind these debts—even though the debts are not listed on the federal government's balance sheet.

Corporate Bonds in the United States

The U.S. market for corporate bonds is the largest corporate bond market in the world, but it is smaller and less liquid than the market for U.S. Treasury securities.[4] Public offerings of corporate debt are underwritten by investment banking firms. The NYSE operates the largest organized market for secondary corporate bonds; it is named the Automated Bond System (ABS). The ABS is designed to provide an active market in the bonds of NYSE-listed firms and some municipal bonds. But the ABS bond prices are not market prices that are determined by supply and demand. **Matrix prices** are used for most of the bonds in the ABS. Matrix prices are based on the price quotations for bonds that have similar coupon rates, maturities, quality ratings, and call provisions. Two problems arise with the NYSE's ABS. First, the ABS does not provide a liquid market or a market that is free from profitable arbitrage opportunities.[5] Second, if a large bond trader (bank, pension fund) gave the NYSE an order to buy or sell many listed bonds at the posted price, the trader would probably find it impossible to buy or sell more than a few of the bonds at that price. The NYSE gives less attention to building its bond market than it does to developing its stock market. In spite of these deficiencies, the ABS is an organized secondary market that lists and trades corporate and government bonds from around the world.

Most corporate bonds in the United States are traded in an over-the-counter (OTC) market. As with the ABS, OTC bond trades in most issues occur infrequently. As a result, OTC bond price quotations in the United States are not highly meaningful. The quoted prices are not meaningful because if a buyer or seller tried to trade more than a few bonds at a quoted price, no one would be willing to take the other side of a large transaction. In either the NYSE's ABS or the OTC market, someone wanting to buy or sell a significant quantity of a particular corporate bond should be prepared to make a series of phone calls in search of a party interested in becoming the other half of the transaction at a negotiated price.

Bond-quality ratings provided by financial service firms (Moody's, S&P, Fitch, IBCA, etc.) assess the probability a bond issuer will default. Bond-quality ratings, the topic of Chapter 22, facilitate trading in corporate bonds. Nevertheless, the U.S. markets for corporate bonds are not highly liquid.

Bond Markets in the United States

Like most industrialized countries, the United States has organized bond markets that operate through domestic stock exchanges and an OTC bond market. Table 19-2 enumerates some

TABLE 19-2   The U.S. Markets for Fixed-Income Securities

Debt Issuers	Underwriter (Facilitators)	Investors
U.S. government	U.S. Treasury (Secondary market makers)	Governments, Pensions, Commercial banks, Insurance companies, Mutual funds, Foreigners, Households
Federal government agencies (FNMA, GNMA, TVA, etc.)	Investment banks (Credit rating agencies, credit and liquidity enhancers, secondary market makers)	Governments, Pensions, Commercial banks, Insurance companies, Mutual funds, Foreigners, Households
Municipalities (states, cities, toll roads, etc.)	Commercial and investment banks (Credit rating agencies, credit and liquidity enhancers, secondary market makers)	Governments, Commercial banks, Insurance companies, Mutual funds, Foreigners, Households
Corporations (AT&T, GM, IBM, etc.)	Investment banks (Credit rating agencies, credit and liquidity enhancers, secondary market makers)	Pensions, Commercial banks, Insurance companies, Mutual funds, Foreigners, Households
Commercial banks (Chase, Citigroup, BankAmerica, etc.)	Commercial and investment banks (Credit rating agencies, credit and liquidity enhancers, secondary market makers)	Pensions, Commercial banks, Insurance companies, Mutual funds, Foreigners, Households
Home buyers, commercial real estate developers	Mortgage banks and portfolio operators (Credit rating agencies, credit and liquidity enhancers, secondary market makers)	Pensions, Commercial banks, Insurance companies, Real Estate Investment Trusts (REITs)
Foreign governments	Investment banks (Credit rating agencies, credit and liquidity enhancers, secondary market makers).	Pensions, Mutual funds, Foreigners, Households
Foreign corporations (SONY, Nestlé, DaimlerChrysler, etc.)	Investment banks (Credit rating agencies, credit and liquidity enhancers, secondary market makers) See Chapter 18.	Pensions, Commercial banks, Insurance companies, Mutual funds, Foreigners, Households

TABLE 19-3	U.S. Treasury's Auction Schedule	
Maturity of Security	Auction Frequency	Date of Auction
3-month T-bills	Weekly	Every Monday
6-month T-bills	Weekly	Every Monday
1-year T-bills	Monthly	Every 4th Thursday
2-year T-notes	Monthly	Last day of month
3-year T-notes	Quarterly	February, May, August, November
5-year T-notes	Monthly	Last day of month
10-year T-bonds	Quarterly	February, May, August, November
30-year T-bonds	Semiannually	February and August

sectors of the U.S. bond market. New debt securities may be issued into two secondary bond markets: (1) the stock exchanges' bond markets, or (2) the OTC bond market. Bond dealers create liquidity by making secondary markets at the stock exchanges and in the OTC market.

U.S. Treasury Securities. The U.S. government is such a large borrower that the U.S. Treasury Department conducts scheduled public auctions of Treasury securities at the times cited in Table 19-3.

Table 19-1 shows that the over-the-counter (OTC) market for U.S. Treasury securities is the largest securities market in the United States. About 40 U.S. Treasury–authorized bond dealers, the U.S. Treasury, the U.S. Federal Reserve System, and about a dozen large commercial banks make a secondary market in U.S. Treasury securities. Table 17-1 in Chapter 17 contrasts the size of the secondary market in Treasury securities with other U.S. financial markets.

Transparency. A securities market is said to be **transparent** when accurate price and volume information is freely available. **Transparency** gives market participants the feeling that fairness prevails. Complaints about high trading costs and a lack of transparency in the U.S. bond market are common.[6] U.S. bond dealers are not required to report their bid-and-ask prices to the public. Electronic help is materializing. A 1999 survey of the 500 largest U.S. Treasury securities investors reported that 21% trade electronically, and that percentage was expected to double within a year.[7]

EXAMPLE   ELECTRONIC BOND MARKETS

TradeWeb. The Internet trading system named TradeWeb got started in 1998. TradeWeb succeeded at getting institutional investors to trade U.S. Treasury securities with each other and with brokerage firms electronically.

BrokerTec Global. BrokerTec set up shop in 1998; it is an online interdealer bond brokerage backed by seven large brokerage firms that include Goldman Sachs and Merrill Lynch.

BondLink. In 1999 California-based Trading Edge (see Web site: www.tradingedge .com) started a trade matching system for bonds on the internet; the system is called BondLink.

BondBook. BondBook is an electronic bond trading system that was set up by Goldman Sachs, Morgan Stanley Dean Witter, Salomon, Deutsche Bank, and Merrill Lynch in 2000. BondBook operates as a central exchange that allows institutional investors and dealers to trade corporate, junk, and municipal bonds anonymously.

Coredeal. The International Securities Market Association (ISMA) set up an electronic bond trading platform named Coredeal in 2000. ISMA, investment banks like J. P. Morgan and UBS Warburg, and several brokerage houses established Coredeal to specialize in trading corporate bonds and to also make a market in government bonds.

Market Axess. In 2000 Bear Stearns, ABN Amro, CSFB, Deutsche Bank, J.P. Morgan, UBS Warburg, Lehman Bros., and Chase started this primary market for high-grade U.S. bonds.

New Components in the Retail Bond Market. While most of the progress in the bond markets is taking place at the institutional level, the retail market is also making headway. In 1998 E*Trade Group Inc., Discover Brokerage Direct, and TreasuryDirect made Internet bond trading available to small investors at transaction costs below 1% of the value of the transaction. The U.S. government's Bureau of the Public Debt operates TreasuryDirect. Visit the Treasury's Web site at: www.publicdebt.treas.gov.

Municipal Bond Markets. Several electronic markets that specialize in municipal bonds also began operations. *MuniAuction* is a privately owned operation that began in 1997. *The MuniCenter* was started in 1999 by Merrill Lynch, Morgan Stanley, Salomon, and Chapdelaine Electronic Brokerage.

The United States can never expect to have the same price transparency and liquidity in its bond markets that its stock markets enjoy. There are about 11,000 individual U.S. stocks, a tiny number in comparison to the 4.5 million bond issues. These bonds range from huge U.S. Treasury issues to small municipal and corporate issues. The vast majority of the outstanding bonds do not trade regularly. Still, the Internet can increase the bond market's transparency and liquidity.

SECTORS OF THE INDUSTRIALIZED WORLD'S BOND MARKETS

Government Borrowing. Figure 1-5A in Chapter 1 shows that federal governments (35%), federal government agencies (14%), and local governments (6%) combined to issue 55% of the world's outstanding debt. In almost every country of the world, the federal bond sector is the nation's largest and most liquid debt market.

Figure 19-1B shows the Japanese federal government is second to the U.S. government in terms of the dollar amount borrowed.[8] Japan issues 20-year coupon-paying bonds, floating-rate bonds, discounted notes, and discounted bills. These Japanese debt securities are similar to the debt securities issued by the U.S. Treasury. Other levels of Japanese government issue federal government agency bonds and local government bonds. Japan has a powerful federal bureaucracy, the Ministry of Finance, which must grant its approval before any of these various government bonds can be issued.

Figure 19-1D and Table 19-1 show that Italy's federal government issued a commanding 72% of that country's outstanding debt. This percentage is not as disproportionate as it may seem, because Italy has federal government agency debt of only 1% and almost no municipal debt outstanding. The U.S. Treasury (21%), U.S. government agencies (27%), and municipal governments (9%) borrow a 57% share of the total U.S. dollar–denominated debt—only 16 percentage points less than Italy's 72% total governmental borrowing.

NAMES FOR FEDERAL GOVERNMENT BONDS

In some cases the aggregate value of the bonds issued by federal governments is so large, and some of these bonds are traded over such a wide area, that they have popular nicknames:

T-bonds are issued by the U.S. Treasury.

OATs stands for Obligations Assimilables du Tresor, issued by the French government.

Bunds are issued by the German government's Deutsche Bank.

Gilts are the bonds issued by the British government's Bank of England.

To make things confusing, British traders use the word *bond* where U.S. traders would use *stock*.

Corporate Bond Sectors in the United States, Japan, Germany, and Italy. Figure 1-5A in Chapter 1 and Table 19-1 show that corporate bonds comprise more than 15% of the global bond market. Figure 19-1 highlights differences between the corporate bond markets in the world, U.S., Japanese, German, and Italian bond markets. Figures 19-1C and 19-1D indicate that the corporate bond sectors in Germany and Italy are unusually small for industrialized nations. These small proportions result from the custom of many European firms to borrow in the Eurobond market and/or obtain long-term bank loans instead of issuing bonds. Japanese businesses also rely on bank borrowing to a significant extent. These business traditions help explain why the corporate bond sectors of these modern nations are small proportions of their national bond markets.

INTERNATIONAL BONDS

International bonds or **crossborder bonds** comprised 13% of the world's aggregate in 1998 and have been a rapidly growing category for years—reflecting an increased willingness of borrowers in the United States, Europe, Asia, and emerging markets to borrow in foreign markets. International bonds are typically issued frequently because they often have short maturities and therefore need to be rolled over frequently.

International bond investors face two main types of political risk: (1) **repatriation-of-funds risk,** the risk that a government blocks payments of principal or interest owed to foreign creditors, and (2) **sovereign risk,** the risk that a government refuses to honor its debts.

International bonds can be categorized into the three following broad market groups:

◆ **Domestic bonds** are issued by a local borrower, denominated in the local currency, and regulated by the local government. (Chapter 5 focused on domestic bonds; this chapter focuses on international bonds.)

◆ **Foreign bonds** are issued in one country, in that country's currency, by a bond issuer from a different country. Foreign bonds are usually traded in the country of issuance and governed by regulations of the country of issuance. Foreign bonds can be subcategorized in terms of the country of issue, as discussed in the next section.

◆ **Eurobonds** are foreign bonds that are underwritten by an international investment banking syndicate and issued in several national markets simultaneously. The currency of denomination for Eurobonds may or may not correspond to the issuer's home currency. The **Eurobond market** encompasses any bond that is not issued in a domestic market, regardless of its currency denomination or the issuer's nationality. Eurobonds are issued by supranational agencies (World Bank, European Investment Bank, Inter-American Development Bank), sovereign governments, government agencies, manufacturing corporations, and financial corporations. Eurodollar bonds that are denominated in U.S. dollars are the largest component of the Eurobond market. Eurobonds and Eurodollar bonds are examined in the following discussion.

FOREIGN BONDS

There are many different categories of foreign bonds:

- ◆ **Yankee bonds** are issued by non-U.S. borrowers within the United States through U.S. investment bankers that register the issue with the SEC.

- ◆ Two types of foreign bonds that are similar to Yankee bonds are issued in Japan. First, non-Japanese borrowers can issue yen-denominated **Samurai bonds** in Japan. Second, **Shogun bonds** are also issued in Japan by non-Japanese borrowers, but they are unlike Samurais because they are not denominated in yen.

- ◆ Non-British entities issue **Bulldog bonds** denominated in British pounds sterling that trade in the U.K.

- ◆ **Matador bonds** are issued in Spain by non-Spanish borrowers.

- ◆ **Carvela bonds** are issued in Portugal by borrowers who are not Portuguese.

- ◆ **Rembrandt bonds** are issued in France by non-French issuers.

Other foreign bonds are issued in other countries as well. Yankee bonds comprise the largest category of foreign bonds.

Practically all U.S. dollar–denominated bonds issued by non-U.S. issuers are either Eurodollar bonds or Yankee bonds.* As mentioned above, Yankee bonds are issued by non-U.S. issuers that employ a U.S. investment banker to register the issue with the SEC and issue the bonds to investors in the United States. Unlike Eurodollar bonds, Yankee bonds are taxed and regulated by the U.S. government. Certain supranational agencies, Canadian provinces (Ontario, Quebec), Canadian utilities (Quebec Hydro), and sovereign governments (Kingdom of Sweden, New Zealand) are large issuers of Yankee bonds. Non-U.S. investors seeking high-quality bonds denominated in U.S. dollars often purchase Yankee bonds because primary and secondary markets for corporate bonds do not exist in their homeland. Corporate bond markets are nonexistent in many countries because some governments encourage domestic firms to borrow from banks rather than issue bonds. The absence of bond-quality rating services (Moody's, Fitch IBCA, and S&P) also inhibits the development of a corporate bond market in some countries. Although the secondary market for corporate bonds is illiquid in the United States, the primary market is active.

THE EUROBOND MARKET

The Eurobond market has been the fastest growing bond market in the world in some recent years. The market for Eurobonds is not the largest bond market in the world, but it is most

---

* A small amount of the Yankee bonds are not denominated in U.S. dollars.

diverse. Eurobonds cover a large number of different countries, instruments, and currencies. They are issued in all the currencies listed in Table 19-1, and others. Eurobonds include the following types of instruments:

◆ Coupon-paying bonds that pay fixed incomes, floating-rate bonds that pay fluctuating incomes, and zero-income bonds that pay no income.

◆ Ordinary bonds that, when they mature, are renewable into new ordinary bonds that have the same term to maturity, coupon rate, and other provisions.

◆ Ordinary bonds that contain embedded options granting the issuer or the buyer the right, when the bond matures, to be renewed into a new issue of floating-rate notes (FRNs).

◆ FRNs that may be exchanged for ordinary bonds at the option of the issuer or the investor.

◆ Convertible bonds.

◆ Bonds with warrants to purchase similar bonds, common stock, or other assets.

◆ Index-linked bonds that have their interest rates or their principal payments tied to some fluctuating market index that is based on the price of gold, the price of oil, a stock market index, or some other price index.

◆ Dual currency bonds that make coupon payments in one currency and principal payments in a different currency. Fannie Mae, for example, has issued yen/dollar dual currency bonds.

The list above is only suggestive; new debt structures are being created as you read. Investment bankers and clever borrowers around the world continually issue new instruments into the Eurobond market.

The Primary and Secondary Markets for Eurobonds

Underwriting syndicates for Eurobond offerings can be large and complex. The syndicate's *lead manager* and several *co-managers,* all from different commercial banks and investment banks headquartered in different countries, form a *management group* that can have from 4 to 30 member firms. The management group assembles an *underwriting group,* having as few as 20 or as many as 300 banks to help finance the new bond issue. Additional firms are added to the underwriting group to create the *selling group.* After the management group, underwriting group, and selling group that make up the **issuing syndicate** completes the offering, they split fees that range from 1.25% to 2.5% of the value of the bond issue.

Since the Eurobond market is neither taxed nor regulated, the time schedule for creating a new issue of Eurobonds is not lengthy. As suggested by Figure 19-2, as little as 6 weeks can elapse from the time the borrower decides to have a public offering and the date when the selling group stops taking purchase orders and pays the issuer for the bonds (the closing date). Public offerings of Eurobonds require less time to complete than the same bond issue carried out under the securities laws of practically any industrialized country. For instance, in the United States securities issuers are required to hire a securities lawyer, file application forms, and wait for advance written consent from the SEC before they can begin to issue bonds—a slow and costly bureaucratic procedure.

After the closing date of a Eurobond issue a tombstone is published, the issuing syndicate gives the issuer the cash proceeds, and public trading begins. A limited amount of advance trading usually begins weeks *before* the closing date. Advance trading in the Eurobond **gray market** begins before the final offering price of the issue is established. The gray market is a forward market for bonds that do not yet exist. Members of the selling group

FIGURE 19-2 The Chain of Events for a Eurobond Issue

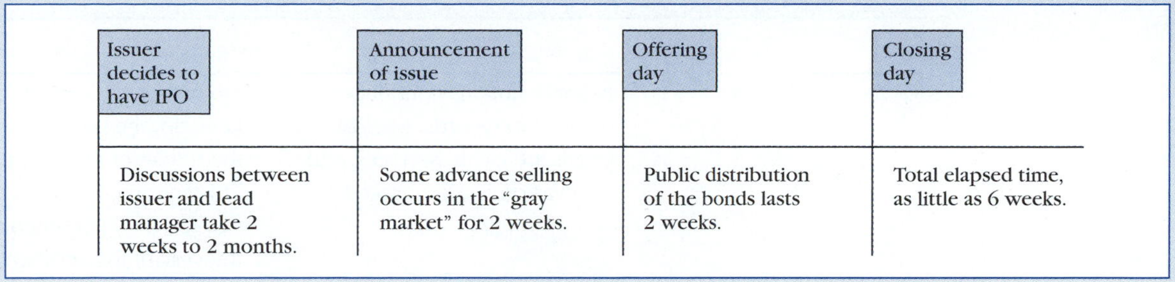

Issuer decides to have IPO	Announcement of issue	Offering day	Closing day
Discussions between issuer and lead manager take 2 weeks to 2 months.	Some advance selling occurs in the "gray market" for 2 weeks.	Public distribution of the bonds lasts 2 weeks.	Total elapsed time, as little as 6 weeks.

The time needed to create a new issue of Eurobonds is short since the Eurobond market is not taxed and not highly regulated. As little as 6 weeks can elapse from the time the borrower decides to raise capital and the date when the selling group closes the issue. It is faster, easier, and cheaper to issue Eurobonds than it is to issue bonds in the United States and deal with the U.S. government.

might sell bonds at conditional prices of "less one-half" in the gray market. "Less one-half" means the member of the selling group is selling the bond(s) for a price that is one-half of 1% below whatever eventually emerges as the bond issue's final offering price. The gray market allows members of the selling group to sell some or all of their portion of the forthcoming issue at a discounted price that is below the yet-to-be-determined issue price. As long as this discounted gray market price exceeds what the member of the selling group pays for the bond, the selling member profits from selling in the gray market.

Eurobonds include both government and corporate bonds. Most Eurobonds are listed on the Luxembourg Stock Exchange, which provides public price quotations. However, few bond transactions occur at the Luxembourg Stock Exchange. Most Eurobond transactions occur in an OTC market from telephone calls between the members of the International Securities Market Association (ISMA)—a self-policing trade association that has members throughout Europe and the United States. ISMA is similar to the NASD in the United States, except that nothing analogous to SEC intervention occurs in the Eurobond market. Freedom from bureaucratic delays, fees, and other types of legislated meddling motivates corporations to issue Eurobonds.

After a Eurobond trader consummates a transaction, the trade is settled within 7 days (it is 2 or 3 days in the United States) through either one of two competing clearing systems. Euroclear is operated by J. P. Morgan's office in Brussels. Cedel, Euroclear's competitor, is headquartered in Luxembourg. Both systems are owned and operated by groups of financial institutions; they handle any currency in which Eurobonds are traded; they both cover about 10,000 different issues of international debt; and they both provide margin accounts for those wanting credit.

Bearer Bonds Versus Registered Bonds

Unless local government regulations prohibit it, any bond issue can be either an issue of registered bonds or bearer bonds. **Registered bonds** send checks for the coupon interest to the registered bond owners whose names are kept on a list. Bond issues that have no list of registered owners' names are called **bearer bonds.** A bearer bond investor must tear off a dated coupon that is attached to their bond certificate as each coupon comes due and cash in the coupon to collect that date's coupon interest. The coupons can be deposited at a

TABLE 19-4	Advantages and Disadvantages of Bearer and Registered Bonds[a]	
	Registered Bonds	Bearer Bonds
Ownership Records	Issuer maintains continuous ownership records. So, lost bonds are easily replaced and tax evasion is discouraged.	No ownership records are kept. So, the bond belongs to the holder of the certificate. This anonymity makes tax evasion easy and encourages thievery of the certificates.
Interest Payments	Issuer mails checks for the interest payments directly to the bond owners The checks may be cashed immediately upon receipt.	Coupons must be clipped off the bond certificate and sent to the issuer to get the check for the coupon interest.
Back Office Considerations	Issuer must hire a transfer agent to maintain ownership records and issue certificates. As a result, redemptions are expedited.	Issuer must maintain operations to process periodic coupon payments. Redemptions are slow, risky, and complicated.

[a]The comparison between bearer bonds and registered bonds is equally applicable for municipal bonds, federal government bonds, corporate bonds, domestic bonds, and foreign bonds.

bank or cashed like checks. Table 19-4 contrasts the features of bearer bonds and registered bonds.*

Since the Eurobond market is neither taxed nor regulated, many Eurodollar bonds are bearer bonds. Income tax evaders, money launderers, criminals, and other deceptive investors prefer to invest in bearer bonds because the owner's identity is unknown.

Eurodollar Bonds

As explained in the discussion of Figure 1-7 in Chapter 1, the market for Eurodollar bonds comprises the largest component of the Eurobond market. **Eurodollar bonds** are U.S. dollar–denominated bonds that are (1) underwritten by an international syndicate of investment bankers, (2) issued and traded outside the jurisdiction of any single country, and (3) issued as bearer bonds. Many of the same organizations issue both Eurobonds and Eurodollar bonds. National governments, supranational agencies (World Bank, European Investment Bank), federal government agencies (Fannie Mae, Ginnie Mae), manufacturing corporations, and financial corporations issue Eurodollar bonds. Corporations in some countries with restrictive governments issue Eurodollar bonds to avoid regulations that do not permit them to issue similar bonds at home. Multinational issuers and investors alike use Eurodollar bonds because they are neither taxed nor regulated. As a result of their nearly complete tax exemption, the interest rates on Eurodollar bonds are usually less than the interest rates on similar domestic bonds denominated in the same currency.

---

* To reduce the opportunities for tax evasion and other deceptive practices, the U.S. government curtailed offerings of bearer bonds by municipalities by removing the tax-exemption for bearer bonds issued after 1981.

ACCRUED INTEREST

The credit markets of the world differ in some ways that are obvious and also in some ways that are not so obvious. One of the subtle ways that bond markets differ is the way they handle accrued interest.

The market price of a bond equals the present value of all of its future coupon interest payments and its principal (par, face value):

$$\begin{pmatrix} \text{Present value} \\ \text{of a bond} \end{pmatrix} = \frac{\text{Coupon}_1}{(1+k)^1} + \frac{\text{Coupon}_2}{(1+k)^2} + \ldots + \frac{\text{Coupon}_T + \text{Par}_T}{(1+k)^T} \qquad (19\text{-}1)$$

where T is the number of time periods until the bond terminates and k is the bond issue's risk-adjusted discount rate (required rate of return). The present value calculated with Eqn. 19-1 is sometimes called the bond's **clean price.**

Bonds may make their coupon-interest payments annually, semiannually, quarterly, or even more frequently. The interest payment dates are stipulated in the terms of the debt issuance contract (indenture contract, deed of trust). When a bond is purchased on any day between its scheduled coupon payment dates, the bond's buyer must compensate the bond's seller for that portion of the coupon payment that was earned but not yet received. This *accrued interest* is calculated as:[9]

$$\begin{pmatrix} \text{Accrued} \\ \text{coupon} \\ \text{payment} \end{pmatrix} = \begin{pmatrix} \text{Coupon payment} \\ \text{for relevant period} \end{pmatrix} \begin{pmatrix} \text{Number of days since last coupon payment was made} \\ \overline{\text{Number of days between scheduled coupon payment dates}} \end{pmatrix} \qquad (19\text{-}2)$$

The invoiced price for a bond normally includes the bond's present value (clean price) plus the accrued interest; this total is called the bond's **invoice price** or **full price** or **dirty price.**

$$\begin{pmatrix} \text{A bond's} \\ \text{dirty price, or} \\ \text{invoice price} \end{pmatrix} = \begin{pmatrix} \text{The present value of all future} \\ \text{cash flows expected from the} \\ \text{bond, or the clean price} \end{pmatrix} + \begin{pmatrix} \text{Accrued} \\ \text{coupon} \\ \text{payment} \end{pmatrix}$$

It is the practice in the United States to quote clean prices in the newspapers and elsewhere, while requiring bond buyers to pay dirty (invoice) prices that are a little higher. Figure 19-3 illustrates the difference between the clean price and the dirty price of a coupon-paying bond through time. Since the accrued coupon interest on a $1,000 bond paying coupons semiannually normally ranges from zero to $100 per bond, the difference between the clean price and the dirty price is not substantial.* Some countries follow different bond invoicing practices.

Dirty Bond Prices Experience an Ex-Coupon Price Drop-off

In a bond market where bond prices are quoted with accrued interest included, if a bond's accrued interest is positive, that dirty bond price is sometimes called a **cum coupon price,** because the coupon is added to the bond's price. A cum coupon (dirty) bond price experiences a sudden price drop-off immediately after the bond pays its coupon—when the accrued interest drops to zero. The first trading day that a bond's accrued interest drops to zero is called the **ex coupon date.** There is no ex coupon price drop-off in the clean price for a bond (published in U.S. newspapers) because clean bond prices do not include accrued interest.

---

* Bonds that are in default trade at flat prices. **Flat prices** contain no accrued interest because defaulted issuers do not make coupon interest payments.

FIGURE 19-3   The Clean and Dirty Prices Fluctuate Together for a $1,000 Bond Paying Semiannual Coupons

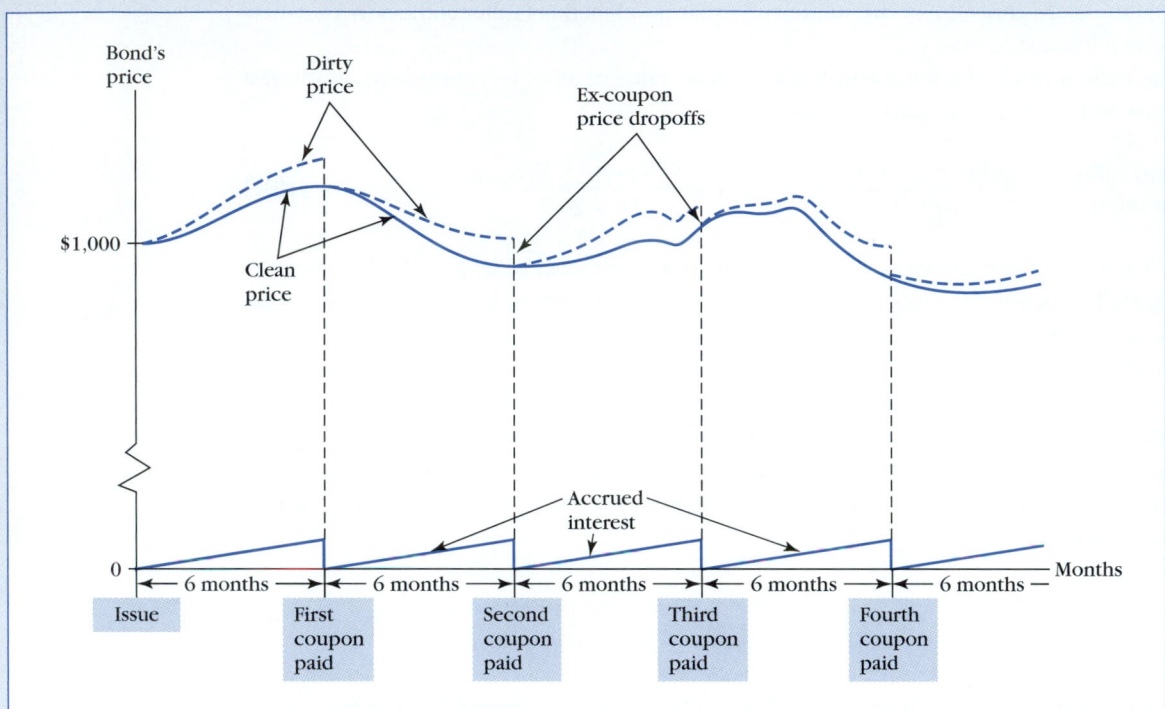

A bond's clean price fluctuates inversely with market interest rates. Accrued coupon interest (illustrated at bottom of figure) is combined with the clean price to obtain the bond's dirty price. Dirty bond prices contain ex-coupon price drop-offs that resemble the ex-dividend cash price drop-offs experienced by common stocks.

Day-counting Conventions

Eqn. 19-2 shows that the **day-count convention** used in computing accrued coupon interest is important.[10] Many money market securities, corporate bonds, and foreign bonds around the world are invoiced using the convention that a year is made up of twelve 30-day months, or a 360-day year. While this day count convention does not align with the calendar year, it is the convention to which millions of investors adhere. At the same time, investors in the United Kingdom, Canada, and Japan use (the actual calendar number of days in) a 365-day year in many of their bond computations.

Some day-count convention must be adopted for each bond computation. If the transaction is sizable, it behooves the parties to the transaction to master the appropriate conventions.

Compounding Conventions

The length of the *compounding period,* or, equivalently, the length of time between coupon payments, has a significant impact on bonds' yields and prices. Eurobonds pay annual coupons, U.S. Treasury bonds pay semiannual coupons, floating-rate notes (FRNs) make quarterly payments, and Ginnie Mae bonds make monthly payments. Figure 19-4 illustrates the

FIGURE 19-4   The Power of Compounding Increases with Frequency of Compounding

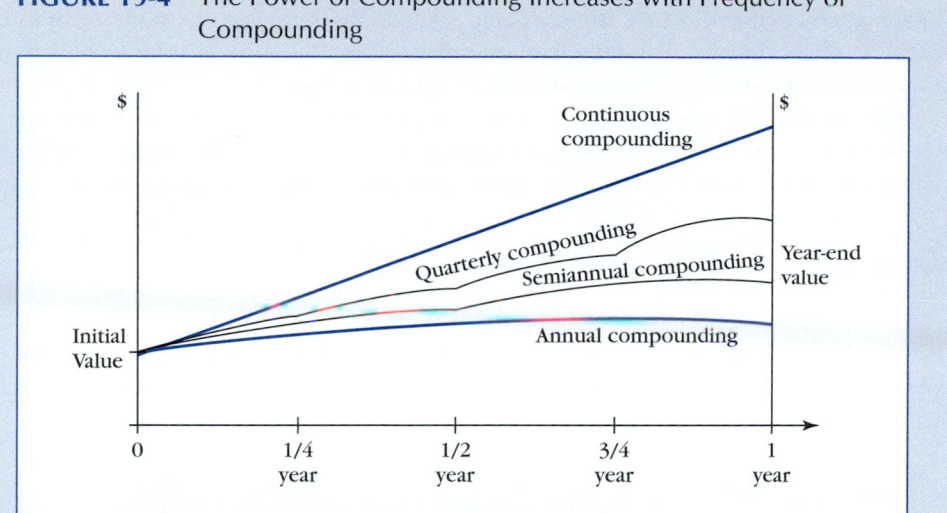

If all other factors are held constant, the interest on the principal and the interest on the interest both accumulate more rapidly as they are compounded more often (the length of the compounding intervals is reduced).

results of different compounding (coupon) intervals. As a result of these different compounding periods, different formulas must be used to calculate the yields-to-maturity (YTM) and prices of these different types of fixed income securities.

THE YIELD-TO-MATURITY (YTM): A FIRST LOOK

In Japan the following simple-interest formula is used to compute a bond's yield-to-maturity (YTM):

$$\begin{pmatrix} \text{Noncompounded} \\ \text{yield-to-maturity} \end{pmatrix} = \begin{pmatrix} \text{Coupon} \\ \text{rate} \end{pmatrix} + \left[\frac{\text{Par} - \text{Current price}}{\text{Years until maturity}} \right] \Big/ (\text{Current price}) \qquad \textbf{(19-3)}$$

$$= \begin{pmatrix} \text{Rate of} \\ \text{cash flow} \end{pmatrix} + \begin{pmatrix} \text{Rate of price appreciation} \\ \text{or depreciation} \end{pmatrix}$$

Eqn. 19-3 is easy to compute and understand.

Unlike the YTM formulas used in other countries, the YTM computed with Eqn. 19-3 involves no compounding (no interest on the interest). This YTM approximates (within, say, 40 basis points or less) the compounded YTM that would be calculated on Wall Street for a bond having the same cash flows. In fact, some American finance textbooks suggest that Eqn. 19-3 be used to approximate compounded YTMs because of its simpler computations. Since a basis point is only $\frac{1}{100}$ of 1%, the discrepancy between the compounded and the noncompounded YTMs might seem insignificant. However, in a multimillion-dollar bond transaction, 1 basis point can be worth thousands of dollars.

The Compounded Yield-to-Maturity (YTM)

Most investors define the YTM to be a compounded rate of return. The **yield-to-maturity (YTM)** is usually defined as the discount rate that equates the present value of all a bond's future cash flows with its current market price (purchase price).*

The well-known present-value formula, Eqn. 19-4, for a bond is used to compute the bond's compounded YTM. Eqn. 19-4 is appropriate for a bond that makes annual coupon payments and has T years until the bond matures and repays its par value (principal, face value).

$$\text{Present value} = \frac{\text{Coupon}_1}{(1 + YTM)^1} + \frac{\text{Coupon}_2}{(1 + YTM)^2} + \cdots + \frac{\text{Coupon}_T + \text{Par}}{(1 + YTM)^T} \tag{19-4}$$

Most bonds in the United States pay semiannual coupons. Semiannual coupons are half the size of annual coupons but are paid twice as often. The YTM of a bond that pays semiannual coupons is computed with Eqn. 19-5:

$$\binom{\text{Present}}{\text{value}} = \frac{\text{Coupon}_1/2}{(1 + YTM/2)^1} + \frac{\text{Coupon}_2/2}{(1 + YTM/2)^2} + \cdots + \frac{\text{Coupon}_{2T}/2 + \text{Par}}{(1 + YTM/2)^{2T}} \tag{19-5}$$

Eqn. 19-5 doubles the number of time periods used in Eqn. 19-4 from T years with annual coupons, to $2T$ 6-month periods with semiannual coupons. Eqn. 19-5 also adjusts the YTM for semiannual compounding by halving it. When the YTM of a fixed-income structure is calculated with Eqn. 19-5, the YTM is sometimes called a **bond equivalent yield.** In the United States and many other places it is the convention to use either Eqn. 19-4 or Eqn. 19-5 to calculate the YTM of practically all annual and semiannual bonds, respectively.

In addition to the Japanese (noncompounded) way and the American (compounded) way, there are other ways to compute the YTM for a bond that pays semiannual coupons. In particular, the **effective YTM (EYTM)** for a bond that pays semiannual coupons is computed with Eqn. 19-6:

$$\binom{\text{Present}}{\text{value}} = \frac{\text{Coupon}_1/2}{(1 + EYTM)^{.5}} + \frac{\text{Coupon}_2/2}{(1 + EYTM)^1} + \frac{\text{Coupon}_3/2}{(1 + EYTM)^{1.5}} + \cdots \tag{19-6}$$

$$+ \frac{\text{Coupon}_T/2 + \text{Par}}{(1 + EYTM)^T}$$

In Eqn. 19-6 the years are cut in half (by using fractional exponents) instead of (as was done in Eqn. 19-5) halving the YTM. Eqn. 19-6 produces a mathematically correct effective YTM that differs slightly from the YTM convention defined by Eqn. 19-5. But, few people compute effective YTMs; it is conventional to compute bond-equivalent yields with Eqn. 19-5.**

---

* The yield-to-maturity (YTM) is typically called the **internal rate of return (IRR)** in managerial finance textbook discussions of capital budgeting. The IRR is defined as the discount rate that equates the present value of all future net cash flows (including the asset's purchase price) to zero.

$$0 = \frac{\text{Net cash flow}_1}{(1 + IRR)^1} + \frac{\text{Net cash flow}_2}{(1 + IRR)^2} + \cdots + \frac{\text{Net cash flow}_T}{(1 + IRR)^T} - (\text{Purchase price})$$

The IRR is identical to the YTM.

** Some books call the effective YTM the **effective annualized return (EAR)**. The following simple relationship between an annual interest rate quoted in the newspaper and the EYTM (or EAR) is computationally convenient. $EYTM = EAR = [1 + (\text{Quoted rate}/N)]^N - 1.0$ where N equals the number of compounding periods per year.

COMPARING A BOND'S CONVENTIONAL AND EFFECTIVE YTMS

EXAMPLE

A $100 par value bond has a 10% coupon rate, pays semiannual coupons, matures in 10 years, and can be purchased for $106.59. Solving the conventional YTM formula, Eqn. 19-5a, we find $YTM = 8.9873\%$.

$$\$106.59 = \frac{\$10/2}{(1 + .089873/2)^1} + \frac{\$10/2}{(1 + .089873/2)^2} + \cdots + \frac{\$10/2 + \$100}{(1 + .089873/2)^{20}} \tag{19-5a}$$

Computing with Eqn. 19-6a, the same bond's effective YTM is $EYTM = 9.1892\%$, which exceeds the bond's conventional YTM by $(9.1892\% - 8.9873\% = .2019)$ about 20 basis points.

$$\$106.59 = \frac{\$10/2}{(1 + .091892/2)^{.5}} + \frac{\$10/2}{(1 + .091892/2)^1} + \cdots + \frac{\$10/2 + \$100}{(1 + .091892/2)^{10}} \tag{19-6a}$$

The denominators of Eqns. 19-5 and 19-6 are where these two yield formulas differ. Equating these two different denominators produces a relationship that sheds light on the difference in the two yield measures.[11]

$$(1 + EYTM) = (1 + YTM/2)^2$$

Solving the equation above for EYTM yields:

$$EYTM = YTM + YTM^2/4 = 0.089873 + (0.089873)^2/4 = .091892 = 9.1892\%$$

These computations show that an investor who purchased the 10-year bond actually earns about $(YTM^2/4 = .002019 =)$ 20 basis points more than the conventional YTM formula indicates. It is comforting to note that this is the same numerical difference that the indirect computations above produced.

Eqn. 19-7 extends the logic embodied in Eqn. 19-5 to bonds that pay coupons quarterly. Quarterly coupons are one-fourth the size of annual coupons and are paid four times as often.*

$$\binom{\text{Present}}{\text{value}} = \frac{\text{Coupon}_1/4}{(1 + YTM/4)^1} + \frac{\text{Coupon}_2/4}{(1 + YTM/4)^2} + \cdots + \frac{\text{Coupon}_{2T}/4 + \text{Par}}{(1 + YTM/4)^{4T}} \tag{19-7}$$

Comparing Various YTMs for a Bond

Because bonds' YTMs are often reported with decimal point precision, some people think the YTM is a highly definitive measure of bond performance. That is not true. Table 19-5

---

* The frequency of compounding can be increased to monthly, daily, and, eventually, to infinitely frequent. The present value of a bond that pays its coupons in a continuous stream (infinitely often) is calculated with Eqn. 19-8:

$$\text{Present value} = (\text{Par})e^{(-YTM)(T\,\text{Years})} + \int_0^{T\,\text{Years}} e^{(-YTM)(t)}(\text{Annual coupon})\,dt \tag{19-8}$$

Continual payments are an intellectually interesting, but an unrealistic, limiting case.

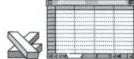

TABLE 19-5   Various YTMs for a $100 Par Value Bond with 10% Coupon Rate, 10-Year Maturity, and a $106.59 Market Price

(A) Conventional YTMs for Various Compounding Intervals

Coupon Frequency	Yield-to-Maturity	Equation Used
Annual	8.9743%	(19-4)
Semiannual	8.9873%	(19-5)
Quarterly	8.9939%	(19-7)
Monthly	8.9983%	Eqn. not shown
Continuous	9.0000%	(19-8)

(B) Various YTMs for Semiannual Coupons

Type of Computation	Yield-to-Maturity	Equation Used
Conventional Semiannual	8.9873%	(19-5)
Effective Semiannual	9.1892%	(19-6)
Japanese Semiannual	9.3817%	(19-3)

compares the different YTMs computed for the same bond under different assumptions about how often the coupon payments are made, and, using different techniques to compute the YTM of the bond that pays semiannual coupons. For the same bond, the lowest YTM is 8.9743% and the highest is 9.341%.

Conditions Required for an Investor to Earn a Bond's Expected YTM

A YTM calculated with any of the preceding formulas is the rate of return the bond investor hopes to get, but may not actually receive. A bond's computed YTM will actually be earned only if several assumptions that are implicit in the formula all work out as planned. If the bond (1) is held to maturity, (2) does not default in the timing or amount of its scheduled payments, and (3) has all of its cash flows immediately reinvested to earn the bond's YTM, then the bond investor will earn the YTM. If one or more of the three assumptions is not fulfilled, the bond will not produce the YTM the investor was promised.*

---

* Consider a bond that has $100 par, sells for $106.59, pays semiannual coupons of $5 (10% coupon rate), and matures in 1.5 years. Substituting these values into Eqn. 19-5 produces:

$$\begin{pmatrix} \text{Present} \\ \text{value} \end{pmatrix} = \frac{\text{Coupon}_1/2}{(1 + YTM/2)^1} + \frac{\text{Coupon}_2/2}{(1 + YTM/2)^2} + \cdots + \frac{\text{Coupon}_{2T}/2 + \text{Par}}{(1 + YTM/2)^{2T}}$$

$$\$106.59 = \frac{\$5}{(1 + YTM/2)^1} + \frac{\$5}{(1 + YTM/2)^2} + \frac{\$5 + \$100}{(1 + YTM/2)^3}$$

Multiplying both sides of the equation above by $(1 + YTM/2)^3$ produces:

$$(\$106.59)(1 + YTM/2)^3 = (\$5)(1 + YTM/2)^2 + (\$5)(1 + YTM/2) + (\$5 + \$100)$$

The equation above highlights three conditions under which the left side equals the right side of the equation: (1) if the bond is held to maturity, (2) no default, and (3) all cash flows are immediately reinvested at the YTM.

TABLE 19-6	Different Reinvestment Rate Assumptions for an 8% Coupon Bond Purchased at Par					
	Interest on Interest					
Assumed Reinvestment Rate, %	Percent of Total Return, %	Amount, $	Coupon Income, $[a]	Capital Gain or Discount	Total Return, $	Total Realized Compound Yield, %
0%	0%	$0	$1600	0	$1600	4.84%
5	41	1096	1600	0	2696	6.64
6	47	1416	1600	0	3016	7.07
7	53	1782	1600	0	3382	7.53
8	58	2201	1600	0	3801	8.00
9	63	2681	1600	0	4281	8.50
10	67	3232	1600	0	4832	9.01

[a]($1,000 par, or face value)(8% coupon rate)(20 years) = ($1,600 coupon income)

SOURCE: Sidney Homer and Martin Leibowitz, *Inside the Yield Book* (Upper Saddle River, NJ: Prentice-Hall, 1972), 22, Table 1.

The Reinvestment Rate Effects a Bond's Realized YTM

As mentioned previously, a bond's YTM is an expected return (promised YTM), which assumes that all interest income is reinvested at the YTM that existed on the day the bond was initially purchased. This assumption is dubious because the bond's income from coupon-interest payments might be reinvested to earn less than the YTM, or the coupon income might be consumed.

Table 19-6 illustrates the effects of different reinvestment rate assumptions on the YTM a bond investor actually realizes. The table shows the compound rate of return realized for a bond paying a coupon rate of 8.0% that is purchased, held until it matures in 20 years, and repays its par value at maturity. Table 19-6 shows a YTM of only 4.84% is realized if the coupon interest is consumed (not reinvested). The bond's YTM is reduced because the investor will not get to earn the *interest-on-the-interest.* In contrast, the same bond has a realized total yield of 9.01% if the coupons are reinvested at 10%. These different realized returns show the importance of the reinvestment opportunities and highlights an often-ignored source of a bond risk. **Reinvestment rate risk** can cause a bond's realized yield to deviate significantly from its promised YTM.

RELATIONSHIPS AMONG A BOND'S YTM, ITS PRICE, AND ITS OTHER RETURN MEASURES

Many investors sell their bonds before they mature and, as a result, actually earn a rate of return that differs from the bond's YTM.

A Bond's Holding Period Return

Eqn. 19-9 defines a **one-period rate of return** that is appropriate for investors who sell a bond before it matures:

$$r = \frac{\text{Price change} + \text{Cash flow (if any)}}{\text{Price at beginning of the holding period}} = \frac{(P_1 - P_0) + CF}{P_0} \tag{19-9}$$

A bond's one-period rate of return is a **holding period return** that can be a positive, zero, or negative during a holding period as the market price of the bond fluctuates. For example, when the market price (present value) of a zero coupon bond rises, the bond's one-period rate of return for that holding period is positive. When the market price of a zero coupon bond remains unchanged, the bond's one-period return for that holding period is zero. And, when the zero coupon bond's price falls, the bond's one-period rate of return for that holding period is negative. The price moves that cause a bond's one-period rate of return to be positive, zero, or negative are determined by fluctuations in the bond's market interest rate (YTM). The YTM is a multi-period (not one period) rate of return.

The Inverse Relationship Between a Bond's Price and Its YTM

The first derivative of a bond's present value formula with respect to that bond's YTM mathematically represents the change in price that results from a small change in the bond's YTM. Eqn. 19-10 is the first derivative of present value Eqn. 19-4.

$$\frac{dP}{d\text{YTM}} = \frac{(-1)(\text{Coupon}_1)}{(1 + YTM)^2} + \frac{(-2)(\text{Coupon}_2)}{(1 + YTM)^3} + \ldots + \frac{(-T)(\text{Coupon}_T + Par)}{(1 + YTM)^{T+1}} \tag{19-10}$$

Since the values of all the cash flows and the YTM in Eqn. 19-10 can be assumed to have positive values, the series of negative integers in the numerator will determine the sign of the entire equation. In other words, Coupon > 0, Par > 0, and $YTM > 0$ implies that the first derivative is negative in sign, $dP/dYTM < 0$. The financial interpretation of this negative first derivative is that the price and YTM of a bond always move inversely. Eqn. 19-10 is depicted graphically in Figure 19-5.

Figure 19-5 illustrates the negative relationship between the present value (price) and YTM of a bond. Eqn. 19-10 states with mathematical accuracy, and Figure 19-5 illustrates the inverse relationship between the present value and the YTM of every bond. This is unambiguous mathematical proof that, if a bond's YTM changes during some short period of time, that bond's price will simultaneously move in the opposite direction.

The inverse relationship between price and YTM exists for all bonds. Figure 19-6 depicts the relationship between the YTM from a long-term U.S. Treasury bond and that T-bond's one-period rates of return computed with Eqn. 19-9. The bond's one-period returns vary directly with the bond's price fluctuations (because the coupon payments are constant).*

Other Measures of Bonds' Yields

A bond's performance can be evaluated in terms of additional features. The yield-to-call, floating rate, and current yield provide additional measures of bond performance.

Yield-to-Call (YTC). Callable bonds have an **embedded option** that the bond issuer may or may not find profitable to exercise. The uncertainty about whether or not the bond will be called forces the investor to evaluate both of the possible future scenarios.

---

* The 1979–82 period that is illustrated in Figure 19-6 portrays an interesting period in monetary policy. Before October 1979 one of the targets of the U.S. Federal Reserve's monetary policy was to smooth market interest rate fluctuations. The Fed temporarily abandoned its smoothing activities and let market interest rates fluctuate freely from October 1979 through the fall of 1982. The temporarily high level of volatility in interest rates that resulted is clearly visible in Figure 19-6. The standard deviation in monthly returns increased almost 50% during the 1979–82 period.

FIGURE 19-5   The Relationship Between a Bond's Price and Its YTM

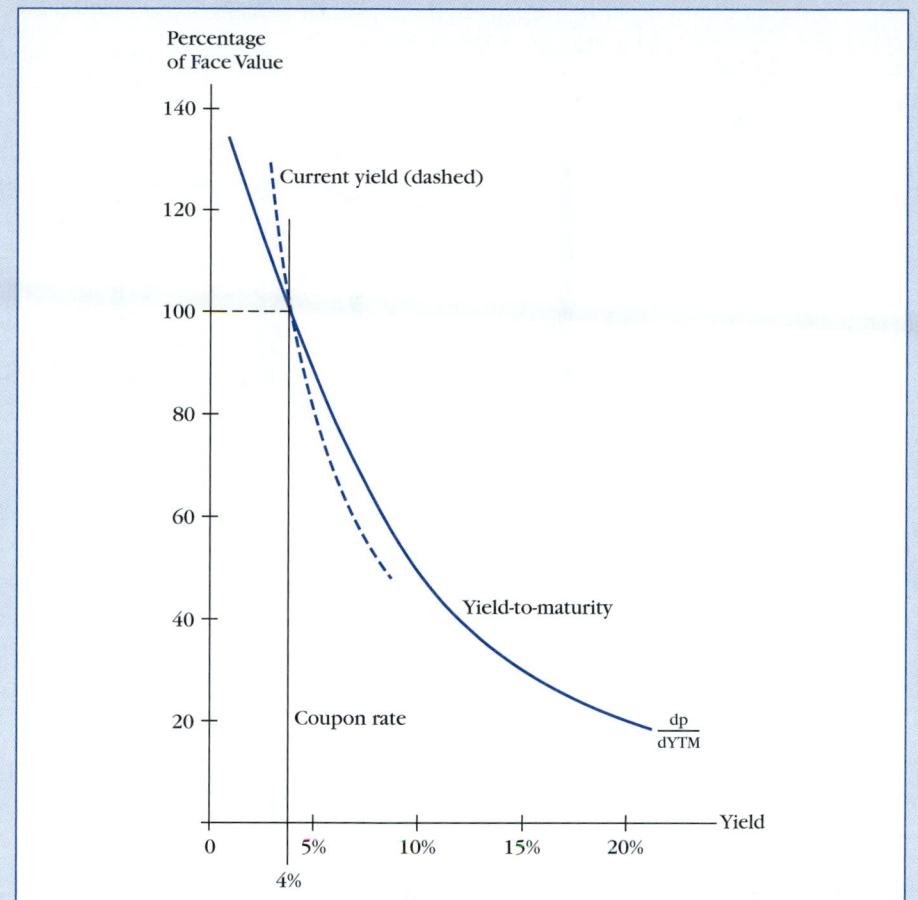

The bond's 4% coupon rate never varies. As the bond's market interest rate (yield-to-maturity) swings between 2% and 20%, the market price of a $100 bond fluctuates inversely in a range between $20 and $130. The bond's market price and YTM move inversely along the solid curve. The bond's current yield [(annual dollar coupon)/(current market price)] moves inversely along the dashed curve.

First, if market interest rates rise it is safe to assume the bond issuer will not find it profitable to exercise the call option. When the bond is not called, it is customary to assume the bond remains outstanding until its maturity date. In the event of this first outcome, the traditional YTM is the appropriate yield measure. Second, consider the possibility that market interest rates decline and that makes it profitable for the bond's issuer to call the bond before it matures. To evaluate this second scenario the bond's YTC must be calculated. The investor never knows in advance which of the two scenarios will occur. The conservative approach is to compute both of these two different yields and then select the lower yield for investment decision-making purposes, because that return represents the minimum yield that the investor can expect to earn.

The YTC is calculated like the YTM. Eqn. 19-5 can be solved for the YTC by setting the terminal time period, T, equal to the bond's time-to-call instead of its time-to-maturity.[12]

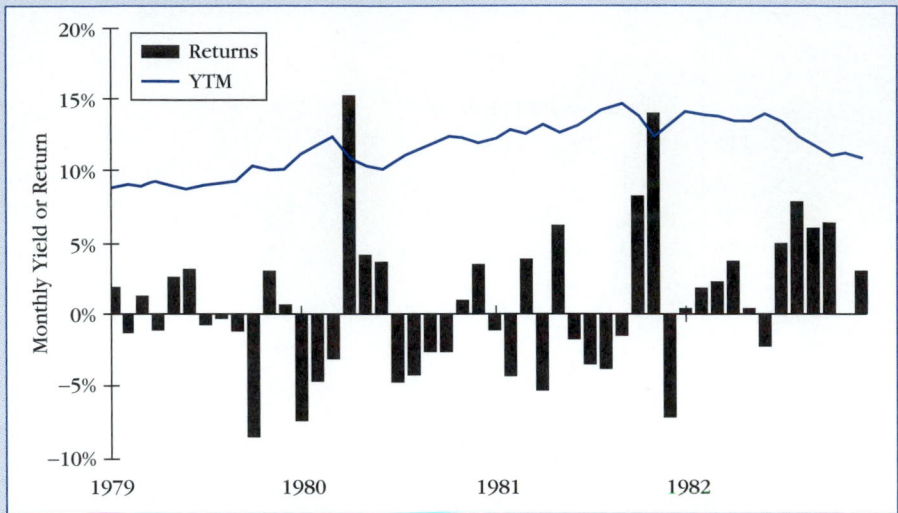

FIGURE19-6 The Inverse Price-YTM Relationship Is Visible in a Graph of One-Period Returns from a Long-Term U.S. Treasury Bond as Its YTM Fluctuates, 1979–82

As a long-term U.S. Treasury bond's YTM fluctuates its market price fluctuates inversely. The inverse Price-Yield relationship is visible in the bar-graph of the T-bond's one-period rates of returns calculated with Eqn. 19-9 as the one-period returns move inversely with the bond's YTM month by month during 1979–82.

SOURCE: Data from *Stocks, Bonds, Bills, and Inflation 1997 Yearbook*, Ibbotson Associates, Chicago. Computations and graph done with EnCorr software from Ibbotson Associates.

EXAMPLE

COMPARING A CALLABLE BOND'S YTC AND YTM

Step One: Compute the YTM. Consider a $10,000 bond paying a 3.5% annual coupon rate for 10 years. Eqn. 19-5 indicates that this bond's present value is $8,140.32 if its cash flows are discounted at a YTM of 6% per year (or 3.0% per 6-month period). The present value of $175 coupons per 6-month period for 20 periods is:

$$\$8,140.32 = \sum_{t=1}^{T=20} \frac{\$175}{(1 + 0.03)^t} + \frac{\$10,000}{(1 + 0.03)^{20}}$$

Step Two: Compute the YTC. Assume the bond has a 7% call premium, which means it is callable at 107% of its par in 5 years (10 semiannual periods). In this case the bond's yield-to-call would be [(4.686% per 6-month period) × (two 6-month periods per year) =] 9.373% at an annual rate. To compute the YTC set $T = 10$ semiannual periods, PV = $10,700 (equals 107% of $10,000 par), and solve for the unknown YTC value. The solution is YTC = 4.686%, or, YTC = 9.372% when it is doubled to restate it at an annual rate.

$$\$8,140.32 = \sum_{t=1}^{T=10} \frac{\$175}{(1 + 0.04686)^t} + \frac{(\$10,000)(1 + 7\%)}{(1 + 0.04686)^{10}}$$

The Conservative Assumption. It would cost the bond issuer the YTC of 9.372% in annual interest expense to call in the callable bond issue before maturity. For decision-making purposes, let us assume the bond will earn its current YTM of 6% if held until maturity. Under this assumption, the bond issuer's cost-minimizing choice is to pay YTM = 6% instead of calling the bond and thereby incurring the higher interest expense of YTC = 9.372%. Summarizing, the bond investor's conservative choice is to assume the bond issuer will make a cost minimizing (profit-maximizing) decision and let the bond mature. Unless additional information becomes available, the investor should make a buy-sell decision based on the YTM = 6% outcome and ignore the unlikely possibility of earning YTC = 9.372%.

Floaters. Most bonds' coupon rates cannot be changed after they are issued, unless the bond is a "floater." A **floater** is a bond with a fixed par and fluctuating (floating) periodic interest payments that vary in accordance with some specified **reference rate.** LIBOR or the U.S. T-bill rate are commonly used as a reference rate. Some prespecified number of basis points is added to the reference rate to establish the floating rate that is used to compute the bond's periodic interest payments. The future values of floating interest rates cannot be known in advance; they can only be forecasted.

Current Yield. Every bond has a non-negative current yield.

$$\text{Current yield} = \frac{\text{Dollars of coupon interest per year}}{\text{Bond's current market price}}$$

The current yield measures the annual cash flow relative to the bond's current market price. Retirees who live on investment cash flows, for instance, are interested in a bond's current yield.

A BOND'S CURRENT YIELD   EXAMPLE

Suppose a 6% coupon bond with $100 par is selling at the price of $90.

$$\text{Current yield} = \frac{\text{Dollars of coupon interest per year}}{\text{Bond's current market price}} = \frac{\$6}{\$90} = 6.666\%$$

Figure 19-5 illustrates how three different interest rate measures interact with the market price of a default-free bond with $1,000 par value, 4% coupon rate, and 20 years until maturity. The one-period rate of return is not shown in this figure because it depends on the beginning-of-period and end-of-period prices of the bond and cannot be illustrated in the figure. The coupon rate does not vary, as shown by the vertical line in Figure 19-5. The YTM and the current yield are positively related and both vary inversely with the bond's price because they are both divided by the price of the bond.

Note that the price-yield curves in Figure 19-5 are *convex* to the origin. The convexity of the price-YTM curve *i*s discussed later in this chapter and other chapters.*[13]

---

*   Convexity is discussed in Chapter 21 of this book. Convexity is measured by the second derivative below. This second derivative is the derivative of the first derivative in Eqn. 19-10.

$$\frac{d^2(\text{Price})}{d(YTM)^2} = \text{Convexity} = \left(\begin{array}{c} \text{The derivative of the slope of} \\ \text{Price} - YTM \text{ curve in Figure 19-5} \end{array} \right)$$

Analyzing the way a bond's YTM and its other yield measures interact with its present value helps us understand high-quality bonds. But, high-yield (low-quality) bonds that sometimes default on their scheduled cash flows can behave differently.

BRADY BONDS AID EMERGING COUNTRIES

Easy credit promoted business development and bank lending in a number of emerging countries during the 1980s. Toward the end of that decade falling commodity prices and recessions in some countries touched off an international debt crisis. Loans with an aggregate par value of more than $200 billion were defaulting. The crisis threatened the international financial system. Many emerging countries vanished from the international financial markets. Billions of dollars of defaulted bank loans, mostly from Latin America, had to be rescheduled and refinanced to revive the economies of the troubled emerging countries. Refinancing the defaulted loans was difficult because bank loans are not marketable securities.

Debtor banks created an organization called the Paris Club to represent their interests. These troubled banks also organized a secondary market for the nonperforming bank loans. The defaulted bank loans being bought and sold were typically valued at less than half of their original face value. This secondary market in nonperforming bank loans allowed debtor banks to recover some of their lost capital and provided financing for the emerging countries. In 1989 Nicholas Brady, then secretary of the U.S. Treasury, suggested what came to be known as the *Brady plan* to deal with these problems.

The Brady plan did not pay off the defaulted bank loans, but it provided a way to finance them until they could be paid off at a later date. By 1997 the Paris Club organized the defaulted bank loans into 15 national categories based on the countries of the defaulted banks. These countries include Argentina, Brazil, Bulgaria, Costa Rica, Czech Republic, Hungary, India, Indonesia, Mexico, Nigeria, Poland, the Philippines, Turkey, Uruguay, and Venezuela. Under the Brady plan an emerging country must get an economic reform plan approved and get loans from the International Monetary Fund (IMF) and the World Bank, and/or some other development bank. The Inter-American Development Bank, the African Development Bank, the Asian Development Bank, and the European Bank for Reconstruction and Development participated in the Brady plan. These development banks bought defaulted bank loans and, in so doing, acquired any collateral that might be backing the loans. The development banks then fashioned repayment plans for the defaulted debt and made them marketable by guaranteeing the repayments. These arrangements allowed the troubled banks in the emerging countries to, essentially, exchange their illiquid defaulted bank loans for liquid Brady bonds. International commercial banks that were the most active lenders to the defaulted banks aided by making active markets in Brady bonds. About $165 billion of Brady bonds were outstanding in 1999, and many were traded in liquid markets. For up-to-the-minute information about Brady bonds and options and futures on Brady bonds visit the Chicago Mercantile Exchange's (CME) Web site at: www.cme.com/market/emerging/bradys.html.

Brady bonds enjoy credit enhancements, but no Brady bonds are 100% guaranteed. Brady bonds can be viewed as sovereign bonds issued by the governments of emerging countries with credit enhancements to increase their liquidity.

Innovative investment bankers have crafted a variety of instruments to make Brady bonds marketable. A single country may issue one or more of the following types of Brady bonds.

1. **The Discount bonds,** or, **principal-reduction bonds,** are issued at a deep discount from the par value of the defaulted debt they replace. The discount equals the debt reduction.

2. **The Par bond,** or **interest-reduction bond,** is a bond whose face value equals the par value of the defaulted debts. They are long-term bonds that usually pay coupon interest. The debt reduction occurs by setting their coupon rates below current market interest rates, which reduces the bond's value. The Par bonds and The Discount bonds usually benefit from principal collateral and rolling-interest guarantees to enhance their credit-worthiness. They are the most popular forms of Brady bonds, but other forms are also outstanding.

3. **Debt-conversion bonds (DCBs)** and **new-money bonds (NMBs)** are typically issued in conjunction under the Brady plan's new-money option to motivate debt holders to invest new money (additional capital) into the emerging country. Each dollar invested in NMBs can be converted into a larger amount (usually about $5 worth) of the more desirable DCBs. This conversion privilege provides the incentive to buy NMBs.

4. **Front-loaded interest-reduction bonds (FLIRBs)** usually have 20 years to maturity and pay low coupon rates during their early years (which provides front loaded debt forgiveness). After several early years of low fixed coupons, the coupon rate increases.

5. **Past-due interest bonds (PDIs)** are issued to pay for interest payments that were omitted in the past. Some issues of PDIs are called floating rate bonds (FRBs) and others are called interest due and unpaid (IDU) bonds.

Financial analysts judge the investment merits of Brady bonds by comparing and contrasting different issues of Brady bonds. The Brady Plan produced three positive outcomes:

1. The emerging nations were able to settle their defaulted bank debts at a reduced cost.
2. Reducing the debt burden of the troubled nations paved the way for renewed economic growth there, and with their trading partners.
3. The troubled nations were able to regain access to the world's capital markets.

Economic renewal plans like the Brady Plan are sometimes criticized for (1) being too costly to the industrialized nations that finance the development banks, and (2) subsidizing financial mismanagement in the troubled nations.

INTERNATIONAL BOND INDEX STATISTICS

Ibbotson Associates used yield-to-maturity data provided by the International Monetary Fund (IMF) to compute market prices of federal governments' bonds. Next, the computed bond prices, bond coupon data, and monthly foreign exchange rate data were used to tabulate one-period rates of return for bonds from different countries. Total returns are computed with Eqn. 19-9. Table 19-7 displays compounded annual average returns (CAR) and standard deviations (SD) that were computed from the one-period rates of return from ten industrialized nations for which consistently defined data has been available for a few recent decades. The statistics in Table 19-7 are reported from the perspective of investors residing in the United States, Britain, Hong Kong, and Germany from 1970 through 1996 inclusive. It is noteworthy that no single bond investment in Table 19-7 appears to be the most risky or least risky, or have the highest return or lowest return, from the different perspectives of investors in the United States, Britain, Hong Kong, and Germany. For instance, what is a good bond investment for a German investor might be a bad investment for an investor in the United States. This lack of a consistent risk or return pattern results from a combination of different components that behave independently.

TABLE 19-7   Summary Statistics for 4 Different Long-Term Government Bond Investments, 1970–96

Investment of:	U.S. $		U.K. Pound		Hong Kong $		German Mark	
	CAR	SD	CAR	SD	CAR	SD	CAR	SD
Australia	8.5%	15.5%	9.9%	18.3%	9.5%	16.4%	5.0%	20.2%
Belgium	11.6%	17.2%	13.0%	14.7%	12.7%	16.2%	8.1%	8.6%
Canada	9.3%	10.4%	10.7%	19.3%	10.3%	13.2%	5.8%	17.0%
France	10.8%	15.6%	12.2%	15.3%	11.8%	15.6%	7.2%	12.2%
Germany	12.0%	14.9%	13.4%	16.7%	13.0%	13.4%	8.4%	8.4%
Japan	12.2%	17.5%	13.7%	18.4%	13.3%	18.3%	8.7%	17.3%
Netherlands	11.7%	14.2%	13.1%	15.8%	12.7%	14.0%	8.1%	8.2%
Switzerland	10.2%	17.1%	11.6%	16.8%	11.2%	16.0%	6.7%	9.8%
United Kingdom	10.2%	22.3%	11.6%	17.2%	11.6%	17.2%	11.3%	23.4%
United States	9.3%	12.2%	10.6%	21.3%	10.3%	14.7%	5.8%	16.8%

CAR = Compund annual return

SD = Standard deviation

SUMMARY: Federal bond returns are from the perspective of investors residing in the United States, Britain, Hong Kong, and Germany. The table contains compound annual returns (CAR) and standard deviations (SD) for each strategy.

SOURCE: Raw data from the International Monetary Fund (IMF) is processed, supplemented, and maintained by Ibbotson Associates in Chicago.

The Components of International Bond Returns

Table 19-8 decomposes the bond returns to the U.S. dollar investor from Table 19-7 into three mutually exclusive components. For investments in each of the countries total returns computed with Eqn. 19-9 are partitioned into a capital appreciation component, a coupon income component, and a foreign exchange component. The foreign exchange component equals the return from the pure investment in the foreign currency. These three components do not add up to equal the compounded annual average returns (CAR) because of approximations.* Table 19-8 shows, for example, Japanese bonds yielded the highest total return to U.S. investors of 12.2% per year from 1970 to 1996. Over half of the U.S. investor's total return from Japanese bonds was from coupon income (6.4%), very little of the total return was from price appreciation (1.0%), and the investment in Japanese yen yielded 4.1%.

The results in Table 19-8 suggest that to achieve superior returns from international bond investments, it is necessary to analyze all three return components. Unless additional information is available, there is no reason to suspect that income from capital appreciation, coupon interest, or foreign exchange from any particular country's bonds will be bad or good.

For example, year-by-year comparison of the national government bond indexes will reveal the largest divergence between two industrialized countries from the point of view of a U.S. investor. More specifically, in 1985 the French government's bond index yielded a total return of 52.7% for a U.S. investor. In 1985 a U.S. investor earned a negative total return of −12.37% from the Australian government bond index. France's high return can be attributed

---

* The components do not add up to the total returns because the CARs are multiplicative, the three components are linear additive sums that are approximations, and furthermore, the rounding errors cumulate.

TABLE 19-8   Components of Investment Returns to U.S.$ Investors from Long-Term Government Bonds, 1970–96

	Capital Appreciation	Income Return	Currency Return	Total Return (US$)
Australia	−1.2%	10.4%	−1.3%	8.5%
Belgium	0.3%	9.1%	1.6%	11.6%
Canada	0.1%	9.6%	−0.9%	9.3%
France	0.3%	9.7%	0.3%	10.8%
Germany	0.5%	7.6%	3.2%	12.0%
Italy	0.1%	12.2%	−3.3%	9.5%
Japan	1.0%	6.4%	4.1%	12.2%
Netherlands	0.3%	8.0%	2.7%	11.7%
Switzerland	0.4%	5.0%	4.2%	10.2%
United Kingdom	0.2%	11.0%	−1.3%	10.2%
United States	0.4%	8.4%	N/A	9.3%

SUMMARY: The table decomposes federal bond returns to U.S. dollar investors into three mutually exclusive components. One-period rate of returns are partitioned into a capital appreciation component, a coupon income component, and a foreign exchange component. The foreign exchange component equals the return from the pure investment in the foreign currency. The components do not add up to the compounded annual average returns (CAR) because approximations were used.

SOURCE: Raw data from the International Monetary Fund (IMF) is processed, supplemented, and maintained by Ibbotson Associates, Chicago.

to (1) a decline in the level of all interest rates in Europe during 1985, and (2) France's retreat from government intervention as the Mitterand administration took control of the nation. Similar effects worked in the opposite direction to reduce the return a U.S. investor could earn from Australian government bonds in 1985. These 1985 events will probably never be repeated. This example illustrates that earning substantial profits and avoiding substantial losses requires research into every factor that determines a security's returns.

Correlations Between International Bond Returns

There are two reasons a bond investor might purchase bonds denominated in a foreign currency. First, international bonds may offer opportunities to enhance a diversified portfolio's returns. Second, multinational diversification can reduce portfolio risk to lower levels than domestic diversification.

Table 19-9 shows there are high positive correlations between pairs of countries like Switzerland and Belgium, France and Austria, Switzerland and Germany, the United Kingdom and Ireland, Switzerland and the Netherlands, and the United States and Canada. These high correlations result from bilateral trade agreements, monetary policies that are often similar, and other commonalities. However, even "sister countries" are not perfectly positively correlated.

The differences between countries are more important for diversification purposes than their similarities. The good news in Table 19-9 is that the returns from foreign bonds do not rise and fall in unison. These differences exist for a number of reasons: the business cycle differs in each country; central bankers of each nation develop different monetary policies; government financing differs; inflation differs in each country; and these factors cause the level and structure of interest rates to differ in each country. Societal trends, foreign policies, and political forces make the nations' bond markets differ even more.

TABLE 19-9 Correlations Between the Total Returns from Long-Term Government Bonds, 1970–96

	Australia	Austria	Belgium	Canada	France	Germany	Ireland	Italy	Japan	Netherlands	New Zealand	South Africa	Switzerland	United Kingdom	United States
Australia	1.00														
Austria	0.22	1.00													
Belgium	0.20	0.86	1.00												
Canada	0.28	0.22	0.25	1.00											
France	0.20	0.82	0.82	0.25	1.00										
Germany	0.20	0.91	0.86	0.28	0.82	1.00									
Ireland	0.24	0.59	0.60	0.27	0.59	0.61	1.00								
Italy	0.17	0.50	0.47	0.22	0.52	0.47	0.46	1.00							
Japan	0.19	0.59	0.59	0.26	0.57	0.59	0.45	0.33	1.00						
Netherlands	0.21	0.88	0.83	0.30	0.83	0.93	0.57	0.47	0.59	1.00					
New Zealand	0.32	0.26	0.27	0.07	0.24	0.23	0.24	0.21	0.23	0.26	1.00				
South Africa	0.21	0.39	0.35	0.06	0.34	0.37	0.29	0.26	0.25	0.34	0.14	1.00			
Switzerland	0.18	0.82	0.77	0.24	0.75	0.83	0.56	0.39	0.61	0.82	0.18	0.31	1.00		
United Kingdom	0.23	0.43	0.46	0.30	0.45	0.47	0.74	0.34	0.40	0.46	0.23	0.23	0.42	1.00	
United States	0.16	0.18	0.22	0.67	0.24	0.26	0.23	0.18	0.21	0.29	−0.05	0.05	0.24	0.21	1.00

SUMMARY: Various long-term federal bonds' monthly rates of return to U.S. dollar investors tend to be positively correlated. The differences that contribute to risk-reducing international diversification exist because the dynamics of the business cycle differ in each country; the central bank of each nation develop different monetary policies; government financing practices differ; the level of inflation differs in each country; and these factors cause the level and structure of interest rates to differ. Divergent societal trends, foreign policies, and political forces also contribute disparities. Note: The Euro will replace several currencies in the table after 2001.

SOURCE: Raw data from the International Monetary Fund (IMF) is processed, supplemented, and maintained by Ibbotson Associates in Chicago.

As a result of these divergent and changing forces, the correlation coefficients in Table 19-9 are not stable through time. In other words, if the correlations in Table 19-9 were calculated over consecutive, nonoverlapping, 5-year intervals (for example, 1971–75, 1976–80, 1981–85, 1986–90, 1991–95), their values would fluctuate 0.10 (or more in some cases) above and below their values over 30 consecutive years. This statistical instability through time complicates the analysis of international bond portfolios and forecasting of future bond prices.

Markowitz Analysis of International Bond Portfolios

Markowitz portfolio theory, introduced in Chapter 14, provides a useful way to analyze the international bond portfolios. Figure 19-7 illustrates a U.S. Treasury bond portfolio (at Point A) and an internationally diversified portfolio made up of long-term government bonds from non-U.S. countries (at Point B). On the curve between points A and B lie an infinite number of portfolios that can be created from the two preceding bond portfolios. The bond portfolio analysis illustrated in Figure 19-7 uses annualized returns that are paid to a tax-free U.S. investor of U.S. dollars (for instance, a U.S. pension fund or mutual fund).

Figure 19-7 illustrates various asset allocations an international bond investor might select. The analysis suggests that a U.S. bond investor can attain a dominant position that reduces portfolio risk (from a standard deviation of 12.1% to 10.2%) and increases the portfolio's expected return (from 9.9% to 10.8%) by passively investing 40% of the portfolio in non-U.S. bonds. Two caveats are appropriate. First, Figure 19-7 is based on historical data that provides no guarantees that future portfolios will perform the same. Second, the portfolio's gains will be reduced by international bond broker's commissions, foreign exchange commissions, transfer fees, and management expenses.

FIGURE 19-7   Markowitz International Portfolio Analysis of Long-Term Government Bond Indexes from a U.S. Investor's Point of View

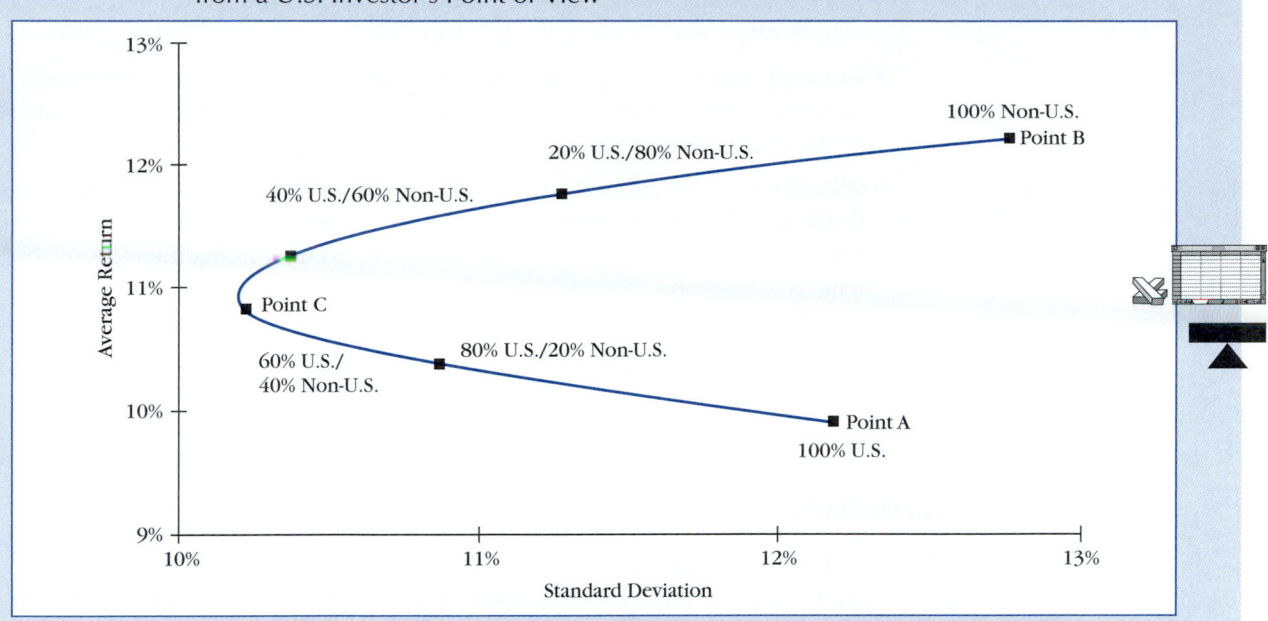

Various long-term federal bonds pretax rates of return to U.S. dollar investors are used to illustrate (Point A) a U.S. Treasury bond portfolio and an internationally diversified portfolio made from non-U.S. countries (Point B). Markowitz portfolio analysis shows a U.S. investor can allocate assets to attain a dominant position that reduces portfolio risk (from a standard deviation of 12.1% to 10.2%) and increases the portfolio's expected return (from 9.9% to 10.8%) by passively investing 40% of the portfolio in non-U.S. bonds (Point C).

SOURCE: Annualized bond index return and foreign exchange data (1970–96), computations, and the graph are from EnCorr software, Ibbotson Associates, Chicago. Kathy D'Elia, Senior Consultant at Ibbotson Associates, prepared the figure and presented it at the Alliance Capital-Ibbotson Associates Research Institute at Alliance Capital's offices in New York City, November 14, 1997.

MANAGING INTERNATIONAL BOND INVESTMENTS ACTIVELY

Figure 19-7 illustrates how an international bond investor can reduce portfolio risk and increase the portfolio's expected return by allocating 40% to foreign bonds in a Markowitz efficient portfolio. These passive improvements are valuable, but insufficient for some investors.

Aggressive investors continually rethink their views of the future and take new positions that will produce large gains if their views are correct. Foreign bond investors can adopt different approaches to aggressive investment management.

◆ **Political analysts** takes a top-down approach to investment analysis and compare the sovereign risks of different countries. Political analysts also study the social and political developments, internal legal systems, and federal budget deficits of nations where investment candidates reside.

◆ **Macro-economists** study the nations' incomes, employment pictures, balance of payments, fiscal policies, monetary policies, and flow of funds to discern which nations are economically strong and which are weak.

- ◆ **Monetary economists** analyze nations' central banks, their monetary policies, their fiscal policies, national banking systems, nations' inflationary environments, and use this information to forecast the level and structure of market interest rates within the nations they study.

- ◆ **Industry analysts** compare financial data from different industries within a country to ascertain which industries are producing profitable products and which industries are producing obsolete products.

- ◆ **Security analysts** are bottom-up financial analysts that focus on the bond issuer's financial condition, protective provisions in the (indenture) contract that governs the bond issue, and the ability of the bond issuer to prosper during the years the bond issue is outstanding.

Aggressive foreign bond investors can pursue one or more of the above approaches to securities research and endeavor to trade actively based on their research findings.

THE BOTTOM LINE

The world bond market is growing, and governments are the largest borrowers in most countries. The untaxed and unregulated Eurobond market is where the most diverse types of bonds are issued, and where the most rapid growth is occurring.

Significant differences exist between the countries' financial conventions. The United States and some other countries publish prices for bonds that equal the present value of the bonds' future cash flows—called clean prices. In other countries the published prices equal the bonds' present values (clean prices) plus any accrued interest—dirty prices. Unless the bond issuer is in default, however, the bond buyer is nearly always billed (invoiced) for the dirty price. Day-counting conventions also differ from country to country, and even differ within countries with the type of bond. In the United States, for example, money market securities are priced using formulas that assume there are 360 days in the year, while U.S. Treasury bonds use formulas based on the 365-day calendar year. To make bond pricing even more complicated for international bond investors, some countries use yield-to-maturity (YTM) formulas that involve compounding, while other countries use formulas that involve no compounding. For example, Japan employs a noncompounded YTM formula.

Bonds pay coupon interest annually, semiannually, quarterly, monthly, and even more frequently. Bonds that make payments more frequently also compound more frequently and, as a result, pay investors more interest-on-interest. The additional income from more interest-on-interest is somewhat offset, however, by the fact that bonds that make more frequent payments expose their investors to more reinvestment risk. If the pre-maturity cash flows from a bond are reinvested at less than the bond's YTM, that bond will actually yield less than the YTM it promised when purchased. Furthermore, if the issuer of a callable bond exercises the embedded call option, that bond's yield-to-call (YTC) will likely be less than its yield to maturity (YTM).

Several different yield measures exist; each is used to gauge different facets of a bond's income-producing capabilities. Investors who buy a bond and hold it until it matures are usually most interested in the bond's YTM. Those who have an investment horizon shorter than the bond's time to maturity are usually most interested in the bond's holding period return (one-period rate of return). Investors who were interested in spending their bond's cash flows are usually most interested in the bond's current yield. Many bonds contain embedded options and, in these cases, the yield-to-call (YTC) or some other yield measure comes into consideration. One of the few things that never changes is the relationship between a bond's price and its YTM—they always move inversely.

Price indexes and/or yield indexes for international bonds can be used to help plan for and analyze multinational investments. International bond indexes can be used to estimate separately the income from capital appreciation, from coupon interest, and from foreign exchange gains in different countries. Bond investors can also use Markowitz portfolio analysis to analyze ways to allocate the assets in a portfolio of multinational bonds.

Bond indexes based on high-quality bonds may be inappropriate for analyzing low-quality bonds. Low-quality bonds and bonds that are in default behave more like common stocks than high-quality bonds. Low-quality bond investors must study the unique circumstances surrounding each individual bond issue.

The Brady Plan generated an array of different packages of defaulted bank loans from emerging market countries. Innovative investment bankers crafted imaginative debt securities to make Brady bonds marketable.

QUESTIONS

Q19-1   (Types of bonds) Define the following: (a) OATS, (b) Bunds, (c) Yankee bonds, (d) Shogun bonds, (e) Bulldog bonds.

Q19-2   (ABS) The NYSE operates an Automated Bond System (ABS) that is designed to provide an active market in the bonds of NYSE-listed firms as well as some additional bonds. Is this system similar, then, to the system used to trade stocks on the NYSE? Explain.

Q19-3   (International bond risks) Define the two major types of political risk faced by international bond investors.

Q19-4   (Categorization of international bonds) How do domestic bonds, foreign bonds, and Eurobonds differ among one another?

Q19-5   (Yankee bonds versus Eurodollar bonds) Discuss the various ways in which Yankee bonds differ from Eurodollar bonds.

Q19-6   (Eurodollar bonds) What are the advantages to a U.S. firm of issuing Eurodollar bonds as opposed to domestic bonds? Why might an American investor prefer to invest in a Eurodollar bond?

Q19-7   (Yield-to-maturity versus yield-to-call) Suppose a callable bond is currently selling at a premium—that is, its market price is greater than its face value—and you believe

that the market rates will be fairly stable over the next few years, or at least until the date that the bond can be called in by the issuing firm. Which is the more relevant yield to consider—its yield-to-maturity or its yield-to-call? Why?

Q19-8   (Reinvestment rate assumption) Tzu-chia purchased a bond of a U.S. corporation that offered a yield-to-maturity of 10%. The bond had 5 years to maturity when Tzu-chia purchased it, and the issuing firm made all its coupon and principal payments as scheduled during Tzu-chia's 5-year holding period. Happily, Tzu-chia accumulated these payments in her savings account that paid a 5% annual rate of return. Tzu-chia noted that interest rates had dropped in the 5 years since she had purchased the bond and was pleased that she was able to earn a 10% average annual rate of return on her 5-year investment. How would you respond to Tzu-chia's claim?

Q19-9   (Brady bonds) Discuss the differences between the following types of Brady bonds: discount bonds, par bonds, debt-conversion bonds, new-money bonds, front-loaded interest-reduction bonds, and past-due interest bonds.

Q19-10   (Currency-hedged foreign bond investments) Explain how an investor would establish a currency-hedged position in a foreign bond investment. Is such a hedge worthwhile? Explain.

PROBLEMS

P19-1   (Clean price versus dirty price) A certain $1,000 bond pays a 10% coupon, with semiannual payments. The bond currently has 2 years, 3 months to maturity. Calculate its (a) clean bond price and (b) its dirty bond price, assuming that the risk-adjusted discount rate is 8%. (Assume the convention of a 360-day year.)

P19-2   (Bond equivalent yield versus effective yield-to-maturity) A bond that has an 8% coupon and makes semi-annual payments has a $1,000 par value and ten years to maturity. It is currently selling for $770.60. Calculate this bond's (a) bond equivalent yield (BEY) and (b) effective yield-to-maturity.

P19-3 (Bond equivalent yield versus effective yield-to-maturity) A bond that pays a 9% coupon, with semiannual payments, has a $1,000 par value, and has 8 years remaining to maturity is selling for $1,058.26. Calculate this bond's (a) bond equivalent yield (BEY) and (b) effective yield-to-maturity.

P19-4 (Reinvestment rate assumption) A Eurodollar bond that pays a 10% coupon and makes annual payments has a $1,000 face value and matures in 12 years. The bond is currently selling for $1,071.60. (a) Calculate this bond's yield-to-maturity. (b) Determine the yield an investor will receive if her reinvestment rate is (i) 0%, (ii) 5%.

P19-5 (Bond pricing and holding period return) Rosemary just purchased a bond that pays interest annually for its par value of $1,000. The bond has a 9% coupon and matures in 20 years. (a) If, 1 year from now, the risk-adjusted discount rate for this bond is 10%, what price can Rosemary expect to receive from the sale of the bond, assuming she has received the first year's interest payment prior to the sale? (b) Calculate Rosemary's holding period return assuming she sells this bond for the price calculated in part (a).

P19-6 (Yield-to-maturity and yield-to-call) A $1,000 bond pays a 12% coupon, with semiannual payments, and matures in 15 years. It is also callable at par plus one year's interest in 7 years. The bond is currently selling for $1,153.72. Calculate its (a) yield-to-maturity and its (b) yield-to-call.

P19-7 (Current yield and yield-to-maturity) A $1,000 bond pays a 10% coupon, makes semiannual interest payments, and matures in 5 years. The bond is selling for $1,081.11. Calculate its (a) current yield and its (b) yield-to-maturity.

P19-8 (Bond yields) Jason just purchased a $1,000 bond that pays of coupon rate of 7% with interest paid annually. The bond matures in 10 years. (a) What price did Jason pay for the bond if the bond's yield-to-maturity is 6%? (b) What is the current yield on Jason's bond? (c) If, 1 year later, Jason's bond is priced to yield 8%, and Jason needs cash and has to liquidate his investment, what would his 1-year holding period return be?

P19-9 (Reinvestment rate assumption) A certain bond pays an 8% coupon, with semiannual payments, has a $1,000 par value and matures in 8 years. (a) If you purchase the bond at par, what is your promised average annual yield for the 8-year holding period? (b) Suppose you can reinvest the coupons at an annual rate of 12%. What will your realized annual return be on this investment?

P19-10 (Different coupon payment schedules) A $1,000 bond pays a 12% coupon, matures in 5 years, and is selling for $1,050. Calculate its yield-to-maturity under the following coupon payment schedule assumptions: (a) annual payments, (b) semiannual payments, and (c) monthly payments.

CFA EXAM QUESTIONS

1. (1999 CFA Sample Exam, Level I) Which of the following is **NOT** a component of call risk for a bond investor?
   A. The cash flow pattern of a callable bond is not known with certainty.
   B. When the issuer calls a bond, the investor is exposed to reinvestment risk.
   C. The value of a callable bond drops when expected interest-rate volatility decreases.
   D. The capital appreciation potential of a callable bond is lower than a noncallable bond.

2. (1998 CFA Sample Exam, Level I) Which of the following statements about yield measures is/are **true**?

   I. Nominal yield measures the current income rate.

   II. Current yield measures the coupon rate.

   III. Realized (horizon) yield measures the expected rate of return for a bond likely to be sold before maturity.
   A. I only.
   B. III only.

   C. I and II only.
   D. I, II, and III.

3. (1997 CFA Sample Exam, Level I) The yield to maturity on a bond is:
   A. below the coupon rate when the bond sells at a discount and above the coupon when the bond sells at a premium.
   B. the interest rate that makes the present value of the payments equal to the bond price.
   C. based on the assumption that all future payments received are reinvested at the coupon rate.
   D. based on the assumption that all future payments received are reinvested at future market rates.

4. (1995 CFA Exam, Level II) When examining the credit worthiness of national governments (sovereigns) or local governments (municipals), an analyst must be aware of both political and economic risks.
   A. Political risk addresses the willingness of a government unit to pay debt service. **Identify** *two* political

risk factors that relate to the analysis of *both* sovereign and municipal debt. **Explain** why *each* factor is significant.

B. Economic risk addresses the ability of a government unit to pay debt service. **Identify** *two* economic risk factors. **Briefly explain** why *each* factor is significant.

C. **Briefly discuss** how *each* of the following *three* factors contributes favorably to the ability of a nation to pay its external debts: (i) Sources of foreign exchange; (ii) Composition of imports, (iii) Composition of exchange partners.

5. (Adapted from a question appearing on the 1994 CFA Exam, Level III) Food Processors Inc. (FPI) is a mature U.S. company reporting declining earnings and a weak balance sheet. Its ERISA-qualified defined-benefit pension plan has total assets of $750 million. However, the plan is underfunded by $200 million by U.S. standards, a cause for concern by shareholders, management, and the Board. The pension portfolio's holdings are equally divided between large-capitalization U.S. equities and high-quality, long-maturity U.S. corporate bonds. For actuarial purposes, the assumed long-term rate of return on plan assets is 9% per year; the discount rate applied to plan liabilities, all of which are U.S.-based, is 8%. As FPI's Treasurer, you are responsible for oversight of the plan's investments and managers and for liaison with the Board's Pension Investment Committee.

The Investment Committee has agreed to consider the addition of non-U.S. securities to the portfolio. You have been asked to discuss with the Committee several aspects of this new direction, the first of which is the matter of currency risk and hedging.

A. **Recommend** whether the currency risk inherent in international investing should or should not be hedged in the FPI situation. **Cite** and **explain** *three* major reasons in support of your conclusion.

The Chairman has become enthusiastic about investing abroad, stating "I believe non-U.S. markets will outperform U.S. markets over the next 5 to 10 years and I expect the dollar to strengthen as well. Therefore, everything will be working in favor of our realizing excellent returns on our international investments over this period."

B. You *disagree* with the Chairman's conclusion. **Justify** your position.

One Committee member has asked, "As world economies become increasingly integrated and more money is committed internationally, won't these trends dramatically affect the dynamics of global investing?"

C. In response to this Committee member, **cite** and **explain** *two* effects on global investment fundamentals that these trends can be expected to produce over time.

FURTHER REFERENCES

Baker, James C. *International Finance: Management, Common Market, and Institutions.* Upper Saddle River, NJ: Prentice-Hall, 1998.

This multinational financial textbook provides a comprehensive 18-chapter review of management procedures, market data, and institutional detail encountered in international transactions. Elementary algebra is supplemented with graphs to create an easy-to-read textbook.

Dixon, Rob and Phil Holmes. *Financial Markets: An Introduction.* London: Chapman and Hall, 1992.

This 9-chapter textbook focuses on investing in Britain and introduces the related discussions about foreign exchange, options, and financial futures. Mathematics is not used in this easy-to-read book.

Giddy, Ian H. *Global Financial Markets.* Lexington, MA: D. C. Heath, 1994.

This 18-chapter textbook provides comprehensive detail about foreign exchange, foreign exchange markets, and foreign exchange relationships. International money markets, capital markets, futures markets, options markets, and commodity markets are discussed. The book is enriched by many informative illustrations.

Shapiro, Alan C. *Multinational Financial Management.* 6th ed. Upper Saddle River, NJ: Prentice-Hall, 1999.

This 22-chapter corporation finance textbook provides a comprehensive review of international financial institutions, foreign currency markets, international risk management procedures, a good discussion of international accounting, international taxes, international banking, and international corporation finance.

Core-Plus Bond Management, Association for Investment Management and Research, AIMR Conference Proceedings, No, 1, Charlottesville, VA.

Investment managers write about a strategy of increasing their allocations to nonbenchmark sectors in order to achieve excess returns, called core-plus fixed-income management, in the informationally efficient U.S. bond market.

Solnik, Bruno. *International Investments,* 4th ed. Reading, MA: Addison-Wesley, 1999.

This 17-chapter textbook about international investing introduces the relevant topics and provides good references where additional detailed studies can be found. Elementary algebra and statistics are used.

ENDNOTES

[1] See Michael Siconolfi, "Salomon's Fattest Pay Didn't Go to CEO," *Wall Street Journal,* 28 March 1994, C1.

[2] Bloomberg's Web site is: www.bloomberg.com.

[3] See Leon T. Kendall and Michael J. Fishman, Editors, *A Primer on Securitization* (Cambridge, MA: MIT Press, 1996). Or, see Scott Y. Peng and Ravi E. Dattatreya, *The Structured Note Market* (Chicago, IL: Probus Publishing, 1995).

[4] For interesting detail about the U.S. bond market, see "Never Cross a Bond Dealer," *Business Week,* 9 March 1998, 84–85.

[5] See Adam K. Gehr and Terrence F. Martell, "Pricing Efficiency in the Secondary Market for Investment-Grade Corporate Bonds," *Journal of Fixed Income* (December 1992): 24–38.

[6] For detailed examples, see Gregory Zuckerman, "The Pricing of Bonds, Long a Big Mystery, Gets Some Scrutiny," *Wall Street Journal,* 10 September, 1998 1.

[7] See Julian Evans, Thomas Marshall, and Tessa Oakley, "A Guide to Consortium Sites," *EUROMONEY,* December 2000, 36–53, London.

[8] For detail about the Japanese bond market, see Chapter IV, entitled "The Bond Market," *Securities Market in Japan* (Tokyo: Japan Securities Research Institute, 1996).

[9] For detail about accrued interest, see Kenneth D. Garbade, *Fixed Income Analytics* (Cambridge, MA: MIT Press, 1996), 11–18, 52. Or, see Bruce Tuckman, *Fixed Income Securities* (New York: Wiley, 1996), 42–44.

[10] For more detail about the many facets of accrued interest and the day-count convention, see Marcia Stigum and Franklin L. Robinson, *Money Market and Bond Calculations* (Burr Ridge, IL: Irwin, 1996), especially Chapter 5.

[11] See Miles Livingston, *Money and Capital Markets,* 3d ed. (Malden, MA: Blackwell Publishers, 1996) 198–200.

[12] For a detailed discussion of callable bonds, see Sidney Homer and Martin L. Leibowitz, *Inside the Yield Book* (Englewood Cliffs, NJ: Prentice-Hall, 1972), Chapters 4 and 14. Also see John Finnerty, "Evaluating the Economics of Refunding High-Coupon Sinking Fund Debt," *Financial Management* (Spring 1983): 5–10.

[13] For more information see F. J. Fabozzi, *Bond Markets, Analysis and Strategies,* 3d ed. (Upper Saddle River, NJ: Prentice-Hall, 1996), Chapter 4. Also see Mark L. Dunetz and James M. Mahoney, "Using Duration and Convexity in the Analysis of Callable Bonds," *Financial Analysts Journal* (May-June 1988): 53–72.

MARKET INTEREST RATES

Earlier chapters explained the one-period rate of return, current yield, coupon rate, and yield-to-maturity (YTM). These interest rates measure a bond's yield from different perspectives. However, the yield-to-maturity (YTM) is the most meaningful interest rate; it is usually what people are talking about when they refer to a bond's market interest rate.

The YTM is the discount rate that determines a bond's market price (present value). The YTM is a common denominator among bonds with different maturities, different issuers, different par values, and different compounding frequencies. Except where otherwise stated, this chapter's discussion of market interest rates focuses on bonds' yields-to-maturity.* YTMs are market-determined interest rates that fluctuate continuously. Meaningful relationships can be discerned in the way market interest rates fluctuate.

This chapter focuses primarily on the YTMs of bills, notes, and bonds issued by the U.S. Treasury. U.S. Treasury bonds are the simplest bonds to discuss because they are free from the bankruptcy risks that complicate corporate bonds. This chapter's discussion is further restricted to U.S. Treasury YTMs that are not obscured by embedded (call, put, conversion) options and to T-bonds that are continuously traded in liquid markets. YTMs from option-free U.S. Treasury bonds are the market interest rates discussed throughout this chapter, except where other bonds are mentioned explicitly.

Figure 20-1 has three panels. Panel (A) illustrates how the market interest rates of two U.S. Treasury bonds tend to rise and fall together. Although the 3-month and 10-year Treasury bonds span considerably different investment horizons, their YTMs are highly positively correlated, $\rho = +0.90$. The Consumers Price Index (CPI) was introduced in Chapter 10. Panel (B) illustrates the CPI's inflation rate, including and excluding the volatile food and energy components. Panel (C) brings

---

* The market interest rate that is the focus of this chapter is the yield-to-maturity (YTM), the discount rate used to find a bond's present value, the cost of capital that is appropriate for a bond, a bond's expected return, and the bond investor's required rate of return. These phrases are synonyms that are used in different contexts.

together elements from (A) and (B) and shows how the YTM from a long-term Treasury bond rises and falls with the rate of inflation. The next section of this chapter discloses logical relationships between the variables in Figure 20-1.

The factors that cause market interest rates to fluctuate can be fit into two categories:

1. ***Undiversifiable Factors***. *Undiversifiable factors have an effect on the market price of every bond in a nation's bond market. For example, the nation's inflation rate, sovereign risk, supply of and demand for credit, and other macroeconomic variables influence the prices of all bonds similarly. These pervasive common factors are what cause all variables in Figure 20-1 to be positively correlated. Undiversifiable interest rate risk factors that cause all market interest rates to rise and fall together are the focus of this chapter.*

2. ***Diversifiable Factors***. *Many changes in bond prices and market interest rates are caused by idiosyncratic changes that are unique to the bond issuer. Changes in and differences between the issuer's default (bankruptcy, credit) risk and embedded (call, put, conversion) options, for instance, are diversifiable risk factors discussed in other chapters. These diversifiable risk factors can cause the YTMs from corporate bonds and municipal bonds to behave differently than the YTMs of Treasury securities.*

THE LEVEL OF MARKET INTEREST RATES

Consider the *level* of all market interest rates. This section ponders questions such as:

◆ Why are all interest rates high or low?

◆ Why are all interest rates rising or falling?

The two questions above refer to market interest rates, or equivalently YTMs. Sometimes we refer to these as simply "interest rates."

Irving Fisher's Theory About the Level of Interest Rates

In 1930 Irving Fisher pointed out that all market interest rates tend to rise and fall with the rate of inflation.[1] Inflation-induced market interest rate movements are said to result from the **Fisher effect** (see Key Definition).

Fisher's Theory in a World of Certainty. Almost all interest rates in the world are stated in nominal money terms rather than real physical terms. Most people don't realize nominal market interest rates include an allowance for inflation. Nominal market interest rates contain an inflation allowance to avoid distortions in the purchasing power of fixed-value financial assets that occurs when inflation alters the nominal market prices of real physical goods. For example, if someone loans $100 for a year at 3% interest, that lender should be repaid $103. If inflation during the year is expected to be at a rate of 10%, E(INF) = 10%, the repayment of $103 will have the purchasing power of (1/1.1 = 90.9% of $103, or) only $93.627.* The lender must charge 3% interest plus a 10% *inflation allowance,* for a total interest rate of

---

* The symbol E denotes the mathematical expectation and the Greek letter delta, Δ, means "finite change." Suppose ΔP measures a finite change in the Consumer Price Index. The symbol $(\Delta P/P)$ is represented by INF in this book. Thus, $E(\Delta P/P) = E(INF)$ stands for the expected rate of inflation rate.

FIGURE 20-1   Market Interest Rates and Inflation in the United States

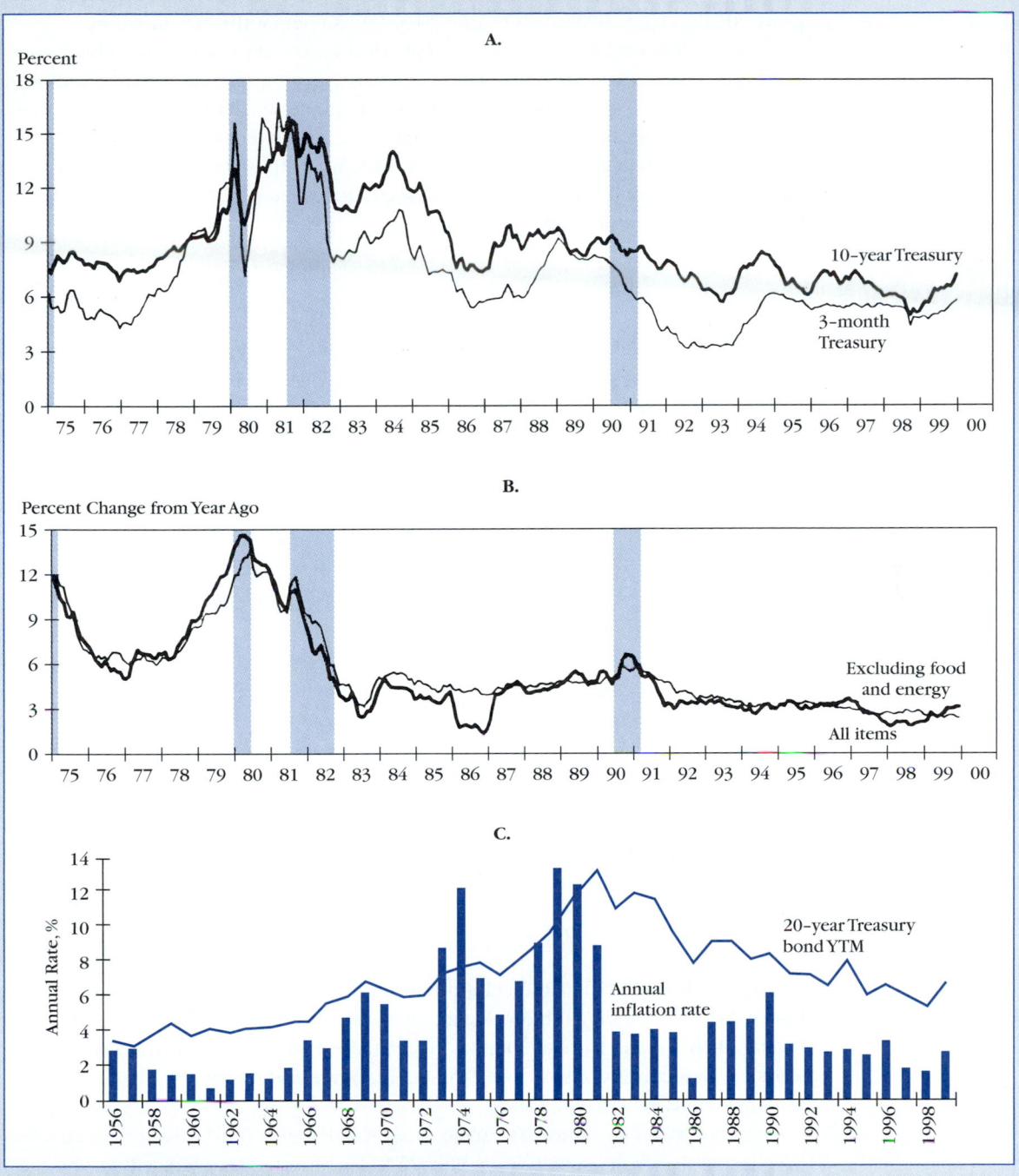

(A) The market interest rates (or YTMs) of a short-term and an intermediate-term U.S. Treasury bond fluctuate together. The 3-month and 10-year Treasury bonds' YTMs are correlated +0.90. The four vertical shaded bands in (A) and (B) delineate official NBER recessions. (B) Inflation measures from the U.S. Consumer Price Index (CPI). The 3-month T-bill is correlated +0.47 with inflation, and the 10-year T-bond is correlated +0.35 with inflation. (C) The market interest rate (T-bond's YTM) fluctuates with the rate of inflation.

SOURCES: *National Economic Trends,* Federal Reserve Bank of St. Louis. Ibbotson Associates, Chicago.

13% per year. In this case, the lender will be repaid $113 [= ($100)(100% + 3% + 10%)] at the end of one year. After allowing for 10% inflation, that $113 will have the same purchasing power that (1/1.1 = 90.9% of $113, or) $102.72 had before the 10% inflation.

The lender's *real return* (in terms of physical goods) at the end of the year is an increase of $2.72 (= $102.72 − $100 =). This 2.72% increase in purchasing power comes from loaning money at a 13% market interest rate during a year in which inflation is 10%. This example shows that lenders need to raise their nominal market interest rates by at least the rate of inflation to maintain the purchasing power of their wealth. Many lenders learn to make these inflation adjustments and, as a result, as Irving Fisher suggested, market interest rates rise and fall with the rate of inflation.

DEFINITION

THE FISHER EFFECT

Irving Fisher observed that all market interest rates tend to rise and fall in a one-to-one correspondence with the rate of inflation. The influence inflation has over nominal market interest rates is summarized in Eqn. 20-1; it is called the Fisher effect.

$$\begin{pmatrix} \text{Nominal, or} \\ \text{Market, interest} \\ \text{rate, } r_t \end{pmatrix} = \begin{pmatrix} \text{Real rate of} \\ \text{interest, } rr \end{pmatrix} + E\begin{pmatrix} \text{Inflation} \\ \text{rate, } INF_t \end{pmatrix} \qquad \text{(20-1)}$$

Eqn. 20-1 treats the real interest rate as a positive constant. For example, $rr = 3\%$ per year.

To see how the Fisher effect works, assume the real rate of interest is $rr = 3\%$. If the rate of inflation is expected to be 10%, $E(INF) = 10\%$, then that expected rate of inflation is added to the real rate to obtain a statistical estimate (forecast) of the nominal market interest rate. In this example Fisher's theory suggests a nominal rate of 13%.

$$r = rr + E(INF) = 3\% + 10\% = 13\%$$

If the expected rate of inflation drops from 10% to 6%, $E(INF) = 6\%$, then that reduced rate of inflation should be added to the real rate to obtain an estimate of the nominal rate of 9%.

$$r = rr + E(INF) = 3\% + 6\% = 9\%$$

Is Fisher's Theory Valid? To quickly assess the validity of Irving Fisher's theory, reconsider Figure 20-1. The 3-month T-bill in Figure 20-1A is correlated +0.47 with the inflation rate in Figure 20-1B, and the 10-year T-bond is correlated +0.35 with the inflation rate. These significant positive correlations between the inflation rate and the two market interest rates are evidence the Fisher effect exists.

Since graphs like Figure 20-1 seem to provide support for the Fisher effect, researchers have tested the theory scientifically. Eqn. 20-1 can be tested statistically by using the simple linear regression equation in Eqn. 20-2.

$$r_t = \alpha + \beta(INF_t) + \varepsilon_t \qquad \text{for } t = 1, 2, 3, \ldots, T \text{ time periods} \qquad \text{(20-2)}$$

The intercept term, the symbol α in Eqn. 20-2, is a statistical estimate of the real rate of return, rr in Fisher's Eqn. 20-1. If Eqns. 20-1 and 20-2 corresponded perfectly: $\alpha = rr$. Since the values of all regression residual terms fluctuate back and forth between positive and negative values (above and below the regression line), the unexplained error term in Eqn. 20-2 has an expected value of zero, $E(\varepsilon) = 0$. In other words, the ε term in Eqn. 20-2 vanishes (averages out to zero) and can be ignored. The regression slope coefficient—the β term in Eqn. 20-2—estimates statistically the impact the rate of inflation has on the concurrent market interest rate. If the one-to-one correspondence between the market interest rate and the inflation rate Irving Fisher hypothesizes is true, the regression slope statistic in Eqn. 20-2 will equal $1, \beta = 1$.

As a result of statistical sampling errors, the statistical estimates of the intercept and slope statistics in Eqn. 20-2 cannot be expected to precisely equal the values Fisher's theory predicts, $\alpha = rr$ and $\beta = 1$. Financial researchers report empirical estimates of the α and β statistics in Eqn. 20-2 are sufficiently close to Fisher's theoretical values to support the Fisher effect.[2] In other words, professional economists and financial analysts think Eqn. 20-2 provides a fairly good, but not perfect, explanation of what makes the level of market interest rates rise and fall. Take another look at Figure 20-1C and judge for yourself.

Realized Real Returns (rrr)

The Fisher effect in Eqn. 20-1 uses the rate of inflation that is *expected* during time period t, $E(INF_t)$, rather than the rate of inflation that is actually *realized* during time period t, denoted INF_t. Experience with surveys of inflation reveals:

- ◆ It is difficult to measure the rate of inflation that is expected.
- ◆ The *expected* and the *realized* rates of inflation during a given time period usually differ, $E(INF_t) \neq INF_t$.

As a result of these problems, financial researchers cannot use Eqn. 20-1 to measure the real interest rate, denoted rr, from market interest rate data. To overcome this difficulty researchers reformulated Eqn. 20-1 from Irving Fisher's theory to become Eqn. 20-3, which differs from Eqn. 20-1 in two respects:

- ◆ Eqn. 20-3 uses the actual (realized) inflation rate instead of an expected inflation rate.
- ◆ Time subscripts are attached to all three variables in Eqn. 20-3 to represent the variables' actual market values observed (realized) during successive time periods.

$$\begin{pmatrix} \text{Realized real} \\ \text{rate of interest} \\ \text{observed during} \\ \text{time period } t,\ rrr_t \end{pmatrix} = \begin{pmatrix} \text{Nominal, or market,} \\ \text{interest rate during} \\ \text{time period } t,\ r_t \end{pmatrix} - \begin{pmatrix} \text{Actual (realized)} \\ \text{rate of inflation during} \\ \text{time period } t,\ INF_t \end{pmatrix} \qquad \textbf{(20-3)}$$

Eqn. 20-3 defines the realized real rate of interest during time period t to be the difference between the actual inflation rate and a market interest rate. This equation corresponds to the economic definition of a *real interest rate* as being an inflation-adjusted interest rate that measures the change in purchasing power earned from some nominal market interest rate.[3] Values of rrr_t measured from market data vary from month to month.[4]

Eqn. 20-4 defines an alternative measure of the realized real rate of interest that is a little more accurate than Eqn. 20-3. To test the similarity of these two equations, U.S. Treasury bill rates and U.S. inflation rates were inserted into both Eqns. 20-3 and 20-4; the two equations yield almost identical rrr_t values. Figure 20-2 illustrates year-by-year rrr_t values computed with Eqn. 20-4. The values fluctuate, and even attain negative values in years when the rate of inflation exceeds the T-bill rate.

$$\begin{pmatrix} \text{Realized real rate of interest} \\ \text{from U.S. Treasury bill} \\ \text{during time period } t,\ rrr_t \end{pmatrix} = \frac{1 + \begin{pmatrix} \text{U.S. T-bill return} \\ \text{during time period } t \end{pmatrix}}{(1 + INF_t)} \qquad \textbf{(20-4)}$$

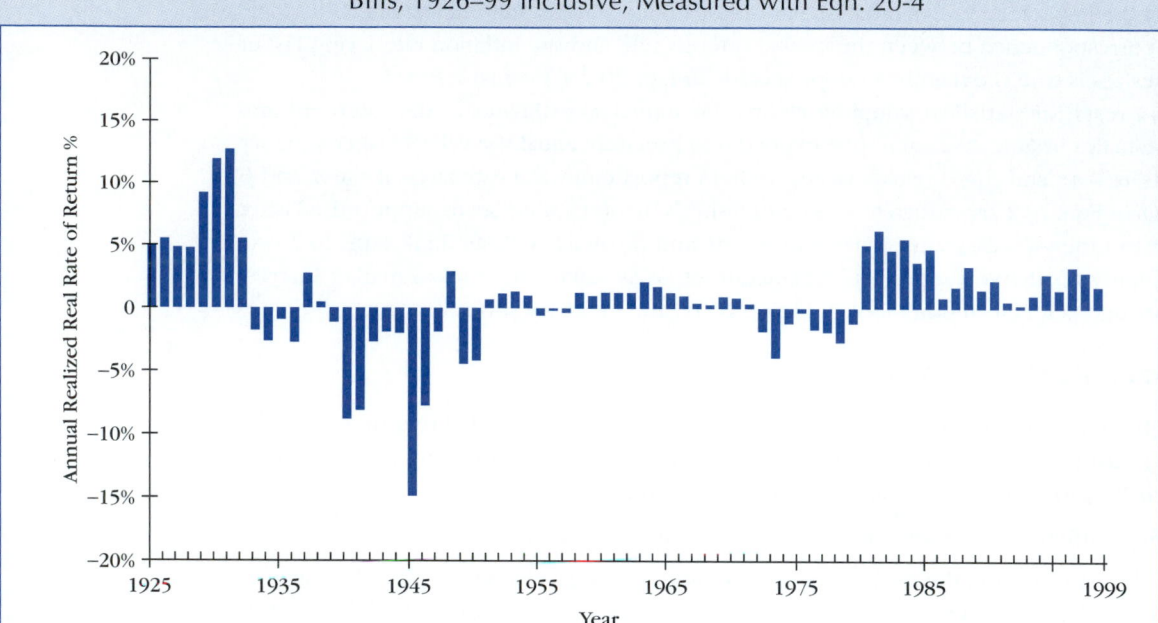

FIGURE 20-2   Annual Realized Real Rates of Return from U.S. Treasury Bills, 1926–99 Inclusive, Measured with Eqn. 20-4

Realized historical U.S. Treasury bill rates and U.S. inflation rates were inserted into Eqns. 20-3 and 20-4; the two equations yielded nearly identical realized real rate (rrr_t) values for each time period. The computed rrr_t values graphed above fluctuate, and even attain negative values in years when the rate of inflation exceeds the T-bill rate. These fluctuating rrr_t values provide evidence that Irving Fisher's *constant* real rate, denoted rr in Eqn. 20-1, is an oversimplification. A more realistic model would contain a real rate that fluctuates with the passage of time.

SOURCE: *Stocks, Bonds, Bills, and Inflation 2000 Yearbook,* published annually by Ibbotson Associates, Chicago, Graph 4-10, p. 88.

Conclusions About Prices and Interest Rates

Financial economists conclude:

1. The level of nominal market interest rates tends to vary directly with large movements in the general price level. But, during a short-run period of several months (or, occasionally, for over a year) the level of market interest rates may not respond at all or, might even move inversely, to movements in the general price level.

2. It is possible to find periods of years when Fisher's Eqn. 20-1 explains movements in nominal market interest rates very well. It is also possible to find periods of years when Fisher's equation has no ability to explain movements in market interest rates. In view of the latter findings, Fisher's Eqn. 20-1 cannot always be relied on for accurate predictions of market interest rates.

3. The constant real rate denoted rr in Fisher's Eqn. 20-1 oversimplifies the fact that the realized real rate, denoted rrr_t, fluctuates through time.

4. Fisher's theory about nominal market interest rates is a valuable intellectual tool that is a useful aid for economic thinkers.

5. Explanatory factors other than the rate of inflation, which are captured statistically in the unexplained residual ε_t in Eqn. 20-2, also impact market interest rates.

Hundreds of economists from around the world study current events and the business cycle and make predictions about market interest rates. Most of these economists agree that the rate of inflation is usually the most important determinant of the level of market interest rates.

Other Factors Influence Market Interest Rates

The Business Cycle. Figures 20-1 and 20-3 illustrate the fluctuations in selected components of the U.S. economy during recent years. Periods of slowing business activity that begin at the *peak* of business activity and last until the *trough* of business activity are called **recessions**. The shaded vertical bands in Figures 20-1 and 20-3 delineate recessions.*

The first three panels of Figure 20-3 show how different components of the *real sector* of the U.S. economy interact through time. Figure 20-3A shows how the real (inflation-adjusted) gross domestic product (GDP), a measure of national income and business activity, falls during every recession. Most of a nation's income is spent on consumption goods (food, clothing, etc.). Figure 20-3B shows that the growth rate in real (inflation-adjusted) consumption expenditures slows during recessions. Sales of durable goods (automobiles, appliances, and similar hard goods) experience more shrinkage than consumption spending during recessions. Figure 20-3C traces the decline in employment and concurrent increase in the unemployment rate that typifies recessions. Figure 20-3C also shows the long-term upward trend in the U.S. labor force.

Fluctuations in the *monetary sector* of the U.S. economy are portrayed in Figures 20-1, 20-3D, and 20-3E. Declining expenditures for consumption goods and other expenditures cause corporate profits to collapse during recessions, as illustrated in Figure 20-3D. Figure 20-3E shows that the stock market is a *leading economic indicator,* which usually collapses several months before the start of a recession and starts rising months before the beginning of the recovery in economic activity (trough of the recession).

One problem with using the stock market as a leading economic indicator is that, in addition to collapsing several months before each recession starts, it collapses at a few other times. For example, on October 19, 1987 the S&P500 index dropped over 20%, but it was several years until the next recession started. Since the stock market occasionally collapses and no recession follows within a few months, the stock market is a flawed leading indicator of economic activity that sometimes issues erroneous signals.

During a period of economic expansion, the unemployment rate falls, business activity quickens, and businesses borrow money to build bigger plants and to finance more inventory. The resulting credit demands bid up interest rates. During economic slowdowns and recessions, unemployment increases, manufacturing activity slows, demand for credit shrinks, and so interest rates usually fall, if all other factors are constant.

Federal Government Borrowing and Crowding Out. President Ronald Reagan pushed major income tax cuts through Congress during his first term in the White House, 1980–84. But Congress did not reduce federal spending in response to the reduced tax revenues. As a result, federal budget deficits of $150 to $200 billion per year occurred regularly during the 1980s. The U.S. Treasury had to sell $150 to $200 billion of additional U.S. Treasury bonds per year to raise the money to pay for the government's deficit spending. These relatively large back-to-back deficits caused fiscal problems for the United States.

During the 1980s businesses and the U.S. Treasury were *competing* to borrow loanable funds as the national economy accelerated out of the 1981–82 recession. The resulting demand for credit exceeded the available supply of loanable funds. Some businesses complained that

---

* Official National Bureau of Economic Research (NBER) peak and trough months are illustrated.

FIGURE 20-3 Selected Economic Indicators from the U.S. Economy, 1974–99, with Recessions as Shaded Vertical Bands

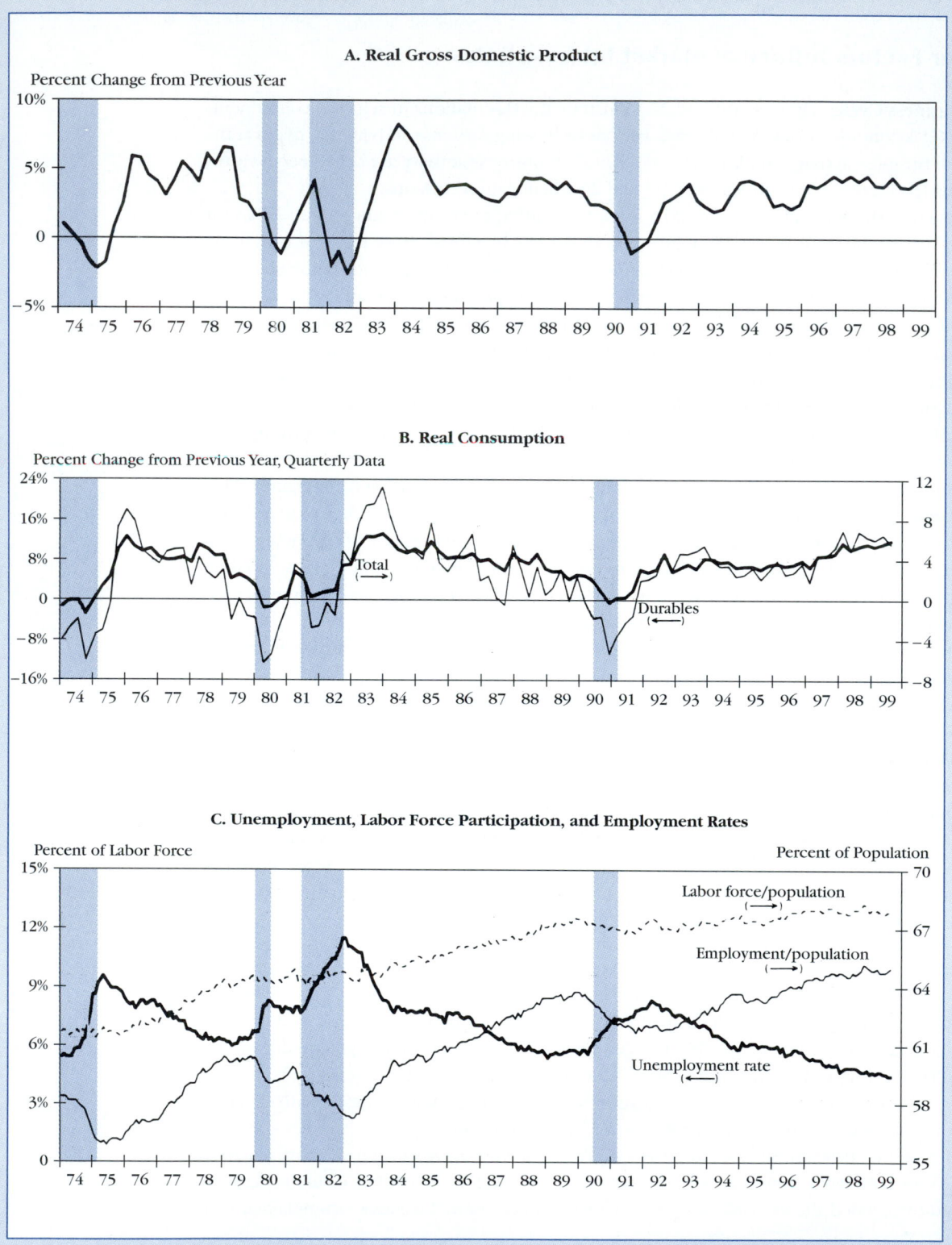

FIGURE 20-3 Selected Economic Indicators from the U.S. Economy, 1974–99, with Recessions as Shaded Vertical Bands *(continued)*

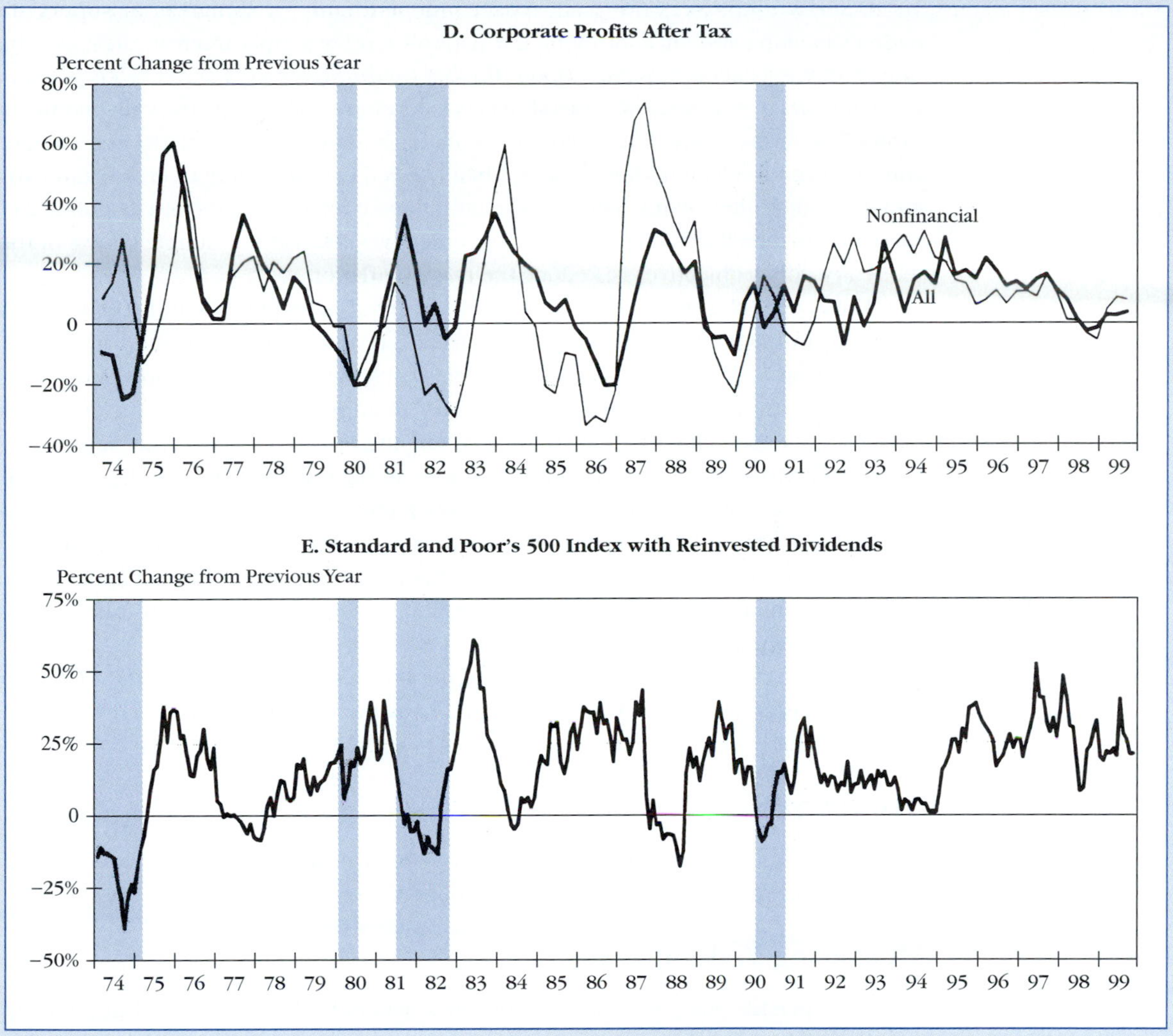

D. Corporate Profits After Tax
Percent Change from Previous Year
80%
60%
40%
20%
0
−20%
−40%
Nonfinancial
All
74 75 76 77 78 79 80 81 82 83 84 85 86 87 88 89 90 91 92 93 94 95 96 97 98 99
E. Standard and Poor's 500 Index with Reinvested Dividends
Percent Change from Previous Year
75%
50%
25%
0
−25%
−50%
74 75 76 77 78 79 80 81 82 83 84 85 86 87 88 89 90 91 92 93 94 95 96 97 98 99

SOURCE: *National Economic Trends,* Federal Reserve Bank of St. Louis.

they were "crowded out" of the credit markets by U.S. Treasury borrowing during 1983–84. This borrowing competition between businesses and the federal government bid up market interest rates during 1983–84 to levels above what they would have been if the government budget was balanced. As a result, and contrary to what Fisher's Eqn. 20-1 would predict, market interest rates rose during 1983–84 even though inflation was declining. (See Fig. 20-1.)

When the demand for credit exceeds the supply of loanable funds, market interest rates tend to get pushed upward. This explains why people sometimes say that market interest rates reflect the "price" of credit.

National Monetary Policy. Every country has a central bank. For example, the Federal Reserve is the U.S. government's central bank, Banco de Mexico is Mexico's, Bundesbank was Germany's central bank until the European Central Bank replaced it at the start of the European Monetary

Union (EMU) in 1999, Britain's is the Bank of England, Egypt has the Central Bank of Egypt, and so on. Central banks make nations' monetary policies and carry them out, hold reserves for the nations' banks, issue currency, and control the nation's supply of money.

U.S. law empowers the "Fed" to act independently of Congress in supervising the nation's banking system, controlling the nation's money supply, interest rates, and the inflation rate. The Federal Reserve's *Open Market Committee* meets about once per month to make monetary policies. The Federal Reserve develops policy objectives (economic targets) for itself in terms of the dollar value of the nation's money supply, the desired inflation rate, and the level of selected interest rates. Then the Fed uses its ability to create and extinguish money in the United States, banking regulations and bank inspectors, and its political clout to carry out its monetary policies (economic objectives). A classic example of one of the Fed's monetary policy objectives is: Reduce the rate of inflation.

The Federal Reserve is the most powerful central bank in the world, it has considerable power to influence the movements of market interest rates. As a result, large investment banking firms and the large commercial banks each have several vice-president/economists assigned to study the Federal Reserve and try to anticipate its impact on market interest rates.[5] Newspapers like the *Wall Street Journal*, the *Financial Times*, the *New York Times*, and the *Economist* continually report rumors about the Fed's actions, because the Fed's actions can have immediate effects on market interest rates around the world. The Federal Reserve is a central bank that has managed to maintain its political independence. Being politically independent helps the Fed be an effective central bank that can fight inflation and maintain economic stability—even when politicians in Congress want to pursue economic goals that might harm the nation.

Inflationary expectations, the phase of the business cycle, the size of the federal deficit and how it is being financed, and the central banks' day-to-day actions are important factors that affect market interest rates.[6]

YIELD SPREADS

Yield spreads measure the difference between two market interest rates. Two different types of yield spreads are discussed in the following sections.

Measuring Yield Spreads

Quality Spread. The yield spread between a default-free U.S. Treasury bond and another, more risky bond that has the same time to maturity is called a **quality spread, credit spread,** or **default risk premium**. A quality spread for a risky bond measured at the *t*th instant in time is:

$$\begin{pmatrix} \text{A quality} \\ \text{yield spread} \end{pmatrix}_t = \begin{pmatrix} \text{Yield on a} \\ \text{risky bond} \end{pmatrix}_t - \begin{pmatrix} \text{U.S. Treasury} \\ \text{bond yield} \end{pmatrix}_t \tag{20-5}$$

Yield spreads like the one in Eqn. 20-5 are called quality spreads because they measure the additional yield that debt investors require risky bonds to pay to induce the investors to buy the risky bonds instead of higher-quality U.S. Treasury bonds.

Horizon Spread. Yield spreads between two bonds of equal quality ratings (usually two U.S. Treasury bonds) that have different terms to maturity are called **horizon spreads** or **maturity risk premiums**.

$$\begin{pmatrix} \text{A horizon} \\ \text{spread} \end{pmatrix}_t = \begin{pmatrix} \text{Yield on a long-} \\ \text{term T-bond} \end{pmatrix}_t - \begin{pmatrix} \text{Yield on a shorter-} \\ \text{term T-bond} \end{pmatrix}_t \tag{20-6}$$

Horizon spreads are rarely negative, because investors normally require a positive horizon-risk premium to induce them to make long-term commitments.

Yield Spreads Open and Close with the Business Cycle

Quality Spreads. The market interest rate data in Table 20-1 shows that quality spreads vary predictably over the business cycle.[7] For example, Column 6 of Table 20-1 shows how the average risk premiums on BBB-grade bonds varied over the business cycle. If other yield spreads were calculated from the data, they would reveal that all risk premiums tend to be larger at economic troughs than at the peaks in economic activity. This cyclical pattern can be used to forecast yield spreads and to establish profitable hedges and spreads between two bonds' yields.

Default risk premiums (quality spreads) are higher at economic troughs for two primary reasons. First, unemployment, fear of job-loss, and risk-aversion are higher during recessions. Therefore, investors demand larger risk premiums to induce them to buy riskier bonds. Second, corporate bond issuers typically experience reductions in their sales and profits during recessions. Since the issuers are more subject to bankruptcy during recessions, investors require larger risk premiums.[8] These cyclical changes in the default risk premiums are another reason why market interest rates fluctuate with the business cycle.

Horizon Spreads. Column 9 of Table 20-1 lists horizon spreads. These maturity risk premiums expand at the troughs of the business cycle, reflecting the widespread expectation that inflation and nominal interest rates will rise during the business expansion that lies ahead.

TABLE 20-1   Average YTMs and a Yield Spread in Percentage Points, at Peaks and Troughs of the Business Cycle[a]

Date	Corporate Bonds				Quality Spread		T-bonds	Horizon Spread	
	(1) AAA %	(2) AA %	(3) A %	(4) BBB %	(5) I-T[a] T-bond %	(6) BBB less I-T[a]	(7) S-T[a] T-bond %	(8) L-T[a] T-bond %	(9) L-T[a] less S-T[a]
August 1957 (peak[b])	4.13	4.27	4.39	5.11	3.84	1.27	3.85	3.68	−0.17
April 1958 (trough[b])	3.63	3.82	4.03	4.82	2.58	2.24	2.22	2.79	0.57
April 1960 (peak)	4.44	4.56	4.75	5.34	4.13	1.21	4.14	4.17	0.03
February 1961 (trough)	4.28	4.40	4.66	5.22	3.74	1.48	3.44	3.78	0.34
December 1969 (peak)	7.65	7.83	8.10	8.67	7.47	1.20	7.85	6.86	−0.99
November 1970 (trough)	7.79	8.31	8.69	9.38	6.52	2.86	6.22	6.51	0.29
November 1973 (peak)	7.76	7.95	8.17	8.67	6.83	1.84	6.98	5.92	−1.06
March 1975 (trough)	8.63	8.86	9.08	9.66	6.92	2.74	6.77	8.05	1.28
January 1980 (peak)	10.98	11.36	11.59	12.12	10.70	1.42	11.09	10.53	−0.56
July 1980 (trough)	10.63	10.96	11.25	12.10	9.72	2.38	9.02	10.21	1.19
July 1981 (peak)	14.11	14.54	14.79	15.74	14.11	1.63	14.62	13.37	−1.25
November 1982 (trough)	10.95	11.33	11.88	13.19	10.09	3.10	9.74	10.30	0.56
July 1990 (peak)	9.03	9.62	9.89	10.45	8.49	1.96	8.21	8.72	0.51
March 1991 (trough)	8.50	9.34	9.54	10.12	7.92	2.20	6.98	8.48	1.50

[a] S-T (I-T, L-T) stands for an average YTM from short-term (intermediate-term, long-term) U.S. Treasury bonds.
[b] Official National Bureau of Economics Research (NBER) Peaks and Troughs.

Horizon spreads shrink at the peak of the business cycle because the nation's bond market expects that inflation and nominal interest rates will decline during the forthcoming recession. Horizon spreads measure the slope of something called "the yield curve."

THE TERM STRUCTURE OF INTEREST RATES (THE YIELD CURVE)

Figure 20-1(A) shows how the *level* of market interest rates rose and fell in the United States. The *level of interest rates* is different from the term structure of interest rates. The **term structure of interest rates** refers to the relationship between years to maturity and YTM for a given bond issuer (typically, U.S. Treasury bonds). The phrase *term structure of interest rates* is a synonym for the **yield curve**.

The hypothetical yield curve for U.S. Treasury bonds graphed in Figure 20-4 is a line-of-best-fit drawn through different Treasury securities that existed one day. Each dot in Figure 20-4 represents a different T-bill, T-note, or T-bond. Yield curves shift position every day. Most days the yield curve changes infinitesimally; on days when more important news arrives it may change significantly. All Treasury securities never lie on the yield curve because the T-bond issues differ with respect to the size of their coupon rate,[*9] call provisions,[**] and tax status.[†]

Since time to maturity and other factors affect a bond's market interest rate, Fisher's Eqn. 20-1 is expanded to become Eqn. 20-7.

$$\begin{pmatrix} \text{Nominal, or} \\ \text{market, interest} \\ \text{rate at time } t, r_t \end{pmatrix} = \begin{pmatrix} \text{Real} \\ \text{interest} \\ \text{rate, } rr \end{pmatrix} + E\begin{pmatrix} \text{Rate of inflation} \\ \text{during time} \\ \text{period } t, INF_t \end{pmatrix} + \begin{pmatrix} \text{Bond issue's} \\ \text{credit, or default,} \\ \text{risk premium} \end{pmatrix} + \begin{pmatrix} \text{Bond issue's} \\ \text{horizon} \\ \text{premium} \end{pmatrix} \quad \textbf{(20-7)}$$

Eqn. 20-7 differs from Eqn. 20-1 in two respects. The first difference is that **credit-risk premiums** were added to Eqn. 20-1. Credit (default, bankruptcy) risk must be considered if bonds issued by corporations and municipalities are considered. Since corporations and municipalities sometimes default, an additional risk premium should be included to compensate investors for assuming this risk. (Credit risk is the topic of Chapter 22.) The second addition to Eqn. 20-1 is that a **horizon-risk premium** is included in Eqn. 20-7. This second factor reflects differences in the term structure (time to maturity) for different bond issues.[10]

Different yield curves exist for the bonds at each level of default risk (quality rating). Figure 20-5 shows several hypothetical yield curves for bonds from different default risk

---

[*] A yield curve created from zero coupon bonds differs from a yield curve created from bonds that pay coupons and are identical in every way except the coupons. The difference between the two yield curves is called **coupon bias** or **coupon effect.** Appendix A to this chapter explains why coupon bias will preclude many bonds from being located on a yield curve that is constructed using yields to maturity (YTMs). The Appendix to this chapter also suggests that by creating a yield curve from *spot rates* (see pp. 622–625), coupon bias can be avoided.

[**] Some issues of Treasury securities are *callable* before their maturity date. Investors require a higher yield to induce them to assume the risk that the bonds might be called before they mature.

[†] The tax status of a bond can affect its YTM in several ways. For example, *flower bonds* are a small subset of all Treasury bonds that the Internal Revenue Service (IRS) will accept at their full face value for payment of federal inheritance taxes. To the extent that flower bonds can be bought at a discount from their face value and given to the IRS before they mature they can provide valuable exemption from inheritance taxes. As a result of this tax exemption flower bonds have lower yields than T-bonds that are similar in all other respects. The *coupon effect* also involves tax considerations. The amount of discount or premium from par included in any taxable bond's purchase price affects its after-tax yield and its price because coupon income is taxed differently than income from price changes. These tax effects explain why some Treasury securities do not lay precisely on the yield curves created from coupon-paying bonds. To avoid *tax bias* only bonds selling at their par values can be used to create a yield curve; the result is called the *par bond yield curve.* Tax-exempt municipal bonds should never be included in the same yield curve as taxable bonds.

FIGURE 20-4   A Hypothetical U.S. Treasury Yield Curve That Exists 1 Day

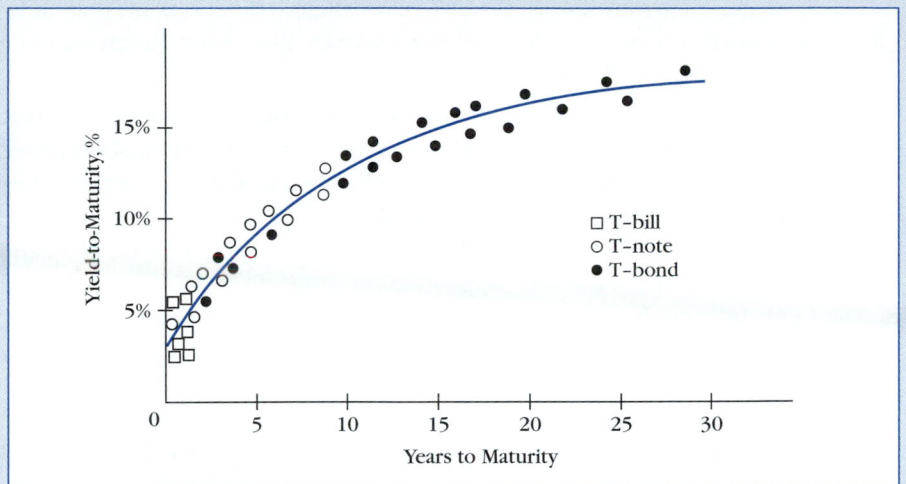

Each issue of U.S. Treasury bonds is represented by one point in the graph. The line-of-best-fit through the points is the yield curve existing that day. The yield curve is the relationship between years to maturity and yield-to-maturity (YTM) for a given bond issuer—typically, for U.S. Treasury bonds. Yield curves continuously shift position to reflect current market conditions.

FIGURE 20-5   Yield Curves for Different Default Classes at a Point In Time

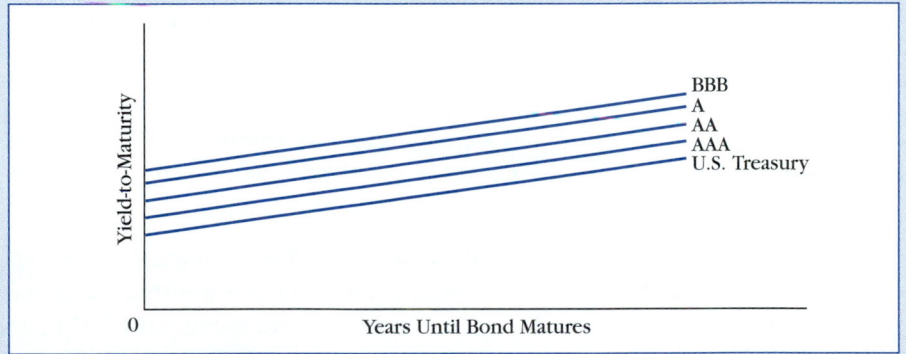

More than one yield curve exists. When hundreds or thousands of bond issues are categorized by default (credit, bankruptcy) risk, a separate yield curve can be drawn for each default-risk category. These different yield curves are approximately parallel; they are separated by yield spreads equal to the default risk premiums between the default-risk (bond quality rating) categories of bonds. These yield curves all change similarly each day in response to current credit market conditions.

categories. The yield curves for the riskier classes of bonds are at a higher level than the yield curves for less risky bonds, due to the credit risk premiums (credit spreads). This chapter confines its attention to the yield curve for U.S. Treasury bonds. By restricting discussion to marketable U.S. government bonds we have, in financial parlance, focused on the *Treasury yield curve.*

THREE THEORIES ABOUT YIELD CURVES

Figure 20-6 illustrates numerous historical yield curves; these yield curves illustrate how the term structure of interest rates varies through time. There are three main theories about what determines the shape of the yield curve:

1. The **horizon premium theory**, or **liquidity premium theory,** asserts that, on average, investors pay a price premium (resulting in lower yields) for short maturities to avoid the higher interest rate risk prevalent in bonds with the longer maturities. Thus, an upward sloping yield curve is considered normal.

2. The **segmentation theory** asserts that the yield curve is composed of a series of independent maturity segments.

3. The **expectations theory** asserts that long-term yields are the average of the short-term yields expected to prevail during the period before a bond matures. This implies that if all investors expect rates to rise in the future, the yield curve will slope upward; if they expect rates to remain unchanged in the future, the yield curve will be horizontal; or, if they expect rates to fall in the future, the yield curve will slope downward.

Each theory is considered separately before all three are integrated.

Horizon Premium Theory

Figures 20-1A and 20-6 show that long-term market interest rates fluctuate less than short-term rates. Although it may be difficult to understand why long-term bonds are riskier than short-term bonds issued by the same issuer, it's true that long-term bonds have more interest rate risk. The market prices of long-term bonds fluctuate more than the prices of short-term bonds even though the market interest rates of the long-term bonds fluctuate less. The large price fluctuations that characterize long-term bonds provides the basis for the *horizon premium hypothesis* (or *liquidity premium hypothesis*) that Rueben Kessel explains:

> *Liquidity preference produces asymmetry in the relationship between short-term and long-term rates at cycle peaks and troughs. It accounts for the failure of short-term rates to exceed long-term rates at peaks by as much as they fall below long-term rates at troughs.*[11]

Advocates of the horizon premium theory take yield curves from each phase of several business cycles and show that the average of short-term T-bond rates is less than the average of long-term Treasury bond rates. Graphically, this means that, on average, the yield curve is upward sloping. Although, on average, the upward slope exists, it does not prove the validity of the horizon premium theory.

Consider four reasons why the horizon premium theory might not hold (that is, why higher rates should be observed for short-term bonds):[12]

◆ With the passage of time short-term rates fluctuate continuously and therefore, investors face reinvestment risk at a series of fluctuating future interest rates.

◆ Increased transaction and information costs required to change frequently in the short-term maturities (instead of in fewer, longer-term bond issues) reduces net returns from such investments.

◆ Investors in long-term bonds can reduce their risk by hedging (that is, by synchronizing their assets and liabilities to mature simultaneously). For instance, long-run funds requirements can be hedged by buying long-term bonds that mature when the investor expects the funds will be needed.

FIGURE 20-6   Yield Curves for High-Grade Corporate Bonds, 1930–82

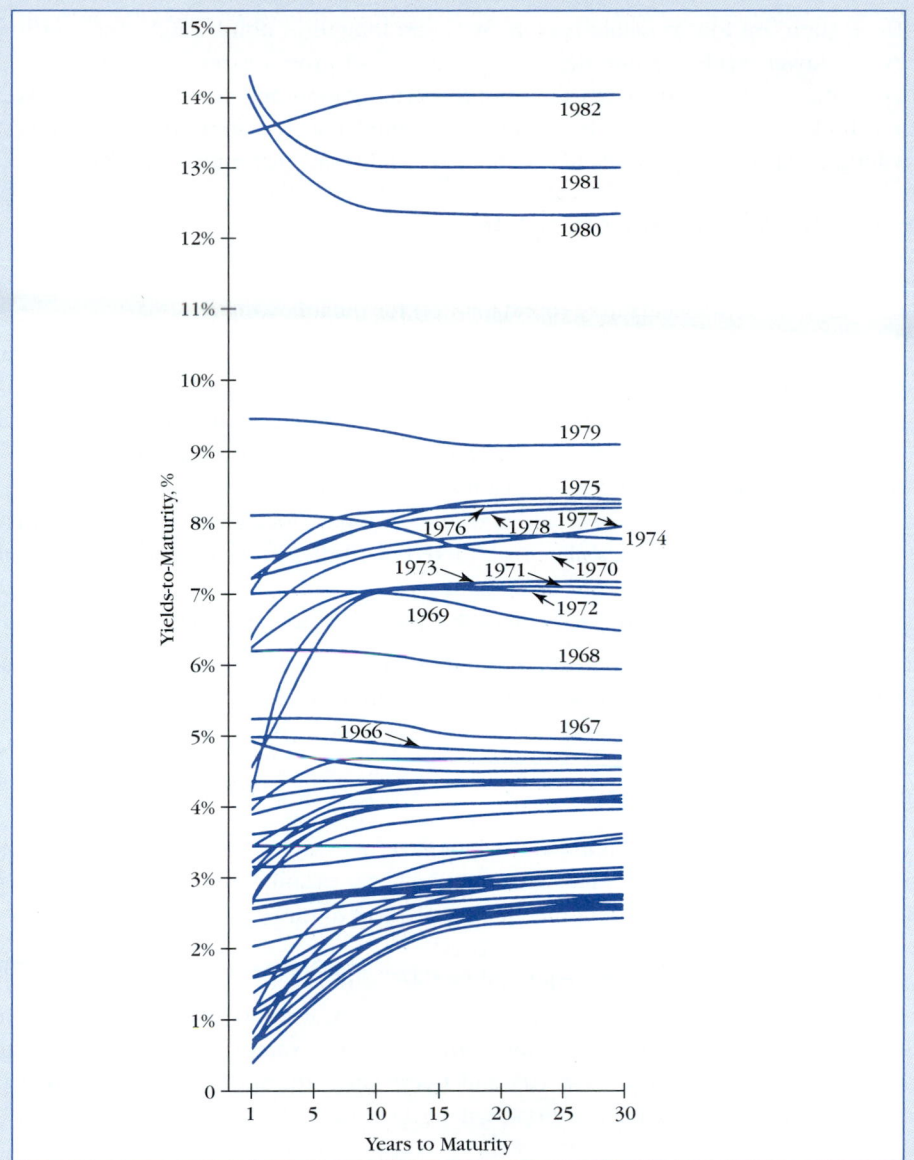

A graph with a tall vertical axis permits many yield curves from different decades to be assembled together. The inclusive graph illustrates how the level and structure of market interest rates fluctuates over a wide range. The level of market interest rates changes with the rate of inflation (Fisher effect) and supply and demand conditions in the nation's credit markets. The structure of market interest rates depends on investors' expectations and the independent supply of and demand for credit that exists at each segment of the yield curve.

SOURCES: David Durand, "Basic Yields of Corporate Bonds, 1900–1942," National Bureau of Economic Research (NBER) Technical Paper 3, Washington, DC, 1942. David Durand, "A Quarterly Series of Corporate Bond Yields, 1952–1957, and Some Attendant Reservations," *Journal of Finance* (September 1958): 348–56. David Durand and Willis J. Winn, "Basic Yields of Bonds, 1926–1947: Their Measurement and Pattern," NBER Technical Paper 6, Washington, DC, 1947. Scudder, Stevens, and Clark. John H. Wood and Norma L. Wood, *Financial Markets* (San Diego: Harcourt Brace Jovanovich, 1985), 630.

◆ The yield curve could slope downward because investors expect lower interest rates in the future than at present.

Here, then, are four possible reasons why the long-term bonds might trade at higher prices and lower yields. Despite these four challenges to the horizon premium theory, the theory contains considerable truth and most financial analysts and economists give it weight in their thinking. Short-term bonds are more like money than long-term bonds, and investors are willing to pay higher prices (and accept lower yields) for that immediate liquidity.

The Market Segmentation Theory

The *market segmentation theory* asserts that lenders and borrowers confine themselves to certain segments of the yield curve (bond market) for the following reasons.

1. Regulations called *legal lists* limit the types of investments that banks, S&Ls, insurance companies, and certain other institutional investors are allowed to make.
2. The high cost of gaining and maintaining information leads investors to specialize in some market segment simply to minimize their information gathering costs.
3. Some institutional investors have liabilities with a fixed maturity structure. For example, life insurance companies and pension funds have long-term liabilities that may be forecast by an actuary. Liabilities with fixed maturities cause investors to *hedge* their liabilities with assets of equivalent maturity.
4. Human beings may have preferences that are not dependent on theories or planning.

Because of these considerations the rates on different maturities tend to be determined independently by the differing supply and demand conditions in the various market segments.* Figure 20-7 shows a simple representation of how the yield curve could be segmented.**

The Expectations Theory

Many financial analysts and economists think of a coupon-paying bond as being a package of zero coupon bonds. Figure 20-8 illustrates how a 3-year default-free bond with a face (par) value of $100 and a 5% annual coupon rate is equivalent to three zero coupons with face values of $5, $5, and $105 that mature 1 year apart.

Viewing an *n*-year coupon-paying bond as a series of *n* zero-coupon bonds shows how the *n*-year bond's YTM can be decomposed into a series of *n* independent rates of return. This insight is useful with the expectations theory.[15] For example, using the simple arithmetic average, if 1-year rates are now 10% and 1-year rates are expected to be 12% next year, then today's interest rate on a 2-year bond will be 11%.

$$11\% \text{ per year} = \frac{10\% + 12\%}{2 \text{ years}} = \text{ average rate over two consecutive 1-year bonds}$$

If we assume that the 1-year forward rate we expect to exist 3 years ahead is 14%, we can calculate the current (spot) rate on a 3-year loan to be the average of the next three consecutive 1-year rates:

---

*   Yield curves are often estimated simply by "eyeballing" a line of best-fit through data points representing bonds in a homogeneous default-risk class. However, scientific methods have also been developed to eliminate coupon bias and taxability bias. Some of the algorithms tend to generate smooth yield curves.

** The pure segmentation theory suggests a complete unwillingness to change from a preferred maturity. The similar *preferred habitat theory* suggests both a preferred maturity and, in addition, a willingness to purchase other maturities when profit opportunities warrant it.

FIGURE 20-7 Illustration of the Segmented Determination of a Yield Curve

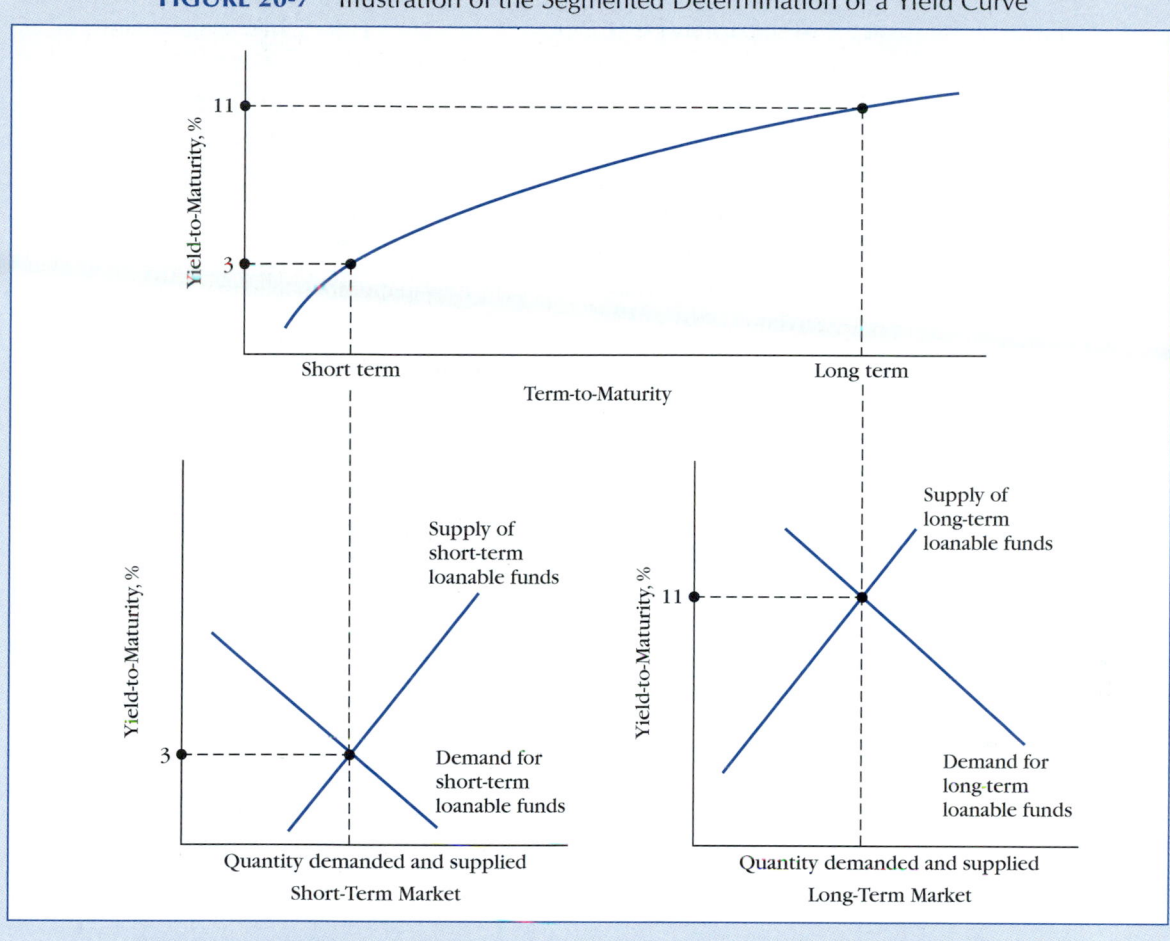

The segmentation theory asserts that the shape of the yield curve is determined by the separate supply of and demand for credit existing at different maturities along the yield curve. The graph illustrates how conditions in the short-term bond market result in a short-term market interest rate of 3%, while different conditions in the market for long-term bonds generate a long-term market interest rate of 11%.

$$12\% \text{ per year} = \frac{10\% + 12\% + 14\%}{3 \text{ years}} = \text{ average rate over three consecutive 1-year bonds}$$

In developing the expectations hypothesis we discuss two types of interest rates—the "spot rate" and the "forward rate."

THE EXPECTATIONS HYPOTHESIS   DEFINITION

A **forward rate**, denoted $_tF_{t+1}$, refers to the yield *expected to exist in the future*. In other words, $_tF_{t+1}$ denotes the market interest rate currently expected in some future 1-year bond that will come into existence at time t. Time t might be the year 2013. It follows that the hypothetical 1-year bond will mature at time $t + 1$, year 2014.

Spot rates, denoted $_0S_t$, refer to the interest rates for bonds that *currently exist* (at $t = 0$) and mature t time periods in the future. These conventions are used in making the rigorous statement of the expectations hypothesis shown at Eqns. 20-8:*

$_tF_{t+n}$ = Forward rate for a loan that starts at future date t and is to be repaid n periods later (at time $t + n$); the forward interest rates are implicit and cannot be observed directly.

Repayment date—the right-hand subscript.

Date the money is loaned—the left-hand subscript.

$_0S_n$ = Spot rate published in the daily newspaper for a loan that starts immediately (time $t = 0$) and is to be repaid (matures) n periods in the future.

Using these mathematical conventions, the expectations theory exists when Eqns. 20-8a, 20-8b, 20-8c, . . . , 20-8n are all true simultaneously and no profitable arbitrage opportunities exist.

$$\left(1 + {_0S_1}\right)^1 = \left(1 + {_0F_1}\right) \tag{20-8a}$$

$$\left(1 + {_0S_2}\right)^2 = \left(1 + {_0F_1}\right)\left(1 + {_1F_2}\right) \tag{20-8b}$$

$$\left(1 + {_0S_3}\right)^3 = \left(1 + {_0F_1}\right)\left(1 + {_1F_2}\right)\left(1 + {_2F_3}\right) \tag{20-8c}$$

$$\left(1 + {_0S_n}\right)^n = \left(1 + {_0F_1}\right)\left(1 + {_1F_2}\right)\left(1 + {_2F_3}\right) \cdots \left(1 + {_{n-1}F_n}\right) \tag{20-8n}$$

FIGURE 20-8   A Coupon-Paying Bond Is Equivalent to a Portfolio of Zero Coupon Bonds

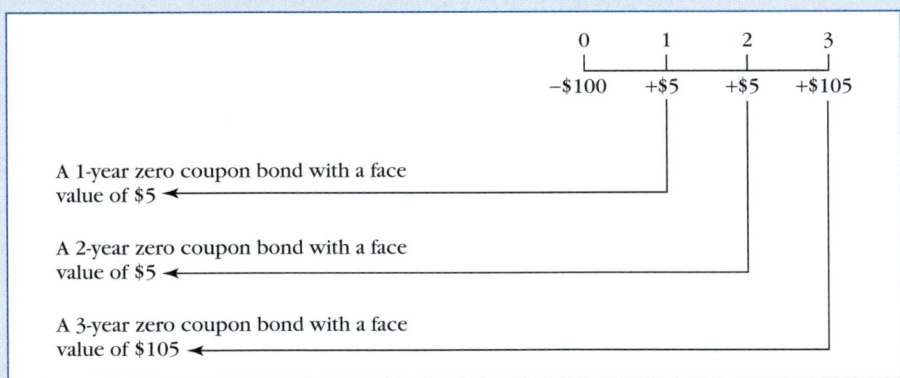

The 3-year bond's first $5 coupon is like a tiny zero coupon bond that has a life of 1 year. The second $5 annual coupon may be viewed as a zero coupon bond with a maturity of 2 years. The 3-year bond's final cash flow can be viewed as a 3-year zero coupon bond with a face value of $105. Treating each cash flow as a separate zero coupon bond eliminates the unrealistic assumption that all coupons are reinvested at the YTM.

---

* Handling coupon-interest payments can be perplexing when formulating a mathematical statement of the expectations hypothesis. The easiest way to deal with this problem is to assume all bonds are zero coupon bonds. This simplifying assumption avoids the coupon bias in the yield curve that is highlighted in Figure 21-8 and analyzed in the Appendix to this chapter.

Spot rates $_0S_n$ exist and can be observed in the daily newspapers. Forward rates $_0F_1, _1F_2,$ $_2F_3, \ldots, _{n-1}F_n$ are implicit interest rates on future bonds that do not yet exist. The implicit (unobservable) future rates can be determined for any future period by algebraically solving the series of Eqns. 20-8 for the desired value of $_tF_{t+n}$. For example, in the year 2010 the implicit market interest rate for a one-period loan that is expected to exist (2013 − 2010 =) 3 years in the future is found by solving Eqn. 20-9 for $_{2013}F_{2014}$ from the spot rates $_{2010}S_{2013}$ and $_{2010}S_{2014}$ obtained from the newspaper in year 2010.

$$1 + {}_{2013}F_{2014} = \frac{\left(1 + {}_{2010}S_{2014}\right)^4}{\left(1 + {}_{2010}S_{2013}\right)^3}$$

$$= \frac{\left(1 + {}_{2010}S_{2011}\right)\left(1 + {}_{2011}F_{2012}\right)\left(1 + {}_{2012}F_{2013}\right)\left(1 + {}_{2013}F_{2014}\right)}{\left(1 + {}_{2010}S_{2011}\right)\left(1 + {}_{2011}F_{2012}\right)\left(1 + {}_{2012}F_{2013}\right)} \qquad \textbf{(20-9)}$$

It is also possible to determine the implicit future rates for multiperiod bonds. For a bond with a life of n periods that starts in period t and ends (matures) in period $t + n$, the yield over the life (of n periods) of this bond can be derived from Eqn. 20-10, where $_tF_{t+n}$ is the market yield for an n-period bond that starts in future period t and matures in the more distant future period $t + n$.

$$\left(\frac{\left(1 + {}_0S_{t+n}\right)^{t+n}}{\left(1 + {}_0S_t\right)^t}\right)^{1/n} = \sqrt[n]{\left(1 + {}_tF_{t+1}\right)\left(1 + {}_{t+1}F_{t+2}\right) \cdots \left(1 + {}_{t+n-1}F_{t+n}\right)} \qquad \textbf{(20-10)}$$

$$= 1 + {}_tF_{t+n}$$

We cannot expect the relations suggested by the expectations hypothesis to be precise because transactions costs (such as sales commissions and taxes) inhibit trading. If transactions costs are small, arbitrage ensures that Eqn. 20-10 will tend to hold. Recall that **arbitrage** (see Chapter 3) is a series of transactions that yields a riskless profit. Arbitrage between maturities will tend to maintain the expectations theory represented in Eqns. 20-8.[16]

Arbitrage Maintains the Expectations Model

Some investors will rearrange their bond portfolios and cause bond prices and yields to be revised according to Eqns. 20-8 because they expect to profit from it. For example, suppose some economic disturbance causes inequality Eqn. 20-11 to emerge. This inequality represents profit opportunities to bond traders who realize it violates Eqn. 20-8.

$$\left(1 + {}_0S_T\right)^T > \left(1 + {}_0F_1\right)\left(1 + {}_1F_2\right) \cdots \left(1 + {}_{T-1}F_T\right) \qquad \textbf{(20-11)}$$

Profit-seekers will purchase the existing long-term bond yielding $_0S_T$. These purchases will continue to drive up its purchase price, P_0, and drive down its yield, $_0S_T$ (as shown by the arrows in the equation below), until Eqn. 20-11 is aligned with Eqns. 20-8.*

---

* Rigorous analysts make a distinction between spot rates and the yield-to-maturity (YTM) of a bond that explains why arbitrage will not maintain inequality Eqn. 20-10 continuously, and why some bonds will never lie exactly on the yield curve. The difference is that a bond's spot rate is a time-weighted (geometric mean) rate of return, while the YTM is a dollar-weighted rate of return (internal rate of return) that differs from the time-weighted rate of return whenever the yield curve is not horizontal at the bond's YTM. The implicit reinvestment rates through time are the key to this difference. Chapter 10 explains the difference between the dollar-weighted and the time-weighted rates of return. The Appendix to this chapter analyzes the economics.

$$\frac{\left(\begin{array}{c}\text{Bond's fixed maturity price} \\ \text{(face value, par) at time } t = T\end{array}\right)}{\left(\begin{array}{c}\text{Bond's purchase} \\ \text{price at time } t = 0\end{array}\right)\uparrow} = \frac{P_T}{\uparrow P_0} = (1 + {}_0S_T\downarrow)^T$$

A simple test that supports the expectations theory of Eqns. 20-8 is to compare the interest rate forecasts inherent in the yield curve of some past date with the record of business activity after that date.[17] Assuming professional investors have worthwhile ideas about the future level of business activity, and also assuming they believe the level of interest rates follows the level of business activity, it then follows directly from the definition of the expectations hypothesis that the yield curve should usually slope up preceding economic expansions and slope downward preceding contractions (recessions). Without recognizing the implicit reasoning, a more common version of the expectations theory would be: Declining business activity during the period of time presented by the yield pattern will result in a negatively sloped yield pattern—or vice versa for a period of time when business activity is accelerating.

The market interest rates (horizon spreads in Column 9 of Table 20-1) support the expectations hypothesis. A yield curve constructed at nearly any cyclical peak slopes downward, and a yield curve drawn at nearly any trough slopes upward. The yield curve for the 1982 recession near the top of Figure 20-6 illustrates an upward sloping yield curve; such yield curves are called *normal yield curves*. The yield curves existing at the economic troughs are upward-sloping yield curves that forecast expectations of rising interest rates; they exist more frequently than the (downward sloping) inverted yield curves.

THE BOTTOM LINE

This chapter focuses on the yields-to-maturity (YTMs) of U.S. Treasury bonds. YTMs from other bonds are considered to a lesser extent. YTMs are market-determined interest rates that fluctuate continuously. The two aspects of YTMs considered in this chapter are the term structure of interest rates (yield curve) and the level of interest rates.

Conclusions About the Term Structure of Interest Rates

There is an undeniable element of logic in each of the three theories about the term structure of interest rates, and each is supported by some empirical data. A combination of all three theories probably furnishes the best description of what actually determines the term structure of interest rates.

Assume the unobservable yield curve denoted *EE* in Figure 20-9 is determined by unobservable expectations. Horizon (liquidity) premiums, which increase with term to maturity, are added on top of this unobservable expectations yield curve *EE*. Thus, the observable yield curve *YY* in Figure 20-9 represents a combination determined by expectations of forward rates and horizon premiums. The *horizon premium* equals the vertical distance between *YY* and *EE*. The horizon premium theory is not invalidated by the occasional observation of a downward-sloping *YY* yield curve. The *YY* yield curve could slope downward, even though increasing horizon premiums are added on top of *YY*, if the underlying *EE* yield curve sloped downward steeply. The curve *EE* symbolizes the *pure expectations theory* and curve *YY* represents the *biased expectations theory* observed in the nominal market interest rates that are published in newspapers.

FIGURE 20-9   A Yield Curve That Is Determined by Expectations and
Horizon Premiums

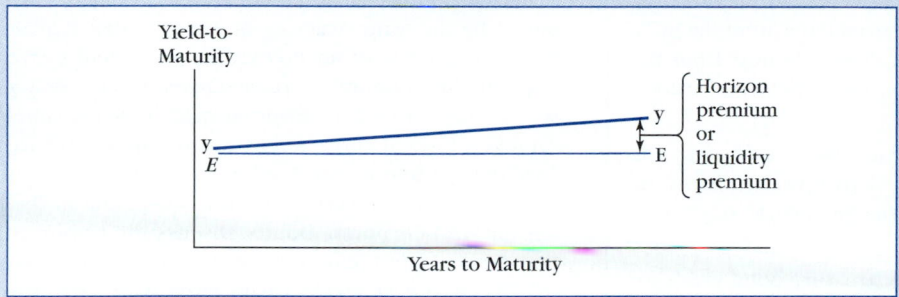

The yield curve denoted *EE* is based on unobservable expectations. Horizon (liquidity)
premiums that increase with term to maturity are superimposed on top of the
unobservable pure expectations yield curve *EE*. A yield curve that is observable in
newspapers is represented by *YY*; it is a combination determined by expectations of
forward rates and bond horizon premiums. The horizon premium is the vertical
distance between *YY* and *EE*. The curve *EE* symbolizes the pure expectations theory and
curve *YY* represents the biased expectations theory observed in the nominal market
interest rates published in newspapers.

The long-term end of the yield curve is determined by investors' expectations and the
horizon premiums needed to induce investors to hold those bonds. The segmentation theory
explains the frequent movements in the short-term end of the yield curve. Almost every day
the U.S. Federal Reserve's Open Market Committee endeavors to control the money supply
and exert pressure on short-term market interest rates by buying and selling millions of dollars of Treasury Bills and similar bonds. The Fed's interactions with the liquidity needs of
commercial banks provide the primary supply and demand forces at work on the short-term
end of the yield curve. The wide and frequent swings in that portion of the yield curve with
less than 1 year to maturity (illustrated in Figure 20-6) are largely attributed to changes in
these supply and demand factors. The effects of these forces on the yield curve are segmented and diminish rapidly in the intermediate and long-term maturities.

Conclusions About the Level of Market Interest Rates

Figure 20-1 documents the positive impact inflation (the Fisher effect) exerts in determining
the level of nominal market interest rates. In addition, shifts in the supply of and demand for
credit can result in faster interest rate changes than changes in inflationary expectations
alone might dictate. Changes in risk-premiums (yield spreads) that occur as the stage of the
business cycle changes can also contribute to movements in the level of market interest
rates.

Since bond prices are strongly affected by market interest rates, forecasting interest rates
is an important task for all bond investors.

QUESTIONS

Q20-1 (Inflation considerations) How should the inflationary concerns of 1-year bond investors differ from the inflationary concerns of investors in 20-year bonds? Does the distinction between the *level* and the *structure* of market interest rates become relevant?

Q20-2 (Yield curve theories) (a) Give two reasons why the yield curve might be expected to slope upward most of the time. (b) Give two reasons why the yield curve might usually slope downward.

Q20-3 (Yield curves) When U.S. Treasury bond yields for a given day are plotted against their years to maturity to draw a yield curve, why do all the data points not lie exactly on the yield curve if it is drawn to be smooth? Does the fact that not all of the data points lie on the yield curve diminish the value of theories about the term structure of interest rates? Explain. What variables can be held constant in the preparation of a yield curve? What variables cannot be held constant in the preparation of a yield curve?

Q20-4 (Introduction to bond duration) Explain why the yields on short-term bonds fluctuate more than the yields on long-term bonds, but the prices of long-term bonds nevertheless fluctuate more than the prices of short-term bonds.

Q20-5 (Hedging strategies) Bond dealers define a *bear hedge* as a transaction in which "a short sale of longs is hedged by going long shorts." This statement means that a short position of long-term bonds is hedged by taking a long position in short-term bonds. Why would a bond dealer enter such a bear hedge? (You can refer to Chapter 3 for an explanation of long and short positions.)

Q20-6 (Term structure of interest rates) The following questions about market interest rates were used on the CFA (Chartered Financial Analysts) Exam. (a) Explain what is meant by the term structure of interest rates. Explain the theoretical basis of an upward sloping yield curve. (b) Explain the economic circumstances under which you would expect to see the inverted yield curve prevail. (*Note:* An inverted yield curve is downward sloping.) (c) Explain "real" rate of interest. (d) Explain the characteristics of the market for U.S. Treasury securities. Compare it to the market for AAA-corporate bonds. Discuss the opportunities that may exist in bond markets that are less than efficient. (e) Over the past several years, fairly wide yield spreads between AAA-corporates and Treasuries have occasionally prevailed. Discuss the possible reasons why this occurred.

Q20-7 (Yield spreads) Differentiate between a quality spread and a horizon spread. How is each measured?

Q20-8 (Factors affecting market rates) Explain how deficit spending by the U.S. government can thwart the Federal Reserve's attempt to keep interest rates low.

Q20-9 (Yield curve theories) Briefly discuss the three main theories regarding the shape of the yield curve.

Q20-10 (Quality spreads) Consider the following two bonds.

Bond	Rating	Coupon	Years to Maturity	Price	YTM
1	A	9%	9	$941.55	10%
2	BBB	10%	10	$951.80	10.8%

You believe that the current yield spread of 80 basis points will narrow to 50 basis points. Which of the two bonds would you prefer to hold, based on this assumption? Why?

PROBLEMS

P20-1 (Forward rates) Assume 4-year bonds are currently yielding 7% and 3-year bonds are yielding 6%. What is the implied yield for 1-year bonds starting 3 years from now? Show your work. *Hint:* Use the expectations theory.

P20-2 (Yield-to-maturity) What is the yield-to-maturity (YTM) of a zero coupon bond with a face value of $1,000 if it is selling for $880 and it has 5 years until it matures?

P20-3 (Bond pricing) What should the price be for a $10,000 face value bond with 7 years to maturity if it pays coupons of 9% annually and has a YTM of 8%?

Use the following data for Problems 20-4 through 20-7.

Bond	Maturity, years	YTM
W	1	8.0%
X	2	9.0%
Y	3	10.5%
Z	4	12.0%

P20-4 (Forward rates) Calculate the implied 1-year forward rate at the start of Year 2.

P20-5 (Forward rates) Calculate the implied 1-year forward rate at the start of Year 3.

P20-6 (Forward rates) Calculate the implied rate for a 3-year bond at the start of Year 2.

P20-7 (Forward rates) Calculate the implied rate for a 2-year bond at the start of Year 3.

P20-8 (Forward rates) If a 15-year Treasury bond is yielding 12% and a 5-year U.S. Treasury bond is yielding 8%, what is the expected return on a 10-year bond starting at the end of Year 5?

P20-9 (Yield-to-maturity and forward rates) Assume the following zero-coupon bonds are available:

Bond Price	Maturity, years
$935	1
870	2
800	3
750	4

(a) Determine the YTM for each bond. (b) Determine the 1-year forward rate at the beginning of Year 3.

P20-10 (Locking in forward rates) Using the information given in Problem 20-9, explain how an investor could lock in the 1-year forward rate for Year 3 at the start of Year 1.

P20-11 (Yield-to-maturity) Using the information given in Problem 20-9, determine the YTM for a 3-year bond at the start of Year 2.

P20-12 (Fisher equation) If the real rate of return is 3%, $RR = 0.03$, what inflation forecast is implied by the yield curve given in Problem 20-9?

P20-13 (Forward rates) Using the information given in Problem 20-9, determine the 1-year forward rate beginning in Year 2.

P20-14 (Forward rates) The YTM on a 10-year bond is 10.5%. If the YTM on a 9-year bond is 10.25%, what is the implied 1-year forward rate for Year 10?

P20-15 (Forward rates) Suppose the YTM on an 11-year bond is 10.6%. If the YTM on the 9- and 10-year bonds are 10.25% and 10.5%, respectively, determine the forward rate on a 2-year bond starting in Year 10.

CFA EXAM QUESTIONS

1. (1997 CFA Sample Exam, Level I) Which of the following statements about the term structure of interest rates is **true**?
   A. The expectations hypothesis indicates a flat yield curve if anticipated future short-term rates exceed current short-term rates.
   B. The expectations hypothesis contends that the long-term rate is equal to the anticipated short-term rate.
   C. The liquidity premium theory indicates that, all else being equal, longer maturities will have lower yields.
   D. The market segmentation theory contends that borrowers and lenders prefer particular segments of the yield curve.

2. (1999 CFA Sample Exam, Level I) An analyst gathers the following information:

Years to Maturity	Spot rate
1	5.00%
2	6.00%
3	6.50%

Based on the data above, the 1-year implied forward rate 2 years from now is *closest* to:
   A. 6.25%.
   B. 7.01%.
   C. 7.26%.
   D. 7.51%.

3. (The following question is adapted from a question appearing on the 1996 CFA Exam, Level II.) The shape of the U.S. Treasury yield curve appears to reflect two expected Federal Reserve reductions in the Federal funds rate. The first reduction of approximately 50 basis points (*bp*) is expected 6 months from now and the second reduction of approximately 50 *bp* is expected 1 year from now. The current U.S. Treasury term premiums are 10 *bp* per year for each of the next 3 years (out through the 3-year benchmark.)

   You agree that the two Federal Reserve reductions described above will occur. However, you believe that they will be reversed in a single 100 *bp* increase in the Federal Funds rate $2\frac{1}{2}$ years from now. You expect term premiums to remain 10 *bp* per year for each of the next 3 years (out through the 3-year benchmark.)
   A. **Describe** the shape of the Treasury yield curve out through the 3-year benchmark.
   B. **State** which term structure policy supports the shape of the U.S. Treasury yield curve described in Part A. **Justify** your choice.

4. (1990 CFA Exam, Level III) The following are the average yields on U.S. T-bonds at two different points in time.

Time to Maturity	Yield-to-Maturity	
	January 15, 19XX	May 15, 19XX
1 year	7.25%	8.05%
2 years	7.50%	7.90%
5 years	7.90%	7.70%
10 years	8.30%	7.45%
15 years	8.45%	7.30%
20 years	8.55%	7.20%
25 years	8.60%	7.10%

A. *Assuming* a pure expectations hypothesis, **define** a forward rate. **Describe** how you would calculate the forward rate for a *3-year* U.S. T-bond *2* years from May 15, 19XX, using the *actual* term structure above.

B. **Discuss** how each of the *three* major term structure hypotheses could explain the January 15, 19XX term structure shown above.

C. **Discuss** what happened to the term structure over the time period *and* the effect of this change on U.S. T-bonds of 2 years and 10 years.

D. Assume that you invest *solely* on the basis of yield spreads, and in January 19XX acted upon the expectation that the yield spread between 1-year and 25-year U.S. Treasuries would return to a more typical spread of 170 basis points. **Explain** what you would have done on January 15, 19XX, and describe the result of this action based upon what happened between January 15, 19XX and May 15, 19XX.

5. (1994 CFA Exam, Level II) Table 1 below shows the characteristics of two annual pay bonds from the same issuer with the same priority in the event of default, and Table 2 below displays spot interest rates. Neither bond's price is consistent with the spot rates.
Using the information in Tables 1 and 2, **recommend** *either* Bond A *or* Bond B for purchase. **Justify** your choice.

Table 1 Bond Characteristics

	Bond A	Bond B
Coupons	Annual	Annual
Maturity	3 years	3 years
Coupon rate	10%	6%
Yield-to-maturity	10.65%	10.75%
Price	98.40	88.34

Table 2 Spot Interest Rates

Term	Spot Rates (Zero Coupon)
1 year	5%
2 year	8%
3 year	11%

FURTHER REFERENCES

Caks, John. "The Coupon Effect on Yield to Maturity," *Journal of Finance* (March 1977): 103–15.

Carleton, Willard and Ian A. Cooper. "Estimation and Uses of the Term Structure of Interest Rates," *Journal of Finance* 31, no. 4 (September 1976): 1067–68.

Culbertson, J. A. "The Term Structure of Interest Rates," *Quarterly Journal of Economics* (November 1957): 485–517; also, J. B. Michaelson, "Comment," *ibid.* (February 1963): 166–74; and J. A. Culbertson, "Reply," *ibid.* (November 1963): 691–96.
   This series of nonmathematical articles articulates the viewpoint of classic advocates of the segmentation theory.

Fabozzi, Frank J. *Bond Markets, Analysis and Strategies,* 4th ed. (Englewood Cliffs, NJ: Prentice-Hall, 2000).
   This popular college finance textbook describes bond markets and surveys modern interest rate theory.

Fisher, Lawrence and R. L. Weil. "Coping with the Risk of Interest Rate Fluctuations," *Journal of Business* 44 (October 1971): 408–31.

Garbade, Kenneth D. *Fixed Income Analytics.* Cambridge, MA: The MIT Press, 1996.
   This scholarly book uses advanced mathematics to analyze the market prices of bonds and interest rate derivatives.

Livingston, Miles. *Money and Capital Markets,* 3d ed. Malden, MA: Blackwell Publishers, 1996.
   This financial economics textbook uses algebra and a few paragraphs of calculus, supplemented with numerical examples to make complicated issues clear.

ENDNOTES

[1] See Irving Fisher, *Appreciation and Interest* (New York: Macmillan, 1896), 75–76. Also see Irving Fisher, *The Theory of Interest* (New York: Macmillan, 1930).

[2] For empirical support of Fisher's theory, see William E. Gibson, "Interest Rates and Inflationary Expectations: New Evidence," *American Economic Review* (December 1972): 854–65. In addition, see E. F. Fama, "Short-Term Interest Rates as Predictors of Inflation," *American Economic Review* (June 1975): 269–82. Also see C. R. Nelson and G. W. Schwert, "Short-Term Interest Rates as Predictors of Inflation: On Testing the Hypothesis That the Real Rate of Interest Is a Constant," *American Economic Review* (June 1977): 478–86. Darby suggested that income taxes modified Eqn. 20-1. See M. R. Darby, "The Financial and Tax Effects of Monetary Policy on Interest Rates," *Economic Inquiry* 13 (June 1975): 266–82.

[3] For an empirical study of realized real rates showing: (a) the real rate is not constant, and (b) the real rate is sometimes negative, see Steven C. Leuthold, "Interest Rates, Inflation and Deflation," *Financial Analysts Journal* (January–February 1981): 28–41. In later research, Fama reported that the real rate fluctuated with business activity. See E. Fama and M. Gibbons, "Inflation, Real Returns and Capital Investment," *Journal of Monetary Economics* 9, no. 3 (1982): 297–323.

[4] A noteworthy view was published by A. H. Gibson, "The Future Course of High Class Investment Values," *Bankers Magazine* (January 1923): 15–43. John Maynard Keynes noted the contradiction between Gibson's graph and Irving Fisher's interest rate theory and called it the "Gibson Paradox." See J. M. Keynes, *A Treatise on Money* (New York: Macmillan, 1930). For an analysis of Irving Fisher's inflation model and the preceding articles, see Robert J. Shiller and Jeremy J. Siegel, "The Gibson Paradox and Historical Movements in Real Interest Rates," *Journal of Political Economy* 85, no. 5 (1977): 891–907.

[5] See Alex D. Patelis, "Stock Return Predictability and the Role of Monetary Policy," *Journal of Finance* 52, no. 5 (December 1997): 1951–72.

[6] Securities brokers, in general, and, in this context, bond brokers encourage investors to switch bonds so that the brokers can earn trading commissions. For an analysis of the profitability of bond swaps see Sidney Homer and Martin L. Leibowitz, *Inside the Yield Book* (Englewood Cliffs, NJ: Prentice-Hall, 1972), Table 29.

[7] Roll and Ross report a statistically significant relationship between common stock returns and the (orthogonalized) market interest rate yield spreads (and several other economic variables too). See Richard Roll and Stephen Ross, "The Arbitrage Pricing Theory Approach to Strategic Portfolio Planning," *Financial Analysts Journal* (May–June 1984): 14–29.

[8] See Lawrence Fisher, "Determinants of Risk Premiums on Corporate Bonds," *Journal of Political Economy* (June 1959): 217–37. See also George E. Pinches and Kent A. Mingo, "A Multivariate Analysis of Industrial Bond Ratings," *Journal of Finance* (March 1973): 1–18. In addition to the risk premiums that investors demand that vary over the business cycle, the current supply of and demand for loanable funds also affects yield spreads; see Ray C. Fair and Burton G. Malkiel, "The Determination of Yield Differentials Between Debt Instruments of the Same Maturity," *Journal of Money, Credit and Banking* (November 1971): 733–49.

[9] For other discussions of coupon bias, see John Caks "The Coupon Effect on Yield to Maturity," *Journal of Finance* (March 1977): 103–15. More recently, see Bruce Tuckman, *Fixed Income Securities* (New York: Wiley, 1996), 36–39. In addition, see Suresh Sundaresan, *Fixed Income Markets and Their Derivatives* (Cincinnati, OH: South-Western, 1997), 173. Furthermore, see Miles Livingston, *Money and Capital Markets,* 3d ed. (Malden, MA: Blackwell Publishers, 1996), 191–201. Also, see Kenneth D. Garbade, *Fixed Income Analytics* (Cambridge, MA: MIT Press, 1996), 139–40. Also see Gerald Bierwag, *Duration Analysis* (Cambridge, MA: Ballinger Press, 1987), 228, 233.

[10] For information about which econometric model has the highest goodness-of-fit statistics for estimating the yield curve empirically, see Robert Ferguson and Steven Raymar, "A Comparative Analysis of Several Popular Term Structure Estimation Models," *The Journal of Fixed Income* 7, no. 4 (March 1998): 17–33.

[11] R. Kessel, *The Cyclical Behavior of the Term Structure of Interest Rates,* National Bureau of Economic Research, Occasional Paper No. 91, 1965.

[12] Franco Modigliani, Richard Sutch, et al., *Supplement to Journal of Political Economy* (August 1967). Also see B. P. Malkiel, *The Term Structure of Interest Rates* (Princeton, NJ: 1966) for a discussion of the liquidity premium hypothesis.

[13] See S. W. Dobson, "Estimating Term Structure Equations with Individual Bond Data," *Journal of Finance* (March 1978): 75–92. Also see A. Vasicek and H. Gifford Fong, "The Tax Adjusted Yield Curve," *Journal of Finance* (June 1975): 811–30. Some algorithms generate more disjointed estimates of the yield curve; see J. H. McCulloch, "Measuring the Term Structure of Interest Rates," *Journal of Business* (January 1971): 19–31.

[14] See Franco Modigliani and Richard Sutch, "Innovations in Interest Rate Policy," *American Economic Review* 56 (May 1966): 178–97.

[15] For more discussion of additional yield curve theories, see Miles Livingston, *Money and Capital Markets,* 3d ed. (Malden, MA: Blackwell, 1996), Chapter 12.

[16] Cox, Ingersoll, and Ross (CIR) have shown that different versions of the expectations theory, that had traditionally been considered to be equivalent, are inconsistent with each other when interest rates fluctuate randomly. Essentially, a combination of uncertainty and Jensen's Inequality is used to drive a wedge between different risk premium measures. CIR use stochastic calculus to show that in a continuous time arbitrage pricing framework only one formulation of the expectations theory is compatible with equilibrium. See

John C. Cox, Jonathan E. Ingersoll, and Stephen A. Ross, "A Re-Examination of Traditional Hypotheses About the Term Structure of Interest Rates," *Journal of Finance* 36 (September 1981): 769–99.

John Wood estimated that the problem CIR highlight is numerically small and probably not statistically significant to those doing empirical work. See J. H. Wood and N. L. Wood, *Financial Markets* (New York: Harcourt Brace Jovanovich, 1985), 647–50. Campbell considered CIR's model and argued in support of the simpler term structure theory that is normally tested empirically. See John Y. Campbell, "A Defense of Traditional Hypotheses About the Term Structure of Interest Rates," *Journal of Finance* 41, no. 1 (March 1986): 183–93. For these and other reasons the CIR model will not be discussed further.

[17] Several studies support the ability of the yield curve to predict business activity. See Arturo Estrella and Gikas Hardouvelis, "The Term Structure as a Predictor of Real Economic Activity," *Journal of Finance* (June 1991): 555–76. Also see Joseph G. Houbrich and Ann M. Dombrosky. "Predicting Real Growth Using the Yield Curve," *Economic Review* (1996 Quarter 1): 26–35. In addition, see Frederic S. Mishkin, "What Does the Term Structure Tell Us About Future Inflation?" *Journal of Monetary Economics* (January 1990): 77–95. Also, see Charles I. Plosser and K. Geert Rouwenhorst. "International Term Structures and Real Economic Growth," *Journal of Monetary Economics* (February 1994): 135–55.

[18] W. T. Carleton and Ian A. Cooper, "Estimation and Uses of the Term Structure of Interest Rates," *Journal of Finance* 31, no. 4 (September 1976): 1067–83.

[19] For a numerical example of how to construct a spot rate yield curve, see Frank J. Fabozzi, *Bond Markets, Analysis and Strategies,* 3d ed. (Englewood Cliffs, NJ: Prentice-Hall, 1996), Chapter 5.

Alternative Formulations of the Yield Curve*

The present value of a bond (P) may be represented in terms of the bond's yield-to-maturity (YTM), or spot (S) rates of interest from the yield curve, or forward rates (F) from the yield curve, respectively, as shown in Eqn. 20A-1. The spot and forward interest rate conventions were explained in Table 20-2.

$$P = \sum_{t=1}^{n} \frac{CF_t}{(1 + YTM)^t} = \sum_{t=1}^{n} \frac{CF_t}{(1 + S_t)^t} = \sum_{t=1}^{n} \frac{CF_t}{\prod_{i=1}^{t}(1 + F_i)^t} \qquad (20A\text{-}1)$$

Eqn.(20A-1) makes the same statement in three different ways. Expanding each of the three bond price formulas above to the first two time periods' results in Equations 20A-2, 20A-3, and 20A-4:

$$P = \frac{C_1}{1 + YTM} + \frac{C_2}{(1 + YTM)^2} + \cdots \qquad (20A\text{-}2)$$

$$P = \frac{C_1}{1 + {}_0S_1} + \frac{C_2}{(1 + {}_1S_2)^2} + \cdots \qquad (20A\text{-}3)$$

$$P = \frac{C_1}{1 + {}_0F_1} + \frac{C_2}{(1 + {}_0F_1)(1 + {}_1F_2)} + \cdots \qquad (20A\text{-}4)$$

Spot and Forward Rates

To begin with, let us ignore dollar quantities and instead focus on the relationships between the three interest (or discount) rates denoted F, S, and YTM. The spot rate is the geometric mean of the forward rates. Eqns. 20A-5, 20A-6, and 20A-7 show equivalent definitional relationships between the spot and forward rates:

$$(1 + {}_0S_t)^t = (1 + {}_0F_1)(1 + {}_1F_2) \cdots (1 + {}_{t-1}F_t) \qquad (20A\text{-}5)$$

$${}_0S_t = \sqrt[t]{(1 + {}_0F_1)(1 + {}_1F_2) \cdots (1 + {}_{t-1}F_t)} - 1.0 \qquad (20A\text{-}6)$$

$$(1 + {}_{t-1}F_t) = \frac{(1 + {}_0S_t)^t}{(1 + {}_0S_{t-1})^{t-1}} \qquad (20A\text{-}7)$$

---

* This Appendix originated as a teaching note written by Professor Jonathan E. Ingersoll at Yale University. Professor David F. Babbel at the Wharton School of Finance added examples. This book's coauthors are indebted to Professors Ingersoll and Babbel for their permission to alter and reprint their teaching note.

Compare and contrast the spot and forward rates with the YTM. A bond's YTM is the weighted average of forward rates where weights are determined in accordance with the size of the cash flows occurring at each point in time. An arithmetic example clarifies this discussion.

Assume the existence of a $1,000 par value bond with three years remaining to maturity, with an annual coupon of $100. This bond's cash flows are $CF_1 = \$100$, $CF_2 = \$100$, and $CF_3 = \$1,100$. Suppose that the forward rate term structure is: $_0F_1 = 0.10$, $_1F_2 = 0.11$, and $_2F_3 = 0.15$ for the three periods in which the cash flows occur. The spot rates in Table 20A-1 are computed from these assumed numerical values.

TABLE 20A-1   Calculations for the Spot Rates

In the first time period the spot rate and future rates are the same:

$$1 + {_0F_1} = 1 + {_0S_1} = 1.10$$

or after subtracting 1:

$$_0F_1 = {_0S_1} = 0.10 = 10.0\%$$

For the second period's spot rate:

$$\sqrt{(1 + {_0F_1})(1 + {_1F_2})} - 1.0 = {_0S_2}$$

or substituting in values:

$$\sqrt{(1.10)(1.11)} - 1.0 = {_0S_2} = 0.104988688 = 10.4988688\%$$

For the third period:

$$\sqrt[3]{(1 + {_0F_1})(1 + {_1F_2})(1 + {_2F_3})} - 1.0 = S_3$$

or:

$$\sqrt[3]{(1.10)(1.11)(1.15)} - 1.0 = {_0S_3} = 0.119793223 = 11.9793223\%$$

After computing the price of the bond, the YTM can be determined to be the discount rate that equates the present values of all the cash flows to the bond's price. That value is $YTM = .11817851 = 11.817851\%$. The present value of the same bond is calculated below using the various discount rates discussed in this Appendix.

Calculating Present Values

Using the spot or forward rates of interest from the numerical example in Table 20A-1, the present value of the bond paying a coupon of $100 per year for 3 years is computed in Table 20A-2. The YTM associated with that price is also calculated in Table 20A-2.

Tables 20A-3 and 20A-4 show how the present value and the associated YTM was calculated for 2-year and 1-year bonds, respectively. The different yield curves that are embedded in the numerical examples above are examined below.

The Term Structure of Interest Rates

The *term structure of interest rates* is, broadly, a relationship between time to maturity and interest rates. The interest rates used in portraying the term structure of interest may be YTMs, or spot rates, or forward rates.

Term structures of interest should be formulated in terms of spot rates or forward rates of interest, since the YTM changes if the size of the coupon changes. As Carleton and Cooper pointed out:

> *As many people have shown, the concept of yield-to-maturity . . . is an ambiguous concept. For a conventional bond (if not for some hybrid financial contracts or real asset purchase), the expected cash flow pattern implies a unique yield-to-maturity as a solving—or internal—rate of return. Its economic meaning is*

TABLE 20A-2 Calculations for the Present Value and the Associated YTM for $100 Coupon—3-, 2-, and 1-Year Bonds

3-Year Bond

$$P_0 = \frac{\$100}{1.10} + \frac{\$100}{(1.1)(1.11)} + \frac{\$1100}{(1.1)(1.11)(1.15)}$$

$$= \frac{\$100}{1.1} + \frac{\$100}{(1.104988688)^2} + \frac{\$1100}{(1.119793223)^3}$$

$$= \$90.9091 + \$81.9001 + \$783.32921 = \$956.2031$$

The YTM that is derived from the price of $956.2031 is calculated and found to be YTM = 0.11817851 = 11.817851%, after rounding off:

$$P_0 = \frac{\$100}{1.11817851} + \frac{\$100}{1.11817851^2} + \frac{\$1100}{1.11817851^3}$$

$$= \$89.4312 + 78.9793 + 786.7908 = \$956.2031$$

TABLE 20A-3 2-Year Bond

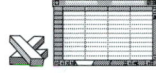

$$P_0 = \frac{\$100}{1.1} + \frac{\$1100}{(1.1)(1.11)}$$

$$= \frac{\$100}{1.1} + \frac{\$1100}{(1.104988688)^2}$$

$$= \$90.9091 + \$900.90090 = \$991.801$$

The YTM that is derived from the price of $991.801 is calculated and found to be YTM = 0.104754 × 100 = 10.4754%:

$$P_0 = \frac{\$100}{1.104754} + \frac{\$1100}{1.104754^2}$$

$$= \$90.51788 + 901.2837 = \$991.801$$

TABLE 20A-4 1-Year Bond

$$P_0 = \frac{\$1100}{1.1} = \$1000$$

$$\frac{\$1100}{1000} = 1.1 = 1 + 10\% = 1 + YTM$$

The YTM that is derived from the price of $1000 is easily seen to be 10%.

moot, however, inasmuch as reinvestment of intermediate cash flows at the solving rate is implied. To borrow a concept from capital budgeting literature, the price of an asset equals its present value only in the sense that its cash flows have been discounted at the market's return requirements. It is true that associated with each bond is a derived yield-to-maturity, but that does not give us license to say that yield-to-maturity is a market-required rate, exogenous to the individual bond in question.[18]

The term structures of interest rates (yield curves) under three different formulations is graphed in Figure 20A-1. The most commonly graphed term structure is the lowest of the three—the YTM curve. Unfortunately, the YTM curve is the least informative of the three term curves and is ambiguous as well. The YTM yield curve depends on the cash flow stream. The forward rate and the spot rate yield curves are both independent of the timing of cash flows. For different bonds that have coupons of $100 and $500, the calculations are shown in Table 20A-5.

Consider a bond selling for $1,932.3078 and having an annual coupon of $500. The YTM on this $500 coupon bond will be 11.51% if it matures in 3 years. However, the bond maturing in 3 years with $100 per year coupons analyzed above with spot and forward rates has a YTM of 11.82%. Table 20A-5 shows other YTMs for these two hypothetical bonds with varying terms to maturity. This contrast between 3-year bonds with different coupons illustrates why we cannot determine the correct "market yield-to-maturity" independent of a particular bond and why the YTM is not unique over dates. On the other hand, the term structure of interest using either the spot or forward rates of interest applies to any financial instrument, regardless of the size or timing of the cash flows.[19] Figure 20-8 suggests this problem can be resolved by treating a coupon-paying bond as a portfolio of zero coupon bonds.

The key to the differences highlighted in this discussion is the differences in the implicit reinvestment rate assumptions that underlie each different formulation of the problem. The YTM calculations implicitly assume that all cash flows are immediately reinvested at the YTM until the bond's maturity—a dubious assumption. It is more realistic to assume that any cash flows are reinvested at future rates.

TABLE 20A-5 Different YTMs for Differing Maturities with Two Different Bonds

Time Periods Until Maturity	$t = 1$	$t = 2$	$t = 3$
Present value of $100 coupon bond given future rates	$1000.00	$991.80	$956.19
YTM of $100 coupon bond	0.10	0.1047	0.1182
PV of $500 coupon bond given future rates	$1363.64	$1683.05	$1932.31
YTM of $500 coupon bond	0.10	0.1042	0.1151

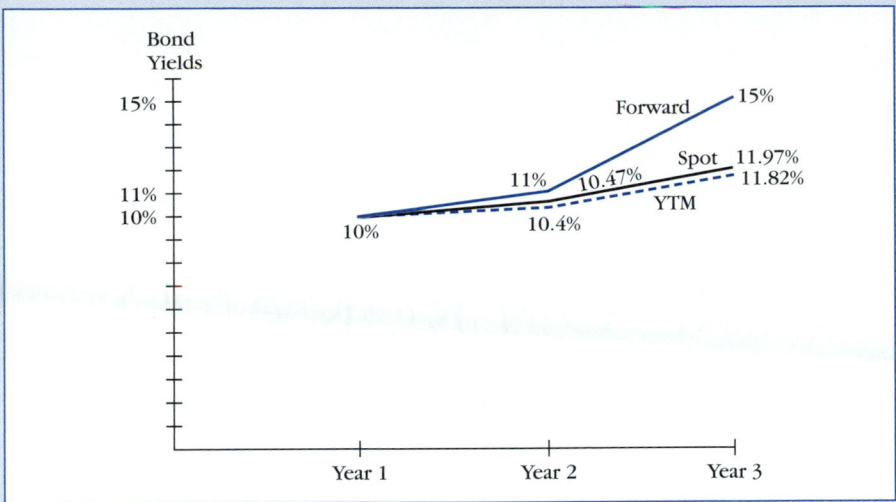

FIGURE 20A-1 Three Different Yield Curves for the Same
10% Coupon Bond

The most commonly graphed term structure of interest rates (yield curve) is the lowest of the three in the graph—the YTM curve. Unfortunately, the YTM curve is the least informative of the three yield curves. The YTM curve is ambiguous because it depends on the cash flow stream and dubious reinvestment assumptions that underlie the cash flows. The forward rate and the spot rate yield curves are both independent of the timing and amount of the cash flows. The argument can be made that, although the graph would be unconventional, the yield curve should be formulated in terms of spot rates or forward rates of interest, since the YTM changes if the size of the coupon changes.

HORIZON RISK AND INTEREST RATE RISK

This chapter analyzes default-free bonds to see how their prices are affected by fluctuating market interest rates and their times until maturity. U.S. Treasury bonds are analyzed because they are easier to analyze than bonds that might default. (Corporate bonds, municipal bonds, common stock, preferred stock, and other securities that might default are not considered.) Credit (default, bankruptcy) risk is the topic of the next chapter. To keep the discussion simple, call, put, conversion, and prepayment options are not discussed.

*As mentioned in Chapter 2, the time remaining until a bond matures (expires) and repays its principal is called its **time horizon**, or simply the bond's **horizon. Horizon risk** is a component of the total risk that increases with the bond's time horizon. Formulas for measuring a bond's time horizon and its horizon risk are considered.*

*Chapter 19 discussed the yield-to-maturity (YTM). Chapter 20 reviewed forces that cause a bond's YTM to fluctuate. This chapter uses what we learned about market interest rates in Chapters 19 and 20 to investigate interest rate risk. A bond's **interest-rate risk** increases directly with the size of the price (present value) fluctuations the bond experiences when the bond's market interest rate (YTM, discount rate) rises and falls. Formulas giving precise measures of a bond's interest rate risk are presented.*

THE PRESENT VALUE OF A BOND

The present value of a bond is:

$$\left(\begin{array}{c}\text{Present}\\\text{value}\end{array}\right) = \frac{\text{Coupon}_1}{(1+\text{Discount rate})^1} + \frac{\text{Coupon}_2}{(1+\text{Discount rate})^2} + \ldots + \frac{\text{Coupon}_T+\text{Par}}{(1+\text{Discount rate})^T} \quad \textbf{(21-1)}$$

where:

The **discount rate** is a market interest rate that fluctuates inversely with the bond's present value (price). This discount rate is the bond's yield-to-maturity (YTM).

A bond's **par value** equals its principal (face value). The par and the date when it is due to be repaid (maturity date, expiration date) are printed on each bond and cannot be changed.

A bond's annual **coupon** payment equals the bond's coupon rate times its par.

COMPUTING THE PRESENT VALUE OF A TREASURY BOND | **EXAMPLE**

A $1,000 U.S. Treasury bond that pays an annual coupon rate of 5% makes one annual payment of $50 [= ($1,000)(5%)] on the last day of each year of its 12-year life.

$$\text{Present value} = \frac{\$50}{(1 + 0.10)^1} + \frac{\$50}{(1 + 0.10)^2} + \ldots + \frac{\$50}{(1 + 0.10)^{11}} + \frac{\$50 + \$1000}{(1 + 0.10)^{12}} \quad \textbf{(21-1a)}$$

Eqn. 21-1a tell us that at a discount rate of 10% the T-bond's present value is $659.315.

The information needed to value bonds with the present value formula is easy to obtain: The bond's par, its coupon interest payments, and the dates of these payments are printed on the bond. These fixed values do not imply the bond's market price (present value) is fixed.

To get a sense of why bond prices vary, revisit Figure 20-1 in Chapter 20, which illustrates fluctuating market interest rates—the primary variable causing the prices of default-free bonds to fluctuate. Figures 19-5, 19-6, and Eqn. 19-10 in Chapter 19 convey information about the inverse relationship between a bond's price and its market interest rate.

Table 21-1 contains tabulated values for the 12-year U.S. Treasury bond with a $1,000 par that pays annual coupons of 5% per year from our example above and Figure 21-1 illustrates this *price-yield relationship.* Figure 21-1 and Table 21-1 show that as the bond's YTM falls below its coupon rate, the bond's present value (price) rises above its par (face) value. Conversely, as the bond's YTM rises above its coupon rate, its present value falls below its par value.

The size of the fluctuations in a bond's price that result from a change in its YTM depends on the bond's time horizon (remaining life) and its coupon rate.

COUPON AND HORIZON EFFECTS

Chapter 20 examined the fluctuating market interest rates that rise and fall in response to changing conditions. Coupon-paying bonds have coupon rates that are fixed when the bond is issued and can never be changed. The difference between a bond's invariant coupon rate and its fluctuating YTM has implications for the bond's price behavior.

Par Versus Price

Table 21-2 lists four categories of coupon payments that characterize the general relationship between a bond's coupon rate and its YTM. Table 21-3 shows the present values (prices) of four bonds that all have 12 years to maturity and pay different coupon rates of 15%, 10%, 5%,

TABLE 21-1   Price-Yield Relationship for a $1,000 Par Bond with 12 Years to Maturity and a 5% Coupon Paid Annually

Bond Price	Discount Rate
$1,450.20	1%
$1,317.26	2%
$1,199.08	3%
$1,093.85	4%
$1,000.00	5%
$916.16	6%
$841.15	7%
$773.92	8%
$713.57	9%
$659.32	10%
$610.46	11%
$566.39	12%
$526.59	13%
$490.57	14%
$457.94	15%
$428.32	16%
$401.39	17%
$376.88	18%
$354.53	19%
$334.12	20%
$315.45	21%
$298.35	22%
$282.66	23%
$268.24	24%
$254.98	25%
$242.75	26%
$231.47	27%
$221.04	28%
$211.38	29%
$202.43	30%
$194.13	31%
$186.40	32%
$179.21	33%
$172.51	34%
$166.25	35%
$160.40	36%
$154.92	37%
$149.78	38%
$144.96	39%
$140.43	40%

SUMMARY: Computers are good for solving the present value equation repetitively over a range of successive discount rates (yields-to-maturity). Such computations reveal an inverse price-yield relationship between a bond's present value (market price) and its yield-to-maturity (YTM, discount rate, market interest rate). These (YTM, PV) pairs are graphed in Figure 21-1. Eqn. 21-1a shows computations for the point with YTM = 10% and PV = $659.315.

FIGURE 21-1   Illustration of the Price-Yield Values from Table 21-1 for a $1,000 Par Bond with 12 Years to Maturity and a 5% Coupon Paid Annually

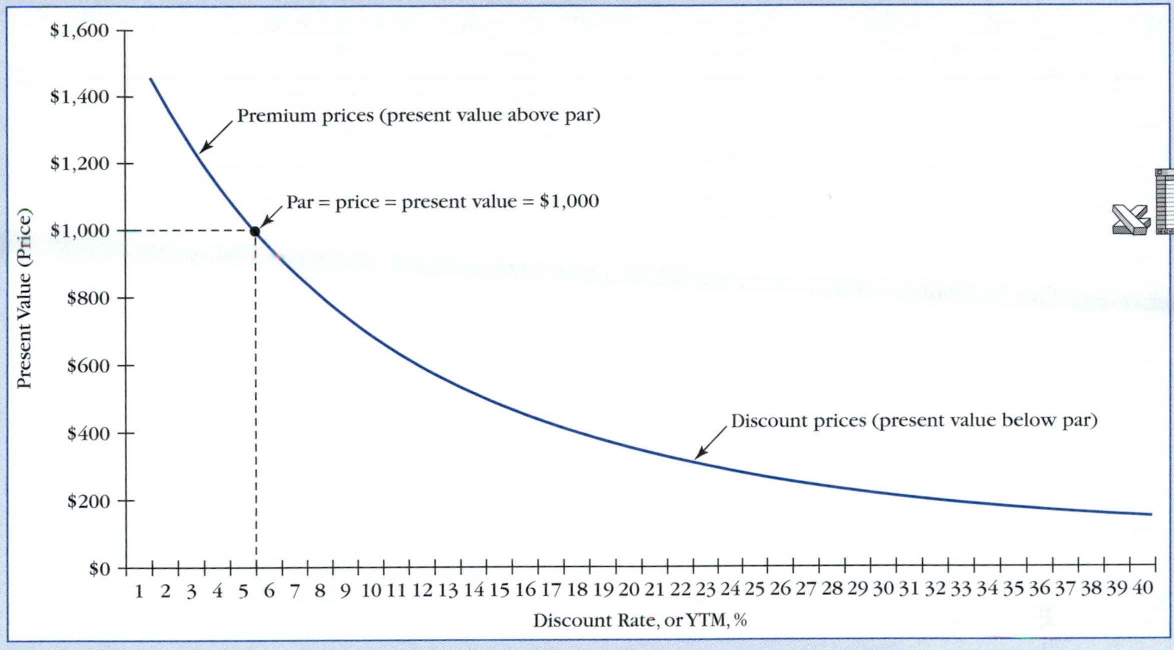

This 5% coupon bond's price-yield relationship illustrates the general inverse mathematical linkage between a bond's present value (price) and its yield-to-maturity (YTM, discount rate).

TABLE 21-2   Pricing Relationships for Bonds from Four Different Categories of Coupons

Coupon and Price Relationships

Price Category	Yield Relationship	Price Relationship
Premium bond	YTM < Coupon rate	Price > Par
Par bond	YTM = Coupon rate	Price = Par
Discount bond	YTM > Coupon rate	Price < Par
Zero coupon bond	Zero coupons	Price < Par

and zero. As the YTMs of the four bonds in Table 21-3 fluctuate, the relationship between the bonds' prices and their par values varies as indicated in Table 21-2.

Premiums and Discounts. For default-free coupon-paying bonds, the relationship between a bond's coupon rate and its YTM is the sole factor that determines whether the bond's market price lies above or below par. When a bond's YTM falls below its coupon rate, that bond's market price rises above par and the bond sells at a *premium* above par. Whenever a bond's fluctuating YTM happens to equal its coupon rate, a second equality occurs simultaneously—the bond's market price equals its *par*. When a bond's market interest rate (YTM) fluctuates above its coupon rate, the bond's price falls to a *discount* price that is below its par value.

TABLE 21-3   Price-Yield Relationships for Four Different $1,000 Par Bonds That All Have 12 Years to Maturity and Have Coupon Rates of 15%, 10%, 5%, and Zero

Discount Rate	Zero Coupon Bond	5% Coupon Bond	10% Coupon Bond	15% Coupon Bond
1%	$887	$1,450	$2,013	$2,576
2%	$788	$1,317	$1,846	$2,375
3%	$701	$1,199	$1,697	$2,194
4%	$625	$1,094	$1,563	$2,032
5%	$557	$1,000	$1,443	$1,886
6%	$497	$916	$1,335	$1,755
7%	$444	$841	$1,238	$1,635
8%	$397	$774	$1,151	$1,528
9%	$356	$714	$1,072	$1,430
10%	$319	$659	$1,000	$1,341
11%	$286	$610	$935	$1,260
12%	$257	$566	$876	$1,186
13%	$231	$527	$822	$1,118
14%	$208	$491	$774	$1,057
15%	$187	$458	$729	$1,000
16%	$168	$428	$688	$948
17%	$152	$401	$651	$900
18%	$137	$377	$617	$856
19%	$124	$355	$585	$816
20%	$112	$334	$556	$778
21%	$102	$315	$529	$743
22%	$92	$298	$505	$711
23%	$83	$283	$482	$681
24%	$76	$268	$461	$653
25%	$69	$255	$441	$627
26%	$62	$243	$423	$603
27%	$57	$231	$406	$581
28%	$52	$221	$390	$560
29%	$47	$211	$376	$540
30%	$43	$202	$362	$521
31%	$39	$194	$349	$504
32%	$36	$186	$337	$488
33%	$33	$179	$326	$472
34%	$30	$173	$315	$458
35%	$27	$166	$305	$444
36%	$25	$160	$296	$431
37%	$23	$155	$287	$419
38%	$21	$150	$279	$407
39%	$19	$145	$271	$396
40%	$18	$140	$263	$386

A bond's par value equals its market value when the bond's YTM equals its coupon rate.

SUMMARY: A lower coupon rate means that more of the bond's present value lies in later payments. Delayed payments imply more interest-rate risk. If all other factors are held constant, bonds that pay low coupon rates involve more interest-rate risk (wider bond price fluctuations) than similar bonds that pay higher coupon rates. The interest rate risk visible in the table does not illustrate this inverse relationship with the coupon rates because all other factors are not held constant. The present values are varying because both the coupon rate and the discount rate are changing.

OID Bonds. The coupon rates of some bonds (**zero coupon bonds,** or **zeros**) are fixed at zero. As illustrated in Figure 5-4 (p. 100), price discounts below par are the largest for newly issued zeros because they are priced at a deep **original-issue discount (OID)**. Since zeros pay no coupon interest, the only income investors get from zeros is the capital gains that occur as the bond's market price rises from its OID price to its higher maturity value (par).

Convexity in the Price-Yield Relationship

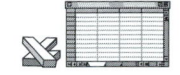

The four curves in Figure 21-2 illustrate the price-yield pairs listed in Table 21-3. At the low discount rates (say, YTM = 1%) the prices of the four bonds shown in Figure 21-2 are far apart. But the prices (present values) converge toward zero as the discount rate rises. The range of prices for zero coupon bonds are less than the price ranges for similar coupon-paying bonds because the price (present value) of a zero never exceeds par.

The shape of a bond's price-yield relationship conveys information about the bond's interest rate risk. **Interest-rate risk** can be defined as the variability of return (bond price fluctuations) caused by fluctuating market interest rates.

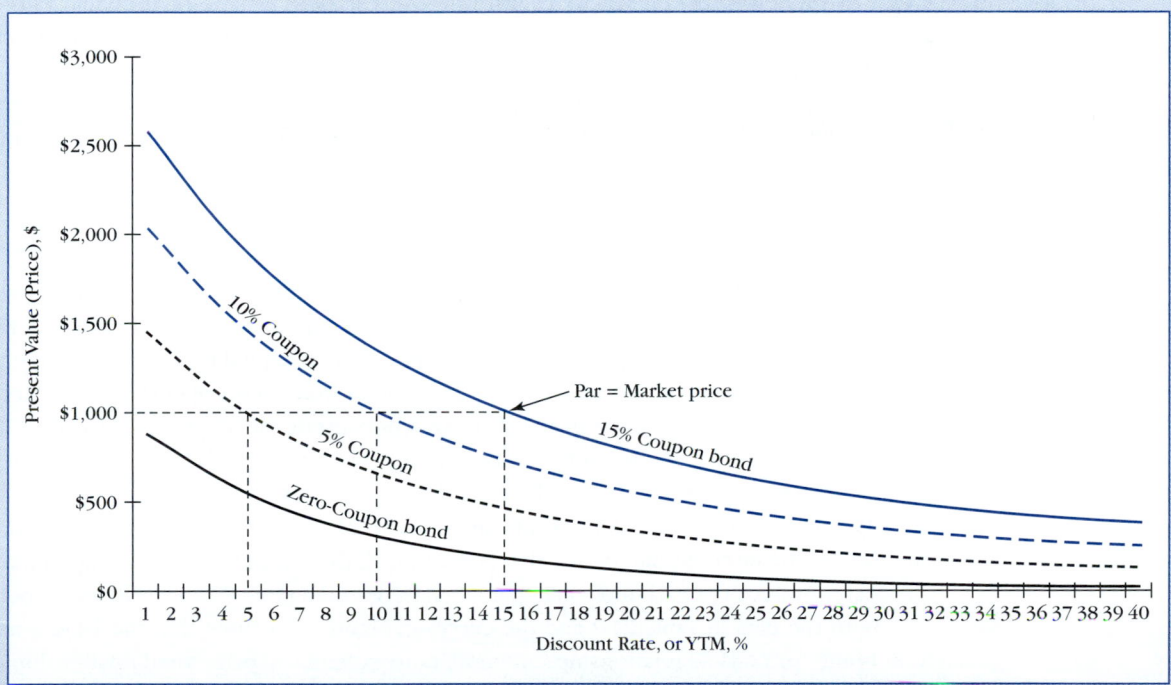

FIGURE 21-2 Contrasting the Price-Yield Relationships of 12-Year Bonds with Four Different Coupon Rates Over a Range of Discount Rates (or YTMs)

The four curves are not parallel, but they never intersect. At the low discount rates (say, YTM = 1%) the prices of the four bonds are far apart. But the prices (present values) converge toward zero at the higher discount rates. The range of prices for the zero-coupon bonds are less than the price ranges for similar coupon-paying bonds because the present value of a zero never exceeds par. Interest-rate risk is the variability of return (bond price or present value fluctuations) caused by fluctuating market interest rates (YTMs). The shape of a bond's price-yield relationship conveys information about the bond's interest rate risk.

Price-yield relationships possess varying degrees of convexity. Perusal of different price-yield relationships suggests that bonds with longer maturities and/or lower coupon rates are usually more convex (bowed) than bonds with shorter maturities and/or higher coupon rates. If one bond has a price-yield relationship that is more convex than a second bond's price-yield relationship, and all the other factors are identical, the bond with more convexity is more desirable. A complex *coupon effect* makes it difficult to make generalities.

The Coupon Effect

The **coupon effect** deals with the impact of a coupon-paying bond's coupon rate on that bond's YTM. To isolate the coupon effect, consider a default-free bond that matures in n years. The law of one price tells us this bond's present value (price) must be same whether it is computed using spot interest rates (S) as in Eqns. 20-8 and 20A-3, or using the bond's yield-to-maturity (YTM) as in Eqns. 19-4 and 20A-2.

$$P = \frac{CF_1}{(1 + YTM)^1} + \frac{CF_2}{(1 + YTM)^2} + \cdots + \frac{CF_n + Par}{(1 + YTM)^n} \qquad \text{(19-4)}$$

$$P = \frac{CF_1}{(1 + {}_0S_1)} + \frac{CF_2}{(1 + {}_1S_2)^2} + \cdots + \frac{CF_n + Par}{(1 + {}_{n-1}S_n)^n} \qquad \begin{array}{l}\textbf{Spot rates from}\\ \textbf{Eqn. 20-8}\end{array}$$

The two equations above show that if the bond's two present values are equal, the bond's YTM must be some average of the spot interest rates $S_1, S_2, \ldots, S_{n-1}, S_n$. The value of the YTM depends on the term structure of interest rates (shape of the yield curve, the coupon reinvestment rates), the size and timing of the coupons, and the bond's time horizon (number of coupons). In other words, a bond's coupons help shape its YTM.

Lower coupons mean that more of a bond's value lies in its later payments that involve more interest-rate risk. As a result, a bond that pays a low coupon rate involves more interest-rate risk than a similar bond that pays a higher coupon rate.

The Horizon Effect

If all other things are equal, bonds with longer horizons are riskier than bonds that have shorter horizons. To become familiar with this **horizon effect,** three default-free bonds that pay 5% annual coupon rates are analyzed. One is the 12-year bond analyzed in the first example in this chapter. This 12-year bond is contrasted to a 2-year bond, both identical in every way except for the difference in maturities (horizons). And we will contrast the 12-year bond with a 22-year bond that is identical to the other two bonds in every way except its longer time horizon. Table 21-4 lists the present values of these three bonds as their YTMs (discount rates) vary from 1% to 40%. Figure 21-3 graphically depicts the data in Table 21-4. The three price-yield relationships intersect at the discount rate of 5%. That is because all three bonds have 5% coupon rates and the present value of every bond equals par when its discount rate (YTM) equals its coupon rate.

Both the data in Table 21-4 and the curves in Figure 21-3 show that the 12-year and 22-year bonds' price-yield relationships are more convex than the price-yield relationship of the 2-year bond. Table 21-5 summarizes the three bonds' characteristics. The differences between the 2-year, 12-year, and 22-year bonds are horizon effects; the bonds that have longer life spans have price-yield relationships that are more convex and these bonds give rise to more interest rate risk than similar bonds with shorter horizons. The horizon effect can be explained intuitively by noting that most of the value in a bond with a long horizon lies in distant future payments that involve more interest rate risk.

TABLE 21-4	Price-Yield Relationships for Three Different $1,000 Par Bonds That Have Coupon Rates of 5% but Have Maturities of 2, 12, and 22 Years		
Discount Rate	2-Year Bond	12-Year Bond	22-Year Bond
1%	$1,079	$1,450	$1,786
2%	$1,058	$1,317	$1,530
3%	$1,038	$1,199	$1,319
4%	$1,019	$1,094	$1,145
5%	$1,000	$1,000	$1,000
6%	$982	$916	$880
7%	$964	$841	$779
8%	$947	$774	$694
9%	$930	$714	$622
10%	$913	$659	$561
11%	$897	$610	$509
12%	$882	$566	$465
13%	$867	$527	$426
14%	$852	$491	$393
15%	$837	$458	$364
16%	$823	$428	$339
17%	$810	$401	$316
18%	$796	$377	$297
19%	$783	$355	$279
20%	$771	$334	$264
21%	$758	$315	$250
22%	$746	$298	$237
23%	$735	$283	$226
24%	$723	$268	$215
25%	$712	$255	$206
26%	$701	$243	$197
27%	$690	$231	$189
28%	$680	$221	$182
29%	$670	$211	$175
30%	$660	$202	$169
31%	$650	$194	$163
32%	$640	$186	$158
33%	$631	$179	$153
34%	$622	$173	$148
35%	$613	$166	$144
36%	$604	$160	$140
37%	$596	$155	$136
38%	$588	$150	$132
39%	$579	$145	$129
40%	$571	$140	$126

SUMMARY: The 2-, 12-, and 22-year bond prices (present values) all vary inversely with the discount rate (yield-to-maturity), but the bonds with longer horizons experience more horizon risk (wider price fluctuations) than the shorter-term bonds.

FIGURE 21-3 The Price-Yield Relationships for Three Bonds That Pay 5% Coupon Rates and Have Maturities of 2, 12, and 22 Years Illustrate Horizon Effects

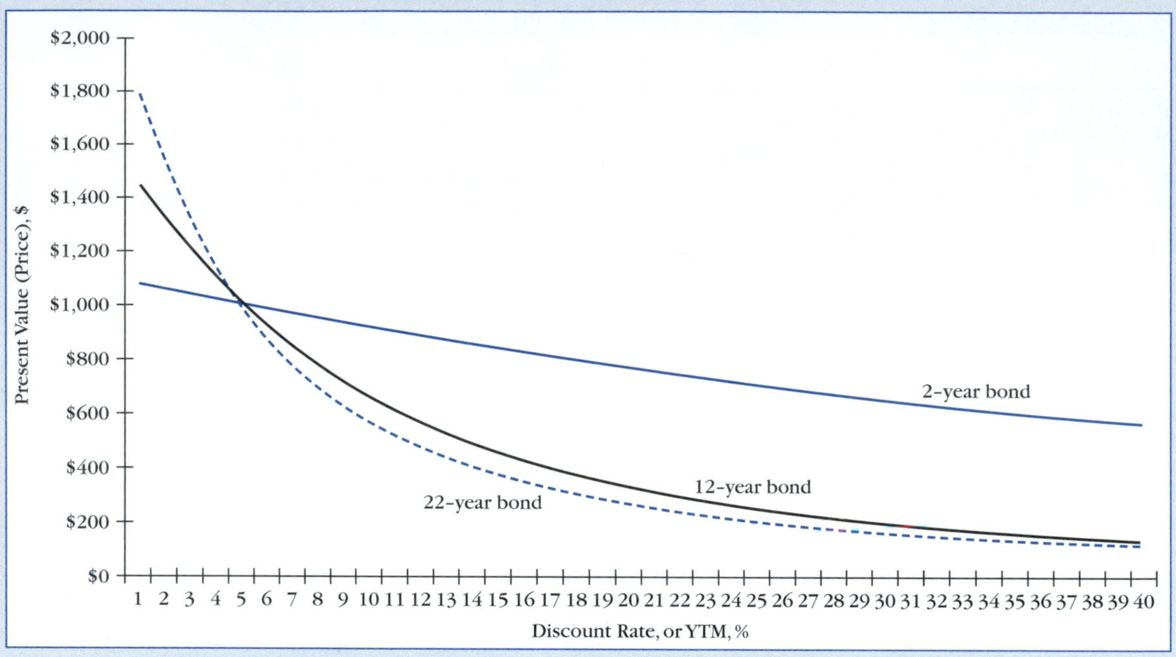

Both the 12-year and 22-year bonds' price-yield relationships are more convex than the price-yield relationship of the 2-year bond. The differences between the 2-year, 12-year, and 22-year bonds exemplify horizon effects, bonds that have longer life spans have price-yield relationships that are more convex and involve more interest rate risk (bond price fluctuations) than similar bonds that have shorter horizons.

TABLE 21-5 Horizon Conclusions Drawn from Table 21-4 and Figure 21-3

	2-Year Bond	12-Year Bond	22-Year Bond
Price Changes as YTMs Range from Zero to 40%	Price ranges from $1,100 to $571 = $529 range	Price ranges from $1,600 to $140 = $1,460 range	Price ranges from $2,100 to $126 = $1,974 range
Convexity	Slight	Significant	Substantial
Interest Rate Risk	Slight	Significant	Substantial

HEDGING FIXED-INCOME INSTRUMENTS

Since coupon-paying bonds and investments in home mortgages both make fixed annual payments to their investors, they are often called *fixed-income instruments.* This section's title refers to bonds and mortgages as fixed-income instruments to focus attention on the periodic cash flows from these investments.

Someone who invests in a default-free fixed-income security (U.S. Treasury bond) or a U.S. government–insured home mortgage is exposed to several different types of interest rate risk. This section considers two kinds of interest rate risk: "reinvestment risk" and "price fluctuation risk."

Reinvestment Risk

Reinvestment risk is variability of return from reinvesting a bond's coupons or a mortgage investment's periodic payments at market rates of interest that fluctuate unpredictably. Reinvestment risk can be avoided by investing in a zero coupon bond or a **balloon mortgage** that returns all the principal and all the interest income to the investor in a single balloon payment at maturity.

ZERO COUPON BONDS HAVE NO REINVESTMENT RISK

EXAMPLE

James Clark paid $318.63 for a zero coupon bond with a face (par) value of $1,000 that matures in 12 years. When Jim receives his interest income and principal repayment in a single $1,000 balloon payment at the end of 12 years, he will earn a rate of return (compound interest rate, YTM) of 10%.

$$\$318.63 = \frac{\$1,000}{(1.10)^{12}} = \frac{\left(\begin{array}{c}\text{Repay principal}\\\text{or par of }\$1,000\end{array}\right)}{(1 + YTM)^{12\,\text{years}}}$$

During the decade Jim owns his zero, market interest rates (YTMs) will fluctuate above and below the YTM of 10%. Nevertheless, Jim will experience no reinvestment risk because his bond makes no coupon interest payments that need to be reinvested prior to the bond's balloon payment at maturity.

Figure 21-4 contrasts the cash flow profiles of a zero coupon bond and a coupon-paying bond. Because zeros generate no cash flows before they mature, they have no reinvestment risk. Another way of looking at this is the YTM that a zero promises will equal the investor's realized YTM if the bond is held to maturity and does not default. In contrast, investors buying

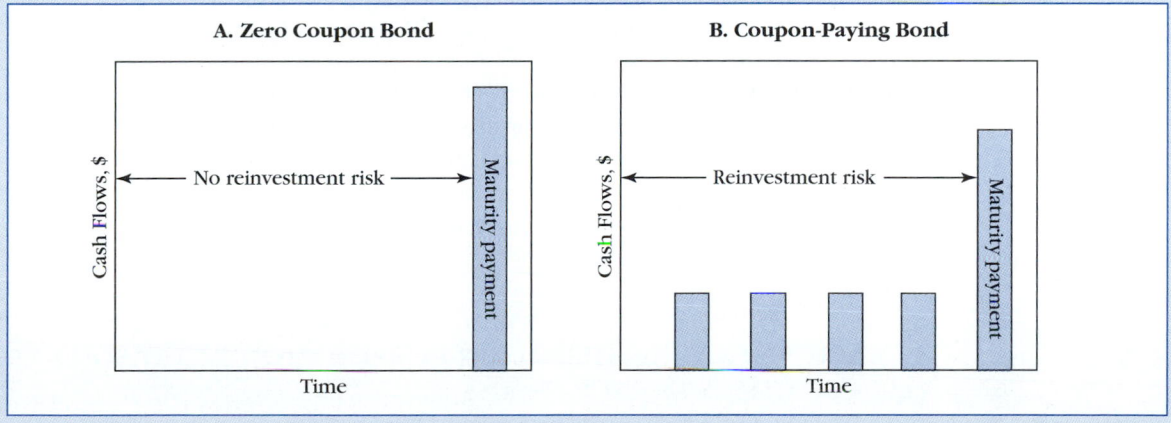

FIGURE 21-4   Cash Flow Profiles from (A) A Zero Coupon Bond and (B) A Coupon-Paying Bond

Because zero coupon bonds generate no cash flows before they mature, they have no reinvestment risk. In contrast, investors buying bonds that make periodic coupon payments must reinvestment those cash payments at a series of varying and uncertain interest rates.

bonds that make periodic coupon payments (or repayments of the principal) must reinvestment those cash flows at a series of fluctuating market interest rates.

Hedging Bond Price Fluctuation Risk

Both zero coupon bonds and coupon-paying bonds expose investors to price fluctuation risk. The numerical examples we looked at earlier in this chapter demonstrate that there can be wide price swings—some adverse—for default-free bonds. It is rational behavior for risk-averse investors to hedge their bond investments to reduce their exposure to price fluctuation risk.

Hedging is a risk-reduction strategy. A hedge is a combination of investments that an investor assembles to avoid or reduce risk. The cost of hedging is that the hedged position (portfolio of investments) usually earns a lower rate of return than an unhedged position. As explained in Chapter 3, most hedges involve a combination of long and short positions that offset (cross cancel) whatever gains and losses the long or short position might earn.

Eqns. 21-2 and 21-3 define the holding-period returns from a long position and a short position in bonds:

$$\begin{pmatrix} \text{One-period return from} \\ \text{long bond position} \end{pmatrix} = \frac{\begin{pmatrix} \text{Ending} \\ \text{price} \end{pmatrix} - \begin{pmatrix} \text{Beginning} \\ \text{price} \end{pmatrix} + \begin{pmatrix} \text{Coupon interest,} \\ \text{if any} \end{pmatrix}}{(\text{Beginning of period purchase price})} \quad (21\text{-}2)$$

$$\begin{pmatrix} \text{One-period return from} \\ \text{a short bond position} \end{pmatrix} = \frac{\begin{pmatrix} \text{Beginning} \\ \text{price} \end{pmatrix} - \begin{pmatrix} \text{Ending} \\ \text{price} \end{pmatrix} - \begin{pmatrix} \text{Coupon interest,} \\ \text{if any} \end{pmatrix}}{(\text{Beginning of period sale price})} \quad (21\text{-}3)$$

A **perfect hedge** occurs when simultaneous long and short positions of equal value yield returns that completely offset (counteract) each other.

$$\begin{pmatrix} \text{One-period return from} \\ \text{a long bond position} \end{pmatrix} + \begin{pmatrix} \text{One-period return from} \\ \text{a short bond position} \end{pmatrix} = \begin{pmatrix} \text{One-period return} \\ \text{from a perfect hedge} \end{pmatrix} = 0$$

$$\frac{\begin{pmatrix} \text{End} \\ \text{price} \end{pmatrix} - \begin{pmatrix} \text{Beginning} \\ \text{price} \end{pmatrix} + (\text{Coupon})}{(\text{Beginning of period price})} + \frac{\begin{pmatrix} \text{Beginning} \\ \text{price} \end{pmatrix} - \begin{pmatrix} \text{Ending} \\ \text{price} \end{pmatrix} - (\text{Coupon})}{(\text{Beginning of period price})} = 0 \, (21\text{-}4)$$

Perfect hedges like Eqn. 21-4 earn returns of zero. Because a perfect hedge has no variability of return, it is a riskless position. To construct a perfect hedge, it is necessary to find a long position (an asset) and a short position (a liability) that are exactly offsetting.

Figures 21-1, 21-2, and 21-3 provide information helpful in creating a hedge to reduce the Palmer Corporation's exposure to interest rate risk.

EXAMPLE

FUNDING (HEDGING) THE PALMER CORPORATION'S DEBT SO AS TO ELIMINATE ITS INTEREST RATE RISK

Figure 21-5A illustrates the price-yield relationship for a $1,000 debt (liability) the Palmer Corporation must pay off in 6.79 years. The Palmer Corporation's chief financial officer (CFO) considered the *maturity matching strategy* of buying a default-free bond with a par value of $1,000 that matures in 6.79 years; such an asset would mature at the correct time

FIGURE 21-5   Contrasting the Price-Yield Relationship from Palmer's Liability with Those from Three Different Bonds: (A) Palmer's Liability; (B) Brett's Bond, (C) Colt's Bond; (D) Dart's Bond

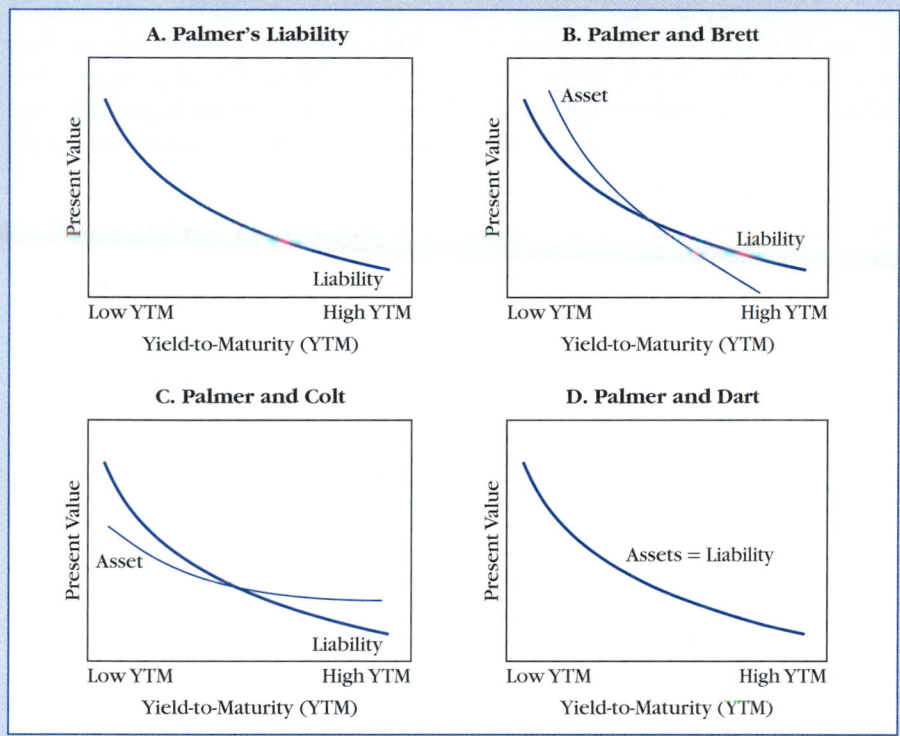

Continuously fluctuating market interest rates cause the present value of Palmer's liability to fluctuate inversely in an unpredictable manner, as shown in (A). (B) and (C) show that Brett and Colt Corporations' bonds provide imperfect hedges for Palmer's interest rate risk. But the Dart Corporation's bond provides a perfect hedge for Palmer's interest-rate risk. (D) shows that Dart's price-yield relationship is identical to the price-yield relationship of Palmer's liability. Combining Palmer's liability (debt, maturing bond) with a long position in Dart's bond (the best asset) results in a perfectly hedged portfolio of debts.

and in the amount needed to pay off Palmer's $1,000 liability. Not surprisingly, the CFO was unable to find a bond that matured in precisely 6.79 years. Longer-term bonds were therefore considered.

Palmer's CFO narrowed the list of investment candidates down to three different high-grade corporate bonds that all have the same current market price, all have par values of $1,000, and all mature in 10 years. If market interest rates remain unchanged, a $1,000 investment in either the Brett Corporation's bond (the asset in Figure 21-5B), the Colt Corporation's bond (the asset in Figure 21-5C), or the Dart Corporation's bond (the asset in Figure 21-5D) could be purchased and held to pay off Palmer's $1,000 debt (liability). When Palmer's liability comes due for payment in 6.79 years either the Brett, Colt, or Dart bond could be liquidated to pay the debt. However, if market interest rates change during the next 10 years, things might not work out smoothly, because the prices of the three bonds would each react differently to changing market interest rates.

Figure 21-5B shows that if market interest rates are low when the 6.79 years are up, the present value (market price) of the Brett Corporation's bond will exceed the value of Palmer's liability. Or, if market interest rates are high, the market price of the Brett bond's price will fall below the value of Palmer's liability. Comparing the two price-yield relationships in Figures 21-5B and 21-5C indicates that the reverse is true for the Colt Corporation's bond. Figure 21-5D shows as market interest rates fluctuate only the Dart Corporation's bond has a market price that always equals the present value of Palmer's liability. Among the three alternative price-yield relationships in Figure 21-5A, B, and C, only the Dart bond provides a perfect hedge.

Derivation of Formula for Macaulay's Duration (MAC)

Embedded in Figure 21-5 are the parameters needed to construct hedges (combinations of bonds) that minimize investors interest rate risk. The slopes of the four price-yield relationships in Figure 21-5 measure the price (present value) sensitivity of the assets and liabilities to fluctuating market interest rates (YTMs). These slopes equal the change in the present value, computed with Eqn. 21-1, resulting from a small change in the bond's discount rate (market interest rate, YTM). Coincidentally, the first derivative of a bond's present value formula, Eqn. 21-1, with respect to its discount rate (YTM) also measures the change in present value that results from a small change in the bond's discount rate (YTM).

$$\frac{dP}{d(YTM)} = \frac{(-1)(\text{Coupon}_1)}{(1 + YTM)^2} + \frac{(-2)(\text{Coupon}_2)}{(1 + YTM)^3} + \ldots + \frac{(-T)(\text{Coupon}_T + \text{Par})}{(1 + YTM)^{T+1}} \tag{21-5}$$

This can be rearranged by factoring out a [1/(1 + YTM)] term.

$$\frac{dP}{d(YTM)} = \left(\frac{1}{1 + YTM}\right)\left(\frac{(-1)(\text{Coupon}_1)}{(1 + YTM)^1} + \frac{(-2)(\text{Coupon}_2)}{(1 + YTM)^2} + \ldots + \frac{(-T)(\text{Coupon}_T + \text{Par})}{(1 + YTM)^T}\right) \tag{21-5a}$$

Concentrating on the sum in the brackets on the far right of Eqn. 21-5a, the negative integers in parentheses are the time periods ($t = 1, 2, \ldots, T$), each multiplied by -1. The sum in the brackets is the weighted-average number of (negative) time periods until the bond matures. The present values of the cash flows $\left(\frac{(\text{Coupon}_t)}{(1 + YTM)^t}\right)$ are the weights attached to each negative time period ($-t$). Overall, Eqn. 21-5a measures the price change in a bond that results from a tiny change and its YTM, denoted *d(YTM)*. Eqn. 21-5a is rewritten more compactly as a summation:

$$\frac{dP}{d(YTM)} = \left(\frac{1}{(1 + YTM)}\right)\left(\sum_{t=1}^{t=T}\frac{(-t)(\text{Cash flow}_t)}{(1 + YTM)^t}\right) \tag{21-5b}$$

Multiplying both sides of Eqn. 21-5b by (1/P) results in:

$$\frac{dP}{d(YTM)}\left(\frac{1}{P}\right) = \left(\frac{1}{1 + YTM}\right)\left(\sum_{t=1}^{t=T}\frac{(-t)(\text{Cash flow}_t)}{(1 + YTM)^t}\right)\left(\frac{1}{P}\right) \tag{21-5c}$$

Eqn. 21-5c is rearranged equivalently as Eqns. 21-6 and 21-6a. Eqns. 21-6 and 21-6a are a measure of the time structure of a bond called the bond's **modified duration (MOD)**. MOD measures the percentage change in a bond's price that results from a small change in its YTM.

$$\binom{\text{Modified}}{\text{duration}} = \frac{dP}{d(YTM)}\left(\frac{1}{P}\right) = \frac{dP/P}{d(YTM)} \approx \frac{\Delta P/P}{\Delta(YTM)} \tag{21-6}$$

$$= \left(\frac{1}{1 + YTM}\right)\left(\sum_{t=1}^{t=T}\frac{(-t)(\text{Cash flow}_t)}{(1 + YTM)^t}\right)\left(\frac{1}{P}\right) \tag{21-6a}$$

Multiplying Eqns. 21-6 and 21-6a by $(1 + YTM)$ creates another measure of a bond's time structure that is called Macaulay duration (MAC).

$$\binom{\text{Macaulay}}{\text{duration}} = \binom{\text{Modified}}{\text{duration}}(1 + YTM) = \frac{dP/P}{d(YTM)/(1 + YTM)} \approx \frac{\Delta P/P}{\Delta(YTM)/(1 + YTM)} \tag{21-7}$$

$$= \left(\frac{1}{P}\right)\left(\sum_{t=1}^{t=T}\frac{(-t)(\text{Cash flow}_t)}{(1 + YTM)_t}\right) \tag{21-7a}$$

Macaulay's duration (MAC) measures the percentage change in a bond's price associated with (that results from) a small percentage change in its YTM. In addition to measuring a bond's response to a change in its market interest rate, MAC and MOD are similar measures of a bond's time structure. MAC tells the average number of years the investor's money is invested in the bond. MOD gives the average number of modified (slightly longer) years the investor's money is invested in the bond.

CALCULATING A BOND'S MACAULAY DURATION (MAC) AND MODIFIED DURATION (MOD)

EXAMPLE

Consider a $1,000 par bond with YTM = 5%; a 10% coupon rate that is paid annually, 3 years until maturity $(T = 3)$, which is selling for a market price of $875.657. This bond's present value (PV) is calculated with Eqn. 21-1.

(1) Year, t	(2) Cash Flow	(3) Discount = $1/(1 + YTM)^t$	(4) = (Col. 2) × (Col. 3) PV of Cash Flows
$t = 1$	Coupon = $50	$0.9091 = 1/(1.10)^1$	$45.455
$t = 2$	Coupon = $50	$0.8264 = 1/(1.10)^2$	$41.322
$t = 3 = T$	Par + Coupon = $1,050	$0.7513 = 1/(1.10)^3$	$788.881
			Bond's PV = $875.657

MAC is calculated below using the values from the present value calculations above.

(1) Year Count, t	(2) PV of Cash Flow from Column (4) Above	(3) Each Cash Flow's PV as Fraction of PV (price)	(4) = (Col. 1) × (Col. 3) t Weighted by Cash Flow
$t = 1$	$45.455	0.05191	$(t = 1)(0.05191) = 0.05191$
$t = 2$	41.322	0.04718	$(t = 2)(0.4718) = 0.09438$
$t = 3 = T$	788.881	0.90090	$(t = 3)(0.90090) = 2.7027$
		1.0	2.84899 years = MAC

Macaulay duration for the 3-year bond is 2.84899 years.[1] This value of MAC is the weighted average number of years $(t = 1, t = 2,$ and $t = 3)$ using the relative present values of the three cash flows in Column 3 as weights.

MAC and MOD are similar measures of a bond's time structure. The bond's modified duration is: $(\text{MOD}) = (\text{MAC})/(1 + YTM) = (2.84899 \text{ years})/(1.10) = 2.5899$ modified years

MACAULAY DURATION (MAC)

The time horizon of a bond has traditionally been years to maturity. However, bonds and other fixed-income instruments have other time dimensions. MOD and MAC are two measures of a bond's time structure that add to the information provided by the bond's time to maturity.

In 1938 F. R. Macaulay suggested studying the time structure of a bond by measuring its average term to maturity (length of investment).[2] Macaulay's duration (MAC) may be defined as the weighted average number of time periods (for example, years) till the investor's cash flows occur, with the relative present values of each cash flow used as the weights. Conceptually useful definitions of MAC are provided in Eqns. 21-7b and 21-7c.

$$\text{MAC} = \frac{\sum_{t=1}^{T}\left(\dfrac{(t)(\text{Cash flow}_t)}{(1 + YTM)^t}\right) + \dfrac{(T)(\text{Par})}{(1 + YTM)^T}}{\text{Present value } (PV) = \text{Price}} \tag{21-7b}$$

$$\text{MAC} = \frac{\sum_{t=1}^{T}\left(\dfrac{(t)(\text{Coupon}_t)}{(1 + YTM)^t}\right)}{PV} + \frac{\left(\dfrac{(T)(\text{Par})}{(1 + YTM)^T}\right)}{PV} \tag{21-7c}$$

$$\text{MAC} = \left(\frac{1}{PV}\right)\sum_{t=1}^{T}\left[\begin{array}{c}\text{Time period of}\\ \text{the cash flow is } t\end{array}\right] \times \left[\text{Weight for } t \text{ is}\left(\frac{(\text{Cash flow}_t)}{(1 + YTM)^t}\right)\right] \tag{21-7d}$$

Consider Eqn. 21-7c and how it applies to zero coupon bonds and you can see an important property of Macaulay duration. For zero coupon bonds all the coupons are zero and, as a result, the weights attached to the coupons' time periods become zero, $\left(\dfrac{\text{Coupon}_t}{(1 + YTM)^t}\right) = 0$. As a result, for zero coupon bonds Macaulay's duration always equals the number of years until the bond matures, MAC $= T$.

STUDY CHECK

MACAULAY DURATION

QUESTION: What generalization can be made about the relationship between Macaulay duration (MAC) and time to maturity (T) for coupon-paying bonds?

ANSWER: The presence of coupons makes all coupon-paying bonds have values of Macaulay duration (MAC) that are less than their time to maturity (T). Concisely, MAC $< T$ for coupon bonds.

The various forms of Eqn. 21-7 may be used to calculate Macaulay duration for a single bond, a diversified portfolio of bonds, or any other asset or liability that has one or more cash flows.

Contrasting Time Until Maturity and Duration

Macaulay duration for every bond is less than or equal to its term to maturity, MAC $\leq T$. If a bond's only cash flow is made to repay the principal at maturity, the bond's term-to-maturity is identical to its duration. In other words, for zeros: MAC $= T$. For a bond that pays coupons, MAC will be less than the bond's term to maturity: MAC $< T$.

Summaries of Relationships Between MAC and Time to Maturity, *T*

For Every Bond	Zeros Vs. Coupons	Discount Vs. Premium Bonds
$MAC \leq T$	$MAC_Z = T$ for zero coupon bonds	$MAC_Z = T$ for OID zeros
$MAC \leq T$	$T = MAC_Z > MAC_{Coupon}$ for coupon bonds	$T = MAC_Z > MAC_{Discount}$ for discount bonds
$MAC \leq T$	$T = MAC_Z > MAC_{Coupon}$ for coupon bonds	$T = MAC_Z > MAC_{Discount} >$ $MAC_{Par \& Premium}$ for par and premium bonds

In the numerical example above the annual coupons of $50 caused the 3-year bond to have an average term to maturity of MAC = 2.84899 years. Earlier and/or larger cash flows shorten a bond's duration. These general patterns can be perceived by studying Eqns. 21-7b and 21-7c and Table 21-6 and Figure 21-6. Table 21-6 shows the duration of different bonds that have a YTM of 6.0%. Figure 21-6 illustrates relationships between the term-to-maturity and MAC for different bonds.

Table 21-7 shows duration and convexity statistics for the same bonds analyzed in Table 21-4 and Figure 21-3, to illustrate the horizon effect. The statistics in the bottom half of Table 21-7 point up positive relationships between bonds' years to maturity and both their durations and their convexities.

Table 21-8 presents duration and convexity statistics for the same bonds that were analyzed above in Table 21-3 and Figure 21-2 to numerically delineate the coupon effect. The statistics in Table 21-8 show how bonds' durations are inversely related to their coupon rates.[3]

MACLIM Defines a Boundary for Macaulay Duration

The following equation can be used to calculate a limiting value for a bond's Macaulay duration.

$$\text{MACLIM} = \frac{1.0 + YTM}{YTM} = \frac{1.0}{YTM} + 1.0 \tag{21-8}$$

Looking at the bottom row of Table 21-6, for example, we see MACLIM equals 17.667 years if YTM = 6.0%. The horizontal dashed line in Figure 21-6A illustrates the MACLIM value for a particular bond.

TABLE 21-6   Durations for a Bond with 6% YTM at Various Times to Maturity

Years-to-Maturity, *T*	Coupon Rate = 2%	Coupon Rate = 4%	Coupon Rate = 6%	Coupon Rate = 8%
T = 1 year	MAC = 0.995 year	MAC = 0.990 year	MAC = 0.985 year	MAC = 0.981 year
T = 2 years	MAC = 4.756 years	MAC = 4.558 years	MAC = 4.393 years	MAC = 4.254 years
T = 10 years	MAC = 8.891 years	MAC = 8.169 years	MAC = 7.662 years	MAC = 7.286 years
T = 20 years	MAC = 14.981 years	MAC = 12.980 years	MAC = 11.904 years	MAC = 11.232 years
T = 50 years	MAC = 19.452 years	MAC = 17.129 years	MAC = 16.273 years	MAC = 15.829 years
T = 100 years	MAC = 17.567 years	MAC = 17.232 years	MAC = 17.120 years	MAC = 17.064 years
T = ∞	MAC = 17.667 years	MAC = 17.667 years	MAC = 17.667 years	MAC = 17.667 years

SOURCE: L. Fisher and R. L. Weil, "Coping with the Risk of Interest Rate Fluctuations: Returns to Bondholders from Naive and Optimal Strategies," *Journal of Business* (October 1971): 418.

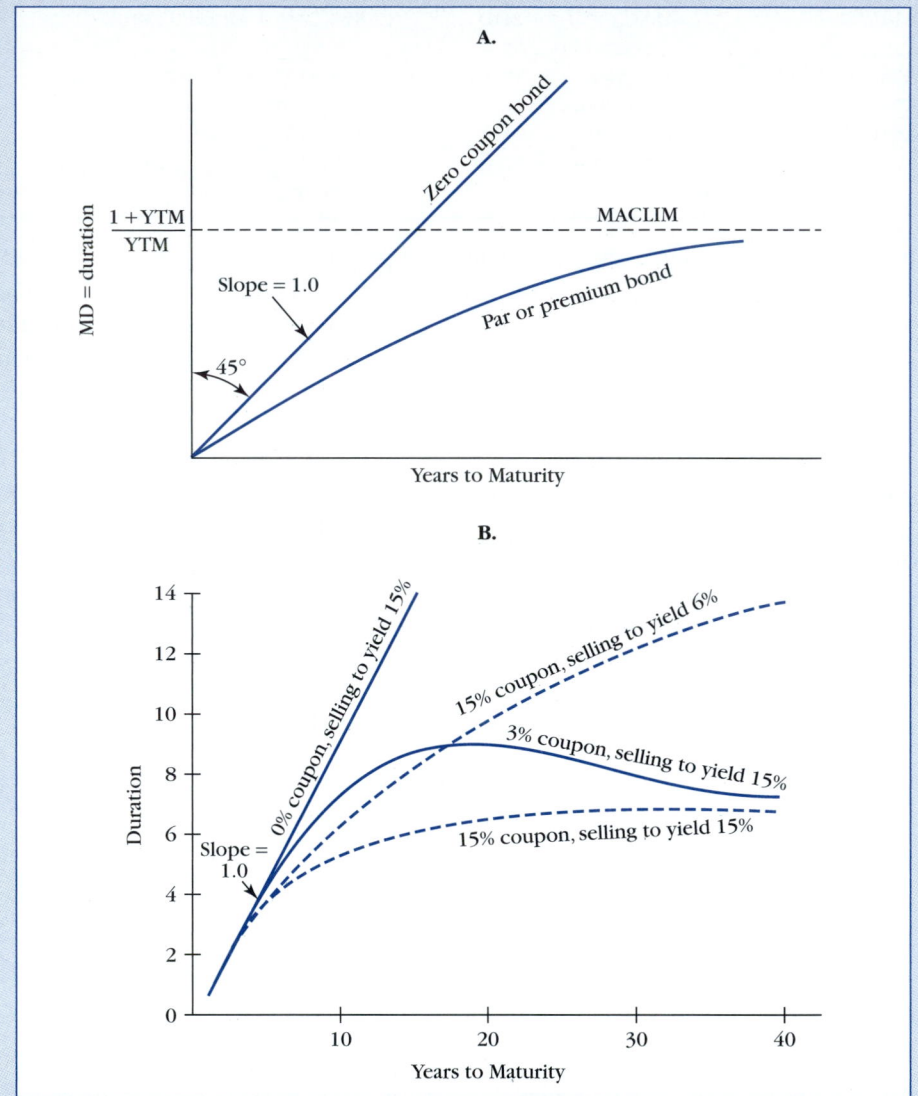

FIGURE 21-6   Various Relationships Between Time-to-Maturity and Macaulay Duration (MAC)

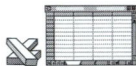

Every bond has Macaulay duration less than or equal to its years to maturity, MAC ≤ T, regardless of whether or not it pays coupons. Zero coupon bonds' only cash flow is repayment of principal at the bond's maturity and the bond's term-to-maturity is identical to Macaulay duration; MAC = T. For bonds that pay coupons, MAC will be less than the bond's term to maturity; MAC < T.

TABLE 21-7   Duration and Convexity Data on Bonds

Data on the 5% Coupon Bonds in Table 21-4 and Figure 21-3 (from Table 21-5)

	2-Year Bond	12-Year Bond	22-Year Bond
Price Changes as	Price ranges from	Price ranges from	Price ranges from
YTMs Range from	$1,100 to $571 =	$1,600 to $140 =	$2,100 to $126 =
Zero to 40%	$529 range	$1,460 range	$1,974 range
Interest Rate Risk	Slight	Significant	Substantial
Convexity	Slight	Significant	Substantial

The Four Rows of Data Below Evaluated at YTM = 10%

	2-Year Bond	12-Year Bond	22-Year Bond
Present Value	PV = $913.22	PV = $659.32	PV = $561.42
Macaulay Duration	MAC = 1.95 Years	MAC = 8.58 Years	MAC = 11 Years
Modified Duration	MOD = 1.77 Years	MOD = 7.80 Years	MOD = 10 Years
Convexity	0.02	0.21	0.58

TABLE 21-8   Statistics on 12-Year Bonds Used in Table 21-3 and Figure 21-2 to Demonstrate the Coupon Effect, Evaluated at YTM = 10%

	Zero-Coupon Bond	5% Coupon Bond	10% Coupon Bond	15% Coupon Bond
Present Value	$318.63	$659.32	$1,000.00	$1,340.68
Macaulay Duration	12 Years	8.58 Years	7.50 Years	6.96 Years
Modified Duration	10.91 Years	7.80 Years	6.81 Years	6.33 Years
Convexity	0.10	0.21	0.20	0.19

There are three things about the MACLIM value to keep in mind. First, Macaulay duration for a perpetual bond (such as a British Consul) is equal to MACLIM, irrespective of the bond's coupon rate.

Second, for a coupon bond selling at or above its par, MAC increases with the bond's term to maturity and converges on MACLIM as the bond's term to maturity approaches infinity. This smooth convergence is illustrated in Figure 21-6A.

Third, for a coupon bond selling at a discount price (below par), MAC reaches a maximum before the bond's maturity date reaches infinity and then retreats downward toward the limiting value of MACLIM.

Many people consider MAC to be a better measure of a bond's horizon structure than years to maturity because MAC reflects both the dollar amount and timing of every cash flow, rather than merely the length of time until the final payment occurs.

Duration Provides a Linear Approximation to the Curvilinear Price-Yield Relationship

Figure 21-7 compares and contrasts the price-yield relationships from three different bonds. Bonds A and B both have positive convexity, but Bond B's price-yield relationship is more

FIGURE 21-7   Price-Yield Relationships for Bonds with Positive, Zero, and Negative Convexity

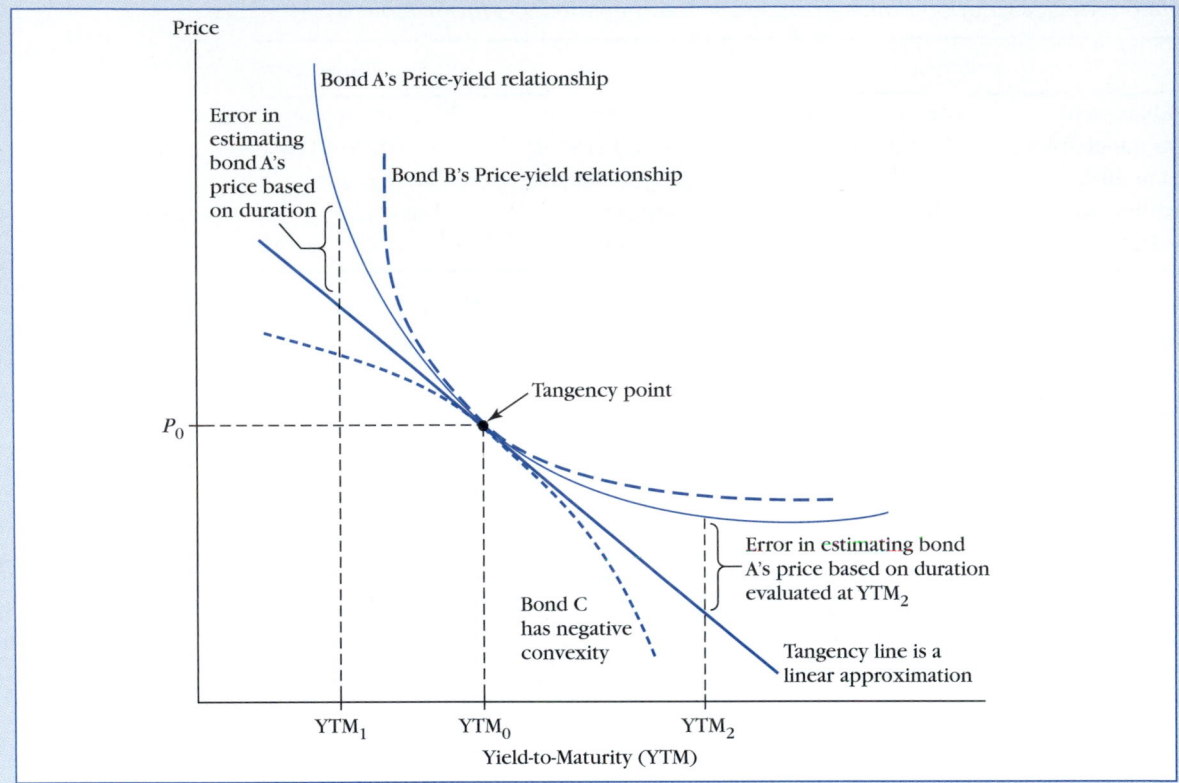

Bonds A and B both have positive convexity, but Bond B has more convexity than Bond A. Bond C has negative convexity. When evaluated at their tangency point, Bonds A, B, and C all have identical measures of duration. The straight line through the tangency point is a linear approximation to the curvilinear price-yield relationships and it grows increasingly inaccurate as it extends farther away from the tangency point. The slope of the straight line measures duration.

convex than Bond A's. Bond C has negative convexity (concavity). Negative convexity is caused by embedded options, a type of option that is discussed others chapters.[*]

When evaluated at the point where the curves for Bonds A, B, and C are tangent to the straight line, all three bonds have identical durations. The slope of the straight line in Figure 21-7 measures the duration of the three different price-yield relationships evaluated at their tangency point. This straight line is a linear approximation to the three curvilinear price-yield relationships, and the approximation grows increasingly inaccurate as it extends farther away from the tangency point.[4]

INTEREST RATE RISK

Elementary economics courses tell us that all *elasticities* measure the percentage change in one quantity with respect to the percentage change in another quantity. A bond's *interest rate risk* can be defined to be the percentage change in the bond's price divided by the per-

---

[*] Embedded options are discussed in the Appendix to Chapter 9 and in Chapter 28.

centage change in market interest rates (in particular, the bond's YTM). A bond's *interest rate elasticity,* denoted *EL* in Eqn. 21-9, measures the bond's interest rate risk.[*5]

$$EL = \frac{\text{Percent change in bond's price}}{\text{Percent change in } (1 + YTM)} \qquad \textbf{(21-9)}$$

$$EL = \frac{\Delta p/p}{\Delta YTM/(1 + YTM)} < 0 \qquad \textbf{(21-9a)}$$

A bond's price elasticity with respect to a change in interest rates (*EL*) is always be a negative number, since a bond's price and its YTM (market interest rate) move inversely.

EVALUATING A BOND'S EL

EXAMPLE

Consider a 2-year bond that has a 10% coupon rate and sells at its par value of $1,000. This bond's present value (price) equals its par value.

$$P = \frac{\$100}{1.10} + \frac{\$100 + \$1,000}{(1.10)^2} = \$90.909 + \$909.091 = \$1,000$$

Suppose the market interest rate (YTM) of this $1,000 bond rises from 10% to 11%. As a result, the bond's price drops from $1,000 to $982.87:

$$\frac{\$100}{1.11} + \frac{\$100 + \$1,000}{(1.11)^2} = \$90.09 + \$892.78 = \$982.87$$

The bond's present value decrease of $17.13 (= $1,000 − $982.87) equals a 1.713% drop from its $1,000 price:

$$\text{Percent price change} = \frac{\Delta P}{\text{Beginning price}} = \frac{-\$17.13}{\$1,000} = -0.01713 = -1.713\%$$

The increase in the bond's YTM from 10% to 11% is a rise of approximately 9/10 of 1%:

$$\text{Percent change in } YTM = \frac{\Delta YTM}{1 + YTM} = \frac{+0.01}{1.10} = +0.0090909 \approx \frac{9}{10} \text{ of } 1\%$$

Substituting these values into Eqn. 21-9 tells us the bond's interest rate elasticity (*EL*) is: −1.90:

$$EL = \frac{\Delta P/P}{\Delta YTM/(1 + YTM)} = \frac{-0.0173}{0.00909} = -1.90 \qquad \textbf{(21-9b)}$$

An elasticity measure of −1.90 means that a change in the bond's YTM of about 9/10 of 1% will cause an inverse percentage change in the bond's price that is 1.90 times larger. In other words, the bond's price decline of 1.713% [= 0.01713 = (−1.90)(9/10 of 1%)] was exactly what Eqn. 21-9 predicted.

---

[*] The uppercase Greek letter delta, Δ, denotes a finite change. If we analyze infinitesimally small changes, then differential calculus can be used to show that:

$$\text{MAC} = \frac{dp}{p} \times \frac{1.0 + YTM}{d(YTM)} = \frac{dp}{p} \bigg/ \frac{d(YTM)}{1 + YTM} = \text{Elasticity} < 0$$

A bond's price elasticity with respect to a change in its YTM can be calculated with Eqn. 21-9. Or, the formula for MAC, Eqn. 21-7, can also be used to calculate the bond's elasticity. The two formulas produce identical values. To see the relationship between the two approaches, reconsider the preceding example.

MAC for the 2-year bond that has a 10% coupon rate and sells at its par value of $1,000 is calculated here with Eqn. 21-7c, it equals the weighted average of years $t = 1$ and $t = 2$.

$$\text{MAC} = [(t = 1)(\$90.909/\$1000)] + [(t = 2)(\$909.091//\$1000)] \tag{21-7c}$$

$$= (t = 1)(0.090909) + (t = 2)(0.909091) = 1.90 \text{ years}$$

This 2-year bond's 1.90 years of MAC equals its price elasticity of 1.90 that was calculated in Eqn. 21-9b. We will not go into the mathematics here, but it can be shown that, in general, MAC $= EL$.

$$\left[\frac{\Delta P}{P}\right] = EL\left[\frac{\Delta \text{YTM}}{1 + \text{YTM}}\right] \tag{21-10}$$

$$= \text{MAC}\left[\frac{\Delta \text{YTM}}{1 + \text{YTM}}\right] \tag{21-10a}$$

Eqn. 21-10 is derived simply by solving Eqn. 21-9a for the percentage price change, denoted $\Delta P/P$. Substituting MAC in place of EL results in Eqn. 21-10a.

Eqns. 21-10 and 21-10a show that either a bond's elasticity or MAC determines the size of the percentage price change that occurs when a bond's YTM changes.* It is reassuring to discover that our measure of bond's interest rate risk, denoted EL, happens to equal our measure of the same bond's time structure, denoted MAC. Interest rate elasticity and Macaulay duration are equally good benchmarks of interest rate risk. In addition, they are also fairly good measures of a bond's total risk because the *systematic fluctuations* in market interest rates affect all bonds simultaneously and are the main source of price fluctuation risk in high-quality bonds.

PROBLEMS WITH DURATION

Criticisms have been aimed at duration. This section reviews the criticisms and considers competing duration measures.

Duration Wandering and Portfolio Rebalancing

As shown in Figure 21-6, a bond's duration does not decrease in one-to-one correspondence with the passage of time. Furthermore, Figure 21-8 shows how market interest rates interact with a bond's coupon rate to impact durations. As a result of complications like these, bonds

---

* MAC and EL will give slightly different numerical values under two conditions. (1) Eqn. 21-9 is a *point elasticity* formula. Substantial changes in the interest rate will be explained a little better with a formula for *arc elasticity*. (2) MAC assumes that the *yield curve is flat,* since the same invariant YTM is used to discount each time period's cash flow. If the slope of the yield curve shifts substantially this change can have a small effect on the MAC calculation.

Some analysts prefer to use **modified duration**, denoted MOD:

$$\text{Modified duration} = \text{MOD} = \frac{\text{MAC}}{1.0 + \text{YTM}}$$

FIGURE 21-8   The Market-Determined YTM and the Coupon Rate Have an Impact on a Bond's Duration

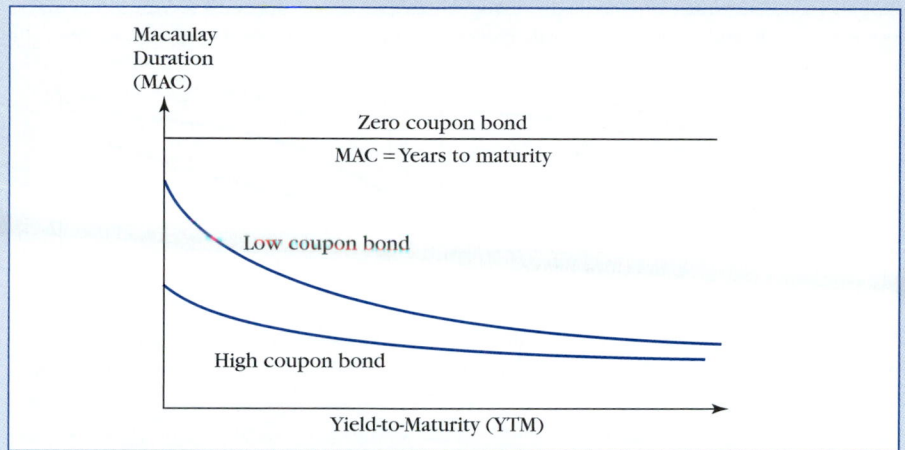

The Macaulay duration of a zero coupon bond always equals the bond's time until the bond matures, $MAC_z = T_z$. Fluctuating market interest rates (changes in the zero's YTM) do not change the duration of a zero. In contrast, the durations of coupon bonds tend to move inversely with changes in the bond's YTM. The durations of low coupon and high coupon bonds tend to react inversely to different degrees in response to changing YTMs. These different changes occur because the YTMs of coupon-paying bonds are impacted by the coupon effect. The coupon effect is capable of changing the YTM of a coupon-paying bond and this effect feeds through the bond's YTM and, in turn, changes the bond's duration.

experience a type of interest rate risk called **duration wandering.** Duration wandering can force the manager of the bond portfolio to rebalance the portfolio to achieve the desired duration.

Changes in the Term Structure of Interest Rates

Stochastic process risk is caused by shifts in the term structure of interest rates. Figure 21-9 illustrates three different categories of yield-curve shifts. Fixed income managers can deal with stochastic process risk by mathematically deriving duration measures that depend explicitly on the type of movement that is expected in the term structure of interest rates. However, if the shift in the yield curve incorporated into the duration measure is inappropriate, a surprising change in interest rate risk is possible.[6] The following section discusses various duration measures that analysts have developed in an effort to deal with stochastic process risk.

Alternative Duration Measures

Macaulay Duration (MAC).   MAC is the simplest and most popular of several competing measures of duration.[7] The simplicity of MAC relies on two implicit assumptions: (1) The yield curve is horizontal at the level of the bond's YTM, and (2) the yield curve experiences only parallel shifts, as illustrated in Figure 21-9A. Macaulay and other researchers have proposed alternatives to the MAC to align these simplifying assumptions more closely with reality.

FIGURE 21-9   Different Categories of Shifts in the Yield Curve: (A) Additive Shift, (B) Multiplicative Shift, (C) Term-Dependent Shift

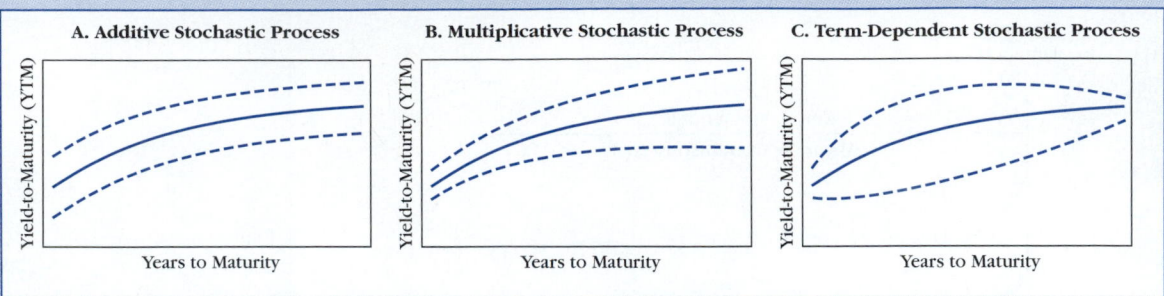

Yield curves (term structures of interest rates) can be modeled mathematically. Each measure of duration is based on some underlying mathematical model of the yield curve. For example, Macaulay duration (MAC) uses one YTM value throughout the bond's life. As a result, using Macaulay duration is equivalent to assuming the yield curve is always horizontal—a painfully simple assumption. Yield curves are said to involve stochastic process risk because market interest rates that fluctuate randomly operate through a process involving spot rates and forward rates to continually reshape the yield curve. An additive shift (straight up or down) is the simplest stochastic shock to model in a yield curve model or a measure of duration. More complicated stochastic processes are more difficult to work with mathematically, but they may be more realistic.

Fisher-Weil Duration (FWD). Macaulay originally proposed two duration measures. In addition to the MAC measure described above, he also proposed a duration measure that embodied the forward interest rates from the term structure of interest rates. Lawrence Fisher and Roman Weil worked extensively with both duration measures that Macaulay proposed, so we will refer to Macaulay's second measure as Fisher-Weil duration (FWD).[8]

$$\binom{\text{Fisher-Weil}}{\text{duration, FWD}} = (1)\left(\frac{\text{Cash flow}_1/(1 + r_1)}{P}\right) + (2)\left(\frac{\text{Cash flow}_2/(1 + r_1)(1 + r_2)}{P}\right) \quad \textbf{(21-11)}$$

$$+ \cdots + (T)\left(\frac{\text{Cash flow}_T/(1 + r_1)(1 + r_2)\cdots(1 + r_T)}{P}\right)$$

For most bonds the FWD measure and the MAC measures produce similar but not identical duration values. However, the FWD measure is conceptually superior to the MAC measure because FWD considers each time period's forward interest rate (denoted r_t in FWD) that is expected to occur when that period's cash flow occurs.* The FWD brings the term structure of interest rates into the analysis, while the simpler MAC measure implicitly assumes that the yield curve is always horizontal at the bond's YTM. Since the MAC formula is simpler to use, and empirical research indicates that no significant advantages are gained by bringing the term structure of interest rates into the analysis, MAC is more popular than FWD.

Modified Duration (MOD). Eqn. 21-13 defines modified duration.

---

* Forward rates were denoted $_1F_{t+1}$ in Chapter 20; the symbol refers to a 1-year yield expected to exist in the future between time periods t and $t+1$.

$$\begin{pmatrix} \text{Modified} \\ \text{duration, MOD} \end{pmatrix} = \frac{dP/P}{d(\text{YTM})} \approx \frac{\Delta P/P}{\Delta(\text{YTM})} \qquad\qquad \textbf{(21-12)}$$

MOD measures the percentage price change in a bond that occurs in response to a small change in the market interest rate; the denominator represents this infinitesimally small change, $d(YTM)$. MOD differs from MAC because MAC measures the percentage change in a bond's price that results from a *percentage* change in the market interest rate; MAC's denominator is $d(YTM)/(1+YTM)$. MOD and MAC are complementary tools that can both be used in slightly different applications.

Cox, Ingersoll, and Ross (CIR) Duration. CIR also proposed a single-factor measure of duration. CIR used stochastic calculus to formulate an interest rate–generating function and then derived a complex duration model.[9] Like FWD, CIR duration offers no significant advantage over MAC, CIR duration is more difficult to compute than MAC, and, therefore, CIR duration has never become as popular with investment managers as MAC.

Testing MAC, FWD, and CIR Duration. Financial researchers have tested the competing measures of duration referred to as MAC, FWD, and CIR. One study concluded:

> the evidence suggests that the Macaulay measure of duration performs reason-ably well in comparison to its more sophisticated counterparts and, because of its simplicity, appears to be cost-effective.[10]

Other researchers have reached the same conclusion.

Other Models. MAC, FWD, CIR, and many other measures are called *one-factor models* because they are based on the fluctuations in a single interest rate. Other authors are developing more complex immunization strategies.[11] Various researchers have been active in the development of *two-factor interest rate risk models*. The two-factor models usually use a short-term and a long-term interest rate as their two factors.[12] Three-factor models have also been developed. Each of the alternative duration measures mentioned above implies a different duration strategy. No single model is superior under all circumstances; each one is superior in the environment it is modeled to reflect. However, the complex models do not provide significantly better solutions than simpler models that are easier to use and, therefore, none of the multi-index models has become popular.

HORIZON ANALYSIS

A bond buyer's *investment horizon* often differs from the *maturity horizons* of the bonds that are investment candidates. These horizon differences mean the investor should perform a **horizon analysis** that involves computing the **horizon return** for every bond that is an investment candidate. A bond's horizon return is its total return, including cash flows and price changes, over whatever investment horizon is relevant. The horizon return incorporates expectations of future market interest rates and reinvestment rates over the investment horizon. Comparing horizon returns permits the investor to evaluate several potential bond investments over the planned investment horizon. The horizon return is more relevant than bonds' YTMs.

Unfortunately, some investors prefer to use the readily available YTM rather than compute a horizon return. These investors object to the horizon return because it requires a forecast about future yields and reinvestment rates. A conscientious investor should prepare different scenarios about future interest rates and reinvestment rates and evaluate a bond's performance over the investment horizon under each scenario. Horizon analysis can be used to evaluate different investment candidates, several bond switches (swaps), and various investment strategies. Different scenarios can be analyzed to develop a probability distribution of returns over the investment horizon.

Contingent immunization is a combination of active management and hedging that is designed to cover an investment horizon of several years.[13] Contingent immunization makes provisions to ensure that fixed-income assets earn at least some minimum **safety net return** or, if possible, a higher return. The bond portfolio manager is given discretion to actively manage a portfolio as long as it earns a return that exceeds the safety net return. If the portfolio suffers some temporary losses, the manager can continue actively managing it as long as the safety net return over some prespecified planning horizon is exceeded. But, if the safety net return is violated, active management is terminated abruptly and the remaining assets are frozen in a hedged position (immunized) to assure that at least the safety net return is achieved.

THE BOTTOM LINE

This chapter can be summarized by setting forth some axioms about bond prices and risk management.

The Behavior of Bond Prices

Axioms about the way bond prices behave can be discerned from this chapter's figures and discussions of duration and elasticity, as well as other issues in chapters 20 through 21:

Bond Price Axiom 1: A bond's price moves inversely to its YTM as these two random variables fluctuate along the bond's price-yield relationship.

Bond Price Axiom 2: Horizon risk refers to the fact that, if all other factors are held constant, a bond's interest rate risk usually increases with the length of time remaining until it matures.*

Bond Price Axiom 3: As the time remaining until a bond matures increases, that bond's interest rate risk increases at a diminishing rate. In other words, horizon risk increases at a diminishing rate as the time to maturity is increased.

Bond Price Axiom 4: The price change that results from an equal-sized increase or decrease in a bond's YTM is asymmetrical.** For any given maturity, a decrease in YTM causes a price rise that is larger than the price loss that results from an equal increase in YTM.†

Bond Price Axiom 5: When the yield curve is not horizontal, coupon-paying bonds are influenced by the size of their coupon rates. This coupon effect refers to the fact that the

---

* Axiom 2 is not true for very long-term bonds that are selling at a discount. However, it is true for all other bonds, and it is not far off the mark for the long-term discounted bonds.

** Axiom 4 assumes yields change from the same starting value whether they move up or down.

† Taking the second derivative of present value Eqn. 21-1 results in the formula for a bond's **convexity**.

$$\frac{d^2P}{d(YTM)^2} = \sum_{t=1}^{T} \frac{t(t+1)CF_t}{(1+YTM)^{t+2}} > 0$$

where CF_t represents the cash flow in time period t. The numerical value of this derivative decreases as the YTM increases; that explains the asymmetric price movements mathematically. Convexity is useful in explaining the bond price axioms and improving hedges (immunizations).

amount and timing of coupon payments can affect the YTM and interest-rate risk of bonds.

Duration Axioms

Macaulay duration and modified duration are measures of a bond's interest rate risk, measures of the time structure of a bond, and, for any given bond they have numerical values that are similar but not identical.

Duration Axiom 1: Duration considers all cash flows and measures the average length of time that funds remain tied up in an investment.

Duration Axiom 2: Macaulay duration equals years to maturity for a zero coupon bond. Macaulay duration is less than years to maturity for a coupon-paying bond. For any particular bond, modified duration has a smaller value than Macaulay duration.

Duration Axiom 3: Duration always varies directly with the bond's years to maturity for zero coupon bonds, bonds priced at a premium over par, and bonds selling at par. Duration usually, but not always, varies directly with the bond's years to maturity for bonds that are priced at a discount from par.

Duration Axiom 4:   If all other factors are held constant, the duration of a coupon-paying bond varies inversely with its yield to maturity. If all other factors are held constant and the yield curve is not horizontal, a bond's duration also varies inversely with its coupon rate. Duration measures the simultaneous impacts that a bond's YTM and its coupon rate have on the bond's interest-rate risk.

Duration Axiom 5: Macaulay duration equals a bond's interest rate elasticity. A small algebraic manipulation can change a bond's modified duration to equal that bond's interest rate elasticity and its Macaulay duration.

Duration Axiom 6: Duration can be used to obtain good linear forecasts of the way a bond's price moves in reaction to a change in its YTM. However, this forecast is an approximation that is only accurate for small changes in the bond's YTM, because the true price-yield relationship is curvilinear instead of linear.

Duration Axiom 7: As the number of years until a bond matures increases, Macaulay duration for that bond approaches a limiting value equal to $(1+\text{YTM})/\text{YTM}$.

Axioms About Interest-Rate Risk

Interest-rate risk is that portion of total risk that is caused by fluctuating market interest rates.

Interest-Rate Risk Axiom 1: For any given bond, interest-rate risk usually increases directly with Macaulay duration, modified duration, the bond's interest rate elasticity, and the number of years until the bond matures.

Interest-Rate Risk Axiom 2: Hedging is an interest rate risk management procedure that can use the duration of assets (long positions) and the duration of liabilities (short positions) to reduce or eliminate interest-rate risk in a portfolio of bonds or other fixed-income securities.

Interest-Rate Risk Axiom 3: Option-free bonds enjoy a risk-reducing curvature in their price-yield relationships that is called positive convexity. However, some bonds have embedded (call, put, early redemption) options that cause them to have a negative convexity that increases their interest-rate risk.

Interest-Rate Risk Axiom 4: If it is expected that a bond will be liquidated before its maturity date, the investor should focus on that bond's horizon return instead of its yield to maturity.

QUESTIONS

Q21-1 (Duration and coupon rates) What is the relationship between a bond's coupon rate and its duration? Explain.

Q21-2 (Duration and term to maturity) What is the relationship between a bond's term to maturity and its duration? Explain.

Q21-3 (Duration and changing YTMs) What happens to a coupon-paying bond's duration if the bond's YTM rises?

Q21-4 (Duration and time structure of cash flows) "Duration does not correspond with the exact date of any particular cash flow that a default-free bond may experience. Therefore duration is a worthless measure of the time structure of a bond's cash flows." True, false, or uncertain? Explain.

Q21-5 (Macaulay versus Modified duration) Both the Macaulay and the Modified duration measures were discussed in this chapter. How do the two measures differ?

Q21-6 (Applying the principal of duration) Consider the following three bonds:

Bond	Coupon Rate	Years to Maturity
1	zero	15
2	10%	15
3	12%	10

Which bond would a bond portfolio manager prefer to have in his portfolio if he anticipates an increase in interest rates? Why?

Q21-7 (MACLIM) Provide the equation that is used to calculate a limiting value for a bond's Macaulay duration and explain its meaning.

Q21-8 (Horizon analysis) What is horizon analysis? What is the advantage of this type of analysis? What difficulty is involved in performing horizon analysis?

Q21-9 (Convexity) What is meant by a bond's convexity? Why might an investor prefer a bond that has positive convexity?

Q21-10 (Contingent immunization) What is contingent immunization? What is its purpose, and how is it effected?

PROBLEMS

P21-1 (Macaulay duration) What is the duration of a bond that has a YTM of 6% and a perpetual maturity? Show your calculations. *Hint:* There is a short-cut formula for perpetuities in this chapter. See Figure 21-6 and Table 21-6.

P21-2 (Macaulay duration and elasticity) Calculate the present value and Macaulay duration for a bond paying an 8% coupon rate annually on its $1,000 face value if it has 8 years until its maturity and has a YTM of 9%. Show your computations. What is this bond's interest-rate elasticity?

P21-3 (Macaulay duration and elasticity) Reconsider the bond described in Problem 21-2 above. Assume the bond's YTM was 8% and re-calculate its present value, Macaulay duration, and elasticity. What can you conclude from this problem about the relationship between (a) the level of market interest rates and (b) interest-rate risk?

P21-4 (Macaulay duration) Consider the following data on three U.S. Treasury bonds that pay interest semiannually:

Bond	Coupon Rate	Years Until Maturity	Yield-to-Maturity	Macaulay's Duration
A	10.0%	2.0	10.0%	?
B	10.0	3.0	10.0	?
C	0	3.0	10.0	?

(a) Calculate the Macaulay duration for each bond. (b) Explain why the three bonds above have different durations, using intuitive economics rather than pure mathematics.

P21-5 (Macaulay duration) Assume that the U.S. Treasury issued a bond that pays coupons of 10% semiannually for 15 years. (a) What will be the price of the bond 2 years after its issue date if the market rate of interest is 12%? (b) What will this bond's Macaulay's duration be 2 years after it is issued?

P21-6 (Macaulay duration) Assume that the U.S. Treasury issued a bond that pays coupons of 10% semiannually for 15 years. (a) What will be the price of the bond 5 years after its issue date if the market rate of interest is 8%? (b) What will this bond's Macaulay's duration be 5 years after it is issued?

P21-7 (Yield-to-maturity) A U.S. Treasury bond that has a $1,000 face value and pays a 12% coupon semiannually is currently selling for $856. (a) If the bond issue has 14 years until maturity, what is its YTM? (b) What is this bond's YTM if it is selling for $1,150?

P21-8 (Yield-to-maturity and Macaulay duration) Calculate the YTM and Macaulay's duration for the two Treasury bonds below.

Year	Bond 1 Cash Flows	Bond 2 Cash Flows	Prices
0	−$1000	−$1000	Purchase prices
1	100	0	
2	100	0	
3	100	0	
4	100	0	
5	100	0	
6	1100	1700	Selling prices

P21-9 (Yield curves and rates of return) Gerald Jones purchased a 10% coupon semiannual bond of the Farr Corporation at par value that had 10 years to maturity. Immediately after Jones purchased the bond, interest rates on bonds of this risk level rose to 12% and remained there until the bond was sold at the end of the fifth year. If the yield curve remained flat during the 5-year period that Jones owned the bond and he reinvested all of his coupon interest, what rate of return did he earn over his 5-year investment? Ignore taxes.

P21-10 (Yield curves and rates of return) Using the information in Problem 21-9, calculate the return Jones would earn if he sold the bond in 3 years.

P21-11 (Yield curves and rates of return) Using the information in Problem 21-9, calculate the return Jones would earn if the interest rate fell to 8% right after he purchased the bond and then remained there for his 5-year investment horizon.

P21-12 (Effect of changing interest rates on duration) Determine the duration of the bond in Problem 21-9 just after it was purchased when it had 10 years until it matured. Find the duration both (a) before the bond's YTM rose above 10% and (b) after the interest rate changed to 12%.

CFA EXAM QUESTIONS

The following two questions are adopted from the 1997 CFA Exam, Level I:

1. Which of the following bond has the longest duration?
   A. 8-year maturity, 6% coupon.
   B. 8-year maturity, 11% coupon.
   C. 15-year maturity, 6% coupon.
   D. 15-year maturity, 11% coupon.

2. A bond with annual coupon payments has the following characteristics:

Coupon Rate	Yield-to-Maturity	Macaulay Duration
8%	10%	9

   The bond's modified duration (in years) is:
   A. 8.18.
   B. 8.33.
   C. 9.78.
   D. 10.00.

3. (1998 CFA Sample Exam, Level I) Convexity of bonds increases in importance when interest rates are:
   A. low.
   B. high.
   C. expected to change very little.
   D. less than the coupon rate on the bond.

4. (1996 CFA Exam, Level III) One common goal among fixed-income portfolio managers is to earn high incremental returns on corporate bonds versus government bonds of comparable durations. The approach of some corporate-bond portfolio managers is to find and purchase those corporate bonds having the largest initial spreads over comparable-duration government bonds. John Ames, HFS's fixed-income manager, believes that a more rigorous approach is required if incremental returns are to be maximized.

Table IX below presents data relating to one set of corporate/government spread relationships present in the market at a given date:

TABLE IX   Current and Expected Spreads and Durations of High-Grade Corporate Bonds (1-Year Horizon)

Bond Rating	Initial Spread over Governments	Expected Horizon Spread	Initial Duration	Expected Duration 1 Year from Now
Aaa	31 b.p.	31 b.p.	4 years	3.1 years
Aa	40 b.p.	50 b.p.	4 years	3.1 years

Recommend purchase of *either* Aaa *or* Aa bonds for a one-year investment horizon given a goal of maximizing incremental returns. Show your calculations. (Base your decision *only* on the information presented in Table IX above.)

5. (1996 CFA Exam, Level II) The shape of the U.S. Treasury yield curve appears to reflect two expected Federal Reserve reductions in the Federal Funds rate. The first reduction of approximately 50 basis points (BP) is expected 6 months from now and the second reduction of approximately 50 BP is expected 1 year from now. The current U.S. Treasury term premiums are 10 BP per year for each of the next 3 years (out through the 3-year benchmark). Kent Lewis, an economist, also expects two Federal Reserve reductions in the Federal Funds rate, but believes that the market is too optimistic about how soon they will occur. Lewis believes that the first 50 BP reduction will be made 1 year from now and that the sec-

ond 50 BP reduction will be made $1\frac{1}{2}$ years from now. He believes that the market will adjust to reflect his beliefs when new economic data is released over the next 2 weeks.

Assume you are convinced by Lewis' argument, and are authorized to purchase either the 2-year benchmark U.S. Treasury or a Cash/3-year benchmark U.S. Treasury barbell weighted to have the same duration as the 2-year U.S. Treasury.

Select an investment in *either* the 2-year benchmark U.S. Treasury (bullet) *or* the Cash/3-year benchmark U.S. Treasury barbell. Justify your choice.

FURTHER REFERENCES

Bierwag, G. O. *Duration Analysis, Managing Interest Rate Risk.* Cambridge, MA: Ballinger Press, 1987.

This mathematical monograph discusses interest rate risk in a comprehensive manner. The book begins by defining the YTM and proceeds logically to explain interest-rate risk and increasingly sophisticated methods to manage interest-rate risk.

Bierwag, G. O., George G. Kaufman, and Alden Toevs. "Duration: Its Development and Use in Bond Portfolio Management," *Financial Analysts Journal* (July-August 1983): 15–35.

An easy-to-read survey of the research that led to duration as a useful tool for bond portfolio managers. Only a little elementary algebra is used.

Fabozzi, Frank J. *Bond Markets, Analysis and Strategies,* 4th ed. Englewood Cliffs, NJ: Prentice-Hall, 2000.

This popular college finance textbook describes bond markets and surveys modern interest rate theory.

Fisher, Lawrence and Roman L. Weil. "Coping with the Risk of Market-Rate Fluctuations: Returns to Bondholders from Naive and Optimal Strategies," *Journal of Business* (October 1977): 408–31.

This study investigates the effectiveness of immunization in reducing interest-rate risk. Portfolio management with a shifting term structure of interest rates is simulated. Only elementary algebra is used.

Haugen, R. A. and D. W. Wichern. "The Elasticity of Financial Assets," *Journal of Finance* (September 1974): 1229–40.

Algebra and differential calculus are used to derive both the duration and elasticity measure of interest-rate risk from the present value model of security valuation. Bankruptcy risk is also considered in the analysis so that it is relevant for both stock and bond valuation.

Hopewell, M. H., and G. G. Kaufman. "Bond Price Volatility and Term to Maturity: A Generalized Respecification," *American Economic Review* (September 1973): 749–53.

Differential calculus is used to show that Macaulay's duration is a measure of interest risk for bonds.

Livingston, Miles. *Money and Capital Markets,* 3d ed. Malden, MA: Blackwell Publishers, 1996.

The 23 chapters of this textbook discuss monetary economics, bond pricing, yield curves, various fixed-income securities, default risk, tax issues, financial futures, and financial engineering. The discussion contains many insightful examples and graphs.

Tuckman, Bruce. *Fixed Income Securities.* New York: Wiley, 1996.

This 18-chapter book focuses on bond pricing, the yield-to-maturity, yield curves, duration, interest-rate options, interest-rate futures, interest-rate swaps, and mortgage-backed securities. Algebra and a little calculus are used.

ENDNOTES

[1] For a computationally simple MAC formula, see Gabriel Hawawini, Chapter Two, "On the Mathematics of Macaulay's Duration," *Bond Duration and Immunization Early Developments and Recent Contributions* (New York: Garland Publishing Company, 1982). See also Jess H. Chua, "A Closed Form Formula for Calculating Bond Duration," *Financial Analysts Journal* (May-June 1984): 76-78.

[2] See F. R. Macaulay, *Some Theoretical Problems Suggested by the Movement of Interest Rates, Bond Yields and Stock Prices in the United States Since 1856,* National Bureau of Economic Research (New York: Columbia, 1938). See also J. R. Hicks, *Value and Capital,* 2nd ed. (New York: Oxford, 1965), 186. Hicks discovered duration independently of Macaulay at an earlier date.

[3] See Joel R. Barber, "A Note on Approximating Bond Price Sensitivity Using Duration and Convexity," The *Journal of Fixed Income* 4, no. 4 (March 1995): 95-98.

[4] See Shantaram P. Hegde and Kenneth P. Nunn, Jr. "Non-Infinitesimal Rate Changes and Macaulay Duration," *Journal of Portfolio Management* 14, no. 2 (winter 1988): 69-73.

[5] See Paul A. Samuelson, "The Effect of Interest Rate Increases on the Banking System," *American Economic Review* (March 1945): 16-27. More recently, see M. H. Hopewell and G. G. Kaufman, "Bond Price Volatility and Term to Maturity: A Generalized Respecification," *American Economic Review* (September 1973): 749-53. See also Robert Haugen and D. W. Wichern, "The Elasticity of Financial Assets," *Journal of Finance* (September 1974): 1229-40.

[6] Immunization, rebalancing immunized portfolios, and dealing with the stochastic process risk that results from changes in the yield curve that affect bonds' durations are discussed by Robert R. Reitano, "Non-parallel Yield Curve Shifts and Stochastic Immunization," *Journal of Portfolio Management* 22, no. 2 (winter 1996): 71-78. Also see G.O. Bierwag, George G. Kaufman, and Alden Toevs, "Duration: Its Development and Use in Bond Portfolio Management," *Financial Analysts Journal* (July-August 1983): 15-35.

[7] For a study that advocates the simplicity and popularity of MAC, see N. Bulent Guletkin and Richard J. Rogalski, "Alternative Duration Specification and the Measurement of Basis Risk: Empirical Tests," *Journal Business* 57, no. 2 (1984): 241-64.

[8] See Lawrence Fisher and Roman L. Weil, "Coping with the Risk of Market Interest Rate Fluctuations: Returns to Bondholders from Naive and Optimal Strategies," *Journal of Business* (October 1971): 408-31.

[9] John C. Cox, Jonathan E. Ingersoll, and Steve Ross, "Duration and the Measurement of Basis Risk," *Journal of Business* 52 (January 1971): 51-61.

[10] Competing measures of duration are discussed by G.O. Bierwag, George G. Kaufman, and Alden Toevs, "Duration: Its Development and Use in Bond Portfolio Management," *Financial Analysts Journal* (July-August 1983): 15-35. Also see Patrick W. Lau, "An Empirical Examination of Alternative Interest Rate Risk Immunization Strategies," Unpublished Ph.D. dissertation, University of Wisconsin, 1983. Lau conducts empirical tests of immunization strategies that are based on different definitions of duration and also concludes that Macaulay's duration is more cost-effective than the FWD or CIR measures.

[11] See Frank J. Fabozzi, *Bond Markets, Analysis and Strategies,* 3d ed. (Englewood Cliffs, NJ: Prentice-Hall, 1996); for a discussion of "dollar duration" see Chapter 4. For a discussion of "effective duration," see pp. 343-45.

[12] See M. J. Brennan and E. S. Schwartz, "A Continuous Time Approach to the Pricing of Bonds," *Journal of Banking and Finance* 3 (1979): 133-55. Also see M. J. Brennan and E. S. Schwartz, "Conditional Predictions of Bond Prices and Returns," *Journal of Finance* 35, no. 2 (May 1980): 405-16. See also M. J. Brennan and E. S. Schwartz, "An Equilibrium Model of Bond Pricing and a Test of Market Efficiency," *Journal of Financial and Quantitative Analysis* (September 1982): 301-29. For a discrete time two-factor model see G. O. Bierwag, G. G. Kaufman, and Cynthia M. Latta, "Bond Portfolio Immunization: Tests of Maturity, One and Two-Factor Duration Matching Strategies," *Financial Review* (May 1987): 203-20.

[13] See Martin L. Leibowitz and Alfred Weinberger, "The Uses of Contingent Immunization," *Journal of Portfolio Management* (fall 1981): 51-55.

CREDIT RISK

Bonds, bank loans, mortgages, accounts receivables, and other debts are sometimes called **credits.** *Bond investors, bank loan departments, and others that extend credit are exposed to credit risk. Credit risk is the portion of an investment's total variability of return resulting from changes in the ability of the borrower to pay off debts.*

This chapter examines four levels of credit risk:

- *First, at the catastrophic level, a* bankruptcy *is a financial funeral.*

- *Second, less ruinous but still very serious, is a significant* default. *A significant default occurs when a firm unavoidably fails to make a scheduled debt payment. A significant default is a step on the pathway to bankruptcy.*

- *Third, a corporation experiences* **rating migration** *when Moody's or Standard & Poor's or some other credit rating agency changes its credit rating. Bankruptcies, significant defaults on scheduled debt payments, and rating migrations are observable* **credit events**.

- **Credit migrations** *are the fourth and least disastrous type of credit risk. Credit migrations involve credit changes that are so small they are difficult to measure. This type of credit risk occurs when lenders quietly buy or sell a credit because they suspect the borrower's financial condition is changing. Credit migrations manifest themselves as continuous price fluctuations of modest proportions.*

Bankruptcies are examined first. After bankruptcies and significant defaults have been reviewed, the remainder this chapter turns to smaller and more common sources of credit risk and to tools for managing them.

CORPORATE BANKRUPTCY

An organization that is unable to meet its obligations because its checking account is overdrawn is *insolvent.* A highly profitable company might become temporarily insolvent simply

CHAPTER 22   CREDIT RISK   **657**

because of cash management problems that do not necessarily constitute a significant default. If the value of a firm's assets falls below its liabilities, that firm is said to be insolvent in the bankruptcy sense. If an insolvent company fails to pay a liability on time, the firm is said to be in *default*. If payment is not forthcoming fairly quickly, creditors usually file lawsuits. Although details differ from case to case, the typical bankruptcy situation begins with out-of-court negotiations. If an out-of-court settlement between the debtor and creditors cannot be reached, either the insolvent company asks the court to declare it bankrupt or its creditors ask the bankruptcy court to declare the defaulting firm bankrupt. Few unpaid debts are forgotten.

An important question addressed in bankruptcy hearings is whether or not the firm should be declared bankrupt and have its assets liquidated at a public bankruptcy auction. The bankruptcy court judge decides whether the auction proceeds would exceed what is likely to be obtained if the firm continues operating. Firms that are merely insolvent are not declared bankrupt. If the bankruptcy judge believes the insolvent firm is having difficulties that are temporary, the court will grant the troubled firm additional time to pay its liabilities, protect the insolvent firm from actions taken by its creditors during the court-mandated *credit extension*, and thereby help the firm avert bankruptcy.

U.S. Bankruptcy Law Specifies a Procedure and a Priority of Claims

Chapter 7 of the U.S. *Federal Bankruptcy Reform Act of 1978* stipulates the following three steps for liquidating a bankrupt corporation.

Step One. A petition for bankruptcy is filed in federal court. A minimum number of creditors may file an involuntary petition against a defaulting corporation. Or the corporation itself may file a voluntary petition requesting that it be declared bankrupt. A troubled firm might want a bankruptcy court to grant it protection from creditors under the bankruptcy law; thus it asks the bankruptcy court to declare it bankrupt while the firm endeavors to overcome its problems.

Step Two. If the bankruptcy judge rules that the firm is hopelessly bankrupt, a trustee is elected by the creditors. Under the supervision of the bankruptcy court, the bankruptcy trustee supervises liquidation of the assets of the bankrupt firm.

Step Three. After the assets are liquidated and the administrative costs are paid, the trustee distributes the proceeds from the bankruptcy auction to the creditors and stockholders.

The Absolute Priority Rule (APR) in U.S. Federal Bankruptcy Law

If the assets of a firm are liquidated at a bankruptcy auction in the United States, the auction proceeds are paid out according to the following absolute priority rule (APR):

Priority 1. The attorney's fees and court costs associated with the bankruptcy proceeding are paid first.

Priority 2. If any funds remain after the attorneys are paid, any expenses incurred between the filing of an involuntary bankruptcy petition and the appointment of the trustee are paid.

Priority 3. Any remaining proceeds from the bankruptcy go to pay back wages, up to a maximum of $2,000 per worker.

Priority 4. After back wages are paid, if any liquidation proceeds remain, past-due contributions that the bankrupt firm owes to its employee pension plan are made.

Priority 5. Whatever just consumer claims might be outstanding are paid from any liquidation funds that still remain.

Priority 6. Any remaining liquidation proceeds are used to pay back taxes to federal, state, and/or local governments.

Priority 7. If any proceeds from the bankruptcy auction are left at this stage, creditors holding secured loans are paid. Mortgage lenders and other collateralized creditors are paid when their collateral is liquidated. The secured creditors typically receive 53.8% of the money owed to them by the bankrupt firm. General (unsecured) creditors are paid next. General creditors include raw material suppliers and public utilities that extended credit to the firm without obtaining any collateral. On average, general creditors receive about 38 cents of every dollar owed to them by the bankrupt corporation.[1]

Priority 8. Preferred stockholders are paid if any auction proceeds are left at this stage of the payoffs. Four cents on each dollar paid for preferred stock is a normal payment for this category of creditor.

Priority 9. Common stockholders are paid last; they almost always receive nothing.[2]

If the financial strength of a corporation weakens, the absolute priority rule has a predictable impact on the price behavior of the troubled firm's securities. Common stock prices typically decline more than the prices of the preferred stock of a troubled corporation. The price of the firm's preferred stock usually falls more than the price of the firm's debenture bonds but less than the common stock's price. The prices of uncollateralized bonds (debentures) fall more than the prices of collateralized bonds but less than the preferred stock.[3] These price behaviors reflect the absolute priority rule governing corporate bankruptcies in the United States.

The objective of U.S. bankruptcy law is to save the firm, if possible. However, providing government subsidies or protections for ailing companies is considered to be undesirable and counterproductive in the U.S. system of competitive free enterprise. Thus, if the bankruptcy judge thinks the firm can somehow save itself, he or she may, instead of declaring it bankrupt, entertain proposals for reorganizing the firm. In a **reorganization** a group of creditors might be given real estate, a fleet of trucks, or other assets as payment in kind (PIK) if they drop their money claims. Top management might be dismissed and a new top management team appointed. The bankruptcy judge might declare the corporation's common stock to be null, void, and worthless. If the existing common stock is declared void, the corporation's preferred stock could be downgraded to become the new common stock. The existing bonds might be downgraded to become the new preferred stock; this reduces the troubled firm's interest expense. Few reorganizations require all these drastic changes to keep the firm operating.

U.S. capitalism is a Darwinian system that uses bankruptcy to eliminate inept business managers and remove obsolete products from the market. Competition allocates most resources in the United States, not the government. To see how bankruptcy law in the United States impacts the market price fluctuations of securities, we offer the following example.

Boston Chicken on the Precipice of Bankruptcy in 1998–99

It is the possibility of default, rather than actual bankruptcy decree, that causes the most investor losses. Consider the case of a restaurant chain that went to the brink of bankruptcy.

In 1993 Boston Chicken Corporation's (ticker BOSTQ) common stock went public and was listed on NASDAQ. To provide capital to finance rapid growth, the restaurant company issued debentures in 1994. Management at the firm's Golden, Colorado headquarters expanded the menu to include roast chicken, roast turkey, baked ham, meatloaf, fresh vegetables, salads, and side dishes to reach a larger market. BOSTQ renamed their Boston Chicken restaurants Boston Market restaurants to reflect the broader menu. Their meals could be eaten in the restaurants, but a lot were take out. In 1996 BOSTQ's management decided to use its wider product offering to compete with fast-food giants like McDonald's and Burger King. BOSTQ's carryout fast-meal restaurant chain expanded rapidly and profits grew. By 1998 the Boston Chicken Corporation had 1,143 Boston Market restaurants operating in 33 states plus the District of Columbia.

At the initial public offering in 1993, BOSTQ's common stock sold for $20 per share. The stock reached $42 per share late in 1996 as profits increased. Management decided not to pay cash dividends; they wanted to reinvest all earnings in the firm to finance expansion.

Not content with its rapidly growing restaurant chain, Boston Chicken Corporation's management diversified into other areas. Boston Chicken acquired a 54% stake in the largest chain of bagel stores in the United States, Einstein/Noah Bagel, which operated 570 bagel shops in 1999. Boston Chicken also reached a licensing agreement with the H. J. Heinz Corporation (ticker HNZ), which it licensed to produce and market a line of Boston Market packaged food entrees for royalty fees based on sales of the products.

The Boston Chicken Corporation expanded too rapidly. The complex menu made the restaurants difficult to operate and their attractive locations were costly to maintain. Many franchise holders who operated restaurants were losing money. BOSTQ loaned money to troubled franchise holders to keep those restaurants open. BOSTQ's profits were inflated in 1997 as unprofitable restaurant owners used money borrowed from BOSTQ to pay franchise fees to BOSTQ. In 1998 $900 million of loans to restaurant owners soured as sales slowed. BOSTQ's profits turned into large losses. In October 1998 BOSTQ filed for Chapter 11 bankruptcy as protection while it continued to operate. Management closed about 230 unprofitable Boston Chicken restaurants in 1998. The stock's price fell to less than $1 per share. NASDAQ delisted BOSTQ stock and it became difficult to get the firm's financial statements. The Boston Chicken Corporation's debenture bonds fell from over $100 in 1997 to $4 per bond in 1999. Table 22-1 summarizes this financial roller-coaster ride.

In December 1999 McDonald's took over BOSTQ for $173 million plus the assumption of certain debts. BOSTQ retained its 54% stake in the chain of Einstein/Noah bagel shops. BOSTQ's common stock and bond holders lost practically everything they invested.

Table 22-1 shows that BOSTQ's bond prices fluctuated between $119 and $4; these bond price fluctuations are the essence of credit risk. The remainder of this chapter investigates bond price fluctuations and bond quality ratings.

SECURITIES QUALITY RATINGS

The second column of Table 22-1 lists the quality ratings of Boston Chicken's bonds. **Junk bonds** are any bonds rated below the BBB category by Standard and Poor's, or equivalently,

TABLE 22-1   Boston Chicken Investors Ride Dangerous Roller Coaster, 1993–99

Date	Bond Rating	Bond Price, $100 par	Bond's Yield to Maturity, YTM	Common Stock Price	Quarterly Earnings (Loss) per Share	Quarterly Cash Dividend, per Share
December 1993	Stock's initial public offering (IPO)			$18	$0.04	Nil
March 1994	B	$100	4.5%	19.25	0.065	Nil
June	B	96	4.79%	19.875	0.085	Nil
September	B	$85\frac{1}{32}$	6.93%	21	0.11	Nil
December	B	73	9.69%	$17\frac{3}{8}$	0.12	Nil
March 1995	B	75	9.13%	$16\frac{1}{4}$	0.23	Nil
June	B	92	5.52%	$24\frac{1}{8}$	0.07	Nil
September	B	$100\frac{1}{32}$	4.18%	$26\frac{1}{8}$	0.17	Nil
December	B	$119\frac{1}{64}$	1.68%	$32\frac{1}{8}$	0.19	Nil
March 1996	B	$125\frac{1}{16}$	0.96%	34	0.24	Nil
June	B	$117\frac{3}{64}$	1.76%	$23\frac{1}{2}$	0.24	Nil
September	B	$128\frac{1}{8}$	0.48%	$35\frac{1}{4}$	0.26	Nil
December	B	$125\frac{7}{8}$	0.61%	$35\frac{7}{8}$	0.27	Nil
March 1997	B	$110\frac{3}{4}$	2.34%	$30\frac{1}{2}$	0.32	Nil
June	B	76	8.91%	14	0.25	Nil
September	B	$75\frac{1}{32}$	9.22%	$14\frac{3}{4}$	0.16	Nil
December	B	49	19.34%	$6\frac{7}{16}$	(4.05)	Nil
March 1998	B	$38\frac{1}{32}$	26.63%	5	(4.38)	Nil
June	CCC	$17\frac{3}{64}$	52.43%	$1\frac{5}{8}$	(1.71)	Nil
September	CC	$7\frac{3}{64}$	78.19%	$\frac{3}{4}$	(3.84)	Nil

October 1998—Management filed for the bankruptcy court's protection from creditors while it continued to operate the business.

Date	Bond Rating	Bond Price, $100 par	Bond's Yield to Maturity, YTM	Common Stock Price	Quarterly Earnings (Loss) per Share	Quarterly Cash Dividend, per Share
December	CC	$4\frac{3}{64}$	89.32%	$\frac{5}{16}$	NA	Nil
March 1999	CC	$4\frac{13}{64}$	141.63%	$\frac{45}{64}$	NA	Nil
June	CC	$4\frac{16}{64}$	159.88%	$\frac{41}{64}$	NA	Nil
September	CC	$4\frac{32}{64}$	179.03%	$\frac{13}{64}$	NA	Nil

In December 1999 McDonald's acquired Boston Chicken Corporation for $173 million and assumed certain debts.

NA = Not Available

Notes about bond issues: Subordinated Debentures issued 02/01/94, 4.5% coupon rate, maturing 02/01/2004 reported above. Another April 1997 bond issue is not reported.

below Baa by Moody's. **Speculative bonds** is a synonym for junk bonds. BOSTQ's low bond quality ratings are common among weak firms and start-ups.[4] Boston Chicken's bond ratings dropped from B in 1994–97 to CCC in June 1998. As Boston Chicken neared bankruptcy its bonds dropped further to CC in September 1998. By the time the firm filed for bankruptcy in October 1998 its securities were nearly worthless. Securities brokers euphemistically refer to junk bonds as **high-yield bonds** because they must promise high yields-to-maturity (YTMs) to induce risk-averse investors to buy them. The bottom of column 4 in Table 22-1 adds meaning to the phrase "high-yield bonds."

When a credit-rating service like Standard & Poor's, Moody's, or Fitch IBCA changes the quality rating assigned to a security, the change is publicly reported (a credit event) in business periodicals. The next section analyzes the determinants of quality ratings.

Definitions of Quality Ratings

Financial services employ bond analysts to study thousands of different corporations, analyze their financial situations, and assign quality ratings to each bond issue. Table 22-2 explains the quality ratings assigned to bond issues by various rating agencies. Different agencies sometimes give slightly different ratings for the same security. If two financial services do give the same security different ratings, the divergent ratings are called a **split rating.** The few split ratings that do occur are rarely more than one rating grade apart.

Financial analysts have studied hundreds of different bonds and their quality ratings over several decades and computed the percentage of firms in each bond quality rating that default. Table 22-3 summarizes some of this research; the table shows only moderate annual rates of default during normal years. The default rates were the highest during the Depression era of the early 1930s. The percentage of poorly rated firms that defaulted was larger than that of firms rated high in each period sampled. This finding suggests that the quality ratings the financial services sell to their subscribers are helpful in assessing the probability that a bond issuer will default.

TABLE 22-2   Ratings from Credit-Rating Services

Moody's	Standard & Poor's	Duff & Phelps	Fitch	Best's	Dun & Bradstreet	Description
Aaa	AAA	AAA	AAA	A++	5A1	Maximum safety
Aa	AA	AA	AA	A	4A1	High quality
A	A	A	A	B++	5A2	Medium-grade investment bonds
Baa	BBB	BBB	BBB	B	4A2	Low-grade investment bonds
Ba	BB	BB	BB	C++	5A3	High-grade junk bonds
B	B	B+	B	C+	4A3	Junk bonds
Caa	CCC	B	CCC	C	4A4	Speculative junk
Ca	CC	B−	CC	D	4A4	Very speculative junk
C	C	CCC	C	E	3A	Gambling on bankruptcy
D	D	DD	D	F	NR	Defaulted

TABLE 22-3   Average 1-Year Default Rates for Different Bond Rating Categories

Period	AAA	AA	A	BBB
1920–29	0.12%	0.17%	0.20%	0.80%
1930–39[a]	0.42	0.44	1.94	3.78
1920–39	0.30	0.30	1.1	2.3
1950–79	0	0	0	0
1970–90	0	0.04%	0.01%	0.17%

[a]Includes Depression years.

SOURCES: W. B. Hickman, *Corporate Bond Quality and Investor Experience* (Washington, DC: National Bureau of Economic Research, 1958). Gordon Pye, "Gauging the Default Premium," *Financial Analysts Journal* (January-February 1974): 49–52. Jerome S. Fons and Andrew E. Kimball, "Corporate Bond Defaults and Default Rates, 1970–90," *The Journal of Fixed Income* 1, no. 1 (June 1991): Table 3, p. 44.

Average Returns Vary with Quality Ratings

Economic theory presumes that rational people are risk-averse. Economic models assume that risk-averse investors refuse to buy issues of high-risk securities unless they pay higher rates of return than similar issues of lower-risk securities. This fundamental assumption is confronted with empirical data below.

Table 22-4 shows average bond yields during the periods 1955–69, 1970–79, 1980–89, and 1990–99. The fact that the average market YTMs increase with the riskiness of the bonds' ratings in every sample period provides evidence that bond investors are risk-averse. Figure 22-1 illustrates the unstable nature of the relationship between risk and corporate bond yields that existed at different times. Changes in the Federal Reserve's monetary policy, the U.S. Treasury's fiscal policy, the supply of and demand for loanable funds, and other factors cause the relationship between market interest rates and bonds quality ratings to shift minute by minute every day.[5] Figures 20-1 and 20-3 in Chapter 20 illustrate these changes through time.

In addition to changes in credit market conditions, the financial condition of the debt issuers also changes. Table 22-5 presents a transition matrix for bond quality ratings that documents changes in the issuers' status. The factors in Figure 22-1 and Table 22-5 interact to create a complex relationship between a corporate bond's yield to maturity, the quality rating of a corporate bond, and the probability that the bond's quality rating will change.

A Merrill Lynch vice president named Leland Crabbe is an analyst who formulates corporate bond strategies. After analyzing years of shifting risk-return relationships like those illustrated in Figure 22-1, Mr. Crabbe in 1994 hypothesized that the **corporate credit curves** in Figure 22-2 represented equilibrium credit spreads toward which the bond market tended at that time. He and some other corporate bond traders use the yield curve for U.S. Treasury bonds as a foundation; they add the corporate credit spreads like those illustrated in Figure 22-2 to the U.S. Treasury bond yield curve, consider a transition matrix like the one in Table 22-5 to provide an allowance for credit rating migration, and consider other factors as well as they devise corporate bond trading strategies. To maximize the likelihood of profitable trading, the Treasury yield curve, corporate credit spreads, and transition probabilities must all be updated continuously.

Some bond investors and speculators interested in profiting from the price movements of bonds invest in high-yield (junk, speculative) bonds. Even without a credit event, the prices of junk bonds can gyrate in a manner that attracts ambitious speculators.

TABLE 22-4   Average YTMs for Bonds with Different Quality Ratings over Various Sample Periods

Bond Index	1955–69 Average YTM	1970–79 Average YTM	1980–89 Average YTM	1990–99 Average YTM
Long-term U.S. Treasury bonds	4.1%	7.3%	10.6%	7.0%
AAA corporate bonds	4.6	8.2	11.1	7.1
AA corporate bonds	4.7	8.4	11.5	7.2
A corporate bonds	4.8	8.6	11.8	7.4
BBB corporate bonds	5.3	9.2	12.4	7.9

SOURCE: *Standard & Poor's Trade and Securities Statistics.*

FIGURE 22-1   The Risk Structure of Corporate Bonds YTMs Fluctuates with Credit Market Conditions

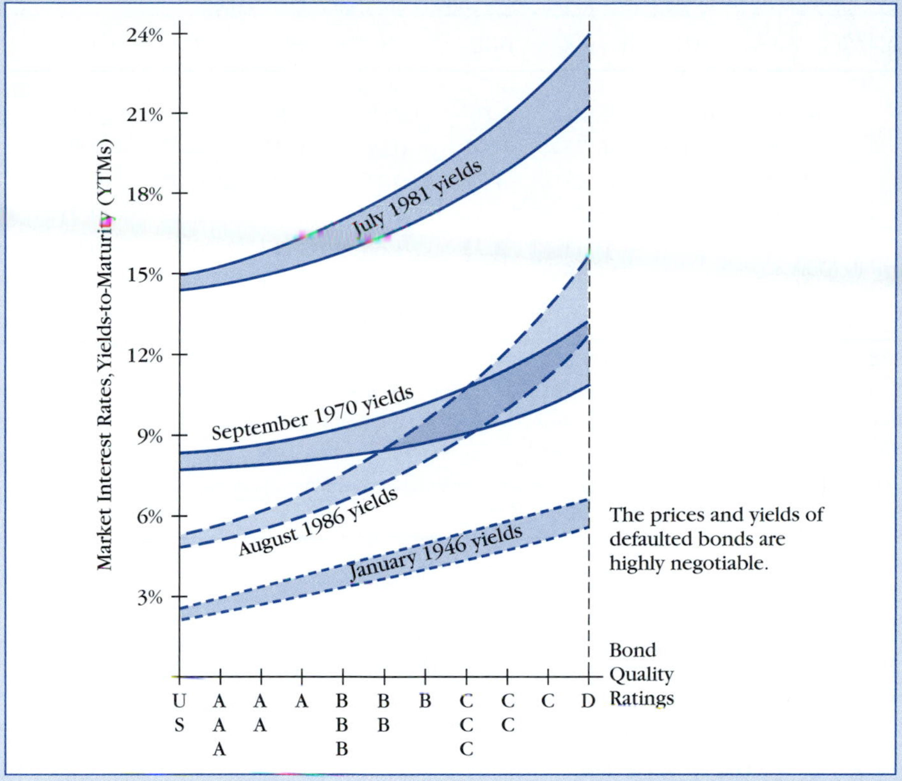

The level and structure (yield curve) for default-free U.S. Treasury bonds is always changing. The credit spreads (default risk premiums, yield spreads) that are added to the underlying default-free interest rates fluctuate, too. In spite of these constant changes, investors always demand higher market interest rates (yields-to-maturity) from bonds that are more likely to default.

Junk Bond Investing

Prior to 1977, respectable investment banking firms refused to underwrite issues of junk bonds. When an issuer of investment grade bonds fell on hard times and its bond ratings dropped below the BBB level, the bonds were called *fallen angels.* A bond trader at Drexel Burnham Lambert named Michael Milken altered this snobby behavior by starting to underwrite *original-issue junk.* More than any other single person, Milken created the junk bond industry. Milken's junk bond public offerings of junk bonds were so profitable that, almost singlehandedly, his operations propelled the growth of Drexel Burnham Lambert from a lackluster brokerage in the 1970s to a large and respectable investment banking firm in the 1980s. Drexel was paying Milken millions of dollars per week when they fired him in 1989 because government lawyers sued him for failure to disclose adequate information. Without Milken, Drexel Burnham Lambert soon went bankrupt. By that time even the most elite investment banking firms were underwriting original issue junk. Thanks to Mike Milken, the total dollar value of all junk bond issues in 1986 was about 20% of the aggregate value of all corporate bond issues underwritten that year.[6]

TABLE 22-5   Average 1-Year Transition Rates (in %) for Corporate Bond Rating Migrations Between Different Quality Categories, Averaged over 1981–99

Initial rating:	AAA	AA	A	BBB	BB	BB	C	D	NR[a]
AAA	89.61	6.61	0.40	0.10	0.03	0.00	0.00	0.00	3.24
AA	0.58	88.65	6.55	0.61	0.05	0.11	0.02	0.01	3.42
A	0.06	2.28	87.48	4.72	0.47	0.21	0.01	0.04	4.73
BBB	0.03	0.24	5.05	83.04	4.33	0.80	0.12	0.21	6.18
BB	0.03	0.10	0.43	6.43	74.68	7.13	0.99	0.91	9.30
B	0.00	0.1l	0.28	0.49	5.36	73.81	3.48	5.16	11.33
CCC	0.14	0.00	0.28	1.12	1.54	9.13	53.09	20.93	13.76

[a]NR means Not Rated, because the rating was withdrawn.

S&P continually updates the probabilities that a bond issue begins and ends the year with any given pair of credit (quality, default) ratings. For instance, of the bonds that begin the year with a rating of A, on average, 87.48% will end that year with a rating of A.

SOURCE: Standard & Poor's, *Ratings Performance 1999: Stability and Transition,* New York City, February 2000, Table 8, p. 12.

FIGURE 22-2   Representative Credit Spreads Imposed over a Hypothetical U.S. Treasury Yield Curve That Is Flat 5%

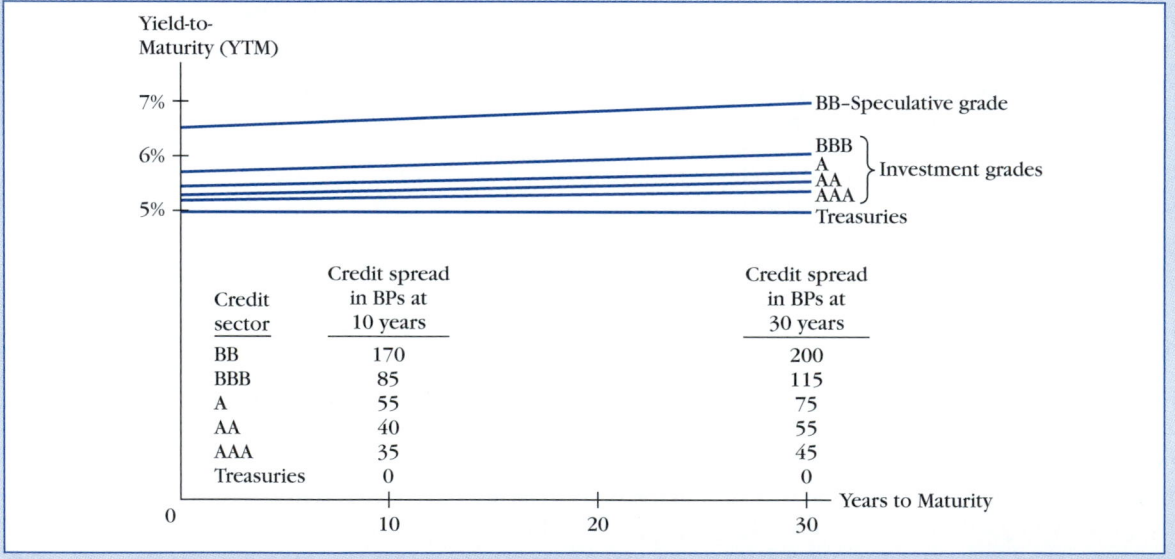

Credit spreads are yield spreads that measure market-determined default-risk premiums. Market interest rates (yields-to-maturity, YTMs) from speculative grade bonds exceed the YTMs from equal-maturity U.S. Treasury bonds more than the YTMs from investment grade bonds exceed the YTMs from equal-maturity U.S. Treasury bonds. Credit spreads widen at the longer maturities. Credit spreads open and close continuously.

SOURCE: Adapted from Leland E. Crabbe, "A Framework for Corporate Bond Strategy," Merrill Lynch, Global Fixed Income Research Department, New York City, September 16, 1994, Table 3. The article is reproduced in its entirety in *Chartered Financial Analysts Candidates Level III Readings,* a booklet published by the Association for Investment Management and Research, ISBN 1-879087-68-5, 1996, pp. 170–81.

It was difficult to adequately research junk bonds during the early 1980s because the junk bond industry was so new it had not generated sufficient data for in-depth investigations. When additional junk bond data accumulated and was investigated, the default rates turned out to be worse than originally believed. As shown in Table 22-6, over one-fifth of the junk bonds that are more than 8 years old default. Many of the junk bond issues that did not default early in their life are exchanged, as part of a corporate reorganization, for other securities that ultimately default. As a result, the cumulative default rates that a buy-and-hold investor could expect were considerably higher than the one-year default rates in Table 22-5.[7] Factors that influence an issuer's probability of default are reviewed in the following section.[8]

Using MDA to Discriminate Between Bankruptcy Candidates

It is costly for institutional investors to employ security analysts to periodically review numerous financial ratios from hundreds of companies; many automated the task to cut costs. This section presents a statistical tool called **multiple discriminant analysis** (MDA) that some institutional investors use to analyze the creditworthiness of thousands of companies frequently at modest cost. This application highlights the roles that both financial ratios and statistical analysis can play in credit analysis. A linear multiple discriminant analysis function of the general form shown below can be used to classify an observation on the basis of a set of associated independent variables, where $i = 1, 2, \ldots, N$ observations (firms).

$$Z_i = b_1 x_{1i} + b_2 x_{2i} + b_3 x_{3i} + b_4 x_{4i} + b_5 x_{5i}$$

The dependent variable Z in the MDA function takes on values that symbolize qualitative categories. If company i is bankrupt Z_i is set to zero, $Z_i = 0$, and $Z_i = 1$ represents a non-bankrupt firm. Ed Altman published a bankruptcy study that used MDA to analyze five financial ratios from N different companies.

TABLE 22-6   Cumulated Average Annual Default Rates for Corporate Bonds from Different Quality Rating Categories

Year	1	2	3	4	5	6	7	8	9	10	11	12	13	14	15
Investment Grade Bonds															
AAA	0.00	0.00	0.04	0.08	0.13	0.22	0.33	0.52	0.59	0.67	0.67	0.67	0.67	0.67	0.67
AA	0.01	0.04	0.11	0.21	0.33	0.49	0.64	0.76	0.84	0.90	0.94	0.98	0.98	0.98	0.98
A	0.04	0.11	0.18	0.31	0.47	0.63	0.82	1.02	1.25	1.48	1.68	1.78	1.84	1.88	1.92
BBB	0.21	0.48	0.77	1.28	1.81	2.34	2.73	3.09	3.37	3.63	3.81	3.94	4.09	4.20	4.27
Speculative Grade Bonds															
BB	0.91	2.82	5.00	7.04	8.82	10.68	11.71	12.78	13.71	14.42	15.19	15.55	15.84	15.84	15.84
B	5.16	10.90	15.36	18.60	20.95	22.65	24.08	25.32	26.29	27.13	27.54	27.76	27.83	27.83	27.83
CCC	20.93	28.04	33.35	36.83	40.67	41.83	42.64	42.86	43.63	44.23	44.23	44.23	44.23	44.23	44.23

More than 20% of all the bonds that were rated below BBB (junk bonds) that were more than 8 years old defaulted. Many of the junk bonds that did not default during the first 8 years after their issuance were exchanged, as part of a reorganization, for other securities that did default. As a result, cumulative default rates for a buy-and-hold investor were considerably higher than the 1-year default rates in Table 22-5.

SOURCE: Standard & Poor's, *Ratings Performance 2000: Stability In Transition,* February 2000, New York City, Table 3, p. 10.

Altman chose to discriminate between failed and nonfailed companies using the financial ratios shown in the MDA function at Eqn. 22-1:[9]

$$Z_i = 0.033 \left(\frac{\text{EBIT}}{\text{Total assets}} \right)_i + 0.999 \left(\frac{\text{Sales}}{\text{Assets}} \right)_i + 0.006 \left(\frac{\text{Aggregate market value of all equity}}{\text{Book value of debt}} \right)_i \quad \text{(22-1)}$$

$$+ \, 0.014 \left(\frac{\text{Retained earnings}}{\text{Total assets}} \right)_i + 0.012 \left(\frac{\text{Net working capital}}{\text{Total assets}} \right)_i + e_i$$

EBIT stands for earnings before interest and taxes, and e_i is an unexplained residual that has an expected value of zero, $E(e_i) = 0$. Using a sample of 33 bankrupt firms and 33 nonbankrupt firms, Altman was able to classify 52 of the 66 firms (52/66 = 79%) correctly.

The MDA function determines a Z-score for each firm based on the company's financial ratios in Eqn. 22-1. The average Z-score for the bankrupt firms in Altman's sample was $Z = -0.29$. The average value for nonbankrupt firms was $Z = 5.02$. Figure 22-3 suggests two normal probability distributions of Z-scores for bankrupt and nonbankrupt firms. These two probability distributions overlap slightly where MDA cannot discriminate and, as a result, some firms are misclassified.

Multiple discriminant analysis (MDA) can be viewed as a low-cost replacement for financial analysts. Alternatively, MDA may be used to supplement the work done by financial analysts.

Standard & Poor's uses human analysts to assign bond-quality ratings instead of statistical classification procedures. The next section reviews financial ratios that S&P financial analysts use to assign quality ratings to bond issues.

FIGURE 22-3   Probability Distributions of Z-Scores for Bankrupt and Nonbankrupt Firms

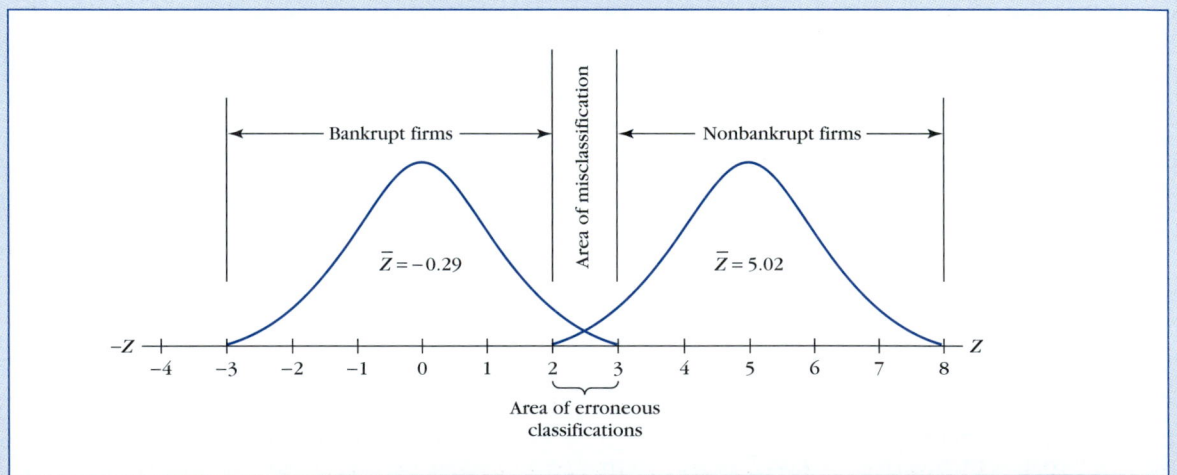

Altman's MDA function was used to compute Z-scores for each firm based on the companies' financial ratios. The average Z-score for the bankrupt firms was $Z = -0.29$ and for nonbankrupt firms the average was $Z = 5.02$. The figure suggests two separate normal probability distributions of Z-scores for bankrupt and nonbankrupt firms. When MDA cannot discriminate between the bankrupt and nonbankrupt firms these two probability distributions overlap and some firms are misclassified.

FINANCIAL RATIOS HELP DETERMINE BOND QUALITY RATINGS

The three most important categories of information considered when a credit analyst assigns a quality rating to a bond issue are:

- The level and trend of the issuer's financial ratios[10]
- The issuer's significance and size
- The protective provisions in the indenture contract that establish the terms of the bond issue

Later discussions consider the way the issuer's significance and size impact its credit risk and review the way the issuer's protective provisions affect its credit risk. This section focuses on the way financial ratios like those explored in Chapter 4 are used to rate the quality of corporate bonds. Table 22-7 lists eight ratios that the Standard and Poor's Corporation

TABLE 22-7   Standard & Poor's Formulas for Eight Key Ratios

Two Coverage Ratios:

$$1. \text{ EBIT interest coverage} = \frac{\text{Earnings from continuing operations before interest and taxes}}{\text{Gross interest incurred before subtracting (1) capitalized interest and (2) interest income}}$$

$$2. \text{ EBITDA interest coverage} = \frac{\text{Earnings from continuing operations before interest, taxes, depreciation, and amortization}}{\text{Gross interest incurred before subtracting (1) capitalized interest and (2) interest income}}$$

Two Cash Flow Ratios:

$$3. \frac{\text{Funds from operations}}{\text{Total debt}} = \frac{\text{Net income from continuing operations + depreciation, Amortization, deferred income taxes, and other noncash items}}{\text{Long-term debt plus current maturities, commercial paper, and other short-term borrowings}}$$

$$4. \text{ Free operating cash flow/total debt} = \frac{\begin{array}{c}\text{Funds from operations} - \text{capital expenditures}, - (+) \\ \text{The increase (decrease) in working capital (excluding changes in cash,} \\ \text{marketable securities, and short-term debt)}\end{array}}{\text{Long-term debt plus current maturities, commercial paper, and other short-term borrowings}}$$

Two Profitability Ratios:

$$5. \text{ Pretax return on capital} = \frac{\text{Pretax income from continuing operations + interest expense}}{\begin{array}{c}\text{Sum of (1) average of beginning of year and end of year current} \\ \text{Maturities, long-term debt, noncurrent deferred taxes, and equity and} \\ \text{(2) average short-term borrowings during year as disclosed in footnotes}\end{array}}$$

$$6. \text{ Operating income/sales} = \frac{\begin{array}{c}\text{Sales minus cost of goods manufactured (before depreciation and amortization),} \\ \text{selling, general and administrative, and research and development costs}\end{array}}{\text{Sales}}$$

Two Financial Leverage Ratios:

$$7. \text{ Long-term debt/capitalization} = \frac{\text{Long-term debt}}{\text{Long-term debt + shareholders' equity (including preferred stock) plus minority interest}}$$

$$8. \frac{\text{Total debt}}{\text{Capitalization}} = \frac{\text{Long-term debt plus current maturities, commercial paper, and other short-term borrowings}}{\begin{array}{c}\text{Long-term debt plus current maturities, commercial paper, and other short-term borrowings} \\ \text{+ shareholders' equity (including preferred stock) plus minority interest}\end{array}}$$

SOURCE: Standard & Poor's, *Corporate Rating Criteria,* 1997, p. 114.

(S&P) uses in formulating its bond-rating criteria. Note that the first two ratios in the table are coverage ratios.

Coverage Ratios

Some bond analysts argue that the single most important category of financial ratios in determining the quality rating of an issue of corporate bonds is coverage ratios. As explained in Table 4–8 (p. 77), *coverage ratios* measure how many times the issuing company's earned income *covers* the interest charges and other costs related to a bond issue. At the simplest level, a coverage ratio of 1 indicates that the issuing firm has just enough income to pay its interest expense. This is important because it reflects the probability that the firm defaults on its interest payments. Table 22-8 summarizes guidelines a security analyst uses to evaluate coverage ratios.

Bond analysts consider not only the issuer's coverage ratios, but also the stability and trend of the issuer's earnings. An upward earnings trend suggests that better times may lie ahead. A flat trend portends little change. A downward trend may cause bond-raters to lower the bond issuer's quality ratings.

Coverage ratios may be calculated on either pretax or after-tax earnings. Some bond analysts include lease payments and sinking fund payments with interest payments and calculate a coverage ratio called the *times-fixed-charges-earned ratio.* This ratio produces lower values than the ratios in Table 22-8 because deducting lease and/or sinking fund payments lowers the ratio's value. When different versions of a ratio are encountered, compare them. Different variations of the same ratio can be useful. But only *consistently defined* ratios are comparable.

The top two lines of Table 22-9 show median values of the first two coverage ratios defined in Table 22-7. The numerical values in the table fluctuate through the years in a cyclical fashion as business activity alternates between recession and boom. Table 22-9 reveals important aspects of S&P's bond-rating criteria.

Cash Flow Ratios

As mentioned in Chapter 4, corporations generate **cash flows.** Bond analysts use a conservative definition of cash flows. First, a firm's after-tax earnings from continuing operations provide cash. Second, **depreciation** and **amortization** allocate the cost of the asset over its useful productive life; they do not represent actual cash outlays for repairs. Since depreciation and amortization are noncash expenses, they provide an additional source of cash.

TABLE 22-8   Coverage Ratios and Quality Ratings

Coverage Ratio	Stability of Earnings	Quality Rating
6 and over	Cyclical	Investment grade
4 and over	Stable	Investment grade
3 to 6	Cyclical	Medium grade
2 to 4	Stable	Medium grade
Under 3	Cyclical	Speculative grade
Under 2	Stable	Speculative grade

SOURCE: Jerome B. Cohen, Edward D. Zinbarg, and Arthur Zeikel, *Investment Analysis and Portfolio Management,* 4th ed. (Homewood, IL: Irwin, 1982), 481.

TABLE 22-9	Median Values of Eight Ratios for U.S. Issuers of Industrial Long-Term Debt That Are Rated by Standard & Poor's, 1994–96						
Name of Ratio (denomination)[a]	AAA	AA	A	BBB	BB	B
1 EBIT[b] interest coverage (times)	16.05	11.06	6.26	4.11	2.27	1.18
2 EBITDA[c] interest coverage (times)	20.3	14.94	8.51	6.03	3.63	2.27
3 Funds from operations/total debt (%)	116.4	72.3	47.5	34.7	18.4	10.9
4 Free operating cash flow/total debt (%)	76.8	30.5	18.8	8.4	2.4	1.2
5 Pretax return on capital (%)	31.5	23.6	19.5	15.1	11.9	9.1
6 Operating income/sales (%)	24.0	19.2	16.1	15.4	15.1	12.6
7 Long-term debt/capital (%)	13.4	21.9	32.7	43.4	53.9	65.9
8 Total debt/capitalization (%)	23.6	29.7	38.7	46.8	55.8	68.9

[a]See Table 22-7 for definitions of the ratios.
[b]EBIT stands for earnings before interest and taxes.
[c]EBITDA stands for earnings before interest, taxes, depreciation, and amortization.

SOURCE: Standard & Poor's, *Corporate Rating Criteria,* 1997, p. 112.

Ratio 3 in Tables 22-7 and 22-9 is found by totaling the two cash flow items immediately above and dividing this total cash flow by the firm's total debt. Solvency cannot be maintained in the long run unless this cash flow ratio has a value that exceeds the firm's average rate of interest expense.[*11] The fourth ratio in the tables is a cash flow ratio that is based on free cash flow (p. 68) instead of funds from operations.

Profitability Ratios

Bond raters and other credit analysts track the profitability of bond issuers because profitability is an indicator of a firm's health. The fifth ratio in Tables 22-7 and 22-9 is a profitability gauge called the *pretax rate-of-return on long-term capital ratio.* The sum of pretax income and interest expense in the numerator of the fifth ratio equals the total amount the firm has available to pay its interest expenses. The pretax return on capital ratio states this measure of the firm's income as a percentage of its permanent capital. The resulting ratio's value is useful for comparison with current interest rates. If the value of this ratio does not exceed current interest rates, the company is probably not earning enough to pay its interest expense—a condition that usually leads to low bond-quality ratings.

The operating-income-to-sales ratio, the sixth ratio in Tables 22-7 and 22-9, can reveal a weakness in a firm's earning power. As explained in Chapter 4, *operating income* is a firm's pretax earnings before depreciation and amortization expenses, selling and administrative expenses, and research and development costs are deducted to obtain the firm's taxable income. Dividing operating income by sales gives the percentage of every sales dollar available to pay overhead expenses and make a contribution to profit. If this ratio is relatively low, that usually means the firm should either raise its sales price per unit, cut its direct manufacturing (operating) costs, or both.

---

* Financial Accounting Board Statement No. 95 went into effect in 1988 and, for the first time, required businesses to include a Statement of Cash Flows (rather than merely a Statement of Changes in Financial Position) when issuing a complete set of financial statements.

Financial-Leverage Ratios

Companies that borrow funds are using *financial leverage*. If a firm uses too much financial leverage, its fixed interest expense will be so high that, if profits fall slightly, the firm might not earn enough to pay its contractual interest expense. This problem moves the troubled firm toward bankruptcy court, and it is the reason bond raters are interested in evaluating the indebtedness of issuing firms. The last two ratios in Tables 22-7 and 22-9 measure the bond issuer's financial leverage.

The *long-term debt-to-capitalization* ratio is calculated to determine what fraction of the firm's permanent capital might be due for immediate repayment. The words *capital* and *capitalization* refer to a firm's permanently committed capital funds. A conservative definition of the capitalization would be the sum of the firm's long-term debt, preferred stock, and stockholders' equity. A liberal definition of capital could also include the firm's permanently maintained current liabilities (continuously revolving accounts payable). The ratio of *total debt to capitalization* is a similar leverage ratio.

The absence of liquidity ratios and turnover ratios in Tables 22-7 and 22-9 does not detract from the usefulness of these ratios; rather, their absence suggests their indirect influence on bond quality ratings.[12] As mentioned, the economic significance and size of the issuing firm are also important determinants of credit risk.

THE ECONOMIC SIGNIFICANCE AND SIZE OF THE ISSUER

When credit analysts assess the financial condition of a security issuer, they consider more than the company's financial ratios. The issuing firm's size, its competition, its importance in its own industry, and related factors are also considered to evaluate its strengths and weaknesses.

The Issuer's Industry

To discern important facts about the industry in which a bond issuer operates, S&P bond analysts study several key points:[13]

1. **Position in the economy.** Is the firm in the capital-goods sector (such as machinery production), the consumer-durables sector (such as appliances or automobile production), or the consumer-nondurables sector (such as food manufacturing)?
2. **Life cycle of industry.** Is the industry (product) in a growth, stable, or declining phase?
3. **Competitive nature.** What is the nature and intensity of the competition in the industry? Is it on a regional, national, or international basis? Is the competition based on price, quality of product, distribution capabilities, public image, or some other factor? Is the industry regulated (as in broadcasting), which can provide some competitive protection?
4. **Labor situation.** Is the industry unionized? If so, are labor contracts negotiated on an industry-wide basis, and what is the recent negotiating history?
5. **Supply factors.** Does the industry generally have some control of its key raw materials, or is it dependent on questionable sources?
6. **Volatility.** Is there an involvement with rapidly developing or changing technologies? Is there a dependence upon a relatively small number of major contracts (as, for instance, is sometimes the case in the defense industry)?

7. **Major vulnerabilities.** Is the industry likely to be a prime target for some form of political pressure? Are substantial environmental expenditures likely to be incurred? Are near-term energy shortages possible? Does ease-of-entry create tough competition in the industry?

Answers to these questions inform the credit analyst about the industry's growth potential, problems that may plague the industry, and the stability of the industry's sales. The analyst can then move on to consider the issuer's competitive situation within its industry. The points must be investigated *in this order* for a meaningful evaluation.

The Issuer's Competitors

Key questions that S&P's bond raters consider when evaluating the competition that a bond issuer or other borrower faces are listed below. The questions are primarily about the *borrowing firm* in order to restrain the research from becoming an aimless and costly inquiry into endless details about each of the borrower's competitors. Research costs can be controlled by only inquiring into how the competition affects the *bond issuer.*

1. **Market share.** Does the company have a large enough portion of the market share (be it regional, national, or international) to influence industry dynamics significantly? This may be especially important in a market dominated by only a few producers. Does the company have the opportunity to exercise price leadership? Does the company offer a full range of products or have proprietary products or enjoy some special niche in the market?

2. **Technological leadership.** Is the company usually among the first with new developments, or is it typically a follower? How do research and development expenditures compare with the industry average?

3. **Production efficiency.** Is the company a relatively low-cost producer? Are its facilities newer or more advanced than the average? Is it more or less vertically integrated than the average? If mandated expenditures (such as for pollution control) are required, has the company already complied to a greater or lesser extent than its competitors? Does the company face any labor problems that are more onerous than its competitors?

4. **Financial structure.** How does a company's use of leverage and various types of financing vehicles compare with that of others in the industry?

After credit analysts answer these questions, they focus on the last phase of their analysis: studying the new issue's indenture contract. Credit analysts evaluate protective provisions designed to enhance the safety of an investment in the issuer's bonds.

PROTECTIVE PROVISIONS IN A CORPORATION'S INDENTURE

The *Trust Indenture Act of 1939* requires that U.S. bond investors' rights be spelled out in an **indenture contract** that accompanies every issue of corporate bonds. *Protective provisions* spelled out in the indenture can raise the quality rating for an issue by one, or occasionally two, letter grades if a strong bond issuer grants liberal protective provisions. These provisions are less important than the issuer's earning power, however. All the protective provisions in the world will not garner a high quality rating for a firm that faces future losses.

Bond issuers commonly provide the following types of protective provisions to ensure the safety of the bondholder's investment:

1. The issuer pledges specific assets as collateral.
2. The issuer subordinates competing legal claims on its assets and/or income.
3. The issuer provides a sinking fund to ensure that the bonds are paid off as promised.
4. The issuing firm's management promises to operate the firm in ways that will protect the bondholders.

Bank loan applicants are sometimes asked to give the lending bank similar protective provisions in writing to obtain the desired loan—especially if the credit is long-term. Let us consider these provisions in more detail.

Collateral Provisions

A **collateral provision** in a bond indenture specifies that certain assets owned by the bond issuer become the property of the bond investors if the issuer defaults on the bond issue's interest or principal payments. Many bond issues have no collateral provision. If all other factors are equal, bond issues that provide collateral are rated approximately one letter grade higher—if the collateral is in good condition and is marketable.

Debentures are bonds that have no assets pledged (zero collateral). If the bond issuer goes bankrupt, debenture owners become *general creditors.* As Table 22–10 suggests, it is common for general creditors to be repaid only about 38% of every dollar owed when a bankruptcy settles. To avoid this risk investors can buy mortgage bonds, for example, to obtain a collateralized investment. Mortgage bonds have a prior claim on specific collateral in the event of bankruptcy.

Collateral is not provided to investors for free. A collateral provision increases the credit's market price slightly, and it lowers the credit's market interest rate (effective rate of return) correspondingly. So, by investing in collateralized bonds, the investor gives up some cash in order to get more safety—a risk-return tradeoff.

Subordination Provisions

To make safety-conscious (highly risk-averse) investors more willing to buy bonds, the indenture can include a *subordination clause* that places other bond issues or specified creditors in an inferior (junior, lower-priority) legal position with respect to claims on the bond issuer's assets if the issuer defaults.

The *after-acquired property clause* is an example of a subordination clause. This clause states that if the bond issuer acquires additional assets after a first mortgage bond (or other collateralized bond) is outstanding, the new assets will automatically become part of the collateral pledged to support the first mortgage bond's. Such a clause increases the first mortgage bondholders' collateral if the firm acquires newer assets against which the first mortgage bond owners hold no explicit claim.

Sinking-Fund Provisions

A sinking-fund provision requires the bond issuer to make scheduled payments into a **sinking fund.** Sinking-fund provisions typically require that the issuer's sinking-fund deposits be held by a third party (such as a commercial bank) that uses the funds to repurchase the issuer's outstanding bonds or preferred stock.

A sinking fund assures bondholders that their chances for repayment increase with the passage of time. After a number of years' sinking-fund payments have been used to retire some of the issuer's outstanding bonds, bond rating agencies may acknowledge these pre-

TABLE 22-10	Average Recovery Rates for Defaulted Bonds Categorized by Seniority and Collateral	
Seniority Class	Mean Recovery Rate, %	Standard Deviation, %
Senior secured	53.80%	26.86%
Senior unsecured	51.13%	25.45%
Senior subordinated	38.52%	23.81%
Subordinated	32.74%	20.18%
Junior subordinated	17.09%	10.90%

SOURCE: Lea V. Carty and Dana Lieberman, "Defaulted Bank Loan Recoveries," Moody's Investors Service, Global Credit Research, Special Report November 1996.

maturity bond purchases by raising the issue's quality rating. An improved quality rating increases the bond's market price.*

Recovery risk is the risk that an investor will not be able to recover the full face value of an investment from the obligor if the obligor defaults on the obligation. The **recovery rate** is the percentage of an asset's face value that a creditor recovers after it defaults. After a credit defaults, the recovery rate depends on the seniority and collateral supporting the credit. Table 22-10 summarizes the recovery rates that occurred under various protective provisions and, essentially, quantifies the effectiveness of the protective provisions. The recovery rates are averages tallied over hundreds of different defaulted bond issues.

Other Protective Provisions

Some indenture contracts forbid the issuer to sell off assets in order to lease them back. **Sale-and-leaseback agreements** free capital invested in plant and equipment so the capital may be spent. Meanwhile, the use of the asset is assured because the seller of the asset contracts to rent it as part of the agreement. Bondholders want provisions against sale-and-leaseback agreements that (a) deplete the borrower's assets available to serve as collateral, and/or (b) encumber future cash flows with contractual lease payments.

Debt test clauses are common in speculative-grade bonds. These provisions constrain the issuer's ability to create additional debt and thereby protect bondholders in two ways. First, they limit the issuer's ability to undertake rapid expansion, which is a risky undertaking. Second, if the issuer should go bankrupt, such clauses limit the number of creditors that are competing for the remaining assets.

Negative pledge clauses limit the issuer's ability to pledge assets as collateral for any future borrowings. This protects existing creditors from the possibility of competing with bankruptcy claims that might arise from future issues of collateralized bonds.

Prohibitions against the sale of subsidiary corporations allow the issuer to sell major subsidiaries only if they use the proceeds to repay previously outstanding debt. This protects creditors from losing important sources of income or collateral the borrower's subsidiaries might possess.

---

* A sinking fund can work to the detriment of unsuspecting bondholders in two significant respects. First, some sinking-fund provisions provide that bonds may be redeemed at stipulated dates or by random selection before the issue matures. Thus, an investor may have gone to the trouble of evaluating a bond issue and purchasing a bond at what is considered to be an attractive yield-to-maturity (YTM) only to have the investment called away by a sinking fund prematurely. Second, issues with sinking funds pay lower yields because they offer their bondholders greater safety. This is another example of a risk-return tradeoff.

Other Protective Devices

High and volatile interest rates spawned a wide variety of protective devices. Some of the better known devices include:

1. *Zero coupon bonds* that protect bond investors from reinvestment risk.
2. *Put bonds* contain embedded put options allowing the bonds' owners to put the bond back to the borrower at a preset price, if that should become advantageous for the creditor.
3. *Foreign-currency bonds* are issued in the United States, but they pay coupons and/or principal in a foreign currency to protect overseas investors from foreign exchange risk or avoid certain kinds of governmental intervention.
4. *Adjustable-rate bonds,* also called *floating-rate bonds,* pay a coupon that is indexed to some economic benchmark. For instance, a commercial bank that issued AA-rated floating rate bonds might index these bonds to pay a coupon rate that is reset every 6 months to 30 basis points above the 3-month T-bill rate.*[14]
5. *Inflation-linked bonds* are issued by the U.S., British, and other federal governments. The coupons and/or principal of these bonds is linked to a price level index to protect the investors from purchasing power risk.

It should now be apparent that an almost unlimited variety of provisions can be inserted into a bond's indenture.[15] The ingenuity with which risk-averse creditors encumber borrowers is refreshing. But nothing is given away for free. Every protective provision bondholders obtain tends to reduce the rate of return they can expect from their bonds. There are rare exceptions to this rule, but the natural economic order requires a tradeoff of risk for return.

CREDIT RISK AND QUALITY RATING CHANGES

The data in Table 22-1 shows how the Boston Chicken Corporation's bond-quality ratings, bond prices, and stock prices all declined as the firm moved toward bankruptcy during 1997–98. The data in Table 22-1 suggest that investors in a deteriorating corporation should be able to manage their losses by observing the falling quality ratings and selling their securities before the firm goes bankrupt. This next section reviews the timing of security price movements for corporations that experience bond rating changes.

Weinstein Analyzes Bond Rating Changes. Mark Weinstein analyzed the monthly market price changes of 132 different bond rating changes.[16] Weinstein studied bond prices to determine if they reacted to quality-rating changes with a lead, a lag, or a combination of leads and lags or if they reacted at all. Weinstein reported that (1) bond prices experienced a statistically insignificant price reaction during the month in which their rating was changed, and (2) bond prices accomplished most of their price reaction to a rating change during the year *preceding* the announcement of the rating change. Stated differently, it appears that Standard & Poor's and Moody's quality-rating changes follow rather than lead the movements in bond prices. The implication of this finding is that credit analysts and bond investors should consider doing their own financial research rather than relying on the bond quality ratings from Moody's or S&P.

---

* Adjustable-rate bonds involve some interesting possibilities because, for instance, if the financial condition of an AA-grade issuing bank deteriorated sufficiently for its floating-rate bonds to be downgraded to A-grade, then the bond market might expect 50 basis points over the 3-month T-bill rate from this issue. As a result, the A-rated bonds would sell at a discount unless the bank's financial condition improved.

Stock Price Reactions to Bond Reratings. Paul A. Griffin and Antonio Z. Sanvicente (GS hereafter) analyzed 63 downgradings and 65 upgradings of bond ratings in order to estimate the impact of these changes on the market prices of the corporations' common stock.[17] GS analyzed the stock prices' monthly rates of return to detect unusual common stock returns associated with the change in the corporations' bond ratings.

GS reported that: (1) corporations' stock prices did experience statistically significant price reactions to quality rating migrations in bonds issued by the same corporation, (2) most of the stock price reaction occurred in the 11 months prior to the announcement of the bond rating change, and (3) the stock price reactions in the month that the rating change occurred were only marginally significant. In other words, GS report that Weinstein's bond research findings are supported by their stock price data.

Hand, Holthausen, and Leftwich (HHL). More recently, John Hand, Robert Holthausen, and Richard Leftwich (HHL) analyzed daily excess bond returns associated with forecasts in S&P's Credit Watch List, which forewarns of bond upgradings and downgradings that appear likely.[18] Average bond price changes of -1.39% for downgrades and $+2.25\%$ for upgrades were associated with S&P's and Moody's ratings changes at the time these changes received advance warning in the Credit Watch. Excluding reratings that were accompanied by forewarnings in the Credit Watch from their sample decreased the average price changes. The prices of investment-grade bonds reacted to rating changes less than the prices of speculative grade bonds. The stock price changes associated with bond rating changes were found to be similar in size to the bond price changes for bond downgrades, but smaller for bond upgrades. HHL's finding that news warnings about rating changes caused larger price changes than the actual bond rating changes is noteworthy.

Anticipatory Prices. Weinstein; Pinches and Singleton;[19] Griffin and Sanvicente; and Hand, Holthausen and Leftwich reported that adjustments in the prices of bonds and stocks issued by companies experiencing bond quality rating changes occurred *before* the rating change. In other words, the security prices tend to *anticipate* the announcement of a rating change. This anticipatory price behavior is the result of aggressive security analysis work.

Goh and Ederington (GE). Studies reporting negative stock price moves in response to downgrading the issuer's bonds motivated Goh and Ederington (GE) to investigate whether these negative stock price reactions should be expected for all bond downgradings, or only some.[20] GE reported different stock price reactions from bond downgradings that occurred for various reasons. Some rating changes are anticipated by market participants and those anticipations shape the way the stock price reacts to the downgrading. GE report that downgrades associated with deteriorating financial prospects convey new negative information to the capital market, but that downgrades due to changes in firms' leverage do not.

Datta, Datta, and Patel on IPOs. Sudip Datta, Mai Iskandar Datta, and Ajay Patel (DDP) examined initial trading day and after-market price performance of corporate bond offerings.[21] They find that initial public offerings (IPOs) of speculative grade bonds tend to be underpriced like equity IPOs. In contrast, investment grade bonds tend to be overpriced. IPOs of investment grade debt are typically issued by exchange listed firms and underwritten by prestigious investment banking firms. The less glamorous junk bonds are typically issued by over-the-counter firms and are likely to be handled by less prestigious underwriters. DDP's analysis reveals that bond rating, the market listing of the issuer, and the prestige of the investment banker are significant determinants of the returns from bond IPOs.

Hite and Warga. Gailen Hite and Arthur Warga (HW) examined 1,200 upgrades and downgrades from the 1985 through 1995.[22] They report that (1) bond prices experience larger

price adjustments when downgraded than they do from an upgrade, (2) upgrades into the investment grade category and downgrades that remove the bond from the investment grade category are more significant than other rating changes, (3) samples of rating changes that are not contaminated by other rating changes within 6 months reveal that the market reacts reliably as much as 6 months before the rating change and continues to react for 6 months after the rating change in the anticipated direction, and (4) although a split rating occurs occasionally, Moody's and S&P tend to rate bonds similarly.

The previous studies indicate that bond quality rating services do not provide as much information as credit investors need. Furthermore, the rating changes generally follow, rather than lead, the changes in the bond issuers that caused the bond rating changes. In response, credit investors developed new tools to analyze credit migration.

ANALYSIS OF RATING MIGRATION RISK

Figure 22-4 illustrates three bonds experiencing credit quality migration. Risk managers sometimes assess price volatility by using a statistic called **value-at-risk,** or simply **VaR.** VaR is a measure of the maximum potential change in value that will occur over a specified time horizon with some prespecified confidence level (probability).[23] The time horizon used in preparing VaR estimates may be a trading day, a month, or a year. Let us consider the variance in value computations for a bond.

A BBB-Grade Bond's Variance in Value

Assume the BBB-grade bond in Figure 22-4 is a 5-year bond with a 6% coupon rate. This bond will pay four annual coupons of $6 before it matures and repays its principal plus the fifth (last) coupon. The five annual discount rates for each of the eight different quality ratings should be obtained from the eight corporate bond yield curves and used to compute the present values of the BBB-grade bond's probabilistic cash flows. These present values and the probabilities for each of the eight possible quality outcomes are shown in Table 22-11. Figure 22-5 illustrates eight probabilistic bond values for a 1-year analysis of the BBB-grade bond's rating possibilities.

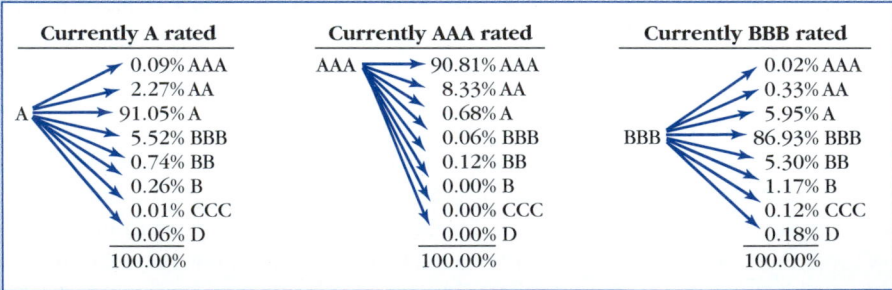

FIGURE 22-4 Three Examples of Credit Quality Migration over a 1-Year Risk Horizon

The credit-rating agencies can revise the credit-quality rating of a bond issuer or other borrower at any time. Large revisions are less likely than small credit migrations. The most likely outcome is no change.

SOURCE: J. P. Morgan, *CreditMetrics—Technical Document,* New York, April 2, 1997, p. 24, Chart 2.2. Reproduced with written permission.

TABLE 22-11   Computation of Variance in Value Due to a BBB-Grade Bond's Rating Migration over a 1-Year Horizon

$$VAR(PV) = \sum_{Rating=1}^{8} (1/8)(PV - E[PV])^2$$

Year-End Quality Rating	Probability of State (%)	New Bond Value plus Coupon ($)	Probability Weighted Value ($)	Difference of Value from Mean ($)	Probability Weighted–Difference Squared
AAA	0.02	109.37	0.02	2.28	0.001
AA	0.33	109.19	0.36	2.1	0.0146
A	5.95	108.66	6.47	1.57	0.1474
BBB	86.93	107.55	93.49	0.46	0.1853
BB	5.30	102.02	5.41	(5.06)	1.3592
B	1.17	98.10	1.15	(8.99)	0.9446
CCC	0.12	83.64	1.10	(23.45)	0.6598
Default	0.18	51.13	0.09	(55.96)	5.6358
			Mean = $107.09		Variance = 8.9477
					Standard deviation = $2.99

Computation of the standard deviation in value for the BBB-grade bond is based on the bond's annual cash flows under each scenario, separate yield curves for the eight credit quality ratings that are possible, and the probabilities for each of the eight quality ratings. J. P. Morgan's CreditMetrics maintains and continually updates this information in a databank for numerous bonds.

SOURCE: J. P. Morgan, *CreditMetrics—Technical Document,* New York, April 2,1997, p. 28, Chart 2.5. Reproduced with written permission.

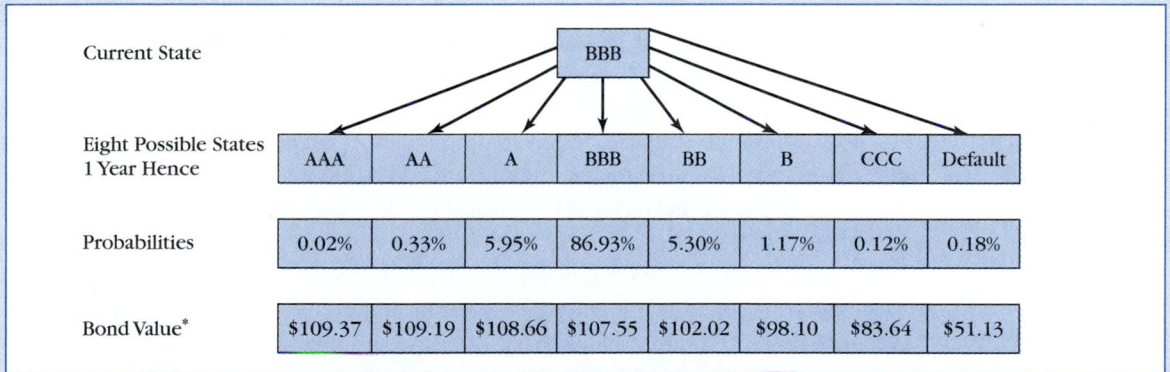

FIGURE 22-5   Probabilistic Values for BBB Bond over 1-Year Risk Horizon

CreditMetrics computed the eight bond values in Table 22-11 with a separate yield curve for the stream of cash flows that are expected in each state. This illustration summarizes possible rating migrations and their probabilities from Table 22-11.

[a]CreditMetrics computes each of the eight present values with a different yield curve that is appropriate for the cash flows that occur in that state.

Credit Derivatives Usually Have Skewed Probability Distributions

Figure 22-6 illustrates the probability distribution for the BBB-grade bond's eight possible outcomes. Unlike bond returns, stock market returns are normally distributed in a symmetric bell-shaped curve that is fully described by the mean and variance. Figure 22-6A and B contrasts credit-risk outcomes that are typically skewed to the left with the normal probability distribution from a common stock.

Security designers and credit-risk managers have developed tools to manage portfolios of credit instruments that have skewed probability distributions.

Analyzing a Portfolio of Credit Derivatives

Most portfolios benefit from risk-reducing diversification. Diversification also reduces credit risk. But the Markowitz portfolio-analysis model must be extended to embrace the characteristics of credit derivatives.

Portfolios of credit derivatives typically include a number of individual probability distributions that are negatively skewed. Powerful theorems from mathematical statistics called the Law of Large Numbers and the Central Limit Theorem show how this asymmetry is reduced in a diversified portfolio. Figure 28-7A in Chapter 28 (p. 841) utilizes Pascal's triangle to intuitively show how a basic random variable that is not symmetrically distributed becomes normally distributed. But some asymmetry can still remain to complicate portfolio analysis and make measuring a portfolio's dollar values problematical.

Some of the probability distributions of the underlying credit derivatives are continuous and some are discrete. Credit-risk managers have developed unique formulas to measure the needed statistics. Such formulas make it possible to compute the mean and variance of a portfolio of credit derivatives.[24] But asymmetric probability distributions require the formulation of new investment selection techniques.

THE BOTTOM LINE

When valuing a bond it is difficult to determine the value of the discount rate. Bond quality ratings can be helpful in determining an appropriate value for the discount rate. Standard and Poor's and other bond-rating services use financial ratios like those in Table 22-9 to aid them in assigning a quality rating to a bond issue. Protective provisions in the bond issue's indenture and the issuer's size and economic significance are also considered when assigning credit ratings and determining the appropriate discount rate.

The relationship between the appropriate discount rate and a bond's quality rating changes continuously through time, as shown in Figures 22-1 and 22-2. Continuously changing Federal Reserve monetary policies, U.S. Treasury fiscal policies, the supply and demand for loanable funds, and many other factors cause the credit markets to fluctuate constantly. Nevertheless, the risk-return relationship is always positive.

Bond ratings purveyed by services like Fitch IBCA, Standard and Poor's, and, Moody's are validated by (1) market data which shows that the highest-grade bonds offer the lowest market-interest rates, (2) the fact that bond-quality ratings are written into the investment guidelines handed down by most state governments and the U.S. federal government, and, (3) bond issuers pay thousands of dollars annually to have their bonds rated by the financial service corporations.

Empirical evidence raised some questions about whether the bond ratings determined the market yields, or whether the reverse is true. Stock and bond price movements that anticipate quality-rating changes suggest that the market prices sometimes guide the rating agencies in determining quality ratings.

FIGURE 22-6   Two Different Probability Distributions; (A) Probability
Distribution of Values for BBB-Grade Bond and
(B) Comparing Normal Probability Distribution with a
Credit Derivative's Skewed Probability Distribution

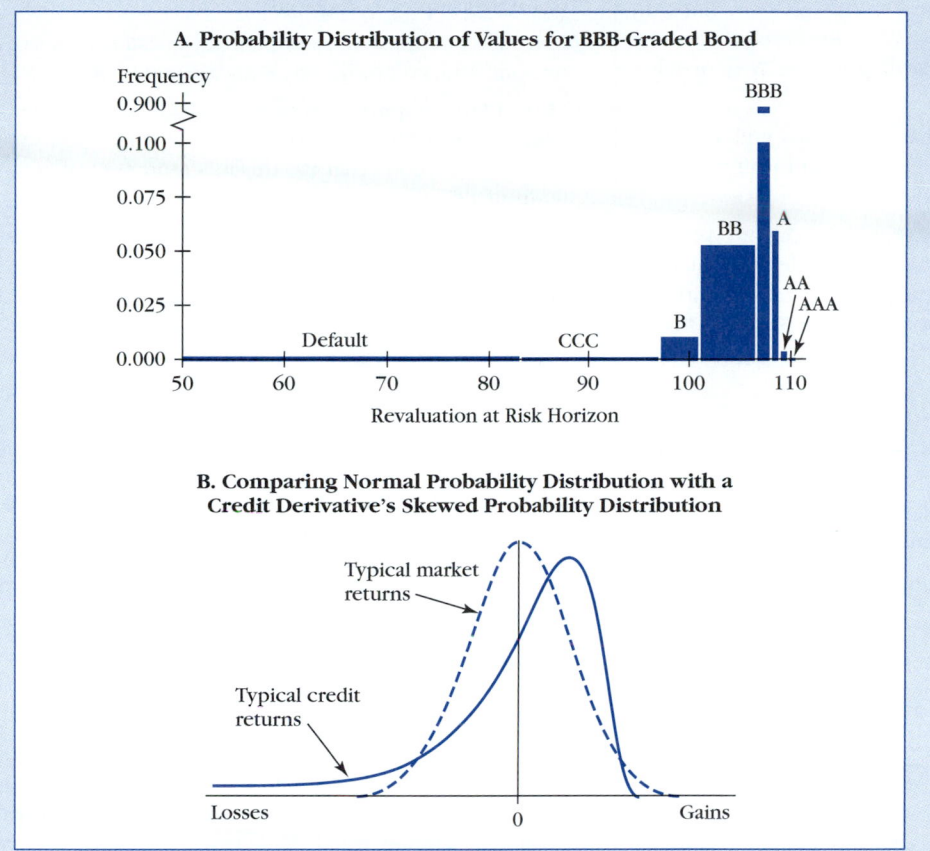

A. Probability Distribution of Values for BBB-Graded Bond

**B. Comparing Normal Probability Distribution with a
Credit Derivative's Skewed Probability Distribution**

Credit-risk outcomes are typically skewed to the left (negatively skewed), as shown in
(A). (B) contrasts the more typical symmetric probability distribution of stock market
returns that can be adequately described by their mean and variance with the
asymmetric (negatively skewed) probability distribution of bond values.

SOURCE: J. P. Morgan, *CreditMetrics—Technical Document,* New York, April 2,1997, Charts
1.1 and 1.2, pp. 7, 11. Reproduced with written permission.

Inadequate information provided by credit rating services like Moody's, Fitch IBCA, and,
Standard and Poor's motivated other financial service providers to create additional tools to
analyze credit risk. For example, the J. P. Morgan Company in New York City has developed
CreditMetrics and the KMV Corporation in San Francisco has created the Credit Monitor to
analyze credit migration.

QUESTIONS

Q22-1   (Sinking funds) Compare and contrast investing in
home mortgages to investing in collateralized bonds with a
sinking fund.

Q22-2   (Bond ratings) Weinstein's study of bond price movements showed that gains could be earned by buying corporate bonds on the day their quality rating was upgraded.
True, false, or uncertain? Explain.

Q22-3 (Bond ratings) Why might you (or Professors Griffin and Sanvicente) suspect that when a corporation has its bond rating changed this event might affect the market price of its common stock?

Q22-4 (Bond ratings) Do you think that bond rating agencies like Standard & Poor's and Moody's give any heed to the monetary policies of the Federal Reserve when they assign quality ratings to outstanding issues? Why or why not?

Q22-5 (Bankruptcy) Under what conditions will an insolvent firm avoid bankruptcy? Will a bankrupt firm necessarily be liquidated? Why or why not?

Q22-6 (Agency conflicts) In Chapter 3, the DuPont Analysis was introduced. An examination of it revealed that, all else equal, a firm's return on equity will be increased with an increase in the amount of debt a firm uses. Suppose that a firm's management does just that—issues new debt of the same seniority as existing debt—in order to increase the return on equity. Who are the winners and who are the losers in this scenario? Explain.

Q22-7 (Bankruptcy law) What are the priority of claims when bankruptcy is declared?

Q22-8 (S&P ratings) What are the key questions considered by bond raters employed by Standard and Poor's?

Q22-9 (After-acquired property clause) Explain what the after-acquired property clause is. How would you expect the yield on a bond that has this indenture provision to differ from a similar bond without such a provision?

Q22-10 (Bond provisions) Put bonds gained in popularity in the early 1980s. Consider the risk-return tradeoff and discuss why the put bond's attractiveness increased during this time period.

PROBLEMS

P22-1 (Priority claims) The Treadwater Corporation has the following existing capital structure:

Liabilities and Equity Claims	Book Value
Secured bondholders	$ 60,000,000
General unsecured creditors	$ 40,000,000
Preferred stockholders	$ 50,000,000
Common stockholders	$100,000,000
Total claims	$250,000,000

The trustee for the bankruptcy reorganization plan has valued Treadwater as a going concern at $150 million and has proposed the following new capital structure for the reorganized firm:

Debentures	$ 40,000,000
Subordinated debentures	$ 40,000,000
Preferred stock	$ 20,000,000
Common stock	$ 50,000,000
Total	$150,000,000

Assuming the court accepts this plan, how will the new securities be distributed among the old security holders?

P22-2 (Priority claims) The following information is found on the balance sheet of the Tipler Corporation:

	Book Value
Assets	$30,000,000
Liabilities	
Notes payable to banks	$10,000,000
Subordinated notes	$ 5,000,000
General creditors	$ 7,000,000
Total liabilities	$22,000,000
Common stockholders equity	$ 8,000,000

The notes are subordinated to the bank loan. Tipler's value as a going concern has been estimated to be $5 million. What will each class of creditor and the stockholders receive if the firm's assets are liquidated for $15 million?

P22-3 (Priority claims) Using the information provided for the Tipler Corporation in Problem 22-2, determine what each class of creditors and the stockholders would receive if the firm's assets are liquidated for $25 million.

P22-4 (Value-at-risk) A certain A-rated bond has 3 years to maturity and pays a 9% coupon annually. Annual discount rates for eight different quality ratings have been obtained from the corporate bond yield curves associated with each rating level, and are as follows:

Rating	Year 1	Year 2	Year 3
AAA	6.0%	6.5%	6.8%
AA	6.3%	6.8%	7.1%
A	6.8%	7.3%	7.6%
BBB	7.3%	7.8%	8.1%
BB	10.0%	10.5%	11.0%
B	12.0%	12.8%	13.5%
CCC	15.0%	16.0%	17.5%
Default	20.0%	25.0%	30.0%

Additionally, the following probabilities have been assigned to each of the following ratings for the A-rated bond:

Rating	Probability
AAA	0.0005
AA	0.0155
A	0.8500
BBB	0.1320
BB	0.0010
B	0.0006
CCC	0.0003
Default	0.0001
	1.0000

Calculate the variance in value due to the A-grade bond's credit-quality rating migration.

P22-5 (Credit-rating changes and bond prices) Assume that the A-rated bond described in Problem 22-4 was downgraded to a BBB-rating at the end of the first year. Assume, also, that the term structure provided in Problem 22-4 remains the same. At what price would you expect the bond to sell at the end of Year 1?

P22-6 (Altman's Z-score) The following balance sheet and income statement information is provided for the Roche-Haight Corporation:

Sales	$40,000,000
EBIT	$ 4,000,000
Net income	$ 3,000,000
Current assets	$ 5,000,000
Total assets	$25,000,000
Current liabilities	$ 3,000,000
Long-term debt	$11,000,000
Common stock	$ 5,000,000
Retained earnings	$ 6,000,000

There are 3 million shares of common stock outstanding with a market price of $12 a share. Calculate the Z-score for Roche-Haight. Based on your answer, how would you assess the likelihood that Roche-Haight will become insolvent? *Computational hint:* When calculating the Z-score, use percentages without the percentage sign attached. For example, if a certain ratio is 20%, use 20 in your calculation rather than 20% or 0.20.

P22-7 (Altman's Z-score) The table below contains five ratios describing the financial conditions of the Bain Corporation, Smith Incorporated, and Upson Limited Company. Insert these ratio values into Altman's multiple discriminant analysis (MDA) model (Eqn. 22-1) to compute a Z-score for each firm. Which, if any, of the three firms do you predict will go bankrupt? (Use the criteria illustrated in Figure 22-3.) *Computational hint:* When calculating the Z-score, use the percentage terms as numbers without the percentage signs attached. For example, use 41 in the MDA equation instead of 41% or 0.41 to compute the Z-score.

Ratio	Bain	Smith	Upson
Working capital/			
Total assets	− 6%	41%	10%
Retained earnings/			
Total assets	−63%	36%	14%
EBIT/Total assets	−32%	15%	−20%
Equity market			
value/Book value			
of total liabilities	40%	248%	150%
Sales/Total assets	1.5 times	1.9 times	1.7 times
Z-score	?	?	?

The following information on Pioneer Manufacturing Corporation is provided for Problems 22-8 through 22-10:

Pioneer Manufacturing Corporation
Income Statement
for the year ending December 31, 20XX

Revenues	$150,000,000
Depreciation and amortization	1,200,000
Other operating expenses	136,000,000
EBIT	$ 12,800,000
Interest expense	1,650,000
Earnings before tax	$ 11,150,000
Tax (@ 34%)	3,791,000
Net income	$ 7,359,000

Pioneer Manufacturing Corporation
Balance Sheet
as of December 31, 20XX

Cash and cash equivalents	$25,500,000
Accounts receivables	15,000,000
Inventories	11,200,000
Other current assets	8,300,000
Total current assets	$60,000,000
Net fixed assets	7,000,000
Total assets	$67,000,000
Accounts payable	$10,000,000
Notes payable	3,550,000
Other current liabilities	8,000,000
Total current liabilities	$21,550,000
Long-term debt	16,000,000
Total liabilities	$37,550,000
Common equity	$29,450,000
Total liabilities and equity	$67,000,000

P22-8 (Coverage ratios) Calculate Pioneer's EBIT interest coverage ratio and its EBITDA interest coverage ratio. Compare your numbers to the median values provided in Table 22-9. Based on these two ratios only, what bond rating might you expect Pioneer to receive?

P22-9   (Cash flow ratios) Calculate the funds from operations/total debt ratio for Pioneer. What does this ratio indicate regarding Pioneer's ability to maintain solvency in the long run?

P22-10   (Financial leverage ratios) Calculate Pioneer's long-term debt to capitalization ratio and its total debt to capitalization ratio. (Assume all current liabilities are permanently maintained.) Industry averages are as follows:

	Industry average
Long-term debt to capitalization	28.2%
Total debt to capitalization	50.0%

How do you assess Pioneer's financial leverage position relative to the industry?

CASES

1. (CFA exam question) Georgia-Pacific Corporation, a large forest products manufacturer, had two AA-rated, $150 million par amount, intermediate term debt issues outstanding in 1985.

	10.10% Notes	**Floating-Rate Notes**
Maturity	1990	1987
Issued	6/12/80	9/27/79
at par to yield	10.10%	12.00%
Callable: (beginning on)	6/15/86	10/01/84
at	100	100
Sinking fund	None	None
Current coupon	10.10%	16.90%
Changes	Fixed	Every 6 months 0.75% above 6-month Treasury bill rate
Range since issued	—	16.90–12.00%
Current price	$73\frac{3}{8}$	97
Current yield	13.77%	17.42%
Yield-to-maturity	15.87%	—
Price range since issue	100-72	102–93

Assume it is 1985. Based on the above data answer the following questions. (a) State the minimum coupon rate of interest at which the Company could sell a Fixed Rate issue at par due in 1990. Assume the same indenture provisions as the 10.10% notes and disregard any tax considerations. (b) Give two reasons why the Floating Rate Notes are not selling at par (offering price). (c) State and justify whether the risk of call is high, moderate, or low for the fixed rate issue. (d) Assuming a decline in interest rates is anticipated, identify and justify which issue would be most appropriate for an actively managed bond portfolio where total return is the primary objective. (e) Explain why yield-to-maturity is not valid for the floating rate note. (f) If interest rates remain stable or increase prior to maturity, identify which issue will have the higher realized compound yield and give the reason.

2. (Reorganization versus liquidation) The Apex Tobacco Corporation has produced and sold snuff and chewing tobacco for over 100 years, but dipping snuff and chewing tobacco have fallen in popularity. Declines in sales and rising production costs resulted in a large deficit at the end of 2000. Apex's financial statements document the dire circumstances into which the firm has fallen:

Apex Tobacco Corporation
Balance Sheet
as of December 31, 2000
(Amounts in thousands of dollars)

Current assets	$375	Current liabilities	$450
Fixed assets	$375	Long-term debt (unsecured)	$225
		Capital stock	$150
		Retained earnings (deficit)	($ 75)
Total assets	$750	Total liabilities and net worth	$750

Apex Tobacco Corporation
Selected Financial Data: 1997–2000

Year	Sales	Net Profit After Tax, Before Fixed Charges
1997	$2,625	$262.5
1998	$2,400	$225.0
1999	$1,425	($ 75.0)
2000	$1,350	($112.5)

External appraisers suggested that the company would have a liquidation value of about $600,000. Management concluded that, as an alternative, a reorganization was possible with an additional investment of $300,000. Management was confident that the firm could undertake the manufacture of new smoking products, such as long, slim cigars for women; cigarette papers of varying colors for the roll-your-own market; Turkish water pipes (or hookahs); and stylish, small pipes for customers who wish to smoke less than the normal full bowl. Outside consultants concluded that this broadened product line could be produced and marketed readily through Apex's existing marketing channels and that new investment of $300,000 was needed. The consultants also forecast that the additional investment would restore earnings to $125,000 a year after taxes and before fixed charges.

Apex's common stock sells at about eight times its earnings per share. Management is negotiating with a local investment group to obtain the additional equity investment of $300,000. If the funds are obtained, the holders of the long-term debt would be issued one-half of the common stock in the reorganized firm in place of their present debt claims. New shares of stock would also be issued to sell to the new investors in Apex so that the old stockholders' voting power and potential earnings per share would be diluted or "watered down" after the reorganization.

Should the stockholders and creditors agree to the reorganization or should they force bankruptcy and liquidation of the firm's assets at auction?

CFA EXAM QUESTIONS

1. (1999 CFA Sample Exam, Level I) A "Fallen Angel" bond is *best* defined as a bond issued:
   A. below investment grade.
   B. at an original issue discount.
   C. as investment grade, but declined to speculative grade.
   D. as a secured bond, but the collateral value declined below par value.

2. (This question is adapted from a question appearing on the 1996 CFA Exam, Level II) PowerTool is the largest U.S. manufacturer of industrial hand tools. Its sales force is strong but clients have complained that marketing is weak. The industrial tool business is mature, with little or no future expected growth.

   PowerTool has acquired Fenton Manufacturing, a small, innovative company whose sales are entirely in the retail tool market. The retail tool market is expected to grow at a 5% annual rate.

   Fenton recently developed a patented line of rechargeable home power tools that displayed strong potential in test markets. Fenton expects this line to generate 50% of its sales within 5 years, but lacks a sales force to market this product line. Jerry Fenton, the company's founder, recently retired.

   You are a private investor with a large investment in PowerTool bonds and wish to determine the effect of the acquisition of Fenton on PowerTool's bonds.

   Table IX presents financial ratios and debt ratings of PowerTool and Fenton prior to the merger, and pro forma ratios of the combined company following the acquisition.

Table IX—Financial Ratios and Debt Ratings June 1, 1996

Company	Total Debt to Total Capital	Pretax Interest Coverage	Operating Cash Flow to Total Debt	Debt Rating
PowerTool	30%	6.2X	50%	A+
Fenton	72%	2.1X	8%	Not rated
Combined	42%	5.4X	40%	To be determined

A. Explain how *each* of the following *three* ratios should be used to evaluate a firm's financial risk:
   i. Total Debt to Total Capital
   ii. Pretax Interest Coverage
   iii. Operating Cash Flow to Total Debt
   PowerTool has issued debt with the following covenants, which continue in force after its acquisition of Fenton.

Dividend Test Covenant
PowerTool may not pay any cash dividend or repurchase shares if such payment would result in total debt-to-capital in excess of 50%.

Put Option Covenant
If PowerTool's debt rating falls below A, bondholders have the right to redeem the bonds at a price of 105 plus accrued interest within 60 days following the change in rating.

B. Discuss the impact of *each* of the *two* debt covenants as described above on PowerTool's financial flexibility following its acquisition of Fenton.
   i. Dividend Test Covenant, *and*
   ii. Put Option Covenant.
   Use only the information provided for Part A to answer the following question.

C. Discuss, *from the PowerTool bondholders' point of view, two* advantages and *two* disadvantages to PowerTool of the acquisition of Fenton, with regard to the following product lines:
   i. industrial tool business, and
   ii. retail tool business.
   Powertool debt has not yet been re-rated following the acquisition of Fenton. PowerTool bonds are currently trading at a price comparable to "A" rated bonds.

   Table X displays financial ratios used to determine bond ratings.

Table X—Bond Rating Criteria
June 1, 1996

Debt Rating	Total Debt to Total Capital	Pretax Interest Coverage	Operating Cash Flow to Total Debt
AA	26%	8.8X	75%
A	37%	4.6X	44%
BBB	48%	2.5X	29%

D. Recommend whether you should *hold* or *sell* the PowerTool bonds. Support your recommendation with *four* reasons drawn from the introduction and Tables IX and X and your answers to Parts A through C of Problem 2.

3. (1998 CFA Exam, Level II) Jane Berry is a fixed-income analyst at an investment management firm. She has been following the developments at two companies, Sturdy Machines and Patriot Manufacturing, which are both U.S.-based industrial companies that sell their products worldwide. Both companies operate in cyclical industries.

Sturdy Machines' profits have suffered from a rising dollar and a slump in its business. The company has said that major cuts in its operating expenses are likely to be necessary if it is to make a profit next year. On the other hand, Patriot Manufacturing has been able to maintain its profitability and enhance its balance sheet, as shown in Table 5.

Table 5—Financial Information

Ratio	1995	1996	1997
Sturdy Machines			
Cash flow/total debt (%)	37.3	31.0	33.0
Total debt/capital (%)	38.2	40.1	41.3
Pretax interest coverage (X)	4.2	2.3	1.1
Patriot Manufacturing			
Cash flow/total debt (%)	34.6	38.0	43.1
Total debt/capital (%)	40.0	37.3	34.9
Pretax interest coverage (X)	2.7	4.5	6.1

Berry has been monitoring the bonds of these companies for possible purchase. She notices that a rating agency recently downgraded the senior debt of Sturdy Machines from A1 to A2 and upgraded the senior debt of Patriot Manufacturing from A3 to A2.

Berry has received the following yield quotes from a broker:

Sturdy Machines 7.50% due June 1, 2008, was quoted at 7.10%.

Patriot Manufacturing 7.50% due June 1, 2008 was quoted at 7.10%.

Recommend which bond Berry should buy. Justify your choice with *two* factors from Table 5 and *two* qualitative factors from the discussion above.

FURTHER REFERENCES

Dattatreya, Ravi E. and Frank J. Fabozzi. *Active Total Return Management of Fixed Income Portfolios,* Rev. ed. Burr Ridge, IL: Irwin, 1995.

This book provides a comprehensive review of bond analysis, analyzing bonds with embedded options, mortgage-backed securities, and interest rate derivatives.

Das, Satyajit Ed. *Credit Derivatives: Trading and Management of Credit and Default Risk.* New York: Wiley, 1998.

This book of readings is written by chapter authors that are expert in different credit derivatives. Helpful chapters about accounting, legal, and tax issues are included.

Francis, Jack Clark, Joyce Frost, and J. Gregg Whittaker. *Handbook of Credit Derivatives.* Burr Ridge, IL: Irwin, 1999.

This edited book of readings contains chapters written by experts in different aspects of credit analysis and credit derivatives. Most of the chapters are about credit derivatives and how to use them. Additional chapters about accounting, legal, and tax issues are included.

J. P. Morgan. *CreditMetrics—Technical Document,* New York, April 2, 1997.

This half-inch-thick paperback users' manual explains CreditMetrics computations and tools in an easy-to-read fashion. The document may be obtained from RiskMetrics, Wall Street, New York City.

Kaiser, Kevin M. J. "European Bankruptcy Laws: Implications for Corporations Facing Financial Distress," *Financial Management* 25, no. 3 (autumn 1996): 67–85.

The paper summarizes, compares, and contrasts bankruptcy law in the United States, the United Kingdom, France, and Germany. These laws are viewed from a financial perspective, rather than from an attorney's perspective. Information asymmetries, conflicts of interest, economic incentives, and the options open to a liquidity constrained firm are examined.

Livingston, Miles. *Bonds and Bond Derivatives*. Oxford, England: Blackwell, 1999.

This easy-to-read textbook begins with time value of money issues, contains chapters about various credit instruments, and concludes with informative chapters about financial derivatives.

Sundaresan, Suresh. *Fixed Income Markets and Their Derivatives*. Cincinnati: Southwestern, 1997.

This textbook reviews the various markets for credit instruments and different quantitative tools that are available to analyze credit instruments. Chapter 15, entitled "Risk Management," delves into credit risk.

Tavakoli, Janet M. *Credit Derivatives*. New York: Wiley, 1998.

This little book contains an introduction to credit instruments, credit risk analysis, and credit derivatives.

ENDNOTES

[1] See Table 22-10 (p. 673) for some detail about Lea V. Carty and Dana Lieberman, "Defaulted Bank Loan Recoveries," Moody's Investors Service, Global Credit Research, Special Report November 1996.

[2] For more details about bankruptcy, see Edward I. Altman, *Corporate Financial Distress* (New York: Wiley, 1983).

[3] See Frank Fabozzi, Jane Tripp Howe, Takashi Makabe, and Toshihide Sudo, "Recent Evidence on the Distribution Patterns in Chapter 11 Reorganizations," *The Journal of Fixed Income* 2, no. 4 (March 1993): 6-23.

[4] See Corolyn E. Clarke, Paul L. Foster, and Waqar I. Ghani, "Differential Reaction to Bond Downgrades for Small Versus Large Firms: Evidence from Analysts' Forecast Revisions," *The Journal of Fixed Income* 7, no. 3 (December 1997): 94-99.

[5] For a classic empirical investigation of the determinants of the yield spreads between different issues of bonds, see Lawrence Fisher, "Determinants of Risk Premiums on Corporate Bonds," *Journal of Political Economy* 67, no. 3 (June 1959): 217-37.

[6] Edward I. Altman, "The Anatomy of the High-Yield Bond Market," *Financial Analysts Journal* (July-August 1987): 13, Table I. For a factual and informative article about Mr. Milken, see "Who Did More for Mankind, Mother Teresa or Mike Milken?," *Business Week,* March 2, 1998, page 28.

[7] For details see Edward I. Altman and Scott A. Nammacher, "The Default Rate Experience on High-Yield Corporate Debt," *Financial Analysts Journal* 41, no. 4 (July-August 1985): 25-41. Also see M. E. Blume and D. B. Keim, "Lower-Grade Bonds: Their Risks and Returns," *Financial Analysts Journal* 43, no 4 (July-August 1987): 26-33. The Altman-Nammacher and Blume-Keim studies impart a positive view of junk bond investing. For a less positive view, see M. I. Weinstein, "A Curmudgeon's View of Junk Bonds," *Journal of Portfolio Management* (Spring 1987): 76-80. For highly informative negative information, see Paul Asquith, David W. Mullins, and E. D. Wolff, "Original Issue High-Yield Bonds: Aging Analysis of Defaults, Exchanges and Calls," *Journal of Finance* 44, no. 4 (September 1989): 923-52. Later, Altman reported statistics that were considerably less favorably disposed toward junk bond investing; see Edward I. Altman, "Measuring Corporate Bond Mortality and Performance," *Journal of Finance* 44, no. 4 (September 1989): 909-22.

[8] See Herbert S. Wagner III, "The Pricing of Bonds in Bankruptcy and Financial Restructuring," *The Journal of Fixed Income* 6, no. 1 (June 1996): 40-47. For details about municipal bond analysis consult Sylvan G. Feldstein, Frank J. Fabozzi, Irving M. Pollack, and Frank G. Zarb, *The Municipal Bond Handbook,* Vols. I and II (Homewood, IL: Dow-Jones-Irwin, 1983).

[9] Edward I. Altman, "Financial Ratios, Discriminant Analysis, and the Prediction of Corporate Bankruptcy," *Journal of Finance* (September 1968): 589-609. Also see E. I. Altman, *Corporate Financial Distress* (New York: Wiley, 1983): see Chapter 3, especially p. 106.

[10] G. E. Pinches and K. A. Mingo, "A Multivariate Analysis of Industrial Bond Ratings," *Journal of Finance* (March 1973): 1-32. Pinches and Mingo showed how to use factor analysis and multiple discriminant analysis to assign bond-quality ratings with a high degree of accuracy. See also Robert S. Kaplan and Gabriel Urwitz, "Statistical Models of Bond Rating: A Methodological Inquiry," *Journal of Business* 52, no. 2 (April 1979): 231-62. Kaplan and Urwitz developed a model that estimates bond ratings. However, they also reported that a common multiple regression model is nearly as accurate at classifying bond issues' ratings as their more sophisticated model.

[11] See J.J. Mahoney, M.V. Sever, and J.A. Theis, "Cash Flow: FASB Opens the Floodgates," *Journal of Accountancy* (May 1988) 27–38.

[12] For detailed numerical examples of financial ratio calculations, consult a book about that topic, such as Leopold A. Bernstein, *Financial Statement Analysis,* 6th ed. (Burr Ridge, IL: Irwin McGraw-Hill, 1998). In addition, see Robert C. Higgins, *Analysis for Financial Management,* 5th ed. (Burr Ridge, IL: Irwin McGraw-Hill, 1998). Also see George Foster, *Financial Statement Analysis,* 2nd ed. (Englewood Cliffs, NJ: Prentice-Hall, 1986).

[13] This discussion draws on Standard & Poor's, *Corporate Rating Criteria,* 1997, and on *Standard & Poor's Rating Guide* (New York: McGraw-Hill, 1979).

[14] For more details about adjustable-rate bonds see Frank J. Fabozzi, *Floating Rate Instruments* (Chicago, IL: Probus Publishing, 1986).

[15] For more detailed analysis of bond indentures and protective provisions, see Mitchell Berlin and Jan Loeys, "Bond Covenants and Delegated Monitoring," *Journal of Finance* 43, no. 2 (June 1988): 397–412. See also T.H. Ho and R.F. Singer, "Bond Indenture Provisions and the Risk of Corporate Debt," *Journal of Financial Economics* 10 (December 1982): 375–406. Also see C.W. Smith and J.B. Warner, "On Financial Contracting: An Analysis of Bond Covenants," *Journal of Financial Economics* 7 (June 1979): 117–61.

[16] See Mark I. Weinstein, "The Effect of a Rating Change Announcement on Bond Prices," *Journal of Financial Economics* 5, no. 3 (December 1977): 329–50. Weinstein used matrix prices (that is, estimated prices) rather than data from actual transactions.

[17] P.A. Griffin and A.Z. Sanvicente, "Common Stock Returns and Rating Changes: A Methodological Comparison," *Journal of Finance* 37, no. 1 (March 1982): 103–19. GS actually employed three different methods to gauge the effects of a bond rating change on the issuer's stock. Also see George Pinches and Clay Singleton, "The Adjustment of Stock Prices to Bond Rating Changes," *Journal of Finance* 33, no. 1 (March 1978): 29–44. More recently, see Fayez A. Elayan, Brian A. Maris, and Philip J. Young, "The Effect of Commercial Paper Rating Changes and Credit-Watch Placement on Common Stock Prices," *Financial Review* 31, no. 1 (February 1996): 149–67.

[18] See John Hand, R.W. Holthausen, Richard W. Leftwich, "The Effect of Bond Rating Agency Announcements on Bond and Stock Prices," *Journal of Finance* 47, no. 2 (June 1992): 733–52.

[19] See George Pinches and Clay Singleton, "The Adjustment of Stock Prices to Bond Rating Changes," *Journal of Finance* 32, no. 1 (March 1978): 29–44.

[20] See Jeremy C. Goh and Louis H. Ederington, "Is a Bond Rating Downgrade Bad News, Good News, or No News for Stockholders?" *Journal of Finance* 48, no. 5 (December 1993): 2001–08.

[21] See Sudip Datta, Mai Iskandar Datta, and Ajay Patel, "The Pricing of Initial Public Offers of Corporate Straight Debt," *Journal of Finance* 52, no. 1 (March 1997): 379–96.

[22] See Gailen Hite and Arthur Warga, "The Effect of Bond-Rating Changes on Bond Price Performance," *Financial Analysts Journal* (May-June 1997): 35–51.

[23] For more information about value at risk, see Phillippe Jorion, *Value At Risk* (Burr Ridge, IL: Irwin, 1997). Also see Suresh Sundaresan, *Fixed Income Markets and Their Derivatives* (Cincinnati: South-Western, 1997): 582–94.

[24] See Jack Clark Francis, Joyce Frost, and J. Gregg Whittaker, *Handbook of Credit Derivatives* (Burr Ridge, IL: Irwin, 1999). Chapters 5 and 6 contain mathematical pricing models and related tools. For example, a formula to compute the correlation between binary events like defaulted and nondefaulted is presented.

PART 6

EQUITY

SHARES

EQUITY VALUATION—A MICRO VIEW

*Eqns. 3-4, 3-5, 3-6, and 3-7 and the Coca-Cola Example in Chapter 3 introduced common stock valuation. This chapter extends those examples by presenting a microeconomic theory of equity valuation focused on one share of stock. Various versions of the **dividend-discount model** (DDM) are used to analyze shares of preferred and common stock. Market data from corporations and from the Standard and Poor's 500 Stocks Composite Index (S&P500) are used to illustrate time paths and relationships between corporate cash dividends, earnings, and stock prices. This is the first of four chapters on equity valuation.*

DIVIDENDS AND DIVIDEND-DISCOUNT MODELS (DDMS)

Many corporations pay more than one kind of cash dividends:

- **Regular cash dividends** are the most common type; they are usually paid quarterly. Most companies rarely decrease their regular cash dividends. Most firms hold their cash dividend payments constant or increase them gradually over the years.

- **Extra dividends** are cash dividends that may or may not be repeated in the future. A few corporations pay an extra dividend at the end of the fiscal year if the firm had an unusually profitable year.

- **Special dividends** are extraordinary cash dividends that may never be repeated. If a corporation won a law suit with a substantial cash settlement, for example, some of that cash might be used to pay a special cash dividend.

- **Liquidating dividends** are cash payouts that occur when all or part of the business is liquidated.

Payment Models for Cash Dividends Per Share

The following timeline lays out the stream of cash dividends from one share of preferred or common stock.

Cash dividend per share, DIV_t	DIV_1	DIV_2	DIV_3	. . .	DIV_∞
Quarterly or annual time periods	$t = 1$	$t = 2$	$t = 3$	. . .	$t = \infty$

Most issues of preferred stock pay regular cash dividends that remain constant forever, $DIV_1 = DIV_2 = DIV_3 = DIV_4 = DIV_5 = \ldots = DIV_\infty$. Common stock dividends involve more uncertainty. The board of directors makes a separate decision about each quarter's common stock cash dividend. Eqn. 23-1 is a cash *dividend-per-share model.*

$$DIV_t (1 + g_t) = DIV_{t+1} \qquad (23\text{-}1)$$

Eqn. 23-1 implies the following single-period cash *dividend growth rate:*

$$\text{One-period growth rate} = g_t = (DIV_t - DIV_{t+1})/(DIV_{t+1})$$

As mentioned above, many preferred stock cash dividend payments have growth rates of zero, $g = 0$. Most corporations' common stock cash dividends per share grow at about 2% per year, $g = 2\%$. Over the past decade Coca-Cola's cash dividends grew at the unusually high rate of about $g = 15\%$ per year.* Some corporations reduce their cash dividend payments. These negative growth rates in cash dividends, $g < 0$, usually occur when either of two events occur. First, unprofitable operations may render the firm unable to make cash dividend payments. Apple Computers stopped paying dividends when it was having difficulties during the mid-1990s, for example, and it never resumed. Second, at the other extreme, extremely profitable operations may cause the firm to retain all of its earnings to finance its growth via retaining earnings rather than using earnings to pay cash dividends. Microsoft, Cisco, America Online, Oracle, and MCI WorldCom are examples of profitable companies that never paid cash dividends and perhaps never will. For corporations that choose to pay cash dividends, Eqn. 23-1a presents an alternative cash-dividend-per-share payments model that can be used when the rate of growth remains fairly constant through time.

Cash dividends, DIV_t	DIV_0	$DIV_1 = DIV_0(1 + g)^1$	$DIV_2 = DIV_0(1 + g)^2$	$DIV_3 = DIV_0(1 + g)^3$	
Time period, t	$t = 0$	$t = 1$	$t = 2$	$t = 3$	**(23-1a)**

Few corporations have a policy of paying cash dividends that grow at a constant growth rate forever. Nevertheless, the simple Eqn. 23-1a does a good job of tracking many corporations.

The Present Value of a Stream of Constant Cash Dividends

It is reasonable to assume that a well-managed corporation will live forever. As old executives retire, new ones are brought up through the ranks. Mergers, acquisitions, and research and development (R&D) can provide new products to sustain the firm. As a result, if the corporation is well managed, an equity share is worth the present value of a stream of cash flows that should continue forever. These considerations are summarized in the cash dividend discount model (DDM) in Eqn. 23-2:

---

* Coca-Cola has paid cash dividends every year since 1920. These cash dividends have been increased almost every year for decades. Coca-Cola's consistently liberal cash payouts attracts a clientele of investors that values dependable cash flows highly. Coca-Cola's earnings per share (EPS) have sometimes grown more rapidly. Coca-Cola has been slowly reducing its cash dividend payout ratio while increasing the cash dividend per share.

$$P_0 = \sum_{t=1}^{\infty} \frac{DIV_t}{(1+k)^t} \qquad (23\text{-}2)$$

$$= \frac{DIV_1}{(1+k)^1} + \frac{DIV_2}{(1+k)^2} + \frac{DIV_3}{(1+k)^3} + \cdots + \frac{DIV_\infty}{(1+k)^\infty}$$

where P_0 is the present value of the share's future cash dividends which, in equilibrium, equals the market price of the share. The symbol k represents a risk-adjusted discount rate, or, equivalently, the issuer's cost of equity capital, or, equivalently, the investor's required rate of return.[1]

Assuming that cash dividends grow at a constant perpetual rate allows us to substitute Eqn. 23-1 into Eqn. 23-2:

$$P_0 = \sum_{t=1}^{\infty} \frac{DIV_t}{(1+k)^t} \qquad (23\text{-}2)$$

$$= \sum_{t=1}^{\infty} \frac{DIV_0(1+g)^t}{(1+k)^t} \quad \text{since } DIV_t = DIV_0(1+g)^t \qquad (23\text{-}3)$$

Algebraically rearranging Eqn. 23-3 results in the mathematically equivalent Eqn. 23-4.*

$$P_0 = \frac{DIV_0(1+g)}{k-g} = \frac{DIV_1}{k-g} \qquad (23\text{-}4)$$

Model-Building Assumptions

We assume $k > g$ to solve Eqn. 23-4 for positive stock prices. This is a realistic assumption. The stock market realizes a company's growth rate and its riskiness tend to rise and fall together. As a result, the stocks' market prices adjust so that their risk-adjusted cost of capital (discount rate) rises with their growth rate, but k is always greater than g.

Do not confuse a short-run event with long-run equilibrium. For instance, suppose a corporation's cash dividends in year t were increased substantially while its cost of equity capital was temporarily low, $k_t < g_t$. This 1-year (temporary) condition does not violate the assumption that $k > g$ because the symbols k and g in Eqn. 23-4 are long-run averages (equilibrium values).

For the sake of simplicity, this chapter ignores taxes, external financing for the firm, and assumes the stock is not complicated by options. Taxes could be added to the model without great difficulty. And it is fairly simple to expand the model to include debt financing. Allowing for executive stock options and warrants that increase the number of shares outstanding and dilute the per share earnings and dividends is more difficult. If all of these realities were incorporated into the model, the valuation formulas would be complicated and difficult to interpret. In order to keep our valuation models easy to understand, we assume these complications don't exist.

---

*   Let the symbols b and z be defined so that $b = DIV_1/(1+k)$ and $z = (1+g)/(1+k)$. These conventions allow us to rewrite Eqn. 25-3 as: $P_0 = b(1+z^1+z^2+z^3+...)$. Multiplying both sides of the previous equation by z results in: $P_0z = b(z^1+z^2+z^3+...)$. Subtracting the second equation from the first equation results in the following difference: $P_0\{1-z\} = b$, which implies: $P_0 = b/\{1-z\}$. Substituting for b and z yields: $P_0 = b/\{1-z\} = \{DIV_1/(1+k)\}/\{1 - (1+g)/(1+k)\}$, which can be solved to obtain: $P_0 = DIV_1/(k-g)$.

VALUING A SHARE OF BATTEL STOCK—INITIAL SITUATION

EXAMPLE

The Battel Corporation paid annual cash dividends of $2 per share; its cost of equity capital was 10% per annum, $k = 10\%$; and, its cash dividends were growing at a rate of $g = 2\%$ per year. Under these circumstances Eqn. 23-4a tells us that Battel's stock was worth $25.50 per share.

$$P_0 = \frac{DIV_0(1 + g)}{k - g} = \frac{DIV_1}{k - g} = \frac{(\$2.00)(1.02)}{0.10 - 0.02} = \frac{\$2.04}{0.08} = \$25.50 \text{ per share} \qquad \textbf{(23-4a)}$$

VALUING A SHARE OF BATTEL STOCK WITH INTERNATIONAL EXPANSION   **EXAMPLE**

Suppose Battel's management considers distributing its product in Europe. This year's cash dividends are not changed by this development; they are still $DIV_0 = \$2.00$. But the firm's growth rate is expected to rise from $g = 2\%$ to $g = 4\%$ if Battel operates in Europe. Because of increased risk exposure from the foreign operations, the corporation's cost of equity capital is expected to increase permanently from $k = 10\%$ to $k = 11\%$. As a result of these contemplated developments Battel's value per share is expected to increase to $29.71 per share.

$$P_0 = \frac{DIV_0(1 + g)}{k - g} = \frac{DIV_1}{k - g} = \frac{(\$2.00)(1.04)}{0.11 - 0.04} = \frac{\$2.08}{0.07} = \$29.71 \text{ per share} \qquad \textbf{(23-4b)}$$

Table 23-1 and Table 2-3 in Chapter 2 suggest simple guidelines for determining the appropriate discount rate to compute a stock's present value. Chapter 15 provided more comprehensive valuation models.

The Present Value of a Stock for Finite Holding Periods

Some people ask if the DDM is relevant if a stock is sold after a few years. To answer this question, Eqn. 23-2 was shortened to Eqn. 23-5, which represents the present value of a stock that is purchased, held for 3 years, and then sold:

$$P_0 = \frac{DIV_1}{(1 + k)^1} + \frac{DIV_2}{(1 + k)^2} + \frac{DIV_3}{(1 + k)^3} + \frac{P_3}{(1 + k)^3} \qquad \textbf{(23-5)}$$

P_3 represents the present value of the share when it is sold 3 years in the future. The sale date of 3 years was selected arbitrarily; this example can easily be generalized to cover the sale of the share after 2, 3, 4, 5, or any other number of years.

The time subscript $t = 0$ represents the current time period (now). The P_3 term in Eqn. 23-5 represents the stock's price (present value) 3 years from now. More specifically, P_3 represents the present value of all dividends from Year 4 to infinity, as shown in Eqn. 23-6:

$$P_3 = \frac{DIV_4}{(1 + k)^1} + \frac{DIV_5}{(1 + k)^2} + \frac{DIV_6}{(1 + k)^3} + \cdots + \frac{DIV_\infty}{(1 + k)^\infty} \qquad \textbf{(23-6)}$$

TABLE 23-1	Larger Discount Rates Used for Riskier Companies	
Stock's Quality Rating	Description of Risk (Corporate Examples)	Appropriate Discount Rate[a]
AAA	Maximum safety, bluest of the blue chips (Abbot Labs, Bristol-Myers Squibb, Exxon, GE, Johnston & Johnston, Nestle, Pfizer, Royal Dutch/Shell)	8%
AA	High-quality, established blue chip (McDonald's, Wells Fargo, Warner-Lambert, PepsiCo, Procter & Gamble)	10%
A	Medium grade investment bonds, established top-50 firms (PaineWebber, Sara Lee, Enron, Hershey Foods, United Technology, Coca-Cola, Tyco)	12%
BBB	Low-grade investment bonds, established top-100 firms (Delta Airlines, Weyerhaeuser Co., Peoplesoft, Sun Microsystems, DuPont, Tosco, Waste Management, Wendys, Zale)	14%
BB	High-grade speculation, FORTUNE 500 firms (J. C. Penney, Qualcomm, Texas Instrument, GM, Unisys, American Standard, Levi Strauss)	16%
B	Speculative FORTUNE 1000 firms (U.S. Airways, Amerada Hess, W.R. Grace, A&P Tea Co., Georgia-Pacific, Allied Waste, Federal Mogul)	18%
CCC	Speculation, very risky (Classic Cable, PSINet, Revlon)	20%
CC	Very speculative, junk bond issuer (Advanced Micro Devices, Silicon Graphics, NEXTEL, National Semiconductor, Edison International)	22%
C	Gambling on bankruptcy (Allied Waste, RSL Communications, Universal Broadband Networks, both Southern California Edison and Pacific Gas & Electric during 2001 deregulation crisis in California)	24%
D	Defaulted (Boston Chicken, Irridium, GST Telecommunications, ICG Communications, AMF Bowling, Northpoint Communications, Claridge Hotel, Daewoo, Pets.com, Bugle Boy, Grand Union, Lernout & Hauspie)	26%
Not rated	Gambling on a small new local firm (Joe's Bar & Grill, Mom & Pop's Deli)	50%

[a] The discount rates in Table 23-1 are appropriate for normal markets. The appropriate discount rate will be higher than normal during periods of bearish market activity and lower than normal during bullish periods. A security's quality rating and its discount rate can change rapidly and frequently.

To show how the constant DDM encompasses situations in which a share is sold after being held 3 years, Eqn. 23-6 is substituted into Eqn. 23-5 to obtain Eqn. 23-7.*

$$P_0 = \frac{DIV_1}{(1+k)^1} + \frac{DIV_2}{(1+k)^2} + \frac{DIV_3}{(1+k)^3} + \frac{DIV_4}{(1+k)^{3+1}} + \frac{DIV_5}{(1+k)^{4+1}} + \cdots + \frac{DIV_\infty}{(1+k)^\infty} \qquad \textbf{(23-7)}$$

Since Eqns. 23-2 and 23-7 are identical, this proves that the DDM includes, as a special case, selling the share of stock before infinity. P_0 includes P_3 and P_3 includes future capital gains. The elegantly simple DDM does not ignore capital gains or retained earnings; it considers retained earnings and capital gains implicitly.

---

* The following identity may be helpful if you work through the algebra of combining Eqns. 23-5 and 23-6.
$$\frac{DIV_{t+3}/(1+k)^t}{(1+k)^3} = \frac{DIV_{t+3}}{(1+k)^t(1+k)^3} = \frac{DIV_{t+3}}{(1+k)^{t+3}}$$

FIGURE 23-1   The Time Paths of Four Different Types of Growth in a Stock's Cash Dividends Per Share

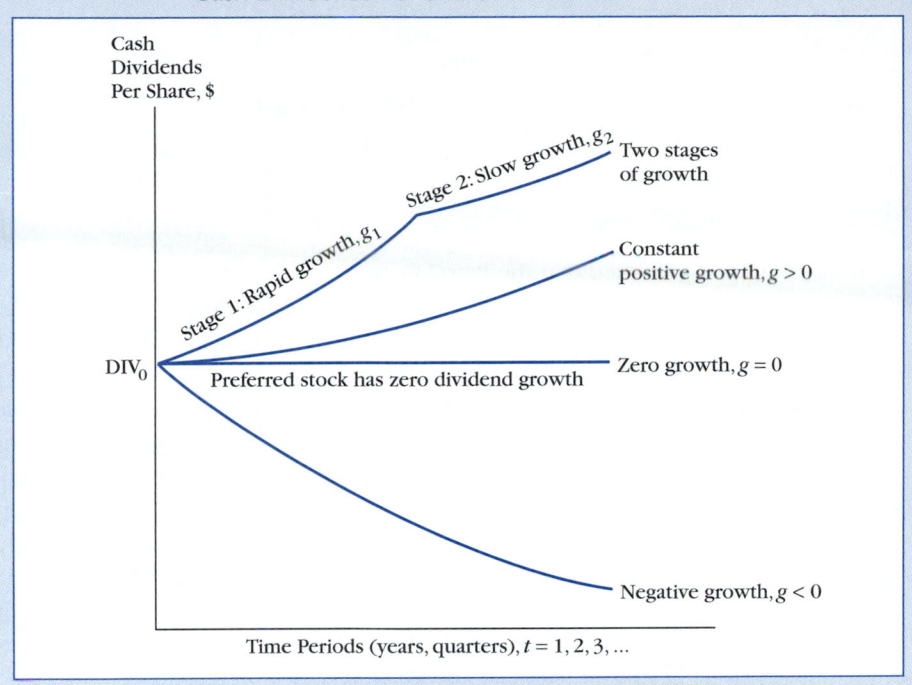

Cash dividends per share are usually paid out of earnings per share; so, if a corporation experiences a long-run earnings decline its cash dividends will probably be reduced too, $g < 0$. Preferred stock pays a constant annual cash dividend; its dividend growth rate is zero, $g = 0$. The typical corporation's cash dividend payments increase between 1% to 4% per year, $g > 0$. Some corporations experience different stages of growth. For example, a corporation might experience an initial stage of rapid growth (g_1), followed by a second stage of slower growth (g_2), where $g_1 > g_2 > 0$.

The Two-Stages-of-Growth DDM

A corporation's common stock might be categorized into one of the four different types of cash dividends per share growth patterns:

1. Two stages with different positive growth rates in each, denoted g_1 and g_2
2. One constant positive growth rate, $g > 0$
3. Zero growth (as with preferred stock), $g = 0$
4. One constant negative growth rate, $g < 0$

Figure 23-1 illustrates these four different types of cash dividend growth patterns.

Eqn. 23-3 is the DDM that assumes one constant growth rate forever. Eqn. 23-3 could be used to value a common stock that had the second, third, or fourth growth patterns illustrated in Figure 23-1. Alternatively, Eqn. 23-3 could be reformulated to embrace the two stages of growth illustrated at the top of Figure 23-1.[2]

Consider a corporation that grows at an initial growth rate of g_1 for T years and then grows at a different growth rate called g_2 from year $T + 1$ to infinity. The first and second stages of growth can last either a short time or a long time, and the two rates of growth can be positive or nonpositive. If the first stage of growth lasts a short time, then the second stage of growth must last a long time, or vice versa. Eqn. 23-8's two-stages-of-growth DDM computes the present value of a share of the stock.

$$P_0 = \sum_{t=1}^{T} \frac{\text{DIV}_0(1 + g_1)^t}{(1 + k)^t} + \sum_{t=T+1}^{\infty} \frac{\text{DIV}_0(1 + g_1)^T(1 + g_2)^t}{(1 + k)^t} \tag{23-8}$$

$$= \sum_{t=1}^{T} \frac{\text{DIV}_0(1 + g_1)^t}{(1 + k)^t} + \frac{P_T}{(1 + k)^T} \quad \text{where} \quad P_T = \frac{(\text{DIV}_T)(1 + g_2)}{k - g_2} \tag{23-8a}$$

EXAMPLE

A DIFFERENT VIEW OF BATTEL'S GROWTH

Earlier in this chapter we learned that the Battel Corporation initially paid annual cash dividends of $2.00 per share; its cost of equity capital was 10% per annum, and its cash dividends were growing at a rate of 2% per year, $g = 0.02$. Under these circumstances the present value of Battel's stock was $25.50 per share. (See Eqn. 23-4a, p.691.)

As mentioned in the previous example, Battel is contemplating distributing its products in Europe. This year's cash dividends would not be changed by the European development ($\text{DIV}_0 = \$2.00$), but Battel's future growth rate is expected to rise temporarily.[3] Suppose European distribution caused Battel's growth rate to rise to 4% for 4 years ($g_1 = 0.04$ during Stage 1), and then fell back to its previous growth rate of 2% per year ($g_2 = 0.02$ during Stage 2). The top curve in Figure 23-1 illustrates such a two-stage dividend growth path. Further suppose that exposure to international risks permanently increases Battel's cost of equity capital from 10% to 11%. As a result of these developments Battel's value per share is expected to decrease to $24.28 per share, as shown below.

PV of Stage 1. The present value of Battel's first 4 years of cash dividends is $6.81576.

Year	Growth Rate	Annual Cash Dividend	Present Value Factor, $k = 11\%$	Present Value of Cash Dividend
$t = 1$	4.0%	$2.08	0.9009	$1.87387
$t = 2$	4.0%	$2.1632	0.8116	$1.75570
$t = 3$	4.0%	$2.2497	0.73119	$1.64496
$t = 4$	4.0%	$2.3397	0.65873	$1.54123
				$6.81576

PV of Stage 2. The present value of a stream of cash dividends that begins at $2.339 in $t = 4$ and grows at 2% per year into perpetuity is $26.516.

$$P_4 = \frac{\text{DIV}_4(1 + g)}{k - g} = \frac{\text{DIV}_5}{k - g} = \frac{(\$2.339)(1.02)}{0.11 - 0.02} = \frac{\$2.386}{0.09} = \$26.516 \text{ per share}$$

The present value of P_4 discounted at a rate of $k = 11\%$ is $P_0 = \$26.516/(1 + 11\%)^4 = \$17.4669$.

Total PV. The present value of all future cash dividends is $24.282.

$$\underbrace{\begin{pmatrix} \text{Total} \\ \text{PV,} \\ \$24.28 \end{pmatrix}}_{P_0 = \sum_{t=1}^{T=4} \frac{(\text{DIV}_0 = \$2)(1.04)^t}{(1.11)^t}} = \overbrace{\begin{pmatrix} \text{PV of Stage 1,} \\ \$6.815 \end{pmatrix}}^{} + \overbrace{\begin{pmatrix} \text{PV of Stage 2,} \\ \$17.467 \end{pmatrix}}^{\left(\frac{\text{DIV}_5}{k - g}\right)/(1 + 11\%)^{4 \text{ years}}} \tag{23-8b}$$

Eqn. 23-8b indicates that the 4-year spurt in growth that Battel obtains from its European distribution is insufficient to overcome the added international risk that pushes the firm's discount rate up to 11%. As a result, Battel's share price is expected to fall slightly from $25.50 per share to $24.28 if it begins distributing in Europe. The increase in cash dividends during Stage 1 is evidence that a profitable increase in sales occurred. Expanding internationally also increased the firm's riskiness, which drove up the discount rate (required rate of return). The firm's present value dropped because the negative impact from the risk increase overpowered the positive impact from the sales increase.

A Common Criticism of the DDM

Critics of the DDM say that it is not practical to use the model because the future cash dividends cannot be forecasted accurately. This criticism is false for some corporations and true for others. A simple extrapolation is adequate to obtain a forecast of most corporations' cash dividends per share.

For example, Coca-Cola is a large corporation that manufactures and distributes different beverages in 200 different countries. In spite of these complexities, in most years it is not terribly difficult to forecast Coke's cash dividend payments with modest accuracy.

STUDY CHECK

FORECASTING COKE'S CASH DIVIDENDS

Use the decade of Coca-Cola's cash dividends per share listed in Table 5-5 in Chapter 5 to draw a time-series graph of the first half of that decade of historical cash dividends. Then, see how well you can forecast the second half of the decade of dividend payments by simply extrapolating the first 5 years of data.

While the critics of the DDM are usually willing to concede that cash dividends 5 or 10 years ahead can be forecasted without great difficulty, they like to point out that simple extrapolation cannot forecast 50 or 100 years ahead. While it is true that simple extrapolation cannot forecast cash dividends 50 or 100 years ahead, the long-range accuracy of these forecasts is not terribly important. The table below shows that a dollar that is received 50 or 100 years ahead has a present value near zero.

Number of Years (time periods, t) in the Future When $1 is Received	Present Value (PV) of $1 Discounted at a Rate of 10%
$t = 10$	$PV = \$1/(1.1)^{10} = \$0.3855 \cong 39¢$
$t = 25$	$PV = \$1/(1.1)^{25} = \$0.0923 \cong 9.2¢$
$t = 50$	$PV = \$1/(1.1)^{50} = \$0.0085 < 1¢$
$t = 100$	$PV = \$1/(1.1)^{100} = \$0.00007 < 1/100$ of $1¢$

This table understates the point because it uses a low 10% discount rate. A higher discount rate is appropriate for the equity issued by most corporations.

The table of present value computations above has important implications for the DDM. The first implication is that it is only essential to forecast cash dividends accurately for 10 years ahead in order to use the constant-growth-rate DDM, because that first decade of cash flows creates much of the stock's present value. The second implication is that cash dividends received during Years 11 through 30 only need to be forecast within plus or minus—

say, 40% of their actual values—since their present values are tiny. And, the third point implied from the present value computations is that all of the cash dividends received from Year 31 through infinity have a present value of only $1 or $2. In other words, it is not worthwhile to work hard at forecasting cash dividends that will be received 50 or 100 years in the future.

It is more difficult to forecast the erratic dividends paid by small companies than it is to forecast the stable dividends paid by the larger corporations. Since the small companies are riskier, however, a higher discount rate is used to find a present value of their cash flows. The present value computations above are replicated below using a higher 16% discount rate, to allow for the additional riskiness found in the smaller corporations.

Number of Years (time periods, t) in the Future When $1 Is Received	Present Value (PV) of $1 Discounted at a Rate of 16%
$t = 10$	$PV = \$1/(1.16)^{10} = \$0.2266 \cong 23¢$
$t = 25$	$PV = \$1/(1.16)^{25} = \$0.0245 \cong 2.5¢$
$t = 50$	$PV = \$1/(1.16)^{50} = \$0.0006 \cong 6/100$ of $1¢$
$t = 100$	$PV = \$1/(1.16)^{100} = \$0.0000003 < 3/100,000$ of $1¢$

The computations above show that when 16% is used as a discount rate the importance of accurate long-range forecasting is diminished further. For small corporations, defaulted corporations, and other high risk corporations that are discounted at high discount rates, it is only necessary to forecast cash dividends accurately for several years.

Forecasting

While discounting reduces the need for highly accurate long-run forecasts, it does not make forecasting an easy business. Experienced financial analysts have found that it is advisable to present assessments of an asset's value with some humility. For example, it would be smarter to say a share of XYZ stock is worth $30, plus or minus a margin for error of 20%, than to simply assert that a share of XYZ stock is worth $30.

Structural Changes in the Payment of Cash Dividends

Financial managers use corporate earnings for the three types of outlays:

A growing number of corporations are taking earnings that used to be paid out as cash dividends and using those funds to buy back their own outstanding common stock.[4] For example, IBM started buying back its shares in 1974 by purchasing $1.4 billion worth of its own stock. Coca-Cola started a share repurchase program in 1984 and has purchased more than one billion shares of its own stock so far; these purchases represent 31% of the shares that were outstanding in 1984. American Express, Bank America, Bristol-Myers Squibb, Chase

TABLE 23-2   Uses of a Corporation's Earnings

	Cash dividends—earnings paid out to the owners
Plus:	Retained earnings—earnings reinvested in the firm
Plus:	Share buybacks—earnings used to repurchase outstanding shares
Equals:	Total earnings—the corporation's net income

Manhattan Bank, Citigroup, Eastman Kodak, Pfizer, McDonald's, Walt Disney, Wells Fargo, and other corporations have each announced plans to buy back more than $1 billion of their own stock. Share buybacks cause reverse dilution that tends to increase the corporation's earnings per share while, at the same time, the buybacks bid up the corporation's stock price. Figure 23-2 illustrates the impact that share repurchase programs have had on the portfolio of diversified stocks making up the S&P500 index.

The cash dividend payout ratio and the cash dividend yield that Figure 23-2 illustrates for the S&P500 stocks were moving down as the S&P500 stock prices moved up during the 1980s and 1990s. These divergent trends result from the growing number of corporations that are taking earnings that were previously used to pay cash dividends and using the funds to bid up the market price of their shares through share repurchases. This new trend in corporations' cash dividend policies altered the relationship between the prices of common stocks and their cash dividends per share in a way that undermines the use of the traditional DDM. The constant growth rate DDM is still mathematically and economically correct, but its predictive powers is diminished by these changes. The next section shows the constant

FIGURE 23-2   S&P500 Index, Its Payout Ratio, Its Cash Dividend Yield, and Its Cash Dividend Per Share, 1935–2000

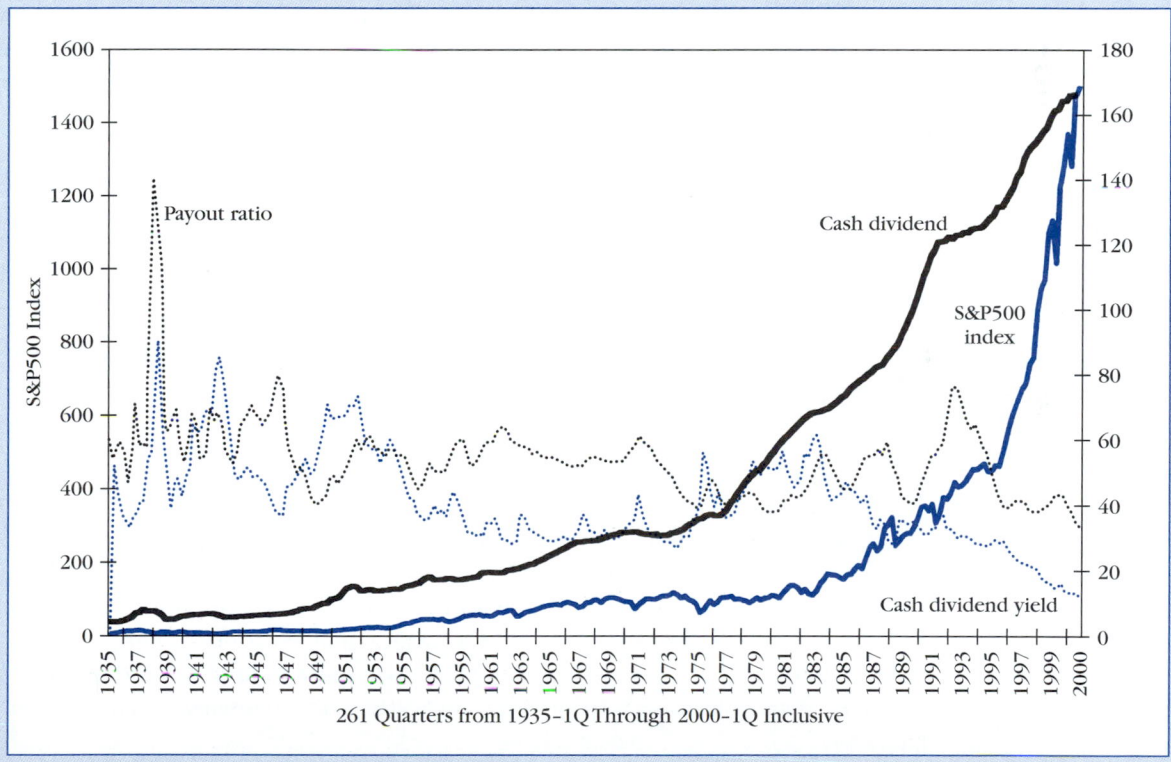

The Standard & Poor's 500 stocks index of cash dividends per share has crept up smoothly for decades. Cash dividends have not kept pace with the rise in the Standard & Poor's 500 stocks price index during the 1980s and 1990s. During the last two decades an increasing number of corporations have taken earnings that could have been used to pay cash dividends and used the funds to repurchase their own shares of common stock. As a result, the cash dividend payout ratio and the cash dividend yield of the Standard & Poor's 500 stocks trended slightly downward during the 1980s and 1990s. While the cash dividend payout ratio has trended downward during the 1980s and 1990s the S&P500 has been bid up by corporate share buybacks and other factors.

growth rate DDM can continue to be useful by restating the model in terms of earnings per share.

RESTATING A SHARE'S PRESENT VALUE IN TERMS OF ITS EARNINGS

Most corporations have cash dividend policies that change little from year to year. For example, page 36 of Coca-Cola's 1997 Annual Report says:

> *In 1997, our dividend payout ratio was approximately 34% of our net income. To free up additional cash for reinvestment in our high-return beverages business, our Board of Directors intends to gradually reduce our dividend payout ratio to 30% over time.*

This statement of Coca-Cola's future cash dividend policy can be represented by a retention rate (RR) of RR = 70% in the models introduced in the following discussion.

Modeling the Relationship Between Earnings and Dividends

A corporation's **retention rate (RR)** measures the proportion of its earnings the corporation retains instead of paying out as cash dividends. Eqn. 23-9 is a cash dividends per share model that defines dividends per share to be equal to the **payout ratio,** $(1 - RR)$, times earnings per share (EPS).

$$\text{DIV}_t = (1 - \text{RR})\text{EPS}_t \qquad\qquad \textbf{(23-9)}$$

Eqn. 23-9 highlights the fact that sustainable cash dividend payments come from corporate earnings.

A corporation can use its per share retained earnings of $[(\text{RR})(\text{EPS})]$ dollars to either repurchase its own shares or reinvest within the firm and earn the firm's return on equity (ROE). The firm's reinvested earnings can finance internal growth at a rate of $g = [(\text{RR})(\text{ROE})]$ per period, as shown in Eqn. 23-10:

$$\text{EPS}_t = \text{EPS}_0(1 + g)^t = \text{EPS}_0[1 + (\text{RR})(\text{ROE})]^t \qquad\qquad \textbf{(23-10)}$$

Profitable corporations can earn a positive ROE by either investing the retained earnings internally in profitable projects, or by repurchasing some of the firm's outstanding shares. Share repurchases increase earnings per share because, after the share buyback, the firm's aggregate earnings are spread over a smaller number of outstanding shares—this is **reverse dilution.**[5] As long as the retention rate is a positive constant fraction, $RR > 0$, dividends per share will change each period as indicated in the following equivalent versions of Eqn. 23-11:

$$\text{DIV}_t = (1 - \text{RR})[1 + (\text{RR})(\text{ROE})]^t(\text{EPS}_0) \qquad\qquad \textbf{(23-11)}$$

$$\text{DIV}_t = (1 - \text{RR})(1 + g)^t(\text{EPS}_0) \qquad\qquad \textbf{(23-11a)}$$

$$\text{DIV}_t = (1 - \text{RR})(\text{EPS}_t) \qquad\qquad \textbf{(23-11b)}$$

Eqns. 23-11, 23-11a, and 23-11b show how cash dividend per share (DIV) relates to the corporation's earnings per share, EPS; retention rate, RR; and, return on equity (ROE).

The Reformulated Present Value Model

When some fraction RR of earnings are retained to earn a return of ROE in the firm, the present value of a share of stock can be determined by substituting Eqn. 23-11 into Eqn. 23-3 to obtain Eqn. 23-12.

$$P_0 = \sum_{t=1}^{\infty} \frac{DIV_0(1+g)^t}{(1+k)^t} \qquad\qquad (23\text{-}3)$$

In Eqn. 23-12 the cash dividends per share, DIV_t, are restated in terms of the earnings per share by substituting $(EPS_t)(1 - RR)$ in place of DIV_t.

$$P_0 = \sum_{t=1}^{\infty} \frac{(EPS_0)(1 - RR)\{1 + [(RR)(ROE)]\}^t}{(1+k)^t} \qquad\qquad (23\text{-}12)$$

Eqns. 23-3 and 23-12 are identical since $\{(EPS_t)(1 - RR)\}\{1 + [(RR)(ROE)]\}^t = \{DIV_0\}\{1 + g\}^t$.

Eqn. 23-12 may be rewritten equivalently as Eqn. 23-12a since $g = [(RR)(ROE)]$:

$$P_0 = \sum_{t=1}^{\infty} \frac{(EPS_0)(1 - RR)(1+g)^t}{(1+k)^t} \qquad\qquad (23\text{-}12a)$$

Since $DIV_0 = (EPS_0)(1 - RR)$, Eqn. 23-12 may be rewritten equivalently as Eqns. 23-13 and 23-13a. Rearranging Eqns. 23-13 and 23-13a results in Eqn. 23-4a, which was introduced earlier in this chapter.

$$P_0 = \sum_{t=1}^{\infty} \frac{DIV_0[1 + [(RR)(ROE)]]^t}{(1+k)^t} \qquad\qquad (23\text{-}13)$$

$$= \sum_{t=1}^{\infty} \frac{DIV_0(1+g)^t}{(1+k)^t} \qquad\qquad (23\text{-}13a)$$

$$= \frac{DIV_1}{k - g} \qquad\qquad (23\text{-}4a)$$

One advantage of the DDM is that it may be rewritten equivalently in many ways. Eqns. 23-2, 23-4a, 23-12, 23-13, and 23-13a are all useful representations of the same model. Eqn. 23-12 explicitly depicts the relationship between earnings per share, EPS; dividend policy, as measured by RR; the firm's internal profitability, represented by ROE; the firm's risk-adjusted cost of capital, k; and the firm's growth rate, g, in determining the value of its common stock.

The valuation models above define all the variables on a per-share basis. These models may be used to value the entire corporation by multiplying the per-share quantities times the number of shares outstanding.

Dividend Policy Is Irrelevant for Most Firms

Substituting $(EPS_1)(1 - RR)$ for DIV_1 into Eqn. 23-4a yields Eqn. 23-14.

$$P_0 = \frac{(EPS_1)(1 - RR)}{k - g} \qquad\qquad (23\text{-}14)$$

Eqn. 23-14 is useful for studying the way that dividend policy impacts the value of a share. Dividend policy is represented by RR in Eqns. 23-14a and 23-15.

A **normal firm** that has an internal rate of return on new investments equal to the firm's risk-adjusted discount rate is analyzed in Eqn. 23-15. The fact that most corporations have an internal rate of return on equity that equals the firm's risk-adjusted discount rate, ROE = k, is used to derive Eqn. 23-15 from Eqn. 23-14a.

$$P_0 = \frac{EPS_1(1 - RR)}{k - g} = \frac{EPS_1(1 - RR)}{k - [(RR)(ROE)]} \quad \text{since } g = [(RR)(ROE)] \tag{23-14a}$$

$$P_0 = \frac{EPS_1(1 - RR)}{k(1 - RR)} \quad \text{if ROE} = k \tag{23-15}$$

$$P_0 = \frac{EPS_1}{k} \tag{23-15a}$$

Eqn. 23-15a shows that regardless of the firm's initial earnings per share, EPS_0, or riskiness (which determines k), the firm's value is not affected by dividend policy. In other words, *when ROE = k, dividend policy is irrelevant* since the firm's dividend policy (represented by RR) cancels out of Eqn. 23-15. Nobel laureates, Merton H. Miller and Franco Modigliani (MM), were the first to show that dividend policy had no effect on the value of most firms.[6]

We know that cash dividend payments can affect stock prices when they convey valuable information about the expectations and intentions of the corporation's board of directors to investors, because they give outsiders a valuable **signal**.[7] But, it is possible to redefine the model to include the idealistic economic assumption that the stock market is perfectly efficient. This idealistic assumption implies all information is fully impacted into prices. In such a model, by assumption, it is impossible for cash dividend policy to convey information (issue signals) about which investors were not already informed. This simplifying assumption was made by Modigliani and Miller when they first derived the MM valuation model. Review the efficient markets evidence presented in Chapter 8 and determine the best way to define the valuation model.

Eqn. 23-15a also provides proof that capitalizing earnings is equivalent to capitalizing dividends when two factors occur. First, the earnings must be properly restated to conform to the discount rate that is used. Second, ROE = k. Note that when ROE = k the quantity $1/k$ becomes the price-earnings ratio (or earnings multiplier).[8]

Dividend Policy Affects the Values of Growth Firms and Declining Firms

The relationship between a firm's internal rate of return, ROE, and its discount rate, k, is crucial in determining the impact dividend policy has on common stock prices.

Growth Stocks Should Not Pay Cash Dividends. Firms that earn an internal rate of return higher than their cost of capital (discount rate) are growth firms. **Growth firms** have ROE > k and they can maximize their value by retaining all earnings for internally financed investments. Paying cash dividends reduces the value of a true growth stock. For example, in the past Coca-Cola, Cisco, Microsoft, and Intel were growth stocks because these corporations enjoyed remarkable market penetration powers and were highly profitable. During the 1990s enviable positions allowed Coca-Cola, Cisco, Microsoft, and Intel to raise capital at a cost of k percent per year and reinvest it at a higher rate of ROE percent per year. Firms that enjoy such profitable investment opportunities should reinvest all their earnings. Microsoft, Cisco,

America Online, Oracle, and MCI WorldCom adhere to this view: These corporations never pay cash dividends. For various reasons, about 20% of the 500 corporations that make up the S&P500 index paid no cash dividends in 2000, and that percentage increases slightly each year.

Although economic theory suggests paying cash dividends is not stock-price-maximizing behavior for growth firms, we observe growth firms like Coca-Cola and Intel paying dividends. These cash dividend payments can be attributed to market imperfections. For example, some states have laws that require life insurance companies, banks, pension funds, and/or other financial intermediaries to invest in common stocks that have been paying consistent cash dividends. These legislated market imperfections cause stocks that have paid cash dividends in recent years to be on what is called the **legal list.** Laws forbidding investment in common stocks that pay no cash dividends artificially increase institutional investors demand for dividend-paying stocks. It is rational behavior for some growth firms to respond to this unnatural (legislated) demand for dividend-paying stocks by paying cash dividends.

Declining Firms Should Pay Liquidating Cash Dividends. Firms that do not possess profitable investment opportunities within the firm are called **declining firms.** A firm typically declines because its product becomes obsolete, its sales shrink, and investing in the firm is not profitable. Examples of declining firms can be found in the buggy-whip industry after the automobile became popular in the 1930s. Also, manufacturers of home-movie projectors suffered product obsolescence during the 1980s when VCR machines became popular. Since declining firms have no profitable investment opportunities, their internal rates of return on equity remain below their cost of capital, ROE $<$ k. In this case, the optimal cash dividend policy is for the firm to pay out all of its declining earnings to its shareholders. In other words, the management of a declining firm will maximize its owners' wealth by liquidating the corporation and paying one big final cash dividend as soon as it becomes clear that the firm's ROE will remain below k in the years ahead.

For Normal Firms, Dividend Policy Is Irrelevant. The vast majority of firms have few growth opportunities; they have few internal investments that offer ROE $>$ k. These *normal firms* operate in a static economic equilibrium where the rate of return from their internal investments equals their cost of capital, ROE $=$ k. For these firms, dividend policy has no effect on the value of their equity shares. The value of the normal corporation's shares are unchanged whether the firm pays zero cash dividends or pays out 100% of its earnings.*

THE NORMAL CORPORATION'S PRESENT VALUE IS CONSTANT FOREVER BECAUSE ROE = K   **EXAMPLE**

Table 23-3 illustrates how the Normal Corporation's stock price and cash dividend grow at g = 10% per year but have the same present value of $50 per share forever. This example assumes: (a) the internal rate of return on equity is ROE $=$ 15%; (b) the capitalization rate is also k $=$ 15%; and, (c) the cash dividends grow at g $=$ [(RR)(ROE)] $=$ [(0.666)(15%)] $=$ 10% per year because two-thirds (RR $=$ 0.666) of each year's earnings per share are retained for internal investment that earns ROE $=$ 15%.

---

* Taking the derivative of the stock price in Eqn. 23-14a with respect to the retention rate yields:

$\delta P / \delta RR = [(EPS)(ROE - k)] / \{k - [(ROE)(RR)]\}^2$

Evaluating this derivative reveals that if ROE $>$ k, then P rises directly with RR, or, $\delta P / \delta RR > 0$. But, if ROE $<$ k, then P varies inversely with RR, or, $\delta P / \delta RR < 0$. If ROE $=$ k, then P does not depend on RR and we can conclude that dividend policy is irrelevant.

Table 23-3 Multiperiod Financial Analysis of the Normal Corporation's Future Per Share Stock Prices and Cash Dividends

			Future Value at g = 10%		*PV of Per Share Data at k = 15%*		
Terminal Time Period, T Years	Annual Cash Dividend Payment, DIV_t	Stock's Market Price, P	PV of the Cumulative Cash Dividend	+	PV of the Future Price	=	PV of Year T's Total
T = 0	NA[a]	$50.00	NA	+	$50.00	=	$50
T = 1	$2.50 (t = 0)	55.00	$2.18	+	47.82	=	50
T = 2	2.75 (t = 1)	60.50	4.26	+	45.74	=	50
T = 3	3.03 (t = 2)	66.55	6.25	+	43.76	=	50
T = 4	3.33 (t = 3)	73.20	8.15	+	41.85	=	50
T = 5	3.66 (t = 4)	80.53	9.97	+	40.03	=	50
T = 10	5.89 (t = 9)	129.68	17.94	+	32.06	=	50
T = 20	15.29 (t = 19)	336.37	29.44	+	20.56	=	50
T = 50	266.80 (t = 49)	5,869.55	44.58	+	5.42	=	50
T = 100	31,319.57 (T = 99)	689,030.62	49.41	+	0.59	=	50
T = ∞	∞	∞	50.00	+	0.0	=	50

[a]Not applicable.

Although yearly dollar values in Table 23-3 change every year the Normal Corporation's present value is constant at $50 per share forever. The cost of capital for its outstanding common stock is 15% and the stock provides its investors 15% rate of return every year.

Cost of capital = Required rate of return

$$\begin{pmatrix} \text{Corporation's} \\ \text{cost of equity} \\ \text{capital, } k = 15\% \end{pmatrix} = 5\% + 10\% = \frac{DIV_1}{P} + g$$

$$= \begin{pmatrix} \text{Annual cash} \\ \text{dividend} \\ \text{yield, } 5\% \end{pmatrix} + \begin{pmatrix} \text{Rate of annual} \\ \text{price} \\ \text{appreciation, } g = 10\% \end{pmatrix} = \begin{pmatrix} \text{Investors'} \\ \text{required rate of} \\ \text{return, ROE} = 15\% \end{pmatrix}$$

The aggregate physical size of the Normal Corporation and the aggregate dollar value of its outstanding common stock increases every year, but the present value of the Normal Corporation (aggregate and per share) never changes because ROE = *k*.

THE PRICE-EARNINGS RATIO

Fundamental common stock analysts utilize a well-known procedure to estimate the value of a share of common stock. They prepare an estimate of a stock's earnings per share and an estimate of the stock's price-earnings ratio and, then, they multiply these two quantities to obtain their estimate of the share's value:*

---

* Since the right-hand side cancels out to equal the left-hand side, a nonfinancial person might think Eqn. 23-16 was merely a tautology, P = (EPS)(P/EPS).

Although EPS and P/EPS are interrelated, Eqn. 23-16 is not a tautology because EPS and P/EPS are separate random variables that are determined by interrelated but different processes.

$$\begin{pmatrix} \text{Estimated} \\ \text{value per} \\ \text{share} \end{pmatrix} = \begin{pmatrix} \text{Estimated} \\ \text{earnings} \\ \text{per share} \end{pmatrix} \begin{pmatrix} \text{Estimated} \\ \text{price-earnings} \\ \text{ratio} \end{pmatrix} \qquad \text{(23-16)}$$

Figures 23-3A and B use quarterly values of the S&P500 index to compare the three stock valuation variables in Eqn. 23-16.

Fluctuations in Stock Prices, Earnings, and the Price-Earnings (P/EPS) Ratios

Figure 23-3A shows that over six decades the S&P500 stock prices and the earnings from the S&P500 tended to rise together. Comparing Figures 23-2 and 23-3A reveals that earnings fluctuate much more than the smoothly rising cash dividends.

Trending, Trendless, and Mean-Reverting Patterns. Common stocks prices and cash dividends have trended upward decade after decade. Figure 23-3B shows that while the S&P500 stocks price index trended upward the S&P500 price/earnings ratio fluctuated without a trend. A pattern is discernible in Figure 23-3B, however. The S&P500 price/earnings ratio exhibits *mean-reversion;* after a large move up or down it tends to revert back toward its long-run average value.

FIGURE 23-3A   S&P500 Index and S&P500 Earnings

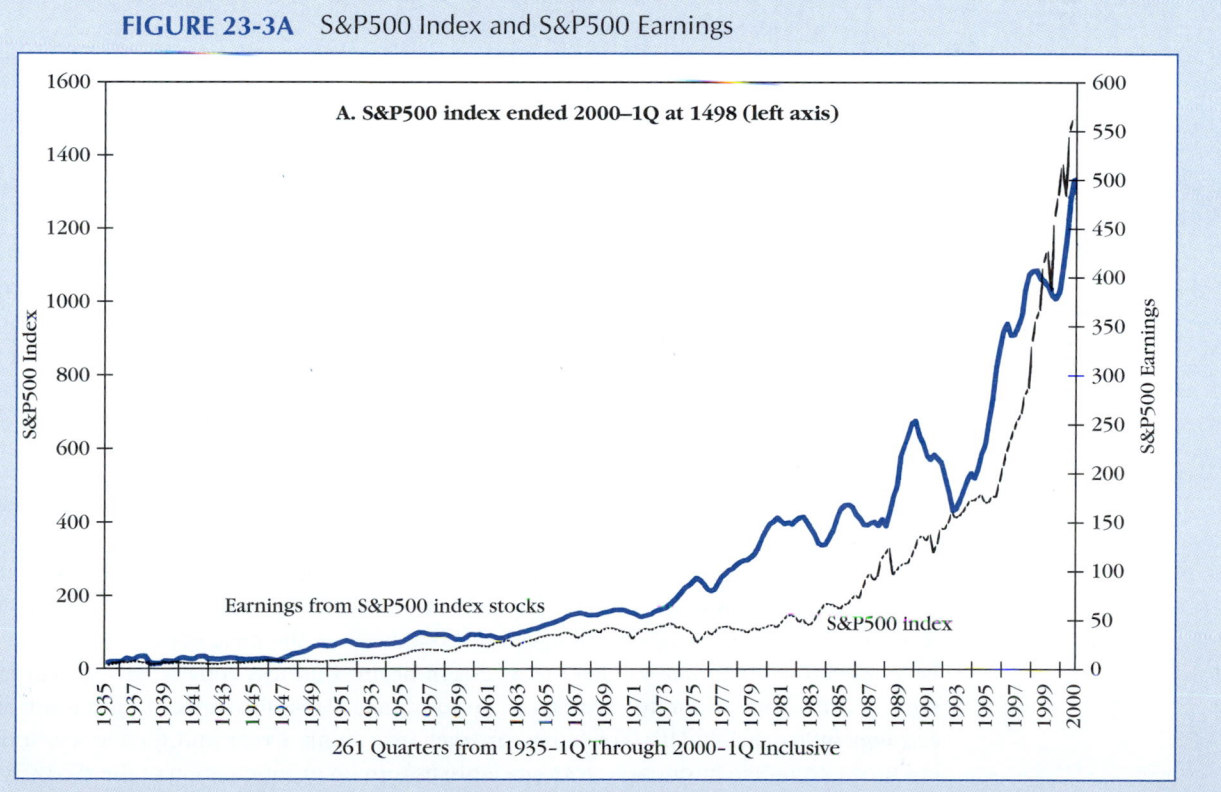

During 1990–91 the S&P500 earnings fell while stock prices continued to rise, but that was an anomaly. Over 66 years stock prices and earnings have usually risen together. Comparing Figures 23-2 and 23-3A reveals that stock prices and earnings have tended to move together more closely than stock prices and cash dividends.

FIGURE 23-3B   S&P500 Index and S&P500 Index's P/E Ratio

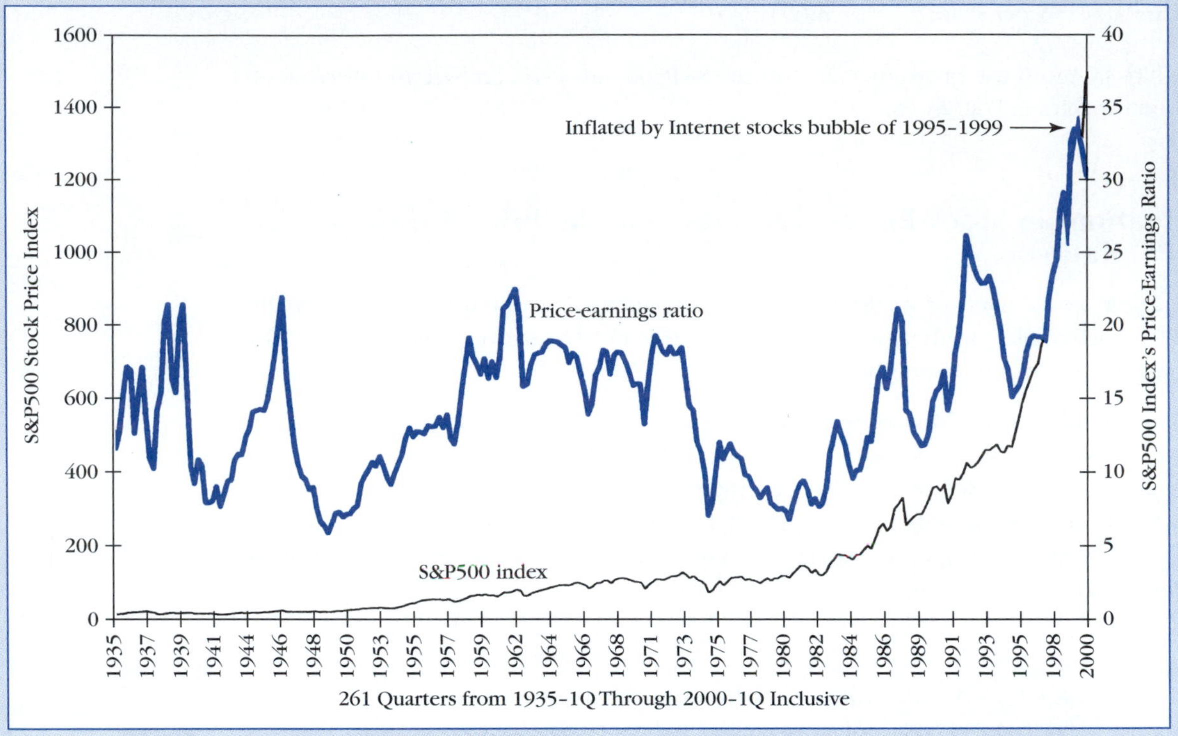

While the S&P500 stocks price index trended upward the S&P500 price-earnings ratio fluctuated without any trend. The S&P500 price-earnings ratio, nevertheless, exhibits two discernible patterns. First, the S&P500 price-earnings ratio tends to rise and fall during bull and bear markets, respectively. Second, after large moves up or down the S&P500 price-earnings ratio tends to revert back toward its long-term mean.

Statistical Aggregation Problems.   The S&P500 index data in Figures 23-3A and B is from a diversified portfolio of 500 stocks. Aggregation smoothes out (averages over) tendencies that are visible when the stocks are viewed individually. If time-series graphs of the prices of individual common stocks, their earnings per share, and their price-earnings ratios from dozens of different corporations were examined, the following two tendencies which cannot be seen in the aggregated (averaged) S&P500 index data would become discernible.

Business Cycle Fluctuations.   When a nation's business activity increases month-after-month *bull market* conditions emerge as increasing business activity pushes up the earnings of most corporations, price-earnings ratios rise as optimism becomes more prevalent, and the prices of most stocks advance each trading day. Months later, in anticipation of a forthcoming recession, stock prices begin crashing a few months before the peak in business activity as a *bear market* starts to unfold.[9] As the recession begins business activity falls off, corporate sales decline, and corporate earnings begin to plunge. Pessimism spreads and most price-earnings ratios shrink. The typical bear market lasts about a year and then, a few months before the trough in business activity, stock prices turn up in anticipation of the recovery and forthcoming expansion. Most corporations' price-earnings ratios tend to move with the corporation's earnings through the business cycle. At the same time, corporations' price-earnings ratios tend to move inversely with the corporation's earnings in response to temporary disturbances.

Reactions to Predictable and/or Temporary Earnings Fluctuations. Some companies experience seasonal fluctuations that are repetitive and predictable. Some retail department stores, for example, experience more sales during the month of December than they experience during the other 11 months of the year combined. The earnings per share of these retail department stores tend to be highly seasonal. The stock prices of seasonal corporations do not typically fluctuate seasonally, however, because their price-earnings ratios move inversely to offset their temporary and predictable seasonal earnings fluctuations. Corporations' price-earnings ratios not only move inversely to offset seasonal earnings fluctuations, they also move inversely to offset other temporary earnings fluctuations. For instance, when a corporation's earnings plunge because of a labor strike, if the stock market perceives the problem to be temporary, the corporation's stock price may not decline at all as the corporation's price-earnings ratio moves inversely to offset the earnings plunge.

Analyzing the Price-Earnings (P/EPS) Ratio

Dividing both sides of Eqn. 23-4 by the stock's expected earnings per share (EPS_1) creates Eqn. 23-17.

$$P/EPS_1 = \frac{DIV_1/EPS_1}{k - g} \tag{23-17}$$

$$= \frac{\text{Payout ratio}}{k - g} \tag{23-17a}$$

$$= \frac{(1 - RR)}{k - g} \text{ since } (1 - RR) = \text{Payout Ratio} \tag{23-17b}$$

Eqns. 23-17, 23-17a, and 23-17b are **static equilibrium models** that change slowly.[10] Eqn. 23-17 shows that, in equilibrium, a stock's price-earnings ratio has three primary determinants.

1. A risk-adjusted discount rate that exceeds the stock's average growth rate, k.
2. A growth rate, g.
3. A cash dividend payout ratio, $DIV_1/EPS_1 = (1 - RR)$.

These three determinants are considered separately. This chapter's Table 23-1 and Table 2-3 in Chapter 2 show how the risk-adjusted discount rate, k, rises and falls with the riskiness of the common stock issuer. This fact, combined the fact that k is in the denominator of Eqn. 23-17, causes the price-earnings ratio to move inversely with the issuer's riskiness.*

Since the growth rate has a negative sign and is in the denominator of Eqn. 23-17, we can see that the price-earnings ratio moves directly with the issuer's growth rate.**

Eqn. 23-17b is rearranged to show how the stock issuer's cash dividend payout ratio affects the stock's price-earnings ratio:

---

* Taking the first derivative of the price-earnings ratio in Eqn. 23-17 with respect to the risk-adjusted discount rate yield: $\delta(P/EPS)/\delta k = [(P/EPS)(-k)]/(k - g)^2 < 0$. By definition, we know that: $\delta k/\delta(\text{risk}) > 0$. These two derivatives combine to imply the conclusion that the price-earnings ratio reacts inversely to changes in the riskiness of the issuer: More concisely, we conclude that: $\delta(P/EPS)/\delta(\text{risk}) < 0$.

** Taking the first derivative of the price-earnings ratio in Eqn. 23-17 with respect to the growth rate yields: $\delta(P/EPS)/\delta g = [(P/EPS)(g)]/(k - g)^2 > 0$.

$$P/EPS_1 = \frac{(1 - RR)}{k - g} \tag{23-17b}$$

$$= \frac{(1 - RR)}{k - [(RR)(ROE)]} \text{ since } g = [(RR)(ROE)] \tag{23-17c}$$

$$= \frac{(1 - RR)}{k(1 - RR)} \text{ if ROE} = k \tag{23-17d}$$

$$= \frac{1}{k} \tag{23-17e}$$

Normal firms were defined to be those that had ROE = k. Eqn. 23-17e shows that when ROE = k the issuer's cash dividend policy, represented by RR, cancels out of the price-earnings ratio. In other words, even though the numerators of Eqns. 23-17 and 23-17 equal the payout ratio, the payout ratio has no effect on the price-earnings ratio of stock issued by a normal firm. Eqn. 23-17d aligns with Eqn. 23-15a, which showed that dividend policy has no impact on the prices of stocks issued by normal firms.

The empirical evidence in Figure 23-4 throws light on the mathematical analysis of the price-earnings ratio. Only one relationship is observable in Figure 23-4; the S&P500 cash dividend yield moves inversely with the S&P500 price-earnings ratio. This inverse relationship is an aberration resulting from the fact that the S&P500 index in the numerator of the S&P500 price-earnings ratio is identical to the denominator of the S&P500 cash dividend yield. Besides this meaningless peculiarity, the Standard & Poor's 500 data in Figure 23-4 reveals no discernible relationship between the S&P500 price-earnings ratio, its cash dividend payout ratio, its cash dividends per share index, or its cash dividend yield during the 1935–2000 period. The market data in Figure 23-4 supports the Modigliani-Miller theorem, mentioned previously, which asserts that the cash dividend policy of a normal firm has no effect on the value of its equity shares.

EXAMPLE   COMPARATIVE STATICS WITH THE BATTEL CORPORATION'S PRICE-EARNING RATIO

Reconsider the Battel Corporation. This year's cash dividends are DIV_0 = $2.00; the firm's growth rate is g = 2%. Earlier in this chapter we saw that if the corporation's cost of equity capital is k = 10%, its initial value is $25.50 per share (see Eqn. 23-4a, p. 691). Assume Battel's expected earnings per share are EPS_1 = $3.00. Under these circumstances, Battel's price-earnings ratio is 8.5:

$$P/EPS = \frac{DIV_1/EPS_1}{k - g} = \frac{\$2.04/\$3.00}{0.10 - 0.02} = \frac{.68}{0.08} = 8.5 \text{ times} \tag{23-17}$$

If we suppose Battel is going to distribute to Europe, the firm's growth rate is expected to rise from g = 2% to g = 4%. Because of increased risk exposure, the corporation's cost of equity capital is expected to rise from k = 10% to k = 11%. As a result of these developments Battel's value per share increases to $29.71 per share.

$$P_0 = \frac{DIV_0(1 + g)}{k - g} = \frac{DIV_1}{k - g} = \frac{(\$2.00)(1.04)}{0.11 - 0.04} = \frac{\$2.08}{0.07} = \$29.71 \text{ per share} \tag{23-4b}$$

Under these international assumptions, a share of Battel's stock should sell for about 9.7 times its earnings.

$$P/EPS = \frac{DIV_1/EPS_1}{k - g} = \frac{\$2.04/\$3.00}{0.11 - 0.04} = \frac{.68}{0.07} = 9.7 \text{ times} \qquad (23\text{-}17)$$

Price-Earnings (P/EPS) Ratios of Stocks That Pay No Cash Dividends

Corporations that pay no cash dividends are problematic for the DDM, because cash dividends are the only cash flows in the model. Microsoft Corporation, for example, which pays zero cash dividends as a matter of corporate policy, does not fit easily into the DDM. This problem can be surmounted by reformulating the DDM in terms of earnings. After all, profitable companies that pay no cash dividends still have earnings and price-earnings ratios.

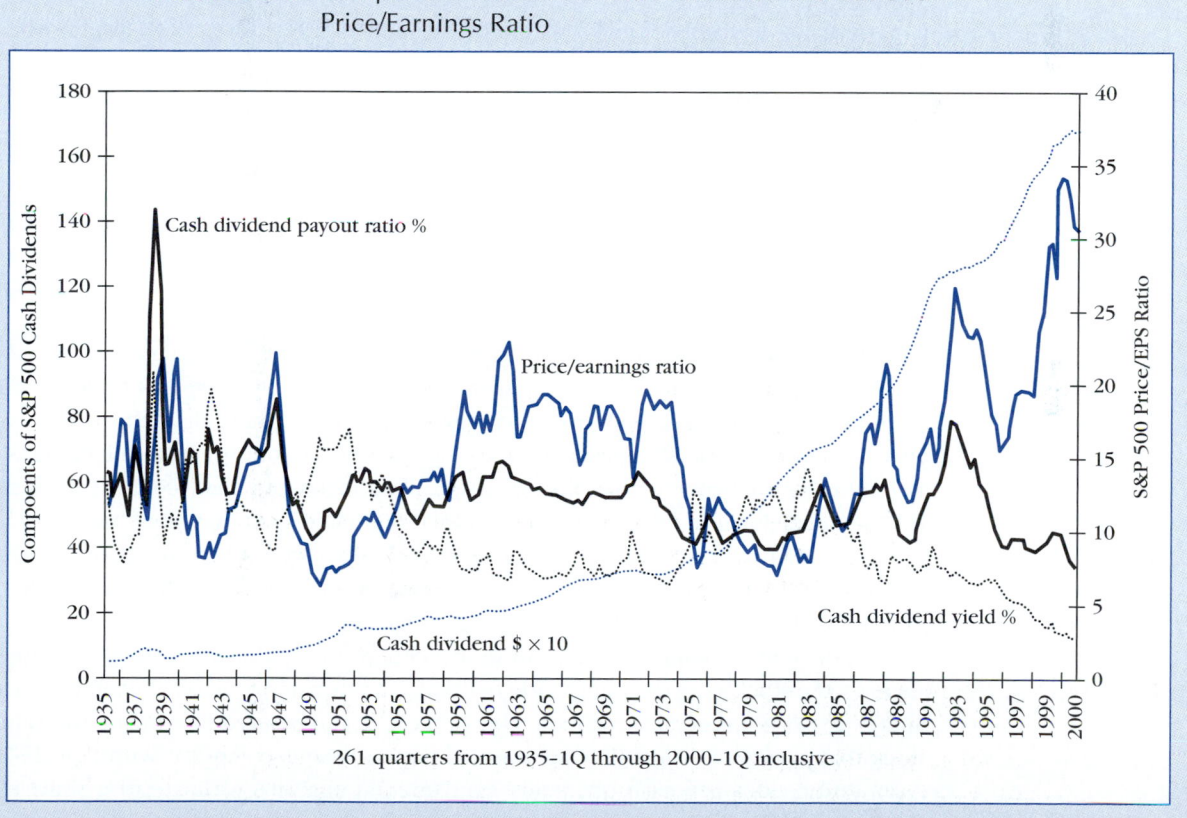

FIGURE 23-4   Components of S&P500 Cash Dividends and S&P500 Price/Earnings Ratio

261 quarters from 1935-1Q through 2000-1Q inclusive

The S&P500 price-earnings ratio demonstrates mean reverting behavior as it fluctuates trendlessly. The S&P500 cash dividend payout ratio exhibits some mean reversion too, with a slight downward trend. In contrast, the S&P500 cash dividends per share move upward smoothly. The cash dividend components seem to have no meaningful relationship with the volatile price-earnings ratio.

Eqn. 23-17 can be reformulated for profitable corporations that pay zero cash dividends. More specifically, Eqn. 23-17 can be used to *attribute* values to the payout ratio of a profitable corporation that pays zero cash dividends, as the following example demonstrates.

EXAMPLE

IMPUTING A PRICE-EARNINGS RATIO TO THE MICROSOFT CORPORATION, WHICH NEVER PAYS CASH DIVIDENDS

The values below are based on Microsoft's 1995–99 average cost of equity capital, $k = 40\%$; earnings per share growth rate, $g = 36\%$; and price-earnings ratio, P/EPS = 40 times.

$$\text{P/EPS} = \frac{\text{DIV}_1/\text{EPS}_1}{k - g} \qquad (23\text{-}17)$$

$$\text{P/EPS} = \frac{\text{Imputed}\left(\text{DIV}_1/\text{EPS}_1\right)}{k - g} \qquad (23\text{-}18)$$

$$40 = \frac{\left(\begin{array}{c}\text{Inputed} \\ \text{payout ratio}\end{array}\right)}{.40 - .36} \qquad \textbf{(23-18a) for Microsoft}$$

Solving Eqn. 23-18a to find Microsoft's imputed payout ratio yields a value of 160%.

$$\left(\begin{array}{c}\text{Imputed} \\ \text{payout} \\ \text{ratio}\end{array}\right) = (\text{P/EPS})(k - g) = (40 \text{ times})(.40 - .36) = 1.6 = 160\% \quad \textbf{(23-18b) for Microsoft}$$

Microsoft's imputed payout ratio of 160% in Eqn. 23-18b is much larger than most payout ratios—most are in the range of 30% to 50%. More commonly, payout ratios in excess of 100% occur when a corporation that pays cash dividends consistently experiences an unexpected steep drop in earnings.

The imputed value of 160% from Eqn. 23-18b suggests the stock market valued $1 of Microsoft earnings at $1.60. This lofty assessment could be interpreted as evidence that the stock market places a high value on Microsoft's policy of retaining all its earnings to finance growth internally instead of paying cash dividends. Since $1 of capital gains income is taxed at a lower income tax rate than $1 of cash dividend income in many countries, it is reasonable to conclude the stock market values a dollar of retained earnings more highly than it values a dollar of cash dividends. In any event, Eqn. 23-18 shows how to adapt the DDM to derive a theoretical model for the price-earnings ratio of companies like Microsoft, Cisco, America Online, and Oracle that never pay cash dividends.

Fundamental common stock analysts' procedure of multiplying a stock's earnings per share by the stock's price-earnings ratio to obtain an estimate of the share's value, as set forth in Eqn. 23-16, is a venerable tradition. This procedure can be used to estimate the value of a stock that pays zero dividends, if an imputed payout ratio is computed with Eqn. 23-18. If a corporation does pay cash dividends, fundamental analyst's estimate of a share's value obtained with Eqn. 23-16 can be compared with an estimate of the same stock's value that was obtained with the DDM, Eqn. 23-4. These two valuation models will probably yield similar but different estimates of the value of a stock. If the two estimates differ, in working to determine why they differ, the security analysts may be able to make the two estimates converge on a single improved estimate of the security's value.

COMPARING TWO DIFFERENT ESTIMATES OF COKE'S COMMON STOCK VALUE

EXAMPLE

Coca-Cola's common stock paid annual cash dividends of 64 cents per share in 1999. In 1999 KO's cost of capital was $k = 20.7\%$ per annum for equity, and its cash dividend growth rate was $g = 19.7\%$ per year over the previous decade. The DDM indicates Coke's stock was worth $64 per share in 1999.

$$P_0 = \frac{DIV_1}{k - g} = \frac{\$0.64}{0.207 - 0.197} = \frac{\$0.64}{0.01} = \$64 \text{ per share} \tag{23-4}$$

In 1999 the Coca-Cola Corporation paid out 65.3% of its earnings in the form of cash dividends, $DIV_1/EPS_1 = 64/98 = 0.653$. Substituting these values into Eqn. 23-17 suggests that Coca-Cola's stock is worth 65.3 times its earnings per share in 1996.

$$P/EPS = \frac{DIV_1/EPS_1}{k - g} \tag{23-17}$$

$$= \frac{.653}{.207 - .197} = 65.3 \text{ times}$$

Multiplying Coke's price-earnings ratio of 65.3 times its 1999 earnings per share of $0.98, as suggested by Eqn. 23-16, produces a fundamental analyst's estimated value of $63.99 per share for 1999.

$$\begin{pmatrix} \text{Estimated} \\ \text{value per} \\ \text{share, \$63.99} \end{pmatrix} = \begin{pmatrix} \text{Earnings per} \\ \text{share, \$0.98} \end{pmatrix} \begin{pmatrix} \text{Estimated} \\ \text{price-earnings} \\ \text{ratio, 65.3 times} \end{pmatrix} \tag{23-16a}$$

The fundamental analyst's estimate of $63.99 per share is remarkably close to the DDM's estimate of $64. If these two estimates had differed significantly, it would be worthwhile for security analysts to investigate the difference. As a matter of fact, the market price of Coca-Cola's common stock actually fluctuated between a low of $47.31 and a high of $70.88 during 1999.

The (*k-g*) Spread

The numerical values of k and g used in the perpetual constant growth DDM Eqn. 23-4 and the price-earnings ratio model Eqn. 23-17 play important roles in determining the security analyst's estimate of what an equity share is worth. However, the difference between k and g can be more important than the individual values of k and g. For instance, reconsider the tiny **(k-g) spread** of 0.01 [$= (.207 - .197)$] in the denominator of the DDM that was used to estimate the value of the Coca-Cola's common stock in the example above. The value of Coke's stock would have been the same if the k and g values had been $k = .31$ and $g = .30$, as long as the difference yielded a (k-g) spread of 0.01. The (k-g) spread is a metric that is worthy of further consideration.

To see where the (k-g) spread comes from, reconsider the perpetual constant growth DDM, Eqn. 23-4:

$$P_0 = \frac{DIV_1}{k - g} \tag{23-4}$$

Solving Eqn. 23-4 for the cash dividend yield produces Eqn. 23-19:

$$DIV_1/P_0 = (k - g) = \text{The } (k - g) - \text{spread} \tag{23-19}$$

Eqn. 23-19 contains two interesting pieces of information. First, it tells us that the perpetual constant growth DDM implies that a stock's (k-g) spread should equal the stock's cash dividend yield, DIV_1/P_0.[11] It is interesting to consider Eqn. 23-19 in light of the steady decline of the S&P500 cash dividend yield since 1983 that is illustrated in Figure 23-2. If the S&P500 cash dividend yield continues its steady decline in the future, Eqn. 23-19 suggests the (k-g) spread could narrow further in the years ahead. If the (k-g) spread continues to narrow this implies higher price-earnings ratios and larger capital gains.

The second bit of information we can obtain from Eqn. 23-19 is about the tradeoff between a common stock's cash dividend yield, DIV_1/P_0, and the rate at which that stock yields capital gains, g. To see the second implication, assume k remains constant in Eqn. 23-19. As long as k remains constant, the stock issuer's cash dividend yield and the rate of capital gains must move inversely to keep from violating the equation. If Eqn. 23-19 is not violated and the cash dividend yield continues to fall as illustrated in Figure 23-2, the rate of capital gains will have to rise by an equal amount in order for k to remain fixed in value. This rising value of g for the S&P500 in Eqn. 23-19 comprises another suggestion that, under the assumed conditions, a stock market that pays more capital gains and less cash dividends might lie ahead.

FINANCIAL ANALYSIS THROUGH TIME

Although the perpetual constant growth DDM is a static equilibrium model, it can be used to track the evolution of an all-equity firm through time. Reformulating this one-period model by including time subscripts links an investment in a share of common stock to the share's underlying assets and earnings. Moving the model through time highlights the fact that the firm's assets, earnings, and dividends all grow at the constant growth rate g. Table 23-4 traces the results from investing in one share of stock for 3 years.

The bottom row of Table 23-4 contrasts stock and flow variables. Assets are **stock variables** that exist at discrete points in time; they can be acquired in an instant and sold just as quickly. In contrast, sales revenues, purchases of raw material, and income are **flow variables** that occur gradually over time and are measured as rates of flow during a set period of time. Stock variables and flow variables interact. For example, if sales revenues exceed costs the company generates an income flow that can be used to purchase larger stocks of assets or pay out as a flow of cash dividends.

ANALYSIS OF GROWTH INVESTING

The versatile DDM may be used to analyze growth stocks. Consider an established firm that will earn EPS_1 per year perpetually if it never buys any new assets. Suppose this firm retains $(RR)(EPS_1)$ dollars from Year 1's ($t = 1$) earnings to buy a new asset that earns a fixed perpetual return of ROE. Starting in Year 2 ($t = 2$) the new asset will earn $(ROE)(RR)(EPS_1)$ dol-

TABLE 23-4   Stocks and Flows Associated with One Share of Common Stock Change in Accordance with the DDM

	Beginning-of-Year Assets Per Share	Annual Earnings Per Share (EPS)	Year's Cash Dividend Per Share	End-of-Year Value on an Equity Share
$t=0$	Zero	Zero	Zero	Initial investment, $P_0 = \$50$
$t=1$	To get started, initial cash of $P_0 = \$50$ is used to purchase: $Assets_0 = \$50$	$EPS_1 = (ROE)(Assets_0)$ $\$7.50 = (15\%)(\$50)$	$DIV_1 = (1-RR)(EPS_1)$ $\$2.50 = (.333)(\$7.50)$	$P_1 = \dfrac{DIV_2}{k-g} = Assets_0(1+g)$ $\$55 = (\$2.75)/(15\%-10\%)$
$t=2$	$Assets_1 = (Assets_0)[1+g]$ $= (Assets_0)[1+(RR)(ROE)]$ $= \$55$	$EPS2 = (ROE)(Assets_1)$ $= (EPS_1)[1+g]$ $= \$8.25$	$DIV_2 = (1-RR)(EPS_2)$ $= (DIV_1)[1+g]$ $= \$2.75$	$P_2 = \dfrac{DIV_3}{k-g} = Assets_0(1+g)^2$ $\$60.50 = (\$3.025)/(15\%-10\%)$
$t=3$	$Assets_2 = (Assets_0)[1+g]^2$ $= (Assets_0)[1+(RR)(ROE)]^2$ $= \$60.50$	$EPS_3 = (ROE)(Assets_2)$ $= (EPS_1)[1+g]^2$ $= \$9.075$	$DIV_3 = (1-RR)(EPS_3)$ $= (DIV_1)[1+g]^2$ $= \$3.025$	$P_3 = \dfrac{DIV_4}{k-g} = Assets_0(1+g)^3$ $\$66.55 = (\$3.3275)/(15\%-10\%)$
Stock or flow?	A growing stock of assets, not a flow of assets.	A growing income flow, not a stock of income	An annual cash flow, not a stock of cash.	A growing stock of value, not a flow of value.

ROE = 15% = Return on equity
RR = Retention Rate = 0.666 = (1−Payout ratio)
g = 10% = Growth rate = (ROE)(RR) < k

k = 15% = Cost of equity capital = [(DIV/P) + g] > g
$Assets_t$ = Dollar value of assets per share at beginning of year t
P_t = Dollar value of an equity share at end of year t

The one-period discounted dividend model (DDM) has time subscripts added and is used to trace the relationship between an investment in a share of common stock and that share's assets, earnings, and cash dividend payments. The corporation's assets are stock variables that exist at points in time, they can be acquired and sold in an instant. In contrast, sales revenues, purchases of raw material, and income are flow variables that occur throughout a time period and are measured on the basis of a flow per period. The numerical example uses values from Table 23-3.

lars per year. Finally, after the first year is past, assume the firm pays out 100% of its earnings in every following year. The present value of an equity share in this firm equals:

$$P_0 = \frac{(EPS_1)(1-RR)}{(1+k)^1} + \frac{(EPS_1)+(ROE)(RR)(EPS_1)}{(1+k)^2} + \frac{(EPS_1)+(ROE)(RR)(EPS_1)}{(1+k)^3} + \cdots \qquad \textbf{(23-12b)}$$

Separating Earnings. The earnings in the numerator of Eqn. 23-12b can be separated into two components:

1. Perpetual annual earnings from the old assets, denoted EPS_1,
2. Perpetual annual dollar earnings of $(ROE)(RR)(EPS_1)$ per year from the new assets begin in the second year and continue forever.

This separation permits Eqn. 23-12b to be rewritten as Eqn. 23-12c:

$$\left(\begin{array}{c}\text{PV of}\\\text{one share}\end{array}\right) = \left(\begin{array}{c}\text{PV of earnings from}\\\text{the old assets}\end{array}\right) +$$

$$P_0 = \frac{EPS_1}{(1+k)^1} + \frac{EPS_1}{(1+k)^2} + \frac{EPS_1}{(1+k)^3} + \cdots$$

$$\cdots + \frac{EPS_1(-RR)}{(1+k)^1} + \frac{(ROE)(RR)(EPS_1)}{(1+k)^2} + \frac{(ROE)(RR)(EPS_1)}{(1+k)^3} + \cdots \qquad \textbf{(23-12c)}$$

$$-\left(\begin{array}{c}\text{PV of cost}\\\text{of new asset}\end{array}\right) + (\text{PV of earnings from new asset})$$

NPV of the New Asset. The **net present value, NPV,** of an investment equals the present value of its cash flows minus the cost of the asset. In the case above, the NPV of the new asset acquired at the end of Year 1 ($t = 1$) equals the present value of its constant perpetual cash flows, denoted $\left(\dfrac{EPS_1(ROE)(RR)}{k}\right)$, minus the new asset's cost of $(RR)(EPS_1)$ dollars.

$$\begin{pmatrix} NPV_0 \text{ of} \\ \text{new asset} \\ \text{at } t = 0 \end{pmatrix} = \frac{1}{1 + k}\begin{pmatrix} NPV_1 \text{ of} \\ \text{new asset} \\ \text{at } t = 1 \end{pmatrix} = \frac{1}{1 + k}\left(\overbrace{\frac{EPS_1(ROE)(RR)}{k}}^{\begin{pmatrix} PV \text{ of perpetual} \\ \text{cash flows} \end{pmatrix}} - \overbrace{(RR)(EPS_1)}^{\begin{pmatrix} Cost \text{ of the} \\ \text{new asset} \end{pmatrix}}\right)$$

New assets increase the owners' equity only if they have positive NPVs.

Total Value. Substituting the NPV above into the right-hand-side of Eqn. 23-12c yields Eqns. 23-12d and 23-12e:

$$P_0 = \frac{EPS_1}{k} + \frac{1}{1 + k}\left(\frac{EPS_1(ROE)(RR)}{k} - (RR)(EPS_1)\right) \qquad \text{(23-12d)}$$

$$P_0 = \frac{EPS_1}{k} + \frac{NPV_1}{1 + k} \qquad \text{(23-12e)}$$

$$\begin{pmatrix} \text{Total} \\ PV_0 \text{ per} \\ \text{share} \end{pmatrix} = \begin{pmatrix} PV_0 \text{ of earnings} \\ \text{from old assets} \end{pmatrix} + \begin{pmatrix} NPV_0 \text{ of growth opportunity} \\ \text{from the new asset} \end{pmatrix}$$

A growth firm might purchase additional new assets every year. If new assets are purchased in future years, the NPVs of new assets purchased in years $t = 1, t = 2, t = 3, \ldots,$ $t = \infty$ are denoted NPV_1, NPV_2, NPV_3, $\ldots$, NPV_∞. Eqn. 23-12e is extended to Eqn. 23-12f to include the possibility that new assets are purchased in future years:

$$P_0 = \frac{EPS_1}{k} + \sum_{t=1}^{\infty}\frac{NPV_t}{(1 + k)^t} \qquad \text{(23-12f)}$$

$$\begin{pmatrix} \text{Total} \\ PV_0 \text{ per} \\ \text{share} \end{pmatrix} = \begin{pmatrix} PV_0 \text{ of earnings} \\ \text{from old assets} \end{pmatrix} + \begin{pmatrix} NPV_0 \text{ of growth opportunities} \\ \text{from future investments} \\ \text{in new assets} \end{pmatrix}$$

Eqn. 23-12f makes it clear that no matter how much of a firm's earnings are retained and reinvested within the firm to finance growth, the value of its equity shares will not be increased unless retained earnings are invested in projects with positive NPVs.[12]

Growth Stock Investing. As mentioned in Chapter 8 (pp. 206–212), empirical evidence documents a widespread tendency for long-run investments in value stocks to outperform growth stocks. This tendency constitutes an anomaly in the semistrong theory of efficient markets.

Eqn. 23-12e throws some light on the value versus growth stock anomaly. Perhaps the growth stocks do not perform as well as the value stocks in the long run because the earnings that growth firms retain to finance internal growth is spent on projects that have zero or negative NPVs. In other words, many growth firms may be growing physically larger, but the present value of their owners' shares is not growing. If $k =$ ROE, this implies NPV $= 0$. Table 23-3 (p. 702) provides a numerical example of how a normal corporation can grow larger without increasing the present value of the owners' shares because ROE $= k$.

Security Analysis. The preceding analysis suggests that security analysts endeavor to assess the profitability of the firm's investment opportunities. If the firm has no marketing advantages over its rivals, no cost advantages, and is not protected by barriers to entry, the security analysts should be highly suspicious of any share valuations that significantly exceed the value of the assets in place.

A Reality Check: INSIDER TRADING   ETHICS

Suppose your Uncle Jack hints that his mining company has made a big discovery. If you buy stock before the announcement, are you guilty of insider trading? Even so, is it really wrong?

   Insider trading is defined as trading stock on the basis of material, nonpublic information. This definition does not consider who is covered (unlike Uncle Jack, you are not an insider) or how the information is acquired (suppose you deduced it from delivering documents as a bicycle courier). The first persons to hear the announcement will quickly buy. What's wrong with getting a jump on them? Surprisingly, the answers to these questions are controversial.

   One argument for legally prohibiting insider trading is to prevent *unfairness* in the market. The market rewards people who seek out new information, but insiders have an unfair advantage if the information is nonpublic. Allowing insiders to exploit this unfair advantage would undermine confidence in the market.

   A second argument is that insider trading is a kind of *fraud* because corporations have an obligation to disclose market-moving information in a timely manner. Trading by insiders before a disclosure is like selling a house without revealing hidden termite damage. Insider trading is prosecuted under SEC Rule 10b-5, which prohibits fraud in the market.

   The standard legal argument is that insider trading utilizes information that a person has *misappropriated* from a corporation. Until it is disclosed, inside information belongs to the company, and an insider has a fiduciary duty not to use that information for personal benefit. The harm is done not to the market or other traders, but to the corporation. Some economists argue that insider trading ought to be permitted because it increases market efficiency by registering information more quickly. However, this argument overlooks the harm to corporations if fiduciary duties are not enforced.

   The courts follow this *misappropriation theory.* Consequently, an inside trader must owe a fiduciary duty to the source of the information. This includes your Uncle Jack. However, you still might be prosecuted for insider trading if you know that your Uncle Jack is violating a duty to his company.

                                        John R. Boatright, *Professor of Business Ethics*

THE BOTTOM LINE

The DDM resembles the present value model used to value bonds, but differs conceptually because equities involve more uncertainty. Most of this added uncertainty comes from the cash flows. A common stock's cash dividends are not spelled out clearly for years into the future in an indenture contract like a bond's coupon interest payments. Bonds and stocks are similar in the sense that both have risk-adjusted discount rates that equal a risk-free rate plus a risk premium. But, again, there is more uncertainty in equities than in bonds. Equity returns contain all the risk premiums the bonds have, plus an equity risk premium.

Although a corporation's board of directors may legally stop paying cash dividends at any time, they rarely elect to do so. Most corporations endeavor to pay cash dividends that grow slowly over time, and they hardly ever reduce regular cash dividends. As a result, the constant growth model does an adequate job of forecasting many corporations' cash dividends per share:

$$\text{DIV}_t (1 + g)^k = \text{DIV}_{t+k}$$

The simple constant growth model does a better job of forecasting dividend payments 10 or 20 years ahead than it does at forecasting for 50 or 100 years into the future. But since the present value of dividends received 50 or 100 years in the future is tiny, long-run forecasting errors are not necessarily a fatal problem. It is more difficult to forecast the cash dividends of small, risky corporations than it is to forecast the dividends from larger, older corporations. However, this increased forecasting difficulty is offset by the fact that the riskier companies are discounted at a higher discount rates which, in turn, reduces the need for long-range forecasting accuracy with the riskier small firms.

The perpetual constant growth DDM is popular because forecasting future cash dividends is difficult. This model generates a forecast of future dividends and, at the same time, computes their present value in one simple model. The model also yields valuation insights. For example, it can be manipulated to show that the firm's return on equity must exceed its risk-adjusted cost of capital, ROE > k, for growth to add to investors' wealth.

The perpetual constant growth DDM is sensitive to the assumed growth rate. The two-stages-of-growth model was developed to allow for a transition from an initial growth rate to a second growth rate that differs from the initial growth rate.

The perpetual constant growth DDM can be divided by earnings per share (EPS) to derive a model that explains stock's price-earnings ratios in equilibrium:

$$P_0 = \frac{\text{DIV}_1}{k - g} \tag{23-4}$$

$$P/\text{EPS}_1 = \frac{\text{DIV}_1/\text{EPS}_1}{k - g} \tag{23-17}$$

Eqn. 23-17 shows that the price-earnings ratio varies directly with both the stock's payout ratio (DIV/EPS) and its growth rate (g), and inversely with the stock's risk-adjusted discount rate (k). For stocks that pay no cash dividends, an imputed payout ratio must be used with Eqn. 23-18a:

$$P/\text{EPS}_1 = \frac{\left(\begin{array}{c} \text{Imputed} \\ \text{payout ratio} \end{array} \right)}{k - g} \tag{23-18a}$$

The DDM's balance sheet implications can be used to link one time-period's investment in a share of common stock to that share's portion of the firm's assets, earnings, and dividends. The firm's assets, earnings, and dividends all grow at the same rate g. Assets are *stock variables* that can be acquired and liquidated instantly. In contrast, sales revenues, purchases of raw material, and income are *flow variables* that occur gradually over time. The stock and flow variables within a firm interact. For example, if sales revenues are less than costs the company can suffer losses (a negative flow) that necessitates liquidating some of the firm's stock of assets.

A multiperiod formulation of the perpetual constant growth DDM that focuses on earnings per share yields insights into the difference between investing in growth stocks and value stocks. The analysis of growth stock investing showed that no matter how much of a firm's earnings are retained to finance growth internally, the present value of the corporation's equity shares will not appreciate unless the earnings that are retained are invested in projects with positive net present values (NPVs). This explains how a growth firm might be growing physically larger, but not appreciate in value as rapidly as some value stocks.

QUESTIONS

Q23-1 (Sustainable growth rate) Use the perpetual constant growth DDM to delineate the maximum rate at which an equity share can grow, assuming that the issuer does not use debt financing.

Q23-2 (Required rate of return) Why is the discount rate used in the DDM sometimes called the required rate of return?

Q23-3 (Payoff from retained earnings) Will every dollar of earnings that a corporation retains to finance its growth internally lead to a dollar of price appreciation in the firm's common stock (capital gains income)? To keep your answer simple, ignore all taxes.

Q23-4 (Specified holding period) Does the price that an investor should be willing to pay for a stock depend on that investor's expected holding period for the stock? Explain.

Q23-5 (Dividends and stock price) What should happen to the price of a growth stock if the retention rate is increased? What should happen to the price of a normal firm's stock if the retention rate is increased? (Assume all new investment is financed internally.) Explain.

Q23-6 (k-g spread) If the difference between the required rate of return on a stock and the expected growth rate of the stock widens, what does this imply about the dividend yield of the stock? Assuming that the required rate of return remained constant, what does this imply about the expected future price of the stock (i.e., capital gain income)? Explain.

Q23-7 (Perpetual constant growth model) To employ the constant growth model, it must be assumed that the required rate of return is greater than the expected growth rate on the stock. Does this assumption seem logical? Explain.

Q23-8 (Forecasting dividends) The perpetual constant growth model assumes that the expected growth rate of dividends will continue to exist even 50 to 100 years into the future. Since we cannot truly be sure of this, the model is not very reliable, even for a firm that can be expected to experience this growth rate for, say, the next 15 years. True or false. Explain.

Q23-9 (Dividend policies) Explain why, if a growth firm's value will increase if the firm retains all of its earnings, we observe some growth firms that pay out dividends.

Q23-10 (Growth firms) Consider the following information on Stocks X and Y and Z:

	Stock X	Stock Y	Stock Z
Required return (k)	15%	15%	15%
ROE (assumed constant)	15%	12%	18%
Retention rate	50%	20%	50%
Expected dividend (DIV_1)	$1.10	$2.00	$1.00

Which of the three stocks would be considered a true growth stock? Which is the stock of a normal firm? Why?

PROBLEMS

P23-1 (Perpetual DDM) A firm reported that it paid dividends of $0.70 a share this year. A financial analyst has determined that the firm's growth rate in dividends will continue at its historical rate of 8% a year indefinitely and has estimated that an investor should require a 20% return on the firm's stock, based on its riskiness. What is the fair market price of the stock that is implied by his estimates?

P23-2 (Estimated holding-period price) What if an investor planned to hold the stock in Problem 23-1 for only 2 years? Use the DDM to determine what price this investor should be willing to pay for the stock.

P23-3 (Two stages of growth) An analyst has estimated that a certain firm will experience an extremely high growth rate of 30% a year for the next 2 years, after which the growth rate is expected to decline to a more moderate 12% a year when competitive pressures exert an influence. The firm has announced that it expects to pay its first dividend of $0.30 a share next year, and the analyst has determined that the required rate of return should be 18%. At what price should this stock be selling?

P23-4   (DDM components) Consider the following information for two stocks, M and N:

	Stock M	Stock N
ROE (assumed constant)	12%	12%
Retention rate (assumed constant)	60%	30%
Required return	12%	12%
Expected dividend (DIV_1)	$1.00	$1.75

Which stock will be more sensitive to the spread between the required return and the growth rate? Why?

P23-5   (Imputed payout ratio) The Fledgling Airline Corporation reported earnings per share of $0.95 for 1999. It paid no dividends, and the required return on its equity is 30%. The firm had an average price-earnings ratio in 1999 of 10.52. Its growth rate is estimated to be 21%. What is its imputed payout ratio?

P23-6   (Growth rate estimates) Assume the growth rate for Fledgling Airlines in Problem 23-4 were revised upward to 28% due to a recent Justice Department ruling in its favor. What would happen to Fledgling's price-earnings ratio, assuming the imputed payout ratio in Problem 23-4 remained unchanged?

P23-7   (Price-earnings ratio) The Pliant Corporation currently has a price-earnings ratio of 6.21, which is well below the industry average of 15X. However, there has been a management shakedown and analysts are expecting that Pliant's price-earnings multiple will increase to the industry average this year. Earnings are expected to be $2.25 per share for the firm. What is the estimated price per share based on this information?

P23-8   (Sustainable growth rate) The CellOptics Corporation reported $1.2 million in net income last year and pays out 20% of its earnings as dividends. Its sales were $22 million on total assets of $15 million. The firm uses all equity financing. What is its sustainable growth rate?

P23-9   (Perpetual DDM) A firm's dividend payout ratio is expected to remain at its present level of 40% and earnings per share are expected to be $3.50 in the coming year, based on an estimated growth rate of 12%, which is expected to continue indefinitely. If the required rate of return is 16%, at what price should this firm's stock sell?

P23-10   (Investment opportunities) The Trimark Corporation is expected to have earnings per share of $3.00 next year and its current market price is $20. The firm has a dividend payout ratio of 60%. The remainder is invested in projects that earn a rate of return of 15%. This is expected to continue indefinitely. (a) What required rate of return is implied by the perpetual DDM model? (b) By what amount does the current market value ($20) exceed what it would be if all the firm's earnings were paid as dividends?

CFA EXAM QUESTIONS

The following three questions are adopted from the 1999 CFA Sample Exam, Level I:

1. Which of the following assumptions does the constant growth dividend discount model require?

   I. Dividends grow at a constant rate.

   II. The dividend growth rate continues indefinitely.

   III. The required rate of return is less than the dividend growth rate.

   A. I only.
   B. III only.
   C. I and II only.
   D. I, II, and III.

2. An analyst gathers the following information about a company:

1997 net sales	$10,000,000
1997 net profit margin	5.0%
1998 expected sales growth	−15.0%
1998 expected profit margin	5.4%
1998 expected common stock shares outstanding	120,000

   The analyst's estimate of the company's 1998 earnings per share should be *closest to:*

   A. $3.26.
   B. $3.72.
   C. $3.83.
   D. $4.17.

3. An analyst estimates the earnings per share and price-to-earnings ratio for a stock market series to be $43.50 and 26 times, respectively. The dividend payout ratio for the series is 65%. The value of the stock market series is *closest* to:

   A. 396.
   B. 735.
   C. 1131.
   D. 1866.

4. (1997 CFA Exam, Level II) The Soft Corporation (SC) is planning to acquire a slower growth competitor, which will materially increase SC's sales volume. The company to be acquired has pretax margins that are approximately the same as those of SC. SC plans to issue $300 million in long-term debt to finance the entire cost of the acquisition.

   A. Discuss how SC's potential acquisition might *decrease* its valuation based on a constant-growth dividend discount model. Be sure to comment on *each* of the *three* factors in such a model.

   B. Discuss *two* reasons why SC's potential acquisition might *increase* the P/E multiple investors are willing to pay for SC.

5. (Adapted from the 1995 CFA Exam, Level II) Your supervisor has asked you to evaluate the relative attractiveness of the stocks of two very similar chemical companies. Litchfield Chemical Corp. (LCC) and Aminochem Company (AOC). Both firms have a June 30 fiscal year end. You have compiled the data in Table 1 for this purpose. Use a 1-year time horizon and assume the following:

   Real gross domestic product is expected to rise 5%;

   S&P 500 expected total return of 20%;

   U.S. Treasury bills yield 5%; and

   30 year U.S. Treasury bonds yield 8%.

   A. Calculate the value of the common stock of LCC and AOC using the constant growth dividend discount model. Show your work.

   B. Calculate the expected return over the next year of the common stock of LCC and AOC using the capital asset pricing model. Show your work.

   C. Calculate the internal (implied, normalized, or sustainable) growth rate of LCC and AOC. Show your work.

   D. Recommend LCC *or* AOC for investment. Justify your choice by using your answers to A, B, and C and the information in Table 1.

Table 1

	Litchfield Chemical (LCC)	Aminochem (AOC)
Current stock price	$50	$30
Shares outstanding (millions)	10	20
Projected earnings per share (fiscal 1996)	$4.00	$3.20
Projected dividend per share (fiscal 1996)	$0.90	$1.60
Projected dividend growth rate	8%	7%
Stock beta	1.2	1.4
Investors' required rate of return	10%	11%
Balance sheet data (millions)		
Long-term debt	$100	$130
Stockholders' equity	$300	$320

6. (1998 CFA Exam, Level III) Joe Brown, an analyst at Global Alpha Investors (GAI), is reviewing the empirical evidence on historical U.S. equity market returns. Brown finds that value stocks (which he defines as stocks with low price-to-book ratios) outperformed growth stocks (stocks with high price-to-book ratios) in many recent time periods. Julia Smith, chief investment officer at GAI, offers two alternative explanations for these results: (a) investors perceive value stocks to be riskier than growth or (b) investors misprice stocks relative to their earnings growth prospects.

   Discuss how *each* of the *two* explanations given by Smith could account for the findings that value stocks have outperformed growth stocks in many recent periods.

ENDNOTES

1 The foundation for the perpetual DDM was laid by John Burke Williams, *The Theory of Investment Value* (Amsterdam: North-Holland Publishing, 1964). The first edition was published in 1938.

2 For a discussion of two-stages-of-growth and three-stages-of-growth DDMs, see Nicholas Molodovsky, "Common Stock Valuation—Principles, Tables, and Applications," *Financial Analysts Journal* (November-December 1969). Alternatively, see Ibbotson Associates, *Stocks, Bonds, Bills, and Inflation, 1999 Yearbook,* Valuation Edition, Chicago, pp. 27–28. For software to compute the two-stages-of-growth DDM and three-stages-of-growth DDM see, Jack Clark Francis, *Investments Analysis Software* (New York: McGraw-Hill, 1994), Chapters 11 and 12.

3 For an analysis of growth, see William J. Hurley and Lewis D. Johnson, "A Realistic Dividend Valuation Model," *Financial Analysts Journal* (July-August 1994): 50–54. Also see Charles C. Holt, "The Influence of Growth

Duration on Share Prices," *Journal of Finance* 7, no. 3 (September 1962): 465-75. In addition, see David Durand, "Growth Stocks and the Petersburg Paradox," *Journal of Finance,* 12, no. 3 (September 1957): 348-63. The last two articles are classics.

4 See Ramasastry Ambarish, Kose John, and Joseph Williams, "Efficient Signaling with Dividends and Investments," *Journal of Finance* 42 (1987): 321-43. Also see M. Brennan and A. V. Thakor, "Shareholder Preferences and Dividend Policy," *Journal of Finance* 45 (1990): 993-1018. In addition, see M. Miller and K. Rock, "Dividend Policy Under Asymmetric Information," *Journal of Finance* 40 (1985):1031-51. Furthermore, see Chris Innes, Peter B. Blanton, Nomo Nomo-Ongolo, and Cindy Sieden, *Stock Buybacks— Strategy and Tactics,* Salomon Brothers, New York City, February 1997. See Deborah J. Lucas and Robert L. McDonald, "Shareholders Heterogeneity, Adverse Selection, and Payout Policy," *Journal of Financial and Quantitative Analysis* 33, no. 2 (June 1998): 233-54. More recently, see M. Jagannathan, C. P. Stephens, M. S. Weisbach, "Financial Flexibility and the Choice Between Dividends and Stock Repurchases," *Journal of Financial Economics* 57, no. 3: 309-54.

5 If the issuer acquires its own shares at a price that is too high the share repurchase might be dilutive. For an insightful discussion of these and related share repurchase issues, see Deborah J. Lucas and Robert L. McDonald, "Shareholders Heterogeneity, Adverse Selection, and Payout Policy," *Journal of Financial and Quantitative Analysis* 33, no. 2 (June 1998): 233-54.

6 This section draws from the classic article by Merton H. Miller and Franco Modigliani, "Dividend Policy, Growth and the Valuation of Shares," *Journal of Business* 34, no. 4 (October 1961): 411-33.

7 See P. Asquith and D. W. Mullins, "The Impact of Initiating Dividend Payments on Shareholders' Wealth," *Journal of Business* (January 1983): 77-96. Also see J. A. Brickley, "Shareholder Wealth, Information Signaling and the Specially Designated Dividend," *Journal of Financial Economics* (August 1983): 187-209. See also T. E. Dielman and H. R. Oppenheimer, "An Examination of Investor Behavior During Periods of Large Dividend Changes," *Journal of Financial and Quantitative Analysis* (June 1984): 197-216. All of these studies document statistically significant cash dividend announcement effects that resulted from *signals* the market perceived to be implied by unusual cash dividend payments.

8 For background see Myron J. Gordon, *The Investment, Financing, and Valuation of the Corporation* (Homewood, IL: Irwin, 1962). For an enlightening discussion of the conditions under which capitalizing earnings is equivalent to capitalizing dividends, see Diran Bodenhorn, "On the Problem of Capital Budgeting," *Journal of Finance* 14 (December 1959): 473-92.

9 The National Bureau of Economic Research (NBER) is a respected group of economists that studies business cycles and other economic topics. The NBER designates the month in which each business cycle peaks and troughs. To avoid uncertainty, most economists and financial analysts utilize official NBER peaks and troughs in their research.

10 For a discussion of P/EPS models for stocks with finite growth, see J. Gordon and Myron Gordon, "The Finite Horizon Expected Return Model," *Financial Analysts Journal* 53, no. 3 (May-June 1997): 52-61. Also see Morris G. Danielson, "A Simple Valuation Model and Growth Expectations," *Financial Analysts Journal* 54, no. 3 (May-June 1998): 50-57. For an empirical study using a similar model that is based on less restrictive assumptions see Patricia M. Fairfield, "P/E, P/B, and the Present Value of Future Dividends," *Financial Analysts Journal* 50, no. 4 (July-August 1994): 23-31.

11 For a discussion of the cash dividend yield, see Michael Rozeff, "Dividend Yields Are Equity Risk Premiums," *Journal of Portfolio Management* 11, no. 1 (Fall 1984): 68-75.

12 For an enlightening discussion of the present value of growth opportunities (PVGO), see Richard A. Brealey and Stewart C. Myers, *Principles of Corporate Finance,* 5th ed. (New York: McGraw-Hill, 1996), Chapter 4, pp. 67-71.

MEASURING
EARNING POWER

Chapter 23 reviewed Modigliani and Miller's (M&M's) Nobel prize-winning dividend irrelevance theorem that showed that the cash dividend policy of a normal firm has no effect on the value of its stock. Without violating M&M's dividend irrelevance theorem, this chapter shows how changes in a firm's cash dividend payments can cause short-term stock price changes. The chapter also shows that the issuer's earnings per share are a very important determinant of the value of an equity share. Empirical evidence is reviewed to illustrate how stock prices anticipate changes in a corporation's earnings and, also, how they behave after the earnings are announced. Before discussing earnings, let us reconsider cash dividends.

Ex-dividend stock price drop-offs are a rational way for an efficient market to process cash flow information without violating the M&M dividend irrelevance theorem. The next section considers other ways cash dividend payments cause stock price changes.

THE INFORMATION CONTENT OF CASH DIVIDENDS

John Lintner interviewed corporate boards of directors and studied the way they arrive at their cash dividend payment decisions. Lintner reported:[1]

1. Corporations' boards of directors typically develop long-run target cash dividend payout ratios. As mentioned in Chapter 23, for example, page 36 of Coca-Cola's 1997 Annual Report says that Coke's "Board Of Directors intends to gradually reduce our dividend payout ratio to 30% . . ."
2. Most corporations "smooth" their cash dividend payments so that they follow the long-run trend in the corporation's earnings. As a result, short-term changes in a corporation's earnings usually have little impact on its cash dividend payments.
3. Corporations' boards of directors are reluctant to change their regular cash dividend payments. Most directors are loath to vote for a decrease unless it is required to keep the firm alive. Small, infrequent increases are popular.

The cash dividend payment policies above are determined after consideration of relevant information.

Asymmetric Information

The cash dividend payment policies above are shaped by inside information available to the board of directors. An **information asymmetry** exists because the board of directors has valuable inside information that is not available to external investors. A corporation board uses this inside information when it allocates the corporation's earnings to pay cash dividends, repurchase the firm's outstanding stock, and/or retain earnings to finance internal growth. M&M's dividend irrelevance theorem shows that the value of most firms cannot be affected by their board's cash dividend decisions. However, the M&M theorem does not mean a corporation's cash dividend payment has no **information content**; external investors who do not have access to inside information scrutinize corporations' cash dividend payments for **signals** that have valuable information content.[2]

Reactions to Cash Dividend Payments

Paul Healy and Krishna Palepu (H&P) investigated 131 corporations that initiated cash dividend payments and 172 corporations that omitted regular cash dividend payments. To see if the directors' decisions passed along information content of any value, H&P studied the stock prices of the corporations for the 60 days before and 20 days after the dividend announcements. The corporations that initiated cash dividend payments experienced average earnings growth rates of 43% in the year before they began paying dividends.[3] In the 4 years after the cash dividends were initiated, the average corporation experienced another 164% increase in earnings. These findings suggest that, on average, boards of directors initiate cash dividend payments when they believe that the higher payments can be sustained in the future. Stated differently, investors can interpret the commencement of cash dividend payments to be a signal from the board of directors that the corporation's future earnings prospects are favorable.

H&P also discovered that when corporations announce they are going to omit a regular cash dividend payment, on average, their stock price experiences an abnormal decrease of 9.5%. Furthermore, their earnings continued to fall over the next four quarters. In contrast, when a corporation announces an increase in its cash dividend payment, its stock price experiences an abnormal average increase of 4%. Clearly, the market interprets cash dividend omissions as signals of forthcoming bad news.

Other researchers who analyzed increases and decreases in regular cash dividend payments reach similar conclusions.[4] The dividend findings reported here do not contradict M&M's dividend irrelevance theorem. The findings only mean that, on average, the market correctly imputes informational content to changes in corporations' cash dividend policies. Taken alone, cash dividend payments are meaningless.[5] The stock prices rise (fall) because the market expects the corporation's earnings to increase (decrease).

Many investors want more information than they can get from corporation's annual reports and public announcements. Investors are particularly eager to get forecasts of a corporation's future earnings because, as this chapter shows, the information has a large impact on stock prices. As a result, financial service corporations have sprung up specifically to provide forecasts of corporation's earnings per share.

FORECASTING EARNINGS PER SHARE

Moody's, Standard & Poor's, Value Line, and many brokerage houses publish forecasts of earnings per share for hundreds of issues of common stock. A securities analyst specializing in stocks in that particular industry usually prepares each corporate forecast.

Surveys of Forecasts

Three corporations that specialize in providing consensus forecasts of earnings collect multiple forecasts:

1. Institutional Brokers Estimate System, called I/B/E/S, headquartered in New York City, has been in the earnings forecasting business since 1971. I/B/E/S gathers financial data on 18,000 companies in 48 countries.
2. Zacks Investment Research, headquartered in Chicago, has been in business for over a decade and compiles similar data from thousands of firms.
3. First Call is a financial research subsidiary of The Carson Group in New York City.

I/B/E/S and Zacks employees make periodic phone calls to professional securities analysts, financial analysts, and investors at mutual funds, banks, and brokerage houses around the world and solicit their forecasts of corporations' earnings per share for 4 quarters of future earnings and up to 5 years of annual earnings. They analyze these earnings forecasts and publish the high, low, average, and median earnings the experts forecast for each firm and each future time period. The data is updated frequently so that it represents current estimates of the continuously changing consensus forecast. Zacks and I/B/E/S compute a statistical measure of dispersion of the forecasts to measure the uncertainty and differences of opinion that exists among forecasters. They also provide an earnings growth rate for each corporation, the adjustment factors for stock splits, the number of forecasters surveyed in each period, per share cash dividends, and per share stock prices.

Zacks or I/B/E/S subscribers may choose to have the data they purchase on paper, on diskettes, on computer tapes, sent via electronic mail, or they may pay for the privilege of being able to interrogate the I/B/E/S or Zacks database 24 hours per day. Subscribers may purchase data about a single company, industry average data for one or more industries, data on all the companies in a single industry, data on all the companies listed on a stock exchange, all the forecasts of one or more security analysts who is of particular interest, or information conforming to other criteria.

First Call's Internet site provides news, chat rooms, information on insider trading, earnings information, price quotes, graphs of prices over time, financial research on companies and mutual funds, and other financial information.

How Expert Are the Experts?

Financial economists analyze the I/B/E/S and Zacks databases to study the earnings forecasts from many different securities analysts; they reach certain general conclusions *about the forecasters.*[6] First, the forecasters tend to overestimate earnings per share. Second, the forecasters tend to revise their forecasts downward to improve their accuracy as the earnings announcement date draws near. Third, the forecasters seem to be reluctant to say negative things about the security issuers. Fourth, the forecasters issue many more buy than sell recommendations. It has been suggested that the reason for the last two characteristics is that the security analysts are reluctant to say anything that might antagonize a potential client of their employers.

Every year the October issue of a monthly publication entitled *Institutional Investor* contains survey results from about 2,000 money managers. The money managers are asked

to evaluate the individual security analysts they know. Based on the survey results, the staff at *Institutional Investor* compiles a list of the "best" security analyst for each of over 60 industries. The security analysts who are selected each have their picture and a short biography published, and the magazine declares them to be members of that year's "*Institutional Investor* (II) All-American Research Team." Several astute observers have suggested the members of II's All-Star team have total annual compensations over $1 million.

Scott E. Stickel compared the forecasts from the member of II's All-American Research Team with the earnings forecasts of other security analysts.[7] His statistical analysis indicated that the members of the All-American Research Team did no better than other security analysts, and he hypothesized that a good personality might be as important as good analytical skills in attaining membership on II's All-American Research Team.

Several financial economists compared the earnings forecasts created by sophisticated mechanical models with the forecasts prepared by professional security analysts. Lawrence D. Brown and Michael S. Rozeff report that from 1971 through 1975 the forecasts of earnings published in *Value Line Investment Survey* modestly outperformed their mechanical model.[8] Patricia C. O'Brien reports that from 1975 through 1982 the analysts' earnings forecasts she obtained from the I/B/E/S databank outperformed the auto-regressive model she tested.[9]

Whisper Earnings

Whisper earnings are forecasts of earnings per share that circulate among securities analysts and traders on Web sites, television programs, and in the financial press. These unofficial forecasts of earnings per share reflect the expectations of various market participants. Bagnoli, Beneish, and Watts (BBW) report that the whisper forecasts are, on average, more accurate than surveys of institutional forecasts.[10] BBW's report abnormal profits from trading on the "whispers."

There is no consensus about whose earnings forecast is best. But, there is widespread agreement that earnings forecasts are useful in determining whether a company's earnings are either surprisingly good or surprisingly bad.

SURPRISING CHANGES IN EARNINGS AFFECT STOCK PRICES

Henry Latané and Charles Jones (LJ) suggested that surprisingly good or surprisingly bad changes in a corporation's earnings caused significant stock price changes.[11] They developed a model to measure the amount of surprise in pleasant or disappointing earnings announcements. Eqn. 24-1 defines what LJ called the **standardized unexpected earnings**, or **SUE**, for a corporation:

$$\mathrm{SUE}_{i,t} = \frac{(\text{Actual quarterly EPS})_{i,t} - (\text{Forecasted quarterly EPS})_{i,t}}{\text{Standard deviation of the forecasting error}_i} \tag{24-1}$$

$$= \frac{\text{Forecasting error}_{i,t}}{\text{Earnings uncertainty}_i}$$

SUE Numerator. The numerator of Eqn. 24-1 measures the *forecasting error* for corporation *i* that can be observed after the *t*th quarter's earnings are announced publicly. The numerator equals the difference between the *i*th corporation's reported accounting earnings and the consensus earnings forecast from I/B/E/S or Zacks or some other forecast. The size and sign of this forecasting error measures the surprise that occurs when the earnings are announced.

SUE's Denominator. As the forecasting error is being determined the standard deviation of past forecasting errors is computed for the denominator of Eqn. 24-1. Dividing each forecasting error by this standard deviation creates an index number. Normalizing or standardizing the SUE facilitates comparisons between different companies and different time periods.

COMPARING THE SUES FROM CORPORATIONS A AND B   EXAMPLE

If Corporations A and B both had forecasted earnings per share of $2.00 and actual earnings of $3.00, they would have identical forecasting errors of $1.00. Suppose Corporation A was a predictable public utility whose forecasting errors had a small standard deviation of 50 cents. In contrast, Corporation B is a technology firm with volatile earnings and a standard deviation of $2.00. The SUE values of these two firms differ substantially.

$$SUE_{A,t} = \frac{(\text{Actual EPS})_t - (\text{Forecasted EPS})_t}{\text{Standard deviation of errors}_A} = \frac{\$3.00 - \$2.00}{0.50} = 2.0 \tag{24-1a}$$

$$SUE_{B,t} = \frac{(\text{Actual EPS})_t - (\text{Forecasted EPS})_t}{\text{Standard deviation of errors}_B} = \frac{\$3.00 - \$2.00}{\$2.00} = 0.5 \tag{24-1b}$$

Since both SUEs are positive, the investors in both corporations are pleasantly surprised to find out that their stock's actual EPS exceeded its forecasted value. But, Eqns. 24-1a and 24-1b show that investors in stock A were much more pleasantly surprised by its earnings than were the investors in stock B, even though both securities had identical forecasting errors. The forecasting error of $+$1$ is a more pleasant surprise to the investors in A than to the investors in B because earnings $1 above the forecast are more unusual for a public utility whose earnings do not fluctuate much (have a small standard deviation).

The Foster-Olsen-Shevlin (FOS) Event Study

George Foster, Chris Olsen, and Terry Shevlin analyzed the way a particular *event* affects stock prices. The event Foster-Olsen-Shevlin (FOS) analyzed is the public announcement of a corporation's quarterly earnings. FOS used Eqn. 24-1 to compute the SUE values for 2,053 corporations over 32 quarterly earnings announcements.[12] After (2,053 stocks $\times$ 32 quarters =) 65,696 SUE values were calculated, these values were arrayed in descending order, and assigned to one of ten size Decile portfolios. Decile Portfolio 1 contained the 10% (either 6,569 or 6,570) most negative SUE values—this portfolio contains the worst news. Decile Portfolio 10 contained the 10% largest positive SUE values—a portfolio of the best surprises. The SUE values in Decile Portfolios 2 through 9 are arrayed along a continuum between good and bad news. The average abnormal returns from the stocks measured over three different time periods surrounding each announcement event are shown in Figure 24-1 for each decile portfolio.

Since earnings announcements are the events FOS analyze, all earnings announcement days are designated as Day zero. Figure 24-1A illustrates the decile portfolio returns measured over the $[-60, 0]$ time period, which begins 60 days before the earnings were announced ($t = -60$) in the *Wall Street Journal* and includes the announcement date ($t = 0$). Figure 24-1B

FIGURE 24-1 Abnormal Common Stock Returns During Three Different Time Periods Surrounding Quarterly Earnings Announcement Dates

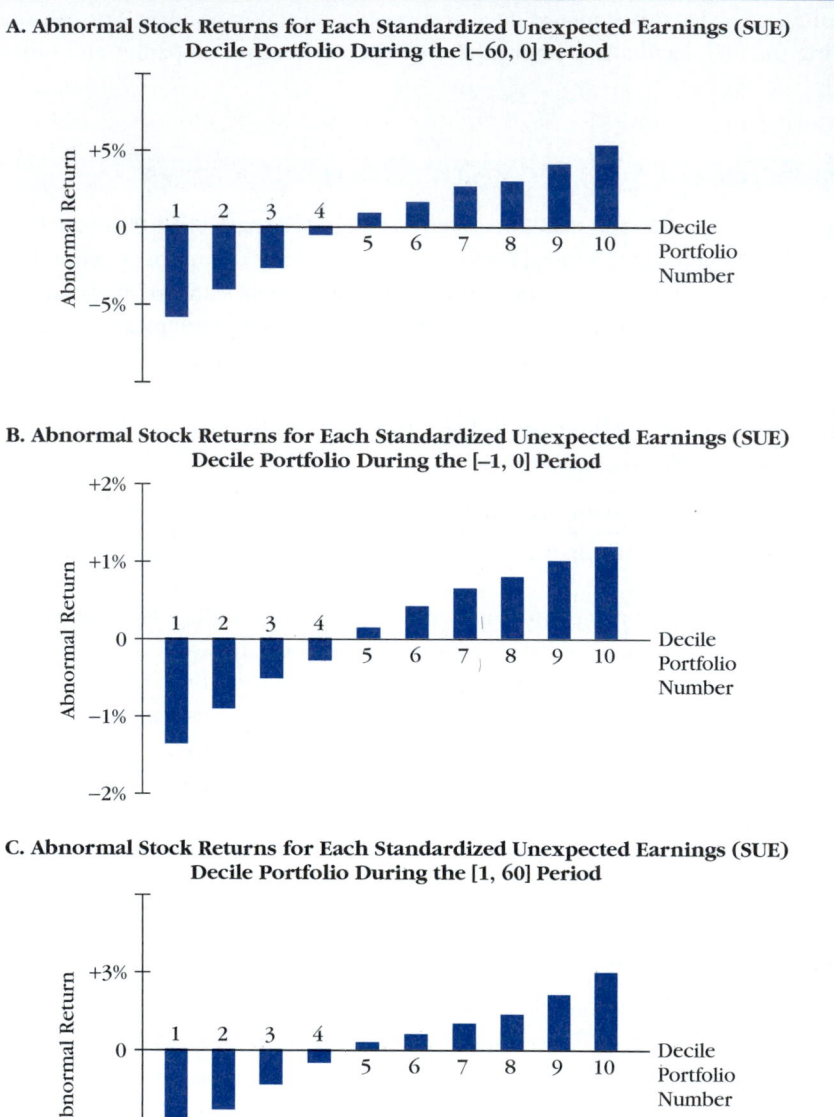

A. Abnormal Stock Returns for Each Standardized Unexpected Earnings (SUE) Decile Portfolio During the [−60, 0] Period

B. Abnormal Stock Returns for Each Standardized Unexpected Earnings (SUE) Decile Portfolio During the [−1, 0] Period

C. Abnormal Stock Returns for Each Standardized Unexpected Earnings (SUE) Decile Portfolio During the [1, 60] Period

Standardized unexpected earnings (SUEs) from earnings announcements were arrayed and sorted into decile portfolios each quarter. Figure 24-1A, B, and C illustrates similar direct relationships between the size and sign of the surprise measured by the average standardized unexpected earnings (SUEs) value and the size and sign of the stocks' abnormal returns.

SOURCE: George Foster, Chris Olsen, and Terry Shevlin, "Earnings Releases, Anomalies and the Behavior of Security Returns," Accounting Review, 59, no. 4 (October 1984): 574–603.

shows the decile portfolios' returns measured over the $[-1, 0]$ period, which covers 2 days—one day before the earnings announcement and the announcement date. Figure 24-1C displays the ten decile portfolios' average returns measured over the $[1, 60]$ period—from the day after the earnings announcement through the following 60 days.

Interpreting the Results

Figure 24-1A, B, and C illustrates similar direct relationships between the size and sign of the unexpected earnings surprise and the size and sign of the stocks' abnormal returns. Figure 24-1A shows that when corporations announce unexpectedly good earnings (Portfolios 9 or 10), averaged over thousands of observations from different corporations and different years, their stock prices tend to increase *prior to the announcement date*. When corporation announce unexpectedly poor earnings (Portfolios 1 or 2), Figure 24-1A shows that their stocks' prices tend to decrease over the same $[-60, 0]$ period. Essentially, Figure 24-1A provides evidence that, on average, the stock market correctly *anticipates* earnings changes before they are announced and responds to these expectations in a rational manner.

The day before the announcement and the event date comprise the $[-1, 0]$ time span. During these two days, Figure 24-1B shows that larger earnings surprises in either direction result, on average, in larger price reactions in the same direction. In other words, even at the "last minute," the stock prices tend to react rationally to new information.[13]

Figure 24-1C documents an anomaly in the *efficient markets theory*.* Figure 24-1C illustrates that the direct relationship between the earnings surprises and the abnormal stock returns documented in Figures 24-1A and 24-1B continues for 2 months *after* the earnings are announced. For instance, an investor in Decile Portfolio 10 can expect to accumulate abnormal gains of 3.23% during 2 months after the unexpectedly good earnings are made public. This finding suggests that an investor could earn abnormal returns simply by looking at the quarterly earnings announcements in the *Wall Street Journal* and, based on the sign and size of the SUE, taking either a long or a short position in Decile Portfolio 10 or 1, respectively. This comprises an anomaly in the semi–strongly efficient markets hypothesis because public information can be used to earn abnormally high returns. Stock prices should reflect all public information in semi–strongly efficient markets.

The FOS study of stock price reactions to earnings announcements reviewed above suggests two conclusions. First, the study leaves little doubt that earnings expectations are a very important determinant of stock prices. Second, it is probable that even more compelling results could have been attained if better measures of earnings had been utilized. The studies cited here were all based on the earnings reported by the corporation's own accountants. The next section discusses ways to obtain better estimates of a company's earning power.

AMBIGUITIES IN ACCOUNTING EARNINGS

Earnings per share are not easy to measure. **Generally accepted accounting principles (GAAP)** leave ample room for interpretation. The latitude the accountant may follow in deriving a firm's income is wide. The accountant needs some leeway to select an accounting procedure that most clearly reports the true economic consequence of a business transaction. Yet accountants sometimes produce income statements that financial analysts, security analysts, and investors alter to obtain estimates of a firm's true economic income. Distorted income statements often result from (1) the accountant's use of an accounting procedure

---

* The efficient markets theory was introduced in Chapter 3 and discussed further in Chapter 8.

that is inappropriate for the relevant economic transaction and/or (2) accrual accounting techniques that do not link revenues and expenses to the time period in which the cash flows actually occurred and/or (3) pressure on the accountant from the firm's management to "window-dress" the financial statements.

Contrasting Two Income Statements for the Same Firm in the Same Year

Table 24-1 shows two income and expense statements for the same company for the same year. These two statements are identical in every way except for some accounting procedures used to prepare them. Income statement B tends to minimize taxable income. Income statement A is presumed to be a true representation of the firm's economic income. The accounting procedures followed in developing Income statements A and B both conform with GAAP. Both income statements are correct on the basis of accounting practices, but only Income statement A provides a true picture of the economic results of the firm's operations.

   The seven items where Statements A and B differ are keyed at the right margin of Table 24-1. The keyed items are discussed below, each highlights points where confusion and deception can enter into an accountants' earnings measurements.

TABLE 24-1   Two Income Statements for the Same Company in the Same Year Prepared with GAAP (in thousands)

Item	Statement B, $		Statement A, $		Key to Explanations
Sales revenue		$9,200		$11,000	(1)
less: Returns and allowances		−1000		−1000	
Net sales		$8200		$10,000	
Beginning inventory	$2000		2000		
Purchases and freight in	6000		6000		
Net purchases	$8000		8000		
less: Ending inventory	−2000		−3000		(2)
Cost of goods sold		6000		5000	
Gross margin		2200		5000	
Operating expenses					
Selling costs	1500		1500		
Depreciation	500		300		(3)
Pension	100		20		(4)
Other expenses	200		50		(5)
Amortization of goodwill	110		30		(6)
Contingent liabilities	90		40		(7)
Salaries	200		200		
Bonuses	100		100		
Total operating expenses		−2800	2240	−2240	
Net operating expenses		(600)		2760	
less: Interest		−100		−100	
Income (loss) before taxes		(700)		2660	
less: Federal taxes (33%) (refund)		(233)		−887	
Net income (loss) from operations		(467)		1773	

Sales (1). Statement A includes under sales revenue both cash sales and current sales made on installment contracts. Assume the hypothetical firm actually factors its accounts receivable as soon as they arise and thus realizes the cash proceeds of the installment contract sales immediately. Statement B does not recognize the credit sales until the customer's final cash payment is actually received and the factoring company has no potential bad debt claims against the firm. Both practices of installment sales recognition are in accordance with GAAP. However, the procedure shown in Statement A is the true reflection of the sales revenue.[14]

Inventory (2). Statement A used the FIFO (first in, first out) method of inventory valuation while B used the LIFO (last in, first out) method. During periods of inflation the FIFO method tends to result in higher reported profits. Contrasting examples of LIFO and FIFO accounting is informative.

ACCOUNTING FOR WIDGETS WITH LIFO AND FIFO   EXAMPLE

Suppose that 1-ton widgets are the inventory items and it is the company's policy to carry one widget in inventory at all times. Assume that, early in the accounting year represented in Table 24-1, the cost of widgets rose from $2,000 apiece to $3,000. The inventory is valued at cost, so the beginning inventory value of the inventory of one widget is $2,000 whether LIFO or FIFO is used. This value is shown in Tables 24-1 and 24-2.

If we assume the newest widgets are used in production, then the LIFO method is appropriate to value the inventory. Thus, during the inflationary accounting period when widget prices rose 50%, the value of the inventory was constant. That is, while 50% inflation transpired the value of the widget in ending inventory is assumed to remain unchanged. This means that, relative to the year's ending market prices of $3,000 per widget, LIFO undervalues ending inventory, overestimates the cost of goods sold, and, underestimates the company's income during inflation. Table 24-2 depicts this LIFO process.

TABLE 24-2   LIFO Inventory Accounting During Inflation (Statement B)

	Inventory Value
Beginning inventory (one widget at $2000)	$2000
plus: Purchases (two widgets at $3000 each)	+$6000
Cost of goods available for sale	$8000
less: Ending inventory (one widget at $2000)	−$2000 (undervalued)
Cost of goods sold	$6000 (overvalued)

If FIFO had been used, the ending inventory (of one widget purchased for $3,000) would be valued at $3,000 and the cost of goods sold in Table 24-2 would be $5,000.

Some consideration of the inventory methods reveals that FIFO incorporates inventory capital gains or losses into regular income, while LIFO does not. Thus, FIFO often causes profit to be more volatile than LIFO. FIFO is assumed to be the most realistic method of inventory valuation in this case for two main reasons. First, it was initially assumed that the manufacturer sold the oldest items in inventory first. Second, profits and losses on the inventory are reflected in reported income as they occur. As a result the second reason, FIFO is the least advantageous for tax purposes during inflation.

Not only does the LIFO versus FIFO decision have an impact on each year's income, switching from one of these inventory valuation techniques to the other can also result in significant one-time earnings distortions. Some companies try to avoid these problems by keeping two sets of books. One set of accounting statements is for public display and the other is kept for decision making within the firm and is confidential. Comparing the federal income taxes a company reports in its published financial statements to the appropriate proportion of its reported pre-tax income is a good way for a securities analyst to detect if the company keeps two sets of books that differ substantially.*[15]

Depreciation (3). Several depreciation schedules may be used to prepare financial statements:

1. Straight-line method
2. Units of production method
3. Double declining balance method
4. Sum-of-the-digits method
5. Modified Accelerated Cost Recovery System (MACRS)

The third, fourth, and fifth methods are accelerated methods of depreciation. The second method may be used to accelerate depreciation during a period of rapid production.

EXAMPLE   CONTRASTING DIFFERENT DEPRECIATION GUIDELINES

Consider an asset that costs $1,000 and has an expected life of 3 years with no salvage value. By use of the straight-line method, depreciation is constant at $333.33 for each of 3 years.

$$\$333.33 \text{ per year} = \frac{\$1,000}{3 \text{ years}} = \frac{\text{Cost} - (\text{Salvage value})}{\text{Years of life}}$$

Using the sum-of-the-digits method, the annual depreciation starts large and diminishes each year, because a decreasing fraction is multiplied by the cost of the asset (a stable amount) to determine each year's depreciation, as shown in Table 24-3. The numerator of this fraction decreases by 1 each year. As shown in Table 24-3, the numerator represents the number of years left in the life of the asset. The denominator of the fraction remains stable. If the life expectancy of an asset is T years, the denominator will be $T(T + 1)/2$. In the case of $T = 3$ years, the denominator works out to be $3(4)/2 = 6$ years.

TABLE 24-3   Sum-of-the-Digits Depreciation Calculations for an Asset with a 3-Year Life

Year, T	Depreciation as Fraction of Cost	Sum-of-the-Digits Annual Dollar Depreciation
1	$\dfrac{T}{T(T + 1)/2} = \dfrac{3}{6}$	$500.00
2	$\dfrac{T - 1}{T(T + 1)/2} = \dfrac{2}{6}$	$333.33
3	$\dfrac{T - 2}{T(T + 1)/2} = \dfrac{1}{6}$	$166.66
Totals:	1	$1000.00

---

* Some companies keep one set of books for management decision-making purposes and a different set of books to show to the Internal Revenue Service (IRS). Presumably the books for management reflects the firm's true economic earnings.

Assuming that no new technology or unusually heavy use is likely to depreciate the value of the firm's assets before they are worn out, the straight-line depreciation used in Statement A is more honest (but less desirable for tax purposes) than the accelerated sum-of-the-digits depreciation procedure employed in Statement B. Regardless of which depreciation method the executives use for decision-making purposes, the U.S. government's Internal Revenue Service (IRS) requires U.S. firms to use MACRS to compute federal income taxes.

All types of *accelerated depreciation* increase depreciation costs in the early years of a new asset's life, thereby decreasing the firm's reported accounting income and net taxable profit when the asset is new. Accelerated depreciation postpones taxes on income. Postponed taxes provide an interest-free loan from the government. The total depreciation expense is unchanged; only its timing is altered. As item 3 in Table 24-1 shows, accelerated depreciation can affect any particular year's reported accounting income significantly.

The IRS requires most firms use the Modified Accelerated Cost Recovery System (MACRS). MACRS is an economically unrealistic, rigidly defined, highly accelerated depreciation method. MACRS represents the federal government's effort to encourage U.S. executives to invest more in new machinery by giving rapid tax write-offs on businesses investments.*

Pension Costs (4). As explained in Chapter 13, the Employment Retirement Income Security Act (ERISA) of 1974 governs pension funds in the U.S. ERISA divides pension funds into two categories: (A) *defined contribution pension plans,* and (B) *defined benefit pension plans.*

Defined contribution pension plans require the employer to deposit some specified amount (the defined contribution) into a permanently segregated pension fund that is only for employees' retirement benefits. If the employer-pension fund manager makes some bad investments that lose all the money in the pension fund, the employer need not pay for those losses. As a result, liabilities for under-funded pension obligations never appear on employers' balance sheet with defined contribution pension plans.

A defined benefit pension plan arises when the employer promises to pay every qualified retiree a pension. This promise creates a legally enforceable liability on the employer's balance sheet. Liabilities are not created by defined contribution pension plans because they promise no specific pension payments to any retiree.

Most employers hire actuarial consultants each year to estimate the present value of the employer's legal liability to its workers under the provisions of the defined benefit pension plan. To prepare their estimates the actuaries make assumptions about the number of employees who will work long enough to qualify for pensions. Further assumptions must be made about the employees' salary levels when they retire, the number of employees who will have legally vested pension claims against the employer but will quit before they reach retirement age, and how many years the retired employees are expected to collect their pensions before they die.[16] After the present value of the employer's pension liability has been estimated the employer must determine how much of that year's earnings to set aside in the segregated pension fund to fund (cover, pay) its estimated pension liability.

Financial Accounting Standards Board (FASB) Statement 87 limits the latitude employers can use in reporting their pension fund's assets, liabilities, costs, and policies. FASB 87 requires employing firms to disclose in a footnote to their financial statements the firm's pension accounting and funding policy, the pension charge for the year, and any underfunded pension liability the company might have.

---

* The IRS mandates a disparity between the two depreciation techniques it requires for tax reporting and the depreciation used in public reported accounting statements. The IRS requires firms to depreciate their assets for tax purposes using the Accelerated Cost Recovery System (ACRS) if the asset was acquired between 1980 and 1987. For assets acquired after 1986 either the straight line method or the MACRS is required.

If a pension fund's assets are less than its liabilities, the fund has a *pension deficit*. A *pension surplus* occurs when a pension's assets exceed its liabilities. Over 90% of the defined benefit pensions in U.S. corporations enjoy a surplus position.* FASB 87 requires that the firm must show a balance sheet liability if it has a pension deficit that exceeds 10% of its pension assets; a liability of this size cannot merely be reported in a footnote.** ERISA requires that pension liabilities be paid off with deductions from the employer's earnings as soon as possible.[†]

Assume that the company in Table 24-1 has a defined benefit pension plan. Statement B reflects a large pension expense deduction and Statement A reports a small deduction. The large deduction in Statement B might result because the employer wants to make a larger than necessary pension fund contribution to accomplish one or more of the following goals: (1) to minimize its income tax payments, (2) smooth down (level out) unusually large earnings for that particular year, and/or (3) accumulate surplus assets in its pension fund to minimize the chance the pension becomes underfunded if a bear market decreases the market value of the pension assets.[††] To accomplish any of these objectives, the employer could urge its actuaries to make high pension cost estimates to make the large deductions shown in Statement B appear necessary. However, if the firm has a youthful labor force with few workers near retirement age, Statement A's treatment of pension costs is more accurate.[17]

Expensing Versus Capitalizing (5).   There are many items that the accountant may either write off as current expenses or capitalize and then amortize over a period of years. For example, motion-picture production costs, oil well exploration costs, the cost of an advertising campaign, and many other items are not clearly either an expense or an asset purchase. Such outlays comprise matters of managerial discretion for the financial analyst to scrutinize. Prior to the issuance of FASB Statement 2, companies were entitled to either capitalize research and development (R&D) outlays or expense them. The rules now prohibit capitalizing R&D outlays.[18]

Statements A and B differ because some outlays that were expensed on statement B were capitalized on statement A. The securities analyst should scrutinize these entries in comparing the two income statements to determine if firm's accounting executive handled the transaction appropriately. A securities analyst who believes that the outlays should be capitalized, should adjust downward the item entitled "Other expenses" in Statement B.

Amortization of Goodwill (6).   Goodwill is an intangible asset. It equals the amount by which the purchase price paid for an acquired company exceeds that company's book value. Typically, goodwill arises because an acquired company has compelling potential for growth, a recognized brand name, and/or valuable customer loyalty which is not reflected in the depreciated value of its assets on the balance sheet.

Goodwill may be amortized over a period of up to 40 years.[19] However, the situation that contributes to the goodwill may exist for a shorter period of time. Statement A uses a

---

* The largest pension deficits in the United States are in government-funded pensions, like the Social Security system, which do not fall under ERISA's jurisdiction.

** More specifically, an additional liability must be created if the pension fund sponsor's accumulated obligations to employees exceed the fair value of the pension fund's assets.

[†] If the rate of return that the actuary uses to calculate the present value of the firm's pension liability is unrealistically high, then the pension plan's liabilities will be reduced to unrealistically low levels, and the firm's pension costs can be reduced on the income statement. However, the company may then have to make large cash contributions in the future to pay for whatever pension funding deficits materialize later.

[††] FASB 87, now called Statement of Financial Accounting Standards 87 (SFAS 87), does not permit a corporation sponsoring a pension fund to show any pension surpluses as assets on the balance sheet. Shrewd corporate raiders will nevertheless ferret out such pools of corporate wealth when they select corporations as targets for leveraged buyouts.

long amortization period for goodwill to reduce the acquiring firm's costs and increase its bottom line (taxable income).

Contingent Liabilities (7). A *contingent liability* is a potential obligation that will occur in the future if certain conditions arise.[20] Contingent liabilities typically arise from pending litigation or from parent company guarantees of a subsidiary's debt.

SFAS 5 requires a company to disclose a contingent liability in a footnote to the financial statement if the liability cannot be reasonably forecasted. If the liability can be forecasted, the company is directed to recognize it as a contingent liability on its balance sheet. These provisions grant the accounting executive wide discretionary powers that are proportional to the amount of the liability. In Statement A the firm's contingent liability is honestly assessed at less than half the value used in Statement B.

Effects on Accounting Income. Table 24-1 summarizes differences in accounting procedures and shows the numeric impact of each on accounting income. Statement B indicates the firm received a $233,000 federal income tax refund to offset its reported losses. In contrast, Firm A paid $887,000 in federal income taxes.[21] This difference in the income taxes makes it hard to believe that the two statements are computed for the same company in the same year and that the underlying business transactions are identical. Nevertheless, the firm could find certified public accountants (CPAs) to certify either of the income statements shown in Table 24-1.

Table 24-1 pinpoints ways devious business managers and accountants can manipulate a company's accounting income. It would be difficult and unlikely for any firm to accomplish all the distortions discussed above in a single year. Table 24-1 is designed to highlight points investors should be skeptical about when they read a firms' reported income statement.

The Quality of Earnings

Quality of earnings refers to the accuracy with which a company's accounting earnings reflects its true earning power. Reported accounting earnings that accurately depict the true economic income generated by a company are high quality earnings—even if they happen to be losses. At the opposite end of the quality continuum, accounting earnings that result from special items and/or an inappropriate choice of GAAP accounting methods are low quality earnings, even if they appear are highly profitable.[22]

Common stock analysts wish that the GAAP produced an earnings number that could be used with confidence in a price-earnings valuation model.[23] Unfortunately, ambiguities may creep into a firm's income and expense statements that lower the quality of the firm's earnings per share (EPS).

More than one measure of EPS may be reported if a company has convertible securities, warrants, stock options, or other contracts that permit the number of shares of common stock outstanding to be increased in future periods.* Moreover, income or losses caused by extraordinary events will result in additional EPS measures being reported. These alternative measures of EPS cause complications.

Potential Dilution of Earnings Per Share (EPS).[24] An increase in the future number of outstanding shares of common stock may dilute a corporation's future EPS. Such an increase in

---

* Technically speaking, EPS on the common stock is net income after *reported* taxes (but reported taxes can differ from the amount of taxes that must be paid) less preferred stock dividend payments divided by the weighted average number of shares of common stock outstanding. To compute the weighted average number of shares outstanding, the weights are determined by the length of time the shares are outstanding. For example, if there were 1.2 million shares outstanding for the first 8 months of the reporting year and 1.5 million shares in the last 4 months, then the weighted average number of share is 1.3 million: (1.2 million shares) $\times$ (8/12) + (1.5 million shares) $\times$ (4/12) = 1.3 million shares.

the outstanding shares can occur if (1) management elects to sell more shares, (2) contracts give various parties options to purchase common stock from the corporation, and/or (3) a corporation exchanges common stock for debt to reduce its debt-equity ratio.

Examples of contracts that grant option to purchase common stock from the corporation include convertible bonds, convertible preferred stock, employee stock options, and warrants to purchase common stock.

If the potential dilution attributable to the existence of convertible security contracts may result in an EPS decline of less than 3%, the potential dilution need not be reported. But, for those corporations in which the diluting impact on EPS is greater than 3%, EPS must be presented two ways. First, dilution that considers only *common stock equivalents* is used to determine EPS.* This first required measure is called *basic EPS.* Second, the maximum potential dilution of EPS must be reported. This second measure is termed *diluted EPS.*

Extraordinary Gains and Losses. Security analysts attempt to estimate the future "normal" earnings of the companies they investigate. However, certain events may disrupt or distort the "normal" stream of income. For example, a company might report a considerable loss because it closed down an unprofitable division, or a firm may win a legal judgment in which a substantial award is received. How should such unusual events be reported on the income statement?

Some accountants argue that extraordinary items should be reported on the income statement for the current period. The opposing view is that extraordinary items would distort income and hence such gains or losses should be added to or subtracted from retained earnings rather than included in income. The controversy was virtually ended in 1966 with the issuance of Accounting Principles Board (APB) Opinion No. 9, "Reporting the Results of Operations." This Opinion requires that extraordinary items be reported separately in the income statement, net of taxes. The exception to this reporting rule is *prior period adjustments,* which paragraph 23 of the opinion defines as:

> *those material adjustments which (a) can be specifically identified with and directly related to the business activities of particular prior periods, and (b) are not attributable to economic events occurring subsequent to the date of the financial statements for the prior period, and (c) depend primarily on determinations by persons other than management, and (d) were not susceptible to reasonable estimation prior to such determination. Such adjustments are rare in modern financial accounting.*

FASB No. 16 went on to limit prior periods adjustments to (i) the correction of an error in a published statement, and (ii) adjustments that result from income realized as tax benefits from pre-acquisition loss carry-forwards of a purchased subsidiary.

Stringent requirements for an item to be classified as *extraordinary* were established in APB Opinion No. 30.[25] The opinion requires that the item be both unusual in nature and not expected to recur in the foreseeable future.** Two examples of extraordinary items are losses

---

* **Common stock equivalents** are defined as options or warrants to purchase common stock and certain convertible securities. For a convertible security to be considered a common stock equivalent, the current yield of the security at the time of issuance has to be less than two-thirds of the prime interest rate when the security was issued. Common stock equivalents may be used when the result will be a decline in a loss per share.

** The SEC requires a company to file Report Form 8-K within 10 days after the close of any month in which any significant problem arises; extraordinary items can fall under this requirement. The SEC requirements were extended in 1982. Now the 8-K must also be filed promptly to report the following: (1) changes in control of the corporation and how these changes occurred; (2) information about mergers, acquisitions, and dispositions; (3) bankruptcy or receivership judgments affecting the corporation; (4) changes in the corporation's certifying accountant; (5) resignation of any corporate directors; and, (6) additional financial information, to include pro forma financial information on acquired subsidiaries.

due to a major casualty, such as a flood, and losses due to an expropriation of business assets by foreign governments. Three examples of transactions or events that are not included as extra-ordinary items are (1) the write-down of inventory, (2) gains or losses due to foreign exchange fluctuations, and (3) gains or losses from the disposition of a segment of the business.[26]

Since the Income and Expense Statement can be manipulated in a misleading manner, security analysts are forced to investigate an array of "Footnotes to Accounting Statements" and FASBs to answer the fundamental question: "What is the stock's earning power?"

CASH FLOWS

Cash flows provide an estimate of true income because cash flows are not obscured by accrual accounting, depreciation, amortization, the establishment of accounting reserves, and other accounting conventions. Cash flow from operations (CFO) is a well-known measure.[27]

Cash Flow from Operations (CFO)

The phrase **cash flow from operations (CFO)** is descriptive; it measures cash flows that arise when goods and/or services are produced and distributed by a firm. The value of a firm's CFO can be obtained from three alternative sources. First, FASB 95 requires U.S. companies to publish a Statement of Cash Flows with their Balance Sheet and Income and Expense Statement. The CFO is the first section in the Statement of Cash Flows. Since many countries of the world do not require Statements of Cash Flows, other sources are needed. Second, the CFO can be compiled by an accountant or financial analyst from the common stock issuer's Statement of Sources and Uses. The CFO can be computed simply by listing the elements that generate cash and the expenses that use cash. Third, the framework outlined in Table 24-4 can be used to calculate CFO indirectly from a company's Income and Expense Statement.

Most firms' accounting incomes are not highly positively correlated with their cash flow from operations (CFO).[28] The column on the right-hand side of Table 24-4 shows the keys that were used to explain the differences between Income and Expense Statements A and B for the firm introduced in Table 24-1. Table 24-4 unravels the disparities between Income Statements A and B by showing: (1) the firm's CFO was unambiguously determined to be $3,060,000, and (2) the same CFO can be obtained from either of the two income statements in Table 24-1.[29] Since Statements A and B in Table 24-1 generate different net incomes but the same CFO, some investors ask: "Should we eliminate this ambiguity by computing the present value of a common stock's CFO per share instead of the present value of its dividends per share or earnings per share?"

It would be not be logical to compute the present value of a common stock's CFO if the company uses financial leveraged because CFO includes cash flows generated from using debt capital as well as the cash outlays required to service the debt. However, the Statement of Cash Flows contains other cash flow measures that are appropriate to use in valuing the firm's equity.

A Firm's Statement of Cash Flows

Figure 24-2 depicts the general layout of the Statement of Cash Flows and shows the relationship between its four major components. Coca-Cola's Statement of Cash Flows at Figure 4-3 in Chapter 4 (p. 69), for example, follows this format. The statement reports of the net amount of cash flows from the operations (CFO), investing, the financing activities of the firm, and the net change in the firm's aggregate cash position.

TABLE 24-4 Converting Accrual Accounting for Income to Cash Flow Accounting (in thousands)

Item	Statement B	Statement A	Key to Explanation
Determine cash inflows from operations			
Start with sales revenues	$9,200	$11,000	(1)
plus: Decrease (−increase) in accounts receivable	+1,800	0	
Cash collections on sales	$11,000	$11,000	
plus: Other revenues (+ or − adjustment for noncash items)	−1,000	−1,000	
Total cash inflows from operations	$10,000	$10,000	
Deduct cash outflows from operations			
Start with cost of goods sold* (excluding depreciation, amortization, etc.)	−$6,000	−$5,000	
less: Operating expenses (including depreciation)	−2,800	−2,240	
plus: Depreciation (add back since it is not a cash outlay)	+500	+300	(3)
Other expenses (including interest)			
plus: Increase (−decrease) in inventories	+1,000	0	(2)
plus: Decrease (−increase) in accounts payables	0	0	
plus: Increase (−decrease) in prepaid expenses	0	0	
plus: Decrease (−increase) in accrued liabilities	0	0	
plus: Pension expense adjustment	+80	0	(4)
plus: Other expenses adjustment	+150	0	(5)
plus: Amortization of goodwill adjustment	+80	0	(6)
Contingent liabilities adjustment	+50	0	(7)
Total cash outflows for operations	−$6,940	−$6,940	
Net total: Cash flow from operations (CFO)	$3,060	$3,060	

SOURCE: Adapted from Leopold A. Bernstein and John J. Wild, *Financial Statement Analysis,* 6th ed. (New York: Irwin/McGraw-Hill, 1998), Exhibit 7A.1, p. 374. Also see L.A. Bernstein and M. M. Makay, "Again Now: How Do We Measure Cashflows From Operations?" *Financial Analysts Journal* 41, no. 4: 74–77.

Sometimes firms engage in activities that involve no direct cash investment. For example, a firm might enter into a barter transaction. A convertible bond might be converted into common stock. Or, a firm might acquire a piece of troubled real estate merely by agreeing to take over the remaining payments. In the United States such transactions must be clearly disclosed in a footnote to the financial statements or in a supplementary schedule or report. The Statement of Cash Flows, combined with the relevant footnotes or supplementary reports, contains the information needed to determine what cash flows are available to equity shareholders.

The change in a firm's cash position during a period is a comprehensive measure that includes cash flow from operations (CFO) as well as the effects of cash dividends; purchases of outstanding stock; the firm's financial arrangements; the firm's investments and its investment income or loss; changes in certain (on and off) balance sheet items; and some footnote items such as changes in the firm's pension surplus, reserves, and accruals. A Statement of Cash Flows can pinpoint similarities and disparities between reported accounting income and the firm's true economic income.

FIGURE 24-2   Breakdown of a Firm's Statement of Cash Flows

Firm's Activity	Cash Inflows		Cash Outflows		Net Cash Flows
Operating	Cash inflows from sales of goods and services	–	Cash paid for operating goods and services	=	Cash flow from operations, or cfo
Investing	Cash received from sales of property, plant equipment, and/or other investments	–	Cash paid for acquisition of property, plant, equipment, and/or other investments	=	Cash flow from investing
Financing	Cash received from issue of debt or capital stock (if relevant)	–	Cash paid for dividends and reacquisition of debt or capital stock (if relevant)	=	Cash flow from financing (if relevant)
Other	Cash received from foreign exchange transactions, etc. (if relevant)	–	Cash paid for foreign exchange transactions, etc. (if relevant)	=	Cash flow from other activities (if relevant)
TOTAL:					Net change in cash for the period

SOURCE: Adapted from Clyde P. Stickney, *Financial Reporting and Statement Analysis,* 3rd ed., Dryden Press, 1996, Ft. Worth, TX, Figure 1-3, page 20.

Cash Flows Available to Equity Shareholders

Cash flows available to equity shareholders are a firm's *leverage-free cash flows.* The Financing section of the Statement of Cash Flows contains the information about any debt financing in which the firm might be involved. This information is used to adjust the firm's CFO to obtain its leverage-free cash flows.

A firm's debt service costs (cash required to service debt) net of tax effects, minus the net cash outflow for investing, plus (minus) any increase (decrease) in debt financing, measures the combined effects of leverage on the firm. These combined leverage effects must be deducted from the firm's CFO to determine its leverage-free cash flows. The present value of the leverage-free cash flows can be computed by using the firm's cost of equity capital (required rate of return on equity) as a risk-adjusted discount rate.*

---

* Modigliani and Miller (M&M) have taught us that the value of a firm is independent of its capital structure. In light of this teaching, at first it may seem inappropriate to include changes in debt financing when valuing a firm. It is appropriate because debt servicing charges affect the amount of cash flows available to the common stockholders. When computing a present value the security analyst must use a leverage-adjusted cost of equity capital to compensate for the impact that leverage has on the firm's cash flows available to equity shareholders.

The Difference Between Cash Flows Available to Equity Shareholders and Economic Income

ECONOMIC INCOME

The **economic income,** or *economic earnings,* of a firm during a given period equals the maximum amount of consumption opportunities that can be withdrawn from the firm during the period without diminishing the consumption opportunities available in the future.[30]

Accounting income provides an upward biased estimate of the true economic income of most firms because the firm's net income contains retained earnings that that are not available for consumption. The firm's cash flow available to shareholders measures the consumption opportunities that are available to the firm's owners. These leverage-free cash flows contain deductions for whatever investments the firm's management feels are needed to maintain the firm's future earning power (and owners' consumption opportunities) undiminished. Thus, the present value of the cash flows available to equity shareholders on a per share basis is an acceptable measure of the share's value,[31] where k is a leverage-adjusted (risk-adjusted) cost of equity capital:

$$\begin{pmatrix} \text{Present value} \\ \text{of cash flows} \\ \text{per share} \end{pmatrix} = \sum_{t=1}^{\infty} \frac{\begin{pmatrix} \text{Cash flow available to equity} \\ \text{shareholders on a per share basis} \end{pmatrix}}{(1 + k)^t} \tag{24-2}$$

Per share CFO is not an acceptable estimate of the cash flows available to equity shareholders. If the firm uses borrowed funds, the CFO must be cleansed of debt servicing costs, tax effects arising from the borrowed funds, and any net cash flows arising from increases or decreases in the debt financing. These leverage-free cash flows should be discounted at what the firm's cost of equity capital would be if it had no debt.

Problems with Cash Dividends

The present value of cash dividends per share provide an estimate of the value of an equity share because, like cash flows available to equity shareholders, cash dividends are a consumable quantity that is left after the firm retains some of its accounting earnings to maintain its future earning power (and the owners' future consumption opportunities) undiminished. But, the present value of cash dividends per share it is not a valid estimate of the value of an equity share for three categories of corporations:

1. **Share Repurchasing Firms.** A growing number of firms pay cash dividends that are below the level of cash dividends the firm has the potential to pay. For example, Coca-Cola, IBM, and many other corporations pay cash dividends and also use another portion of their earnings to buy back some of the corporation's own common stock. The *treasury stock* that is acquired tends to cause *reverse dilution* of the issuer's earnings per share, cash dividends per share, and value per share.
2. **Growth Firms.** Growth firms can invest internally at a rate of return that exceeds their cost of capital, $k < r$. For example, Microsoft, Cisco, America Online (AOL), Oracle, MCI WorldCom, and many other growth firms pay no cash dividends.

3. **Declining Firms.** Declining firms have no internal investments that pay a rate of return as large as the firm's cost of capital, $k > r$. During the 1930s, for instance, buggy-whip manufacturers were declining firms. Declining firms can maximize their owners' wealth by liquidating the firm and paying one large liquidating dividend. Optimal liquidation occurs rarely because of an agency problem, management is not willing to give up their positions to maximize their employers' (the firm's owners', the principals') wealth.

The present value of cash dividends per share is not the most popular way to estimate the value of an equity share because (1) computing the present value of the cash flows per share available to equity shareholders avoids the three problems listed above, and (2) many fundamental common stock analysts prefer to multiply an appropriate price/earnings ratio times their estimate of a share's normalized EPS.

THE BOTTOM LINE

Asymmetric information exists because external investors do not have access to inside information available to a corporation's board of directors. Although the M&M dividend irrelevance theorem shows that the value of normal corporation is unaffected by the board's cash dividend decisions, the theorem does not mean that a corporation's cash dividend payment cannot have valuable informational content. External investors study corporations' cash dividend payments for signals about the future intention of the corporation's board of directors. External investors are interested in gaining information about the corporation's future earnings power, because earnings are an important determinant of a stock's price.

Institutional Brokers Estimate System (I/B/E/S), Zacks Investment Research, and First Call are corporations that specialize in compiling quarterly earnings forecasts. Earnings forecasts not only have value as forecasts, they are also valuable in determining if a corporation's announced earnings are surprisingly good or are surprisingly bad when compared to the consensus forecast for that firm.

Foster, Olsen, and Shevlin (FOS) compared corporations' forecasted EPS with their actual EPS and computed standardized unexpected earnings (SUEs). Thousands of SUEs were tabulated from the quarterly earnings announcements of different firms in different years. The SUEs were arrayed to create decile portfolios. The performances of these decile portfolios are illustrated in Figure 24-1. Figure 24-1A shows that, averaged over thousands of announcements, stock prices tend to increase in the months *prior* to the announcement date if earnings are surprisingly good and decrease *prior* to the announcement date if earnings are surprisingly bad. Figure 24-1B shows that the largest good and bad earnings surprises result in the largest positive and negative price changes as stock prices react to the announcement of new earnings information. Figure 24-1C documents an anomaly in the efficient markets hypothesis. Figure 24-1C shows that the direct relationship between the earnings surprises and the abnormal stock returns that was documented in Figures 24-1A and 24-1B continues for 2 months *after* the earnings are announced. This lagged response should not occur in a semi–strongly efficient market.

Generally accepted accounting principles (GAAP) leave ample room for interpretation. The accountant needs some leeway to select an accounting procedure that most clearly reports the true economic consequence of a business transaction. Some accountants use too much latitude, sometimes they produce income statements that financial analysts, security analysts, and investors must alter to obtain estimates of a firm's true economic income. Distorted income statements often result from (1) the accountant's use of an accounting procedure that is inappropriate for the relevant economic transaction, (2) accrual accounting techniques that do not link revenues and expenses to the time period in which the cash flows actually occurred, and/or (3) pressure on the accountant from top management to "window-dress" the corporation's financial statements.

The phrase *quality of earnings* refers to the accuracy with which the accounting earnings for a company reflects the firm's true economic income. Some financial analysts have become discouraged with the quality of earnings reported by accountants and they began to use corporations' cash flows, instead of accounting earnings, to measure the companies earning power. A firm's cash flows provide an estimate of its true income because cash flows are not obscured by accrual accounting, depreciation, amortization, the establishment of accounting reserves, and other complex accounting conventions. Eqn. 24-2 shows how to compute the present value of the cash flows available to equity shareholders on a per share basis.

Some security analysts prefer to use the present value of the cash flows available to equity shareholders instead of the present value of cash dividends per share to estimate a share's value. Multiplying EPS times an appropriate price/earnings ratio, which fundamental stock analysts have been doing for decades, is still also a popular way to estimated a share's value.

QUESTIONS

Q24-1 (Dividend irrelevance theorem) True, false, or uncertain: A firm's stock price increases with the announcement of a dividend increase and falls with the announcement of a dividend decrease. Explain.

Q24-2 (Inventory valuation) Which of the two inventory valuation techniques, FIFO or LIFO, will result in a higher cost of goods sold during periods of inflation? Which one will result in the higher net income?

Q24-3 (Depreciation methods) True, false, or uncertain: Since a depreciable asset will be fully depreciated over its useful life to a value of zero, the method of depreciation that a firm uses is irrelevant.

Q24-4 (Goodwill) Why might the goodwill deduction on a firm's income statement not be a true reflection of the firm's actual cost?

Q24-5 (Fully diluted EPS) What is the difference between the primary EPS and the fully diluted EPS that is reported on a firm's income statement?

Q24-6 (Extraordinary items) Classify each of the following items as either ordinary or extraordinary according to APB

rules: (a) bad debt losses, (b) write-off of obsolete inventory, (c) destruction of a building by a hurricane, (d) loss from the sale of a division, (e) expropriation of the assets of a business by a foreign government, (f) loss due to foreign currency translations.

Q24-7 (Cash flow from operations) Explain why an increase in accounts receivable is deducted from sales revenues and a decrease is added to sales revenues in arriving at cash flow from operations (CFO). Likewise, explain why a decrease in accounts payable would be deducted while an increase in accounts payable would be added back to determine cash flow from operations.

Q24-8 (Economic income) In what way does accounting income overstate the true economic income of a firm?

Q24-9 (Leverage-free cash flows) How is the cash flow available to equity shareholders determined?

Q24-10 (FOS event study) Summarize the results of the Foster-Olsen-Shevlin event study on quarterly earnings announcements. Do their results support the efficient market hypothesis? Why or why not?

PROBLEMS

P24-1 (SUE) Consider the following information on two stocks, X and Y:

	Stock X	Stock Y
Actual quarterly EPS	$2.00	$3.00
Forecasted quarterly EPS	$2.30	$3.50
Standard deviation of forecasting error	$0.70	$1.66

Which stockholders, those of Firm X or those of Firm Y, received the more unpleasant surprise?

P24-2 (Inventory valuation) Calumet Corporation orders its inventory in quantities of 500 units at a time. In January, the firm paid $10 a unit for its purchase. In May, when Calumet reordered, the price was $11 a unit, and by September, Calumet had to pay $12 a unit for its 500 units. During the year, Calumet sold 1,200 units at a price of $20 each. Calculate the firm's ending inventory balance and its cost of goods sold under both the FIFO and the LIFO inventory valuation methods.

P24-3 (Depreciation) The Inmar Corporation purchased an asset with a 5-year life for $10,000. Calculate the annual depreciation that would be expensed under both the (a) straight-line method and (b) the sum-of-the-digits method.

P24-4 (Cash flow from operations) The following balance sheet and income statement information is provided for the Canton Corporation:

Calculate the cash flow from operations (CFO) for Canton Corporation for 20 × 2.

P24-5 (Cash flows from investing) Using the information provided in Problem 24-4, calculate the cash flows from investing activities for Canton Corporation.

P24-6 (Cash flows from financing) Using the information provided in Problem 24-4, calculate the cash flows from financing activities for Canton Corporation.

P24-7 (Cash flows from operations) Use the following information to determine the cash flows from operations for INFONEXT Corporation:

Canton Corporation
Balance Sheet
as of December 31
(amounts in thousands)

	20 × 2	20 × 1
Cash	$ 460	$ 100
Accounts receivable	950	900
Inventory	1,700	1,000
Total current assets	$ 3,110	$ 2,000
Gross plant, property and equipment	$12,000	$11,000
less accumulated depreciation	5,000	4,500
Net fixed assets	$ 7,000	$ 6,500
Total assets	$10,110	$ 8,500
Accounts payable	$ 600	$ 500
Accrued expenses	400	200
Total current liabilities	$ 1,000	$ 700
Long-term debt	4,000	3,500
Total liabilities	$ 5,000	$ 4,200
Common stock	$ 2,000	$ 2,000
Retained earnings	3,110	2,300
Total liabilities and equity	$10,110	$ 8,500

Income Statement
for the years ending December 31
(amounts in thousands)

	20 × 2	20 × 1
Sales	$10,000	$8,000
less Cost of goods sold[a]	6,000	5,000
Gross profit	$ 4,000	$3,000
less General selling and administrative expenses	1,500	1,200
Operating profit	$ 2,500	$1,800
less Interest expense	400	350
Earnings before tax	$ 2,100	$1,450
Taxes (@ 40%)	840	580
Earnings after tax	$ 1,260	$ 870
less common stock dividends	450	400
Addition to retained earnings	$ 810	$ 470

[a]includes depreciation expense of $500 in 20 × 2 and $400 in 20 × 1.

INFONEXT CORPORATION
Balance Sheet
as of December 31
(amounts in thousands)

	20 × 2	20 × 1
Cash	$ 800	$ 500
Accounts receivable	1,050	1,200
Inventory	1,550	1,000
Total current assets	$ 3,400	$ 2,700
Gross plant, property, and equipment	$17,300	$16,200
less accumulated depreciation	10,600	9,800
Net plant, property, and equipment	$ 6,700	$ 6,400
Total assets	$10,100	$ 9,100
Accounts payable	$ 720	$ 600
Accrued expenses	400	500
Total current liabilities	$ 1,120	$ 1,100
Long-term debt	1,500	1,800
Common stock	$ 3,000	$ 3,000
Retained earnings	4,480	3,200
Total liabilities and equity	$10,100	$ 9,100

Income Statement
for the years ending
December 31
(amounts in thousands)

	20 × 2	20 × 1
Sales	$22,000	$20,000
less Cost of goods sold	14,300	13,000
Gross profit	$ 7,700	$ 7,000
less Other operating expenses		
Selling costs	1,200	1,000
Depreciation	800	600
Other expenses	700	500
Total other operating expenses	$ 2,700	$ 2,100
Earnings before interest and taxes	$ 5,000	$ 4,900
less Interest expense	1,200	1,000
Earnings before taxes	$ 3,800	$ 3,900
less Taxes (@ 40%)	1,520	1,560
Net income	$ 2,280	$ 2,340
less Common stock dividends	1,000	1,000
Addition to retained earnings	$ 1,280	$ 1,340

P24-8 (Cash flows from investing) Use the information provided in Problem 24-7 to determine the cash flows from investing activities for INFONEXT Corporation.

P24-9 (Cash flows from financing) Use the information provided in Problem 24-7 to determine the cash flows from financing activities for INFONEXT Corporation.

P24-10 (Free cash flow and firm value) Calculate the free cash flow available to equity holders for the INFONEXT Corporation, using the information provided in Problem 24-7. INFONEXT has 500,000 shares outstanding and its cost of equity capital is 15%. If the free cash flow is assumed to be a perpetuity, what is the value per share of INFONEXT?

CFA EXAM QUESTIONS

1. (1999 CFA Sample Exam, Level I) An analyst gathers the following data:

   1,000,000 common shares outstanding (no change during the year).

   $6,500,000 net income.

   $500,000 preferred dividends paid.

   $600,000 common dividends paid.

   $60 average market price of common stock for the year.

   100,000 warrants outstanding exercisable at $50.

   The company's diluted earnings per share is *closest* to:
   A. $5.45.
   B. $5.90.
   C. $6.00.
   D. $6.39.

2. (1999 CFA Sample Exam, Level I) Which of the following *correctly* classifies (as operating or investing cash flow) interest received, dividends received, and interest paid?

	Interest Received	Dividends Received	Interest Paid
A.	Operating	Operating	Operating
B.	Operating	Operating	Investing
C.	Operating	Investing	Investing
D.	Investing	Investing	Investing

3. (1997 CFA Sample Exam, Level I) For a material item to be classified as an extraordinary item on the income statement, the item must be:
   A. estimated and probable.
   B. current and unusual in frequency.
   C. probable and infrequent in nature.
   D. unusual in nature and infrequent in occurrence.

FURTHER REFERENCES

Bernstein, Leopold A. and John J. Wild, *Financial Statement Analysis,* 6th ed. New York: Irwin/McGraw-Hill, 1998.

   Chapters 6 and 7 of this perennial best-selling textbook focus on earnings.

Stickney, Clyde P. *Financial Reporting and Statement Analysis,* 3d ed. Ft. Worth, TX: Dryden Press, 1996.

   Chapter 2 introduces cash flow accounting and Chapter 11 shows how to use cash flows to value an equity share. Virtually no math is used in this textbook.

ENDNOTES

1   See John Lintner, "Distribution of Incomes of Corporations Among Dividends, Retained Earnings, and Taxes," *American Economic Review* 46 (May 1956): 97–113.

[2] See Stephen A. Ross, "The Determination of Financial Structure: The Incentive Signaling Approach," *Bell Journal of Economics* 8, no. 1 (spring 1977): 203–40. More recently, the dividend information hypothesis has been formalized by, among others, M. H. Miller and K. Rock, "Dividend Policy Under Asymmetric Information," *Journal of Finance* 40 (1985): 1031–51. See the references in Miller and Rock for other relevant research.

[3] See Paul M. Healy and Krishna G. Palepu, "Earnings Information Conveyed by Dividend Initiations and Omissions," *Journal of Financial Economics* 21 (1988): 149–75.

[4] See Joseph Aharony and Itzhak Swary, "Quarterly Dividend and Earnings Announcements and Stockholders Returns: An Empirical Analysis," *Journal of Finance* 35, no. (March 1980): 1–20.

[5] The theory of cash dividend policy is laid out by Merton H. Miller and Franco Modigliani, "Dividend Policy, Growth and the Valuation of Shares," *Journal of Business* (October 1961): 411–33. This theory was advanced by Eugene F. Fama and H. Babiak, "Dividend Policy: An Empirical Analysis," *Journal of the American Statistical Association* 63 (December 1968): 1132–61.

   The following empirical studies mostly reach the conclusion that cash dividends have a positive but marginally significant effect on the market value of equity shares. (1) Black, F., and Scholes, M. "The Effects of Dividend Yield and Dividend Policy on Common Stock Prices and Returns," *Journal of Financial Economics* 1 (May 1974): 1–22. Insignificant cash dividend effects are reported. (2) Blume, M., "Stock Returns and Dividend Yields: Some More Empirical Evidence," *Review of Economics and Statistics* (November 1980): 567–77. Stocks that pay zero cash dividends are reported to earn abnormally high returns. (3) Brennan, M.J. "Taxes, Market Valuation and Corporate Financial Policy," *National Tax Journal* 23 (1970): 417–27. (4) Elton. E. J., and Gruber, M. J. "Marginal Stockholder Tax Rates and the Clientele Effect," *Review of Economics and Statistics* 52 (February 1970): 68–74. The effects of income taxes on cash dividends are estimated empirically. (5) Litzenberger, R. H., and Ramaswamy, K. "Dividends, Short Selling Restrictions, Tax-Induced Investor Clienteles and Market Equilibrium," *Journal of Finance* 35 (May 1980): 469–81. (6) Litzenberger, R.H., and Ramaswamy, K. "The Effect of Personal Taxes and Dividends on Capital Asset Prices," *Journal of Financial Economics* 7 (June 1979): 163–95. A positive and significant relationship between dividend yield and common stock returns is reported. (7) Miller, M.H., and Scholes, M. "Dividends and Taxes," *Journal of Financial Economics* 6 (December 1978): 333–64. Also see Miller and Scholes, "Dividends and Taxes: Some Empirical Evidence," *Journal of Political Economy* 90, (1982): 1118–41. Insignificant empirical results are reported in the latter article. (8) Ofer, A.R. and D.R. Siegel, "Corporate Financial Policy, Information, and Market Expectations: An Empirical Investigation of Dividends," *Journal of Finance* 42 (September 1987): 889–911. (9) Sharpe, W. F., and Sosin, H. B. "Risk, Return and Yield, New York Stock Exchange Common Stocks, 1928–69," *Financial Analysts Journal* 32 (March-April 1976): 33–42.

[6] See John C. Groth, Wilbur G. Lewellen, Gary Schlarbaum, and Ronald C. Lease, "An Analysis of Brokerage House Recommendations," *Financial Analysts Journal* 35, no. 1 (January-February 1979): 32–40. Also see Werner F. De Bondt and Richard H. Thaler, "Do Security Analysts Over React?" *American Economic Review* 80, no. 2 (May 1990): 52–57. In addition, see the references in these articles.

[7] See Scott E. Stickel, "Reputation and Performance Among Security Analysts," *Journal of Finance* 47, no. 5 (December 1992): 1811–36.

[8] See Lawrence D. Brown and Michael S. Rozeff, "The Superiority of Analysts' Forecasts as Measures of Expectations: Evidence from Earnings," *Journal of Finance* 33, no. 1 (March 1978): 5–11.

[9] See Patricia C. O'Brien, "Analysts Forecasts as Earnings Expectations," *Journal of Accounting and Economics* 10, no. 1 (January 1988): 53–83.

[10] See Mark Bagnoli, Messod D. Beneish, and Susan G. Watts, "Whisper Forecasts of Quarterly Earnings Per Share," *Journal of Accounting and Economics,* forthcoming 2000.

[11] See Henry A. Latané and Charles P. Jones, "Standardized Unexpected Earnings—1971–77," *Journal of Finance* 34 (June 1979): 717–24. Also see Charles P. Jones, Richard J. Rendleman, and Henry A. Latane', "Stock Returns and SUEs During the 1970s," *Journal of Portfolio Management* (winter 1984): 18–22.

[12] See George Foster, Chris Olsen and Terry Shevlin, "Earnings Releases, Anomalies and the Behavior of Security Returns," *Accounting Review* 59, no. 4 (October 1984): 574–603. The study is also discussed by George Foster, *Financial Statement Analysis* (Englewood Cliffs, NJ: Prentice-Hall, 1986); see Chapters 8 and 11, especially pp. 383–84, 392, and 396–97. For an interesting psychological theory about these empirical results, see Kent Daniel, David Hirshleifer, and Avanidhar Subrahmanyam, "Investor Psychology and Security Market Under- and Overreactions," *Journal of Finance* 53, no. 6 (December 1998): 1839–85.

[13] For evidence that "good news" tends to be announced earlier than expected, while "bad news" tends to be announced later than expected, see V. V. Chari, R. Jagannathan, and A. Ofer, "Seasonality in Security Returns: The Case of Earnings Announcements," *Journal of Financial Economics* 21, no. 1 (May 1988): 101–21. In addition, the "timeliness" of the announcement (defined to be the difference between the expected announcement date and the actual announcement date) tends to affect the size of the abnormal return. Furthermore, around earnings announcement dates trading volume tends to pick up and security prices become more volatile. Also see G. Foster, *Financial Statement Analysis* (Englewood Cliffs, NJ: Prentice-Hall, 1986), 377–86.

[14] The SEC responded to problems like this with *Accounting Series Release No. 95,* which has the descriptive title: "Accounting for Real Estate Transactions Where Circumstances Indicate That Profits Were Not Earned at the Time the Transactions Were Recorded." In a related matter, APB Opinion No. 21 required companies to record transactions resulting in notes receivable at the fair market value instead of the face value of the note. See APB Opinion No. 21, "Interest on Receivables and Payables," AICPA, New York, 1971. For additional

GAAP opinions about how sales should be recognized see *Statements of Financial Accounting Standards* (SFAS) 66 and 67, Financial Accounting Standards Board, Norwalk, CT.

[15] For a detailed explanation of a multimillion-dollar inventory valuation switch that the Chrysler Corporation used in 1970, see Abraham Briloff, *Unaccountable Accounting* (New York: Harper & Row, 1972), 36–39. This excellent book is full of actual examples that use people's names and give actual dates. Several accounting firms and corporations mentioned in the book sued Professor Briloff to intimidate him. Luckily, the truth is a perfect defense against libel and slander suits.

[16] For a discussion of estimating an employer's pension liabilities see D. Don Ezra, "How Actuaries Determine the Unfunded Pension Liability," *Financial Analysts Journal* (July-August 1980). See also Richard A. Ippolito, "The Economic Burden of Corporate Pension Liabilities," *Financial Analysts Journal* (January-February, 1986). Also see Gerald I. White, "A User's Guide to FAS 87," *CFA Readings in Financial Statement Analysis,* 2nd ed. (Charlottesville, VA: 1990).

[17] For discussion of pension funds see Jay Vawter, "Determination of Portfolio Policies: Institutional Investors," *Managing Investment Portfolios,* Ed. John L. Maginn and Donald L. Tuttle, sponsored by The Institute of Chartered Financial Analysts (Boston: Warren, Gorham & Lamont, 1983), 67–84.

[18] FASB No. 2, "Accounting for Research and Development Costs," Norwalk, CT: (October 1974). An exception to the rule is material, equipment, or facilities that have "alternative future uses." For a list of activities that should be included in R&D and examples of activities that should be excluded, see paragraphs 9 and 10 of FASB 2. Also see Baruch Lev and Theodore Sougiannis, "The Capitalization, Amortization, and Value Relevance of R&D," *Journal of Accounting and Economics* (February 1996): 107–38.

[19] See "Intangible Assets," *Opinions of the Accounting Principles Board, No. 17* (New York: American Institute of Certified Public Accountants, 1970), paragraph 29. Also see Philip E. Fess and Carl S. Warren, *Accounting Principles,* 16th ed. (Cincinnati: South-Western, 1990), 406–07.

[20] See "Accounting for Contingencies," *Statement of Financial Accounting Standards, No. 5* (Norwalk, CT: Financial Accounting Standards Board, 1975). Also see Philip E. Fess and Carl S. Warren, *Accounting Principles,* 16th ed. (Cincinnati: South-Western, 1990), 479–80.

[21] FASB 96, "Accounting for Income Taxes," December 1987, provides guidelines about reporting income taxes and tax liabilities.

[22] See Jeremy J. Siegel, *Stocks for the Long-Run,* 2nd ed. (New York: McGraw-Hill, 1998), 163. Also see John J. Wild, "The Audit Committee and Earnings Quality," *Journal of Accounting, Auditing, and Finance* (spring 1996): 247–76.

[23] See Fischer Black, "The Magic in Earnings: Economic Earnings Versus Accounting Earnings," *Financial Analysts Journal* (November-December 1980):19–24.

[24] Based on APB Opinion No. 15, "Earnings per Shares," AICPA, New York, 1969.

[25] APB Opinion No. 30, "Reporting the Results of Operations," AICPA, New York, 1973.

[26] The accounting rules for reporting the impact of foreign exchange fluctuations on earnings were set forth in FASB statement No. 8, "Accounting for the Translation of Foreign Currency Transactions and Foreign Currency Statement," AICPA, Stamford, Connecticut, 1975. For a summary of the statement see David Norr, "Currency Translation and the Analyst," *Financial Analysts Journal* (July-August 1976): 46–54. In the article immediately following David Norr's, John K. Shank discusses the pitfalls of FASB Statement No. 8. See John K. Shank, "FASB Statement 8 Resolved Foreign Currency Accounting—or Did It?" *Financial Analysts Journal* (July-August 1976). Rita M. Rodriquez has examined the impact of FASB No. 8 on a sample of large U.S. Multinationals; see her "FASB No. 8: What Has It Done to Us," *Financial Analysts Journal* (March-April 1977): 40–47. She found that there was no significant impact on the earnings of the companies in her sample. More recently, FASB No. 52 has been issued to modify FASB 8. FASB Statement 52 revises the accounting requirements for translation of foreign currency transactions and foreign currency financial statements. Stated simply, FASB 52 adopts the functional currency approach and requires each financial statement to be stated in its functional foreign currency before being translated into dollars. In contrast, FASB 8 specified the dollar as the measuring unit for all entities.

[27] See Leopold A. Bernstein and John J. Wild, *Financial Statement Analysis,* 6th ed. (New York: Irwin/McGraw-Hill, 1998); Chapter 7 addresses cash flows. Also see L.A. Bernstein and M. M. Makay, "Again Now: How Do We Measure Cash Flows from Operations?" *Financial Analysts Journal* 41, no. 4: 74–77. Alternatively, see George Foster, *Financial Statement Analysis* (Englewood Cliffs, NJ: Prentice-Hall, 1986), Table 3.4, p. 63. In addition, see Clyde P. Stickney, *Financial Reporting and a Statement Analysis,* 3d ed. (Dryden Press, 1996), Chapters 1 and 7.

[28] See Robert E. Bowen, David Burgstahler, and Lane A. Daley, "Evidence on the Relationship Between Earnings and Various Measures of Cash Flow," *Accounting Review* (October 1986): 713–25.

[29] For an enlightening story about the differences between reported earnings and book values of companies like Alcoa, Affiliated Publishing, First Boston, Merrill Lynch, Union Carbide, and Capital Cities/ABC, see "The Many Ways of Figuring Financial Results," *Business Week* (April 11, 1988): 131. The article also compares and contrasts the accounting philosophies of the Value Line and the Standard & Poor's financial service corporations.

[30] Milton Friedman, *A Theory of the Consumption Function* (Princeton, NJ: Princeton, 1957).

[31] For a discussion that is supportive of this approach to equity valuation, see Clyde P. Stickney, *Financial Reporting and Statement Analysis,* 3d ed. (Ft. Worth, TX: Dryden Press, 1996), 578–79.

STOCK VALUATION ISSUES

Chapters 23 and 24 investigated the determinants of the value of a share of stock. This chapter looks into the determinants of the value of a nation's entire stock market—which is another perspective on what determines the value of one share of stock. This chapter also considers special groups of equities. Industry analysis, technology stocks, patents and inventions, and inactively traded stocks are explored.

The efficient market theory in Chapter 8 suggests that most securities are priced fairly. If the strongly efficient markets model is descriptive of reality, the security analysis tools in this chapter are not worth learning. Alternatively, if the security analysis tools in this chapter are worth learning, then why should we have bothered studying the strongly efficient markets theory in Chapter 8? It turns out that this chapter and Chapter 8 are both worthwhile reading, but sometimes they contradict each other because the market is not always efficient. If this chapter's investment rules were always true, we could simply write a computer program that could separate the good investments from the bad ones. Life is rarely that simple. This chapter explains guidelines and suggests when to apply them.

The first section of this chapter considers the relationship between the inflation rate and stock market returns. Two centuries of U.S. data are analyzed.

The second section adapts financial ratios from Chapter 23 to make judgments, at any point in time, about whether stock prices in the United States are too high or too low. In determining whether the stock market is over- or underpriced Standard and Poor's 500 Stocks Composite Index is used as a market indicator. You could use the Dow-Jones Industrial Average if you think that is a better indicator of the U.S. stock market—or a stock market index for one industry if you want to analyze a single industry. The market valuation guidelines presented in this chapter are useful for market timing decisions. Market data on the price-earnings ratio and the cash dividend yield from the S&P500 index are reviewed.

The later parts of this chapter consider how industry analysis fits into the security valuation process. The industry life cycle model is reviewed. Aggregated financial statements from all the firms in an industry are considered.

The last sections of this chapter give special consideration to unusual categories of stocks. Internet stocks are analyzed. Call option theory is adapted to value up-and-coming situations, and the price-to-book-value (PBV) ratio is evaluated.

THE IMPACT OF INFLATION ON EQUITY PRICES

Compared to the last 200 years, the last 30 years have been a period of high inflation for many countries. Inflation will probably continue to be a problem in the years ahead because most nations' governments will continue to spend more than they collect in taxes. Deficit spending forces governments to borrow. It is common for federal governments to pay their debts (buy their bonds) by increasing the nation's money supply (printing money, monetizing debt). Monetizing a nation's debt is inflationary because more money winds up chasing the same amount of physical goods. Since most voters support deficit spending, this inflationary process goes on as long as the inflation rate does not get high enough to incur the voters' wrath.

As we enter the 21st century the United States finds itself in an unusual situation. Federal budget surpluses that allow the country to reduce its national debt without significantly increasing its money supply will make it easier for the United States to keep inflation under control.

Most governments measure inflation through a consumers' price index (CPI) like the one you saw in Chapter 10. The direct relationship between the rate of inflation and market interest rates (nominal interest rates) was represented by Irving Fisher's model, Eqn. 20-1, in Chapter 20 (p. 598). How bond prices (present values) move inversely to changes in market interest rates was explained in Chapter 21. Because market interest rates tend to rise and fall with the inflation rate, and bond prices move inversely with interest rates, it follows that bond prices will move inversely to the inflation rate if everything else is held constant. The next section compares this monetary theory with the empirical evidence about the relationship between inflation and common stock prices.

What Stock Market Data Tell Us About Inflation

People who say inflation is good for the stock market believe corporations benefit from it: They think that as corporations raise the prices of the products they sell, because they have previously entered into long-term contracts with their raw material suppliers and labor unions, their costs do not increase. The supposed result is a boost in corporate profits and stock prices.

The preceding scenario cannot be true for several reasons:

1. Consumers resist price increases.
2. Corporations also enter into long-term contracts to sell their products at fixed prices and thus inflation can hurt them.
3. Generally accepted accounting procedures do not contain inflation adjustments for depreciation allowances. As a result, the cash flows from depreciation become inadequate to pay for equipment renewal during inflationary periods.

These three issues cause many corporations to suffer from inflation. It is possible that investors who believe the stock market reacts positively to inflation may not understand the difference between *nominal returns* and *real returns*.

Table 25-1 provides statistics from over two centuries of U.S. data that summarize the impact of inflation on the stock market. Table 25-1A lists six categories of inflation and shows the average real common stock total rate of return under each category of inflation. At the lowest extreme is *extraordinary deflation,* which is defined to be inflation rates of −4.00% and lower. *Moderate deflation* has the second lowest rate of inflation; it includes inflation rates between −3.99% and −1.00%. *Price stability* is said to exist when the inflation rate is near zero—or between −0.99% and +0.99%. *Moderate inflation* is defined to occur at a rate from 1.00% to 3.99% per year. Inflation rates from 4.00% to 7.99% are called *high inflation.* The highest inflation category, called *extraordinary inflation,* encompasses inflation rates of 8.00% and above.

Table 25-1A reports above average returns from the stock market during price stability, moderate deflation, and extraordinary deflation; these three categories include all rates of inflation of 0.99% and below. The stock market returns were average during years categorized as moderate inflation. Real returns were far below average during the high inflation years. The stock market performed worse during periods of extraordinary inflation: The average real returns were negative when inflation was at the highest rates. The returns were more volatile during the postwar years (1946–97), but the pattern was the same over two centuries (1790–1997).

Table 25-1B uses the same two centuries of data in Table 25-1A to create four different categories of inflation. Table 25-1B is based on the year-to-year *changes* in the inflation rate, not on the inflation rate itself. Rapidly accelerating inflation (the largest year-to-year increases) caused the lowest real total returns, on average. The highest average real total returns occurred when inflation was rapidly decelerating (the largest year-to-year decreases). The patterns were the same in the long run and the short run.

Other Empirical Observations About Inflation

If we compare the average real returns over different sample periods, only minor differences are revealed. Averaging over the inflationary periods and the deflationary periods in the United States separately (see bottom of Table 25-1), for instance, the stock market's real returns are about the same in the long run, 1790–1997, as in more recent years, 1946–97. In the short-run stock price changes (returns from stocks) move inversely with the rate of inflation. However, in the long run, stock prices adjust to inflation so that their long-run average real returns and inflation-adjusted prices are unaffected by inflation.

Around the world, stock market prices and returns tend to move inversely with the inflation rate. In Japan, for example, two very bearish years for the stock market, 1973 and 1990, occurred during periods of rising inflation. In contrast, Japan's stock market turned in its highest stock market returns when the country's inflation rate was falling, for example, during the mid-1980s. A similar inverse relationship between inflation and stock prices is discernible in the United Kingdom, Germany, and other countries.

Two Yardsticks for Timing the Stock Market

Common stocks' price/earnings ratios and cash dividend yields may be used like index numbers. Figures 25-1A and C suggest a historical tendency for these two financial ratios to fluctuate between upper and lower horizontal boundaries most of the time. In Figures 25-1A and C one of these boundary lines is interpreted to be a *buy line* and the other boundary line is called a *sell line.* The buy and sell signals from Figure 25-2A, and the separate buy and sell signals from Figure 25-1C, are traced through to the S&P500 price index in Figure 25-1B to be compared and evaluated.

TABLE 25-1   Inflation Rate Changes and Equity Returns, 1790–1997 and 1946–97

	Long Run: 1790–1997		Postwar Years: 1946–97	
	Number of Years	Arithmetic Mean Real Total Return	Number of Years	Arithmetic Mean Real Total Return
Six ranges of inflation				
Extraordinary deflation				
−4.00% and below	33	14.03%	0	N/A
Moderate deflation				
−3.99% to −1.00%	23	12.25%	1	20.59%
Price stability				
−0.99% to 0.99%	34	12.28%	5	25.28%
Moderate inflation				
1.00% to 3.99%	64	11.20%	26	12.44%
High inflation				
4.00% to 7.99%	31	5.39%	12	8.36%
Extraordinary inflation				
8.00% and above	23	−4.64%	8	−10.35%
All years	208		52	
Four categories of inflation changes from previous year				
Rapid deceleration				
down 5.00% or more	34	14.88%	4	11.81%
Low deceleration				
down 0.01% to 4.99%	71	12.02%	24	16.95%
Low acceleration				
up 0.00% to 4.99%	72	7.11%	21	2.75%
Rapid acceleration				
up 5.00% or more	30	1.52%	3	−7.92%
All years	208		52	
Means		**1790–1997**		**1946–97**
Arithmetic mean		9.33%		9.39%
Geometric mean		7.48%		7.81%

SUMMARY: Annual stock market returns vary inversely with the rate of inflation. Table 25-1A shows that, on average, the U.S. stock market's highest real (inflation-adjusted) returns occurred during periods of extraordinary deflation. During periods of extraordinary inflation, the real total returns are negative. Table 25-1B shows that, on average, the highest real total stock market returns occurred when inflation was rapidly decreasing. But when inflation was accelerating rapidly, the average real total returns were the smallest. The average real total returns over two centuries at the bottom of the table are very similar to the returns from the last five decades. This means that, in the long-run, stock prices react and adjust to fluctuating rates of inflation.

SOURCES: 1790–1824: Roger G. Ibbotson and Gary P. Brinson, *Global Investing* (New York: McGraw-Hill, 1993), Chapter 12.
1825–1870: William N. Goetzmann and Roger G. Ibbotson, "An Emerging Market: The NYSE from 1815 to 1871," Yale School of Management, December 16, 1994.
1871–1925: Jack W. Wilson and Charles P. Jones, "A Comparison of Annual Common Stock Returns: 1871–1925 with 1926–85," *Journal of Business* 60, no. 2 (1987): 1926–1997: *Stocks, Bonds, Bills and Inflation,* Ibbotson Associates, Chicago.
Also, see Steven C. Leuthold, *The Myths of Inflation and Investing* (Crain Books, 1980).

FIGURE 25-1A   Buy-Sell Guidelines for S&P500 Cash Dividend Yield

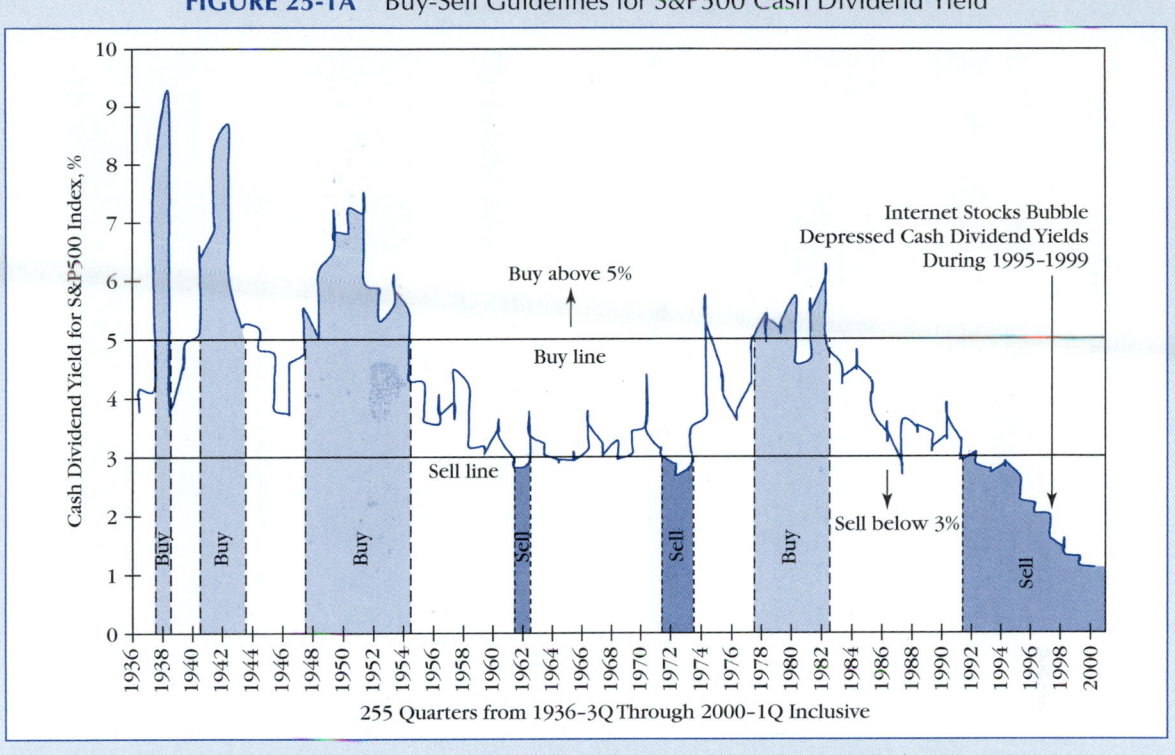

When the average cash dividend yield (Annual cash dividend/Current market price) from the 500 stocks in the S&P500 index rises above 5%, the U.S. stock market has usually fallen. As a result, some investors interpret a 5% cash dividend yield from the S&P500 to be a buy signal. These investors also suggest that the horizontal line at 3% in (A) is a sell signal. These trading signals are traced through to the S&P500 price index illustrated in (B).

The S&P500 Cash Dividend Yield

Cash dividends change slowly and gradually, while stock prices are more volatile. Some common stock investors study the cash dividend yield (annual cash dividends divided by the current market price) for trading signals. They interpret cash dividend yield values above 5% for the S&P500 index illustrated in Figure 25-1A to mean the U.S. stock market is underpriced. These investors interpret a 5% cash dividend yield from the S&P500 to be a *buy signal;* it is illustrated by the horizontal line at 5% in Figure 25-1A. Similarly, some investors interpret the horizontal line at 3% in Figure 25-1A to be a *sell signal.* It is believed that the S&P500 index's cash dividend yield cannot fall far below 3% unless a large proportion of the common stocks are overpriced.

Figure 25-1A shows that when the cash dividend yield soared above 5% in 1937–38 and again in 1941–42, these peaking cash dividend yields were interpreted by many as signals to buy. A glance at Figure 25-1B shows that 1938 and 1942 were good times to buy stocks. Trading points can be traced from Figure 25-1A by connecting vertical lines from Figure 25-1A to simultaneous points in Figure 25-1B to identify the buy and sell points on the S&P500 price index.

The S&P500 Price-Earnings Ratio

Figure 25-1C illustrates buy and sell signals derived from the price/earnings ratio for the S&P500 index. Some investors believe that when the stocks in the S&P500 index are selling

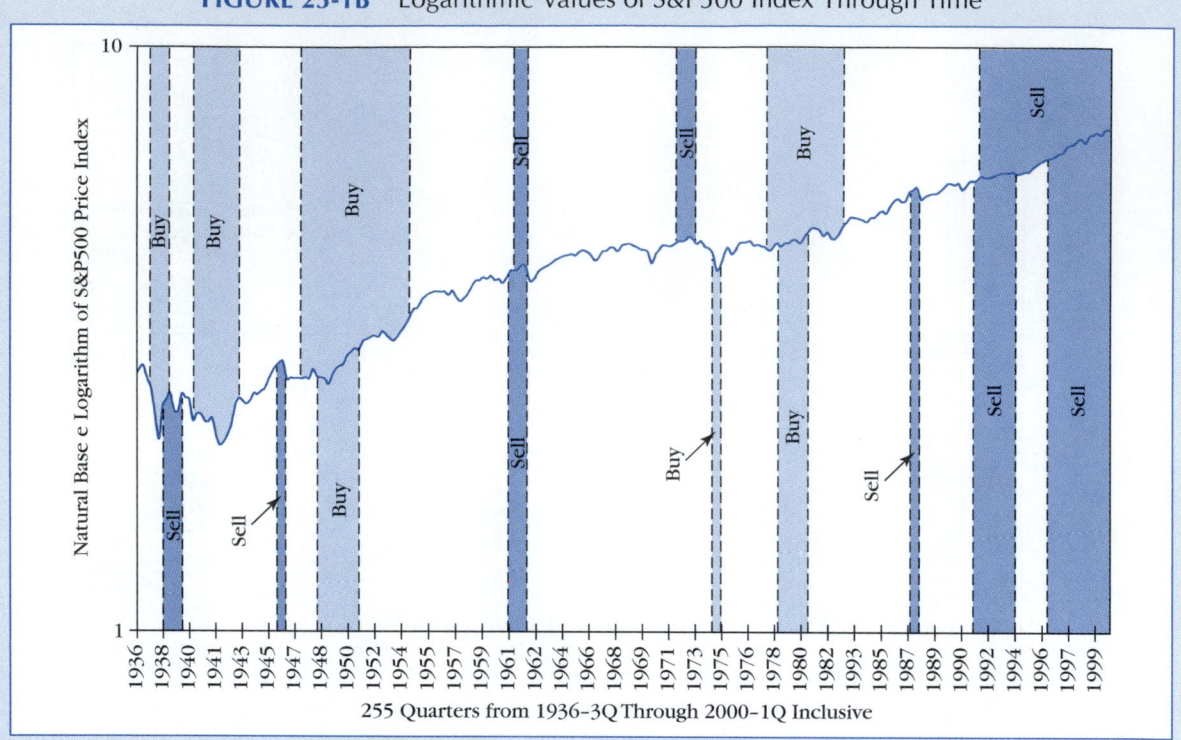

FIGURE 25-1B   Logarithmic Values of S&P500 Index Through Time

To ascertain the profitability of interpreting a 5% cash dividend yield from the S&P500 in (A) to be a buy signal, and 3% to be a sell signal, these trading signals are traced from (A) to the S&P500 price index graph in (B).

To determine the profitability of treating an average S&P500 price-earnings ratio below 8 times earnings as a buy signal and a price-earnings ratio above 19 times as a sell signal, these trading signals are traced from (C) to the S&P500 price index graphed in (B).

at less than eight times their earnings, the U.S. stock market is underpriced. They see the S&P500 price-earnings ratio of eight in Figure 25-1C as a signal to buy. These investors also believe that when the stocks in the S&P500 index are selling at more than 19 times their earnings, the stock market is overpriced. The price-earnings ratio of 19 in Figure 25-1C is illustrated as a horizontal line labeled as a signal to sell. For instance, when the S&P500 price-earnings ratios went above 19 during 1987, the ratio was issuing a profitable sell signal before the well-known international stock market crash on October 19, 1987. These buy and sell signals can be traced from Figure 25-1C to Figure 25-1B by drawing vertical lines to identify the suggested trading points on the S&P500 price index.

Assessing the Buy-Sell Guidelines

Prior to 1991, the buy-sell recommendations generated from Figures 25-1A and B were sometimes profitable and sometimes unprofitable. There are a few investors who blindly follow every buy and sell signal illustrated in Figures 25-1A, B, and C. Some investors act only when the S&P500 price-earnings ratio and the S&P500 cash dividend yield are both giving the same signal to buy or sell. Some investors prefer to use cash dividend yields that differ from 5% and 3% as the basis for their trading decisions. And some investors use price-earnings ratios that differ from 19 and 8 as their guidelines for selling and buying.

FIGURE 25-1C   Buy-Sell Guidelines for S&P500's Price-Earnings Ratio

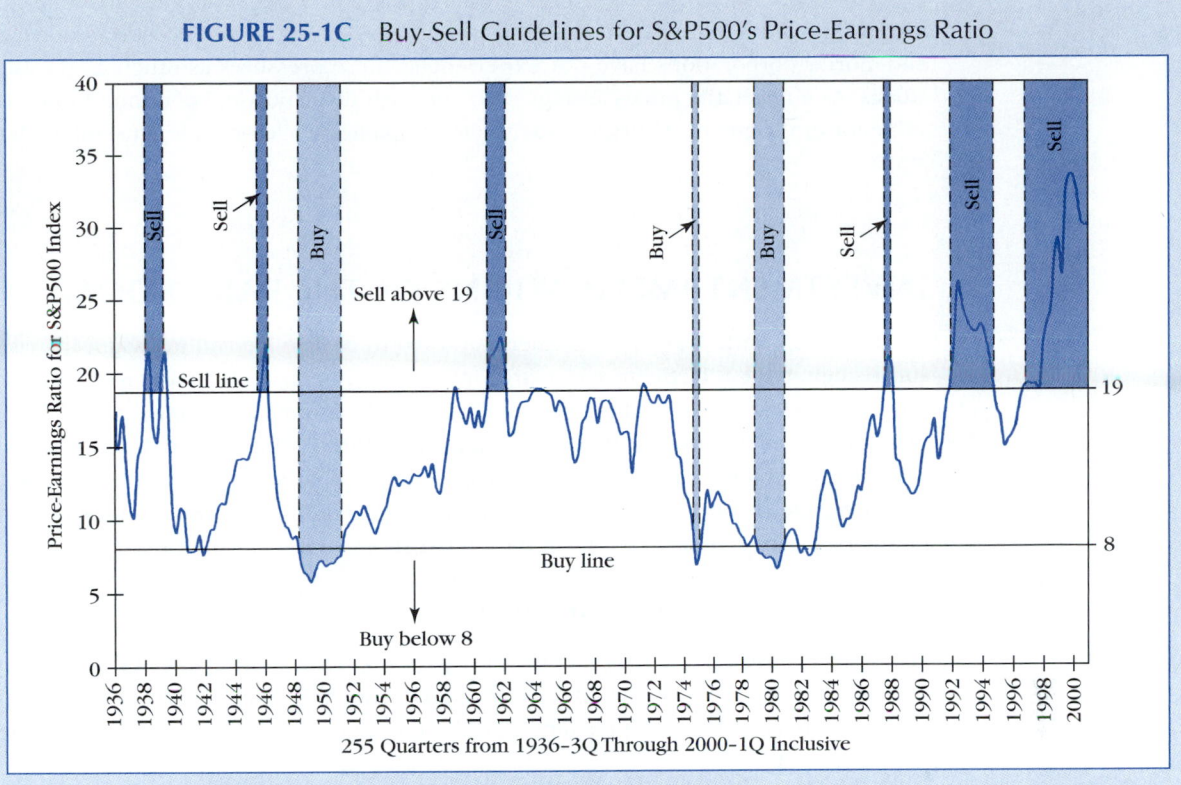

Some investors believe that when the stocks comprising the S&P500 index are selling, on average, at less than 8 times their annual earnings, the U.S. stock market is underpriced. These investors see the horizontal line at a P/E ratio of 8 in (C) as a signal to buy. Similarly, the horizontal line at a price-earnings ratio of 19 is a sell signal. To ascertain the profitability of these trading signals we trace them through to the S&P500 price index in (B).

One advantage of the buy or sell suggestions illustrated in Figures 25-1A, B, and C is that they are simple. Another advantage is that these suggestions can find some support in the valuation theories reviewed in Chapter 23.

Problems with the Buy-Sell Guidelines

During 1938 the S&P500 price-earnings ratio issued a sell signal, while at the same time the S&P500 cash dividend yield was issuing a buy signal. Contradictory signals like this highlight the fact that the guidelines in Figures 25-1A, B, and C can be wrong.

The S&P500 price-earnings ratio in Figure 25-1C started issuing a sell signal in 1992 that discontinued temporarily in 1995, resumed in 1997, and continued for years after 1997. Figure 25-1A shows that the S&P500 cash dividend yield started issuing a sell signal in 1992 that continued for years. At the same time these two sell signals were being issued, the S&P500 and other stock price indexes continued to rise. After 1992 the S&P500 index, the S&P500 price-earnings ratio, and the S&P500 cash dividend yield were affected by:

1. A demographic factor called the "baby boom"
2. The growing trend for corporations to buy back their own common stock
3. Rising labor productivity in the United States
4. The addition of Internet and computer software stocks to the S&P500 index

These four factors raised the price-earnings ratio and lowered the cash dividend yield for the S&P500 index in the years after 1992, as illustrated in Figure 25-1. Most traditional bricks-and-mortar corporations have not experienced these pressures as much as the Internet stocks. As a result, the price-earnings ratio and cash dividend yield continue to be of some value for evaluating many bricks-and-mortar companies while being less useful for Internet stocks.

INVESTMENT IMPLICATIONS OF THE BABY BOOM

At the end of World War II, U.S. soldiers returned to civilian life and many got married. Not surprisingly, the U.S. birthrate saw a large increase beginning in 1946 and remaining at high levels until 1962. This was the "baby boom." The baby boom babies have caused significant reallocations of resources within the United States throughout their lives, and their impact will continue to be felt in the decades ahead as they strain the nation's retirement resources. The life-cycle theory of savings is helpful in understanding the implications of the baby boom for recent economic events in the United States.

The Life-Cycle Theory of Savings

Figure 25-2 illustrates the *life-cycle theory of savings* for a representative (average, typical) consumer; it begins when a child is emancipated from his or her parents and becomes economically independent and presumes that the typical consumer is happier if his or her life-

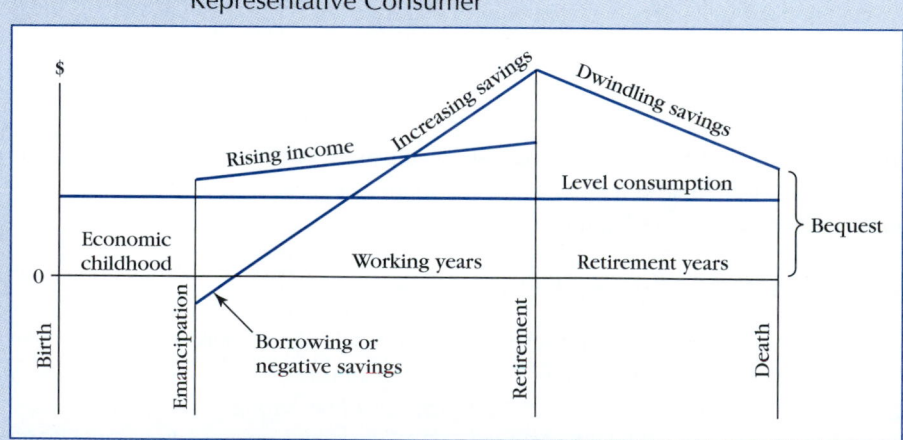

FIGURE 25-2 The Life-Cycle Theory of Savings for a Representative Consumer

The life-cycle theory of savings begins when a child is emancipated from his or her parents. The typical child begins life as a representative consumer who endeavors to allocate his or her consumption smoothly over their lifetime. The typical consumer's annual income begins low and rises to a peak when the consumer retires. Young consumers typically dis-save (borrow) to finance purchases of automobiles and a home. However, as the representative consumer matures his or her annual income typically rises and it becomes possible for the consumer to accumulate more savings each year. When the consumer retires, the income stops, and the accumulated savings begin to be consumed. Savings remaining when the consumer dies become a bequest to heirs.

time allocation of consumption goods are apportioned fairly equally through the lifetime.[1] Consumption that is presumed to be level from year to year is financed by annual incomes that peak when the consumer reaches retirement. Young consumers typically borrow (incur negative savings, dis-save) because their beginning annual incomes are less than their annual outlays for consumption goods. As our representative consumer matures, his or her annual income rises, debts incurred while younger are repaid, and savings begin to accumulate. The representative consumer's savings peak at retirement. During the retirement years the savings diminish as consumption is financed by savings withdrawals (liquidating investments). Whatever savings remain when the consumer dies are a bequest to heirs.

Zhiwu Chen's 1990 Forecast

When summed up over millions of baby boomers in the United States, the life cycle theory of savings for the representative consumer has stock market implications. A 1990 Yale doctoral dissertation by Zhiwu Chen appears to be the first research to link the life-cycle theory of savings and the baby boom.[2] Based on the life-cycle theory of savings, Chen predicted that millions of aging baby boomers would allocate a significant portion of their savings to equity investments, and he traced the implications of this behavior to common stock prices. Chen's findings were published in a 1994 paper he coauthored with Gurdip Bakshi.[3]

The Bakshi-Chen paper hypothesized that when the baby boomers reached approximately 49 years of age they would allocate an increasing portion of their income to savings and stock market investing to finance their retirement needs. As a result, high levels of annual stock market investing should continue until the youngest baby boomers reach retirement age. In other words, the Bakshi-Chen paper forecasted that bullish stock market conditions would begin in about 1995 (when the oldest baby boomers became 49 years old) and would start to decline in about 2012 (when the youngest baby boomers reach 65 and retire), as indicated in Table 25-2A.

Table 25-2B shows that the 1926–94 average total return was 11.2% per year from the S&P500 index. Then, a raging bull market started in U.S. stocks in 1995. The 1995–99 average annual total return from the S&P500 index was 28.6%, substantially above the 1926–94 average return of 11.2% per annum. Dr. Chen's baby boom forecast seems to be off to a good start.

The Bakshi-Chen lifetime theory of savings can also be used to predict the point during the 2010–20 decade when the flow of unusually large savings (stock market investing) will

---

TABLE 25-2   Some Investment Implications of the Baby Boom: (A) Implied Actions and (B) Average Returns

(A) Delineating Some Implications of the Baby Boom

Event	Beginning of Event	End of Event
Baby Boom	Birth rate rises in 1946	Birth rate falls in 1962
Add: Age	Add: Retirement saving starts at 49	Add: Retirement starts at 65
Saving Years	Heavy investing begins in 1995	Liquidation begins in 2012

(B) Contrasting Two Average Rates of Return from the S&P500 Index

Years	1926–94	1995	1996	1997	1998	1999
Year's total return from S&P500	NA	37.5%	23.1%	33.4%	28.6%	21.0%
Average annual total return	11.2%			28.6%		

reverse direction. After the baby boomers retire they will consume their lifetime savings until they die a few decades later. In other words, unless additional considerations become relevant, a long bull market may be followed by a long bear market as pensions funds, mutual funds, and other financial intermediaries experience continuous annual outflows from approximately 2012 until 2042.

The demographic findings reported in the Bakshi-Chen paper help rationalize the unusually high price-earnings ratios, low cash dividend yields, and bullish stock market conditions (illustrated in Figure 25-1) during the late 1990s.

INVESTMENT IMPLICATIONS OF COMMON STOCK BUYBACKS

At the same time the baby boomers were starting to finance their retirements by making annual multibillion-dollar investments in the stock market, corporate share buybacks started rising sharply too. In 1997 and 1998 the amount spent on common stock repurchases by large public corporations exceeded the cash dividend payments to the owners of those corporations. Repurchasing stock by large nonbank public corporations more than tripled between 1994 and 1998, reaching nearly $150 billion. Between 1994 and 1998, cash dividend payments rose a more modest 35%, to about $115 billion. This dramatic growth in stock buybacks and the simultaneous shrinking cash dividend payout ratios modified the role of the traditional cash dividend yield in equity valuation, as illustrated in and Figure 25-1A and summarized in Table 25-3.

INCREASING LABOR PRODUCTIVITY AND WHAT IT IMPLIES FOR INVESTMENT

The productivity of a nation's labor force can be measured in terms of output per hour of work.

$$\left(\begin{array}{c} \text{Output} \\ \text{per hour} \end{array}\right) = \frac{\text{A nation's aggregate real national output}}{\text{Aggregate hours worked by the nation's labor force}} = \left(\begin{array}{c} \text{Labor} \\ \text{productivity} \end{array}\right)$$

During the 1980s the U.S. productivity of labor had been growing between approximately 1% to 2% each year because the capital-to-labor ratio climbed (which means more and newer machines per worker), the education of the labor force improved, and new technology emerged more rapidly. In 1990s, wider implementation of computers and the Internet accelerated the growth rate in labor productivity in the United States to the higher range of 2% to 3% per year (and even more in some years) as shown in Figure 25-3.

TABLE 25-3	Uses of a Corporation's Net Income (After-tax earnings)		
Traditional Uses			More Recent Uses
			Share buybacks
	Cash dividends	plus:	Cash dividends
plus:	Retained earnings	plus:	Retained earnings
Equals:	Total earnings	Equals:	Total earnings

FIGURE 25-3   Accelerating Average Annual Nonfarm Output Per Hour of Labor in United States

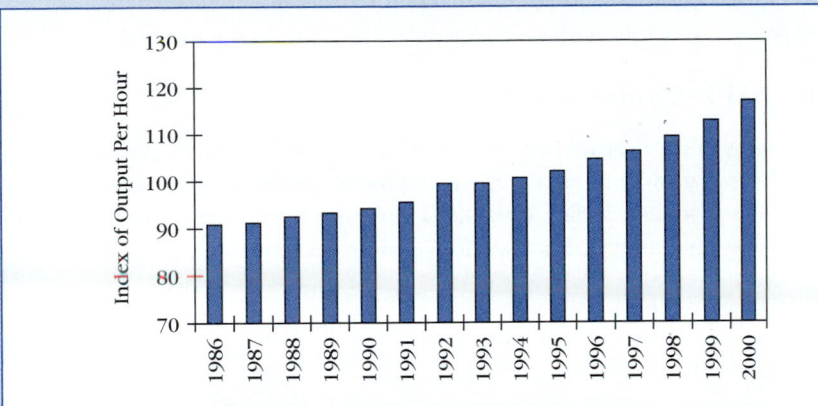

Labor productivity is measured in terms of output per hour of work. During the 1980s the productivity of labor grew slowly in the range from about 1% to 2% per year in the United States. In the 1990s wider implementation of improved computer technology and the Internet accelerated the growth rate in labor productivity in the United States to the range from about 2% to 4% per year.
Source: U.S. Department of Labor, Series PRS85006093

If raw materials prices remain constant, increases in a nation's labor productivity (output per hour worked) leads to reduced unit labor costs. Since increases in labor productivity leads to reduced unit labor costs, if all other factors are held constant, it may be concluded that increases in labor productivity are anti-inflationary.

INCREASING LABOR PRODUCTIVITY IS ANTI-INFLATIONARY   **EXAMPLE**

Suppose that in one particular year in the United States raw materials prices remain constant, wages rise 2% a year, and output per hour worked increase 3%. If wages rise 2% in a year when output per hour worked increases 3%, then unit labor costs fall by 1% that year.

    2% per year rise in wages

−3% increase in output per hour worked

−1% change in unit labor cost

CONCLUSION: The falling unit labor costs in the example above are anti-inflationary (even though the workers got 2% pay raises).

The rate of inflation for a whole nation is usually measured by a consumer price index (CPI) that includes goods and services from many different industries. The inflation rates in different industries vary around the nation's overall average rate of inflation. As a result of these differences in inflation, and other industry influences as well, the next section focuses on the industries within a country separately instead of only looking at the country as a whole.

INDUSTRY ANALYSIS

Because a single product usually defines an industry, all the companies in an industry usually profit or suffer losses together. This pattern makes it worthwhile to determine if an *industry* is likely to be profitable before bothering to analyze the *firms* in the industry.

The Product Life-Cycle Model

Many products, firms, and industries pass through a life cycle of four stages: (1) introduction of a new product, (2) rapid growth in sales of the new product, (3) slowing growth as the product matures, and (4) the product's decline. Figure 25-4 illustrates the four stages of the *product life-cycle model.* Because an industry comprises firms that produce the same product, this theory is

FIGURE 25-4   The Product Life-Cycle Model

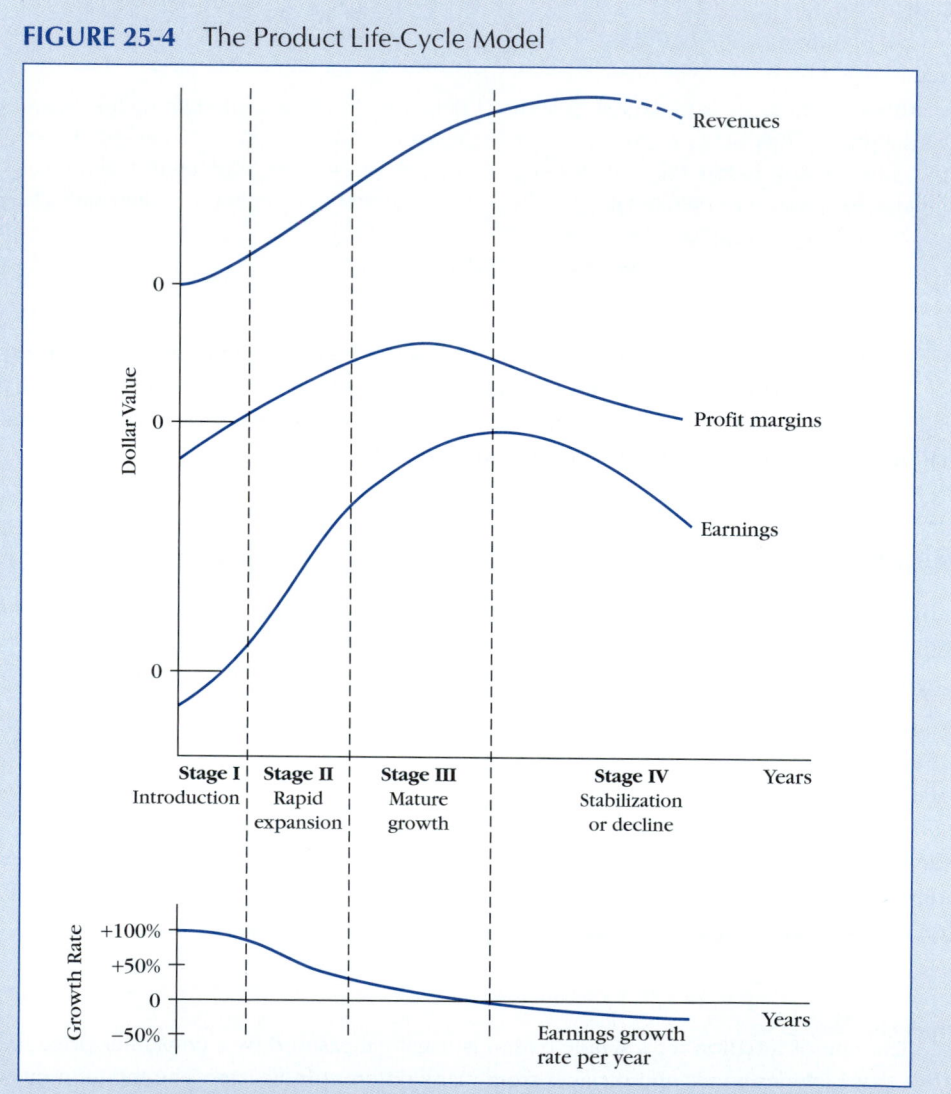

The development of many products, firms, and industries passes through a four-stage life-cycle. The duration of a life cycle varies from product to product. If a product conforms to the life-cycle model, the model contains valuable investment implications.

also called the *industry life-cycle model*. Table 25-4 enumerates various attributes that the product and the firms in the industry experience during each stage of the product's life cycle.

The nature of the product determines the duration of the industry's life cycle. Music groups that produce hits for youthful audiences provide numerous examples of short product life cycles. It is typical for an unheard of musical group to attain "top ten" status on the sales charts, earn millions within months, and be forgotten one year later. In contrast, Frank Sinatra, the Beatles, the Rolling Stones, the Beach Boys, and a precious few other musical groups have been able to maintain star status for several decades. Surpassing the duration of hit musicians, the Coca-Cola Corporation is more than a century old and is still growing.

In 1886, a pharmacist and a bookkeeper in Atlanta, Georgia created Coca-Cola syrup. In 1891, Asa Candler acquired complete ownership of Coca-Cola syrup by investing $2,300. Mr. Candler registered the name with the U.S. patent office, started expanding the business nationwide, incorporated the business, began paying cash dividends, and started selling shares to stockholders in 1892. Coca-Cola grew and achieved worldwide fame. Today Coca-Cola is a mature product that has been in Stage 3 of its product life cycle for over 100 years. It remains to be seen if Coca-Cola's product life cycle can span two centuries.

Although there is considerable ambiguity about the duration of a product's life cycle, the life-cycle model is still an important piece of equipment in many security analysts' toolboxes. The first step in using the life-cycle model, is to locate the product (or firm, or industry) on the life cycle curve in Figure 25-4. Its location suggests where it is going and provides implications about the value of an investment. For example, since Coca-Cola is in the third stage of its product life cycle, the model tells the security analysts to look for signs that Coke's sales are starting to decline. If Coca-Cola's growth rates dropped with sufficient consistency to qualify the firm to reach Stage 4, the value of its stock would collapse to a fraction of what it was when Coke enjoyed the consistent positive growth rates that characterize Stage 3.

TABLE 25-4   Characteristics of the Product and the Competing Firms During Each Stage of the Product Life-Cycle Model

	Stage 1: Product Introduction	Stage 2: Emerging Growth	Stage 3: Mature Growth	Stage 4: Declining Growth
Product's Stage of Life	Pioneering	New	Widely accepted	Becoming obsolete
Product's Price Per Unit	High	High, but falling	Competitive	Low and declining
Sales Revenues	Beginning from zero	Rising rapidly	Rising slowly	Declining
Number of Competing Producers	One, or a few	Few, but growing	A number of stable firms	Decreasing
Producer's Profits	Losses due to development costs	Rising rapidly	Starting to decline gradually	Declining
Producer's Solvency	Near bankruptcy	Profitable, but barely solvent	Profitable and solvent	Highly solvent
Producer's Cash Dividends	None	None, or small and initial	Growing payments	Level or declining payments

SUMMARY: The illustration of the product (or industry, or firm) life cycle model in Figure 25-4 summarizes numerous developments that can help investors recognize profitable trades.

The product life-cycle theory is of no value in trying to analyze commodities, fads, and most speculative situations. However, the life-cycle model can be useful to investors that compare products and industries, and are willing to invest in new companies.

Financial Analysis of an Industry

Federal governments around the world compile industrial data for census and tax purposes. Trade associations collect data on their member firms, other firms in the same industry, and competing industries to prepare reports for their members, for advertising, and for lobbying. The Standard & Poor's Corporation, Moody's Investors Services, and many other financial service corporations collect and update company data and industrial data to be sold to subscribers.

Standard & Poor's provides stock price indexes on 103 U.S. industries that extend back as far as 1967, and on many international indexes. S&P compiles industry stock price indexes, industry balance sheets, industry income statements, and industry financial ratios for 87 industrial industries, 13 technology industries, 4 transportation industries, 2 utility industries, 10 financial industries, and other narrowly defined industry groups.[4]

Standard & Poor's Industrial Stocks Index is the largest component of the S&P500 Stocks Composite Index. The S&P Industrial Stocks Index is made up from 87 narrowly defined industrial indexes that are made up from about 400 underlying industrial stocks (the number of firms fluctuates slightly through time).

Figure 25-5 reproduces a page from *Standard & Poor's Analysts Handbook* showing several year's balance sheets, income statements, and financial ratios for one of S&P's many industrial indexes. This industry index is based on a sample of ten soft drink manufacturers. Figure 25-6 is also from the **Handbook;** it shows several years of per-share financial data on S&P's nonalcoholic beverage stocks index from 1966 through 1998. An investor considering taking positions in Coca-Cola, Pepsi-Cola, or some other soft drink manufacturer, for example, would want to study S&P's Non-Alcoholic Beverage Industry Index to determine if the reasons for this industry's superior performance over the past decade can be expected to continue.

THE INTERNET STOCKS BUBBLE

During the late 1990s the U.S. stock market split into two sectors—the technology stocks and the nontechnology stocks. The bull market that characterized the last half of the 1990s surged on until 2000 for the technology stocks, leaving many good nontechnology stocks behind. This section considers various aspects of this optimistic bubble.

Cash dividend yields plunged and price/earnings ratios soared as stock prices surged to new highs between 1995 and 2000. This bull market can be attributed to six factors. First, interest rates dropped sharply during the 1980s and 1990s; this drop set the stage for lower discount rates that pushed up present values. Second, equity risk premiums (measured by: $r -$ RFR) declined as the U.S. economy racked up the longest economic expansion on record and investors' risk aversion diminished. This declining risk-aversion helped reduce discount rates further. Third, earnings grew at faster rates during the 1990s. As a result of these three factors, for most stocks the quantity $P = d_1/(k - g)$ rose because the quantity $(k - g)$ shrank to a tiny value. Fourth and fifth, as mentioned earlier in this chapter, both the baby boomers and stock buybacks channeled additional millions of dollars into stock market purchases. And, sixth, the productivity of labor in the United States kept increasing.

The S&P500 index entered the new millennium with a price-earnings ratio that was twice as high as normal and its cash dividend yield that was only half the size of its historical average value. A closer look at the individual stocks comprising the S&P500 index reveals

FIGURE 25-5   Financial Data from S&P's Non-Alcoholic Beverage Stocks Index, 1993–98

BEVERAGES (NON-ALCOHOLIC)
Per Share Data - Adjusted to Stock Price Index Level
Average of Stock Price Index, 1941 - 1943 = 10

INCOME ACCOUNT—

	1998	1997	1996	1995	1994	1993
SALES	760.41	798.46	861.06	805.79	731.96	629.08
COSTS & EXPENSES	569.33	631.33	689.44	644.03	586.50	503.16
OPERATING INCOME	191.08	167.13	171.62	161.76	145.46	125.93
OTHER INCOME	NA	NA	NA	NA	NA	NA
TOTAL INCOME	NA	NA	NA	NA	NA	NA
DEPRECIATION	45.38	26.79	37.92	33.88	32.08	28.02
INTEREST	22.78	13.79	16.09	15.87	13.91	12.36
SPECIAL ITEMS	-2.37	8.08	-12.92	-8.84	0.29	0.23
MINORITY INTEREST	NA	NA	NA	NA	NA	NA
INCOME TAXES	32.56	47.66	35.27	36.08	33.72	29.61
NET INCOME	94.05	103.03	78.52	76.43	71.20	61.05
PREFERRED DIVIDENDS	0.02	0.00	0.00	0.00	0.00	0.00
SAVINGS FR. COM. STK. EQUIV.	0.00	0.00	0.00	0.00	0.00	0.00
COMMON EARNINGS	94.03	103.03	78.52	76.43	71.20	61.05
COMMON DIVIDENDS	38.08	36.66	32.66	28.71	25.63	22.14
BALANCE AFTER DIVIDENDS	55.95	66.37	45.86	47.72	45.58	38.91

FINANCIAL RATIOS—

	1998	1997	1996	1995	1994	1993
CURRENT RATIO	0.69	1.00	0.90	0.90	0.90	0.80
QUICK RATIO	0.39	0.70	0.70	0.70	0.70	0.70
DEBT TO TOTAL ASSETS (%)	24.00	24.00	24.00	24.00	27.00	25.00
DEBT TO TOTAL EQUITY (%)	83.29	NA	78.00	76.00	85.00	81.00
DEBT TO TOTAL CAPITAL (%)	58.00	46.00	40.00	NA	NA	NA
TIMES INTEREST EARNED	11.14	19.60	8.10	8.10	8.50	8.30
INVENTORY TURNOVER	4.64	6.60	22.50	22.30	22.10	19.70
TOTAL ASSETS TURNOVER	1.02	1.10	1.20	1.20	1.20	1.10
PROFIT MARGIN (%)	15.34	20.93	19.93	20.07	19.87	20.02
RETURN ON TOTAL ASSETS (%)	15.06	15.12	10.95	11.35	11.23	10.59

ASSETS—

	1998	1997	1996	1995	1994	1993
CASH & EQUIVALENT	37.65	81.86	41.93	46.80	49.54	47.36
RECEIVABLES	90.53	67.17	75.83	69.16	58.65	50.48
INCOME TAX REFUND	0.00	0.00	0.00	0.00	0.00	0.00
INVENTORIES	40.64	30.17	38.26	36.07	33.10	31.90
OTHER CURRENT ASSETS	47.34	39.76	NA	NA	NA	NA
TOTAL CURRENT ASSETS	216.15	218.95	198.14	182.96	168.62	155.04
NET PROPERTY, PLANT, & EQUIP	263.46	178.34	241.07	236.29	228.85	203.01
INV. & ADV. TO UNCONS. SUBS.	127.55	81.15	79.93	67.07	38.36	34.51
INTANGIBLES	158.34	120.68	140.68	141.80	139.20	136.51
OTHER ASSETS	NA	NA	NA	NA	NA	NA
TOTAL ASSETS	758.20	666.15	717.27	673.27	633.92	576.51

LIABILITIES —

	1998	1997	1996	1995	1994	1993
NOTES PAYABLE	121.21	45.86	56.73	51.22	44.79	62.08
CURRENT PORTION OF LTD	36.80	NA	1.73	9.19	0.58	0.31
ACCOUNTS PAYABLE	62.45	58.65	64.68	60.41	53.99	48.41
INCOME TAX PAYABLE	19.25	29.10	25.47	28.45	32.57	31.20
ACCRUED EXPENSES	45.68	21.10	NA	NA	NA	30.92
OTHER CURRENT LIABILITIES	74.40	62.47	42.58	38.70	34.66	16.79
TOTAL CURRENT LIABILITIES	331.04	207.73	217.49	209.31	187.85	189.70
LONG TERM DEBT	237.61	108.81	173.17	160.46	168.14	142.94
DEFERRED INCOME TAX	118.50	34.88	35.41	34.57	35.25	34.14
INVESTMENT TAX CREDIT	0.00	0.00	0.00	0.00	0.00	0.00
MINORITY INTEREST	NA	3.79	NA	NA	NA	NA
OTHER LIABILITIES	71.05	57.64	63.82	57.57	44.37	33.36
PREFERRED STOCK	0.81	0.00	0.00	0.00	0.00	0.00
COMMON STOCK	22.23	23.44	22.39	7.36	7.26	7.14
CAPITAL SURPLUS	90.71	47.81	36.58	37.99	33.37	30.39
RETAINED EARNINGS	510.54	469.71	388.95	340.53	296.29	248.95
LESS TREASURY COST	338.21	287.65	224.52	174.51	138.61	110.11
TOTAL LIABILITIES	758.20	666.15	717.27	673.27	633.92	576.51

NA - Not Available
NM - Not Meaningful
CF - Combined Figure

SOURCE: Standard & Poor's *Analysts Handbook,* New York City, published annually.

that some traditional bricks-and-mortar stocks were high-priced, and almost all Internet stocks were overpriced.

The U.S. stock market experienced a correction that started early in 2000. By the end of that year investors had given back many of the handsome gains acquired during the 1995–99 bull market. Internet and other technology stocks investors were the biggest losers.

Clicks Versus Bricks

During the raging bull market for technology stocks during 1995–99 many investors claimed Dot.com companies differed from traditional bricks-and-mortar companies in several ways:

1. Many bricks-and-mortar companies forecast sales by extrapolating historical sales of their same products, but the Internet companies create faster grow by inventing new products.
2. The typical bricks-and-mortar company endeavors to increase profit by cutting costs, because raising selling prices significantly is not feasible. Some Dot.com companies have no trouble charging higher prices as they struggle to meet growing demand.
3. Most bricks-and-mortar companies are burdened by the fixed interest expense of debt, but many Dot.coms have no debt. Many Dot.coms raise capital by issuing common stock that pays no cash dividends.

FIGURE 25-6   Per Share Financial Data from S&P's Non-Alcoholic Beverage Stocks Index, 1966–98

BEVERAGES (NON-ALCOHOLIC)

Per Share Data — Adjusted to stock price index level. Average of stock price indexes, 1941-1943=10

Year	Sales	Oper. Profit	Profit Margin %	Depr.	Income Taxes	Cash Flow	Dil. Earn. Per Share	% of Sales	Div. Per Share	% of Earn.	Price High (1941-43=10)	Price Low	Price Close	P/E Ratio High	P/E Low	P/E Close	Div. Yield % High	Low	Close	Total Return Index	Book Value Per Share	Price % Return	Price to Book Ratio	Working Capital	Capital Expenditures
1966	30.25	5.44	17.98	1.00	2.06		2.26	7.47	1.26	55.75	58.19	46.59	78.88	25.75	20.62	34.90	2.70	2.17	1.60	...	11.67	19.37	6.76	5.46	2.73
1967	32.70	5.95	18.20	1.17	2.19		2.47	7.55	1.38	55.87	80.44	55.43	89.71	32.57	22.44	36.32	2.49	1.72	1.54	...	11.39	21.69	7.88	5.75	2.32
1968	35.61	6.56	18.42	1.14	2.66		2.73	7.67	1.51	55.31	97.61	74.77	98.81	35.75	27.39	36.19	2.02	1.55	1.53	...	12.43	21.96	7.95	5.08	2.77
1969	40.41	7.16	17.72	1.24	3.00		2.96	7.32	1.69	57.09	101.88	82.37	103.30	34.42	27.83	34.90	2.05	1.66	1.64	...	13.55	21.85	7.62	4.47	3.15
1970	46.09	7.87	17.08	1.33	3.15		3.41	7.40	1.82	53.37	104.19	80.07	149.50	30.55	23.48	43.84	2.27	1.75	1.22	...	14.46	23.58	10.34	5.81	3.43
1971	50.37	8.73	17.33	1.44	3.55		3.89	7.72	1.96	50.39	150.21	102.16	182.40	38.61	26.26	46.89	1.92	1.30	1.07	...	16.95	22.95	10.76	7.47	2.68
1972	56.31	9.64	17.12	1.55	3.92		4.40	7.81	2.02	45.91	183.25	142.45	148.60	41.65	32.38	33.77	1.42	1.10	1.36	...	19.69	22.35	7.55	8.55	3.33
1973	65.67	10.57	16.10	1.74	4.22		4.92	7.49	2.24	45.53	182.90	141.76	148.60	37.17	28.81	30.20	1.58	1.22	1.51	...	21.76	22.61	6.83	9.76	3.86
1974	78.04	10.35	13.26	1.85	3.81		4.61	5.91	2.58	55.97	146.85	59.05	66.35	31.85	12.81	14.39	4.37	1.76	3.89	...	23.84	19.34	2.78	12.21	4.66
1975	87.45	12.90	14.75	2.05	5.03		5.66	6.47	2.86	50.53	115.19	68.10	105.60	20.35	12.03	18.66	4.20	2.48	2.71	...	27.74	20.40	3.81	13.07	3.77
1976	96.06	14.89	15.50	2.24	5.96		6.89	7.17	3.35	48.62	118.80	102.55	107.30	17.24	14.88	15.57	3.27	2.82	3.12	...	31.30	22.01	3.43	14.96	5.94
1977	110.70	17.24	15.57	2.74	6.56	10.57	7.83	7.07	3.87	49.43	107.98	96.90	105.30	13.79	12.38	13.45	3.99	3.58	3.68	...	35.20	22.24	2.99	14.55	8.68
1978	131.17	19.47	14.84	3.26	7.01	11.89	8.63	6.58	4.47	51.80	127.59	98.58	112.50	14.78	11.42	13.04	4.53	3.50	3.97	...	39.33	21.94	2.86	13.49	10.76
1979	152.95	21.68	14.17	3.97	7.20	13.98	10.01	6.54	5.10	50.95	146.66	90.42	95.26	11.65	9.03	9.52	5.64	4.37	5.35	...	42.95	23.31	2.22	12.51	11.41
1980	177.47	24.21	13.64	4.61	7.93	14.96	10.35	5.83	5.57	53.82	102.93	79.39	96.73	9.94	7.67	9.35	7.02	5.41	5.76	...	47.41	21.83	2.04	14.02	12.24
1981	193.30	26.86	13.90	5.39	8.54	16.95	11.58	5.99	5.98	51.64	116.64	98.01	111.50	10.07	8.46	9.63	6.10	5.13	5.36	...	52.92	21.88	2.11	15.53	11.99
1982	195.77	27.03	13.81	5.63	8.86	15.82	10.23	5.23	6.44	62.95	152.84	99.96	143.60	14.94	9.77	14.04	6.44	4.21	4.48	...	48.90	20.92	2.94	14.26	11.93
1983	213.51	29.06	13.61	7.28	8.47	18.13	12.45	5.83	7.03	56.47	158.75	132.42	154.70	12.75	10.64	12.43	5.31	4.43	4.54	...	52.70	23.62	2.94	18.96	14.31
1984	217.22	31.50	14.50	6.25	8.60	19.31	12.44	5.73	7.06	56.75	186.17	144.48	180.20	14.97	11.61	14.49	4.89	3.79	3.92	...	55.53	22.40	3.25	18.47	15.84
1985	240.68	36.44	15.14	9.30	9.86	25.87	16.62	6.91	7.74	46.57	264.85	177.62	259.80	15.94	10.69	15.63	4.36	2.92	2.98	...	59.78	27.80	4.35	26.71	20.99
1986	264.37	44.01	16.65	12.20	11.59	32.88	20.72	7.84	8.12	39.19	392.53	240.82	317.80	18.94	11.62	15.34	3.37	2.07	2.56	...	56.70	36.54	5.60	17.35	18.93
1987	286.85	46.47	16.20	10.61	12.56	33.46	22.88	7.98	8.78	38.37	460.29	330.56	344.60	20.12	14.45	15.06	2.66	1.91	2.55	...	66.69	34.31	5.17	7.48	20.16
1988	348.14	58.89	16.92	12.83	14.15	40.57	27.77	7.98	9.89	35.61	413.25	332.06	413.30	14.88	11.96	14.88	2.98	2.39	2.39	...	59.45	46.71	6.95	d2.21	18.60
1989	382.27	70.49	18.44	15.05	16.16	47.88	32.84	8.59	11.45	34.87	701.39	408.89	680.10	21.36	12.45	20.71	2.80	1.63	1.68	...	22.23	...	30.59	d3.08	22.19
1990	447.17	83.74	18.73	17.73	19.29	56.87	39.15	8.76	13.35	34.10	848.79	603.06	824.33	21.68	15.40	21.06	2.21	1.57	1.62	...	40.81	95.93	20.20	d13.44	29.79
1991	498.58	94.28	18.91	20.30	21.68	63.46	43.15	8.65	16.04	37.17	1280.72	764.78	1280.72	29.68	17.72	29.68	2.10	1.25	1.25	...	59.80	72.16	21.42	13.92	37.03
1992	563.42	109.91	19.51	24.07	23.49	75.35	51.28	9.10	18.40	35.88	1458.55	1173.47	1413.08	28.44	22.88	27.56	1.57	1.26	1.30	...	30.82	...	45.85	d8.72	42.88
1993	629.08	125.93	20.02	28.02	29.61	89.07	61.05	9.70	22.14	36.27	1480.71	1269.94	1464.78	24.25	20.80	23.99	1.74	1.50	1.51	...	39.87	...	36.74	d34.66	45.42
1994	731.96	145.46	19.87	32.08	33.72	103.29	71.20	9.73	25.63	36.00	1594.21	1230.37	1549.39	22.39	17.28	21.76	2.08	1.61	1.65	1715.01	59.11	...	26.21	d19.23	51.32
1995	805.79	161.76	20.07	33.88	36.08	110.30	76.43	9.49	28.71	37.56	2429.21	1473.08	2280.43	31.78	19.27	29.84	1.95	1.18	1.26	2560.74	69.57	...	32.78	d26.35	50.58
1996	861.06	171.62	19.93	37.92	35.27	117.42	78.52	9.12	32.66	41.59	3064.84	2242.90	2961.64	39.03	28.56	37.72	1.46	1.07	1.10	3364.34	82.71	94.93	35.81	d19.35	57.09
1997	798.46	167.13	20.93	26.79	47.66	129.82	103.03	12.90	36.66	35.58	4013.90	2933.51	3815.08	38.96	28.47	37.03	1.25	0.91	0.96	4378.64	132.63	77.68	28.76	11.22	45.95
1998	760.41	191.08	21.10	45.38	32.56	139.43	93.58	10.74	38.95	40.07	4851.57	3191.16	3964.46	49.91	32.83	40.78	1.22	0.80	0.98	4594.24	126.12	34.08	31.43	8.91	63.37

SOURCE: Standard & Poor's *Analysts Handbook,* New York City, published annually.

4. When the bricks-and-mortar companies grant pay raises, those rewards add to the firms' fixed costs. Many Dot.coms do not give many pay raises—they increase employees incentives by giving stock options that involve no fixed costs.

5. Bricks-and-mortar companies typically struggle to maintain their historical share of the same market. The Dot.coms strive to dominate their market because they appreciate the winner-take-all nature of the Internet.

Each year from 1995 through 1999 more people came to believe the list above and, as a result, the prices of most Internet stocks were bid higher. With Internet stocks making a larger and larger component of the S&P500 index, the feeding frenzy in Internet stocks fueled the rising S&P500 price index values, rising price-earnings ratios, and falling cash dividend yields visible from 1995 through 1999 in Figure 25-1.

The Internet stocks bubble burst in March 2000. The list of irrationally exuberant factors listed above came under wide spread scrutiny, the prices of most Internet stocks started to plummet from the peak they reached early in 2000, price-earnings ratios tumbled downward, and many Internet companies went out of business. Normalcy began to enter into Internet stock valuations as people started to assess technology stocks the same way they had always valued nontechnology stocks.

Although the Internet stocks bubble of 1995–99 was characterized by excessive optimism, financial analysts discerned an insightful economic feature of the industry: Internet companies enjoy economies of scale that ensure many firms will not survive. Within each specialty area of the Internet one company usually emerges as the triumphant winner.

Winner-Take-All

A hidden order exists within the Internet's dynamic complexity. The first firm to successfully enter a new niche on the World Wide Web may or may not reap great rewards. But, what is more certain, latecomers will face serious difficulties in getting their share of that market. The Internet is a self-organizing system in which a few Web sites have many pages, but many sites have very few pages. Furthermore, a few sites are very popular and have many visitors, but many sites have very few visitors. Similarly, a few Web sites enjoy huge market prices, but most Web sites are not worth nearly as much, as illustrated in Figure 25-7.

The winner-take-all nature of the Internet is easy to understand. The popularity of the first Web site in any particular market niche is determined by a social process in which Web site referrals come from friends, relatives, and acquaintances. A combination of social networking and Web surfing delivers initial traffic to a new Web site. After an Internet visitor uses a Web site once, they tend to return to the same site to minimize their search costs. Later, newer competing Web sites often link themselves to an already established Web site in

FIGURE 25-7   The Size Rankings of Total Market Value Tends to Determine the Total Market Value of Web Site Companies

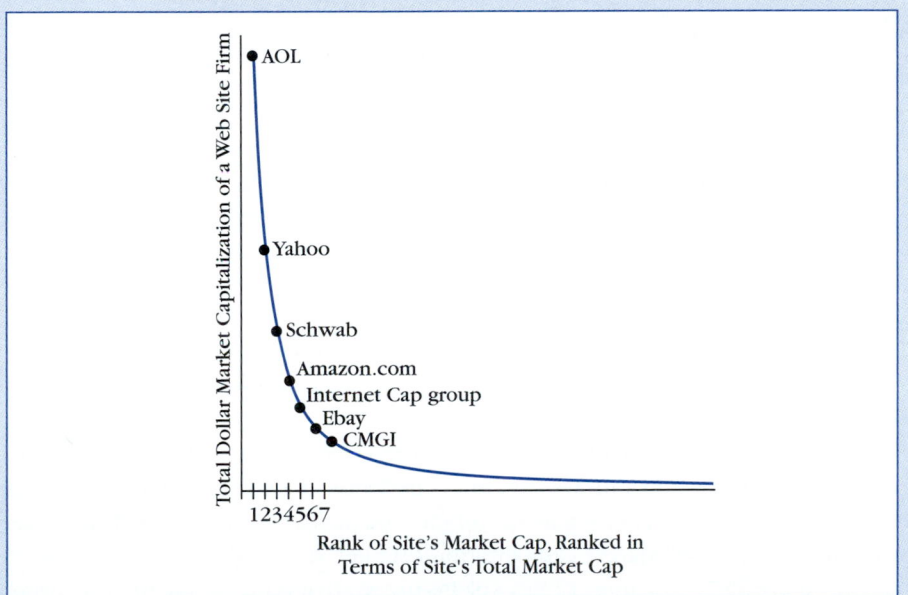

The rank of a Web site company's market value explains that site's total market capitalization (aggregate dollar value) according to the following power law formula.

$$\begin{pmatrix} \text{Market} \\ \text{cap of} \\ \text{site } i \end{pmatrix} = \begin{pmatrix} \text{Market} \\ \text{cap of most} \\ \text{valuable site} \end{pmatrix} \left[\frac{1}{(\text{Size ranking of market cap of site } i)^{\text{Power}}} \right] + \begin{pmatrix} \text{Unexplained} \\ \text{forecasting} \\ \text{error for firm } i \end{pmatrix}$$

If the exponent's value is Power = 1.01, that implies the third most valuable Web site company (Rank = 3) is worth ($\frac{1}{3^{1.01}} = 0.3297 =$) 33% as much as the site with the largest market capitalization. The formula's forecasting errors are small. The formula explains over 98% of the variance in the market caps of Web site companies. In terms of market capitalizations, the Internet exhibits winner-takes-all tendencies.

SOURCE: Michael Mauboussin, Alexander Schay, and Stephen Kawaja, "Absolute Power," Credit Suisse First Boston, New York City, December 11, 1999, Figure 3.

hopes of snaring visitors away from the established Web site. This scheme usually backfires—an established Web site will usually pull visitors away from a new Web site that offers less features. This results in a rich-get-richer phenomenon, in which the most popular sites become even more popular. Investors and venture capitalists complete this winner-take-all process by bidding up the prices of the most popular Web site companies.

The Power Law

Eqn. 25-1 defines a power law that models the Internet's winner-takes-all tendencies, where $i = 1, 2, 3, \ldots, N$ firms. The model also does a good job of explaining the total market capitalizations of a large and diverse sample of Internet companies.

$$\begin{pmatrix} \text{Market} \\ \text{capitalization} \\ \text{of firm } i \text{ in \$} \end{pmatrix} = \begin{pmatrix} \text{Market} \\ \text{capitalization} \\ \text{of largest firm, \$} \end{pmatrix} \Bigg/ \begin{pmatrix} \text{Rank of market} \\ \text{capitalization} \\ \text{for firm } i \end{pmatrix}^{\text{Power}} + \begin{pmatrix} \text{Unexplained} \\ \text{forecasting error} \\ \text{for firm } i \end{pmatrix} \quad \textbf{(25-1)}$$

In 1999, when America Online (AOL) was the largest (size ranking #1) Internet firm, the model explained AOL's [(Number of shares outstanding) $\times$ (Price per share) =] total market value as follows:

$$\begin{pmatrix} \text{Market} \\ \text{cap of AOL,} \\ \$204,385 \end{pmatrix} = \begin{pmatrix} \text{Market} \\ \text{capitalization of} \\ \text{the largest firm,} \\ \$204,385 \end{pmatrix} \Bigg/ \begin{pmatrix} \text{Rank of market} \\ \text{capitalization} \\ \text{for AOL is 1} \end{pmatrix}^{1.01} + (0) = (\$204,385)/(1)^{1.01} + (0)$$

The model predicted second-ranking Yahoo would be worth $(1/2^{1.01} = 0.4965 =)49.65\%$ as much as AOL, but Yahoo's market cap was actually \$6,942 less than Eqn. 25-1 forecasted:

$$\begin{pmatrix} \text{Market} \\ \text{cap of Yahoo,} \\ \$93,055 \end{pmatrix} = \begin{pmatrix} \text{Market} \\ \text{capitalization of} \\ \text{the largest firm,} \\ \$204,385 \end{pmatrix} \Bigg/ \begin{pmatrix} \text{Rank of market} \\ \text{capitalization} \\ \text{for Yahoo is 2} \end{pmatrix}^{1.01} + (-\$6,942)$$

On the date the regression model was fit the third largest Internet firm was Schwab, the fourth was Amazon.com, the fifth was Internet Cap Group, the sixth was Ebay, CMGI was seventh, and over 100 other firms were in the sample. The power rule model explained over half the variation in the total market capitalization (market value) of these firms. Eqn. 25-1 is graphed in Figure 25-7.* The power rule explains the relative values of the Internet firms very well, but gives no clue as to whether the market prices of all Internet stocks are too high or too low.

It is possible to obtain statistical estimates of the power law model (Eqn. 25-1), separately for different industries and/or industry subgroups. Power rule rankings for electronic brokerage firms, electronic airline reservation services, electronic bookstores, electronic toy stores, electronic flower services, and other subsamples of e-commerce firms appear to support the concept.

---

* Power law formulas are linear in the logarithms. Eqn. 25-1 was estimated as a simple regression of the form: $y = a + bx + e$ where $y = \text{Log(Mkt.Cap.}i)$, $x = \text{Log(Rank of firm }i)$, $a = \text{Log(Mkt.Cap.Largest.Firm)}$, and $b = 1.01$. To be exact, $b = 1.0124$ and $R^2 = .986$ on the date the model was estimated. This log-log model is linear. For background, see Lada Adamic and Bernardo Huberman, "The Nature of Markets in the World Wide Web," from the proceedings of Computing in Economics and Finance, May 6, 1999, or, see the Web site of the Xerox Palo Alto Research Center.

Slippery Slopes Around the Winner's Peak

Amazon.com's Chief Executive Officer Jeffrey Bezos left his career as a rising young star on Wall Street to found the firm in Seattle in 1995. Amazon started as an Internet bookstore. Sensing the winner-takes-all possibilities of the Internet, Bezos expanded Amazon's business into music, videos, toys, video games, electronics, auctions, electronic greeting cards, gifts, and other areas. Although Amazon.com Inc. registered losses every year, the 35-year-old Bezos sought rapid development by spending millions annually on software development, new warehouses, larger inventories, more accounts receivable, and a growing marketing budget. Amazon went public on NASDAQ in 1997 at $1.50 per share. As shown in Figure 25-8, by 1999 AMZN was trading at over $100 per share. While AMZN's stock soared, so did its losses. Amazon.com's annual per share losses were 3 cents in 1996, 12 cents in 1997, 42 cents in 1998, and $2.20 in

FIGURE 25-8   Amazon.com Trades on NASDAQ Under the Ticker Symbol AMZN

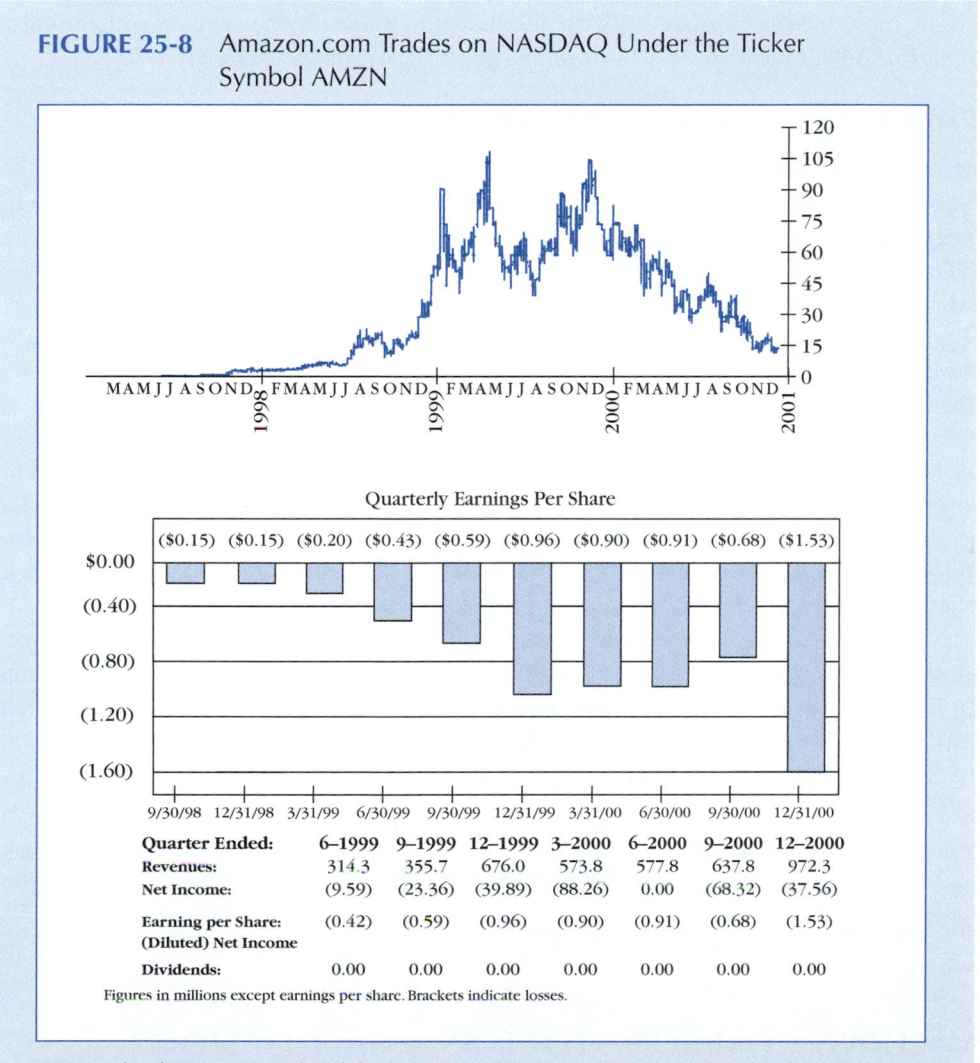

Quarter Ended:	6–1999	9–1999	12–1999	3–2000	6–2000	9–2000	12–2000
Revenues:	314.3	355.7	676.0	573.8	577.8	637.8	972.3
Net Income:	(9.59)	(23.36)	(39.89)	(88.26)	0.00	(68.32)	(37.56)
Earning per Share: (Diluted) Net Income	(0.42)	(0.59)	(0.96)	(0.90)	(0.91)	(0.68)	(1.53)
Dividends:	0.00	0.00	0.00	0.00	0.00	0.00	0.00

Figures in millions except earnings per share. Brackets indicate losses.

During the first 2 years of its life the price of Amazon.com's stock soared as the firm's losses grew larger each year. AMZN investors watched the firm's revenues grow rapidly during the late 1990s and hoped to be winners in the Internet's winner-takes-all game. After 3 years of losses, investor enthusiasm began to wear thin in 2000.

1999. While the losses mounted, investors kept bidding up the stock's price because they believed Amazon.com was turning into a lucrative Internet company. The feeding frenzy that pushed up AMZN's price up was based on investors' expectations that years of profits would follow the losses incurred to achieve the rapid initial growth. Investors' faith was reaffirmed during 1997–99 by large annual sales increases. In 2000 AMZN suffered small sales declines and laid off 1,500 people as the firm's initial losses begin to look like they might become perennial losses. As a result, during 2000 the stock price fell as investors continued to liquidate.

In a winner-take-all environment it is richly rewarding to be the winner, but it is not an easy position to maintain. The Internet industry is a technology business, and technology changes fast. If what the leading e-commerce firm is offering becomes uncompetitive and the firm slips into second place, Eqn. 25-1 tells us its market capitalization will be approximately halved.

Chapter 23's discussion of growth stock valuation applies to Internet stocks too. Eqn. 23-12f in Chapter 23 (p. 712) separates the present value of a firm's old assets from the net present value (NPV) of new assets the firm acquires. Eqn. 23-12f shows us that a good acquisition must have a positive NPV to increase the value of the firm. In other words, Amazon.com must eventually deliver profits or Mr. Bezos will be unemployed.

Price-Earnings Ratios for Internet Stocks

Many Internet companies pay no cash dividends, and, like Amazon.com, some have never reported any earnings. These data make it difficult to use traditional financial ratios like the price-earnings ratio and cash dividend yield. Mr. Chip Morris, the portfolio manager of the multi-billion-dollar T. Rowe Price Science and Technology mutual fund in Baltimore, Maryland, devised what he calls the *practical price-earnings ratio* to estimate the value of the technology stocks.[5] The first four steps in Table 25-5 explain how to calculate a practical price-earnings ratio. America Online (AOL) data from June 1999 (before the Time-Warner acquisition) are used in the example. Since AOL had earnings per share (EPS) of 34 cents per share in 1999, Step 5 in Table 25-5 multiplies the EPS times the stock's practical price-earnings ratio to obtain an estimate of what a share of the stock was worth. AOL's stock price fluctuated from $32 to $115 per share (after adjusting for a 2-for-1 split) during 1999. During the summer of 1999, when AOL's stock's market price was above its estimated value of $43.40 per share, the stock was overpriced and should have been sold (or sold short). When AOL's price was below its estimated per share value of $43.40, the stock was underpriced and was a good investment candidate.

Mr. Morris also recommends the *price-earnings-to-growth rate multiple,* which measures how much investors are paying for projected growth. The lower the value of this multiple, the better the stock's profit potential. The most desirable Internet stocks usually trade at 2.4 to 2.6 times their underlying growth rate. Based on Mr. Morris's forecasted growth rate of 52.6% for AOL, the stock had a multiple of 2.4 times in June 1999:

$$\text{Price-earnings-to-growth rate} = \frac{(\text{Price-earnings ratio})}{(\text{Estimated growth rate})} = \frac{\text{P/E} = 127.6 \text{ times}}{g = 52.6\%} = 2.4 \text{ times}$$

Investors need tools to evaluate new business models.

VALUING COMMON STOCK AS A CALL OPTION

Chapter 9 introduced call options. This section shows how to use the call option model to value speculations, special situations, patents, and the debt and equity of a leveraged company. Bankruptcy law provides logical reasons for applying option theory to value securities issued by a leveraged company.

TABLE 25-5	How to Find a Practical Price-Earnings Ratio for an Internet Stock	
The Steps	**Sample Numbers for AOL, June 1999**
Step 1: Compute the firm's market capitalization (number of shares outstanding times the price per share).	(1,086 million shares) × ($110 per share) = $119,460 million = $119,460,000,000 = Market capitalization on June 30, 1999.
Step 2: Multiply sales from the most recent quarter by 4 to find the current annual rate of sales.	($1,376.25 million quarterly sales) × (4 quarters) = $5,505,000,000 sales at annual rate for 1999.
Step 3: Divide the firm's market capitalization by annualized sales to get a price/sales ratio.	$119,460 Million/$5,505 Million = 21.7 times
Step 4: Divide the price/sales ratio by your estimate of the largest plausible net profit margin to get the practical price/earnings ratio.	21.7 times/17% = 21.7/.17 = 127.6 times
Step 5: Multiply your estimate of a normal EPS times the practical price-earnings ratio to find the stock's value per share.	(EPS = 34 cents) × (127.6 times) = $43.40 per share

SOURCE: Adapted from "How a Tech-Fund Star Picks His Plays," *Business Week,* 14 June 1999, 166. Also, *T. Rowe Price Report,* Summer 1999, Baltimore, MD, pp. 1–4.

Bankruptcy Law. According to the bankruptcy law in most countries, the stockholders of a bankrupt company are entitled to whatever assets the corporation has left after all the firm's debts are paid. If total liabilities exceed the firm's total assets, the creditors get to keep the assets as partial payment and the stockholders get nothing. This legal framework aligns with a call option model in which a company's creditors own the company and sell a call option on the firm's assets to the firm's owners (common stockholders). The exercise price of this call option equals the face (par) value of the firm's total debt. If the owners (stockholders) exercise this option they call in the firm's total assets, but they must pay all of the company's liabilities to keep its assets. If all the firm's assets are insufficient to repay all the firm's debts, the common stockholders' call option will be allowed to expire worthless and unexercised and the stockholders forfeit all claims on the bankrupt firm to the firm's creditors. Within this framework bankruptcy can be viewed as a decision by the owners (stockholders) not to pay off the firm's total liabilities and, in so doing, forfeit the right to exercise their call on the assets of their insolvent company.

Conflicts of Interest. There are several different inherent conflicts of interest between those who own a company (stock investors) and those who loan the firm money (creditors and bond investors). One case of such divergent economic motivations can be demonstrated when the protective provisions in a bond issue's indenture contract are analyzed in terms of the call option valuation model.

Bond investors typically benefit from a provision in the bond issue's indenture requiring that coupon-interest payments be paid at a series of scheduled dates. If one scheduled coupon payment is missed, the bond owners can sue the corporation in bankruptcy court and force the stockholders to pay the firm's debts (the bonds' coupons). When this happens, essentially, the bond investors are exercising an option to call in the company's assets before the principal payment is due. If the stockholders cannot or do not want to make a scheduled coupon payment, the bondholders gain control of the corporation. These provisions for coupon payments may be interpreted as evidence that the owners (stockholders) have a call option on the company that is an American call and not a European call. If the bond owner's coupon-interest claims could somehow be delayed until the bond matured, the owner's call option would be a European call. This is one inherent conflict of interest between the owners and creditors of a firm; other similar conflicts exist.[6]

The Springdale Corporation: A Hypothetical Valuation Case

Suppose the Springdale Corporation financed the purchase of its plant and equipment with an issue of mortgage bonds that has a principal (face) value of $D = \$30$ million. Also suppose Springdale's total assets, $A = \$50$ million, are pledged as collateral for this bond issue. For simplicity, assume the debts all have the same maturity date and that protective provisions in the indenture prohibit the corporation from paying any cash dividends until all debts are repaid.*

The owners of mortgage bonds have a *senior claim* on (high priority legal entitlement to) the assets of the corporation. The common stockholders have the most *junior claim* on (low priority entitlement to) the corporate assets if the firm goes bankrupt. Figure 25-9 shows how, when the options expire, the intrinsic values of these claims is determined by the market value of the Springdale Corporation's total assets.

Compare the call writer's position in Figures 9-4A and 9-7A in Chapter 9 (p. 246, 257) with Figure 25-9A. Figure 25-9A illustrates how the mortgage bond owners are like the writers of a call with an exercise price of zero.** This call option has the constraint that the maximum payoff equals Springdale's total debt of $D = \$30$ million.

The total value of all the Springdale Corporation's outstanding stock is illustrated in Figure 25-9B. Because common stockholders have limited liability, their equity is worthless until the market value of the corporation's total assets exceeds the corporation's total debts (until $A > \$30$ million $= D$).

The corporation is presumed to have N shares of common stock selling at a to-be-determined price of P dollars per share. When Springdale's debts come due, the stockholders' options exercise price must be paid. When the debts are due, the total value of the claims against the Corporation's assets adds up:

$$\begin{pmatrix} \text{Firm's} \\ \text{total} \\ \text{assets, } A \end{pmatrix} = \begin{pmatrix} \text{Aggregate debt} \\ \text{owed creditors,} \\ D = \$30 \text{ million.} \end{pmatrix} + \left(\begin{Bmatrix} \text{Number of} \\ \text{outstanding} \\ \text{common} \\ \text{shares, } N \end{Bmatrix} \times \begin{Bmatrix} \text{Price per} \\ \text{share of} \\ \text{stock, } P \end{Bmatrix} \right) \quad \textbf{(25-2)}$$

$$= \begin{pmatrix} \text{Aggregate debt,} \\ D = \$30 \text{ million} \end{pmatrix} + \left(\text{Total equity} \right) \quad \textbf{(25-2a)}$$

When the corporation's debts mature, if the assets happen to be worth less than its debts ($A < \$30$ million $= D$), then the common stock is worthless ($P = 0$). But if the value of the Springdale Corporation's assets exceeds the value of its total indebtedness ($A > \$30$ million

---

* The prohibition against cash dividend payments until the debts are fully paid grows out of another conflict of interest between the firm's owners and its creditors. This prohibition prevents stockholders from draining the assets out of the corporation via cash dividend payments for themselves so the creditors get less if the corporation goes bankrupt.

* The mortgage bond owners in Figure 25-9A are more like covered, rather than uncovered, call writers. The bond investors have a position that is equivalent to holding the company's assets in a long position and simultaneously writing a call with an exercise price that equals the total debt of D. Covered call writing is addressed in Chapter 28.

FIGURE 25-9   Using Call Option Theory to Estimate the Value of Claims
Against a Corporation: (A) Mortgage Bond Investors;
(B) Equity Investors

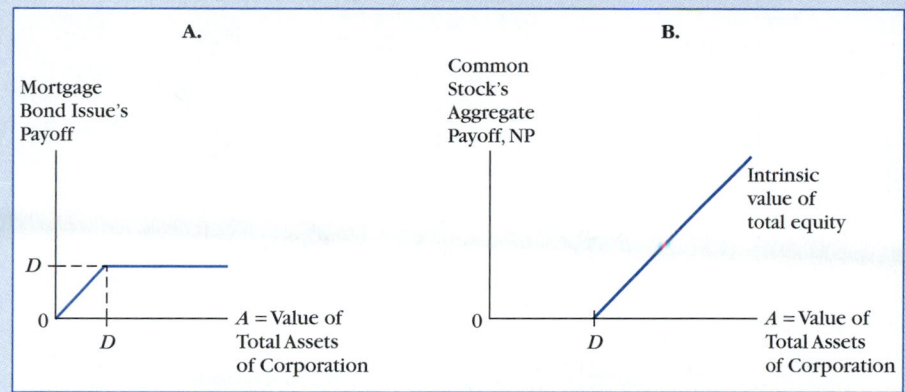

If the equity owners pay off the corporation's total debt of *D* dollars, essentially, they exercise their option to call in (to buy) the corporation's total assets. If the equity owners do not pay the corporation's debts, they are giving the corporate assets to the debt holders that offered them the option to pay *D* dollars for those assets. If the corporate assets are worth more than the corporate debt, *A* > *D*, it will be profitable for the stockholders to pay *D* dollars to the holders of the corporation's debt. If the corporate assets are worth less than the debt, *A* < *D*, it will be advantageous for the stockholders to let the option expire unexercised.

= *D*), the value of a share of common stock is positive. Eqn. 25-3 is the model suggested by option theory for calculating the intrinsic value per share of the common stock when the firm's debts come due.

$$\text{Intrinsic value per share of stock} = P = \frac{\text{MAX}[0, A - D]}{N} \tag{25-3}$$

MAX[0, *A* − *D*] stands for the maximum value of either zero or *A*−*D*.

The maturity value of the Springdale Corporation's mortgage is defined in Eqn. 25-4. In aggregate, the mortgage bonds are equal to either the principal amount of the bond issue, denoted *D*, or the total value of the corporation's assets, *A*, whichever is less.

Total dollar value of mortgage bond issue = MIN[*D*, *A*]   **(25-4)**

MIN[*D*, *A*] represents the minimum value of either *D* or *A*.

Option Theory and the Prices of Corporate Securities

Figure 25-10 delineates the intrinsic values of the Springdale Corporation's securities. Call option theory tells us when we consider the riskiness of the optioned assets (see Figure 9-8 in Chapter 9, p. 258) and different times until expiration of the option, options will have time premiums that push their prices (premiums) above their intrinsic values. Chapter 9 introduces options' time values and shows how to develop estimates for the values of a corporation's debt and equity that are more accurate than the intrinsic values illustrated in Figure 25-9.[7]

FIGURE 25-10   Using Call Option Pricing Theory to Value the Equity and Debt of a Corporation at Expiration of the Debt

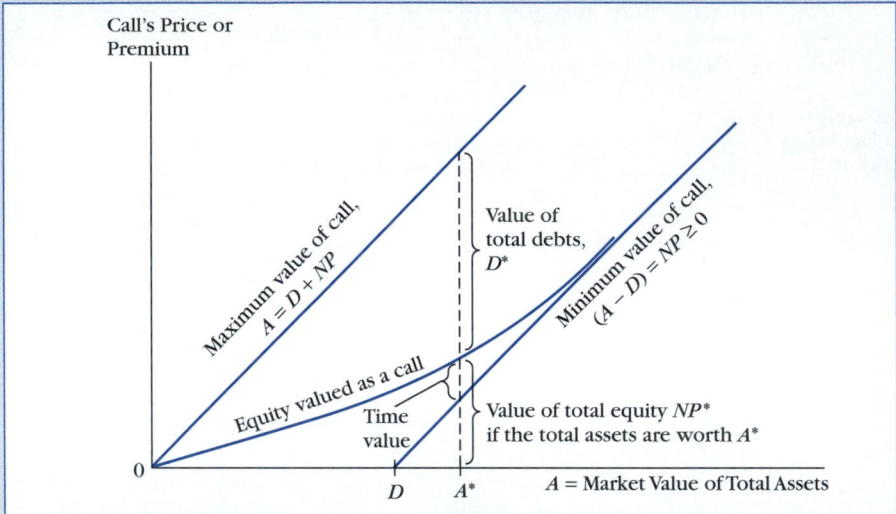

Springdale's total debt is equivalent to the exercise price of the stockholders' call option. The 45-degree line rising out of the exercise price, denoted *D* on the horizontal axis, equals the intrinsic (minimum) value of the stockholder's call on the corporation's assets over a range of plausible asset values. The curve coming out of the origin delineates the aggregate market value of Springdale's outstanding stock, denoted *NP*. (This value can be computed with the Black-Scholes call pricing formula.) The value of the corporation's equity exceeds the intrinsic value of the stockholder's call on the total assets by an amount equal to the option's time value.

If common stock is valued as a call option on the corporation's assets, Figure 25-10 provides the model for valuing the debt and equity securities of the Springdale Corporation defined by Eqns. 25-2 through 25-4. The 45-degree line out of the origin in Figure 25-10 traces the maximum aggregate value boundary for all of the Springdale Corporation's outstanding debt and equity securities. This maximum value limit means that the call on a corporation's debt and equity securities cannot be worth more than the total assets of *A* dollars.

The Springdale Corporation's total debt is equivalent to the exercise price of the stockholders' call option. The 45-degree line rising out of the exercise price, point *D* on the horizontal axis, traces out the intrinsic (minimum) value of the stockholder's call on the corporation's assets.

The curve coming out of the origin in Figure 25-10 equals the aggregate market value of the Springdale Corporation's outstanding common stock, denoted *NP* (and can be computed with the Black-Scholes call pricing formula).[8] The value of the corporation's equity exceeds the intrinsic value of the stockholder's call on the corporate assets by an amount equal to the time value of the option. Eqn. 9-11 in Chapter 9 (p. 256) defines the time value of a call option.

Let's attach numerical values to the variables with asterisks and work through an example. The model shown in Figure 25-10 indicates that if the value of the Springdale Corporation's total assets remains constant at $A^* = \$50$ million, any change in the value of the Corporation's equity is offset by an opposite but equal change in the value of the Corporation's total debt. More specifically, for total assets of A^* dollars the following balance sheet identity is appropriate.

$$\begin{pmatrix} \text{Total} \\ \text{assets, } A^* \end{pmatrix} - \begin{pmatrix} \text{Aggregate debt owed} \\ \text{to creditors, } D^* \end{pmatrix} = \begin{pmatrix} \text{Total equity of} \\ \text{the corporation} \\ \text{equals } N \text{ times } P^* \end{pmatrix} \qquad \text{(25-2a)}$$

USING ADDITIONAL FACTS TO VALUE THE SPRINGDALE CORPORATION'S SECURITIES

EXAMPLE

Consider additional facts about the Springdale Corporation. The Corporation has total assets of $A^* = \$50$ million, a $D^* = \$30$ million mortgage bond issue that must be repaid in one year, and the interest rate on the mortgage bonds is (RFR =) 6%. The market value of the Springdale's total assets will vary directly with the variance of: VAR = 0.04 (or, equivalently, a standard deviation of 0.2).

Is the Springdale Corporation's total equity worth ($A^* - D^* = \$50 - \$30 = NP =$) \$20 million? No, there is an additional consideration. The Nobel prize–winning Black-Scholes call-option formula can be used to trace out the call price curve coming out of the origin of Figure 25-10. This curve indicates that the Springdale Corporation's total equity will be worth \$21.75 million because Springdale's equity contains \$1.75 million worth of time value. This \$1.75 million of *time value* is added to the \$20 million of intrinsic value in the Springdale's equity for reasons that are explained in Chapter 28.

The call-option valuation model illustrated in Figure 25-10 can be used to analyze bond and common stock investments. For instance, changing the riskiness of the endeavor in which the corporate assets are being employed, changing the amount of corporate debt, changing the maturity date of the firm's debt, and other considerations can be analyzed explicitly by using the Black-Scholes call pricing model. These factors will change the value of the corporations' outstanding debt and equity as illustrated in Figure 25-10.*[9]

Option theory can be used to value investment opportunities. Insights can be obtained into pure speculations, companies that are being reorganized by a bankruptcy court, leveraged buyouts (LBOs), management buyouts (MBOs), merged firms, emerging new firms, patents, new technologies, and other special situations.

VALUING AN UNUTILIZED PATENT

EXAMPLE

BACKGROUND: Assume you are the chief executive officer of Microsoft. Also suppose that a professor of computer science from Carnegie-Mellon University offers to sell you a patent on a piece of important computer software he created.

A product's patent grants its owner the right to develop and distribute a product monopolistically. It is difficult to compute the discounted present value of an undeveloped software product. QUESTION: What is this patent worth?

ANSWER: The professor's patent is a call option on the underlying software product, as outlined in Figure 25-11. The total initial investment (payment to the professor, plus product development costs, plus marketing costs, plus legal costs) needed to get the project operating may be viewed as being the call option's exercise price. The U.S. Patent Office grants patents that do not expire for 20 years. The probability distribution of expected present values from the project will have a large impact on the option's value.

---

*   Chapters 9 and 28 of this book discuss factors that determine option values; the Black-Scholes model is the major topic in Chapter 28.

FIGURE 25-11 The Call-Option Pricing Model Can Be Used to Estimate the Value of a Product Patent

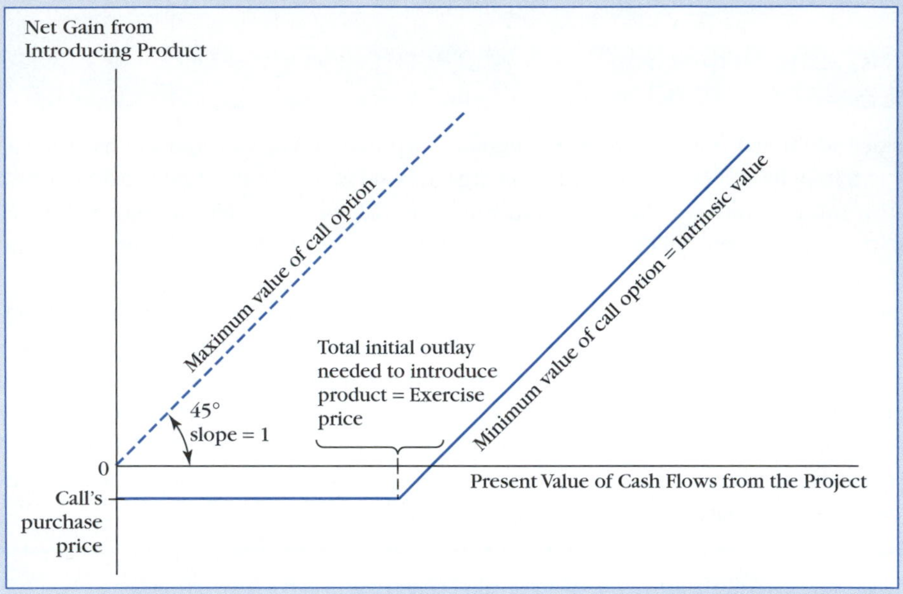

A product patent can be viewed as a call option on the underlying product. The total investment (payment for the patent, product development costs, marketing costs, legal costs) to get the project operating may be viewed as being the call option's exercise price.

ETHICS

A REALITY CHECK: PRINCIPAL-AGENT RELATIONSHIPS INVOLVE ILLEGAL OR UNETHICAL AGENCY COSTS

The owners of a business are the **principals** of the firm. Employees with decision-making powers (such as a hired president, hired vice-presidents, or a securities broker) are **agents** that are employed to maximize the principals' (owners', stockholders') wealth. The agents listed below are operating in an unethical fashion to enrich themselves by extracting agency costs from their principals.

Principals	Agents	Agency costs	Legal?
Investors	Securities brokers	Broker **churns** (turns over the account needlessly) for commission income.	No
Stockholders	Hired top executives who own no stock	Unproductive **perquisites** such as chauffeur driven autos, inflated salaries, secluded retreats, and private jet planes for executives.	Yes
Stockholders	Hired top executives who own no stock	The cost of going private in a management buyout (MBO) may be a stock price depressed by unethical mismanagement.	Yes
Stockholders	Hired top executives who own no stock	**Greenmail** is paid by a corporation to keep away potential buyers so incompetent managers can keep their jobs	Yes

Principals	Agents	Agency costs	Legal?
Stockholders	Hired top executives who own no stock	**Poison pills** and **golden parachutes** to protect inept top managers are paid for with stockholders' money.	Yes
Stockholders	Hired top executives who own no stock	**Classified common stock** can be used to let voting managers reelect themselves even when incompetent.	Yes

Churning is an agency cost that is illegal. Extravagant executive perquisites, MBOs, greenmail, poison pills, golden parachutes, and some uses of classified stock are unethical, but they are legal. These unethical abuses of the principal-agency relationship sometimes result in special situations that can be profitable investments. Ethical investors might be able to buy a corporation cheap if it is mismanaged by extravagant or incompetent executives. It can be profitable to replace incompetents who are protected by greenmail or golden parachutes or poison pill agreements and then resell the stock at a higher price. Ethical investors can also buy stock at a depressed price that is held down by executives trying to pull off a management buyout (MBO). Investors can replace the unscrupulous MBO-seeking managers that are depressing the firm's stock price. Ethical investors can also organize a stockholders' revolt against classified common stock that perpetuates bad management and, perhaps, profit from a reorganization.

Jack Clark Francis

THE PRICE/BOOK VALUE RATIO

A common stock's *book value per share* is found by subtracting total liabilities from total assets and dividing the difference (the corporation's net worth) by the number of shares of common stock. In a new company, the assets' book values often equal their purchase prices and provide fair estimates of their current market values. If a new company is not publicly owned, or, if it is publicly owned but its shares are not traded actively, book values can be useful in estimating the firm's value.

Book values are determined by economic events and accounting conventions. In contrast, a common stock's market price is primarily shaped by the market's assessment of its earning power. The relationship between a common stock's market price and its book value has always attracted the attention of investors.

Some investors say that when the price of a stock is well below its book value, the stock may be underpriced. And a stock may be overpriced when its price is significantly higher than its book value. The *price to book value (PBV) ratio* highlights such discussions.

$$\text{PBV ratio} = \text{Price/book value ratio} = \frac{\text{Market price per share for stock } i \text{ at time } t}{\text{Book value per share for stock } i \text{ at time } t} \qquad \textbf{(25-5)}$$

During the 1990s Eugene Fama and Kenneth French, Jeffrey Pontiff and Larry Schall, and other researchers suggested that in certain formulations the PBV ratio had significant explanatory power over common stock prices and returns.[10] The Fama-French empirical tests used portfolios formed for statistical grouping purposes. In 1995 Dongcheol Kim pointed out that using individual assets in empirical tests offers several advantages that were not available when using portfolios of assets to minimize the errors in variables problem.[11] Findings published by Kim and others cast some clouds over the role of the PBV ratio.

Analysis of the PBV Ratio

The constant growth dividend discount model (DDM) from Eqn. 23-4 in Chapter 23 asserts a share of stock is worth P_0, where:

$$P_0 = \frac{DIV_1}{k - g} \tag{25-6}$$

The next time period's cash dividends per share, DIV_1, can be restated in terms of this period's earnings per share, EPS_0, by using the stock's retention rate (RR) and growth rate, g, as follows:

$$DIV_1 = (1 - RR)(EPS_1)$$

$$DIV_1 = (1 - RR)(1 + g)(EPS_0) = (\text{Payout ratio})(1 + g)(EPS_0)$$

where (1-RR) = Payout ratio

Substituting the equation above into Eqn. 25-6 results in:

$$P_0 = \frac{(\text{Payout ratio})(1 + g)(EPS_0)}{k - g} \tag{25-7}$$

Since EPS_0 equals the return on equity (ROE) times book value (BV) per share, $EPS_0 = (ROE)(BV_0)$, Eqn. 25-7 can be rewritten:

$$P_0 = \frac{(\text{Payout ratio})(1 + g)(ROE)(BV_0)}{k - g} \tag{25-7a}$$

Dividing both sides of Eqn.(25-7a) by BV_0 redefines the PBV ratio in terms of the ROE.

$$\text{PBV ratio} = \frac{P_0}{BV_0} = \frac{(\text{Payout ratio})(1 + g)(ROE)}{k - g} \tag{25-8}$$

The numerator of Eqn. 25-8 shows that, if all other factors are fixed, a higher ROE increases the stock's PBV ratio. The denominator of Eqn. 25-8 shows that a higher ROE also increases the PBV ratio indirectly, since $g = (RR)(ROE)$.

Over- and Underpriced Stocks

Eqn. 25-8 explains the tendency for firms with high ROEs to have stock prices well above their book values and also for firms with low ROEs to have stock prices that are below their book values. Table 25-6 summarizes these two tendencies and considers two other possibilities.

When a firm has a high PBV ratio and a low ROE at the same time, it is reasonable to suspect the stock might be overpriced. Conversely, it is likely that a stock is underpriced when the issuer has a low PBV ratio and a high ROE. This logic can be carried a step further by computing PBV/ROE ratios to control for differences in firms' ROEs. The investment desirability of stocks should tend to vary directly with the size of their PBV/ROE ratios.

The logic of Eqn. 25-8, Table 25-6, and the PBV/ROE ratio overlook the important fact that *expected* earnings have a larger impact on stock prices than *historical* accounting measures. Zero and negative ROE values can also complicate the computations. In spite of these problems, the PBV ratio can provide a helpful tool for screening or ranking investment candidates.

TABLE 25-6 Four Possible PBV and ROE Relationships for a Stock

NORMAL PRICING:	OVERPRICED:
High PBV High ROE	High PBV Low ROE
UNDERPRICED:	NORMAL PRICING:
Low PBV High ROE	Low PBV Low ROE

Tobin's q Ratio

James Tobin suggested a ratio that is similar to the PBV ratio.[12]

$$\text{Tobin's q ratio} = \frac{\text{Market value of a firm's assets}}{\text{Replacement value of the firm's assets in place}} \qquad (25\text{-}9)$$

Tobin's q ratio differs from the PBV ratio in two respects. First, the numerator of Eqn. 25-9 includes the aggregate market value of all equity and all debt, not only the equity. Second, the q ratio is not tied as closely to accounting conventions as the PBV ratio. Tobin's q ratio can help detect mis-priced securities in a highly inflationary environment that has inflated asset prices, and in areas where technological advancements have reduced the cost of replacing existing assets.

THE BOTTOM LINE

Popular folklore claims that inflation spurs the stock market to higher levels. Table 25-1 summarizes two centuries of empirical data about the relationship between annual stock market returns and the concurrent inflation rate in the United States. Table 25-1 shows that, contrary to the folklore, inflation tends to have a negative impact on concurrent stock prices and returns in the short run. In the long run, over at least one complete business cycle, inflation has no lasting impact on common stock returns.

Dr. Zhiwu Chen's 1990 demographic analysis provides an explanation of the high average annual return of 28.6% the S&P500 index earned during 1995–99. A paper that was published by Bakshi and Chen in 1994 hypothesized that when the baby boomers started reaching 49 years of age in 1995 they would allocate a large portion of their income to stock market investments to finance their retirements. This demographically determined influx of cash provides a plausible explanation for the high 28.6% average annual rate of return in Table 25-2 and, also, for the unusually low cash dividend yield and unusually high price/earnings ratio for the S&P500 index that was observed during the late 1990s (Figure 25-1). Increasingly popular common stock buybacks and rising labor productivity during the last half of the 1990s provide additional explanations for the higher-than-expected 28.6% rate of return during 1995–99, the unusually low cash dividend yield, and the unusually high price/earnings ratio for the S&P500 index that period. The technology industry also added some zest to the longest bull market in the history of the United States.

Most common stock analysts considered industry analysis to be an important part of their analysis of individual common stock issuers. The industry life cycle or, equivalently, the product life cycle, is useful in anticipating important developments that determine the future value of a product, firm, or industry. Governments, trade associations, and financial service firms provide data that facilitates utilizing the life cycle model to analyze a product, firm, or industry.

The computer software industry is comprised of companies that are like natural monopolies because they have high start-up costs and small per unit costs. This cost structure tends to create a winner-takes-all business environment. The power rule model rationalizes the high market capitalizations of some Internet companies. The winners in the software business do not enjoy secure monopolies. The winner's peak is surrounded by slippery slopes. Newer technology in the hands of a competitor can result in a new winner.

Traditionally, stocks issued by bricks-and-mortar corporations were priced in accordance with projections of the bricks-and-mortar corporation's past earnings. The new technology companies are different; many have no earnings history. The prices of stocks in fast-growing Internet corporations are bid up by investors' expectations of future profits. For example, during the late 1990s Amazon.com's stock price soared while the corporation's losses continued to grow larger each year.

The call option model introduced in Chapter 9 can be adapted to assess the values of unusual equity positions. The total equity, the total debt, and the total market capitalization of a company can be formulated as components of a call option's value. Product patents, start-up business, new technologies, and speculative opportunities may also be valued with the call-option model.

Book values can be used to help determine the value of a company that is not actively traded. If a corporation stock is actively traded and the price of a stock lies far below its book value, the stock may be underpriced. And, an actively traded stock may be overpriced when its price is considerably higher than its book value. Comparing stocks' market prices and their book values often focuses on the stocks' price/book value (PBV) ratios. If stocks' PBV ratios are considered in conjunction with their returns on equity (ROEs), the combined information can be useful in discovering under- and overpriced stocks.

QUESTIONS

Q25-1   (Timing tools) Discuss how some investors use the cash dividend yield and the price-earnings ratio on the S&P500 to attempt to time the market. Are there any disadvantages to doing so?

Q25-2   (Bakshi-Chen forecast) Zhiwu Chen and Gurdip Bakshi published a paper in which they used demographics and the life-cycle theory of savings to forecast what the market will do through the year 2040. Discuss their conclusions.

Q25-3   (Internet companies) Discuss the ways in which the new Dot.com companies differ from the more traditional firms.

Q25-4   (Power rule) True, false, or uncertain. The power rule is useful in determining the fair market value of Internet firms. Explain.

Q25-5   (Inflation and stock returns) What have empirical studies concluded regarding the relationship between inflation and stock market returns in the United States?

Does this relationship seem to exist in foreign markets as well?

Q25-6   (Product life-cycle model) Discuss the attributes associated with an industry that is characterized as being in the mature growth stage (stage three) of the industry life cycle.

Q25-7   (Life-cycle theory of savings) Discuss the rapid growth of equity mutual funds in the 1990s in the context of the life-cycle theory of savings. What conclusion might you draw regarding their continued growth?

Q25-8   (Valuing common stock as a call option) Explain the rationale behind using a call option model to determine a value for a firm's equity.

Q25-9   (Product life cycles) Do you think it is necessarily the case that an industry or product always progresses from stage one (product introduction) to stage four (declining growth) over the years? Can you think of any industry that might have moved backward in the product life-cycle model?

Q25-10   (PBV/ROE ratios) Explain how the relationship between a firm's price/book value ratio and its ROE may be used to determine underpriced or overpriced securities. What problems can occur when using this method for ranking investment candidates?

PROBLEMS

P25-1   (Practical price/earnings ratio) The following information pertains to the stock of Amazon.com, as of December 31, 1999:

Sales (most recent quarter)	$676,042,000
Price per share	$76.125
Shares outstanding	340.8 million

Amazon.com reported negative earnings, but assume that you have estimated a plausible net profit margin for the firm of 0.5%. Calculate the practical price/earnings ratio for the firm.

P25-2   (Practical price/earnings ratio) The following information pertains to the stock of Yahoo!, Inc., as of December 31, 1999:

Price per share	$432.6875
Shares outstanding	263.2 million
Sales (most recent quarter)	$201,083,000
Year-end EPS	$0.21
Net profit margin for 1999	10.4%

a. Calculate the practical price/earnings ratio for Yahoo!, Inc., assuming that you believe the 1999 net profit margin is the largest plausible number to use and that the year-end EPS is your estimate of the normal EPS for the firm.
b. Based on your answer to part (a), would you have considered Yahoo!, Inc. a good investment candidate on December 31, 1999?

P25-3   (Price/earnings-to-growth ratio) Analysts are estimating a growth rate of 55.04% for the stock of Yahoo!, Inc. Calculate its price/earnings-to-growth rate multiple. What does this suggest about the desirability of Yahoo's stock at the end of 1999?

P25-4   (Practical price/earnings ratio) The following information pertains to the stock of eBay as of December 31, 1999:

Price per share	$125.1875
Shares outstanding	129.3 million
Sales (most recent quarter)	$73,919,000
Net profit margin for 1999	4.8%
1999 EPS	$0.10

a. Calculate eBay's practical price/earnings ratio, assuming that you believe the 1999 net profit margin is the largest one plausible and that the firm's 1999 EPS figure is your estimate of a normal EPS for the firm.

b. Based on your answer to part (a), was eBay overpriced, underpriced, or correctly priced on December 31, 1999.

c. If your answer to part (b) was "overpriced," how do you justify the popularity of the stock?

P25-5   (Price/earnings-to-growth ratio) Given the practical price/earnings ratio calculated in Problem 25–4, what would eBay's expected growth rate have to have been to make its stock desirable at its December 31, 1999 level?

P25-6   (Power law model) The market capitalizations for the stocks of Amazon.com, eBay, Yahoo, and AOL as of February 14, 2000 are presented below:

Stock	Market capitalization
Amazon	$25.282 billion
eBay	$19.845 billion
AOL	$125.4 billion
Yahoo	$87.132 billion

Using the power law model and the size rankings for these stocks presented in the chapter, determine which of these stocks appear to be overvalued or undervalued relative to the number one size-ranked AOL stock.

P25-7   (Valuing stock as a call option) Assume that the Castle Pines Corporation (CPC) has financed its plant and equipment with an issue of mortgage bonds that have a face value of $50 million. Castle Pines' total assets are $80 million and are pledged as collateral for the mortgage bonds. (Assume, too, that the debts all have the same maturity date and that the payment of dividends is prohibited until all debts are repaid.) CPC has 5 million shares outstanding.

a. What is the exercise price on the call option owned by the stockholders of Castle Pines?

b. If, on the maturity date of the bonds, the value of the firm's assets is $100 million, what is the intrinsic value per share of the stock of CBC?

c. What is the total dollar value of the mortgage bond issue on the maturity date of the bonds if the value of the firm's assets is $100 million?

P25-8   (Valuing stock as a call option) Now assume that the value of the assets of Castle Pines Corporation is $40 million on the maturity date of the bond issue.

a. Recalculate the intrinsic value per share of the firm's stock and the total dollar value of the debt issue.

b. Suppose that, instead, the bonds have two years to mature and that the value of the assets of CPC is $40 million. Would you expect its stock price to be zero? If not, is this a flaw in the model provided by Eqn(25–2)? Explain.

P25-9 (PBV ratio) The following information pertains to Hasbro, Inc., as of December 30, 1999:

Book value per share	$9.59
Price per share	$18.625
Beta	0.96
Dividend payout ratio	18.5%
ROE	14.17%

The relevant risk-free rate was 5.1%, and the estimated market risk premium was 9.8%.

a. Calculate the Price/Book Value ratio for Hasbro.

b. Use the constant growth dividend discount model to estimate the price per share of Hasbro's stock.

c. Note the great discrepancy between the market price of Hasbro on December 30, 1999 ($18.625) and the price calculated in part (b). Discuss some possible reasons for this.

P25-10 a. (PBV ratio) Given the information supplied for Hasbro in Problem 25–9, what is the implied expected growth rate at its December 30, 1999 price per share of $18.625.

b. How does the number calculated in part (a) compare to the growth rate used in Problem 25–9(b)?

CFA EXAM QUESTIONS

1. (1999 CFA Sample Exam, Level I) The decline stage of the industry life cycle is *most likely* characterized by:
   A. slowly growing sales.
   B. a search for product differentiation.
   C. a rapidly increasing return on equity.
   D. an emphasis on production efficiencies.

2. (1997 CFA Sample Exam, Level I) According to Porter, which of the following are competitive forces that determine the intensity of competition within an industry?

   I. Rivalry among existing competitors.

   II. Threat of new entrants.

   III. Threat of substitute products.

   IV. Bargaining power of buyers and suppliers.

   A. I and IV only.
   B. II and III only.
   C. I, II, and III only.
   D. I, II, III, and IV.

3. (1998 CFA Exam, Level II) Janet Ludlow is preparing a report on U.S.-based manufacturers in the electric toothbrush industry and has gathered the information shown in Table 1 and Exhibit 1.

   Ludlow's report concludes that the electric toothbrush industry is in the maturity (i.e., late) phase of its industry life cycle.

   A. Select and justify *three* factors from Table 1 that *support* Ludlow's conclusion.

Table 1 Ratios for Electric Toothbrush Industry Index and Broad Stock Market Index

Year	1992	1993	1994	1995	1996	1997
Return on equity						
Electric toothbrush industry index	12.5%	12.0%	15.4%	19.6%	21.6%	21.6%
Market index	10.2	12.4	14.6	19.9	20.4	21.2
Average P/E						
Electric toothbrush industry index	28.5x	23.2x	19.6x	18.7x	18.5x	16.2x
Market index	10.2	12.4	14.6	19.9	18.1	19.1
Dividend payout ratio						
Electric toothbrush industry index	8.8%	8.0%	12.1%	12.1%	14.3%	17.1%
Market index	39.2	40.1	38.6	43.7	41.8	39.1
Average dividend yield						
Electric toothbrush industry index	0.3%	0.3%	0.6%	0.7%	0.8%	1.0%
Market index	3.8	3.2	2.6	2.2	2.3	2.1

Exhibit 1—Characteristics of the Electric Tooth-brush Manufacturing Industry

- *Industry Sales Growth* - Industry sales have grown at 15%–20% per year in recent years and are expected to grow at 10%–15% per year over the next 3 years.

- *Non-U.S. Markets* - Some U.S. manufacturers are attempting to enter fast-growing non-U.S. markets, which remain largely unexploited.

- *Mail Order Sales* - Some manufacturers have created a new niche in the industry by selling electric tooth-brushes directly to customers through mail order. Sales for this industry segment are growing at 40% per year.

- *U.S. Market Penetration* - The current penetration rate in the United States is 60% of households and will be difficult to increase.

- *Price Competition* - Manufacturers compete fiercely on the basis of price, and price wars within the industry are common.

- *Niche Markets* - Some manufacturers are able to develop new, unexploited niche markets in the United States based on company reputation, quality, and service.

- *Industry Consolidation* - Several manufacturers have recently merged, and it is expected that consolidation in the industry will increase.

- *New Entrants* - New manufacturers continue to enter the market.

B. Select and justify *three* factors from Exhibit 1 that *refute* Ludlow's conclusion.

FURTHER REFERENCES

Damodaran, Aswath. *Investment Valuation.* New York: Wiley, 1996.

Tools for valuing many different types of investments are suggested in this 24-chapter book. No mathematics beyond algebra is used. Helpful graphs and numerical examples are plentiful.

Stocks, Bonds, Bills, and Inflation: 1999 Yearbook, Valuation Edition, Ibbotson Associates, Chicago, published annually.

The topic of this 6-chapter book is common stock valuation techniques. Tables of empirical data and graphs are used to analyze equity valuation problems and evaluate possible solutions. A modest amount of algebra is used.

ENDNOTES

1 See Franco Modigliani, "Life Cycle, Individual Thrift, and the Wealth of Nations," *American Economic Review* 76 (June 1986): 297–312. Also see F. Modigliani and R. Brumberg, "Utility Analysis and the Consumption Function: An Interpretation of Cross-Section Data," K. Kurihara, ed. *Post-Keynesian Economics* (New Brunswick, NJ: Rutgers University Press, 1954).

2 See Zhiwu Chen, "Changing Tastes and Asset Pricing in Multiperiod Economies," Ph.D. dissertation, Yale University, School of Management, 1990.

3 See Gurdip Bakshi and Zhiwu Chen, "Baby Boom, Population Aging, and Capital Markets," *Journal of Business* 67, no. 2 (April 1994): 165–202. Zhiwu Chen's 1990 research reached the popular press after its veracity was established. See William Sterling and Stephen Waite, *Boomernomics* (New York: Ballantine Books, 1998). Bakshi and Chen are not cited in this book.

4 Standard & Poor's Corporation sells the 1-inch thick annual *Analysts Handbook.* The *Handbook* contains stock price indexes and tables of financial data on 103 industries annually from 1967 through the present. Contact the Standard & Poor's Corporation, 25 Broadway, New York, NY 10004, phone 212-208-8000. The expensive *Handbook* and other data are available free in public libraries.

5 See Robert Barker, "How a Tech-Fund Star Picks His Plays," *Business Week,* 14 June 1999, 166.

6 Black and Scholes were the first to suggest using their option pricing model to value stocks and bonds. See Fischer Black and Myron Scholes, "The Pricing of Options and Corporate Liabilities," *Journal of Political Economy* (May-June 1973); see the section entitled "Common Stock and Bond Valuation," pp. 649–52.

7 See Eqn. 9–11 (p.256). The implications of option theory for the prices of corporate securities has been investigated by F. Black and J. Cox, "Valuing Corporate Securities: Some Effects of Bond Indenture

Provisions," *Journal of Finance* 31 (May 1976): 351–78. Also see Thomas Ho and Ronald Singer, "Bond Indenture Provisions and the Risk of Corporate Debt," *Journal of Financial Economics* 10 (March 1982): 375–406.

8 To review numerical examples of how to price corporate securities using the Black-Scholes call pricing model, see S. A. Ross and R. W. Westerfield, *Corporate Finance,* (St. Louis: Mosby, 1988), 521–28. For a more recent discussion that does not use the Black-Scholes model, see S. A. Ross, R. W. Westerfield, and Jeffrey Jaffe, *Corporate Finance,* 4th ed. (Chicago: Irwin, 1996), 591–96. Or, to price corporate securities using the Black-Scholes model see R. A. Brealey and S. Myers, *Principles of Corporate Finance,* 5th ed. (New York: McGraw-Hill, 1996), 564–66. More recent editions of these corporation finance textbooks do not use the Black-Scholes model to price corporate securities.

9 See Robert Merton, "On the Pricing of Corporate Debt," *Journal of Finance* (May 1974): 449–70. Also see Eduardo S. Schwartz and Mark Moon, "Rational Pricing of Internet Companies," *Financial Analysts Journal* 56, no. 3 (May-June 2000): 62–75.

10 See Eugene F. Fama and Kenneth R. French, "The Cross-Section of Expected Stock Returns," *Journal of Finance* 47 (1992): 427–65. E. F. Fama and Kenneth R. French, "Common Risk Factors in the Returns on Bonds and Stocks," *Journal of Financial Economics* 33 (1993): 3–56. E. F. Fama and Kenneth R. French, "The SML Is Wanted, Dead or Alive," Working paper, University of Chicago, 1995. See James L. Davis, 1994, "The Cross-Section of Realized Stock Returns: The Pre-COMPUSTAT Evidence," *Journal of Finance* 49: 1579–93. Also see Jeffrey Pontiff and Lawrence D. Schall, "Book-to-Market Ratios as Predictors of Market Returns," *Journal of Financial Economics* 49, no. 2 (August 1998): 141–60.

11 See Dongcheol Kim, "The Errors-in-Variables Problem in the Cross-Section of Expected Stock Returns," *Journal of Finance* 50 (1995): 1605–34. Also see Dongcheol Kim, "A Re-examination of Firm Size, Book-to-Market, and Earnings-Price in the Cross-Section of Expected Stock Returns," *Journal of Financial and Quantitative Analysis* 32, no. 4 (December 1997): 463–89. Another possible flaw in the Fama-French methodology is analyzed by Wayne E. Ferson, Sergei Sarkissian, and Timothy Simin, "The Alpha Factor Asset Pricing Model: A Parable," *Journal of Financial Markets* 2, no. 1 (February 1999): 49–68.

12 See James Tobin, "A General Equilibrium Approach to Monetary Theory," *Journal of Money, Credit, and Banking* (February 1969): 15–29. For empirical estimates of *q* see E. B. Lindberg and S. A. Ross, "Tobin's q Ration and Industrial Organization," *Journal of Business* (January 1981): 1–33.

TECHNICAL ANALYSIS

There are three main approaches to analyzing stocks. Chapters 7 and 13–16 introduced risk-return analysis, *Chapters 3 and 23–25 reviewed* fundamental analysis. *This chapter focuses on a third approach,* technical analysis. *Technical analysis is used to forecast the prices of stocks, bonds, commodities, foreign exchange, security market indexes, and market interest rates.*

Some **technical analysts,** *or* technicians, *believe it is not worthwhile to analyze the issuing company's earnings, its products, forthcoming legislation that might affect the firm, or perform other aspects of fundamental analysis. These technical analysts believe all this information is summarized in one number—the market price of the security. Other technicians use both technical analysis and fundamental analysis.*

Technical analysts focus their attention on charts of market prices and transactions statistics. They are sometimes called chartists *because most use price charts. Technicians believe that the charts and market statistics they study reveal all the public information and the unknown secrets that cause securities trades. Some chartists ignore accounting transactions, financial ratios, patents that are granted, mergers, and executive changes. In sharp contrast to the fundamental analysts, technicians study* patterns *in security prices as they seek to discern the market* impact *of the facts fundamental analysts study, the effect of buyers accumulating positions and sellers liquidating positions, the market's "psychology," and whatever else might be moving market prices.*

Most technical analysts use only charts of various financial variables to forecast security prices, but an increasing number use quantitative (statistical) tools too. Professional technical analysts employ dozens of different techniques. This chapter explores some of the more prominent technical tools they use. First, however, we will review the concepts that are at the core of technical analysis.

THEORETICAL FOUNDATION OF TECHNICAL ANALYSIS

Technical analysis is based on the premise that security prices are determined by supply and demand. A classic book by Edwards and Magee[1] articulated the basic assumptions underlying technical analysis:

1. Market value is determined by the interaction of supply and demand.
2. Supply and demand are governed by numerous factors, both rational and irrational.
3. Despite minor fluctuations in the market, security prices tend to move in trends that persist for an appreciable length of time.
4. Changes in a trend are caused by the shifts in supply and demand.
5. Shifts in supply and demand, no matter why they occur, can be detected sooner or later in charts of market transactions.
6. Some chart patterns tend to repeat themselves.

Essentially, technical analysts believe that patterns of market action recur and can therefore be used for predictive purposes.

Chapters 23 through 25 of this book explained how fundamental analysts estimate the *value* of shares of stock. Technical analysts estimate *prices* instead of values. They tend to ignore fundamental valuation facts such as a firm's riskiness and earnings growth rate in favor of various barometers of supply and demand they have devised. A classic technical analysis book lyrically asserts that:[2]

> *It is futile to assign an intrinsic value to a stock certificate. One share of United States Steel, for example, was worth $261 in the early fall of 1929, but you could buy it for only $22 in June 1932. By March 1937, it was selling for $126 and just one year later for $38. . . . This sort of thing, this wide divergence between presumed value and actual value, is not the exception; it is the rule; it is going on all the time. The fact is that the real value of a share of U.S. Steel common is determined at any given time solely, definitely and inexorably by supply and demand, which are accurately reflected in the transactions consummated on the floor of the . . . Exchange.*
>
> *Of course, the statistics which the fundamentalists study play a part in the supply and demand equation—that is freely admitted. But there are many other factors too. The market price reflects not only the differing fears and guesses and moods, rational and irrational, of hundreds of potential buyers and sellers, as well as their needs and their resources—in total, factors which defy analysis and for which no statistics are obtainable, but which are nevertheless all synthesized, weighted and finally expressed in one precise figure at which a buyer and seller get together and make a deal (through their agents, their respective brokers). This is the only figure that counts.*
>
> *In brief, the going price as established by the market itself comprehends all the fundamental information which the statistical analyst can hope to learn (plus some which is perhaps secret to him, known only to a few insiders) and much else besides of equal or even greater importance.*

This quotation makes some strong assertions as it articulates the spirit of technical analysis.

Most technical analysts do not accuse fundamental analysts of being wrong or illogical. In fact, many security analysts use both fundamental and technical security analysis tools. However, the technical analysis purists assert the superiority of their methods over fundamental analysis by pointing out that technical analysis is easier, faster, and can be simultaneously applied to more stocks. Many technical analysts find fundamental analysis simply too troublesome to bother with. First, they point out that even if a fundamental analyst does find an underpriced security, he or she must wait and hope that the rest of the market recognizes the security's true value and bids its price up. Second, technical analysts cite the inadequacy of the accounting statements (see Chapter 24) which forms the basis for much fundamental analysis. Third, fundamental analysis is hard work. Finally, technical analysts point out that earnings growth-rate forecasts, management evaluations, and price-earnings multipliers used by fundamental analysts involve ambiguities.

These claims may be true. However, if technical analysis cannot predict security prices satisfactorily, the fact that it is easier to learn or simpler to use is unimportant. What, then, are the tools of technical analysis?[3]

THE DOW THEORY

The Dow Theory is a classic technical tool. It was originated by Charles Dow, founder of the Dow Jones Company and editor of the *Wall Street Journal,* in a series of articles published around 1900. Mr. Dow died in 1902, and William Hamilton, who became editor of the *Journal,* developed the Dow Theory further in a book he published a 1922 entitled *The Stock Market Barometer.* In 1932 the Dow Theory was formalized in a book entitled *Dow Theory,* authored by Charles Rhea (the theory was given its name by Mr. Rhea and staff members at the *Journal*). The Dow Theory is still the basis for much work done by technical analysts.

What Is the Dow Theory?

The Dow Theory is a trend-following strategy that presumes the market moves in persistent bull and bear market trends. The theory is typically used to delineate trends in the market as a whole, but it is also used for individual securities and commodities. Dow theorists define three types of movements in a market index or security price they are analyzing:

1. **Primary trends** are commonly called bear or bull markets. Delineating primary trends is the goal of the Dow Theory.
2. **Secondary movements** are market collapses or upward surges that last only a few weeks or months. Secondary movements are sometimes called **corrections.**
3. **Tertiary moves** are simply little daily fluctuations. The Dow Theory asserts that daily fluctuations are meaningless random wiggles. Nonetheless, the chartist should plot the daily prices in an effort to discern the latest development in the important primary trend.

Figure 26-1 illustrates a *line chart* that a Dow theorist might develop. Line charts can be constructed by plotting the closing price for each day and connecting the daily points with a continuous line. A line chart could also be constructed from the opening, or high, or low price for each day; being consistent is important. The meaningless daily fluctuations are not present in Figure 26-1. The distracting tertiary moves were smoothed away by plotting a moving 3-day average price (denoted $M3DAP_t$ for day t) instead of plotting each day's individual price.

$$M3DAP_t = \frac{P_t + P_{t-1} + P_{t-2}}{3 \text{ days}} \tag{26-1}$$

Figure 26-1 shows an upward primary trend, or *bull market,* existing from period t to the peak price which occurred just before day $t + j$. On trading day $t + j$ an *abortive recovery* occurs, signaling a change in the direction of the market's primary movement. An abortive recovery begins when a secondary movement fails to rise above the preceding top.

FIGURE 26-1   A Line Chart of Daily Prices Covering Several Hypothetical Years Annotated with Dow Theory Signals

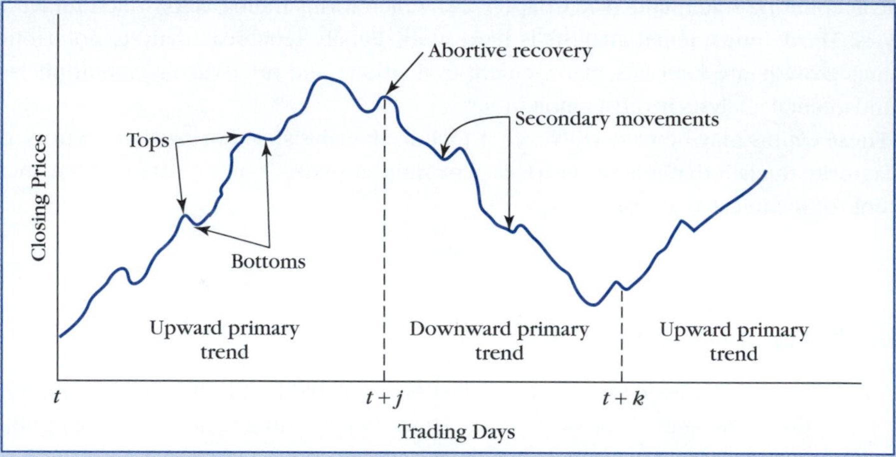

A moving 3-day average price is plotted each day to smooth over meaningless random daily wiggles (called tertiary moves). The smoothed line chart traces out (1) primary trends called bear markets or bull markets, and (2) secondary movements that last a few months and are called corrections. Ascending tops (and bottoms) are components of bull markets, and descending tops (and bottoms) occur during bear markets.

Before $t + j$, all the tops are ascending; after the abortive recovery, the tops are descending as a *bear market* begins. The bear market continues until just before day $t + k$. At $t + k$, a secondary movement fails to reach a new bottom, signaling the start of a new bull market. Most Dow theorists do not believe that the emergence of a new primary trend has been *confirmed* until the pattern of ascending or descending tops occurs in both the industrial and transportation stock price averages.[4]

Testing the Dow Theory

Stephen Brown, William Goetzmann, and Alok Kumar (BGK hereafter) formulated an event study to test the ability of the Dow Theory to predict future movements in the Dow-Jones Industrial Average (DJIA). BGK analyzed 255 of William Hamilton's editorials from the *Wall Street Journal* from the early 1900s. Each of Hamilton's editorials is treated as an event. BGK use the feature vector analysis (FEVA) methodology developed by Kumar and McGee to delineate the trend shapes (FEVA *features*) in the DJIA that prevailed when each of Hamilton's 255 *Journal* articles were published (events occurred).[5] In other words, neural net estimation was used to identify optimal trading rules during 1902–29 sample period.

The BGK cluster analysis of the *Wall Street Journal* events (FEVA features) reveals that William Hamilton's forecasts are based on at least four discernible patterns in the DJIA's movements during the 40 days before and after his *Journal* articles:

1. Recent downward trends in the DJIA are sell signals.
2. DJIA falls from recent peaks are sell signals.
3. Recent upward trends in the DJIA are buy signals.
4. Recoveries from recent declines in the DJIA are buy signals.

When Hamilton's *Wall Street Journal* articles were interpreted as either a buy signal or a neutral signal, a hypothetical portfolio was fully invested in the DJIA. When an article was interpreted as a sell signal, the hypothetical portfolio was fully invested in cash that earned no interest.

Hamilton's Dow Theory–based trading rules were tested over 17,457 out-of-sample trading days from 1930 to 1997. BGK conclude that ". . . although the Dow Theory appears to have some power to predict returns in the post-sample period, normal trading frictions would preclude using the theory to generate large excess returns, particularly in the most recent period."[6] Summarizing, it seems that the Dow Theory is a useful way for a financial analyst to organize his or her thinking about trends, but it is not likely to be a tool that enables the analyst to "get rich quick."

BAR CHARTS

Technical analysts construct several different types of charts. Figure 26-1 is an example of a **line chart**. Figure 26-2 is a bar chart. **Bar charts** use one vertical bar to summarize one trading day's price movements. Each bar spans the distance from the day's highest price to the day's lowest price, and a small cross on each bar marks the closing price.

Line charts and bar charts usually have bar graphs along the bottom of the charts showing the *volume of shares traded.* Figure 26-2 illustrates volume data. Next to the market prices, trading volume is the second most important statistic technicians follow. As an example of how technical analysts relate stock price moves and the volume of shares traded, consider a pattern called the "head-and-shoulders" formation.

A Head-and-Shoulders Top Pattern Within a Bar Chart

A head-and-shoulders top (HST) is a series of reversals that is supposed to signal that a security's price, a commodity's price, or a market price index has reached a top and will decline in the future. Figure 26-2 shows how the market action comprising a HST can be broken down into four components:

1. **Left shoulder.** A period of heavy buying pushes the price up to a new peak before a lull in trading allows the price to slip back down.
2. **Head.** A spurt of buying activity bids the price up to a new high, and then another lull in trading allows the price to fall back below the top of the left shoulder.
3. **Right shoulder.** A moderate rally lifts the price somewhat but fails to push prices as high as the top of the head before another decline begins.
4. **Confirmation (or Breakout).** The price falls below a straight line, called the *neckline,* that is tangent to the bottoms (or tops) of the left and right shoulders. When the price drops below the neckline this is called a *breakout* and it is supposed to be a sell signal that precedes further price declines.

Other Patterns

Technical analysts have described numerous patterns that they believe will indicate the direction of future price moves. Triangles, pennants, flags, channels, rectangles, double tops, triple tops, wedge formations, and diamonds are only some of the patterns for which chartists search. Some chartists employ very complex charts and/or search for very intricate patterns. *Point-and-figure charts* and the *Elliot Wave Theory* are the names of some of these more elaborate charting techniques. Anyone with a rich imagination can conceive new patterns and interpret them as they see fit.

FIGURE 26-2   A Bar Chart of a Head-and-Shoulders Top Formation

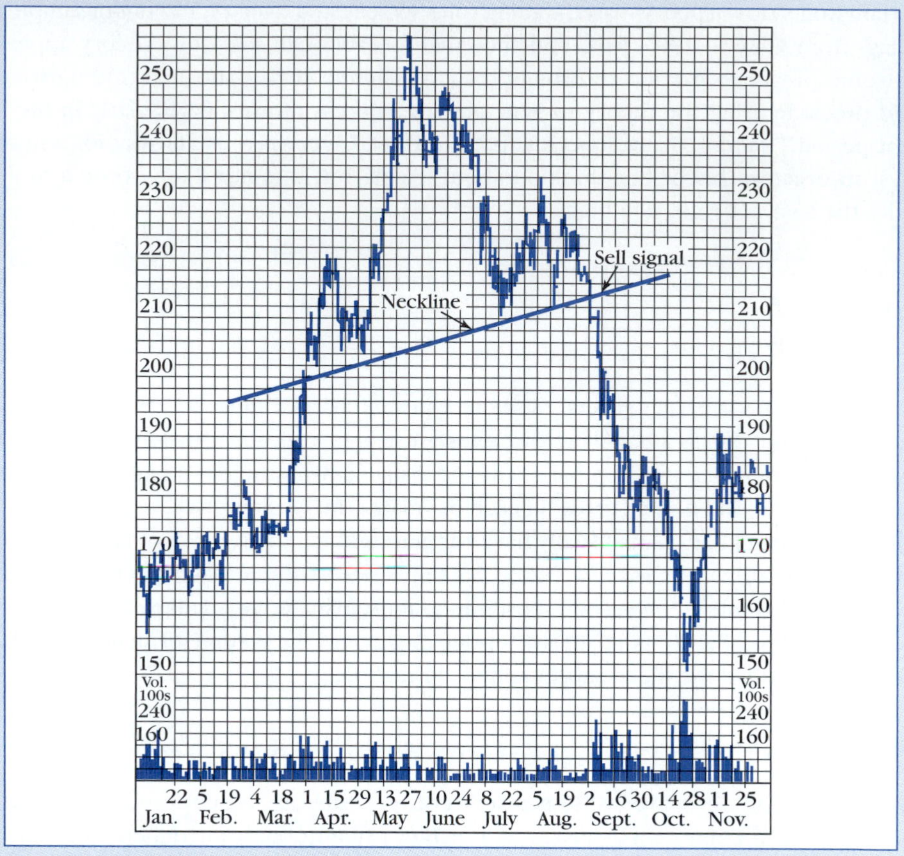

The head-and-shoulders formation is a reversal pattern that frequently occurs after a long trend. It typically takes several months to form the left shoulder, the head, and then the right shoulder of the formation. A signal to trade occurs when the neck line is penetrated.

CHARTING THE VOLUME OF SHARES TRADED

Many daily newspapers publish data about the total volume of shares traded during the previous trading day. Figure 26-3 shows an excerpt from a typical financial newspaper giving the volume of shares traded data on the NYSE.

Technicians say volume measures the intensity of investors' feelings. They do not study trading volume by itself, however. Volume is studied in conjunction with some price action. There is a Wall Street adage that "it takes volume to move a stock's price." This adage explains why stock price chartists study volume data in an effort to better understand specific stock price movements. But the cause-and-effect relationship between the volume of shares traded and the price change in the traded security is difficult to unravel.[7] The next section shows how information about the volume of trading is used by technicians to clarify the meaning of resistance and support levels.

---

*   As explained in Chapter 3 (pages 51–53), security transactions are sometimes grouped into two categories: (a) *information trading* and (b) *liquidity trading.* Sometimes a large volume of liquidity (or noise) trading can take place without causing any price change.

FIGURE 26-3   Data About the Shares Traded on One Day

STOCK MARKET DATA BANK   6/19/00

MAJOR INDEXES

—†12-MO— HIGH	LOW		DAILY HIGH	LOW	CLOSE	NET CHG	% CHG	†12-MO CHG	% CHG	FROM 12/31	% CHG
DOW JONES AVERAGES											
11722.98	9796.03	30 Industrials	10597.44	10440.11	x10557.84	+ 108.54	+ 1.04	− 258.14	− 2.39	− 939.28	− 8.17
3515.99	2263.59	20 Transportation	2687.55	2669.00	2680.67	+ 7.48	+ 0.28	− 747.55	− 21.81	− 296.53	− 9.96
333.30	269.20	15 Utilities	328.16	322.99	323.56	− 2.59	− 0.79	− 3.21	− 0.98	+ 40.20	+ 14.19
3324.42	2751.55	65 Composite	3056.90	3030.35	x3049.04	+ 16.05	+ 0.53	− 209.94	− 6.44	− 165.34	− 5.14
364.71	285.95	DJ US Total Mkt	346.07	338.03	345.55	+ 5.79	+ 1.70	+ 37.82	+ 12.29	+ 3.99	+ 1.17
NEW YORK STOCK EXCHANGE											
663.12	576.17	Composite	655.94	649.14	654.35	+ 4.67	+ 0.72	+ 17.41	+ 2.73	+ 4.05	+ 0.62
843.24	728.87	Industrials	830.29	820.29	828.13	+ 3.21	+ 0.39	+ 38.43	+ 4.87	− 0.08	− 0.01
519.96	461.53	Utilities	512.01	505.87	511.33	+ 5.46	+ 1.08	+ 18.10	+ 3.67	+ 0.18	+ 0.04
540.03	353.51	Transportation	395.36	392.25	393.30	+ 0.84	+ 0.21	− 135.51	− 25.63	− 73.40	− 15.73
575.19	442.71	Finance	541.22	529.20	538.98	+ 9.35	+ 1.77	− 19.30	− 3.46	+ 22.37	+ 4.33
STANDARD & POOR'S INDEXES											
1527.46	1247.41	500 Index	1488.98	1459.00	1486.00	+ 21.54	+ 1.47	+ 137.00	+ 10.16	+ 16.75	+ 1.14
1917.64	1544.13	Industrials	1853.28	1815.66	1850.47	+ 26.30	+ 1.44	+ 225.49	+ 13.88	+ 8.55	+ 0.46
276.52	215.62	Utilities	273.21	268.91	269.46	− 2.91	− 1.07	+ 4.00	+ 1.51	+ 42.24	+ 18.59
503.02	369.50	400 MidCap	503.03	492.89	503.02	+ 6.41	+ 1.29	+ 92.31	+ 22.48	+ 58.35	+ 13.12
223.58	168.96	600 SmallCap	211.02	207.41	211.02	+ 2.45	+ 1.17	+ 30.73	+ 17.04	+ 13.23	+ 6.69
323.37	262.26	1500 Index	315.83	309.70	315.32	+ 4.51	+ 1.45	+ 31.65	+ 11.16	+ 6.43	+ 2.08
NASDAQ STOCK MARKET											
5048.62	2490.11	Composite	3990.79	3825.69	3989.83	+ 129.27	+ 3.35	+1359.55	+ 51.69	− 79.48	− 1.95
4704.73	2163.77	Nasdaq 100	3935.33	3730.77	3933.70	+ 146.34	+ 3.86	+1665.04	+ 73.39	+ 225.87	+ 6.09
2841.00	1480.60	Industrials	2108.47	2033.09	2107.88	+ 50.65	+ 2.46	+ 543.92	+ 34.78	− 131.09	− 5.85
2365.99	1602.08	Insurance	1779.02	1752.61	1764.37	+ 6.07	+ 0.35	− 556.32	− 23.97	− 131.91	− 6.96
1871.69	1340.36	Banks	1530.94	1491.13	1529.05	+ 32.78	+ 2.19	− 313.98	− 17.04	− 162.24	− 9.59
2964.66	1300.68	Computer	2349.36	2248.58	2348.71	+ 84.10	+ 3.71	+1000.83	+ 74.25	+ 23.31	+ 1.00
1230.06	571.45	Telecommunications	891.16	856.42	891.08	+ 23.88	+ 2.75	+ 204.98	+ 29.88	− 124.32	− 12.24
OTHERS											
1036.40	765.27	Amex Composite	936.98	930.51	934.22	− 1.62	− 0.17	+ 168.52	+ 22.01	+ 57.30	+ 6.53
813.56	646.79	Russell 1000	789.94	774.59	788.47	+ 12.27	+ 1.58	+ 86.66	+ 12.35	+ 20.50	+ 2.67
606.12	408.90	Russell 2000	522.79	510.05	522.79	+ 9.05	+ 1.76	+ 73.35	+ 16.32	+ 18.04	+ 3.57
844.78	667.03	Russell 3000	816.30	800.45	815.11	+ 12.78	+ 1.59	+ 91.38	+ 12.63	+ 21.80	+ 2.75
472.95	394.35	Value-Line(geom.)	418.06	415.12	418.06	+ 2.15	+ 0.52	− 42.43	− 9.21	− 12.98	− 3.01
14751.64	11446.60	Wilshire 5000			13856.79	+ 222.21	+ 1.63	+1512.26	+ 12.25	+ 44.12	+ 0.32

†-Based on comparable trading day in preceding year.

MOST ACTIVE ISSUES

NYSE	VOLUME	CLOSE	CHANGE
Honeywell	20,651,300	40 1/16	− 8 11/16
LucentTch	15,591,400	60 11/16	+ 11/16
Motorola	15,581,100	33 7/16	− 5/8
AT&T	14,610,400	34	+ 5/8
Xerox	11,698,500	20 11/16	+ 7/16
EMC Cp	11,468,900	81 3/4	+ 2 1/2
MicronTch	10,750,400	80 5/8	+ 3
Compaq	10,641,900	27 5/8	+ 3/16
NortelNtwks	10,419,400	68 3/4	+ 15/16
BankAm	10,311,300	48 5/8	+ 1 1/16
Nokia	10,175,200	61 1/2	+ 3
AmOnline	10,034,400	54 7/16	− 1/4
GenElec	9,775,600	51 5/16	+ 1/16
PhilipMor	8,936,300	25 13/16	+ 1/4
Pfizer	8,259,200	47 1/8	− 3/4
NASDAQ			
Rambus	48,074,100	91 1/4	+ 7 7/8
CiscoSys	33,805,700	68 15/16	+ 1 1/8
Intel	29,431,900	136 1/2	+ 10 7/16
DellCptr	27,283,300	49 9/16	+ 2 1/16
OracleCp	25,186,000	86	+ 4 1/8
WorldCom	23,107,400	42	+ 1
Microsoft	22,109,800	73 11/16	+ 1 1/8
EricsnTel	15,499,200	21 11/16	+ 5/16
JDS Uniphs	14,335,300	127 5/16	+ 7 1/8
PwrwaveTch	13,258,400	45 1/8	− 4 5/8
Qualcomm	13,029,400	65 3/16	− 9/16
CovadComm	12,258,100	18 5/16	− 1/8
SunMicrsys	11,816,700	95 7/16	+ 4 1/8
AMEX			
NASDAQ100	20,013,800	97 13/16	+ 3 5/8
SPDR	5,056,600	148 3/8	+ 1 3/4
NaborsInd	1,590,100	40 3/16	− 1 1/16
GreyWolf	1,124,100	4 5/8	− 5/16
TWA	1,063,800	2 5/8	− 1/4

DIARIES

NYSE	MON	FRI	WK AGO
Issues traded	3,371	3,359	3,396
Advances	1,413	1,298	1,381
Declines	1,455	1,586	1,515
Unchanged	503	475	500
New highs	74	74	67
New lows	66	67	45
zAdv vol (000)	476,831	360,154	305,195
zDecl vol (000)	351,670	679,235	377,561
zTotal vol (000)	916,126	1,207,766	751,972
Closing tick[1]	−80	+44	−114
Closing Arms[2] (trin)	.72	1.54	1.13
zBlock trades	19,967	21,866	14,643
NASDAQ			
Issues traded	4,616	4,571	4,661
Advances	1,979	1,780	1,505
Declines	1,957	2,106	2,591
Unchanged	680	685	565
New highs	52	49	62
New lows	73	68	52
Adv vol (000)	916,500	731,915	326,195
Decl vol (000)	386,300	619,034	878,220
Total vol (000)	1,328,553	1,392,387	1,224,663
Block trades	n.a.	18,108	12,628
AMEX			
Issues traded	733	731	729
Advances	279	250	262
Declines	297	316	312
Unchanged	157	165	155
New highs	20	8	13
New lows	21	23	5
zAdv vol (000)	27,676	27,648	8,563
zDecl vol (000)	9,247	14,731	24,992
zTotal vol (000)	37,841	44,196	35,265
Comp vol (000)	53,034	61,066	51,685
zBlock trades	n.a.	836	730

SOURCE: *Wall Street Journal*, 20 June 2000, C2.

Support and Resistance Levels

A **resistance level** is a market price at which one may expect an increase in the supply of a security or commodity offered for sale. Resistance levels are sometimes called **ceilings** above which a price cannot rise; they are also called *peaks*. In contrast, a **support level** is the price at which one may expect an increase in demand for a security or commodity. Support levels are sometimes referred to as **floors** beneath which a price is not expected to fall; they are also called **troughs.** Figure 26-4 is a line chart illustrating several support and resistance levels that occur as the price of a stock trends upward.

The price of the stock in Figure 26-4 rises until it meets selling resistance at resistance level A. Then the price retreats until it finds buying support at support level B. How should we interpret these price actions?

Suppose there was daily trading volume plotted along the horizontal axis of Figure 26-4 that showed a moderate surge in trading at point A and, in addition, a larger surge in trading at point B that was three times larger than the surge of volume at point A. Combining this volume information with the price actions in Figure 26-4 allows us to surmise that at point B some bullish new information caused buying pressure at price level B to be strong enough to overpower the previous resistance at price level A. If a technician had the trading volume information she might have anticipated that the strong buying surge which started at point B would drive the price up past resistance level A to the higher resistance level C. It would be difficult to anticipate the stock's price advance to resistance level C without the large surge in daily trading volume we assumed took place at point B.

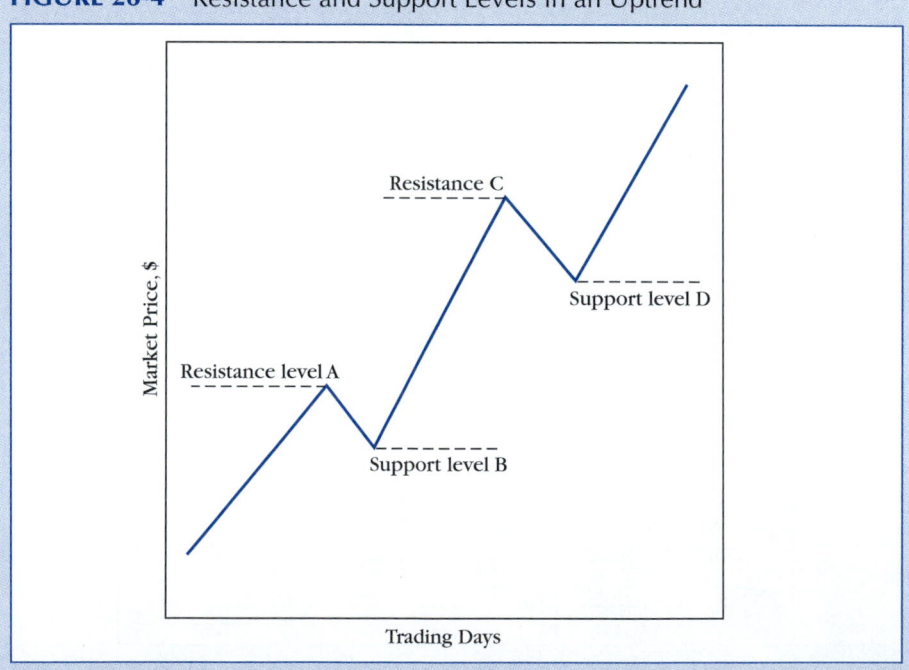

FIGURE 26-4   Resistance and Support Levels in an Uptrend

Resistance levels are temporary ceilings above which a price is not expected to rise; they are also called peaks. In contrast, a support level exists where demand for a security is expected to place a temporary floor beneath that price.

Congestion Areas

The ascending peaks and troughs in Figure 26-4 trace a sharp uptrend. The support and resistance lines in the bar graph of Figure 26-5 depict two periods when no trends exist. The price fluctuates in the first **congestion area** between $40 and $50 trendlessly for a number of trading days. Then the security's price rises through the old $50 resistance level. The old resistance level becomes the new support level. Essentially, the price moves up from congestion area #1 between $40 and $50 to the higher congestion area #2 and fluctuates aimlessly between $50 and $60.

Technical analysts are unable to give reasons for price actions like those illustrated in Figure 26-5. They might hypothesize, for example, that in congestion area #1 investors thought of the stock as being a 40-something dollar stock. As a result there was price resistance at $50 and price support at $40, until investors changed their opinions and started thinking of the stock as being a 50-something dollar stock. After investors started thinking of the stock as being a 50-something dollar stock, its price moved up into congestion area #2 and fluctuated between $50 and $60. Such subjective hypotheses cannot be proven or disproven.

When a security's price is fluctuating trendlessly in a congestion area, the price can penetrate either the support line or the resistance line. A **trading range breakout** (TRB) that penetrates the support line is interpreted as a sell signal. When the resistance line is penetrated, that trading range breakout (TRB) is a signal to buy. When one of these breakouts is accompanied by a surge in volume, the signal is considered to be more emphatic.

Brock, Lakonishok, and LeBaron (BLL) analyzed 90 years of daily Dow Jones Industrial Average (DJIA) data from 1897 through 1986. They examined several different TRB rules and reported that the technical analysis trading rules provided significant forecast power over the DJIA's daily returns.[8] Bessembinder and Chan tested the findings of BLL over a more recent long sample period (1926–91) and reported similar, but less profitable, trading results.[9] The BLL study and the study by Bessembinder and Chan did not use volume data. Bessembinder and Chan included cash dividend income, which BLL had ignored, and implemented other refinements. Both studies analyzed TRBs over 50, 150, and 200 trading days and found that, after trading commissions were deducted, the returns from TRBs were only

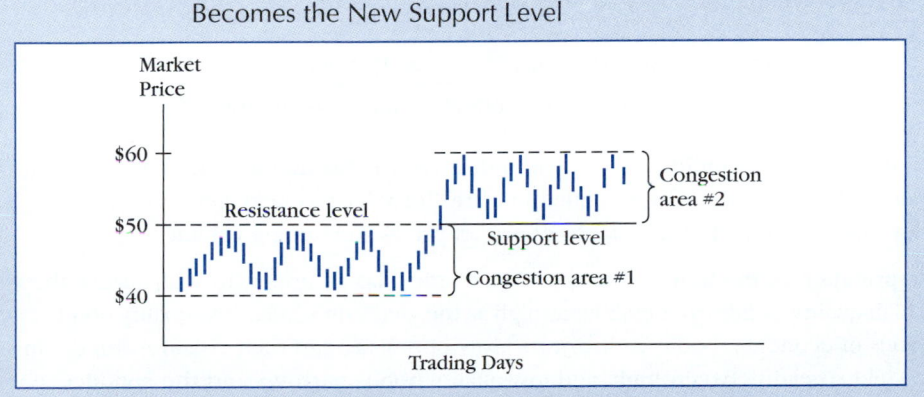

FIGURE 26-5   A New Congestion Area Emerges as the Old Resistance Level Becomes the New Support Level

The price fluctuates trendlessly in a congestion area between $40 and $50 for a number of trading days, and then moves to a higher congestion level between $50 and $60.

slightly larger the riskless rate of interest. Furthermore, the modest profitability of TRBs in the more recent decades was less than it was in the more distant past.

Selling Climaxes and Speculative Blowoffs

Technicians watch volume closely when supply and demand are out of balance and, as a result, the price is moving. If high volume occurs on days when prices move up, the market is considered to be bullish. High volume on days when prices are falling is a bearish sign. If the same price changes occurred on low trading volume, technicians would considered them to be of lesser importance.

There is one occasion when falling prices and high volume are considered bullish. When technicians feel the end of a bear market is near, they watch for a high volume of selling as the last of the bearish investors liquidates their holdings—this is called a **selling climax.** A selling climax is supposed to eliminate the last of the bearish sellers who drive prices down and clear the way for bullish investors to start bidding prices upward.

Some technicians also look for a **speculative blowoff** to mark the end of a bull market. A speculative blowoff occurs when a high volume of buying pushes prices up to a peak and exhausts the enthusiasm of bullish speculators; this makes way for a bear market to begin. Technicians sometimes explain a speculative blowoff by saying "a bull dies with a bang, not a whimper."

The Confidence Index

As they forecast securities prices and other factors, technical analysts observe various quantities. To help them obtain "a feel for the market's temperament" technicians have created market measures of prices and trading volumes. The "confidence index" is one of these measures.

The confidence index is the ratio of high-grade bond yields to low-grade bond yields. This ratio tends to reveal how willing investors are to take investment risks. When bond investors grow more confident about the strength of the national economy, they shift their holdings from high-grade to lower-grade bonds in order to obtain the higher yields. This change bids up the prices of low-grade bonds, lowers their yields relative to high-grade bonds, and increases the confidence index.

Calculating the BCI. *Barron's* weekly financial newspaper publishes figures on the confidence index regularly in its "Market Laboratory" section. The **Barron's confidence index,** or BCI, is the ratio of the average yield from *Barron's* list of the 10 high-grade bonds over the average yield of the Dow Jones 40-bond index.

$$BCI_t = \frac{\text{Average yield of } Barron's \text{ 10 high-grade bonds at time } t}{\text{Average yield of Dow Jones 40 bonds at period } t \text{ (lower grade bonds)}}$$

Although *Barron's* confidence index is widely used, it has no intrinsic superiority over any other confidence index that is defined similarly. Technicians create graphs of the confidence index that are similar to their graphs of market prices and trading volumes.

Interpretation of the Index. The confidence index has an upper limit of 1, since the yields on high-quality bonds can never be as high as the yields on similar low-quality bonds. During periods of economic boom, as investors grow optimistic and their risk-aversion diminishes, the yield spread between high- and low-quality bonds narrows and the confidence index rises. A rising confidence index is interpreted by chartists as an indication that the managers of the "smart money" are optimistic. On the assumption that the wisdom of these investors will be borne out, confidence index technicians predict that the stock market will follow the leadership of the "smart" money managers. Some confidence index technicians claim that the confidence index leads the stock market by several months. Thus, an upturn in the confidence index is supposed to foretell rising optimism and rising prices in the stock market. Conversely, a fall in the index is expected to precede a drop in stock prices.

Interestingly, the BCI was at historically high levels and rising prior to the famous October 19, 1987 international stock market crash. This misleading buy signal turned out to be very costly for those technicians that followed it.

There is no question that the confidence index is positively correlated with the stock market over a complete business cycle. This is not unique; many economic variables are positively correlated with the stock market. Like most other technical indicators, the confidence index is not always a leading indicator; sometimes it is a lagging indicator, and sometimes it issues erroneous signals. Speaking generally, no technical indicator should be used without confirming evidence from other indicators.[10]

MOVING AVERAGE ANALYSIS

Figure 26-6 shows bar charts of the Dow-Jones Industrial Average (DJIA) and the Standard & Poor's 500 (S&P500) composite stocks index. Daily volume on the NYSE is plotted along the bottom of the chart. Figure 26-6 also contains a separate moving average line for each of the two stock market indicators that fluctuates smoothly.

Moving-average technicians, or rate-of-change technicians, as they are also called, like to compute the moving average of a price they are following. The **moving average** is used to provide a smoothed, stable reference point against which the more volatile daily fluctuations can be gauged. Moving-average analysis is used for individual securities, market indices, commodity prices, interest rates, foreign exchange rates, or anything.

Construction of a Moving-Average Chart

Some technicians who perform moving-average analysis use a 150-day (30-week) moving average of closing prices. The moving average changes each day as the most recent day is added and the 151st day is dropped. To calculate a moving 150-day average price, denoted $M150DAP_t$ for the S&P500 on day t, the following formula is employed:

$$M150DAP_t = \frac{1}{150}\left(\text{S\&P500}_t + \text{S\&P500}_{t-1} + \cdots + \text{S\&P500}_{t-149}\right) \qquad \textbf{(26-2)}$$

Figure 26-6 shows the 30-week (150 trading days) moving average of the DJIA and Standard & Poor's index of 500 composite stocks as lines traced out by tiny dots.

Comparing the moving 3-day average price of the Eqn. 26-1 with the moving 150-day average price of Eqn. 26-2 suggests the widely different purposes for which moving averages are used. Moving averages computed over short time spans follow the daily price more closely and are therefore more volatile than moving averages computed over longer time spans.

The relationship between the daily market prices and the moving average provide trading directions for technicians.

Interpreting Charts with a Moving Average

When the daily prices penetrate the moving-average line, technicians interpret that as a signal to take action. For example, when the daily price moves downward through the moving average, they frequently fail to rise again for many months. Thus, a downward penetration of a

FIGURE 26-6   Bar Charts of Stock Market Indexes Plotted with Their Moving
Average Lines and the Volume of Trading

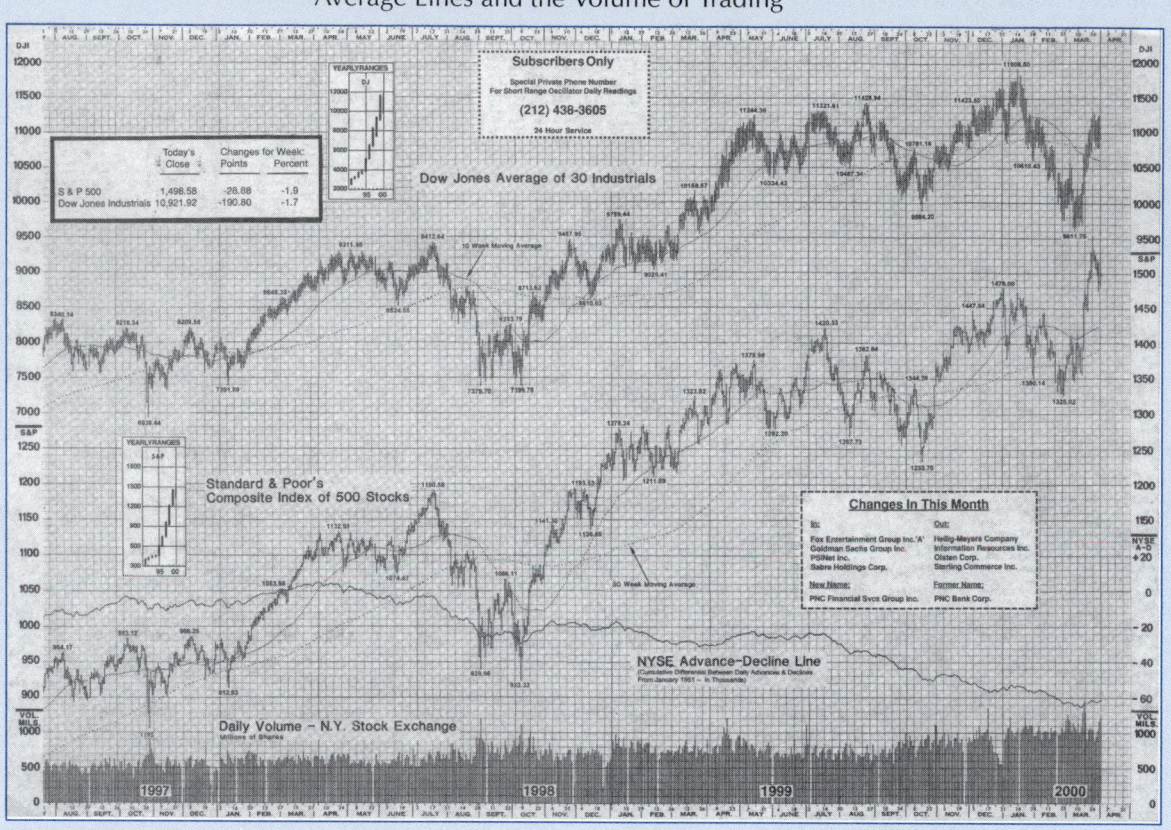

Bar Charts of the Dow-Jones Industrial Average (DJIA) and the S&P500 index are plotted with their 10-week and
30-week moving average lines. The daily volume of trading on the NYSE is plotted at the bottom of the graph.

SOURCE: *Daily Action Stock Charts,* 31 March 2000, Trendline Division, Standard and Poor's, 55 Water Street,
New York, NY 10041

flattened moving average suggests it is time to sell. Figure 26-6 provides an example of such a
sell signal in August 1998. When actual prices are above the moving average but the difference
is narrowing (see June–July 1998), this is a signal that a bull market may be nearing an end.

Moving-average analysts recommend buying a stock when: (1) the moving-average line
flattens and the stock's price rises up through the moving average line, (2) the price of a
stock temporarily falls below a moving-average line that is rising, and (3) a stock's price that
is above the moving-average line falls but turns around and begins to rise again before it ever
penetrates the moving-average line from above.

Moving-average technicians recommend selling a stock when: (1) the moving-average
line flattens out and the stock's price drops downward through the moving-average line,
(2) a stock's price temporarily rises above a moving-average line that is declining, and (3) a
stock's price falls downward through the moving-average line and turns around to rise but
then falls again before penetrating the moving average line from below.

The buy and sell signals initiated by a moving-average trading system vary with the
length of time over which the moving average is calculated. Moving averages calculated over
very short time spans of only a few days tend to touch off many unprofitable trades.

Instead of drawing charts by hand, some technicians subscribe to a chart drawing service that delivers up-to-date charts to the subscriber. The Trendline chart in Figure 26-6 is an example of a commercially prepared chart. Other technical analysts buy years of historical daily prices and load the data into their own personal computer (PC). The PC can be used to draw charts or to simulate trading. Some technicians simulate trading by issuing computer instructions to manage hypothetical trades inside their PC that are based on historical price and volume data. Technicians with PCs can employ multiple technical analysis techniques and compare their results from these different tools before they decide how they want to trade.

Empirical Tests of Moving-Average Rules and Congestion Areas

Brock, Lakonishok, and LeBaron (BLL) reported that trading rules based on moving averages provided significant forecast power over the DJIA.[11] Bessembinder and Chan replicated BLL's investigation of the DJIA over the more recent period from 1926 to 1991 and reported less profitable, but similar, results.[12] The study by Bessembinder and Chan considered factors like cash dividends and trading commissions, which were overlooked by BLL. Franklin Allen and Risto Karjalainen (AK) used a new tool called *genetic algorithms* to analyze daily data on the S&P500 index from 1926 to 1995.[13] Genetic algorithms are computer programs that search data, adapt to changes in the data, and seek optimum techniques to forecast the data based on the principles of natural evolution. AK considered transactions costs but omitted cash dividends. AK's genetic algorithms delineated a wide range of different price patterns in the empirical data, and some of the patterns resembled moving averages of various lengths.

The BLL, Bessembinder and Chan, AK, and other studies all found sample periods a few years in length during which moving-average trading rules yielded significant profits.[14] However, they also reported many sample periods during which moving-average trading rules yielded significant losses. After transactions costs were considered, none of the studies reported high levels of profitability over sample periods of several decades for any moving-average trading rule. Summarizing, it seems that moving-average trading rules can aid an investor, but they are not worth an expensive price.

Technical analysts have identified many price patterns. Fulcrums, inverse fulcrums, compound fulcrums, compound inverse fulcrums, wedges, inverted wedges, V formations, inverted V formations, extended V formations, saucers, inverse saucers, delayed endings, and pennants are some of the shapes for which they search. These patterns are not rigidly defined. New patterns may be perceived, named, and discussed at will.

BEHAVIORAL FINANCE

The efficient market theory argues that security prices should fluctuate randomly as profit-seekers cause them to adjust quickly to the random arrival of new information. As explained in Chapter 8, this theory suggests that securities market prices will not move in the discernible patterns discussed by technical analysts.

Bounded rationality occurs in economics when a decision-making process falls short of profit maximization because inadequate knowledge is available or the decision-makers have limited perceptive abilities. *Behavioral finance* is a psychology-based branch of economics that focuses on bounded rationality. Behavioral finance focuses on human frailties that limit people's ability to maximize profits and that, in turn, result in anomalies in the efficient markets theory. Overconfidence, framing, hindsight bias, and the base-rate fallacy are four human foibles discussed in behavioral finance.

Overconfidence occurs when an individual overestimates his or her abilities or knowledge. Behavioral finance uses the concept of overconfidence to explain the high volume of securities trading, the high percentage of the unprofitable trades that take place in financial markets, and the millions of people who buy lottery tickets when the chance of winning is practically nonexistent.

A psychological **frame** is composed of the acts, outcomes, and contingencies associated with a decision-maker's perception of a particular choice. For example, an investor with a gain-oriented frame might define a bear market as a year during which less than 5% of the stocks listed on the NYSE experience price increases. Alternatively, an investor with a loss-oriented frame could define a bear market to be a year when 95% or more of the stocks listed on the NYSE suffer from price collapses. This framing tends to cause the gain-oriented investors to be risk-averters while the loss-oriented investors tend to be risk-seekers.

When you give news to someone who is interested in a topic about which you have recent information, sometimes they respond by saying that's-what-I-thought, or, I knew-it-all-along. This human frailty is called **hindsight bias**. Some people tend to erroneously believe they could have predicted the correct outcome after the actual outcome has been explained to them. Hindsight bias contributes to overconfidence and leads to decisions that fail to maximize the investor's profit.

The **base-rate fallacy** occurs when someone who is making a probabilistic inference ignores population statistics or insightful sample information. The base rate fallacy leads to decisions that have bounded rationality.

Behavioral finance is a body of psychological concepts and empirical data that documents the human frailties mentioned above.[15] Behavioral economists argue that these behaviors cause investors to have learning lags and cause securities prices to react gradually to the arrival of new information. These consistent departures from rational profit-maximizing behavior are supposed to cause anomalies in the efficient market hypothesis and result in the security price patterns discussed by technical analysts.

ETHICS   A REALITY CHECK

Arbitration in the Investment Industry

Unfortunately, some investors entrust their nest egg to a broker only to have it consumed by dishonest or incompetent trading. Justice requires that victims be compensated for their losses. For this, arbitration generally works better than litigation, but the process is widely criticized.

A 1994 report by the National Association of Securities Dealers (NASD) identifies four areas of concern: the requirement of compulsory arbitration, the competence and objectivity of arbitrators, the "hardball" legal tactics of securities firms, and the permissibility of punitive damages.

Securities firms often require investors to sign a predispute arbitration agreement (PDAA). One critic argues, "investors should not be forced to make the Faustian bargain of signing away rights to litigate in order to invest in our financial markets." Some investors are not aware of signing a PDAA or the implications of doing so. The courts have held that PDAAs are legally enforceable as long as arbitration is reasonably effective in enforcing investor rights. The NASD reports recommends that investors be fully informed about compulsory arbitration.

Investors complain that some arbitrators are inattentive to the proceedings, ignorant of proper procedure, capricious in their rulings, and biased in favor of the industry. Arbitrators for their part feel overburdened, undercompensated, and inadequately trained. The NASD report recommends the development of professional arbitrators and greater reliance on other methods of dispute resolution.

Securities firms sometimes litigate the terms of a PDAA, thereby forcing investors into court. There they encounter "hard ball" legal tactics from firms seeking to avoid heavy punitive damages. The industry opposes the permissibility of punitive damages by arguing that arbitration is designed to compensate investors, not punish firms. But investors contend that in accepting mandatory arbitration, they should not also give up a right (punitive damages) that they would otherwise have in court. A compromise, recommended by the NASD report, is placing a reasonable cap on punitive damages.

John R. Boatright, *Professor of Business Ethics*

THE BOTTOM LINE

This chapter provides a sampling of technical analysis tools. Technical analysis tools attempt to detect and use price patterns.[16] Technical analysis assumes that when shifting prices are detected, they are the result of gradual shifts in supply and demand rather than a series of instantaneous shifts that all coincidentally happened to be moving in the same direction. Since these shifts are expected to continue as the price gradually reacts to information, the price change pattern is extrapolated to predict further price changes.

Many financial economists believe that technical analysis cannot predict market prices. The disbelievers suggest that security markets are efficient markets that impact new information into security prices instantaneously.[17] As a result, these financial economists believe that security prices are a random walk that occur in reaction to the random arrival of new information. When a security's price moves in the same direction for several days, those who believe that securities markets are efficient interpret these moves as a series of independent changes in supply or demand, which coincidentally happen to move the price in the same direction. They assert that technical analysts are wrong in believing that supply and/or demand adjust gradually, causing trends that may be used for predicting future prices. Evidence provided by disbelieving financial economists was examined in Chapter 8 and other chapters of this book.

QUESTIONS

Q26-1 (Technical analysis tools) Consider the following list of factors and indicate which of the factors would be ignored by a technical analyst: (a) risk, (b) growth rate, (c) historical prices, (d) financial ratios, (e) trading volume.

Q26-2 (Dow theory) Define the three types of movements on which the Dow theory is based.

Q26-3 (Dow theory) According to the Dow theory, what is the significance of an *abortive recovery* that follows a series of ascending tops?

Q26-4 (Moving averages) How is the moving average used in analyzing stock prices? Can the moving average be meaningfully calculated in different ways? Explain.

Q26-5 (Technical analysis indicators) Which of the technical indicators discussed in Chapter 26 gave the clearest and most unambiguous forewarning of the October 1987 international stock market crash? Explain.

Q26-6 (Confidence index) (a) What is the confidence index supposed to measure? (b) Does the confidence index have any limit on its upper value? Why or why not? (c) What relevance does this measure of bond inventors' confidence have for common stock investors?

Q26-7 (HST stages) Discuss the four stages associated with a head and shoulders top (HST) pattern.

Q26-8 (Charting) Define the phrases *speculative blowoff* and *selling climax*. What do these concepts have in common?

Q26-9 (Technical analysis tools) Are the technical analysis tools presented in the chapter useful for analyzing individual securities, market indexes, or both? Explain.

Q26-10 (Technical analysis tools) "Experienced technical analysts usually have one favorite tool that they follow closely to the exclusion of others." Is the statement true, false, or uncertain? Explain.

PROBLEMS

P26-1 (Support and resistance levels) Consider the following 14 days of data for the Hemmel Corporation's common stock. On which day do you think the market received important new information that affected the value of Hemmel's stock?

Day	Closing Price	Volume of Shares Traded
1	$29.25	1,000
2	$31.125	11,000
3	$32.50	3,000
4	$33.125	2,000
5	$33.75	500
6	$32.875	2,000
7	$32.125	1,000
8	$31.50	1,000
9	$31.75	12,000
10	$33.125	500
11	$34.50	2,000
12	$34.00	3,000
13	$33.75	2,000
14	$32.625	500

P26-2 (Moving averages) (a) Calculate a 5-day moving average from the Hemmel Corporation's closing price data from Problem 26-1. *Note:* You will only be able to calculate nine moving average prices, since it is impossible to calculate the average for the first 4 days. (b) Over what range does Hemmel's price vary? (c) Over what range do the moving average values of Hemmel's prices vary?

P26-3 (Confidence index) Consider the spectacular stock market crash of October 1987 and answer the questions pertaining to the following data:

P26-4 (Confidence Index) Assume you collected the following data for a 5-year period:

Years	1	2	3	4	5
Average Yield of Barron's 10 High-Grade Bonds	8%	7.8%	8.5%	9%	9.1%
Average Yield of Dow Jones 40-Bond Index	10%	10.1%	11%	12%	12.5%
Return on S&P 500 Index	15%	16%	15.5%	16.5%	17%

(a) Calculate the confidence index for each year. (b) How might chartists interpret this trend?

P26-5 (Moving averages) The following are the close prices for the DJIA in June 1999:

Date	Close Price
June 1	10596.26
June 2	10577.89
June 3	10663.69
June 4	10799.84
June 7	10909.38
June 8	10765.64
June 9	10690.29
June 10	10621.27
June 11	10490.51

(a) Calculate the 3-day moving average for June 3 through June 11. (b) What day might a chartist designate as the beginning of a bear market?

	January	February	March	April	May	June	July	August	September	October	November	December
Yields-to-Maturity												
T-bond	6.97	7.12	7.05	7.80	8.52	8.29	8.24	8.47	9.16	9.30	8.65	8.72
AA	8.86	8.82	8.78	9.31	9.81	9.70	9.64	9.83	10.48	10.62	9.97	10.08
A	9.07	8.94	8.91	9.39	9.91	9.89	9.90	10.16	10.77	10.98	10.51	10.59
BBB	9.47	9.50	9.42	9.55	10.44	10.38	10.42	10.61	11.25	11.55	10.99	11.06
Standard & Poor's 500 Composite Stocks Index												
S&P 500	265	281	293	289	289	301	310	329	319	280	245	241

(a) Do you think the Federal Reserve's monetary policy might have played a role in the October 1987 crash? (b) Construct a Confidence Index (CI) from the interest rate data above. (c) Did the CI you constructed give any indication of the October 1987 stock market crash? (d) If your CI gave any indications of the October 1987 were they leading, coincident or lagging indications? (e) If your CI failed to give a clear-cut leading indication of the October 1987 market crash, should you abandon technical analysis?

P26-6 (Bar chart) Use the following data to construct a bar chart for Texaco:

Date (1999)	High	Low	Close
June 4	64.25	62.6875	64.25
June 3	64.6875	62	62.3125
June 2	65.125	64	64.5
June 1	65.25	62.9375	64.1875
May 28	65.875	62	65.5
May 27	63.5625	62.25	62.875
May 26	65.9375	63.6875	65.25

Date (1999)	High	Low	Close
May 25	65.5	62.8125	63.0625
May 24	66.125	63.4375	63.625
May 21	66.875	64	66.125
May 20	65.1875	63.5	64.375
May 19	65	63.5	64
May 18	66.1875	64	64.0625
May 17	66.0625	66.0625	66.0625
May 14	66.75	66.75	67.6875
May 13	69.875	67	69.125
May 12	70.0625	66.8125	69
May 11	69.375	64.5	68.625
May 10	69.25	65.5	65.875

Date	Close Price	Volume
May 14	65.25	2,881,200
May 17	67.125	3,149,000
May 18	68.75	5,347,500
May 19	68.4375	2,804,200
May 20	67.9375	2,060,800
May 21	68	3,151,100
May 24	66.8125	2,819,200

On which day do you think the market received important, new information that would affect the price of Coca-Cola's stock?

P26-7 (Moving averages) (a) Use the data provided for the close prices in Problem 26-6 for Texaco to calculate 5-day moving averages for May 21 through June 4, 1999. (b) Use the same data to calculate 10-day moving averages for the same period. (c) What differences exist between the two different moving averages you calculated in parts (a) and (b)?

P26-8 (Line charts) Obtain the close prices for the Nasdaq Composite Index for January 2, 2001 through February 16, 2001 from the following Web site: finance.yahoo.com. Use the data to prepare a line chart.

P26-9 (Support and resistance levels) Consider the following price and volume data that is provided for the Coca-Cola Corporation for May 1999:

P26-10 (Relative strength) Many technical analysts compute relative strength ratios, using either monthly or weekly data. The ratio is calculated as the price of the stock divided by the value of a specific index. (a) Use the following monthly data provided for the Coca-Cola Corporation and the S&P 500 index to calculate Coca-Cola's relative strength ratios. (b) What is the prevalent trend in Coca-Cola's relative strength in the last half of 1998?

	Close Price	
Month (1998)	**Coca-Cola**	**S&P 500 Index**
June	85.5	1133.84
July	80.5	1120.67
August	65.125	957.28
September	57.625	1017.10
October	67.5625	1098.67
November	70.0625	1163.63
December	67	1229.23

CFA EXAM QUESTIONS

The following three questions are adopted from the 1997 CFA Sample Exam, Level I:

1. Technical analysis is best characterized by which of the following sets of assumptions?
   A. Security prices adjust rapidly to new information, and liquidity is provided by securities dealers.
   B. Security prices adjust rapidly to new information, and market prices are determined by the interaction of supply and demand.
   C. Security prices adjust gradually to new information, and liquidity is provided by securities dealers.
   D. Security prices adjust gradually to new information, and market prices are determined by the interaction of supply and demand.

2. Which of the following would be a *bullish* signal to a technical analyst using contrary opinion rules?
   A. Mutual funds have a relatively small cash position.
   B. A large proportion of speculators expect the price of stock index futures to rise.
   C. The ratio of the Nasdaq Stock Market volume to New York Stock Exchange volume is relatively high.
   D. The ratio of odd-lot short sales to total odd-lot sales is relatively high.

3. When technical analysts say a stock has good relative strength, they mean the:
   A. ratio of the price of the stock to a market index has trended upward.
   B. recent trading volume in the stock has exceeded the normal trading volume.

C. total return on the stock has exceeded the total return on other stocks in the same industry.

D. stock has performed well compared with other stocks in the same risk category as measured by beta.

4. (Adapted from the 1995 CFA Exam, Level II) **Briefly discuss** the implications of the efficient market hypothesis for investment policy as it applies to technical analysis in the form of charting.

FURTHER REFERENCES

Achelis, Steven B. *Technical Analysis: From A To Z.* Burr Ridge, IL: Irwin Professional Publishing, 1995.

This useful book reviews different aspects of technical analysis.

Edwards, R. D., and John Magee, Jr. *Technical Analysis of Stock Trends,* 5th ed. Springfield, MA: Stock Trends Service, 1966.

This classic book has been used for years by technical analysts. It is easy-to-read and many different techniques are explained.

Jiler, William L. *How Charts Can Help You in the Stock Market.* New York: Trendline, 1962.

This book on charting explains many techniques and gives illustrated examples.

Pring, Martin J. *Technical Analysis Explained,* 2d ed. New York: McGraw-Hill, 1985.

This comprehensive book elucidates a large number of technical analysis techniques that are used with individual stocks, bonds, commodities, and market averages. Helpful illustrations are provided.

Shaleen, Kenneth H. *Volume and Open Interest,* rev. ed. Burr Ridge, IL: Irwin Professional Publishing, 1997.

This book's focus on trading activity measures, such as the volume of shares traded and the open interest of contracts that are open, makes it unique.

ENDNOTES

[1]   R. D. Edwards and John Magee, Jr., *Technical Analysis of Stock Trends,* 7th ed. (Springfield, MA: John Magee, 1997), 106.

[2]   Ibid.

[3]   Although this chapter focuses on charting security prices, technical analysis of other market indicators and other types of financial instruments is also widely practiced. For an admiring report about technical analysis in foreign exchange markets see Christopher J. Neely, "Technical Analysis in the Foreign Exchange Market: A Layman's Guide," *Review* [Federal Reserve Bank of St. Louis] 79, no. 5 (September-October 1997): 23–38.

[4]   An empirical test of the Dow Theory that is supportive was published by David A. Glickstein and Rolf E. Wubbels, "Dow Theory Is Alive and Well," *Journal of Portfolio Management* (April 1983): 28–31. Statistically speaking, the Dow Theory is based on trends that can be measured by serial correlation (or auto correlation) coefficients that are significantly different from zero. In 1988 Fama and French reported statistically significant trends in security prices measured over 3- to 5-year time periods. The longer-term serial correlations they reported measure the type trends on which the Dow Theory and some other technical analysis theories are based. See E. F. Fama and K. R. French, "Permanent and Temporary Components of Stock Prices," *Journal of Political Economy* 96, no. 2 (April 1988): 246–73.

[5]   See Stephen J. Brown, William M. Goetzmann, and Alok Kumar, "The Dow Theory: William Peter Hamilton's Track Record Reconsidered," *Journal of Finance* 53, no. 4 (August 1998): 1311–33. The FEVA methodology was developed by Alok Kumar and Victor McGee, "FEVA (Feature Vector Analysis): Explicitly Looking for Structure and Forecastability in Time Series Data," *Economic and Financial Computing* (winter 1996): 165–89.

[6]   See Stephen J. Brown, William M. Goetzmann, and Alok Kumar, "The Dow Theory: William Peter Hamilton's Track Record Reconsidered," *Journal of Finance* 53, no. 4 (August 1998): 1329–30.

[7]   Research into the implications of the volume of shares traded includes Prem C. Jain and Gun-Ho Joh, "The Dependence Between Hourly Prices and Trading Volume," *Journal of Financial and Quantitative Analysis* 23, no. 3 (September 1988): 269–84. Also see J. M. Karpoff, "The Relation Between Price Changes and Trading Volume: A Survey," *Journal of Financial and Quantitative Analysis* 22 (March 1987): 109–26. See also G. E.,

Tauchen, and M. Pitts, "The Price Variability-Volume Relationship on Speculative Markets," *Econometrica* 51(March 1983): 485-505. More recently, see David Easley and Maureen O'Hara, "Adverse Selection and Large Trade Volume, The Implications for Market Efficiency," *Journal of Financial and Quantitative Analysis* 27 (1992): 185-208.

8   W. Brock, J. Lakonishok, and B. LeBaron, "Simple Technical Trading Rules and the Stochastic Properties of Stock Returns," *Journal of Finance* (December 1992): 1731-64.

9   Hendrik Bessembinder and Kalok Chan, "Market Efficiency and the Returns to Technical Analysis," *Financial Management* 27, no. 2 (summer 1998): 5-17.

10   The confidence index is a yield spread that credit analysts call a credit spread. The confidence index also turns up as a significant explanatory factor in the arbitrage pricing theory model used to manage money by Roll and Ross. See Nai-Fu Chen, Richard Roll, and Stephen A. Ross, "Economic Forces and the Stock Market: Testing the APT and Alternative Asset Pricing Theories," *Journal of Business* 59, no. 3 (July 1986): 383-403.

11   W. Brock, J. Lakonishok, and B. LeBaron, "Simple Technical Trading Rules and the Stochastic Properties of Stock Returns," *Journal of Finance* (December 1992): 1731-64.

12   Hendrik Bessembinder and Kalok Chan, "Market Efficiency and the Returns to Technical Analysis," *Financial Management* 27, no. 2 (summer 1998): 5-17.

13   Franklin Allen and Risto Karjalainen, "Using Genetic Algorithms to Find Technical Trading Rules," *Journal of Financial Economics* 51, no. 2 (February 1999): 245-71.

14   See Jennifer Conrad and Gautam Kaul, "An Anatomy of Trading Strategies," *Review of Financial Studies* 11, no. 3 (fall 1998): 489-519. Conrad and Kaul, for example, reports a momentum strategy that was profitable during the 1926-47 subperiod, but not during other periods.

15   For financial examples, see Mark W. Riepe and Daniel Kahneman, "Aspects of Investor Psychology," *Journal of Portfolio Management* 24, no. 4 (summer 1998): 52-65. For more psychological discussions, see Richard H. Thaler, *The Winner's Curse* (Princeton, NJ: Princeton University Press, 1992).

16   See Andrew W. Lo, Harry Mamaysky, and Jiang Wang, "Foundations of Technical Analysis: Computational Algorithms, Statistical Inference, and Empirical Implementation," *Journal of Finance* 55, no. 4 (August 2000): 1705-65. The paper shows that modern computational techniques can recognize some of the patterns discussed by technical analysts, but no profitable trading strategies are reported.

17   See Eugene F. Fama, "The Behavior of Stock Market Prices," *Journal of Business* (January 1965): 34-105. Also see Eugene F. Fama, "Efficient Capital Markets: A Review of Theory and Empirical Work," *Journal of Finance* (May 1970): 383-417. For a reassertion of the efficient markets theory that attributes its anomalies to chance results, see Eugene F. Fama, "Market Efficiency, Long-Term Returns, and Behavioral Finance," *Journal of Financial Economics* (September 1998): 283-306.

PART 7

DERIVATIVES and Alternative INVESTMENTS

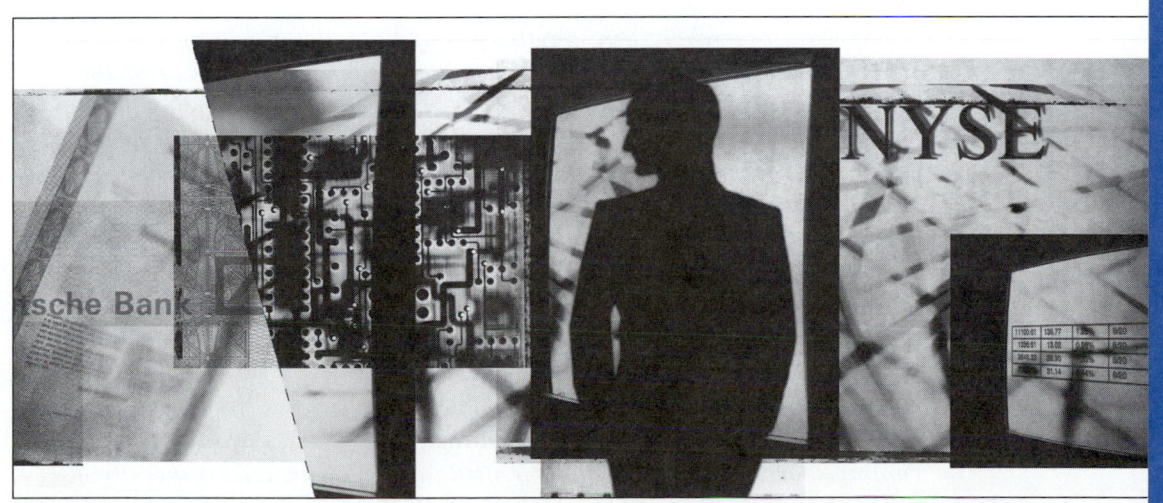

FUTURES

A futures contract specifies the commodity, the future date when the commodity will be delivered to the contract owner, the price that must be paid at delivery, the delivery quantity, and related details, as discussed in Chapter 9. Tables 9-1A, B, C, D, and E in Chapter 9 (pp. 231–233) list futures exchanges around the world and the contracts they trade.

*Futures contract traders can take either of two positions. The first possibility is a **long futures position** that entitles the buyer to take delivery of the commodity at the contracted date and price. Alternatively, the commodity trader can initiate a **short futures position,** which obligates the short seller to deliver the commodity at the contracted date and price. Many short sellers do not own the underlying commodity when they sell short; in these cases the short seller must do one of three things:*

- *Buy back the short position*
- *Buy a similar futures contract to deliver to fulfill the short position*
- *Buy the underlying commodity to deliver when the short position's delivery date arrives*

Speculators rarely buy anything and hold it for a long time. A trader who buys a speculative long position expects the price of the underlying commodity will rise so the position can be quickly sold for a gain. A trader with a speculative short position expects the price of the contracted commodity to fall before the delivery date. If the market price of the commodity declines, quickly covering (buying back) the short contract (delivery obligation) at the new lower price results in a gain for the short seller. If the price expectation of either a long or short speculator is wrong, the erroneous party suffers a loss. Figures 9-1A and B in Chapter 9 (page 234) contrast the gain-loss graphs for long and short positions.

Speculators are not the only people using futures. Investors take longer-term positions in a futures contract, or in a succession of futures contracts, or in a portfolio of diversified futures contracts. Furthermore, risk-averse hedgers and arbitrageurs use futures contracts to establish hedges.

MECHANICS OF COMMODITIES TRADING

Commission brokers, also called **floor brokers,** execute trades at commodity exchanges for people who are not members of the exchange. Nonmembers pay the brokers commissions for executing their trades.* Another type of exchange insiders, who trade only for their own accounts, are called **locals.** Trading between locals and commission brokers increases the market's liquidity.

Traditional commodity exchanges have *trading rooms,* each containing several *trading rings,* also known as *trading pits.* Each commodity listed at an exchange is traded in an assigned pit. Commission brokers and locals who want to buy or sell futures go to a trading room, step into a trading pit, and indicate by *open outcry* their intention to transact. Unlike the NYSE, most commodity futures exchanges do not use specialists or other market makers to consummate trades. When a buyer and seller settle on contract terms, they hand slips of paper to clerks that immediately post the price of the transaction to a large electronic *commodity board* on the trading room wall. This board automatically forwards all prices to brokerage houses, other exchanges, and financial news services around the world.

Orders to buy and sell come into a futures exchange in the form of messages to the commission brokers from their customers. The commission brokers walk to the a trading pit, execute the requested trade, and notify their customer of the results within minutes after the request was submitted.

The physical commodities that underlie the futures contracts are bought and sold in **cash markets, physicals markets,** or **actuals markets.** Grain elevators and stockyards where farmers sell grain and livestock are examples of physicals markets; the NYSE and foreign exchange dealers provide examples of the physicals markets for financial commodities. Commodity futures are not traded in the markets where the physical commodities are traded. (Can you imagine finding cattle walking around in an air-conditioned trading room at the Chicago Mercantile Exchange?) Futures contracts are financial instruments that are traded at **futures exchanges.** In some countries, a futures exchange is connected to a stock exchange, or an options exchange.

Futures contracts that are due for delivery within 1 month are not called futures contracts; they are called **spot contracts.** For example, a futures contract that has 12 months to its maturity (delivery) date when it was originated will be called a futures contract only during the first 11 months of its life. The contract will be called a spot contract during the last month of its life. Spot and futures contracts are traded together at futures exchanges.

In the Pits

Modern futures contracts are governed by a set of legal contract provisions, rules, regulations, and exchange bylaws. It would be unwieldy to put all this information onto individual fill-in-the-blanks futures contracts and carry these contracts onto the trading floor. It is more convenient to use **trading cards** to represent the futures contracts. A different color trading card is used for each commodity. When a buyer and seller consummate a transaction, they jot down the price, delivery month, and quantity on separate trading cards, and hand these cards to trading clerks.**

---

* Commission brokers execute orders for the public and for their own accounts as well—this is called **dual trading.** Dual trading can involve a conflict of interest. To avoid such conflicts of interest, most exchanges forbid commission brokers to execute an order for one of their clients that might change the price of a commodity in which they are holding a position for their own account.

** Fees from sales of price quotations comprise about one-third of the income of the typical securities or futures exchange. Transactions fees and membership dues are other major sources of income for an exchange.

TABLE 27-1	Prices for 5 Delivery Months—Commodity Board for Chicago Wheat (cents per bushel)				
	December	March	May	July	September
Lifetime High and Low	490-311	499-350	491-366	749-344	484-360
Previous Day's Close	370	$377\frac{1}{4}$	379	355	$363\frac{3}{4}$
Today's Open	$371\frac{1}{2}$	377	$378\frac{3}{4}$	353	362
Today's High	372	379	379	353	362
Today's Low	$368\frac{3}{4}$	$377\frac{1}{4}$	377	$350\frac{1}{2}$	361
Most Recent Price	369	379	378	350	$361\frac{1}{4}$

The Commodity Board

For any commodity, futures contracts exist that have different **delivery months.** In the United States the delivery months are selected by the commodity exchanges, subject to the approval of the Commodity Futures Trading Commission (CFTC). The prices of the futures contracts on a commodity are different for each different delivery month. Commodity futures prices are listed for each delivery month on a **commodity board** like the one shown in Table 27-1.

To maintain a feel for the direction of the market futures, traders watch the commodity board, they observe the action in the pits where they trade, and, when they are not trading, they read the news that might affect commodity prices as it comes into the futures exchange's wire service machines. Some traders use fundamental analysis, some use technical analysis, and some use both types of analyses.

Price Fluctuation Limits

Futures exchanges enforce minimum price fluctuations, called **ticks,** to prevent haggling over insignificantly small changes. A typical tick size equals a fraction of one penny per bushel of grain, per pound of potatoes, per ounce of gold, or whatever is relevant. All price changes must differ from the existing price by at least one tick.

Commodity exchanges enforce *maximum daily price fluctuations,* called **limit moves,** to prevent potentially destabilizing price changes. A *limit up (limit down)* move typically equals several cents above (below) that day's opening price. Commodity boards like the one in Table 27-1 report the day's price fluctuations. If a commodity's price experiences a limit move, trading in that commodity is halted and, for the remainder of that day, trading cannot occur at any price that differs from the opening price by more than the daily limit. Trading as usual is resumed the next day, but the price cannot change the next day by more than the daily limit or trading will be halted again.

EXAMPLE   CORNERING SILVER

The maximum price fluctuation limits seldom halt trading. Yet when the wealthy Hunt brothers tried to corner the silver market they drove the price from $9 per ounce in mid-1979 to $35 per ounce in 1980. When the Hunts were unable to continue buying all the silver in the world that became available, their attempt to corner the silver market failed. Silver prices collapsed to $9 per ounce in 1981. Several *limit up* moves in late 1979 and early 1980, and several *limit down* moves in late 1980 and early 1981, and locked traders into their positions.

When silver would make a limit move on the first trade of the day and also on the first trade of the next day, trading would be suspended for 2 consecutive days while the changing prices bankrupted some helpless traders. Adverse limit moves are futures traders' worst nightmare.

Some economists say daily price fluctuation limits are valuable tools that contribute to market stability. Other economists argue that these price fluctuation restrictions distort the natural forces of supply and demand and misallocate resources when they come into play. While most people agree that the maximum daily price fluctuation limits increase price stability, there is a perennial debate about whether the price change limits do more harm than good.[1]

Clearing House Guarantees

Every commodity exchange has a **clearing house.** Every futures contract is transferred through it. A clearing house inserts itself between the buyer and seller in every transaction and uses its wealth to guarantee the performance of every transaction. Clearing houses make themselves middlemen by paying the seller the contracted price for the agreed-upon quantity and simultaneously selling an identical futures contract to the buyer at the same price. The clearing house keeps track of the purchase and sale prices of each transaction and communicates with each buyer and seller separately.* Delivery responsibility is reassigned by the clearing house each time a speculator, investor, hedger, or arbitrageur resells a contract to the next buyer.

The clearing house keeps track of all transactions during each trading day so it can calculate the net position of each trader at the end of each day. It collects a tiny fee from each contract and accumulates these monies in a guarantee fund. The clearing house creates market liquidity by using the funds in its guarantee fund to assure the performance of every contract (even if one counterparty to the contract defaults).** The clearing house guarantee frees futures traders from checking each other's credit every time they trade and, thereby, makes futures contracts liquid. Clearing houses quickly execute all transactions and, later, sue the defaulting counterparties to collect damages.

The Mechanics of Trading Commodity Futures

Commodity traders usually start by opening a trading account with a **futures commission merchant,** also called a *commodities broker,* at a brokerage firm that deals in commodities. The brokerage firm may employ a member of a commodity exchange, or it may arrange with one or more floor traders who are members of a commodity exchange to execute trades for the brokerage.

Some full-service brokerage firms (like Merrill Lynch, Pierce, Fenner, and Smith, for instance) employ commodities brokers to assist the general public in trading futures. Firms

---

* The traders on the floor of a commodity exchange make it a point to know the names of the other sides of all of their trades in order to expeditiously clear up any mistakes—called **out trades**—before the clearing house steps in as middleman. By knowing the other party to an out trade, the trader can negotiate a settlement. Such direct negotiation avoids inconvenient arbitration of the out trade that can be costly.

** The members of a commodity exchange are required to buy stock in their clearing house and support its guarantee fund by keeping deposits there.

like Goldman Sachs assist wealthier futures traders.* In the commodity futures business there are also discount brokers; they do not provide free research and similar services. Because they do not, these brokers charge commissions that are a fraction of the full-service brokerage charge for the same transaction. Lind-Waldlock & Company and Jack Carl Futures are well-known discount commodities brokerages, but dozens of other discounters exist.

Contract Units. Futures contracts for each commodity are only available in standard quantities called **units**. Examples: on the Chicago Board of Trade one futures contract of soybean meal specifies 100 tons to be the unit for that contract, the T-bond contract calls for one Treasury bond that has a $100,000 face value and an 8% coupon rate to be the contract unit, and the wheat contract specifies 5,000 bushels as the contract unit. Table 9-1 in Chapter 9 (pp. 231–233) lists the unit specifications for futures contracts from exchanges around the world. The unit sizes are also defined above the price quotations for each futures contract in the newspaper excerpt at Figure 9-2 in Chapter 9 (p. 241).

To trade futures, the trader gives the broker an order to either short futures (sell futures) or buy futures (purchase a long position), states the number of units, specifies the asked for sales or the bid price for purchases, and indicates the desired delivery month. People who buy or sell futures must either pay cash in advance, or, pay the *initial margin requirement* of 3% to 10% when the order is given to the broker. Margined traders do not have to pay for the remainder of their transaction until the delivery occurs. Deliveries occur rarely; most futures traders liquidate their contracts before the delivery date.

Reversing Out of a Position. Before a delivery date arrives, over 90% of contracts are closed out (eliminated). A contract can be eliminated by **reversing out** of the position. Futures buyers reverse out of (close out, eliminate, liquidate) a long position by selling the futures before its delivery date. A short seller reverses out of a short position by buying a contract (taking a long position) like the one they sold short. These reversing trades leave the trader with a net position of zero at the clearing house.

Reversing a Purchase	Reversing a Short Sale
First, buy a long futures position	First, sell futures short
+ Before delivery, sell an identical long position	+ Before delivery, buy an identical contract
Equals: No remaining position	Equals: No remaining position

In addition to reversing out of a position, a trader can **roll out** a long or short position (extend its time horizon) by trading the position for an identical position that has a later delivery date.[2]

Delivery and Settlement. Futures exchanges typically give the short futures position alternatives to as to where to make delivery, when to make delivery, and what quality level to deliver. Agricultural commodities, for example, may typically be delivered at any one of a few different warehouses surrounding the futures exchange. If the short seller delivers to a warehouse that is far from the commodity futures exchange, a penalty, in the form of price discounts that are prespecified in the futures contract, is subtracted from the contracted deliv-

---

* A few large, prestigious commercial banks (such as Morgan Guaranty) and investment banks (like Morgan Stanley and Goldman Sachs) refuse to let any client open an account with less than a $1 million initial deposit. Investment banks that have retail brokerage operations operate much differently. Retail brokers like Merrill Lynch, Pierce, Fenner, and Smith will open new accounts as small as $3,000. As a result of these policies, Merrill has thousands of small clients while the more prestigious firms have fewer, but wealthier, clients.

ery price. The penalties for distant deliveries are enough to pay for shipping the commodity to the futures exchange.

Short sellers may select from several different days in the delivery month; these are specified in the futures contract. When the short seller is ready to deliver the commodity, she or he must send a **notice of intention to deliver** to the futures exchange specifying the delivery day and place.

Short sellers in agricultural commodities are typically required to deliver physical commodities that meet quality standards specified in the futures contract. Some financial futures can only be settled in cash. *Cash settlement* is required when it would be troublesome to deliver the commodity—for example, a basket of the 500 different stocks specified in the S&P500 index contract.

Open Interest

The **open interest** measures the number of futures contracts of a specific type that are outstanding at a given moment. Commodity futures traders watch the open interest each day because it measures the public's interest in a commodity. Several national newspapers publish the commodity futures prices and the open interest for many different futures.

On the day when a new futures contract starts trading, the open interest advances from zero to 1 when the first contract is sold. During the early months of a contract's trading life (1 year for most futures contracts), the volume of trading increases and many more contracts are opened than closed. The open interest rises to a peak about midway through the life of a futures contract. As the contract's delivery date nears, speculators who do not want to take delivery of the commodity reverse out of their positions. These reversals continue to shrink the open interest as the delivery date nears. The small number of contracts that remain open on the delivery date are extinguished by deliveries as the open interest drops back to zero. The typical pattern of a futures contract's lifetime open interest is shown in Figure 27-1.

Table 9-6 in Chapter 9 (p. 242) shows how to compute the *volume of contracts traded* and the open interest for one contract. The volume of contracts traded and the open interest in a futures contract both measure the public's interest in that contract; they are highly positively correlated with each other through the life of the contract. Figure 9-2 in Chapter 9 (p. 241) displays a newspaper excerpt showing price quotations; the daily volume and the open interest for each contract are shown beneath its quoted prices.

Electronic Markets

In 1990 a new German futures exchange, Deutsche Terminborse (DTB), sometimes called Eurex, began trading. By 1998 the DTB had stolen the world's highest volume futures contract, the Euro-BUND contract, from the mighty London International Financial Futures Exchange (LIFFE). Some observers attributed this remarkable intermarket victory to DTB's electronic trading platform, suggesting it was the beginning of the end for open outcry trading in the pits.

In 1997 the Sydney Futures Exchange—and in 1999 LIFFE—shut down open outcry trading and switched to electronic trading. The Chicago Board of Trade, CBOT, is the world's oldest and largest futures market. In 1998 the Cantor Financial Futures Exchange, CFFE, opened an electronic market attack on the CBOT by starting to trade two of the CBOT's contracts with the highest trading volume.

Hundreds of experienced workers, who know nothing about computers, are being automated out of their jobs by technological developments at commodity exchanges and brokerage houses around the world.

FIGURE 27-1 Graph of the Open Interest over the Life of a Hypothetical Futures Contract

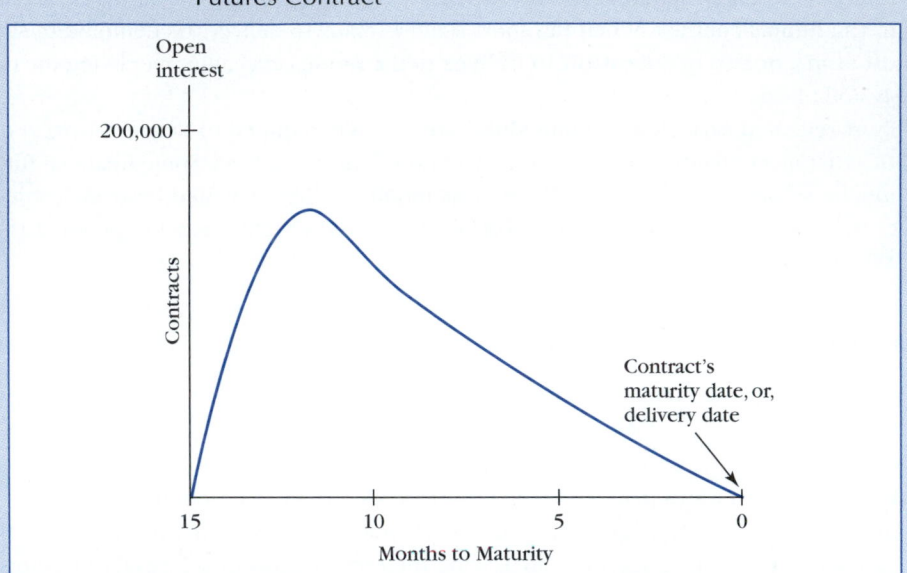

The open interest in a contract begins at zero. Open interest usually rises rapidly during the early months of the contract's life and gradually shrinks back to zero when the contract's delivery date arrives.

REGULATING FUTURES

The **Commodity Futures Trading Commission, CFTC, Act of 1974** established the CFTC and gave it authority to license futures exchanges and approve futures contracts. All futures contracts and changes to existing contracts in the United States must be approved by the CFTC. To gain approval the contract must fulfill a useful economic purpose. Usually, this means it must serve the needs of hedgers and speculators alike.

The CFTC looks after the public interest. The CFTC promotes the disclosure of essential information by requiring that current prices be continuously made available to the public. The CFTC also requires futures traders to disclose the size of their positions when they exceed certain levels; this information warns others of forces that might destabilize prices. The CFTC also licenses dealers who offer services to the public. Dealers are investigated and they must meet minimum capital requirements. The CFTC deals with complaints brought by the public and ensures that appropriate disciplinary action is taken. It has the authority to force exchanges to take disciplinary action against members who are in violation of exchange rules. The CFTC's Web site is: www.cftc.gov

The National Futures Association. The National Futures Association (NFA) was formed in the United States in 1982. The NFA is a self-regulating trade group that was created to get some of the regulatory responsibilities of the CFTC shifted to the futures industry itself. Its objective is to prevent fraud and ensure that futures markets operate in the best interests of the general public. The NFA requires its members to pass an exam. It is authorized to monitor trading and take disciplinary action and has set up an efficient system for arbitrating disputes between individuals and its members. The NFA's Web site is: www.nfa.futures.org

Jurisdictional Turf Battles. From time to time governmental bodies, such as the Securities and Exchange Commission (SEC), the Federal Reserve Board, and the U.S. Treasury Department, have asserted their jurisdictional right over some aspect of futures trading. These federal bodies are concerned about the effects of futures trading on the spot markets for securities such as stocks, Treasury bills, and Treasury bonds. The SEC currently has veto power over new stock or bond index futures contracts. However, the basic responsibility for all futures and options on futures rests with the CFTC.

PRICES AND PRICING RELATIONSHIPS

A market for a storable commodity is said to be *normal* when that commodity's futures price exceeds its spot price by an amount that is sufficient to cover the **carrying charges** incurred to store the commodity for future delivery. This normal carrying charge relationship induces profit-seeking speculators to buy commodities when their prices are low (typically, at a crop's harvest) and store the goods for later sales when prices are higher. Speculators' purchases when prices are low and sales when prices are high helps allocate both commodity prices and consumption smoothly over time.

The difference between the futures and spot prices of a commodity at a given moment is called the **basis.**

$$\text{Basis}_t = \text{futures price}_t - \text{spot price}_t \tag{27-1}$$

If futures exceed spot prices, the difference is called a *premium*. If the spot price exceeds the futures price, the future is said to be at a *discount* to the spot price.*

When the futures price (*FP*) is less than the spot price (*SP*), an **inverted market** occurs, $FP < SP$. A grain market may get inverted, for example, when the current supply of grain is very low, keeping spot prices high, but the growing crop is expected to yield such a large harvest that grain futures prices are low because the market is anticipating a bumper crop.**[3]

Price Convergence

As mentioned in Chapter 9, the **Convergence Principle** states that, as a futures contract approaches its expiration date, the futures price draws closer and finally converges with the commodity's spot price. Convergence of futures and spot prices on the delivery date is one of the few things we can predict with certainty as the fluctuating prices move closer together. To see why convergence must occur, reconsider **arbitrage.**

To see how the appropriate arbitrage works, we ignore carrying costs and transactions costs for simplicity. We will consider the two arbitrage processes that are possible when: (1) futures prices exceed spot prices, and (2) spot prices exceed futures prices.

---

* Some authors define the basis as shown in Eqn. 27-1a. As a result, the basis is negative in normal market conditions and has an absolute value equal to the carrying costs.

$$\text{Basis} = \text{spot price} - \text{futures price} \tag{27-1a}$$

** Commodities like fresh eggs, fresh potatoes, live cattle, and, some people would say, Treasury Bills, are unstorable. The theory of carrying costs is irrelevant for these *nonstorable* commodities and, as a result, spot prices often exceed futures prices. For *storable* commodities, just before harvest time when current supplies are short but a bumper crop is forthcoming, inverted markets sometimes occur.

(Process 1) If futures prices exceed spot prices (a normal market). When the futures price is above the spot price, traders can earn arbitrage profits as follows:

- Step 1. Sell a futures contract short.
- Step 2. Buy the physical commodity underlying the futures contract.
- Step 3. Deliver the underlying physical commodity to fulfill the maturing short futures contract.

These three steps generate arbitrage profit equal to the excess of the futures price over the spot price. As traders continue to execute the three-step arbitrage opportunity, profit from the short position are caused by continued short selling that drives the futures price downward.

(Process 2) If spot prices exceed futures prices (an inverted market). If the futures price is below the spot price, anyone interested in acquiring the underlying commodity will find it profitable to buy a long futures position and wait for delivery. As these futures buyers wait for delivery, similar purchases by other profit-seekers will make the long position profitable because the purchases will bid up the futures price.

Figure 27-2 illustrates convergence of futures and spot prices. The futures price is above the spot price just prior to the delivery month (the normal market condition) in Figure 27-2A. The futures price is below the spot price shortly before the delivery month (an inverted market) in Figure 27-2B.*

The futures price converges with the spot and cash prices because a futures contract turns into a spot contract in the delivery month. And, as the delivery date nears, the spot contract also provides delivery of the underlying physical commodity. On the last permissible delivery date (when the futures contract ceases to exist), the futures price converges with the spot price and the basis shrinks to zero, as illustrated in Figure 27-3.

FIGURE 27-2   Futures Price and Spot Price Converge as Delivery Month Nears: (A) In a Normal Market, and (B) In an Inverted Market

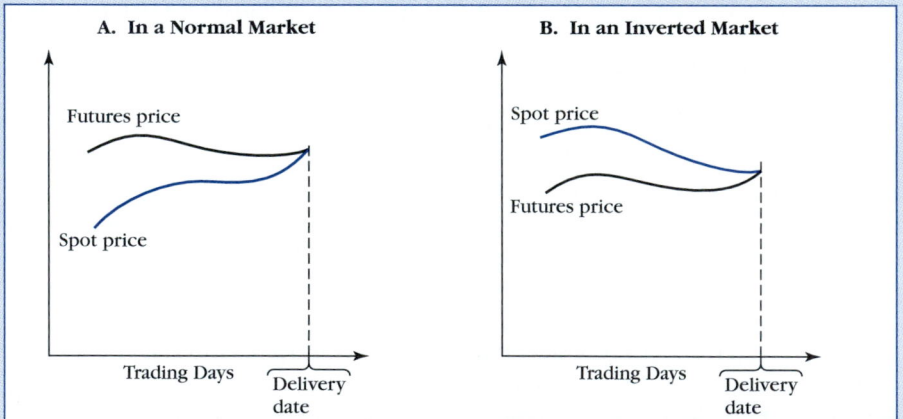

Under normal market conditions and, also, when inverted market conditions occur, the spot and futures prices converge on the contract's maturity (delivery) date.

---

* The futures price of platinum on the New York Mercantile Exchange is an increasing function of time to maturity. In contrast, the futures price of copper on the New York Commodity Exchange is a decreasing function of time to maturity. For hogs, the pattern is mixed. Sometimes the futures price for hogs is an increasing, and sometimes it is a decreasing, function of time to maturity. In other words, normal backwardation and forwardation (contango) are both observable phenomena.

FIGURE 27-3 The Prices of Spot and Futures Covary Together and Converge at the Contract's Maturity, While the Prices of Cash and Futures Covary Together but Do Not Quite Converge for Storable Physical Commodities

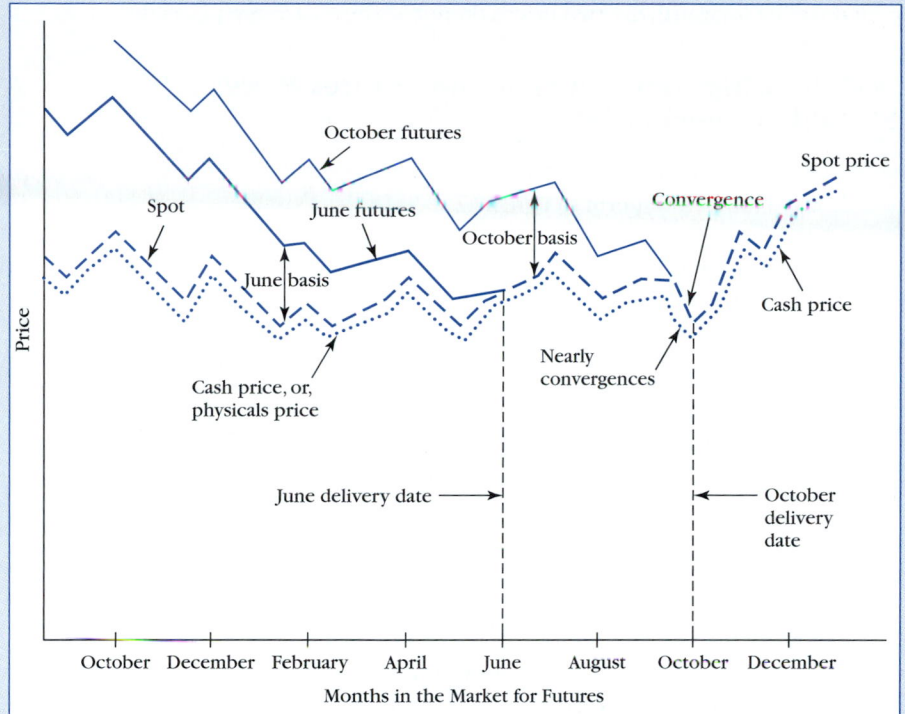

The spot price and futures price of a contract are highly positively correlated through time. The spot and futures prices converge at the contract's maturity (delivery) date. For storable physical commodities, the cash market (physicals) price and futures price are highly positively correlated as they fluctuate together and converge at the contract's maturity, but sometimes they do not converge completely.

Actually, futures prices do not always converge with the cash (physicals) price because of problems such as:

Convergence Problem 1: Consider three facts. First, Farmer Smith's grain harvest is sold at the cash (physicals) market in Tulsa, Oklahoma. Second, the Kansas City Board of Trade requires physical delivery on its futures contracts be made in Kansas City. Third, transportation costs between Tulsa and Kansas City of one cent per bushel complicate the price determination process for Farmer Smith's grain. As a result of facts like these, the convergence of futures and spot prices may not be to the penny for commodities involving shipping costs.

Convergence Problem 2: The agricultural commodities that are available for immediate delivery may have a quality level different from that of commodities that are acceptable to fulfill a futures contract's delivery requirements. Small discrepancies between what the futures buyer needs and what the futures exchange accepts for delivery can complicate determination of the settlement price.

Convergence Problem 3: Carrying costs may complicate price determination.* After a contract matures and some deliveries are made, the futures price and the cash price are still affected by carrying costs because many futures traders roll their hedges forward rather than make or take delivery. The cash and the future prices move closer together on a futures contract's delivery date but, because delivery on some contracts is postponed (rolled forward), the two prices do not always converge perfectly.

The Relationship Between Spot and Futures Prices for Storable Commodities

Commodities can be stored for future delivery. Under normal conditions the market prices for storable commodities conform to Eqn. 27-2.

$$\begin{pmatrix} \text{Futures price} \\ \text{at time } t, FP_t \end{pmatrix} \leq \begin{pmatrix} \text{Spot price at} \\ \text{time } t, SP_t \end{pmatrix} + \begin{pmatrix} \text{Carrying} \\ \text{cost, } CC \end{pmatrix} \qquad (27\text{-}2)$$

The carrying cost equals about 3 cents per bushel per month for grain commodities and the total carrying cost is computed as

$$\begin{pmatrix} \text{Carrying} \\ \text{cost, CC} \end{pmatrix} = \left[\begin{pmatrix} \text{Monthly} \\ \text{carrying} \\ \text{cost} \end{pmatrix} \times \begin{pmatrix} \text{Number of months} \\ \text{the inventory} \\ \text{is carried} \end{pmatrix} \right].$$

The only carrying cost (CC) for most financial commodities is the interest expense to finance the securities inventory.

The inequality in Eqn. 27-2 means futures prices cannot rise above the spot price plus the carrying cost. This inequality results from the fact that, simply by paying the carrying cost, current inventories can be carried into future months.

Inequality (Eqn. 27-2) can be extended to explain the difference between the prices of two futures contracts on the same storable commodity that have different delivery dates. Inequality (Eqn. 27-3) can be used to estimate the *price spread* between the near-futures and the distant-futures contracts on the same underlying commodity.

$$\begin{pmatrix} \text{Price of} \\ \text{the distant} \\ \text{future, } FP_2 \end{pmatrix} \leq \begin{pmatrix} \text{Price of} \\ \text{the near} \\ \text{future, } FP_1 \end{pmatrix} + \left[\begin{pmatrix} \text{Carrying cost} \\ \text{per item per} \\ \text{month, } CC \end{pmatrix} \times \begin{pmatrix} \text{Number of months difference} \\ \text{between the expiration dates} \\ \text{of the two contracts, } t_1 - t_2 \end{pmatrix} \right] \qquad (27\text{-}3)$$

The time subscript t_2 represents the *distant-future* and the subscript t_1 represents the *near-future*. The quantity $(t_2 - t_1)$ is the time difference between the expiration dates of the two futures contracts in the inequality: $FP_2 \leq FP_1 + (CC)(t_2 - t_1)$

If inequality (Eqn. 27-3) became reversed, arbitrageurs would quickly restore it by simultaneously performing the following transactions:

- Step 1. Buy a long position in the near-futures contract that provides for delivery in period t_1.

- Step 2. Take a short position in the distant-future contract for delivery much later, at time t_2;

---

* The futures prices for financial futures can be identical to cash prices because (1) transportation costs are essentially zero for financial instruments, and (2) there are no quality differences between the financial instruments delivered against futures contracts and those traded in the cash markets. However, carrying costs (fluctuating interest expenses) for financial futures that are rolled forward can complicate price determination to deter perfect price convergence.

- Step 3. Take delivery at time t_1 at price FP_1 and store the commodity for CC cents per month.
- Step 4. At time t_2 deliver the stored commodity at a price of FP_2 to reap a riskless profit.
- Step 5. Repeat this transaction as many times as you can profit from it. The riskless profit will exist until inequality (Eqn. 27-3) is restored.

This five-step arbitrage process keeps Eqn. 27-3 from being violated.*

The One-Period Returns from Futures

The one-period rate of return from purchasing a futures contract in period t and selling it in period $t + 1$ is

$$r_t = \frac{FP_{t+1} - FP_t}{FP_t} = \text{percentage price change} \tag{27-4}$$

The price of the futures contract in period t is FP_t. Eqn. 27-4 ignores commissions, taxes, and other transactions costs for simplicity. These transactions costs should be deducted from the numerator to compute the holding period return *net* of transactions costs.[4]

Margin Requirements

Most futures traders do not invest the full amount represented in the denominator of Eqn. 27-4; they only make small down payments called the **initial margin.**** Minimum margin requirements are set by the commodity exchanges to accomplish three objectives. First, margin requirements are performance bonds that help maintain the financial integrity of futures contracts. Second, margin deposits are down payments (equity investments) for traders who want to borrow money to take larger (leveraged) positions. Third, minimum margin requirements control the pyramiding of debt (excessive borrowing) that could contribute to a market crash.

Initial minimum margin requirements of 3% to 10% for futures are common.[†] Two types of adverse price fluctuations are possible with futures: (1) the underlying commodity's price can fall with a margined long futures position, or (2) the underlying commodity's price can rise with a margined short futures position. Either type of adverse price movement can cause the trader to receive a **margin call** from the broker. A margin call occurs when the broker demands that the trader pay additional margin money within a day or two. The additional margin money that is required is called *maintenance margin* money.

Maintenance margin payments restore the trader's margin (equity) when adverse price fluctuations diminish it below the minimum margin requirement. For example, if a speculator buys a futures contract long position with 10% initial margin and then the commodity's price falls 5%, half the speculator's initial margin (equity in the position) is wiped out. In this case the broker might ask the futures trader to meet the maintenance margin requirement. If the trader does not pay the **variation margin** (maintenance margin) quickly, the broker will

---

*   Stock index arbitrage with futures contracts is discussed on pp. 820–824 of this chapter. Stock index arbitrage provides another application of this arbitrage process.

** Commodity brokerages define a client's *margin* to be equal to the equity value in the client's account. The equity equals the sum of the following amounts: (1) cash (2) cashlike securities (namely, U.S. Treasury bills that are left on deposit at the broker's office) and (3) the net total of the unrealized gains on open positions less the unrealized losses (that is, net "paper profits" that may be positive or negative).

†   Common stock initial margin minimum requirements, set by the Federal Reserve Board, are currently 50%— they have varied from 50 to 75%. It is inappropriate to compare the sizes of stock market margins and commodity margins because, unlike commodity traders, stock traders do not usually have to mark to the market daily.

liquidate the futures contract being held as collateral for the loan. To reduce the losses and ill-feelings that can result from a margin call, the clearing house requires its broker-members to make all of their accounts **mark to the market** each trading day. A futures account is marked to the market when it meets the minimum maintenance margin (variation margin) requirement associated with the current market price.*[5]

Marking to the Market Daily with Cash and/or T-Bills

The daily mark-to-the-market guidelines require futures traders to be ready to make cash contributions to their accounts on the days when adverse price fluctuations diminish their margin below the minimum requirement. The same futures traders can make cash withdrawals from their accounts on days when their holdings benefit from advantageous price moves. Some futures traders prefer to leave excess margin in their accounts in the form of cash or interest-bearing Treasury bills, rather than deal with daily cash inflows and outflows as the market value of their account fluctuates.

Ed Elton, Martin Gruber, and Joel Rentzler estimated the cost of using interest-bearing T-bills to mark to the market.[6] Because the cost is small, they suggested that leaving excess margin in an account is worthwhile. Maintaining excess margin reduces margin calls and makes it easier to manage cash inflows and outflows that result from fluctuating market prices.

HEDGING

Losses from an adverse price move may be reduced, and perhaps even eliminated, by hedging. Unfortunately, hedging also reduces the gains from favorable price moves. **Hedging** may be defined as arranging for a short position to offset a similar long position, or as arranging for a long position to offset a similar short position. The closer the dollar values of the long and short positions, the closer together the maturity dates of the long and short positions, and the higher the correlation between the long and short positions, then the more perfect will be the resulting hedge. Figures 3-2 and 3-5 in Chapter 3 (pp. 49, 56) analyzes hedges and Tables 9-4 and 9-5 in Chapter 9 (pp. 239, 240) review a selling hedge with futures. We now reconsider the selling hedge and the perfect hedge and contrast them with the buying hedge.

The Perfect Hedge

Hedges are made out of long and short positions (shown in Figure 9-1 in Chapter 9, p. 234). Someone who owns identical long and short (perfectly offsetting) positions on the same underlying commodity or other asset has a **perfect hedge**. Price fluctuations cannot affect the market value of a perfectly hedged position. The owner of a perfectly hedged futures position is contractually bound to earn zero gains and losses of zero. Risk-averters use perfect hedges to protect them during intimidating periods when volatility is high.

Few futures hedges are actually perfect. "Basis risks" that are investigated later in this chapter introduce elements of risk into every hedge involving futures.

Buying Hedges

A *buying hedge* is sometimes called a *long hedge* because the hedger buys a long position in the futures contract. A buying hedge is a purchase of futures to protect the buyer from a loss

---

*   Maintenance margins are approximately 75% of the initial margins at most commodity brokerage firms, but this relationship varies from broker to broker. However, any time the customer's equity falls below the required maintenance margin, the customer receives a margin call.

caused by a price rise. Breakfast cereal manufacturers that buy grains, shoe manufacturers that buy hides, jewelry manufacturers that buy silver and gold, and other commodity users can use buying hedges to protect themselves from the risk of a price increase in their raw material.[7] When the price of a commodity they want to purchase in the future is low, they buy a long position in the futures contract at that low price. The buyer of the futures contract holds the contract until it matures because it guarantees future delivery of the needed goods at a low price on a delivery date they selected when they purchased the futures contract. The short position that offsets the long futures contracts are the manufacturer's commitments to deliver (short positions in) breakfast cereal, shoes, jewelry, or other finished goods in the future.

Selling Hedge

A *selling hedge* is sometimes called a *short hedge* because it uses a short position in a futures contract to avoid a loss from a price decline on a commodity that is held in inventory. For example, *mortgage banking* firms originate mortgages (make home loans) and carry (temporarily invest in an inventory of) mortgages until they can be resold to a long-term mortgage investor like Fannie Mae (FNMA) or Ginnie Mae (GNMA). Essentially, mortgage bankers own long positions in physical mortgages that are subject to interest-rate risk.

Suppose a mortgage banker believes the Federal Reserve is going to raise interest rates. The present value of a mortgage (collateralized bond) moves inversely with the market interest rate. To protect the mortgage banking firm from losses if the market prices of the mortgage falls, the mortgage banker can take a short position in futures on mortgages to hedge (offset any change in) the value of its inventory of mortgages. Selling mortgage or long-term Treasury bond futures short hedges the mortgage banker's selling risks. The speculator who buys the mortgage future that the mortgage banker sold short assumes the risks of a drop in mortgage prices.[8]

Basis Risks

A hedge can reduce a commodity owner's losses from adverse price changes, but there are other risks inherent in every hedge. A **basis risk** arises when the offsetting long and short positions used to construct a hedge do not converge to the same market value as their delivery dates approach. Consider four types of basis risks:

1. **Quantity risk.** At the Kansas City Board of Trade (KCBT) a unit of wheat is 5,000 bushels. If a pasta factory wants to hedge 8,000 bushels of wheat, the unit specified in the KCBT wheat contract does not align with that inventory. Because futures are standardized contracts that cannot be tailored, the unhedged portion of the wheat inventory will remain at risk (unhedged, exposed).

2. **Quality risk.** Pasta is made from durum wheat. A pasta manufacturer cannot make spaghetti from the hard red spring wheat listed at some exchanges. Alternatively, an undesirable grade of the commodity may be the *cheapest to deliver.* This basis (quality) risk can be costly to the futures buyer who receives an unsatisfactory grade of the commodity on the contract's delivery date.

3. **Location risk.** The KCBT wheat futures prices are based on wheat delivered in Kansas City. Futures buyers incur shipping costs and/or delays if they are given delivery at an inconvenient location.

4. **Expiration date risk.** The delivery months for KCBT wheat futures are March, May, July, September, and December. Wheat futures providing for delivery in Kansas City in other months do not exist. As a result, a hedger might be forced to utilize a futures contract that provide an inconvenient delivery month. Such a contract could result in additional storage expenses or other costs.

Such basis risks prevent most hedges from being perfect hedges. Hedging can reduce the price change risks. But the remaining basis risks can be so substantial that some speculators earn their livings by *trading on the basis.* This occurs when a futures trader seeks to profit by trading on changes in pricing spreads they anticipate. Basis traders enter into imperfect hedges and speculate on the changes in the *differences* between the prices of their long and short positions, rather than directly on the individual prices.[9]

Spreading with Futures

Spreads are trading strategies that employ a combination of long and short futures positions that partially offset each other. For a **two-legged spread,** the long futures position is one leg of the spread and the short futures position forms the other. Three-legged spreads clearly are more complex.

Calendar Spreads. Suppose a trader uses Eqn. 27-3 to determine that the amount by which the far-term futures price exceeds the nearer-term futures price exceeds (the basis is larger than) the carrying cost between two contracts that are identical in every way except their delivery dates. This trader may seek to profit from these misaligned prices by entering into a **calendar spread.** The trader will *leg into the spread* by purchasing the near-futures contract for one leg of the spread and selling short the distant-futures contract for the other leg. If the pricing spread between these two futures (the basis) narrows, the calendar spread will be profitable.

Intercommodity-Spread. The T-bill–Eurodollar spread, called a *TED-spread,* is an **intercommodity spread.** The TED-spread uses offsetting positions in Treasury bill futures and Eurodollar futures to gain from interest rate differentials between the two contracts that appear to be temporarily out of line.

Soybean Crush Spread. There is a mathematical relationship between how much soybean meal and how much soybean oil can be produced when soybeans are crushed. This mathematical formula can be rearranged to yield a pricing relationship between soybean meal, soybean oil, and soybeans. Soybean traders employ an intercommodity spread called the *crush spread* to speculate on misaligned prices between soybeans and the soybean derivatives. Crush spreads can be two-legged or three-legged. For example, there are three legs to a crush spread if the trader buys long futures positions in both the meal and the oil and shorts bean futures. If the soybeans were priced too high compared to the prices of the meal and the oil, this three-legged spread would yield profits when the three futures prices move into alignment.

The Economic Effects of Hedging and Spreading

The hedges and spreads outlined above affect market prices. Spreading tends to (1) align the forward interest rates implicit in various interest rate futures contracts with the market interest rates from the yield curve, (2) maintain the basis between spot and futures so it usually equals the carrying cost, and (3) support the law of one price.

The risk-reducing benefits of hedging and spreading are reflected in the way margin requirements are formulated. Commodity brokerages require margins on hedged positions and spreads that are substantially below the margins required for unhedged positions.

THEORIES ABOUT SPOT AND FUTURES PRICE CONVERGE

Financial economists do not agree about how large the basis for a given futures contract should be. Even under normal market conditions, three competing theories exist: normal backwardation, contango (or forwardation), and unbiased expectations.

Normal Backwardation. John Maynard Keynes and John R. Hicks argued that the futures prices (*FP*) for storable commodities should normally be slightly less than the expected spot prices, $E(SP)$, by the amount of a tiny insurance premium they called **normal backwardation.**

$$\begin{pmatrix} \text{Current} \\ \text{futures} \\ \text{price, } FP_t \end{pmatrix} = \begin{pmatrix} \text{Expected} \\ \text{future spot} \\ \text{price, } E(SP)_t \end{pmatrix} - \begin{pmatrix} \text{A tiny positive} \\ \text{insurance} \\ \text{premium} \end{pmatrix} \qquad (27\text{-}5)$$

Normal backwardation converges to zero at the contract's delivery date. Since the expected spot price can never actually be observed and measured, Eqn. 27-5 cannot be tested empirically in a straightforward manner.[10]

Contango. C. O. Hardy argued that the futures price should normally be at a slight premium—instead of a discount—above the expected future spot price.[11] Hardy hypothesized speculators are like gamblers who are willing to pay to gamble. As a result, Hardy expected spot prices to be below what they actually turn out to be in the future. Hardy's hypothesis is summarized by Eqn.(27-6).

$$\begin{pmatrix} \text{Current} \\ \text{futures} \\ \text{price, } FP_t \end{pmatrix} = \begin{pmatrix} \text{Expected} \\ \text{future spot} \\ \text{price, } E(SP)_t \end{pmatrix} + \begin{pmatrix} \text{A tiny positive} \\ \text{insurance} \\ \text{premium} \end{pmatrix} \qquad (27\text{-}6)$$

Hardy's gambling fee is called **contango** or **forwardation**; it converges to zero as the contract nears expiration (its delivery date).

Unbiased Expectations. Whether futures prices normally lie a little above or a little below their expected spot price has been debated for decades. Michael L. Hartzmark, Avraham Kamara, and others published evidence suggesting spot prices should equal futures prices.[12] Eqn. 27-7 formalizes this **unbiased expectations hypothesis**:

$$FP_t = E(SP_t) \qquad (27\text{-}7)$$

Eqn. 27-7 says futures prices are unbiased estimates of the expected future spot prices. Abstracting from the continuous fluctuations that characterize actual market prices, Figure 27-4 illustrates the differences between the Keynes-Hicks theory of normal backwardation, Hardy's theory about people who are willing to pay to gamble, and the unbiased expectations hypothesis.

A number of researchers have conducted empirical tests of forwardation, backwardation, and the unbiased expectations hypothesis. Darrell Duffie reviewed several of these studies.[13] In addition, Fama and French published empirical studies documenting time varying risk premiums (backwardation, forwardation, or other explanatory variables).[14]

UNIVERSAL PRICING PRINCIPLE FOR FORWARDS AND FUTURES

Finance textbooks define the **net present value** (NPV) of an asset to be the present value (PV) of all the asset's future cash flows minus the asset's purchase price.

$$\begin{pmatrix} \text{Net present} \\ \text{value, } NPV \end{pmatrix} = \begin{pmatrix} \text{Present} \\ \text{value, } PV \end{pmatrix} - \begin{pmatrix} \text{Purchase} \\ \text{price} \end{pmatrix} \qquad (27\text{-}8)$$

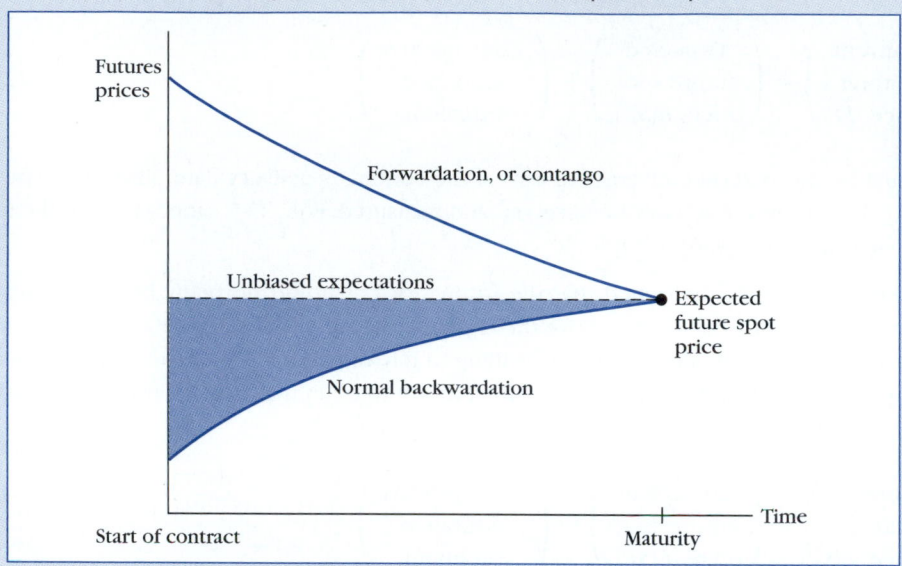

FIGURE 27-4   Three Competing Hypotheses About the Way Futures Prices Converge on the (Unobservable) Expected Spot Price

Keynes and Hicks argued that the current futures prices (*FP*) for storable commodities should normally be slightly less than the expected spot prices, $E(SP)$, by the amount of a tiny negative premium they called normal backwardation.

$$\begin{pmatrix} \text{Current} \\ \text{futures} \\ \text{price, } FP_t \end{pmatrix} = \begin{pmatrix} \text{Expected} \\ \text{future spot} \\ \text{price, } E(SP_t) \end{pmatrix} + \begin{pmatrix} \text{A tiny positive,} \\ \text{zero, or negative} \\ \text{price premium} \end{pmatrix}$$

Hardy argued that the current futures price should normally be slightly (a tiny positive premium) above the expected future spot price. The unbiased expectations hypothesis argues the price premium should be zero, $FP_t = E(SP_t)$.

All forward or futures contracts have NPVs of zero at the time they are purchased.*[15] This section uses these facts to formulate a *universal pricing principle* for forwards or futures.

The PV of Forwards and Futures

After a contract is purchased, the purchase price is a fixed historical value. But after the contract is purchased, the market price of the underlying commodity fluctuates. The contract may take on positive or negative NPVs as the contract's market price and PV fluctuate together after the contract's purchase date.

Since a contract's initial NPV is zero, we can set NPV = 0 and then solve Eqn. 27-8 for the appropriate purchase price of the forward or futures contract.

PV = Purchase price   (27-9)

---

* This book often ignores the cash flows involved when a futures contract is marked to market. When the risk-free interest rate is constant and identical for all maturities (that is, when the yield curve is flat and does not fluctuate), forward prices and futures prices are identical. When the yield curve is not flat and it does fluctuate the difference between forward prices and futures prices are usually small enough to ignore.

We can find the present value (PV) for the futures contract in Eqn. 27-9 by separating the PV into two components: (1) the cash flow, and (2) the discount factor.

$$PV = \frac{\text{Cash flow}}{(1 + \text{Discount Rate})^{\text{YEARS}}}$$

$$= (\text{Cash flow}) \times (\text{Discount factor})$$

If the discount rate is 6.0% and the contract has 3 months (one quarter of a year) until delivery, the *discount factor* is 0.986.

$$\binom{\text{Discount}}{\text{factor}} = \frac{1}{(1 + \text{Discount rate})^{\text{YEARS}}} = \frac{1}{(1 + 6\%)^{0.25}} = \frac{1}{1.0147} = 0.986$$

The discount rate includes the interest expense incurred to finance the inventory, warehousing costs, plus any other carrying costs.

Financial Futures

Pricing Financial Futures. Unlike agricultural commodities, financial futures do not incur physical storage costs like warehousing or insecticide costs. The discount rate for a financial futures contract is the interest rate for a loan to finance the inventory underlying the contract. Because the clearing house's guarantee removes default risk from futures contracts, the risk-free rate (RFR) is the appropriate discount rate for a financial futures contract. The purchase price for a financial future can be computed as:

$$NPV = PV - \text{Purchase price} \qquad \textbf{by definition, Eqn. 27-8}$$

$$\text{Purchase price} = PV \qquad \textbf{since initially NPV = 0, Eqn. 27-9}$$

$$\binom{\text{Purchase}}{\text{price}} = (PV) = \binom{\text{Future}}{\text{cash flow}} \Big/ (1 + RFR)^{\text{YEARS}} \qquad \textbf{by definition of PV}$$

Although the *universal pricing principle* for futures contracts above is applicable to both agricultural and financial futures, the remainder of this chapter focuses on financial futures because of their growing popularity.

The Popularity of Financial Futures. In 1982 the 134-year-old Chicago Board of Trade (CBOT) initiated trading in U.S. Treasury bond futures. As Figure 27-5 shows, the T-bond contract rapidly became one of the CBOT's most successful contracts. Futures exchanges around the world have had similar experiences when they listed financial futures.

PRICING FUTURES CONTRACTS ON U.S. TREASURY BILLS

Futures contracts on discount bonds that pay no income are the simplest kind of financial futures to price. The International Monetary Market (a subsidiary of the Chicago Mercantile Exchange) lists futures contracts on U.S. Treasury bills (introduced in Chapter 5, pp. 94–95) that have $1 million denomination bonds as their unit, and the Chicago Board of Trade lists futures contracts on 30-day Fed funds that have units of $5 million. The pricing model developed in the next section for a forward contract on a T-bill can also be used for futures on any other original issue discount (OID) bond or non-dividend-paying stock.

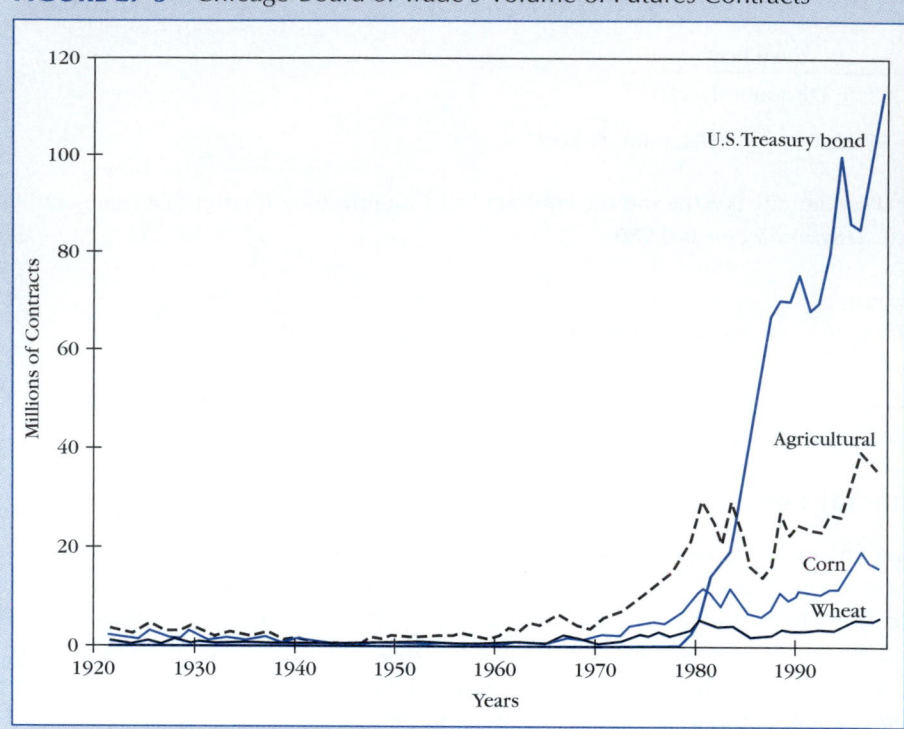

FIGURE 27-5 Chicago Board of Trade's Volume of Futures Contracts

The popularity of financial futures contracts that only began to be traded a few decades ago has soared above the popularity of agricultural futures contracts that have been traded for many decades.

We use what is referred to as *quasi-arbitrage* to price a futures contract on a U.S. Treasury bill. Quasi-arbitrage differs from pure arbitrage because quasi-arbitrage assumes some cash is invested in the security being priced.

In the example that follows, a quasi-arbitrage process is used to create a synthetic financial instrument that replicates the cash flows from an actual T-bill. The law of one price is invoked to permit us to equate the cost of the synthetic T-bill to the cost of the actual T-bill. Then, our equal-cost equation is solved to derive a pricing formula for a forward contract that is embedded in the synthetic T-bill position. Finally, the futures contract is priced to be the same as the forward contract used in the quasi-arbitrage.

A T-bill Example

Suppose an investor wants to buy a T-bill with a face value of $1 million that matures in 180 days. Consider two different purchase plans that could be used to buy two different $1 million T-bills that mature on the same date. Both purchase plans fulfill the investor's desire:

(A) Direct purchase of a T-bill. At $t = 0$ pay a cost of PV dollars to purchase one U.S. Treasury bill with a face value of $1 million that matures at $t = 180$ days and hold that T-bill till it matures.

(B) Indirect purchase of a different T-bill. Simultaneously buy two items. (1) At $t = 0$ pay $F90B/(1 + RFR)$ dollars for an actual T-bill that pays a maturity value of $F90B$ dollars at $t = 90$ and yields an interest rate of RFR. (2) Simultaneously at time $t = 0$ purchase a forward contract that will deliver at time $t = 90$ a second (consecutive) 90-day T-bill that pays a $1 million face value when it matures at $t = 180$. Let $F90B$ dollars represent the delivery price paid at for this second consecutive 90-day T-bill. And also let $F90B/(1+RFR)$ dollars be the present value at $t = 0$ of this forward contract to pay $F90B$ dollars at delivery ($t = 90$) of the second consecutive T-bill.

Table 27-2 contrasts the cash flows from the two purchase plans. The indirect purchase plan is a complicated trading mechanism that was constructed to allow us to derive an implicit pricing formula. Both cash flow arrangements provide the desired $1 million T-bill at the end of 180 days. Since the purchase plans have identical net cash flows, the **law of one price** tells us they should have the same purchase price. Therefore, we equate the purchase prices of the two different purchase plans in Eqn. 27-10:

$$\left(\begin{array}{l}\text{Cost of direct}\\\text{purchase plan}\end{array}\right) = PV = F90B/(1 + RFR) = \left(\begin{array}{l}\text{Cost of indirect}\\\text{purchase plan}\end{array}\right) \qquad \textbf{(27-10)}$$

The two different purchase plans have equal costs (in Eqn. 27-10), both have identical net cash flows (in Table 27-2), and both result in a $1 million T-bill in the investor's hands at $t = 180$. These three things mean the correct forward pricing formula is implicit in Table 27-2 and Eqn. 27-10. In other words, the information in Table 27-2 and Eqn. 27-10 can be used to develop a pricing formula for a futures contract for an original issue discount (OID) bond like a T-bill. These facts suggest that the futures price is a function of the spot and forward prices of the underlying OID bond and the rate of interest. A pricing model follows next.

Economic Forces That Align Prices

If Eqn. 27-10 is violated one or more of the following economic processes will be set in motion to restore the equation:

1. **Arbitrage.** Riskless profits can be earned from selling short the more expensive arrangement and using the proceeds from that short sale to buy the cheaper

---

TABLE 27-2 Cash Flows from Two Alternative 180-Day Investments

Time line → Days in the future:	$t = 0$	$t = 90$	$t = 180$
(A) Direct purchase:			
Buy an actual 180-day T-bill for PV dollars of cash and hold it until it matures at $t = 180$.	PV		$1,000,000
(B) Indirect purchase:			
Buy a homemade T-bill for delivery in 180 days, as described in (1) and (2).			
(1) At $t = 0$ pay cash for a 90-day T-bill	$F90B/(1 + RFR)$	$F90B$	
(2) Purchase 90-day forward contract and then at $t = 90$ take delivery and pay for second consecutive T-bill.		$-F90B$	$1,000,000
Totals: Net cash flows from indirect plan:	$F90B/(1 + RFR)$	0	$1,000,000

arrangement. This arbitrage will continue to be profitable until the two purchase plans have the identical costs indicated in Eqn. 27-10.

2. **Buy the cheapest to deliver (CTD).** Because the two arrangements in Table 27-2 produce identical cash flows, investors will purchase whichever arrangement costs the least. The supply and demand pressures from investors who buy the CTD alternative should bring the costs of the two purchase plans together, as suggested by Eqn. 27-10.

3. **Switching.** If the cost of one of the purchase plans in Table 27-2 differs from the cost of the other at any point in time, investors will replace the more expensive arrangement by switching to the less costly arrangement. This switching keeps Eqn. 27-10 from being an inequality.

Transactions costs can inhibit any of the three economic processes above. The costs of gathering information, telephone expenses, postal fees, brokerage commissions, taxes, and the time and trading effort expended by the investor are costs that should be considered before undertaking any one of these processes. After considering these costs investors sometimes find it profitable to ignore small deviations from Eqn. 27-10. But the transactions costs for financial futures are small and, as a result, significant deviations from Eqn. 27-10 will be profitable to correct.

It matters not which combination of the three economic processes above realigns the prices of the two purchase plans in Table 27-2. Eqn. 27-10 can be used to price T-bill forward contracts in all three cases. Furthermore, an equation that is analogous to Eqn. 27-10 can be constructed to price T-bill futures contracts since futures are so similar to forward contracts. Even though the costs of using forward contracts and futures contracts differ slightly, the economic pressures that form their market prices are the same.

The Cost of Marking to the Market on T-Bill Futures

Mark-to-the-market rules force futures traders meet their minimum margin requirements every trading day to avoid a getting a margin call. Table 9-3 in Chapter 9 (p. 237) explains that forward contracts need not be marked to the market. Operating cost differences between a forward contract and a futures contract arise from the intermediate cash flows futures traders must make to mark-to-the-market.

To estimate the cost of marking to the market, consider a $1 million Treasury-bill future priced to yield 9% interest over a 60-day period; this T-bill will yield a total of [($1 million) × (60 days/360 days) × (0.09) =] $15,000 interest income. Ed Elton, Martin Gruber, and Joel Rentzler statistically estimated the cost of marking to the market for this futures contract to be an average of only $4 per contract. As a fraction of the $15,000 interest income, the $4 cost of marking to the market is insignificant.[16] The cost of marking to the market is a true difference between forward contracts and futures contracts, but in most cases this difference can be safely assumed to be negligible.

Using a Carrying-Cost Model to Price T-Bill Futures

Eqn. 27-2 emphasizes the role of carrying costs in the relationship between spot prices and futures prices. This relationship is especially useful for determining the prices of financial futures because the interest expense of financing an inventory of financial securities is the only carrying cost, and because the spot prices equal cash prices. The spot and cash prices are equal because the quality differences and some of the other basis risks that complicate the prices of agricultural futures are not present with financial futures.

Eqn. 27-11 is a pricing model for a futures contract on an original issue discount (OID) bond based on carrying costs. The only carrying cost for a T-bill is interest expense. The pricing model in Eqn. 27-11 is implied by the information in Table 27-2 and Eqn. 27-10 and by the carrying cost theory.

$$FP_t = SP_t(1 + RFR)^{YEAR} \tag{27-11}$$

where SP_t represents the spot price or cash market price or present value (PV) of the OID bond observed at time t, FP_t is the futures price (for example, $1 million) for the OID bond observed at time t, RFR is an annualized risk-free rate of interest (risk free because futures are guaranteed by a clearing houses), $YEAR$ denotes the number of years (or the fraction of 1 year) until the contract's delivery date.

The formulas in Table 27-2 and Eqn. 27-10 can be solved to obtain an explicit pricing formula for a futures contract for an original issue discount bond that is similar to Eqn. 27-11. The particular pricing formula that is derived will vary with the timing of the transaction. The dollar amount on the invoice from the futures broker may involve some accrued interest and/or interest expense that will complicate things. Essentially, however, Eqn. 27-11 is the pricing formula for a futures contract on any OID bond.[17]

PRICING THE T-BILL PURCHASED BY A DALLAS BANK

EXAMPLE

PROBLEM: Some time ago the National Bank of Dallas purchased a futures contract on a $100,000 one-year Treasury bill that specifies FP = $98,000 delivery price when the contract matures. At this time, the bank's futures contract has 3 months remaining until its maturity date. The current market price of the underlying T-bill is $96,000 in the cash market. Let us use the current market interest rate of 6.0% on 3-month T-bills as the risk-free rate of interest. **TWO QUESTIONS:** (A) What profit can the bank earn by letting its forward contract mature? (B) What profit can the bank earn by selling its forward contract today?

TWO SOLUTIONS: We can compare the current cash market price of the underlying T-bill with the spot price of a futures contract for the immediate delivery of an identical T-bond. In other words, the current price of the T-bill in the cash market is SP = $96,000. Because the bank's futures contract has 3 months until it matures, YEAR = 0.25.

Solution A: To determine the bank's profit from accepting delivery on the T-bill in 3 months, we substitute the values above into Eqn. 27-11:

$$FP_t = SP_t(1 + RFR)^{YEAR} \tag{27-11}$$

$$FP_t - SP_t(1 + RFR)^{YEAR} = \text{Profit in 3 months}$$

$$\$98,000 - \$96,000(1 + 6\%)^{0.25} = \$98,000 - \$97,408.69 = \$591.31 = \text{Profit in 3 months}$$

Solution (A) assumes the bank invests $96,000 at 6% interest for 3 months. At the end of 3 months the bank withdraws [$96,000(1.06)^{0.25} =] $97,408.689 and uses that withdrawal to pay for the T-bill which the futures contract will deliver for a price of FP = $98,000. The difference of ($98,000 − $97,408.69 =) $591.31 is profit received in 3 months.

Solution B: We could rearrange Eqn. 27-11 to find the present value of the bank's profit from selling the futures contract today.

$$FP_t = SP_t(1 + RFR)^{YEAR} \tag{27-11}$$

$$FP_t/(1 + RFR)^{YEAR} = SP_t$$

$$FP_t/(1 + RFR)^{YEAR} - SP_t = \text{Profit today}$$

$$\$98,000/(1 + 6\%)^{.25} - \$96,000 = \$98,000/(1.01467) - \$96,000 = \$96,582.76 - \$96,000$$
$$= \$582.76 = \text{Profit today}$$

Solution (B) is based on the present value of the T-bill that the futures contract entitles the bank to buy in 3 months [$98,000/(1 + 6%)$^{.25}$ = $98,000/(1.01467) = $96,582.76]. This present value is what the futures contract sells for today. Futures contracts are riskless instruments that should be discounted at the risk-free interest rate, because they are guaranteed by a clearing house. Subtracting $96,000 current cash from the current market value of its futures contract yields a difference of ($96,582.76 − $96,000 =) $582.76, which is the bank's profit today.

Equating (A) and (B): Solutions (A) and (B) are identical because today's profit of $582.76 equals the present value of the $591.31 profit that can be received in 3 months. In other words, $582.76 = $591.31/(1 + 6%)$^{.25}$ = $591.31/(1.01467).

PRICING A FUTURES CONTRACT ON A STOCK MARKET INDEX

Figure 9-2 in Chapter 9 (p. 241) and the surrounding discussion offers a reintroduction to stock market index futures. The prices for stock market index futures contracts on different stock market indexes in Figure 9-2 are determined by multiplying the value of each contract's underlying stock index by either 1,000, 500, 250, 100, 50, or 10 times the value of the underlying stock market index. The designer of each stock index futures contract selects whatever multiple they wish. The CME's future on the S&P500 has been the most popular stock market index futures contract in the world for years; it is priced at 250 times the value of the underlying index.

Futures on stock market indexes are primarily used for: (1) speculating, (2) hedging, and (3) index arbitrage. This book contains examples of each. First, the "Lunch with Brenda" case in Chapter 9 provides a numerical example of speculating with the S&P500 stock market index. Second, the "A Domestic Common Stock Mutual Fund's Hedge During a Volatile Period" case in Chapter 12 demonstrates how a mutual fund uses the S&P 500 index futures to hedge. Third, index arbitrage is discussed in the next section.

Index Arbitrage

Index arbitrage is a trading strategy that is based on a stock market index. Much of this arbitrage uses futures contracts on the S&P500 index. At maturity the S&P500 index futures contract's price equals 250 times the price of the underlying S&P500 index because that futures contract's cash settlement price is defined to have that value. However, prior to the maturity date of the S&P500 index futures contract its market price is sometimes not quite equal to 250 times the value of the S&P500 index. For instance, a strong bull market can cause the stock market futures price to rise slightly above 250 times the value of its underlying index. Such disparities violate the law of one price. Index arbitrageurs earn profits by correcting deviations from the law of one price.[18] Consider an example.

Stock Index Arbitrage. Suppose the S&P500 index is at 1290 and at the same time a S&P500 index futures contract that matures in 3 months is trading at 1293. To profit from this price disparity, index arbitrageurs buy the 500 stocks that make up the index in the same proportions they exist in the underlying S&P500 index and, at the same time, sell short the S&P500 index futures contract. These offsetting long and short positions create a hedge that locks in profits equal to the 3-point spread between the S&P500 future at 1293 and the basket of 500 stocks that cost 1290.* The two prices will come into alignment when the S&P500 futures price declines, the market value of the basket of 500 stocks rises, or some combination of both. In addition to gains from these price changes, the arbitrageurs get to keep whatever cash dividends might be paid by the 500 stocks they hold.

Professional index arbitrageurs routinely create S&P500 index hedges worth $10 million or more—usually more. Figure 27-6 is an excerpt from the *Wall Street Journal* containing summary statistics about program trading. The NYSE defines **program trading** to be the simultaneous purchase or sale of at least 15 different stocks with a total market value of $1 million or more. Program trading is done to execute index arbitrage and other derivative-related trading strategies.

Fluctuations in the S&P500 index occurring after the index arbitrageur—"the arb"—establishes an arbitrage position cannot affect whatever profit was already "locked up" in the position. For instance, suppose all 500 stocks in the S&P500 index somehow went bankrupt at once. The resulting 1290 loss on the basket of 500 stocks would be exceeded by the gain of 1293 from the short S&P500 index futures position as the contract's price plunged from 1293 to zero. And, if the S&P500 doubled its value from 1290 to 2580, the 1290 gain from the rising prices of 500 stocks would be 3 points larger than the simultaneous loss of [(ending value of 2580) − (short position at 1293) =] 1287 from the short S&P500 futures position.

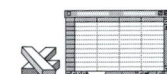

FIGURE 27-6   Periodic Report on Program Trading Activity at NYSE

PROGRAM TRADING

NEW YORK—Program trading in the week ended Feb. 18 accounted for 18.1%, or an average 185.4 million daily shares, of New York Stock Exchange volume.

Brokerage firms executed an additional 81.6 million daily shares of program trading away from the NYSE, mostly on foreign markets. Program trading is the simultaneous purchase or sale of at least 15 different stocks with a total value of $1 million or more.

Of the program total on the NYSE, 19.6% involved stock-index arbitrage, up from 11.9% the prior week. In this strategy, traders dart between stocks and stock-index options and futures to capture fleeting price differences.

Some 66.6% of program trading was executed by firms for their customers, while 31.1% was done for their own accounts, or principal trading. An additional 2.3% was designated as customer facilitation, in which firms use principal positions to facilitate customer trades.

The report includes a special profile of trading whenever the Dow Jones Industrial Average rises or falls more than 220 points from its previous close during any one-hour period. There were no such periods during the week.

Of the five most-active firms, Deutsche Bank Securities, RBC Dominion, Morgan Stanley Dean Witter and TLW Securities executed all or most of their program activity for its customers, as agents. Credit Suisse First Boston executed most of its activity as principal for its own accounts.

NYSE PROGRAM TRADING
Volume (in millions of shares) in the week ended Feb. 18, 2000

Top 15 Firms	Index Arbitrage	Derivative-Related*	Other Strategies	Total
Deutsche Bank Securities	25.1	.....	88.8	113.9
RBC Dominion	54.6	.....	27.4	82.0
Morgan Stanley Dn Wttr	8.8	.....	69.4	78.2
CS First Boston	15.9	0.9	48.4	65.2
TLW Securities LLC	9.6	1.7	51.5	62.8
CIBC World Markets	23.4	.....	39.3	62.7
Salomon Smith Barney	1.7	.....	55.7	57.4
BNP Securities	.....	.....	56.7	56.7
Lehman Brothers	.....	6.2	45.9	52.1
Nomura Securities	29.8	.....	14.6	44.4
Bear Stearns	.....	.....	42.5	42.5
Interactive Brokers	.....	.....	36.4	36.4
W&D Securities	.....	.....	31.4	31.4
Susquehanna Bkrg. Srvs.	3.2	.....	25.6	28.8
Merrill Lynch	5.1	.....	18.4	23.5
OVERALL TOTAL	182.2	10.1	734.8	927.1

*Other derivative-related strategies besides index arbitrage
Source: New York Stock Exchange

The NYSE defines program trading to be the simultaneous purchase or sale of at least 15 different stocks with a total market value of $1 million or more. Index arbitrageurs do a significant portion of the NYSE's program trading.

SOURCE: *Wall Street Journal,* 25 February 2000, C3.

---

*   The construction of the S&P500 index is analyzed in Chapter 10. For more explanation of hedging and arbitrage see Chapters 3 and 15.

Index Arbitrage Algebraic Analysis. There are different formulas representing stock market index arbitrage that can be solved to derive a valuation formula for a futures contract. One possible scenario involves the following two investment routes:

(A) Purchase the stocks directly. Assume: At time $t = 0$ the investor can buy all the stocks that comprise the stock market index at a cost of *PV* dollars; the investor wants to hold these securities until terminal time $t = T$; and, total cash dividends with a present value of *PVD* are received by the investor during that holding period. If the investor sells the rights to all these cash dividends to a collection agent for a cash payment of *PVD* dollars at the time the stocks are purchased the total initial outlay at time $t = 0$ for the basket of stocks is *PV-PVD*. Assume that at time *T* the terminal value of the basket of stocks turns out to be *TVA* dollars.

(B) Purchase the stocks indirectly. Assume: At time $t = 0$ the investor buys a futures contract on the stock market index; this purchase requires *FTB* dollars be paid when the cash settlement is made at terminal time $t = T$; also at time $t = 0$ the investor buys a T-bill that will also mature at time $t = T$ and be worth a face value of *FTB* dollars. The T-bill yields a riskless rate of *RFR* and can be purchased for $FTB/(1 + RFR)$ dollars. The T-bill is left on deposit at the brokerage house to meet the initial margin requirement on the futures contract so that $FTB/(1 + RFR)$ dollars is the total initial outlay for this arrangement. When the T-bill matures at terminal time $t = T$ its proceeds of *FTB* dollars are used to pay for the futures contract's delivery price of *FTB* dollars so the investor gets to keep the terminal value of the index future. Assume the terminal value of the index futures contract turns out to be *TVB* dollars.

Table 27-3 shows the cash flows associated with purchase plans (A) and (B). Stock index futures contracts are written so that the terminal value of the contract equals the terminal value of the underlying basket of stocks. Therefore, arrangements (A) and (B) in Table 27-3 must both be worth the same terminal values, TVA = TVB. Since the two different purchase plans have identical terminal values at time $t = T$, the law of one price should cause their initial costs at time $t = 0$ to be equal. The initial costs of purchase plans (A) and (B) are equated in Eqn. 27-12:

$$PVD - PV = \frac{-FTB}{1 + RFR} \tag{27-12}$$

TABLE 27-3   Cash Flows from Two Alternative Stock Purchase Plans

Time Line → Dates of Transactions:	$t = 0$	$t = T$
(A) Purchase the stocks in the index directly:		
Buy stocks	$-PV$	TVA
Sell present value of cash dividends	PVD	
Totals	$PVD - PV$	TVA
(B) Purchase the stocks in the index indirectly:		
Buy stock index futures on margin		TVB-*FTB*
Buy T-bill	$-FTB/(1 + RFR)$	*FTB*
Totals	$-FTB/(1 + RFR)$	TVB

Solving Eqn. 27-12 for the ratio *FTB/PV* provides an equation that tells us how to value stock index futures contracts.

$$\frac{FTB}{PV} = \left(1 + RFR\right) - \frac{PVD}{PV}\left(1 + RFR\right) \tag{27-12a}$$

The quantity *PVD/PV* is the average cash dividend yield for the basket of stocks over the holding period. Eqn. 27-12a says that the ratio *FTB/PV* should (1) vary inversely with the average cash dividend yield from the basket of stocks, $d(FTB/PV)/d(PVD/PV) < 0$, and, (2) vary directly with the riskless interest rate, $d(FTB/PV)/dRFR > 0$. It is comforting to note that as the delivery date gets nearer the values of *PVD* and *RFR* approach zero so that on the delivery date of $t = T$ the FTB/PV ratio reaches a value of $FTB/PV = 1$.

The stock market index futures valuation model of Eqn. 27-12a was derived without considering whether the cash dividends could be forecast accurately, or what the commission costs would do to the index arbitrage profits. Both problems are minor. Cash dividends can be forecast for a few months into the future with great accuracy because most corporations do not change their cash dividend payments every year. And the commission costs for large trades are tiny—a few cents per share is typical. Sometimes electronic communications networks (ECNs) do trades for free. But an ECN cannot be depended to handle a large transaction quickly. Block traders routinely handle large transactions quickly for a few cents a share. As a result of these low commission costs, Eqn. 27-12a provides a fairly accurate guideline for pricing stock market index futures.

Pricing Futures on a Stock Market Index

The information provided by Table 27-3 and Eqn. 27-12 can be used to price a futures contract on a stock market index. Eqn. 27-12 is analogous to the pricing model for a futures contract on an OID bond in Eqn. 27-11. The particular pricing formula used varies with the stock market index used, the way cash dividends are handled, and the timing of the transaction. Furthermore, the dollar amount on the invoice from the futures broker may involve accrued cash dividends and/or interest expense that will complicate that payment. In any event, Eqn. 27-13 is the general pricing formula for a futures contract on a stock market index, where the exponent YEARS denotes the number of years, or the fraction of 1 year, until the futures contract matures.

$$\begin{pmatrix} \text{Price of futures} \\ \text{contract on a stock} \\ \text{market index at } t = 0 \end{pmatrix} = \begin{pmatrix} \text{Spot price of future on} \\ \text{underlying stock} \\ \text{market index at } t = 0 \end{pmatrix} \left[1 + \begin{pmatrix} \text{Risk-free rate,} \\ \text{for example,} \\ \text{T-bill yield} \end{pmatrix} - \begin{pmatrix} \text{Cash dividend} \\ \text{yield from the} \\ \text{underlying stocks} \end{pmatrix} \right]^{YEARS} \tag{27-13}$$

Note that the cash dividend yield offsets the interest expense and reduces the carrying costs in Eqn. 27-13.

PRICING A 6-MONTH FUTURES CONTRACT ON THE S&P500 INDEX   EXAMPLE

The S&P500 index opened at 1300 today. To place his bet that the S&P500 index will rise to a value of [(1300) × (1+10%) =] 1430 within six months, Thomas buys one S&P500 futures contract that has a spot price of [($250) × (1300) =] $325,000. Assume the cash dividend yield on the portfolio of 500 stocks underlying the S&P500 is 2% per year, and the risk-free rate (RFR) is 6% per year. What will Thomas have to pay for this 6-month S&P500 index future contract today?

SOLUTION: Thomas will have to pay $331,436 for his stock index future.

$$\begin{pmatrix} \text{Price of futures} \\ \text{contract on S\&P500} \\ \text{index today, \$331,436} \end{pmatrix} = \begin{pmatrix} \text{Spot price of the} \\ \text{underlying stock index} \\ \text{future today, \$325,000} \end{pmatrix} \left[1 + \begin{pmatrix} \text{Risk-free} \\ \text{rate, 6\%} \end{pmatrix} - \begin{pmatrix} \text{Cash dividend} \\ \text{yield from the} \\ \text{500 stocks, 2\%} \end{pmatrix} \right]^{YEARS = 0.5}$$

$$\$331,436 = (\$325,000)[1.0198] = (\$325,000)[1 + 6\% - 2\%]^{0.5}$$

In the calculation above the 6% interest expense is a gross carrying charge that is diminished by income from a cash dividend yield of 2% to produce a net carrying charge of (6% − 2% =) 4%, stated at an annual rate.

Using Futures Can Yield Substantial Savings in Commissions

What a portfolio can save in common stock trading commissions alone can justify using futures contracts to hedge a common stock position rather than using the common stock itself to form an offsetting position.

EXAMPLE   REDUCING TRADING COSTS

If $40 million of common stock can be sold and bought back at a total round-turn commission cost of 1%, this transaction would involve $400,000 in commission costs. In contrast, the round-turn commission cost for a futures contract on the Standard & Poor's index is only about $25 per contract. Because 500 of these futures contracts would hedge the $40 million portfolio, the total commission cost of using the futures contracts would be [(500 contracts) × ($25 commission) =] $12,500. The estimated commission savings is ($400,000 − $12,500 =) $387,500. The disadvantage of hedging with futures contracts is that after some months the futures contracts will expire; a new hedge must be established and the $12,500 commission cost must be incurred again if the need for the hedge remains. However, the futures commissions expenses in the example above could be repaid 32 times [($12,500) × (32 transactions) = $400,000] before they added up to the commissions on one round-turn in the underlying stocks.

THE BOTTOM LINE

Futures contracts are bought and sold at commodity futures exchanges, stock exchanges, and options exchanges around the world. Most buyers and sellers are exchange members who meet in trading pits. The bid prices of potential buyers and the asked prices of potential sellers are announced via open outcry in the pits. The futures traders at some exchanges have been "automated out of their jobs" by new electronic technology.

Investors who want to speculate on price changes buy futures contracts, expecting to buy the contract at a price below the contract's selling price, or sell a futures contract short at a price above the price at which they expect to cover that short position (buy back and, thereby, close out their position). Speculators rarely take delivery on their futures contracts.

Hedgers use futures contracts to reduce their risk exposure, not to earn speculative profits. A perfect hedge eliminates risk. But, basis risks are troublesome flaws that make perfect hedges unusual. Speculators and hedgers buy and sell futures contracts from each other as speculators pursue trading profits and hedgers try to avert risk.

Economic theory suggests that futures prices normally exceed spot prices by the amount of carrying charges. However, inverted markets sometimes occur and force futures prices below spot prices. The difference between the spot price and the futures price is called the basis. As a futures contract's delivery date arrives, the basis shrinks to zero as the spot and futures prices converge.

Futures prices (*FP*) for storable commodities should normally be slightly less than the expected spot prices, *E(SP)*, by the amount of an insurance premium Keynes and Hicks called normal backwardation. Hardy disagreed with Keynes and Hicks; he argued that futures prices should normally be at a slight premium over the expected spot prices. More recently, some researchers published evidence suggesting that spot prices are unbiased estimates of futures prices.

A U.S. Treasury bill future provides for delivery of a physical T-bill at the contract's maturity. Futures contracts on stock market indexes like the S&P500 index do not provide a deliverable commodity, they are financial futures that are settled in cash. The carrying cost model was used to price both Treasury bill futures and stock market index futures.

The risk-free rate (RFR) of interest is the only carrying cost for a financial future. As a result, simple carrying cost models are able to price financial futures contracts. The market price of the underlying commodity is the primary factor shaping the prices of futures; carrying costs have a smaller impact of futures prices. Swapping to cheaper contracts, arbitrage, and the desire to deliver the cheapest available underlying instrument were shown to provide support for the law of one price. These factors all work together to determine the continuously fluctuating futures prices.

QUESTIONS

Q27-1   (Short position in futures) Compare and contrast selling a futures contract without owning an inventory in the commodity and selling a common stock short.

Q27-2   (Futures clearing houses) What functions are performed by the clearing house at a commodity exchange?

Q27-3   (Inverted market) Define an inverted market and suggest what might cause one to occur.

Q27-4   (Futures and spot prices) "Futures prices are determined after spot prices are known. Adding carrying costs to spot prices yields futures prices." Is this statement true, false, or uncertain? Explain.

Q27-5   (Speculation) "Speculation is an evil pastime for wealthy playboys. It destabilizes prices and misallocates resources, and it should be made illegal." Is the quotation true, false, or uncertain? Explain.

Q27-6   (Underlying assets) Why do you think there are no futures markets for commodities like coal, raisins, and salt? Does the absence of futures markets mean that no speculation in these commodities occurs?

Q27-7   (Underlying assets) Assume you are hired by the Chicago Board of Trade (CBT) to be a consultant to its New Products Committee. You are directed to do research to discern commodities on which the CBT might advantageously

trade futures contracts. List and explain six criteria you would adopt for screening commodities in order to select high volume candidates in which the CBT might initiate trading.

Q27-8   (Basis) (a) What determines the size and sign of the basis for an agricultural commodity? (b) for a financial future?

Q27-9   (Perfect hedges) What factors prevent hedges from being a perfect hedge? Explain.

Q27-10   (Speculation) Suppose that long-term Treasury bonds are currently yielding higher interest rates than the Treasury notes—that is, the yield curve is sloping upwards. Further assume that you have done economic research that makes you confident that the yield curve will flatten out, causing the yield spread between T-notes and T-bonds to narrow. How can you profit from this flattening of the yield curve if your expectations are borne out?

Q27-11   (Futures markets) "The existence of two almost identical T-bill futures contracts, which are traded at competing commodity exchanges, is economically undesirable because it fragments the market." Is the preceding sentence true, false, or uncertain? Explain.

Q27-12 (Hedging) If someone buys a Treasury bond in a long position and then realizes that the T-bond's price is going to decline because of a previously unforeseen turn in interest rates, what can he do to avoid losses? Describe more than one way to avoid the imminent loss.

Q27-13 (Futures and options) Compare and contrast a long position in futures contracts with owning a call option position of the same size on the same asset. *Note:* You may want to refer to the chapter that discusses call options.

PROBLEMS

P27-1 (Rate of return) Define the one-period rate of return for a commodity investor who purchased a futures contract on margin and gave the commodity broker a U.S. Treasury bill to hold as the margin.

P27-2 (Hedging) Jim Jones expects to harvest 40,000 bushels of soybeans from his farm in September, 20XX. On May 1, 20XX, the September futures price of soybeans is $6.00 per bushel. (a) If Jim believes this is a good price, what should he do to lock in the $6.00 price? (b) Show Jim's position at the September harvest if the futures price of soybeans falls to $5.00 a bushel and the basis is zero. Ignore commission charges and taxes.

P27-3 (Hedging) Ed Franklin grows cotton. As of June, 20XX Ed expects to produce 300,000 pounds of cotton for his September, 20XX harvest. The September futures price for cotton is $0.80 per pound. (a) If Ed decides to hedge one-half of his production, what should he do? (b) What would be Ed's price gain or loss on his cotton if the futures price of cotton falls to $0.60 per pound at harvest time and the basis is zero? Ignore commission charges and taxes.

P27-4 (Hedging) In July, 20XX Mrs. Sample's Syrup Company signed a contract with several food distributors to deliver several truck loads of syrup in November, 20XX at the price agreed on in July. The vice-president of Mrs. Sample Syrup is concerned about the rising price of sugar between now and November. (a) What should the company do to hedge its profit on the syrup sale? Assume that 672,000 pounds of sugar will be needed to produce the syrup and that the current price of sugar is $0.23 per pound. (b) If the price of sugar goes to $0.35 per pound and if Mrs. Sample's Syrup Company does not hedge their position, how much would they lose? Ignore commission costs.

P27-5 (Speculation) Assume it is June 1, 20XX; you expect the price of wheat to increase over the next 3 months. Initial margin requirements call for a minimum of 10% down, and the current price of wheat is $3 per bushel. (a) If you have $10,000 to invest and the margin is 10%, what should you do? Assume a $40 commission per contract. (b) Assume you purchased 6 wheat contracts on June 1, 20XX and then the price of wheat goes to $3.50 per bushel over the next 3 months. What is your rate of return after commission costs? (c) How much will you earn or lose, net of commission costs, if you take the long position on June 1, 20XX and the price of wheat goes to $2.25 per bushel over the next 3 months?

P27-6 (Speculation) In March, 20XX you are bearish on the price of gold over the next 6 months. If you sell 10 gold futures contracts short at the price of $450 per troy ounce, what will you earn if the price of gold goes to $400 per troy ounce over this period of time? Assume a $1500 margin and $35 commission per contract.

P27-7 (Hedging) Assume you are managing a $7.5 million portfolio of common stock and were bearish about the next 6 months. (a) If 6-month futures contracts are available on the S&P500 and the S&P500 index is currently at 150, how can you advantageously use your bearish expectations to hedge your long position in the stock market? (b) What will happen to the overall value of the portfolio if it has been fully hedged and the common stock portfolio declines in value by $1.5 million to a total value of $6 million, and the S&P500 index simultaneously falls to 120?

P27-8 (Speculation) Joe Speculator is bearish on the stock market. (a) What will Joe make if the S&P500 index is currently at 130 and Joe sells ten S&P500 futures contracts short, assuming a 10% initial margin requirement? Assume that 6 months from now the S&P500 index has fallen to 100. (b) How much would Joe have earned if the S&P500 index had increased to 150 in the 6-month period?

P27-9 (Hedging) The Taylor Construction Company recently signed a contract to construct several condos at a fixed price. J. G. Taylor, owner of the company, is fearful of rising lumber prices. (a) What should Taylor do to hedge the firm's lumber position? Assume that 1.5 million board feet of lumber will be necessary and that the current price per 1,000 board feet is $178. The condos are scheduled to be completed in about 8 months. *Hint:* Outside research into lumber contract units is needed. (b) What would be the loss for Taylor Construction Company if the company did not hedge its position and the price of lumber rose to $190 per 1,000 board feet? Ignore commission costs.

P27-10 (Calendar spread) Bill Williamson entered a long position in 1 contract (5,000 bushels) for July corn at $2.20 per bushel and simultaneously sold a December corn contract at $2.32. The spot price on corn at the time was $1.98 per bushel. One month later, the spot price had risen to $2.14 a bushel and July corn was trading at $2.30 a bushel while December corn was trading at $2.40 a bushel. Calculate Bill's gain or loss from this spread position, ignoring commissions.

CFA EXAM QUESTIONS

The following questions were adopted from the 1999 CFA Sample Exam, Level I:

1. The open interest on a futures contract at any given time is the total number of outstanding:
   A. contracts.
   B. unhedged positions.
   C. clearing-house positions.
   D. long and short positions.

2. In futures trading, the minimum level to which an equity position may fall before requiring additional margin is *most accurately* termed the:
   A. initial margin.
   B. variation margin.
   C. cash flow margin.
   D. maintenance margin.

3. A silver futures contract requires the seller to deliver 5,000 Troy ounces of silver. Jerry Harris sells one July silver futures contract at a price of $8 per ounce, posting a $2,025 initial margin. If the required maintenance margin is $1,500, what is the *first* price per ounce at which Harris would receive a maintenance margin call?
   A. $5.92.
   B. $7.89.
   C. $8.11.
   D. $10.80.

4. (1997 CFA Exam, Level II) Mike Lane will have $5 million to invest in 5-year U.S. Treasury bonds 3 months from now. Lane believes interest rates will fall during the next 3 months and wants to take advantage of prevailing interest rates by hedging against a decline in interest rates. Lane has sufficient funds to pay the costs of entering into and maintaining a futures position.
   A. Describe what action Lane should take using 5-year U.S. Treasury note futures contracts to protect against declining interest rates. [No calculations required to answer Part A.]

Assume 3 months have gone by and despite Lane's expectations, 5-year cash and forward markets interest rates have increased by 100 basis points compared with the 5-year-forward market interest rates of 3 months ago.
   B. Discuss the effect of higher interest rates on the value of the futures position that Lane entered into in Part A.
   C. Discuss how the return from Lane's hedged position differs from the return he could now earn if he had not hedged in Part A.

5. (1998 CFA Exam, Level II) Susan Baker is an investor who seeks to arbitrage pricing discrepancies in the marketplace over the next 6 months. She has noted the data in Table 6:

Table 6

Instrument	Spot Price	Futures Price for Contract Expiring in 6 Months	Income from Treasury Note for 6 Months	Finance Charge for 6 Months
U.S. Treasury note deliverable on the futures contract	$101	$100 (invoice price)	$4.50	$2.50

List the components of the arbitrage transaction and calculate the arbitrage profits, if any, that are available to exploit a possible pricing discrepancy. Show your calculations.

6. (1998 CFA Exam, Level III) Jacob Bower has a liability that

   has a principal balance of $100 million on June 30 1998,

   accrues interest quarterly starting on June 30, 1998,

   pays interest quarterly,

   has a 1-year term to maturity, and

   calculates interest due based on 90-LIBOR (the London Interbank Offered Rate).

Bower wishes to hedge his remaining interest payments against changes in interest rates. Bower has correctly calculated that he needs to sell (short) 300 Eurodollar futures contracts to accomplish the hedge. He is considering the alternative hedging strategies outlined in Table 9.

Table 9 Initial Position (6/30/98) in 90-Day LIBOR Eurodollar Contracts

Contract Month	Strategy A (contracts)	Strategy B (contracts)
September 1998	300	100
December 1998	0	100
March 1999	0	100

   A. Explain why strategy B is a more effective hedge than strategy A when the yield curve undergoes an instantaneous nonparallel shift.
   B. Discuss an interest rate scenario in which strategy A would be superior to strategy B.

FURTHER REFERENCES

Black, Fischer, "The Pricing of Commodity Contracts," *Journal of Financial Economics* 3, nos. 1 and 2: 167–79.

> The article shows how to price options on futures.

Duffie, Darrell. *Futures Markets.* Englewood Cliffs, NJ: Prentice-Hall, 1989.

> This advanced textbook presents a rigorous and concise discussion of futures contracts, futures markets, futures options, hedging, and the federal regulatory framework. Mathematical statistics is used. The book also lists some helpful FORTRAN computer codes.

Francis, Jack Clark, William W. Toy, and Gregg Whittaker, eds. *The Handbook of Equity Derivatives,* rev. ed. New York: Wiley, 1999.

> Chapters 1–9 discuss exchange-listed futures, options, and other derivatives. Chapters 10–20 discuss over-the-counter (OTC) equity derivatives. Chapters 21–27 delve into law, taxes, and the design of successful instruments. The book provides a rare look at the OTC derivatives market, which is larger than the market for exchange-listed derivatives. Practically no mathematics is used.

Samuelson, Paul. "Intertemporal Price Equilibrium: A Prologue to the Theory of Speculation," *Weltwirtschaftliches Archiv* 79 (1957): 181–219, reprinted in *Collected Scientific Papers of Paul A. Samuelson,* Vol. II, ed. J. E. Stiglitz (Cambridge, MA: MIT Press, 1966). Chapter 73, pp. 946–84.

> This classic article by the Nobel laureate analyzes the price determinants for storable agricultural commodities.

ENDNOTES

[1] See M. J. Brennan, "A Theory of Price Limits in Futures Markets," *Journal of Financial Economics* 16, no. 2 (1986): 213–33.

[2] For an informative discussion of the trading rules and market-making in a futures market and explanation of some of the rules see William J. Silber, "Market-Maker Behavior in an Auction Market: An Analysis of Scalpers in Futures Markets," *Journal of Finance* 39, no. 4 (September 1984): 937–54.

[3] See Holbrook Working, "Theory of the Inverse Carrying Charge in Futures Markets," *Journal of Farm Economics* 30 (February 1948). To read classic theory about the relationship between spot and futures prices see Holbrook Working, "The Theory of Price of Storage," *American Economic Review* (December 1949): 1254–62. Also see M. J. Brennan, "The Supply of Storage," *American Economic Review* (March 1958), for empirical evidence.

[4] Dusak defines the return as in Eqn. 27-4, Katherine Dusak, "Futures Trading and Investor Returns: An Investigation of Commodity Market Risk Premiums," *Journal of Political Economy* (December 1973): 1387–1406. Fischer Black, in contrast, argues that it is not possible to define the rate of return for a highly leveraged futures contract in "The Pricing of Commodity Contracts," *Journal of Financial Economics* (January 1976). Returns on margined futures contracts are defined by Zvi Bodie and Victor Rosansky, "Risk and Return in Commodity Futures," *Financial Analysts Journal* (May-June 1980): 38–39. Professor Lester Telser argues that margins affect the rates of return, but does not explicitly show how he thinks they should be measured. L. Telser, "Margins and Futures Contracts," *Journal of Futures Markets* 1, no. 2 (1981): 225–54.

[5] Margins are discussed by John C. Hull, *Options, Futures, and Other Derivatives,* 3d ed. (Upper Saddle River, NJ: Prentice-Hall, 1997), 20–23. Chapter 2 includes a detailed numerical example of how maintenance margins are calculated.

[6] See E. Elton, M. Gruber, and J. Rentzler, "Intra-Day Tests of the Efficiency of the Treasury Bill Futures Market," *Review of Economics and Statistics* 66, no. 1 (February 1984): 129–37. The paper analyzes T-bill futures and finds the cost of marking to the market stated as a percentage of the interest income from the position is trivial.

[7] For a theoretical analysis of hedging see L. L. Johnson, "The Theory of Hedging and Speculation in Commodity Futures," *Review of Economic Studies* 27, no. 3: 139–51. More recently, see Ron W. Anderson and Jean-Pierre Danthine, "Hedging and Joint Production: Theory and Illustrations," *Journal of Finance* 35, no. 2 (May 1980): 487–97.

[8] For more details about hedging with financial futures, see Stephen Figlewski, Kose John, and John Merrick, *Hedging with Financial Futures for Institutional Investors* (Cambridge, MA: Ballinger Publishing Company, 1986). Also see Peter Ritchken, *Derivative Markets* Harper Collins College Publishers, New York City, 1996.

[9] In order to invest in commodity futures indirectly, some people buy shares in commodity funds. Evidence suggesting that commodity funds tend to be bad investments has been published by E.J. Elton, M.J. Gruber, and J. Rentzler, "New Public Offerings, Information and Investor Rationality: The Case of Publicly Offered Commodity Funds," *Journal of Business* 62, no. 1 (January 1989): 1–16.

[10] For an early explanation of normal backwardation see J.M. Keynes, *A Treatise on Money,* Vol. II, and also *The Applied Theory of Money* (London: Macmillan, 1924). Also see J.R. Hicks, *Value and Capital,* 2nd ed. (Oxford, England: Clarendon Press, 1946), Chapters IX and X, esp. pp. 136–39.

[11] C. O. Hardy, *Risk and Risk Bearing* (Chicago: University of Chicago Press, 1923), 67–69. Also see C.O. Hardy and L.S. Lyon, "The Theory of Hedging," *Journal of Political Economy* 31, no. 2 (April 1923): 276–87.

[12] See Michael L. Hartzmark, "Returns to Individual Traders of Futures: Aggregate Results," *Journal of Political Economy* 95, no. 6 (1987): 1292–1306. In addition, see Avraham Kamara, "The Behavior of Futures Prices: A Review of Theory and Evidence," *Financial Analysts Journal* 40, no. 4 (July-August 1984): 68–75.

[13] See Darrell Duffie, *Futures Markets* (Upper Saddle River, NJ: Prentice-Hall, 1989), 180–84. Duffie discusses the Martingale and efficient market implications of unbiased expectations.

[14] See Eugene F. Fama and Kenneth R. French, "Commodity Futures Prices: Some Evidence on Forecast Power, Premiums, and the Theory of Storage," *Journal of Business* 60, no. 1 (January 1987): 55–74. Also see Eugene F. Fama and Kenneth R. French, "Business Cycles and the Behavior of Metals Prices," *Journal of Finance* 43, no. 5 (December 1988): 1075–94.

[15] See John C. Hull, *Options, Futures, and Other Derivatives,* 3d ed. (Upper Saddle River, NJ: Prentice-Hall, 1997), Appendix 3A, "Proof That Forward and Futures Prices Are Equal When Interest Rates Are Constant," pp. 76–77.

[16] See E. Elton, M. Gruber, and J. Rentzler, "Intra-Day Tests of the Efficiency of the Treasury Bill Futures Market," *Review of Economics and Statistics* 66, no. 1 (February 1984): 129–37.

[17] See John C. Hull, *Options, Futures, and Other Derivatives,* 3d ed. (Upper Saddle River, NJ: Prentice-Hall, 1997), Chapter 3 provides additional detail about pricing financial futures.

[18] See James Overdahl and Henry McMillan, "Another Day, Another Collar: An Evaluation of the Effects of NYSE Rule 80A on Trading Costs and Intermarket Arbitrage," *Journal of Business* 71, no. 1 (January 1998): 27–53. Also see Robert Neal, "Direct Tests of Index Arbitrage Models," *Journal of Financial and Quantitative Analysis* 31, no. 4 (December 1996): 541–62. In addition, see Craig W. Holden, "Index Arbitrage as Cross-Sectional Market Making," *Journal of Futures Markets* 15, no. 4 (June 1995): 423–55. Also, see Lawrence Harris, George Sofianos, and James E. Shapiro, "Program Trading and Intraday Volatility," *Review of Financial Studies* 7 no. 4 (winter 1994): 653–85.

Futures Options

This appendix introduces the **futures option,** or an *option on a futures contract.* A futures option is a two-tiered financial instrument. The lower (last) tier consists of a futures contract on the underlying asset. A put or call option on the futures contract is positioned above (before) the futures contract. Futures options are like ordinary futures contracts that have been augmented with an option that limits the investor's liability.

Figure 27A-1 is a newspaper excerpt showing one day's price quotations for a few actively traded futures options. The newspaper quotations for futures options reveal there is no consistency in tick sizes. Futures options on stock indexes are priced in pennies. Some futures options on interest rates are priced in pennies, some in 32nds, and others are priced

FIGURE 27A-1 Newspaper Quotations for Futures Options

FUTURES OPTIONS PRICES

Thursday, February 17, 2000

AGRICULTURAL

CORN (CBT)
5,000 bu.; cents per bu.

Strike	Calls-Settle			Puts-Settle		
Price	Mar	May	Jly	Mar	May	Jly
200	21¼	30	38⅞	⅛	¼	1⅜
210	11¼	20½	30½	⅛	1¼	3
220	1⅞	13¼	23½	⅝	3⅜	5½
230	⅛	7⅞	18	8¾	8	10
240	⅛	4½	13¾	18¾	14¼	15¾
250	⅛	2½	10½	28¾	22¼	22⅛

Est vol 15,000 Wd 10,554 calls 5,114 puts
Op int Wed 298,583 calls 189,057 puts

SOYBEANS (CBT)
5,000 bu.; cents per bu.

Strike	Calls-Settle			Puts-Settle		
Price	Mar	May	Jly	Mar	May	Jly
450	58	68¼	79	⅛	1	3½
475	33⅛	45¾	60	⅛	3¼	8½
500	8½	28¼	43¾	½	10½	17
525	¼	16	31	17¼	23½	29
550	⅛	8½	22	42⅛	40½	45¼
575	⅛	4½	16	67	61½	63½

Est vol 10,000 Wd 7,996 calls 4,115 puts
Op int Wed 133,466 calls 68,194 puts

SOYBEAN MEAL (CBT)
100 tons; $ per ton

Strike	Calls-Settle			Puts-Settle		
Price	Mar	May	Jly	Mar	May	Jly
155	11.80	15.75	19.50	0.05	1.65	3.35
160	6.90	12.00	16.00	0.15	3.00	5.05
165	2.25	8.85	13.00	0.75	4.80	6.75
170	0.40	6.25	10.75	3.50	7.15	9.50
175	0.10	4.75	8.75	....	....	....
180	0.05	3.15	7.25	....	....	....

Est vol 2,000 Wd 720 calls 575 puts
Op int Wed 25,545 calls 23,351 puts

INTEREST RATE

T-BONDS (CBT)
$100,000; points and 64ths of 100%

Strike	Calls-Settle			Puts-Settle		
Price	Mar	Apr	Jun	Mar	Apr	Jun
92	2-11	2-18	2-63	0-01	0-37	1-17
93	1-12	1-40	....	0-02	0-58	....
94	0-19	1-05	1-53	0-09	1-23	2-07
95	0-03	0-43	....	0-57	1-61	....
96	0-01	0-26	1-02	1-55	....	3-18
97	0-01	0-14	....	2-54	....	....

Est vol 120,000;
Wd vol 35,286 calls 37,794 puts
Op int Wed 482,787 calls 528,689 puts

T-NOTES (CBT)
$100,000; points and 64ths of 100%

Strike	Calls-Settle			Puts-Settle		
Price	Mar	Apr	Jun	Mar	Apr	Jun
93	1-37	....	2-02	0-01	0-26	0-56
94	0-40	0-60	1-28	0-04	0-49	1-17
95	0-04	0-32	0-63	0-32	1-21	1-51
96	0-01	0-15	0-41	1-29	2-03	2-29
97	0-01	0-07	0-26	2-28	....	3-13
98	0-01	0-03	0-16	3-28	....	....

Est vol 39,000 Wd 15,455 calls 18,407 puts
Op int Wed 321,590 calls 238,175 puts

INDEX

DJ INDUSTRIAL AVG (CBOT)
$100 times premium

Strike	Calls-Settle			Puts-Settle		
Price	Feb	Mar	Apr	Feb	Mar	Apr
103	....	....	....	1.05	16.60	....
104	11.75	29.85	....	2.25	20.35	29.50
105	5.35	24.20	....	5.85	24.70	....
106	1.70	19.20	....	12.20	29.65	37.00
107	0.75	15.40	....	20.85	35.80	....
108	0.35	12.15	....	30.55	42.60	46.25

Est vol 750 Wd 238 calls 737 puts
Op int Wed 8,529 calls 13,463 puts

S&P 500 STOCK INDEX (CME)
$250 times premium

Strike	Calls-Settle			Puts-Settle		
Price	Feb	Mar	Apr	Feb	Mar	Apr
1375	14.60	39.00	66.40	4.10	28.60	38.10
1380	11.10	36.10	63.20	5.60	30.60	39.80
1385	8.00	33.20	....	7.50	32.70	41.60
1390	5.50	30.40	....	10.00	34.90	....
1395	3.60	27.80	....	13.10	37.30	....
1400	2.30	25.20	51.20	16.80	39.60	47.60

Est vol 12,166 Wd 5,877 calls 10,738 puts
Op int Wed 86,968 calls 184,654 puts

A futures option bestows on its owner a long position in either a put or a call option on an underlying futures contract. Sometimes a futures option is more popular than the simpler futures contract or option on the same underlying quantity.

SOURCE: *Wall Street Journal,* 18 February 2000, 18.

in 64ths. Tick sizes for metals, such as silver and gold, are in dimes and nickels. Why tick sizes are so different can be seen by looking at the underlying futures contract. The underlying futures contracts cover agricultural, metallic, financial, and other goods that are listed on different exchanges. These heterogeneous backgrounds result in diverse tick sizes.

Buying a Futures Option

The *buyer* of one futures option may exercise the option to assume either a long (take delivery) or short (make delivery) position on a futures contract. The position assumed depends on whether the investor purchased a put or a call. Purchasing a call option gives the buyer the option to purchase a long, but not a short, position in the future at the exercise price stipulated in the call option. If a put option was purchased, the buyer has the right to exercise that put by establishing a short (not a long) position in the future at the exercise price specified in the put option. These put options and call options must be exercised to obtain a futures position, sold to another investor before they mature, canceled out by an offsetting transaction, or held until they expire and are worthless.

The buyers of put and call options on futures have the right, but not an obligation, to exercise the option they purchased. These options need not be exercised to be profitable. Futures options are marketable financial instruments. The owners of profitable put and call options on futures usually choose to realize their profits by selling the option for a higher price than they paid for it instead of exercising it to obtain the underlying futures position. Table 27A-1 summarizes the alternatives the buyer of a futures option faces.

Writing a Futures Option

Consider the responsibility of the seller (writer) of a futures option. Unlike the option buyer, the option writer has a legal obligation to perform. The option writer's obligation to perform depends on whether a put or a call option was written (sold).

If the writer of one call option on a futures contract is notified that the buyer is exercising the option, that call seller must immediately deliver the specified future. More precisely, the call seller must deliver the optioned futures contract at the exercise price stipulated in the option, and the delivered contract must be fully marked to the market (not inadequately margined) at its delivery. If the writer of the option does not have a long position in the deliverable futures contract, the writer must immediately buy the contract to make the promised delivery.

TABLE 27A-1 Buying Options on Futures Requires a Series of Decisions		
Two-Way Initial Decision	Three-Way Intermediate Decision	Two Delivery Alternatives
Buy a call option on a futures contract	(1) Let option expire worthless (2) Sell futures option for profit (3) Exercise call and get long future's position	(3a) Accept delivery on futures (3b) Reverse out of futures position
Buy a put option on a futures contract	(1) Let option expire worthless (2) Sell futures option for profit (3) Exercise put and get short future's position	(3a) Make delivery on futures (3b) Reverse out of futures position

If the writer of one put option on a futures contract is notified that the buyer is exercising the option, the put seller is obliged to deliver a short position to the put owner at once. In other words, the put writer must deliver a short futures contract at the contracted exercise price.

Rights Versus Obligations for the Option Parties

Options are unilateral (one-way) contracts. Futures contracts are bilateral (two-way) contracts. Anyone who buys a futures option acquires the right—but not the obligation—to assume a long or a short position in a futures contract at the prearranged exercise price any time during the life of the option—if it is an American option. (European options are usually written on forward contracts.) Because option buyers have no obligation to perform, they are not required to mark to the market (cannot receive margin calls) like the sellers of futures options.

In contrast to option buyers, anyone who writes a futures option is committed to deliver a long or a short position (for a call or a put, respectively) in the futures market at the exercise price if the buyer exercises the futures option. Because option writers are required to perform, they are required to deposit an initial margin when a position is opened. This margin requirement is marked to the market daily to reflect changes in the market value of the futures option.

The buyer of an American option on a futures contract may exercise the option at any time before it expires. It only takes a phone call to the buyer's broker, who then notifies the clearing house. The clearing house will proceed to establish a futures position for the buyer—a long position for a call option, or a short position for a put option. At the same time, the seller of the option is obliged to instantly act as a counterparty at the prearranged exercise price.

Futures Options Specifications: A T-Bond Example

The expiration months for options on T-Bond futures are identical to the delivery months on T-Bond futures—March, June, September, and December.

The market prices of both T-Bonds and T-Bond futures are quoted in terms of percentage points followed by thirty-seconds of a percentage point. For example, a T-Bond quoted at 99-16 is worth $99\frac{16}{32}$ or 99.5% of the bond's face value. A $100,000 T-Bond quoted at 99-16 is worth $99,500. With T-bonds each tick (thirty-second of a point) is worth $31.25.

Unlike T-Bond futures, options on T-Bond futures are quoted in sixty-fourths of a percentage point. A premium of 2-16, for instance, represents $2\frac{1}{4}$% of the face value or a premium of $2,250 for a $100,000 T-Bond future.

Determinants of Premiums for a Call on a T-Bond Future

Consider a futures option on a T-bond future that has an exercise price of 90% of face value ($90,000 for a face value of $100,000). Figure 27A-2 illustrates the determinants of this option price. When the underlying T-Bond futures contracts are trading at 92-00 the call option on these contracts has a minimum value or intrinsic value of 2 points, denoted 2-00. The price of this call is 3-00 points ($3,000 for a $100,000 T-Bond) because the option's (93-00 price − 92-00 intrinsic value =) time premium is 1 point above its intrinsic value when the T-Bond future's price is $92,000. The time value premium for an in-the-money call option is calculated as:

$$\begin{pmatrix} \text{Time value premium} \\ \text{over and above the} \\ \text{intrinsic value} \end{pmatrix} = \begin{pmatrix} \text{Call option} \\ \text{premium, or} \\ \text{call's price} \end{pmatrix} + \begin{pmatrix} \text{Exercise} \\ \text{price for} \\ \text{the call} \end{pmatrix} - \begin{pmatrix} \text{Market price of} \\ \text{underlying asset} \end{pmatrix} \text{ if Mkt. Pr.} > \text{Exer. Pr.}$$

$$1 \qquad = \qquad 3 \qquad + \qquad 90 \qquad - \qquad 92$$

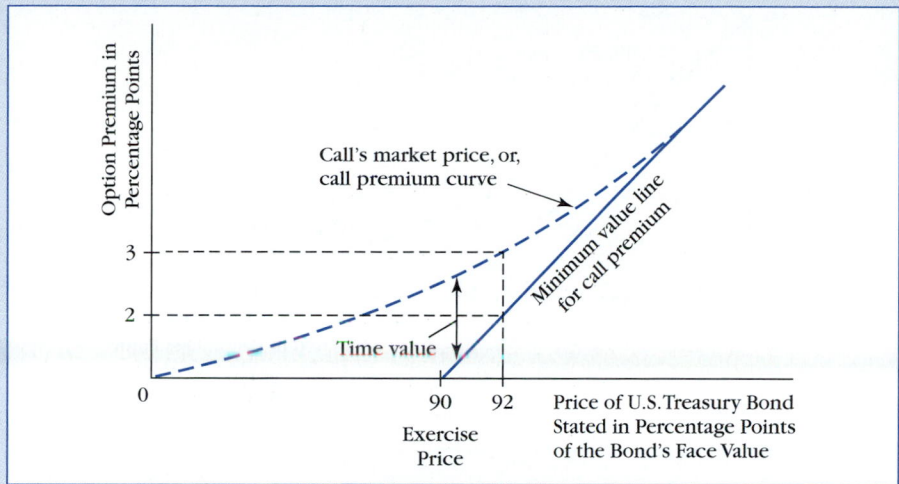

FIGURE 27A-2 Premium Breakdown for Futures Option on a T-Bond

The Treasury bond futures option has an exercise price of 90% of the T-bond's face value. When the underlying T-bond futures contracts are selling at 92.0% of face value the call option on these futures option contracts has a minimum value of 2 points. The price on this call is 3-00 points, which is comprised of an intrinsic value of 2-00 plus a time value premium of 1-00.

Determinants of Premiums for a Put on T-Bond Futures

Figure 27A-3 illustrates determinants of the premium for a put option on a T-Bond future with an exercise price of 90-00. If the underlying T-Bond future is trading at 88-00 ($88,000 for a $100,000 T-Bond) the put option's premium is 3-00 points ($3,000). This 3-00 point market price is comprised of an intrinsic value of 2-00 plus a time value premium of 1-00. The time value premium for an in-the-money put option is calculated as:

$$\begin{pmatrix} \text{Time value premium} \\ \text{in excess of the} \\ \text{intrinsic value} \end{pmatrix} = \begin{pmatrix} \text{Put option's} \\ \text{premium,} \\ \text{or price} \end{pmatrix} + \begin{pmatrix} \text{Market price} \\ \text{of the} \\ \text{underlying} \end{pmatrix} - \begin{pmatrix} \text{Exercise} \\ \text{price for} \\ \text{the put} \end{pmatrix} \text{ if Market price} < \text{Exercise price}$$

$$1 \quad = \quad 3 \quad + \quad 88 \quad - \quad 90$$

The Advantages and Disadvantages of Options on Futures

There are advantages to buying futures options instead of buying the futures contract or the underlying asset.

Limited Liability. Speculators who buy futures options enjoy limited liability. The buyer of a futures option cannot lose more than the premium. In contrast, investors who buy futures contracts directly must pay initial margin and, in addition, mark to the market based on each day's settlement price. If the price of the underlying asset makes a substantial disadvantageous move, the owner of a futures contract could lose much more than an option premium. The buyers of futures options do not obtain this limited liability without giving up something. Futures options do not become profitable until the price of the underlying asset moves far enough in the profitable direction to cover the cost of the option's premium.

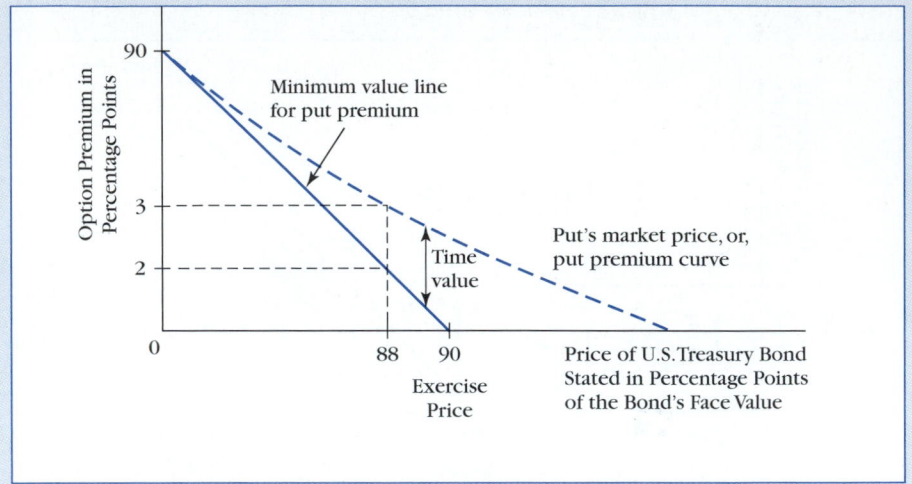

FIGURE 27A-3   Premium Breakdown for Put on T-Bond Future

The premium for a futures option on a T-bond with an exercise price that is 90% of the T-bond's face value depends on several factors. If the underlying T-bond future is trading at 88-00 the put option's premium is 3-00 points, which is comprised of an intrinsic value of 2-00 plus a time value premium of 1-00.

Conserve Cash. Futures options require less cash than might be needed to buy an option on the underlying asset (commodity) directly. This advantage becomes evident when comparing the cost of exercising the two different options. When an option is exercised directly on the underlying asset, the underlying asset must be purchased with cash—a large outlay.* In contrast, someone who exercised an option on a futures contract need only pay the initial margin on the futures contract. However, this low-cost exercise advantage may be worth little to investors who sell the option. If the option is sold, paying the initial margin upon exercise becomes irrelevant.

More Liquid. If an optioned commodity or security is traded infrequently in the cash market, its price is sometimes ambiguous. The price of an option on that infrequently traded asset is, therefore, somewhat ambiguous too. In other words, options on underlying assets that are not actively traded may not always be perfectly liquid (have meaningful current prices).

Suppose a futures contract exists for a commodity or security that is traded infrequently in the cash market. The listing futures exchange will post a price for that futures contract continuously. Therefore, the market price (premium) for an option on that futures contract will be unambiguously defined at all times. As a result, an option on that future may have a more clearly defined price (be more liquid) than (A) an option on the underlying asset that is traded infrequently, and, (B) the underlying asset itself.

---

* Exchange-listed options on some physical commodities are not available in the United States. However, over-the-counter (OTC) options on any commodity can be tailor-made and the price determined by negotiation. But OTC options are less liquid than listed options, and the price determination process can be difficult.

OPTIONS

This chapter explains how put and call prices are affected by six variables:

1. *The price of the underlying asset*
2. *The option's exercise price*
3. *Length of time until the option expires*
4. *Volatility (risk) of the underlying asset*
5. *The risk-free interest rate (RFR)*
6. *Cash flows (such as cash dividends)*

Formulas permit you to compute put and call prices (premiums) from these variables. These option valuation formulas are valid for options on stocks, options on stock market indexes, options on foreign currencies, and options on other underlying assets.

We derive a put-call parity formula showing the relationship between the prices of a put and a call on the same underlying asset. A formula showing the impact of cash dividend payments on options on dividend-paying common stocks is also presented.

One noteworthy feature of the option valuation formulas is the omission of variables that people intuitively think determine option prices. Most people are surprised to learn that investors' expectations about whether the price of the underlying asset is likely to rise or fall has no effect on the prices of puts and calls.

A binomial option-pricing model for valuing calls is presented first, followed by the Black-Scholes call-pricing model and the put-call parity formula. The put-call parity formula is used to determine put prices after call prices have been computed and to determine if the prices of puts and calls are aligned properly. If the underlying asset makes a cash payment, there is a formula to adjust the option price for that cash flow.

*One popular approach to option pricing is called **option replication.** A **replicating portfolio** is created to mimic the price behavior of the option. This replicating portfolio should provide a payout that is identical to the option, involve hedging costs that are identical to the option, and match the option's initial price exactly. If the prices of its components are known, the total cost of the replicating portfolio can be determined.*

> *Then the law of one price is invoked to equate the cost of the replicating portfolio and the price of the option being priced.*
>
> *In the last half of this chapter we use options as building blocks to construct investment strategies. Puts and calls are used to construct a synthetic long position and a synthetic short position in the underlying stock. Spreads, straddles, strangles, and covered call writing are the names of some of the option strategies we review.*

INTRODUCTION TO BINOMIAL OPTION PRICING

This section derives a simple valuation model to determine the premium (price) for a call option. The binomial option-pricing model that is derived assumes that the optioned security will experience either of two possible rates of return over the time being analyzed. Over the holding period (such as a month) either the optioned security's price can go up by $u = (1 + r_u)$ with probability p (up) or go down by $d = (1 + r_d)$ with probability p (down) $= [1.0 - p$ (up)]. Figure 28-1 illustrates an example that assumes the initial price of the optioned asset (for example, an underlying security) is \$45.45 and that this price can fluctuate either up or down by 10% during the next time period.*

To keep the mathematics simple we assume that the optioned security pays no cash flows during the period the underlying asset is optioned. For simplicity income taxes, brokerage commissions, transfer taxes, and margin requirements are ignored. The convention RR is used to represent one plus the risk-free interest rate, $RR = (1 + RFR)$. Finally, it is assumed that the investor can sell short and gain immediate use of the total proceeds from the short sale. These assumptions allow us to write uncomplicated formulas that are easy to understand and simple to manipulate.

The One-Period Binomial Call Pricing Formula

Eqn. 9-3 in Chapter 9 (p. 247) introduced the formula below for the intrinsic value of a call option on its expiration date.

Intrinsic value of a call $= MAX[0, (\{\text{Stock's price}, P\} - \{\text{Exercise price}, XP\}]$ **(28-1)**

FIGURE 28-1 Binomial Price Moves for an Optioned Security

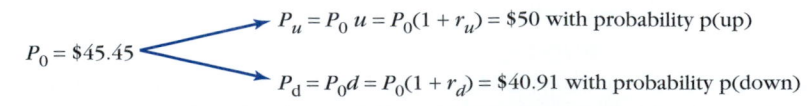

$$P_0 = \$45.45$$
$$P_u = P_0 u = P_0(1 + r_u) = \$50 \text{ with probability p(up)}$$
$$P_d = P_0 d = P_0(1 + r_d) = \$40.91 \text{ with probability p(down)}$$

The initial price of \$45.45 is expected to rise by $r_u = 10\%$ with a probability of p (up) or decline by $r_d = -10\%$ with a probability of $[1 - p$ (up)].

---

* To avoid profitable arbitrage opportunities, the following inequality can never be violated: $u > RR > d$. If $RR < d < u$, for example, an investor could borrow at RR and purchase the security in order to make a riskless profit with zero equity investment. Alternatively, if $RR > u > d$ the riskless investment would dominate two risky assets. If the price of the optioned security rises the exercised call will be worth COP_u.

To continue the example of the security initially priced at $45.45, we assume the option's exercise price (XP) is $40. At expiration a call is worth either zero or the excess of the optioned security's price over the exercise price, whichever is greater. If the price of the optioned security moves up 10% ($u = 1 + r_u = 1 + 10\% = 1.1$) the call option premium (*COP*) will be $10 at expiration, $COP_u = \$10$.

$$COP_u = Max[0, Pu - XP] \tag{28-1a}$$

$$\$10 = Max(0, \$45.45(1.1) - \$40]$$

If the price of the optioned security moves down 10% ($d = 1 - r_d = 1 - 10\% = 0.9$) the expiring call will be worth $COP_d = \$0.91$.

$$COP_d = Max[0, Pd - XP] \tag{28-1b}$$

$$\$0.91 = Max[0, \$45.45(.9) - \$40]$$

Figure 28-2 illustrates the two possible call premiums computed in Eqns. 28-1a and b.

Suppose we create a portfolio with h shares of the optioned security that is financed by borrowing B dollars at a riskless rate of $RR = (1 + RFR) = (1 + 5\%) = 1.05$. This portfolio's initial value is $V_0 = (hP_0 - B)$ dollars. It is called a **self-financing portfolio** because no money, $V_0 = 0$, is invested to get started. The money needed to finance the initial investment of hP_0 dollars is borrowed by issuing (selling) a bond worth B dollars. Money is never added to or withdrawn from this self-financing portfolio. If the investment of hP_0 is ever reduced, for example, the cash proceeds from selling some of hP_0 are used to pay off debt (reduce B). According to the binomial model, the portfolio can have either of the two values illustrated in Figure 28-3 at the end of one holding period.[1]

We now have enough information to determine what the call is worth. To find the call option's premium we find values for B and h that will equate the end-of-period values of the call for each possible state of nature (COP_u and COP_d) to the value of their associated hedge portfolios(V_u and V_d):

$$COP_u = V_u$$

$$COP_d = V_d$$

Expanding the two equations above yields:

$$Max[0, P_0u - XP] = COP_u = V_u = [huP_0 - RRB]$$

$$Max[0, P_0d - XP] = COP_d = V_d = [hdP_0 - RRB]$$

FIGURE 28-2   Call Premiums Fluctuate Directly with the Price of the Optioned Security

$COP_u = Max[0, P_0u - XP] = Max[0, P_u - XP]$ with probability p (up)

COP_0

$COP_d = Max[0, P_0d - XP] = Max[0, P_d - XP]$ with probability $1 - p$ (up)

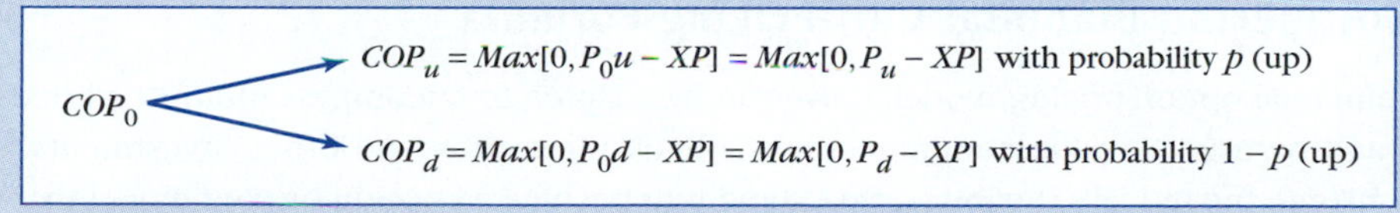

The call option's initial premium (price) of COP_0 is expected to rise to COP_u with a probability of p (up) or decline to COP_d with a probability of $[1 - p (up)] = p$ (down).

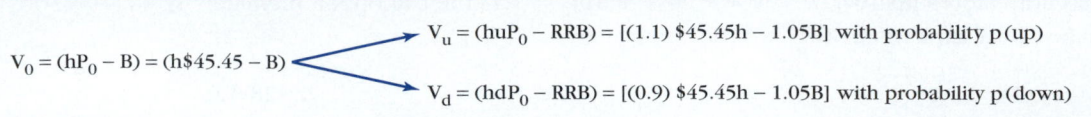

FIGURE 28-3   The Portfolio's End of Period Value Varies Directly with the Price of the Optioned Asset

$$V_0 = (hP_0 - B) = (h\$45.45 - B)$$

$$V_u = (huP_0 - RRB) = [(1.1) \$45.45h - 1.05B] \text{ with probability } p\,(up)$$

$$V_d = (hdP_0 - RRB) = [(0.9) \$45.45h - 1.05B] \text{ with probability } p\,(down)$$

The self-financing portfolio's initial value of V_o is expected to rise to V_u with a probability of p (up) or decline to a value of V_d with a probability of $[1 - p\,(up)]$, as determined by the price moves of the underlying asset.

Although we have suggested numerical values for most of the variables in the two expanded equations above, the values of h and B are still unknown. These two equations in two unknowns can be solved simultaneously to derive Eqns. 28-2 and 28-3. The solved value of h is denoted h^* and called the **hedge ratio** (discussed below). The money to form the leveraged portfolio initially worth V_0 dollars was provided by selling (issuing) a bond worth B^* dollars.

$$h^* = \frac{COP_u - COP_d}{(u - d)P_0} = \frac{COP_u - COP_d}{P_u - P_d} \tag{28-2}$$

$$B^* = \frac{dCOP_u - uCOP_d}{(u - d)RR} = \frac{P_dCOP_u - P_uCOP_d}{(P_u - P_d)RR} \tag{28-3}$$

We showed above that a leveraged portfolio containing h^* shares of a stock (or other securities) costing P_0 can be financed by borrowing B^* dollars and that this portfolio will duplicate the expiration payoffs from a call option. To prevent arbitrage this call must have the same initial cost as the leveraged (replicating) portfolio. Eqn. 28-4 is an equilibrium relation (no buying and no selling situation) that prevents arbitrage. Eqn. 28-4 can also be used as a call-pricing model.

$$\begin{pmatrix} \text{Initial price} \\ \text{of call option} \end{pmatrix} = \begin{pmatrix} \text{Value of the portfolio} \\ \text{containing } h^* \text{ and } B^* \end{pmatrix} \tag{28-4}$$

$$(COP_0) = (h^*P_0 - B^*)$$

Several factors about the call-pricing model above are noteworthy. First, the fluctuating price of the underlying asset, P_0, is a major determinant of a call option's initial price, COP_0. Second, the probabilities p (down) and p (up) have no impact on Eqn. 28-4. In other words, the call-pricing model is *unaffected by expectations*. Third, the model is *risk-neutral*. It is risk-neutral because the call buyer's preferences are not considered—the call has the same value whether a call buyer is risk-averse, risk-neutral, or risk-seeking.

A Multiperiod Binomial Call-Pricing Formula

The binomial option-pricing model above can be adapted to encompass multiple periods of time and be used to value common stocks, bonds, mortgages, and other investments.[2] To demonstrate the model's flexibility, we extend it to become an option-pricing model that has two time periods before expiration. Figure 28-4 shows the three possible prices the optioned asset might attain at the end of time period $t = 2$. Figure 28-5 illustrates the call prices implied by the three prices for the optioned asset shown in Figure 28-4. COP_{du} indicates the call premium that results when the price of the optioned asset goes down in the first period and then up in the second period. Likewise, COP_{uu} and COP_{dd} are the call premiums that result from two consecutive price upticks and down-ticks, respectively, in the price of the optioned security (or other asset).

Figure 28-6 illustrates all the prices of the underlying asset, associated call prices, hedge ratios, and the amounts that would have to be borrowed to establish riskless hedges over two consecutive time periods. The example in Figure 28-6 can be extended to three, four, or any number of time periods. The model can also be enhanced by adding branches representing the payment or nonpayment of cash flows (like cash dividends or coupon interest) and other events that affect the security's price.[3] Essentially, the binomial model can be transformed into a multiperiod option-pricing model. When the binomial call-pricing model employs a very large number of very small time intervals (for example, time periods equal to single trading days) to span a finite period (say, 2 months) the branches in the lattice proliferate and take on the recognizable symmetric forms shown in Figure 28-7.

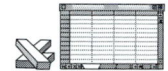

Pascal's Triangle, introduced in the 1600s, is adapted to call pricing in Figure 28-7A.[4] The integers in the left-most column of Figure 28-7A give the number of different prices that could occur at each different branch in a binomial random walk after t time periods. A frequency distribution that is stable through time becomes more apparent as the number of time periods increases. By the time t reaches $t = 7$ the normal probability distribution is emerging clearly in Figure 28-7A. We can anticipate that, after a large number of time periods have passed, the

FIGURE 28-4   Binomial Security Price Moves over Two Time Periods

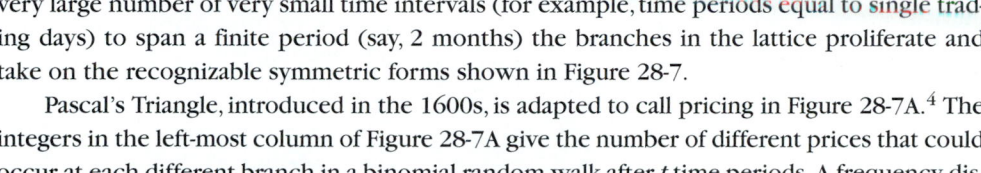

The initial price \$45.45 is expected to rise by $r_u = 10\%$ with a probability of p (up) or decline by $r_d = -10\%$ with a probability of $[1 - p\,(up)] = p\,(down)$ during the first time period, as illustrated in Figure 28-1. During the second period, the asset's market price is expected to rise by $r_u = 10\%$ or decline by $r_d = -10\%$, as it did in time period $t = 1$.

FIGURE 28-5   Call Premium Fluctuations over Two Periods

$t = 0$	$t = 1$	$t = 2$
		$COP_{uu} = Max[0, P_0u^2 - XP] = \$15$
	$COP_u = Max[0, P_0u - XP] = \$11.90$	$COP_{du} = Max(0, Pdu - XP) = \$5$
$COP_0 = \$9.35$	$COP_d = Max[0, P_0d - XP] = \$3.57$	$COP_{uu} = Max[0, P_0d^2 - XP] = 0$

During the first time period the call option's initial premium of COP_0 is expected to rise to COP_u with a probability of p (up) or decline to COP_d with a probability of $[1 - p\,(up)]$, as illustrated in Figure 28-2. During the second time period the call option's premium is expected to rise to $COP_{uu} = \$15$, change to a value of $COP_{du} = COP_{ud} = \$5$, or decline to $COP_{dd} = 0$, as determined by the market price of the underlying asset.

FIGURE 28-6 Lattice of Call Option Values That Follow Price Changes in the Optioned Security over Two Time Periods

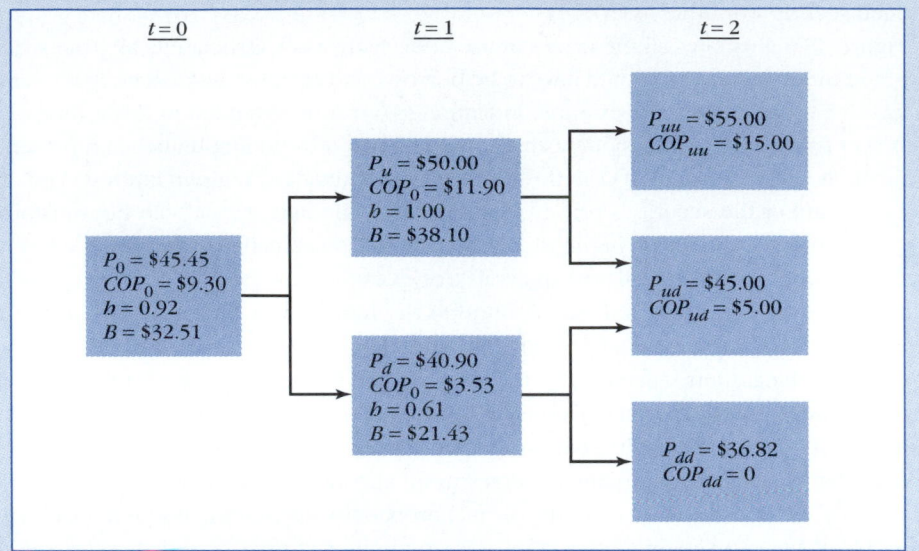

The lattice (tree diagram) traces option values that follow price changes in the optioned security over two consecutive time periods. The hedge ratios and the amounts of money borrowed are also shown.

SOURCE: Peter Ritchken, *Derivative Markets* (New York: Harper Collins, 1996), Exhibit 8.3, p. 193.*

outcomes from a binomial random walk evolve into a continuous time model that has normally distributed outcomes. This tendency forms the basis for equating the binomial option pricing model with the Black-Scholes option pricing model in the next section.[5]

Figure 28-7B illustrates a tree diagram of the possible paths the prices of a market asset might take as it followed a binomial random walk.

THE BLACK-SCHOLES CALL-OPTION-PRICING MODEL

By assuming that assets' continuous rates of return were normally distributed, Fischer Black and Myron Scholes were able to derive a formula to compute call prices.[6] Figure 28-7's illustrations of the outcomes resulting from a binomial random walk suggests intuitively why they used the normal probability distribution of returns. The mathematics used to derive the Nobel prize–winning Black-Scholes model is beyond the scope of this book, but that does not mean we cannot use the model to value call options.

The Black-Scholes Call-Valuation Formula

Black and Scholes used a self-financing (replicating) portfolio like the one introduced above in Figure 28-3 and Eqn. 28-4.

---

* Ritchken goes into details about their results shown in Figure 28-6. Ritchken's book also shows how to value a put option on the same underlying asset.

FIGURE 28-7   A Binomial Random Walk Generates More Outcomes and They Tend to Become More Normally Distributed as the Number of Time Periods (denoted *t*) Increases: (A) Pascal's Triangle, (B) A Tree Diagram (Lattice) of Possible Stock Prices

(A) Pascal's Triangle

Number of Prices at Time t	$t=0$	$t=1$	$t=2$	$t=3$	$t=4$	$t=5$	$t=6$	$t=7$	...
1	1	1	1	1	1	1	1	1	...
2		1	2	3	4	5	6	7	...
3			1	3	6	10	15	21	...
4				1	4	10	20	35	...
5					1	5	15	35	...
6						1	6	21	...
7							1	7	...
8								1	...
Paths to Outcome	$2^0=1$	$2^1=2$	$2^2=4$	$2^3=8$	$2^4=16$	$2^5=32$	$2^6=64$	$2^7=128$	...

(B) A Tree Diagram of Possible Price Outcomes

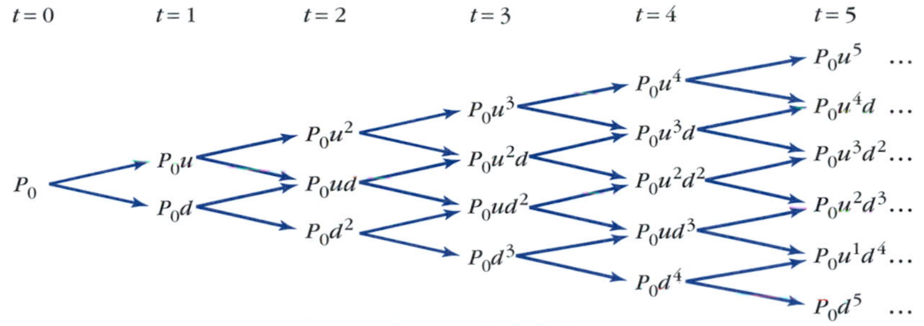

The two diagrams trace binomial random walks (series of two-way outcomes that can't be forecasted and) that generate more outcomes each period. These increasingly numerous outcomes more closely resemble a normal probability distribution as the number of periods increases. After an infinite number of periods (when $t=\infty$), the probability distribution comes together (converges) with the well-known normal bell-shaped curve.

$$COP_0 = (P_0 h - B) \tag{28-4}$$

Black and Scholes assumed the hedge ratio is $h = N(x)$ and the borrowings equaled $B = XP[e^{(-RFR)d}]N(y)$ dollars. Eqn. 28-5 presents the Black-Scholes call-option-pricing model in a form similar to Eqn. 28-4.

$$\text{Call options price }(COP_o) = P_0 N(x) - XP[e^{(-RFR)d}]N(y) \tag{28-5}$$

x and y are defined in Eqns. 28-6 and 28-7.

$$x = \frac{ln(P_0 XP) + [RFR + 0.5VAR(r)]d}{\sigma d^{0.5}} \qquad \text{The value of } x \text{ has no intuitive meaning.} \tag{28-6}$$

$$y = x - \sigma d^{0.5} \qquad \text{The value of } y \text{ has no intuitive meaning.} \qquad \text{(28-7)}$$

ln denotes the natural (base *e*) logarithm with *e* = 2.7183, *d* denotes the fraction of 1 year until expiration of the call (for example, a 6-month maturity means *d* = 1/2), and, *N*(*x*) represents a cumulative normal-density function of the argument *x* (see Table 28-1). *N*(*x*) gives the probability that a value of less than *x* will occur in a normal probability distribution which has a mean of zero and a standard deviation equal to unity. Sample values of *N*(*x*) are:

$$N(-\infty) = 0, \qquad N(0) = .5, \qquad N(+\infty) = 1.0$$

The call prices suggested by the Black-Scholes model are illustrated by the dashed curves in Figure 28-8. The curves in Figure 28-8 trace the call prices generated by the model for different prices of the underlying asset and different assumptions about the length of time until the call matures.

EXAMPLE

USING THE BLACK-SCHOLES MODEL TO PRICE A CALL OPTION

All that is needed to use the Black-Scholes model are (1) a table of natural logarithms (many algebra and statistics books and hand calculators contain natural logarithms), and (2) a table of cumulative normal distribution probabilities. The cumulative normal distribution values for *N*(*x*) and *N*(*y*) are shown in Table 28-1.

For this numerical example of how to use the Black-Scholes call-pricing model, we assume the following data:

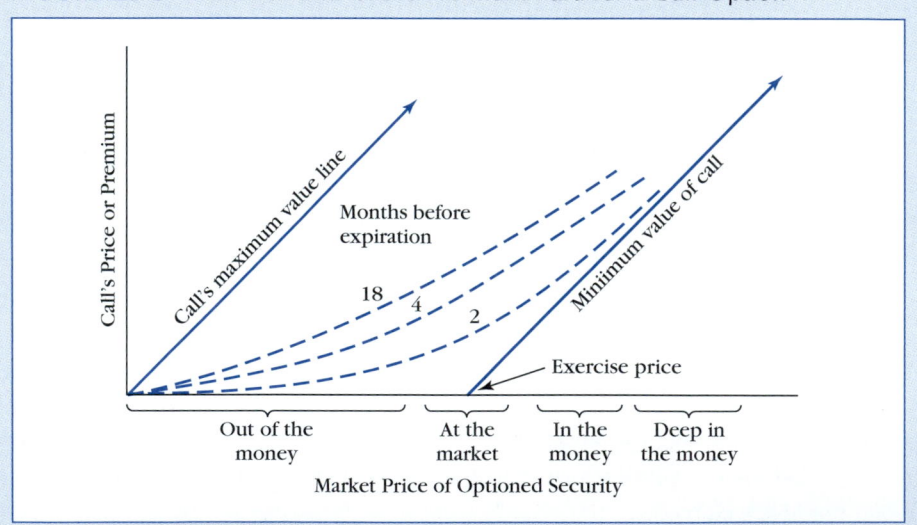

FIGURE 28-8 Determinants of the Premium Paid for a Call Option

A call option's premium, COP, is determined by price of the underlying asset, the time remaining until the option expires, the exercise price, XP, of the option, and the variance (standard deviation, variance, volatility) of the underlying asset's price. The risk-free rate, RFR, of interest and cash flows (such as cash dividend payments, if any) also help determine the price of the call option, but their impacts are not revealed in this figure.

P_0 = \$60 = market price of the underlying asset (such as the share price of an optioned stock)

XP = \$50 = exercise (striking) price

d = .333 = 4 months (one-third of a year) = the time until the option expires and is worthless

R = .07 = 7% = risk-free rate (RFR) stated at an annual rate

VAR(r) = .144 = variance of returns = The riskiness of an investment in the optioned asset. Estimating the risk statistic is discussed further below.

The quantity x is calculated by substituting the numerical values into Eqn. 28-6 to obtain Eqn. 28-8.

$$x = \frac{ln(P_0/XP) + [RFR + 0.5VAR(r)]d}{\sigma\,d^{0.5}} = \frac{ln(\$60/\$50) + [0.07 + .5(0.144)](0.333)}{(0.3794)(0.5773)} = \frac{0.2296}{0.2190} = 1.048 \qquad \textbf{(28-8)}$$

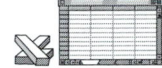

The value of y is evaluated in Eqn. 28-9:

$$y = x - \sigma d^{0.5} = 1.04825 - (0.3794)(0.5773) = 1.04825 - .21907 = .829 \qquad \textbf{(28-9)}$$

Substituting the x and y values above into Eqn. 28-5 yields Eqn. 28-10:

$$COP_0 = P_0N(x) - XP[e^{(-RFR)d}]N(y) = \$60N(1.048) - \$50(anti\ ln\{-0.7\}\{0.333\})N(0.829) \quad \textbf{(28-10)}$$

Looking up the values of the antilog for natural logs and the cumulative normal distribution in tables and completing the calculations indicates that the call is worth \$12.29. If P_0 = \$60 was the price of a share of stock and $VAR(r)$ = .144 was that share's variance, then COP = \$12.29 is the value of a call option on that share of stock.

$$COP_0 = \$60(.853) - \$50(.977)(.796) = \$51.18 - \$38.89 = \$12.29$$

Instead of using data for a share of stock, suppose P_0 = \$60 was the price for 10 ounces of silver and $VAR(r)$ = .144 was silver's variance. In this case COP = \$12.29 would be the value of a call option on 10 ounces of silver that had an exercise price of XP = \$50. The Black-Scholes option-pricing model is a general model that can be used to value stock options, commodity options, or other options.

The Hedge Ratio

An option's **hedge ratio** may be defined to be the fraction of a \$1 change in the option's premium that is caused by a \$1 change in the price of the optioned asset. The hedge ratio is also called *delta,* the *neutral hedge ratio,* the *elasticity,* and the *equivalence ratio.* Graphically speaking, the hedge ratio equals the slope of any one of the dashed call price curves in Figure 28-8 evaluated at a particular point. The figure shows that calls have positive hedge ratios that are never less than zero and never greater than +1.

Hedgers seek the hedge ratio that will totally eliminate changes in the value of their hedged portfolio. Mathematically, this hedge ratio is given by the value of the quantity $N(x)$ in the Black-Scholes call pricing Eqn. 28-5; it is repeated as:

$$N(x) = \delta(COP)/\delta P = \text{Slope of call price curve in Figure 28-8} = \text{Black-Scholes hedge ratio} \quad \textbf{(28-11)}$$

TABLE 28-1   Values of N(x) for Given Values of x for a Cumulative Normal Probability Distribution Function with Zero Mean and Unit Variance

x	$N(x)$	x	$N(x)$	x	$N(x)$	x	$N(x)$	x	$N(x)$	x	$N(x)$
		-2.00	.0228	-1.00	.1587	.00	.5000	1.00	.8413	2.00	.9773
-2.95	.0016	-1.95	.0256	-.95	.1711	.05	.5199	1.05	.8531	2.05	.9798
-2.90	.0019	-1.90	.0287	-.90	.1841	.10	.5398	1.10	.8643	2.10	.9821
-2.85	.0022	-1.85	.0322	-.85	.1977	.15	.5596	1.15	.8749	2.15	.9842
-2.80	.0026	-1.80	.0359	-.80	.2119	.20	.5793	1.20	.8849	2.20	.9861
-2.75	.0030	-1.75	.0401	-.75	.2266	.25	.5987	1.25	.8944	2.25	.9878
-2.70	.0035	-1.70	.0446	-.70	.2420	.30	.6179	1.30	.9032	2.30	.9893
-2.65	.0040	-1.65	.0495	-.65	.2578	.35	.6368	1.35	.9115	2.35	.9906
-2.60	.0047	-1.60	.0548	-.60	.2743	.40	.6554	1.40	.9192	2.40	.9918
-2.55	.0054	-1.55	.0606	-.55	.2912	.45	.6736	1.45	.9265	2.45	.9929
-2.50	.0062	-1.50	.0668	-.50	.3085	.50	.6915	1.50	.9332	2.50	.9938
-2.45	.0071	-1.45	.0735	-.45	.3264	.55	.7088	1.55	.9394	2.55	.9946
-2.40	.0082	-1.40	.0808	-.40	.3446	.60	.7257	1.60	.9452	2.60	.9953
-2.35	.0094	-1.35	.0885	-.35	.3632	.65	.7422	1.65	.9505	2.65	.9960
-2.30	.0107	-1.30	.0968	-.30	.3821	.70	.7580	1.70	.9554	2.70	.9965
-2.25	.0122	-1.25	.1057	-.25	.4013	.75	.7734	1.75	.9599	2.75	.9970
-2.20	.0139	-1.20	.1151	-.20	.4207	.80	.7881	1.80	.9641	2.80	.9974
-2.15	.0158	-1.15	.1251	-.15	.4404	.85	.8023	1.85	.9678	2.85	.9978
-2.10	.0179	-1.10	.1357	-.10	.4602	.90	.8159	1.90	.9713	2.90	.9981
-2.05	.0202	-1.05	.1469	-.05	.4801	.95	.8289	1.95	.9744	2.95	.9984

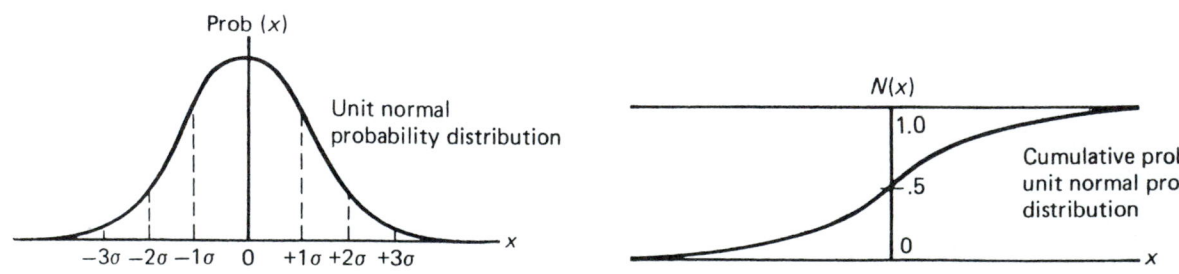

The unit normal probability distribution has a mean of zero and a variance of one and is represented by the convention $N(\bar{x}, \sigma^2) = N(0,1)$. For a given value of x a cumulative normal probability distribution function gives the probability, denoted N(x), that a value of x or lesser value of x will occur.

In terms of the Black-Scholes option-pricing model, the hedge ratio is the ratio of the value of the stock held in a long position, $P_0 N(x)$, divided by the size of the debt needed to finance that investment, $XP[e^{(-RFR)d}]N(y)$ dollars.

Investors can use the hedge ratio to translate the option—either a call or a put—into a fractional equivalent of the underlying instrument. For example, the investor can create a hedged portfolio that has the fraction $(-1)N(x)$ as many shares of the underlying security as the option is worth so, for small price changes, movements in the value of the stock position will be exactly offset by an opposite and equal movement in the value of the option. For instance, suppose a call option on 100 shares of ABC stock is hedged based on the computed value $x = 1.65$, the hedge ratio is $N(1.65) = .9505$. This hedge ratio value means 95.05 shares of ABC should be sold short to establish a perfect hedge against 100 shares held in an offsetting long position.[7] Conversely, someone who is short a 100-share call on ABC would be perfectly hedged with a long position of 95.05 shares of ABC.

Unfortunately, the hedges formed using the hedge ratio are perfect only as long as the price of the optioned asset remains constant. As soon as the price or the variance of returns of the underlying asset changes, the value of $N(x)$ changes and the value of the call option has to be recomputed.

Risk Statistics and Option Values

The investor normally uses his or her own standard deviation of returns as an input statistic to the Black-Scholes option-pricing model. Alternatively, the investor can insert a call option's current market price (premium) as an input statistic to the Black-Scholes option-pricing model and then solve the model to find the standard deviation (volatility) that is *implied* by the call option's market price.[8] Table 28-2 contains some *implied risk statistics.* Comparing Tables 28-2a, 28-2b, and 28-2c reveals significant changes in the implied risk statistics of various optioned assets through time. Implied volatility statistics (standard deviations) differ from the historical risk statistics, although the two statistics tend to have similar values and to rise and fall together as the months pass.

Figure 9-8 in Chapter 9 (p. 258) shows that, as the riskiness of the underlying security increases, the prices of calls and puts on the asset increase. The figure illustrates the cause and effect relationship between risk and call prices for the ABC and XYZ Corporations. The exercise prices of the calls on ABC and XYZ stocks have been set equal to their expected stocks prices in Figure 9-8, $E(P) = XP$; this implies that both calls have a 50-50 chance of ending up either out-of-the-money (if $P < XP$) or in-the-money (if $P > XP$). Figure 9-8C shows that the call on XYZ is worth more than the call on ABC because XYZ is riskier. Puts and calls are both more likely to become profitable to exercise when the volatility of the underlying asset rises.

Table 28-2 showed how risk statistics change with the passage of time.[9] One way to obtain current risk statistics is to estimate the variance using recent empirical returns and then subjectively to adjust the empirically estimated variance to reflect expected changes in the optioned security's risk. Table 28-3 presents some annualized variances for optioned stocks that were appropriate during January 2000.

THE PUT-CALL PARITY FORMULA

The **put-call parity formula** is an arbitrage-free (partial equilibrium) relationship between the prices of a put and a call on the same underlying security, if the two options have identical exercise prices and identical times to maturity. To see how this relationship is derived, consider a portfolio containing a share of stock purchased for P_0 dollars, a call on the same stock has been sold short (written), and a put on the same stock that has the same exercise price as the call has been purchased. As shown in the two-outcomes box below (p. 847), the value of each quantity depends on whether the price of the optioned stock is above (right column) or below (left column) the options' exercise price.

TABLE 28-2   Implied Volatilities for Four Underlying Assets Derived from Options' Market Premiums Using Black-Scholes Model: (A) 1 Year, (B) Over 3 Years, (C) Over 10 Years

	Eurodollar	Japanese Yen	S&P500	Live Cattle
(A) 1 Year, 1998				
High	13.9%	24.7%	44.1%	27.6%
90 Percentile	12.0%	18.9%	31.5%	20.1%
50 Percentile	9.6%	15.2%	20.3%	15.4%
10 Percentile	8.2%	12.5%	16.6%	11.8%
Low	7.1%	11.4%	15.4%	10.9%
(B) Over 3 Years, 1996–98				
High	21.2%	24.7%	44.1%	32.8%
90 Percentile	15.4%	17.2%	25.3%	18.4%
50 Percentile	11.5%	11.2%	18.2%	14.0%
10 Percentile	8.7%	7.2%	13.0%	11.6%
Low	7.1%	6.6%	10.5%	9.8%
(C) Over 10 Years, 1989–98				
High	37.6%	24.7%	44.1%	32.8%
90 Percentile	23.8%	14.2%	21.9%	16.9%
50 Percentile	15.6%	10.5%	14.8%	12.3%
10 Percentile	10.0%	8.0%	10.5%	9.6%
Low	7.1%	6.6%	8.4%	7.8%

The implied volatilities above are annualized standard deviations that measure the risk of an optioned asset. The implied volatilities of four underlying assets derived from options' market premiums using Black-Scholes model (A) over a single year, (B) over 3 years, and (C) over 10 years are not stable through time. Changing volatilities reflect changes in the market's perception of the risk of the underlying asset.

SOURCE: "1999 Volatility Reference Guide," CME Traders Corner, March 3, 2000, Chicago Mercantile Exchange (CME), Chicago, IL; Web site address is: *www.cme.com/market/options*

TABLE 28-3   Historical Volatility Statistics for Optioned Stocks

Optioned Stock (Ticker Symbol)	Variance of Returns	Standard Deviation
Amazon.com (AMZN)	114.31	10.69% (high)
American Telephone & Telegraph (T)	45.06	6.71%
Coca-Cola (KO)	45.67	6.75%
General Motors (GM)	51.60	7.18%
Sysco Corp. (SYY)	65.26	8.08%
Microsoft (MSFT)	50.00	7.07%
Wrigley (WWY)	30.70	5.54% (low)

Each asset has risk statistics that reflect the amount of volatility in that asset's market price. The statistics above suggest Amazon.com's Internet business is a high-risk business and manufacturing Wrigley's chewing gum is a low-risk business.

SOURCE: Market Statistics Summary for January 2000, observed March 3, 2000, Chicago Board of Options Exchange (CBOE), Chicago, IL; Web site address is: *www.cboe.com/tools/statistics*

Portfolio of 3 Positions	Position Value when Options Expire	
	If P < XP	**If P > XP**
1) Long position on underlying stock	P	P
2) Short a call option (sell call)	0	XP − P
3) Long a put option (buy put)	XP − P	0
The portfolio's two total values:	XP	XP

The two different sums in the left and right columns of the box above both have total values
of XP dollars—regardless of whether P is larger or smaller than XP. In other words, the portfolio is perfectly hedged to a fixed value of XP dollars regardless of whether the option is in
the money (P > XP) or out of the money (P < XP).

To value this portfolio, consider two facts.

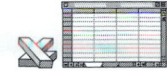

- The portfolio in the two-outcomes-box above is worth the present value of the
  option's exercise price, $(XP)/(1 + RFR)^d$, under either outcome.

- The portfolio must also be worth the combined prices paid for the share of optioned
  stock (P) plus the price of the put (POP), less the price for which the short call
  (COP) was sold. In other words, the portfolio is worth: $(P + POP − COP)$ dollars.

Equating the two quantities listed above results in the put-call parity equation.

$$\left(\begin{array}{c}\text{Stock's}\\\text{price, }P\end{array}\right) + \left(\begin{array}{c}\text{Purchase price}\\\text{of put, }POP\end{array}\right) - \left(\begin{array}{c}\text{Call option's}\\\text{premium, }COP\end{array}\right) = \left(\begin{array}{c}\text{Excercise}\\\text{price, }XP\end{array}\right)/(1 + RFR)^d \quad \textbf{(28-12)}$$

Pricing Put Options

We determined the price of a call option by using either the binomial call-pricing model or
the Black and Scholes formula. This book has not yet shown a model for valuing put
options.[10] The put-call parity equation can be used to determine the value of a put *after* the
value of a call on the same security has been determined.[11]

As mentioned above, the put-call parity equation is a relationship between the price of a
put and the price of a call on the same underlying stock for options with identical times to
maturity. Eqn. 28-12 is restated in terms of the put option's price:

$$\left(\begin{array}{c}\text{Purchase price}\\\text{of put, }POP\end{array}\right) = \left(\begin{array}{c}\text{Call option's}\\\text{premium, }COP\end{array}\right) + \left(\begin{array}{c}\text{Exercise}\\\text{price, }XP\end{array}\right)/(1 + RFR)^d - \left(\begin{array}{c}\text{Stock's}\\\text{price, }P\end{array}\right) \quad \textbf{(28-12a)}$$

The same numerical values from the example using Black-Scholes Eqns. 28-8, 28-9, and
28-10 to price a call are employed here to determine the value of a put option on the same
asset. The price of the optioned stock is P = $60; the exercise price is XP = $50; d = .333;
R = .07; and, VAR(r) = .144. The Black-Scholes model placed a value on this 4-month call,
COP = $12.29. The value of a 4-month put is calculated by substituting the appropriate
values into Eqn. 28-12a:

$$\left(\begin{array}{c}\text{Purchase price}\\\text{of put,}\\POP = \$1.18\end{array}\right) = \left(\begin{array}{c}\text{Call option's}\\\text{premium,}\\COP = \$12.29\end{array}\right) + \left(\begin{array}{c}\text{Exercise}\\\text{price,}\\XP = \$50\end{array}\right)/(1.07)^{.333} - \left(\begin{array}{c}\text{Stock's}\\\text{price,}\\P = \$60\end{array}\right) \quad \textbf{(28-12b)}$$

Eqn. 28-12b shows that if all variables in the put-call parity are known except the put's
premium, the formula can be solved to determine that price. We see POP = $1.18 if the put
has the same 4-month time to expiration as the call.

Eqn. 28-12 can also be rearranged to find the price the call when the values of all other variables in the put-call parity are known.

Checking Alignment of Put and Call Prices on an Underlying Stock

The Chicago Board of Options Exchange (CBOE), American Stock Exchange (AMEX), Philadelphia Stock Exchange (PHIX), Pacific Stock Exchange (PSE), and other options exchanges around the world that are listed in Table 9-1F of Chapter 9 trade puts and calls on actively traded stocks. When prices are posted for both the put and call on the same underlying stock, the put-call parity formula can be used to determine if these put and call prices are aligned properly. If put and call prices on the same stock are not aligned, arbitrage profits can be earned by correcting the pricing discrepancy.

EXAMPLE   **ARE A PUT AND A CALL ON COCA-COLA'S STOCK PRICED CORRECTLY?**

On July 13, 2000 the market price of Coca-Cola's common stock was $57. On that date calls on Coke stock with an exercise price of $60 and 1 month to expiration were selling for $1.625. The analogous puts were selling for $4.125, and the 3-month (8.33% of 1 year) Treasury bills were yielding a risk-free rate of 6%. We can insert these values into the put-call parity equation:

$$\binom{\text{Purchase price}}{\text{of put, } POP} = \binom{\text{Call option's}}{\text{premium, } COP} + \binom{\text{Exercise}}{\text{price, } XP}\Big/(1 + RFR)^d - \binom{\text{Stock's}}{\text{price, } P}$$

The put-call parity equation shows that, on a per share basis, either the put was underpriced by 21 cents or the call was overpriced by 21 cents.

$$\binom{\text{Pricing error}}{\substack{\text{of 21 cents} \\ \text{per share}}} + \binom{\text{KO put's}}{\substack{\text{price,} \\ POP = \$4.125}} = \binom{\text{KO call}}{\substack{\text{premium,} \\ COP = \$1.625}} + \binom{\text{Put and call's}}{\substack{\text{exercise prices,} \\ XP = \$60}}\Big/(1.06)^{0.0833} - \binom{\text{KO's}}{\substack{\text{share price,} \\ P = \$57}}$$

Commissions, income taxes, and other transactions costs eat into the profits from correcting the 21 cents per share option-pricing error. The put-call parity formula pinpoints pricing errors but, since it ignores the transactions costs from the arbitrage, it does not tell us if the arbitrage will generate a profit net of the transactions costs.[12]

THE EFFECTS OF CASH DIVIDEND PAYMENTS

When a corporation's board of directors declares that the stockholders of record are eligible to receive a cash dividend, that stock's market price adjusts to the announcement. The first trading day after the cash dividend is paid is called the **ex-dividend date;** that is when the stock begins trading without the cash dividend attached. On the ex-dividend date the stock's market price adjusts on the opening trade by starting to trade at a price that is reduced by the amount of the cash dividend payment. This **ex-dividend stock price dropoff** occurs because buyers of a stock that is trading ex-dividend are not entitled to receive the cash dividend and, so, they should no longer pay for it.[13]

The ex-dividend stock price drop-off decreases the value of any call options on the stock, and increases the value of any put options.* Because cash dividend payments affect option prices, they should be considered in determining when to sell or exercise an American option. As European calls can be exercised only on their maturity date, their exercise date is a moot point.**

Figures 28-8 (p. 842) and 28-9 illustrate the minimum call boundary and the Black-Scholes value curve for an American call option that has not yet expired. An option's intrinsic value line is the minimum value of the call if it is exercised before it expires, or what it will be worth on its expiration day. The vertical distance between the minimum value (intrinsic value) line and the price curve measures the **time value** in the option's price.

The Decision to Exercise. A call is said to be "dead" after it expires because it has no remaining value. The price curves trace out the option's price if it is not exercised and not expired—if it is still "alive." An American call is always worth more alive than dead. Figure 28-9 is used to illustrate some considerations involved in deciding whether to exercise an American call before the underlying stock starts trading ex-dividend.

If a call on a stock with a pre–cash-dividend has a stock price of P^d, the call option's price of COP^d lies along the price curve in Figure 28-9. When the optioned stock starts trading ex-dividend, its price drops from P^d to P^e. The option's price will not usually fall as much as the optioned stock price if the option is alive (because the slope of the price curve is less than $+1$). The Black-Scholes formula can be used to price calls on live stocks. At an ex-dividend market price for the optioned stock of P^e, the value of the live call is COP^e. If the option's value before it trades ex-dividend exceeds its value ex-dividend value by more than the amount of the cash dividend, $(COP^d - COP^e) > DIV$, then the call should be exercised before it trades ex-dividend to capture the cash dividend while it is still embedded in the stock's price.[14] Sometimes it is optimal to exercise an American call immediately prior to an ex-dividend date.

Computations with the Cash Dividend. The present value of a cash dividend per share, DIV, that is expected to be received with certainty 1 year ahead is $DIV/(1+RFR)$. Because a cash dividend payment causes a stock price ex-dividend price drop-off that causes the call's price to drop too, the present value of the cash dividend payment should be deducted from the underlying stock price in the Black-Scholes option pricing model.

$$COP^e = [P_0 - DIV/(1 + RFR)]N(x) - XP[e^{(-RFR)d}]N(y) \tag{28-5a}$$

Eqn. 28-5a is the Black-Scholes option-pricing model with a cash dividend adjustment of $DIV/(1+RFR)$ included to compute the ex-dividend price of the call.

---

* **Payout-protected options** have their contractual terms adjusted so the option value is unaffected by cash dividends. Most options listed on organized exchanges are not payout protected. Specialists at many stock exchanges and brokerage houses automatically reduce open orders for stock by the amount of the dividend on the ex-dividend date. Some over-the-counter options partially protect the call option owner from losses resulting from cash dividend payments by reducing the option's exercise price by the amount of the cash dividend per share whenever a cash dividend is paid.

** Cash dividend stock price drop-offs cause small discontinuities in the tree diagrams used with the binomial option-pricing model. But these small price path drop-offs do not reduce the value of the binomial option-pricing model.

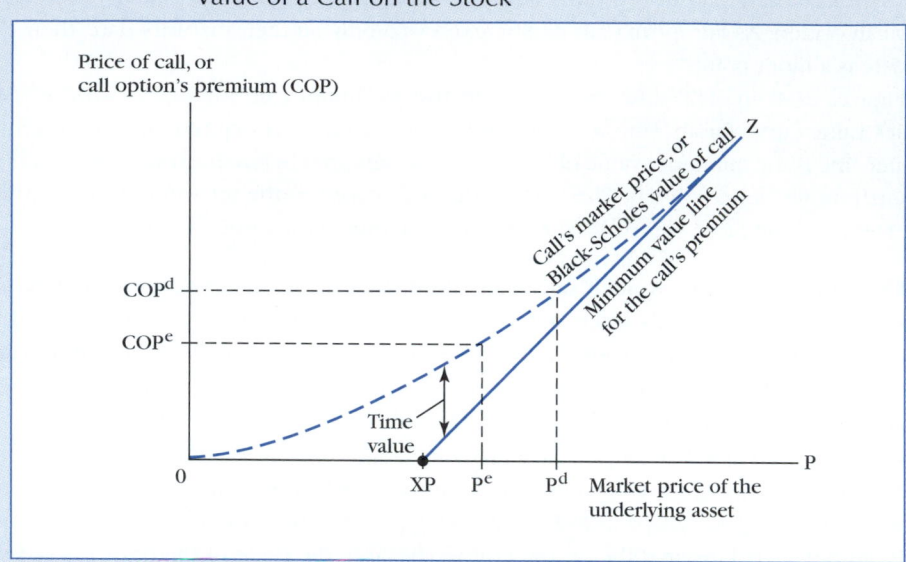

FIGURE 28-9   The Optioned Stock's Ex-Dividend Price Dropoff Affects the Value of a Call on the Stock

The intrinsic value line traces out the minimum value of a call option's price (COP). The price curve traces out COPs computed with the Black-Scholes call option-pricing formula. The vertical distance between the intrinsic value line and a price curve measures that time value embedded in the COP.

On the first day after a stock begins trading ex-dividend, its market price drops off by the amount of the cash dividend paid. An ex-dividend stock price drop-off causes the associated COP to decrease simultaneously.

EXAMPLE   CALL OPTION PREMIUM AFTER A CASH DIVIDEND ADJUSTMENT

Using the same data used with the Black-Scholes call-pricing example earlier in this chapter gives us: $P_0 = \$60, XP = \$50, d = .333, RFR = .07$, and $VAR(r) = .144$. In addition, suppose the stock is expected to pay a cash dividend per share of $DIV = \$2$ 1 year in the future with certainty. The present value of this cash payment is $DIV/(1+RFR) = \$2/(1.07) = \$1.869$ inserted into Eqns. 28-5a and b.

$$COP^e = [P_0 - DIV/(1 + RFR)]N(x) - XP[e^{(-RFR)d}]N(y) \tag{28-5a}$$

$$= [\$60 - \$1.869]N(1.048) - \$50(anti\ ln\{-0.7\}\{0.333\})N(0.829) \tag{28-5b}$$

$$= [\$60 - \$1.869](.853) - \$50(.977)(.796) = \$49.5857 - \$38.89 = \$10.69$$

The call was priced at $12.29 in the earlier example without any cash dividend. The call's ex-dividend premium has decreased by $1.60 (= $12.29 − $10.69) because of a $2 cash dividend payment that as a present value of $1.869. The put-call parity formula can be used to convert this cash-dividend-adjusted call price to the ex-dividend price for a put with similar provisions on the same underlying stock.

OPTIONS MARKETS

The Chicago Board Options Exchange (CBOE) was founded in 1973; today it is the largest options exchange in the world. The American Stock Exchange (AMEX) is a stock exchange and is also the second largest options exchange in the world. The Philadelphia Stock Exchange (PHIX), the oldest stock exchange in the United States, also lists currency options on a half dozen foreign currencies and equity options on dozens of common stocks. The Pacific Stock Exchange (PSE) supplements its stock exchange activities with an options market. Many other stock exchanges around the world trade options. Table 9-1F in Chapter 9 (p. 233) lists the world's options exchanges. In addition to these easily identifiable options exchanges, international banks around the world operate a huge over-the-counter options market. The OTC market's volume of currency options and interest rate options far exceeds the volume of the options listed at exchanges.

The CBOE, AMEX, PHIX, and PSE clear their option transactions through the *Options Clearing Corporation (OCC)*. The OCC is headquartered in Chicago and operates in those U.S. cities where option exchanges it services are located. It is owned by the exchanges it services. The SEC regulates the OCC and the markets for options on common stock. The CFTC oversees futures trading in the United States. The CFTC also has jurisdiction over options on agricultural goods.

In 2000 the International Securities Exchange (ISE), with the permission of the SEC, began operating. The ISE has no trading floor; it is an electronic exchange. The ISE is backed by a group of brokerage firms that includes Morgan Stanley Dean Witter, Ameritrade, E*Trade Group, Knight Trading Group, and other brokerages that hope to gain cost savings from the ISE. The ISE has no traditional open-outcry trading floor; it competes electronically with the CBOE, AMEX, PHIX, and PSE by listing options on most of the same stocks listed on these traditional options exchanges.

SYNTHETIC POSITIONS CAN BE CREATED FROM OPTIONS

A deliberate plan sometimes goes through a series of transactions that results in a unexpected outcome.

The Synthetic Long Position

An options trader who simultaneously writes (sells, shorts) a put and buys (takes a long position in) a call on the same underlying security at about the same exercise prices creates a position that is the economic equivalent to owning a long position in the underlying stock. Stated differently, buying a call and selling a put on the same security creates a *synthetic long position* in the optioned security similar to a buy-and-hold position in the security. Consider Figures 9-4A (buying a call) and 9-5B (writing a put) from Chapter 9 (p. 246, 250) and you will see that when these two options have about the same exercise price and are combined; this merger creates a synthetic long position with the same gain-loss potentials as the long position in Figure 28-10.

CONTRASTING LONG POSITIONS IN PHELPS STOCK

EXAMPLE

Phelps Corporation's common stock is currently selling at $40 per share. Suppose a 6-month call on Phelps with a $40 exercise price is purchased for $5 per share, and, an 8-month Phelps put with an exercise price of $40 is written to gain premium income of $5 per share. These two options create a synthetic long position that is compared to an actual long position in Phelps stock in Table 28-4 for a 100-share transaction.

FIGURE 28-10   The Components of a Synthetic Long Position: (A) Long Call, (B) Short Put, (C) Synthetic Long, (D) Ordinary Long Position

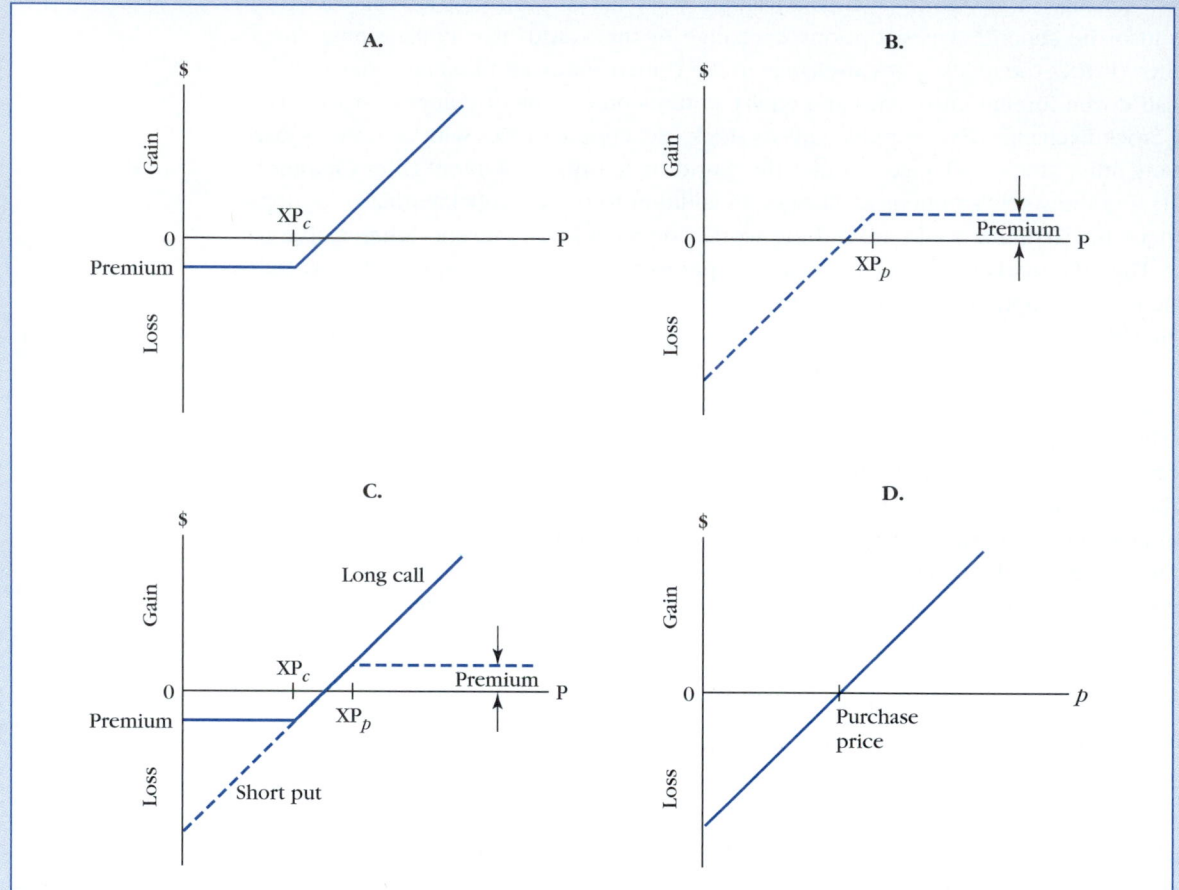

A long position can be created via financial engineering. Purchasing a call and writing a put with about the same exercise prices on the same underlying stock creates a synthetic long position in that stock.

TABLE 28-4   **Contrasting Actual and Synthetic Long Positions in Phelps Stock**

Possible Prices of Phelps Stock at Expiration of Options	Results from 6-Month Call with $40 Exercise Price Costing $5	Results from $5 Put Written with $40 Exercise Price	Result from Two Option Positions Combined	Result from the 100-Share Long Position at $40
$30	−$500	−$500	−$1,000	−$1,000
$35	−$500	0	−$500	−$500
$40	−$500	+$500	0	0
$45	0	+$500	+$500	+$500
$50	+$500	+$500	+$1,000	+$1,000
$55	+$1,000	+$500	+$1,500	+$1,500

If the prices of a put and a call on Phelps stock are not equal, the synthetic long position would not be equivalent to the actual long position. The put-call parity relationship showed that, if their exercise prices and maturity dates are equal, a put is worth less than a call on the same stock. To make the put and call prices in Table 28-4 both equal $5 it is necessary to assume the put on Phelps stock had more time to maturity than the call. However, different maturities cause a problem. For example, when a 6-month call expires, an 8-month put will have 2 months of remaining life. When that time arrives, the investor must buy a 2-month call on Phelps stock to maintain the synthetic long position. The cost of buying a 2-month put or call on Phelps stock makes that synthetic long position more costly to maintain than an ordinary long position in the underlying stock. In addition, the synthetic long strategy will incur more commission costs than simply buying the stock.

Some investors would find a synthetic long position more desirable than a straightforward long position because the synthetic position requires less initial cash investment, and investing less funds creates more financial leverage.*[15] An undesirable feature is that the owner of a synthetic long position does not collect cash dividends or coupon interest from underlying securities, because no securities exist with a synthetic position. The final undesirable feature of the synthetic long position is that when the options expire additional option prices (premiums) must be paid to re-establish the synthetic position.

The Synthetic Short Position

Selling (shorting, writing) a call and simultaneously buying a put with a similar exercise prices on the same underlying stock creates a *synthetic short position.* This can be seen by combining Figures 9-4B (selling a call) and 9-5A (buying a put) from Chapter 9 to create the arrangement illustrated in Figure 28-11.

A synthetic short position is often more desirable than a traditional short position in the same stock for three reasons. First, the option position is superior because the call that was sold should bring the call writer more premium income than is spent to pay for the put's premium.**[16] Second, the synthetic short sale offers more leverage. Short sales require an initial margin of about 50%. The synthetic short position involves a smaller initial investment than an actual short sale, as shown:

Deposit: About 20% of the optioned stock's price

Plus: The call premium received

Minus: The put premium paid

Total: An amount that is less than 50% of the actual short stock position

---

* If the put and call maturities are identical the put-call parity relationship shows that the premium paid to purchase the call will normally exceed the premium income from selling the put. As a result, ignoring margin requirements, there is a negative net cash flow to establish a synthetic long position.

** If the put and call maturities are identical, the premium paid for the put will normally be less than the premium income from selling the call. As a result, ignoring margin requirements, a positive initial net cash inflow can be obtained from a synthetic short position.

FIGURE 28-11   The Components of a Synthetic Short Position: (A) Short Call, (B) Buy Put, (C) Synthetic Short Position, (D) Normal Short Position

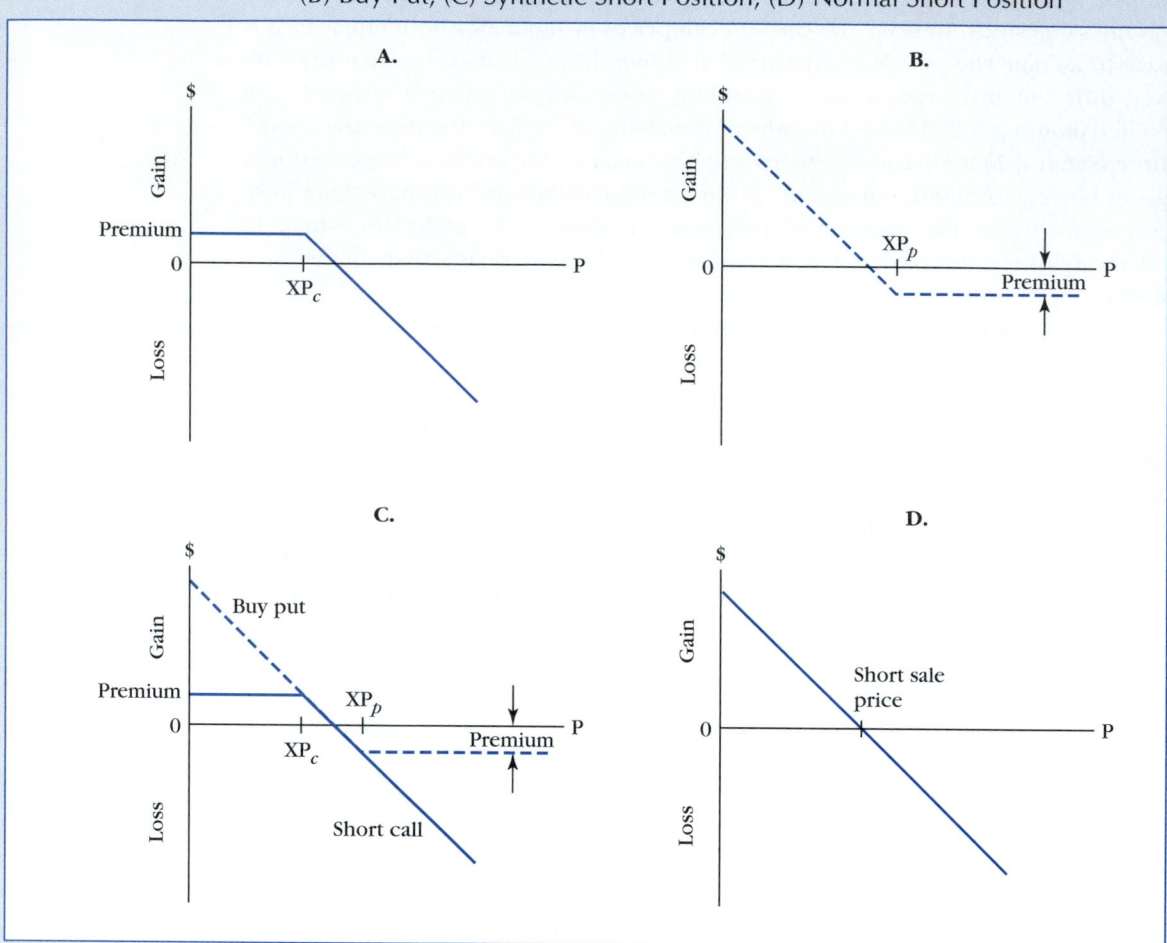

A synthetic short position in a stock can be created by writing a call and simultaneously buying a put with similar exercise prices on that stock.

Third, the synthetic short seller does not have to pay cash dividends on the optioned stock, whereas the short seller would have to pay cash dividends from his or her own pocket on the borrowed stock.

The disadvantage inherent in any option position is that options expire and more money must be spent to purchase new options to reestablish the position. Another disadvantage of the synthetic short position is that the investor has a short call position that could accumulate unlimited losses if the price of the underlying stock rose high enough.

Other Synthetic Positions

Many different investment positions can be created synthetically by combining options. In some cases, a synthetic investment position is more desirable than the position created by purchasing the investment.

WRITING COVERED CALLS

If an investor writes a call option against securities they already own, they are said to have written a **covered call.** The securities already owned cover the call writer's exposure to potential loss. For example, an investor might own 100 shares of a stock and write (sell) a call against those stocks. If the price of the optioned stock rises and the call owner decides to exercise the call, the covered call writer can avert a loss that would be incurred if the shares had to be purchased by delivering the already owned shares. If the covered call writer's interest expense and commissions incurred in covering the position are less than the premiums received for writing the call, both the call writer and the call buyer can gain from the stock's price rise. If the call writer is covered with securities purchased on margin, a large rate of return can be earned on the invested capital (initial margin minus call premium).

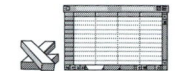

All covered call positions are not profitable, however. If the price of the optioned security falls, then the call buyer pays the premium to the covered call writer for doing nothing while the covered call writer loses on the long stock position. At least the call writer's security price losses are partially offset by the call premium income.[17] Figure 28-12 contrasts writing covered calls with writing calls uncovered.

A call-option writer who does not own the underlying security is said to be *writing naked,* or *writing against cash,* or *writing uncovered.* Figure 28-12A depicts the gain-loss graph for a naked call writer. The naked call buyer's gains equal the naked call writer's losses. A comparison of the call writer's exposure to loss in Figures 28-12A and 28-12B shows that writing calls naked is risky if the price of the optioned security is likely to rise and writing calls covered is risky if the price of the optioned security is likely to fall. The covered-call writer's position in Figure 28-12B is equivalent to the naked put writers position illustrated in Chapter 9's Figure 9-5B (p. 250).

Federal margin requirements for uncovered option writers demand initial margins of 15% or more. In contrast, a covered-call writer who has the optioned securities in a deliverable position at his or her broker's office will be able to deliver the optioned securities and, as a result, is not required to put up additional margin money to write a covered call. Because

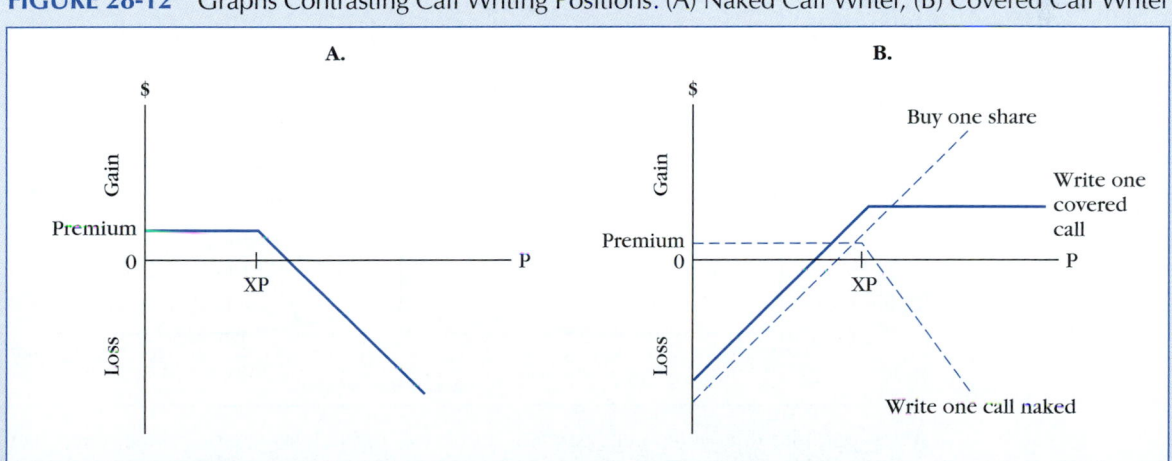

FIGURE 28-12   Graphs Contrasting Call Writing Positions: (A) Naked Call Writer, (B) Covered Call Writer

The covered call position is created by selling a call on an underlying stock the call writer already owns. A covered call writer's position is economically equivalent to a put writer's position.

covered-call writers must maintain an investment of at least the minimum maintenance margin money required to purchase their covering positions, the leverage is not infinite.

Some investors write covered calls to reshape their probability distribution of returns. Figure 28-13 contrasts the option writer's probability distributions from (A) a stock with no options and (B) writing covered calls on the same stock.[18] Covered call writers gain the most from their call writing when the price of their optioned stock remains at its exercise price and the option expires unexercised; when that happens the option writer gets to keep both the call writing premium and the underlying stock. Figure 28-13 shows that if the price of the stock advances significantly, the covered call writer would have been better off not to have written the option because the appreciating securities will be called away at the option's low exercise price. If the underlying stock's price rises, the call writer's income is limited to the call premium received. If the price of the underlying stock declines, the covered call writer suffers a loss in market value that is partially offset by the premium income.

STRADDLES

A **straddle** is created by purchasing an equal number of puts and calls on the same underlying asset. These puts and calls must all have the same exercise price and same maturity. The

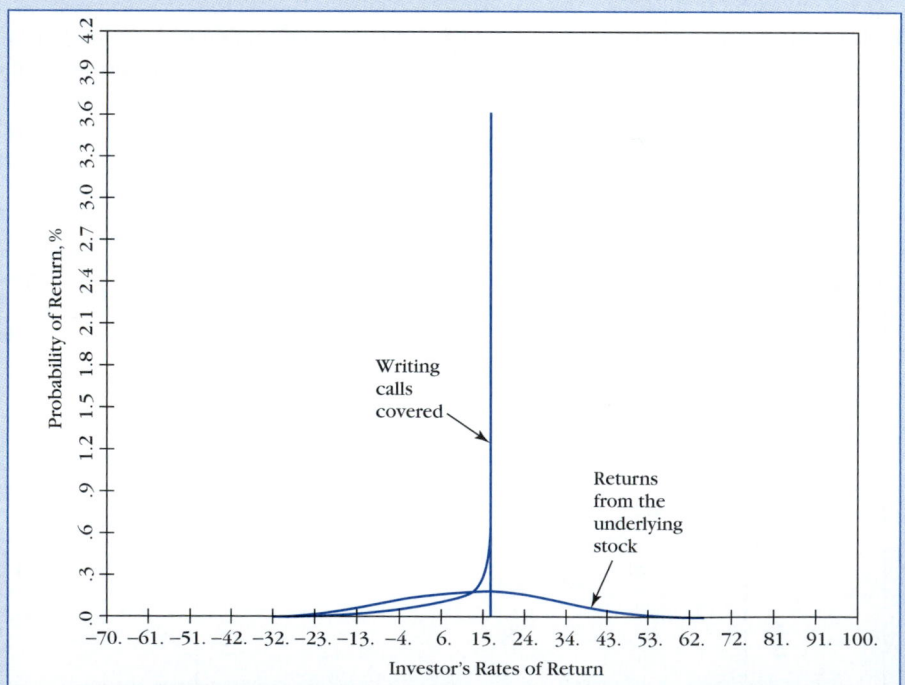

FIGURE 28-13   Contrasting the Probability Distributions of Returns: (A) The Underlying Stock without Any Options; (B) Covered Call Writing (Stock and Option)

A portfolio of covered calls contains much less positive skewness (upside gain) than a naked long position in the optioned (underlying) asset.

SOURCE: Richard M. Bookstaber and Roger G. Clarke, Option Strategies for Institutional Investment Management (Reading, MA: Addison-Wesley, 1983), Figure 5-2, p. 78.

straddle buyer pays a total premium equal to the sum of the premiums for the puts and calls purchased separately. Straddle buyers are willing to invest this sum if they believe the price of the optioned security will fluctuate substantially. As shown in Figure 28-14A, a speculator who buys a *long straddle position* can profit if the price of the optioned asset makes either a large upward price move, a large downward, or large moves both upward and downward. Straddles are a useful strategy for the stock of a corporation that is a takeover candidate or during other periods of high price volatility.

There are an infinite number of break-even points for a long straddle position. The largest single downside price move needed to breakeven equals the sum of the put and call options' prices. As a limiting case on the upside, the price of the optioned asset must rise by at least as much as the sum of the put and call options' prices to break even. There are an infinite number of other combinations of smaller price increases and decreases that will generate enough profits from both the put and the call to break even.

$$\begin{pmatrix} \text{Aggregate profitable price movements in one} \\ \text{or both directions needed to break even} \end{pmatrix} = \begin{pmatrix} \text{Put} \\ \text{premium} \end{pmatrix} + \begin{pmatrix} \text{Call} \\ \text{premium} \end{pmatrix}$$

The buyer of a long straddle believes the underlying stock has the potential for enough price fluctuations to make the straddle profitable before expires. Although losses may occur from a large proportion of straddle purchases that are held to expiration, there is only a small probability of losing the aggregate premium outlay.

The *short straddle position* is opposite but symmetric to the long straddle position. Straddle writers are sufficiently confident the optioned security's price will not vary significantly before the options mature that, with the premium as an inducement, they are willing to contract to pay if the underlying asset's price fluctuates appreciably. There is often a good chance that a stock's price remains unchanged for a brief period. During these periods of

FIGURE 28-14   Position Graphs for a Straddle: (A) Straddle Buyer; (B) Straddle Writer

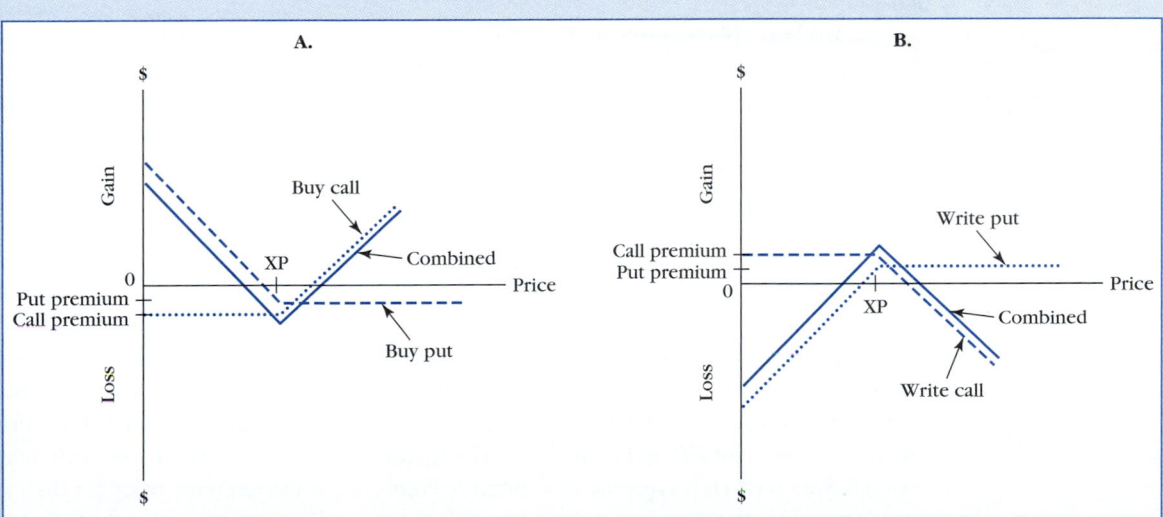

The owner of a long straddle can earn profits that increase with the price volatility of the optioned asset. The owner of a short straddle position (straddle writer) enjoys the maximum gain if the market price of the optioned security is invariant.

price stability potential straddle writers must be careful not to succumb irrationally to the offer of large premiums. The probability that a straddle writer gets to keep 100% of the premium income is small.

The gain-loss graph for a straddle writer is illustrated in Figure 28-14B. Since a straddle is equivalent to a put and call at the same exercise price, the position graphs in Figure 28-14 are merely combinations of Figures 9-4 and 9-5 in Chapter 9 for the case when the put and the call have identical exercise prices.

SPREADS

A **spread** is the purchase of one option and sale of another option that is similar but different.* An option spread can be created from either two puts or two calls, but not from both puts and calls. These options may have either differing maturities or different exercise prices.

Spreading Vocabulary

The way the option prices are listed in the newspaper quotations provides an explanation of the names given to different kinds of option spreads.

As Figure 9-3 in Chapter 9 (p. 244) shows, newspapers list all options with the same expiration dates in vertical columns. That's why spreads involving options with different exercise prices but the same expiration date are called **vertical spreads.**

Horizontal spreads include those combinations of options having different expiration dates but the same exercise price. They are called horizontal spreads because different options that all have the same exercise prices are listed in horizontal rows in the newspapers. Horizontal spreads are also called *time spreads* and *calendar spreads*.

Diagonal spreads include mixtures of vertical spreads and horizontal spreads from the newspaper quotations. They include options in which both the expiration dates and the exercise prices differ. Regardless of whether they were purchased or written, any option spread fits into one of the three categories: a vertical spread, a horizontal spread, or a diagonal spread.

A different approach to categorizing option spreads is based on whether the total price of the spread generates net cash inflows or outflows for the spreader. Spreads that generate premium income that exceeds their related costs are called **credit spreads. Debit spreads** initially cost the investor a net cash outflow. The paragraphs below define various spreads that fit in the categories suggested here.

Strangles

A **strangle** uses a put and a call, typically with the same expiration date, but with different exercise prices. A strangle is a horizontal spread that is like a straddle with an exercise price that is "points away" (different) from the current market price of the underlying security. Figure 28-15 shows the gain-loss graphs for the buyer and the writer of a strangle; note the similarity to the straddle illustrated in Figure 28-14. The exercise price for the put portion of the strangle is point XP_P in Figure 28-15. The market price of the optioned security when the strangle was written is typically near point S. Point XP_C is the exercise price for the call por-

---

*   Spreads may also be created by using options, futures contracts, and/or options on futures contracts. Futures contracts are used to create intercommodity spreads, intracommodity spreads, intermarket spreads, cross spreads, and other types of spreads. Futures contracts are the topic of Chapters 9 and 27.

FIGURE 28-15   Position Graphs for a Strangle

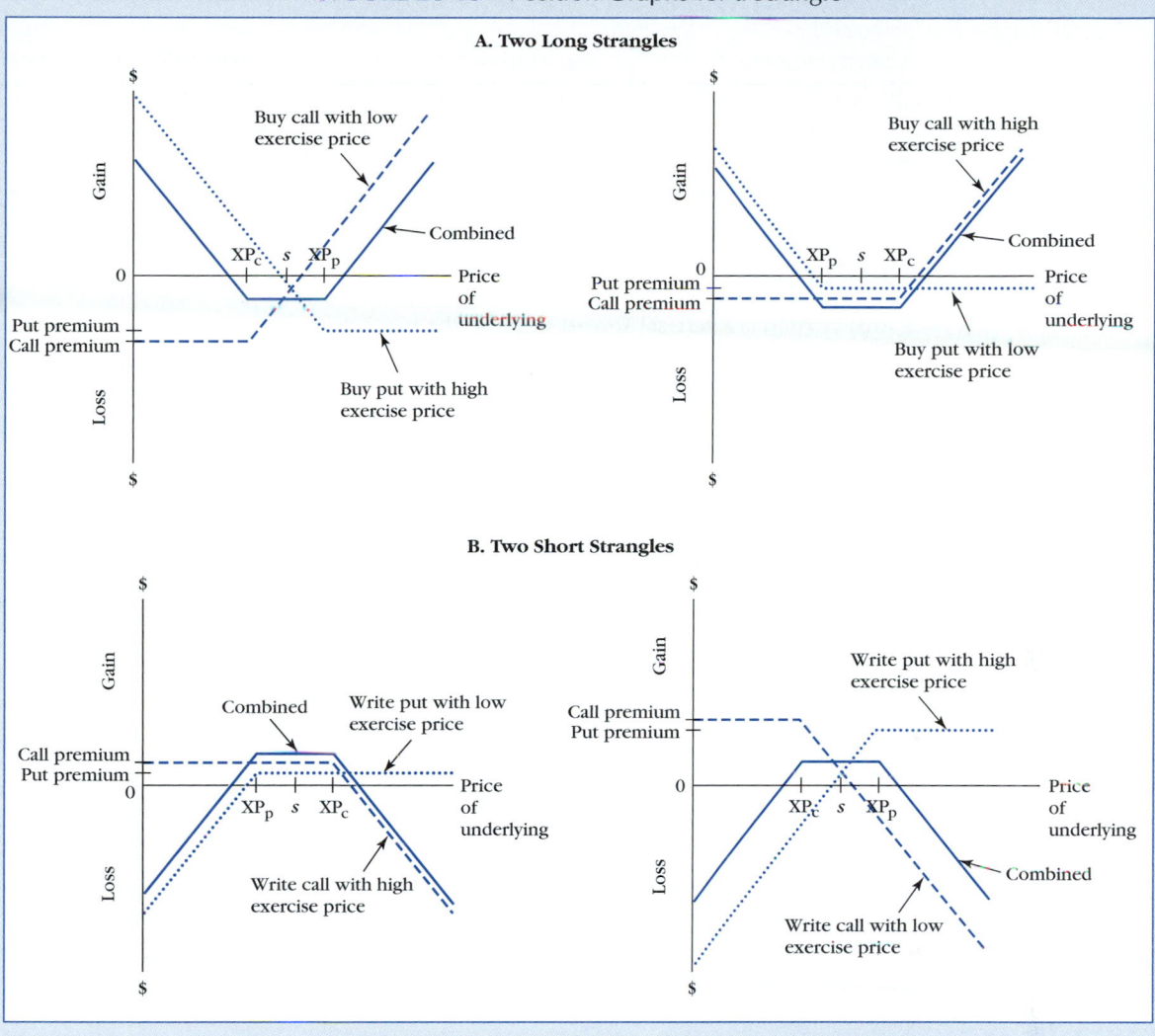

There is more than one way to construct any given strangle. The owner of a long strangle can gain from large fluctuations in the price of the underlying, but these large price fluctuations would create losses for a short strangle position.

tion of the strangle. The premiums for a strangle involve a smaller total outlay than the total premiums on the straddle because the market price of the security that is optioned with a strangle must rise or fall more than if it were optioned with a straddle for the option buyer to profit. The payoffs for a long strangle are delineated in Table 28-5.

A *long strangle* is a debit transaction because the component options must all be purchased—no premium income from option writing is involved. The reverse is true of the short strangles. *Short strangles,* or *reverse strangles,* are credit transactions that reap premium income without incurring any initial outlays for premiums. The premium income from strangles that are out-of-the-money is small, but so is the chance a strangle writer ever has an option being exercise against him or her.

TABLE 28-5   Payoffs at the Expiration of a Long Strangle Position

Price of the Underlying Asset, P	Payoff from Put	Payoff from Call	Strangle's Total Payoff
$XP_P \geq P$	$XP_P - P$	0	$XP_P - P$
$XP_C > P > XP_P$	0	0	0
$P > XP_C$	0	$P - XP_C$	$P - XP_C$

Bull Spread

A **bull spread** is a vertical spread, because the two calls comprising it have the same expiration date. A bull spread is a debit transaction because selling the call generates less cash inflow than the call purchase requires. As a result, there is a net cash outflow from the investor's brokerage account when a bull spread is initiated. Figure 28-16 illustrates the gain-loss graphs for two different bull spreads.

The bull spread in Figure 28-16A involves buying a put and writing another put that is similar in every respect, except that the written put has the higher exercise price. The bull spread in Figure 28-16B is constructed by buying one call and writing another call that is similar, but the written call has the higher exercise price.

Bull spreads are for people who believe the price of the optioned stock will rise, but won't rise a lot. As Figure 28-16 shows, the only upward security price moves that are profitable occur between the exercise prices of the two calls (the range between XP_1 and XP_2). The option strategist can incur losses if the price of the underlying security falls below the lowest exercise price (security's price $< XP_1$), but these losses are limited to the option's price. The gains are not affected by price movements above the highest exercise price (secu-

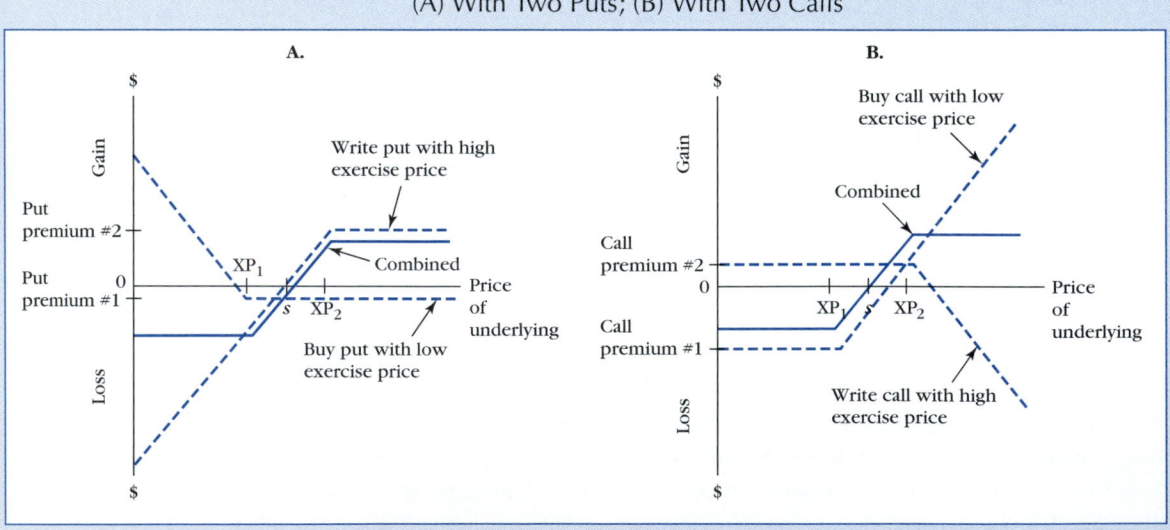

FIGURE 28-16   Position Graphs for Two Different Bull Spreads: (A) With Two Puts; (B) With Two Calls

The owner of a bull spread gains from upward price moves that occur between the exercise prices of the two options (in the range: $XP_1 <$ Optioned Security's Price $< XP_2$).

rity's price $> XP_2$) and the losses are not affected by price movements below the lowest exercise price (security's price $< XP_1$).

Bear Spreads

A *put bear spread* can be established by writing a put and, at the same time, buying a put that has a higher exercise price on the same underlying security. Figure 28-17A illustrates a put bear spread. A bear spread is a *vertical spread* because both options compromising it usually have the same expiration date. Figure 28-17B illustrates a *call bear spread* created by selling a call and simultaneously buying a call with a higher exercise price on the same stock. Figure 28-17B illustrates a *net credit spread* because the premium income from selling the call with the lower exercise price normally exceeds the cost of the call purchased with the higher exercise price.

Bear spreads and bull spreads both have limited gain-loss potentials. Only asset price declines between the exercise prices of the two options are profitable for a bear spread. Additional gains or losses are not possible if the price of the optioned security moves below the lower exercise price (security's price $< XP_1$) or above the higher exercise price (security's price $> XP_2$) in Figure 28-17. Cautious investors like bear spreads because their losses are limited if the investor's expectations are wrong.[19]

Butterfly Spreads

A **butterfly spread** is a combination of a bull spread and a bear spread on the same underlying security. Figure 28-18 depicts the gains and losses for the long and short butterfly spreads. The *long butterfly spread* will maximize its profit potential if the price of the optioned asset does not fluctuate from XP_B. Figure 28-18A shows the worst possible outcome for a long butterfly spread occurs if the price moves both below XP_A and above XP_C

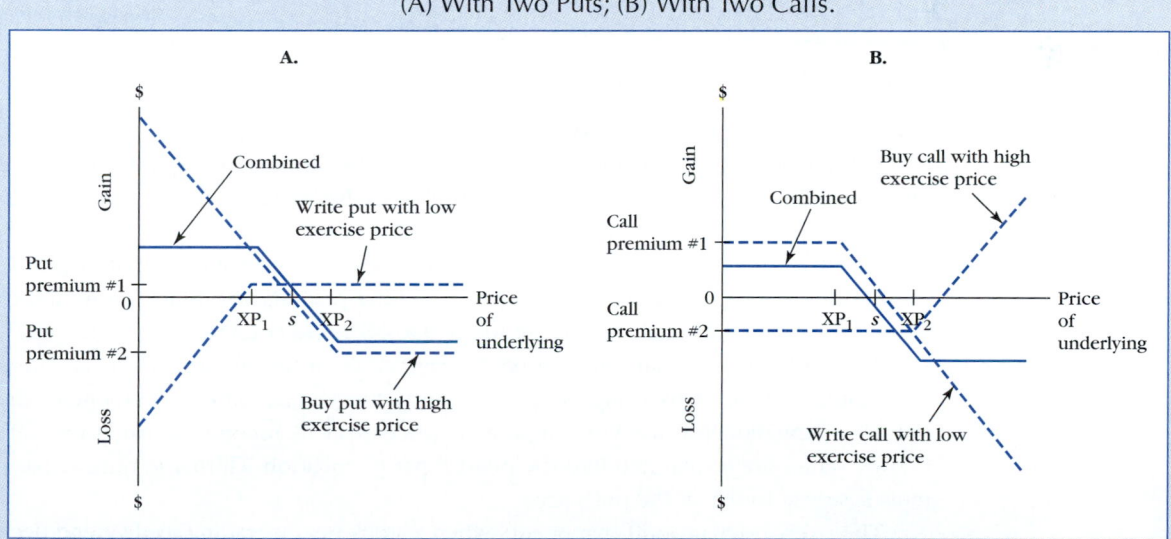

FIGURE 28-17   Position Graphs for Two Different Bear Spreads: (A) With Two Puts; (B) With Two Calls.

Bear spreads can earn limited gains and losses for price fluctuations in the range between the two exercise prices: $XP_1 <$ (Optioned Security's Price) $< XP_2$.

FIGURE 28-18   Position Graphs for a Butterfly Spread: (A) A Long
Butterfly Spread; (B) A Short Butterfly Spread

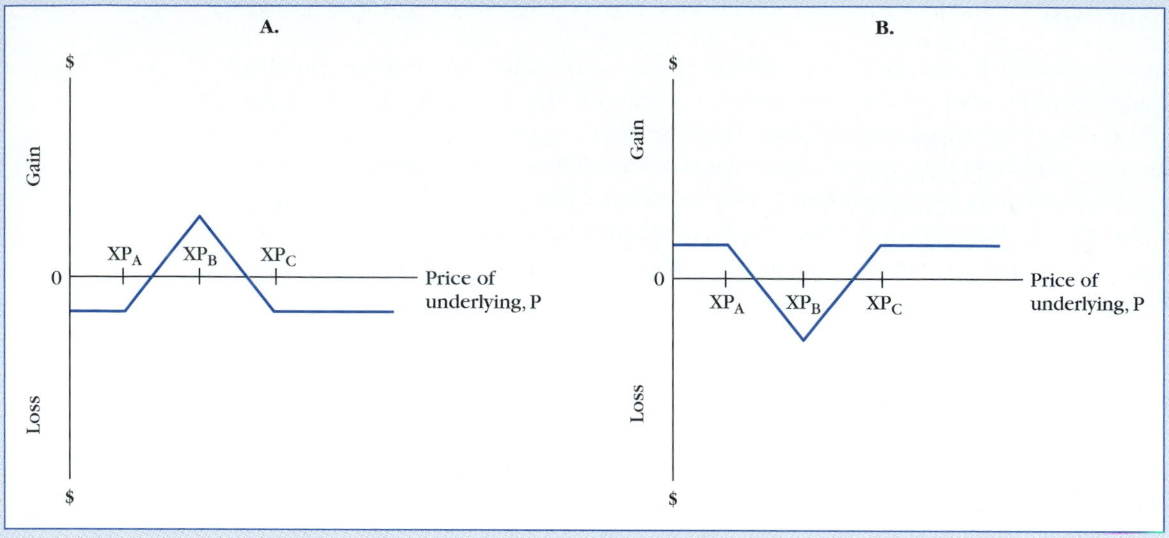

The owner of a long butterfly spread enjoys the maximum gain if the price of the optioned asset does not fluctuate. In contrast, the short butterfly spread is profitable if the price of the optioned asset fluctuates very far in either direction.

The *short butterfly spread* in Figure 28-18B is profitable if the price of the price of the optioned asset experiences large price fluctuations up and/or down. Butterfly spreads can be created in different ways, from various combinations of puts and calls. It is left as an exercise for the reader to determine the construction of long and short butterfly spreads.[20]

THE BOTTOM LINE

Option pricing theory can be divided into two parts.

Binomial option pricing models are mathematically simple models that have been developed to deal with a broad class of valuation problems that include options, stocks, bonds, and other risky financial claims.

The Black-Scholes call-pricing model was the first closed-form option-pricing model. In the limiting case of an infinite number of tiny time periods, the binomial model can be shown to be mathematically equivalent to the Black-Scholes continuous time model.

The value of European puts can be determined from the price of a similar call on the same underlying asset by using the put-call parity formula as follows. First, one of the call-option-pricing models is used to compute the price of a call. Second, the call price and other known values are substituted into the put-call parity equation. Third, the put-call parity formula is solved to obtain the put's price.

The stock price dropoff that occurs when a stock begins trading ex-dividend decreases the value of call options on the stock and increase the value of put options on the stock. It is necessary to adjust the put and call option premiums (prices) on dividend paying stocks to obtain ex-cash dividend option premiums.

Puts and calls can be viewed as building blocks that are used to build other, more complex, structures. Synthetic long and short positions can be created from combinations of put and call options. It is useful to think of puts and calls this way to be able to decompose, analyze, alter, and recombine investment positions. Such conceptualization facilitates the creation of new structures and strategies.

By combining puts and calls in various ways, it is possible to create investment positions that will be profitable if the price of the underlying asset rises, falls, fluctuates up and down, or never changes. The number of different straddles, spreads, and other combinations that can be created from puts and calls is infinite.

Puts and calls are also useful conceptual tools for security analysts. The prices of some investments contain embedded options that are not obvious to the untrained observer. Delineating embedded options sometimes yields a better understanding of the opportunities within an investment. Seeing a security as a combination of options, or options and other investments, permits the analyst to evaluate that security as a combination of simpler elements that may be easier to value on a piece-by-piece basis.

QUESTIONS

Q28-1 (Option premiums) What are the main factors determining put and call premiums?

Q28-2 (Put-call parity) Explain how you could replicate the expiration date payoff from a long position in an asset by taking positions in calls and puts.

Q28-3 (Black-Scholes model) Consider the Black-Scholes formula presented in Eqn. 28-5. How can you interpret the $N(x)$ and $N(y)$ terms? *Hint:* Consider what the value of the option would be if both $N(x)$ and $N(y)$ are close to zero; then consider what it would be if both terms were close to one.

Q28-4 (Put-call parity) Is there any kind of basic relation between the prices of puts and calls on the same security that might be expected to exist permanently? Explain.

Q28-5 (Option premiums) Compare and contrast the intrinsic value with the time value for (a) a call option and (b) a put option.

Q28-6 (Option premiums) If the XYZ Corporation was confronted with tough new foreign competition that reduced its profit margins and sales, what effect do you expect this would have on the premiums charged for (a) calls and (b) puts on XYZ's stock?

Q28-7 (Hedge ratio) True, false, or uncertain: An investor who utilizes the hedge ratio presented in the Black-Scholes model, $N(x)$, to establish a perfect hedge will be guaranteed a return equal to the risk-free rate at the expiration of the option.

Q28-8 (Put-call parity) True, false, or uncertain: If the put-call parity model suggests that the fair value of a put option is $2, given the market price of an identical call option, but you observe that the put is selling for $1½ you can conclude that the put option is underpriced.

Q28-9 (Put-call parity versus Black-Scholes model) Compare and contrast the put-call parity model with the Black-Scholes model in determining the value of a call option.

Q28-10 (Binomial option pricing model) True, false, or uncertain: The hedge ratio, h, that is used in the binomial option pricing model will be lower, the more in-the-money the call option is.

PROBLEMS

P28-1 (Option pricing) Determine the value of (a) a call and (b) a put on a common stock with the following characteristics: Standard deviation of returns = 0.16, Exercise price = $40, Risk-free rate = 0.10, Current price = $42, Time to maturity = 6 months.

P28-2 (Put-call parity model) You observe that the price of a call option on Titan Industries stock, with an expiration date 6 months from now, is $3\frac{1}{2}$. The strike price on the

option is $50, and Titan is currently selling for $52 a share. An identical put on Titan Industries is selling for $1. If the annual risk-free rate is 5%, are these options correctly priced relative to one another?

P28-3 (Hedge ratio) As an investor you are bullish on the stock of the XYZ Company. Consequently, you purchase ten 6-month XYZ calls with an exercise price of $50 for $2600. The current price of XYZ stock is $50. How much would XYZ stock need to increase in price in 6 months for you to make a 10% annual rate of return on your investment? Ignore commission charges and taxes.

P28-4   (Option pricing) The total market value of the Azore Corporation's assets is $90,000. Azore has a $110,000 issue of zero-coupon bonds maturing in 1 year. The riskless rate of interest is 9.5%. The standard deviation of returns on Azore's stock is 0.4, or equivalently, the variance is 0.16. (a) Calculate the value of all common stock shares outstanding in the Azore Corporation using the Black-Scholes call-option-pricing model. (b) Why might Azore's stock have a positive value when the firm's debts of $110,000 exceed its total market value?

P28-5   (Hedge ratio) Jean Samples recently purchased a 3-month European call on the stock of the Miller Corporation for $5. This call has an exercise price of $80, and the current price of Miller's stock is $83. (a) At what price must Miller's stock sell for at maturity for Ms. Samples to break even? (b) Determine the price at which Miller's stock must sell in order for Ms. Samples to earn a 20% annual rate of return on the money she has invested in the calls.

P28-6   (Black-Scholes model) Using the information given in Problem 28-5, determine the value of the call today assuming a $1.00 cash dividend will be paid at the end of 1 month and the price of the stock stays at $83. Assume the riskiness of Miller's stock is $Var(r) = 0.16$, and the risk-free rate is $RFR = 10\%$.

P28-7   (Black-Scholes model) The current price of Alison Engine Corporation common stock is $50. A call on Alison's stock has a $3 premium and an exercise price of $50. If the call has 3 months until maturity, what standard deviation of returns on the firm's stock is consistent with the above values? Assume the risk-free rate is 9.0%.

P28-8   (Black-Scholes model) The stock of the BBB Company is currently selling for $65. A 3-month call option on the stock with an exercise price of $60 has a premium of $6.20. The standard deviation of returns on BBB stock has been estimated to be 0.18. Currently, the 3-month T-bill rate is ten percent. (a) Is the option overvalued, undervalued, or priced correctly? (b) If you have confidence in your analysis how would you react to your findings in (a)?

P28-9   (Black-Scholes model and put-call parity) The common stock of the ZBZ Corporation has a current price of $40 and a standard deviation of returns of 0.40. Assume a risk-free rate of 8%. (a) Using the Black-Scholes model, determine the price of a 4-month call option that has a strike price of $35. (b) Determine the value of a put on ZBZ's stock that also has a striking price of $35.

P28-10   (Hedge ratio) After a quarterly cash dividend of $1.00 per share is paid, the market price of an optioned stock drops off $1.00 when it starts trading ex-dividend. The T-bill rate is 10%, the hedge ratio (or delta) is $N(x) = 0.9$, and the standard deviation of the optioned stock is 0.12. How will the premium for a call option on this stock react to the cash dividend price dropoff? *Hint:* Beware of sophistry.

CFA EXAM QUESTIONS

1. (1997 CFA Sample Exam, Level I) In the Black-Scholes option valuation formula, an increase in a stock's volatility (all else being constant):
   A. decreases the associated put option value.
   B. increases the associated call option value.
   C. may decrease or increase the option value, depending on the level of interest rates.
   D. does not change either the put or call option value because put-call parity holds.

2. (1997 CFA Exam, Level II) Current equity call prices for Furniture City are contained in Table 20. In reviewing these prices Jim Smith, CFA notes discrepancies between several option prices and basic option pricing relationships.

Table 20   Closing Prices Furniture City Equity Call Options—May 30, 1997

		Expiration Month			
Close	Strike	June	July	August	September
$119\frac{1}{2}$	110	$8\frac{7}{8}$	$12\frac{1}{2}$	15	18
$119\frac{1}{2}$	120	$1\frac{1}{2}$	$3\frac{3}{4}$	3	$4\frac{1}{4}$
$119\frac{1}{2}$	130	1	$2\frac{1}{4}$	$2\frac{7}{8}$	5

Identify *three different* apparent pricing discrepancies in Table 20. **Identify** which of the basic option-pricing relationships *each* discrepancy violates. *Note:* The fact that option contracts do not always trade at the same time as the underlying stock should *not* be identified as a discrepancy.

3. (1998 CFA Exam, Level II) Joel Franklin is a portfolio manager responsible for derivatives. Franklin observes an American-style option and a European-style option with the same strike price, expiration, and underlying stock. Franklin believes that the European-style option will have a higher premium than the American-style option.

   A. Critique Franklin's belief that the European-style option will have a higher premium.

   Franklin is asked to value a 1-year European style call option for Abaco Ltd. common stock, which last traded at $43.00. He has collected the information in Table 7.

Table 7

Closing Stock Price	$43.00
Call and Put Option Exercise Price	45.00
1-Year Put Option Price	4.00
1-Year T-Bill Rate	5.50%
Time to Expiration	One year

B. Calculate, using put-call parity and the information provided in Table 7, the European-style call option value. **Show** your work.

C. State the effect, if any, of *each* of the following *three* variables on the value of a call option. (No calculations required.)

   i. an increase in short-term interest rate.

   ii. an increase in stock price volatility.

   iii. a decrease in time to option expiration.

FURTHER REFERENCES

Black, F. and M. Scholes, "The Pricing of Options and Corporate Liabilities," *Journal of Political Economy* (June 1973): 637–54.

   A seminal paper that developed a mathematical pricing model for options.

Cox, John C. and Mark Rubinstein. *Options Markets.* Englewood Cliffs, NJ: Prentice-Hall, 1985.

   A comprehensive review of option theory and the mathematics of options.

Hull, John. *Options, Futures, and Other Derivative Securities,* 3rd ed. Englewood Cliffs, NJ: Prentice-Hall, 1997.

   This textbook contains substantial information about options. Graphs are used to supplement the small amount of calculus in the book.

McMillan, Lawrence G. *Options as a Strategic Investment,* 3rd ed. New York: New York Institute of Finance, 1993.

   This easy-to-read book contains no formulas and very few graphs. The book teaches option trading by leading the reader through simple numerical examples that are realistic, clear, and illustrative.

Ritchken, Peter. *Derivative Markets,* New York: Harper Collins, 1996.

   Numerous graphs and numerical examples make this textbook easy-to-read in spite of the fact that it utilizes some advanced mathematics.

ENDNOTES

[1] See Mark Rubinstein and Hayne E. Leland, "Replicating Options with Positions in Stock and Cash," *Financial Analysts Journal* (July-August 1981): 63–74.

[2] See David P. Jacob, Graham Lord, and James A. Tilley, "A Generalized Framework for Pricing Contingent Cash Flows," *Financial Management* 16, no. 3 (autumn 1987): 5–14. The article shows how investment bankers use the binomial option pricing model to value GNMA mortgage-backed securities.

[3] For a discussion of valuing options on stocks that pay cash dividends within a lattice framework see John Hull, *Options, Futures, and Other Derivatives* (Upper Saddle River, NJ: Prentice-Hall, 1997), Sections 15.3 through 15.5, pp. 352–60. Trinomial trees are also introduced.

[4] Several statistics textbooks explain Pascal's Rule in conjunction with the binomial model. Pascal's Rule is used to generate Pascal's Triangle of Figure 28-7A, to count the number of combinations from binomial

models, and for other applications. A lucid example is provided by John C. Cox and Mark Rubinstein, *Options Markets* (Englewood Cliffs, NJ: Prentice-Hall, 1985), Chapter 5.

5 See John C. Cox, Stephen A. Ross, and Mark Rubinstein, "Option Pricing: A Simplified Approach," *Journal of Financial Economics* 7 (September 1979): 229–63. Also see Richard J. Rendelman Jr. and Brit J. Barter, "Two-State Option Pricing," *Journal of Finance* 34, no. 5 (December 1979): 1093–1110. See also P. P. Boyle, "A Lattice Framework for Option Pricing with Two State Variables," *Journal of Financial and Quantitative Analysis* 23 (March 1988): 1–12.

6 See F. Black and M. Scholes, "The Pricing of Options and Corporate Liabilities," *Journal of Political Economy* (May-June 1973): 637–54. The Black-Scholes model was derived by assuming the optioned security's prices are log-normally distributed so that the continuously compounded one-period rates of return $r_{it} = ln(p_{it}/p_{i,t-1})$ are normally distributed with a constant known variance. Gary L. Gastineau and Albert Mandansky developed a competing option valuation model that does not assume stock prices are lognormally distributed. This model is described briefly by Gary L. Gastineau, "An Index of Listed Option Premiums," *Financial Analysts Journal* (May/June 1977): 70–75, see especially the Appendix. Or, see G. L. Gastineau, *The Options Manual,* 3d ed. (New York: McGraw-Hill, 1988), Chapter 7.

7 The hedge ratio is discussed by Peter Ritchken, *Derivative Markets* (New York: Harper Collins, 1996), 229–31.

8 See H. Latane and R. J. Rendelman Jr., "Standard Deviation of Stock Price Ratios Implied in Option Prices," *Journal of Finance* (May 1976): 369–81.

9 For a discussion of estimating risk statistics see Michael Parkinson, "The Extreme Value Method for Estimating the Variance of the Rate of Return," *Journal of Business* 53, no. 1 (January 1980): 61–67. See also in the same issue Mark B. Garman and Michael J. Klass, "On the Estimation of Security Price Volatilities from Historical Data," 67–78.

10 See M. Parkinson, "Option Pricing: The American Put," *Journal of Business* (January 1977): 21–36. See also, M. Brennan and E. Schwartz, "The Valuation of American Put Options," *Journal of Finance* (May 1977): 449–62.

11 The parity between put and call premiums is explained by Hans R. Stoll, "The Relationship between Put and Call Option Prices," *Journal of Finance* (December 1969): 801–24. The Black-Scholes model values European calls and, by working through the put-call parity formula, can be used to accurately value European puts. However, this procedure will yield only approximate values for American puts.

If American options are being priced the following research can be useful. See R. Geske, "A Note on an Analytic Valuation Formula for Unprotected American Call Options on Stocks with Known Dividends," *Journal of Financial Economics* 7 (1979): 375–80. See also R. Whaley, "On the Valuation of American Call Options on Stocks with Known Dividends," *Journal of Financial Economics* 9 (1981): 207–11. In addition, see R. Geske, "Comments on Whaley's Note," *Journal of Financial Economics* 9 (June 1981): 213–15.

12 See Drew Wagner, David M. Ellis, and David A. Dubofsky, "The Factors Behind Put-Call Parity Violations of S&P 100 Index Options," *Financial Review* 31, no. 3 (August 1996): 535–52. Also see Avraham Kamara and Thomas W. Miller Jr., "Daily and Intradaily Tests of European Put-Call Parity," *Journal of Financial and Quantitative Analysis* 30, no. 4 (December 1995): 519–39.

13 See Rakesh Bali and Gailen L. Hite, "Ex Dividend Day Stock Price Behavior: Discreteness or Tax-Induced Clienteles?" *Journal of Financial Economics* 47, no. 2 (February 1998): 127–59.

14 Rational call-premium adjustments to reflect the payment of cash dividends and other factors were analyzed by Robert C. Merton, "The Theory of Rational Option Pricing," *Bell Journal of Economics and Management Science* (spring 1973): 141–83. An exact method was suggested by Richard Roll, "An Analytic Valuation Formula for Unprotected American Call Options on Stocks with Known Dividends," *Journal of Financial Economics* 5 (1977). See R. Geske, "A Note on an Analytic Valuation Formula for Unprotected American Call Options on Stocks with Known Dividends," *Journal of Financial Economics* 7 (1979): 375–80. Also see R. E. Whaley, "Valuation of Americans Call Options on Dividend Paying Stocks: Empirical Tests," *Journal of Financial Economics* 10 (March 1982): 29–58.

15 For a numerical example see L. G. McMillan, *Options as a Strategic Investment,* 3d ed. (New York: New York Institute of Finance, 1993), 301–03.

16 For a numerical example see L. G. McMillan, *Options as a Strategic Investment,* 3d ed. (New York: New York Institute of Finance, 1993), 303–04.

17 For an extended discussion of covered call writing and the margin requirements on covered call writing, see L. G. McMillan, *Options as a Strategic Investment,* 3d ed. (New York: New York Institute of Finance, 1993), Chapter 2.

18 For a discussion of how the options strategist can reshape the probability distribution of returns attainable from the various options, see Richard M. Bookstaber and Roger G. Clarke, *Option Strategies for Institutional Investment Management* (Reading, MA: Addison-Wesley, 1983).

19 For an extended discussion of bear spreads see John Hull, *Options, Futures, and Other Derivative Securities,* 3d ed. (Englewood Cliffs, NJ: Prentice-Hall, 1997), 181–83 and 457. Alternatively, see Lawrence G. McMillan, *Options as a Strategic Investment,* 3d ed. (New York: New York Institute of Finance, 1993), Chapters 8 and 22.

20 For details about butterfly spreads see John Hull, *Options, Futures, and Other Derivative Securities,* 3d ed. (Englewood Cliffs, NJ: Prentice-Hall, 1997), 183–85 and 457. Alternatively, see Lawrence G. McMillan, *Options as a Strategic Investment,* 3d ed. (New York: New York Institute of Finance, 1993), Chapters 10 and 23.

ALTERNATIVE INVESTMENTS

In a book about collecting, Rigby and Rigby point out that: "Henry VIII, specializing in wives and tapestries, acquired six items in the first category and 2,000 in the latter."[1] Taking a different approach than King Henry, this chapter focuses on financial investments.

First we look at the risk-and-return statistics on real estate used for residential, commercial, and farming purposes, and, real estate investment trusts (REITs). Domestic and off-shore hedge funds are then discussed. Precious metals are covered as well, and we analyze the investment characteristics of gold bullion and physical silver.

REAL ESTATE

There are four main types of real estate investments:

1. **Residences.** Over 60% of the total market value of U.S. real estate rests in owner-occupied single-family homes. Investments in single-family homes peaked at 33% of the average U.S. household's total assets in 1985 and declined to 27% in 1998.[2]

2. **Business real estate** includes office buildings, apartment buildings, hotels, shopping centers, industrial property, and raw land. Comingled real estate equity funds (CREFs), life insurance companies, and pension funds are the major owners of these investments.

3. **Farms** are businesses typically occupied and operated by their farmer-owners. Income is derived from rents and crop sales, and additional capital appreciation income (depreciation) from changes in the price of the property.

4. **Real estate investment trusts,** or **REITs,** are commercial investment portfolios that are patterned after closed-end investment companies. REITs are exempt from income taxes if more than 75% of their investments are in real estate and/or mortgages and if their cash dividend payout ratio exceeds 95% of their annual income every year. *Equity REITs* own portfolios in which more than 75% of the assets are equity positions in real estate. Equity REITs manage the properties, and shareholders receive rental income and income from capital appreciation if property is sold for a gain. *Mortgage REITs* own portfolios in which more than 75% of the assets are mortgages.

Mortgage REITs lend money to builders and make loan collections; shareholders receive interest income and capital appreciation income from improvement in the prices of loans. REITs securitize illiquid real estate assets; their shares are listed on stock exchanges and over-the-counter. REITs may leverage themselves.

Returns from Real Estate Investments

The *total return (TR)* from all types of real estate equals the sum of the income returns, if any, plus the capital appreciation (or minus any deterioration) returns. We use monthly market data from the NYSE, AMEX, and Nasdaq to analyze the financial performance of REITs.

Because residential, farm, and business real estate transactions occur infrequently, investors are not able to get market data from very many actual transactions. Appraised real estate values are used instead of data from market transactions.

Smoothing. The statistics in the far-right column of Table 29-1 show much higher serial correlations (auto-correlations) for the residential, farm, and business real estate returns in (A) than for the market-determined returns in (B) and (C). Furthermore, the standard deviations in (A) are smaller than standard deviations for the market-determined data in (B) and (C). The high serial correlations and low standard deviations in (A) are products of a "smoothing process" that accompanies many real estate appraisals. There is a lack of agreement among real estate appraisers about whether they should be estimating prices that fluctuate with the market's liquidity or whether they should be estimating values. Those appraisers who choose to be value estimators instead of price estimators smooth over the temporary problems that cause market prices to fluctuate. To see the economic implication of this behavior, consider the market price obtained from a single-family residence that had to liquidated within 48 hours. In a such a rapid sale, it is easy to imagine a selling price that equaled half of the house's appraised value. Appraisers ignore such realistic events and produce appraised values that fluctuate much less.

Average Returns. Over the 1972–99 sample period shown in Table 29-1, all categories of real estate investments had smaller (geometric and arithmetic) mean returns than the S&P500 (large cap) stock market index, the small cap stocks index, and the commodity futures index. If we take the low standard deviations in (A) at their face value, these diminutive risk statistics could provide an economic rationale for real estate assets to provide lower average returns than the riskier stock market. However, the higher standard deviations for the REITs in (B), which are computed from market prices rather than an appraised values, remind us that the standard deviations in (A) are biased downward by the appraisal process.* Other considerations that are unique to real estate investments further complicate attempts to explain the real estate returns.

EXAMPLE   BUYING A SINGLE-FAMILY RESIDENCE

Consider purchasing a $150,000 home. If the home buyer is employed, has a good credit record, and can make a 20% down payment (20% × $150,000 = $30,000), a bank will probably grant a $120,000 mortgage loan to be paid off over the next 30 years at 8% interest, in equal monthly installments of $880. Table 29-2 shows a hypothetical budget for this home purchase.

---

* The smoothing process places a downward bias on the standard deviations which makes the Sharpe ratio (see Chapter 16) a misleading measure of performance for real estate investments. In addition, the correlations between smoothed real estate values and instantaneous security market prices are downward biased.

TABLE 29-1   Performance Statistics from Real Estate and Alternative Asset Classes, 1972–99

	Geometric Mean, %	Arithmetic Mean, %	Standard Deviation, %	Serial Correlation
(A) Real Estate Assets				
Business R.E. TR[a]	8.8	9.0	6.3	0.8
Business R.E. Income Return	7.4	7.4	1.6	0.8
Business R.E. Cap App	1.2	1.3	5.8	0.8
Residential R.E. TR	13.7	13.7	4.3	0.7
Residential R.E. Income Return	6.7	6.7	0.5	0.9
Residential R.E. Cap App	7.0	7.1	4.2	0.7
Residential R.E. Market Value	8.7	8.8	4.9	0.7
Farm R.E. TR	10.5	10.9	9.0	0.8
Farm R.E. Income Return	5.2	5.2	0.5	0.8
Farm R.E. Cap App	5.4	5.7	8.7	0.8
Farm R.E. Market Value	5.5	5.9	9.5	0.7
(B) Real Estate Investment Trusts (REITs)				
NAREIT-All TR	8.7	10.9	21.2	0.2
NAREIT-All Income Return	9.3	9.3	2.1	0.5
NAREIT-All Cap App	−0.9	1.2	19.7	0.2
NAREIT-Equity TR	12.0	13.3	17.3	0.2
NAREIT-Equity Income Return	8.6	8.6	2.5	0.2
NAREIT-Equity Cap App	3.0	4.3	16.3	0.2
NAREIT-Mortgage TR	3.1	7.0	28.5	0.2
NAREIT-Mortgage Income Return	11.3	11.3	2.6	0.4
NAREIT-Mortgage Cap App	−7.9	−4.4	25.9	0.2
(C) Alternative (Non–Real Estate) Asset Classes				
U.S. T-Bond TR	8.7	9.3	12.5	−0.2
U.S. T-Bill TR	7.8	7.8	3.4	0.6
Gold TR	7.0	11.1	34.1	0.3
Silver TR	5.0	15.5	72.5	−0.1
AAA Corp Bond TR	8.6	9.0	10.1	0.0
S&P500 Index TR	14.1	15.3	16.4	−0.1
U.S. Small Stk TR	15.4	17.6	22.6	0.1
Commodity TR	11.3	13.9	24.4	0.3
Commodity Futures TR	15.1	16.4	20.0	0.0
Commodity Spot Price TR	2.0	3.9	20.2	0.2
U.S. Inflation	5.2	5.2	3.4	0.7

[a]Total return (TR) = Income return + Capital appreciation (Cap App) return

The business, residential, and farm real estate in (A) earn total returns (TRs) that are significantly below the stock market returns in (C). Economic theory suggests these lower TRs could be occurring because the real estate in (A) has lower standard deviations (less risk) than the stock market. Unfortunately, this risk-based explanation is flawed because the appraisal process biases downward the standard deviations from real estate so a comparison with market-determined stock market statistics is not meaningful.

TABLE 29-2 Budget for Purchase of a $150,000 Home with $30,000 Down	
Monthly Payments:[a]	
Mortgage[b]	$880
Real estate taxes	203
Heat, lights, and water	160
Home insurance	40
Repairs and upkeep	120
Total monthly payments	$1403
Monthly savings:[a]	
Income tax reduction[c]	$300
Price appreciation[d]	500
Equity accumulation[e]	83
Total monthly savings	$883
Excess of monthly payments over savings ($1,403 − $883)	$520 per month

[a] Monthly values rounded to the dollar.

[b] A $120,000 mortgage at a fixed rate of 8% for 30 years.

[c] $797 of the $880 monthly mortgage payment is interest expense. This $797 interest and the $203 real estate tax are both tax-deductible. If you are in the 30% income tax bracket, you save 30% of $1,000 (= $797 + $203), or $300 per month in income taxes.

[d] Assume 4% per year price appreciation, or ($150,000 times 4% =) $6,000 appreciation in the first year (or $500 per month).

[e] $996 of the $120,000 loan will be paid off in the first year, which represents $83 per month of equity accumulation (apart from the price appreciation).

Table 29-2 indicates that even if the price of the new home rises 4% per year, the home purchase will *decrease* its owner's wealth by $520 per month in the first year. To justify purchasing the home, this wealth loss of $520 per month should be less than the monthly rental payments on a similar home. Moreover, the home buyer should remember that the estimated capital gain of $6,000 per year cannot be spent while the buyer owns the home. This accumulating capital gain and the accumulating equity in the home will not be available until the home is sold.

The price appreciation and the equity accumulation associated with the home purchase are like savings programs that allow no withdrawals. The $300 monthly income tax savings is the only actual reduction in cash outflows that results from the home purchase. Therefore, the home-buyer must be prepared to make cash payments of ($1,403 − $300 =) $1,103 per month. Considering the income and expense figures above, and the illiquidity of a home investment (home owners typically pay 6% sales commission to buy and 6% to sell), buying a home is a long-term investment that earns a modest rate of return and limits the investor's flexibility. It is necessary to consider the home owner's "psychic" income (pride, bragging rights, status) to rationalize most home purchases.

General Advantages and Disadvantages. Real estate investing involves several disadvantages:

1. Most parcels of real estate are not easy to divide into smaller pieces. As a result, real estate investing involves *large idiosyncratic risks* for most investors because the properties are a relatively large part of the investor's total portfolio. Owners of single-

family residences and the large institutional investors that buy shopping centers both experience this problem.

2. The *cost of acquiring information is high* because every piece of real estate is unique, and some flaws may not become evident until after the property is owned for a while.

3. Real estate brokers charge *high commissions.* Commissions of 6% of an asset's market value to buy and another 6% to sell are common.

4. Real estate involves substantial *maintenance (repair) and management (rental administration) costs* that are not incurred by securities investors.

5. Real estate investors are exposed to the risk of *neighborhood deterioration.* This problem is likely to result from conditions that are beyond the investor's control.

6. Valuable income tax deductions available to real estate investors are accompanied by the *political risk* that arises when voters question the continuation of these tax subsidies.

On the other hand, real estate investors enjoy certain advantages that tend to increase real estate prices:

1. To the extent that the law allows mortgage interest, property taxes, and other expenses to be tax deductible, real estate owners benefit from valuable *tax subsidies.*

2. Mortgage loans permit most real estate borrowers, if they wish, to utilize more *financial leverage* than is available to securities investors. Initial margins of 20% are common with real estate.

3. Real estate investors exercise some *controls* over their property that permits an advantageous decision, such as expanding or modernizing, to increase the market value of the property. In contrast, an investor who owns $150,000 worth of Coca-Cola stock has virtually no voice in the management of the corporation.

4. The typical owner of a single-family residence obtains *psychic income from home ownership* that inflates the values of these properties above what they are worth based on their investment merits alone.

5. Multiple real estate investments can provide *geographic diversification.* Geographically disparate real estate investments tend to be uncorrelated with each other and with non–real estate investments. Substantial geographic distance is not necessary to achieve risk reducing geographic diversification. For instance, the prices of suburban homes can be rising while, in the same city, the prices of inner city houses are falling. Furthermore, the value of family farms located just outside the city limit may be uncorrelated with the prices of residential properties in the suburbs and the inner city.

6. High positive correlations between all types of real estate prices and inflation document the fact that real-estate is a good *inflation hedge.*

7. The *low standard deviations* in (A) of Table 29-1 are appealing. However, we should be skeptical about this advantage because we know these risk statistics are biased downward by the smoothing process associated with real estate appraisals.

Conclusions About Real Estate

The market value of most physical real estate is positively correlated with the rate of inflation. Real estate REITs and mortgage REITs are investments in financial, not physical, assets. Financial investments in real estate interact with inflation differently than investments in physical real estate. REITs tend to be negatively correlated with inflation. Financial assets (REITs, bonds, common stocks) do not hedge inflation in the same way as physical assets (real estate, gold, silver). Sometimes financial assets, especially bonds, are poor inflation hedges.

California house prices were rising at a rate of 3% a month in 1978 and falling at the same rate in 1990. Extreme values like these are smoothed out in the reports produced by real estate appraisers and, as a result, the standard deviations of return in (A) of Table 29-1 can be downward biased.

Real estate is a complex investment with a list of advantages and disadvantages that every investor weights differently. These advantages and disadvantages, combined with the uniqueness of each piece of real estate, make it difficult to reach all-encompassing conclusions about real estate investing.

Real Estate on the Internet

Considering high real-estate brokerage commissions, the unique nature of every parcel, and flaws that are difficult to discern in advance, real estate research is an expensive, labor-intensive process. The Internet, however, brings cost-cutting transparency and liquidity to the market. Dozens of Web sites list millions of homes and other properties for sale, along with neighborhood data, and provide financial links to mortgage lenders. A few of the real estate Web sites are listed here.

- *www.homeadvisor.com* The Microsoft Network's large Web site contains home listings from over 100 Multiple Listing Services (MLSs), linkages to over a dozen mortgage lenders, and school and neighborhood data for the United States. Information about buying, financing, and repairing homes is also provided.

- *www.homegain.com* Enter the city, state, and street address of a home in the United States and this site immediately gives you an appraisal of the home.

- *www.homepricecheck.com* As above, give this site a city, state, and street address in the United States and it comes back with an appraisal of the home's value.

- *www.homeseekers.com* This site provides information about U.S. homes in English, Spanish, or French.

- *www.homestore.com* This site is connected to *realtor.com, homebuilder.com,* and *springstreet.com* and lists rental apartments in cities across the United States.

- *www.mortgagebot.com* This on-line mortgage lender provides current mortgage interest rate quotes and estimates of closing costs by county. You can apply for a mortgage and get it approved on line.

HEDGE FUNDS

Hedge funds are actively managed portfolios that hold positions in publicly traded securities. Unlike U.S. mutual funds, U.S. hedge funds are not regulated by the Investment Company Act of 1940. Most hedge funds are organized as limited partnerships, but some operate as limited liability corporations.

Hedge fund managers usually run their portfolios aggressively for a fixed fee ranging from 1% to 2% of the value of the assets managed per year, plus 5% to 25% of each year's profits. This fee structure and permissive governmental regulations encourage hedge fund managers to manage their portfolio's aggressively. Hedge funds often have investors that require their portfolio's manager to make a significant investment of personal money in the fund. This gives the portfolio manager an added incentive for achieving high returns and avoiding losses.[3]

The Hedge Fund Industry

National Securities Markets Improvement Act (NSMIA) of 1996. The NSMIA allows hedge funds more leeway than the Investment Company Act grants mutual funds. The law allows hedge funds to use leverage, sell short, buy put and call options, trade futures contracts, use other derivatives, buy shares in other investment companies, take concentrated positions in a few assets, and take an active role in the governance of corporations in which they invest.

Before the NSMIA was enacted, domestic hedge funds were limited to a maximum of 99 investors. The NSMIA allows a hedge fund to have as many as 500 investors and remain unregulated. Since hedge funds are prone to take risky positions, the law allows them to accept money only from experienced individual investors who have a minimum of $5 million to invest. The law requires institutional investors to have at least $25 million to invest.

Types of Hedge Funds. U.S. investors divide hedge funds into two categories—domestic funds and offshore funds. **Domestic hedge funds** must register with the SEC and are subject to the modest regulations imposed by the NSMIA. Almost all domestic hedge funds have their main offices in the United States. **Offshore hedge funds** are headquartered outside the United States, are not required to register with the SEC, and are largely unregulated.

Since the hedge fund industry is not tightly regulated, and many hedge funds are not even registered, it is difficult to estimate the size of the industry. Between 2,000 and 3,000 hedge funds are thought to have managed between $100 and $140 billion in 1996, and about 45% of these hedge funds were offshore funds.

Offshore hedge funds are typically located in tax havens such as Bermuda, the British Virgin Islands, the Bahamas, the Cayman Islands, and Luxembourg. Many domestic hedge funds in the United States have an offshore *sister fund* set up to invest in the same securities as the U.S.-based sister fund, and these sister funds are managed similarly. The offshore fund provides non-U.S. investors the opportunity to avoid taxation, and allows the domestic U.S. hedge fund to have more than 500 investors without coming under U.S. government regulation.

The High-Water Mark. Hedge fund managers are typically paid a fixed fee of about 1% of the value of the assets managed per year, plus about 20% of each year's gains above a base value. Most hedge funds use their total asset value at the beginning of the year as a *high-water mark,* or *base value.* Incentive fees of 5% to 25% of any gains above this base value are paid to the fund manager; 20% is typical. If the hedge fund loses money in one year, that fund's manager must make up the losses in the next year to qualify for incentive pay. In other words, in the year after a hedge fund suffers losses, these losses must first be made up to reach the high-water mark (base value) on which that year's incentive fees are based.

If a hedge fund suffers large losses for one or two consecutive years, the provision of incentive fees only above the high-water mark causes many hedge fund managers to become discouraged about their future bonuses and quit. Furthermore, it is difficult to keep old investors and get new investors after a hedge fund suffers large losses. These two forces cause a high attrition rate among hedge funds. About 20% of the existing hedge funds go out of business every year.

To keep investors from fleeing as soon as a hedge fund starts to perform poorly, some hedge funds require a 1-year *lock-up period* during which new investors may not withdraw funds. Investors who have been in the fund longer than 1 year may make withdrawals, but many hedge funds allow their investors to withdraw funds on only one designated date each quarter.

Turnover Among Hedge Funds. Column 4 of Table 29-3 shows the number of funds no longer available for sampling each year (recall the attrition rate discussed above). Columns 2, 5, and 6 show that the number of hedge funds available for study, and their assets, have been

TABLE 29-3 Sample Statistics from the Hedge Funds

(1) Year	(2)[a] Number of Offshore Funds Sampled	(3)[b] Number of Advisors for Sampled Funds	(4) Number of Dropped or Defunct Funds	(5) Number of New Funds	(6) Aggregate Capitalization of Sampled Funds, U.S.$
1988–89	78 funds	98 advisors	NA	NA	$ 4,721,256,000
1989–90	108	137	17	47	6,153,900,000
1990–91	142	155	19	53	11,466,358,100
1991–92	176	210	27	61	18,876,303,000
1992–93	265	316	23	112	39,064,117,965
1993–94	313	363	58	108	35,419,454,000
1994–95	399	450	65	152	40,345,412,365

[a]Only offshore funds were sampled. Most offshore hedge funds are a sister fund to a similarly managed domestic hedge fund based in the United States, so the sample should be representative of the combined offshore and domestic hedge fund industry.
[b]Some funds have more than one advisor.

SOURCE: Stephen J. Brown, William N. Goetzmann, and Roger G. Ibbotson, "Offshore Hedge Funds: Survival and Performance, 1989–95," *Journal of Business* 72, no. 1 (January 1999): 91–117, Table 1.

growing rapidly in recent years. These changes cause continual annual turnover in the hedge fund industry. If the failing funds are not included in the sample of data that is analyzed, survivorship bias results.

The Performance of Hedge Funds

Managed Account Reports (MAR) Inc., a hedge fund database firm, categorizes hedge funds based on statements that each portfolio publishes about its investment objective. Table 29-4 defines MAR's seven major categories of hedge fund investment goals, and several subcategories. Table 29-5 provides performance statistics from hedge funds in each of the seven categories listed in Table 29-4.

Although no category of hedge funds shown in Table 29-5 is able to demonstrate superiority over the market indexes or over other categories of hedge funds, three categories appear to be inferior performers. The fund-of-funds, market neutral, and short sales portfolios seem to do more harm than good for their investors.

Comparison of the investment objective statements published by the individual hedge funds with their actual individual performances (information that is not published here) reveals some discrepancies. U.S. law requires mutual funds and hedge funds to publish statements of their investment goals, but lack of penalties for deviating from these published statements gives portfolio managers considerable leeway in changing their goals, and some of them do so frequently. These deviations create a moral hazard for unsuspecting investors.

The Role of the Portfolio Manager. The unregulated environment in which hedge funds operate, the way hedge funds reward portfolio managers for taking large risks, and the use of lock-up periods are all pieces of evidence documenting the faith hedge fund investors place in their portfolio managers. An investment in a hedge fund is, essentially, a bet on the skills of the portfolio manager.

That faith, and the unregulated environment, grants hedge fund managers considerable freedom. They can travel down avenues forbidden to mutual fund managers and change direction frequently. As a result, applying Sharpe's style analysis[4] to monthly hedge fund

TABLE 29-4   Categories of Hedge Fund Investment Objectives

Event Driven:

Distressed Securities—Manager focuses on securities of companies in reorganization and bankruptcy, ranging from senior secured debt to the common stock of the company.

Risk Arbitrage—Manager simultaneously buys stock in a company being acquired and sells stock in its acquirers.

Global:

International—Manager pays attention to economic change around the world (except the United States) but more bottom-up oriented in that managers tend to be stock-pickers in markets they like. Uses index derivatives to a much lesser extent than macro managers.

Emerging—Manager invests in less mature financial markets of the world, e.g., Hong Kong, Singapore, Pakistan, India. Because shorting is not permitted in many emerging markets, managers must go to cash or other markets when valuations make being long unattractive.

Regional—Manager focuses on specific regions of the world, e.g., Latin America, Asia, Europe.

Global Macro:

Opportunistic trading manager that profits from changes in global economies, typically based on major interest rate shifts. Uses leverage and derivatives.

Market Neutral:

Long/short stocks:—Half long/half short. Manager attempts to lock-out or neutralize market risk. In theory, market risk is greatly reduced but it is very difficult to make a profit on a large diversified portfolio so stock picking is critical.

Convertible arbitrage—Manager goes long convertible securities and short the underlying equities.

Stock index arbitrage—Manager buys a basket of stocks and sells short stock index futures, or the reverse

Fixed income arbitrage—Manager buys T-bonds and sells short other T-bonds that replicate the bond purchased in terms of rate and maturity.

Short Sales:

Manager takes a position that stock prices will go down. Used as a hedge for long-only portfolios and by those who feel market is approaching a bearish trend.

U.S. Opportunistic:

Value—Manager focuses on assets, cash flow, book value, out-of-favor stocks.

Growth—Manager invests in growth stocks; revenues, earnings, and growth potential are key.

Short term—Manager holds positions for a short time frame.

Fund of Funds:

Capital is allocated among a number of hedge funds, providing investors with access to managers they might not be able to discover or evaluate on their own. Usually has a lower minimum than a hedge fund.

SOURCE: Carl Ackermann, Richard McEnally, and David Ravenscraft, "The Performance of Hedge Funds: Risk, Return, and Incentives," *Journal of Finance* 54, no.3 (June 1999), Figure 1, p. 843. Reproduced from a hedge fund database firm named Managed Account Reports (MAR) Inc., and distributed through LaPorte Asset Allocation System.

TABLE 29-5   Hedge Fund Performance Statistics for All Funds and for Seven Subcategories of Funds

(1) Type of Hedge Funds	(2) No. of Years Sampled[a]	(3) No. of Funds	(4) Mean Return, %	(5) Median Return, %	(6) Standard Deviation of Returns, %	(7) Minimum Return, %	(8) Maximum Return, %
Total Sample							
	2	547	9.2%	8.9%	11.9%	−38.4%	69.3%
	4	272	14.7%	13.9%	9.2%	−16.3%	58.1%
	6	150	14.6%	13.4%	7.8%	−1.1%	47.4%
	8	79	16.1%	15.0%	8.7%	−1.9%	39.8%
Event-Driven Funds							
	2	56	11.1%	11.6%	7.2%	−16.2%	35.4%
	4	34	15.8%	16.3%	4.7%	7.3%	26.2%
	6	27	14.7%	13.2%	7.7%	3.9%	43.6%
	8	11	17.9%	15.0%	7.8%	11.5%	39.8%
Fund of Funds							
	2	118	3.2%	3.6%	7.9%	−14.7%	33.7%
	4	57	10.2%	10.2%	8.2%	−13.4%	27.0%
	6	22	12.6%	10.1%	6.5%	5.0%	32.3%
	8	6	11.4%	10.1%	3.2%	9.3%	18.4%
Global Funds							
	2	104	5.7%	5.9%	13.1%	−32.5%	68.3%
	4	44	17.1%	15.7%	10.1%	0.7%	44.5%
	6	27	15.3%	15.1%	7.5%	−11%	28.0%
	8	16	19.3%	17.4%	9.6%	7.0%	39.5%
Global Macro Funds							
	2	61	9.8%	9.1%	14.6%	−38.4%	69.3%
	4	35	14.9%	16.7%	8.7%	−16.3%	37.0%
	6	23	18.0%	15.8%	8.7%	2.8%	43.0%
	8	14	20.5%	19.5%	7.1%	6.9%	35.4%
Market Neutral Funds							
	2	72	9.9%	8.9%	9.3%	−10.1%	44.7%
	4	27	9.8%	9.6%	4.4%	3.4%	24.0%
	6	19	10.4%	9.9%	2.9%	5.7%	16.1%
	8	9	8.0%	7.8%	2.9%	3.2%	12.4%
Short Sales Funds							
	2	7	5.6%	3.6%	9.3%	−4.9%	23.9%
	4	5	2.8%	3.6%	5.5%	−4.0%	9.1%
	6	1	N/A[b]	N/A	N/A	N/A	N/A
	8	1	N/A	N/A	N/A	N/A	N/A
U.S. Opportunistic Funds							
	2	129	16.0%	14.3%	11.5%	−16.6%	67.3%
	4	70	19.2%	18.2%	9.6%	−4.5%	58.1%
	6	32	15.3%	14.5%	8.7%	−0.4%	47.4%
	8	23	14.9%	16.5%	8.7%	−1.9%	38.5%

SOURCE: Carl Ackermann, Richard McEnally, and David Ravenscraft, "The Performance of Hedge Funds: Risk, Return, and Incentives," *Journal of Finance* 54, no. 3 (June 1999): Table III, p. 847.

[a]All sample periods end on December 31, 1995.   [b]N/A Short Sales Funds stands for "Not Available" because only one fund was in the category.

returns reveals frequent changes in hedge funds' exposures to different risk factors. This dynamic activity complicates performance measurement and evaluation. To make matters worse, news stories about one unusual portfolio manager can give investors the wrong impression of the hedge fund industry.

The Quantum Fund. George Soros's Quantum Fund is a well-known hedge fund that is noteworthy in several respects. First, the Quantum Fund has operated for three decades—an unusually long life for a hedge fund. Second, at one time the Quantum Fund was the largest hedge fund in existence—a multibillion-dollar portfolio. And third, it earned compound annual returns of over 30% for more than two decades—a lengthy period for a large portfolio to attain such high compounded returns. The Quantum Fund also had some very bad years.

Hedge Fund Returns. Table 29-6 shows annual net rates of return and fee data for the hedge funds in Table 29-3. Most of the equal-weighted arithmetic mean returns in Column 3 of Table 29-6 exceed the median returns in Column 5 because the frequency distribution of hedge fund returns is skewed to the right. This positive skewness occurs because the maximum returns in Table 29-6 go as high as +296.9%. But, since it is impossible to lose more than 100%, a portfolio's return is bounded below at −100%.

Most of the value-weighted arithmetic mean returns in Column 4 of Table 29-6 exceed the equal-weighted arithmetic mean returns in Column 3 because the superior performance of a few large hedge funds increased the value-weighted returns. In addition, funds earning poor returns experience shrinking total assets and thus have small weights.

The wide ranges between each year's maximum return (Column 6) and minimum return (Column 7) in Table 29-6 highlight the riskiness of hedge fund investing. A representative sample of common stock mutual funds would show less variability of return because the Investment Company Act limits mutual funds' ability to make concentrated investments, use leverage, and employ derivatives.

We've seen that the portfolio manager's incentive fees in Column 9 of Table 29-6 are typically computed as a contractually stipulated fraction (about 20%) of whatever positive

TABLE 29-6   Annual Rate of Return and Fee Data from Hedge Funds Sampled

(1) Year	(2) No. of Funds in Sample	(3) Arithmetic Equal Weighted Mean Return[a]	(4) Arithmetic Value Weighted Mean Return[a]	(5) Median Return[a]	(6) Maximum Return[a]	(7) Minimum Return[a]	(8) Average Annual Fee	(9) Average Incentive Fee
1988–89	78	18.08%	NA	20.30%	57.3%	−33.6%	1.744%	19.755%
1989–90	108	4.36	16.37%	3.80	85.9	−30.7	1.647	19.519
1990–91	142	17.13	36.95	15.90	94.6	−53.4	1.786	19.548
1991–92	176	11.98	36.99	10.70	92.4	−24.4	1.809	19.344
1992–93	265	24.59	41.94	22.15	155.6	−30.3	1.621	19.096
1993–94	313	−1.60	−7.03	−2.00	105.1	−49.8	1.644	18.753
1994–95	399	18.32	23.05	14.70	296.9	−40.3	1.551	118.497

SOURCE: Stephen J. Brown, William N. Goetzmann, and Roger G. Ibbotson, "Offshore Hedge Funds: Survival and Performance, 1989–95," *Journal of Business* 72, no. 1 (January 1999): 91–117, Table 1.

[a] The reported returns are net after fees are deducted.

return the hedge fund earned. In a few cases the incentive fee is a contractual fraction of an excess return above the interest rate paid by a U.S. Treasury bond.

Risk-Adjusted Return Measures. There is a popular perception that hedge funds undertake large risks to generate high rates of return. In fact, Brown, Goetzmann, and Ibbotson report that over a 7-year sample period the average hedge fund earned a lower average rate of return (13.26%) than the S&P500 index (16.47%) over the same period. Furthermore, the average hedge fund experienced a lower standard deviation of returns than the S&P500 index (9.07% compared to 16.32%). The average betas for the hedge funds are also low. Using both the equal-weighted and the value-weighted hedge fund returns, the hedge fund beta coefficients were 0.33 and 0.43, respectively.

When risk and return are considered at the same time, performance of the hedge funds is better than that of the S&P500 index. Both the equal-weighted and the value-weighted hedge fund indexes had SHARPE values (see Eqn. 16-3 in Chapter 16, p. 483) exceeding the S&P500 index. Further, the equal-weighted and the value-weighted hedge fund indexes had positive Jensen's alphas (see Eqn. 16-10 in Chapter 16, p.488) of 5.7% and 16.6%, respectively. These values support the conclusion that there is a positive risk-return tradeoff in the hedge fund industry.

Ackermann, McEnally, and Ravenscraft's Comparisons. Hedge funds are organized to align the interests of the portfolio manager and the portfolio's investors. Hedge fund managers receive most of their pay in the form of incentive fees that reward achieving what the owners want; they tend to invest in their own fund, which gives them an interest in the fund's success; and many of them are general partners who have legal liability for any extreme losses the portfolio might incur. These features provide better incentives for hedge fund managers than are available for mutual fund managers. In addition, U.S. securities law gives hedge fund managers more investment leeway than it allows mutual fund managers. These organizational differences motivated Ackermann, McEnally, and Ravenscraft (AMR) to compare the performance of hedge funds and mutual funds.

AMR concluded that:"The combination of incentive alignment and investment flexibility gives hedge funds a clear performance advantage over mutual funds." When AMR compared the SHARPE measures from mutual funds with those from hedge funds, they reported modest superiority for the hedge funds.

AMR went on to compare the performances of their hedge fund sample with eight different securities market indexes. Their results were mixed. The winner in this comparison varied with the time period, the hedge fund category, and the securities market index used for the comparison. However, AMR concluded that: ". . . hedge funds are unable to consistently beat the market when absolute or total risk-adjusted returns are used." Summarizing, it seems that the hedge funds slightly outperformed the mutual funds, but neither group of portfolios were able to outperform representative market indexes.

Survivorship Bias. Most hedge fund industry performance statistics are probably exaggerated because of survivorship bias. The last annual return from a defunct hedge fund must be omitted from the sample if the fund ceases operations part way through the year—and there are usually several such funds each year. Presumably, defunct hedge funds were terminated because they are unable to reach the high-water mark incentive pay. Deleting the last year in the lives of these defunct funds upward biases the average returns of the funds that remain to be sampled that year.

Hedge Funds on the Internet

Several Web sites publish information about hedge funds:

◆ *www.hedgeworld.com*   HedgeWorld Limited (HFL), based in Bermuda, publishes hedge fund news and basic performance data at no cost to the viewer. More sophisticated analytical tools and additional historical information are available for a fee. HFL's hedge fund data on 2,200 hedge funds and 1,700 hedge fund managers around the world are supplied by London-based TASS Investment Research.

◆ *www.hedgefundcenter.com*   Hedge Fund Center (HFC) provides educational information about hedge funds, links to other sources of hedge fund information, and a message board.

◆ *www.hedgefund.net*   Hedge Fund Net (HFN) posts information on over 1,000 hedge fund managers, provides educational information about hedge funds, posts hedge fund index data, has links to other sources of hedge fund information, and has a message board.

GOLD BULLION AND PHYSICAL SILVER

Before paper money existed, gold and silver were currencies. Their portability and durability makes them useful as a medium of exchange, and their scarcity ensures they have value everywhere in the world. When a nation suffers an economic collapse (depression), its federal government fails, or it is defeated in a war, gold is the asset its citizens seek.

The Gold Standard.   Any nation that chooses to operate under the **gold standard** is obligated to exchange its money for a fixed amount of gold. Except for temporary departures during wars, the United States and Britain operated under the gold standard during the 1800s and 1900s. Figure 29-1 shows that the price of gold remained fixed during most decades of the 19th and 20th centuries. The United States created the Federal Reserve in 1913, and Federal Reserve Notes (U.S. paper money), for instance, could be redeemed for a specified quantity of gold.

The gold standard helps accomplish three worthwhile national objectives. First, it keeps the lid on the nation's money supply. Second, it keeps the nation's politicians from spending too much. Keeping a nation's spending and money supply under control accomplishes the third objective—it controls the nation's inflation rate .

In the United States The Great Stock Market Crash of 1929 marked the beginning of The Depression, which caused several years of economic suffering around the globe during the 1930s. In an attempt to spend their way out of The Depression, Britain abandoned the gold standard in 1931 and the United States abandoned it in 1933. These two actions caused a jump in the price of gold during the 1930s that can be seen in Figure 29-1.

Demonetizing Gold.   Although the right to redeem U.S. dollars for gold was denied to U.S. citizens after 1933, a few years later, after The Depression started to bottom out, the Federal Reserve quietly reinstated the gold standard for the central banks of other nations. After 1936 any central bank in the world could redeem U.S. dollars for $35 per ounce through the Federal Reserve System but private individuals couldn't.

During 1970 the market price of gold rose to $40 an ounce, and millions of U.S. dollars were being exchanged for gold daily. Fears arose about the U.S. gold supply being exhausted. On August 15, 1971 President Nixon announced that the United States was abandoning the gold standard, and the country has not resumed it. Figure 29-1 illustrates how the price of gold shot up from $35 an ounce after being freed in 1971. After 1971 the price of gold was determined by the market forces of supply and demand.

Silver Prices in the United States   The *Coinage Act of 1965* ended the U.S. government's use of silver to make dimes and quarters, and was the first step toward demonetizing silver in the

FIGURE 29-1 Indexes of Nominal Prices for Gold, Silver, Two Portfolios of Diversified U.S. Common Stocks, and the Cost of Living 1800–1999 Inclusive

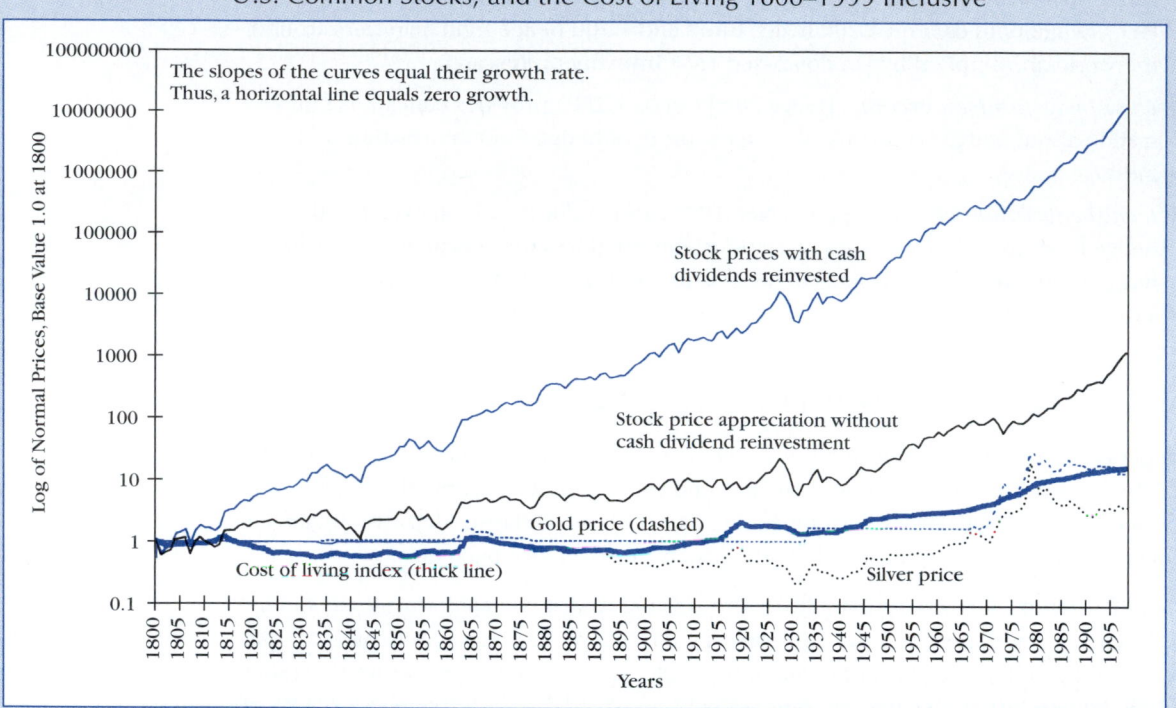

The market prices of gold, silver, two highly diversified portfolios of U.S. common stocks, and a cost-of-living index, with no adjustments for taxes and other transaction costs, are all indexed to a base value of Log(1) in 1800. The purchasing power of silver declined slightly over the sample period, while the price of gold tended to stay near the cost of living. Ignoring year-to-year fluctuations, common stocks provided a better long-run hedge against inflation than gold or silver.

United States. When the U.S. Treasury stopped supporting the price of silver at $1.29 per ounce in 1967, it jumped to $1.87 per ounce and began to fluctuate. In 1968 the Secretary of the U.S. Treasury declared that the paper currency called *silver certificates* were no longer redeemable in silver, which demonetized silver in the United States.

Physical silver was used in a number of industrial applications (jewelry, manufacturing film) and was actively traded on commodity exchanges around the world. By the mid-1970s its price had reached $5 per ounce. Figure 29-1 shows that some investors made millions when silver briefly soared to $50 per ounce in 1980, as the Hunt family of Texas sought to corner the silver market. Later in 1980 many silver investors (including the Hunts) lost millions when the Hunt family's vast wealth proved insufficient to buy all the silver for sale in the huge international silver market. Since 1983, the market price of silver has fluctuated between $4 and $10 per ounce.

Besides value as money, silver also has, as noted, value as a raw material. As a result of differing supply and demand forces, the price of silver has not remained as highly positively correlated with the price of gold during the 1900s as it was during the 1800s. Although silver and especially gold still possess some of the qualities of money, today they should both be viewed as commodities whose prices fluctuate freely.

Market price indexes for gold, silver, two diversified portfolios of U.S. common stocks, and the Consumers Price Index (CPI) for the United States are compared in Figure 29-1. The purchasing power of silver declined slightly, while gold prices tended to stay about even with inflation over the two centuries illustrated in Figure 29-1. Although stock prices are negatively correlated with inflation during sample periods of less than 1 year, these are short-term reactions. Common stocks are uncorrelated with inflation during longer periods and have provided a better long-run inflation hedge than gold or silver.

Gold and Monetary Policy. Although the gold standard provided economic stability for the world during the 1800s and 1900s, few tears were shed when the United States abandoned it on August 15, 1971. The U.S. stock market jumped 4% on the day after President Nixon abandoned the gold standard.

Demonetizing gold removes a powerful constraint on inflationary growth in a nation's money supply. Most politically unstable nations can benefit from a gold standard, because it keeps their political leaders from expanding the nation's money supply in an inflationary manner to pay for projects that are frequently only designed to buy popularity or power. After the leader has been deposed, high inflation often remains to cripple the nation's economy. A stable political system helped bring the U.S. money supply and inflation rate under control.

During the 1900s Milton Friedman taught central bankers and government administrators how a nation's money supply should be controlled—a feat for which he was received the Nobel prize.[5] To help keep inflation under control, in 1975 the U.S. Congress passed a law requiring the Federal Reserve to routinely publish its money supply growth policies for the months ahead. In 1979 Paul Volcker was appointed Chairman of the Federal Reserve Board, and he established firm controls on the U.S. money supply. Since Volcker's Chairmanship ended, the Federal Reserve Board's Open Market Committee has not hesitated to restrict the money supply, raise market interest rates, and carry out other unpopular actions needed to keep inflation under control. As a result, the U.S. gold standard "died a peaceful death" in 1971 and has been missed by few.

Investing in Gold or Silver. The inflation-adjusted rates of return from gold bullion and physical silver are near zero. After allowing for the costs of acquisition, storage, and insurance, the real returns from investing in these precious metals are negative. If a short-term investor has to choose between gold, silver, and financial securities, the securities usually offer the best choice. Money market securities offer the same zero real returns as gold and silver, but with better liquidity and fewer risks. Short-term price speculators can close transactions more quickly and cheaply using futures contracts on gold or silver than by trading in the physical metals. However, gold bullion and physical silver offer investors two attractive features: catastrophe insurance and diversification.

Public catastrophes can be caused by an "act of God," an economic collapse, hyperinflation, or other causes. The purchasing power of money falls rapidly during most catastrophes. Gold and silver are a portable store of value and a medium of exchange that tends to become money during periods of crisis. For these reasons, investments in gold and silver have value as catastrophe insurance.

Figure 29-1 shows that the prices of gold and silver are not highly correlated with securities prices. This quality gives these metals the capacity to reduce risk in a diversified portfolio that is heavily invested in securities. Because they are global commodities that are not highly influenced by local events, gold and silver are particularly useful in reducing a portfolio's political risk.

THE BOTTOM LINE

Investors looking for assets with unique returns that are likely to reduce their portfolio's overall risk exposure may invest in new asset classes uncorrelated with their traditional positions.

Low correlations between alternative investments and traditional bond and stock investments enable investors to diversify away some uncertainty about the terminal value of their portfolio. Investors should appreciate that a low historical average return or a failure to achieve a high historical average return from an alternative investment is not evidence of a poor investment, just as a stock's low historical return is not evidence it will be a poor investment in the future.

Real estate is a special type of passive investment. A passive investor who buys real estate may not remain completely passive; the investor must perform maintenance (repairs) and/or manage (rent) the asset. Tax deductibility of mortgage interest and property taxes provide government subsidies for real estate investors. But high transactions costs tend to make real estate illiquid.

Hedge fund investors co-mingle their funds in a pool and hire a portfolio manager—usually an aggressive manager—to manage their hedge fund portfolio. Hedge fund managers are normally paid an annual management fee of about 1% of the market value of the assets managed, plus incentive pay of about 20% of each year's gains—if any gains over the year's high-water mark are earned. The aggregate market value of a hedge fund at the beginning of each year equals that year's high-water mark. If a hedge fund manager suffers losses, those losses must be made up before the portfolio manager reaches the high-water mark upon which future incentive payments are based. If a hedge fund earns enough consecutive losses to make it unlikely that the portfolio manager will be able to surpass the high-water mark in the future, that hedge fund is usually dissolved at considerable loss to its investors.

Gold bullion and physical silver are precious metals that possess the same qualities as money. Although many countries used these metals as money for centuries, in recent years most countries have demonetized their currencies. Today gold and silver are commodities whose prices are determined by supply and demand.

QUESTIONS

Q29-1   (REITs) What are REITs? What is the difference between an equity REIT and a mortgage REIT?

Q29-2   (Real estate investments) True, false, or uncertain: The historical statistics indicate that investments in real estate are very low risk when compared to the S&P500 index, the small cap stocks index, and the commodity futures index.

Q29-3   (Real estate investments) Discuss the advantages of investing in real estate. Discuss the disadvantages.

Q29-4   (Hedge funds) What are hedge funds and how do U.S. hedge funds differ from U.S. mutual funds?

Q29-5   (Sister funds) What is a "sister fund," and what advantages does it offer investors?

Q29-6   (Hedge funds) True, false, or uncertain: While hedge funds are extremely risky, they tend to outperform the S&P500 index on a risk-adjusted basis.

Q29-7   (Hedge funds) Discuss the differences between domestic hedge funds and offshore hedge funds.

Q29-8   (Gold bullion) True, false, or uncertain: Over the long run, gold provides a much greater inflation hedge than either common stocks or silver.

Q29-9   (Gold bullion and physical silver investments) What two advantages do investments in gold bullion and physical silver offer investors?

Q29-10   (Correlation coefficient for silver and gold prices) Explain why the price of silver is no longer highly positively correlated with the price of gold, as was the case in the 1800s.

PROBLEMS

P29-1   (Risk diversification with REITs) Use the information provided in Table 29-1 to calculate the expected return and risk of a portfolio that is invested equally in an equity REIT and the S&P500 index. The correlation coefficient for the returns on equity REITs and the S&P500 index is 0.3.

P29-2 (Risk diversification with gold) Use the information provided in Table 29-1 to calculate the expected return and risk of a portfolio that is invested equally in the S&P500 index and gold. The correlation coefficient for the returns on the two investments over the 1972–99 period was −0.4.

P29-3 (Risk diversification using gold and silver) Use the information provided in Table 29-1 to calculate the expected return and risk of a portfolio that is invested in 25% gold, 25% silver, and 50% in the S&P500 index. The correlation coefficients are as follows:

$$\rho_{S\&P,gold} = -0.4$$
$$\rho_{S\&P,silver} = -0.1$$
$$\rho_{gold,silver} = 0.8$$

P29-4 (Risk diversification) Compare your answers to Problems 29-2 and 29-3. How do you explain the differences in the results?

P29-5 (Real returns) Use the information in Table 29-1 to calculate the compounded annual real return on each of the following investments: equity REITs, mortgage REITs, gold, silver, U.S. treasury bills, and the S&P500 index. Which provided the highest compounded annual real return over the 1972–99 period? Which provided the lowest?

P29-6 (Real estate investments) Gabe and Ginny Herschel are interested in buying a $270,000 home. The required down payment is 20%, and the interest rate on a 30-year, fixed-rate mortgage is 9%. What would their monthly mortgage payment be, assuming they make only the minimum down payment?

P29-7 (Real estate investments) Develop an amortization schedule for the first year of payments using the informa-

tion in P29-6. *Note:* You may need to review the preparation of an amortization schedule, which should have been covered in a prerequisite course.

P29-8 (Purchase budget) Gabe and Ginny expect their home to appreciate at a rate of 5% a year. They have also estimated the following:

Annual real estate taxes: $2,600

Monthly insurance cost: $70

Average monthly gas, electricity, and water: $200

Average monthly cost of repairs and upkeep: $50

Gabe and Ginny are in the 28% marginal tax bracket. Use the above information, in addition to the information in Problems 29-6 and 29-7, to develop a budget for the purchase of the $270,000 home.

P29-9 (Monthly cash outflow for real estate) Based on your calculations for Problem 29-8, what will Gabe and Ginny's monthly cash outflow be?

P29-10 (Hedge fund incentives) A certain hedge fund had a net asset value of $575 billion at the beginning of 20X1. The manager of the fund receives a fixed fee of 1% of the value of the assets plus an incentive fee of 20% of the gains above the net asset value at the beginning of the year. The net asset value of the fund at the beginning of the following 2 years were:

20X2	$525 billion
20X3	$565 billion

What incentive fee will the fund's manager receive in 20X1 and 20X2?

CFA EXAM QUESTIONS

1. (1997 CFA Exam, Level I) Which of the following is the *most valid* justification for including real estate as part of an investment portfolio?
   A. Low correlation of real estate with stocks and bonds.
   B. Low management and information costs.
   C. Low project-specific risk.
   D. High liquidity.

2. (1998 CFA Exam, Level I) *All* of the following statements about real estate investment trusts (REITs) are generally true *except:*
   A. The shares of REITs are traded only on the New York Stock exchange.
   B. REITs must keep at least 75% of their assets in real estate investments.

   C. REITs are required by law to pay out 95% of their income as dividends.
   D. REITs yield a return at least 1–2 percentage points above money market funds and about the same return as high-grade corporate bonds.

3. (1997 CFA Exam, Level III) Robin Quon is reviewing two indexes that measure real estate investment performance. One index is composed of equity real estate investment trusts (the EREIT Index), and the other is composed of commingled real estate funds (the CREF Index). Both indexes are broadly diversified and hold similar types of properties from the same geographical areas in roughly comparable amounts. Quon has noted, however, that the performances of the two indexes have

been noticeably different. In discussing the possible reasons for the difference, he states, "With CREFs, there are transaction barriers, in that the minimum investment in a CREF may be too large for some investors." Identify and discuss *two other* reasons that might account for the difference in the performance of the two indexes.

4. (Adapted from the1994 CFA Exam, Level III) Food Processors Inc. (FPI) is a mature U.S. company reporting declining earnings and a weak balance sheet. Its ERISA-qualified defined-benefit pension plan has total assets of $750 million. However, the plan is underfunded by $200 million by U.S. standards—a cause for concern by shareholders, management, and the Board.

The average age of plan participants is 45 years. FPI's annual contribution to the plan and the earnings on its assets are sufficient to meet pension payments to present retirees. The pension portfolio's holdings are equally divided between large-capitalization U.S. equities and high-quality, long-maturity U.S. corporate bonds. For actuarial purposes, the assumed long-term rate of return on plan assets is 9% per year; the discount rate applied to plan liabilities, all of which are U.S.-based, is 8%. As FPI's Treasurer, you are responsible for oversight of the plan's investments and managers and for liaison with the Board's Pension Investment Committee.

The investment policy for FPI's plan includes a commitment "to invest a portion of the assets in appropriate equity real estate." The Committee is aware that real estate has been a disappointing investment over the past decade, but wonders if the time may be near to begin a purchase program. A local real estate consultant you invited to discuss the subject with the Committee has made the following statement:

"Everyone knows that real estate is much less risky than common stocks and is a sure hedge against inflation. The data prove it. Adding real estate as a plan asset automatically improves diversification and long-run returns. You don't need to think about real estate in a 'portfolio' context; all that matters is the property deals you make. Putting together a combination of 'good buys' will deliver what you want from real

estate, regardless of what securities the portfolio holds. Real estate is different from stocks and bonds, and different rules apply."

5. (1994 CFA Exam, Level II) You have been recently appointed chief investment officer of a major charitable foundation. Its large endowment fund is currently invested in a broadly diversified portfolio of stocks (60%) and bonds (40%). You believe that the addition of other asset classes to the endowment portfolio would improve the portfolio by reducing risk and enhancing return. You are aware that depressed conditions in U.S. real estate markets are providing opportunities for property acquisition at levels of expected return that are unusually high by historical standards. You believe that an investment in U.S. real estate would be both appropriate and timely, and have decided to recommend a 20% position be established with funds taken equally from stocks and bonds.

Preliminary discussions revealed that several trustees believe real estate is too risky to include in the portfolio. The Board Chairman, however, has scheduled a special meeting for further discussion of the matter and has asked you to provide background information that will clarify the risk issue.

To assist you, the following expectational data have been developed:

Asset Class	% Return	% Standard Deviation	Correlation Matrix			
			U.S. Stocks	U.S. Bonds	U.S. Real Estate	U.S. T-Bills
U.S. Stocks	12.0	21.0	1.00			
U.S. Bonds	8.0	10.5	0.14	1.00		
U.S. Real Estate	12.0	9.0	−0.04	−0.03	1.00	
U.S. Treasury Bills	4.0	0.0	−0.05	−0.03	0.25	1.00

Your understanding of capital market theory causes you to doubt the validity of the expected return and risk for U.S. real estate. Justify your skepticism.

FURTHER REFERENCES

Schneeweis, Thomas and Joseph F. Pescatore, Eds. *The Handbook of Alternative Investment Strategies.* New York: Institutional Investor Inc., 1999.

This book contains 22 chapters written by experts in their respective fields. The chapters cover common stock investing, hedge fund investing, trading futures contracts, commodity investments, real estate investing, venture capital investing, credit derivatives, and risk-return analysis of alternative investments.

Francis, Jack and Roger Ibbotson, "Empirical Risk-Return Analysis of Real-Estate Investments in the United States 1972–1999," *The Journal Of Alternative Investments*, Institutional Investor, New York City, Summer 2001, pages 33–39.

The real estate statistics published in this chapter, plus additional real estate statistics (such as a correlation matrix) that are not published in this chapter, are published in this article. All statistics are computed from the same sample.

ENDNOTES

[1] See Douglas Rigby and Elizabeth Rigby, *Lock, Stock, and Barrel: The Story of Collecting* (Philadelphia: Lippincott, 1944), 225.

[2] See Joseph Tracy, Henry Schneider, and Sewin Chan, "Are Stocks Overtaking Real-Estate in Household Portfolios?" *Current Issues,* 5, no. 5 (April 1999): Table 1, Chart 1. The decline in the proportion invested in real estate can be attributed to a concurrent increase in common stock holdings, measured at market value, that rose from 10% of total assets in 1985 to 28% in 1998.

[3] See Stephen J. Brown, William N. Goetzmann, and Roger G. Ibbotson, "Offshore Hedge Funds: Survival and Performance, 1989-95," *Journal of Business* 72, no. 1 (January 1999): 91-117. Also see Carl Ackermann, Richard McEnally, and David Ravenscraft, "The Performance of Hedge Funds: Risk, Return, and Incentives," *Journal of Finance* 54, no. 3 (June 1999): 833-74. And see William Fung and David A. Hsieh, "Empirical Characteristics of Dynamic Trading Strategies: The Case of Hedge Funds," *Review of Financial Studies* 10 (1997): 275-302.

[4] See William F. Sharpe, "Asset Allocation: Management Style and Performance Management," *Journal of Portfolio Management* 18, no. 2 (Winter 1992): 7-19.

[5] See Milton Friedman, *A Program for Monetary Stability* (New York: Fordham University Press, 1959).

PRESENT VALUE TABLES

TABLE A.1 Present Value of $1: PVIF $= 1/(1+k)^t$

Period	1%	2%	3%	4%	5%	6%	7%	8%	9%	10%	12%	14%	15%	16%	18%	20%	24%	28%	32%	36%
1	.9901	.9804	.9709	.9615	.9524	.9434	.9436	.9259	.9174	.9091	.8929	.8772	.8696	.8621	.8475	.8333	.8065	.7813	.7576	.7353
2	.9803	.9612	.9426	.9246	.9070	.8900	.8734	.8573	.8417	.8264	.7972	.7695	.7561	.7432	.7182	.6944	.6504	.6104	.5739	.5407
3	.9706	.9423	.9151	.8890	.8638	.8396	.8163	.7938	.7722	.7513	.7118	.6750	.6575	.6407	.6086	.5787	.5245	.4768	.4348	.3975
4	.9610	.9238	.8885	.8548	.8227	.7921	.7629	.7350	.7084	.6830	.6355	.5921	.5718	.5523	.5158	.4823	.4230	.3725	.3294	.2923
5	.9515	.9057	.8626	.8219	.7835	.7473	.7130	.6806	.6499	.6209	.5674	.5194	.4972	.4761	.4371	.4019	.3411	.2910	.2495	.2149
6	.9420	.8880	.8375	.7903	.7462	.7050	.6663	.6302	.5963	.5645	.5066	.4556	.4323	.4104	.3704	.3349	.2751	.2274	.1890	.1580
7	.9327	.8706	.8131	.7599	.7107	.6651	.6227	.5835	.5470	.5132	.4523	.3996	.3759	.3538	.3139	.2791	.2218	.1776	.1432	.1162
8	.9235	.8535	.7894	.7307	.6768	.6274	.5820	.5403	.5019	.4665	.4039	.3506	.3269	.3050	.2660	.2326	.1789	.1388	.1085	.0854
9	.9143	.8368	.7664	.7026	.6446	.5919	.5439	.5002	.4604	.4241	.3606	.3075	.2843	.2630	.2255	.1938	.1443	.1084	.0822	.0628
10	.9053	.8203	.7441	.6756	.6139	.5584	.5083	.4632	.4224	.3855	.3220	.2697	.2472	.2267	.1911	.1615	.1164	.0847	.0623	.0462
11	.8963	.8043	.7224	.6496	.5847	.5268	.4751	.4289	.3875	.3505	.2875	.2366	.2149	.1954	.1619	.1346	.0938	.0662	.0472	.0340
12	.8874	.7885	.7014	.6246	.5568	.4970	.4440	.3971	.3555	.3186	.2567	.2076	.1869	.1685	.1372	.1122	.0757	.0517	.0357	.0250
13	.8787	.7730	.6810	.6006	.5303	.4688	.4150	.3677	.3262	.2897	.2292	.1821	.1625	.1452	.1163	.0935	.0610	.0404	.0271	.0184
14	.8700	.7579	.6611	.5775	.5051	.4423	.3878	.3405	.2992	.2633	.2046	.1597	.1413	.1252	.0985	.0779	.0492	.0316	.0205	.0135
15	.8613	.7430	.6419	.5553	.4810	.4173	.3624	.3152	.2745	.2394	.1827	.1401	.1229	.1079	.0835	.0649	.0397	.0247	.0155	.0099
16	.8528	.7284	.6232	.5339	.4581	.3936	.3387	.2919	.2519	.2176	.1631	.1229	.1069	.0930	.0708	.0541	.0320	.0193	.0118	.0073
17	.8444	.7142	.6050	.5134	.4363	.3714	.3166	.2703	.2311	.1978	.1456	.1078	.0929	.0802	.0600	.0451	.0258	.0150	.0089	.0054
18	.8360	.7002	.5874	.4936	.4155	.3503	.2959	.2502	.2120	.1799	.1300	.0946	.0808	.0691	.0508	.0376	.0208	.0118	.0068	.0039
19	.8277	.6864	.5703	.4746	.3957	.3305	.2765	.2317	.1945	.1635	.1161	.0829	.0703	.0596	.0431	.0313	.0168	.0092	.0051	.0029
20	.8195	.6730	.5537	.4564	.3769	.3118	.2584	.2145	.1784	.1486	.1037	.0728	.0611	.0514	.0365	.0261	.0135	.0072	.0039	.0021
25	.7798	.6095	.4776	.3751	.2953	.2330	.1842	.1460	.1160	.0923	.0588	.0378	.0304	.0245	.0160	.0105	.0046	.0021	.0010	.0005
30	.7419	.5521	.4120	.3083	.2314	.1741	.1314	.0994	.0754	.0573	.0334	.0196	.0151	.0116	.0070	.0042	.0016	.0006	.0002	.0001
40	.6717	.4529	.3066	.2083	.1420	.0972	.0668	.0460	.0318	.0221	.0107	.0053	.0037	.0026	.0013	.0007	.0002	.0001	*	*
50	.6080	.3715	.2281	.1407	.0872	.0543	.0339	.0213	.0134	.0085	.0035	.0014	.0009	.0006	.0003	.0001	*	*	*	*
60	.5504	.3048	.1697	.0951	.0535	.0303	.0173	.0099	.0057	.0033	.0011	.0004	.0002	.0001	*	*	*	*	*	*

*The factor is zero to four decimal places.

Table A.2 Present Value of an Annuity of $1 Per Period for n Periods:

$$\text{PVIFA} = \sum_{t=1}^{n} \frac{1}{(1+k)^t} = \frac{1 - \dfrac{1}{(1+k)^n}}{k}$$

Number of Payments	1%	2%	3%	4%	5%	6%	7%	8%	9%	10%	12%	14%	15%	16%	18%	20%	24%	28%	32%
1	0.9901	0.9804	0.9709	0.9615	0.9524	0.9434	0.9346	0.9259	0.9174	0.9091	0.8929	0.8772	0.8696	0.8621	0.8475	0.8333	0.8065	0.7813	0.7576
2	1.9704	1.9416	1.9135	1.8861	1.8594	1.8334	1.8080	1.7833	1.7591	1.7355	1.6901	1.6467	1.6257	1.6052	1.5656	1.5278	1.4568	1.3916	1.3315
3	2.9410	2.8839	2.8286	2.7751	2.7232	2.6730	2.6243	2.5771	2.5313	2.4869	2.4018	2.3216	2.2832	2.2459	2.1743	2.1065	1.9813	1.8684	1.7663
4	3.9020	3.8077	3.7171	3.6299	3.5460	3.4651	3.3872	3.3121	3.2397	3.1699	3.0373	2.9137	2.8550	2.7982	2.6901	2.5887	2.4043	2.2410	2.0957
5	4.8534	4.7135	4.5797	4.4518	4.3295	4.2124	4.1002	3.9927	3.8897	3.7908	3.6048	3.4331	3.3522	3.2743	3.1272	2.9906	2.7454	2.5320	2.3452
6	5.7955	5.6014	5.4172	5.2421	5.0757	4.9173	4.7665	4.6229	4.4859	4.3553	4.1114	3.8887	3.7845	3.6847	3.4976	3.3255	3.0205	2.7594	2.5342
7	6.7282	6.4720	6.2303	6.0021	5.7864	5.5824	5.3893	5.2064	5.0330	4.8684	4.5638	4.2883	4.1604	4.0386	3.8115	3.6046	3.2423	2.9370	2.6775
8	7.6517	7.3255	7.0197	6.7327	6.4632	6.2098	5.9713	5.7466	5.5348	5.3349	4.9676	4.6389	4.4873	4.3436	4.0776	3.8372	3.4212	3.0758	2.7860
9	8.5660	8.1622	7.7861	7.4353	7.1078	6.8017	6.5152	6.2469	5.9952	5.7590	5.3282	4.9464	4.7716	4.6065	4.3030	4.0310	3.5655	3.1842	2.8681
10	9.4713	8.9826	8.5302	8.1109	7.7217	7.3601	7.0236	6.7101	6.4177	6.1446	5.6502	5.2161	5.0188	4.8332	4.4941	4.1925	3.6819	3.2689	2.9304
11	10.3676	9.7868	9.2526	8.7605	8.3064	7.8869	7.4987	7.1390	6.8052	6.4951	5.9377	5.4527	5.2337	5.0286	4.6560	4.3271	3.7757	3.3351	2.9776
12	11.2551	10.5753	9.9540	9.3851	8.8633	8.3838	7.9427	7.5361	7.1607	6.8137	6.1944	5.6603	5.4206	5.1971	4.7932	4.4392	3.8514	3.3868	3.0133
13	12.1337	11.3484	10.6350	9.9856	9.3936	8.8527	8.3577	7.9038	7.4869	7.1034	6.4235	5.8424	5.5831	5.3423	4.9095	4.5327	3.9124	3.4272	3.0404
14	13.0037	12.1062	11.2961	10.5631	9.8986	9.2950	8.7455	8.2442	7.7862	7.3667	6.6282	6.0021	5.7245	5.4675	5.0081	4.6106	3.9616	3.4587	3.0609
15	13.8651	12.8493	11.9379	11.1184	10.3797	9.7122	9.1079	8.5595	8.0607	7.6061	6.8109	6.1422	5.8474	5.5755	5.0916	4.6755	4.0013	3.4834	3.0764
16	14.7179	13.5777	12.5611	11.6523	10.8378	10.1059	9.4466	8.8514	8.3126	7.8237	6.9740	6.2651	5.9542	5.6685	5.1624	4.7296	4.0333	3.5026	3.0882
17	15.5623	14.2919	13.1661	12.1657	11.2741	10.4773	9.7632	9.1216	8.5436	8.0216	7.1196	6.3729	6.0472	5.7487	5.2223	4.7746	4.0591	3.5177	3.0971
18	16.3983	14.9920	13.7535	12.6593	11.6896	10.8276	10.0591	9.3719	8.7556	8.2014	7.2497	6.4674	6.1280	5.8178	5.2732	4.8122	4.0799	3.5294	3.1039
19	17.2260	15.6785	14.3238	13.1339	12.0853	11.1581	10.3356	9.6036	8.9501	8.3649	7.3658	6.5504	6.1982	5.8775	5.3162	4.8435	4.0967	3.5386	3.1090
20	18.0456	16.3514	14.8775	13.5903	12.4622	11.4699	10.5940	9.8181	9.1285	8.5136	7.4694	6.6231	6.2593	5.9288	5.3527	4.8696	4.1103	3.5458	3.1129
25	22.0232	19.5235	17.4131	15.6221	14.0939	12.7834	11.6536	10.6748	9.8226	9.0770	7.8431	6.8729	6.4641	6.0971	5.4669	4.9476	4.1474	3.5640	3.1220
30	25.8077	22.3965	19.6004	17.2920	15.3725	13.7648	12.4090	11.2578	10.2737	9.4269	8.0552	7.0027	6.5660	6.1772	5.5168	4.9789	4.1601	3.5693	3.1242
40	32.8347	27.3555	23.1148	19.7928	17.1591	15.0463	13.3317	11.9246	10.7574	9.7791	8.2438	7.1050	6.6418	6.2335	5.5482	4.9966	4.1659	3.5712	3.1250
50	39.1961	31.4236	25.7298	21.4822	18.2559	15.7619	13.8007	12.2335	10.9617	9.9148	8.3045	7.1327	6.6605	6.2463	5.5541	4.9995	4.1666	3.5714	3.1250
60	44.9550	34.7609	27.6756	22.6235	18.9293	16.1614	14.0392	12.3766	11.0480	9.9672	8.3240	7.1401	6.6651	6.2402	5.5553	4.9999	4.1667	3.5714	3.1250

Table A.3   Future Value of $1 at the End of n Periods: $FVIF_{k,n} = (1 + k)^n$

Period	1%	2%	3%	4%	5%	6%	7%	8%	9%	10%	12%	14%	15%	16%	18%	20%	24%	28%	32%	36%
1	1.0100	1.0200	1.0300	1.0400	1.0500	1.0600	1.0700	1.0800	1.0900	1.1000	1.1200	1.1400	1.1500	1.1600	1.1800	1.2000	1.2400	1.2800	1.3200	1.3600
2	1.0201	1.0404	1.0609	1.0816	1.1025	1.1236	1.1449	1.1664	1.1881	1.2100	1.2544	1.2996	1.3225	1.3456	1.3924	1.4400	1.5376	1.6384	1.7424	1.8496
3	1.0303	1.0612	1.0927	1.1249	1.1576	1.1910	1.2250	1.2597	1.2950	1.3310	1.4049	1.4815	1.5209	1.5609	1.6430	1.7280	1.9066	2.0972	2.3000	2.5155
4	1.0406	1.0824	1.1255	1.1699	1.2155	1.2625	1.3108	1.3605	1.4116	1.4641	1.5735	1.6890	1.7490	1.8106	1.9388	2.0736	2.3642	2.6844	3.0360	3.4210
5	1.0510	1.1041	1.1593	1.2167	1.2763	1.3382	1.4026	1.4693	1.5386	1.6105	1.7623	1.9254	2.0114	2.1003	2.2878	2.4883	2.9316	3.4360	4.0075	4.6526
6	1.0615	1.1262	1.1941	1.2653	1.3401	1.4185	1.5007	1.5869	1.6771	1.7716	1.9738	2.1950	2.3131	2.4364	2.6996	2.9860	3.6352	4.3980	5.2899	6.3275
7	1.0721	1.1487	1.2299	1.3159	1.4071	1.5036	1.6058	1.7138	1.8280	1.9487	2.2107	2.5023	2.6600	2.8262	3.1855	3.5832	4.5077	5.6295	6.9826	8.6054
8	1.0829	1.1717	1.2668	1.3686	1.4775	1.5938	1.7182	1.8509	1.9926	2.1436	2.4760	2.8526	3.0590	3.2784	3.7589	4.2998	5.5895	7.2058	9.2170	11.703
9	1.0937	1.1951	1.3048	1.4233	1.5513	1.6895	1.8385	1.9990	2.1719	2.3579	2.7731	3.2519	3.5179	3.8030	4.4355	5.1598	6.9310	9.2234	12.166	15.916
10	1.1046	1.2190	1.3439	1.4802	1.6289	1.7908	1.9672	2.1589	2.3674	2.5937	3.1058	3.7072	4.0456	4.4114	5.2338	6.1917	8.5944	11.805	16.059	21.646
11	1.1157	1.2434	1.3842	1.5395	1.7103	1.8983	2.1049	2.3316	2.5804	2.8531	3.4785	4.2262	4.6524	5.1173	6.1759	7.4301	10.657	15.111	21.198	29.439
12	1.1268	1.2682	1.4258	1.6010	1.7959	2.0122	2.2522	2.5182	2.8127	3.1384	3.8960	4.8179	5.3502	5.9360	7.2876	8.9161	13.214	19.342	27.982	40.037
13	1.1381	1.2936	1.4685	1.6651	1.8856	2.1329	2.4098	2.7196	3.0658	3.4523	4.3635	5.4924	6.1528	6.8858	8.5994	10.699	16.386	24.758	36.937	54.451
14	1.1495	1.3195	1.5126	1.7317	1.9799	2.2609	2.5785	2.9372	3.3417	3.7975	4.8871	6.2613	7.0757	7.9875	10.147	12.839	20.319	31.691	48.756	74.053
15	1.1610	1.3459	1.5580	1.8009	2.0789	2.3966	2.7590	3.1722	3.6425	4.1772	5.4736	7.1379	8.1371	9.2655	11.973	15.407	25.195	40.564	64.358	100.71
16	1.1726	1.3728	1.6047	1.8730	2.1829	2.5404	2.9522	3.4259	3.9703	4.5950	6.1304	8.1372	9.3576	10.748	14.129	18.488	31.242	51.923	84.953	136.96
17	1.1843	1.4002	1.6528	1.9479	2.2920	2.6928	3.1588	3.7000	4.3276	5.0545	6.8660	9.2765	10.761	12.467	16.672	22.186	38.740	66.461	112.13	186.27
18	1.1961	1.4282	1.7024	2.0258	2.4066	2.8543	3.3799	3.9960	4.7171	5.5599	7.6900	10.575	12.375	14.462	19.673	26.623	48.038	85.070	148.02	253.33
19	1.2081	1.4568	1.7535	2.1068	2.5270	3.0256	3.6165	4.3157	5.1417	6.1159	8.6128	12.055	14.231	16.776	23.214	31.948	59.567	108.89	195.39	344.53
20	1.2202	1.4859	1.8061	2.1911	2.6533	3.2071	3.8697	4.6610	5.6044	6.7275	9.6463	13.743	16.366	19.460	27.393	38.337	73.864	139.37	257.91	468.57
21	1.2324	1.5157	1.8603	2.2788	2.7860	3.3996	4.1406	5.0338	6.1088	7.4002	10.803	15.667	18.821	22.574	32.323	46.005	91.591	178.40	340.44	637.26
22	1.2447	1.5460	1.9161	2.3699	2.9253	3.6035	4.4304	5.4365	6.6586	8.1403	12.100	17.861	21.644	26.186	38.142	55.206	113.57	228.35	449.39	866.67
23	1.2572	1.5769	1.9736	2.4647	3.0715	3.8197	4.7405	5.8715	7.2579	8.9543	13.552	20.361	24.891	30.376	45.007	66.247	140.83	292.30	593.19	1178.6
24	1.2697	1.6084	2.0328	2.5633	3.2251	4.0489	5.0724	6.3412	7.9111	9.8497	15.178	23.212	28.625	35.236	53.108	79.496	174.63	374.14	783.02	1602.9
25	1.2824	1.6406	2.0938	2.6658	3.3864	4.2919	5.4274	6.8485	8.6231	10.834	17.000	26.461	32.918	40.874	62.668	95.396	216.54	478.90	1033.5	2180.0
26	1.2953	1.6734	2.1566	2.7725	3.5557	4.5494	5.8074	7.3964	9.3992	11.918	19.040	30.166	37.856	47.414	73.948	114.47	268.51	612.99	1364.3	2964.9
27	1.3082	1.7069	2.2213	2.8834	3.7335	4.8223	6.2139	7.9881	10.245	13.110	21.324	34.389	43.535	55.000	87.259	137.37	332.95	784.63	1800.9	4032.2
28	1.3213	1.7410	2.2879	2.9987	3.9201	5.1117	6.6488	8.6271	11.167	14.421	23.883	39.204	50.065	63.800	102.96	164.84	412.86	1004.3	2377.2	5483.8
29	1.3345	1.7758	2.3566	3.1187	4.1161	5.4184	7.1143	9.3173	12.172	15.863	26.749	44.693	57.575	74.008	121.50	197.81	511.95	1285.5	3137.9	7458.0
30	1.3478	1.8114	2.4273	3.2434	4.3219	5.7435	7.6123	10.062	13.267	17.449	29.959	50.950	66.211	85.849	143.37	237.37	634.81	1645.5	4142.0	10143.
40	1.4889	2.2080	3.2620	4.8010	7.0400	10.285	14.974	21.724	31.409	45.259	93.050	188.88	267.86	378.72	750.37	1469.7	5455.9	19426.	66520.	*
50	1.6446	2.6916	4.3839	7.1067	11.467	18.420	29.457	46.901	74.357	117.39	289.00	700.23	1083.6	1670.7	3927.3	9100.4	46890.	*	*	*
60	1.8167	3.2810	5.8916	10.519	18.679	32.987	57.946	101.25	176.03	304.48	897.59	2595.9	4383.9	7370.1	20555.	56347.	*	*	*	*

*FVIFA > 99,999

Table A.4 Sum of an Annuity of 1$ Per Period for n Periods:

$$FVIFA_{k,n} = \sum_{t=1}^{n}(1+k)^{t-1} = \frac{(1+k)^n - 1}{k}$$

Number of Periods	1%	2%	3%	4%	5%	6%	7%	8%	9%	10%	12%	14%	15%	16%	18%	20%	24%	28%	32%	36%
1	1.0000	1.0000	1.0000	1.0000	1.0000	1.0000	1.0000	1.0000	1.0000	1.0000	1.0000	1.0000	1.0000	1.0000	1.0000	1.0000	1.0000	1.0000	1.0000	1.0000
2	2.0100	2.0200	2.0300	2.0400	2.0500	2.0600	2.0700	2.0800	2.0900	2.1000	2.1200	2.1400	2.1500	2.1600	2.1800	2.2000	2.2400	2.2800	2.3200	2.3600
3	3.0301	3.0604	3.0909	3.1216	3.1525	3.1836	3.2149	3.2464	3.2781	3.3100	3.3744	3.4396	3.4725	3.5056	3.5724	3.6400	3.7776	3.9184	4.0624	4.2096
4	4.0604	4.1216	4.1836	4.2465	4.3101	4.3746	4.4399	4.5061	4.5731	4.6410	4.7793	4.9211	4.9934	5.0665	5.2154	5.3680	5.6842	6.0156	6.3624	6.7251
5	5.1010	5.2040	5.3091	5.4163	5.5256	5.6371	5.7507	5.8666	5.9847	6.1051	6.3528	6.6101	6.7424	6.8771	7.1542	7.4416	8.0484	8.6999	9.3983	10.146
6	6.1520	6.3081	6.4684	6.6330	6.8019	6.9753	7.1533	7.3359	7.5233	7.7156	8.1152	8.5355	8.7537	8.9775	9.4420	9.9299	10.980	12.135	13.405	14.798
7	7.2135	7.4343	7.6625	7.8983	8.1420	8.3938	8.6540	8.9228	9.2004	9.4872	10.089	10.730	11.066	11.413	12.141	12.915	14.615	16.533	18.695	21.126
8	8.2857	8.5830	8.8923	9.2142	9.5491	9.8975	10.259	10.636	11.028	11.435	12.299	13.232	13.726	14.240	15.327	16.499	19.122	22.163	25.678	29.731
9	9.3685	9.7546	10.159	10.582	11.026	11.491	11.978	12.487	13.021	13.579	14.775	16.085	16.785	17.518	19.085	20.798	24.712	29.369	34.895	41.435
10	10.462	10.949	11.463	12.006	12.577	13.180	13.816	14.486	15.192	15.937	17.548	19.337	20.303	21.321	23.521	25.958	31.643	38.592	47.061	57.351
11	11.566	12.168	12.807	13.486	14.206	14.971	15.783	16.645	17.560	18.531	20.654	23.044	24.349	25.732	28.755	32.150	40.237	50.398	63.121	78.998
12	12.682	13.412	14.192	15.025	15.917	16.869	17.888	18.977	20.140	21.384	24.133	27.270	29.001	30.850	34.931	39.580	50.894	65.510	84.320	108.43
13	13.809	14.680	15.617	16.626	17.713	18.882	20.140	21.495	22.953	24.522	28.029	32.088	34.351	36.786	42.218	48.496	64.109	84.852	112.30	148.47
14	14.947	15.973	17.086	18.291	19.598	21.015	22.550	24.214	26.019	27.975	32.392	37.581	40.504	43.672	50.818	59.195	80.496	109.61	149.23	202.92
15	16.096	17.293	18.598	20.023	21.578	23.276	25.129	27.152	29.360	31.772	37.279	43.842	47.580	51.659	60.965	72.035	100.81	141.30	197.99	276.97
16	17.257	18.639	20.156	21.824	23.657	25.672	27.888	30.324	33.003	35.949	42.753	50.980	55.717	60.925	72.939	87.442	126.01	181.86	262.35	377.69
17	18.430	20.012	21.761	23.697	25.840	28.212	30.840	33.750	36.973	40.544	48.883	59.117	65.075	71.673	87.068	105.93	157.25	233.79	347.30	514.66
18	19.614	21.412	23.414	25.645	28.132	30.905	33.999	37.450	41.301	45.599	55.749	68.394	75.836	84.140	103.74	128.11	195.99	300.25	459.44	700.93
19	20.810	22.840	25.116	27.671	30.539	33.760	37.379	41.446	46.018	51.159	63.439	78.969	88.211	98.603	123.41	154.74	244.03	385.32	607.47	954.27
20	22.019	24.297	26.870	29.778	33.066	36.785	40.995	45.762	51.160	57.275	72.052	91.024	102.44	115.37	146.62	186.68	303.60	494.21	802.86	1298.8
21	23.239	25.783	28.676	31.969	35.719	39.992	44.865	50.422	56.764	64.002	81.698	104.76	118.81	134.84	174.02	225.02	377.46	633.59	1060.7	1767.3
22	24.471	27.299	30.536	34.248	38.505	43.392	49.005	55.456	62.873	71.402	92.502	120.43	137.63	157.41	206.34	271.03	469.05	811.99	1401.2	2404.6
23	25.716	28.845	32.452	36.617	41.430	46.995	53.436	60.893	69.531	79.543	104.60	138.29	159.27	183.60	244.48	326.23	582.62	1040.3	1850.6	3271.3
24	26.973	30.421	34.426	39.082	44.502	50.815	58.176	66.764	76.789	88.497	118.15	158.65	184.16	213.97	289.49	392.48	723.46	1332.6	2443.8	4449.9
25	28.243	32.030	36.459	41.645	47.727	54.864	63.249	73.105	84.700	98.347	133.33	181.87	212.79	249.21	342.60	471.98	898.09	1706.8	3226.8	6052.9
26	29.525	33.670	38.553	44.311	51.113	59.156	68.676	79.954	93.323	109.18	150.33	208.33	245.71	290.08	405.27	567.37	1114.6	2185.7	4260.4	8233.0
27	30.820	35.344	40.709	47.084	54.669	63.705	74.483	87.350	102.72	121.09	169.37	238.49	283.56	337.50	479.22	681.85	1383.1	2798.7	5624.7	11197.9
28	32.129	37.051	42.930	49.967	58.402	68.528	80.697	95.338	112.96	134.20	190.69	272.88	327.10	392.50	566.48	819.22	1716.0	3583.3	7425.6	15230.2
29	33.450	38.792	45.218	52.966	62.322	73.639	87.346	103.96	124.13	148.63	214.58	312.09	377.16	456.30	669.44	984.06	2128.9	4587.6	9802.9	20714.1
30	34.784	40.568	47.575	56.084	66.438	79.058	94.460	113.28	136.30	164.49	241.33	356.78	434.74	530.31	790.94	1181.8	2640.9	5873.2	12940.	28172.2
40	48.886	60.402	75.401	95.025	120.79	154.76	199.63	259.05	337.88	442.59	767.09	1342.0	1779.0	2360.7	4163.2	7343.8	22728.	69377.	*	*
50	64.463	84.579	112.79	152.66	209.34	290.33	406.52	573.76	815.08	1163.9	2400.0	4994.5	7217.7	10435.	21813.	45497.	*	*	*	*
60	81.669	114.05	163.05	237.99	353.58	533.12	813.52	1253.2	1944.7	3034.8	7471.6	18535.	29219.	46057.	*	*	*	*	*	*

*FVIF > 99.999

GLOSSARY

Absolute Priority Rule (APR) A mandate protecting the interests of creditors when a business goes bankrupt. The law requires that all creditors must be paid in full before any of the bankrupt business's common stockholders receive any of the liquidation proceeds.

Absolute Purchasing Power Parity A version of the law of one price applied to international finance. It says that foreign exchange rates must adjust so the cost to purchase a given basket of goods is the same in every country.

Agent Someone the principal (owner) authorizes to make decisions governing the principal's assets. For example, a stock broker or a corporation's president.

Alpha A risk-adjusted measure of excess returns from an investment. Sometimes called Jensen's Alpha.

American Depository Receipts (ADRs) A document that provides evidence of an ownership share in a foreign corporation. It is denominated in U.S. dollars.

American Options Options that can be exercised on any trading day of their life, up to and including the expiration date.

AMEX The American Stock Exchange in New York City.

Amortization A non-cash expense item, like depreciation, that allows deductions for the wear and tear of an asset.

Arbitrage The type of hedge that occurs when simultaneous purchases and sales of identical (or similar) assets are made with a profitable price or yield differential. It often involves buying a long position and selling a short position in the same security.

Arbitrage Opportunity A hedged portfolio that can be acquired at a cost of zero and will have a positive value with certainty when the position is liquidated.

Arbitrage Pricing Theory (APT) An equilibrium model which uses several undiversifiable risk factors to determine an asset's expected return.

Arbitrageurs A person or entity performing arbitrage; typically, a sophisticated investor.

Arithmetic Mean Return (AMR) An arithmetic average rate of return that involves no compounding.

Ask (Offer) Price The lowest price any potential seller is willing to accept.

Asset Allocation An approach to investing that focuses on determining the mixture of asset classes that is most likely to provide a combination of risk and expected return that is optimal for the investor.

Asset Class A grouping of securities with similar characteristics and properties. For example, growth stocks or value stocks.

Auto Correlation See Serial Correlation.

Average Either a weighted or unweighted mean.

Balance Sheet A document reflecting a company's assets, liabilities, and stockholders' equity at one point in time.

Bankers Acceptance (BA) An agreement between two banks to finance an international transaction. One international bank promises to pay another international bank after an international shipment is received by the bank's customer and the loan to finance the shipment or transaction matures.

Barron's Confidence Index (BCI) This ratio of high-grade average bond yields divided by low-grade average bond yields measures investors' degree of market optimism.

Base Year (Base Period) A past year that is selected to serve as the starting point for an index; it imparts perspective to a time-series of index numbers.

Basis The difference between the futures and the spot price of a commodity at a given moment, it decreases toward zero as the delivery date approaches.

Basis Point (BP) A BP is one-hundredth of 1%.

Basis Risks The risks that cause offsetting long and short positions used to construct a futures hedge not to converge to the same market value as the delivery date approaches. These risks occur, for example, when the desired and actual delivery time, delivery quality, or delivery location differ.

Bearer Bonds Bonds issued into the owners' possession that have no list of registered owners' names. Different from Registered Bonds.

Bearish A pessimistic security market condition that exists when most investors expect the prices of most traded securities to decline. Or, one investor can be bearish about a single security.

Beta An index of undiversifiable risk that is usually measured by regressing an asset's returns onto the simultaneous returns from a market index (market portfolio). In finance, one of several quantitative risk surrogates. In statistics, a regression slope coefficient.

Bid Price The highest price a potential investor is willing to pay.

Block Positioners Special brokers/dealers who routinely process block transactions without causing the market price of the issue to change significantly.

Block Trade A single transaction that involves 10,000 or more shares.

Bond Equivalent Yield (BEY) A money-market interest rate that is adjusted to make it comparable to a bond's yield to maturity.

Book Entry Basis When U.S. Treasury bills are sold at public auction, the transaction is recorded in a computer and the investor receives a receipt instead of the securities.

Book Value The accounting value of that asset on paper or on a balance sheet.

Brady Bonds Consolidated restructured debt obligations composed of defaulted credits from lesser developed countries (LDCs) that were created by Secretary of State Brady during the 1980s. They include Conversion Bonds (DCBs), Front-Loaded Interest-Reduction Bonds (FLIRBs), Interest Reduction Bonds, New Money Bonds (NMBs), Debt Conversion Bonds (DCBs), Past-Due Interest (PDI) Bonds, Par Bonds, and Discount Bonds.

Brokers Commissioned salespeople that are usually employed by a dealer; they contribute to market liquidity by buying and selling from their employer's inventory of securities.

Brokers Call Rate The fluctuating market interest rate paid for margin loans.

Bullish An optimistic market condition that exists when most investors expect the prices of most traded securities to rise. Or, one investor can be bullish about a single security.

Bull Spread A debit transaction because selling the call generates less cash inflow than the call purchase requires. Bull spreads are for people who believe the price of the optioned stock will rise, but not by a lot.

Business Cycle The average business cycle lasts seven years from peak to peak or from trough to trough, but they can last over a decade or less than seven years.

Calendar Spread An equal number of options are purchased and sold, and both options have the same exercise price. Also called a time spread or a horizontal spread.

Callable A bond that may be called in by the issuer before its maturity date.

Callability Risk Variability of return that reflects the possibility the security may be redeemed (called in) by its issuer before its scheduled maturity date.

Capital Asset Pricing Model (CAPM) See Security Market Line (SML).

Capital Market Line (CML) The most desirable asset allocation line (AAL). The most desirable risky portfolios that can be generated by borrowing and lending at the riskless rate of interest.

Carrying Charges Expenses incurred to store a commodity for future delivery.

Cash Account A brokerage account that requires the investor to pay cash for the securities. Cash accounts provide no margin.

Cash Dividend Yield A stock's annual cash dividend payment divided by its current market price per share.

Cash Flows Common stock dividends, coupon interest from bonds, rental income, or other investment income. Alternatively, an asset's cash inflows and/or outflows.

Cash Flow From Operations (CFO) Cash flows that arise when goods and/or services are produced and distributed in the natural course of operating a firm.

Cash-Flow-to-Long-Term-Debt Ratio A ratio measure of how much cash is available to pay interest on debts that need not be repaid within one year.

Cash Market A market where physical goods are traded. For example, a stock exchange, a grain elevator, or a bond market. Not a derivatives market.

Cash Settlement An arrangement to deliver cash rather than the underlying commodity when some futures contracts mature.

Ceiling A resistance level that tends to prevent further price rises; also called a peak price.

Central Limit Order Book (CLOB) A book in which limit orders to buy and sell from competing market-makers are collected.

Certificates of Deposit (CDs) Pieces of paper documenting savings that cannot be bought and sold (traded) in a secondary market.

Characteristic Line A time-series regression line for one asset that is used to estimate its diversifiable and undiversifiable risk statistics.

Churning An illegal activity in which a broker turns over a client's account to generate commission income for the broker with little regard for whether the client profits from the trades.

Classified Common Stock Stock that has voting power or cash dividend payments, but not both in the same stock. Typically called Class A and Class B shares.

Clean Price A bond's present value. A bond's invoice (dirty) price less any accrued interest.

Clearing House An organization within a stock exchange, commodity exchange, futures exchange, or options exchange that processes every transaction. It is the buyer in every sale and a seller to every purchaser. The clearing house also guarantees delivery for every transaction.

Closed-End Investment Company A publicly traded investment portfolio that differs from a mutual fund because its price fluctuates away from its net asset value per share and, also, it is not allowed to sell additional shares or redeem its original shares.

Collateral Assets pledged as security by a bond issuer to increase the likelihood that lenders get repaid.

Collateral Trust Bonds Bonds issued by a company that pledges securities it owns as collateral for the issue.

Commercial Paper Unsecured loans (money market securities) issued by large companies and finance companies that promise to repay a set amount within one year.

Commission Brokers Members of a commodity or securities exchange who execute transactions for non-members to earn brokers fees.

Commodity Board A sign posted above a trading pit that lists futures prices for each delivery month.

Commodity Futures Trading Commission (FTC) Act of 1974 A U.S. law that established an independent federal agency to oversee futures exchanges and futures contracts.

Common Market A group of nations that band together to foster cross-border trade with the expectation that this will spur their economic welfare.

Common-Sized Balance Sheet A balance sheet in which every item's value is stated as a percentage of total assets.

Common-Sized Statements Financial statements that state the value of each item as a percentage of some common denominator (such as total assets or sales).

Common Stock A security that evidences an ownership share in a corporation.

Common Stock Equivalents Options or warrants to purchase common stock, and certain convertible securities.

Competitive Advantage Individual talents, advanced education, expertise, contacts, and/or access to valuable information that enables an investor to trade profitably.

Compounded Rate of Return A rate of return that includes multi-period compounding (interest on the interest).

Congestion Area A trading range within which a security's price fluctuates. It lies above the support level and below the resistance level.

Confirmation A price move that breaks through a resistance level, support level, or neckline and comprises a signal to buy or sell. Also called a breakout.

Consolidated Quotations System (CQS) A national system in the U.S. that reports bid and asked prices from national stock exchanges, regional stock exchanges, and some over-the-counter markets.

Consumer Price Index (CPI) A national price index based on the prices of 300 goods and services that most urban consumers buy.

Contango An increment added to a futures price to cover the carrying costs until delivery occurs at the scheduled settlement date. Also called Forwardation.

Contingent Immunization A fixed-income portfolio management system that allows the portfolio manager to trade actively until they perform poorly. If the portfolio performs poorly, active management is no longer permitted and hedging (immunization) is used to reduce the portfolio's risk.

Convergence Principal A basic tendency for spot and futures prices to come closer together as they move closer to maturity.

Convertible Bond A bond that can be converted into a pre-specified number of shares of common stock if certain conditions are met.

Convertibility Risk Variability of return that grows from the possibility that a bond or preferred stock might be converted into the issuing corporation's common stock.

Corporate Bonds Senior debt securities issued by a corporation.

Correction A move in stock prices that lasts several weeks. The Dow Theory calls corrections secondary movements.

Cost of Capital Interest payments on borrowed money, cash dividend payments to stockholders, and other payments made to induce investment. Also called the required rate of return, risk-adjusted rate of return, and expected return in different contexts.

Counterparties The buyer and seller of a derivative.

Coupon Effect The subtle impact that coupon interest has on a bond's yield to maturity and price.

Coupon Yield A bond's annual coupon interest payment divided by its current market price.

Coupons Periodic interest payments that are specified in a bond issue's indenture contract.

Coupons-Paying Bonds Bonds that are originally issued at their face value and promise coupon interest payments.

Covered Call A call option that is written (sold) by a party that also owns the underlying security. Different than a naked (uncovered) call.

Credits Bonds, bank loans, mortgages, accounts receivable, and other debts.

Credit Event Bankruptcy or a rating change.

Credit Migration The credit risk (bond price fluctuations) that result when investors perceive the debt issuer's financial condition is changing.

Credit Risk Variability of return associated with the possibility of bankruptcy. Also called default risk.

Credit Risk Premiums Yield spreads between bonds with different quality ratings. Also called Credit Spreads and Quality Spreads.

Credit Spread See Credit Risk Premiums.

Crossborder Bonds International bonds.

Cross Correlation An index number between $+1$ and -1 that measures how separate series covary.

Cross-Sectional Comparisons Assessments based on the relative merits of different items.

Cum Coupon Price The price of a coupon-paying bond that includes accrued interest. Also called a Dirty Price.

Cumulative Cash Dividends Preferred stock cash dividends that are owed to investors even after the stock's issuer misses annual payments.

Cumulative Voting Exists when a corporation allows its stockholders to have as many votes as shares owned multiplied times the number of directors being elected.

Current Ratio A solvency ratio that equals current assets divided by current liabilities.

Day Counting Conventions Widely accepted practices specifying the number of days (usually 365 or 360) assumed to be in a calendar year for the purposes of calculating particular bond market interest rates.

Day Order An order to trade that cancels automatically unless it is executed on the day it was issued.

Day Trade Buying and selling a security in the same day.

Dealer A person or company that buys and sells securities from an inventory of securities they own and manage. A market-maker that employs commission brokers.

Declining Firms Companies whose prospects are limited because they do not possess profitable investment opportunities within the firm (because, for example, of product obsolescence).

Debentures Corporate bonds that have no assets or collateral pledged to back them.

Debit Balance A margin account at a brokerage that is in a net borrowed position.

Debit Spreads Horizontal or vertical spreads that cost the investor a net cash outflow to establish. Different than credit spreads.

Debt Test Clause A provision that protects existing bondholders by constraining the issuer's ability to create new debt.

Delivery Months Several designated months each year during which deliveries are made on specific futures contracts.

Default-Free Bonds A bond issue by an entity that is widely perceived to be highly likely to make all scheduled payments on time and in full. For example, U.S. Treasury bonds.

Default Premium Also called a Risk Premium, a Default Risk Premium, or a Quality Spread, it is a yield spread over and above market interest rates on default-free bonds with a similar maturity that is paid by a bond issuer that might default to induce investors to accept the possibility of default.

Defined Benefit Pension Plan A pension fund that creates legal liabilities for the employer (pension sponsor) by promising to pay retired employees explicitly defined pension benefits.

Defined Contribution Pension Plan A pension fund that creates no liabilities for the employer (pension sponsor) because it does not promise to pay retired employees any explicitly defined pension benefits. They are sometimes called Profit-Sharing Plans because the employer is only required to contribute a percentage of profits, if any materialize, into the pension plan.

Dependent Variable The y variable in the regression model: $y = a + bx + e$. The y values are determined by x, the independent variable. The one-period rates of return from an investment in the characteristic line are a dependent variable, for example.

Depreciation A non-cash business expense that is deducted from taxable income to provide an allowance for an asset's wear and tear. Similar to amortization.

Derivatives Financial instruments, like futures contracts and options, that derive their market values from specified underlying values. For example, derivatives on the S&P500 derive their market values from the value of that stock market index.

Diagonal Spreads Option positions involving different options quoted on different lines and in different columns of the newspapers' tables of options price quotations.

Differencing Interval Assumed time span (holding period) between repetitive purchases and sales that are hypothesized to occur to compute a series of one-period rates of return for an investment.

Dirty Price See Invoice Price. Different from the Clean Price.

Discount Rate An interest rate used to compute a present value.

Diversifiable Risk Variability of return caused by inventions, management errors, discoveries, new customers, lost customers, lawsuits, acts of God, and other idiosyncratic events that are statistically independent. Over a diversified sample of securities these idiosyncratic events tend to add up to zero.

Dollar Denominated Securities Securities whose prices and cash flows are stated and paid in dollars.

Domestic Bonds Bonds issued by a local borrower, denominated in the local currency, and regulated by the local government.

Domestic Hedge Fund A local hedge fund that must register with the SEC and is subject to the modest regulations imposed by the National Securities Markets Improvement Act (NSMIA) of 1996. Some operate in conjunction with an off-shore (sister) hedge fund.

Domestic Political Risk Variability of return caused by changes in environmental regulations, zoning requirements, local fees, local licenses, and local taxes.

Dominant Assets Assets that have the maximum expected return in their risk-class. These assets are usually portfolios, not individual assets.

Dow Theory A technical analysis theory that believes market price movements can be broken into three separate components: (1) primary moves are a bull or bear market that can last for years; (2) secondary moves include surges and collapses that last a few weeks; (3) tertiary moves are meaningless random daily wiggles.

Dual Trading Commission brokers that execute orders for the public and also for their own accounts. This common U.S. practice creates conflicts of interest.

DuPont Analysis Decomposes the return on equity (investment) ratio into component ratios that yield insights.

Duration See Macaulay's Duration.

Duration Wandering Fixed-income hedges must be rebalanced sometimes because duration changes continuously (the value wanders).

Dynamic Asset Allocation (DAA) Changes to asset class weights made in response to changes in the current market conditions.

Earnings Before Interest and Taxes (EBIT) Also called operating income, it measures the income from a firm's routine operations. Extraordinary income and the effects of leverage and taxes are not included.

Earnings Per Share (EPS) A corporation's total income divided by the number of common shares outstanding. An important determinant of a share's value.

Economic Union A common market (group of nations) that has adopted a single common currency, and perhaps more ambitious goals.

Economic Income The maximum amount of consumption opportunities that can be withdrawn during a period of time without diminishing future consumption opportunities.

Effective yield-to-maturity (EYTM) Also called the effective annualized return (EAR), this yield-to-maturity formula utilizes fractional exponents to represent fractions of years.

Efficient Frontier The set of dominant portfolios in $[\sigma, E(r)]$ space. All portfolios that have: (1) the maximum return in their risk-class, and/or, (2) the minimum risk at their level of return.

Efficient Market A market in which a security's price tends to equal its value. The market may be strongly efficient, semi-strong efficient, or weakly efficient. Also called Informational Efficiency and Pricing Efficiency.

Electronic Communications Network (ECN) A computer program that provides a securities distribution channel to compete with securities exchanges, other securities markets, and other ECNs.

Electronic Order-Working System A sophisticated (smart) electronic communication network that makes decisions as it searches for ways to execute trades.

Embedded Option Attached or detachable options (such as call or conversion options) that are components of a security's value.

Emerging Markets Securities markets that are, typically, small, new, have low turnover, and are located in countries where below-average incomes prevail.

Employee Retirement Income Security Act (ERISA) of 1974 This U.S. law stipulates vesting, funding, investing, payment, and reporting requirements that are designed to protect retired workers' pensions.

Enhanced Indexing An indexed portfolio management system that has been modified to include the portfolio manager's idea of how to outperform the index.

Equal Weighting System A portfolio or investment index weighting system that assigns equal weights to every asset. Designed to provide a no-skill (random selection) standard of portfolio performance.

Equity Owner's net worth. The first money invested in a new corporation and the last money paid out from a bankrupt corporation.

Equity Risk Premium An additional rate of return (yield spread) paid to attract investors to participate in an equity financing.

Eurobonds Bonds underwritten by an international investment banking syndicate and issued into several different nations simultaneously. The currency of denomination may differ from the issuer's home currency.

Eurobond Market Anyplace in the world where Eurobonds are traded.

Eurodollars U.S. dollar denominated bank deposits made into foreign banks.

Eurodollar Bonds Bearer bonds that are denominated in U.S. dollars and underwritten by an international syndicate of investment banks and are to be traded outside the jurisdiction of any single country.

European Options Options traded in non-European countries and in Europe that may be exercised only on their expiration date.

Exchange Rate The price of one country's currency stated in terms of another country's currency. The price of foreign exchange.

Ex-Coupon Date The first day a bond trades after making a coupon interest payment. The bond's dirty (invoice) price experiences a drop-off because accrued interest falls to zero that day.

Exit Fees See Redemption Fees.

Expectations Theory A yield curve theory which asserts that long-term bond yields are the average of the short-term interest rates expected to prevail during the bond's life.

Expected Return A weighted average rate of return that uses the probabilities of each outcome for weights, denoted $E(r)$.

Expected Utility The happiness (utility) that is expected to be derived from some outcome involving chance, denoted $E(U)$.

Extra Dividends An unusual cash dividend payment that reflects an extraordinary circumstance (such as an unusually profitable year).

Factor Betas In arbitrage pricing theory (APT), they are index numbers (statistical coefficients) measuring undiversifiable risks from different risk factors.

Fed A nickname for the Federal Reserve Board in Washington, D.C. The monetary authority (central bank) that controls the U.S. commercial banking system, money supply, market interest rates, and inflation.

Federal Bankruptcy Act A U.S. law governing reorganizations and bankruptcies. It stipulates an absolute priority rule (APR) which specifies the priority of creditors' claims that must be paid with the proceeds from a bankruptcy auction before the equity owners can be paid anything.

Federal Funds Also called "Fed funds," they are overnight loans between commercial banks. Their continuously fluctuating money market interest rate is called the "Fed funds rate."

Fed Wire A wire transfer system used to transfer funds between commercial banks; it is operated by the Federal Reserve System.

Fiduciary A person, company, or other organization that manages other people's (principals') money and has a legal obligation to be a good agent.

Fiduciary Responsibility The legal responsibility of an agent to act in the better interest of the principal.

Financial Statement Analysis Scrutinizing a company's financial statements from different perspectives to determine the firm's strengths and weaknesses. Financial ratios are used.

Fisher Closed An equation Irving Fisher proposed to explain the relationship between nominal interest rates, real interest rates, and inflation to in a single country. See Fisher Effect.

Fisher Effect The inflation rate has a direct impact on nominal interest rates. As stipulated in the Fisher Closed equation, market interest rates rise and fall in, roughly, a one-to-one correspondence with the rate of inflation.

Fisher Open An equation Irving Fisher proposed to explain the relationship between nominal interest rates, real interest rates, and inflation in two different countries. An extension of the Fisher Closed equation.

Fixed-Income Securities Debt securities issued by governments and businesses. For example, bonds that pay fixed coupon rates.

Flat Prices Defaulted bonds that are not making their interest payments and, hence, have no accrued interest.

Floater A bond with a fixed par value and fluctuating periodic interest rate payments that vary in accordance with some specified rule that is based on a reference (market) interest rate.

Floating-Rate Bond See Floater.

Floating-Rate CDs Buyers of large denomination certificates of deposit (CDs) can purchase an instrument with either a fixed or floating rate of interest. See Floater.

Floor Brokers See Commission Brokers.

Floor The price level at which a price support either exists or seems to exist. A low level below which prices do not fluctuate.

Flow Variables Sales revenues, purchases, income, and other values that occur and are measured over a specified time interval. Different than a stock variable.

Foreign Bonds Bonds that are issued in one country, in the currency of the issuing country, by a bond issuer from a different country. Foreign bonds are usually traded in the country of issue and are governed by the issuing country's regulations.

Foreign Country Risk The variability of return that international investors face because of fluctuations in the foreign exchange rates, differences in language and culture, time differences, and related international dissimilarities.

Foreign Exchange Risk Traditionally, it was the risk that a country's government decreed that its currency would be exchanged for a different amount of gold in the future than it was in the past. More generally, it is the variability of return that international investors face because foreign exchange rates fluctuate.

Forwardation See Contango.

Forward Contract A bilateral agreement obliging the buyer to purchase a specific commodity or security from the seller on a given future date for a specified price and, also, obliging the seller to make delivery under the terms of the contract. These illiquid contracts are not listed or traded in any secondary market; they are the historical forerunner of futures contracts.

Forward Market A place where forward contracting is routine business. For example, the informal interbank foreign exchange market provides both a cash market and a forward market.

Forward Price (FP) The price for goods to be delivered in the future, but not for current delivery.

Forward Rate The foreign-exchange rate or interest rate for a future delivery, but not for current delivery.

Fourth Market Telephone and other communication networks where securities traders negotiate block trades without the normal dealer services (such as research, credit, and safekeeping of the securities).

Full-Service Brokerage Firm A securities brokerage firm that takes buy/sell orders, extends margin credit to customers, holds clients' securities in safekeeping, collects cash dividends and interest, and gives free research advice.

Full Disclosure Revealing all information that is relevant to a financial transaction. A requirement of U.S. securities law that is not found in many other countries.

Fundamental Common Stock Analysis The venerable practice of studying a corporation and other facts about the environment in which it operates in order to forecast its earnings per share and determine an appropriate price-earnings ratio. The earnings per share is then multiplied by the price-earnings ratio to determine the intrinsic value per share of that corporation's stock.

Futures Commission Merchant (FCM) A salesperson who sells futures contracts to earn commission income.

Futures Contract An agreement between the buyer and seller to exchange some agricultural or financial commodity at a pre-specified price on some pre-arranged future delivery date. These contracts are listed and traded at futures exchanges.

Futures Exchange A securities market where futures contracts are listed and traded; the underlying commodity may not be traded there.

General Creditors Suppliers that sell raw materials to a company on credit without the benefit of collateral. In the event of bankruptcy, the claims of general creditors are junior to those of collateralized creditors.

Generally Accepted Accounting Principles (GAAP) Principles and procedures that are espoused and used widely by professional accountants in the preparation of financial statements.

Geometric Mean Return (GMR) A compounded multi-period rate of return that is never larger than the non-compounded arithmetic mean rate of return (*AMR*). Concisely, $GMR \leq AMR$. The *GMR* is sometimes called the time-weighted rate of return.

Global Depository Receipts (GDRs) Marketable securities not denominated in U.S. dollars that provide evidence that shares of a foreign corporation back the GDR. Similar to the U.S. dollar-denominated American Depository Receipts (ADRs).

Good Till Canceled (GTC) Order A trading order given to a broker that remains in effect until it is canceled.

Gold Exchange Standard The policy of a federal government to purchase any amount of its currency for a specified amount of gold.

Gray Market An informal forward market for new securities that are to be issued in the near future.

Growth Firms In valuation theory, companies that can earn an internal rate of return that exceeds their cost of capital, $r > k$. For example, IBM, Microsoft, Coca-Cola.

Growth Stock Investors Investors who like to invest in popular stocks that have high price-earnings ratios (growth stocks).

Great Crash A huge U.S. market crash that began in September 1929 and kept the U.S. stock market depressed well into the 1930s.

Head and Shoulders Top (HST) A complex pattern (left shoulder, head, right shoulder, and then breaking through the neckline) perceived by technical analysts to be a sell signal. The opposite of the head and shoulders bottom (HSB) pattern.

Hedge Funds Actively managed investment portfolios that are not as closely regulated as mutual funds.

Hedging An investment position or combination of positions undertaken to reduce risk. Offsetting positions are used to reduce or eliminate one or more types of risk, usually at the expense of expected return.

Hedge Ratio For options, it is the fraction of $1 change in the option's premium that is caused by a $1 change in the price of the optioned asset. Also called delta. Mathematically, it is: d(premium)/d(price of underlying) = slope of the premium curve. For futures contracts, it is the ratio of long futures contracts to short futures contracts that is required to offset a particular risk.

Heteroscedasticity Occurs when the variances (standard deviations) computed from a population vary from one sample to the next. The absence of homoscedasticity.

Holding Period The time between the purchase and sale of a security. Also called the investment horizon.

Holding Period Return See One-Period Rate of Return.

HOLDRS Investment portfolios constructed and marketed by Merrill Lynch.

Holiday Effect Daily returns before holiday weekends are usually larger than the average daily returns. An anomaly in the efficient markets theory.

Homogeneous Markets Countries that have highly positively correlated economic activity and do not restrict cross-border trade or investing have homogeneous markets.

Homoscedasticity If different samples drawn from the same population all have the same variances, the population is homoscedastistic. A condition that, in most statistical work, is more desirable than heteroscedasticity.

Horizon The length of time an investment is expected to be held.

Horizon Analysis Astute financial investigation in which a bond's yield to maturity is computed under different scenarios. For example, different reinvestment rate assumptions or different holding periods are evaluated.

Horizon Premium An additional increment of rate of return (yield spread) that induces investors to make investments with long horizons rather than short-term investments.

Horizon Premium Theory Assets that, on average, investors pay a premium price (resulting in lower yields) for short maturities to avoid the higher interest rate risk present in the long-term bonds.

Horizon Return A bond's total return (cash flows plus price changes) over the relevant investment horizon (which may differ from the bond's maturity date).

Horizon Spread Yield spread between equivalent bonds that have different times to maturity. Sometimes called a duration premium.

Horizontal Spread Option spreads that involve buying and selling equal numbers of different options that all have the same exercise price. Also called a Calendar Spread or a Time Spread.

Illiquidity Premium See Liquidity Premium.

Imperfect Hedge A hedge comprised of different sized investments in the long and short positions. Alternatively, a hedge in which the short sale price differs from the long position's purchase price.

Income And Expense Statement This financial statement starts with a company's sales revenues, lists the firm's deductible expenses, and the bottom line is the profit or loss for that reporting period.

Indenture A contract that the Trust Indenture Act of 1939 requires for every issue of corporate bonds. This long, detailed contract states the terms of the bond issue (face value, coupon rate, maturity date) and protective provisions (collateral, sinking fund) of the bond issue.

Index Arbitrage A trading strategy that employs long and short positions in a futures contract and the underlying assets in order to profit from temporary price discrepancies (tracking errors) between the futures contract and the underlying assets. Index arbitrage on the S&P500 index, for example, is popular.

Index Funds Passively managed portfolios that invest in the same securities used to create a security price index. The Vanguard S&P500 index fund, for example, is the largest common stock index fund.

Indifference Curves Curves representing different combinations of goods (or risk and return characteristics) that all deliver the same level of happiness. Also called Utility Isoquants.

Individual Retirement Account (IRA) Personal pensions that provide deferred income taxes if the investor abides by federal rules governing deposits and withdrawals.

Industry Analysis Studying groups of companies that all produce the same product (industries) to ascertain which are good and bad investment candidates.

Industry Risk Variability of return caused by events that affect competing companies. Product obsolescence and changes in the foreign competition are examples of industry risks.

Information Asymmetry Exists when some groups have valuable investment information that is unavailable to other groups. For example, a corporation's board of directors (insiders) has valuable information that is denied, or released after some delay, to outside investors.

Information Content Some actions contain signals that can convey information. For example, when a board of directors announces a cash dividend increase this action signals (contains the suggestion), but does not explicitly proclaim, an increase in the company's permanent earning power.

Informational Efficiency Refers to the extent to which a securities market uses information to align prices with values. Differs from operational efficiency.

Information Traders Active investors that discover material information and use it as a basis for trading. Different from the liquidity traders.

Initial Margin Down payments (up-front equity investment) paid into margin accounts to increase the likelihood later payments will be made.

Initial Public offering (IPO) A corporation's first public issue of common stock.

Insider Trading Illegal buying or selling of securities that is based on material non-public information.

Insider Trading Sanctions Act of 1984 This U.S. securities law provides for penalties of treble damages, fines up to $1 million, and jail sentences of as much as 10 years for insider trading.

Issuing Syndicate A group of investment bankers operating under the Agreement Among Underwriters that governs one issue; it includes the Underwriting Group and the Selling Group.

Instinet A fourth market firm with offices around the world.

Institutional Investors Pensions, mutual funds, trust departments of commercial banks, life insurance companies, foundations, and similar professional organizations that manage large portfolios of investments. Different from small private, household, or amateur investors.

Interest Rate Risk Variability of return caused by changes in market interest rates.

Intermarket Trading System (ITS) Electronic trading network that links the various U.S. stock markets and facilitates trading in different markets.

International Bonds These cross-border bonds can be broken down into the three broad market groups: domestic bonds issued locally in a country that the investor views as being a foreign country; foreign bonds are issued in one country, in that country's currency, by a foreign bond issuer; and Eurobonds.

International Risk Premium An additional increment of return that investors require to induce them to undertake risks that are unique to international investing.

Intertemporal Instability Statistics that vary because they are computed from samples drawn from different time periods.

Intrinsic Value A security's fundamental value. For common stocks, it is estimated by multiplying earnings per share times the appropriate price-earnings ratio.

Inverted Market A commodity market condition that occurs when a commodity's spot prices exceeds its futures price. Sometimes called backwardation.

Investment Bankers Bankers that create primary markets by finding investors for new issues of securities. Also called underwriters.

Investment Company A business organization that markets its equity shares to the investing public, commingles the monies from these share sales into a single pool, uses the pooled funds to invest in a diversified list of securities, and charges its owners an annual fee to manage the portfolio. See Investment Company Act of 1940.

Investment Company Act of 1940 A U.S. securities law that governs open-end investment companies (mutual funds), close-end investment companies, and unit investment trusts.

Invoice Price A bond's dirty price. A bond's clean price plus its accrued interest. Different than the bond's present value.

January Effect On average, common stocks (especially small cap stocks) earn significantly higher average monthly rates of return during January than in any other month of the year.

Junk Bonds Bonds rated below the BBB category by Standard & Poor's, or, equivalently, rated below Baa by Moody's.

k-g Spread The denominator in the following share valuation formula: $P = DIV/(k - g)$

Law of One Price An economic law which states that identical goods should sell at the same price in all markets, except for differences that can be attributed to transportation costs between the markets.

LEAPS Equity options called Long-Term Equity Anticipation Securities (LEAPS) have maturities as long as 30 months.

Legal List Refers to a hypothetical list of securities that are permissible investments for institutional investors, according to various state laws. For example, some states forbid state banks from investing in common stocks that have not paid consecutive cash dividends for five years.

Leveraged Portfolios Portfolios that contain securities with weights that are positive (representing investing) and securities with weights that are negative (for borrowing). Also called borrowing portfolios.

Leverage Ratios Financial ratios measuring how much a company finances its operations with borrowed money.

Lien A creditor's legal claim on property that may be seized if specified obligations are not paid.

Limited Liability If a corporation goes bankrupt, its creditors may not make claims on shareholders' personal assets because stockholder liability is limited to the price paid for the common stock.

Limit Move The maximum daily price fluctuation a commodity exchange will permit a commodity to experience before trading is stopped for the rest of that trading day.

Limit Order An investor's order to buy a security with a restriction on the maximum price to be paid, or, an order to sell which stipulates the minimum price to be received. See Limit Order Book.

Limit Order Book (LOB) A book in which a market-maker records limit orders. See Limit Order.

Liquidating Costs Price discounts given and/or sales commissions paid to speed a sale.

Liquidating Dividend An unusual cash dividend payment that occurs when all or part of the business is liquidated.

Liquidity Premium An additional increment in the rate of return that investors require to induce them to buy an illiquid asset. Also called the liquidity risk premium.

Liquidity Risk Variability of return that results because an asset is not easily marketable and the liquidation costs may be high.

Load Fee One-time front-end sales commission paid to buy mutual funds; U.S. law limits load fees to a maximum of 8.5% of the purchase price.

Local A floor trader or market-maker at a futures exchange or other securities market.

London Interbank Offer Rate (LIBOR) A money-market interest rate at which British banks buy and sell short-term loans. Analogous to the Fed Funds Rate in the U.S.

Long Position The owner of securities is said to have (own) a long position in the securities. Inverse of a Short Position.

Long-Run Asset Allocation See Strategic Asset Allocation.

Macroeconomics The study of a nation's income, fiscal policies, monetary policies, capital markets, and labor markets. Different than microeconomics (theory of the firm).

Maintenance Margin Requirement The rule that a margin call will be made if and when the price of an asset decreases by an amount viewed as being dangerous to the margin lender. Usually less than the initial margin requirement.

Maloney Act of 1938 The U.S. law governing the over-the-counter (OTC) market.

Management Fee Management and administration fees charged by money managers. For example, the average common stock mutual fund management fee in the U.S. is 1.4% of the market value of the assets managed per year.

Management Risk Variability of return caused by good and bad decisions made by the issuer's management.

Margin The equity in an investor's brokerage account.

Margin Account A brokerage account which permits the investor to buy securities with borrowed money.

Margin Call Results when an adverse security price move results in a phone call requiring the investor to post additional margin money to avoid having the position liquidated by the brokerage house.

Margin Fraction (MGFR) The down payment (investors equity) stated as a percentage of the security's market value.

Margin Risk Variability return resulting from the use of borrowed funds (margin money).

Market A meeting place or a communications network that places buyers and sellers in contact so they can transact business.

Market Capitalization Price per share multiplied times the number of shares outstanding. Also called market cap.

Market Impact Cost The change in price between the time an order is given to the broker and the time the order is executed. One of the costs of buying liquidity.

Market-Maker A security dealer that stands ready to make purchases at its bid price and thereby increase its inventory of securities, or, decrease its inventory by selling at its asked (offer) price. Specialists, for example, are monopolistic market-makers at the NYSE.

Market-On-Close Order An investor's order to buy and sell that can only be executed at the day's closing price.

Market Order An investor's order telling the broker to buy or sell a specified security as soon as possible at the current market price.

Market Portfolio This theoretical portfolio is uniquely desirable because it is used to construct the Capital Market Line (CML). It contains every asset in the world in the proportion in which it exists.

Market Segmentation Barriers to entering a market that lead to violations of the law of one price. Listing requirements and membership requirements help segment securities exchanges. Nation's securities markets are segmented by language differences, different time zones, different currencies, and government restrictions.

Market Turnover (MTO) Ratio MTO can be computed as follows: MTO = (Purchases + Sales)/(Beginning Value + Ending Value). If MTO equals 25%, about one-fourth of the portfolio was sold and replaced during the time period. Other MTO ratios are also used.

Market Value Weighting A portfolio or securities market index weighting system that weights the individual securities in proportion to their current market values.

Markowitz Diversification A mathematical algorithm that considers the return, standard deviation, and correlation of every asset simultaneously in order to delineate a group of efficient portfolios that each have the maximum expected return at their level of risk.

Matrix Prices Not market-determined prices; the prices of infrequently traded securities that are determined from the prices of other securities that possess similar characteristics.

Maturity Risk Premium See Horizon Spread.

Mean Reversion A process in which a random variable (such as a stock's price) tends to revert to its average value after temporarily fluctuating to an extreme value. See Time Diversification.

Macaulay's Duration (MAC) A formula that measures two characteristics of a bond: (1) the time structure of its cash flows; and (2) the bond's interest rate risk (interest elasticity).

Modified Duration (MOD) A measure used with fixed-income securities that is similar to Macaulay's Duration.

Monetary Economics Focuses on a nation's central bank, monetary policies, national banking system, interest rates, inflation, and other national factors.

Money Illusion A naive tendency to focus on nominal money amounts rather than on real (inflation-adjusted) quantities.

Money Market A communications network where professional traders execute multi-million dollar transactions in various debt securities that mature in less than one year.

Money Market Securities Highly liquid debt securities that mature in less than one year. For example, U.S. Treasury bills, commercial paper, and bankers acceptances.

Moral Hazard A situation in which one party does not bargain in good faith in order to gain unfairly at the expense of others.

Mortgage Bond A bond issue secured (collateralized) with a lien on real estate or buildings.

Moving Average An average that changes continuously as more recent data is added and the oldest data is deleted from the computations.

Multiple Discriminant Analysis (MDA) A statistical tool that can derive a numerical score from qualitatively defined explanatory variables.

Municipal Bonds Bonds issued by the states, cities, and other municipalities that enjoy exemption from federal income taxes on their coupon interest payments. Sometimes called munis.

Mutual Funds A popular nickname for open-end investment companies, as defined under the Investment Company Act of 1940.

NASD National Association of Securities Dealers; a trade association for brokers and dealers in the over-the-counter (OTC) securities market.

Nasdaq National Association of Securities Dealers Automated Quotations; an OTC securities market that centralizes bid and asked prices from competing market-makers in a centralized computer system.

National Association of Securities Dealers See NASD.

National Quotation Bureau (NQB) A market-making system that lists OTC securities not traded actively enough to be included in Nasdaq's national daily list.

NAVPS See Net Asset Value Per Share (NAVPS).

Negative Pledge Clause A protective provision in a bond issue's indenture contract that limits its ability to pledge assets as collateral.

Negotiable Certificates of Deposit Also called Negotiable CDs; depository receipts from a commercial bank that evidences deposits of $100,000 or more, with provisions to discourage early withdrawals. They are actively traded in a liquid secondary market.

Net Present Value (NPV) The present value of an asset's future cash flows minus the asset's purchase price. Concisely, $NPV = PV - Cost$.

Net Worth The book value of the owner's equity on a company's balance sheet.

Nominal Rates of Return Rates of return that are not inflation-adjusted (not real returns). Rates of return published in news media.

Normal Asset Mix See Strategic Asset Allocation.

Normal Firm In valuation theory, one of many companies that has an internal rate of return on new investments equal to its cost of capital, $r = k$.

NYSE New York Stock Exchange.

Objective Probability Distribution A probability distribution that is based on historical (not subjective) data.

Odd Lot A common stock transaction involving less than 100 shares. Less than a round lot.

Off-Balance-Sheet Financing Borrowing that is expedited by using misleading financial statements that omit some affiliated (indirect) debts; a popular bid practice of the U.S. Treasury.

Off-Shore Hedge Funds Hedge funds headquartered outside the U.S. that do not have to register with the SEC; they are sometimes linked to a domestic sister fund that is registered with the SEC.

One-Period Rate of Return The holding period return, denoted r, below for a stock or bond: $r =$ (Price Change + Cash Flow, if any)/(Purchase Price).

Open-End Investment Companies Investment companies that are allowed to sell additional shares and/or redeem shares. Popularly called mutual funds.

Open-End Mortgage A mortgage permitting some additional debt to be issued on the same collateral.

Open Interest The number of futures contracts that have been opened but not yet eliminated since trading in the contract began. An activity measure.

Open Outcry A price negotiation procedure used at some securities exchanges; it involves shouting and hand signals that can be observed by others on the trading floor.

Operational Efficiency A securities market that endeavors to minimize participants' transactions costs.

Operating Income A measure of a company's earnings from its ordinary, day-to-day operations. Also called earnings before interest and taxes (EBIT).

Opportunity Cost A non-cash (implicit) cost that equals the difference between what was actually earned and what could have been earned in the highest-paid alternative use of the resource.

Option A two-party agreement to buy or sell shares of stock within a stipulated time for a pre-determined exercise price.

Options Clearing Corporation (OCC) The clearing house for options transactions executed at the Chicago Board of Options Exchange, American Stock Exchange, Philadelphia Stock Exchange, Pacific Stock Exchange, and Philadelphia Stock Exchange. Office of the Comptroller of the Currency (OCC) has same acronym.

Option Replication A procedure used to value an unpriced option by creating a synthetic but equivalent structure which can be valued, and then using the law of one price to impute the value to the unpriced option.

Order-Crossing Network An electronic communications network (ECN) that endeavors to find and match buy and sell orders.

Original Issue Discount (OID) Bonds Debt securities that are originally issued at discounted prices; they provide price appreciation (implicit income) instead of coupon interest income.

Over-the-Counter (OTC) Market An informal network of brokers and dealers that trade securities. For example, the NASD and Nasdaq.

Payout Ratio The percent of its net income a corporation pays out as cash dividends.

Par Value An arbitrary face value assigned to a bond or share of stock.

Payment-In-Kind (PIK) The investor may be repaid with the underlying securities instead of cash, which is sometimes a tax advantage.

Pension Sponsor The employer that pays for the pension fund.

Perfect Hedge Occurs when simultaneous long and short positions offset each other perfectly.

Perfectly Efficient Price The market price reflects everything that is knowable about the security and, as a result, that price equals the security's value. Also called a strongly efficient price.

Physicals Market The market where the (underlying) physical goods are bought and sold. For example, a grain elevator where farmers sell their harvest, but not the futures exchange where agricultural futures contracts are traded.

Policy Asset Allocation See Strategic Asset Allocation.

Political Analysis Studying the sovereign risk, social and political developments, legal system, and federal budgets of different countries to assess the desirability of making investments in them.

Portfolio Insurance Purchasing protective puts to hedge against adverse price movements.

Preferred Stock An ownership security that receives (cumulative or non-cumulative) cash dividends, but only has voting power under special circumstances.

Present Value The current value, after discounting all cash flows to reflect the time value of money.

Price Discount A price reduced to below a security's face (par) value. Bank discount pricing is a special pricing mechanism used for money-market securities.

Price-Earnings Ratio A common stock's price per share divided by its earnings per share (EPS). Also known as the stock's earnings multiplier.

Price Index A statistical indicator designed to summarize pricing conditions. For example, the Consumers Price Index or the S&P500 Index.

Primary Market The market for new issues of securities where investment bankers sell IPOs. Later, the securities are traded in a secondary market.

Primary Trends The Dow Theory's label for bull and bear markets.

Principal The owner (principal) who hires an agent to help manage the owner's assets. For example, securities brokers and mutual fund managers act as agents for the investors (principals) that own the securities.

Private Placement Selling an entire issue of stock or bonds to one or a few institutional investors and/or wealthy individuals. SEC registration not required.

Probability Distribution of Returns A list or graph of all possible rates of return and the probabilities assigned to each. Can be subjectively or objectively derived.

Profit-Sharing Plan A defined contribution pension fund to which the employer/sponsor is obliged to pay a fixed percentage of each year's profit, if any profits are earned.

Prospectus A booklet that fully discloses all relevant information about a securities issuer which the SEC requires be given to prospective investors before they invest.

Protective Provisions Stipulations written in the indenture contract that are designed to protect the interests of the bond investors. For example, collateral, sinking fund, and other provisions.

Proxy In investments, a proxy statement is a legal document that entitles another person (the proxy, or stand-in) to temporarily exercise the stockholder's voting power with respect to the voting affairs of the corporation that issued the stock.

Purchasing Power Risk Variability of return caused by changes in the rate of inflation. The possibility that purchasing power will be lost because the cash flows associated with a fixed income investment (such as a bond or savings account) are not free to increase with the rate of inflation.

Put-Call Parity Formula An arbitrage-free relationship between the prices of a put and call on the same underlying asset, in which the two different options have identical exercise prices and times to maturity.

Quadratic Programming (QP) A mathematical algorithm invented by Harry Markowitz. A computer program to perform QP minimizes a quadratic risk function (the variance-covariance matrix) subject to linear constraints. In investments work, the typical linear constraints are: (1) the weights sum to one, and, (2) the portfolio's weighted average return equals some designated value [for instance, $E(r_p) = 12\%$]. The set of dominant portfolios comprising the efficient frontier are delineated by varying the value of $E(r_p)$.

Quality of Earnings Refers to the degree of accuracy with which the company's accounting earnings reflect the firm's true economic income.

Quality Spread The yield spread between a risky bond and a default-free bond. Also called a default risk premium.

Quick Ratio A firm's current assets, with the exception of inventory, which are divided by current liabilities. A solvency ratio.

Random Variable A series of independent and identically distributed values that reflect the outcomes from a stochastic process. For example, the monthly rates of return from an investment in a share of Coca-Cola stock.

Rate of Inflation In the U.S., the percentage change in the Consumers Price Index (CPI) measured at an annual rate is the most popular measure. Other price indexes may be used.

Rating Migration A publicly observable credit event that occurs when a financial service (like S&P, Moody's, or Fitch) changes the quality rating of a bond issue. Small credit migrations are not credit events.

Real Rate of Return This inflation-adjusted rate of return is computed by dividing (or, less accurately, subtracting) the rate of inflation out of the nominal rate of return.

Recovery Rate The percentage of an asset's face value a creditor recovers if the asset defaults.

Redemption Fees Exit fees charged when an investor liquidates. Fees investment managers charge to discourage liquidation.

Reference Rate An observable rate of interest, such as LIBOR or the 1-year T-Bill rate. Periodic interest rate payments are sometimes defined to equal a Reference Rate plus a fixed number of basis points (BPs). For example, an indenture contract may stipulate that the semiannual interest payment on a floating-rate bond is to be reset semiannually at LIBOR + 400 BPs.

Reg ATS An SEC regulation allowing alternative trading systems (ATS) in the U.S. to register as stock exchanges. For example, Archipelago ECN and Island ECN applied to the SEC.

Regular Cash Dividends Periodic cash dividend payments made by a corporation that do not change much from year to year.

Registered Bonds Investors in these bonds have their names and addresses in a list that is maintained by that bond issue's registrar. Different than bearer bonds.

Reinvestment Risk Variability of return from reinvesting (plowing back cashflows from) a consecutive series of bond coupons (or other fixed income payments) into a series of new and different fixed income investments that each pay different and unpredictable market interest rates.

Relative Frequency Distribution A probability distribution based on objective historical observations.

Repatriation-of-Funds Risk The risk that a government blocks payments of principal or interest owed to foreign investors.

Replicating Portfolio A portfolio created to mimic the price behavior of an unpriced financial instrument. The replicating portfolio should provide a pattern of payouts that is identical to the duplicated unpriced financial instrument and is also made up from components that have discernible market prices. The law of one price can then be invoked to assign the total value of the components in the replicating portfolio to the unpriced financial instrument.

Repurchase Agreement (Repo) Agreements that are actively traded in the money markets which allow their issuers to sell and then, a day or two later, buy back (repurchase) specified securities at a slightly higher price. The price change equals the interest payment on these collateralized loans.

Required Rate of Return The minimum rate of return an investor must earn to increase the investors' wealth. In different contexts, it is also called the cost of capital, cut-off rate, risk-adjusted discount rate, and expected return.

Residual Claim The legal claim held by stockholders (equity investors). For example, bankruptcy law specifies that stockholders have the last claim on the (residual) assets of a bankrupt corporation after all other bills have been paid. Similarly, accounting conventions define the income available to stockholders to be the residual income that remains after all the firm's expenses have been paid.

Residual Error The idiosyncratic portion left unexplained by a statistical model. For example, the epsilon, e_t, in the characteristic regression line: $r_{j,t} = a + br_{M,t} + e_t$

Resistance Level A price level at which one may expect an increase in the supply of a security or commodity that is offered for sale. Sometimes called a price ceiling.

Retained Earnings (RE) On a corporation's income and expense statement, retained earnings equals net income minus any cash dividend payments and, also, minus any funds spent on share buybacks. An accumulation of past years' retained earnings is also shown as an equity component in the net worth section of a corporation's balance sheet.

Retention Rate (RR) The percentage of a corporation's net income that is retained for investment within the firm. Retained earnings stated as a percentage of net income.

Return on Assets (ROA) A corporation's annual net income stated as a percentage of its total assets.

Return on Equity (ROE) A corporation's annual net income stated as a percentage of its net worth (book value, owners equity).

Revenue Bonds Limited obligation bonds issued by a municipality. The interest and principal on these bonds must be repaid from revenues from the project the bond issue financed. For example, revenue bonds issued to pay for the construction of a toll road must be repaid by using toll revenues from that highway.

Risk Variability of return. Total risk may be decomposed into meaningful components.

Risk-Adjusted Discount Rate A rate of return (discount rate) that provides an appropriate inducement to entice investors to accept the level of risk in an investment. In different contexts, it is also called the required rate of return, cost of capital, or expected return.

Risk-Free Rate (RFR) The interest rate that provides an appropriate rate of return from a default-free (riskless, guaranteed) investment. For example, the U.S. Treasury bill interest rate.

Risk-Return Analysis An approach to financial analysis that focuses on mean (average) returns, variances (standard deviations) of returns, and correlations (covariances) between the returns from different assets.

Risk Premium An additional increment of return that investors expect to receive to compensate them for accepting the risks inherent in a risky investment. Fisher's inflation premium and credit risk premiums (quality spreads) provide two examples of risk premiums.

Round Lot A common stock transaction measured in hundreds of shares; larger than an odd lot.

Runs Test A statistical randomness test that counts the numbers of changes in a series of numbers that move consistently in the same direction. The numbers of positive runs, zero runs, and negative runs are then each totaled to see if they equal the number of runs that should be found in an equal-sized table of random numbers.

Sample Dependent Statistics Statistics that vary from one sample to the next. Heteroscedasticity, for example, can cause statistics to be sample dependent.

Sampling Error The difference between the value of a statistic and the quantity (population parameter) that statistic is designed to estimate.

Secondary Market A market in which investors trade outstanding securities. Contrast with Primary Market.

Secondary Movements According to the Dow Theory, they are either upward price surges or market collapses that last only a few weeks or months.

Secured Debt Collateralized debt. Debts that are issued with a legal contract that pledges specific assets will be made available to redeem the debt; this pledge reduces potential losses for investors.

Securities Act of 1933 A federal law that requires securities issuers in the U.S. to make full disclosure of the relevant facts (provide prospectuses) and prohibits fraud. It was supplemented by the Securities Exchange Act of 1934.

Security Analysts Financial analysts who focus on stocks, bonds, and related securities. Some security analysts are fundamental analysts, some are risk-return analysts, some are technical analysts, and some use a combination of these tools.

Securities Exchange Act of 1934 A federal law that established the SEC to enforce the Securities Act of 1933, gave the SEC power over securities exchanges, and prohibited fraud and price manipulation.

Securities and Exchange Commission (SEC) A department within the U.S. government that was established by the Securities Exchange Act of 1934 to supervise the securities industry. The SEC employs hundreds of lawyers that bring charges against securities law violators.

Securities Fraud Enforcement Act of 1988 Provides insider trading penalties up to three times any damages that may have been caused, fines up to $1 million, and up to 10 years' imprisonment.

Security Market Line (SML) A financial theory which uses undiversifiable (beta or covariance) risk to explain assets' expected returns. Also called the Capital Asset Pricing Model (CAPM).

Securitization A process which takes illiquid accounts receivable (such as mortgages), commingles these loans into a single pool, and sells asset-backed securities with varying degrees of liquidity and safety (different tranches of bonds) to finance the asset pool.

Segmentation Theory Asserts the yield curve is composed of a series of independent maturity segments.

Self-Financing Portfolio A portfolio that takes the proceeds from a short sale and uses those funds to buy a long position of equal value. A no-money-invested portfolio.

Selling Climax Sometimes occurs at the end of a bear market, when a high volume of selling clears the way for bullish investors to start bidding up prices.

Self-Regulating Organization (SRO) A trade association that governs its members and hands out punishments for misconduct; often undertaken to avoid being governed by a regulatory bureaucracy. For example, the NASD.

Semi-Strong Prices Security market prices that reflect all public information.

Separate Trading of Registered Interest and Principal of Securities (STRIPS) A program to market coupon-paying U.S. Treasury bonds in which one T-Bond is viewed as being a portfolio of zero-coupon bonds. Each individual coupon payment and the principal repayment are all marketed as separate zero-coupon bonds.

Serial Correlation A correlation coefficient that measures the extent to which lagged values in a time-series of data covary with more recent values. Also called Auto Correlation.

Short Interest The aggregate number of shares brokers have listed in their accounts as being sold short; usually below 5% of the total number of shares traded on the NYSE.

Short Position The position that results when the selling party sells something it does not own. The short-seller typically borrows what is needed to make delivery in the future.

Short-Term Bonds Bonds sold by a corporation or government that mature in the near future. Some highly-liquid financial instruments that mature in less than one year (for example, T-Bills) are money market securities.

Signals Cash dividend payments, debt versus equity financing decisions, stock buyback announcements, and other decisions by management may contain intentional or inadvertent indicators of top management's intentions or confidence. Such signals are said to have information content.

Sinking Fund A protective provision in an indenture contract that requires a bond issuer to set aside money in a segregated account (called a Sinking Fund) and use the funds to repurchase the outstanding bonds.

Size Premium An additional increment of return (risk premium) that investors expect to receive to induce them to buy securities issued by smaller, less well-known firms. Also called a small stock premium.

Sovereign Risk Variability of return caused by the possibility that a foreign government does not honor its debts.

SPDRs Standard & Poor's 500 Depository Receipts (SPDRs) are S&P 500 Index funds (portfolios) that are traded actively and continuously on the AMEX. Similar to but different from an S&P 500 Index mutual fund.

Special Dividends Extraordinary cash dividend payments that may never be repeated.

Speculation A purchase (or short sale) made with the expectation that a short-term price change will permit the position to be closed out at a profit in the near future.

Speculators Aggressive traders who expose themselves to price fluctuation risk with the expectation of earning trading profits.

Speculative Blowoff At the end of the bull market, a high volume of buying pushes prices up to an unsustainable peak that sets the stage for the bear market selling to begin.

Speculative Bonds See Junk Bonds.

Split Rating An unusual event that occurs when S&P and Moody's, or some other bond ratings' service, assigns different quality ratings to the same bond issue.

Spot Contract A futures contract that matures in one month or less and, therefore, by convention, ceases to be called a futures contract.

Spot Market A market where physical goods or spot contracts are traded.

Spot Price The price of a financial instrument that is available for a cash delivery. A price in the spot market.

Spot Rates The current interest rates on bonds that exist today and mature in the future. Interest rates that can now be purchased in the cash market for bonds. Similarly, the current foreign-exchange rates for a future's contract on a currency.

Spread (1) The difference between the yields or prices of two financial instruments or two positions. (2) A bid-asked spread is a market-maker's (dealer's) payment for providing liquidity. (3) A trading strategy that is designed to profit from a widening or narrowing in a yield spread or price differential.

Specialists Market-makers at an organized securities exchange.

Standardized Unexpected Earnings (SUE) A normalized measure of the difference between the actual and expected values of a stock's earnings per share.

Standard of Comparison A benchmark used for performance evaluation.

Standard Deviation A statistic that measures dispersion about the expected value. Square root of the variance. In finance, one of several quantitative risk surrogates.

Standard & Poor's 500 Depository Receipts See SPDRs.

Static Equilibrium Model An economic model in which supply and demand are equal so there is no tendency for change.

Stochastic Process Risk Risks arising from changes in the term structure of interest rates. For example, the risk duration wandering occurs.

Stock Dividend Occurs when a corporation issues its own shares to pay a dividend to its shareholders, instead of paying a cash dividend. Similar to a Stock Split.

Stock Split A change in the unit of account that occurs when a corporation reallocates its earnings, dividends, and voting power among its shares. Similar to a stock dividend.

Stock Variable Cash, raw materials, accounts receivable, or any other variable that can be carried in "inventory." Different than a flow variable.

Stop Order An order to trade that includes a stop price. When the securities market price attains or passes through the stop price, the stop order becomes a market order.

Straddle An option position that is created by purchasing an equal number of puts and calls with identical exercise prices on the same underlying asset.

Strangle A long put and a long call, or, a short put and a short call, on the same underlying asset. The put and call usually have the same maturities but different exercise prices.

Strategic Asset Allocation (SAA) The portion of an asset allocation plan that identifies the asset classes and their proportions in the normal mix for a long-run (equilibrium) portfolio.

STRIPS See Separate Trading of Registered Interest and Principal of Securities.

Subjective Probability Distribution A probability distribution that is based on guesstimates of the outcomes rather than being based on objective historical data.

Superfluous Diversification An uneconomical effort to diversify that spreads the investment funds over so many different investments it is impossible to manage the portfolio well. It often results from the portfolio manager's desire to maximize management fee collections and leads to managing more money than can be managed effectively.

Support Level The price level at which one might expect an increase in demand for a security or commodity. Also called a "floor" beneath the price.

Syndicate In finance, a group of bankers that form a temporary alliance to underwrite and distribute an initial public offering (IPO).

Tactical Asset Allocation (TAA) Policies that govern dynamic asset reallocations that are designed to profit from temporary market disequilibriums. A plan about how to deviate from the Strategic Asset Allocation (SAA) when it becomes temporarily advantageous to deviate.

Technical Analysis Involves several different approaches to security analysis and market analysis that utilize graphs and market statistics to detect meaningful patterns in market data. Technical analysts believe that these meaningful patterns have valuable predictive powers. See the Dow Theory and the Head and Shoulders pattern for examples.

Term Structure of Interest Rates The relationship between years to maturity and yield-to-maturity (YTM) for a given issuer's (most commonly, U.S. Treasury) bonds. Also called the Yield Curve.

Third Market An over-the-counter (OTC) market where exchange-listed stocks are traded.

Tick The minimum security price change permitted at a securities exchange. For example, the NYSE reduced its tick size from 12.5¢ to 1¢ when it decimalized in 2001.

Time Diversification If an investment's return is extremely high or low during one time period and the returns tend to revert back toward the mean return during later periods, this mean-reversion process tends to smooth out (average away) some of the short-term fluctuations and, in so doing, reduces the risk of long-term investing. See mean reversion.

Times-Interest-Earned Ratio A coverage ratio that measures how many times a firm's annual earnings covers (pays for) debt-servicing charges such as interest, sinking fund payments, or lease payments.

Time-Series Comparison The evaluation and assessment of one series of sequential data that is observed over different sample periods. Different than cross-sectional comparisons.

Time Value Money saved in an FDIC-insured (riskless) savings account earns interest income that causes the value of the invested money to grow with certainty as time passes. As a result, invested money has time value rather than a fixed value.

Time-Weighted Rate of Return Refers to Geometric Mean Return (GMR).

Tombstone In finance, a display ad that investment bankers place in a newspaper or magazine to announce an initial public offering (IPO).

Total Returns (TR) Returns that include income from both cash flows (cash dividends, coupon interest) and price changes.

Tracking Stock A special class of stock that is somehow linked to a segment or division of the issuing corporation.

Trading Cards Separate cards are used for every commodity pit transaction to document the details (price, quantity, delivery month) of each transaction.

Trading Range Breakout (TRB) When the market price of the security passes through (breaks out of) the top (bottom) of a trading range, that price move can be interpreted as a signal to buy (sell).

Transactions Fees Brokerage commissions, taxes, transfer fees, or other costs that are generated by securities trading.

Transfer Agent A designated third party (usually a bank) that facilitates transactions between the buyer and seller of shares and maintains records.

Treasury Inflation-Protected Securities (TIPS) An inflation-adjusted U.S. Treasury bond that is designed to diminish its investors' purchasing power risk.

Treasury Notes Coupon-paying U.S. Treasury bonds with initial maturities of one to seven years. Shorter maturities than U.S. Treasury bonds.

Treynor's Performance Index An investment performance evaluation tool that considers both the average return and beta risk from an investment and reduces these two statistics into a single value that gauges the desirability of the investment.

Trough The bottom point in a cycle.

Trust Indenture Act of 1939 A securities law requiring corporate bonds issued in the U.S. to be accompanied by an indenture contract specifying the amount and dates of all cash flows, all protective provisions, and a trustee to enforce the protective provisions.

Two-Legged Spread A spread that has two legs (components). For example, a two-legged spreader might leg into a near-futures position for one leg and a far-futures position for the other leg.

Unbiased Expectations Hypothesis The belief that the Expectations Theory alone (without, for instance, a liquidity premium) determines the shape of the yield curve.

The "Underlying" The underlying quantity (stock price, market index value, commodity price) from which an option (or other derivative) derives its value.

Underwriter In finance, an investment banker that underwrites IPOs.

Undiversifiable Risk Variability of return caused by systematic market forces that affect many securities simultaneously.

Unified Gift and Inheritance Tax A federal tax on estates in excess of $1 million.

Unit Investment Trust (UIT) A special type portfolio defined by the Investment Company Act of 1940. The law does not permit UITs to issue or redeem shares, or actively trade the securities in their portfolio, during their lives.

Utility In economics, happiness. Economics is based on the assumption that happiness (utility) increases with wealth.

Utility Isoquants See Indifference Curves.

Value A measure of an asset's economic worth that may differ from its market price.

Variance In mathematics, a statistic that measures dispersion about the expected value. The standard deviation squared. In finance, one of several different quantitative risk surrogates.

Variance-Covariance Matrix In mathematical statistics, an NxN symmetric matrix that contains a quadratic formula. In finance, a formula used to measure the elements of risk in a diversified portfolio of N investment candidates.

Variation Margin See Maintenance Margin Requirement.

Vertical Spreads A spread involving either two puts or two calls with different exercise prices but the same expiration date. Sometimes called a money spread.

Volume of Contracts The number of futures contracts that have been opened since a contract began trading and have not yet expired or been closed out (unwound, sold). A measure of trading activity.

Weakly Efficient Prices Market prices that reflect all historical information.

Whip-sawed Occurs when an unfortunate trader buys during a small rise that is immediately followed by a larger price fall that throws him for a loss. Alternatively, it also occurs when an unfortunate trader sells during a small drop and then watches with regret as a larger price rise follows immediately after his sale.

Whisper Earnings Forecasts of earnings per share that circulate among securities analysts, traders on Web sites, and in the financial press.

X Percent Filter Rule The following mechanical trading rule: If the price of a security rises by x percent, buy and hold the security until its price reaches a peak and then drops by x percent. After a security's price drops by x percent, liquidate any long positions that may be held and sell the security short. Maintain that short position until the price of the security rises by x percent.

Yield In finance, it could refer to an interest rate, a stock's cash dividend yield, or a bond's coupon yield.

Yield Curve See Term Structure of Interest Rates.

Yield-To-Maturity (YTM) The discount rate that equates the present value of all cash flows to the asset's (usually, a bond's) current market (purchase) price.

Zero-Coupon Bond A bond that never pays coupon interest. Also simply called a zero.

Zero Sum Game A game involving chance, or a risky investment, in which one counterparty's gains equal the other counterparty's losses. For example, the counterparties in most derivatives transactions are participating in a zero sum game.

INDEX

Absolute Priority Rule (APR), 27, 657–58
absolute purchasing power parity, 519
accounting income, 729, 731, 736
Accounting Principles Board (APB) opinions, 732
accounting with LIFO and FIFO, example
of, 727
accrued interest in bonds, 573, 574
Ackermann, McEnally, and Ravenscraft
(AMR) performance comparison of
hedge and mutual funds, 878
active investment managers, 54
activity ratios (see turnover ratios)
adjustable-rate bonds (floating-rate
bonds), 674
after-acquired property clause, 672
agency bonds, 102
alternative minimum tax (AMT), 392
Altman, Ed, 665
Altman study of bankruptcy, 665–66
Amazon.com Internet firm, 760, 761–62
ambiguities in accounting earnings, 725,
727, 732, 737
amortization of goodwill and, 730–31
confusion and deception and, 726–28
contingent liabilities and, 731
contrasting two income statements for,
726–31
convertible security contracts and, 732
distorted income statements and, 725–26
earnings per share (EPS) potential dilution and, 731–32
expensing vs. capitalizing and, 730
extraordinary gains and losses and,
732–33
Financial Accounting Statements Board
(FASB) and, 729, 730, 732, 733
income statement accounting procedures and, 726–28
inventory methods and, 727–28
pension costs and, 729–30
quality of earnings and, 731–33
taxation and, 727, 729
American call, 764, 849
American Depository Receipts (ADRs),
138, 530, 545–47
American Municipal Bond Assurance
Association (AMBAC), 108

America Online (AOL) Internet firm, 760
American options, 245
American Stock Exchange (AMEX), 126,
245, 347, 348, 349, 851
Amihud, Yakov, 447
amortization, 668
analysis of rating migration risk, 676
anticipatory prices, 675
arbitrage, 38, 55, 60
convergence and, 805
expectations theory and, 613
index arbitrage, 820–23
and the law of one price, 58–59, 817,
825
opportunity, defined, 456
stock index arbitrage, 820–21
Arbitrage Pricing Theory (APT), 450, 452,
462–63, 465, 466
APT line, 453
APT model, 455–56
arbitrage opportunity in, 456
Arbitrage Portfolio Theory model,
458–61
arbitrageurs and, 453, 463
cross-sectional regression in, 463–64
empirical tests of, 463–66
factor betas in, 451
homogeneous expectations in, 463
implications of APT theory, 455–56,
458, 460
k-dimensional APT hyperplane, 461
long/short positions in, 455–56
market portfolio and, 463, 465
mathematical APT, 457–58, 474
one-factor model in, 450–53
overpriced and underpriced assets,
454
risk factors in, 464
Ross and Roll (RR) empirical study, 464
vs. Security Market Line (SML) theory,
462–63
self-financing position in, 457
two-factor model of, 456–61
arbitrageurs, 58, 143, 348, 454, 525,
820–21
Archipelago Exchange, 150
arithmetic mean return (AMR), 24–25, 34,
281, 314, 317

arithmetic mean return vs. geometric
mean return, 283–84
Arizona Stock Exchange (AZX), 149–50,
155
assessing values of securities, 45–46
asset allocation, 369, 370, 371, 376, 379
(see also asset allocation process)
adverse market movements and, 374–75
asset classes of, 6, 22, 366, 373
benchmark portfolio and, 372
Brinson, Hood, Beebower (BHB) study
of, 382–83
constrained asset allocation, 372–73,
376–77
dynamic asset allocation (DAA), 380
expectations of investor in, 371–72
explicit investment policy statements
and, 372
foundations, endowments and, 371
fundamental security analysis and, 375
historical market index statistics and,
376
Ibbotson-Kaplan (IK) study of, 383–84
investor's time horizon and, 368–69, 626
large transactions and, 379
long-run asset allocation, 376
market impact costs and, 379
Markowitz portfolio theory and, 377,
415–20
normal asset mix in, 376
numerical policy statement and,
373–74
optimizer and, 380
performance reports and feedback in,
379
risk-return analysts in, 372, 375
shadow asset mix in, 382
simple asset allocation, 376
small transactions in, 379
strategic asset allocation (SAA), 367,
376, 377, 380
tactical asset allocation (TAA), 367, 377,
380
tax exemption and, 371
tax situation of investor and, 369–70
technical analysis, 375, 382
written statement of investment goals
for, 370, 372–75

Asset Allocation Line (AAL), 427, 428, 438
  and capital market line (CML), 438
  combining with Markowitz's efficient frontier, 420–21
  index of investment desirability and, 419–20
  and Markowitz 5th concept, 415–21
  risk-free rate of interest (RFR) and, 415–17
asset allocation process, 367–80
  phase 1—creating a written policy statement, 368–75
  phase 2—managing the money, 375–80
asset mix (normal), 377
asset-turnover ratio, 76
Association for Investment Management and Research (AIMR), 16, 50
assumptions underlying portfolios theory, 440–41
asymmetric information, 20, 737
authorized investment trusts (see unit investment trusts (UITs))
Automated Bond System (ABS), 564
average rates of return (computing), example of, 25, 281–82
Avraham, Kamara, 813

Baby boom, 750–52
Bagnoli, Beneish and Watts (BBW) report on whisper forecasts, 722
Bakshi, Gurdip, 751
Bakshi-Chen lifetime theory of savings, 751–52, 756, 771
balance sheet, 66, 87, 766–67
balance sheet (common size), 70
Bali, Rakesh, 866
balloon mortgage, 635
banker's acceptances (BAs), 96
Bank of America, 16
Bank of New York, 349, 545
bankruptcy, 27, 28–29, 108, 110, 120
  bond investors and, 763–64
  Boston Chicken Corporation, example of, 659
  and call option of common stockholders, 763
  corporate bankruptcy, 656–59
  coupon-interest claims and, 763–64
  law, 762, 763
  managing losses in, 674
  market price fluctuations and, 659–60
  mortgage bonds and, 763
  stockholders and, 763–64
Banz, Rolf, 205
Banz empirical study of small company stocks, 205
Banz, Reinganum and Keim report on average returns, 448

bar charts, 781
Barclary, Holderness, Pontiff (BHP) closed end fund report, 477
Barclary, Michael J., 477
Barclay's Global Investors (BGI), 349, 350, 360
Barron's, publication, 273
Barron's confidence index (BCI), 786–87
base rate fallacy, 790
basic random variable of investments, 34
basis point (BP), 28, 299
Basu, Sanjoy, 448
bearer bonds, 571
bearer securities, 111
Beebower, Gilbert L., 382
behavioral finance, 789–90
Bessembinder and Chan study of the DJIA, 785, 789
beta economics, 177–78, 448–49
Bezos, Jeffrey, 761
bid-asked spreads (trading fees), 102, 151
bounded rationality, 789
Black-Scholes call pricing formula, 766, 767, 840–45, 862
Black-Scholes model example, 842–43
block positioners, 141, 155, 379
block trade, 13, 141, 155
Bloomberg, Michael, 561
Bloomberg Corporation, the, 144, 147, 561
Boatright, John R., 20, 29, 50, 110, 153–55, 501, 713, 791
Bodie, Jaffe and Mandelker, and Nelson empirical study on inflation, 289
BondBook electronic bond market, 566–67
bond index funds, 359–60
bond investment management (international), 589–90
BondLink electronic bond market, 566
bond price behavior axioms, 650–51
bond quality rating, 659–62, 663, 676
  average returns and, 662
  bond analysts and, 661
  corporate credit curves and, 662
  credit market conditions and, 662
  credit-rating services, 660–61
  credit risk and changes in, 674–75
  relationship between appropriate discount rate, 678
  risk-aversion and, 662
  split rating in, 661
bonds, 14, 313, 631–32, 635, 641–41, 643
  (see also global bonds)
  adjustable-rate bonds (floating-rate bonds), 674
  asked/offer price, 106
  average returns vs. quality ratings, 662
  bid price of, 106

callable, 102, 266–67, 313
call provisions of, 100, 267
collateral trust and, 109
components of default premium, 313
computing present value of, 41
contrasting time until maturity with duration of, 640–41, 643
convertible bonds, 100–101, 267
convexity in price-yield relationship, 641, 643
corporate bonds, 14, 28, 108, 120, 317, 327, 564–65
coupon effect on, 631–632
coupon-paying bonds, 98, 99, 103, 106, 627, 629, 763–64
coupon payment, 41, 627, 632
current yield, example of, 583
debenture bonds (debentures), 109, 658, 659, 672
debt test clauses in, 673
default free, 626
default premium in, 28, 312–13, 313, 327
discount rate in, 41, 627, 632
duration axioms for, 651
duration wandering, interest rate risk and, 647
electronic bond markets, 566–67
embedded call option in, 100, 266–67, 580–81, 590
European call, 862
features of, 99–101
Fisher-Weil (FWD) duration measure of, 648
floating-rate bonds, 99, 583
foreign currency bonds, 674
general-obligation (GO) bonds, 107, 120
high-grade corporate bond funds, 359
high-yield, 660 (see also junk bonds)
horizon analysis of, 632, 635, 649
horizon premium in, 28, 312
horizon return on, 649
index funds of, 359
inflation-linked bonds, 674
inflation premium in, 312
insured municipal bonds, 107–8
interest rate risk of, 626, 631, 644–46
intermediate-term U.S. Treasury bonds, 28
investment horizon vs. maturity horizons of, 649
issuer significance and size, 670–71
junk bonds, 359, 659–60, 663, 665
limited-obligation bonds, 107
long-term corporate bonds, 28, 120
long-term Treasury bonds, 28, 312, 318
Macaulay's duration (MAC) and, 640–44, 651

bonds *(continued)*
  marketable U.S. Treasury securities, 101–2
  markets for in the U.S., 565–66
  matrix prices of, 564
  maturities of, 100
  modified duration (MOD) in, 638–39, 648–49
  mortgage bond funds, 359
  mortgage bonds, 764
  municipal bonds (munis), 106–7
  new-money bonds (NMBs), 585
  nonconvertible, 101
  non-marketable U.S. Treasury securities, 101
  option to call, 763–64
  original-issue discount (OID) bonds, 101, 103, 120, 631
  par value, 41, 101, 113, 627
  par *vs.* price, 627, 629, 631
  past-due interest bonds (PDIs), 585
  premium/discount to face value of, 99
  premiums and discounts in, 629
  present value of a bond, 41, 626–27
  price behavior axioms of, 650–51
  price elasticity of, 646
  price quotations via newspaper, 104–5
  price-yield relationship in, 632, 643–44
  principal (corpus) of, 103
  put bonds, 674
  quality rating of, 659–62, 667, 674–75
  rating agencies for, 77, 565
  ratios and quality ratings in, 667–70
  recovery risk in bonds, 673
  retired prematurely, 267
  revenue bonds, 107
  risk-free rate (RFR) and, 28, 415, 416, 417, 427, 428
  safety net return goal and, 650
  sales-and-leaseback agreements of, 673
  savings bonds, 101
  secondary markets in, 566
  secured/collateralized bonds, 108–9
  senior claim of mortgage bonds, 764
  short-term bond interest rates, 608
  sinking fund (bond redemption), 101, 120
  Standard & Poor's bond rating, 659
  stock price adjustments and, 675
  systematic fluctuations of market interest rates of, 646
  tax-exempt funds, 359, 394
  term-to-maturity of, 640
  total bond default premium, 312
  transparency of U.S. bond market, 566
  U.S. Treasury and, 14, 24–26, 94, 101, 103, 359
  unsecured bonds, 109
  yield-to-call (YTC), 580–81, 590

  yield-to-maturity (YTM) of, 41, 106, 575–76, 579–80, 590, 595
  zero coupon bonds (zeros), 98, 103, 629, 631
book-to-market effect, 209–10
book-to-market equity (B/V) ratio, 448, 449
book value, 87, 113, 772
Boston Chicken Corporation bankruptcy (1998–1999), 659, 674
Boucrelle, Cyril, 542
bounded rationality, 789
Brady, Nicholas, 584
Brady bonds, 584–85, 591
Brinson, Gary, 382
Brinson, Hood, Beebower (BHB) investigation of asset allocation, 382–83
Brinson, Singer, Beebower investigation of asset allocation, 382
British bond, defined, 568
Brock, Lakonishok, and LeBaron (BLL) report on moving averages, 789
Brock, Lakonishok, and LeBaron (BLL) study of the DJIA, 785
brokerage services, 126, 132, 133–34, 155, 161
  discount brokers, 129
  electronic brokers, 129–30
  full-service brokers, 128–29
  margin requirements, 234–35, 809–10
  and personal financial information, 371
  trading on margin, 132–34, 155
  transacting with, 130–31
BrokerTec Global electronic bond market, 566
Brown, Stephen, 780
Bulldog bonds, 569
bull market (1990s), 756
Bundesbank of Germany, 603
Burmeister, Edwin, 449
business cycle, 162, 601, 704
buybacks, investment implications of, 752, 756
buy-sell guidelines, 748–50
  advantage of, 749
  buy and sell signals in, 748
  Internet stocks and, 749–50
  problems with, 749–50
  S&P500 and, 748, 749
buy-sell rules under certainty, 45, 50

Cadbury Schweppes, 73
calculus, 433–35, 649
callable bonds, 102, 580–81, 582–83
callable convertible corporate bond, example of, 267
call buyer and writer, defined, 242–43
call option of common stockholders, 763

call option theory, 762, 763–67
Canada, 6, 574
Candler, Asa, 755
Cantor Financial Futures Exchange (CFFE), 803
capital, 9–10
  cost of, 29, 34, 700, 701
  financial, 8, 9–10
  human, 8, 10, 12, 413
  real, 8, 10–11
Capital Asset Pricing Model (CAPM), 437, 440–41
capital gains tax, 392–93
capitalization, 670
Capital Market Line (CML), 438–39, 440–41
capital market securities, 98, 327
capital market theory, 444, 462–63
Capual, Rowley and SHARPE (CRS) portfolio analysis, 211
Carleton and Copper on term structure, 622
Carson Group, the, 721
Carvela bonds, 569
cash dividend
  computations with, 849
  discount model (DDM), 688, 689–90, 693–94
  effects of payments of, 848–50
  ex-dividend stock price dropoff, 848–49, 862
  problems with cash dividends, 736–37
  yield of, 747, 756
cash dividends information content
  asymmetric information, 720, 737
  boards of directors and, 719, 720
  decreases in, 719
  earnings per share forecasting, 721–22
  forecasting error and, 722–23
  forecasts and, 720–22
  Healy and Paplepu (H&P) study of, 720
  increase, decrease of stock prices, 720
  Lintner study of decisions concerning, 719
  Miller and Modigliani (M & M) dividend irrelevance theorem, 719, 720, 737
  payments and, 719
  policies determinants and, 720
  quality of earnings and, 731–33
  reactions to, 720
  short-term changes and, 719
  signals in, 720
  standardized unexpected earnings (SUEs) and, 722
  statement of cash flows and, 733–35
  Stickel (Scott E.) statistical analysis of forecasts and, 722
  whisper earnings forecasts of earnings per share, 722

cash flow, 40, 42, 63–64, 668, 669, 733–36
  available to equity shareholders, 735
  cash dividends and, 736–37
  equity shareholders *vs.* economic income in, 736
  extraordinary gains and losses, 732
  from operations (CFO), 733
  in Arbitrage Pricing Theory (APT), 450, 460
  in bonds, 41
  defined, 67
  leverage-free cash flow, 735
  operating income and, 669
  ratios in finance, 77–78
  statement of cash flows and, 733–34
cash market, 512, 799
cash settlement, 230, 353
central limit order book (CLOB), 142
Central Limit Theorem, 677
certificates of deposit (CDs), 95–96
Chan, Louis K.C., 449
characteristic line, 169–71
  asset returns and, 172
  dependent variable and, 172
  econometric problems with, 448–49
  estimating statistics of, 172–73
  in first-pass regressions, 447–48
  interpretation of, 176
  in Jenson's model, 488–89
  regression line in, 172
  residual error in, 175, 201–2
  of stock splits and dividends, 200–202
Charles Schwab & Company, 129
chartists, 777, 781, 782
Chase Bank, 16, 518
Chen, Zhiwu, 751
Chicago Board of Trade (CBOT), 235, 245, 802, 803
Chicago Board Options Exchange (CBOE), 245, 851
Chicago Mercantile Exchange (CME, "the Merc"), 236, 351
Chicago Stock Exchange (CHX), 145
Chrysler Credit Corporation, 97
churning, 110, 129, 768, 769
Citibank, 518, 545
classified common stock, 114–15, 769
clean price, defined, 573
clearing house, 230, 801
Clearing House Interbank Payments System (CHIPS), 508
closed-end investment companies, 333, 341
CMGI Internet firm, 760
Coca-Cola Corporation, 54, 65, 66, 689, 709, 755
  analysis of sales and competition, 72–73
  analyzing a call on its stock, 247–48

annual report of, 698, 719
  balance sheet of, 67
  cash flows statement of, 67–68
  coefficient of determination for, 178
  collection period of, 75
  common-sized balance sheet of, 70
  comprehensive income of, 68–69
  and consolidated financial statements, 87
  covariance, correlation in stock of, 406
  coverage ratios of, 77
  current ratio of, 74
  DuPont Analytical framework and, 81
  earnings per share (EPS) of, 80–81, 737
  equity-turnover ratio of, 76
  establishing financial ratio guidelines, 75–76
  expected rate of return, 162, 164
  forecasting cash dividends in, 695
  future cash dividend policy of, 698
  global sales and, 545
  income and expense statement of, 396
  leverage ratios with value of, 78
  operating income of, 76
  profitability ratios for, 79, 80
  quick ratio for, 74
  solvency (or liquidity) ratio for, 74–75
  Standard & Poor's stock report and, 85–86
  stock splits of, 200
  trademark of, 87
  turnover ratio for, 74
  undiversifiable proportion of total risk, 179
  Web site address for, 70
Coinage Act (1965), 879–80
collateral provisions in debentures, 672
collection period, 75
commercial paper market, 97
commission brokers (floor brokers), 799
commodities trading
  agricultural commodities in, 802, 803
  arbitrage and, 805–6
  basis risk in, 805, 824
  calendar spreads in, 812
  cash (actuals physicals) markets in, 799
  clearing house, 801
  commission brokers (floor brokers) in, 799
  commodity board, 800
  Commodity Futures Trading Commission (CFTC) Act (1974) and, 804
  convergence principle in, 203, 805
  crush spread, 812
  delivery and settlement in, 802–3
  electronic markets and, 803, 824
  exchanges for, 799
  futures commission merchant (commodities broker), 801

  hedging and, 810–11, 824
  initial margin requirement for, 802, 809
  intercommodity spread, 812
  inverted market in, 805
  limit moves in, 800
  locals in, 799
  maintenance margin, 809
  margin call in, 809
  mark to the market in, 810, 818
  maximum price fluctuation limits, example of, 800–801
  National Futures Association (NFA) and, 804
  premium in, 805
  price convergence and, 805–8
  price relationships in, 805–10
  reversing out of a position, 802
  spot contracts, 799
  spreads in, 812
  storable commodities prices and, 808–9, 813, 824, 825
  technology and, 803, 824
  ticks (minimum price fluctuations) in, 800
  two-legged spread, 812
Commodity Futures Trading Commission (CFTC) Act (1974), 241, 242, 804
common-sized income and expense statement, 70
common stock, 28, 109, 349, 448, 732
  bankruptcy and, 110
  bearer securities, 111
  book value, 113
  book value per share, 769
  buybacks, investment implications of, 752
  call option of stockholders, 763
  cash dividend payments, 112
  Class A and B, 114–15
  classified common stock, 769
  coupon-interest claims in, 763–64
  cumulative voting with, 111
  dividend policy impact on, 700
  dividends payments and, 689
  fundamental common stock analysis, 702–3
  impact of dividend policy on, 700
  inflation-adjusted returns for, 316–17
  initial public offerings (IPO) of, 116, 349
  junior claim of common stockholders, 764
  limited liability of, 764
  preemptive right in, 111–12
  price quotations via newspaper, 113–14
  proxy, 111
  registered securities, 111
  registrar of, 111
  right to information, 112
  right to stock certificate, 110–11

common stock *(continued)*
 splits and dividends of, 113, 199–200
 stockholder's rights, 110–11
 transfer agent, 110
 underlying, 243
 valuing as a call option, 762–67
 voting rights of, 111
common stock equivalents used to determine EPS, 732
competitive advantage (in investing), 45–46, 256
compounded rate of return, 281
compounding conventions in bond market, 574–75
computing and interpreting financial ratios, 73–80
 for cash flow ratio, 77–78
 for coverage ratios, 76–77
 for financial leverage ratios, 78–79
 present value of a bond, 41, 627
 for profitability ratios, 79–80
 for solvency (or liquidity) ratios, 74
 for turnover ratios, 74–75
confidence index, 786–87
Conrad, Jennifer, 193
Consolidated Quotation System (CQS), 143, 150
consolidated statements, 87
constant dividend discount model, 772
Consuls (perpetual bonds), 42, 643
Consumer Price Index (CPI), 270, 279, 287, 290, 595, 744
contango, 813
contingent immunization, 650
contingent liabilities, 731
contrasting different depreciation guidelines, example of, 728
contrasting time until maturity with duration of bonds, 640–41, 643
convergence principle, 239, 805
convertible securities, 100–101, 267
convexity in price-yield relationship in bonds, 631–32
Coredeal electronic bond market, 567
corporate bankruptcy, 656–59
 and the Absolute Priority Rule (APR), 657–58
 common stock and, 658
 debenture bonds and, 658
 default and number of creditors, 657
 involuntary/voluntary, 657
 judge's discretion, 657–58
 preferred stock and, 658
 reorganization and, 658
 trustee in, 657
 and U.S. capitalism, 658–59
 U.S. Federal Bankruptcy Reform Act (1978) steps for liquidation, 657
corporate bond markets, 569

corporate bonds, 14, 28, 108, 120, 317, 327, 564–65
corporate cash flow (straightforward), defined, 77
corporations providing consensus forecasts of earnings, 721
correctly priced, defined, 45
cost of capital (discount rate), 29, 34, 700, 701
counterparties, 229, 260, 348
coupon effect in bonds, 632
coupon-interest, 98
coupon payment of bonds, 41, 627, 632
coupon rate, 99, 627
covariance, defined, 309
coverage ratios, 73, 76, 77, 78, 668
covered arbitrage, example of, 524–25
covered interest-rate parity, 524
Cox, Ingersoll and Ross (CIR) single-factor measure of duration, 649
credit analysis, 665
credit derivatives
 analyzing a portfolio of, 676–77
 asymmetric probability distributions of, 677
 Markowitz portfolio-analysis model and, 677
CreditMetrics, 679
credit migrations, 656, 679
credit risk
 bankruptcy, 28–29, 108, 110, 120, 656–59
 cash flow ratios in, 668–69
 categories of information for bond quality rating, 667
 corporate bankruptcy and, 656–59
 corporate credit curves and, 662
 coverage ratios in, 670
 credit migrations and, 656, 679
 debt test clauses and, 673
 financial ratios and, 667–70
 foreign currency bonds and, 674
 and indenture contract, 671
 inflation-linked bonds and, 674
 junk (speculative) bonds and, 660
 multiple discriminant analysis (MDA) of, 665–66
 negative pledge clauses of issuers and, 673
 protective devices for, 674
 and quality rating changes, 674–75
 quality ratings and, 659–66, 671
 rating migration and, 656, 676, 674–76
 recovery risk and, 673
 significant default and, 656, 659
 size of issuer and, 670–71
 split rating in, 661
 Standard & Poor's financial ratios and, 666–68

value-at-risk and, 676
 variance in value and, 676
 zero coupon bonds (zeros) and, 674
credit spread in yield measuring, 604, 662
cross-section regression (CRS), 449
cum coupon price of bonds, 573
cumulative average returns (CARs), 4, 203–05
cumulative cash dividends, 116–17, 119, 120
cumulative voting, example of, 111
currencies market
 absolute purchasing power parity in, 519
 arbitrage-free equilibrium condition of, 525
 arbitrageurs and, 525
 cash market (physicals market), 512
 common market and, 510
 covered interest-rate parity, 524
 customs union in, 526
 economic union and, 510
 equilibrium conditions, simplified summary of, 525
 European Central Bank (ECB) and, 511–12
 European Monetary Union (EMU) in, 510–12
 exchange rate, 508
 expectations hypothesis in, 514
 expected premium or discount in, 514
 Fisher's two inflation-based theories for, 522–23
 forward premuims and discounts in, 514
 forward price (FP) in, 512
 gold exchange standard and, 509
 hyperinflation and, 510
 inflation and, 509
 interest-rate parity, 523–24, 526, 527
 law of one price in, 519
 parity relationships in, 519–20, 522–24, 526–27
 rate movements in, 510
 relative purchasing power parity (relative PPP), 519–20, 526–27
 size of, 508
 spot market, 512
 telecommunications networks and, 508
 trading books and, 518
 uncovered interest-rate parity in, 523
currency devaluation/revaluation, 509–10
current (spot) rate of interest, 610–11, 612, 613

DaimlerChrysler, 6
Datta, Mai Iskandar, 675
Datta, Sudip, 675
Datta, Datta and Patel (DDP) study of initial public offerings (IPOs), 675

Davis, James, 449

day-counting conventions for bonds, 574, 590

day order, 132

death benefit, 392

debenture bonds, 109, 672

DeBondt, Werner, 192

debt balance, 161

debt-conversion bonds (DCBs), 584

debt test clauses in bonds, 673

decile portfolios, 205, 723, 725, 737

declining firms, 701, 737

default-free bonds, 28, 626

default risk premium, 604

deficit spending, 744

defined-benefit pension funds, 369

defined-contribution pension fund, 369

definition boxes
  agents, 768
  American call, 764
  arbitrage, 57, 450
  arbitrage opportunity, 456
  bearish, 47, 305
  block positioners, 141
  bonds, 568
  British bond, 568
  bullish, 47, 305
  business cycle, 162
  buy-sell rules under the assumption of certainty, 45
  call buyer, 242
  call writer, 243
  capital market line (CML), 438–39
  cash flows, 67
  characteristic line, 169
  churning, 129
  clean price, 573
  convergence principle, 239
  corporate cash flow (straightforward), 77
  correctly priced, 45
  covariance, 309
  cross correlations, 309
  down-tick, 348
  economic income (economic earnings), 736
  electronic communication network (ECN), 146
  electronic order-working system, 147
  European call, 764
  filter rule, 190, 372
  financial capital, 8
  Fisher effect, 598
  floater, 583
  forward rate, 611
  free lunch theorem, 219
  futures option, 830
  generalized free lunch theorem, 220
  gilts, 568

growth managers, 208

hedge funds, 872

human capital, 8

index arbitrage, 820

informational efficiency, 125

insider, 214

insider trading, 713

Instinet, 145

interest rate risk, 631

intertemporal stability, 308

investment, as defined by U.S. Treasury, 5

law of one price, 450

leverage, 352

market, 125

money market securities, 93

one-period rate of return, 20

one round lot, 242

operational efficiency, 125

option, 228

overpriced, 45

performance presentation standard (PPS), 373

present value model, 40

present value of a perpetuity, 41

prices indexes, 20

principal, defined, 20, 768

put option, 243

real capital, 8

recessions, 601

risk arbitrage, 59

runs, 193

security market line (SML), 442

selling short against the box, 57

spot rate, 612

stock variables, 714

T-Bonds, 568

time value of money, 37

underpriced, 45

undiversifiable risk, 290

utility, 422

value managers, 207

value of investment, 37

variable annuities, 391–92

yield-to-maturity (YTM), 576

delta ratio, 843

depreciation, 228, 668, 728, 744

Depression era, 298, 661, 879

derivatives, 228, 260, 677

Deutsche Termiborse (DTB), 803

diluted EPS, 732

dirty price of bonds, 573, 590

discount bonds (principal-reduction bonds), 584

discount rate (bonds), 41, 627, 632

discount rate of return, 39–40

diversifiable risk, 399

diversification (naive), 399

dividend-per-share model, 689

dividend policy impact on common stock, 700

dividends, types of, 688

domestic bonds, 568

domestic hedge funds, 873

dominance principle, 168, 169, 427

Dow, Charles, 779

Dow Jones, 144, 273

Dow Jones Industrial Average Dow (DJIA), 271, 272
  Bessembinder and Chan study of, 785
  Brock, Lakonishok, and LeBaron (BLL) study of, 785
  DJIA divisor, 274–75
  DJIA points, 274–75
  DJIA vs. S&P500, 290
  flaws in, 273
  indicator of stock market value, 743
  maintaining the DJIA, 278
  point, 275
  price-weighting system, 275
  S&P500 vs. DJIA, 277–78, 279
  stock splits and the DJIA divisor, 274

Dow-Jones Industrial Average Model New Deposit Shares (DIAMONDS), 349, 360

down-tick, defined, 348

Dow Theory, the, 779–81
  Brown, Goetzman, Kumar (BKG) test of, 780
  line chart of, 779
  primary trends of, 779
  secondary movements (corrections) of, 779
  tertiary moves of, 779
  testing of, 780–81

Drexel Burnham Lambert, 663

dual listings of exchange-listed stocks, 145

Duff and Phelps financial ratings company, 84, 93

Dun & Bradstreet financial ratings company, 84

DuPont Analytical framework, 81–82, 83

duration axioms in bonds, 651

Dutch auction, 119, 136

dynamic asset allocation (DAA), 380

earnings before interest and taxes (EBIT), 76, 78, 666

earnings multiplier (see P/E ratio)

earnings per share (EPS), 80, 731

earnings per share (EPS) potential dilution, 731–32

earnings per share forecasting, 721–22

earnings-price (E/P) ratio, 449

Ebay Internet firm, 760

econometric analysis of empirical data, 447–48

econometrics, 308–9

economic assumptions (idealistic), 700
economic equilibrium, 437
economic forces aligning prices, 817–18
  arbitrage, 817
  buy the cheapest to deliver (CTD), 818
  switching, 818
  transactions costs and, 818
economic income (economic earnings),
    defined, 736
economic theory, 421, 662, 701, 825
Economist, publication, 604
Electronic Data Gathering Analysis and
    Retrieval (EDGAR), 69–70
effective YTMs, example of, 577
effects of stock splits and stock divi-
    dends, 199–201
efficiency ratios (*see* turnover ratios)
efficient markets theory, 55, 56, 188–89,
    725, 743, 789
  semi-strong hypothesis, tests of, 197–99
  strong hypothesis, tests of, 213–18
  weakly efficient hypothesis in, 190–97
elasticities, 644
elasticity ratio, 843
electronic bond markets, 120, 566–67
electronic communication network
    (ECN), 146–47, 150, 155
  defined, 146
  electronic order-working system,
    147–49
  smart systems in, 148–49
electronic order-working system, defined,
    147
electronic stock exchanges, example of,
    149
Elton, Ed, 810
Elton, Gruber, Rentzler study of mark to
    the market, 810
embedded option of callable bonds,
    580–81, 590
emerging markets, 10, 321–27, 539–40,
    561
empirical tests (criticisms of), 465–66
Employee Retirement Income Security
    Act (ERISA), 33, 370, 371, 729
English banks, 96
enhanced indexing, defined, 345
equilibrium relationship between infla-
    tion and exchange rates, 520, 522
equity capital (world)
  market capitalization and, 9
  market price in, 10
  stock markets and, 9–10
  U.S. equity market in, 10
equity derivatives, 228
equity market (U.S.), 10, 13, 15
equity risk premia, 313–15
equity securities, 109, 120
equity shareholders cash flows, 735, 738

equity-turnover ratio, 76
equity valuation, 691, 694–95, 704, 708,
    732
  cash dividend discount model (DDM)
    for, 695
  cash dividend growth rate in, 689
  cash dividends, share buyback in,
    696–97
  cash dividends, types of, 688
  cash dividends and share buyback, 752,
    756
  common stock and, 689
  declining firms and, 701, 737
  determinants of price-earnings ratio, 705
  dividend discount model (DDM) and,
    688
  dividend discount models (DDMs) and,
    688–90, 692, 697–98, 707, 714–15
  dividend-per-share model, 689
  flow variables in, 714–15
  fluctuations in P/EPS ratios and, 703
  forecasting asset value and, 696
  fundamental common stock analysis
    and, 702–3, 708
  future cash dividends, 695
  growth firms and, 700–701, 736
  impact of dividend policy on common
    stock, 700
  irrelevant dividend policy, 699–700
  issue signals and, 700, 720
  market imperfections and, 701
  Miller and Modigliani (M & M) valuation
    model of dividend policy, 700
  model-building assumptions in, 690–91
  modeling relationship between earnings
    and dividends, 698
  net present value (NPV) in, 712, 813
  normal firms and, 700, 701, 719
  payment models for cash dividends per
    share, 688–89
  payout ratio in, 81, 698
  payout ratio *vs.* cash dividend, 705–6
  predictable/temporary earnings fluctua-
    tions in, 705
  preferred stock and, 689
  present value of cash dividends per
    share in, 736
  present value of share in terms of earn-
    ings, 698
  present value of stock for finite holding
    periods, 691–92
  price-earning (P/EPS) ratios of stock
    with no cash dividends in, 707–8
  quality of earnings, 731–33, 738
  relationship between common stocks
    and cash dividends in, 697
  retention rate (RR) for, 81, 698
  return on equity (ROE) for, 81, 83, 698,
    699, 770

reverse dilution of, 698
Standard & Poor's 500 indicators and,
    703, 704
stock variables in, 714–15
two stages of growth dividend discount
    model (DDM) for, 693–96
equivalence ratio, 843
errors-in-variables (EVI), 449
Erunza, Vihang, 549
Erunza, Hogan and Hung (EHH) study of
    U.S. stock market indexes, 549
estate planning, 395
ethics in investment, 344, 712–13
  access to information and, 153
  arbitration and, 790–91
  churning and, 768–69
  classified common stock and, 769
  conflicts of interest in, 20
  fairness in, 20, 153
  fraud, 713
  fraud and manipulation, 153
  fund managers ethical issues, 500–501
  golden parachutes and, 769
  greenmail and, 768, 769
  individual investor and, 110
  insider trading and, 713
  the law and ethics, 50
  manipulation of income and expense
    statement, 733
  moral hazard of, 110
  mutual funds and, 337
  pension funds and, 33–34
  poison pills and, 769
  principal, agent relations and, 20, 768
  unfairness and, 713
Eurobond market, 569–70
Eurobonds, 14, 568, 570–71
  Cedel clearing house for, 571
  compounding conventions of, 574
  Euroclear clearing house for, 571
  Eurodollar bonds and, 569, 572
  gray market in, 570–71
  issuing syndicate in, 570
  Luxembourg Stock Exchange listing of,
    571
  margin accounts for, 571
  and over-the-counter (OTC) sales, 571
  public offerings of, 570
Euro CDs, 96, 97
Eurodollar bonds, 572
Eurodollar CDs, 96
Eurodollars, 97, 510–11
Euromoney, magazine, 531
European Association of Securities
    Dealers Automated Quotations
    (EASDAQ), 150
European Bank for Reconstruction and
    Development, 584
European call (of bonds), 764, 849, 862

European Central Bank (ECB), 511–12, 603

European Monetary System (EMS), 510
  interaction of currencies, 510

European Monetary Union (EMU), 510–11, 526, 561, 603

European options, 245

evaluating a bond's EL, example of, 645

event studies in semi-strong tests, 198

exchange-trade funds (ETFs), 347–50
  cloning SPDRs and, 349
  derivatives and, 348
  market-on-close prices and, 347
  MidCap SPDRs and, 349
  payment-in-kind (PIK) and, 348
  SPDRs advantages over traditional S&P500 index funds in, 348
  Standard & Poor's Depository Receipt (SPDR) in, 347
  TIP 35 and, 350
  Toronto Stock Exchange (TSE) and, 350
  traditional S&P500 index funds vs. SPDRs in, 347–48
  unit investment trust (UIT) in, 347–48
  World Equity Benchmark Shares (WEBS) and, 350–51

ex-dividend stock price dropoff, 848–49

exercising a call, example of, 248

exercising a put, example of, 255

expectations theory of yield curves, 608

expected rate of return, 162–64

explanatory power of price to book ratio, 769

explicit/implicit interest payment, 99, 120

extra dividends, 688

fallen angels (see junk bond investing)

Fama, Eugene, 449, 769

Fama, Fisher, Jensen, Roll (FFJR) stock split study, 200–201

Fama and Schwert empirical study on inflation, 289

Fama-French book-value-to-market equity (B/V) contradiction, 449

Fama-French empirical tests of price to book value ratio, 769

Fannie Mae (FNMA), 14, 102, 564, 811

feature vector analysis (FEVA) methodology, 780

Federal Bankruptcy Act, 108

Federal Deposit Insurance Corporation (FDIC), 95

federal funds loans (fed funds), 96

Federal Home Loan Mortgage Corp. (FHLMC), 102

federal income tax, 106, 118, 728

Federal National Mortgage Association (FNMA), 14, 102, 564

Federal Reserve (the Fed), 96, 603, 662, 678, 805
  Board of Governors, 132
  and the gold standard, 879
  independence of, 604
  monetary policy objective, 604
  Open Market Committee, 604, 615, 881

Fidelity Investments, 129

Fidelity Magellan Fund, 481, 491

Fidelity mutual funds, 16, 340, 341

fiduciary, 20, 33

fiduciary duties, 713

fill or kill order (FOK), 131–32

Financial Accounting Statements Board (FASB), 68, 729, 730, 732

financial analysis problems, 84–87
  accounting income (vague definition), 84–85
  inflationary distortions, 84, 290

financial analysis through time, 710

financial capital, defined, 8

financial engineers, 440–41

financial futures, 260, 361, 815, 825

financial information providers, 144

financial instruments, 228

financial interior decorators, 410

financial leverage ratios, 670

financial ratio guidelines (establishing), example of, 75

financial services industry, 16, 20

financial statements (see also ambiguities in accounting earnings)
  analysis of, 66, 84
  analyzing, interpreting ratios in, 81–84
  balance sheet and, 66, 87, 766–67
  book value and, 87
  capitalization and, 79
  cash flow ratio in, 78–79
  cash flow statement and, 67–69
  common-sized statements in, 70–72
  comprehensive income of, 68–69
  computing, interpreting financial ratios, 73–80
  consolidated statements and, 87
  contingent liabilities, 731
  coverage ratios and, 73, 76–77
  cross-sectional standards of, 84
  depreciation schedules of, 728
  DuPont Analytical framework and, 81–82, 83
  financial analysis problems in, 84–87
  financial leverage ratios in, 78–79
  financial ratios categories, 73
  full disclosure requirement of, 69
  growth ratios in, 73
  income and expense statement of, 66–67, 76, 77

and the Internet, 69–70
  interpreting ratios, 77, 83–84
  leverage ratios in, 73
  payout ratio in, 81
  per share data in, 73
  price-earnings ratio (P/E) in, 81
  profitability ratios in, 73, 79
  ratio definition differences in, 77
  retention rate (RR) in, 81
  risk analysis ratios in, 73
  and Securities Act (1933), 69
  and Securities and Exchange Act (1934), 69
  solvency (or liquidity) ratios in, 73, 74
  sources of, 69–70
  turnover ratios in, 73, 74–75
  types of, 66

Financial Times, 604

Financial Times Stock Exchange (FT-SE) "Footsie," 198, 199, 322

First Call consensus forecasts, 721, 737

first in, first out (FIFO) inventory valuation method, 727

Fisher, Irving, 522, 596

Fisher, Lawrence, 648

Fisher and Lorie study of portfolios, 401

Fisher effect, defined, 598

Fisher's two inflation-based theories, 522–23

Fisher-Weil duration (FWD) measure of bonds, 648

Fitch financial ratings company, 84, 93, 565, 569, 660, 678

fixed and adjustable dividends, 118

fixed-income instruments, 634

fixed-income securities, 120, 359, 641
  balloon mortgage and, 635
  bond price behavior axioms in, 650–51
  contingent immunization in, 650
  coupon interest in, 98
  coupon-paying bonds in, 99, 106, 627, 629
  duration axioms in, 651
  explicit/implicit interest payments in, 99
  interest rate axioms in, 651–52
  original issue discount (OID) bonds and, 99
  recovery risk in, 673
  reinvestment risk in, 635
  safety net return of, 650
  U.S. securities and, 120
  zero coupon bonds (zeros) and, 98

"flight to safety," 374

floater, defined, 583

floating-rate bonds, 99

floating-rate notes (FRNs), 574

fluctuation of security's value, 51, 60

fluctuations in P/EPS ratios, 703

Ford Motor Credit Corporation, 97

forecasting cash dividends, 714

forecasting small *vs.* large company dividends, 696

foreign bonds, 568, 569, 674

foreign exchange, 515–16

absolute purchasing power parity, 519

components of investor's total return in, 516

information risk in, 534

interest-rate parity, 523–25

liquidity risk in, 531–32

market makers in, 512

parity relationships in, 526–27

relative purchasing power parity (PPP), 519–23

risk analysis (example of), 515–16

risk undertaken by international investors, 516–18

sovereign risk in, 530–31, 552, 568

special securities for, 530

transaction elements in, 512, 514, 516–18

forward and future contract users, 230

forward contract, 228, 229, 260

forward discount, 514

forward rate, defined, 611

forwards and futures, universal pricing principle for, 813–15

Foster, George, 723

Foster-Olsen-Shevlin (FOS) event study, 725, 737

Foster-Olsen-Shevlin (FOS) on effecting stock prices, 723

foundations and endowments, 369, 371

Francis, Jack Clark, 448, 769, 884

Freddie Mac (FHLMC) investments, 14, 102, 564

free lunch theorems, 219–20

free-market capitalism, 137

French, Kenneth, 449, 769

front-loaded interest-reduction bonds (FLIRBs), 585

full disclosure requirements, 136–37

full faith and credit bonds (*see* general-obligation (GO) bonds)

fundamental analysts *vs.* technical analysts, 778–79

fundamental common stock analysis, 702, 708

fundamental security analysis, 65, 375, 778

funding (hedging) to eliminate interest rate risk, 636–38

fungible, 229

future cash dividends, 695

futures commission merchant (commodities broker), 801

futures contract, 198, 228, 798, 824

cash settlement in, 230, 233, 260

characteristics of, 229–30

clearing house for, 230, 241–42, 801

and commissions savings, 824

on commodities, 230

contract pricing, example of, 823–24

contract units, 802

convergence principle, 203, 805

delivery date in, 229, 230

delivery months in, 800

delivery unit in, 235

expected spot prices (ESP), 825

financial futures, 260, 361, 815, 825

fluctuating prices of, 230

vs. forward contracts, 230

forward prices (FP), 825

Gwilym, Buckle, Clarke, and Thomas (GBCT) study of, 198, 199

hedging and, 238–40, 810–11

Hicks, Keynes futures prices argument, 813, 825

initial margin in, 235, 237, 260, 352–53, 802

law of one price and, 817, 825

leverage of, 236–37, 260, 352

London International Financial Futures Exchange (LIFE) and, 198

long futures positions in, 234, 798

long positions in, 233, 234, 235, 243, 260

maintenance margin (variation margin) in, 235, 809–10

margin requirements in, 234–35, 809–10, 856

mark to the market in, 810

open interest and, 240, 803

open outcry negotiation of, 230, 799, 824

option on (futures option), 830–34

overlay in, 358

perfect hedges and, 56, 239–40, 810, 824

physical commodities underlying, 799

prices, data in newspapers, 240

put or call option position in, 831

regulation of, 241–42

reversing out of a position, 802

on the S&P500 index, 351–53

selling hedge and, 238–39

short futures positions of, 234, 798

short positions in, 233, 234, 260

speculation with, 235, 236

spot contracts in, 799

stock market index pricing, 820–24

tick size in, 235

trading cards in, 799

trading futures, 230

volume of contracts in, 240

futures exchanges, 228, 799

futures option, 830–34

advantages, disadvantages of options on, 833–34

buyer option, 831

limited liability in, 833

rights *vs.* obligations in, 832

seller (wrtiter) responsibility, 831–32

specifications in, 832

writing of, 831–32

gain-loss positions, 49–50, 245–47, 251

gains and losses (extraordinary), 732

gambling *vs.* investment, 4, 5, 424–25

general creditors, 109

general creditors of debentures, 672

General Electric Credit Corporation (GECC), 97

generalized free lunch theorem, defined, 220

generally accepted accounting procedures (GAAP), 66, 84, 725, 731, 737, 744

General Motors Acceptance Corporation (GMAC), 97

general obligation (GO) bonds, 107, 120

generation-skipping transfer tax, 396

genetic algorithms, 789

geometric mean return (GMR), 25, 281–83

geometric *vs.* arithmetic mean return, 283–84

Gibbons, Michael, 449

gilts, defined, 568

Ginnie Mae (GNMA), 14, 102, 564, 574, 811

glamour stocks, 208

global bond market, 10–11, 102, 560, 585

accrued interest in, 573, 574

aggregate value of bond issues, 561

Automated Bond System (ABS) and, 564

bearer bonds *vs.* registered bonds in, 571–72

categories of international bonds, 56, 561, 568–69

clean price in, 573, 590

components of international bond returns, 586–87

corporate bond sectors in, 568

currency of issue in, 561

day-counting conventions in, 574, 590

embedded call option in, 580–81, 590

emerging markets and, 561

Eurobond market, 569, 590

Eurodollar bonds, 569, 572

European call, 764, 849

European Monetary Union (EMU) and, 561

European puts, 862

federal bond sector of, 567

floater, defined, 583

international bond categories, 568–69

international bond index statistics, 585–89

global bond market *(continued)*
  one-period rate of return in, 579–80
  political risk in, 568, 587, 589
  reference rate in, 583
  repatriation-of-funds risk in, 568
  secondary markets and, 566
  sovereign risk in, 568
  structured finance (securitization) in, 564
  transparency of U.S. bonds in, 567
  U.S. dollar denominated debt and, 563, 567
  and U.S. government agency bonds, 563–64
global bonds
  aggressive investment management of, 589–90
  bond-quality rating agencies for, 565
  Brady bonds, 584–85, 591
  Bulldog bonds, 569
  Carvela bonds, 569
  components of bond returns in, 586–87
  compounded yield-to-maturity (YTM), 576, 578, 590
  compounding conventions in, 574–75
  conditions for earning bond's expected YTM, 578
  Consuls (perpetual bonds), 42, 643
  corporate bonds (U.S.), 564
  correlations between international bond returns, 587–88
  crossborder bonds, 568
  cum coupon price, 573
  debt-conversion bonds (DCBs) in, 585
  discount bonds (principal-reduction bonds) in, 584
  domestic bonds in, 568
  Eurobonds in, 568–69
  foreign bonds, analysis of, 590
  foreign bonds in, 568
  front-loaded interest-reduction bonds (FLIRBs) in, 585
  index statistics of, 584–88
  industrial analysts approach to management of, 589
  invoice/dirty price, 573, 590
  macro-economic approach to management of, 589
  major sectors of market for, 14
  Markowitz analysis of international bond portfolios and, 588, 589, 591
  Matador bonds, 569
  matrix prices, 564–65
  new-money bonds (NMBs) and, 585
  over-the-counter (OTC) market and, 564–65
  par bonds (interest-reduction bond), 585
  past-due interest bonds (PDIs), 585

political analysis approach to management of, 589
  present-value formula in, 573, 576
  price/yield indexes for, 591
  reinvestment rate effects on YTM and, 578
  reinvestment rate in, 579
  Rembrandt bonds, 569
  Samurai bonds, 569
  security analysts approach to management of, 589
  Shogun bonds, 569
  Yankee bonds, 569
  yield-to-call (YTC) of, 580–81, 590
  yield-to-maturity (YTM) of, 575–76, 579–80, 590, 595
Global Depository Receipts (GDRs), 530, 545, 547–48 *(see also* global investing)
global equilibrium conditions, 550, 552
global investing
  American Depository Receipts (ADRs) and, 545–47
  categories of international investment companies, 548
  computing impact of two-country correlations, 539–40
  correlation coefficients between countries, 542–44, 552–53
  depository receipts for diversification, 545–48
  diversification study of, 549
  diversifying across industries, 536
  efficient frontier and, 540–41
  emerging markets and, 540–41
  foreign investors disadvantage in, 552
  Global Depository Receipts (GDRs) and, 547–48
  home bias in, 550
  illiquid assets in, 531
  information risk in, 534, 536
  international arbitrage pricing theory (IAPT) and, 550, 552
  international diversification via multinational corporations (MNCs) and, 544–45
  international mutual funds and, 547, 552
  international security market line (ISML) and, 549–50, 552
  liquidity risk, 531, 533
  market segmentation in, 536
  Markowitz portfolio theory and, 537, 540, 552
  mutual funds and, 530
  risk and, 530–31, 533, 534, 539–40, 552
  risk premiums in, 550, 551
  risk-reducing diversification need, 542
  Solnik's diversification study of, 536–37
  sovereign risk in, 530–31

Global Investment Performance Standards (GIPS), 374
global stock market, 6, 126, 155 *(see also* international stock markets)
Goetzmann, Will, 327, 780
Goetzmann and Ibbotson, 497–99
Goh and Ederington (GE) study of bond downgradings, 675
gold and monetary policy, 881
gold and silver investing, 881, 882
golden parachutes, 769
Goldman Sachs investment bank, 16, 128, 130, 801, 802
gold standard, 509, 879
good till canceled (GTC) order, 132
goodwill amortization, 730–31
Government National Mortgage Association (GNMA), 14, 102, 564
Great Crash (of market), 297, 879
greenmail, 768, 769
Griffin, Sanvicente (GS) study of stock price reaction to bond rerating, 675
gross domestic product (GDP), 451, 452
gross national product (GNP), 7–8
growth and value stocks, 208, 209, 211, 213
growth firms, 208, 700–701, 710–11, 736
growth ratios, 73
growth ratios *vs.* value management, 208
growth stock investing, 712–13, 715
growth-value anomaly, 206, 208
Gruber, Martin, 810
Gwilym, Buckle, Clarke, and Thomas (GBCT) study of futures contract, 198

Hamao, Yasushi, 449
Hamilton, William, 779
Hand, Holthausen, Leftwich (HHL) study of excess bond returns, 675
Hand, John, 675
Handa, Puneet, 449
Hands, Kothari, Wasley (HKW) and Kim study of the errors-in-variables (EIV), 449
Hardy, C.O., 813
Hardy futures prices argument, 813
Harris, Lawrence, 193–94
Hartzmark, Michael L., 813
head-and-shoulders top (HST) pattern, 781
Healy, Paul, 720
Healy and Paplepu (H&P) study of cash dividend payments, 720
hedge funds, 872, 882
  Ackermann, McEnally, and Ravenscraft (AMR) performance comparison of hedge and mutual funds, 878

hedge funds (continued)
  base value (high-water mark) in, 873, 882
  Brown, Goetzmann, and Ibbotson report on, 878
  Managed Account Report (MAR) Inc. and, 874
  performance of, 874–78
  portfolio manager's role in, 874, 877, 878, 882
  Quantum Fund and, 877
  sister fund in, 873
  survivorship bias and, 878
  turnover of, 873–74
  types of, 873
hedge ratio, 838, 843–45
hedging, 38, 55–57, 60, 260, 608, 638–40
  basis risk in (types of), 811–12
  bond price fluctuation risk, 636
  buying hedges, 810–11
  currency hedging, 359
  to eliminate interest rate risk, 635–36
  with futures, 238–40, 354–55
  futures overlay and, 352–53
  imperfect hedge (arbitrage position), 56, 57
  index options and, 353
  Macaulay's duration (MAC) and, 640–44, 651
  market segmentation theory and, 610
  option and, 243, 245, 353–59
  perfect hedges, 56–57, 239–40, 810, 824
  portfolio insurance (protective puts), 354–55
  as risk-reduction strategy, 636, 638
  S&P Depository Receipt (SPDR) and, 348
  selling hedges (short hedge), 238–39, 811
  and spreading, 812
heteroscedasticity in a standard deviation, 308–9
Hicks, John R., 813, 825
high-yield bonds, 660
hindsight bias, 790
historical return and risk interpretation, 27–29
Hite, Gailen, 675, 866
Hite, Warga (HW) study of bond upgrades, downgrades, 675–76
Hogan, Ked, 549
Holderness, Clifford G., 477
HOLDing company Depository ReceiptS (HOLDRS) funds, 349–50
holding period, 15
Holthausen, Robert, 675
home ownership and taxation, 394
homogeneous expectations, 440, 446, 463
homogeneous markets, 536

homoscedasticity, 308 (see also intertemporal stability)
Hood, L. Randolph, 382
horizon effect on bonds, 632
horizon premium hypothesis of yield curves, 608, 610
horizon premium in bonds, 28, 312
horizon return of bonds, 649
horizon risk, 626
horizon spreads in yield measuring, 604
human capital, 8, 10, 12
Hung, Mao-Wei, 549
hurdle rate of return, 29, 34
hyperinflation, 289–90, 510

Ibbotson and Geotyman 497–99
Ibbotson Associates, 318, 481, 585
Ibbotson-Kaplan (IK) study of asset allocation, 383–84
Ibbotson seven basic indexes, 296–97
  analyzing total returns (TRS) from, 303–5
  historically derived inflation premiums, 315–18
  10-year average returns for basic U.S. indexes, 302–3
idealized uncertainty, 440
illiquid assets, 371, 531, 569
imperfect hedge (arbitrage position), 56, 57
implicit interest payments, 99, 101
imputed payout ratio of cash dividends, 708
income and expense statement, 66–67, 76, 77
indenture contract (deed of trust), 108, 713
  after-acquired property clause, 672
  collateral provisions in, 672
  debentures in, 672
  general creditors in, 672
  protective provisions of, 671
  sinking fund provisions, 672–73
  subordination provisions in, 672
  types of protective provisions in, 672
index
  adjustments in, 278
  arithmetic mean return (AMR) and, 281, 283–84
  business cycle and, 605
  compounded rate of return and, 281
  Consumer Price Index (CPI) and, 270, 279, 287
  empirical research and, 289–90
  geometric mean return (GMR) and, 281, 283–84
  index numbers in, 271
  maintenance of, 278–79
  multi-period historical returns and, 284–85

  one-period return and, 279–81
  price indexes, defined, 270
  sample changes, 278
  securities index, 296
  time-weighted rate of return and, 281
  unsatisfactory securities in, 278
  usefulness of, 290
index arbitrage, 820–23
indexed common stock portfolios, 120
  enhanced indexing in, defined, 345
  tracking errors in, 345
  transaction costs vs. tracking errors, 346–47
index funds, 55, 333, 339–40
  vs. actively managed portfolios, 342, 344
  management fees of, 339–40
index numbers, 271
index options, 353
individual investors, 13, 15, 214
individual retirement account (IRA), 370, 391
individual vs. institutional investors, 13
industrial analysis, 754–56, 772
industry ratios, 84
inflation, 87, 289, 290, 299, 327, 394
  vs. bond prices, 744
  vs. common stock prices, 744
  and common stock returns, 771
  corporate profits and, 744, 771
  and the currencies market, 509
  exchange rates equilibrium relations and, 520, 522
  extraordinary deflation/deflation, 745
  Fama and Schwert empirical study of, 289
  impact on equity prices, 744–50
  and labor productivity, 753
  and level of interest rates, 599
  moderate deflation, 745
  negative impact of, 771
  nominal market interest rates and, 596
inflation-adjusted
  common stock returns and, 316–17
  government bond returns, 318
  long-term corporate bond returns, 317
  real rate of return, 369, 745
  U.S. Treasury Bill returns and, 318
inflation-induced market interest rate movements, 596
inflation-linked bonds, 674
informational efficiency, defined, 125
information and the value of securities, 190, 198, 219
information-signaling hypothesis, 200
information traders, 52
initial minimum margin requirement, 132, 260, 809
initial public offering (IPO), 4, 134, 341
  investment bankers and, 155

inside information, 20, 125, 214, 216–17

insider trading, 214, 713

Instinet, 145–146, 148

Institutional Brokers Estimate System (I/B/E/S) consensus forecasts, 721, 737

Institutional Investor, magazine, 531, 721–22

institutional investors, 13, 14, 15, 475–76

insured municipal bonds, 107–8

integrated asset allocation, 380

interest payments, implicit *vs.* explicit, 120

interest rate, 600–601
  in bonds, 631, 634
  elasticity of, 645
  parity in, 523–24
  term structure changes in, 647
  volatility of, 299

interest rate risk
  axioms about, 651–52
  in bonds, 626, 644–46
  Cox, Ingersoll and Ross (CIR) duration measure of, 649
  defined, 631
  Fisher-Weil duration (FWD) measure, 648
  investment and, 649–50
  Macaulay's duration (MAC) and, 640–44, 646, 647, 651
  Macaulay's duration (MAC) *vs.* MACLIM and, 641, 646
  modified duration (MOD) in, 638–39, 648–49

Intermarket Trading System (ITS), 143, 150

intermediate-term government bond index, 298

intermediate-term U.S. Treasury bonds, 28

internal rate of return, 700

Internal Revenue Service (IRS), 393, 396, 729

international arbitrage pricing theory (IAPT), 550, 552

international bond categories, 568–69

International Finance Corporation (IFC), 125

International Monetary Fund (IMF), 584, 585

international mutual funds, 552

international risk premiums, 550, 551

International Securities Exchange (ISE), 851

International Security Market Line (ISML), 552

international stock market crash (1987), 748

international stock market index funds, 350–51
  iShares, 350–51, 359

MSCI indexes, 350
  World Equity Benchmark Shares (WEBS), 350

international stock markets, 318–27, 548
  emerging markets in, 10, 321–22, 325–27
  emerging *vs.* developed markets, criteria for, 322–323
  index funds and, 350–51
  market indexes and, 322–23
  Morgan Stanley Capital International (MSCI) indexes, 319, 322–23, 327
  portfolio diversification and, 318, 325
  risk and return in, 323, 327
  vs. U.S. stock markets, 319

Internet, the, 69–70
  bond trading on, 567
  British securities information Web site address, 551
  Coca-Cola Corporation Web site address, 70
  CreditMetrics Web site address, 676
  Credit Monitor Web site address, 676
  CreditRisk+ Web site address, 676
  Credit Suisse First Boston Web site address, 676
  derivatives markets Web site addresses, 231
  Discover Brokerage Direct on, 567
  E*Trade Group Inc. on, 567
  E-Crossnet, 147
  European Monetary Union (EMU) informational Web site address, 511
  European stocks, IPOs, market news Web site address, 551
  First Call Web site address, 721
  foreign exchange rate data Web site address, 511
  hedge fund information on, 878–79
  Hoover's On Line Web site address, 70
  I/B/E/S Web site address, 721
  informational Web site address Brady bonds, options, futures, 584
  insider trading data on, 214
  International Monetary Fund (IMF) Web site address, 551
  Internet Final Network Web site address, 721
  investment bankers on, 136
  Investment Insurance International Web site address, 551
  Investment Management and Research (AIMR) Web site address, 374
  Latin American stocks, bonds, Global Depository Receipts (GDRs) Web site address, 551
  Merrill Lynch Web site address, 350

Moody's Investors Services Web site address, 676
Morgan Stanley Capital International (MSCI) indexes Web site, 323
  MuniAuction on, 567
  MuniCenter, the, 567
  mutual funding investing data site, 477
  National Futures Association Web site address, 804
  Prentice-Hall Web site, 16
  PR Newswire Web site address, 70
  real estate investment Web site addresses, 872
  SEC's Electronic Data Gathering Analysis and Retrieval (EDGAR) System on, 69–70
  statistics from, 180
  TreasuryDirect on, 567
  U.S. Treasury Web site address, 567
  Web site addresses for financial information, 70
  worldwide economic and political data Web site address, 551
  Yahoo!Finance Web site address, 70, 551
  Zacks Investment Research Web site address, 721

Internet stocks, 756–62
  Amazon.com and, 760, 761–62, 772
  baby boomers and, 756
  vs. bricks-and-mortar companies, 757–58, 772
  irrational factors in, 756, 757–58
  market capitalization (total cap) and, 760, 762
  power rule model in, 760, 772
  practical price-earnings ratio in, 762
  price-earnings ratios (P/E) for, 762
  price-earnings-to-growth rate multiple for, 762
  risk aversion and, 756, 757
  S&P500 index and, 756–57, 758
  stock buybacks and, 756
  Web site market prices, 759, 760
  winner-take-all nature of, 758, 759–60, 762, 772

intertemporal stability of volatility, 307–9, 308

inventory turnover guidelines, 76

investment, U.S. Treasury definition of, 5

investment banks, 134–36
  electronic investment bankers, 136
  functions of investment bankers, 134–35
  initial public offerings (IPOs) and, 134
  private placement and, 135
  secondary markets and, 137–38

investment companies, 341
  categories (international), 548

Investment Company Act (1940), 332–33, 347, 348, 476, 477

investment indexes
  cross correlations, 309, 310–11, 327
  Ibbotson's seven basic indexes, 296–97, 302, 303, 305
  intrinsic value (exercise value), 245, 247, 248, 353
  investment *vs.* individual securities categories, 296
  large-company stock index, 297
  serial correlation (autocorrelation), 309–10, 327
  small-company stock index and, 297
  U.S. indexes 10-year average return, 302–3
  U.S. Treasury Bill index, 298
investments
  agents and fiduciaries in, 20
  arithmetic mean return (AMR) for, 24–25
  asset classes of, 22
  bankruptcy law and, 27–28, 108
  basic random variable of investments, 34
  behavior of investors, 40
  conflicts of interest in, 20
  definition of, 5
  determining present value of, 38
  estimating value of, 37
  interpreting historical return and risk, 27–29, 161
  measuring historical returns in, 22–25, 161
  one-period rate of return in, 20–22, 34, 39
  rate of return in, 18
  realized returns in, 29, 34
  required rate of return, 29, 34
  risk of, defined, 26
  risk premium, 28, 34
  risk rankings, 27
  terminal value of, 18–19
investment tax results, example of, 393
Investment Technology Group (ITGs), 146
investors
  behavior of, 40, 45
  determinants of investor utility, 426
  and ethics, 110
  individual *vs.* institutional investors, 13
  investor's goal, 18
  passive investors, 361
  preferences, 169
  rate of return and, 18
  rational investors and utility theory, 423
  risk aversion, 180, 181, 398, 423–24, 426, 662, 751, 757
  risk-loving investors, 424–25
Investor's Liquidity Network (ILN), 147
invoice price of bonds, 573, 590

iShares, 360, 537, 548–49, 552
Island ECN, 146–47, 150

J.P. Morgan, 130, 545, 546, 567, 571, 679
Jack Carl Futures, 802
Jack White & Company, 129
Jaffe, Jeffrey F., 216–17
January effect, 194, 196, 218
Janus mutual funds, 16
Japan, 6, 10, 211, 333, 574
Japan RAM Monitors This Week, newsletter, 461
JIWAY cross-border European stock market, 150
Jones, Charles, 722
Jorion, Philippe, 327
junior claim of common stockholders, 764
junk bond investing, 663, 665
junk bonds, 359, 659–60

Kansas City Board of Trade (KCBT), 811
Kaul, Gautan, 193
Keogh plans, 379
Kessel, Rueben quoted, 608
Keynes, John Maynard, 813, 825
k-g spread, the, 709–10
Kim, Dongcheol, 449, 769
Kinney, William, 194
KMV Corporation, 679
Kothari, S.P., 449
Kuznets, Simon, 12

labor productivity, 752–53
Lakonishok, Josef, 449
Lanstein, Ronald, 449
largest investors in the world, 13
last in, first out (LIFO) inventory valuation method, 727
Latané, Henry, 282, 722
Latané and Jones (LJ) standardized unexpected earnings (SUE), 722–23
law of large numbers, 677
law of one price, 58, 143, 450, 460, 518, 632, 817, 825
Leftwich, Richard, 675
legal lists, 610, 701
Lehman Brothers Aggregate Bond Index, 360
letter stock, 370
leverage (financial), 236–37, 352
leverage-free cash flows, 735
leverage ratios, 73, 87
  total-debt-to-equity ratio, 78–79
  total-debt-to-total-asset ratio, 78
life-cycle theory of savings, 750–51
life insurance, 392
limited-obligation bonds, 107
limit order, 131, 155

limit order book (LOB), 139, 142, 149
Lintner, John, 719
Lin-Waldlock & Company, 802
liquidating dividends, 688
liquidity, 155
  in actively managed mutual funds, 344
  in asset allocation, 371
  of assets categories, 151
  "flight to safety" and, 374
  futures contracts and, 230
  hypothesis of, 200
  long-term capital gains and, 395–96
  money market securities and, 96
  of old assets, 379
  premium in, 151
  ratios of, 73, 74, 75
  risk and, 180, 531, 534, 552
  secondary markets and, 566
  and the Security Market Line (SML), 447
  traders, 51–52
  transaction costs and, 151, 153
liquidity premium theory of yield curves, 608
Litzenberger, Robert, 449
Lo, Andrew, 193
lock-up period, 370
logarithmic scale, 22
London, England, 6
London Interbank Offer Rate (LIBOR), 96–97, 119, 583
London International Financial Futures Exchange (LIFFE), 198, 803
long positions, 46, 49–50, 56, 57, 60, 237
  in options, 233, 234, 235, 260, 352
long-run asset allocation, 377
long-run equilibrium, 690
long-term capital gains, 392, 393, 395–96
long-term capital's pretax rate of return (LTCPTROR), 80
long-term corporate bonds, 28, 120
Long-term Equity Anticipation Securities (LEAPS), 243
long-term government bond index, 298
long-term U.S. Treasury Bonds, 28, 627
Lorie, James, 401
Luxembourg Stock Exchange, 571

Macaulay's duration (MAC), 640, 646, 647, 651
  contrasting time until maturity and duration, 640–41
  derivation of formula
  vs. MACLIM, 641, 643
  and modified duration (MOD), example of, 639
MacBeth, James, 449
MacKinlay, Craig, 193
Malkiel, Burton, 213, 495
Maloney Act (1938), 142

management buyout (MBO), 768, 769

mandatory disclosure, 153

margin account, 49, 132, 161

margin calls, 133–34

margin fraction (MGFR), 161

margin risk, 180

market, defined, 125

marketable U.S. Treasury securities, 101–2

Market Access electronic bond market, 567

market capitalization (total cap), 9, 10, 125, 126, 205

market impact of buying, selling, 151, 371

market imperfections, 701

market interest rates
  bankruptcy and, 606
  biased expectations theory and, 614
  business cycle and, 601
  Carleton and Copper on term structure, 624
  convexity in price-yield relationship and, 631–32
  credit-risk premiums in, 606
  default risk (quality rating) and, 606
  default risk premium in, 604, 605
  discount rate in, 627
  diversifiable factors in, 596
  duration and, 646–47
  expectation hypothesis in, 611–14
  expectations theory of yield curves and, 608
  expected *vs.* realized rate of inflation, 599
  factors influencing, 596, 601, 603–4
  federal government borrowing, effect on, 601–3
  Fisher effect on, 596, 598–99, 603, 615
  forward rate in, 611, 622, 624
  horizon (liquidity) premiums in, 606, 608, 610, 614
  horizon spreads in, 604, 605–6
  inverted yield curves in, 614
  liquidity premium hypothesis in, 608
  market segmentation theory, 610
  maturity risk premiums in, 604
  measuring yield spreads in, 604–5
  nominal market interest rates and, 596, 597
  par value in, 627
  prices and interest rates conclusions for, 600–601
  profit-seekers in, 613–14
  pure expectations theory in, 614
  quality spread, 604, 605
  realized real returns (rrr) in, 599
  risk of bonds and, 631
  risk-premiums (yield spreads) changes in, 615

segmentation theory of yield curves and, 608, 615

short-term bond interest rates and, 608

spot rate in, 610–12, 613, 622, 624

systematic fluctuations of, 646

term structure of interest rates (yield curves) in, 606–7, 614–15, 622, 624

theories concerning yield curves and, 608–10

undiversifiable factors in, 596

yield curve alternative formulations and, 621–24

yield spreads in, 604–6

market interest rates (nominal), 596

market-makers, 139

market-on-close orders, 132, 347

market order, 131

market portfolio, 172, 444–45

market risks, 180

mark-to-the-market rules, 818

Markowitz portfolio theory, 377, 377–78, 398, 403, 410–13
  analysis of a two-asset portfolio with, 406–7
  analysis using diversification in, 409–410, 428
  Asset Allocation Line (AAL) in, 415–20, 420–21
  Capital Asset-Pricing Model (CAPM) and, 440
  decision variables and, 403
  dominant portfolios and, 413–14, 427, 428
  efficient frontier of, 404, 413, 420–21, 427, 428, 437, 477, 540
  expected return and, 403–4
  fundamental concepts of, 427–28
  international investing and, 537, 540
  leverage portfolios (borrowing portfolios) in, 411
  limitations of, 433
  linear return and risk formulas in, 416
  Markowitz diversification, 402–3, 440
  more than two assets analysis and, 410
  negatively correlated investments and, 414
  negative weights and, 410–13, 417
  opportunity set of, 413
  perfectly correlated returns and, 407–8
  perfectly negatively correlated returns and, 409
  positive weights in, 428
  quadratic programming (QP) and, 410, 437
  risk and, 404–6
  risk-free rate (RFR) and, 415, 416, 417, 427, 428, 438
  Security Market Line (SML) and, 437–38

short selling and, 410–12, 414–15

variance-covariance matrix (portfolio risk equation) and, 405–6, 427

weight (participation level) and, 403

Matador bonds, 569

Matrix pricing of bond, 564–65

maturity risk premiums in yield measuring, 604

maximizing return or wealth, example of, 19

McElroy, Marjorie, 449

McGraw-Hill, 144

mean reverting, 305, 380, 703

Mendelson, Haim, 447

Merrill Lynch, 16, 126, 128, 130, 350, 801

Metropolitan Insurance Company, 16

Meulbroek, Lisa, 217

Milken, Mike, 663

Miller, Merton H., 700

Miller and Modigliani (M & M) dividend irrelevance theorem, 700, 719, 720, 737

model-building assumptions of equity valuation, 698

Modified Accelerated Cost Recovery System (MARCS), 729

Modified duration, 638–39, 648–49

Modigliani, Franco, 700

Monday effect, 193–94, 218, 219

monetizing debt, 744

money illusion, 288, 317

money market securities, 93, 119, 137
  banker's acceptances (BAs) and, 96
  vs. capital market securities, 98
  cash equivalents and, 93
  certificates of deposit (CDs) and, 95–96
  commercial paper and, 97
  credit ratings and, 93–94
  Eurodollar CDs and, 97
  explicit *vs.* implicit interest payment in, 120
  federal funds loans (fed funds) and, 96
  maturity of, 93, 98
  nonrated issuers of, 94
  reference rate and, 97
  repurchase agreements (repos), 97
  T-Bills, 21, 22, 28, 94–95, 101, 120

Montgomery, David, 289

Moody's financial information company, 77, 84, 93, 94, 678
  bond quality ratings and, 565, 569, 660
  discount brokers and, 129
  municipal bonds ratings and, 108
  quality rating changes and, 674

Moosa, Hasbrouck, and Gultekin study of stocks, 289

moral hazard, 110, 481

Morgan Stanley Capital International (MSCI), 211, 517, 534, 540
  for non-U.S. stock markets, 319, 322–23
  as surrogate for world market portfolio, 550
  World Equity Benchmark Shares (WEBS) and, 360
Morgan Stanley Dean Witter, 128, 130, 350
Morris, Chip, 762
mortgage-backed securities, 564
mortgage bond funds, 359, 764
moving average chart interpretation, 787–89
multinational corporations (MNCs), 530, 544
multiple discriminant analysis (MDA), 665–66
muni bond insurance companies, 108
Municipal Bond Insurance Association (MBIA), 108
Municipal Bond Markets (electronic bond market), 567
municipal bonds (munis), 106–7, 394
  alternative minimum tax (AMT) and, 394
  general-obligation (GO) bonds and, 107, 120
  insured municipal bonds, 107–8
  limited-obligation bonds and, 107, 120
  and muni bond insurance companies, 108
Muriel Siebert, 129
mutual fund hedge during volatile period, example of, 352
mutual fund investing, 208, 333–41, 495
  alpha, explanation of, 489–90
  analyzing performance statistics of, 491, 493–94
  appraisal ratio in, 491
  asset allocation line (AAL) in, 484–85, 493–94
  betas and standard deviation in, 479
  bond index funds and, 359–60
  characteristic line and, 488–89
  characteristics of, 335–36
  contingent deferred sales charges (CDSCs) and, 337
  deferred income taxes and, 393
  disbursed capital gains in, 336
  distribution fees in, 337
  economies of scale in, 339
  evaluating timing decisions in, 496–97
  factor analysis of, 480–81
  failure of, 341
  fees in, 336–37, 339–40
  goal statements of, 478–80
  hedge in, 352–53
  income tax and, 336
  index funds and, 55, 60, 340

index funds vs. actively managed portfolios in, 342, 344
international funds, 548–49
Internet data on mutual funding investing, 477
inverse correlation between expenses and returns, 495
and the Investment Company Act of 1940, 333
Jenson's alpha measure of, 491, 502
load fees, 337
management fees in, 337, 339–40
Markowitz efficiency and, 478–79
Midas Fund, 495
net asset value per share (NAVPS) of, 335, 336, 341, 476–77
net rate of return for expenses (determination of), 337
no-load funds for, 337, 477
performance measurement tools for, 213–14, 495, 501–2
portfolio turnover and, 340–41
quantitative style analysis and, 481
quantity discounts in, 338, 339
redemption fees in, 337
reinvestment and, 336
required goal statements in, 333
risk-adjusted returns of, 483, 501
rolling style analysis of, 481
Rydex family of, 356–58
S&P500 index and, 342
Sharpe's portfolio performance measure and, 482-83, 491, 494, 501
SHARPE, TREYNOR and Alpha values of, 491, 494, 495, 502
single-period rate of return, 336
small or foreign companies and, 338
survivorship bias in, 497
taxation and, 344–45

Nasdaq-100 Shares, 349, 360
National Association of Securities Dealers (NASD), 50, 142, 371, 790
National Association of Securities Dealers Automated Quotation (Nasdaq), 126, 142–43, 149, 155
  and the American Stock Exchange (AMEX), 143
  bid-ask quotations and, 142
  national daily list, 144
national best bid or offer (NBBO), 142
National Futures Association (NFA), 804
National Quotation Bureau (NQB), 144
National Securities Markets Improvement Act (NSMIA), 873
negative pledge clauses of issuers, 673
net long term capital gain, 393
net rate of return from a mutual fund, example of, 337–38

net worth (book value), 66, 772
neutral hedge ratio, 843
new-money bonds (NMBs), 585
New York Stock Exchange (NYSE), 126, 140–41, 149, 155, 178
  Automated Bond System (ABS) of, 564
  bid-ask spread in, 139
  block trade and, 141
  decimalization in, 139
  floor brokers, 139
  listing requirements, 140–41
  market-makers, 139
  membership of, 138
  operations of, 138
  program trading definition, 821
  specialists, 139
New York Stock Exchange Fact Book (1999), 52
New York Times, 604
noncumulative cash dividends, 118
non-marketable U.S. Treasury securities, 101
normal backwardation, 813
normal corporation's present value, example of, 700–701, 719

OATs, defined, 568
objective probability distributions, 166
Obligations Assimilables du Tresor (OATs), 568
odd lot trade, 13
Official Summary of Insider Transactions, SEC publication, 214, 216
off-shore hedge funds, 873
Olsen, Chris, 723
one-period rate of return, 20–22, 34, 39, 159, 279
  for bonds, 579–80
  calculations of, 160–61
  defined, 20
  holding period (for bonds), 580
  for an index, 279–81
one-period return from a share of Coca-Cola stock, example of, 20–21
one-period return from a U.S. Treasury Bond, example of, 21
open-end investment companies, 333, 477
open interest, 803
open outcry negotiation, 230, 260, 799, 824
operating income, 669 (see also earnings before interest and taxes (EBIT))
operational efficiency, defined, 125
opportunity cost, 29, 34, 151
opportunity set, 413
options
  advantages of, 253–54
  bear spreads (vertical spreads) in, 861

options *(continued)*
  binomial option pricing, 836–40, 862
  Black-Scholes call-valuation formula, 840–45
  bull spreads (vertical spreads) in, foriginal-issue
  call option premium after dividend adjustment, 850
  call option using Black-Scholes model, 842–43
  covered calls in, 855
  ex-dividend price drop-off and, 862
  financial leverage of, 253
  hedge ratio in, 843–45
  intrinsic value, 849
  limited liability of, 252, 260
  vs. long, short positions, 260
  long position (synthetic) in, 851–52
  market price of underlying asset of, 259
  markets for options, 245, 851
  over-the-counter (OTC) market volume, 851
  put-call parity formula, 845, 847–48, 862
  replicating portfolio, 835, 840
  straddle position in, 856, 857
  strangle in, 859
  time value in option price, 256, 766, 849
  uncovered option writers, 855–56
  underlying stock and, 253–55
  wash sales and, 393
  zero sum game in, 252, 256, 260
Options Clearing Corporation (OCC), 242, 851
option theory and prices of corporate securities, 674, 765–66
order crossing networks, example of, 146–47
original-issue discount (OID) bonds, 99, 101, 103, 631, 818
over and underpriced stocks, 39, 42, 43, 44, 45, 770, 772
overconfidence, 790
overseas investments, example of, 358–59
over-the-counter (OTC) stock, 114, 141, 144, 145, 155

Pacific Stock Exchange (PSE), 851
PaineWebber, 128
Palepu, Krishna, 720
par bonds (interest-reduction bond), 585
Paris Club, the, 584
par value of bonds, 41, 101, 113, 627, 629, 631
par value of common stocks, 113
Pascal's triangle, 677, 839
passive investment management, 55, 361

past-due interest bonds (PDIs), 585
Patel, Ajay, 675
patterns, 781
paying for order flow, 145
payment-in-kind (PIK), 348
payment models for cash dividends per share, 688–89
payout ratio, 81, 698
pension funds, 371, 729–30
  401K's, 390
  403B's, 390
  analyzing large pension funds, 382–84
  defined benefit pension plan, 33, 369, 729, 730
  defined contribution plans, 33, 34, 369, 729
  Employee Retirement Income Security Act (ERISA), 370, 371
  expense deductions of, 730
  Financial Accounting Standards Board (FASB) Statements and, 730
  individual retirement account (IRA), 370–371, 390, 391, 393
  Keogh plans, 379
  largest investors in the world, 31
  overfunding, 33
  pension costs, 729
  pension deficit, 729, 730
  present value of employer's legal liability for, 729
  profit-sharing plans, 369
  sponsor of, 31, 369
PepsiCo, 73
P/E ratio (earnings multiplier), 81
per capita gross domestic product (GDP), 7
perfect hedge, 56–57, 239–40, 810, 824
performance of standard S&P 500 composite index, example of, 280
performance presentation standard (PPS), 373, 374
periodic call market, 149
permanent capital, 80, 669
perpetual constant growth dividend discount model (DDM), 709, 714, 715
perpetual stocks and bonds, 41
per share data, 73
personal taxes, 390–91
Philadelphia Stock Exchange (PHIX), 851
physicals markets, 512, 799
poison pills, 769
policy asset allocation, 377
Pontiff, Jeffrey, 477, 769
portfolio
  arbitrage portfolio, 455–56
  benchmark portfolio, 372
  dominant, 413–14, 427
  efficient, 377, 404, 440, 442
  holding for tax purposes, 344–45

international diversification of, 318, 325, 549
  lending, 417
  leverage portfolios (borrowing portfolios), 411, 417
  market portfolio, 439, 444–45
  Markowitz efficient, 377, 441
  minimum risk, 433
  perfectly hedged, 56–57
  replicating, 360, 835
  risk aversion and, 398
  turnover and taxes of, 392
portfolio analysis (*see also* Markowitz portfolio theory)
  alpha, explanation of, 489–91
  assumptions underlying portfolio theory, 440–41
  average risk and, 399
  Capital Market Line (CML) in, 438–39
  CML, SML and CAPM assumptions in, 440–41
  computing impact of two-country correlations on portfolio's variance, 539
  diversifiabile risk in, 399
  diversifying across industries, 400–401
  efficient portfolio and, 377, 404, 433–35, 440, 442
  evaluating timing decisions in, 496–97
  factor analysis of, 480–81
  vs. financial interior decorators, 410
  homogenous expectations (idealized uncertainty) in, 440
  investment desirability index for, 419–20
  Jenson's model for, 488, 491
  leverage (borrowing) portfolios and, 411
  management style and, 480–81
  Markowitz analysis with more than two assets for, 409–10
  minimum portfolio variance, finding, 433–35
  naïve diversification in, 399
  perpetual growth rate (estimating value of share), 43, 44, 709
  portfolio management and, 401
  quantitative style analysis, 481
  random diversification in, 398, 399–400
  regression analysis in, 447–48, 449, 451, 463–64, 481
  return generating process and, 451, 461
  reward-to-variability ratio in, 420–21
  risk-adjusted return and, 483
  risk and, 428
  risk-free rate (RFR) and, 28, 415, 416, 417, 427, 428, 438, 483
  risk premium and, 483
  rolling style analysis, 481

portfolio analysis (continued)
  Sharpe's portfolio performance measure, 482–83
  Sharpe's statistical model analyzing portfolio manager's style, 480–81
  SHARPE, TREYNOR, and Alpha investment performance measures, 491, 502
  simple diversification in, 399–400, 442, 536
  superfluous diversification and, 401–2
  Treynor and Mazuy evaluation of market timing and, 496–97
  TREYNOR portfolio performance measures and, 486, 488
  TREYNOR, SHARPE and Alpha investment performance measures, 502
  of two-country diversification, 537, 539, 541
  two-pass regression methodology in, 449, 463–64
  undiversifiable risk and, 399, 437
  utility theory and, 422–27, 428
portfolio analysis (mathematical), 433–35
  Lagrangian objective function, 433
  Markowitz portfolio theory and, 433
  minimization solution procedure, 433
  three-security portfolio calculus minimization, 434
  two Lagrangian constraints, 433
  weights sum to unity, 433
portfolio analysis (utility theory of), 422–27
  decision-making and, 426
  determinants of investor utility in, 426
  expected utility and, 423
  and happiness/unhappiness, 422, 423
  holding period in, 422
  indifference curves, 423–24, 427
  rational investors and, 423, 424
  risk-averse investors and, 423–24
  risk-loving investors and, 424–25
portfolio diversification (international), 318, 325, 537, 549
portfolio rebalancing and duration wandering, 646–47
POrtfolio System for Institutional Trading (POSIT), 146
positive horizon risk premium, 605
power law model, 760
practical price-earnings ratio, 762
precious metals, 10
predispute arbitration agreement (PDAA), 790–91
preemptive right, 111–12
preferred stock, 109, 118, 119
  call feature of, 119
  vs. common stock/bonds, 116

  cumulative cash dividends of, 115–17, 119
  dividends payments and, 689
  fixed and adjustable dividends in, 118
  noncumulative dividends of, 118
  par value of, 118–19
  redemption of, 119
  rights of, 116, 118
  and taxation of corporate income, 118
premiums
  common stock premium, 28
  default risk and, 28, 312, 313, 327
  equity risk premium, 28, 313–15
  horizon premium, 28, 312
  illiquidity premium, 447
  inflation premium, 312
  interest rate (impact on), 259
  international risk premium, 550
  in option contract, 245, 256, 259, 353
  puts and calls, 256, 260, 267
  risk and, 18, 28, 34, 302
  size premium and, 28
  small-stock premium, 28
  total bond default, 312
present value
  of a bond, 626–27
  of cash dividends, 736–37, 738
  of forwards and futures, 814–15
  of investment, 37
  model, 37, 40, 50
  of a perpetuity, defined, 41
  present value of stream of constant cash dividends, 689–90
  share of stock reformulated, 699
  of stock for finite holding periods, 691–92
price
  anticipatory prices, 675
  bond price behavior axioms, 627, 650–51
  bond prices vs. interest rates, 744
  clean bond price, 573, 590
  comparing difference between price and value, 52–53
  consensus value estimate, 52
  dirty bond price, 573, 590
  forward price (FP), 512
  inflation and, 744
  information and, 53–54, 187
  invoice price of bonds, 573
  matrix price, 564
  movements of, 188–89
  over-priced asset, 39, 42, 43, 44–45
  perfectly efficient price, 53, 187, 188
  price-earnings ratio (P/E), 81, 762
  pricing efficiency categories, 188
  pricing inefficiencies and profit, 188
  randomness and, 188, 193, 197
  runs tests of, 193

  semi-strongly efficient price, 53, 187, 188
  serial correlation and, 192–93, 372
  volatility, 676
  weakly efficient price, 53, 187, 188, 193, 196
price-earnings ratios (P/EPS), 705, 707–8
price-earnings-to-growth rate multiple, 762
price elasticity of bonds, 646
price to book value (PBV) ratio, 208–9, 211, 769–72
price-value interaction, 51
price-yield relationship in bonds, 643–44
pricing futures on stock market index, 823–24
PriMark Corporation, 214
primary securities, 93
Primex electronic auction system, 150
principal, defined, 20, 768
prior period adjustment, 732
probability distribution
  construction of, 166
  of returns, 162, 165, 180
  skewness in, 185–86, 677
  stability of, 166–68
profitability ratios, 73, 79–80, 670
profit-sharing plans, 369
prospectus, 136–37
protective puts to hedge during volatility, example of, 354
proxy, 111
Prudential Insurance Company, 16
purchasing power parity (PPP), 7
purchasing power risk, 287–90
put bonds, 674
puts and calls, 256, 834, 863
  alignment of on underlying stock, 848–49
  analyzing a call, example of, 247
  cash payments of puts, 254
  characteristics of, 242–43
  and correctly priced stock, example of, 848
  defined, 242–3
  exercise price in, 259, 849
  futures contract and, 830
  futures option and, 831
  gain-loss for put writer, 251
  index options and, 353
  intrinsic value (exercise value) in, 245, 247, 248, 353, 849
  premium (price) in, 256, 260, 835
  protective puts, 354–55
  put bear spread in, 861–62
  put-call parity formula, 845, 847
  short sale vs. put buying, 255
  synthetic positions in, 851–54
  and T-Bond futures, 833
  variables effecting, 835

quadratic programming (QP), 410, 437
quality of earnings, 731–33, 738
quality rating of bonds, 659–62, 674–75
quality spread in yield measuring, 604
Quantum Fund, 877
Quick & Reilly, 129

Ramaswamy, Krishna, 449
RAM Monitors This Week, newsletter, 461
random diversification, 398, 400
random numbers, 310, 465
rate of return, 18, 20–22, 39, 180, 440 (*see also* one-period rate of return)
 average rate of return (measuring), 24–26
 compounded, 281
 concepts in, 34
 cross correlations of, 310
 on equity (ROE), 80, 698, 699, 770
 equivalent pretax/after-tax and, 394
 expected rate of return, 162, 445
 geometric mean return (GMR), 25, 281–83
 historical returns and, 22–25, 161
 hurdle rate of return, 29, 34
 hyperinflation and, 289–90
 inflation and, 289, 290
 internal rate of return, 700
 from long positions, 46
 long-term capital's pretax rate of return (LTCPTROR), 80
 major types of investment and, 27–29
 mean reverting returns and, 305, 380
 measuring historical returns, 22–25, 161
 in mutual funds, 337
 nominal rate of return, 288, 290, 312
 one-period rate of return, 22
 of puts and calls, 256–57, 259
 real rate of return, 288–89, 290, 311
 required rate of return, 29–31
 risk premiums in, 18, 27, 302
 serial correlation (autocorrelation), 310–11
 short sale and, 46–47, 50, 60, 255, 410–12, 414–15
 standard deviation in, 26–27, 165, 181, 299
 T-Bond returns and, 21–22
 time diversification and, 305
 time-weighted, 281
 variance in, 165, 404
rating migration, 656, 676
ratio analysis
 asset-turnover, 76, 87
 bond quality ratings and, 667–70
 book-to-market equity (B/V), 448, 449
 cash flow ratios, 77, 87, 668–69
 categories of, 73

consistently defined ratios, 668
coverage ratios, 87, 668
current ratio, 76
 difference in definitions of, 77
earnings-price (E/P), 449
efficiency/activity, 76
elasticity ratio, 843
equity-turnover, 76
financial leverage ratios, 670
fluctuations in P/EPS ratios, 703
interpreting ratios with standards of comparison, 83–84
inventory-turnover, 76
leverage ratios, 87
long-term debt-to-capitalization ratio, 670
multiple discriminant analysis (MDA) of, 665–66
practical price-earnings ratio, 762
pretax rate-of-return on long-term capital ratio, 669
price to book value ratio, 208–10, 769–71
profitability ratios, 87, 668, 674
quick ratio, 76
solvency (or liquidity) ratios, 73, 74, 75
Standard & Poor's financial ratios, 666–68
time-series comparisons of, 83–84
times-fixed-charges-earned ratio, 668
times-interest-earned, 76
turnover ratios, 73, 87
real estate investment, 44, 289, 871–72, 882
 advantages, disadvantages of, 870–71
 average returns and, 868
 market data and, 868
 single-family residence purchase, example of, 868, 870
 total returns (TR) in, 868
 types of, 867–68
real interest rate, 599
realized capital gain or loss, 344
realized real returns (rrr), 599
realized returns, 29, 34
real rate of return, 288–89, 290, 311, 745
recessions, 8, 601
recovery risk in bonds, 673
reference rate for bonds, 583
Reg ATS exchanges, 150–51
registered securities, 111, 571
regular cash dividends, 688
Reid, Kenneth, 449
Reinganum, Marc, 205, 448
reinvestment return component of total returns, 303–5
relative frequency distributions, 166
relative purchasing power parity (relative PPP), 519–20

Rembrandt bonds, 569
Rentzler, Joel, 810
repatriation-of-funds risk, 568
replicating portfolio, 360
repurchase agreements (repos), 97
required rate of return, 29, 30, 31, 34
residual claim, 28
residual variance (diversifiable risk), 169, 177–78, 179
retention rate (RR), 81, 698
return (historical) and risk interpretation, 27–29
return on assets (ROA), 79–80, 81, 87
return on equity (ROE) formula, 81, 83, 698, 699
returns (bullish and bearish), 305–7, 399, 406, 756
Reuters, 144, 561
revenue bonds, 107
reverse dilution of shares, 698, 736
reward-to-variability ratio, 420
Rhea, Charles, 779
right to information, 112
risk
 assessing risk, 26
 and average returns, 301–2
 bankruptcy law and, 27–28, 108
 beta variance of, 169, 177–78, 181
 counterparty risk, 229
 currencies market risk, 516–18
 default risk in bonds, 108–9
 defined, 26
 diversifiable risk, 399
 diversifiable/undiversifiable, 169, 178–79, 181
 efficient portfolios and, 440
 equity risk premia, 313–15
 estimates, 164–65, 440
 expiration date risk, 811
 factors in, 180
 foreign exchange risk analysis, 509, 515–16
 horizon effect on bonds, 632
 interest rate risk of bonds, 631
 international diversification of portfolio and, 325, 539
 and investor preferences, 169
 measuring of, 26–27
 in optioned stocks, 256–57, 259
 partitioning assets' total risk, 178
 political risk, 568
 portfolio and, 398
 premiums and, 18, 28, 34, 40, 302, 464, 483
 purchasing power risk, 287–90
 quality risk, 811
 quantity risk, 811
 rankings of, 27
 rate of return and, 440

risk *(continued)*
  repatriation-of-funds, 568
  and return relationship, 307–9
  risk-return analysts, 375
  sources of, 165
  sovereign risk, 530–31, 552, 568
  standard deviation in, 26, 165, 181, 440
  standard error in, 179
  stochastic process risk, 647
  U.S. Treasury Bills and, 28–29
  underwriting, 134–35
  undiversifiable risk, 290, 399, 437
  and variability of return, 159
  zero coupon bonds (zeros) and, 635
risk-adjusted cost of capital (discount rate), 690
risk-adjusted discount rate, 40
risk arbitrage, defined, 59
risk-free rate (RFR), 28, 416, 427, 428, 825
  borrowing, lending at, 415, 438, 483
  in hypothetical mutual funds, 484–85
  in SHARPE's performance index, 483
riskless assets, 415
risk premiums, 18, 28, 34, 40, 302, 464, 473, 550, 551
risk-return relationship, 307–9, 672, 678
Ritter, Jay R., 4
Roll, Richard, 464
Rosenberg, Barr, 449
Ross, Stephen, 450
round lot trade, 13
Rozeff, Michael, 194
runs, defined, 193
Rydex family of mutual funds, 356–58

safety net return, 650
sales-and-leaseback agreements, 673
Salomon High Grade Long-Term Bond Index, 360
Salomon Smith Barney (SSB), 128, 153, 560
Salomon Smith Barney (SSB) weekly risk attribute model (RAM), 461
Samurai bonds, 569
Sanvicente, Antonio Z., 675
scale order, 131
Scandinavian countries, 7
Schall, Larry, 769
Schwab Internet firm, 760
Schwartz, Robert, 13
secondary markets for securities, 95, 137–38, 566, 569
secret trading, 145
Section 20 subsidiary corporation, 545–46
secured/collateralized bonds, 108–9
  blanket mortgage, 108

collateral trust, 109
  mortgage bonds, 108
  open-end mortgage, 109
Securities Act (1993), 19, 112
securities analysts, 46, 53–54, 180, 181, 665
  active investment management and, 54–55
  efficient markets and, 55
  passive investment management and, 55
Securities and Exchange Act (1934), 19, 214
Securities and Exchange Commission (SEC), 136, 142, 143, 153
  EDGAR Online address, Electronic Data Gathering Analysis and Retrieval (EDGAR) System, 69–70
  FreeEDGAR address, 70
  futures contracts and, 805
  insider trading and, 217
  Official Summary of Insider Transactions SEC publication, 214, 216
  and the Options Clearing Corporation (OCC), 851
  Reg ATS rule of, 150
securities and price fluctuation, 45–46
securities index, 296
security issuers economic significance and size, 670–71
Security Market Line Theory (SML), 181, 462, 488–89, 552
  vs. Arbitrage Pricing Theory (APT), 437, 462–63
  assumptions of, 447, 462–63
  assumptions underlying CML, SML and CAPM, 440–41
  bases of, 449
  borrowing and lending in, 438, 445
  and the Capital Asset Pricing Model (CAPM), 437, 440–41
  Capital Market Line (CML) and, 438–39, 440–41
  CML and SML assumption relaxation, 445–47
  contradictions in, 448–49
  criticisms and tests of the SML, 447–49
  defined, 442
  econometric analysis of, 447–48
  econometric problems with, 448–49
  empirical data analysis of, 447–48
  equilibrium portfolio theory, 461
  errors-in-variables (EIV) problem in, 449
  heterogeneous expectations (common investment horizon) of, 446
  vs. historical data, 445
  homogeneous expectations (idealized uncertainty), 440, 446

indivisibilities in, 447
  liquidity of investments and, 447
  market portfolio and, 439, 444–45, 448
  Markowitz portfolio theory and, 437
  numerical estimate, example of, 444
  overpriced assets, 444
  rationale, 441–43
  restatement of, 443
  risk-return space in, 437–40
  Security Market Line restatement, 442–44
  separation theorem in, 440
  support for, 449
  tax rates and, 446
  theoretical SML, 449
  and transaction costs, 445
security price indicators, 271
segmentation theory of yield curves, 608, 615
SelectNet, 146
Select Sector SPDRs, 349
self-financing portfolio, 837
self-regulating organizations (SROs), 50, 142, 150
selling climax, 786
selling short against the box. defined, 57
senior claim of mortgage bonds, 764
Separate Trading of Registered Interest and Principal of Securities (STRIPS), 103, 106
Seyhun, H. Nejat, 217
SFAS 5 and contingent liabilities, 731
Shanken, Jay, 449
share repurchasing firms, 736, 752
Sharpe, William, 420
Sharpe's portfolio performance measure, 482–83
Sharpe's statistical model analyzing portfolio manager's style, 480–81
SHARPE, TREYNOR and Alpha values, 491, 494, 495
Shevlin, Terry, 723
Shogun bonds, 569
short positions, 46–49, 50, 56, 57, 60, 255
  and investment opportunities, 414–15
  margin money, 49
  market price rise and, 49
  negative weights and, 410–12
  options and, 233, 234, 260
  short interest, 50
short sellers, 60, 412
short-term bond interest rates, 608
short-term capital gains, 393
Siegel, Laurence, 289
Siegel, Montgomery study of pretax returns, common stock, 289
silver (physical), 879–80
simple diversification, 399–400, 536
Singer, Brian D., 382

single parameter portfolio performance index, 483

sinking fund (bond redemption), 101, 120

sinking fund provisions in debentures, 672-73

size premium, 28

skip-day convention, 95

small-company stocks, 28

small-stock premium, 28

small *vs.* large company dividends, forecasting, 696

smart systems, example of, 148

Society for Worldwide Interbank Financial Telecommunications (SWIFT), 508

Solnik, Boucrelle, Yann Le Fur (SBL) study of international correllations, 542

Solnik, Bruno, 536

solvency (or liquidity) ratios, 73, 74, 75

Sony Corporation, 6, 14

Soros, George, 877

sources of risk, 165

sovereign risk, 530-31, 552, 568

SP/BARRA Growth and Value Index Funds, 210, 211

special dividends, 688

speculating on common stock IPOs, example of, 4

speculation, 260, 398
  carrying charges of storable commodity and, 805
  currency traders and, 525
  futures contract and, 798, 824
  high-yield (junk, speculative) bonds, 662
  index options and, 353
  initial public offering (IPO) and, 4
  vs. investment, 4, 5, 15
  long straddle position and, 857
  and options, 243, 245
  Standard & Poor's Depository Receipt (SPDR) and, 348

speculation, example of, 235

speculative blowoff, 786

speculative bonds (*see* junk bonds)

speculators, 235

spot and futures price theories, 812-13, 825

spot contracts, 799

spot market, 512

spot price (SP), 512

spot rate, defined, 612

stability of probability (relative frequency) distributions, 166-68

Standard & Poor's 500 Stocks Composite Index (S&P500), 55, 170, 211, 270, 271
  buy and sell signals in, 747-48
  cash dividend yield and, 747

equal weights, 276

factors affecting, 749-50

financial ratios of, 666-68, 670-71

futures contract on, 351-53

index, 278-79, 299, 340, 360, 697, 703

index futures speculation, 236

as indicator of stock market value, 743

indicators, 273, 275, 703, 704, 771

Industrial Stocks Index, 758

and Internet stock, 750

MidCap 400 stocks index, 349

price-earnings ratio, 747-48

and stock splits, 277

Vanguard Index Trust 500 Portfolio and, 342

Standard & Poor's Analysts Handbook, publication, 756

Standard & Poor's Depository Receipt (SPDR), 347, 348, 360

Standard & Poor's financial ratings company, 129, 569, 660, 674, 678
  bond quality ratings and, 77, 565
  company/industrial data subscriptions, 756
  financial ratios and, 84
  insured municipal bonds and, 107-8
  money market securities and, 93

standard deviation, 26-27, 181, 398, 399, 404
  heteroscedasticity of, 308-9
  of interest rates, 299
  statistical analysis and, 165

standardized unexpected earnings (SUEs), 722-23

statement of cash flows, 733-34

static equilibrium model of price-earnings ratio, 705

statistical aggregation problems, 704

statistical analysis, 308-9
  aggregation problems in, 704
  alpha (regression intercept term) in, 178
  analysis of margined investment returns, 161
  arbitrage pricing theory line and, 453-55
  basic random variable in, 159-61
  beta and residual variance, 169
  beta coefficient, 177-78, 181, 481, 485-86
  carrying-cost model for T-Bill futures, 818-19
  characteristic line in, 169-71, 176, 447-49, 488-89
  characteristic line's residual errors, 175, 201-2
  characteristic line's statistics (estimating), 172-73
  coefficient of determination in, 178
  computations with cash dividends, 849

computing a stock's alpha and beta, 175-76

computing impact of two-country correlations on portfolio's variance, 539

computing returns over multiple periods, 285-86

constructing probability distributions, 166

correlation coefficient in, 177, 309, 406

covariance of returns, 176, 327, 404-5, 406

cross correlations and, 309

cross-section regression (CRS), 449

delta, 843

econometric problems with characteristic line, 448-49

errors-in-variables (EIV) problem, 449

expected rate of return and, 162

factor analysis, 480-81

factor betas in, 464

first pass time-series regressions, 463

for forwards and futures, 814, 815

genetic algorithms, 789

hedge ratio, 838, 843-45

heteroscedasticity in a standard deviation, 308-9

homoscedasticity in a standard deviation, 308

intertemporal stability and, 308, 448

k-dimensional APT hyperplane, 461

linear return and risk formulas, 416

market portfolio and, 172, 444-45, 463, 465

multiperiod binomial call-pricing formula, 838-40

neutral hedge ratio, 843

one-period binomial call pricing formula, 836-38

partitioning asset's total risk, 178

probability distribution of returns in, 162, 180

sample dependent betas, 448

sample selecting in, 162

second-pass cross-sectional regression, 463-64

serial correlation (autocorrelation) and, 309-10

SHARPE, TREYNOR and Alpha values, 491, 494, 495

skewness of probability distribution, 185-86

stability of probability distributions, 166-67, 166-68

standard deviation and, 165

statistics from the Internet, 180

of stock splits and dividends, 199-203

two statistics theorems for, 436

unrealistic values in, 164

statistical analysis *(continued)*
variance-covariance matrix (portfolio risk equation), 427
variance of asset's rate of return, 165, 404–5
Sterling 3-Month Interest rate, 198
Stickel, Scott E. statistical analysis of earnings forecasts, 722
stochastic process risk, 647
stock exchanges (evolving), 149–50
stock flow variables, defined, 714
stockholders' options, 764
stock index arbitrage, 820–21
stock market average, 271
Stock Market Barometer, The, 779
stock market collapsing, 601
stock market index
intercountry correlations of, 539–40
pricing futures on, 820–24
stock market indexes options, 353–59
stock market indicator construction, 271–78
base year (base period) in, 271
contrasting two stock market indicators, 273–78
DJIA points and, 274–75
DJIA *vs.* S&P500, conclusions, 765–66
equal weighting in, 272
first principles for, 271–73
market value-weighting system, 272
representative samples in, 271–72
S&P500, 275
S&P weights and, 276
small samples and, 273
standard of comparison (benchmarks), 271
stock splits and the DJIA divisor in, 274
stock splits and the S&P500 in, 277
timeliness of, 273
total returns (TR) in, 272
uniform definition in, 272–73
stock options
American options and, 245
break-even point in, 247
characteristics of, 243, 245
European options and, 245
ex-dividend date and, 259
ex-dividend price drop-off and, 259, 849
exercise price (strike price) of option, 245
expiration of option, 243
gain-loss positions in, 245–47
hedging and, 243, 245, 355
interest rates impact on premiums in, 259
intrinsic value of, 245, 247, 248
intrinsic value of call writer's position in, 248, 764
Long-term Equity Anticipation Securities (LEAPS) in, 243

option exchanges, 243
premium (price) of, 245, 256, 353
put options and, 243, 354
seller (short options) and, 243
sell option in, 243
short position (synthetic) of, 852–54
short straddle position, 856
underlying asset price in, 243
underlying asset risk, 256–57, 259, 260
stock price reaction to bond reratings, 675
stock purchase warrants *(see* warrants)
stocks
bond reratings and, 675
book value and, 87, 773
cash dividend growth rate of, 689
cash dividend payments of, 720
constant rate of growth valuation, 63–64
convertible, 267
day-of-week effects on, 193–94
and the Dow Jones Industrial Average (DJIA), 273–75
earnings per share (EPS) of, 80, 737
equity risk premia, 313–15
equity risk premium and, 28
equity securities and, 109
estimating value of share, 42–43
ex-dividend date stock dropoff, 848–49
expected returns from Small Cap issuer, 314–15
Fama and French (F&F) analyze, 208–9
forecasting earnings per share, 721–22
Foster-Olsen-Shevlin (FOS) event study and, 723, 725, 737
glamour stocks, 208
growth and value stocks, 208, 209, 211
growth stock investing, 712–13, 715
insider information and, 20, 214
insider trading and, 216–17
interrelationship between January and size effects on, 205–6, 218
January effect on, 194, 196, 218
letter stock, 370
liquidating, effect of, 353
long-horizon return from, 314
long-term capital (permanent-capital/ capitalization) of, 80
over and underpriced stocks, 770, 772
partitioning financial ratios of, 208
per share data (common stock) of, 80–81
S&P500 indicators and, 273, 275, 276
size effect (small *vs.* large companies), 205
stock certificate, right to, 110–11
stock dividend payments and, 689
stock market average and, 271
total returns (TR) in, 272–73, 303–4, 314–15
tracking stocks, 116

transactions costs of, 151–53
treasury stock, 736
unexpected earnings surprise, 722–25
value and growth stocks, characteristics of, 208
whisper earnings and, 722
stock splits and dividends, 199–203
characteristic line's residual errors in, 201
conclusions about stock splits, 203
cumulative average residuals (CARs) of, 203
effects of, 199–201
event month and, 201
Fama, Fisher, Jensen, and Roll (FFJR) study of, 200–201
S&P500 and stock splits, 277
total value and, 199–200
stock values, comparing two different estimates of, 709
stop orders, 131
storable commodities, 808–9, 813, 828
strategic asset allocation (SAA), 377
street name, 111
subjective probability distribution, 166
subordination provisions in debentures, 672
SuperECN, 147
survivorship bias, 497, 878
Switzerland, 7, 211
systematic fluctuations of market interest rates (bonds), 646

T.Rowe Price Science and Technology mutual fund, 762
tactical asset allocation (TAA), 367, 377
taxation and investments
after taxable income, 390
after-tax evaluation and, 393
agency bonds and, 102
alternative minimum tax (AMT), 392
capital gains/losses tax treatment, 392–393, 396
corporate income taxation, 118, 396
estate taxes *vs.* income taxes, 395–96
exclusion ($1 million) in, 395–96
generation-skipping transfer tax, 396
gift taxes and, 396
home ownership and, 394
letter stock and, 370
lock-up period and, 370
long-term capital gains, 392
municipal bonds (munis) and, 394
net long-term capital and gain, 393
ordinary income and, 392, 393
personal taxes and, 390–91
retirement plans and, 393

taxation and investments *(continued)*
  short-term capital gains and, 393
  tax-managed funds, 392
  Unified Estate and Gift Tax, 396
  Unified Gift and Inheritance Tax, 370
  Unified Transfer Tax (estate tax), 394–96
  wash sale and, 393
tax-exempt funds, 394
tax-sheltered annuity (*see* variable annuity)
T-bill-Eurodollar spread, 812
T-Bills (*see* U.S. Treasury bills)
T-Bonds (*see* U.S. Treasury bonds)
technical analysis, 190, 375, 791
  assumptions underlying, 778–79
  bar charts and, 781
  Barron's confidence index (BCI), 786–87
  base-rate fallacy and, 790
  bounded rationality and, 789
  congestion areas, 785
  and the Dow Theory, 779–81
  filter rules in, 190
  vs. fundamental analysts, 778–79
  holiday effect, 194, 218
  January effect in, 194, 195, 205–6, 218
  moving average analysis in, 787–89
  overconfidence and, 790
  patterns and, 781, 789
  psychological frame in, 790
  runs tests in, 193
  selling climax and, 786
  serial correlation (autocorrelation) in, 191–93, 309–10, 327, 372
  speculative blowoff, 786
  supply and demand in, 791
  support and resistance levels in, 784
  trading range breakout (TRB), 785
  and volume, 782, 786
  weakly efficient market hypothesis anomalies in, 193–96, 218–19
technology industry, 757–60, 771
technology stocks *vs.* nontechnology stocks, 756–58
telecommunications, 6, 155
Tennessee Valley Authority (TVA), 14
Term CDs, 96
terminal value, 18–19
term repos, 97
term structure of interest rates, 622, 624
Thaler, Richard, 192
third market in United States, 145
tick, 139, 348
time diversification, 305
time-interest-earned ratio, 76, 77
time-series comparisons, 84, 87
times-fixed-charges-earned ratio, 668
time value of money
  cash flows and, 41

definition of, 37
determining present value for, 38
equivalent models for, 39
multiperiod models for, 40
one-period models for, 38–40
present value model for, 40
present value of a perpetuity and, 41
terminal time period in, 40
yield-to-maturity (YTM) of bonds and, 41, 106, 575–76, 579–80, 590
time-weighted rate of return, 281
timing the stock market, 745
T-notes (*see* U.S. Treasury notes)
Tobin, James, 771
Tobin's q ratio, 771
Tokyo Stock Exchange (TSE), 126
tombstone, 116, 134, 570
Toronto Index Participation (TIP), 350
Toronto Stock Exchange (TSE), 350
total debt to capitalization, 670
total-debt-to-equity ratio, 78–79
total returns (TR) in, 868
tracking errors, 345, 346–47, 360–61
tracking stocks, 116
Tradebook, 147
Tradepoint electronic exchange, 150
TradeWeb electronic bond market, 566
trading (in secrecy), 145
trading cards, 799
trading futures, 230
trading on margin, 132–34
trading range breakout (TRB), 785
transaction costs, 151–53, 161, 818
  direct/indirect, 151
  international survey of, 153
  and small coporations' stocks, 153
  total transaction costs, 151
transfer agent, 110
transparent market, 149, 566
Treasury inflation-protected securities (TIPS), 106
treasury stock, 736
trending, trendless and mean-reverting patterns, 703
Treynor, Jack, 485
Treynor index of portfolio performance, 485–86
Treynor and Mazuy evaluation of market timing, 496–97
TREYNOR, SHARPE and Alpha investment performance measures, 491, 502
Trust Indenture Act (1939), 108, 671
turnover ratios, 73, 87
types of preferred stock, 119

U.S. Depression (1929–1933), 298, 661, 879

U.S. dollar-denominated financial asset risk, 287
U.S. Federal Agency Securities, 102–3, 106
U.S. Federal Bankruptcy Law absolute priority rule (APR), 657–58
U.S. Federal Bankruptcy Reform Act (1978), 657
U.S. government Consumer Price Index (CPI), 270, 279, 290
U.S. government securities, 10, 101–6
  marketable securities, 101–2
  nonmarketable securities, 101
  price quotations via newspaper, 104
U.S. interest rates, 299
U.S. Internal Revenue Service (IRS), 118
U.S. savings bonds (series EE and HH), 101
U.S. stock market, 13
U.S. tax law, 370
U.S. Treasury, 24–26, 94, 583, 662, 805
  bond issuing agencies, 14
  bond market and, 563, 567
  borrowing, 601, 602
  and the Federal Reserve's Open Market Committee, 615
  hypothetical yield curve of, 606
  inflation-indexed securities, 106
  interest rate risk in bonds, 608, 632, 634
  intermediate-term bonds, 28, 318
  long-term bonds, 28, 298, 608, 627
  marketable securities, 101–2
  nonmarketable issues, 101
  price-yield relationship in bonds, 627
  public auctions of securities, 566
  Separate Trading of Registered Interest and Principal of Securities (STRIPS), 103
  silver certificates and, 880
  Treasury inflation-protected securities (TIPS), 106
  as world's largest borrower, 563
  yield curve and, 607
  yield curve for bonds, 608
  yield curve of securities, 606
  yields-to-maturity (YTMs) of bonds, 614, 627
  zero coupon bonds (zeros), 98, 103, 120, 610, 631, 635, 765–66
U.S. Treasury bills (T-Bills), 21, 22, 28, 40, 120, 311, 415
  bank discount of, 94
  bid yield of, 95
  bill index, 298
  book entry basis of, 94
  carrying-cost model for T-Bill futures, 818–19
  cost of marking to the market, 818
  denominations of, 94
  indirect purchase of, 816–17

U.S. Treasury bills (T-Bills) *(continued)*
inflation-adjusted returns for, 318
price quotations of, 94–95
pricing futures contracts on, 815–16, 825
pricing T-Bill purchase, example of, 819–20
public auctions of, 94, 566
skip-day convention in, 95
U.S. Treasury bonds (T-Bonds)
and bankruptcy risk, 595
bond fund, 359
callable, 102
computing present value of, 627
coupons of, 103
fractional price quotations of, 101–2
futures options and, 832–33
maturity period of, 102
one-period return for, 21
principal (corpus) of, 103
stripping of, 103
zeros and, 103
U.S. Treasury notes, 102
UBS Warburg, 567
unbiased expectations hypothesis of future prices, 813
uncovered interest-rate parity, 523
underfunding pensions, 33
underlying value, 228, 243
under-priced asset, 39
underwriting IPO corporate bonds, example of, 317–18
underwriting syndicate, 134–35
undiversifiable factors in market interest rates, 596
undiversifiable risk, 290, 399, 437, 466
unexpected earnings surprise, 722–25
Unified Gift and Inheritance Tax, 370, 394–96
Union Bank of Switzerland (UBS), 211
United Kingdom, 6, 211, 333, 574
United States, 6, 10
unit investment trust (UIT), 333, 342, 347–48
unit trusts (*see* open-end investment companies)
unsecured bonds, 109
using different discount rates, example of, 39
utility, defined, 422

value and growth stocks, characteristics of, 208
value-at-risk (VaR), 676
value investing *vs.* growth stock investing, 211
Value Line financial ratings company, 84
Value Line Investment Survey, publication, 214

value managers, defined, 207
value of a share of stock (estimating), example of, 42–43
value of investment, defined, 37
value of real estate investment (estimating), example of, 44
value of securities and information, 190, 198, 219
value of share of perpetual preferred stock (estimating), example of, 44
value of share of stock with constant perpetual growth rate (estimating), example of, 43
valuing an unutilitzed patent, example of, 767
valuing a share, example of, 691
valuing common stock as a call option, 762–67
American *vs.* European call in, 764
bankruptcy law and, 762, 763
Black-Scholes call pricing formula for, 766, 767
bondholders *vs.* stockholders and, 763–64
call option model in, 762, 763, 767, 772
conflict of interest in, 763–64
coupon-interest claims and, 763–64
junior claim of common stockholders in, 764
limited liability in, 764
mature debts and, 764
mortgage bonds and, 764
option theory and prices of corporate securities in, 765–66
senior claim of mortgage bonds and, 764
stockholders and, 763, 764
time values *vs.* intrinsic values in, 765
valuing corporation's securities using additional facts, 767
Vanguard 500 Index Fund, 495
Vanguard Brokerage Services (VBS), 129
Vanguard Index Trust 500 Portfolio, 338, 340, 342, 347, 361, 495
Vanguard mutual fund, 210, 211
Vanguard Total Bond Market Portfolio (VTBMP), 360
variable annuities, 391–92
variance and standard deviation of returns, 26–27
variance-covariance matrix (portfolio risk equation), 427
variance in value of a bond, 676
Vickers Stock Research Corporation, 214
volatility
hedging and, 352, 354
of interest rates, 299

intertemporal stability of, 307–9
price assessment and, 676

Wall Street Journal, 102–3, 273, 355, 604, 723
and the Dow Theory, 779
editorials in, 780
quarterly earning announcements in, 725
reproduced article, 305, 381
Warga, Arthur, 675
warrant pricing, example of, 265
warrants
detachable, 266
exercise price of, 265
intrinsic value *vs.* intrinsic value of a call, 265–66
warrant agreement, 266
wash sale, 393
Wasley, Charles, 449
wealth accumulation, 19, 299, 299–301
wealth maximization, 19, 34, 38, 166, 282–83, 301
Web sites of exchanges and investment bankers, 136
weekend effect, 193, 196
Weekly Insider Report, 214
Weil, Roman, 648
whip-sawed, 131
whisper earnings forecasts, 722
Winston, Mark, 674
Winston study of bond prices, 674
World Bank, 584
World Equity Benchmark Shares (WEBS), 350–51
world income map, 7
worldwide electronic trading book, example of, 518
writing covered calls, 855–56

x percent filter rule, 190, 372

Yahoo! Internet firm, 760
Yankee bonds, 569
Yankee CDs, 96
yield curve alternative formulations, 621–24
yield curve theories, 608, 610–14
yield spreads in market interest rates, 604–6
yield-to-call (YTC), 580–81, 590
yield-to-maturity (YTM) of bonds, 41, 106, 575, 590
bond performance and, 577
and bond quality ratings, 662
bond's coupon rate and, 627, 629, 631
comparing various YTMs, 577–78
compounded, 576
conditions required to earn expected YTM, 578

yield-to-maturity (YTM) of bonds
    (continued)
  conventional and effective YTMS, 577
  conventions in calculation of, 576
  coupon effect in bonds, 632
  defined, 576
  discount rate of bonds and, 632
  duration axioms in bonds and, 651
  effective YTM, 576
  high-yield bonds and, 660

vs. horizon return, 649–50
importance of, 595
inverse relationship with price, 580,
    590, 591
Macaulay's duration (MAC) and,
    638–39
premiums and discounts factor in,
    629
present-value formula for, 576, 627
price behavior axioms, 650–51

and reinvestment rate, 579
and U.S. Treasury yield curve, 662

Zacks Investment Research consensus
    forecasts, 721, 737
zero collateral (*see* debenture bonds)
zero coupon bonds (zeros), 98, 103, 610,
    631, 635
zero sum game, 252, 256, 260

RISK-RETURN FORMULAS USED IN VARIOUS CHAPTERS

$$r_t = \frac{(P_1 - P_0) + \text{Cashflow (if any)}}{P_0} = \text{One} - \text{period return}$$

$$AMR = \bar{r} = \left(\frac{1}{T}\right)(r_1 + r_2 + \ldots + r_T) = \text{Arithmetic Mean Return}$$

$$GMR = \sqrt[T]{(1 + r_1)(1 + r_2)\ldots(1 + r_T)} - 1 = \text{Geometric Mean Return}$$

$$E(r) = \sum_{t=1}^{T} p_t\, r_t = p_1 r_1 + p_2 r_2 + \ldots + p_T r_T = \text{Expected return}$$

$$\sigma^2 = VAR(r) = \left(\frac{1}{T}\right)\sum_{t=1}^{T}(r_t - \bar{r})^2 = \text{Variance of returns}$$

STATISTICAL FORMULAS FROM CHAPTER 7

$$COV(r_i, r_m) = \left(\frac{1}{T}\right)\sum_{t=1}^{T}[r_{i,t} - E(r_i)]\,[r_{m,t} - E(r_m)] = \rho_{i,m}\sigma_i\sigma_m = \text{Covariance}$$

$$\rho_{i,M} = \frac{COV(r_i r_M)}{\sigma_i \sigma_M} = \text{Correlation between } i \text{ and } M$$

$$SKEW = \sum_{i=1}^{i=N} p_i[r_i - E(r)]^3 = \text{Skewness}$$

PORTFOLIO ANALYSIS FORMULAS

$$\sum_{i=1}^{N} x_i = 1 = 100\% = \text{Sum of the investment weights}$$

$$E(r_i) = \sum_{i=1}^{N} x_i\, E(r_i) = \text{A portfolio's expected rate of return}$$

$$VAR(r_p) = \sum_{i=1}^{N}\sum_{j=1}^{N} x_i x_j \sigma_{ij} = \text{A portfolio's variance of returns}$$

$$(\text{Terminal wealth, } W_T) = (\text{Beginning wealth, } W_0)(1 + r)^T$$

$$U(W_T) = \text{Log}(W_T) = \text{Logarithmic utility of terminal wealth}$$

$$U(r) = \text{Log}(r) = \text{Logarithmic utility of returns}$$

$$E[U(r)] = \sum_i p_i U(r_i) = \text{Expected utility of returns}$$

BOND AND INTEREST RATE RISK FORMULAS

$$PV = \frac{CF_1}{(1 + k)^1} + \frac{CF_2}{(1 + k)^2} + \frac{CF_3}{(1 + k)^3} + \ldots + \frac{CF_T}{(1 + k)^T} = \text{Present value}$$

Solve for Yield To Maturity (YTM):
$$PV_0 = \sum_{t=1}^{T}\frac{CF_t}{(1 + YTM)^t}$$

$$\begin{pmatrix}\text{Modified} \\ \text{duration,} \\ \text{MOD}\end{pmatrix} = \left(\frac{1}{1 + YTM}\right)\left(\frac{1}{P}\right)\left(\sum_{t=1}^{t=T}\frac{(-t)(Cashflow_t)}{(1 + YTM)^t}\right) \approx \frac{\Delta P/P}{\Delta(YTM)}$$

$$\begin{pmatrix}\text{Macaulay} \\ \text{duration,} \\ \text{MAC}\end{pmatrix} = \begin{pmatrix}\text{Modified} \\ \text{duration,} \\ \text{MOD}\end{pmatrix}(1 + YTM) = \left(\frac{1}{P}\right)\left(\sum_{t=1}^{t=T}\frac{(-t)(Cashflow_t)}{(1 + YTM)^t}\right)$$

$$EL = \frac{\text{Percent change in bond's price}}{\text{Percent change in }(1 + YTM)} = \frac{\Delta p/p}{\Delta YTM/(1 + YTM)} = MAC < 0$$

$$\text{Convexity} = \frac{d^2 P}{d(YTM)^2} = \sum_{t=1}^{T}\frac{t(t + 1)CF}{(1 + YTM)^{t+2}} + \frac{T(T + 1)m}{(1 + YTM)^{T+2}} > 0$$

$m = $ Number of times per year payments (compounding) occurs
$INF = (CPI_{t+1} - CPI_t)/CPI_t = $ Inflation rate in CPI
$rr = $ Real rate of interest $= r - INF$

OPTION FORMULAS

Intrinsic value of a call $= \text{MAX}[0, (\text{Stock price} - \text{Exercise price})]$

$$\begin{pmatrix}\text{Intrinsic value} \\ \text{of a warrant}\end{pmatrix} = \text{MAX}\left[0, \left\{\left\langle\begin{pmatrix}\text{Price of} \\ \text{stock}\end{pmatrix} - \begin{pmatrix}\text{Exercise} \\ \text{price}\end{pmatrix}\right\rangle\begin{pmatrix}\text{Number} \\ \text{of shares}\end{pmatrix}\right\}\right]$$

Intrinsic value of a put $= \text{MAX}[0, (\text{Exercise price} - \text{Price of stock})]$

Put-Call parity below:

$$\begin{pmatrix}\text{Stock's} \\ \text{price, } P\end{pmatrix} + \begin{pmatrix}\text{Purchase price} \\ \text{of put, } POP\end{pmatrix} - \begin{pmatrix}\text{Call option's} \\ \text{premium, } COP\end{pmatrix} = \begin{pmatrix}\text{Exercise} \\ \text{price, } XP\end{pmatrix}/(1 + RFR)^d$$